STATISTICAL VIEW

OF THE

UNITED STATES,

EMBRACING

ITS TERRITORY, POPULATION—WHITE, FREE COLORED, AND SLAVE—MORAL AND SOCIAL CONDITION, INDUSTRY, PROPERTY, AND REVENUE; THE DETAILED STATISTICS OF CITIES, TOWNS AND COUNTIES;

BEING A

COMPENDIUM OF THE SEVENTH CENSUS,

TO WHICH ARE ADDED

THE RESULTS OF EVERY PREVIOUS CENSUS, BEGINNING WITH 1790, IN COMPARATIVE TABLES, WITH EXPLANATORY AND ILLUSTRATIVE NOTES, BASED UPON THE SCHEDULES AND OTHER OFFICIAL SOURCES OF INFORMATION.

By J. D. B. DeBOW,

SUPERINTENDENT OF THE UNITED STATES CENSUS.

WASHINGTON:

A. O. P. NICHOLSON, PUBLIC PRINTER.

1854.

IN THE HOUSE OF REPRESENTATIVES,

JANUARY 12, 1854.

Resolved, That there be printed, for the use of the House of Representatives, by the Publi Printer of the House, one hundred thousand copies of a compendium of the Seventh Census to be arranged by the Superintendent of the Census, embracing the population by towns an counties; the ratio tables of population; tables of nativities, births, marriages and deaths of the deaf, dumb, blind, insane and idiotic; of schools and colleges; of aggregates of occu pations; of churches; of newspapers and libraries, and of agricultural products, with illus trative notes and comparative tables: ***Provided,*** The said compendium shall be printed i royal octavo form, and not exceed four hundred pages.

CENSUS OFFICE, *Washington, Sept.* 1, 1854.

TO THE HON. R. MCCLELLAND,
Secretary of the Interior.

In the volume which is now handed you—though restricted in size by the order of Congress—will be found a very full compendium of the Census Statistics of the United States from the earliest period, together with all of the tables embraced in the quarto publication of 1850, with the few exceptions noted below. To these have been added a large amount of information collected for the first time from the returns and from other official sources, with illustrative notes and ratio and comparative tables.

In lieu of the classification of ages by counties and their subdivisions, the births, marriages and deaths, the church and school statistics by counties, and the occupations by States, I have inserted as of wider interest, county tables in the following particulars—of population, white, free colored and slave, native and foreign, male and female, in 1850, with the aggregate in 1840, and the changes of county organization within that time; of college, private school and public school scholars, with the revenues appropriated to each; the total educational income; the illiterate; the number of persons within the school age, and the actual average of scholars in the year; of the number of farms; and the capital, product and amount of labor in manufactures, mining and the mechanic arts. The occupations and the number of births, marriages and deaths are given in States and in great sections of the Union, and the specific ages and nativities in all the leading cities.

The tables embraced in the volume have been examined and revised, involving in most cases a re-examination of the returns, during which care was taken to exhaust, by way of illustration, for certain cities, counties, or States, every source of information embodied in them. This would have been done for the whole Union had time and the means at my disposition admitted. As it was, however, the time and labor actually expended will, I trust, be amply repaid in the results. Never before has so large a part of the census material, collected by such expensive machinery, been made available by the government, for popular use, in compact and systematic form.

The statistics of manufactures and of mortality, which alone remain of the census, will be ready for publication by the meeting of Congress, and can be included if desired in a volume of the size of the present.

For other suggestions in relation to the experiences of this office and the history of the census system of the United States, I beg to refer you in particular to the Introductory Chapter.

Your obedient servant,

J. D. B. DEBOW.

UNITED STATES—1854.

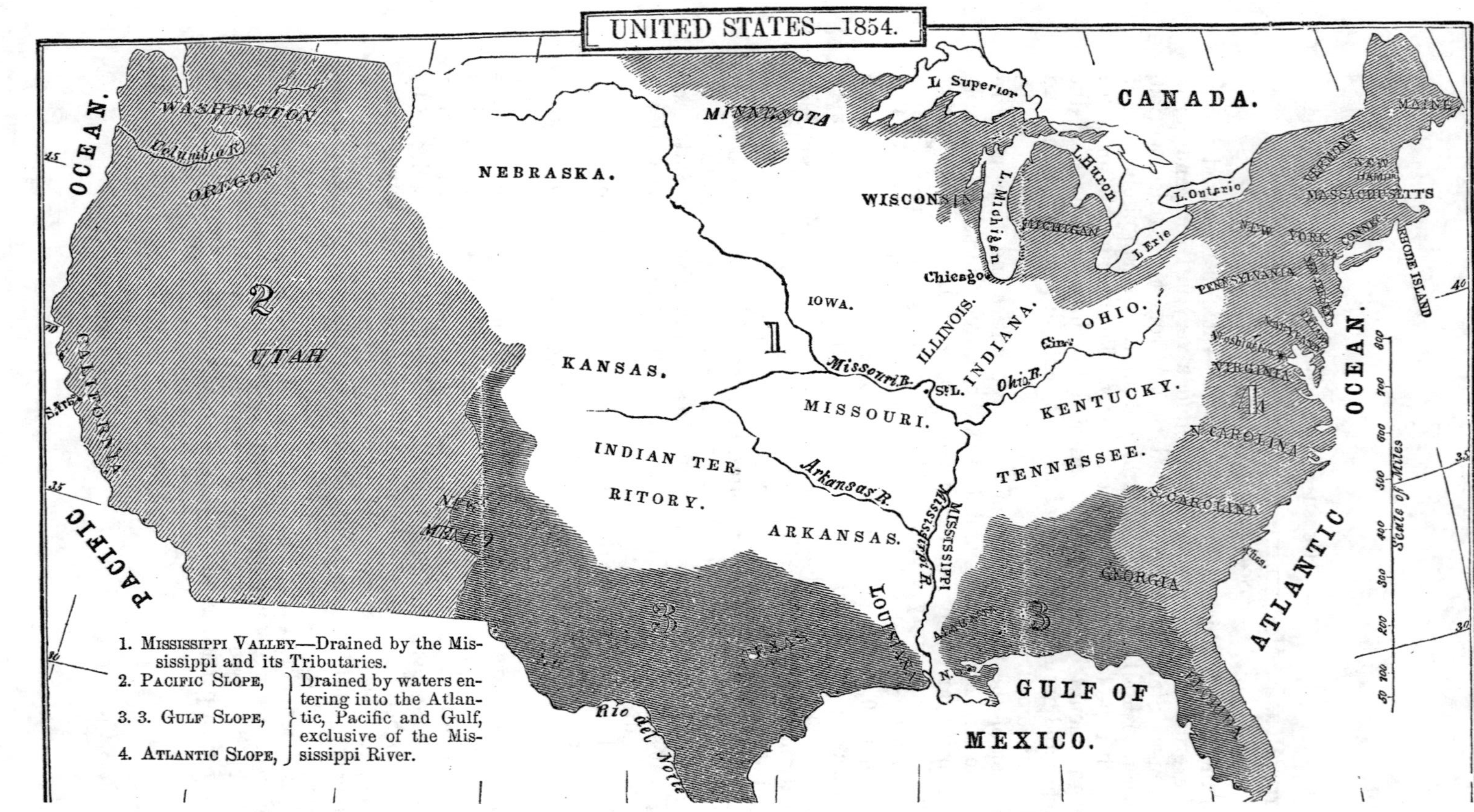

1. Mississippi Valley—Drained by the Mississippi and its Tributaries.
2. Pacific Slope,
3. 3. Gulf Slope,
4. Atlantic Slope,

} Drained by waters entering into the Atlantic, Pacific and Gulf, exclusive of the Mississippi River.

INDEX.

INDEX.

INDEX.

INTRODUCTORY REMARKS.

ORIGIN—HISTORY AND USES OF STATISTICAL INVESTIGATIONS—ADVANTAGES OF THE CENSUS—THE UNITED STATES AND FOREIGN CENSUS AND STATISTICAL SYSTEMS—SYSTEMS IN THE SEVERAL STATES AND LARGE CITIES OF THE UNION—STATISTICAL BUREAUS—CENSUS EXPERIENCE AND PROPOSED SCHEDULES FOR FUTURE ENUMERATIONS—CENSUS LEGISLATION AND EXPENDITURE AT EACH PERIOD—MACHINERY OF THE CENSUS OFFICE—FUTURE IMPROVEMENT—MODE OF PUBLISHING THE RESULTS.

In every country, and almost at all periods, the exigencies of revenue or of military service must have rendered occasionally necessary some sort of estimation of the numbers of the people. Among the Greeks and Romans inquiries in regard to population were often pressed to a considerable extent, yet the science of statistics, as now understood, may be said to belong altogether to the present age. Achenwall, of Prussia, who lived about the middle of the last century, has the credit of having given form and name to this important branch of knowledge, and is said to have left the full development of its principles to be carried out by his pupil, Schlözer. Other writers followed each other in rapid succession, until Sir John Sinclair at last introduced the term into Britain, and the Society of Universal Statistics was founded in 1829, in France. The transactions of this Society, arranged under the several divisions, give a better idea of the scope of the science of statistics than could be otherwise expressed. They include—

1*st*. *Physical and Descriptive Statistics*—embracing topography, hydrography, meteorology, population, man physically, hygiene, and the sanitary state. 2*d*. *Positive and Applied Statistics*—embracing animal and vegetable productions, agriculture, industry, commerce, navigation, state of the science, general institutions, literature, language and the fine arts. 3*d*. *Moral and Philosophical Statistics*—including the forms of religious worship, legislative and judicial powers, public administration, finance, the marine, military and diplomacy.

The importance of correct information regarding the age, sex, condition, occupation and numbers of a people, their moral and social state, their education and industry, is now universally recognized among the enlightened of all civilized nations. Where this information can be had for periods running back very far, and for many countries, it furnishes the material for contrasts and comparisons the most instructive, and for deducing the soundest rules in the administration of Government, or in promoting the general welfare of society.

Statistics are far from being the barren array of figures ingeniously and laboriously combined into columns and tables, which many persons are apt to suppose them. They constitute rather the ledger of a nation, in which, like the merchant in his books, the citizen can read, at one view, all of the results of a year or of a period of years, as compared with other periods, and deduce the profit or the loss which has been made, in morals, education, wealth or power.

Are the results objected to upon the score of being imperfect, or in some respects unreliable? Let the objection be admitted, and is it necessary to grope in absolute darkness because it is impossible to have absolute truth? If the census of a people, for example, cannot be received implicitly, does it become proper and right to have no data whatever? Are men acting upon this principle in other matters? Is not a large and valuable mass of human knowledge derived entirely from approximations? If there cannot be faith in the results of a census, can there be in those of imports and of exports, returned at the custom-houses, or by the registries of the several ports, or in the returns of the popular elections? Without doubt the degree of accuracy of a census may be very great or very small—dependent upon the pains which has been bestowed, the qualifications of the parties employed in taking, or afterwards combining it, and the intelligence of the masses of the people. The chances of error are countless at almost every step. In Europe, where the system is thought to be comparatively perfect, and where the best talent is always employed, the chances of error will be as great, perhaps from the want of general intelligence in the people and in their fear of taxation, as in the United States, where the people are generally informed, but the census system is bad, and the enumerators are worse. Hence there is little practical difference in the results in either case. Moreover, the imperfections of the census are believed to be exaggerated. All intention to deceive must of course be excluded, and a faithless performance of duties can be easily detected by the exposure to the public view, of the returns in the several neighborhoods where they are made, which is invariably required. There is, besides, an equal chance that errors will compensate or balance each other, and those that remain will not greatly impair the result. Admitting the latter to be the case, and that it is a question, what proportion the children of a State, under one year of age, bear to the whole population of that State? Let the population be 1,000,000, and the children 25,000, or two and a half per cent. If the marshal has entered 500 of these children erroneously—which would be a great amount of error certainly—the ratio will only be affected to the extent of the one twentieth of one per cent.; a very trifling fraction. However deficient the census system of the United States has been, any one who will take the trouble to compare the results upon certain points, will perceive how strikingly and truly the several enumerations harmonize—a confirmation, at least, of their general accuracy, whatever the particular errors which may be pointed out.*

An enlightened people will not object to the apparent exposure of their affairs, involved in a census, (that exposure, after all, amounting to very little, since the Government is pledged against the use of the material, except in the aggregate, and merging all individuality,) when satisfied that the great object is the promotion of the public welfare, and is disconnected from any plans of legislative spoliation. This is evidenced in the fact that every census has descended into more particulars than the last, and found the people more willing to respond. The publication and general comprehension of the results increase the public zest for more. This will be seen hereafter in referring to the State and city census, and other local reports, becoming every where so frequent and so full. Satisfied that there is a great purpose to be subserved, the people always acquiesce. Though seemingly impertinent, at first sight, to be interrogated in regard to their age, their place of birth, their occupation, and degree of education, if they are married or single, if there is a deaf or a dumb person in their family, if they own real estate, if they cultivate land, and how much of it, what crops they are producing, if any of their household have been born or have died within the year, yet, when twenty millions of people have responded to these questions, and their answers have been digested into tables, and made public, the idea of impertinence falls at once to the ground. By questions, such as these, they perceive, can be ascertained

* The remarkable uniformity in the proportions of the sexes as shown in the table on page 49, is an illustration in point. For every 100 males in 1790, there were 96.4 females; in 1800, 95.3; 1810, 96.2; 1820, 96.8; 1830, 96.4; 1840, 95.6; and in 1850, 95; the results of immigration, composed as it is largely of males, being exactly indicated.

for cities and States, the proportion of the sexes to each other, indicating the capacity for industry or development; the productive power, duration of life, degree of health or mortality, the migration of population and its homogeneous or heterogeneous elements, the occupations which yield the greatest and the least results, or are more favorable to longevity, the extent of education imparted, or to which it is neglected, how the soil is parcelled out, in what cultivated and how much is the distributive share of wealth to each individual, in the several localities. The examples are few out of a multitude presenting themselves. Who will then deny its great importance to information of this character, or, refuse his cheerful co-operation in obtaining it? The extensive publication given to the results of the present census—320,000 bound volumes having been already ordered at different times, to say nothing of countless other abstracts—will take a copy into almost every family, where it must become, to some extent, the subject of conversation and discussion. It is not easy to estimate the effect which this will have in diffusing true notions of the nature and character of the census, and in inciting the people and the enumerators to greater alacrity and more accuracy in their future reports.

In the United States a general census has been taken every tenth year, beginning with 1790, the leading results of which are digested in the present volume. The *first* of this series included but five particulars—the white males over and under 16, the white females, the slaves, and all other free persons, "except Indians, not taxed." The *second*—1800—retained the same divisions of class, and distinguished the white males and females into ages, under 10, between 10 and 16, 16 and 26, 26 and 45, and of 45 and over. The *third*—1810—was identical with the second, but a schedule of manufactures was ordered to be added, showing the capital, labor, material used in manufactures, and the kind and value of the product. The *fourth*—1820—divided the whites as the second had done, but added a column for the white males between 16 and 18, and another for foreigners not naturalized, with blanks for those of the population employed in agriculture, in commerce, or in manufactures. This census regarded also, for the first time, the ages of the free colored and slaves, male and female; under 14, between 14 and 26, between 26 and 45, and 45 and upwards. A schedule of manufactures, similar to, but an improvement on, that of 1810, was appended. By an oversight the column for "all other persons," by which was previously meant the "free colored," was retained, although this class was specifically mentioned, and the error has given rise to subsequent difficulties. The *fifth* census—1830—divided the white males and females into ages quinquennially until 20, and decennially afterwards to 100, &c.; divided the colored and slaves, male and female, into those under 10, between 10 and 24, 24 and 36, 36 and 55, 55 and 100, 100 and upwards; added columns, for the first time, of white and colored deaf and dumb, under 14 years of age, between 14 and 25, of 25 and upwards, and for the blind in the aggregate; also a column for aliens not naturalized. No returns of manufactures were embraced. The *sixth* census—1840—followed the divisions of age, sex and color in the fifth, and the divisions for the deaf, dumb and blind, but added columns for the insane and idiotic, at public or private charge, the universities and colleges, academies and schools, students and scholars, scholars at public charge, and adult whites who cannot read and write. It also embraced, as a part of the general schedule, more full particulars of industry than had been previously obtained.

These enumerations were published, within one, two, or three years, severally, from the time when they were made, but in such a manner as unfitted them for general use, understanding, or reference, and with very little tabular system and accuracy. A complete set of them does not exist in the public departments at Washington, and one or two are nearly, if not entirely, out of print. A new edition of these decennial reports, uniform with the quarto volume of 1850, considering the heavy outlay they required, and that they are the only existing records of the facts, especially recommends itself. The whole could be embraced in a small type, and by condensation, into a single volume.

The *Seventh* census—or that of 1850—began a new era, by adopting six instead of one or two schedules. The first related to the *Free Inhabitants*, embracing the number of dwellings and families, and introduces the principle of recording the name and sur-name of every free person, old or young, in the Union, with their sex, and exact age, from one month upwards; their color, as white, black, or mulatto; their nativity, as born in the State or in some other State or country, at home or abroad; their condition, as married or single; their education, as attending school in the year, or over 20 years of age and unable to read and write. The deaf and dumb, blind, insane, idiotic, pauper or convict, and the owners of real estate were also noted.

The second schedule, *Slaves*, included the names of slaveholders, the sex, color, and specific age of the *slave*, the fugitive, and manumitted, the deaf and dumb, blind, insane, and idiotic.

The third, *Mortality*, gave the names of such persons as had died within the previous year, their age, sex, color, (white, black or mulatto,) whether free or slave, married or widowed, their specific place of birth, at home or abroad, the month of their decease, the occupation of the person, the duration of the sickness, and the cause of death. Remarks upon topography, &c., accompany these schedules, and were made by the enumerators.

The fourth, *Agriculture*, embraced the name of every farmer or planter, and all of the particulars included in the agricultural tables of this volume.

The fifth, *Manufacturing Industry*, with the name and location of every person or establishment producing over $500 annually; the quantity, kind, and value of raw material used; the motive power, and labor employed, male and female, the rate and amount of wages, the quantity, kind, and value of productions, leaving the marshals to enter them in detail.

The sixth, *Social statistics*, included real and personal estate in each county or town; the several kinds and amounts of taxes levied; the schools, libraries, newspapers; religious, criminal, pauper, and wages statistics as they are now published; and the facts—if the crops were average or not? which of them if any were short, and to what extent, and the average annual crop?

These schedules as well as those of every previous decade may be consulted with the instructions that accompanied them, by reference to the introduction of the Quarto Census, where they are collected and published; nearly all the points of instruction have however, been referred to in their proper places in the present volume.

Objections were raised in 1840 to the searching nature of the industrial investigations, and several counties in Virginia, Georgia, Alabama, and Louisiana, as there was no penalty attached, refused peremptorily to answer them. It was asked by a leading journal "Is this federal prying into the domestic economy of the people a precursor to direct taxes? Is nothing to escape its inquisitors or its tax gatherers? Is it worthy of the dignity and high functions of the federal government to pursue such petty investigations?" Such objections were rarely raised in 1850, and in but two or three cases was it necessary to call in the services of the district attorney to enforce the requisitions of the law.

The schedule of the census of 1840 originated in Congress, and was carried through without opposition, upon a suggestion of the President in his annual message, that "the decennial enumerations might be extended so as to embrace authentic statistical returns of the great interests especially entrusted to or necessarily affected by the legislation of Congress."

As the time for taking the last census approached, the whole subject began to be agitated again in Congress. It was proposed at the session of 1848 to revive the schedules of 1840, omitting only the minute, and as it was thought, objectionable inquiries. Against such a course protests were made by statisticians in and out of Congress, and N. Capen of Massachusetts, suggested the appointment of commissioners for taking the census, and in a letter to a senator from Massachusetts published among the official documents, recommended that a board of inquiry be appointed to examine and report upon the particulars which should properly be embraced, sketching himself some of the leading outlines. The act of 3d March, 1849, establishing the Census Board was the result. Mr. Shattuck, of Boston, made, also, a similar suggestion to the board when constituted. In his own language:

* * "A Central Board of three persons, as Commissioners, should be organized at Washington. It might be denominated the Central Statistical Department, or Bureau, or Commission, or any other appropriate name. These men should be appointed not for their political opinions, but for their scientific attainments and knowledge of the matters they are to investigate. They should have the whole management of planning and carrying into execution all matters relating to the Census. Similar Commissions, should be appointed by this Central Board, with the consent of the governors of each state, of three competent persons in each state; and this state commission should appoint district commissions in their state, and see that all the facts sought should be obtained in their respective states and districts. By this machinery a more perfect collection of facts could be obtained than in any other way. The National, State, and District Statistical Bureaus, acting in concert with each other, would act intelligently and cheaply, and would accomplish far more and with greater accuracy than by any plan heretofore adopted."

The Census Board consisted of the Secretary of State, the officer previously entrusted exclusively with the census, the Postmaster General, as it was conceived possible the machinery of the Post Office Department might prove adequate to the requisitions of the census, or at least greatly auxiliary, and the Attorney General whose legal advice would at times be necessary. There was then no Department of the Interior, to which when created the whole charge of the work was entrusted. A secretary was appointed, who remained in charge of the census over three years, preparing several reports, of which large editions were published.

At the ensuing session of Congress a special committee upon the census was raised in the Senate which went to work assiduously in preparing the schedules, unassisted as they alleged by any suggestions from the board, but with some unofficial ones from its secretary. Pending the discussion upon the plan which the committee proposed, another was submitted by the board, very full in its details and embracing some of the same points, which was adopted. Mr. Shattuck, who was invited to visit Washington near the close of the year 1849, gave the benefit of his great experience and statistical knowledge in the preparation of the plan, (being afterwards assisted in the same labors by Archibald Russell of New York.) The general act for taking the census was passed substantially as it was drawn up by him, except as to the rate of compensation and the ratio of representation. The instructions to marshals, prepared by him, were also adopted, but with a few modifications. The feature of recording the name and description of every person enumerated, was proposed by this gentleman, and was first adopted in the Boston census of 1845. Neither the blanks for "real estate owned," nor for married within the year, were his. He drew up the mortality schedule, by request, though against his own advice,* and also furnished the schedule of social statistics and that in part of slaves.

* See Shattuck's Report on the State Census of Massachusetts, 1850—also Sanitary report of Massachusetts, 1850, pp. 126-133, appendix 375. A more limited census had been originally recommended by this gentleman, Dr. Jarvis, and others in a memorial to Congress. The Census Board reported to Congress, March 19, 1850, as follows:

"At the request of the secretary of the board, during the autumn we invited the assistance of two other persons, who had bestowed much attention on the subject, to an examination of the work and its arrangement previous to its final adoption; and after a full consideration of all their suggestions, we then agreed upon a full set of schedules, and ordered them to be delivered to the printer we had employed for the purpose of printing them.

"After thus terminating our labors, in obedience to the law, we requested the persons we had employed to assist us, in connexion with the secretary of the board, to submit for our approval a set of instructions to the marshals, necessary to carry into effect the objects we had in view in making the schedules."

The plan of the Senate committee was very extended, embracing ten schedules and a multitude of particulars. Some reference to it may be of future value.

SCHEDULE 1. *Those engaged in Agriculture*—embracing the head of the family's name, his place of birth, if out of the state; his male and female apprentices, those in his house who cannot read and write, and those of all of the usual ages, under 5, of 5 and 10, &c., male and female, and the ages of the male and female slaves: Heads of families of the free colored, their ages and sex as of the white: Aliens in the family, name of the head, male aliens under and over 21 years of age, female aliens under and over 18 years of age.

SCHEDULE 2. *Those in Mechanic Arts*—the same particulars as in agriculture, except that the name of the business was added, the number of journeymen, the yearly wages paid to them, the number of laborers engaged in the shop or business, the stone, brick or wood houses wholly or partially built.

In regard to the six schedules which were at last adopted, though they are conceded to be a great improvement upon any previous ones, several particulars were omitted, which ought to have been included, at the expense of others much less important. The adoption of so many schedules, whatever merits they individually have, was calculated to make the work unnecessarily cumbersome and expensive, without securing by any means greater or more certain results. On the contrary, it precluded the possibility of some very valuable comparisons, and made unattainable information easily secured by another arrangement. For example: if a slave existed in a non-slaveholding State, he would not by the schedules be returned, nor can any of the facts relating to slaveholders now be ascertained—such as, their nativity, age, occupation, education, &c.; nor can the deaths of individuals be associated with families, and with the remainder living in families, without almost impracticable labor. The schedules are otherwise admirable.

It will not be out of place to suggest, as the result of experience acquired during eighteen months familiarity with the returns, an outline for the next decennial census, which may possibly afford some aid also to those who are engaged in framing the forms for State and city enumerations, now becoming almost annual.

It is suggested that there be but two schedules hereafter—one of POPULATION, and the other of PRODUCTION. These, with proper instructions to the enumerators, will include all of the information embraced at present in six, and a great deal besides, in a form much more compact and less expensive.

SCHEDULE 3. *Those engaged in Commerce*—the same particulars as the last, including clerks and the wages paid to them.

SCHEDULE 4. *Those not engaged in Agriculture, Arts, or Commerce*—treated as those in agriculture.

SCHEDULE 5. *The Idiots, Lunatics, Deaf and Dumb, Blind and Paupers*—male or female, their ages, and the age when lunacy was discovered, and the occupation of the party: The sex, age and occupation of Deaf and Dumb and Blind and Idiots. The same for slaves and free colored, and whether the party were supported by public charity, or by friends or by his own means. Paupers, foreign or native not affected as above at public charge in the last year.

SCHEDULE 6. *Agricultural Statistics*—name of the farmer, his improved and unimproved land, his laborers over 15 years old employed in tillage. The other particulars of crops, &c., as in the present volume, except that turnips, indigo, fodder, number of hogs and sheep slaughtered, houses built, were added to the list of products.

SCHEDULE 7. *Manufactures when other power is used than that of the man himself*—name of the owner, president or superintendent; grist mills—number of pairs of stones; saw mills—number of saws employed, quantity of lumber, planks, &c., in feet made per annum; cotton gins; wool carding machines; cotton mills—number of spindles employed, number of bales of cotton annually consumed, quantity of yards made per annum, quantity of cotton goods or number of yards made per annum; mills for the manufacture of wool, pounds of wool of domestic growth annually consumed, pounds of wool of foreign growth annually consumed, quantity of cloth, cassimeres, &c., in yards, made per annum; forges and rolling mills—quantity of blooms made per annum, quantity of bar iron made per annum, quantity of railroad iron, quantity of boiler iron, quantity of other description of iron; anthracite furnaces; charcoal furnaces—quantity of castings and pig metal made per annum; silk manufactories—quantity of goods produced annually; hemp and flax manufactories—quantity of goods produced annually; founderies, and what articles engaged in manufacturing—quantity of articles and value made per annum; glass works—quantities and kinds and value of glass manufactured per annum, capital invested in the manufactory, dividends declared, number of males employed under 18 years of age, number of males employed over 18 years of age, number of females employed under 15 years of age, number of females employed over 15 years of age, average wages paid to men per annum, average wages paid to boys per annum, average wages paid to women per annum, average wages paid to girls per annum; water, principal agent in propelling machinery, horses ditto, number of horses, mules or oxen employed; locomotive manufactories; machine shops and hands employed and value of annual productions.

SCHEDULE 8. *Mining Interests*—owner, superintendent or manager's name; gold mines—number of laborers employed, quantity of ounces raised preceding year; silver mines—number of laborers employed, quantity of ounces raised; lead mines—number of laborers employed, number of pounds smelted during preceding year, value of the lead per pound at the furnace; copper mines—number of laborers employed, number of pounds made during preceding year, price per pound at the mines; copperas mines—number of laborers employed, number of pounds made during preceding year; salt springs or wells, or furnaces to evaporate sea water—number of hands employed, number of bushels made during preceding year, value per bushel at the furnace; coal mines, (anthracite;) coal mines, (bituminous;) coal mines, (cannel)—cost of machinery in working mines, number of tons raised during preceding year, value per ton at the mine, number of laborers employed.

SCHEDULE 9. *Colleges, &c.*—this schedule adds to the one which was adopted the name of the pastor and the number of male and female communicants of churches, the number of historical societies and of lunatic asylums.

SCHEDULE 10. *Internal Improvements, Railroad, Canals, &c.*—name of improvement, miles finished, cost, locks in line, lift of locks, income from passengers, persons employed, wages paid, dividends, fare per mile, freight per mile.

SCHEDULE I.—POPULATION.	
1.	Dwelling Houses in the order of visitation.
2.	Families in the order of visitation.
3.	Name of every person whose usual place of abode on the first day of June was in this family, or who has died in it in the year preceding such date.
4.	Age of the person.
5.	Sex.
6.	Color—White, Black, Mulatto, or Domesticated Indian. Free or Slave.
7.	Occupation—if a male over 15 years of age.
8.	Relation to the head of the family, as wife, child, apprentice or servant.
9.	Married, unmarried, or widowed.
10.	Married within the year.
11.	Born within the year.
12.	Number of children now living away from the parents.
13.	Number of months attending school or college in the year.
14.	Over 20 years of age and unable to read and write.
15.	Place of birth, in the town, county or State, or in what other State or country, (in the United States or abroad.)
16.	Years resident of present locality—if a foreigner, also the year of immigration to the United States.
17.	If a native voter or naturalized foreigner.
18.	If confined to bed or room by illness, and how long.
19.	Disease, if died within the year.
20.	If Deaf and Dumb, Deaf alone, Blind, Insane or Idiotic, or Pauper, or partially receiving public relief, Pensioner or Convict.
21.	If a Fugitive or Manumitted Slave.
22.	If an owner of real estate and the amount owned.
23.	If the person has built a house during the year, of stone, brick or wood, and its cost.

This schedule condenses three into one: that of Free, of Slaves, and of Deaths. The number of columns and the expense of paper, printing and copying will be reduced one-half or two-thirds, whilst every fact, except only the month of decease, and that may be embraced if necessary, will be included, with a number of additional ones. Every untenanted or unfinished house should be noted upon the margin of the returns, and also such as are used for boarding houses, hotels, asylums, colleges, jails, barracks, etc. Column 3. There will be no greater difficulty in separating the living and the dead upon the returns than is now experienced in separating the deaf and dumb, &c. 4. The ages under one year should be given in months; those between 1 and 3 years in quarters of a year, as recommended by Quetelet; those of 3 years and over in years. 6. The introduction of Slaves and of Indians domesticated does not at all complicate this column. Domesticated Indians are reckoned by the New York census. 8. The omission of this head from the present schedule was a cardinal defect, and closed the door upon a multitude of valuable facts. It is included in the British and Boston census. 9. This column is equally important, and is a new one. 11. Another proposed column, though these facts may be deduced, with some pains, from the column of ages. 12. New, also, and essential to any correct reasonings upon the extent of families, the number of children to each, etc. 14. Perhaps it would be better to indicate every person over 10 years of age who cannot read and write, and then those over 20 can be deduced for comparison with previous returns. 15. Changed from the present so as to denote whether the party was born in the town, city or county of his residence, or in another part of the same State, etc. (embraced in Boston and English census.) 17. Valuable for statistical purposes, and especially so in vital statistics. 17, 18. The United States census of 1820 and 1830 included naturalized foreigners. 18. It might be well to know the number of persons actually confined from illness, as an important element in the sanitary statistics. This column, in case of deceased persons, will show the number of days or months they have been sick. 19. Perhaps it would be better to say died within one month, as it is next to impossible for persons to report from memory facts for a whole year. In this case a separate column for month of decease is obviated. 20. The deaf ought to be taken as well as the deaf and dumb, as explained in this volume. Insane and idiotic should not be separated, as they are popularly confounded; and persons receiving partial relief ought to be distinguished from paupers. Pensioners of the United States, if included as was once or twice done, would put an end to many of the frauds so frequent upon the Government. 23 refers to houses *owned* by the party.

SCHEDULE II.—PRODUCTION.

Name of corporation, company or individual producing articles to the value of $500, on his own account or as employer.	Name of business, manufacture or product, or if engaged in agriculture or farming, etc.	Capital invested in real and personal estate in the business, or disposition, value, and other statistics of land and agriculture.	Raw material used, including fuel, or farming stock.			Kind of motive power, machinery, structure or resource.	Average number of hands employed.		Average wages paid monthly without board.		Annual product.		
			Quantity.	Kind.	Value.		Male.	Female.	Male.	Female.	Quantity.	Kind.	Value.
1.	2.	3.	4.			5.	6.		7.		8.		

The schedule of Industry for 1850, with slight alterations, will answer perfectly for all mechanical, manufacturing, mining, agricultural and commercial interests. The directions should be printed at the top. If the interest be agricultural, under division 3 would be included the acres cultivated, the acres occupied, the new land taken into cultivation, the acres in each of the crops and in pastures, the value of the farm and of its implements and machinery. Under division 4 the number of each description of live stock. Column 5 will show any mills in use on the farm. Column 6, all persons over 12 years of age actually employed on the farm. Column 7, blank on a slave interest. 8 to include *bushels*, *pounds*, &c. of each of the following articles, or any others, (dispensing with hhds., tons and bales, which lead to confusion and incompleteness, as experience has shown,) wheat, rye, corn, oats, rice, tobacco, cotton, wool, peas and beans, Irish potatoes, sweet potatoes, barley, buckwheat, fruit, wine, market gardens, butter, cheese, hay, clover, other grass seed, hops, hemp—dew and water-rotted, flax, flax-seed, silk cocoons, sugar—cane or maple, molasses, beeswax and honey, home-made manufactures, &c.

There is no greater propriety in ruling out separate columns for each agricultural product or article of live stock, than in having such columns for the articles of raw material used, or of annual products in the manufacturing schedule. There were no such columns in that schedule, and aggregates from the returns are as simple and as easily comprehended without them. All that is necessary is to print at the head of the schedules a list of such articles as the enumerators will be instructed to call over. A great many columns will increase the space to be occupied, and increase also the chances of error by making it more probable that facts will fall out of their proper division. Not one man in fifty will furnish an entry for half of the blanks in the present agricultural schedule.*

These schedules include all that at present require six, excepting only the valuation of real and personal estate, the amount of taxes, the cost of pauperism, and the average crop per acre; facts which an intelligent superintendent could procure easily from the State reports or from correspondence with the county officers, as has been done before with but little expense. The schools, colleges, &c., and their means of support, can all be obtained when the schoolmaster is called upon for enumeration, or when the school or college is visited. The entries may be made upon the back of the returns. If a private teacher, and not a school teacher, the fact should be stated. Facts for churches can be obtained when the clergyman is called upon, as also for Sunday school scholars and libraries. Those for newspapers and periodicals, together with a copy of the paper, on calling upon the editor: from librarians obtain the number of volumes. Particulars are thus obtained for the British census and the difficulties which present themselves, (such as a clergyman with several churches or a church with several clergymen, &c.,) can be easily obviated by careful and well digested instructions. "Public paupers" and "criminals," are all in schedule 1, and arranged much better. The "cost of labor" "Seasons," etc., are in schedule 2.

But however perfect may be the schedules of a census, if a corresponding perfection is not found in the machinery for taking it in the field, and for aggregating and combining it, and deducing the results in the office, little advantage will be gained upon the score of accuracy or of sound science. These two subjects, therefore—the enumerators and collators, will receive a moment's attention.

The Enumerators. The persons who have been entrusted with the work in the United States at every census, have been, in general, found (so low was the rate of compensation,) among those who were willing to undertake it, rather than among those who would have been selected for their especial fitness. Political service has also entered into the element of qualification. That the latter should have great weight, is not surprising, considering how the appointments are provided for, but so ample was the remuneration in 1850 that capacity might well have been secured. An examination of the returns and the correspondence of the office will

* Americans resident abroad should be ascertained through the State Department. Circumstances giving a temporary enlargement to the population of a neighborhood, such as the construction of a rail road, canal, etc. ought also to be noted. In many of the old and thickly settled States, the English plan of enumeration in a single day, and by means of householder's schedules, left in advance to be filled up by heads of families, on the day preceding the census is practicable, and recommends itself for accuracy and perhaps for economy. The time is very far off, it is feared, when it can be applied with any advantage for the general census throughout all the States and Territories of the Union.

show that capacity was as often the exception as the rule. It would be better to entrust the work to the regular officers of each county, employed by them for assessments and taxation purposes, or in general, for taking the census as will be seen hereafter, provided for by local authority. There are no counties without such officers, and it may be safely assumed that if not always among the most educated, they will at least have the advantage of some previous familiarity with the business upon which they are employed and recognize an accountability that may affect their future positions. If the fact however explained, that these persons are a part of the recognized tax machinery, might be supposed to interfere with their receiving correct returns, the recourse must then be had to a better system of appointments requiring proof of education and experience and some general knowledge of statistical investigations. In Great Britain the census has been entrusted to the overseers of the poor, the parochial school masters, or to the office of the Registrar-General and his subordinates, all of them permanent.

The Office. Unless there is machinery in advance at the seat of Government no census can ever be properly taken and published. There is a peculiar education required for these labors which neither comes from zeal or genius, but is the result only of experience. They are the most irksome and trying imaginable, requiring inexhaustible patience and endurance, and baffling almost every effort after accuracy. Long familiarity can alone secure system, economy and certainty of result. This office machinery exists in all European countries where statistics are the most reliable, but there has been none of it in the United States. Each census has taken care of itself. Every ten years some one at Washington will enter the hall of a department, appoint fifty or a hundred persons under him, who, perhaps, have never compiled a table before, and are incapable of combining a column of figures correctly. Hundreds of thousands of pages of returns are placed in the hands of such persons to be digested. If any are qualified it is no merit of the system. In 1840 returns were given out by the job to whoever would take them. In 1850, such was the pressure of work, that almost any one could at times have had a desk. Contrast this with the English system and reflect that one individual, as hereafter remarked, presided over the census of 1801, '11, '21 and '31. In Washington, as soon as an office acquires familiarity with statistics, and is educated to accuracy and activity, it is disbanded, and even the best qualified employee is suffered to depart. The government may rely upon paying heavily for the experience which is being acquired. Even the head of the office, whatever his previous training, must expect, if faithful, to learn daily; and it is not going too far to say that a matter of one or two hundred thousand dollars is the difference between the expense which a census would cost, conducted by an office which has had the experience of a previous one, (even if partly or entirely in new hands, which might often be desirable, since the machinery, as in other offices, would be kept up,) and an office without such experience. This can be demonstrated if required. Half of that amount would sustain an office of several persons from census to census and defray all of the expenses of an annual or biennial report after the closing of the regular one, which itself would be executed with despatch, with greatly less force, and with a more economical and wiser application of labor. The permanent force would have no other interest than the prompt execution of the work.

The establishment of a regular statistical Office is therefore suggested, as a matter of economy, and essential to the proper execution of the census. In it would be collected—and they could be obtained without expense by exchange—official statistical reports, upon any subject whatever, published by every city, town, county, or State in the Union, or in any other part of the world. The absence of such documents in Washington was severely felt during the whole progress of the present census, although the former Superintendent obtained many by a visit to Europe, and others were subsequently sent by Mr. Vattemare, of Paris, and Mr. Hübner, of Berlin, and by the several states and cities which politely furnished such as were especially asked. All of this created labor and delay. The office ought also to be provided with a complete statistical library, and with all the leading statistical journals in the world, together with maps, charts, &c. The returns of immigration and of foreign consuls could be sent to it, especially such as are in answer to circulars that were lately prepared in obedience to a call of Congress. A digest of such material, published annually or semi-annually, in a small and compact volume, would keep up the results of the general census to date, and shed no little light upon the industry and general and comparative wealth of the country. It would have charge of the manuscript volumes of every census, and respond to calls made by Congress in regard to them, or upon other kindred matters. Duties somewhat similar to these were performed by Mr. Porter for the English Government, and a Bureau of Statistics, as will be seen hereafter, exists in most of the European governments..

Such a bureau is recommended, also, in each of the States; and it would be the means of corresponding with the Central office, furnishing very much of the material to be aggregated by it. It has been proposed in South Carolina,* Rhode Island, Virginia, and Illinois, and was actually established in Louisiana,† but failed for the want of adequate legislation, after reports had been published upon about half of the parishes. The city of New York has such a bureau. In every State there are the materials for one with but little expense, if properly organized. The various local census, assessments of property and production, reports on

*A special committee of the legislature of South Carolina, in the session of 1848, after having ably shown in a variety of instances how little information existed in regard to the resources of that State, declare: "There are facts and considerations which, properly exhibited, would prove the necessity of providing some such organization as would lead to a correct understanding of these important matters; and the insufficiency of the matters here presented only serves to show conclusively that we have been heretofore neglectful of those means of information which are calculated to elicit correct apprehensions of our advantages and duties. The establishment of an efficient bureau of statistics will be the means of collecting and disseminating statistical information touching all the interests of the State, of the most valuable kind." The Governor, in his annual message to the legislature of the same State, says, "I recommend the careful collection of statistical information on all the branches of industry. By the possession of facts and materials, lucidly arranged and methodized, we shall be furnished with complete data as to the present state of the population, white and colored, their agriculture, commerce, navigation, manufactures, trade, finance, health, and indeed of whatever may be interesting or instructive."

† The following Circular was prepared by the author of this Report and issued from the Bureau of Statistics of the State of Louisiana: with some modifications it will be applicable to any of the States.

I. Time of *settlement* of your parish or town; dates of oldest land grants; number and condition of first settlers; whence emigrating; other facts relating to settlements and history.

II. *Indian names* in your vicinity; what tribes originally; what relicts or monuments of them; if Indians still in what condition?

III. *Biography*, anecdotes, &c., of individuals distinguished in your vicinity in the past for ingenuity, enterprise, literature, talents, civil or military, &c.

IV. *Topographical description* of your parish, mountains, rivers, ponds, animals, quadrupeds, birds, fishes, reptiles, insects, &c., vegetable growths, rocks, minerals, sand clays, chalk, flint, marble, pit coals, figments, medicinal and poisonous substances, elevation above the sea, nature of surface, forests, or undergrowth, what wells and quality of well water, nature of coasts, does the water make inroads, mineral springs, caves, &c.

V. *Agricultural description* of parish; former and present state of cultivation; changes taking place; introduction of cotton, sugar, rice, indigo, tobacco, grains, fruits, wines, &c., &c.; present products; lands occupied and unoccupied, and character of soil; value of lands; state of improvements; value of agricultural products; horses, cattle, mules, hogs, and whence supplied; profits of agriculture, prices of products; new estates opening; improvements suggested in cultivation and new growths; improvements in communication, roads, bridges, canals, &c.; kind and quantity of timber; fuel, &c.; state of the roads, summer and winter; kind of enclosures, and of what timber; manures; natural and artificial pastures; agricultural implements used; fruit trees, vines and orchards; modes of transportation; extent of internal navigation; levees, &c.; modes of cultivating and manufacturing sugar in use.

VI. Instances of *longevity* and *fecundity;* observations on diseases in your section; localities, healthful or otherwise; statistics of diseases; deaths; summer seats, &c.

VII. *Population* of your parish; increase and progress, distinguishing white and black; Spanish, French, American or German origin; foreigners, classes of population; number in towns; growth of towns and villages, &c.; condition, employment, ages; comparative value of free and slave labor; comparative tables of increase; marriages, births, &c.; meteorological tables of temperature, weather, rains, &c.

VIII. *Education and Religion.*—Advantages of schools, colleges, libraries enjoyed; proportion educated at home and abroad; expense of education; school returns; churches or chapels in parish, when and by whom erected; how supplied with clergy; how supported and attended, oldest interments; church vaults, &c.

IX. *Products in Manufactures and the Arts.*—Kinds of manufactures in parish; persons employed; kind of power; capital; wages; per centum profit; raw material; sugar and cotton; machinery and improvements; kind and value; manufacturing sites, &c.

X. *Commercial Statistics.*—Value of the imports and exports of the State with each of the other States of the Union, as far as any approximation may be made, or data given; growth and condition of towns; increase in towns, &c.

XI. *General Statistics.*—Embracing banking, rail roads, insurances, navigation, intercommunication; learned and scientific societies; crime, pauperism, charities, public and benevolent institutions; militia, newspapers, &c.; application of parish taxes; expenses of roads, levees, &c.; number of suits decided in different courts; expenses and perfection of justice; number of parish officers, lawyers, physicians, &c.

XII. Date, extent, consequences, and other circumstances of droughts, freshets, whirlwinds, storms, lightnings, hurricanes, or other remarkable physical events, in your section, from remote periods; other meteorological phenomena; changes in climate, &c., &c.

XIII. Literary productions emanating from your neighborhood; your associations, if any; what manuscripts, public or private records, letters, journals, &c., or rare old books, interesting in their relation to the history of the State, are possessed by individuals within your knowledge.

XIV. Add any other matters of interest.

schools, asylums, penitentiaries, boards of health and commerce, furnish abundant details. Hundreds of other facts could be ascertained when the local assessments are made, with little if any more cost. The State and city census should be made to correspond, as far as possible, with the national, and be provided for at some intervening period. At present they are often taken in the same year, thus entailing a great waste of labor. The time is at hand when the several State governments should look to this matter; and as it was deemed important for European statisticians to meet in convention in order to bring about uniformity in their several systems, the States should also secure uniformity. A meeting of persons properly appointed by each, and fitted for the duties, would be the means of maturing some practical plan of co-operation.

In 1845 the subject of a statistical bureau was before Congress, and two very able and elaborate reports were made in its advocacy. A bill was introduced providing for the collection of material relating to all the great Industrial interests of the country to be published in an annual report by the Secretary of the Treasury, who was authorized to constitute an office of several persons for the purpose. The Secretary himself recommended that authority be given him to appoint a chief of the bureau with an appropriate salary, two assistants, and one clerk. "A statistical bureau," he says, "properly organized and supported, will be able to respond promptly and correctly to all calls by Congress for information on statistical subjects, save great waste of time and money, and furnish information highly interesting and useful to the great body of the people." The result of the movement, however, was a failure, in consequence of a single clerk only, with a small salary, being detached for the service.

What the agricultural department of the Patent Office is doing for agriculture, it is proposed that this office shall do for the great Industrial interests; gathering and combining their results, and developing them in connexion with the movement of population, and the growth or decline of cities and states.

Before closing these remarks, it will be proper to show what is now accomplished by the several foreign and State governments, as well as by the larger cities, in regard to statistical investigations. The information will be valuable, and has been obtained from official reports; and for our country, from replies made to circular letters directed to the Secretaries of State and leading geologists and statisticians in every part of the Union.

The decennial system of enumeration adopted in the United States has been imitated by *Great Britain,* beginning with the census of 1801. In *Denmark* a statistical central commission exists, which published eighteen large volumes of statistics between 1835 and 1849; subsequently ten volumes have been published by a central bureau. In *Bavaria* there is a statistical bureau. In *Austria* one was established in 1828, and besides the yearly statistics, there have been published in the last four years monthly and quarterly reports of foreign statistics, including the report of consuls. In *France* every ministry publishes its own statistics, though some have special bureaus. Those of Finance and Commerce have published thirteen volumes on finance, population, industry, &c. Individual effort is combined with official by establishing in every district statistical commissions which fill up the blanks, &c. To the commissions are assigned the reports on population, foundlings, beggars, &c. A census has been published every five years beginning with 1841. In *Saxony* a statistical bureau exists which has published three volumes. In *Spain* the census is rarely taken; M. Madoz prepared a Statistical and Geographical Dictionary of Spain in sixteen volumes by sending commissions into every part of the country. There are frequent statistical reports in relation to *Cuba.* In *Sardinia,* in 1820, a commission to collect statistics was established, with which thirty-seven juntas, of six members each, corresponded; four large volumes have been published. In *Holland* a statistical bureau was established in 1826, which published several volumes. A census was published in 1840; there is now no general bureau. In *Wurtemburg* a bureau has published thirty-three volumes. In *Switzerland* detailed reports have been received since 1830 from nearly all the cantons. *Zurich* has a census of population made two hundred and twenty years ago. In *Portugal* there was a census in 1838, 1843, 1849, and 1851. In *Russia* there is a system of registration of births, &c., and occasionally a census has been ordered. In *Sweden* a board of table commission digests the returns of population supplied by the clergy. The census considers the people as having subsistence, or less or more than subsistence. In *Norway* there is a census by the magistrates in the towns, and rectors in the country; and inquiries extend to productions, occupations, deaf and dumb, &c. The *Prussian* census is taken every three years; that of 1849 gives ages, sex, faith, occupation, deaf and dumb, &c., education, schools, churches, asylums, dwellings, and families. There are lists of population in Prussia running back to 1748. In 1805 a statistical bureau was established, and eleven volumes have been published by it, as, also, every fortnight a statistical journal. In *Belgium* the town and country population are distinguished; the sex, ages, married, widowed, occupation, faith, language, number of floors or parts of the house, gardens, protection against fire, degree of instruction, &c. The early population of *England* was in much dispute until Mr. Rickman, in 1836, addressed a letter to the clergy and obtained their returns as far back as 1570. The census of 1801, 1811, 1821, and 1831, were each superintended by Mr. Rickman, clerk of the House of Commons, and the business of the enumeration was conducted by the overseers of the poor in England and Wales, and the parochial schoolmasters in Scotland. In 1841 and 1851 the duty devolved upon the Registrar-General and his subordinates. The census was taken in one day, and in 1851 employed 38,740 persons as enumerators.

The first census of Great Britain included the sex, but not the age; also the number of houses and the occupations; the second made some improvements in the mode of recording the occupations; the third carried out the plan, but distinguished the ages quinquennially and decennially; the fourth effected important changes in the mode of ascertaining occupations, (a subject full of difficulty at all times,) calculated areas, &c.; the fifth embraced the general features of the sixth and last, which is worthy of minute consideration.

Of the sixth census of Great Britain, 1851, four bulky quarto volumes have been published by the Registrar-General, Major Graham, assisted by Dr. Farr and Horace Mann. Each of the fourteen divisions of the empire is prepared separately, and is illustrated by handsome district and county maps and other drawings, indexes, &c. The volumes include the number of the people, distinguishing male and female; the number of houses occupied, unoccupied, and building; the statistics of public worship, with a condensation of every previous census. In other volumes the ages of the population will be given, their birth-place, condition as regards marriage and occupation, the returns of schools, colleges, and other institutions; the number of blind, deaf and dumb, etc.

"The inquiries undertaken at the census of 1851 were of a far more extensive character than those pursued at any previous enumeration, for it was resolved to exhibit not only the statistics of parishes, and of parliamentary and municipal boroughs, but also of such other large towns in England and Scotland as appeared sufficiently important for separate mention, and the statistics of all the ecclesiastical districts and new ecclesiastical parishes which, during the last forty years, had been created in England and Wales. In addition, also, to the inquiry concerning the occupation, age, and birth-place of the population, it was determined to ascertain various relationships, such as husband, wife, son, daughter,—the civil condition, as married, unmarried, widower or widow,—and the number of blind, or deaf and dumb. Moreover, the design was formed of collecting statistics as to the accommodation afforded by the various churches and other places of public worship throughout the country, and the number of persons generally frequenting them; also as to existing educational establishments, and the actual number of scholars under instruction.

The local machinery by which the objects thus contemplated were to be obtained, differed considerably in England and Scotland. In England and Wales the *registration districts*, which, for the most part, are conterminous with the *unions*, were made available for enumerating the population. Of these districts there were 624, each having a superintendent registrar; and these were divided into 2,190 sub-districts, each having a local registrar of births and deaths. Under the supervision of their 624 superintendents, the 2,190 registrars were directed to form their sub-districts into *enumeration districts*, according to certain instructions.

The number of such enumeration districts in England and Wales was 30,610, each district being the portion assigned to one enumerator, who was required to complete his enumeration in one day.

In Scotland, which is, unfortunately, without any system of registration, the census was taken through the agency of the sheriffs of counties, and the provosts, or other chief magistrates of royal and parliamentary burghs. The sheriffs generally assigned their functions to the sheriff's substitute, who appointed a fit person, generally the parochial schoolmaster, in each parish, to divide it into enumeration districts, and to superintend the proceedings of the census therein. The same course was adopted by the provosts of burghs within their respective jurisdictions, which, for the occasion included the *parliamentary* limits of the burgh in cases where that boundary extended beyond the royalty. The number of parishes in Scotland including those in royal and parliamentary burghs, were 1,010, and that number of dividers, or superintendents were appointed. The number of enumeration districts formed by them throughout Scotland was 7,873.

In the Islands of the British seas dividers of parishes were appointed, in like manner, by the respective Lieutenant-Governors, and 257 enumeration districts were similarly formed.

Public institutions, such as work-houses, prisons, asylums, hospitals, and the like, were treated as districts of themselves, provided they contained upwards of 200 inmates.

In this manner the whole surface of Great Britain and of the small adjacent islands was divided into suitable districts, and an equal number of enumerators appointed. Thus provision was made for obtaining an account of all persons residing on *land* within the above named territory, on the night of the 30th March.

The first step taken by the enumerators was to deliver to every occupier of a house or tenement a *householder's schedule.* Upon this schedule inquiry was made as to the name, relation to head of family, condition, sex, age, occupation and birth-place of every person in Great Britain, and also as to how many of them were blind, or deaf and dumb. For the use of the poorer native population of Wales, a certain number of forms were printed in the language of that country. The total number of schedules forwarded from the Census Office was 7,000,000, weighing some 40 *tons,* or if the blank enumeration books and other forms are included, upwards of 52 tons. The schedule was to be filled up on the night named. No one present on that night was to be omitted, and no person absent was to be included, except *miners, potters,* and other work people usually engaged at their labor during the night, and regularly returning home in the morning; or *policemen* and others on night duty. Persons *travelling* were enumerated at the hotels or houses at which they arrived on the following morning.

At the same time that these schedules were distributed, the enumerators delivered forms for collecting information respecting places of worship, scholastic establishments, and miscellaneous institutions, but it was optional with the respective parties to decline making these returns if they thought proper.

When a house was uninhabited, or in progress of building, the enumerators made a note of such a case upon the schedule last collected, by which means the unoccupied houses and houses in course of erection, were enumerated. The number of *inhabited* houses were indicated by the number of householder's schedules filled up.

Having collected all the schedules, filling up those which the parties neglected or were unable to fill, and copied them into books prepared on an uniform plan, the enumerators summed the various totals in their respective districts. The totals thus obtained expressed the number of persons who were *inmates of dwelling-houses* on the night of the census, with the special addition of certain classes on night duty; but several classes had yet to be enumerated, viz., the persons who, on the night named, slept or abode in barges, or boats remaining stationary on canals or small streams; in barns, sheds, and the like; and in tents or in the open air. The number of these in each district were estimated by the respective enumerators; the estimate, however, was not to include people in coasting or other sea-going vessels, as they would be dealt with by other means yet to be described. Where, for some extraordinary reason, a large number of persons belonging to a neighborhood were absent from it, or a large number of strangers were present, the enumerator was required to note the fact on the return.

The enumerators were allowed one week for the transcription of the contents of the householder's schedules into the enumeration book, and for the completion of the various summaries and estimates. The schedules and book, together with the returns relating to schools and places of worship, were then forwarded to the respective registrars, and the duties of the 38,740 enumerators terminated. The census returns were now in the hands of 3,220 registrars, or dividers of districts.

The registrars immediately commenced a careful and systematic examination and revision of the documents described, directing their attention, according to instructions, to nine specially defined points in respect to them. They then prepared a summary of the statements of the enumerators in their respective districts, and transmitted them, together with the enumeration books, to the superintendent-registrar, for a further revision by that officer, forwarding the householders' schedules and returns for places of worship and schools direct to the census office. With the completion of these duties, for which a fortnight was allowed, the functions of the 3,220 registrars, or dividers of districts, ceased. The summaries and enumeration books (as far as England and Wales were concerned) were now in the hands of 624 superintendent-registrars.

The chief duties of the superintendant-registrars were to expedite the investigation, but they had also further to revise the summaries and enumeration books, and to transmit them to the Census Office, there to undergo a still further revision before the commencement of the abstracts.

A complete enumeration was thus effected of all persons resident upon the *land* of Great Britain, and on canals and small streams; but, as before mentioned, an important portion of the population remained yet to be reached, viz., persons on board vessels in harbors and navigable rivers, and those at sea in ships belonging either to the royal navy or to the merchant service. As, however, only a certain portion of the persons on board vessels can be properly described as *residents in the country*, those only who slept on board vessels actually lying in harbor, or in the navigable rivers of the interior, on the night of the 30th of March, were included in the population of Great Britain; but the numbers of those at sea in vessels engaged in the home trade; those absent in ships bound to foreign parts; and those in the royal navy, were recorded as valuable collateral information. Considerable arrangements were requisite to enemerate these.

The enumeration of persons on board vessels in harbors, and in the navigable rivers of the interior, was accomplished by the officers of the customs. The officers of the respective ports left a schedule on board every ship in port or in dock in Great Britain and Ireland, on the night of the census, and on the following morning collected the returns, filled up by the respective masters. Ships engaged in the home trade, and being *at sea* on the night of the census, were supplied with forms either before their departure or on their return, which were collected as they arrived in British ports. The ports on the coasts of the United Kingdom are 122 in number, and are subdivided into 253 sub-ports. The seamen abroad on the night of the 30th of March, in vessels belonging to the British merchant service, were traced to all parts of the world by means of the registry of merchant seamen, and enumerated from the lists under the superintendence of the Registrar of merchant seamen. The seamen in the royal navy and the royal marines were returned by the officers in command, in conformity with instructions issued by the Lords of the Admiralty.

By the machinery explained, all that was necessary in regard to the census of Great Britain was accomplished; but further valuable returns were obtained, presenting a view, in a collective form, of certain important *classes* of the community already enumerated among the general population; as, for instance, the army at home and in the colonies, or on board ship *in transitu;* half-pay officers and pensioners; the civil service; the civilians and European troops in the East India Company's service, and British subjects of European origin not in the Company's service, the latest returns of the population of the colonies; and through the intervention of the Secretary of State for Foreign Affairs, the number of British subjects in the several States of Belgium, France, Greece, Russia, Sardinia, Saxony, Turkey, the two Sicilies, China, Persia, Egypt and Mexico.

In two months from the taking of the census, the householders' schedules, amounting to about 4,300,000 distinct returns, and the enumeration books, nearly 39,000 in number were received at the census office; and the result of the enumeration being obtainable from the *summaries* forwarded with the books, a *rough* statement of the total population and number of houses was transmitted on the 7th of June, ten weeks from the night of the census, to the Secretary of State, and at once made public.

With the view to secure accuracy in the census, it was considered an indispensable process to examine every total and summary throughout the enumerators' returns; accordingly a minute revision of the whole was undertaken, involving the examination and totaling of more than 20 *millions* of entries, contained on upwards of 1,250,000 pages of the enumerators' books; and thus the figures forming the groundwork of the abstracts to be prepared of the numbers of the people, their occupations, birth-places, and condition as regards marriage, were finally settled and determined." [See Compendium of British Census.]

Having taken a rapid survey of the United States and European census and statistical system, some remarks will be appropriate upon that of the several States and cities of the Union.

Alabama.—There is a census every six years, the last being in 1850, which cost $9,594, and was taken by persons appointed by the court of each county. Assessments are made every year. Reports on penitentiary and other subjects annual. Explorations have been made by Mr. Tuomey and Mr. Bromby, upon the inexhaustable coal fields of the State, and others by Mr. Hale, of Mobile. Traces of copper, sulphurate of lead and antimony were discovered.

Arkansas.—A census every four years; last in 1854, and embraced population divided into sex and certain ages; acres in cotton and grain, production of cotton, wheat, corn and oats. Cost of census $10,000. Assessments annual by sheriffs. Partial geological explorations have been made.

Connecticut.—There is no regular census. Assessments annual by a board of assessors, acting upon the reports of parties; includes real and personal property taxable, annual reports upon banks, deaf and dumb and insane, schools, rail roads,

&c. with great minuteness. Reports upon the geology of the State were made by Professor Percival, and also by Professor Shepard.

California.—A State census was taken, with many particulars, in 1852. Cost $80,000. Another is provided for by law in 1855. The assessment of property annual. Regular reports of hospitals, &c. Geological report of J. B. Trask, published by the Legislature in 1853.

Florida.—Census in every ten years—last 1845; expense $2,237.59; taken by assessors and collectors of counties; includes all classes of population. Assessments annual by regular assessors, and children between five and eighteen ascertained at the same time. Regular reports upon the State lands from State engineer and geologist.

Georgia.—Census every seven years—last in 1852; cost $25,000; embraced white males between six and sixteen, females six and fifteen, total male and female, total colored and slave, families, deaf, dumb, blind, lunatics, &c. Population returned 935,000, exclusive of three counties. Assessments annual through tax receivers. Biennial reports by the governor on State institutions. Education reports annual. Census takers appointed by county courts. An appropriation was made many years ago for a geological survey under Dr. Cotting, which was, however, not carried through. A partial report was printed, but not circulated. It is said a granite vein penetrates and in some places passes through the gneiss, mica and talcose slates in Columbia county about six miles above Richmond, and from this point to the south-eastward gneiss, mica slate, talcose slate and chloride slate formations exist. On these rest beds of clay, underlaid with beds of gravel. Animal remains occur lower in the valley. Fine particles of gold have been found in the gravel beds. Iron and manganese are the predominating colorings in the sand and gravel. The slate contains veins of arroganite, beds of spidote and small beds of limestone with specimens of sulphuret of iron and sulphuretted copper.

Iowa.—Census every two years by the constitution—latest in 1852 and 1854; expense paid by counties; taken by township assessors, who assess property every year. Annual reports upon education, &c. Last census embraced males and females, voters, militia, foreigners not naturalized, deaf, dumb, blind, &c. Each town and village to be separated. For the geology of Iowa, see Owen's report on the Northwest.

Illinois.—Census every ten years—last in 1845. Cost $9,738; taken by commissioners appointed by county courts. Assessments of personal property annual, of real, biennial. Regular reports upon education, &c. A geological survey is now in progress, with an appropriation of $10,000, under Dr. J. G. Norwood, and has extended over a considerable portion of the State. The work of Dr. Owen may also be consulted. A survey of Northern Illinois some years ago was published in Silliman's Journal.

Indiana.—Census every six years—last in 1853; cost about $4,000. Taken by townships. Assessors include white males over 21. Assessment every year of personal, and every five years of real property. Regular reports from State board of agriculture, and annual returns of farm and mechanical products, also of education, deaf and dumb, blind, insane, &c. The governor has frequently recommended a statistical bureau.

Kentucky.—There is no regular census. Regular reports are made on internal improvements, public institutions, deaf and dumb, blind and lunatic asylums, &c. A geological survey of Kentucky has recently been commenced by Dr. D. D. Owen, the State geologist. Operations were begun in the south-western part of the State, and between the mouth of Tradewater and Anvil Rock, a distance of about eight miles, eleven beds of coal, thick enough to be worked to advantage, have been found. These beds vary from two to five feet. Eleven others have been discovered, varying from four inches to two feet, and Dr. O. thinks, from indications he has seen, that there are probably six other beds from two and a half to five feet thick, lying above the part of the coal measures he has examined.

Louisiana.—A regular census taken—latest in 1853; embracing white, free colored and slave, number of electors, white males between 18 and 45. The State reports of education and of public institutions, banks, internal improvements, hospitals, asylums, annually, are very complete. A bureau of statistics was established a few years ago, as previously adverted to. A geological, botanical and natural history survey of the State was partially made a few years ago at large expense, but the reports were not published and are lost.

Maryland.—There is no stated time for a census. Assessments every ten years provided for by counties and cities. Surveys have been made by Ducatel and Alexander, which were published by the State. There are other reports by Dr. Higgins, State chemist. In regard to the geology of Maryland it is stated that the Eastern Shore is free from mountain chains or elevated table lands, the highest elevation being less than 100 feet above tidewater level, and the entire region almost wholly unexplored. Shell marl abounds everywhere, containing innumerable varieties of fossil shells, tombs of the Moluscæ of a former world (Consult Lyell's map of United States.) Near the estuaries of the Chesapeake are extensive banks of oyster shells. The Eastern Shore is devoid of coal and iron formations and limited in water power, consequently it must remain agricultural. Tradition and observation maintain that the land is being gradually elevated.

Maine.—No census. Assessments at least every ten years by mayors, selectmen and assessors, who note also the males over twenty. Reports upon prisons, reform schools, asylums, &c. The third annual report of the geology of Maine was published in 1839.

Massachusetts.—This State is in advance of every other in the extent and accuracy with which it presses statistical investigations, and is worthy of all praise. Nothing is too minute to escape attention, and among her citizens are the first statisticians of America. Census every ten years, 1840, 1850, &c.; very full; taken by assessors of towns. Assessment every ten years, or as often as the Legislature requires. The last in 1850. Very complete reports are published occasionally upon industry, manufactures, public health, &c., and annually of births, marriages and deaths, hospitals, crime, reform schools, prisons, the poor, children under fourteen supported by towns, agriculture, education, banks, insurance, rail roads, &c. These works are handsomely issued, and are doing much for the advancement of statistical knowledge. An invaluable sanitary survey of the State has been issued.

Michigan.—Census every ten years; last in 1854, taken by marshals appointed by the Executive in each county. Annual assessments by persons properly elected. A manuscript report of survey, by Dr. Houghton, unpublished, is in possession of Prof. Douglass, of the medical college of Ann Arbor.

Missouri.—A census every four years; the last in 1852; cost $7,000. Taken by sheriffs. Annual assessments by regularly elected officers. Regular reports of deaf and dumb, blind and insane, asylums incorporated, internal improvement companies, schools, &c. A geological survey has been ordered but no progress made.

Mississippi.—Census generally every six or eight years; last in 1853. Cost three cents per head. Embraced whites, males and females. Total returned 288,718. Assessment every four years. Number of slaves taxable in 1853, 303,000. Regular reports from universities, penitentiary, &c. The census taken by assessors of counties, includes whole free white. Personal property assessed annually. A geological survey is in progress by Prof. Wailes, State Geologist, and a report will probably be published soon.

Minnesota.—Returns of population and militia regularly made by the assessors of taxes. This is general in the Territories, and a census is usual before the formation of a State government.

New Hampshire.—No regular census; last in 1783, embracing inhabitants, houses, barns and acres of land. School, agricultural and similar reports regularly. See transactions of the State Agricultural Society.

New Jersey.—No State census in this century. No State taxes assessed. County and township taxes assessed by township assessors. Reports on education, asylums, &c. Report by H. D. Rogers, State Geologist in 1840.

New York.—A census every ten years; latest in 1845. Taken by a marshal in each election district, which is not to exceed 500 voters. Blanks are furnished by the State. Expenses met by the counties. Particulars embraced very minute, and more than a hundred in number, to wit: nativities, voters, aliens, foreigners, naturalized, unmarried or married, births, deaths, paupers, militia, education, religion, manufactures, agriculture, crops and land in cultivation, deaf, dumb, blind, &c., occupations, &c. This is the most complete census of any State. The assessments of property are annual, and annual reports are made on canals and their trade, asylums, railroads, schools, colleges and academies. Geological surveys of the State have been partially made, and their results published by the State Agricultural Society. The legislature has made liberal appropriations for general surveys of the State; scientific men have been engaged to explore the *field* as well as the *mine*. The State and county agricultural societies, with their annual productions, are exciting a happy and noble influence in promoting scientific and practical agriculture, in the increase of crops, the breeding of stock, the drainage of wet lands, the reclamation of barren patches, the general improvement of farms, and the development of the mineral resources of the State.*

North Carolina.—No census taken; assessments once in ten years of the real estate only; the last nearly ten years ago. A geological report has been published by the State.

Ohio.—Census every fourth year; last in 1851, and includes white males above twenty-one and white and colored children between five and twenty-one; annual assessments of personal property; every six years for real; assessors elected in districts, and ascertain yearly the acres in wheat and corn and their yield; regular reports upon benevolent institutions, schools, penitentiaries, &c. The whole State, with few exceptions, lies on a substratum of secondary limestone, considerable alluvion, lime, sand stone, and much iron. Clays mixed with protoxide of iron, potash, and soda, valuable for vegetable productions. The State contains great quantities of vegetable mould, and an abundance of limestone.

Pennsylvania.—No census ever authorized; assessments triennially for real and annually for personal property. The first partial survey of Pennsylvania was made in 1836 by Professor Henry D. Rodgers; in 1851 the legislature passed an act for the publication of his survey. Some few counties have had surveys made independently of the State action. Professor Rodgers' survey was conducted for a period of six years, but little progress has been made in the publication of the results.

Rhode Island.—No census; no county taxes; the rateable property of the State was last estimated in 1849 by a committee of eleven persons. There are regular reports upon prisons, schools, banks, railroads, public health, births, marriages, and deaths. An effort was made to establish a bureau of statistics. A report upon the geology of the State was made by Dr. Charles T. Jackson. See also the report of a committee on the Cumberland coal mines.

South Carolina.—Census every ten years; latest in 1849; number of the white inhabitants and the deaf and dumb only taken. Cost, $8,989 for 280,000 people. Assessment of personal estate annual, of real, fixed by the legislature and remains permanent, the party only determining whether his land be of the first, second, or third quality. In regard to geology, an act of the legislature was passed in 1842, authorizing the Governor to appoint a person to survey the State. Mr. Ruffin, of Virginia, was selected, who commenced the work. His attention was principally directed to the extensive marl beds and calcareous deposits abounding in the lower portions of the State, and which could be made available for agri-

* The Industrial Exhibition of New York employed itself in making a collection, under the superintendence of Professor Silliman, the leading object of which was to present a geological view of the mineralogical and mining wealth of the country, and at the same time to illustrate its geology.

cultural purposes. His report was made in 1843. He resigned, and Professor Tuomey was selected to continue the work, his report being published in 1844, and a final report in 1848. Nothing of consequence has been done since, excepting the labors of Professor F. S. Holmes in exploring bays, islands, &c. of the coast. Fossils collected were to have been published in figure, but were omitted. These fossils have since been presented to the Charleston Cabinet of Natural History. The valuable Transactions of the State Agricultural Society have been published by the legislature.

Texas.—Census by constitution every eight years, embracing all free inhabitants, and the number of qualified electors; expense two cents for each white inhabitant, and one cent for each slave and free person of color. The latest census in 1850, when taken, embraced white males of eighteen and under forty-five, children under eighteen and over twelve, over six and under twelve, under six; slaves, colored. Census taken by the regular collectors and assessors of taxes; assessments of taxable property annual; annual reports on penitentiary, schools, railroads, the attorney general's office, &c. The last legislature established a school system, and $2,000,000 United States bonds, together with one-tenth of the whole taxation, were set apart for it.

Tennessee.—Census decennially, qualified voters enumerated; the latest in 1851, taken by Commissioners elected for each county. Expense $4,500 for 150,000 voters; assessments annually by similar commissioners. Reports are made on the penitentiary, lunatic and other asylums, internal improvements, geology, banks, &c. every two years. Surveys were made by Dr. Troost, who submitted eight or ten partial reports to the legislature. Before his death his report was presented to Professors Aggasiz and Hall for revision, and will be published by the Smithsonian Institution. [Consult Silusian Basin of Middle Tennessee, 1851.]

Virginia.—Census every fifth year after the national census by the late constitution. Provision not yet carried into effect. It is to include population and such statistics as may be prescribed by law; assessments irregularly for real, and by special act for personal property annually; a permanent rate is fixed for real estate; regular reports upon public institutions, internal improvements, and education. A bill is now pending in the legislature for a statistical bureau. Professor Rodgers was engaged several years since to survey the State. He submitted annual reports (1836 to 1841) which are published in the journal of the House of Delegates; he has not issued his final report, the legislature not having made an appropriation for its publication. The mineralogy of Virginia is receiving some attention from a number of miners, who are examining different localities for economic purposes.

Vermont.—No regular census provided for; the last was taken in 1771, and was but partial. Real estate is appraised every five years by regular appraisers, personal every year, including everything but household furniture, fuel, and provisions necessary for life. Annual reports are made on banks, railroads, asylums, prisons, and schools; the latter suspended during the last two years. Thompson's Natural History of the State contains a sketch of its geology. Four annual reports have been made by Professor Adams, State geologist. Roofing and writing slate, granite, marble, limestone for quick lime, soapstone, manganese, &c., are abundant and of fine quality in the State.

Wisconsin.—Census every ten years from and after 1855; the last was taken in 1848; annual assessments, and reports upon deaf and dumb, blind, insane, &c., the penitentiary, public schools, &c. For geology of the State, see Owens' Report, 1839, 1849, 1853, of Iowa, Wisconsin, and Minnesota, published by order of Congress, and also Lapham's Wisconsin. An appropriation for a geological survey was made by the legislature in 1852, and Mr. Daniels was appointed to conduct it.*

* For other data upon the geology of the States, see American Journal of Sciences, (Silliman's,) for proceedings of the meetings of American Geologists, Nos. 39, 41, 43, 45, 47; American Geology, No. 35; Geological Surveys No. 40; Geology of Massachusetts, Nos. 1, 32, 36; N. American Review, 42, 46; Geology of New York, (Silliman) Nos. 31, 36, 40, 42, 46, 48; 2d Series, 1 and 3; Geology of Northern States, N. A. Review, No. 11; of Western States, (Silliman,) No. 42. The successful investigation of American Geology was begun

In a volume little larger than the quarto, and in the same type with this compendium, it was possible to have embraced the whole material of the census, that which has been published, and that which is still buried in the returns together with two hundred pages of comparative and illustrative notes. Without such notes the tables of a census cannot be understood, or at least, without great labor and will often lead even the most careful examiner astray.†

in 1807 by Mr. McClure. In 1814 De Witt Clinton urged in New York a geological, mineralogical botanical, zoological and agricultural survey, the results of which were published in a magnificent series of volumes, at the expense of half a million of dollars. North Carolina has the merit of having sent the first geologist into the field, Prof. Olmstead, whose report was prepared in 1825. The subject is now introduced into many of the leading colleges, together with that of agricultural chemistry. In addition to the State and Federal Census, the larger cities obtain annual or periodical statistics of their population and wealth. In *New Orleans* there is a census of voters every five years, the last being in 1852, which embraced 13,401 names at an expense of $2,600. The State assessments of real estate are adopted for municipal purposes. Annual reports from the Board of Health, from schools, and commercial statistics are very complete. *Indianapolis*: Census every year by assessors. Assessments also annual and reports of common schools. *Cleveland*, latest census in 1853—cost $76.00. Total population 31,214. Assessment of personal property annual, real every six years. *Augusta*, Georgia, latest census 1852, cost $200, total population 15,000, particulars embraced, white, colored and slave, male and female; whites between 6 and 15 and 16. *Richmond*, Va., assessment of real estate every four years, none of personal. *Wilmington*, Del., last census 1853, population 16,163, embraced also statistics of manufactures. *Chicago*, census nearly every year, last 1853, taken by special commissioners and embraced dwellings, families, schools, churches, native and foreign, white and colored. Total population 60,652, cost $1,000. *Charleston*, S. C., latest census, 1848, two regular assessors; a board in 1854 raised the valuation of real estate to $23,000,000. Statistics of health complete. In 1848 an elaborate statistical volume was published by the city. *Lowell*, Mass., a census is taken once or twice in ten years, latest in 1850, cost $150, and included the number of families, children between 5 and 15 and foreigners. There are regular reports of births, marriages, &c., and of manufactures. *Portland*, Maine, latest census 1854. *New Haven*, last census 1845, total population 17,674. New Haven, Fair Haven and Westville, make up the town of New Haven. *Detroit*, assessments annual, reports on education, etc. *Milwaukie*, Wis.—the board of trade in 1853 published an extended report of commerce and manufactures. *Providence*, R. I.—Assessment annual, last census 1845. *St. Louis*.—Census every two years, last in 1852, taken by regular assessors and included color, sex, age and school children; cost $1,000. Assessment annual, and full commercial statistics published annually. *Baltimore*, no city census is taken; regular reports are published upon health and public schools, etc. *Cincinnati*, no city census except of children. Real estate assessed every six years, personal every year. Board of health and other statistical and commercial reports annual. *Memphis*, Tennessee, assessment annual, value of real and personal estate 1854, $7,116,500. Last census 1854, total population 12,687 persons. Annual reports on education, etc.

The above are all the replies that were received to a circular from the office. Of the larger cities omitted it may be asserted that their statistics are equally full. In *Boston* the statistical reports are frequent and thorough and the census descends into numerous and important details. That of 1850 was especially complete. The census of Boston, published in 1846 by Mr. Shattuck, by public authority, was an invaluable statistical document. In *New York* a statistical bureau has been established; and reports upon population, health, industry, education, etc., are issued, which are worthy of imitation every where. The city of *Philadelphia* has lately provided for a report upon its manufactures. Its health reports are annual.

† A plan, something like the following, would have presented the greatest advantages, though a great deal of discretion must necessarily be allowed to the head of the office.

I. *Sub-Divisions of Counties Alphabetically*—Population, white, free colored and slave, (disregarding age or sex,) of every place whatever, found in the schedules.

II. *Counties alphabetically*—The total population of each county at every census from 1790 with the date of formation.

III. *Counties*—Statistics of every county in 1850 precisely as published in this Compendium, adding the deaf and dumb, &c., births, marriages, deaths, and real and personal estate.

IV. *Counties*—Detailed population of counties in 1850.

Counties.	White. Free colored. Slave. Total.	Divided into males and females, and into the ages as now classified.	Counties.	Total Blacks. " Mulattoes. " Native born pop. " Foreign " "	Divided into males and females, and into the ages as now classified.

V. *Towns and Cities Alphabetically*—Of over 2,000 population, each arranged as the counties in No. IV.

VI. *Cities*—Of over 10,000 with occupations, specific nativities, houses with one family; one to two, two to five families, &c.

VII. *Cities*—Of over 10,000 by every census, white, colored and slave, male and female.

VIII. *States*—Population of States and Territories at each census, white, colored and slave, male and female.

IX. *States*—Population of States and Territories between certain ages, as under 15; 15 and 30; 30 and 45; 45 and 60; and over 60.

X. *States*—Considered as in Table IV.

XI. *States*—Occupations in each State.

XII. *States*—Specific nativities of the population of each State.

XIII. *States*—Statistics of each with more full particulars of education, newspapers, libraries, real estate holders, persons occupying under five acres, 5 to 20; 20 to 50; 50 to 100, &c.; producing under and over certain quantities of leading crops; natives and foreigners, white, blacks and mulattoes, holding real estate, &c.

XIV. *United States*—Specific ages of the population of the United States in the aggregate, as of 1 year, two years, &c., to the highest ages. They should be taken from the returns, in this manner.

XV. *United States*—Aggregate Statistics of the United States combined as in this compendium, with Statistics of States and Sections and Cities, upon such points as have not yet been aggregated from the returns, except in a few particular cases. Ratio tables.

Appendix I.—*Manufacturing Statistics* of each county and large town, as they are prepared in the office.

Appendix II.—*Mortality* tables, condensed upon the plan of the Massachusetts Reports by Counties and towns.

The States should be printed as in the Compendium, alphabetically, though prepared in the order of Sections, each Section being added and the results appended at the foot of the Table. Thus, New England, etc., slaveholding States, non-slaveholding, etc. The Tables can then be cut up and pasted in the alphabetical order. The work should be illustrated by diagrams.

General Notes.—The U. S. marshals, the governors of territories and assistants under them have always been employed. The district of each enumerator in the last census was not to exceed, when practicable, 20,000 persons. The marshals have always received a fixed compensation, varying from $100 to $2,500 or $3,000, and the assistants from 1 to 2 cents for each inhabitant enumerated, with an increase in the way of mileage in sparsely settled neighborhoods. The mileage by the last census was fixed at 10 cents per mile, to be ascertained by multiplying the square root of the number of houses visited by the square root of the number of miles in the district. For each inhabitant 2 cents were allowed, for each death 2 cents, each farm 10 cents, each manufacturing establishment 15 cents. For social statistics 2 per cent. on the earnings for population. For copies 8 cents per page. An addition of 100 per cent. was allowed California. The mileage rule in 1850 came as near expressing the number of miles travelled as any which could be devised. If the district embraced 100 square miles and the number of dwellings was 10,000, the result would be expressed by 10×100=1,000. In other words it was assumed that the district would have been traversed ten times in order to call at every house, which would be very nearly the fact. The clerical duties previous to 1850 were for the most part performed by marshals and their assistants. Accuracy has in general been secured by the oaths of these officers and by the penalties affixed. Parties were also compelled to answer under penalty. The returns are required to be exposed for inspection and the originals in 1850 were to be deposited in the county court, one copy to be sent to the Secretary of State at home, and one to the Secretary of the Interior. It is now provided that future census enumerations shall follow that of 1850 if no other law be passed, and a permanent system of representative numbers has been adopted, as will be seen in another place. The Secretary is also authorized to order a new census hereafter in any instance where there is a failure of returns.

Comparative Expense of the National Census 1840 *and* 1850, *to each State and individual.*

States and Territories.	Enumerating Whites, Free Col'd. & Slaves.				To Marshals and assistants for all statistics.			
	Aggregate.		Each individual.		1840.		1850.	
	1840.	1850.	1840.	1850.	Aggregate.	Pr. head	Aggregate.	Pr head
			Cents.	Cents.		Cents.		Cents.
Alabama	$15,481.54	$22,564.00	2.62	2.92	$19,532.50	3.31	$30,209.90	3.92
Arkansas	7,854.90	8,427.00	8.05	4.01	9,910.44	10.16	11,372.80	5.42
California	....	6,927.00	....	7.48	....	....	7,597.45	†8.20
Columbia, Dist. of	....	1,530.00	....	2.96	....	....	1,862.25	3.60
Connecticut	8,569.09	9,612.00	2.76	2.59	10,811.35	3.49	14,389.30	3.88
Delaware	2,449.54	2,834.00	3.14	3.10	3,090.43	3.96	4,000.65	4.37
Florida	3,278.71	4,676.00	6.02	5.35	4,136.61	7.59	5,497.45	6.29
Georgia	24,706.30	27,210.00	3.57	3.00	31,171.15	4.51	36,537.05	4.03
Illinois	21,505.53	26,734.00	4.56	3.14	27,133.57	5.70	39,541.60	4.64
Indiana	17,536.58	28,687.00	2.56	2.90	22,125.32	3.23	44,455.20	4.50
Iowa	2,530.19	7,245.00	5.87	3.77	3,192.34	7.40	9,839.30	5.17
Kentucky	28,261.93	28,904.00	3.62	2.94	35,656.63	4.57	41,831.35	4.26
Louisiana	13,499.55	15,167.00	3.83	2.93	17,031.93	4.83	18,722.55	3.62
Maine	13,590.73	16,906.00	2.71	2.90	17,146.70	3.42	25,474.55	4.37
Maryland	10,925.05	15,461.00	2.32	2.65	13,783.97	2.93	20,998.20	3.60
Massachusetts	14,576.39	24,345.00	1.95	2.45	18,390.47	2.49	34,193.85	3.44
Michigan	8,630.80	13,022.00	4.07	3.27	10,889.24	5.13	19,029.45	4.79
Mississippi	19,651.03	17,817.00	5.23	2.94	24,793.04	6.60	23,891.55	3.94
Missouri	17,161.30	21,786.00	4.47	3.19	21,651.82	5.64	31,322.35	4.59
New Hampshire	10,390.91	8,992.00	3.65	2.83	13,109.60	4.61	14,237.65	4.43
New Jersey	9,229.74	12,844.00	2.47	2.62	11,644.28	3.12	18,422.20	3.76
New York	57,865.56	77,525.00	2.38	2.50	73,006.30	3.01	114,474.95	3.70
North Carolina	17,775.17	26,419.00	2.36	3.04	22,422.21	2.98	36,487.60	4.20
Ohio	35,347.26	52,711.00	2.33	2.66	44,596.17	2.93	78,700.30	3.97
Pennsylvania	50,405.43	60,453.00	2.92	2.61	63,613.33	3.69	88,829.75	3.84
Rhode Island	2,389.60	3,969.00	2.19	2.69	3,014.86	2.77	5,384.95	3.65
South Carolina	28,321.89	17,941.00	4.76	2.68	35,732.61	6.01	23,747.65	3.55
Tennessee	28,479.71	29,923.00	3.43	2.98	35,931.79	4.33	42,619.15	4.25
Texas	....	11,442.00	....	5.38	....	....	13,756.35	6.47
Vermont	7,843.16	8,938.00	2.69	2.85	9,894.97	3.39	13,998.35	4.46
Virginia	36,604.46	42,149.00	2.95	2.96	46,182.01	3.72	56,876.15	4.00
Wisconsin	2,810.88	10,273.00	9.08	3.36	3,545.70	11.46	14,001.30	4.58
Territ's. Minnesota	....	1,516.00	....	24.95	....	....	1,569.75	25.83
Territ's. New Mexico	....	5,525.00	....	8.98	....	....	6,405.45	10.47
Territ's. Oregon	....	3,419.00	....	25.72	....	....	3,620.80	27.24
Territ's. Utah	....	1,283.00	....	11.27	....	....	1,458.10	12.81
	Extra pay to California marshals and assistants						8,424.00	†9.10
Total	517,672.93	675,176.00	3.03	2.91	653,141.34	3.83	963,781.25*	4.15

Remarks.—The census of 1790 cost $44,377.28 or cts. 1.13 to each head enumerated or cts. 9.6 to each sq. mile.

"	1800	" 66,109.04	" 1.25	"	"	" 11.3	"	"
"	1810	" 178,444.67	" 2.46	"	"	" 22.2	"	"
"	1820	" 208,525.99	" 2.16	"	"	" 23.0	"	"
"	1830	" 378,545.13	" 2.94	"	"	" 39.2	"	"
"	1840	" 833,370.95	" 4.88	"	'	" 77.8	"	"
"	1850	" 1,362,500.00	" 5.87	"	"	" 59.4	"	"

The preceding table, will show the expense incurred upon each national census in the aggregate and to the individual. It has reference to the whole amount expended, inclusive of printing and binding, except for the census of 1850. The cost of printing and binding in 1840 reached $184,629. It is not yet ascertained for the present census. The amounts in the large table are exclusively of office work, which in 1840 cost but about $40,000 and in 1850 over $300,000. In the former instance the marshals performed the most of such labors which was taken into consideration in their pay, and in the latter instance they performed very little. The cost to each individual may be compared with that incurred by the States and cities for their own enumerations as shown when upon those subjects.

The schedules of the United States census, 1850, embraced about 640,000 medium pages, and will make 800 or 1,000 volumes. Those of 1840 are bound in 350 volumes; those of 1830 in 150 volumes. The earlier schedules are unbound. Three thousand reams of blanks were sent out by express in 1850, and returned by mail between the 29th August, 1850, and 17th February, 1852. The weight in tons was one hundred. They were uninjured, except a few in California destroyed by fire. In 1840 a million of blanks were distributed. The number of marshals in 1850 was 45, assistants 3,231. In 1840 marshals and assistants 2,087. Whenever the schedules were incomplete the assistants were written to and part of their pay retained until the corrections were made if important. The principle should be more stringently adhered to hereafter.

* Per head in 1850, exclusive of the extra pay to California marshals and assistants, 4.12.

† Per head in 1850 in California, including the extra pay, as above, 17.30.

STATISTICAL VIEW OF THE UNITED STATES,

BASED UPON THE SEVERAL OFFICIAL RETURNS, FROM THE EARLIEST PERIOD,

AND EMBRACING A

COMPENDIUM OF THE CENSUS OF 1850.

THE subjects to be illustrated and discussed in the present volume admit of the following convenient distribution:

I. TERRITORY.
II. POPULATION.
III. MORAL AND SOCIAL CONDITION.
IV. INDUSTRY.
V. PROPERTY, REVENUE, TAXATION, etc.
VI. STATISTICAL DETAIL OF CITIES, TOWNS AND COUNTIES.

I. TERRITORY, embracing a comparison of States with each other and with the Union, the area of the United States at the several Census periods, the geographical distribution of areas, etc.

II. POPULATION, considered as

WHITE.
FREE COLORED.
SLAVE.
AGGREGATE.

The facts for the several subdivisions or chapters of population, whether considered as native or foreign born, will be treated in the following order, combined in each particular with appropriate ratio and comparative tables.

1. Aggregrate Number.
2. Families and Dwellings.
3. Sex.
4. Age.
5. Births, Marriages and Deaths.
6. Deaf and Dumb, Blind, Insane, &c.
7. Occupations.
8. Nativities.

The free colored and slaves, wherever practicable, will be separated into 1st, BLACK; and 2d, Mixed or MULATTO; and a table of Indian population at several periods, will be added.

III, V, VI. These heads sufficiently explain themselves.

IV. INDUSTRY, including

1. Agriculture.
2. Manufactures.
3. Commerce.
4. Internal Improvements.

The separate consideration of each of the classes which make up the population of the United States, is indispensable to any correct statistical reasonings in regard to it, and should be as far as possible secured in the tables of every Census. No set of truths can be applicable alike to classes so differently situated and of such distinct organization. How these classes compare with reference to the family relation and to the occupancy of dwellings, with reference to the predominance of the male or the female, with reference to age or to vital and industrial power, what are the ratios of births to marriages and deaths, how the people are employed, are they of native or foreign extraction, are they born in the State of residence or in some other of the States,—these are all questions of vital importance to the socialist who would reform abuses—to the moralist who would trace the sources of vice, to the economist who would develop those of wealth and power, to the physician laboring in the cause of science, and to the statesman legislating soundly for the present and the future.

PART I.

TERRITORY.

The territorial limits of the United States include that portion of the continent of North America, extending from the Atlantic to the Pacific ocean, which is bounded by the British possessions on the North, and by the Gulf of Mexico and the Mexican Republic on the South.

The superficial area of the Union, according to a computation made by the Topographical Bureau at the close of 1853, and subsequently reviewed and amended, amounted on the first of January, 1854, to *two millions nine hundred and thirty-six thousand, one hundred and sixty-six square miles*, being somewhat more than one-third of the area of the continent of North America.

The treaty of 1854 with Mexico settles the boundaries of the two republics as follows. "Retaining the same dividing line between the two Californias as already defined and established according to the 5th article of the treaty of Guadalupe Hidalgo, the limits between the two Republics shall be as follows: Beginning in the Gulf of Mexico, three leagues from land, opposite the mouth of the Rio Grande, as provided in the 5th article of the treaty of Guadalupe Hidalgo; thence, as defined in the said article up the middle of that river to the point where the parallel of 31 deg. 47 min, north latitude crosses the same; thence due west one hundred miles; thence south to the parallel of 31 deg. 20 min. north latitude; thence along the said parallel of 31 deg. 20 min. to the 111th meridian of longitude west of Greenwich; thence in a straight line to a point on the Colorado river, twenty English miles below the junction of the Gila and Colorado rivers; thence up the middle of the said river Colorado, until it intersects the present line between the United States and Mexico."

TABLE I.—*Area of North America, exclusive of the West Indies.*

Territory.	Sq. miles.	Sq. miles.
United States, as ascertained by the Topographical Bureau	....	2,936,166
British America, New Britain†	2,598,837	
British America, Upper and Lower Canada‡	346,860	
British America, Nova Scotia, New Brunswick, Cape Breton, &c	104,701	
		3,050,398
Mexico	....	1,038,834
Central America	....	203,551
Russian America‖	....	394,000
Danish America, (Greenland,)§	....	380,000
Total square miles	....	**8,002,949

† According to Balbi's estimate of the area of North America. Another estimate gives New Britain but 1,800,000 square miles.

‡ McCulloch. The late Canadian census gives 242,482 square miles as the area over which jurisdiction is actually extended.

‖ Guibert gives 962,500 kilometres carrés, or 371,611 square miles.

§ Greenland from present information would appear to be a trilateral island, 1,500 miles long and 600 miles in its greatest breadth. Its area, therefore, cannot be greater than we state above. Guibert gives the area of Danish America 3,861 square miles, and McCulloch only 170, meaning only that portion which has been explored.

** The area of the continent of North America is variously estimated by geographers at from five to seven millions of square miles. Guyot ("Earth and Man") estimates it at 5,472,000, and that of Europe at 2,688,000, exclusively of islands. The following tables have been carefully compiled from the latest official sources. Where these were wanting recourse has been had to Guibert ("*Dictionnaire Geographique*,") and the Gotha "*Almanach.*" In the quarto volume of the Census the figures for Europe were entirely adopted from McCulloch, and differ in several particulars as well as in the aggregate from those which are now given. It is needless to say that exactness cannot be expected in such calculations, but only the best approximation.

TABLE II.—*Territorial Extent of European and South American States, &c.*

STATES.	Area in sq. miles.	STATES.	Area in sq. miles.
Russia (in Europe)	2,120,397	Hesse Darmstadt	3,230
Austria	257,368	Mecklenberg Schwerin	5,907
France	207,145	Oldenburg	2,422
Great Britain	121,912	Nassau	1,785
Prussia	107,921	Other German States	10,166
Spain	182,270	Naples and Sicily	44,401
Turkey	210,585	Sardinia and Piedmont	29,276
Sweden and Norway	293,313	Papal States	15,892
Belgium	11,390	Tuscany	8,511
Portugal	36,510	Parma and Lucca	2,380
Holland	12,601	Modena	2,316
Denmark	22,533	Andorre	191
Bavaria	29,637	San Marino	22
Hanover	14,734	Swiss Confederation	14,950
Wurtemberg	7,522	Greece	17,900
Saxony	5,750	Ionian Islands	999
Baden	5,918		
Hesse Cassel	3,740		3,811,594

TABLE II.—*Continued.*

STATES.	Area in sq. miles.	STATES.	Area in sq. miles.
WEST INDIES.		SOUTH AMERICA.	
San Domingo	29,000	Venezuela	417,605
Spanish { Cuba	42,383	New Grenada	381,543
Spanish { Porto Rico	3,865	Ecuador	318,750
British. Trinidad	2,020	Bolivia	374,480
British. Jamaica	6,250	Peru	580,550
British. Leeward Islands	864	Chilé	130,115
British. Windward Island	778	Argentine Confederation	641,956
British. Bahamas	3,982	Uruguay	164,125
British. Turks Island and Caicos	434	Paraguay	76,500
French { Guadaloupe	631	Brazil	2,762,500
French { Martinique	382	Guiana, British	96,000
Dutch West Indies	600	Guiana, Dutch	38,500
Danish West Indies	192	Guiana, French	27,560
Swedish West Indies	25	Patagonia	300,000
	91,406		6,310,184

The limits of the United States when their independence was achieved (1783) did not exceed 820,680 square miles. Louisiana, purchased from France in 1803, and Florida from Spain in 1819, added respectively an extent of 899,579 and 66,900 square miles. In 1842 and 1846 the Northern boundary was settled by treaties with Great Britain, confirming the rights of the United States to 308,052 square miles, included in the Territory of Oregon, &c. In 1846 Texas was annexed, with an area of 318,000 square miles, and by a treaty soon afterwards with Mexico an area of 522,955 additional square miles was incorporated. Thus did the territory of the United States double itself in the first twenty years of its existence, and thus has it increased over three-fold in less than sixty years. The figures are given upon the authority of a statement prepared at the Topographical Bureau for the Census office, and annexed. The new treaty with Mexico, if ratified by the Senate, will add a fraction more and swell the aggregate to about 3,000,000 square miles.*

TABLE III.—*Territorial increase of the United States.*

Territory.	Sq. Miles.
Area of the United States at the peace of 1783	†820,680
The purchase of Louisiana added (about)	†899,579
(The limits were indefinite; those here assumed are the boundaries of the treaty of 1819, with the exception of Florida and parts of Mississippi and Alabama.)	
The acquisition of Florida, (treaty of 1819,) added	66,900
Admission of Texas, (Emory's map of 1844,)	318,000
Oregon treaty	308,052
Treaty with Mexico‡	522,955
Total	2,936,166

The territorial extent of the Republic is, therefore, nearly ten times as large as that of Great Britain and France combined; three times as large as the whole of France, Britain, Austria, Prussia, Spain, Portugal, Belgium, Holland, and Denmark, together; one-and-a-half times as large as the Russian empire in Europe; one-sixth less only than the area covered by the fifty-nine or sixty empires, states, and Republics of Europe; of equal extent with the Roman empire, or that of Alexander, neither of which is said to have exceeded 3,000,000 square miles.‖

Considered in lesser divisions, the calculations of the Topographical Bureau show the existence of an interior valley drained by the waters of the Mississippi and its tributaries, nearly as large as the slopes of the Pacific and Atlantic proper together, and one-third larger than the whole domain of the Republic upon the adoption of the present Constitution, (1789.)

* The treaty has been ratified but with a reduction of the contemplated area to 27,500 square miles, making the total area of the Union July 1st, 1854, 2,963,666 square miles.

† These estimates are lower than those usually made. Morse, in his Gazetteer estimates the area of the Union in 1783 at 1,000,000 square miles, and Major Stoddard, who took possession of Louisiana under the treaty and prepared a very valuable history of it, considers the area to be 1,307,260. These, of course, were but vague estimates, subject to after correction. Again, Oregon has generally been estimated at 341,463, Texas 402,907, California 448,691. *De Bow's Industrial Resources, Vol.* 3, *Art. U. S.*

‡ The Mesilla Valley is included in the computation.

‖ Voltaire, "*Histoire de Russie,*" Chap. 1.

TABLE IV.—*Area of each slope and ratio to the total area of the U. States.*

Territory.	Area in sq. miles.	Ratio of area of each slope to total area of U. S.
Pacific slope	766,002	26.09
Atlantic slope proper	514,416	17.52
Northern Lake region	112,649	3.83
Gulf region,	325,537	11.09
Atlantic, Lake and Gulf east and west of the Mississippi	952,602	32.44
Mississippi valley, drained by the Mississippi and its tributaries	1,217,562	41.47
Atlantic, including Northern Lake	627,065	21.35
Mississippi valley and Gulf or Middle region	1,543,099	52.55
Total	2,936,166	

Thus, over two-fifths of the national territory is drained by the Mississippi and its tributaries, and more than one-half is embraced in what may be called its *Middle Region.* One-fourth of this total area belongs to the Pacific, one-sixth to the Atlantic proper, one-twenty-sixth to the Lakes, one-ninth to the Gulf, or one-third to the Atlantic, including the Lakes and the Gulf.*

A calculation made at the office of the Coast Survey in 1853, gives for the total main shore line of the United States, (exclusively of bays, sounds, islands, &c.,) 12,609 statute miles. If all of these be followed, and the rivers entered to the head of tide water, the total shore line will be swelled to 33,069 miles.

TABLE V.—*Shore Line of the United States in Statute Miles.*

COASTS.	Main shore, including bays, sounds, &c.	Proportion of each part of coast to total.	Islands.	Proportion.	Rivers to head of tide.	Proportion.	Total.	Proportion.	Ocean line in steps of ten miles.	Continental shore line of States North of Virginia.	Continental shore line of States South of Maryland.
	Miles.	Per cent.	Miles.	Pr. ct.	Miles.	Pr. ct.	Miles.	Pr. ct.	Miles.	Miles.	Miles.
Atlantic coast.	6,861	54.41	6,328	68.44	6,655	59.35	19,844	60.01	2,059	907	1,256
Pacific coast..	2,281	18.09	702	7.59	712	6.35	3,695	11.17	1,405	....	....
Gulf coast....	3,467	27.50	2,217	23.97	3,846	34.30	9,530	28.82	1,643	....	1,764
Total	12,609	100.00	9,247	100.00	11,213	100.00	33.069	100.00	5,107	907	3,020

* From the charts prepared some years ago by Col. Gilpin, of Missouri, it will be perceived that a circle described from the forks of the Kansas river, west of Missouri, will touch New Orleans and Galveston, or the Gulf frontier, and the 49th parallel of latitude, our northern boundary, making these points equidistant from the centre. On a larger circle, with the same centre, the points of equidistance will be San Francisco, in California, Fort Vancouver on the Columbia, in Oregon, Quebec and Boston upon the Atlantic, Hudson's Bay on the extreme north, and Havana, Vera Cruz and the city of Mexico on the extreme south. The various great basins, declivities and table lands on the continent he estimates as follows: Mississippi basin 1,123,100 square miles; St. Lawrence 475,400; Hudson's Bay 1,077,200; Mackenzie basin 898,500; Pacific declivity 420,000; Atlantic declivity 270,700 square miles.

Mr. Darby, in his "Geographical Dictionary," gives the following aggregates: Valley of the Ohio 200,000 square miles; Valley of the Mississippi proper 180,000; Valley of the Missouri 500,000; and the Valley of the Lower Mississippi 330,000: total 1,210,000 square miles.

Lieut. Maury compares the basins of the Old World with those which are drained into the Gulf of Mexico and Caribbean seas.

Mediterranean in Europe	1,160,000
Nile	520,000
Euphrates	196,000
Indus	312,000
Ganges	432,000
Irrawaddy	331,000
Others of India	173,000
Of Western Europe, Rhine, &c	730,000
Total of Mediterranean India and W. Europe	3,854,000

Basin of Mississippi	982,000
Basins in Florida and Texas	529,000
Mexico and Central America	300,000
Amazon	1,796,000
Orinoco and all others of the Caribbean sea,	700,000
Total of Gulf and Caribbean sea	4,298,000
	3,854,000
Difference in square miles	444,000

Lieut. Maury remarks "the area of all the valleys which are drained by the rivers of Europe which empty into the Atlantic, all the valleys that are drained by the rivers of Asia which empty into the Indian ocean, and of all the valleys that are drained by the rivers of Africa and Europe which empty into the Mediterranean, does not cover an extent of territory as great as that included in the valleys drained by the American rivers alone, which discharge themselves into one central sea."

Dr. Patterson, of Philadelphia, made the centre of *representative population* of the Union in 1840 in the north-western extremity of Virginia, and states that it had travelled westward since 1790, when it was in Baltimore county, Md., 182 miles in very nearly the same parallel of latitude.

The main shore line of the Atlantic including Bays, &c., is twice that of the Gulf, three times that of the Pacific and more than equal to that of the Pacific and Gulf combined. The Southern States have three times as much sea coast as the Northern.

The extent of shore line is an important element in determining the commercial character of a nation. In this regard Europe is more favored than any other portion of the earth, and North America next; the former having, according to Guyot ("Earth and Man") only 156 miles, and the latter 228 miles of surface to one mile of coast (the United States having 241) whilst South America has 376, Africa 623 and Asia 459 miles.

The table which follows furnishes three measurements, viz:

1st. *The Coast Line*, i. e. sea coast, bays, islands, &c., "as if an adometer wheel were passed over the high water line," and the results are for the Atlantic coast........ 12,359 miles.
The rivers to head of tide have not been measured, but from a former table the length total is *both shores*........ 6,655 "
For the Gulf of Mexico, the coast line is........ 5,744 "
Length of rivers to head of tide, from same table........ 3,846 "
2d. *Coast line, exclusive of islands and rivers* to head of tide.
For the Atlantic........ 6,017 "
" Gulf........ 3,551 "
3d. *Coast line, exclusive of bays, islands*, &c., &c., except Massachusetts bay—Atlantic........ 2,163 "
Do. do. do. Gulf........ 1,764 "

These results are somewhat greater than those of Table V., and are believed to be nearer the truth by the amount of the difference.

TABLE VI.—*The results of measurements of Coast and Shore line of the United States as required by the Superintendent of the Census Bureau from the Coast Survey of July* 12, 1854, *are as follows, in statute miles:*

STATES.	Shore line including bays, islands and all irregularities.	Shore line except islands.	Continent line viz: shore line except islands, bays, &c.	REMARKS.
				Measurements taken on best maps of the Coast Survey Archives:
Maine........	2,486	784	278	Measured on Greenleaf's map of Maine, as correct as possible, but the great irregularities of coast prevent a correct result.
New Hampshire....	49	41	18	Measured on Garrigain's map of N. H., generally correct and compared with Smith's map.
Massachusetts......	886	622	286	Measured on Borden's map of Mass., generally correct as compared with Smith's map.
Rhode Island.......	320	245	45	Measured on Smith's and Mitchell's maps.
Connecticut........	262	240	104	Measured on Coast Survey off shore charts.
New York..........	980	50	none	do. do. do. do.
New Jersey.........	540	300	120	do. do. do. do.
Delaware..........	118	106	23	Measured on F. Lucas' map of Md., Ches. Bay and C. S. Sketches and Charts.
Maryland..........	509	411	33	Measured on F. Lucas' map of Md., Ches. Bay and C. S. Sketches and Charts.
Northern Atlantic.	6,150	2,799	907	From N. E. boundary to State line between Md. & Va.
Virginia...........	654	348	116	Measured on F. Lucas' map of Md. & C. S. maps.
North Carolina.....	1,641	1,089	320	Measured on Brazier's map of N. C., and compared with Smith's.
South Carolina......	756	267	220	Measured on Smith's map and compared with Mitchell's.
Georgia............	684	480	128	do. do. do. do.
Florida East Coast..	2,474	1,034	472	Measured on map of Topographical Engineers.
Southern Atlantic.	6,209	3,218	1,256	From State line between Md. and Va. to S. extremity of Florida.
Total Atlantic....	12,359	6,017	2,163	
Florida West Coast.	1,562	883	674	Measured on map of Topographical Engineers.
Alabama...........	315	247	58	Measured on Smith's map and compared with Mitchell's.
Mississippi.........	287	225	88	do. do. do. do.
Louisiana.........	2,250	1,256	552	Measured on Gerdes' Reconnoissances and Smith's map.
Texas............	1,330	940	392	Measured on Blunt's and Smith's map.
Total Gulf........	5,744	3,551	1,764	
Total South Atlantic and Gulf.........	11,953	6,769	3,020	
Total Pacific, from boundary of San Diego to the mouth Frazer's river*....	3,251	2,533	1,343	Measured on Alden's Reconnoissances.

* Or 1,343 miles of shore line of contingent coast on the Pacific; 483 miles of shore line of bays; 707 miles of shore line from Cape Flattery to Frazer's river; 414 miles of shore line of islands in the Pacific, and 304 miles of shore line of islands from Cape Flattery to Frazer's river. The Atlantic and Gulf States were measured also on Burr's maps and Blunt's coast charts.

The following table will show the distances between some of the leading points of the United States by the nearest mail routes. That a better judgment may be formed of the extent of the country, they are compared with nearly equidistant foreign cities.

TABLE VII.—*Comparative Distances—American and Foreign Cities.*

American Cities.	Distance in miles.	Nearly equidistant American and Foreign Cities.	Distance in miles.
Pittsburg to Boston	616	Paris to Vienna	625
New York to Mobile	1,476	Paris to St. Petersburg	1,510
Philadelphia to Pensacola	1,443	St. Petersburg to Constantinople	1,430
Boston to Nashville	1,590	London to Constantinople, (land route)	1,499
Albany to Richmond	506	Paris to Berlin	540
New York to Charleston	790	London to Vienna	760
New York to Cleveland, (Ohio)	671	Paris to Rome	700
Boston to Galveston, (Texas)	2,256	Stockholm (Sweden) to Madrid*	2,160
New York to Astoria, (land route)	3,523	London to Ispahan Persia*	3,580
New York to Astoria, (via Cape Horn)	17,500	Liverpool to Canton, (via Cape of Good Hope)	18,000
New York to Astoria, (via Panama)	6,260		
New York to San Diego, Cal. (land route)	3,732	London to Delhi, (Hindostan)*	5,337
Charleston to Hartford	900	New York to Bremen, (across Atlantic)	3,800
New York to New Orleans	1,640	London to Rome	910
Falls of St. Anthony to mouths of Mississippi river	2,200	London to Constantinople, (by land)*	1,490
		Stockholm (Sweden) to Tunis (Africa)*	2,200
Sources of Mississippi to mouths of Mississippi	2,986	St. Petersburg to Thebes (Egypt)*	2,800
		St. Petersburg to Madrid*	2,100
Pittsburg to New Orleans via river	2,175		

The citizen of the United States arriving at New Orleans from New York has passed over a distance more than equal to that separating London from Constantinople, or Paris from St. Petersburg. If he has taken the land route to Astoria his travel will be nearly as great as from New York to Bremen; if the water route, he will have made a voyage nearly equal to one from London to Canton.

The United States consist at the present time (1st July 1854,) of thirty-one independent States and nine Territories, including the District of Columbia, whose areas will be found in the table annexed, prepared at the Topographical Bureau. It is the only official statement. There were, in 1850, sixteen hundred and twenty county divisions included within the organized States and Territories, but it is impossible to give any satisfactory statement of their areas. By reference to the statistical tables of these counties at the end of the volume, it will be found how liable they are to changes, and also what changes were actually effected between 1840 and 1850.

* Estimated.

NOTE.—The following statement of the river navigation and shore line of the United States was prepared by Colonel Abert, of the Topographical Engineers, at the request of the Treasury Department, December 7th, 1845. It has since been completed to date. The head of tide-water is assumed as the limit of steam navigation, as impeding falls or rapids are encountered at that point, above which many rivers are adapted to steam navigation, but to what extent is not sufficiently known. The shore line of rivers to head of tide-water from

Maine to Texas is		10,501	miles.
Rivers of Texas		1,210	"
Lower Mississippi, islands and bayous		8,372	"
Upper Mississippi and tributaries		2,736	"
Big Black, Yazoo and bayous		1,190	"
Red river and tributaries		4,924	"
Arkansas river and tributaries		3,250	"
Missouri river and tributaries		7,830	"
Ohio river and tributaries		7,342	"
Total		47,355	"
Add rivers on the Pacific—Sacramento	600		
San Joaquin	600		
Oregon	460		
Umpqua	50		
	—	1,710	
Total river shore line in the United States in 1854, including both banks		49,065	miles.
Frontier line of United States on British Possessions		3,303	"
Do. do Mexico (1848)		1,456	"
Shore line of northern lakes, including bays, sounds, and islands (American)		3,620	"
Shore line of northern lakes, including bays sounds, and islands (British)		2,629	"

TABLE VIII.—*Area of the States and Territories of the United States.**

State or Territory.	Area in sq. miles.	Per cent. of total area.	Rank of States, &c. territorially.	State or Territory.	Area in sq. miles.	Per cent. of total area.	Rank of States, &c. territorially.
Alabama	50,722	1.73	20	Missouri	67,380	2.29	11
Arkansas	52,198	1.78	18	Nebraska Territory	335,882	11.44	1
California	155,980	5.32	7	New Hampshire	9,280	0.32	34
Columbia, District of	60	....	40	New Mexico Territory	207,007	7.05	4
Connecticut	4,674	0.15	37	New York	47,000	1.60	23
Delaware	2,120	0.07	38	New Jersey	8,320	0.28	35
Florida	59,268	2.02	13	North Carolina	50,704	1.73	21
Georgia	58,000	1.98	14	Ohio	39,964	1.36	27
Illinois	55,405	1.89	16	Oregon Territory	185,030	6.30	5
Indiana	33,809	1.15	29	Pennsylvania	46,000	1.57	24
Indian Territory, (south of Kansas)	71,127	2.42	10	Rhode Island	1,306	0.04	39
Iowa	50,914	1.73	19	South Carolina	29,385	1.01	31
Kansas	114,798	3.91	9	Tennessee	45,600	1.55	25
Kentucky	37,680	1.28	28	Texas	237,504	8.09	3
Louisiana	41,255	1.40	26	Utah Territory	269,170	9.17	2
Maine	31,766	1.08	30	Virginia	61,352	2.10	12
Maryland	11,124	0.38	32	Vermont	10,212	0.35	33
Massachusetts	7,800	0.26	36	Washington Territory	123,022	4.19	8
Michigan	56,243	1.91	15	Wisconsin	53,924	1.84	17
Minnesota Territory	166,025	5.65	6	Total	2,936,166		
Mississippi	47.156	1.61	22				

The Territory of Nebraska constitutes *one-ninth;* Utah, *one-eleventh;* Texas, *one-twelfth;* New Mexico, *one-fourteenth;* Oregon, *one-sixteenth;* Missouri and Virginia, a little more than *one-fiftieth* each; South Carolina, *one-hundredth;* Massachusetts, *one three hundred and eightieth;* and Rhode Island, *one-two thousand three hundredth* part of the national area.

The following table will show the area included within the several geographical divisions which are named.

TABLE IX.—*Area of the several great divisions of the United States.*

Area included in	Square miles.	Per cent. of total area.	Area included in	Square miles.	Per cent. of total area.
The States	1,464,105	49.86	The ten largest States	857,254	29.20
The Territories	1,472,061	50.14	The twenty-one smallest States	606,851	20.66
Non-slaveholding States, not territories	612,597	20.86	East of the Mississippi	865,576	29.48
Slaveholding States, not territories†	851,508	29.00	Between the Mississippi and Rocky Mountains	1,200,381	40.88
New England States	65,038	2.21	West of the Mississippi	2,070,590	70.52
Middle States	114,624	3.90	North of latitude 36° 30′	1,970,077	67.10
Southern States	258,709	8.81	South of latitude 36° 30′	966,089	32.90
Southwestern States	474,435	16.15	West of the Rocky Mountains	870,209	29.64
Northwestern States	395,319	13.46	East of the Rocky Mountains	2,065,957	70.36

The States and the Territories have, at the present time, about an equal area. The slaveholding States have 851,508 square miles, and the non-slaveholding States, 612,597. There are 865,576 square miles east of the Mississippi, 2,070,590 west, 1,200,381 intermediate between the Mississippi and the Rocky Mountains, and 870,209 west of the Rocky Mountains. North of the old Missouri compromise line, there is an area of 1,970,077 square miles, and 966,089 south of it.

* Some of the areas in this table will be found to differ very materially from those published in the quarto census, page xxxiii. They were made up in that instance from previous census publications and from the reports of the General Land Office. As no two statements hitherto made in geographies, gazetteers, etc., can be found to agree, it seemed fit to have the whole matter referred to a proper and competent authority for settlement, and none could be more so than the U. S. Topographical Bureau. Col. Abert, the head of that department was kind enough to have all of the computations made from the map of Colton, (1844) and from the Topographical Bureau map of the country west of the Mississippi; and, in a note of June 7th, 1854, says: "You will perceive the total area is still less than that formerly sent from this office. As these results are necessarily approximate, it is not to be expected from the imperfections of the maps, that the same results precisely will be arrived at by different persons and methods. The discrepancy between the total here given for the States, and that of table XII. of the quarto census, (made up from the popular sources of information,) is principally in the following. The Indian Territory is there given, 187,171, Nebraska, 136,700, North-west Territory, 528,725. Total, 852,596, instead of 521,807 in the present table. Are not the two first included in the third in table XII?"

The areas for California, Texas and the Territories west of the Mississippi were computed for Table XII. of the quarto census, from Disturnell's map, commonly known as the "Treaty Map." Since the publication of that of the Topographical Bureau, the other is deemed valueless, and the discrepancies, though great, will illustrate the comparative accuracy of the two authorities.

† And District of Columbia.

There are six States and Territories larger, as large or a little less only than that of either of the powers of France, Great Britain, Austria, Prussia, Spain or Turkey. Eight of the largest States have an area as large as the remaining twenty-three States. Whilst the New England States have about one-fortieth of our territory, the Middle States have one-twenty-fifth, the Southern States one-eleventh, the North-western, one-seventh, and the South-western one-sixth, in round numbers. As these great divisions will be frequently referred to in this volume, and tables will be presented in regard to them, it is proper to explain* (see note) what they are always intended to embrace, unless the contrary be expressly stated.

Now that the States and Territories have increased and are increasing so greatly in number, difficulties of arrangement continually occur, and it is almost impracticable to adopt any which will be convenient for reference, easy of designation, and readily suggestive of contrasts and comparisons. For all of the detailed tables in this work, it has been deemed best to follow the alphabetical order of arrangement, except for the Territories, instead of the method by geographical position or by the date of admission into the Union. These last methods are complex and embarrassing, and ought to be abandoned. Where the object is a *classification* of States *geographically*, the methods in use are equally at fault. Thus, Kentucky and Missouri are forcibly separated from Tennessee and Arkansas, and thrown with the North-west to be associated with California and with Oregon and the other Territories. Maryland and the District of Columbia are combined with Pennsylvania and New York to form the Northern or Middle States, though in fact they belong to the South. Other difficulties may be stated, and they will increase with the settlement of the country. Cannot some method be proposed, which, whilst it shall not obliterate the old distinctions now so much in use, will admit as elements of classification the great geographical divisions of the country, the Lakes, the Valley, the Gulf, the Atlantic, the Pacific, and also such as are political or social, as States or Territories, slaveholding or non-slaveholding States, &c? After some reflection, and not a few abortive efforts, the arrangement on page 38 is suggested, which, it is believed, will combine all the proposed advantages, and be of very simple comprehension and reference.

PART II.

POPULATION.

CHAPTER I.—COLONIAL POPULATION.

There was no general enumeration of the people of the United States earlier than the census of 1790, although conjectural estimates of population, more or less accurate, are to be found among the records of the colonial period, and are valuable in the absence of other material. Several of these are annexed. Upon the basis of the increase which was afterwards ascertained, (viz: for the colored population between 1790 and 1800, being at that time least disturbed by immigration,) the total population in 1775 would have been 3,490,740, including 479,155 slaves, the population in 1749, 1.467,539, including 261,833 slaves; the population in 1701, 390,299. But this mode of calculation would be very fallacious for extremely early periods.†

*1. New England States. Maine, New Hampshire, Vermont, Massachusetts, Rhode Island and Connecticut.

2. Middle States. New York, New Jersey, Pennsylvania, Delaware, Maryland and the District of Columbia.

3. Southern States. Virginia, North Carolina, South Carolina, Georgia and Florida.

4. South-western States. Alabama, Mississippi, Louisiana, Texas, Arkansas and Tennessee.

5. North-western States. Kentucky, Missouri, Illinois, Indiana, Ohio, Michigan, Wisconsin, Iowa, California and the Territories, (in questions of area the two last are excluded.)

6. The Slaveholding States include Delaware, Maryland, Virginia, North Carolina, South Carolina, Georgia, Florida, Alabama, Mississippi, Louisiana, Texas, Arkansas, Missouri, Kentucky and Tennessee, in all fifteen States, besides the District of Columbia.

7. The Non-Slaveholding States include Maine, New Hampshire, Vermont, Massachusetts, Rhode Island, Connecticut, New York, New Jersey, Pennsylvania, Ohio, Michigan, Indiana, Illinois, Wisconsin, Iowa and California; in all sixteen.

† In 1775 Congress recommended the several Assemblies of the Colonies to ascertain the number of their inhabitants. In 1782 the journals state that "such enumerations have not been made." The recommendation was repeated in 1783, but a committee declared in 1785 that they could not ascertain how many of the States had complied. The estimates in the text are taken from Holmes' Annals. In the documents of the Congress of 1775, the estimate reaches 3,000,000. Holmes says that Dr. Humphreys, in his "Historical Account of the Society for the promulgation of the Gospel," is authority for the figures in the column of 1701, but that Dr. Stiles had assigned them specifically to that year. Beverly gives to Virginia, in 1704, 60,000 souls. In 1755, the population of Massachusetts was estimated at 234,000; that of Connecticut, at 133,000; of Rhode Island at 35,929; of New Hampshire at 34,000. Connecticut, in 1756, contained 128,212 whites, and 3,587 blacks; in 1774, 191,392 whites and 6,464 blacks. Rhode Island, in 1748, contained 29,755 whites, and 4,373 blacks. Maryland, in 1755, contained 107,208 souls, including 3,592 mulattoes, and 42,764 negroes. The estimates in the tables for the colonies in 1701 and 1749, include generally, it is believed, all classes. In South Carolina, however, in 1701, the negroes are omitted. Dr. Shattuck gives Boston (in 1742) 16,382 inhabitants, including 1,374 colored, of whom, in 1754, 989 were slaves. In 1765 the total colored population was 811. (See chapter on Slave Population.)

TABLE X.—CLASSIFICATION OF STATES AND TERRITORIES OF THE UNITED STATES.

		STATES AND TERRITORIES.	NEW CLASSIFICATION.																	OLD CLASSIFICATION.						
			GEOGRAPHICAL.												POLITICAL.											
			Northern States, &c.					Southern States, &c.					Total.		Non-slaveholding States.	Slaveholding States.										
			North-eastern.	Northern interior.	Northwest	Total northern.	Per ct. of the whole northern.	South-eastern.	Southern interior.	Southwest	Total southern.	Per ct. of the whole southern.	Area.	Per ct. of the whole U. States.		Northern tier.	Southern tier.	Total States.	Territories.	New England.	Middle States.	Southern.	Southwestern.	Northwest, including Territories.	Lake States.	Gulf States.
			Square miles.	Square miles.	Square miles.	Square miles.		Square miles.	Square miles.	Square miles.	Square miles.		Square miles.		P. ct.	P. ct.	P. ct.	P. ct.	P. ct	P. c.	P. c.	P. c.	P. ct.	P. ct.	P. c.	P. ct.
EASTERN.	North.	Me., N. H., Vt., Mass. Conn. and R. I.	65,038				5.13							2.22	2.22			2.22		2.22						
		N. Y., Pa. and N. J.	101,320				8.00							3.45	3.45			3.45			3.45					
	South.	Del., Md. and D. C.						13,304				0.80		0.45		0.45		0.45			0.45					
		Va., N. C., S. C., and Georgia						199,441				11.94		6.79			6.79	6.79								
		Florida						59,268				3.55		2.02			2.02	2.02				8.81				2.02
		Total 17 eastern States, &c	Total	north-	eastern	166,358	13.13	Total	south-	eastern	272,013	16.29	438,371	14.93												
INTERIOR.	North.	Ind., Ill. and Iowa		140,128			11.07							4.77	4.77			4.77								
		Ohio, Mich. Wis.		150,131			11.85							5.11	5.11			5.11							5.11	
		Nebraska and Minn.		501,907			39.63							17.10					17.10					26.98		
	South.	Kentucky, Missouri.							105,060			6.29		3.58		3.58		3.58						3.58		
		Arkansas, Tennessee							97,798			5.86		3.33		3.33		3.33								
		Ala., Miss., La. and Texas							376,637			22.56		12.83			12.83	12.83					16.15			14.85
		Kansas, Indian Terr.							185,925			11.14		6.33					6.33					6.33		
		Total 18 middle States, &c	Total	north	middle	792,166	62.55	Total	south	middle	765,420	45.85	1,557,586	53.05												
WESTERN.	N.	Oreg'n, Washing'n			308,052									10.49					10.49					10.49		
	S.	California								155,980		9.34		5.34	5.31			5.31						5.31		
		New Mexico, Utah								476,177		28.52		16.22					16.22					16.22		
		Total 5 Western States, &c	Total	north	wes'rn	308,052	24.32	Total	south-	wes'rn	632,157	37.86	940.209	32.02												
		Grand total of 40 States, &c.	166,358	792,166	308,052	1,266,576	43.14	272,013	765,420	632,157	1,669,590	56.86	2,936,166	100.00	20.86	*7.36	21.64	*49.86	50.14	2.22	3.90	8.81	16.16	†68.91	5.11	16.87

* Total Slaveholding States, 29.00. † Excluding California and the Territories only, 13.46.

The classification divides the country, first, into three great sections; the *East* on the Atlantic; the *West*, on the Pacific; and the *Interior*, embracing the Valley of the Mississippi, etc. Each of these divisions has its own *South* and its own *North*, designated as Northern Atlantic, Southern Interior, Northern Pacific, etc. Combining the North of each, the *true* Northern States result, in none of which the institution of Slavery exists. Combining the South of each in the same way, every State having slave institutions will be included, and all of the Territories in which Slavery exists or may exist, and California which is sufficiently Southern. The arrangement shows also the *Gulf* States and the *Lake* States, considering as the latter only those having the largest lake frontier, though others have a less extent or have intimate lake interests. It preserves, too, all of the old distinctions, separating where necessary the States from the Territories, and admits of a ready adjustment in its proper place of States to be formed from territory present or future.

By the classification, the Northern States and Territories constitute 43.14 per cent of the Union, and the Southern 56.86 per cent.; the Eastern States 14.93 per cent.; the Middle States 53.05 per cent.; the Western States 32.02 per cent.; the North-eastern, 5.67 per cent; the South eastern, 14.93 per cent.; the Northern Interior, 26 98 per cent.; the Southern Interior, 26,07 per cent.; the North-western, 10.49 per cent.; the South-western, 21.53 per cent.; the non-Slaveholding States, 20.86 per cent.; and the Slaveholding, 20 per cent; of which 7.36 per cent. is in the Northern tier. Thus the Southern States, &c. are a quarter larger than the Northern; the Western, more than twice as large as the Eastern; the Middle, larger than the two together; the South-eastern are nearly twice the North-eastern; the Northern Interior, twice as large as the two together, and about equal to the Southern Interior; the North-western and South-eastern are nearly equal; the South-western is twice as large as either. The Slaveholding States are nearly a third larger than the non-Slaveholding.

TABLE XI.—*Colonial Population.*

COLONIES.	COLONIAL POPULATION.			Increase per cent. first 48 years.	Increase per cent. per annum.	Increase per cent 2d period, 26 yrs.	Increase per cent. per annum.	Increase per cent. in 74 years.	Increase per ct. per ann. in 74 years.
	1701.	1749.	1775.						
Connecticut........	30,000	100,000	262,000	233.33	4.65	162.00	6.23	773.33	10.45
Delaware...........	....	Incl.in Pa.	37,000						
Georgia............	....	6,000	27,000	....	....	350.00	13.46		
Maryland...........	25,000	85,000	174,000	240.00	5.00	104.71	4.00	596.00	8.05
Massachusetts......	70,000	220,000	352,000	214.29	4.46	60.00	2.31	402.86	5.44
New Hampshire......	10,000	30,000	102,000	200.00	4.17	240.00	9.23	920.00	12.43
New Jersey.........	15,000	60,000	138,000	300.00	6.25	130.00	5.00	820.00	11.08
New York...........	30,000	100,000	238,000	233.33	4.86	138.00	5.31	693.33	9.37
North Carolina.....	5,000	45,000	181,000	800.00	16.67	302.22	11.62	3,520.00	47.57
Pennsylvania.......	20,000	250,000	341,000	1,150.00	23.96	36.40	1.40	1,605.00	21.69
Rhode Island.......	10,000	35,000	58,000	250.00	5.21	65.71	2.53	480.00	6.49
South Carolina.....	7,000	30,000	93,000	328.57	6.84	210.00	8.08	1,228.57	16.60
Virginia...........	40,000	85,000	300,000	112.50	2.34	252.94	9.73	650.00	8.78
Whites.............	....	....	2,303,000						
Slaves, estimated....	....	....	500,000						
All classes........	262,000	1,046,000	2,803,000	299.24	6.23	167.97	6.46	969.85	13.11

At the beginning of the revolution the Southern colonies had therefore 812,000 white inhabitants, and the Northern 1,491,000. Connecticut was the fourth State in rank. Massachusetts and Pennsylvania were each a third larger than New York, which was even excelled by Connecticut.

Upon the adoption of the Federal Government in 1789, framed upon the basis of popular representation, more precise and accurate knowledge in regard to the numbers of the people became necessary, and such knowledge is accordingly provided for in the Second Section of the first Article of the Constitution.*

"Representatives and taxation shall be apportioned among the several States which may be included within this Union, according to their representative numbers, which shall be determined by adding to the whole number of free persons (including those bound to service for a term of years and excluding Indians not taxed) three-fifths of all other persons," (meaning slaves.)

CHAPTER II.—POPULATION OF THE UNITED STATES.

THERE have been seven enumerations of the inhabitants of the United States, the periods and aggregate results of which are as follows:

	Number.
Census of 1790	3,929,827
" " 1800	5,305,925
" " 1810	7,239,814
" " 1820	9,638,131
" " 1830	12,866,020
" " 1840	17,069,453
" " 1850	23,191,876

At the close of 1854 the total population of the United States, upon the supposition that its average ratio of increase has been maintained, or nearly so, may be stated in round numbers at **26,500,000.**

The present population of the Union may be said to consist of, *first*—the number who were in the country on the formation of the government in 1789, and their descendants; *second*, of those who have come into the country since that period by immigration, and their descendants, (of this class much will be said under the head of "Nativities;") *third*, of those who have been brought in by annexation, as in Louisiana, Florida, New Mexico, etc., and their descendants. It is sufficient to say of the last class, that Louisiana, when purchased, had 77,000 inhabitants, including 53,000 slaves; Florida about 10,000; California and New Mexico, about 60,000; and that Texas and Oregon only brought back into the Union citizens who had emigrated thither but a short time before. The number of Indians (taxed) domesticated and absorbed in the population, cannot be ascertained. The colonial population was swelled, in 1765, by the extension of the boundary to the Mississippi, and the introduction of 2,000 French residents of the territory incorporated. (Bancroft.†)

* See Introductory Chapter.

† Dr. Dowler, of New Orleans, a profound vital statistician, in a pamphlet upon the influence of republican government upon the extension of population, after showing an extraordinary decline in most of the Cities, States, and Towns of South and Central America and Mexico, remarks that "in three centuries the entire Caucasian race in both Americas south of the United States, has not equalled numerically that portion of the Union lying west of the Alleghany mountains, settled by the present generation, amid the conflicts of prolonged savage wars with the bravest and most sanguinary nations known in all history."

TABLE XII.—*Aggregate Population and Density of the States and Territories.**

STATES.	POPULATION.							DENSITY.	
	1790.	1800.	1810.	1820.	1830.	1840.	1850.	1840.	1850.
Alabama				c127,901	309,527	590,756	771,623	11.65	15.21
Arkansas				14,273	30,388	97,574	209,897	1.87	4.02
California							92,597		.59
Columbia, Dist. of		14,093	24,023	33,039	39,834	43,712	51,687	437.12	861.45
Connecticut	238,141	251,002	262,042	275,202	297,675	309,978	370,792	66.32	79.33
Delaware	59,096	64,273	72,674	72,749	76,748	78,085	91,532	36.83	43.18
Florida					34,730	54,477	87,445	0.92	1.48
Georgia	82,548	162,101	252,433	340,987	516,823	691,392	906,185	11.93	15.62
Illinois			12,282	55,211	157,445	476,183	851,470	8.59	15.37
Indiana		4,875	24,520	147,178	343,031	685,866	988,416	20.28	29.24
Iowa						43,112	192,214	0.85	3.78
Kentucky	73,077	220,955	406,511	564,317	687,917	779,828	982,405	20.70	26.07
Louisiana			76,556	153,407	215,739	352,411	517,762	8.54	12.55
Maine	96,540	151,719	228,705	298,335	399,455	501,793	583,169	15.80	18.36
Maryland	319,728	341,548	380,546	407,350	447,040	470,019	583,034	42.25	52.41
Massachusetts	378,717	423,245	472,040	523,287	610,408	737,699	994,514	94.58	127.50
Michigan			4,762	8,896	31,639	212,267	397,654	3.77	7.07
Mississippi		8,850	40,352	75,448	136,621	375,651	606,326	7.97	12.86
Missouri			20,845	66,586	140,455	383,702	682,044	5.69	10.12
New Hampshire	141,899	183,762	214,360	244,161	269,328	284,574	317,976	30.67	34.26
New Jersey	184,139	211,949	245,555	277,575	320,823	373,306	489,555	44.87	58.84
New York	340,120	586,756	959,049	1,372,812	1,918,608	2,428,921	3,097,394	51.68	65.90
North Carolina	393,751	478,103	555,500	638,829	737,987	753,419	869,039	14.86	17.14
Ohio		45,365	230,760	581,434	937,903	1,519,467	1,980,329	38.02	49.55
Pennsylvania	434,373	602,361	810,091	1,049,458	1,348,233	1,724,033	2,311,786	37.48	50.26
Rhode Island	69,110	69,122	77,031	83,059	97,199	108,830	147,545	83.33	112.97
South Carolina	249,073	345,591	415,115	502,741	581,185	594,398	668,507	20.23	22.75
Tennessee	35,791	105,602	261,727	422,813	681,904	829,210	1,002,717	18.18	21.99
Texas							212,592		0.89
Vermont	85,416	154,465	217,713	235,764	280,652	291,948	314,120	28.59	30.76
Virginia	748,308	880,200	974,622	1,065,379	1,211,405	1,239,797	1,421,661	20.21	23,17
Wisconsin						30,945	305,391	0.57	5.66
Territories.									
Minnesota							6,077		0.04
New Mexico							61,547		0.30
Oregon							13,294		0.07
Utah							11,380		0.04
		5,305,937 aLess 12		9,638,191 aLess 60	b5,318	b6,100			
Total	3,929,827	5,305,925	7,239,814	9,638,131	12,866,020	17,069,453	23,191,876	9.55	7.90

a Deducted to make the totals published incorrectly in those years. *b* Persons on board vessels of war in the United States naval service. *c* A later statement from the State Department for the same year, gave Alabama a total of 144,317.

* By the State Census of Missouri, in 1848, there were 510,435 whites; 1,779 free colored; 76,757 slaves total, 588,971. By the census of 1852, there were 623,319 whites; 2,526 free colored; and 87,172 slaves; total, 713,017. By the State Census of Louisiana there were in 1847, 196,430 whites; free colored 19,842; slaves, 211,483; total, 427,755; and in 1852, 301,103 whites; 23,820 free colored; 261,692 slaves; total, 585,312. By the Census of New York, in 1845, there were 2,560,149 whites, and 44,346 colored; total, 2,604,495. By the Alabama State Census of 1850, there were 434,392 whites, 2,491 free colored, and 340,048 slaves; total 776,931. By the Massachusetts State Census of 1850, the total population was 973,715. The population of California, according to the State Census of 1852, [ordered to be made part of the Census by Congress] was 224,435. [See table near the end of the volume.] The population of Wisconsin in 1836 was 11,683; in 1838, 18,130; in 1842, 44,478; in 1847, 210,546. The white population of South Carolina, by the State Census of 1849, was 280,385.

Much interesting detail, not now published, could be gleaned from the national Census, such as should receive attention at future periods. For example, a hasty view of the returns from three or four States shows: one white person in Cole county, Missouri, pauper, and one in Schuyler county, both females, aged 110 each. In Indiana, one female, black, in Hendricks county, born in Virginia, and a female, black, in Perry county, each aged 113; and another in Wayne county, also born in Virginia, aged 104. In Colleton District, S. C., a female black, aged 111. In Lincoln county, Geo., a blind male white, aged 108; and in Wilkinson county, same State, a female white aged 105. In the parish of Lafayette, La., one female black slave aged 130, not infirm. In North Carolina three male whites aged respectively 108, 110 and 111; two white females aged each 106; one, 108; one, 114; one mulatto male, 106; one mulatto male 120; one black male, 109; one female black, 115; two black females, 110; one black female, 111; one mulatto female, 100; one Indian male, 125; one Indian female, 140. In Fountain county, Indiana, there is a family, four members of which are deaf and dumb; in Greene county, same State, another with five; in Howard county, twins deaf and dumb. In Marshall county, Indiana, there is a family with three boys, now thirteen years old, born at one birth; one of whom is blind. [The Prussian Statistics show in 23 years, 1,689 cases of *three* children at a birth, and 36 cases of *four* children; the males always preponderating.] Four out of five in a family in Weymouth, Mass., are deaf and dumb. Three children in one family in North Brookfield, are deaf and dumb. In Boston, Mass., there is a female who was a mother at eleven years of age, and in 1850 was 25 years old, and had five children living.

It appears from table XII, that although the density of population in all of the States and Territories which were organized in 1840, has increased since that time, yet in consequence of the introduction of new territory, the density of population in the Union at large, has declined from 9.55 persons to a square mile, which it was in 1840 to 7.90 in 1850. A similar decline, and for the same reason, is noticed in 1810 and 1820, from the density of 1800. Although the population of the United States has increased six fold since 1790, the number of persons to a square mile of its territory has not doubled. (See Part I.)

TABLE XIII.—*Density of Population to Square Mile in the United States.*

1790.	1800.	1810.	1820.	1830.	1840.	1850.
4.79	6.47	4.21	5.39	7.20	9.55	7.90

The population of the United States on the first of June, 1850, was twenty-three millions one hundred and ninety-one thousand eight hundred and seventy-six persons, of whom, as will be hereafter seen, nineteen millions five hundred and fifty three thousand and sixty-eight were WHITE, four hundred and thirty-four thousand four hundred and ninety-five were FREE COLORED, and three millions two hundred and four thousand three hundred and thirteen were SLAVES. If to this number be added those who possibly escaped the enumerators from being temporarily abroad or travelling in the country at the time, and were not reported, (those on their way to California were considered as already there,) as belonging to any household, or who were not sleeping in any dwelling house or out house visited—the total number may be safely set down at twenty-three millions two hundred and fifty thousand persons.* There were at that period within the jurisdiction of the Union, (see table hereafter,) *four hundred thousand seven hundred and sixty-four* unrepresented and untaxed INDIANS, swelling the aggregate population under the jurisdiction of the republic in 1850, to *twenty-three millions six hundred and fifty thousand seven hundred and sixty-four persons.*

TABLE XIV.—*Population of the several Geographical Divisions of the Union.*

The different slopes, &c.	1790.	1800.	1810.	1820.	1830.	1840.	1850.*	Per ct.
Pacific slope	....	....	....	....	....	....	117,271	0.5
Mississippi Valley	205,280	582,619	1,337,946	2,419,369	3,794,477	5,983,707	8,641,754	37.2
Atlantic slope	3,708,116	4,687,725	5,824,708	7,013,154	8,633,632	10,097,785	12,729,859	54.8
Gulf, (East of Mississippi)	16,431	35,581	75,582	201,586	426,512	964,448	1,414,598	6.1
Gulf, (West of Mississippi)	....	....	1,578	4,022	11,399	23,513	288,394	1.2
Gulf and Mississippi Valley	221,711	618,200	1,415,106	2,624,977	4,232,388	6,971,668	10,344,746	44.6

By the above table it appears that, whilst the Atlantic States have increased more than three-fold since 1790, the Gulf States, which had then scarcely any existence, have now a population nearly one-half as great as the population of all the States together at that time

* The assistant Marshals were ordered to visit every description of house; to enumerate persons temporarily absent, to include those alive on the first of June, although dead at the time of their visit, and to omit all the living who were born since the first of June. Thus sailors abroad and travellers belonging to the country, were to be included, and the assistants were required to enter from the registers at seaports, Mariners not already enumerated in families. Persons on board every description of vessel were to be taken, unless temporarily or accidentally in the country, and not belonging to it.

The English Census of 1851 gives a total of 82,921 persons not sleeping in houses at the time the census was taken, to wit, 12,924 sleep in barges, 9,972 in barns, 8,277 in tents and open air, 8,575 in vessels in port engaged in inland navigation, 43,173 in sea-going vessels in port. The total number of sailors in tha American merchant marine may be estimated in 1853, at about 112,500. In the United States navy, the number of seamen at the period of the census of 1850, was 7,500, of whom about 6,638 were then out of the country, and of the total number, about 1,360 were of foreign birth, [from a statement prepared for this office by the Secretary of the Navy], a similar report from the War Department, shows the number of the army, 1st June 1850, officers and men, 10,540, two-thirds of the latter or about 7,026 being foreign born. The number of men in the army, navy, &c, of Great Britain in 1853, was 210,474. The number of merchant seamen at home and abroad, 124,744, total, 335,218; of the 225,916 abroad, 13,722 were of colonial or foreign birth. The number of British subjects other than mariners in foreign states, was ascertained in 1851 through the State Department to be 33,775, exclusively of those in other places not ascertained, to wit, in Greece, 1,068, Russia, 2,783, Sardinia, 1,069, Turkey, 611, Two Sicilies, 1,414, China, 649, Persia, 33, Alexandria, 155, Cairo, 85, Tripoli, 23, Belgium, 3,828, France, 20,357, Saxony, 321, Turkey in Asia, 624, Mexico, 755, &c. It would be well for the government of the United States in a similar manner through its consuls and ministers, to obtain this information in regard to its citizens at each census or oftener. At present the number of citizens residing abroad cannot be conjectured unless from the number of native passengers annually returning to the country. It is said that 700 to 1,000 are now residents of Paris. The total number abroad may be supposed at least as large as that of foreigners in the country who are merely passing through it without the intention of remaining, and no doubt it is many times larger. Such foreigners, however, under the instructions to Marshals, would not be enumerated in our schedules. The whole number of foreigners temporarily in Great Britain is not known, though the annual number entering the country did not exceed before 1850, an average of 18,000, swelled in 1851 in consequence of the Great Fair, to 65,233.

The great Interior Valley of the Mississippi has, in sixty years advanced more than forty-fold; the increase being six-fold in the first twenty years and nearly seven-fold in the following forty years. The Gulf region and the Mississippi Valley together, in 1850, have eleven-twentieths of the whole population of the Union. The statistics are calculated upon a close inspection of the maps, including, where necessary, counties only, or fractions of counties, so as to correspond with the divisions indicated by the Topographical Bureau. They will therefore be found to correspond very nearly, if not altogether, with the facts.

TABLE XV.—*Population and Density of Geographical and Other Divisions.*

Divisions.	Population.	Density.	Divisions.	Population.	Density.
The States, exclusively of Territories	23,099,578	15.77	Southern States	3,952,837	15.27
The States, exclusively of Texas and California	22,794,389	21.29	South Western States	3,321,117	7.00
Texas and California	305,189	.77	North West	6,379,923	16.13
The Territories	92,298	.06	North of 36.30	13,626,995	6.91
The Non-slaveholding States	13,434,922	21.91	South of 36.30	9,564,881	9.90
The Slaveholding States	9,664,656	11.35	East of the Mississippi	21,393,954	24.71
New England States	2,728,116	41.94	West of the Mississippi	1,797,922	.87
Middle States	6,624,988	57.79	Pacific slope	117,271	.15
			Mississippi slope	8,641,754	6.98
			Atlantic slope	12,729,859	19.98

The Middle States are therefore the densest portion of the Union, owing, in some degree, to the very large cities existing there. The New England States come next in order; then the North-west; then the South, and lastly the South-west. The non-slaveholding States are twice as dense as the slaveholding States. The States, taken together, have a density of about sixteen to the square mile. Excluding Texas and California, their density is over twenty-one to the square mile. The Territories have one inhabitant only to every sixteen square miles. Texas and California together have less than one to a square mile. Whilst nearly twenty-five persons inhabit a square mile in the region east of the Mississippi, and nearly twenty persons in the Atlantic slope, in the Mississippi valley there are only about seven persons to the square mile; west of the Mississippi, less than one person to the square mile; on the Pacific slope, one person to every six square miles! With the density of the Mississippi valley the United States would have had but 21,000,000 inhabitants; with the density of the Southern States, the number would be nearly 45,000,000; with the density of New England, 123,000,000; and with the density of the Middle States, 170,000,000*

The density of Switzerland approximates nearer than that of any of the countries named in the note to the density of Massachusetts, although still at a large remove. Belgium, the highest on the list, is more than three times as dense as Massachusetts, and nearly ten times as dense as New England. Great Britain is denser than France; and Holland, denser than either, having twice the density of Massachusetts. Brazil, Mexico and Canada are much less dense than the United States. With the density of Sweden and Norway, the least populous of any European States, the United States would embrace forty-five millions of inhabitants; with the density of Russia, over eighty millions; with that of Spain, two hundred millions; of France, five hundred millions; of Britain, six hundred and sixty millions; of Belgium eleven hundred and fifty millions. Twelve times the number of persons now live to the east of the Mississippi as live to the west of it. The non-slaveholding have a third greater population than the slaveholding States. The South has more than the South-west. The Middle States have as much as the Southern, and New England or South-western together, and a little more than the North-west.

The number of representatives assigned to each of the States in the lower House of Congress under the several enumerations, and those that were assigned prior to the first census, together with other facts relating to the origin of States and Territories, are condensed into the table which follows. To understand it fully will require a reference to other pages of the volume in which the population is exhibited by classes.

* TABLE XVI.—*Exhibiting the population and number of inhabitants to the square mile of various American and European Countries.*

Countries.	Population.	Density.	Countries.	Population.	Density.
United States	23,191,876	7.90	Prussia	16,331,187	151.32
Canada	1,842,265	5.31	Spain	14,216,219	78.03
Mexico	7,661,919	7.37	Turkey in Europe	15,500,000	73.60
Central America	2,049,950	10.07	Sweden and Norway	4,645,007	15.83
Brazil	6,065,000	2.19	Belgium	4,426,202	388.60
Peru	2,106,492	3.63	Portugal	3,473,758	95.14
Russia in Europe	60,315,350	28.44	Holland	3,267,638	259.31
Austria	36,514,466	141.88	Denmark	2,296,597	101.92
France	35,783,170	172.74	Switzerland	2,392,740	160.05
England	16,921,888	332.00	Greece	998,266	55.70
Great Britain and Ireland	27,475,271	225.19			

TABLE XVII.—*Representation in Congress—Formation of States and Territories.*†

States and Territories.	Before census.	1790	1800	1810	1820	1830	1840	1850	REMARKS
Alabama	....	....	....	*1	3	5	7	7	From territory ceded to U. S. by South Carolina and Georgia. Admitted Dec. 14, 1819.
Arkansas	....	....	....	....	....	*1	1	2	From territory ceded by France. Admitted June 15, '36.
California	....	....	....	....	....	....	*2	2	From territory ceded by Mexico. Admitted Sept. 9, '50.
Columbia, Dist. of	....	....	....	....	....	....	....	....	From territory ceded by Maryland and Virginia. Established as seat of government July 16, 1790. Alexandria retroceded July 1846.
Connecticut	5	7	7	7	6	6	4	4	One of the thirteen original States. Ratified the Constitution January 9, 1788.
Delaware	1	1	1	2	1	1	1	1	One of the thirteen original States. Ratified the Constitution December 7, 1787.
Florida	....	....	....	....	....	....	*1	1	From territory ceded by Spain. Admitted March 3, '45.
Georgia	3	2	4	6	7	9	8	8	One of the thirteen original States. Ratified the Constitution January 2, 1788.
Illinois	....	....	....	*1	1	3	7	9	Out of territory ceded by Virginia. Admitted Dec. 3, '18.
Indiana	....	....	....	*1	3	7	10	11	From territory ceded by Virginia. Admitted Dec.11, '16.
Iowa	....	....	....	....	....	....	*2	2	From part Wisconsin territory. Admitted Dec. 28, '46.
Kentucky	....	2	6	10	12	13	10	10	From the territory of Virginia. Admitted June 1, 1792.
Louisiana	....	....	....	*1	3	3	4	4	From territory ceded by France. Admitted April 8, '12.
Maine	....	....	....	*7	7	8	7	6	Out of part of territory of Mass. Admitted Mar. 15, '20.
Maryland	6	8	9	9	9	8	6	6	One of the thirteen original States. Ratified the Constitution April 28, 1788.
Massachusetts	8	14	17	20	13	12	10	11	One of the thirteen original States. Ratified the Constitution February 6, 1788.
Michigan	....	....	....	....	....	*1	3	4	From territory ceded by Virginia. Admitted Jan. 26, '37
Mississippi	....	....	....	*1	1	2	4	5	From territory ceded by Georgia and South Carolina. Admitted December 10, 1817.
Missouri	....	....	....	....	*1	2	5	7	From territory ceded by France. Admitted Aug. 10. '21.
New Hampshire	3	4	5	6	6	5	4	3	One of the thirteen original States. Ratified the Constitution June, 21, 1788.
New Jersey	4	5	6	6	6	6	5	5	One of the thirteen original States. Ratified the Constitution December 18, 1787.
New York	6	10	17	27	34	40	34	33	One of the thirteen original States. Ratified the Constitution July 26, 1788.
North Carolina	5	10	12	13	13	13	9	8	One of the thirteen original States. Ratified the Constitution November 21, 1789.
Ohio	....	....	*1	6	14	19	21	21	Out of territory ceded by Virginia. Admit'd Nov. 29, '02
Pennsylvania	8	13	18	23	26	28	24	25	One of the thirteen original States. Ratified the Con stitution December 12, 1787.
Rhode Island	1	2	2	2	2	2	2	2	One of the thirteen original States. Ratified the Constitution May 29, 1790.
South Carolina	5	6	8	9	9	9	7	6	One of the thirteen original States. Ratified the Constitution May 23, 1788.
Tennessee	....	*1	3	6	9	13	11	10	Of territory ceded by N. Carolina. Admit'd June 1, '96.
Texas	....	....	....	....	....	....	*2	2	Independent Republic. Admitted December 29, 1845.
Vermont	....	2	4	6	5	5	4	3	From part of the territory of New York. Admitted March 4, 1791.
Virginia	10	19	22	23	22	21	15	13	One of the thirteen original States. Ratified the Constitution June 26, 1788.
Wisconsin	....	....	....	....	....	....	*2	3	From part of the territory of Michigan. Admitted May 29, 1848.
Territories. Minnesota									Territorial government established March 3, 1849.
New Mexico	[The Territorial governments, when established by Congress and organized, send delegates to that body, who are present at its deliberations with a right of debating but not of voting.]								Formed from territory ceded by Mexico and Texas. Territorial government established Sept. 9, 1850.
Oregon									Territorial government established August 14, 1848.
Utah									Territorial government established September 9, 1850.
Washington									" " " March 2, 1853.
Nebraska									" " " May 30, 1854.
Kansas									" " " May 30, 1854.

* Admitted into the Union after the apportionment under which they are here arranged was made, but before the succeeding census.

† The whole of the thirteen "original States" were settled in the period of one hundred and twenty-five years, which intervened between the landing at Jamestown, Virginia, in 1607, and the arrival of Oglethorpe in Georgia in 1733. Meanwhile Henry Hudson had come to New York [1609]; the Mayflower's colony had landed in Massachusetts [1620]; John Mason had received a grant of New Hampshire in the same year; a patent had issued for Connecticut [1631]; religious differences in Massachusetts had sent settlers to Rhode Island; a title to Maryland had vested in Lord Baltimore [1632]; a cession of Delaware was obtained from the Indians [1640]; the Carolinas had passed into the possession of Clarendon and others, were settled in 1667 or 1668, and divided in two in 1729; and New Jersey had been patented in 1664. During the revolution, and afterwards, Congress held its sessions in Philadelphia, Baltimore, New York, Lancaster, York, Princeton, Annapolis and Trenton. Having been interrupted at Philadelphia the sessions were removed to the halls of the college at Princeton. In 1784 commissioners were appointed to procure a site for the Capitol, between two or three miles square, upon the Delaware river, and erect suitable buildings, but nothing was done by them. In 1789 a bill passed one House of Congress in favor of a location upon the banks of the Susquehanna. The present seat of government, [District of Columbia,] was selected by virtue of acts passed in 1788–89, by Virginia and Maryland ceding ten miles square upon the Potomac under the name of Connogocheague. The first session of Congress was held in the District, November, 1800.

NOTE.—Ratios of Representation 1790 and 1800, 1 to 33,000; 1810, 35,000; 1820, 40,000; 1830, 47,700; 1840, 70,680; 1850, 93,420; act of 1850 fixes the number of members at 233, to which afterwards was added 1 for California; Massachusetts, Rhode Island, Connecticut, Pennsylvania, Maryland, Alabama, Tennessee, Kentucky, Missouri, Indiana, Texas, South Carolina and Georgia, 1 member each for largest fractions. Future ratios of apportionment to be determined by Secretary of Interior, by dividing the number 233 into whole *representative population*, giving States with largest fractions members to make up the total. Members from new States admitted shall be in addition to the 233 until the next census.

Including the Senate, where the representation of each State is equal, it will be seen that the Atlantic States which sent, in 1820, one hundred and ninety-six members to Congress, against sixty-two members sent from the West, sent, in 1850, but one hundred and sixty-seven against one hundred and twenty-nine from the West. In 1800, one hundred and thirty-two members represented slaveholding States, and thirty-seven, only, States without slaves. The present slaveholding States, which had, in 1820, ninety-seven representatives to one hundred and sixty-one from the free States, had in 1850, one hundred and twenty to one hundred and seventy-six from the Free States. Some other tables illustrating the comparative rank of the States, will have place hereafter. The United States, which in 1790 included fifteen States and the District of Columbia, had increased, in 1800 to sixteen States and three Territories, including the District of Columbia; in 1810 to seventeen States and seven Territories; in 1820 to twenty-three States and five Territories; in 1830 to twenty-four States and five Territories; in 1840 to twenty-six States and three Territories; in 1850 to thirty-one States and five Territories; and in 1854 to thirty-one States and eight organized Territories (including the District of Columbia, always.)

In population, therefore, the United States, in 1850, was only exceeded by four of the European powers, namely, Russia, Austria, France, and the British Empire in Europe. It is nearly or quite twice as populous as either Prussia, Spain, Turkey, the whole of the German States, the whole of the Italian States, including Greece and the Swiss republics, and excluding Naples and Sicily. It is nearly three times as large as the kingdoms of Sweden, Belgium, and Portugal combined, and is equal to the aggregate population of twenty-four out of the thirty-seven States into which McCulloch divides Europe. Exclusively of Ireland, it exceeds that of Great Britain by a population nearly equal to that of the State of Pennsylvania. In comparing with the individual States, Portugal and the Netherlands find their counterpart in New York, Sweden and Switzerland in Pennsylvania, and Norway and Denmark in Virginia.*

Thirteen territorial governments have ceased to exist, having been absorbed by the several new States. Their names and the dates at which they were respectively established are as follows:—

Territories.	Established.	Territories.	Established.
Northwest of the Ohio	July 13, 1787	Missouri	June 4, 1812
Indian	May 7, 1800	Alabama	March 3, 1817
Mississippi	May 10, 1800	Arkansas	March 2, 1819
Orleans	March 26, 1804	Florida	March 3, 1819
Louisiana	March 26, 1804	Wisconsin	April 20, 1836
Michigan	January 11, 1805	Iowa	June 12, 1838
Illinois	February 3, 1809		

Having given the aggregate population of the Union at the several census periods, and during its colonial history, it will now be proper to pass to the consideration of the statistics in detail, separating the color, sex, age, nativity, and condition, and condensing the facts and forming the ratios in regard to each under its respective chapter or division. A concluding chapter will embrace the ratio and comparative tables of the total population, native and foreign, and such other facts and discussions as may not be readily or conveniently reducible under the previous heads.

* The Registrar General of Great Britain, in endeavoring to give a clear conception of the enormous number of persons embraced within the empire, indulges, in his report for 1851, in some rather amusing illustrations. He estimates the number of square miles which would be covered by them, if closely packed together; and the number of days they would occupy in passing through the halls of the great Crystal Palace. If a similar indulgence might be allowed, it will be supposed that the aggregate population of the United States in 1850 is to be formed into a single procession, in which each person shall be at a distance of six feet from any other a convenient walking distance. The length of such a procession would be 26,875 miles, more than sufficient to belt the earth itself. Whilst the head of the procession might be located where the waters of the Atlantic form the Chesapeake bay, a portion would be ascending the Rocky mountains, and another descending to the sea on the opposite extremity of the continent. Were the ocean for this purpose considered fordable, a third would be midway of the wide expanse of the Pacific, a fourth admiring the walls of China, a fifth lost in the wilds of Tartary, whilst a sixth, seventh, and eighth would be crossing the deserts of Arabia, viewing the ruins of Palestine, entering Greece, spreading over Germany, France, and Britain, or wending its way across the basin of the Atlantic from the old world back again to the new. The glare of noonday sun lights up the procession in one part, in another it is immersed in the gloom of midnight darkness. The snows of Arctic regions, the blaze of torrid suns, and the genial breezes of the tropics divide empire alike over the ranks of the great procession.

To continue the illustration, the time which it would take this procession to pass a given point on a march of three miles an hour, would be as follows: the free whites alone, 308 days, the men requiring 158 days, and the women 150; native born 273 days, and foreign born 35. The free blacks would require nearly 7 days; the slaves 50 days, and the Indians of the forests about 6 days. The merchants, mechanics, and manufacturers would require 25 days, the farmers 37 days, the laborers 16 days, the sailors and boatmen 40 hours. The children under ten years would occupy 166 days, and the infants in the arms of their nurses, under one year of age, at least 10 days more. Or taking the aggregate of all, an observer would be required to stand throughout every hour of the day and night for three hundred and seventy-three days, to enumerate the persons as they passed.

CHAPTER III.

WHITE POPULATION OF THE UNITED STATES.

1. *Aggregate Number.*—The number of white persons in the United States on the 1st of June, 1850, was ascertained to be 19,553,068, of whom 17,312,533 were native and 2,240,535 foreign born. By reference to the following table the aggregate number, at every census, in the States and Territories will be seen:

TABLE XVIII.—*White Population of the United States.*

STATES AND TERRITORIES.	1790.	1800.	1810.	1820.	1830.	1840.	1850.
Alabama	…	…	…	85,451	190,406	335,185	426,514
Arkansas	…	…	…	12,579	25,671	77,174	162,189
California	…	…	…	…	…	…	91,635
Columbia, District of	…	10,066	16,079	22,614	27,563	30,657	37,941
Connecticut	232,581	244,721	255,279	267,161	289,603	301,856	363,099
Delaware	46,310	49,852	55,361	55,282	57,601	58,561	71,169
Florida	…	…	…	…	18,385	27,943	47,203
Georgia	52,886	101,678	145,414	189,566	296,806	407,695	521,572
Illinois	…	…	11,501	53,788	155,061	472,254	846,034
Indiána	…	4,577	23,890	145,758	339,399	678,698	977,154
Iowa	…	…	…	…	…	42,924	191,881
Kentucky	61,133	179,871	324,237	434,644	517,787	590,253	761,413
Louisiana	…	…	34,311	73,383	89,441	158,457	255,491
Maine	96,002	150,901	227,736	297,340	398,263	500,438	581,813
Maryland	208,649	216,326	235,117	260,223	291,108	318,204	417,943
Massachusetts	373,254	416,793	465,303	516,419	603,359	729,030	985,450
Michigan	…	…	4,618	8,591	31,346	211,560	395,071
Mississippi	…	5,179	23,024	42,176	70,443	179,074	295,718
Missouri	…	…	17,227	55,988	114,795	323,888	592,004
New Hampshire	141,111	182,898	213,390	243,236	268,721	284,036	317,456
New Jersey	169,954	195,125	226,861	257,409	300,266	351,588	465,509
New York	314,142	556,039	918,699	1,332,744	1,873,663	2,378,890	3,048,325
North Carolina	288,204	337,764	376,410	419,200	472,843	484,870	553,028
Ohio	…	45,028	228,861	576,572	928,329	1,502,122	1,955,050
Pennsylvania	424,099	586,094	786,804	1,017,094	1,309,900	1,676,115	2,258,160
Rhode Island	64,689	65,437	73,314	79,413	93,621	105,587	143,875
South Carolina	140,178	196,255	214,196	237,440	257,863	259,084	274,563
Tennessee	32,013	91,709	215,875	339,927	535,746	640,627	756,836
Texas	…	…	…	…	…	…	154,034
Vermont	85,144	153,908	216,963	234,846	279,771	291,218	313,402
Virginia	442,115	514,280	551,534	603,087	694,300	740,858	894,800
Wisconsin	…	…	…	…	…	30,749	304,756
Territories. Minnesota	…	…	…	…	…	…	6,038
Territories. New Mexico	…	…	…	…	…	…	61,525
Territories. Oregon	…	…	…	…	…	…	13,087
Territories. Utah	…	…	…	…	…	…	11,330
					† 5,318	† 6,100	
		4,304,501 * less 12.		7,861,931 *add 6			
Aggregate	3,172,464	4,304,489	5,862,004	7,861,937	10,537,378	14,195,695	19,553,068

TABLE XIX.—*Increase of the Whites.*

	1800.	1810.	1820.	1830.	1840.	1850.
Present slaveholding States	33.94	29.70	28.2	29.35	26.54	34.26
Present non-slaveholding States	36.85	40.43	37.70	36.67	39.10	39.42

The number of whites in the slaveholding States, in 1790, was 1,271,488; in 1800, 1,702,980; in 1810, 2,208,785; in 1820, 2,831,560; in 1830, 3,662,606; in 1840, 4,634,519; and in 1850, 6,222,418.

The number of whites in the present non-slaveholding States, in 1790, was 1,900,976; in 1800, 2,601,509; 1810, 3,653,219; 1820, 5,030,377; 1830, 6,874,772; 1840, 9,561,176; 1850, 13,330,650. The persons engaged in naval service in 1830 and 1840 are divided in proportion between the two sections.

The white population which had been increasing at a declining ratio in the slaveholding States generally between 1790 and in 1840, increased between 1840 and 1850, 34.26 per cent., being a larger ratio than at any previous period. In the non-slaveholding States the ratio in 1840 and 1850 differs but slightly, and is less than it was in 1810, though greater than at other periods.

By the following table, it will be seen that Massachusetts, which was the first State, according to its white population in 1790, has now become the fourth, exactly reversing the course

* Added or deducted to make the aggregates, published incorrectly in those years.
† Persons on board of vessels of war in the United States naval service.

of New York, which has become first from the fourth rank. Virginia has descended from the second to the sixth; South Carolina from the tenth to the twenty-third; whilst Ohio, which in 1800 was the seventeenth, has become the third, and Indiana, which in 1810 was the nineteenth, has become the fifth in rank; Pennsylvania has changed least of any of the States, being always of first, second, or third rank.

TABLE XX.—*Relative Rank of the States and Territories according to their White Population.*

States and Territories.	Whites.						
	1790.	1800.	1810.	1820.	1830.	1840.	1850.
Alabama	....	....	....	18	18	14	15
Arkansas	....	....	....	26	27	25	26
California	....	....	....	....	....	....	29
Columbia, Dist. of	....	18	22	25	26	29	33
Connecticut	6	6	7	10	14	17	18
Delaware	15	16	17	22	24	26	30
Florida	....	....	....	....	28	30	32
Georgia	14	13	15	16	12	12	13
Illinois	....	....	23	23	19	11	7
Indiana	....	20	19	17	10	6	5
Iowa	....	....	....	....	....	27	25
Kentucky	13	11	6	6	7	8	8
Louisiana	....	....	18	20	22	23	24
Maine	....	....	....	9	9	9	11
Maryland	7	7	8	11	13	16	16
Massachusetts	1	2	3	5	5	5	4
Michigan	....	....	24	27	25	21	17
Mississippi	....	19	20	24	23	22	22
Missouri	....	....	21	21	20	15	10
New Hampshire	9	10	14	13	16	19	19
New Jersey	8	9	10	12	11	13	14
New York	4	3	1	1	1	1	1
North Carolina	5	5	5	7	8	10	12
Ohio	....	17	9	4	3	3	3
Pennsylvania	3	1	2	2	2	2	2
Rhode Island	12	15	16	19	21	24	28
South Carolina	10	8	13	14	17	20	23
Tennessee	16	14	12	8	6	7	9
Texas	....	....	....	....	....	....	27
Vermont	11	12	11	15	15	18	20
Virginia	2	4	4	3	4	4	6
Wisconsin	....	....	....	....	....	28	21
TERRITORIES:							
Minnesota	....	....	....	....	....	....	36
New Mexico	....	....	....	....	....	....	31
Oregon	....	....	....	....	....	....	34
Utah	....	....	....	....	....	....	35

The annexed table will show the proportion which the white population of each State sustained to its total population at each of the periods mentioned. It will be seen that while the proportion of this class has been generally gaining at the north and in Virginia, in the South, except Virginia, it has been as generally losing.

TABLE XXI.—*Proportion of White to Total Population of each State.*

States and Territories.	Whites.						
	1790.	1800.	1810.	1820.	1830.	1840.	1850.
Alabama	....	....	....	66.81	61.52	56.74	55.27
Arkansas	....	....	....	88.13	84.48	79.09	77.27
California	....	....	....	....	....	....	98.96
Columbia, District of	....	71.43	66.93	68.44	69.20	70.13	73.41
Connecticut	97.66	97.50	97.42	97.08	97.29	97.38	97.93
Delaware	78.36	77.56	76.18	75.99	75.05	75.00	77.75
Florida	....	....	....	....	52.93	51.29	53.98
Georgia	64.07	62.73	57.60	55.59	57.43	58.97	57.56
Illinois	....	....	93.64	97.42	98.49	99.17	99.36
Indiana	....	93.89	97.43	99.03	98.94	98.96	98.86
Iowa	....	....	....	....	....	99.56	99.83
Kentucky	83.66	81.41	79.76	77.02	75.27	75.69	77.50
Louisiana	....	....	44.82	47.83	41.46	44.96	49.35
Maine	99.44	99.46	99.58	99.69	99.70	99.73	99.77
Maryland	65.26	63.34	61.78	63.88	65.12	67.70	71.68
Massachusetts	98.56	98.48	98.57	98.60	98.85	98.82	99.09
Michigan	....	....	96.98	96.57	99.07	99.67	99.35
Mississippi	....	58.52	57.06	55.90	51.56	47.67	48.76
Missouri	....	....	82.64	84.08	81.73	84.41	86.79
New Hampshire	99.44	99.53	99.55	99.62	99.78	99.81	99.84
New Jersey	92.30	92.06	92.39	92.73	93.59	94.18	95.09
New York	92.36	94.76	95.79	97.08	97.66	97.94	98.42
North Carolina	73.19	70.65	67.76	65.62	64.07	64.36	63.64
Ohio	....	99.26	99.18	99.16	98.98	98.86	98.72
Pennsylvania	97.63	97.30	97.13	96.92	97.16	97.22	97.68
Rhode Island	93.60	94.67	95.18	95.61	96.32	97.02	97.51
South Carolina	56.28	56.79	51.60	47.33	44.37	43.59	41.07
Tennessee	89.44	86.84	82.48	80.40	78.57	77.26	75.48
Texas	....	....	....	....	....	....	72.45
Vermont	99.68	99.64	99.66	99.61	99.69	99.75	99.77
Virginia	59.08	58.43	56.59	56.61	57.31	59.76	62.94
Wisconsin	....	....	....	....	....	99.37	99.79
Territories. Minnesota	....	....	....	....	....	....	99.36
Territories. Oregon	....	....	....	....	....	....	98.44
Territories. Utah	....	....	....	....	....	....	99.56
Territories. New Mexico	....	....	....	....	....	....	99.96

The increase per cent. of the white population in each period of ten years, is shown below for all of the States. The greatest increase in ten years was made in Indiana, which gained 510 per cent. between 1810 and 1820; in Michigan, which gained 574 per cent. between 1830 and 1840, and in Wisconsin, which gained 891 per cent. between 1840 and 1850. But a single case of decrease of whites is to be found in the whole period, to wit: Delaware which lost a fraction between 1810 and 1820.

TABLE XXII.—*Progress of Population.—Increase of the White Population of the United States under each Census from* 1790 *to* 1850.

States and Territories.	1800.	1810.	1820.	1830.	1840.	1850.
	Increase per cent.	Increase per cent.	Increase per cent.	Increase per cent.	Increase per cent.	Increase per cent.
Alabama	....	....	....	122.82	76.03	27.24
Arkansas	....	....	....	104.07	200.62	110.16
California	....	....	....	....	....	....
Columbia, District of	....	59.73	40.64	21.88	11.22	23.75
Connecticut	5.21	4.31	4.65	8.4	4.23	0.28
Delaware	7.64	11.05	*	4.19	1.66	21.52
Florida	....	....	....	....	51.98	68.92
Georgia	92.25	43.01	30.36	56.57	37.36	27.93
Illinois	....	....	367.68	188.28	204.56	79.14
Indiana	....	421.95	510.12	132.85	99.97	43.97
Iowa	....	....	....	....	....	347.02
Kentucky	194.22	80.26	34.05	19.12	13.99	28.99
Louisiana	....	....	113.87	21.88	77.16	61.23
Maine	57.18	50.91	30.56	33.94	25.65	16.26
Maryland	3.67	8.68	10.67	11.86	9.3	31.34
Massachusetts	11.66	11.63	10.98	16.83	20.82	35.17
Michigan	....	....	86.03	264.87	574.91	86.74
Mississippi	....	344.56	83.18	67.02	154.21	65.13
Missouri	....	....	225.00	105.03	182.14	82.78
New Hampshire	29.61	16.67	13.98	10.47	5.69	11.76
New Jersey	14.81	16.26	13.46	16.64	17.09	32.4
New York	77.0	65.22	45.06	40.58	26.96	28.14
North Carolina	17.19	11.44	11.36	12.79	2.54	14.05
Ohio	....	408.26	151.93	61.0	61.8	30.15
Pennsylvania	38.19	34.24	29.26	28.78	27.95	34.72
Rhode Island	1.15	12.03	8.31	17.89	12.78	36.26
South Carolina	40.0	9.14	10.85	8.6	0.47	5.97
Tennessee	186.47	135.39	57.46	57.6	19.57	18.13
Texas	....	....	....	....	....	....
Vermont	80.76	40.96	8.24	19.12	4.09	7.61
Virginia	16.32	7.24	9.34	15.12	6.7	20.77
Wisconsin	....	....	....	....	....	891.1
Territories	....	....	....	....	....	....

2. *Families and Dwellings.*—The number of families into which the white population of the United States is divided, and the dwellings which they occupy, though indicated separately upon the returns, were not taken off in the tables except in combination with the free colored. This was an omission which it is now too late to remedy, and the statistics upon the subject will therefore be postponed to Chapter VI, which treats of the details of aggregate population.

The schedules do not give the relation of the members of the family to its head, as was recommended, and as it is given in Great Britain, Massachusetts, etc. It would then be practicable to ascertain the average number of children to a family, the number of female as well as male servants, the number who are living in the married, single or widowed state, &c. A census cannot be complete without these facts. At present nothing but unsatisfactory approximations can be made from the materials of the office in regard to them, and nothing has, therefore, been attempted.

3. *Sex.*—The number of white males in the United States in 1850 was 10,026,402, and of white females 9,526,666. Of these 8,786,968 males and 8,525,565 females were ascertained to be native born, and 1,239,434 males and 1,001,101 females to be foreign born. The following table will show the number of white males and females at each census from 1790 to 1850.

* Decrease, 0.14.

TABLE XXIII.—*Sex of the White Population of the United States.*

MALES.

STATES AND TERRITORIES.	1790.	1800.	1810.	1820.	1830.	1840.	1850.
Alabama	....	....	....	45,839	100,846	176,692	219,483
Arkansas	....	....	....	6,971	14,195	42,211	85,874
California	....	....	....	....	....	....	84,708
Columbia, District of	....	5,308	8,130	11,171	13,647	14,822	18,494
Connecticut	115,019	121,193	126,373	130,707	143,047	148,300	179,884
Delaware	23,926	25,033	28,006	27,905	28,845	29,259	35,746
Florida	....	....	....	....	10,236	16,456	25,705
Georgia	27,147	53,380	75,846	98,404	153,288	210,534	266,233
Illinois	....	....	6,380	29,401	82,048	255,235	445,544
Indiana	....	2,574	12,570	76,649	175,885	352,773	506,178
Iowa	....	....	....	....	....	24,256	100,887
Kentucky	32,211	93,956	168,805	223,696	267,123	305,323	392,804
Louisiana	....	....	18,940	41,332	49,832	89,747	141,243
Maine	49,132	76,832	115,509	149,195	200,689	252,989	296,745
Maryland	107,254	110,650	120,220	131,744	147,340	158,804	211,187
Massachusetts	182,672	205,494	229,742	252,154	294,685	360,679	484,093
Michigan	....	....	2,837	5,383	18,168	113,395	208,465
Mississippi	....	2,917	12,850	23,286	38,466	97,256	156,287
Missouri	....	....	9,387	31,001	61,405	173,470	312,987
New Hampshire	70,940	91,158	105,782	119,210	131,184	139,004	155,960
New Jersey	86,667	99,525	115,357	129,619	152,529	177,055	233,452
New York	161,822	297,452	474,281	679,551	954,295	1,207,357	1,544,489
North Carolina	147,494	171,648	188,632	209,644	235,954	240,047	273,025
Ohio	....	24,433	119,657	300,607	479,713	775,360	1,004,117
Pennsylvania	217,736	301,467	401,466	516,618	665,812	844,770	1,142,734
Rhode Island	31,844	31,858	35,843	38,492	45,333	51,362	70,340
South Carolina	73,298	100,916	109,587	120,934	130,590	130,496	137,747
Tennessee	16,648	47,180	111,763	173,600	275,066	325,434	382,235
Texas	....	....	....	....	....	....	84,869
Vermont	44,746	79,328	109,581	117,310	139,996	146,378	159,658
Virginia	227,069	262,129	280,038	304,884	347,887	371,213	451,300
Wisconsin	....	....	....	....	....	18,757	164,351
Territ's. Minnesota	....	....	....	....	....	....	3,695
Territ's. New Mexico	....	....	....	....	....	....	31,725
Territ's. Oregon	....	....	....	....	....	....	8,138
Territ's. Utah	....	....	....	....	....	....	6,020

FEMALES.

STATES AND TERRITORIES.	1790.	1800.	1810.	1820.	1830.	1840.	1850.
Alabama	....	....	....	39,612	89,560	158,493	207,031
Arkansas	....	....	....	5,608	11,476	34,963	76,315
California	....	....	....	....	....	....	6,927
Columbia, District of	....	4,758	7,949	11,443	13,916	15,835	19,447
Connecticut	117,562	123,528	128,906	136,454	146,556	153,556	183,215
Delaware	22,384	24,819	27,355	27,377	28,756	29,302	35,423
Florida	....	....	....	....	8,149	11,487	21,498
Georgia	25,739	48,298	69,568	91,162	143,518	197,161	255,339
Illinois	....	....	5,121	24,387	73,013	217,019	400,490
Indiana	....	2,003	11,320	69,109	163,514	325,925	470,976
Iowa	....	....	....	....	....	18,668	90,994
Kentucky	28,922	85,915	155,432	210,948	250,664	284,930	368,609
Louisiana	....	....	15,371	32,051	39,609	68,710	114,248
Maine	46,870	74,069	112,227	148,145	197,574	247,449	285,068
Maryland	101,395	105,676	114,897	128,479	143,768	159,400	206,756
Massachusetts	190,582	211,299	235,561	264,265	308,674	368,351	501,357
Michigan	....	....	1,781	3,208	13,178	98,165	186,606
Mississippi	....	2,262	10,174	18,890	31,977	81,818	139,431
Missouri	....	....	7,840	24,987	53,390	150,418	279,017
New Hampshire	70,171	91,740	107,608	124,026	137,537	145,032	161,496
New Jersey	83,287	95,600	111,504	127,790	147,737	174,533	232,057
New York	152,320	258,587	444,418	653,193	919,368	1,171,533	1,503,836
North Carolina	140,710	166,116	187,778	209,556	236,889	244,823	280,003
Ohio	....	20,595	109,204	275,965	448,616	726,762	950,933
Pennsylvania	206,363	284,627	385,338	500,476	644,088	831,345	1,115,426
Rhode Island	32,845	33,579	37,471	40,921	48,288	54,225	73,535
South Carolina	66,880	95,339	104,609	116,506	127,273	128,588	136,816
Tennessee	15,365	44,529	104,112	166,327	260,680	315,193	374,601
Texas	....	....	....	....	....	....	69,165
Vermont	40,398	74,580	107,382	117,536	139,775	144,840	153,744
Virginia	215,046	252,151	271,496	298,203	346,413	369,645	443,500
Wisconsin	....	....	....	....	....	11,992	140,405
Territ's. Minnesota	....	....	....	....	....	....	2,343
Territ's. New Mexico	....	....	....	....	....	....	29,800
Territ's. Oregon	....	....	....	....	....	....	4,949
Territ's. Utah	....	....	....	....	....	....	5,310

NOTE.—The aggregates do not always correspond exactly with those of Table XXV, as the corrections there made are not noted in this. The differences are but slight.

TABLE XXIV.—*Exhibiting the ratio of white Females to 100 Males at each Census.*

SEX.	1790.	1800.	1810.	1820.	1830.	1840.	1850.
Males	100	100	100	100	100	100	100
Females	96.4	95.3	96.2	96.8	96.4	95.6	95

It appears from the above that the number of white females in the United States, at every census, has been from four to six in a hundred, nearly, less than that of the males, and that the excess of the males has been increasing, though in no very regular manner. In 1850 it was greater than at any other period.

The increase of white males and females and the per centages of the increase of both together, in periods of ten years, are shown in the following table:

TABLE XXV.—*Increase of White Population, Males and Females.*

PERIODS.	Number of males.	Number of females.	Excess of males.	Total free whites.	Increase in each 10, and in 60 years.	Increase per cent. in each 10, and in 60 years.
1790	1,615,625	1,556,839	58,786	3,172,464	....	....
1800	2,204,421	2,100,068	104,353	4,304,489	1,132,025	35.6828
1810	2,987,571	2,874,433	113,138	5,862,004	1,557,515	36.1835
1820*	3,995,133	3,866,804	128,329	7,861,937	1,999,933	34.1169
1830*	5,355,133	5,171,115	184,018	10,526,248	2,675,441	34.0303
Add, for errors of marshal's assistants of New York and Louisiana, and for the naval service, [*vide* Fifth Census]	....	....	....	†11,130		
Total number free whites in 1830	....	....	....	10,537,378		
" " 1840	7,255,534	6,940,161	315,373	14,195,695	3,658,317	34.7175
" " 1850	10,026,402	9,526,666	499,736	19,553,068	5,357,373	37.7394
Total increase in 60 years.	....	....	....	....	16,380,604	516.3370

TABLE XXVI.—*Proportion of White Males to White Females in different sections at the several Census periods.*

Geographical divisions.	Dates.	Males.	Females	Proportion of females to 100 males.	Geographical divisions.	Dates.	Males.	Females.	Proportion of females to 100 males.
New England	1790	494,353	498,428	100.82	Southern States	1840	968,746	951,704	98.24
	1800	605,863	608,795	100.48		1850	1,154,010	1,137,156	98.54
	1810	722,830	729,155	100.87					
	1820	807,068	831,367	103.01	South-Western States	1790	16,648	15,365	92.29
	1830	954,934	978,404	102.46		1800	47,180	44,529	94.38
	1840	1,098,712	1,113,453	101.34		1810	143,553	129,657	90.32
	1850	1,346,680	1,358,415	100.87		1820	291,028	262,488	90.19
						1830	478,288	433,209	90.57
Middle States	1790	597,405	565,749	94.70		1840	731,340	659,177	90.13
	1800	839,430	774,060	92.21		1850	1,069,991	980,791	91.66
	1810	1,147,450	1,091,471	95.12					
	1820	1,496,587	1,448,758	96.80	North-Western States	1790	32,211	28,922	89.79
	1830	1,959,614	1,894,885	96.70		1800	123,880	110,775	89.42
	1840	2,432,067	2,381,948	97.94		1810	319,636	290,698	90.95
	1850	3,186,102	3,112,945	97.70		1820	666,737	608,604	91.28
						1830	1,084,342	1,002,375	92.44
Southern States	1790	475,008	448,375	94.39		1840	2,018,569	1,833,879	90.85
	1800	588,073	561,904	95.55		1850	3,135,333	2,888,080	92.11
	1810	654,102	633,452	96.84					
	1820	733,723	715,577	97.53	Territories and California	1850	134,286	49,329	36.73
	1830	877,955	862,242	98.21					

1830.—Omitted—the number of persons on board of vessels of war in the United States naval service, 5,318; in New York, sexes nor color not designated, 5,602; In Louisiana, ditto, 210; aggregate, 11,130.

1840.—Omitted—the number of persons on board of vessels of war in the United States naval service, 6,100. California admitted into the Union Sept. 9, 1850.

* Between 1820 and 1830, only 9 years and 10 months elapsed in consequence of the change from August to June in the period of enumeration. This remark is applicable to all of the ratio tables and is made once for all.

† These are also apportioned between the sexes.

In New England it will be seen that the females are always in excess, in some cases as much as 3 in 100, as in 1820. In all the other divisions of the Union, males are in excess for every period, the excess being greatest generally in the Southwest, where it is about 100 males to 91 females. In the Territories and California there are nearly three times as many males as females.

4. *Age.**—In 1850, 537,661 white persons in the United States were under one year of age, and 2,358,797 one and under five; 7,234,973 were in youth or between 5 and 20; 7,633,288 were in maturity or between 20 and 50; 1,777,255 were between 50 and 100, (73,798 were between 80 and 100;) and 787, were in extreme old age or 100 and over. In the dependent class under 15 there were 8,002,715; in the producing class between 15 and 60 there were 10,720,175; in the supported class above 60, there were 819,871; of the males between 15 and 60, or those capable in emergency of bearing arms, the number was 5,542,785; the latest enrolments of militia as reported by the War Department, giving only 2,006,456. On a computation there were 4,684,883 white males of twenty-one years of age and upwards. The ages of the native and foreign born population have not been distinguished in the classifications made in the office, although a very important distinction; nor can the number of naturalized foreigners be known from the returns. It is therefore impossible to ascertain the number of persons entitled to the right of suffrage. Still, however, some estimate may be made. Supposing the foreign born males of 21 and over, to be 60 per cent., of the whole foreign born males (the per cent. for the native and foreign being 47) and supposing that half of the foreign born males over 21 are capable of voting somewhere, (these suppositions have reference to the ages of foreigners who arrive and to the fact that they vote at early periods in the new States) the number of such voters would be 371,839; and the number of male foreigners over 21 not capable of voting would also be 371,839. Deduct these from the whole males over 21, and the number of persons actually capable of enjoying the elective franchise; would be 4,313,044, giving to every free native citizen that right. The foreign vote, therefore, (including those who have come into the country from the earliest times) would be but one-twelfth of the total.

A table of the actual votes cast in the different States in the Union at the three last Presidential elections, is annexed, and though it is not official it yet comes from a source entitled to entire credit. A column has been added to show the number of males, native and foreign, of 21 years and over, in the several States in 1852. The number was obtained by ascertaining the number of 21 years and under, and deducting this from the total male whites, then adding for increase for 1850 to 1852 according to the increase in the several States between 1840 and 1850. California and Texas being introduced since 1840, no ratio of increase could be ascertained and therefore the figures are for 1850.

TABLE XXVII.—*Popular vote cast at several Presidential Elections of the United States, compared with the total Male Whites of* 21 *years of age and upwards.*

States.	1852.				1848.			1844.
	Party vote.		Total, including scattering.	White males, 21 and over.	Party vote.		Total, including scattering.	Total vote
Alabama	15,038	26,881	41,919	93,808	30,482	31,363	61,845	63,824
Arkansas	7,404	12,173	19,577	41,371	7,588	9,300	16,888	15,050
California	34,971	39,665	74,736	110,525				
Connecticut	30,359	33,249	66,768	102,936	30,314	27,046	62,365	64,164
Delaware	6,293	6,318	12,673	17,087	6,422	5,910	12,412	12,259
Florida	2,875	4,318	7,193	13,251	4,539	3,238	7,777	
Georgia	16,660	34,705	51,365	112,110	47,544	44,802	92,346	86,267
Illinois	64,934	80,597	155,497	220,619	53,215	56,629	125,648	107,018
Indiana	80,901	95,299	183,134	225,255	69,907	74,745	152,752	140,154
Iowa	7,444	8,624	16,845	68,940	11,178	12,125	24,429	
Kentucky	57,068	53,806	111,139	176,974	67,141	49,720	116,861	119,243
Louisiana	17,255	18,647	35,902	86,590	18,217	15,370	33,588	26,865
Maine	32,543	41,609	82,182	149,162	35,276	40,206	87,660	85,445
Maryland	40,022	35,077	75,153	109,355	37,702	34,528	72,355	68,660
Massachusetts	56,063	46,880	132,936	283,910	61,070	35,281	134,409	132,141
Michigan	33,860	41,842	82,939	112,511	23,940	30,687	65,016	55,572
Mississippi	17,548	26,876	44,424	72,908	25,922	26,537	52,459	44,332
Missouri	28,944	36,642	65,586	157,672	32,671	40,077	72,748	72,574
New Hampshire	16,147	29,997	52,839	86,160	14,781	27,763	50,104	49,187
New Jersey	38,556	44,305	83,211	119,557	40,015	36,901	77,765	76,636
New York	234,882	262,083	522,294	839,398	218,583	114,319	453,399	485,882
North Carolina	39,058	39,744	78,861	117,787	43,519	34,869	78,473	82,519
Ohio	152,526	169,220	353,428	471,842	138,359	154,773	328,479	312,224
Pennsylvania	179,122	198,568	386,214	571,778	185,730	172,186	369,093	335,070
Rhode Island	7,626	8,735	17,005	41,735	6,779	3,646	11,155	12,189
South Carolina†								
Tennessee	58,898	57,018	115,916	155,895	64,705	58,419	123,124	119,947
Texas	4,995	13,552	18,547	41,933	4,509	10,668	15,180	
Vermont	22,173	13,044	43,838	83,289	23,122	10,948	47,907	48,765
Virginia	57,132	72,413	129,545	206,758	45,265	46,738	92,012	95,473
Wisconsin	22,240	33,658	64,712	206,198	13,747	15,001	39,166	
Total	1,383,537	1,585,545	3,126,378	5,097,314	1,362,242	1,223,795	2,877,415	2,711,460

* As to age, the Marshals were instructed to take the specific age at the last birth day previous to the first of June, and if the exact age could not be ascertained, then to give the nearest approximation. Under one year to be given in months.

† Incomplete. In S. Carolina electors are chosen by the legislature; had the vote been popular there, the whole vote for 1852 in the U. States would have reached about 3,170,000. Adding for S. Carolina, and the probable increase of Texas and California, the whole number over 21 in 1852 in the U. States would be about 5,222,314.

TABLE XXVIII.—*Per cent. of the several Ages of the White Population to the total Whites*—1850.

STATES & TERRITORIES.	Under 1.	1 and under 5.	5 and under 10.	10 and under 15.	15 and under 20.	20 and under 30.	30 and under 40.	40 and under 50.	50 and under 60.	60 and under 70.	70 and under 80.	80 and under 90.	90 and under 100.	100 & over.	Unknown.
Alabama	2.86	13.88	15.87	13.88	11.67	16.90	10.77	6.96	4.15	1.96	.80	.23	.04	.01	.02
Arkansas	3.37	15.03	16.27	14.25	11.13	17.53	10.77	6.51	3.22	1.36	.43	.09	.01	.01	.02
California	0.29	1.77	2.28	2.13	5.94	50.60	24.50	8.72	2.41	.50	.09	.03	.01	....	.73
Columbia, District of	2.63	10.66	12.96	11.57	10.67	19.70	13.91	8.65	5.41	2.64	.90	.23	.03	....	.04
Connecticut	2.07	8.84	10.56	10.44	10.47	19.36	13.59	9.94	6.96	4.51	2.33	.78	.08	....	.07
Delaware	2.74	11.68	13.94	12.54	10.92	17.83	12.77	8.51	4.94	2.65	1.14	.26	.03	....	.05
Florida	2.75	13.78	15.80	12.48	10.06	18.02	12.51	7.39	4.40	1.95	.66	.16	.03	....	.01
Georgia	2.91	14.10	16.06	13.95	11.24	16.95	10.28	6.93	4.03	2.25	.92	.30	.05	.01	.02
Illinois	3.14	13.57	15.35	13.34	10.96	17.74	12.11	7.34	4.00	1.70	.54	.11	.01	....	.09
Indiana	3.27	13.70	15.96	13.58	11.33	17.11	10.98	6.88	4.30	1.97	.69	.17	.03	....	.03
Iowa	3.18	14.67	16.13	13.19	10.47	16.86	12.54	7.17	3.72	1.51	.43	.09	.01	....	.03
Kentucky	3.10	13.47	15.36	13.27	11.15	17.62	11.03	7.09	4.22	2.30	1.00	.31	.05	.01	.02
Louisiana	2.70	11.86	12.97	10.94	9.05	21.65	16.64	8.36	3.64	1.46	.47	.11	.02	.01	.12
Maine	2.40	10.60	12.77	12.31	11.50	17.14	11.95	9.15	6.03	3.56	1.80	.59	.06	....	.14
Maryland	2.88	11.57	13.06	11.94	10.34	18.74	13.44	8.65	5.13	2.76	1.15	.30	.04	....	....
Massachusetts	2.33	9.13	10.34	9.86	10.65	21.23	14.46	9.67	6.05	3.71	1.81	.58	.06	....	.12
Michigan	2.74	12.35	14.99	12.54	10.75	17.38	12.95	8.66	4.57	2.17	.71	.14	.02	....	.03
Mississippi	2.93	14.45	16.20	13.93	10.82	17.18	11.25	6.82	3.86	1.72	.62	.15	.02	....	.05
Missouri	3.31	13.61	15.37	13.39	10.90	18.28	12.12	7.05	3.73	1.59	.50	.12	.01	....	.02
New Hampshire	1.92	8.48	10.78	10.79	11.26	18.00	12.53	10.17	7.46	4.83	2.67	.96	.13	....	.02
New Jersey	2.76	11.20	13.04	11.84	10.76	18.33	12.68	8.71	5.55	3.21	1.41	.44	.04	....	.03
New York	2.47	10.58	12.21	11.07	10.78	20.25	13.58	8.96	5.39	2.95	1.29	.38	.04	....	.05
North Carolina	2.87	12.62	14.50	13.25	11.20	17.30	11.05	7.64	4.95	2.82	1.31	.40	.06	.01	.02
Ohio	2.87	12.80	14.72	12.88	11.16	17.76	11.64	7.69	4.55	2.59	1.02	.26	.03	....	.03
Pennsylvania	2.79	12.19	13.80	12.04	10.68	18.43	12.27	8.28	5.07	2.84	1.20	.33	.03	....	.05
Rhode Island	2.46	9.58	10.56	10.25	10.43	20.74	14.27	9.48	6.06	3.76	1.78	.56	.06	....	.01
South Carolina	2.35	12.77	14.78	13.46	11.02	17.23	11.22	7.71	4.98	2.72	1.23	.41	.08	.01	.03
Tennessee	3.03	13.69	15.71	14.04	11.75	17.00	10.21	6.79	4.12	2.22	1.03	.32	.05	.01	.03
Texas	3.09	14.13	15.34	12.86	10.33	18.67	12.64	7.34	3.62	1.36	.39	.09	.01	.01	.12
Vermont	2.10	9.89	12.15	11.52	10.93	16.95	12.45	9.92	6.72	4.26	2.26	.76	.08	....	.01
Virginia	2.65	12.56	14.55	13.12	10.91	17.33	11.33	7.92	5.02	2.84	1.28	.39	.06	.01	.03
Wisconsin	3.41	13.42	13.85	11.14	9.43	19.13	14.67	8.13	4.33	1.82	.50	.10	.01	....	.06
Territories. Minnesota	2.78	12.44	11.91	9.29	7.55	28.47	16.08	7.00	3.01	1.03	.33	.08	.03	....	....
Territories. New Mexico	2.00	12.30	14.18	11.42	11.41	20.47	11.77	7.13	4.67	2.76	.93	.52	.14	.07	.23
Territories. Oregon	2.37	13.27	14.07	10.77	9.18	24.28	14.43	6.55	3.26	1.13	.16	.02	.01	....	.50
Territories. Utah	3.81	15.30	12.04	12.07	11.70	19.02	12.00	8.09	3.75	1.71	.47	.04	....	....	....
Total	2.75	12.06	13.83	12.28	10.89	18.55	12.36	8.13	4.90	2.67	1.15	.34	.04	....	.05

By the table of ages it will be seen that the age of nineteen nearly divides the whites into two parts—that nearly two-fifths of the whole are between the ages of twenty and fifty, and less than one-tenth over fifty; whilst more than one-half are under twenty years of age.

TABLE XXIX.—*Ages and Ratio to the White Population.*

Ages.	Number.	Ratio per cent. to total.
Under one year of age	537,661	2.750
One and under five	2,358,797	12.064
Five and under twenty	7,234,973	37.002
Twenty and under fifty	7,633,288	39.039
Fifty and under eighty	1,703,457	8.712
Eighty and under one hundred	73,798	.377
One hundred and over	787	.004
Unknown	10,307	.053
Total	19,553,068	
Males twenty-one* and over	4,684,883	23.96
Males fifteen and under sixty†	5,542,785	28.35

* Including eight-tenths of males of "unknown" ages (5722.)

† Including seven-tenths of males of "unknown" ages (5007.) The unknown ages are for the most part adults.

TABLE XXX.—*Ages of the White Population by the Census of* 1830, 1840 *and* 1850.

STATES.	Under 1.	Under 5.			5 and under 10.			10 and under 15.			15 and under 20.			20 and under 30.			30 and under 40.		
	1850.	1830.	1840.	1850.	1830.	1840.	1850.	1830.	1840.	1850.	1830.	1840.	1850.	1830.	1840.	1850.	1830.	1840.	1850.
Alabama	12,216	44,104	70,528	71,440	30,283	55.019	67,690	23,221	44,605	59,204	19,460	34,133	49,763	31,897	57,029	72,092	19,958	34,492	45,919
Arkansas	5,472	5,802	16,715	29,857	3,918	12,184	26,388	3,120	9,946	23,108	2,497	7,774	18,049	4,847	14,413	28,431	2,907	8,446	17,463
California	270	....	....	1,894	....	....	2,091	....	....	1,947	....	....	5,446	....	....	46,367	....	....	22,446
Columbia, District of	998	4,515	•4,648	5,043	3,326	3,526	4,917	3,134	3,663	4,391	3,365	3,805	4,049	5,661	5,921	7.473	3,569	3,979	5,278
Connecticut	7,500	37,303	37,274	39,598	34,834	34,309	38,344	34,363	33,234	37,907	32,487	33,196	38,013	52,706	53,217	70,289	34,545	39,166	49,329
Delaware	1,953	9,391	9,690	10,264	8,110	7,816	9,918	7,573	6,985	8,923	6,565	6,441	7,768	10,992	11,429	12,689	6,385	7,018	9,086
Florida	1,297	3,739	4,696	7,801	2,584	3,708	7,458	1,996	2,968	5,889	1,712	2,627	4,750	3,618	6,608	8,505	2,384	4,020	5,905
Georgia	15,165	63,985	84,338	88,707	46,299	65,979	83,760	36,572	53,129	72,749	31,638	43,292	58,582	50,880	66,401	88,400	30,130	41,799	53,596
Illinois	26,541	36,263	93,138	141,360	24,753	72,191	129,905	19,270	59,558	112,860	15,823	48,954	92,698	27,167	91,403	150,044	15,675	54,104	102,426
Indiana	31,980	77,285	136,865	165,887	56,005	111,262	155,932	43,944	89,019	132,687	35,740	73,503	110,673	54,855	115,178	167,134	33,607	70,273	107,298
Iowa	6,093	....	8,462	34,245	....	6,100	30,959	....	4,663	25,309	....	4,243	20,095	....	9,996	32,348	....	5.175	24,064
Kentucky	23,563	104,951	114,709	126,144	80,512	90,264	116,919	66,419	76,488	101,064	58,640	65,818	84,916	87,849	101,235	134,179	49,752	60.814	84,017
Louisiana	6,888	15,768	27,553	37,175	12,595	21,131	33,205	10,274	15,608	27,960	9,034	15,165	23,118	17,388	34,397	55,298	11,981	24,211	42,505
Maine	13,956	66,524	78,717	75,614	56,418	70,129	74,295	49,589	61,735	71,596	44,748	55,680	66,891	70,581	84,431	99,735	43,960	58,910	69,541
Maryland	12,021	46,093	52,601	60,367	38,131	40,551	54,574	35,213	35,911	49,915	33,798	34,567	43,228	56,645	61,049	78,337	34,832	40,075	56,145
Massachusetts	22,993	80,177	92,626	112,997	70,525	80,411	101,845	68,005	74,803	97,163	67,240	77,429	104,912	119,116	150,535	209,162	73,596	101,607	142,542
Michigan	10,824	5,766	37,885	59,615	4,392	31,143	59,231	3,591	24,637	49,531	2,981	21,706	42,454	6,929	41,465	68,677	4.138	27,889	51,152
Mississippi	8,673	15,237	37,777	51,407	10,737	27,492	47,899	8,760	22,394	41,186	7,276	17,573	32,004	12,468	34,548	50,794	7,722	19,842	33,277
Missouri	19,573	26,092	67,197	100,163	18,694	50,375	90,962	14,263	40,901	79,262	11,404	33,736	64,549	19,938	60,102	108,197	12,205	35,457	71.767
New Hampshire	6,097	37,966	36,394	33,004	34,311	33,993	34,212	32,262	32,618	34,267	29,670	31,120	35,741	45,755	46,849	57,180	31,386	35,050	39,780
New York	75,216	309,945	368,499	397,706	270,155	312,632	372,139	233,689	274,729	337,525	206,908	267,508	328.743	345,651	458,118	617,208	217,658	302.076	413.875
New Jersey	12,837	49,008	56,332	64,968	41,683	46,970	60,695	38,012	42,313	55,126	33,907	39,009	50,060	52,818	62,566	85,345	33,854	42,083	59,032
North Carolina	15,851	90,524	90,050	85,652	70,214	72,232	80,200	59,369	61,119	73,299	52,850	51,784	61,955	81,064	81,888	95,648	47,576	50,160	61,093
Ohio	56,195	186,284	282,307	306,579	146,541	226,781	287,682	121,457	187,991	251,736	103,773	166,303	218,215	156,864	266,485	347,150	93,240	161,743	227,610
Pennsylvania	62,946	229,800	291,266	338,204	188,918	232,921	311,523	162,462	199,494	271,891	149,089	186,517	241,256	237.257	306,427	416,239	144,776	192,285	277,111
Rhode Island	3,544	13,356	13,625	17,327	11,428	11,759	15,200	10,613	11,679	14,743	10,938	11,689	15,000	17,628	20,711	29,844	11,135	13,936	20,526
South Carolina	6,452	48,823	48,467	41,509	39,302	38,101	40,577	32,129	32,443	36,974	29,083	28,410	30,262	44,030	44,881	47,307	27.407	27,245	30,807
Tennessee	22,926	114,975	129,866	126,507	88,341	104,834	118,887	69,600	86,816	106,269	59,863	70,183	88,964	87,952	103,019	128,626	48,656	61,920	77,308
Texas	4,763	....	....	26,534	....	....	23,624	....	....	19,802	....	....	15,909	....	....	28,765	....	....	19,470
Virginia	23,741	128,204	134,594	136,107	101,769	105,749	130,172	85,223	89,818	117,440	77,426	80,738	97,653	122,955	129,262	155,051	72,995	81,223	101,358
Vermont	6,571	43,034	42,165	37,560	38,038	37,946	38,077	34,467	34,228	36,094	31,535	32,743	34,258	49,387	47,231	53,112	32,037	35.759	39,028
Wisconsin	10,403	....	5,155	51,293	....	3,485	42,197	....	2,592	33,946	....	2,544	28,739	....	9,041	58,288	....	4,771	44,724
Territ's. { Minnesota	168	....	....	919	....	....	719	....	....	562	....	....	456	....	....	1,719	....	....	971
Territ's. { New Mexico	1,233	....	....	8,798	....	....	8,727	....	....	7,027	....	....	7,020	....	....	12,596	....	....	7,242
Territ's. { Oregon	310	....	....	2,047	....	....	1,841	....	....	1,409	....	....	1,202	....	....	3,177	....	....	1,889
Territ's. { Utah	432	....	....	2,166	....	....	1,364	....	....	1,368	....	....	1,325	....	....	2,155	....	....	1,359
Total	537,661	1,894,914	2,474,139	2,896,458	1,532,816	2,010,993	2,704,128	1,308,590	1,716,087	2,402,129	1,169,450	1,548,190	2,128,716	1,874,898	2,575,835	3,627,561	1,148,066	1,645,528	2,416,939

TABLE XXX.—*Ages of the White Population.—Continued.*

STATES.	40 and under 50.			50 and under 60.			60 and under 70.			70 and under 80.			80 and under 90.			90 and under 100.			100 and upwards.			Unknown.
	1830.	1840.	1850.	1830.	1840.	1850.	1830.	1840.	1850.	1830.	1840.	1850.	1830.	1840.	1850.	1830.	1840.	1850.	1830	1840	1850	1850.
Alabama	10,724	20,967	29,697	6,324	10,671	17,685	3,060	5,293	8,339	1,023	1,844	3,402	291	478	969	48	92	187	13	34	29	98
Arkansas	1,404	4,466	10,557	735	1,999	5,227	316	880	2,206	100	275	692	21	65	151	4	7	20	....	4	10	30
California	....	....	7,989	....	....	2,211	....	....	457	....	....	83	....	....	23	....	....	8	....	....	....	673
Columbia, District of	2,048	2,539	3,280	1,196	1,519	2,051	517	725	1,001	169	264	341	57	62	87	5	3	13	1	3	....	17
Connecticut	24,809	28,218	36,092	17,096	19,913	25,281	12,202	12,947	16,386	6,914	7,655	8,452	2,099	2,470	2,835	237	245	311	8	12	6	256
Delaware	4,083	4,290	6,054	2,683	2,611	3,519	1,239	1,519	1,886	465	588	813	99	153	185	15	14	24	1	7	2	38
Florida	1,244	1,897	3,486	683	884	2,079	295	376	920	102	122	313	20	30	77	7	5	13	1	2	2	5
Georgia	17,969	26,186	36,233	10,763	14,418	21,016	5,747	7,919	11,710	2,107	3,126	4,776	558	898	1,522	128	166	268	30	44	55	198
Illinois	8,377	28,521	62,072	4,900	15,269	33,828	1,984	6,601	14,410	657	1,985	4,577	167	441	938	20	74	109	5	15	15	792
Indiana	19,334	41,645	67,223	10,812	24,548	42,039	5,435	11,230	19,241	1,839	4,038	6,763	452	987	1,667	74	127	273	17	23	26	311
Iowa	....	2,491	13,752	....	1,192	7,141	....	459	2,892	....	124	832	....	18	165	....	....	24	....	1	1	54
Kentucky	31,442	38,008	53,963	20,342	22,716	32,137	11,568	12,668	17,520	4,780	5,617	7,614	1,274	1,595	2,344	216	267	357	42	54	59	180
Louisiana	6,614	12,039	21,358	3,280	5,276	9,296	1,556	2,097	3,733	539	733	1,194	151	183	275	41	45	59	10	19	21	294
Maine	28,730	39,972	53,238	18,558	24,855	35,104	11,860	15,111	20,723	5,325	8,274	10,471	1,734	2,315	3,443	231	294	329	5	15	13	820
Maryland	21,912	25,103	36,154	13,548	15,117	21,449	7,095	8,275	11,517	2,916	3,334	4,792	787	951	1,257	117	159	177	21	24	17	14
Massachusetts	50,367	63,270	95,308	33,464	41,954	59,633	23,308	26,077	36,550	12,748	14,860	17,787	4,288	4,869	5,755	520	570	590	5	19	13	1,193
Michigan	1,958	14,385	34,221	1,048	7,836	18,068	404	3,344	8,579	99	1,074	2,793	30	168	556	9	23	67	1	5	7	120
Mississippi	4,158	10,285	20,154	2,578	5,539	11,409	1,068	2,505	5,093	338	847	1,828	81	226	453	18	36	67	2	10	18	129
Missouri	6,360	19,964	41,710	3,438	9,879	22,075	1,693	4,458	9,418	561	1,448	2,971	120	314	689	23	49	87	4	8	23	131
New Hampshire	22,668	27,098	32,282	15,666	18,514	23,671	10,947	12,187	15,342	5,896	7,447	8,461	1,925	2,472	3,051	259	284	402	10	10	11	52
New York	133,186	187,705	273,057	78,847	108,471	164,351	46,498	61,059	89,847	19,679	28,975	39,211	5,234	8,136	11,586	559	901	1,331	52	81	62	1,684
New Jersey	22,050	27,958	40,518	14,360	17,367	25,835	9,163	10,140	14,959	4,181	5,228	6,580	1,120	1,463	2,031	107	149	194	3	10	10	156
North Carolina	31,426	34,913	42,237	21,137	21,806	27,399	11,948	13,119	15,576	4,985	5,773	7,241	1,396	1,703	2,190	296	275	351	58	48	61	126
Ohio	58,658	103,580	150,332	33,956	58,335	88,872	19,076	32,818	50,686	6,547	12,370	19,947	1,671	2,962	5,016	227	373	574	35	74	45	606
Pennsylvania	91,085	125,204	187,009	55,914	75,898	114,551	32,306	41,275	64,038	14,063	19,007	27,057	3,704	5,178	7,379	463	556	741	63	87	51	1,110
Rhode Island	7,536	9,343	13,641	4,983	6,229	8,712	3,383	3,746	5,410	1,912	2,058	2,560	637	731	808	72	79	86	....	2	3	15
South Carolina	16,802	18,277	21,176	11,099	11,166	13,673	5,971	6,227	7,468	2,391	2,861	3,372	649	839	1,117	146	124	211	31	43	29	81
Tennessee	30,372	38,567	51,401	20,467	24,290	31,219	10,084	13,605	16,801	3,962	5,656	7,803	1,199	1,587	2,399	215	235	376	60	49	62	214
Texas	....	....	11,305	....	....	5,569	....	....	2,082	....	....	596	....	....	144	....	....	22	....	....	23	189
Virginia	47,131	54,393	70,861	30,708	33,535	44,889	17,736	19,659	25,435	7,521	8,926	11,462	2,206	2,497	3,508	372	398	517	54	66	63	284
Vermont	21,439	25,624	31,072	14,203	16,594	21,076	9,930	10,877	13,359	4,289	6,012	7,075	1,270	1,835	2,391	135	184	255	7	20	8	37
Wisconsin	....	1,803	24,773	....	914	13,201	....	329	5,540	....	92	1,539	....	17	304	....	4	18	....	2	2	192
Territories. Minnesota	....	....	421	....	....	182	....	....	62	....	....	20	....	....	5	....	....	2	....	....	....	....
Territories. New Mexico	....	....	4,388	....	....	2,872	....	....	1,694	....	....	572	....	....	319	....	....	87	....	....	40	143
Territories. Oregon	....	....	857	....	....	426	....	....	148	....	....	21	....	....	3	....	....	2	....	....	....	65
Territories. Utah	....	....	917	....	....	425	....	....	194	....	....	53	....	....	4	....	....	....	....	....	....	....
Total	723,886	1,038,711	1,588,788	452,788	619,315	958,171	266,389	347,525	521,222	116,108	160,613	224,064	33,240	45,643	65,646	4,564	5,738	8,152	539	791	787	*10,307

* There were 210 in Louisiana, 5,602 in New York and 5,318 in U. S. naval service in 1830; and 6,100 in the same service in 1840, of unknown ages.

TABLE XXXI.—*Proportion of the different ages to the total White Population.*

1790.	AGES.	1800.		1810.		1820.	
		Number.	Ratio.	Number.	Ratio.	Number.	Ratio.
No ages given for the females.	Under 10	1,479,315	34.37	2,016,479	34.40	2,625,790	33.40
	10 and under 16	676,719	15.72	916,405	15.63	1,217,910	15.49
	16 " 26	794,655	18.46	1,109,553	18.93	1,557,401	19.81
	26 " 45	843,283	19.59	1,116,253	19.04	1,502,883	19.12
	45 and upwards	510,517	11.86	703,314	12.00	957,953	12.18
3,172,464	Total	4,304,489	....	5,862,004	....	7,861,937	....

AGES.	1830.		1840.		1850.	
	Number.	Ratio.	Number.	Ratio.	Number.	Ratio.
Under 1	....	....	....	....	537,661	2.75
1 and under 5	....	....	....	....	2,358,797	12.06
Under 5	1,894,914	17.98	2,474,139	17.43	2,896,458	14.81
5 and under 10	1,532,816	14.55	2,010,993	14.17	2,704,128	13.83
10 " 15	1,308,590	12.42	1,716,087	12.09	2,402,129	12.28
15 " 20	1,169,450	11.10	1,548,190	10.91	2,128,716	10.89
20 " 30	1,874,898	17.79	2,575,835	18.14	3,627,561	18.55
30 " 40	1,148,066	10.90	1,645,528	11.59	2,416,939	12.36
40 " 50	723,886	6.87	1,038,711	7.32	1,588,788	8.13
50 " 60	452,788	4.30	619,315	4.36	958,171	4.90
60 " 70	266,389	2.53	347,525	2.45	521,222	2.67
70 " 80	116,108	1.10	160,613	1.13	224,064	1.15
80 " 90	33,240	.31	45,643	.32	65,646	.34
90 " 100	4,564	.04	5,738	.04	8,152	.04
100 and upwards	539	....	791	....	787	....
Unknown	....	....	....	....	10,307	.05
Errors in New York, Louisiana, and sailors in the employ of the United States	11,130	.11	....	....	....	....
Error in Maryland, and sailors in the employ of the United States	....	....	6,587	.05	....	....
Total	10,537,378	....	14,195,695	....	19,553,068	....

The proportion of persons at the different ages given, varies very little for the first, second and third census; about one-third of the population at each period being under 10 years of age, another third between 16 and 26, and the remainder over that age. The number under five has been decreasing since 1830, and constitutes less than one-seventh of the whole. Those between ten and fifteen and fifteen and twenty have also been decreasing, whilst there has been a pretty steady increase in the number of persons at the ages above 20, and under 90. The number of those aged over ninety, has slightly declined in ratio. There were 539 centenarians in 1830; 791 in 1840, and 787 in 1850. To estimate the chances of reaching these ages, their proportion must be known to the whole number alive one hundred years ago, &c. The unknown ages for the whites amounted in 1850, for the whole Union, to 10,307.

It will be seen that for every period under fifteen years of age, the males are in excess in all of the States and Territories in 1850, with only few exceptions, the most remarkable of which are the District of Columbia and Rhode Island. Between fifteen and twenty an excess of females exists in most of the States. The most notable exceptions are those of Vermont, where to each 100 males there are 95.98 females, and California, 100 males to 19 females. From the age of twenty to fifty, the males are in excess, except in some of the Northern States, the Carolinas, &c. For very old persons the excess is with the females, the exceptions being chiefly in the new States. It will be seen that the ages of the females are more generally returned than those of the males. At best the number of unreturned ages constitutes but a small part of the whole, and perhaps results as much from the carelessness of enumerators as from refusals of parties themselves.

TABLE XXX.—*Comparative Ages of Male and Female Whites in 1830, 1840 and 1850.*

AGE.	1830.			Ratio per cent.	1840.			Ratio per cent.	1850.			Ratio per cent.
	Males.	Females.	Total.		Males.	Females.	Total.		Males.	Females.	Total.	
Under 5	972,980	921,934	1,894,914	17.98	1,270,743	1,203,319	2,474,062	17.43	1,472,053	1,424,405	2,896,458	14.81
5 and under 10	782,075	750,741	1,532,816	14.55	1,024,050	986,940	2,010,990	14.16	1,372,438	1,331,690	2,704,128	13.83
10 and under 15	669,734	638,856	1,308,590	12.42	879,530	836,630	1,716,160	12.09	1,225,575	1,176,554	2,402,129	12.28
15 and under 20	573,196	596,254	1,169,450	11.10	756,106	792,223	1,548,329	10.91	1,041,116	1,087,600	2,128,716	10.89
20 and under 30	956,487	918,411	1,874,898	17.79	1,322,453	1,253,490	2,575,943	18.15	1,869,092	1,758,469	3,627,561	18.55
30 and under 40	592,535	555,531	1,148,066	10.89	866,452	779,120	1,645,572	11.59	1,288,682	1,128,257	2,416,939	12.36
40 and under 50	367,840	356,046	723,886	6.87	536,606	502,183	1,038,789	7.32	840,222	748,566	1,588,788	8.13
50 and under 60	229,284	223,504	452,788	4.30	314,528	304,852	619,380	4.36	498,660	459,511	958,171	4.90
60 and under 70	135,082	131,307	266,389	2.53	174,238	173,329	347,567	2.45	264,742	256,480	521,222	2.67
70 and under 80	57,772	58,336	116,108	1.10	80,067	80,565	160,632	1.13	111,416	112,648	224,064	1.15
80 and under 90	15,806	17,434	33,240	.32	21,677	23,962	45,639	.32	31,243	34,403	65,646	.34
90 and under 100	2,041	2,523	4,564	.04	2,508	3,232	5,740	.04	3,653	4,499	8,152	.04
100 and upwards	301	238	539	.01	476	316	792	.01	357	430	.787	
	5,355,133	5,171,115	*10,526,248		7,249,434	6,940,161	14,189,595		10,019,249	9,523,512	*19,542,761	
	* Aliens, &c. in the 9th Ward N. York city, were omitted by the Marshal		5,477	.05	Persons on board vessels of War in U. States service		6,100	.04	* Age unknown—Males		7,153	.04
									" " Femalos		3,154	.01
	Also the inmates of poor house at New Paltz, Ulster county, New York		125									
	Also in the Eastern District of Louisiana		210									
	The whole number of persons on board vessels of war in United States service		5,318	.05								
	Total Population		10,537,378				14,195,695				19,553,068	

By this table it will be seen that the ratio per cent. of the ages under 20 has been declining since 1830 in the Union at large; and that for those over that age for the most part it has been increasing. This must be the result of the large immigration of persons in middle life, and perhaps of that decline in the ratio of natural increase indicated by the less proportion of young children, adverted to by Prof. Tucker. The proportion of the very aged has remained about the same.

TABLE XXXIII.—*Proportion of White Males to Females, for* 1850.

For every hundred males there are in the different States, of the ages mentioned, the following number of females:

STATES AND TERRITORIES.	INFANCY.	YOUTH.			MATURITY.			OLD AGE.					EXTREME OLD AGE.	
	Under 5.	5 and under 10.	10 and under 15.	15 and under 20.	20 and under 30.	30 and under 40.	40 and under 50.	50 and under 60.	60 and under 70.	70 and under 80.	80 and under 90.	90 and under 100.	100 and upwards.	Age unknown.
Alabama	95.5	97.8	96.4	102.7	98.2	84.6	85.8	79.6	83.5	86.7	102.3	81.5	190.0	71.9
Arkansas	95.6	95.8	93.6	99.2	87.1	73.8	74.3	71.2	69.1	67.1	118.8	185.7	66.6	66.6
California	91.7	93.6	71.6	19.1	3.5	4.5	6.0	8.9	17.7	29.6	53.3	33.3	......	0.5
Columbia, Dis. of	95.9	100.6	103.6	121.3	112.1	97.0	99.1	106.1	115.7	156.3	148.5	160.0	......	466.6
Connecticut	97.5	98.7	95.6	105.1	99.4	96.7	101.6	113.4	121.1	128.5	141.4	185.3	50.0	83.5
Delaware	98.3	96.9	94.7	103.6	99.7	97.3	94.9	105.4	114.0	117.9	143.4	166.6	......	58.3
Florida	94.2	95.6	91.3	103.1	78.0	65.9	67.9	63.8	69.1	66.5	92.5	160.0	100.0	25.0
Georgia	93.9	96.4	96.2	105.5	97.0	90.9	92.4	92.9	88.8	95.1	109.9	125.2	96.4	90.3
Illinois	96.5	95.6	92.7	97.4	88.8	79.1	80.5	76.9	80.8	81.1	86.1	98.1	50.0	61.9
Indiana	95.9	95.9	94.4	99.4	92.5	86.7	90.9	78.6	85.1	84.1	91.3	89.5	44.4	73.7
Iowa	96.3	95.1	92.1	101.7	93.6	76.7	76.6	73.5	77.3	79.7	70.1	60.0	......	100.0
Kentucky	95.6	96.1	95.8	101.6	92.5	85.2	88.7	89.1	96.7	90.6	97.3	101.6	110.7	66.6
Louisiana	97.2	96.1	98.2	117.6	79.9	54.8	54.4	64.8	81.6	92.2	118.2	96.6	133.3	16.2
Maine	96.2	97.0	96.6	99.9	93.8	93.5	94.0	98.9	97.4	100.4	104.5	120.8	44.4	33.7
Maryland	98.7	98.0	97.2	108.1	95.0	90.5	92.9	101.4	112.1	121.7	147.4	180.9	142.8	75.0
Massachusetts	98.2	99.1	97.7	114.6	106.4	96.5	99.8	110.4	118.3	128.5	146.4	199.4	225.0	17.4
Michigan	95.6	94.9	94.3	100.1	89.7	81.9	76.2	74.4	78.5	75.3	75.4	59.5	40.0	96.7
Mississippi	93.9	96.2	95.1	101.9	86.9	74.5	77.1	71.1	78.8	88.8	98.6	91.4	157.1	92.5
Missouri	95.7	96.2	95.2	100.1	85.7	75.0	77.1	76.8	80.9	82.1	84.7	74.0	91.6	63.7
New Hampshire	97.3	96.8	96.6	111.2	102.5	103.3	103.8	109.4	113.8	116.6	131.1	166.2	120.0	85.7
New Jersey	97.8	98.2	95.3	106.0	102.2	95.5	93.9	101.8	106.2	110.4	128.6	169.4	150.0	83.5
New York	98.1	98.1	98.4	109.1	99.8	91.1	88.9	92.3	95.6	96.5	102.9	115.3	87.8	43.4
North Carolina	95.1	96.6	95.0	105.3	107.8	108.2	107.9	109.4	117.2	114.0	107.7	160.0	238.8	82.6
Ohio	97.1	97.1	96.5	103.7	94.1	88.8	87.4	91.7	84.5	84.8	88.0	87.5	95.6	73.6
Pennsylvania	97.5	98.2	96.1	106.0	98.7	92.3	91.6	95.3	101.2	105.1	120.6	121.1	155.0	67.1
Rhode Island	99.6	100.2	100.1	109.1	103.6	98.6	105.5	115.2	121.4	143.8	153.2	126.3	......	.....
South Carolina	95.0	97.0	96.2	105.4	101.5	98.3	100.2	98.3	104.1	117.9	126.1	170.5	480.0	107.7
Tennessee	96.1	96.6	95.1	102.7	100.7	98.4	101.2	91.8	96.1	94.7	94.8	108.8	121.4	91.0
Texas	95.5	92.4	91.4	103.0	74.8	60.6	62.9	61.3	67.6	63.2	77.7	144.4	109.0	11.1
Vermont	98.0	95.9	95.2	95.9	93.4	97.4	95.9	97.3	101.2	100.9	95.0	119.8	100.0	42.3
Virginia	96.4	96.1	95.8	104.9	100.0	97.0	96.2	98.3	99.9	106.6	107.7	127.1	125.0	82.0
Wisconsin	96.3	93.8	93.1	97.9	82.5	71.4	72.6	72.9	73.0	73.7	71.7	260.0	100.0	71.4
Territories. Minnesota	102.4	98.0	87.9	102.6	48.9	34.8	45.1	41.0	58.9	17.6	66.6	......	......	.....
Territories. N. Mexico	99.4	98.2	91.0	120.2	99.1	80.8	82.3	76.5	67.7	82.7	64.4	47.4	110.5	0.7
Territories. Oregon	92.5	102.9	96.5	77.5	33.7	40.6	47.0	38.7	37.0	31.2	......	100.0	......	71.0
Territories. Utah	98.5	95.9	100.2	101.0	70.4	78.5	78.7	54.7	94.0	70.9	300.0	......	......	.....

By the annexed table it will be perceived that for 1800, 1810 and 1820, the white females under 10 are fewer than the males, but have been gaining upon them in proportion. This is also the case between ten and sixteen and between twenty-six and forty-five. Above forty-five, though the females are less, the ratios are more uniform. Between sixteen and twenty-six the females are more numerous than the males and increase their advantage. For 1830, and 1840, the females under five, between five and ten, and ten and fifteen, are less than the males, though gaining upon them. Between twenty and seventy the males are still in excess and gain upon the females. Between fifteen and twenty there is a large and growing excess of females, attributable in some slight degree, as Prof. Tucker intimates, to the anxiety of the sex to retain this interesting age. This can be proved in another way.* At all periods over seventy the females preponderate with only two exceptions.

TABLE XXXIV.

Year.	Age.	Males.	Females.	Total.	Year.	Age.	Males.	Females.	Total.
1830	Under 10	1,755,055	1,672,675	3,427,730	1830	20 and 30	956,487	918,411	1,874,898
1840	10 and 20	1,635,521	1,628,756	3,264,277	1840	30 and 40	866,431	779,097	1,645,528
1850	20 and 30	1,869,092	1,758,469	3,627,561	1850	40 and 50	840,222	748,566	1,588,788
1830	10 and 20	1,242,930	1,235,110	2,478,040	1830	30 and 40	592,535	555,531	1,148,066
1840	20 and 30	1,322,440	1,253,395	2,575,835	1840	40 and 50	536,568	502,143	1,038,711
1850	30 and 40	1,288,682	1,128,257	2,416,939	1850	50 and 60	498,660	459,511	958,171

* Those who were under ten at one census should be of ten and under twenty years at the next. In consequence of deaths the number would be less, were there no foreign immigration. Thus there were 3,427,730 under 10 in 1830, and 3,364,277 between ten and twenty in 1840, &c. The numbers between twenty and thirty seem to show a disposition to retain those ages on the part of both sexes.

TABLE XXXV.—*White Males and Females at different Ages in* 1800, 1810, 1820, 1830, 1840, *and* 1850.

AGES.	1800.		1810.		1820.		1800.	1810.	1820.
	Males. p'r cent.	Fem's. p'r cent.	Males. p'r cent.	Fem's. p'r cent.	Males. p'r cent.	Fem's. p'r cent.	Proportion of males to females as 100 to		
1. Whites under 10 years.....	34.66	34.06	34.64	34.14	33.67	33.12	93.6	94.82	95.19
2. 10 and under 16 "	16.01	15.41	15.67	15.6	15.33	15.65	91.67	95.78	98.8
3. 16 " 26 "	17.84	19.12	18.33	19.55	19.43	20.21	102.12	102.62	109.7
4. 26 " 45 "	19.58	19.6	19.15	18.93	19.18	19.05	95.39	95.15	96.12
5. 45 and upwards...........	11.91	11.81	12.21	11.78	12.39	11.97	94.49	92.77	93.5
Total....................	100.00	100.00	100.00	100.00	100.00	100.00	95.3	96.2	96.8
	1830.		1840.		1850.		1830.	1840.	1850.
1. Whites under 5 years.....	18.17	17.83	17.53	17.34	14.68	14.95	94.75	94.7	96.76
2. 5 and under 10 "	14.60	14.52	14.13	14.22	13.69	13.98	95.99	96.38	97.03
3. 10 " 15 "	12.51	12.35	12.13	12.06	12.23	12.35	95.39	95.12	96.00
4. 15 " 20 "	10.70	11.53	10.43	11.41	10.39	11.42	104.02	104.78	104.46
5. 20 " 30 "	17.86	17.76	18.24	18.06	18.64	18.46	96.02	94.78	94.08
6. 30 " 40 "	11.06	10.74	11.95	11.23	12.85	11.84	93.75	89.92	87.55
7. 40 " 50 "	6.87	6.89	7.40	7.23	8.38	7.86	96.79	93.58	89.09
8. 50 " 60 "	4.28	4.32	4.34	4.39	4.97	4.83	97.48	96.92	92.15
9. 60 " 70 "	2.52	2.54	2.40	2.50	2.64	2.69	97.2	99.48	96.88
10. 70 " 80 "	1.08	1.13	1.11	1.16	1.11	1.18	100.98	100.62	101.1
11. 80 " 90 "	.30	.34	.30	.35	.31	.36	110.29	110.54	110.11
12. 90 " 100 "	.04	.05	.04	.05	} .04	0.5 }	123.62	128.87	123.16
13. 100 and upwards..........	.01	....	....	....			79.07	66.38	120.45
14. Age unknown............	....	....	....	....	.07	.03	....	....	44.09
Total....................	100.00	100.00	100.00	100.00	100.00	100.00	96.4	95.6	95.0

5. *Births, Marriages and Deaths.*—The tables of the census which undertake to give the total number of Births, Marriages and Deaths, in the year preceding the first of June, 1850, can be said to have but very little value. Nothing short of a registration system in the States can give the required data satisfactorily, and it has been proved that even where such systems have been best established, difficulties continually arise which require a very long time to be removed. Experience has shown that people will not, or cannot, remember and report to the census taker the number of the facts, and the particulars of them which occur in the period of a whole year to eighteen months prior to the time of his calling. It might be possible to obtain them for a single month.

Births.—Only those persons born within the year and surviving at the end of it, are included in the table of births: in other words it comprises the figures of the column of population under one year of age. It was made up in this manner in the Maryland table, adopted by Congress as the model for this. To arrive at the *true* number of births some laborious calculations become necessary. It will not do to add to the living the number that have died under one year of age, as was done in another place in the Maryland volume: the aggregate becomes then too large. A child who had died two months before the first of June, at the age of eleven months, and so for other parallel cases, would be considered as a death under one year of age, though certainly not a birth within the year. Time does not admit of these precise and laborious calculations, and if it did, as Congress failed to order publication of the details of the deaths, the office has not yet been free to incur the expense of an investigation, which, at the best, considering the deficiencies of the reports, would be only to substitute one approximation for another. The census takers too, in many counties have adopted one year as the lowest designation of age, and for this reason, also, the births are deficient, more especially for slaves.

An experiment made upon Rhode Island, mentioned in the note, gives, for the figures to be added to the births from the death statistics 163.* If this were assumed to be anything of an average for all of the States, the list of births would be increased by 24,473 and make an aggregate of 653,917 for all classes.†

* In Rhode Island out of 353 deaths of children reported as under one year of age, 163 only were born within the year preceding the first of June.

† During the year ending June 1st, 1850, the deaths of persons under one year of age reported in the various States and Territories were respectively as follows: Alabama 2,023, including 1,190 slaves; Arkansas 524, including 134 slaves; California 36; District of Columbia 154, including 11 slaves; Connecticut 705; Delaware 239, including 7 slaves; Florida 147, including 85 slaves; Georgia 2,283, including 1,373 slaves; Illinois 2,270; Indiana 2,269; Iowa 446; Kentucky 2,710, including 808 slaves; Louisiana 1,275, including 538 slaves; Maine 919; Maryland 2,090, including 306 slaves; Massachusetts 2,842; Michigan 856; Minnesota Territory 5; Mississippi 1,839, including 798 slaves; Missouri 1,954, including 273 slaves; New Hampshire 451; New Mexico

The table of *Marriages* in the census includes only the white population in some of the States, in others, the white and free colored. In a few instances, in the first case, free colored marriages have been also noted, and are included. In the other case, though generally included, much less care seems to have been exercised with them than with the whites. The remark is, however, only applicable to the slave States. No comparison of the proportion of the marriages to the total population can be made, as the marriages of slaves are not included. It will be observed that the figures refer to the number of persons married, and are, therefore, twice the number of actual marriages in the year, admitting them all to be returned, which, at a glance, any one can see is far from being the fact.*

In regard to the number of *Deaths*, the returns of the census are not likely to deceive any one, since an attempt to reason from them would exhibit a degree of vitality and healthfulness in the United States unparalleled in the annals of any nation, and demonstrate between county and county and State and State, the most extraordinary differences in sanitary condition. The truth is but a part of the deaths have been recorded, varying for sections from a very small to a very large part of the whole.

The various ratio and detailed tables of Marriages and Deaths, will be embraced under the chapter of aggregate population, since they cannot be separated for the whites. Those of Births being merely the white children under one year of age, as before explained, will be found in the table of ages.

6. *Deaf, Dumb, Blind, Insane and Idiotic.*—The tables which follow will exhibit the total number of white persons returned by the census of 1830, 1840 and 1850 as affected in either of these ways. The statistics have not been collected for any earlier period. The ages of neither class, except the deaf and dumb in 1830 and 1840 have been published, although they would add greatly to the value of the information. It is of little importance for example to know the mere number of blind and idiotic, if they are of extreme old age, and therefore beyond the age of treatment. Upon the age of the person will depend the opportunity or hope of his amelioration. The following tables will show the ages of the deaf and dumb whites in 1830 and 1840, and the ages of the same class of deaf and dumb, blind, insane and idiotic in 1850, for a few of the States. They are the results of an earlier examination, and therefore the aggregates do not correspond with those of the regular tables. The total number of deaf, dumb, blind, &c., whites, will be found in the table which follows. The figures are those that were published in the quarto volume of the census. It was there observed that they differed for 1850 in some respects, owing to re-examination, from those that were previously published, but that such differences were unavoidable, even with the most careful persons, in running over so many millions of names, to select the particular facts. The letters indicating the insane and idiotic could not always be distinguished on the returns. Persons with more than one infirmity, as for example, being deaf and dumb and blind and insane, could be put by different classifiers under either one of those heads it suited. Being considered to belong to only one of the classes, the rule in the earlier examinations was to select the class of greater infirmity. In the later examination the infirmity first named, as a rule, gave character to the person, a rule not more arbitrary, but certainly less liable to different constructions. In 1830 and 1840 the individunl instead of being placed under one of the heads was placed under all of them. As cases of the kind supposed did not in 1850 exceed in 16 States one per cent. of the whole the disturbance from this cause, cannot be very material. In poor-houses, hospitals, &c., it is often difficult to determine from the returns whether the party be pauper only or blind pauper, etc. The dumb are included, but those deaf only, are excluded from the columns of the deaf and dumb. The total number of the deaf reported by the marshals, though they were not instructed to report them, and no doubt generally obeyed their instructions, was 3,050 in the Union.†

Territory 207; New York 6,708; New Jersey 1,081; North Carolina 1,912, including 1,059 slaves; Ohio 4,420; Oregon Territory 5; Pennsylvania 4,977; Rhode Island 353; South Carolina 1,416 including 1,120 slaves; Tennessee 2,545, including 1,028 slaves; Texas 555, including 186 slaves; Utah Territory 41; Virginia 3,150, including 1,565 slaves; Vermont 301; Wisconsin 645.

* The marriages did not necessarily take place in the county, nor even the State of the parties residence.

† "It is not generally understood that a degree of deafness which is little more than a serious social inconvenience when it occurs in middle life, or comes with other infirmities in old age, occurring in infancy, would induce dumbness, or at least disqualify the child for instruction in ordinary schools. The child under ten, who is deaf, will hereafter become mute, at least so far, that he needs and is entitled to the privileges of a special institution for the education of deaf mutes. The man or woman who becomes deaf in mature life, does not therefore become mute. Such cases might, as a part of vital statistics, be noted as well as the cases of those who become blind late in life; but to judge of the probable number of deaf mutes, who require the means of education, the deaf who become so late, should be carefully distinguished from those who are so from birth or infancy. This can be done in another census by merely noting in each case at what age the hearing was lost, and we would suggest this as a very desirable improvement whenever a census of the deaf and dumb is taken." *Dr. Peet.*

TABLE XXXVI.—*Ages of Whites—Deaf and Dumb in* 1830 *and* 1840.

States and Territories.	1830.				1840.			
	Under 14.	14 to 25.	25 and upwards.	Total.	Under 14.	14 to 25.	25 and upwards.	Total.
Alabama	45	25	19	89	72	53	48	173
Arkansas	6	2	2	10	18	11	11	40
Columbia, District of.	4	5	3	12	1	5	2	8
Connecticut	43	152	99	294	60	141	108	309
Delaware	6	15	14	35	18	17	12	47
Florida	2	....	3	5	6	4	4	14
Georgia	50	51	44	145	78	62	53	193
Illinois	23	27	16	66	54	48	53	155
Indiana	49	59	33	141	112	91	94	297
Iowa	....	....	....	....	3	2	5	10
Kentucky	100	113	90	303	120	128	152	400
Louisiana	15	15	19	49	14	17	11	42
Maine	64	60	56	180	47	73	102	222
Maryland	50	31	54	135	43	58	77	178
Massachusetts	56	62	138	256	56	63	154	273
Michigan	4	7	4	15	7	9	15	31
Mississippi	12	10	7	29	25	16	23	64
Missouri	12	5	10	27	48	32	46	126
New Hampshire	32	55	48	135	43	41	97	181
New Jersey	64	71	72	207	33	29	102	164
New York	277	310	255	842	269	362	408	1,039
North Carolina	70	81	79	230	82	80	118	280
Ohio	148	160	118	426	167	198	194	559
Pennsylvania	224	279	255	758	225	225	331	781
Rhode Island	6	22	28	56	15	25	34	74
South Carolina	60	52	62	174	40	41	59	140
Tennessee	59	59	54	172	102	93	96	291
Vermont	39	59	55	153	27	19	89	135
Virginia	132	118	169	419	133	111	209	453
Wisconsin	....	....	....	....	1	4	....	5
	1,652	1,905	1,806	5,363	1,919	2,058	2,707	6,684

TABLE XXXVII.—*Ages of White and Free Colored Deaf and Dumb and Blind, in ten States, in* 1850.

STATES	Deaf and Dumb.								Blind.							
	Under 10.		10 and under 30.		30 and under 70.		70 and upwards.		Under 10.		10 and under 30.		30 and under 70.		70 and upwards.	
	M.	F.	M.	F.	M.	F.	M.	F.	M.	F.	M.	F.	M.	F.	M.	F.
Vermont	12	10	24	19	38	38	1	1	4	3	15	9	43	21	27	16
Virginia	50	44	182	138	84	72	9	2	25	16	80	66	94	90	62	103
South Carolina	20	5	29	32	25	17	.....	1	8	3	15	13	42	26	26	19
Louisiana	19	9	30	15	7	6	2	1	3	3	10	8	15	17	8	3
Tennessee	48	28	98	73	46	39	3	.....	12	9	53	46	89	76	45	55
Arkansas	10	9	26	19	10	9	.....	.....	6	.....	17	8	17	16	5	6
Ohio	82	76	295	247	123	108	3	5	24	34	104	77	171	103	71	69
Michigan	9	15	39	26	13	17	1	1	5	3	19	16	37	21	11	10
Wisconsin	7	7	24	12	10	4	1	.....	4	3	9	6	15	6	6	1
Iowa	11	10	8	7	8	7	.....	.....	5	3	9	5	11	7	3	4

TABLE XXXVIII.—*Ages of White Idiotic and Insane in ten States in* 1850.

STATES.	IDIOTIC.													
	Under 10.		10 and under 20.		20 and under 40.		40 and under 60.		60 and under 80.		80 and upwards.		Total	
	M.	F.	M.	F.	M.	F.	M.	F.	M.	F.	M.	F.	M.	F.
Vermont	14	18	24	25	85	35	36	19	9	11	3	1	171	109
Virginia	62	46	125	90	248	156	98	77	24	15	3	1	560	385
South Carolina	16	13	37	24	58	40	20	18	8	8	......	....	139	103
Louisiana	9	5	24	12	25	16	9	4	......	....	......	....	67	37
Tennessee	35	35	116	85	207	166	69	54	10	10	2	....	439	350
Arkansas	9	5	15	14	24	18	3	3	......	....	......	....	51	40
Ohio	77	57	189	171	363	278	111	81	27	23	2	1	769	611
Michigan	12	11	44	29	43	29	10	4	4	1	......	....	113	74
Wisconsin	9	3	13	14	20	10	3	4	......	....	......	....	45	31
Iowa	7	8	13	19	18	17	6	4	1	....	......	....	45	48
	INSANE.													
Vermont	......	2	3	8	104	74	126	143	40	47	3	2	276	276
Virginia	4	9	16	24	198	144	188	164	84	67	15	9	505	417
South Carolina	......	....	5	4	41	25	48	41	14	12	......	2	108	84
Louisiana	2	2	9	13	49	34	18	9	4	7	1	2	83	67
Tennessee	7	7	36	15	107	80	72	65	29	21	7	7	258	195
Arkansas	4	3	8	2	13	7	12	9	......	1	1	....	38	22
Ohio	19	9	52	50	331	282	226	211	60	81	7	7	695	640
Michigan	3	....	6	7	35	32	22	19	4	5	1	1	71	64
Wisconsin	3	....	1	1	12	11	11	8	......	1	......	....	27	21
Iowa	1	....	5	5	9	7	3	9	1	....	......	....	19	21

TABLE XXXIX.—*Deaf and Dumb, Blind, Insane and Idiotic White Persons in the United States, in* 1830, 1840 *and* 1850.

STATES AND TERRITORIES.	Deaf and Dumb.			Blind.			Insane & Idiotic.*	Insane.	Idiotic.	Total Insane and Idiotic.	Aggregate Deaf and Dumb and Blind.		
	1830.	1840.	1850.	1830.	1840.	1850.	1840.	1850.	1850.	1850.	1830.	1840.	1850.
Alabama	89	173	151	68	113	156	232	201	343	544	157	286	307
Arkansas	10	40	80	8	26	78	45	60	103	163	18	66	158
California	......	......	7	......	......	1	......	2	7	9	......	......	8
Columbia, District of	12	8	17	11	6	15	14	13	10	23	23	14	32
Connecticut	294	309	398	188	143	174	498	464	283	747	482	452	572
Delaware	35	47	48	18	15	25	52	48	74	122	53	62	73
Florida	5	14	13	3	9	15	10	9	28	37	8	23	28
Georgia	145	193	208	150	136	224	294	294	515	809	295	329	432
Illinois	66	155	354	35	86	259	213	236	361	597	101	241	613
Indiana	141	297	533	85	135	341	487	556	925	1,481	226	432	874
Iowa	......	10	59	......	3	50	7	42	94	136	......	13	109
Kentucky	303	400	507	169	236	419	795	502	796	1,298	472	636	926
Louisiana	49	42	82	36	37	72	55	144	106	250	85	79	154
Maine	180	222	265	159	180	198	537	556	575	1,131	339	402	463
Maryland	135	178	197	147	165	215	387	477	275	752	282	343	412
Massachusetts	256	273	356	218	308	457	1,204	1,661	786	2,447	474	581	813
Michigan	15	31	124	5	25	125	39	132	186	318	20	56	249
Mississippi	29	64	79	25	43	112	116	105	136	241	54	107	191
Missouri	27	126	263	27	82	191	202	249	325	574	54	208	454
New Hampshire	135	181	162	105	153	132	486	378	350	728	240	334	204
New Jersey	207	164	184	205	126	178	369	370	406	776	412	290	362
New York	842	1,039	1,256	642	875	1,137	2,146	2,487	1,644	4,131	1,484	1,914	2,393
North Carolina	230	280	389	223	223	379	580	467	615	1,082	453	503	768
Ohio	426	559	905	232	372	630	1,195	1,303	1,344	2,647	658	931	1,535
Pennsylvania	758	781	1,130	475	540	941	1,946	1,865	1,432	3,297	1,233	1,321	2,071
Rhode Island	56	74	62	56	63	61	203	210	110	320	112	137	123
South Carolina	174	140	134	102	133	150	376	224	249	473	276	273	284
Tennessee	172	291	334	176	255	383	699	380	756	1,136	348	546	717
Texas	......	......	49	......	......	61	......	37	93	130	......	......	110
Vermont	153	135	147	51	101	139	398	560	297	857	204	236	286
Virginia	419	453	540	355	426	497	1,048	864	891	1,755	774	879	1.037
Wisconsin	......	5	69	......	9	63	8	54	92	146	......	14	132
Territories. Minnesota	......	......	......	......	......	......	......	1	1	2	......	......	......
Territories. New Mexico	......	......	34	......	......	98	......	11	44	55	......	......	132
Territories. Oregon	......	......	......	......	......	......	......	5	4	9	......	......	......
Territories. Utah	......	......	......	......	......	2	......	5	1	6	......	......	2
Total	5,363	6,684	9,136	3,974	5,024	7,978	14,641	14,972	14,257	29,229	9,337	11,708	17,114

* These were not returned in 1830, and were not given separately in 1840.

Nativities.—The detailed nativities by States (native and foreign being combined for the whites and free colored(will be found in the Chapter of Aggregate Population.

TABLE XL.—*Nativities of White Population.*

States and Territories.	Born in the State		Born out of the State and in the United States.		Born in Foreign Countries.		Unknown.		Aggregate.
	Number.	Ratio.	Number.	Ratio.	Number.	Ratio.	Numb.	Ratio.	
Alabama	234,691	55.03	183,324	42.98	7,498	1.76	1,001	.23	426,514
Arkansas	60,996	37.61	98,950	61.01	1,468	0.90	775	.48	162,189
California	7,696	8.40	61,866	67.51	21,629	23.60	444	.49	91,635
Columbia, Dist. of	18,375	48.43	14,620	38.54	4,913	12.95	33	.08	37,941
Connecticut	284,978	78.49	39,117	10.77	38,374	10.57	630	.17	363,099
Delaware	55,591	78.11	10,326	14.51	5,243	7.37	9	.01	71,169
Florida	19,120	40.51	25,332	53.67	2,740	5.80	11	.02	47,203
Georgia	396,298	75.98	118,268	22.67	6,452	1.24	554	.11	521,572
Illinois	331,089	39.13	399,733	47.25	111,860	13.22	3,352	.40	846,034
Indiana	520,583	53.28	398,695	40.80	55,537	5.68	2,339	.24	977,154
Iowa	41,305	21.53	129,248	67.36	21,014	10.95	314	.16	191,881
Kentucky	580,129	76.19	148,582	19.51	31,401	4.13	1,301	.17	761,413
Louisiana	126,917	49.67	60,641	23.74	67,308	26.34	625	.25	255,491
Maine	514,655	88.46	35,019	6.02	31,695	5.45	444	.07	581,813
Maryland	326,040	78.01	40,610	9.72	51,011	12.20	282	.07	417,943
Massachusetts	679,625	68.97	139,419	14.15	163,598	16.60	2,808	.28	985,450
Michigan	137,637	34.84	201,586	51.02	54,593	13.82	1,255	.32	395,071
Mississippi	135,501	45.82	154,946	52.40	4,782	1.61	489	.17	295,718
Missouri	265,304	44.81	249,223	42.11	76,570	12.93	907	.15	592,004
New Hampshire	258,132	81.31	44,925	14.15	14,257	4.49	142	.05	317,456
New Jersey	361,691	77.70	43,711	9.39	59,804	12.85	303	.06	465,509
New York	2,092,076	68.63	296,754	9.74	655,224	21.49	4,271	.14	3,048,325
North Carolina	529,483	95.74	20,784	3.76	2,565	0.46	196	.04	553,028
Ohio	1,203,490	61.56	529,208	27.07	218,099	11.15	4,253	.22	1,955,050
Pennsylvania	1,787,310	79.15	165,966	7.35	303,105	13.42	1,779	.08	2,258,160
Rhode Island	98,754	68.64	21,221	14.75	23,832	16.56	68	.05	143,875
South Carolina	253,399	92.29	12,601	4.59	8,508	3.10	55	.02	274,563
Tennessee	580,695	76.73	168,966	22.33	5,638	0.74	1,537	.20	756,836
Texas	43,281	28.10	92,657	60.15	17,620	11.44	476	.31	154,034
Vermont	228,489	72,91	50,894	16.24	33,688	10.75	331	.10	313,402
Virginia	813,811	90.95	57,582	6.44	22,953	2.56	454	.05	894,800
Wisconsin	54,312	17.82	139,166	45.66	110,471	36.25	807	.27	304,756
Territ's. Minnesota	1,572	26.04	2,486	41.17	1,977	32.74	3	.05	6,038
Territ's. New Mexico	58,404	94.93	761	1.24	2,151	3.49	209	.34	61,525
Territ's. Oregon	2,301	17.58	9,636	73.63	959	7.33	191	1.46	13,087
Territ's. Utah	1,159	10.23	8,117	71.64	2,044	18.04	10	.09	11,330
Total	13,104,889	67.02	4,174,940	21.35	2,240,581	11.46	32,658	0.17	19,553,068

By comparing the above table with one made up from the British Census of 1841, (the returns for 1851 embracing these particulars not having been yet received,) it will be seen that whilst for our oldest States, such as North Carolina, South Carolina, Virginia, Maryland and Pennsylvania, only 95, 92, 90, 78 and 79 per cent. respectively of the free population (the proportion will not be affected for the slave) were born in the States of their residence, in England there were 96 per cent.; in Ireland 99.58.; in Scotland, 93 per cent. In some of our States such as Wisconsin, Iowa and California the proportion runs down as low as seventeen, twenty-one, and eight per cent. Only sixteen per cent. in England and five per cent. in Ireland resided out of their native counties! The proportion of foreign born was not more than one-tenth of one per cent. in Scotland, one-twentieth of one per cent. in Ireland, and one-fiftieth of one per cent. in England against over eleven per cent. in the United States, thirty-six per cent. in Wisconsin, and twenty-six per cent. in Louisiana, one-half of one per cent. in North Carolina, and three-quarters of one per cent. in Tennessee.

TABLE XLI.—*Nativities of the White Population by Sex.*

States and Territories.	Born in the State.		Born out of the State and in the U. States.		Born in foreign countries.		Unknown.	
	Males.	Females.	Males.	Females.	Males.	Females.	Males.	Females
Alabama	118,012	116,679	95,988	87,336	4,928	2,570	555	446
Arkansas	31,145	29,851	53,266	45,684	989	479	474	301
California	4,532	3,164	59,471	2,395	20,278	1,351	427	17
Columbia, District of	8,924	9,451	6,831	7,789	2,724	2,189	15	18
Connecticut	139,232	145,746	20,242	18,875	19,968	18,406	442	188
Delaware	27,773	27,818	5,195	5,131	2,770	2,473	8	1
Florida	9,684	9,436	14,058	11,274	1,953	787	10	1
Georgia	199,271	197,027	62,452	55,816	4,242	2,210	268	286
Illinois	169,665	161,424	210,225	189,508	63,427	48,433	2,227	1,125
Indiana	264,241	256,342	207,707	190,988	32,692	22,845	1,538	801
Iowa	21,406	19,899	67,278	61,970	11,983	9,031	220	94
Kentucky	293,442	286,687	79,167	69,415	19,461	11,940	734	567
Louisiana	63,664	63,253	36,386	24,255	40,714	26,594	479	146
Maine	260,037	254,618	18,816	16,203	17,534	14,161	358	86
Maryland	160,562	165,478	22,632	17,978	27,813	23,198	180	102
Massachusetts	333,492	346,133	67,511	71,908	81,129	82,469	1,961	847
Michigan	69,998	67,639	106,868	94,718	30,678	23,915	921	334
Mississippi	69,000	66,501	83,730	71,216	3,236	1,546	321	168
Missouri	135,005	130,299	131,224	117,999	46,178	30,392	580	327
New Hampshire	127,150	130,982	20,510	24,415	8,211	6,046	89	53
New Jersey	179,355	182,336	21,905	21,806	32,009	27,795	183	120
New York	1,041,446	1,050,630	156,274	140,480	343,900	311,324	2,869	1,402
North Carolina	260,546	268,937	10,803	9,981	1,583	982	93	103
Ohio	605,329	598,161	273,435	255,773	122,531	95,568	2,822	1,431
Pennsylvania	890,111	897,199	85,834	80,132	165,690	137,415	1,099	680
Rhode Island	48,558	50,196	10,203	11,018	11,531	12,301	48	20
South Carolina	125,545	127,854	7,043	5,558	5,136	3,372	23	32
Tennessee	290,177	290,518	87,519	81,447	3,734	1,904	805	732
Texas	22,396	20,885	51,418	41,239	10,726	6,894	329	147
Vermont	114,626	113,863	25,656	25,238	19,147	14,541	229	102
Virginia	404,331	409,480	31,084	26,498	15,606	7,347	279	175
Wisconsin	26,348	27,964	75,165	64,001	62,231	48,240	607	200
Territories. Minnesota	776	796	1,612	874	1,305	672	2	1
Territories. New Mexico	29,350	29,054	647	114	1,523	628	205	4
Territories. Oregon	1,074	1,227	6,082	3,554	800	159	182	9
Territories. Utah	550	609	4,357	3,760	1,104	940	9	1
Total	6,546,753	6,558,136	2,218,594	1,956,346	1,239,464	1,001,117	21,591	11,067

8. *Occupations.*—These will also be treated of in the chapter of aggregate population, being combined for the white and free colored, and, in some cases, for white, free colored and slaves.

CHAPTER IV.

FREE COLORED POPULATION.

1. *Aggregate.*—The free colored population of the United States in 1850 amounted to 434,495, of whom 275,400 were black, or of unmixed African descent, and 159,095 mulattoes, of mixed African and other blood.* [See table under Slaves.] The distinction was not observed in any census prior to 1850. For some remarks upon free blacks in the colonies, see ante, p. 37.

* Where the proportion is less than one-eighth of African blood the distinction of class begins to be obscured. The Mestizo is the issue of the Indian and the Negro, and has all the disabilities of the mulatto. The free colored are made up of those and their descendants who have been emancipated, either by general law or by individuals; those who are fugitives from slavery and their descendants, with a small admixture of such as have come into the country in a state of freedom and their descendants.

The decrease in the free colored persons of Louisiana, shown in the table, in 1850, is supported by the State census. It seems to be chiefly in New Orleans, where the decline has been 9,321 since 1840, or about one-half. The third municipality alone declined from 8,704 in 1840 to 3,524 in 1850, or nearly two-thirds. The average number of colored persons to a family in the third municipality in 1840 was ten and one-half, and in 1850 five and one-seventh. All of this is very extraordinary, and leads to the conviction that errors were committed in one or the other period, (almost certainly the first,) or that free mulattoes have been passing into the white column, which is not shown, however, in the increase of the whites in that municipality since 1840. The colored persons who are known to have left the city will not account for this decline of one-half, notwithstanding the natural increase.

Table XLII.—*Free Colored Population of the United States.*

States and Territories.	1790.	1800.	1810.	1820.	1830.	1840.	1850.
Alabama	....	....	....	571	1,572	2,039	2,265
Arkansas	....	....	....	59	141	465	608
California	....	....	....	....	....	....	962
Columbia, District of	....	783	2,549	4,048	6,152	8,361	10,059
Connecticut	2,801	5,330	6,453	7,844	8,047	8,105	7,693
Delaware	3,899	8,268	13,136	12,958	15,855	16,919	18,073
Florida	....	....	....	....	844	817	932
Georgia	398	1,019	1,801	1,763	2,486	2,753	2,931
Illinois	....	....	613	457	1,637	3,598	5,436
Indiana	....	163	393	1,230	3,629	7,165	11,262
Iowa	....	....	....	....	....	172	333
Kentucky	114	741	1,713	2,759	4,917	7,317	10,011
Louisiana	....	....	7,585	10,476	16,710	25,502	17,462
Maine	538	818	969	929	1,190	1,355	1,356
Maryland	8,043	19,587	33,927	39,730	52,938	62,078	74,723
Massachusetts	5,463	6,452	6,737	6,740	7,048	8,669	9,064
Michigan	....	....	120	174	261	707	2,583
Mississippi	....	182	240	458	519	1,366	930
Missouri	....	....	607	347	569	1,574	2,618
New Hampshire	630	856	970	786	604	537	520
New Jersey	2,762	4,402	7,843	12,460	18,303	21,044	23,810
New York	4,654	10,374	25,333	29,279	44,870	50,027	49,069
North Carolina	4,975	7,043	10,266	14,612	19,543	22,732	27,463
Ohio	....	337	1,899	4,723	9,568	17,342	25,279
Pennsylvania	6,537	14,561	22,492	30,202	37,930	47,854	53,626
Rhode Island	3,469	3,304	3,609	3,554	3,561	3,238	3,670
South Carolina	1,801	3,185	4,554	6,826	7,921	8,276	8,960
Tennessee	361	309	1,317	2,727	4,555	5,524	6,422
Texas	....	....	....	....	....	....	397
Vermont	255	557	750	903	881	730	718
Virginia	12,766	20,124	30,570	36,889	47,348	49,852	54,333
Wisconsin	....	....	....	....	....	185	635
Territories. Minnesota	....	....	....	....	....	....	39
Territories. New Mexico	....	....	....	....	....	....	22
Territories. Oregon	....	....	....	....	....	....	207
Territories. Utah	....	....	....	....	....	....	24
				233,504 *add 20			
Aggregate	59,466	108,395	186,446	‡233,524	319,599	386,303	434,495

The table in the chapter on Slave Population will show the distribution of Blacks and Mulattoes in the States, whether free or slave, and their proportion to the total of either class of population. The material not having been prepared when the other facts of population were being tabulated, could not now be presented in greater detail without expense and delay. For purposes of comparison, the returns have been subsequently searched for Connecticut, Louisiana, (New Orleans being separated) and New York City, and all of the facts relating to free blacks and mulattoes carefully aggregated, as will appear hereafter.

The increase and decrease per cent. of the free colored population in the great divisions of the Union, are shown as follows.

Table XLIII.—*Increase and Decrease per cent. of the Free Colored Population in Geographical Divisions.*

Geographical Divisions.	1800.	1810.	1820.	1830.	1840.	1850.
New England	31.63	12.54	6.51	.39	6.11	1.71
Middle States	123.88	81.54	22.26	33.90	17.17	11.19
Southern States	57.33	50.43	27.33	29.49	8.05	12.07
Southwestern States	36.01	1,761.91	56.32	64.42	48.51	†19.52
Northwestern States	988.60	330.70	81.29	112.39	84.93	56.10

* Added to make the totals published incorrectly. ‡ Excluding 4632 other persons except Indians untaxed.

† This is a decrease, and the only instance. The immigration of free colored from abroad cannot be ascertained, but is very small. Their emigration is also small, consisting of those who go to Canada—those from Louisiana to France, and those generally to Liberia. By the report of the Colonization Society, made in 1852, it seems that in 32 years, 7,592 persons have been sent to that colony, including 800 to the colony of Maryland, and 1,044 liberated Africans. The "present emigrant population of the colony," is stated at "about six or seven thousand." The emigrants were from Massachusetts 10, Rhode Island 32, Connecticut 30, New York 126, New Jersey 1, Delaware 4, Maryland 489, District of Columbia 101, Virginia 2,409, N. Carolina 872, S. Carolina 372, Georgia 756, Alabama 49, Mississippi 505, Louisiana 234, Tennessee 287, Kentucky 297, Ohio 45, Indiana 30, Illinois 34, Michigan 1, Iowa 3. Slaveholding States, 6,792; non-slaveholding, 457: Born free, 2,720; purchased, 204; emancipated for Liberia, 3,868.

The declining ratio of the increase of the free colored in every section is notable. In New England the increase is now almost nothing. In the South West it is much reduced, owing in some degree to errors in the Louisiana report in 1840. In the Southern States the increase is only one-fourth as great as between 1800 and 1810. The North West shows the heaviest ratios of increase, indicating a large emigration to that quarter.**

TABLE XLIV.—*Manumitted and Fugitive Slaves,* 1850.

States.	Manumitted	Fugitive.	States.	Manumitted	Fugitive.
Alabama	16	29	Missouri	50	60
Arkansas	1	21	Mississippi	6	41
Delaware	277	26	North Carolina	2	64
Florida	22	18	South Carolina	2	16
Georgia	19	89	Tennessee	45	70
Kentucky	152	96	Texas	5	29
Louisiana	159	90	Virginia	218	83
Maryland	493	279			
			Total	1,467	1,011

The increase and decrease per cent. of the free colored population in each period of ten years is shown below for all of the States. The greatest increase in ten years was in Kentucky, 1800, 550 per cent.; in Ohio, 1810, 463 per cent.; in Michigan, 1850, 265 per cent.; in Wisconsin, 1850, 243 per cent.; in Illinois, in 1830, 258 per cent. The least increase occurred in Massachusetts, in 1820, .04 per cent., and in 1850, 4.55 per cent.; in Connecticut, in 1830, 2.58 per cent.; and in 1840, 0.72 per cent.; in Maine, in 1850, 0.07 per cent. In 1800 there was a decrease in two States; in 1820, in seven; in 1830 in two; in 1840 in four; and in 1850, in six. The greatest decrease was in Missouri, in 1820, of 42 per cent., and in Louisiana and Mississippi, in 1850, of 31 per cent. The others were in Rhode Island in the years 1800 and 1820; in Tennessee in 1800; in Delaware, Georgia, Illinois, Maine, Missouri, New Hampshire, in 1820; in New Hampshire and Vermont, in 1830, &c.

TABLE XLV.—*Increase and Decrease per cent. of the Free Colored Population of the United States.*

States and Territories.	1800.	1810.	1820.	1830.	1840.	1850.
Alabama	...	...	...	*175.30	*29.70	*11.08
Arkansas	...	...	...	*138.98	*229.78	*30.75
California	...	...	...	...	...	...
Columbia, District of	...	*225.54	*58.80	*51.97	*35.90	*20.30
Connecticut	*90.28	*21.06	*21.55	*2.58	*0.72	†5.08
Delaware	*112.05	*58.87	†1.35	*22.35	*6.71	*6.82
Florida	...	...	...	...	†3.19	*14.07
Georgia	*156.03	*76.74	†2.10	*41.00	*10.74	*6.46
Illinois	...	...	†25.44	*258.20	*119.79	*51.08
Indiana	...	*141.10	*212.97	*195.04	*97.43	*57.55
Iowa	...	...	...	...	...	*93.60
Kentucky	*550.00	*131.17	*61.06	*78.21	*48.81	*36.81
Louisiana	...	...	*38.11	*59.50	*52.61	†31.52
Maine	*52.04	*18.45	†4.12	*28.09	*13.86	*0.07
Maryland	*143.52	*73.21	*17.10	*33.24	*17.26	*20.36
Massachusetts	*18.10	*4.41	*0.04	*4.56	*22.99	*4.55
Michigan	...	...	*45.00	*50.00	*170.88	*265.34
Mississippi	...	*31.86	*90.83	*13.31	*163.19	†31.91
Missouri	...	...	†42.83	*63.97	*176.62	*66.32
New Hampshire	*35.87	*13.31	†18.96	†23.15	†11.09	†3.16
New Jersey	*59.37	*78.16	*58.86	*46.89	*14.97	*13.14
New York	*122.90	*144.19	*15.57	*53.24	*11.49	†1.91
North Carolina	*41.56	*45.76	*42.33	*33.74	*16.31	*20.81
Ohio	...	*463.50	*148.70	*102.58	*81.25	*45.76
Pennsylvania	*122.74	*54.46	*34.27	*25.58	*26.16	*12.06
Rhode Island	†4.75	*9.23	†1.52	*0.19	†9.07	*13.34
South Carolina	*76.84	*42.98	*49.89	*16.04	*4.48	*8.26
Tennessee	†14.40	*326.21	*107.06	*67.03	*21.27	*16.25
Texas	...	...	...	...	...	...
Vermont	*118.43	*34.64	*20.40	†2.43	†17.13	†1.64
Virginia	*57.63	*59.90	*20.67	*28.35	*5.28	*8.98
Wisconsin	...	...	...	...	...	*243.24

* Increase. † Decrease.

** On the schedules 1,467 slaves are returned in 1850, as emancipated in the slaveholding States during the previous year, increasing the total free colored population by about one in 1,800, and in Maryland by about one in 150. Admitting an equal number emancipated during every year between 1840 and 1850, and one-third of the number emancipated during every year from 1790 to 1840, and 500 annually from 1770 to 1790, (the figures will be considered to fall short of the reality, in remembering that emancipation has been retarded in later years, and that those for 1850 are very low,) the total number emancipated at the South since the Revolution would be set down at 50,000. The number emancipated by *general law* in the other States may be

TABLE XLVI.—*Increase of the Free Colored Population in the Slaveholding and Non-Slaveholding States.*

		1800.	1810.	1820.	1830.	1840.	1850.
Present Slaveholding States.	Free Colored	89.27	76.79	24.92	34.62	18.40	10.49
	Whole Colored	33.11	38.52	30.04	32.23	23.51	27.40
Non-Slaveholding States.	Free Colored	73.94	65.80	31.61	33.66	24.14	14.98
	Whole Colored	23.01	27.19	15.43	15.65	21.80	14.38

The rank which the States held with reference to each other, considered with regard to the free colored population only, at each census, is herewith shown. Maryland, during forty years, has held the first rank. Virginia, which was first in 1790, became third in 1840, and second in 1850. Massachusetts, from the fourth, has become the thirteenth.

TABLE XLVII.—*Relative Rank of the States and Territories with reference to the Free Colored Population.*

States and Territories.	1790.	1800.	1810.	1820.	1830.	1840.	1850.	States and Territories	1790.	1800.	1810.	1820.	1830.	1840.	1850.
Alabama	....	....	....	22	20	20	22	Missouri	....	....	21	25	25	21	20
Arkansas	....	....	....	27	28	28	29	New Hampshire	12	13	18	20	24	27	30
California	....	....	....	....	....	....	24	New Jersey	10	9	7	7	6	7	7
Columbia, District of.	....	14	13	13	13	11	11	New York	6	4	3	4	3	2	4
Connecticut	9	8	10	9	10	13	15	North Carolina	5	7	6	5	5	6	5
Delaware	7	5	5	6	8	9	8	Ohio	....	17	14	12	9	8	6
Florida	....	....	....	....	23	24	25	Pennsylvania	3	3	4	3	4	4	3
Georgia	13	12	15	17	18	19	19	Rhode Island	8	10	12	14	17	18	18
Illinois	....	....	20	23	19	17	17	South Carolina	11	11	11	11	11	12	14
Indiana	....	20	22	18	16	15	10	Tennessee	14	18	17	16	15	16	16
Iowa	....	....	....	....	....	30	32	Texas	....	....	....	....	....	....	31
Kentucky	16	15	16	15	14	14	12	Vermont	15	16	19	21	22	25	27
Louisiana	....	....	9	8	7	5	9	Virginia	1	1	2	2	2	3	2
Maine	....	....	....	19	21	23	23	Wisconsin	....	....	....	....	....	29	28
Maryland	2	2	1	1	1	1	1	Territories. Minnesota	....	....	....	....	....	....	34
Massachusetts	4	6	8	10	12	10	13	Territories. New Mexico	....	....	....	....	....	....	36
Michigan	....	....	24	26	27	26	21	Territories. Oregon	....	....	....	....	....	....	33
Mississsppi	....	19	23	24	26	22	26	Territories. Utah	....	....	....	....	....	....	35

The following table will show the proportion of the free colored population in each State to its total population at each of the periods named. It has decreased in New England notwithstanding its accession from its own slaves, and fugitives from other States, except in Connecticut, where there has been an increase. This increase is notable in other Northern States. In Delaware the free colored from six per cent. in 1790, in 1850 were nineteen per cent. In Maryland from 2.51 per cent. in 1790, were 12 per cent. in 1850. Nearly one-fifth of the inhabitants of the District of Columbia are free colored. In the other Southern States, except North Carolina and Kentucky the proportion is declining. In Louisiana it has declined from nearly 10 per cent. in 1810 to a little over 3 per cent. in 1850, but see note *ante* In nearly all the other States there is a proportionate decline.

TABLE XLVIII.—*Proportion of Free Colored to total Population.*

States, &c.	1790.	1800.	1810.	1820.	1830.	1840.	1850.
Alabama	....	....	....	0.45	0.51	0.34	0.29
Arkansas	....	....	....	0.54	0.46	0.48	0.29
California	....	....	....	....	....	....	1.04
Columbia, District of	....	5.55	10.61	12.25	15.44	19.13	19.46
Connecticut	1.18	2.12	2.46	2.89	2.70	2.61	2.07
Delaware	6.60	12.86	18.08	17.81	20.66	21.66	19.75
Florida	....	....	....	....	2.43	1.50	1.07
Georgia	0.48	0.63	0.71	0.51	0.48	0.40	0.32
Illinois	....	....	4.99	0.92	1.04	0.75	0.64

ascertained by an estimate of their slave population at the periods of emancipation, if it be admitted that all of the slaves received the benefit of the emancipating acts. A liberal estimation will carry the figures to 50,000 or 51,000. By the mode of arranging the returns, the slaves liberated in 1849–1850 are counted still as slaves, and are, no doubt, in many cases, counted again as free colored.

The number of fugitive slaves or those who had absconded during the year 1849–1850, and had not been heard from, was 1,011, by the reports. As might be supposed, the border States, Maryland, Missouri and Kentucky, show the largest proportion, being respectively one in 320, one in 1,450, and one in 2,100. In Georgia and Louisiana the proportion was one in 2,700, and one in 4,000, respectively

TABLE XLVIII—*Continued.*

States, &c.	1790.	1800.	1810.	1820.	1830.	1840.	1850.
Indiana	....	3.34	1.60	0.84	1.06	1.04	1.14
Iowa	....	....	....	....	....	0.40	0.17
Kentucky	0.15	0.33	0.42	0.52	0.71	0.94	1.02
Louisiana	....	....	9.91	7.15	7.74	7.24	3.37
Maine	0.56	0.54	0.42	0.33	0.30	0.27	0.23
Maryland	2.51	5.73	8.92	9.75	11.84	13.21	12.82
Massachusetts	1.44	1.52	1.43	1.31	1.15	1.18	0.91
Michigan	....	....	2.52	3.43	0.82	0.33	0.65
Mississippi	....	2.06	0.59	0.61	0.38	0.36	0.15
Missouri	....	....	2.91	0.56	0.41	0.41	0.38
New Hampshire	0.44	0.47	0.45	0.38	0.22	0.19	0.16
New Jersey	1.50	2.08	3.19	4.54	5.71	5.64	4.86
New York	1.37	1.77	2.64	2.18	2.34	2.06	1.58
North Carolina	1.26	1.47	1.85	2.29	2.65	3.01	3.16
Ohio	....	0.74	0.82	0.84	1.02	1.14	1.28
Pennsylvania	1.51	2.42	2.78	3.06	2.81	2.78	2.32
Rhode Island	5.02	4.78	4.68	4.33	3.66	2.98	2.48
South Carolina	0.72	0.92	1.10	1.36	1.36	1.39	1.34
Tennessee	1.01	0.29	0.50	0.66	0.67	0.66	0.64
Texas	....	....	....	....	....	....	0.19
Vermont	0.30	0.36	0.34	0.39	0.31	0.25	0.23
Virginia	1.71	2.29	3.14	3.48	3.91	4.02	3.82
Wisconsin	....	....	....	....	....	0.59	0.21

TABLE XLIX.—*Sex of the Free Colored Population of the United States at several Census periods.*

STATES AND TERRITORIES.	MALES.				FEMALES.			
	1820.	1830.	1840.	1850.	1820.	1830.	1840.	1850.
Alabama	318	844	1,030	1,056	253	728	1,009	1,209
Arkansas	54	88	248	314	23	53	217	294
California	....	....		872	....	....	....	90
Columbia, District of	1,731	2,645	3,453	4,248	2,317	3,507	4,908	5,811
Connecticut	3,886	3,850	3,891	3,820	4,058	4,197	4,214	3,873
Delaware	6,479	7,882	8,626	9,035	6,479	7,973	8,293	9,038
Florida	....	383	398	418	....	461	419	514
Georgia	854	1,261	1,374	1,375	913	1,225	1,379	1,556
Illinois	262	824	1,876	2,777	244	813	1,722	2,659
Indiana	654	1,857	3,731	5,715	576	1,772	3,434	5,547
Iowa	....	....	93	165	....	....	79	168
Kentucky	1,582	2,652	3,761	4,863	1,359	2,265	3,556	5,148
Louisiana	4,744	7,230	11,526	7,479	6,216	9,480	13,976	9,983
Maine	469	610	720	726	526	580	635	630
Maryland	18,746	24,906	23,187	35,192	20,984	28,032	32,891	39,531
Massachusetts	3,372	3,358	4,654	4,424	3,496	3,690	4,015	4,640
Michigan	169	159	393	1,431	136	102	314	1,152
Mississippi	239	288	715	474	219	231	651	456
Missouri	202	284	883	1,361	174	285	691	1,257
New Hampshire	439	275	248	260	486	329	289	260
New Jersey	6,490	9,501	10,780	11,798	6,119	8,802	10,264	12,012
New York	13,798	21,466	23,809	23,452	16,182	23,404	26,218	25,617
North Carolina	7,395	9,561	11,227	13,298	7,217	9,982	11,505	14,165
Ohio	2,523	4,789	8,740	12,691	2,339	4,779	8,602	12,588
Pennsylvania	15,714	18,377	22,752	25,369	16,460	19,553	25,102	28,257
Rhode Island	1,609	1,548	1,413	1,738	1,989	2,013	1,825	1,932
South Carolina	3,296	3,672	3,864	4,131	3,530	4,249	4,412	4,829
Tennessee	1,526	2,330	2,796	3,117	1,253	2,225	2,728	3,305
Texas	....	....	....	211	....	....	....	186
Vermont	445	426	364	375	473	455	366	343
Virginia	17,970	22,387	23,828	26,002	19,169	24,961	26,024	28,331
Wisconsin	....	....	101	365	....	....	84	270
Territories. Minnesota	....	....	....	21	....	....	....	18
Territories. New Mexico	....	....	....	17	....	....	....	5
Territories. Oregon	....	....	....	120	....	....	....	87
Territories. Utah	....	....	....	14	....	....	....	10
	114,966	153,453	186,481	208,724	123,190	166,146	199,822	225,771

2. *Families and Dwellings.*—The families and dwellings of the free colored have not been classified distinct from those of the whites except in the States and Cities named.

TABLE L.—*Families and Dwellings of Free Colored.*

STATES AND CITIES.	FAMILIES.			DWELLINGS.			Persons to Families.	Persons to Families.	Families to 100 dwellings.	Families to 100 dwellings.
	Mulatto.	Black.	Total.	Mulatto.	Black.	Total.	Mulatto.	Black.	Mulatto.	Black.
Connecticut.........	338	1,095	1,433	326	939	1,265	5.32	5.38	1.04	1.17
Louisiana...........	2,568	858	3,426	2,297	734	3,031	5.48	3.94	1.12	1.17
New York City......	663	2,326	2,989	211	721	932	4.62	4.62	3.14	3.23
New Orleans........	1,468	530	1,998	1,274	429	1,703	5.49	3.59	1.15	1.24

3. *Sex.*—There were, in 1850, in the United States, 208,724 males, and 225,771 females, of the free colored population.

TABLE LI.—*Proportion of Free Colored Males to Females in the several sections of the Union.*

States and Territories.	Dates.	Males.	Females	Females to 100 males.	States and Territories.	Dates.	Males.	Females	Females to 100 males.
New England...	1790	....	....	*	Southern States	1840	40,691	43,739	107.49
	1800	....	....	*		1850	45,224	49,395	109.22
	1810	....	....	*	South-Western States.	1790	....	....	*
	1820	10,220	11,028	107.95		1800	....	....	*
	1830	10,067	11,264	111.89		1810	....	....	*
	1840	11,290	11,344	100.48		1820	6,981	7,964	115.74
	1850	11,343	11,678	102.95		1830	10,780	12,717	117.97
Middle States...	1790	....	....	*		1840	16,315	18,581	113.89
	1800	....	....	*		1850	12,651	15,433	121.99
	1810	....	....	*	North-Western States.	1790	....	....	*
	1820	62,958	68,541	108.87		1800	....	....	*
	1830	84,777	91,271	107.66		1810	....	....	*
	1840	98,607	107,676	109.20		1820	5,392	4,828	89.54
	1850	109,094	120,266	110.24		1830	10,565	10,016	94.80
Southern States.	1790	....	....	*		1840	19,578	18,482	94.40
	1800	....	....	*		1850	29,368	28,789	98.03
	1810	....	....	*					
	1820	29,515	30,829	104.45	Territories and California.	1850	1,044	210	20.11
	1830	37,264	40,878	109.70					

* Sex not designated.

As with the whites, it will be seen that in New England with the free colored the females are always in excess. This excess of free colored females is found at every census in the Middle, Southern and Southwestern States; the reverse of the whites, the excess being from 113 to 121 to the 100 in the Southwest. In the Northwest and the Territories the males preponderate; in the last instance very largely.

TABEL LII.—*Male and Female Free Colored at every Census.*

Sex.	1790.	1800.	1810.	1820.	1830.	1840.	1850.
Males..........	sex	not desig-	nated.	114,966	153,453	186,481	208,724
Females	"	"	"	123,190	166,146	199,822	225.771

The increase of the free colored males and the females, and the per centage of increase of both together, in periods of ten years are shown in the table which follows, including those returned as "other free persons except Indians," &c. distributed in the proportion of male and female.

TABLE LIII.—*Increase of Free Colored Males and Females.*

Year.	Number of males.	Number of females	Excess of females.	All other free except Indians, sex not designated.	Total free colored.	Increase.	Increase per cent.	Free colored to whites as 1 to
1790	....	....	....	59,466	59,466	....	....	53.3492
1800	....	....	....	108,395	108,395	48,929	82.2806	39.7111
1810	....	....	....	186,446	186,446	78,051	72.0006	31.4407
1820	112,734	120,790	8,056	4,632	238,156	51,710	27.7345	33.0117
1830	153,453	166,146	12,693	....	319,599	81,443	34.1973	32.9796
1840	186,481	199,822	13,341	....	386,303	66,704	20.8712	36.7476
1850	208,724	225,771	17,047	....	434,495	48,192	12.4752	45.0018
Total increase of each class in 60 yrs.	....	....	....	....	....	375,029	630.6612	....

The sex of the Blacks has not been classified distinct from that of the Mulattoes, except in the instances below.

TABLE LIV.—*Sex—Blacks and Mulattoes.*

States and Cities.	Males.		Females.		Total.	Per cent. of mulattoes.	Per cent. of blacks.
	Mulattoes.	Blacks.	Mulattoes.	Blacks.		Males.	Males.
Connecticut	880	2,940	918	2,955	7,693	95.86	99.53
Louisiana	6,249	1,230	7,861	2,122	17,462	79.49	57.96
New York city	1,328	4,770	1,735	5,982	13,815	76.54	79.74
New Orleans	3,270	685	4,771	1,235	9,961	68.54	55.47

TABLE LV.—*Proportion of one hundred Free Colored Males to Females*, 1850.

STATES AND TERRITORIES.	INFANCY.	YOUTH.			MATURITY.			OLD AGE.					EXTREME OLD AGE.	Age unknown.
	Under 5.	5 and under 10.	10 and under 15.	15 and under 20.	20 and under 30.	30 and under 40.	40 and under 50.	50 and under 60.	60 and under 70.	70 and under 80.	80 and under 90.	90 and under 100.	100 and upwards.	
Alabama	105.5	90.0	104.7	110.4	159.1	147.1	103.1	96.8	83.7	172.2	100.0	200.0	166.6	.....
Arkansas	91.6	88.5	97.3	179.1	86.0	79.4	56.1	110.0	125.0	75.0	33.3	.....	.....	.....
California	75.0	125.0	181.8	19.4	7.7	4.6	2.7	12.5	.....	.....	.....	.....	.....	.....
Columbia, Dist.	98.1	109.7	114.9	161.6	172.0	143.6	165.1	137.8	176.5	186.5	335.0	550.0	.....	.....
Connecticut	101.8	94.9	103.5	109.9	89.8	99.6	105.9	113.5	109.5	145.9	116.0	140.0	300.0	33.3
Delaware	99.6	97.8	93.0	94.0	114.6	102.1	99.1	106.6	86.7	92.3	130.0	76.4	150.0	33.3
Florida	109.3	127.1	88.7	122.2	110.3	161.3	162.0	168.7	115.0	157.1	133.3	200.0	25.0	.....
Georgia	87.8	91.4	88.6	116.3	148.7	136.6	98.9	159.6	152.2	125.7	225.0	155.5	200.0	.....
Illinois	97.0	98.6	109.9	102.4	96.7	78.4	91.6	72.5	115.6	125.9	122.2	80.0	200.0	200.0
Indiana	95.6	105.5	92.9	99.6	108.6	99.8	92.7	62.7	74.7	91.2	100.	128.5	.....	155.5
Iowa	114.2	96.5	117.6	94,4	105.7	70.8	85.7	83.3	500.0	.....	.....	.....	.....	.....
Kentucky	103.8	96.2	107.5	115.9	118.1	112.6	106.3	96.0	99.7	87.6	109.6	138.8	183.3	125.0
Louisiana	103.9	99.5	97.6	141.7	153.3	163.7	143.8	184.5	244.1	179.0	248.5	409.0	190.9	18.7
Maine	80.0	90.3	77.1	94.2	95.4	80.9	69.5	109.3	103.4	118.1	50.0	.....	.....	.....
Maryland	101.1	103.6	101.4	118.2	125.3	121.3	119.6	107.0	107.4	120.2	136.5	244.4	436.3	.....
Massachusetts	112.1	107.4	101.1	117.5	94.3	97.3	102.9	118.6	122.4	144.2	124.1	228.5	100.0	41.3
Michigan	97.2	96.0	91.7	99.0	86.4	58.7	52.0	51.2	73.3	130.0	300.0	.....	100.0	50.0
Mississippi	101.5	92.9	107.1	86.3	77.7	102.0	117.1	106.4	100.0	52.9	150.0	.....	.....	.....
Missouri	121.2	105.1	110.9	69.3	76.5	96.5	90.0	85.1	87.5	60.8	180.0	400.0	400.0	25.0
New Hampshire	100.0	73.3	95.8	81.8	107.3	109.3	100.0	131.8	80.0	137.5	100.0	100.0	.....	.....
New Jersey	105.4	106.1	94.8	100.7	104.1	100.7	95.3	95.3	107.8	113.2	125.4	121.7	400.0	100.0
New York	104.7	105.0	104.4	124.2	115.8	105.1	100.6	103.0	116.8	132.4	171.0	183.3	116.5	314.2
North Carolina	99.9	96.6	95.1	100.0	117.5	125.9	126.5	105.1	107.4	119.3	115.7	90.9	242.8	.....
Ohio	93.6	101.0	102.6	113.5	105.7	91.9	91.9	94.0	71.1	100.7	88.6	128.5	160.0	122.2
Pennsylvania	103.5	103.9	107.6	124.1	125.6	108.9	104.7	103.1	106.1	120.2	126.6	272.7	166.6	85.7
Rhode Island	93.5	98.4	115.7	106.5	101.6	107.6	114.4	154.2	182.7	127.5	173.3	700.0	.....	100.0
South Carolina	95.5	102.4	97.0	125.3	133.9	133.9	125.7	149.4	143.8	155.3	164.0	162.5	233.3	.....
Tennessee	101.4	104.3	92.5	118.5	109.2	136.1	117.3	84.3	117.0	77.7	96.6	45.4	14.2	400.0
Texas	96.3	71.0	76.0	133.3	85.0	100.0	111.7	64.2	100.0	33.3	200.0	.....	.....	.....
Vermont	58.9	80.9	68.3	142.8	113.6	56.1	112.1	103.8	166.6	125.0	125.0	300.0	100.0	.....
Virginia	97.7	99.6	99.3	112.9	120.0	119.9	112.8	116.0	109.4	123.5	132.8	125.4	175.0	1000.0
Wisconsin	92.6	64.0	148.0	100.0	69.1	53.4	65.3	86.6	25.0	33.3	.....	.....	.....	.....
Territories. Minnesota	.....	.....	100.0	50.0	85.7	100.0	33.3	.....	.....	.....	.....	.....	.....	.....
Territories. N. Mexico	.....	.....	.....	.....	14.2	60.0	.....	.....	.....	.....	.....	.....	.....	.....
Territories. Oregon	78.2	146.1	122.2	90.9	39.4	45.0	125.0	.....	.....	.....	.....	.....	.....	.....
Territories. Utah	25.0	100.0	100.0	66.6	100.0	200.0	.....	.....	.....	.....	.....	.....	.....	.....

4. *Age.*—It will be seen by the table that in the very aged class of free colored there are, in general, a large preponderance of the females, the most signal exception being in Tennessee. But the whole table is worthy of study and reflection.

TABLE LVI.—*Ages of the Free Colored Population of the United States,* 1830, 1840, *and* 1850.

Ages.	1830.			Ratio pr. cent.	1840.			Ratio pr. cent.
	Males.	Females.	Total.		Males.	Females.	Total.	
Under 10 years of age	48,675	47,329	96,004	30.04	56,284	55,062	111,346	28.82
10 and under 24 " "	43,079	48,138	91,217	28.54	52,805	56,592	109,397	28.32
24 " 36 " "	27,650	32,541	60,191	18.83	35,321	41,682	77,003	19.93
36 " 55 " "	22,271	24,327	46,598	14.58	28,274	30,371	58,645	15.18
55 " 100 " "	11,509	13,425	24,934	7.80	13,513	15,753	29,266	7.58
100 and upwards	269	386	655	.21	284	362	646	.17
Total	153,453	166,146	319,599	100.00	186,481	199,822	386,303	100.00

Ages.	1850.			Ratio per cent.
	Males.	Females.	Total.	
Under 5 years of age	30,319	30,502	60,821	14.00
5 and under 10 years of age	28,806	29,246	58,052	13.36
10 " 15 " "	26,061	26,247	52,308	12.04
15 " 20 " "	20,395	23,399	43,794	10.08
20 " 30 " "	35,782	41,765	77,547	17.85
30 " 40 " "	26,153	29,072	55,225	12.71
40 " 50 " "	18,199	19,741	37,940	8.73
50 " 60 " "	11,771	12,582	24,353	5.60
60 " 70 " "	6,671	7,362	14,033	3.23
70 " 80 " "	2,878	3,438	6,316	1.45
80 " 90 " "	1,106	1,512	2,618	.60
90 " 100 " "	319	540	859	.20
100 and upwards	114	229	343	.08
Total	208,574	225,635	*434,209	
* Age unknown—Males 150; Females 136			286	.07
Total			434,495	100.00

TABLE LVII.—*Classification of Ages and Sex of the Free Colored Population of the United States, 1850.*

STATES AND TERRITORIES.	Uuder 1.		1 and under 5.		5 and under 10.		10 and under 15.		15 and under 20.		20 and under 30.		30 and under 40.		40 and under 50	
	Males.	Females	Males.	Females	Males.	Females	Males.	Females	Males.	Females.	Males.	Females.	Males.	Females.	Males.	Females.
Alabama	20	29	143	143	160	144	147	154	115	127	142	226	89	131	95	98
Arkansas	6	5	42	39	35	31	37	36	24	43	43	37	39	31	41	23
California	1	2	3	1	4	5	11	20	72	14	374	29	256	12	111	3
Columbia, District of	125	125	523	511	657	662	534	614	394	637	672	1,156	531	763	367	606
Connecticut	74	72	350	360	434	412	397	411	361	397	815	732	543	541	367	389
Delaware	271	271	1,145	1,140	1,391	1,361	1,232	1,146	1,033	971	1,328	1,522	975	996	683	677
Florida	9	16	55	54	70	89	62	55	36	44	58	64	44	71	29	47
Georgia	44	30	178	165	221	202	203	180	147	171	193	287	131	179	97	96
Illinois	75	65	331	329	376	371	312	343	285	292	551	533	353	277	216	198
Indiana	161	155	772	737	867	915	823	765	627	625	903	981	561	560	400	371
Iowa	3	3	18	21	29	28	17	20	18	17	35	37	24	17	14	12
Kentucky	101	141	545	530	673	648	501	539	396	459	634	749	492	554	460	489
Louisiana	191	213	910	931	1,188	1,182	1,059	1,034	704	998	1,147	1,761	900	1,474	678	975
Maine	26	13	64	59	83	75	83	64	69	65	133	127	105	85	69	48
Maryland	1,017	998	4,422	4,502	4,950	5,131	4,516	4,582	3,396	4,015	5,437	6,816	4,344	5,273	3,030	3,625
Massachusetts	85	114	409	440	459	493	428	433	381	448	944	891	704	685	472	486
Michigan	39	35	177	175	176	169	133	122	105	104	281	243	252	148	146	76
Mississippi	8	6	58	61	57	53	56	60	44	38	90	70	49	50	35	41
Missouri	31	28	110	143	136	143	110	122	114	79	298	228	205	198	151	136
New Hampshire	7	7	22	23	30	22	24	23	22	18	41	44	32	35	26	26
New Jersey	361	358	1,302	1,395	1,484	1,579	1,498	1,421	1,174	1,183	2,018	2,101	1,526	1,538	1,049	1,000
New York	582	539	2,213	2,390	2,666	2,800	2,507	2,619	2,045	2,541	4,556	5,280	3,719	3,911	2,619	2,635
North Carolina	412	385	1,812	1,837	2,138	2,067	1,907	1,815	1,520	1,520	2,195	2,581	1,250	1,574	793	1,003
Ohio	370	319	1,565	1,493	1,793	1,811	1,572	1,613	1,332	1,513	2,324	2,457	1,556	1,431	980	901
Pennsylvania	637	748	2,897	2,911	3,286	3,417	2,900	3,121	2,397	2,975	4,607	5,787	3,480	3,792	2,471	2,589
Rhode Island	37	29	164	159	197	194	159	184	153	163	363	369	287	309	180	206
South Carolina	77	78	571	541	695	712	653	634	395	495	606	812	474	635	283	356
Tennessee	81	83	418	423	483	504	440	407	307	364	455	497	249	339	236	277
Texas	......	2	27	24	38	27	25	19	18	24	40	34	23	23	17	19
Vermont	15	8	41	25	42	34	44	30	28	40	66	75	57	32	33	37
Virginia	695	717	3,403	3,288	3,924	3,911	3,633	3,609	2,637	2,978	4,298	5,159	2,787	3,344	2,014	2,272
Wisconsin	15	6	26	32	50	32	25	37	27	27	81	56	86	46	26	17
Territ's. Minnesota	......	......	......	......	......	2	3	3	4	2	7	6	4	4	3	1
Territ's. New Mexico	......	......	......	1	......	......	......	......	1	......	7	1	5	3	4	......
Territ's. Oregon	......	......	23	18	13	19	9	11	11	10	38	15	20	9	4	5
Territ's. Utah	......	......	4	1	1	1	1	1	3	2	2	2	1	2	......	1
Total	5,576	5,600	24,743	24,902	28,806	29,246	26,061	26,247	20,395	23,399	35,782	41,765	26,153	29,072	18,199	19,741

TABLE LVII.—*Classification of Ages of the Free Colored Population—Continued.*

States and Territories.	50 and under 60.		60 and under 70.		70 and under 80.		80 and under 90.		90 and under 100.		100 and upwards.		Age unknown.		Total.		Aggregate.
	Males.	Fem.	Males.	Fem.	Males.	Fem.	Males.	Fem.	Males.	Fem.	Males.	Fem.	Males.	Fem.	Males.	Females.	
Alabama	63	61	43	36	18	31	13	13	5	10	3	5	....	1	1,056	1,209	2,265
Arkansas	20	22	12	15	12	9	3	1	....	2	....	....	....	....	314	294	608
California	32	4	6	....	2	....	....	....	....	....	....	....	....	....	872	90	962
Columbia, District of	256	353	115	203	52	97	20	67	2	11	....	5	....	1	4,248	5,811	10,059
Connecticut	237	269	147	161	61	89	25	29	5	7	1	3	3	1	3,820	3,873	7,693
Delaware	450	480	310	269	143	132	40	52	17	13	2	3	15	5	9,035	9,038	18,073
Florida	16	27	20	23	7	11	6	8	2	4	4	1	....	....	418	514	932
Georgia	62	99	44	67	35	44	8	18	9	14	2	4	1	....	1,375	1,556	2,931
Illinois	171	124	64	74	27	34	9	11	5	4	1	2	1	2	2,777	2,659	5,436
Indiana	346	217	166	124	57	52	16	16	7	9	....	6	9	14	5,715	5,547	11,262
Iowa	6	5	1	5	....	2	....	1	....	....	....	....	....	....	165	168	333
Kentucky	458	440	335	334	178	156	62	68	18	25	6	11	4	5	4,863	5,148	10,011
Louisiana	370	683	172	420	87	156	35	87	11	45	11	21	16	3	7,479	9,983	17,462
Maine	43	47	29	30	11	13	8	4	3	....	....	....	....	....	726	630	1,356
Maryland	2,104	2,252	1,242	1,334	503	605	175	239	45	110	11	48	....	1	35,192	39,531	74,723
Massachusetts	284	337	129	158	61	88	29	36	7	16	3	3	29	12	4,424	4,640	9,064
Michigan	78	40	30	22	10	13	1	3	....	....	1	1	2	1	1,431	1,152	2,583
Mississippi	31	33	25	25	17	9	4	6	....	1	....	2	....	1	474	456	930
Missouri	108	92	64	56	23	14	5	9	1	4	1	4	4	1	1,[illegible]1	1,257	2,618
New Hampshire	22	29	15	12	8	11	8	8	2	2	1	....	....	....	260	260	520
New Jersey	715	682	407	439	166	188	63	79	23	28	3	12	9	9	11,798	12,012	23,810
New York	1,432	1,476	702	820	268	355	100	171	24	44	12	14	7	22	23,452	25,617	49,069
North Carolina	638	671	337	362	176	210	89	103	22	20	7	17	2	....	13,298	14,165	27,463
Ohio	568	534	413	294	137	138	53	47	14	18	5	8	9	11	12,691	12,588	25,279
Pennsylvania	1,467	1,513	744	790	297	357	120	152	22	60	9	15	35	30	25,369	28,257	53,626
Rhode Island	83	128	58	106	40	51	15	26	1	7	....	....	1	1	1,738	1,932	3,670
South Carolina	188	281	105	151	47	73	25	41	8	13	3	7	1	....	4,131	4,829	8,960
Tennessee	205	173	123	144	72	56	29	28	11	5	7	1	1	4	3,117	3,305	6,422
Texas	14	9	2	2	3	1	1	2	3	....	....	....	....	....	211	186	397
Vermont	26	27	9	15	8	10	4	5	1	3	1	1	....	1	375	343	718
Virginia	1,259	1,461	794	869	349	432	137	182	51	64	20	35	1	10	26,002	28,331	54,333
Wisconsin	15	13	8	2	3	1	3	....	....	1	....	....	....	....	365	270	635
Territ's. Minnesota	....	....	....	....	....	....	....	....	....	....	....	....	....	....	21	18	39
Territ's. New Mexico	....	....	....	....	....	....	....	....	....	....	....	....	....	....	17	5	22
Territ's. Oregon	2	....	....	....	....	....	....	....	....	....	....	....	....	....	120	87	207
Territ's. Utah	2	....	....	....	....	....	....	....	....	....	....	....	....	....	14	10	24
Total	11,771	12,582	6,671	7,362	2,878	3,438	1,106	1,512	319	540	114	229	150	136	208,724	225,771	434,495

TABLE LVIII.—*Ages of the Free Colored Population*, 1850.

STATES AND TERRITORIES.	Under 1.	1 and under 5.	5 and under 10.	10 and under 15.	15 and under 20.	20 and under 30.	30 and under 40.	40 and under 50.	50 and under 60.	60 and under 70.	70 and under 80.	80 and under 90.	90 and under 100.	100 and upwards.	Unknown.	Total.
Alabama	49	286	304	301	242	368	220	193	124	79	49	26	15	8	1	2,265
Arkansas	11	81	66	73	67	80	70	64	42	27	21	4	2			608
California	3	4	9	31	86	403	268	114	36	6	2					962
Columbia, District of	250	1,034	1,319	1,148	1,031	1,828	1,294	973	609	318	149	87	13	5	1	10,059
Connecticut	146	710	846	808	758	1,547	1,084	756	506	308	150	54	12	4	4	7,693
Delaware	542	2,285	2,752	2,378	2,004	2,850	1,971	1,360	930	579	275	92	30	5	20	18,073
Florida	25	109	159	117	80	122	115	76	43	43	18	14	6	5		932
Georgia	74	343	423	383	318	480	310	193	161	111	79	26	23	6	1	2,931
Illinois	140	660	747	655	577	1,084	630	414	295	138	61	20	9	3	3	5,436
Indiana	316	1,509	1,782	1,588	1,252	1,884	1,121	771	563	290	109	32	16	6	23	11,262
Iowa	6	39	57	37	35	72	41	26	11	6	2	1				333
Kentucky	242	1,075	1,321	1,040	855	1,383	1,046	949	898	669	334	130	43	17	9	10,011
Louisiana	404	1,841	2,370	2,093	1,702	2,908	2,374	1,653	1,053	592	243	122	56	32	19	17,462
Maine	39	123	158	147	134	260	190	117	90	59	24	12	3			1,356
Maryland	2,015	8,924	10,081	9,098	7,411	12,253	9,617	6,655	4,356	2,576	1,108	414	155	59	1	74,723
Massachusetts	199	849	952	861	829	1,835	1,389	958	621	287	149	65	23	6	41	9,064
Michigan	74	352	345	255	209	524	400	222	118	52	23	4		2	3	2,583
Mississippi	14	119	110	116	82	160	99	76	64	50	26	10	1	2	1	930
Missouri	59	253	279	232	193	526	403	287	200	120	37	14	5	5	5	2,618
New Hampshire	14	45	52	47	40	85	67	52	51	27	19	16	4	1		520
New Jersey	719	2,697	3,063	2,919	2,357	4,119	3,064	2,049	1,397	846	354	142	51	15	18	23,810
New York	1,121	4,603	5,466	5,126	4,586	9,836	7,630	5,254	2,908	1,522	623	271	68	26	29	49,069
North Carolina	797	3,649	4,205	3,722	3,040	4,776	2,824	1,796	1,309	699	386	192	42	24	2	27,463
Ohio	689	3,058	3,604	3,185	2,845	4,781	2,987	1,881	1,102	707	275	100	32	13	20	25,279
Pennsylvania	1,385	5,808	6,703	6,021	5,372	10,394	7,272	5,060	2,960	1,534	654	272	82	24	65	53,626
Rhode Island	66	323	391	343	316	732	596	386	211	164	91	41	8		2	3,670
South Carolina	155	1,112	1,407	1,287	890	1,418	1,109	639	469	256	120	66	21	10	1	8,960
Tennessee	164	841	987	847	671	952	588	513	378	267	128	57	16	8	5	6,422
Texas	2	51	65	44	42	74	46	36	23	4	4	3	3			397
Vermont	23	66	76	74	68	141	89	70	53	24	18	9	4	2	1	718
Virginia	1,412	6,691	7,835	7,242	5,615	9,457	6,131	4,286	2,720	1,663	781	319	115	55	11	54,333
Wisconsin	21	58	82	62	54	137	132	43	28	10	4	3	1			635
Territories: Minnesota			2	6	6	13	8	4								39
Territories: New Mexico		1			1	8	8	4								22
Territories: Oregon		41	32	20	21	53	29	9	2							207
Territories: Utah		5	2	2	5	4	3	1	2							24
Total	11,176	49,645	58,052	52,308	43,794	77,547	55,225	37,940	24,353	14,033	6,316	2,618	859	343	286	434,495

TABLE LIX.—*Proportion of the different Ages to the Total Free Colored Population.**

1820.			1830.			1840.		1850.		
Ages.	Number	Ratio	Ages.	Number	Ratio	Number	Ratio	Ages.	Number	Ratio
Under 14..	93,557	39.28	Under 10	96,004	30.04	111,346	28.82	Under 1	11,176	2.57
14 and under 26..	52,862	22.20	10 and under 24	91,217	28.54	109.397	28.32	1 and under 5	49,645	11.43
26 and under 45..	50,631	21.26	24 " 36	60,191	18.83	77,003	19.93	5 " 10	58,052	13.36
45 and upwards..	36,474	15.32	36 " 55	46,598	14.58	58,645	15.18	10 " 15	52,308	12.04
All other persons except Indians not taxed......	4,632	1.94	55 " 100	24,934	7.80	29,266	7.58	15 " 20	43,794	10.08
			100 and upwards	655	0.21	646	0.17	20 " 30	77,547	17.85
								30 " 40	55,225	12.71
								40 " 50	37,940	8.73
								50 " 60	24,353	5.60
								60 " 70	14,033	3.23
								70 " 80	6,316	1.45
								80 " 90	2,618	.60
								90 " 100	859	.20
								100 and upwards	343	.08
								Unknown.......	286	.07
Total.........	238,156	.....	....	319,599	.....	386,303	.....	....	434,495	

TABLE LX.—*Ratio of Ages and Sex of Free Colored Population at several periods.*

1. *Proportion of Free Colored Males and Females,* 1820 *and* 1830.

AGES.	1820.			AGES.	1830.		
	Males, per cent.	Females, per cent.	Proportion of males to females as 100 to		Males, per cent.	Females, per cent.	Proportion of males to females as 100 to
Under 14......	42.27	38.00	96.3	Under 10....	31.72	28.49	97.23
14 and under 26......	21.30	23.89	120.15	10 and under 24....	28.07	28.97	111.74
26 " 45......	20.80	22.50	115.91	24 " 36....	18.02	19.59	117.7
45 and upwards......	15.63	15.61	107.09	36 " 55....	14.51	14.64	109.23
				55 " 100....	7.50	8.08	116.64
				100 and upwards....	.18	.23	143.5
	100.00	100.00	107.5		100.00	100.00	108.3

2. *Proportion of Free Colored Males and Females,* 1840 *and* 1850.

AGES.	1840.			AGES.	1850.		
	Males, per cent.	Females, per cent.	Proportion of males to females as 100 to		Males, per cent.	Females, per cent.	Proportion of males to females as 100 to
Under 10.....	30.18	27.55	97.83	Under 5....	14.53	13.51	100.6
10 and under 24.....	28.32	28.32	107.17	5 and under 10....	13.8	12.95	101.53
24 " 36.....	18.94	20.86	118.00	10 " 15....	12.49	11.63	100.71
36 " 55.....	15.16	15.21	107.42	15 " 20....	9.77	10.37	114.73
55 " 100.....	7.25	7.88	116.58	20 " 30....	17.14	18.5	116.72
100 and upwards.....	.15	.18	127.46	30 " 40....	12.53	12.88	111.16
				40 " 50....	8.72	8.74	108.47
				50 " 60....	5.64	5.57	106.89
				60 " 70....	3.20	3.26	110.36
				70 " 80....	1.38	1.52	119.46
				80 " 90....	.53	.67	136.71
				90 " 100....	.15	.24	169.28
				100 and upwards....	.05	.1	200.87
				Unknown	.07	.06	90.67
	100.00	100.00	107.2		100.00	100.00	108.17

* The sex was not distinguished, as before remarked, for the free colored at any Census previous to 1820.

TABLES LXI.—*Ages of the Free Colored Population, separating Blacks and Mulattoes, in the places named, in* 1850.

AGES.	CONNECTICUT.					LOUISIANA.				
	Blacks.		Mulattoes.		Total.	Blacks.		Mulattoes.		Total.
	M.	F.	M.	F.		M.	F.	M.	F.	
Under 1.....	53	51	20	21	145	47	65	144	148	404
1 and under 5.....	266	250	84	110	710	81	89	829	842	1,841
5 " 10.....	325	314	109	98	846	136	130	1,052	1,052	2,370
10 " 15.....	304	305	93	106	808	101	159	958	875	2,093
15 " 20.....	262	297	99	100	758	112	138	592	860	1,702
20 " 30.....	629	561	186	172	1,548	181	241	966	1,520	2,908
30 " 40.....	417	420	126	121	1,084	167	339	733	1,135	2,374
40 " 50.....	287	304	80	85	756	165	305	513	670	1,653
50 " 60.....	190	216	47	53	506	139	269	231	414	1,053
60 " 70.....	125	132	22	29	308	79	202	93	218	592
70 " 80.....	51	71	10	18	150	46	70	41	86	243
80 " 90.....	22	24	4	4	54	20	52	15	35	122
90 " 100.....	5	6	....	1	12	4	23	7	22	56
100 and upwards.....	1	3	....	....	4	10	9	1	12	32
Age unknown	3	1	....	....	4	....	....	14	5	19
Aggregate	2,940	2,955	880	918	7,693	1,288	2,091	6,189	7,894	17,462

AGES.	NEW YORK.					NEW ORLEANS.				
	Blacks.		Mulattoes.		Total.	Blacks.		Mulattoes.		Total.
	M.	F.	M.	F.		M.	F.	M.	F.	
Under 1.....	101	76	51	42	270	50	61	75	77	263
1 and under 5.....	348	419	142	153	1,062	18	11	420	429	878
5 " 10.....	429	483	186	162	1,260	57	74	543	566	1,240
10 " 15.....	421	457	102	152	1,132	35	52	502	499	1,088
15 " 20.....	369	528	91	165	1,153	58	69	282	502	911
20 " 30.....	1,035	1,469	292	449	3,245	111	156	488	949	1,704
30 " 40.....	955	1,121	247	326	2,649	71	227	487	789	1,574
40 " 50.....	635	772	145	157	1,709	106	189	283	424	1,002
50 " 60.....	294	375	48	76	793	82	181	128	280	671
60 " 70.....	130	174	19	29	352	42	121	37	153	353
70 " 80.....	34	73	3	18	128	12	49	15	58	134
80 " 90.....	8	27	2	4	41	8	28	2	24	62
90 " 100.....	1	6	....	1	8	1	20	3	13	37
100 and upwards.....	....	2	....	1	3	4	7	....	5	16
Age unknown	5	2	2	1	10	3	....	18	7	28
Aggregate	4,765	5,984	1,330	1,736	13,815	658	1,245	3,283	4,775	9,961

TABLE LXII.—*Ratio per cent. of Ages of the Free Colored in* 1850.

States and Territories.	Under 1.	1 and under 5.	5 and under 10.	10 and under 15.	15 and under 20.	20 and under 30.	30 and under 40.	40 and under 50.	50 and under 60.	60 and under 70.	70 and under 80.	80 and under 90.	90 and under 100.	100 and over.	Unknown.
Alabama	2.16	12.63	13.42	13.29	10.68	16.26	9.71	8.52	5.48	3.49	2.16	1.15	.66	.35	.04
Arkansas	1.81	13.32	10.85	12.01	11.02	13.16	11.51	10.53	6.91	4.44	3.45	.66	.33	....	....
California	0.31	0.42	0 .94	3.22	8.94	41.89	27.86	11.85	3.74	0.62	0.21	....	....	....	....
Columbia, District of	2.49	10.28	13.11	11.41	10.25	18.17	12.86	9.67	6.06	3.16	1.48	.87	.13	.05	.01
Connecticut	1.90	9.23	11.00	10.50	9.85	20.11	14.09	9.83	6.58	4.00	1.95	.70	.16	.05	.05
Delaware	3.00	12.64	15.23	13.16	11.09	15.77	10.90	7.53	5.14	3.20	1.52	.51	.17	.03	.11
Florida	2.68	11.70	17.06	12.55	8.58	13.09	12.34	8.16	4.61	4.61	1.93	1.50	.65	.54	....
Georgia	2.52	11.70	14.43	13.07	10.85	16.38	10.58	6.59	5.49	3.79	2.70	.89	.78	.20	.03
Illinois	2.58	12.14	13.74	12.05	10.61	19.94	11.59	7.62	5.43	2.54	1.12	.37	.17	.05	.05
Indiana	2.81	13.40	15.82	14.10	11.12	16,73	9.95	6.85	5.00	2.58	0.97	.28	.14	.05	.20
Iowa	1.80	11.71	17.12	11.11	10.51	21.62	12.31	7.81	3.31	1.80	0.60	.30	....	....	....
Kentucky	2.42	10.74	13.19	10.39	8.54	13.81	10.45	9.48	8.97	6.68	3.34	1.30	.43	.17	.09
Louisiana	2.31	10.54	13.57	11.99	9.75	16.65	13.60	9.47	6.03	3.39	1.39	.70	.32	.18	.11
Maine	2.88	9.07	11.65	10.84	9.88	19.17	14.01	8.63	6.64	4.35	1.77	.89	.22	....	....
Maryland	2.69	11.94	13.49	12.18	9.92	16.40	12.87	8.91	5.83	3.45	1.48	.55	.21	.08	....
Massachusetts	2.20	9.37	10.50	9.50	9.15	20.24	15.32	10.57	6.85	3.17	1.64	.72	.25	.07	.45
Michigan	2.86	13.63	13.36	9.87	8.09	20.29	15.49	8.59	4.57	2.01	0.89	.15	....	.08	.12
Mississippi	1.50	12.80	11.83	12.47	8.82	17.20	10.64	8.17	6.88	5.38	2.80	1.07	.11	.22	.11
Missouri	2.26	9.67	10.66	8.86	7.37	20.09	15.39	10.96	7.64	4.58	1.41	.54	.19	.19	.19
New Hampshire	2.69	8.65	10.00	9.04	7.69	16.35	12.89	10.00	9.81	5.19	3.65	3.08	.77	.19	....
New Jersey	3.02	11.33	12.86	12.26	9.90	17.30	12.87	8.60	5.87	3.55	1.49	.60	.21	.06	.08
New York	2.28	9.38	11.14	10.45	9.35	20.04	15.55	10.71	5.93	3.10	1.27	.55	.14	.05	.06
North Carolina	2.90	13.29	15.31	13.55	11.07	17.39	10.28	6.54	4.77	2.54	1.41	.70	.15	.09	.01
Ohio	2.71	12.10	14.26	12.60	11.25	18.91	11.82	7.44	4.36	2.80	1.09	.40	.13	.05	.08
Pennsylvania	2.58	10.83	12.50	11.23	10.02	19.38	13.56	9.44	5.56	2.86	1.22	.51	.15	.04	.12
Rhode Island	1.80	8.80	10.65	9.35	8.61	19.94	16.24	10.52	5.75	4.47	2.48	1.12	.22	....	.05
South Carolina	1.73	12.41	15.70	14.36	9.93	15.83	12.38	7.13	5.24	2.86	1.34	.74	.23	.11	.01
Tennessee	2.55	13.09	15.37	13.19	10.45	14.82	9.16	7.99	5.89	4.16	1.99	.89	.25	.12	.08
Texas	0.50	12.85	16.37	11.08	10.58	18.64	11.59	9.07	5.79	1.01	1.01	.76	.75	....	....
Vermont	3.20	9.19	10.58	10.31	9.47	19.64	12.40	9.75	7.38	3.34	2.51	1.25	.56	.28	.14
Virginia	2.60	12.31	14.42	13.33	10.33	17.41	11.28	7.89	5.01	3.06	1.44	.59	.21	.10	.02
Wisconsin	3.31	9.13	12.91	9.76	8.50	21.58	20.79	6.77	4.41	1.58	0.63	.47	.16	....	....
Territories: Minnesota	....	......	5.13	15.38	15.39	33.33	20.51	10.26	....	....	....	....	....	....	....
Territories: New Mexico	....	4.55	....	......	4.55	36.36	36.36	18.18	....	....	....	....	....	....	....
Territories: Oregon	....	19.81	15.46	9.66	10.14	25.60	14.01	4.35	.97	....	....	....	....	....	....
Territories: Utah	....	20.83	8.33	8.34	20.83	16.67	12.50	4.17	8.33	....	....	....	....	....	....
Total	2.57	11.43	13.36	12.04	10.08	17.85	12.71	8.73	5.60	3.23	1.45	.60	.20	.08	.07

5. *Births, Marriages and Deaths.*—The Births being considered as including only those under one year of age, it will be necessary to refer to that column of the classification of ages. The proportion to the whole free colored population will be one birth to every 39 persons. Separating the black from the mulatto the following will result for two States and two Cities

States and Cities.	Free colored births.			Free colored marriages.		
	Mulattoes.	Blacks.	Total births.	Mulattoes.	Blacks.	Total.
Connecticut	42	104	146	15	2	17
Louisiana	251	150	404	52	....	52
New York city	93	177	270	18	21	39
New Orleans	152	111	263	33	....	33

Marriages.—The free colored marriages were not separated from those of the whites. They seem not to have been noticed at all upon the returns in most of the Slave States. The reports of Registration in the States do not separate the colors. The colored marriages are condensed from the returns for Connecticut &c., as above. There were 117 deaths of blacks and 28 of mulattoes reported in Connecticut; 53 blacks and 177 mulattoes in Louisiana; 28 blacks and 9 mulattoes in Michigan, of the free colored population in 1850. For the other States the mulattoes and blacks are combined in the tables.

6. *Deaf, Dumb and Blind.*—Objection was taken to the statistics of the Deaf and Dumb, Blind, &c., for 1830 and 1840, so far as they relate to the non-Slaveholding States, and a memorial was sent to Congress from several persons in Boston, protesting against their publication. The memorial, a history of which is given on the next page, was referred to the Department of State, and that Department entrusted its examination to a gentleman who had

been charged with the preparation of the census of 1840 for the press.* The Secretary in transmitting his Report, now in manuscript in the office, and dated February 12th, 1845, says:

"On a review of the whole, two conclusions, it is believed, will be found to follow inevitably. The one is that the correctness of the late census in exhibiting a far greater prevalence of the diseases of insanity, blindness, deafness, and dumbness, stands unimpeachable. That it may contain errors, more or less, is hardly to be doubted. It would be a miracle if such a document, with so many figures and entries, did not. But that they have, if they exist, materially affected the correctness of the general result, would seem hardly possible. Nothing but that the truth is so, would seem capable of explaining the fact that, in all the non-Slaveholding States, without exception, the census exhibits, uniformly, a far greater comparative prevalence of these diseases among the free blacks than among the slaves of the other States. They are indeed vastly more so among the most favorable of the former than in the least favorable of the latter."

The leading fact relied upon by the memorialists was the mention of insane, or deaf and dumb colored persons in towns, townships, &c., in the free States, where the census reported no free colored persons at all, or a less number, or only an equal number existing. To this it is answered in the report that the memorialists have reference to uncorrected copies of the census in manuscript in Boston, and not to the corrected originals as published by the State Department. These originals, when consulted, greatly reduce the number of alleged discrepancies. Others of them are explained by the omission of the census takers after entering the colored person in the insane column to enter him again in the population column. The memorialists only extended their examination to the Northern States. The present Superintendent of the Census extended the examination to the Slaveholding States also, and found the same omissions existing there both in 1830 and in 1840, and is of the opinion that they occurred generally throughout the country.† The insane and deaf and dumb &c., of the colored population would therefore bear a larger proportion, as well at the South as the North, according to the published census, to the whole of that class, than was the fact. The memorialists therefore did not meet the whole case. The ratio in the free States where the colored are comparatively few, would of course be more affected by the omissions than in the Slave States, where they are very numerous. The census takers in 1830 and 1840 had the right under the act to locate on the returns persons without a regular place of abode, wherever they might be found, or in any part of the district most convenient, and this accounted for deaf and dumb, &c., colored, appearing sometimes in places where the residents would afterwards deny the existence of any such.

A strong circumstance supporting the census of 1840 grew out of its near correspondence with that of 1830, in the ratio of the affected to the whole colored population. It becomes necessary to suppose that different sets of persons, residents of the localities, without concert, after a lapse of ten years, and with all the checks imposed by the census law, and the publicity required in the exposure of the returns before sending them to Washington, have fallen into the same errors, designedly, which no one can for a moment suppose, or accidentally.

Notwithstanding these explanations, and the very strong support given by one census to the other, there still remains the chance, in either, of insane, or deaf and dumb white persons falling by accident into the colored columns. The chances for this error were equal in every part of the Union, though such an error in the non-Slaveholding States, as before remarked, would have vastly more effect than in the others. For example, a mistake of 1 where the total is 100, will make a difference of one per cent., but where the total is 1,000 it will be but one-tenth of one per cent.

Since the results of the census of 1850 have been ascertained, it is quite probable that the ratios at the North in 1830 and 1840 did suffer for some of the reasons above given, as the three cannot be reconciled upon any other supposition, and the first cannot be attacked upon any ground which would materially invalidate it. If no greater disposition may be supposed among the free colored to withhold the information in 1850 than in 1840 or 1830, the only chance of error would remain of their insane, &c., being accidentally entered under the white column, from the neglect of the marshal to indicate the color of the person. Such omissions [illegible] a few instances occur, increasing the whites and the insane whites, and diminishing the [illegible] and the insane colored, and they will perhaps account for a small part of the decline, o[illegible] the small ratio of the increase in some cases, of free colored at the North.‡

* Feb. 26th, 1844.—Motion made by Mr. Adams, of Mass., in the House, directing inquiries in regard to certain alleged errors in the Census.

May 16th, 1844.—Letter received from the Secretary of State informing the House that no such errors had been discovered.

Jan. 28th, 1845.—Resolution adopted directing the Secretary of State to inform the House of the steps taken to ascertain whether the errors imputed by certain memorialists existed, and whether they were of such a character as to impeach the general correctness of the Census.

Feb. 12th, 1845.—Letter received from the Secretary of State, transmitting a report in relation to alleged errors in the Census report. The letter and report were referred to a select committee from Massachusetts, New York, Pennsylvania, Maine, Indiana, Maryland, North Carolina, South Carolina and Georgia, but no further action seems to have been had upon them.

† For example, taking up at random the first schedules which come to hand. In the schedules of 1830, on page 52, under the head of Edgefield District, S. C., there is one colored deaf and dumb not reported in the total colored; Chesterfield District, page 32, one in the same way, &c., &c. In the schedules of 1840, in Laurens District, S. C., one on page 28; on page 38, one; on page 44, one; in Lexington District, on page 5, one; on page 39, one: in Marion District, on page 3, three; on page 50, one: in Pickens District, on page 2, one: in Missouri, St. Charles county, on page 3, one; in St. Louis county on page 11, one; in St. Ferdinand, one; Stoddard, one; Scott, one; Benton, one, &c., &c. All of these deaf, dumb and blind are reported in families where no colored persons are stated to exist in the population column.

‡ The memorialists, in examining the Census of 1830 and 1840, when descending to particular facts, exposed two notable errors. One in Worcester, Massachusetts, by which a whole institution was entered in the wrong column, and one in Plympton. Both of these are corrected in the tables now published for 1840. Out of 79

Admitting however the census of 1850 to be entirely correct, and the others incorrect, the proportion of the whole colored persons, deaf, dumb and blind, in the non-slaveholding States is one in every 919, and in the Slaveholding States, one in every 1,517. For the insane and idiotic the proportion in the non-Slaveholding States, is one in 709; in the Slaveholding States, one in 1,821. But if errors are admitted in all of the Census, and that they would probably balance each other, a mean of the three shows for the deaf and dumb and blind, insane and idiotic, one in every 505 colored in the non-Slaveholding States, and one in every 1,446 in the Slaveholding States. Such a table will be found in the Chapter of Aggregate Population. The columns for the mean being made up from other similar columns do not express the result exactly, but yet with sufficient approximation.

TABLE LXIII.—*Deaf and Dumb, Blind, &c., Free Colored,* 1850.

States.	Deaf and dumb.	Blind.	Insane.	Idiotic.	Aggregate	States.	Deaf and dumb.	Blind.	Insane.	Idiotic.	Aggregate
Alabama	1	2	2	.....	5	Missouri	.....	3	2	.....	5
Arkansas	.....	1	.....	2	3	New Hampshire	.....	2	.....	1	3
California	.....	.....	.....	.....	.....	New Jersey	5	29	9	13	56
Connecticut	6	12	6	4	28	New York	7	44	34	21	106
Columbia, Dist. of	2	8	9	3	22	North Carolina	7	27	10	28	72
Delaware	4	14	20	14	52	Ohio	10	12	14	17	53
Florida	.....	1	.....	.....	1	Pennsylvania	15	28	49	35	127
Georgia	1	4	2	1	8	Rhode Island	3	6	7	4	20
Illinois	2	5	2	2	11	South Carolina	2	14	4	5	25
Indiana	4	12	7	13	36	Tennessee	2	9	5	5	21
Iowa	.....	.....	.....	.....	.....	Texas	.....	1	.....	.....	1
Kentucky	5	20	2	20	47	Vermont	1	1	.....	2	4
Louisiana	3	20	11	6	40	Virginia	13	85	47	90	235
Maine	1	.....	5	2	8	Wisconsin	.....	.....	.....	2	2
Maryland	38	63	44	48	193						
Massachusetts	2	6	19	5	32						
Michigan	1	.....	1	3	5						
Mississippi	1	.....	.....	2	3	Total	136	429	311	348	1,224

TABLE LXIV.—*Ages of Free Colored Deaf and Dumb, and Blind in* 1850 *in several States.**

States.	Deaf and dumb.								Blind.							
	5 and under 10		10 and under 30		30 and under 70		70 and upwards		Under 10		10 and under 30		30 and under 70.		70 and upwards.	
	M.	F.	M.	F.	M.	F.	M.	F.	M.	F.	M.	F.	M.	F.	M.	F.
Vermont	....	....	....	....	....	1	....	....	....	....	....	....	....	....	....	....
Virginia	1	1	6	5	1	1	2	1	1	2	8	5	27	23	20	35
South Carolina	....	....	....	....	....	1	....	....	1	1	1	....	2	4	2	3
Louisiana	....	....	....	1	2	1	1	....	2	....	4	....	3	4	6	6
Tennessee	....	....	....	2	....	....	....	....	....	1	1	....	2	2	1	3
Arkansas	....	....	....	....	....	....	....	....	....	....	....	....	....	....	....	1
Ohio	....	....	2	....	4	2	....	....	1	....	1	....	4	1	1	4
Michigan	....	....	....	....	....	....	....	1	....	....	....	....	....	....	....	....

specifications of error made by them, eleven were the result of their consulting the Boston copy of the returns, and sixteen others were cases in which there might or might not have been error. Most of the other cases admitted of the explanation in the text. For example, they say: "Deputy Marshal W——— states there were 133 colored lunatics in the family of W———, but on another page he says there are no colored in said family." By referring to the returns in this office, the Marshal appears to be "E———"—and so far from saying there are no colored, he actually returned seven. Again, the memorialists say, "in the family of P———, town of Pepperell, there are sixteen colored lunatics, &c., after it is stated in another place there are no colored persons in the family." The returns show that the marshal did not mention any such colored lunatics, and none are published. They say, again, "that nineteen colored persons were reported deaf and dumb or blind, &c., in Higham and Scituate, and that the overseers of the poor state that no such persons have lived there within twelve years, and that the deputy marshal never reported such persons." By reference to the office reports, it appears that the marshal did return them; that it was not necessary, as before said, that the parties should have lived in the towns mentioned, but if transient persons, might have been entered any where, they accidentally happened to be. Besides, nineteen affections such as blind, &c., do not necessarily indicate nineteen individuals affected, but may only embrace six, as a person is sometimes blind and insane, blind and idiotic, blind, deaf and dumb, &c. Finally, the memorialists say they "have made private inquiries in forty-four towns of Massachusetts, and have not found one colored lunatic or idiot." In another place they admit that the State authorities in the same counties found sixteen at public charge, exclusively of those at private charge. The printed Census gave but forty.

* See corresponding tables of white population, and remarks, p. 58, *et seq.*

TABLE LXV.—*Ages of the Free Colored Idiotic and Insane in* 1850 *in several States.*

States.	Insane Free Colored.														Idiotic Free Colored.													
	Under 10.		10 and under 20.		20 and under 40.		40 and under 60.		60 and under 80.		80 and upwards.		Total.		Under 10.		10 and under 20.		20 and under 40.		40 and under 60.		60 and under 80.		80 and upwards.		Total.	
	m	f	m	f	m	f	m	f	m	f	m	f	m	f	m	f	m	f	m	f	m	f	m	f	m	f	m	f
Vermont																					1						1	
Virginia			3		6	10	7	11	3	5		1	19	27	6	4	14	11	27	27	11	9	5	4	1	1	64	56
South Carolina					1	1		1					1	2	1					2							1	2
Louisiana			2		3	5	1	2		2			6	9	1		1		3	4		3		1			5	8
Tennessee			1	1				2					1	3			2			2							2	2
Arkansas																	1		1								2	
Ohio			2	2	5	3	2	1			1		11	6			2	2	5	6	3	1					10	9
Michigan							1						1				1		2								3	
Wisconsin															1												1	

More minute particulars of the free colored insane, idiotic, &c., will be given under the Chapters treating of "Slaves," and of "Aggregate Population," as the tables have been generally united.

7. *Nativities.*—The tables, except as to two or three leading particulars, are again combined with those of the whites.

TABLE LXVI.—*Nativities of the Free Colored Population of the United States.*

States and Territories.	Born in the State.		Born out of the State and in the U. States.		Born in foreign countries.		Unknown.	
	Males.	Females	Males.	Females.	Males.	Females.	Males.	Fem.
Alabama	758	883	279	310	5	6	14	10
Arkansas	165	128	138	159	1	2	10	5
California	60	9	641	68	161	12	10	1
Columbia, District of	2,580	3,417	1,655	2,386	3	2	10	6
Connecticut	2,945	3,132	685	666	127	40	63	35
Delaware	8,467	8,465	559	570	7	3	2	....
Florida	357	447	46	53	15	14	....	....
Georgia	1,223	1,358	133	170	12	24	7	4
Illinois	1,308	1,356	1,396	1,267	16	16	57	20
Indiana	2,593	2,556	3,073	2,958	19	16	30	17
Iowa	24	28	140	140	1	....	....	.....
Kentucky	3,732	3,936	1,106	1,186	8	11	17	15
Louisiana	6,821	8,381	387	892	238	687	33	23
Maine	449	479	178	98	81	49	18	4
Maryland	34,485	38,871	571	531	103	95	33	34
Massachusetts	2,719	2,980	1,348	1,339	232	194	125	127
Michigan	452	338	898	745	53	57	28	12
Mississippi	317	323	144	121	3	3	10	9
Missouri	842	788	492	451	15	7	12	11
New Hampshire	165	174	84	83	8	....	3	3
New Jersey	9,978	10,451	1,655	1,454	86	58	79	49
New York	17,680	19,895	5,089	5,277	379	326	304	119
North Carolina	12,939	13,879	333	275	13	3	13	8
Ohio	6,093	6,293	6,451	6,211	57	37	90	47
Pennsylvania	17,603	20,165	7,367	7,796	151	161	248	135
Rhode Island	1,129	1,377	563	520	42	28	4	7
South Carolina	3,994	4,623	68	74	69	130	....	2
Tennessee	2,500	2,640	584	634	7	8	26	23
Texas	92	71	79	92	39	22	1	1
Vermont	234	218	117	103	14	13	10	9
Virginia	25,710	28,090	266	218	15	17	11	6
Wisconsin	100	67	255	199	3	3	7	1
Territories. Minnesota	7	7	14	11	....	....	....	.....
Territories. New Mexico	7	4	10	1	....	....	....	.....
Territories. Oregon	47	62	23	12	50	13	....	.....
Territories. Utah	2	2	12	8	....	....	....	.....
Total	168,577	185,893	36,839	37,078	2,033	2,057	1,275	743

TABLE LXVII.—*Nativities of the Free Colored.*

States, District and Territories.	Born in the State.	Ratio per cent.	Born out of the State and in the United States.	Ratio per cent.	Born in Foreign countries.	Ratio per cent.	Unknown.	Ratio per cent.	Aggregate.
Alabama	1,641	72.45	589	26.00	11	.49	24	1.06	2,265
Arkansas	293	48.19	297	48.85	3	.49	15	2.47	608
California	69	7.17	709	73.70	173	17.98	11	1.15	962
Columbia, District of	5.997	59.62	4,041	40.17	5	.05	16	.16	10,059
Connecticut	6,077	79.00	1,351	17.56	167	2.17	98	1.27	7,693
Delaware	16,932	93.69	1,129	6.25	10	.05	2	.01	18,073
Florida	804	86.27	99	10.62	29	3.11	....	....	932
Georgia	2,581	88.06	303	10.34	36	1.23	11	.37	2,931
Illinois	2,664	49.01	2,663	48.99	32	.59	77	1.41	5,436
Indiana	5,149	45.72	6,031	53.55	35	.31	47	.42	11,262
Iowa	52	15.62	280	84.08	1	.30	....	....	333
Kentucky	7,668	76.60	2,292	22.89	19	.19	32	.32	10,011
Louisiana	15,202	87.05	1,279	7.33	925	5.30	56	.32	17,462
Maine	928	68.44	276	20.35	130	9.59	22	1.62	1,356
Maryland	73,356	98.17	1,102	1.47	198	.27	67	.09	74,723
Massachusetts	5,699	62.88	2,687	29.64	426	4.70	252	2.78	9,064
Michigan	790	30.58	1,643	63.61	110	4.26	40	1.55	2,583
Mississippi	640	68.82	265	28.49	6	.65	19	2.04	930
Missouri	1,630	62.26	943	36.02	22	.84	23	.88	2,618
New Hampshire	339	65.19	167	32.12	8	1.54	6	1.15	520
New Jersey	20,429	85.80	3,109	13.06	144	.60	128	.54	23,810
New York	37,575	76.58	10,366	21.12	705	1.44	423	.86	49,069
North Carolina	26,818	97.65	608	2.21	16	.06	21	.08	27,463
Ohio	12,386	49.00	12,662	50.09	94	.37	137	.54	25,279
Pennsylvania	37,768	70.43	15,163	28.28	312	.58	383	.71	53,626
Rhode Island	2,506	68.28	1,083	29.51	70	1.91	11	.30	3,670
South Carolina	8,617	96.17	142	1.59	199	2.22	2	.02	8,960
Tennessee	5,140	80.04	1,218	18.97	15	.23	49	.76	6,422
Texas	163	41.06	171	43.07	61	15.37	2	.50	397
Vermont	452	62.95	220	30.64	27	3.76	19	2.65	718
Virginia	53,800	99.02	484	.89	32	.06	17	.03	54,333
Wisconsin	167	26.30	454	71.50	6	.94	8	1.26	635
Territories. Minnesota	14	35.90	25	64.10	....	....	....	....	39
Territories. New Mexico	11	50.00	11	50.00	....	....	....	....	22
Territories. Oregon	109	52.66	35	16.91	63	30.43	....	....	207
Territories. Utah	4	16.67	20	83.33	....	....	....	....	24
Total	354,470	81.58	73,917	17.01	4,090	.94	2,018	.47	434,495

TABLE LXVIII.—*Nativities of the Free Colored Population in Connecticut and Louisiana, and in the cities of New York and New Orleans.*

PLACE OF BIRTH.	CONNECTICUT.			LOUISIANA.			NEW YORK.			NEW ORLEANS.		
	Blacks.	Mulattoes.	Total.	Blacks.	Mulattoes.	Total.	Blacks.	Mulattoes.	Total.	Blacks.	Mulattoes.	Total.
Alabama	2	......	2	16	46	62	4	1	5	13	41	54
Arkansas	......	......	......	......	4	4	......	......	......	......	......	......
Columbia, District of	5	......	5	7	23	30	......	......	......	6	21	27
Connecticut	4,671	1,406	6,077	......	3	3	242	77	319	......	......	......
Delaware	9	1	10	......	1	1	159	30	189	......	1	1
Florida	1	3	4	8	26	34	4	7	11	8	20	28
Georgia	11	8	19	5	13	18	18	14	32	2	11	13
Indiana	......	......	......	......	1	1	......	1	1	......	1	1
Illinois	......	......	......	6	11	17	......	......	......	......	5	5
Kentucky	1	......	1	31	77	108	10	4	14	21	57	78
Louisiana	2	......	2	2,488	12,714	15,202	22	5	27	1,303	6,820	8,123
Maine	1	......	1	......	1	1	10	4	14	......	......	......
Maryland	67	14	81	56	45	101	580	170	750	27	47	74
Massachusetts	141	47	188	4	7	11	111	30	141	2	7	9
Mississippi	1	......	1	30	59	89	8	3	11	9	50	59
Missouri	......	......	......	3	16	19	2	......	2	3	14	17
New Hampshire	......	......	......	......	1	1	4	......	4	......	1	1
New Jersey	80	15	95	2	......	2	1,234	246	1,480	1	......	1
New York	447	125	572	12	32	44	6,469	1,887	8,356	10	31	41
North Carolina	13	4	17	22	41	63	81	23	104	10	10	20
Ohio	......	1	1	3	20	23	7	9	16	3	19	22
Pennsylvania	75	38	113	10	33	43	513	169	682	9	33	42
Rhode Island	118	41	159	......	1	1	46	9	55	......	1	1
South Carolina	6	5	11	40	47	87	62	33	95	17	32	49
Tennessee	......	......	......	17	27	44	2	......	2	8	20	28
Texas	......	......	......	8	15	23	......	......	......	......	......	......

TABLE LXIX.—*Continued.*

PLACE OF BIRTH.	CONNECTICUT.			LOUISIANA.			NEW YORK.			NEW ORLEANS.		
	Blacks.	Mulattoes.	Total.	Blacks.	Mulattoes.	Total.	Blacks.	Mulattoes.	Total.	Blacks.	Mulattoes.	Total.
Vermont	2	1	3	....	....	....	6	7	13	....	....	....
Virginia	53	13	66	226	223	449	712	166	878	153	225	378
Germany	....	....	....	1	4	5	....	....	....	1	3	4
Mexico	1	....	1	3	33	36	....	....	....	2	31	33
South America	2	....	2	....	2	2	2	2	4	....	2	2
West Indies	41	11	52	167	494	661	93	54	147	151	496	647
England	2	1	3	....	3	3	16	9	25	....	3	3
France	2	....	2	9	17	26	5	11	16	6	13	19
Ireland	....	....	....	....	6	6	....	....	....	....	6	6
Spain	....	....	....	....	7	7	8	2	10	....	7	7
Portugal	2	....	2	....	....	....	3	5	8	....	....	....
China	1	....	1	....	1	1	....	....	....	....	1	1
Africa	4	1	5	146	10	156	17	....	17	114	7	121
Other countries and unknown	134	63	197	59	19	78	299	88	387	24	22	46
Total	5,895	1,798	7,693	3,379	14,083	17,462	10,749	3,066	13,815	1,903	8,058	9,961

Out of 7,693 free colored persons in Connecticut, 1,798 were mulattoes, of whom 48 were born in the slave States. Out of 13,815 free colored in New York city, 3,066 were mulattoes. Thus, in both instances, the mulattoes constituted less than one-fourth of the free colored population. About one-fifth of the free colored in New York were born in the present slave States.

8. *Occupations.*—These, so far as they have been separated, will be found below.

TABLE LXX.—*Occupations of Free Colored Males over fifteen years, distinguishing Blacks and Mulattoes*—1850.

OCCUPATIONS.	CONNECTICUT.			LOUISIANA.			NEW YORK.			NEW ORLEANS.*		
	Blacks.	Mulattoes.	Total.	Blacks.	Mulattoes.	Total.	Blacks.	Mulattoes.	Total.	Blacks.	Mulattoes.	Total.
Apprentices	....	1	1	1	10	11	2	....	2	....	4	4
Architects	....	....	....	....	1	1	....	....	....	....	1	1
Bakers	....	....	....	....	4	4	3	1	4	....	1	1
Barbers	18	21	39	6	40	46	80	42	122	6	35	41
Barkeepers	1	....	1	....	2	2	2	1	3	....	2	2
Basket makers	8	2	10	....	....	....	....	....	....	....	....	....
Blacksmiths	8	4	12	6	20	26	....	1	1	4	11	15
Boarding house keepers	4	1	5	1	17	18	15	6	21	1	17	18
Boatmen	4	1	5	7	32	39	25	3	28	5	32	37
Bookbinders	....	....	....	....	4	4	....	....	....	....	4	4
Brick makers	1	....	1	....	3	3	....	....	....	....	2	2
Brokers	....	....	....	1	8	9	....	....	....	1	8	9
Butchers	....	....	....	1	24	25	30	3	33	1	17	18
Cabinet-makers	....	....	....	3	21	24	....	....	....	2	17	19
Capitalists	....	....	....	....	4	4	....	....	....	....	4	4
Carriage-makers	1	1	2	....	....	....	....	....	....	....	....	....
Carmen	8	5	13	19	20	39	28	11	39	19	20	39
Carpenters	3	1	4	74	447	521	10	2	12	56	299	355
Cigar-makers	....	....	....	14	155	169	6	2	8	13	143	156
Clerks	1	3	4	....	63	63	3	4	7	....	61	61
Clothiers	1	....	1	1	....	1	....	....	....	....	....	....
Collectors	....	....	....	....	2	2	....	....	....	....	2	2
Colliers	3	2	5	....	....	....	....	....	....	....	....	....
Coachmen	9	7	16	5	7	12	96	11	107	4	6	10
Confectioners	....	....	....	....	....	....	2	....	2		....	....
Cooks	24	10	34	18	19	37	78	17	95	7	18	25
Coopers	2	....	2	18	37	55	7	....	7	17	26	43
Daguerreotypists	1	....	1	....	....	....	....	....	....	....	....	....
Doctors	....	....	....	1	5	6	7	2	9	....	4	4
Druggists	....	....	....	....	....	....	1	2	3	....	....	....
Dyers	2	1	3	....	....	....	....	....	....	....	....	....
Engineers	....	....	....	....	4	4	....	....	....	....	....	1
Farmers	122	24	146	10	148	158	12	12	24	....	....	....
Gardeners	4	1	5	6	7	13	5	2	7	4	5	9
Gunsmiths	2	....	2	....	4	4	1	....	1	....	4	4
Hatters	....	....	....	....	....	....	2	....	2			

* Including Lafayette.

TABLE LXX.—*Occupations of Free Colored—Continued.*

OCCUPATIONS.	CONNECTICUT.			LOUISIANA.			NEW YORK.			NEW ORLEANS.		
	Blacks.	Mulattoes.	Total.	Blacks.	Mulattoes.	Total.	Blacks.	Mulattoes.	Total.	Blacks.	Mulattoes.	Total.
Hostlers	9	1	10		3	3	10	1	11		3	3
Hunters				5	4	9				4	3	7
Ink-makers							5		5			
Jewellers					5	5	2	1	3		5	5
Laborers	914	194	1,108	139	272	411	957	187	1,144	71	108	179
Lawyers							4		4			
Lithographers					1	1					1	1
Mariners	262	54	316	2	20	22	316	118	434	1	9	10
Market-men				8	24	32	13	2	15	6	19	25
Masons	1		1	68	257	325				65	213	278
Mechanics (generally)	4		4	7	51	58	1	1	2	6	46	52
Merchants	1	1	2	8	69	77	2	1	3	6	58	64
Ministers	9	3	12		1	1	12	9	21		1	1
Musicians	3	2	5		4	4	17	7	24		4	4
Music teachers					1	1					1	1
Overseers				3	22	25				1	10	11
Painters	1	1	2	4	26	30	3	1	4	4	24	28
Pedlars	1		1	2	7	9				2	7	9
Pilots					2	2					2	2
Planters				23	221	244					2	2
Powder makers	2		2									
Printers		1	1				2	2	4			
Sailmakers	1		1	1	5	6					2	2
Servants	83	25	108	2	2	4	612	196	808			
Sextons	1		1		1	1	9	3	12		1	1
Ship carpenters	1		1	2	4	6				2	4	6
Shoemakers	28	13	41	18	81	99	18	5	23	16	76	92
Stevedores				1	6	7				1	6	7
Stewards	3	1	4	2	9	11	34	10	44		9	9
Students	1		1		7	7	1		1		7	7
Tailors	2	7	9	3	83	86	18	5	23	3	79	82
Tanners	1		1									
Teachers				1	14	15	6	2	8		12	12
Upholsterers				1	7	8				1	7	8
Other occupations	17	13	30				160	47	207			
Total	1,572	401	1,973	492	2,317	2,809	2,617	720	3,337	329	1,463	1,792

Thus, of the free colored population of New York city, sixty were clerks, doctors, druggists, lawyers, merchants, ministers, printers, students, and teachers, or one in about fifty-five; in New Orleans there were one hundred and sixty-five, or one in eleven, engaged in similar pursuits which may be considered as requiring education. The remainder are mechanics, laborers, and waiters. The "other occupations" include for the most part sweeps, scavengers, etc. Of those engaged in pursuits requiring education, one-third are mulattoes, though the proportion of mulattoes to the whole free colored is between a fourth and a fifth.

In Connecticut there are only twenty individuals engaged in occupations requiring education, or one in one hundred of the whole. In Louisiana the number is one hundred and eighty-five, or one in twelve of the whole free colored. The ratios of black and mulatto may also be studied to advantage in the several occupations.

CHAPTER V.

SLAVE POPULATION OF THE UNITED STATES.

1. *Aggregate Number.*—The number of slaves in the United States in 1850 was 3,204,313. The number in each of the States at this and every previous census will be found in the following table:

TABLE LXXI.—*Slave Population of the United States.*

STATES AND TERRITORIES.	1790.	1800.	1810.	1820.	1830.	1840.	1850.
Alabama	....	....	....	41,879	117,549	253,532	342,844
Arkansas	....	....	....	1,617	4,576	19,935	47,100
California	....	....	....	....	....	....	....
Columbia, District of	....	3,244	5,395	6,377	6,119	4,694	3,687
Connecticut	2,759	951	310	97	25	17	....
Delaware	8,887	6,153	4,177	4,509	3,292	2,605	2,290
Florida	....	....	....	....	15,501	25,717	39,310
Georgia	29,264	59,404	105,218	149,654	217,531	280,944	381,682
Illinois	....	....	168	917	747	331	....
Indiana	....	135	237	190	3	3	....
Iowa	....	....	....	....	....	16	....
Kentucky	11,830	40,343	80,561	126,732	165,213	182,258	210,981
Louisiana	....	....	34,660	69,064	109,588	168,452	244,809
Maine	....	....	....	....	2	....	....
Maryland	103,036	105,635	111,502	107,397	102,994	89,737	90,368
Massachusetts	....	....	....	....	1	....	....
Michigan	....	....	24	....	32	....	....
Mississippi	....	3,489	17,088	32,814	*65,659	195,211	309,878
Missouri	....	....	3,011	10,222	25,091	58,240	87,422
New Hampshire	158	8	....	....	3	1	....
New Jersey	11,423	12,422	10,851	7,557	2,254	674	236
New York	21,324	20,343	15,017	10,088	75	4	....
North Carolina	100,572	133,296	168,824	205,017	245,601	245,817	288,548
Ohio	....	....	....	....	6	3	....
Pennsylvania	3,737	1,706	795	211	403	64	....
Rhode Island	952	381	108	48	17	5	....
South Carolina	107,094	146,151	196,365	258,475	315,401	327,038	384,984
Tennessee	3,417	13,584	44,535	80,107	141,603	183,059	239,459
Texas	....	....	....	....	....	....	58,161
Vermont	17	....	....	....	....	....	....
Virginia	293,427	345,796	392,518	425,153	469,757	449,087	472,528
Wisconsin	....	....	....	....	....	11	....
Territories. Minnesota	....	....	....	....	....	....	....
Territories. New Mexico	....	....	....	....	....	....	....
Territories. Oregon	....	....	....	....	....	....	....
Territories. Utah	....	....	....	....	....	....	26
				1,538,125 * less 87			
Aggregate	697,897	893,041	1,191,364	1,538,038	2,009,043	2,487,455	3,204,313

Of these Slaves in 1850, 2,957,657 were black or of unmixed African descent, and 246,656 were mulatto. The distribution in the different States and many interesting ratios of the two colors will be found in the table following.

The mulattoes in the United States are about one-eighth as numerous as the blacks—the free mulattoes are more than half the number of the free blacks, whilst the slave mulattoes are only about one-twelfth of the slave blacks. Between the States the ratios are very remarkable. Whilst nearly half of the colored in the non-slaveholding States are mulatto, only about one-ninth in the slaveholding States are mulatto, excluding New Jersey. In Ohio and the Territories there are more mulattoes than blacks. In nearly all of the slave States, except Kentucky, Delaware and Missouri, &c., the free mulattoes greatly preponderate over the free blacks. Kentucky, Arkansas, Missouri and Texas have the largest portion of slave mulattoes, and in the District of Columbia they are about one-fourth of the whole.

It will be observed from the above table, that slavery, which in 1790, existed in all of the States, except two, in 1850 did not exist in fifteen States, and that ten States which returned slaves in 1840 returned none in 1850, slave schedules not having been sent to them in that year

* Deducted to make the aggregate, published incorrectly in that year.

TABLE LXXII.—*Black and Mulatto Population of the United States.*

States and Territories.	FREE.			SLAVES.			SLAVE AND FREE.		RATIO OF MULATTOES TO 100 BLACKS		
	Blacks.	Mulattoes.	Total.	Blacks.	Mulattoes.	Total.	Blacks.	Mulattoes.	Free.	Slave.	Total.
Alabama	567	1,698	2,265	321,239	21,605	342,844	321,806	23,303	299.47	6.73	7.24
Arkansas	201	407	608	40,739	6,361	47,100	40,940	6,768	202.49	15.61	16.53
California*	875	87	962	....	......	....	875	87	9.94	......	9.94
Columbia, Dis. of	6,783	3,276	10,059	2,885	802	3,687	9,668	4,078	48.30	27.80	42.18
Connecticut	5,895	1,798	7,693	....	......	....	5,894	1,798	30.51	......	30.51
Delaware	16,425	1,648	18,073	2,207	83	2,290	18,632	1,731	10.03	3.76	9.29
Florida	229	703	932	36,288	3,022	39,310	36,517	3,725	306.99	8.33	10.20
Georgia	1,403	1,528	2,931	359,013	22,669	381,682	360,416	24,197	108.91	6.31	6.71
Illinois	2,930	2,506	5,436	....	......	....	2,930	2,506	85.53	......	85.53
Indiana	5,941	5,321	11,262	....	......	....	5,941	5,321	89.56	......	89.56
Iowa	178	155	333	....	......	....	178	155	87.08	......	87.08
Kentucky	7,381	2,630	10,011	181,252	29,729	210,981	188,633	32,359	35.63	16.40	17.15
Louisiana	3,379	14,083	17,462	224,974	19,835	244,809	228,353	33,918	416.78	8.82	14.85
Maine	895	461	1,356	....	......	....	895	461	51.51	......	51.51
Maryland	61,109	13,614	74,723	82,479	7,889	90,368	143,588	21,503	22.28	9.56	14.98
Massachusetts	6,724	2,340	9,064	....	......	....	6,724	2,340	34.80	......	34.80
Michigan	1,465	1,118	2,583	....	......	....	1,465	1,118	76.31	......	76.31
Mississippi	295	635	930	290,148	19,730	309,878	290,443	20,365	215.25	6.80	7.01
Missouri	1,687	931	2,618	74,187	13,235	87,422	75,874	14,166	55.19	17.84	18.67
New Hampshire	336	184	520	....	......	....	336	184	54.76	......	54.76
New Jersey	20,113	3,697	23,810	232	4	236	20,345	3,701	18.38	1.72	18.19
New York	40,930	8,139	49,069	....	......	....	40,930	8,139	19.89	......	19.89
North Carolina	10,258	17,205	27,463	271,733	16,815	288,548	281,991	34,020	167.72	6.19	12.06
Ohio	11,014	14,265	25,279	....	......	....	11,014	14,265	129.52	......	129.52
Pennsylvania	38,285	15,341	53,626	....	......	....	38,285	15,341	40.07	......	40.07
Rhode Island	2,939	731	3,670	....	......	....	2,939	731	24.87	......	24.87
South Carolina	4,588	4,372	8,960	372,482	12,502	384,984	377,070	16,874	95.29	3.36	4.48
Tennessee	2,646	3,776	6,422	219,103	20,356	239,459	221,749	24,132	142.71	9.29	10.88
Texas	140	257	397	50,458	7,703	58,161	50,598	7,960	183.57	15.27	15.73
Vermont	512	206	718	....	......	....	512	206	40.23	......	40.23
Virginia	18,857	35,476	54,333	428,229	44,299	472,528	447,086	79,775	188.13	10.34	17.84
Wisconsin	338	297	635	....	......	....	338	297	87.87	......	87.87
Territories. Minnesota	16	23	39	....	......	....	16	23	143.75	......	143.75
Territories. N. Mexico	6	16	22	....	......	....	6	16	266.67	......	266.67
Territories. Oregon	45	162	207	....	......	....	45	162	360.00	......	360.00
Territories. Utah	15	9	24	9	17	†26	24	26	60.00	188.89	108.33
Total	275,400	159,095	434,495	2,957,657	246,656	3,204,313	3,233,057	405,751	58.13	8.34	12.55

In the Chapter upon Colonial Population, and in the note, will be found some statistics of the early slave population of the United States. Another statement of the date of 1776 exists, in which the slaves are entered as follows: Massachusetts 3,500; Rhode Island 4,373; Connecticut 6,000; New Hampshire 629; New York 15,000; New Jersey 7,600; Pennsylvania 10,000; Delaware 9,000; Maryland 80,000; Virginia 165,000; North Carolina 75,000; South Carolina 110,000; and Georgia 16,000; total, 502,132.‡

* By State Census of 1852, 1,678 blacks, 578 mulattoes. † Reported on their way to California.

‡ Slavery, which had existed in all of the nations of antiquity and throughout Europe during the middle ages, was introduced at an early day into the colonies. The first introduction of African slaves was in 1620, by a Dutch vessel from Africa to Virginia. Mr. Carey, of Pennsylvania, in his work upon the Slave Trade says, "the trade in negro slaves to the American colonies was too small before 1753 to attract attention." In that year Macpherson ("*Annals of Commerce*") says five hundred and eleven were imported into Charleston, and in 1765–1766 those imported into Georgia, (from their valuation,) could not have exceeded 1,482. From 1783 to 1787 the British West Indies exported to the colonies 1,392, nearly 300 per annum. These West Indies were then the entrepot of the trade, and though they received nearly 20,000 (*Macpherson*) in the period above named, they sent to the colonies but that small number, proving the demand could not have been large. After a close argument from the ratio of increase since the first census, Mr. Carey is enabled to recur back and compute the population at earlier periods, separating the native born from those derived from importations. Setting out with the fact that the *slaves* (blacks) numbered 55,850 in 1714, he finds that 30,000 of these were brought from Africa 30,000

Importations between 1715 and 1750	90,000
" " 1751 " 1760	35,000
" " 1761 " 1770	74,000
" " 1771 " 1790	34,000
" " 1790 " 1808	70,000
Total number imported	333,000

The number since 1790 is evidently too small. Charleston alone, in the four years 1804, 1805, 1806 and 1807, imported 39,075.§ Making, therefore, a correction for such under estimate, and a very liberal increase to Mr.

§ These were consigned to 91 British subjects, 88 citizens of Rhode Island, 10 French subjects and 13 natives of Charleston. (*Census of Charleston*, p. 141, 1849.)

TABLE LXIII.—*Increase and Decrease per cent. of the Slave Population of the several States, at each Census.*

States and Territories.	1800.	1810.	1820.	1830.	1840.	1850.
Alabama	....	....	....	*180.68	*115.68	*35.22
Arkansas	....	....	....	*182.99	*335.64	*136.26
Columbia, District of	....	*66.30	*18.20	†4.04	†23.28	†21.45
Connecticut	†65.53	†67.40	†68.70	†74.22	†32.00	....
Delaware	†30.76	†32.11	*7.94	†26.99	†20.86	†12.09
Florida	....	....	....	....	*65.90	*52.85
Georgia	*102.99	*77.12	*42.23	*45.35	*29.15	*35.85
Illinois	....	....	*445.83	†18.53	†55.68	....
Indiana	....	*75.55	†19.83	†98.42	....	....
Kentucky	*241.02	*99.69	*57,31	*30.36	*10.31	*15.75
Louisiana	....	....	*99.26	*58.67	*53.71	*45.32
Maryland	*2.52	*5.55	†3.68	†4.09	†12.87	*.70
Mississippi	....	*389.76	*92.02	*100.09	*197.31	*58.74
Missouri	....	....	*239.48	*145.46	*132.11	*50.10
New Hampshire	†94.93	....	....	....	†66.66	....
New Jersey	*8.74	†12.64	†30.35	†70.17	†70.09	†64.98
New York	†4.60	†26.18	†32.82	†99.25	†94.66	....
North Carolina	*32.53	*26.65	*21.43	*19.79	*.08	*17.38
Ohio	....	....	....	....	†50.00	....
Pennsylvania	†54.34	†53.39	†73.45	*90.99	†84.11	....
Rhode Island	†59.97	†71.65	†55.55	†64.58	†70.58	....
South Carolina	*36.46	*34.35	*31.62	*22.02	*3.68	*17.71
Tennessee	*297.54	*227.84	*79.87	*76.76	*29.27	*30.80
Virginia	*17.84	*13.51	*8.31	*10.49	†4.40	*5.21

The increase and decrease per cent. of the slaves in each decennial period is shown for all of the States. The greatest increase in ten years was in Illinois, in 1820, 445 per cent.; in Mississippi, in 1810, 389 per cent.; in Arkansas, in 1840, 335 per cent.; in Tennessee in 1800, 297 per cent.; and Kentucky in 1800, 241 per cent. The greatest decrease in ten years was in New York, in 1830, 99 per cent.; Indiana, in 1830, 98 per cent.; in New York in 1840, 94 per cent. The least increase in ten years was in Maryland, in 1800, 2 per cent.; and in 1820, 3 per cent.; in North Carolina in 1840, and Maryland in 1850, less than 1 per cent. Virginia, which had declined 4 per cent, between 1830 and 1840, increased 5 per cent, between 1840 and 1850.

The increase of slaves in the Southern Atlantic States has only averaged about 2 per cent. per annum in fifty years, though averaging 18 per cent. per annum in the Gulf States, &c. for the last twenty years.

Geographical Divisions.	1790.	1820.	1850.	Per cent. per annum.
Atlantic Slaveholding States, including Virginia	530,357	....	1,204,221	2.05
Kentucky, Missouri, Delaware, Maryland, District of Columbia.	123,753	....	394,658	6.6
Gulf States, and including Florida, Arkansas and Tennessee	....	225,481	1,242,251	18.0

Carey's figures, the whole number of Africans at all times imported into the United States would not exceed 375 or 400,000.

Thus, in the United States, the number of Africans and their descendants is nearly eight or ten to one of those that were imported, whilst in the British West Indies there are not two persons remaining for every five of the imported, and their descendants. This is seen from the following: Imported into Jamaica previously to 1817, 700,000 negroes, of whom and their descendants but 311,000 remained after 178 years to be emancipated in 1833. In the whole British West Indies,—imported 1,700,000, of whom and their descenndats 660,000 remained for emancipation. (*Carey.*)

The Continental Congress of 1774 resolved to discontinue the slave trade, in which resolution they were anticipated by the Conventions of Delegates of Virginia and North Carolina. In 1789 the convention to frame the federal constitution, looked to the abolition of the traffic in 1808. On the 2nd of March, 1807, Congress passed an act against importations of Africans into the United States after January 1st, 1808. An act in Great Britain in 1807 also made the slave trade unlawful. Denmark forbid the introduction of African slaves into her colonies after 1804. The Congress of Vienna, in 1815, pronounced for the abolition of the trade. France abolished it in 1817, and also Spain, but the acts were to take effect after 1820. Portugal abolished it in 1818. The slave trade in these instances, continued in despite of the abolition. The average number of slaves, according to the Report of the London Slave Trade Committee, exported from the coast of Africa, averaged 85,000 per annum, from 1798 to 1805; and from 1835 to 1840 there was a total of 135,810; in 1846 and 1847, the import was 84,000 per annum. Between 1840 and 1847, 249,800 were taken to Brazil, and 52,027 into the Spanish colonies, etc. (See Report of Select Committee of the House of Commons, 1850.) In Pennsylvania slavery was abolished in 1780. In New Jersey, it was provisionally abolished in 1784; all children born of a slave after 1804 are made free in 1820. In Massachusetts, it was declared after the revolution, that slavery was virtually abolished by their constitution, (1780.) In 1784 and 1797 Connecticut provided for a gradual extinction of slavery. In Rhode Island, after 1784, no person could be *born* a slave. The ordinance of 1787 forbid slavery in the Territory Northwest of the Ohio, but the census shows that the injunction was disobeyed. The constitutions of Vermont and New Hampshire, respectively, abolished slavery. In New York it was provisionally abolished in 1799, twenty-eight years ownership being allowed in slaves born after that date, and in 1817 it was enacted that slavery was not to exist after ten years, or 1827.

* **Increase.** † **Decrease.**

TABLE LXXIV.—*Relative Rank of the States and Territories at each Census with regard to Slave, and also with regard to the whole Colored Population.*

STATES AND TERRITORIES.	SLAVES.							FREE COLORED AND SLAVES.						
	1790.	1800.	1810.	1820.	1830.	1840.	1850.	1790.	1800.	1810.	1820.	1830.	1840.	1850.
Alabama				9	7	4	4				9	9	5	4
Arkansas				16	14	13	13				21	21	16	15
California														28
Columbia, District of		12	12	14	13	14	15		14	14	16	17	19	20
Connecticut	12	14	16	20	21	19		12	13	16	17	19	21	23
Delaware	9	10	13	15	15.	15	16	8	10	13	14	15	17	19
Florida					12	12	14					16	14	16
Georgia	5	5	5	4	4	3	3	5	5	5	4	4	3	3
Illinois			18	17	17	17				21	22	24	23	24
Indiana		16	17	19	*25	*25			20	23	23	22	22	21
Iowa						20							30	32
Kentucky	7	6	6	5	5	8	9	9	6	6	6	5	8	9
Louisiana			8	8	8	9	7			8	8	8	7	7
Maine					26						24	25	25	27
Maryland	3	4	4	6	9	10	10	2	4	4	5	6	10	10
Massachusetts					27			11	12	15	18	20	20	22
Michigan			20		20					24	27	28	27	26
Mississippi		11	9	10	10	6	5		16	12	11	10	6	6
Missouri			14	11	11	11	11			18	15	13	11	11
New Hampshire	14	17			*24	26		15	17	20	25	27	28	31
New Jersey	8	9	11	13	16	16	17	7	8	11	13	14	15	18
New York	6	7	10	12	19	23		6	7	9	10	11	12	14
North Carolina	4	3	3	3	3	5	6	4	3	3	3	3	4	5
Ohio					23	*24			19	19	19	18	18	17
Pennsylvania	10	13	15	18	18	18		10	9	10	12	12	13	13
Rhode Island	13	15	19	21	22	22		13	15	17	20	23	24	25
South Carolina	2	2	2	2	2	2	2	3	2	2	2	2	2	2
Tennessee	11	8	7	7	6	7	8	14	11	7	7	7	9	8
Texas							12							12
Vermont	15							16	18	22	26	26	26	29
Virginia	1	1	1	1	1	1	1	1	1	1	1	1	1	1
Wisconsin						21							29	30
Territories. Minnesota														35
Territories. New Mexico														36
Territories. Oregon														33
Territories. Utah							18							34

Virginia has always held the first rank, and South Carolina the second, with reference to slave population. North Carolina has descended since 1790 from the fourth to the sixth, and New Jersey from the eighth to the seventeenth.

With regard to the total colored population, the rank of Virginia has also been always first; South Carolina, from the third has become the second; New Hampshire from the fifteenth has become the thirty-first; Tennessee from the fourteenth has become the eighth; and Connecticut from the twelfth, the twenty-third.

TABLE LXXV.—*Ratio of the Slave and total Colored Population to the total Population of each State.*

States and Territories.	Slaves.							Free Colored and Slaves.						
	1790.	1800.	1810.	1820.	1830.	1840.	1850.	1790.	1800.	1810.	1820.	1830.	1840.	1850.
Alabama				32.7	37.9	42.9	44.4				33.1	38.4	43.2	44.7
Arkansas				11.3	15.0	20.4	22.4				11.8	15.5	20.9	22.7
California														1.0
Columbia, District of		23.0	22.4	19.3	15.3	10.7	7.1		28.5	33.0	31.5	30.8	29.8	26.5
Connecticut	1.1	.3	.1					2.3	2.5	2.5	2.9	2.7	2.6	2.0
Delaware	15.0	9.5	5.7	6.2	4.2	3.3	2.5	21.6	22.4	23.8	24.0	24.9	25.0	22.2
Florida					44.6	47.2	44.9					47.0	48.7	46.0
Georgia	35.4	36.6	41.6	43.8	42.0	40.6	42.1	35.9	37.2	42.3	44.4	42.5	41.0	42.4
Illinois			1.3	1.6	.4					6.3	2.5	1.5	.8	.6
Indiana		2.7	.9	.1					6.1	2.5	.9	1.0	1.0	1.1
Iowa													.4	.1
Kentucky	16.1	18.2	19.8	22.4	24.0	23.3	21.4	16.3	18.5	20.2	22.9	24.7	24.3	22.5
Louisiana			45.2	45.0	50.8	47.8	47.2			55.1	52.1	58.5	55.0	50.6
Maine								.5	.5	.4	.3	.3	.2	.2
Maryland	32.2	30.9	29.3	26.3	23.0	19.0	15.5	34.7	36.6	38.2	36.1	34.8	32.3	28.3

* The above numerical rank of New Hampshire and Indiana in 1830, and Ohio and Indiana in 1840, relative to slave population, is arbitrary, each State in both Census reports having returned three slaves.

TABLE LXXV—*Continued.*

States and Territories.	Slaves.							Total Colored.						
	1790.	1800.	1810.	1820.	1830.	1840.	1850.	1790.	1800.	1810.	1820.	1830.	1840.	1850.
Massachusetts	.....	.....	.....	.....	.....	.....	.....	1.4	1.5	1.4	1.3	1.1	1.1	.9
Michigan	.....	.....	.5	.....	.1	.....	.....	.....	.....	3.0	3.4	.9	.3	.6
Mississippi	.....	39.4	42.3	43.4	48.0	51.9	51.0	.....	41.4	42.9	44.1	48.4	52.3	51.2
Missouri	.....	.....	14.4	15.3	17.8	15.1	12.8	.....	.....	17.3	15.9	18.2	15.5	13.2
New Hampshire	.1	.....	.....	.....	.....	.....	.....	.5	.4	.4	.3	.2	.1	.1
New Jersey	6.2	5.8	4.4	2.7	.7	.1	.....	7.7	7.9	7.6	7.2	6.4	5.8	4.9
New York	6.2	3.4	1.5	.7	.....	.....	.....	7.6	5.2	4.2	2.9	2.3	2.0	1.5
North Carolina	25.5	27.8	30.3	32.0	33.2	32.6	33.2	26.8	29.3	32.2	34.3	35.9	35.6	36.3
Ohio	.....	.....	.....	.....	.....	.....	.....	.....	.7	.8	.8	1.0	1.1	1.2
Pennsylvania	.8	.2	.....	.....	.....	.....	.....	2.3	2.7	2.8	3.0	2.8	2.7	2.3
Rhode Island	1.3	.5	.1	.....	.....	.....	.....	6.4	5.3	4.8	4.3	3.6	2.9	2.4
South Carolina	43.0	42.2	47.3	51.4	54.2	55.0	57.5	43.7	43.2	48.4	52.7	55.6	56.4	58.9
Tennessee	9.5	12.8	17.0	18.9	20.7	22.0	23.8	10.5	13.1	17.5	19.6	21.4	22.7	24.5
Texas	.....	.....	.....	.....	.....	.....	27.3	.....	.....	.....	.....	.....	.....	27.5
Vermont	.....	.....	.....	.....	.....	.....	.....	.3	.3	.3	.3	.3	.2	.2
Virginia	39.2	39.2	40.2	39.9	38.7	36.2	33.2	40.9	41.5	43.4	43.3	42.6	40.2	37.0
Wisconsin	.....	.....	.....	.....	.....	.....	.....	.....	.....	.....	.....	.....	.6	.2
Territories. Minnesota	.....	.....	.....	.....	.....	.....	.....	.....	.....	.....	.....	.....	.....	.6
Territories. N. Mexico	.....	.....	.....	.....	.....	.....	.....	.....	.....	.....	.....	.....	.....	.....
Territories. Oregon	.....	.....	.....	.....	.....	.....	.....	.....	.....	.....	.....	.....	.....	1.5
Territories. Utah	.....	.....	.....	.....	.....	.....	.2	.....	.....	.....	.....	.....	.....	.4

The above table indicates the proportion which the slave population and the total colored population of each State bore to the whole population at the several periods named. Whilst the proportion has been increasing for the slaves in the Southern States generally, it has decreased in Virginia, Maryland, the District of Columbia and Missouri. In South Carolina from 43 per cent. it has become 57, and in Georgia from 35 per cent. it has become 42, &c., &c.

In all of the States north of North Carolina, the proportion of total colored has been decreasing, whilst in those South it has been generally increasing, except in Louisiana, where it has declined from 55 per cent. to 50. (See note chap. I.) In Kentucky and Missouri there has been a slight decline. In the North-west, with the exception of Ohio, there has also been a decline.

2. *Dwellings and Families.*—These are not ascertained on the slave schedules. The facts, if known, would compare favorably with those of other classes in most moderate circumstances, and especially with the free colored.

3. *Sex.*—There were 1,602,535 males, and 1,601,778 female slaves in the United States in 1850. The number in each of the States will be seen in this table. There was no distinction made of sex earlier than 1820.

TABLE LXXVI.—*Male and Female Slaves.*

STATES, &C.	MALES.				FEMALES.			
	1820.	1830.	1840.	1850.	1820.	1830.	1840.	1850.
Alabama	21,780	59,170	127,360	171,804	20,099	58,379	126,172	171,040
Arkansas	820	2,293	10,119	23,658	797	2,283	9,816	23,442
Columbia, District of	3,007	2,852	2,058	1,422	3,370	3,267	2,636	2,265
Delaware	2,555	1,806	1,371	1,174	1,954	1,486	1,234	1,116
Florida	....	7,985	13,038	19,804	....	7,516	12,679	19,506
Georgia	75,914	108,817	139,335	188,857	73,740	108,714	141,609	192,825
Kentucky	63,914	82,309	91,004	105,063	62,818	82,904	91,254	105,918
Louisiana	36,566	57,911	86,529	125,874	32,498	51,677	81,923	118,935
Maryland	56,372	53,442	46,068	45,944	51,025	49,552	43,669	44,424
Mississippi	16,850	33,099	98,003	154,964	15,964	32,560	97,208	154,914
Missouri	5,341	12,439	28,742	43,484	4,881	12,652	29,498	43,938
New Jersey	3,988	1,059	303	96	3,569	1,195	371	140
North Carolina	106,551	124,313	123,546	144,581	98,466	121,288	122.271	143,967
South Carolina	130,472	155,469	158,678	187,756	128,003	159,932	168,360	197,228
Tennessee	39,747	70,216	91,477	118,780	40,360	71,387	91,582	120,679
Texas	....	....	....	28,700	....	....	....	29,461
Virginia	258,274	239,077	228,661	240,562	206,879	230,680	220,426	231,966
Other States and Ter.	5,874	566	225	12	5,677	748	230	14
Total	*788,025	1,012,823	1,246,517	1,602,535	*750,100	996,220	1,240,938	1,601,778

* Error in Census of 1820, being plus 87.

TABLE LXXVII.—*Exhibiting the Ratio of Female Slaves to* 100 *Males, at each Census.*

1820.	1830.	1840.	1850.
95.19	98.36	99.55	99.95

The increase of the slaves, male and female, and the per centage of the increase of both together, as well as the increase of the whole colored, will be learned from the following tables, for each period of ten years since 1790.

TABLE LXXVIII.—*Number and Increase of Slaves.*

Census.	Slaves.						
	Number of males.	Number of females.	Excess of males.	Total number of slaves.	Increase in each ten and in 60 years.	Increase per centum in each ten and in 60 years.	Proportion of slaves to free white, as 1 slave to
1790	....	....	....	697,897	....	....	4.5457
1800	....	....	....	893,041	195,144	27.9617	4.8200
1810	....	....	....	1,191,364	298,323	33.4053	4.9204
1820	788,028	750,010	38,018	1,538,038	346,674	29.0989	5.1116
1830	1,012,823	996,220	16,603	2,009,043	471,005	30.6237	5.2450
1840	1,246,517	1,240,938	5,579	2,487,455	478,412	23.8129	6.8622
1850	*1,602,535	*1,601,778	757	3,204,313	716,858	28.8189	7.2377
Total increase of each class in 60 yrs.	....	....	....	....	2,506,416	359.1384	....

TABLE LXXIX.—*Number and Increase of Free Colored and Slaves.*

Census.	Combined Free Colored and Slave Population.						
	Number of males.	Number of females.	Excess.	Number of free colored and slave.	Increase in each ten and in 60 years.	Increase per centum in each 10 yrs. and in 60 years.	Proportion of free colored and slave to the free white as 1 to
1790	....	....	....	757,363	....	....	4.1888
1800	....	....	....	1,001,436	244,073	32.2271	4.2983
1810	....	....	MALES.	1,377,810	376,374	37.5830	4.2546
1820	†902,994	†873,200	29,774	1,776,194	398,384	29.3273	4.4263
1830	1,166,276	1,162,366	3,910	2,328,642	552,448	31.1030	4.5251
			FEMALES.				
1840	1,432,998	1,440,760	7,762	2,873,758	545,116	23.4092	4.9398
1850	1,811,547	1,827,261	15,714	3,638,808	765,050	26.6219	5.3735
Total increase of each class in 60 yrs.	....	....	....	....	2,881,445	379.7058	....

* In Mississippi 578 slaves are returned without distinction as to age or sex. These have been distributed in the columns of slaves in the general proportion of the sexes, viz: 290 males, 288 females.

† In the Census of 1820, 4,632 are returned as "all other persons, except Indians not taxed." These have been generally added to the "free colored," and they are so placed in this table—divided, however, in the general proportion of the sexes, viz: males, 2,232; females, 2,400.

Table LXXX.—*Proportion of Slaves, Male to Female, in different sections at several periods.*

Geographical Divisions.	Years when each Census was taken.	Males.	Females	Proportion as 100 Males to Females.
New England...	1790	....	....	*
	1800	....	....	*
	1810	....	....	*
	1820	55	90	163.63
	1830	11	37	336.36
	1840	9	14	155.56
	1850	....	....	....
Middle States...	1790	....	....	*
	1800	....	....	*
	1810	....	....	*
	1820	71,096	65,044	91.49
	1830	59,344	55,793	94.02
	1840	49,835	47,943	96.20
	1850	48,636	47,945	98.58
Southern States.	1790	....	....	*
	1800	....	....	*
	1810	....	....	*
	1820	531,165	507,046	95.46
	1830	635,661	628,130	98.82
Southern States.	1840	663,258	665.345	100.31
	1850	781,560	785,492	100.50
South-western States.	1790	....	....	*
	1800	....	....	*
	1810	....	....	*
	1820	115,763	109,718	94.78
	1830	222,689	216,286	97.12
	1840	413,488	406,701	98.36
	1850	623,780	618.471	99.15
North-western States.	1790	....	....	*
	1800	....	....	*
	1810	....	....	*
	1820	69,901	68,160	97.51
	1830	95,118	95,974	100.90
	1840	119,927	120,935	100.84
	1850	148,547	149,856	100.88
California and Territories.	1850	12	14	116.67

When slavery existed in New England the females were largely in excess. In 1830 there were over three to one male. In the Middle States the males are always in excess. In the Southern States, since 1830, the male and female have been equal, or nearly so, and the same is true of the North-western States. In the South-west, since 1830, there is a small excess of males; in the Territories, a large excess of females.

Table LXXXI.—*Ages of the Slave Population of the United States*, 1850.

States & Territories.	Under 1.		1 and under 5.		5 and under 10.		10 and under 15.		15 and under 20.	
	Males.	Fem's.	Males.	Fem's.	Males.	Fem's.	Males.	Fem's.	Males.	Fem's.
Alabama	3,992	4,118	25,471	25,687	25,724	25,671	23,190	22,260	18,989	19,871
Arkansas	540	619	3,475	3,573	3,480	3,546	3,389	3,179	2,745	2,765
Columbia, Dist. of	30	41	165	184	208	287	239	341	207	319
Delaware	27	32	155	148	223	178	205	194	219	151
Florida	463	451	2,840	2,918	2,889	2,874	2,507	2,442	1,974	2,087
Georgia	4,730	4,889	27,984	28,070	28,941	28,711	26,834	26,749	21,865	23,072
Kentucky	3,023	3,245	14,952	15,311	16,761	16,828	15,602	15,203	12,370	12,695
Louisiana	2,349	2,591	14,260	14,814	14,874	15,009	13,865	13,410	11.151	11,799
Maryland	1,243	1,203	5,961	5,931	6,902	6,712	6,963	6,400	5,643	5,466
Mississippi	3,611	3,788	22,705	23,417	23,240	23,106	20,666	19,812	16,611	17,087
Missouri	1,365	1,334	6,420	6,684	7,090	6,845	6,492	6,358	5,395	5,400
New Jersey	....	....	....	....	1	2	2	2	5	2
North Carolina	4,022	4,064	21,891	22,043	23,400	23,536	20,711	19,860	15,710	15,800
South Carolina	4,450	4,744	27,019	28,229	27,069	28,131	24,890	24,825	20,521	21,875
Tennessee	3,452	3,609	17,620	18,075	18,647	19,087	17,889	17,252	14,004	14,621
Texas	705	724	4,406	4,366	4,356	4,504	4,152	4,091	3,175	3,442
Virginia	5,341	5,814	32,419	32,687	35,356	34,897	33,883	32,331	25,584	24,659
Utah Territory	....	....	2	3	2	1	1	3	1	2
Total	39,343	41,266	227,745	232,140	239,163	239,925	221,480	214,712	176,169	181,113

* Sex not designated.

TABLE LXXXI.—*Ages of the Slave Population—Continued.*

States & Territories.	20 and under 30.		30 and under 40.		40 and under 50.		50 and under 60.		60 and under 70.	
	Males.	Fem's.	Males.	Fem's.	Males.	Fem's.	Males.	Fem's.	Males.	Fem's.
Alabama	31,658	31,208	19,636	19,514	11,433	11,779	6,368	6,030	3,774	3,451
Arkansas	4,930	4,684	2,528	2,612	1,415	1,421	653	580	378	339
Columbia, Dist. of	239	425	127	245	91	182	55	129	44	70
Delaware	212	243	67	84	31	43	20	22	8	11
Florida	3,878	3,681	2,277	2,312	1,344	1,340	895	798	474	397
Georgia	33,959	34,590	19,146	20,427	12,100	13,006	6,584	6,560	4,585	4,544
Kentucky	19,031	17,627	10,325	10,422	6,520	7,156	3,744	3,985	1,819	2,123
Louisiana	26,047	23,971	20,250	18,415	12,690	10,550	5,955	4,864	3,032	2,388
Maryland	8,092	7,443	4,269	4,500	2,953	2,931	1,926	1,850	1,187	1,175
Mississippi	29,915	30,021	18,565	18,986	9,996	9,933	4,854	4,390	3,139	2,839
Missouri	8,623	7,988	3,902	4,300	2,278	2,779	1,136	1,291	535	632
New Jersey	10	1	....	....	2	9	21	38	27	42
North Carolina	23,969	23,536	13,687	13,927	8,444	8,631	6,814	6,327	3,637	3,606
South Carolina	31,745	33,472	20,583	22,938	13,138	14,518	8,771	8,750	5,426	5,502
Tennessee	21,709	21,064	11,370	11,984	6,550	7,115	4,421	4,468	2,050	2,137
Texas	5,585	5,683	3,131	3,449	1,750	1,878	898	829	373	332
Virginia	39,991	36,974	25,435	24,240	18,416	17,514	12,138	10,850	7,614	6,981
Utah Territory	2	4	2	....	1	....	1	1	....	....
Total	289,595	282,615	175,300	178,355	109,152	110,780	65,254	61,762	38,102	36,569

States & Territories.	70 and under 80.		80 and under 90.		90 and under 100.		100 and upwards.		Age unknown.	
	Males.	Fem's.	Males.	Fem's.	Males.	Fem's.	Males.	Fem's.	Males.	Fem's.
Alabama	1,068	959	338	338	97	93	65	61	1	....
Arkansas	75	88	30	24	11	6	9	5	....	1
Columbia, Dist. of	12	29	4	8	1	3	....	2	....	....
Delaware	6	7	....	2	....	....	1	1	....	....
Florida	141	126	45	45	22	21	15	14	40	....
Georgia	1,399	1,430	480	519	142	162	81	79	27	17
Kentucky	621	913	198	255	61	94	28	53	8	8
Louisiana	937	771	319	225	81	59	57	66	7	3
Maryland	549	510	190	196	41	74	24	31	1	2
Mississippi	825	727	288	243	85	85	47	73	127	119
Missouri	141	220	63	65	25	25	8	9	11	8
New Jersey	17	31	9	7	2	5	....	....	....	1
North Carolina	1,520	1,665	570	658	132	202	66	98	8	14
South Carolina	2,008	2,022	613	638	154	200	81	86	1,288	1,303
Tennessee	719	833	233	287	82	98	31	47	3	2
Texas	100	93	40	34	12	12	6	10	11	14
Virginia	3,028	3,264	958	1,196	263	334	87	184	49	41
Utah Territory	....	....	....	....	....	....	....	....	....	....
Total	13,166	13,688	4,378	4,740	1,211	1,473	606	819	*1,581	1,533

TABLE LXXXII.—*Ratio of Ages of the Slaves in* 1850.

States and Territories.	Under 1.	Ratio per cent.	1 and under 5.	Ratio per cent.	5 and under 10.	Ratio per cent.	10 and under 15.	Ratio per cent.	15 and under 20.	Ratio per cent.
Alabama	8,110	2.36	51,158	14.92	51,395	14.99	45.450	13.26	38,860	11.33
Arkansas	1,159	2,46	7,048	14.96	7,026	14.92	6,568	13.95	5,510	11.70
Columbia, District of	71	1.93	349	9.47	495	13.43	580	15.73	526	14.27
Delaware	59	2.58	303	13.23	401	17,51	399	17.42	370	16.16
Florida	914	2.32	5,758	14.65	5,763	14.66	4,949	12.59	4,061	10.33
Georgia	9,619	2.52	56,054	14.69	57,652	15.11	53,583	14.04	44,937	11.77
Kentucky	6,268	2.97	30,263	14.34	33,589	15.92	30,805	14.60	25,065	11.88
Louisiana	4,940	2.02	29,074	11.88	29,883	12.22	27,275	11.14	22,950	9.37
Maryland	2,446	2.71	11,892	13.16	13,614	15.07	13,363	14.79	11,109	12.29
Mississippi	7,399	2.39	46,122	14.88	46.346	14.96	40,478	13.06	33,698	10.87
Missouri	2,699	3.09	13,104	14.99	13,935	15.94	12,850	14.70	10,795	12.35
New Jersey	....	......	....	......	3	1.27	4	1.69	7	2.97
North Carolina	8,086	2.80	43,934	15.23	46,936	16.27	40,571	14.06	31.510	10.92
South Carolina	9,194	2.39	55,248	14.35	55,200	14.34	49,715	12.91	42,396	11.01
Tennessee	7,061	2,95	35,695	14.91	37,734	15.76	35,141	14.67	28,625	11.95
Texas	1,429	2.46	8,772	15.08	8,860	15.23	8,243	14.17	6,617	11.38
Virginia	11,155	2.36	65,106	13.78	70,253	14.87	66,214	14.01	50,243	10.63
Utah Territory	....	......	5	19.23	3	11.54	4	15.38	3	11.54
Total	80,609	2.52	459,885	14.35	479,088	14.95	436,192	13.61	357,282	11.15

* 578 age unknown—sex not given in Mississippi.

TABLE LXXXII.—*Continued.*

States and Territories.	20 and under 30.	Ratio per cent.	30 and under 40.	Ratio per cent.	40 and under 50.	Ratio per cent.	50 and under 60.	Ratio per cent.	60 and under 70.	Ratio per cent.
Alabama	62,866	18.34	39,150	11.42	23,212	6.77	12,398	3.62	7,225	2.11
Arkansas	9,614	20.41	5,140	10.91	2,836	6.02	1,233	2.62	717	1.52
Columbia, District of	664	18.01	372	10.09	273	7.40	184	4.99	114	3.09
Delaware	455	19.87	151	6.59	74	3.23	42	1.83	19	.83
Florida	7,559	19.23	4,589	11.67	2,684	6.83	1,693	4.31	871	2.22
Georgia	68,549	17.96	39,573	10.37	25,106	6.58	13,144	3.44	9,129	2.39
Kentucky	36,658	17.38	20,747	9.83	13,676	6.48	7,729	3.66	3,942	1.87
Louisiana	50,018	20.43	38,665	15.79	23,240	9.49	10,819	4.42	5,420	2.21
Maryland	15,535	17.19	8,769	9.70	5,884	6.51	3,776	4.18	2,362	2.61
Mississippi	59,936	19.34	37,551	12.12	19,929	6.43	9,244	2.98	5,978	1.93
Missouri	16,611	19.00	8,202	9.38	5,057	5.78	2,427	2.78	1,167	1.33
New Jersey	11	4.66	....	.....	11	4.66	59	25.00	69	29.24
North Carolina	47,505	16.46	27,614	9.57	17,075	5.92	13,141	4.55	7,243	2.51
South Carolina	65,217	16.94	43,521	11.31	27,651	7.18	17,521	4.55	10,928	2.84
Tennessee	42,773	17.86	23,354	9.75	13,665	5.71	8,889	3.71	4,187	1.75
Texas	11,268	19.38	6,580	11.31	3,628	6.24	1,727	2.97	705	1.21
Virginia	76,965	16.29	49,675	10.51	35,930	7.60	22,988	4.86	14,595	3.09
Utah Territory	6	23.08	2	7.69	1	3.85	2	7.69	....	.....
Total	572,210	17.86	353,655	11.04	219,932	6.86	127,016	3.96	74,671	2.33

States and Territories.	70 and under 80.	Ratio per cent.	80 and under 90.	Ratio per cent.	90 and under 100.	Ratio per cent.	100 and upwards.	Ratio per cent.	Age unknown.	Ratio per cent.	Aggregate slaves.
Alabama	2,027	.59	676	.20	190	.05	126	.04	1	.....	342,844
Arkansas	163	.35	54	.11	17	.04	14	.03	1	.....	47,100
Columbia, District of	41	1.11	12	.32	4	.11	2	.05	....	.....	3,687
Delaware	13	.57	2	.09	......	......	2	.09	....	.....	2,290
Florida	267	.68	90	.23	43	.11	29	.07	40	.10	39,310
Georgia	2,829	.74	999	.26	304	.08	160	.04	44	.01	381,682
Kentucky	1.534	.73	453	.22	155	.07	81	.04	16	.01	210,981
Louisiana	1,708	.70	544	.22	140	.06	123	.05	10	.....	244,809
Maryland	1,059	1.17	386	.43	115	.13	55	.06	3	.....	90,368
Mississippi	1,552	.50	531	.17	170	.06	120	.04	824	.27	309,878
Missouri	361	.41	128	.15	50	.06	17	.02	19	.02	87,422
New Jersey	48	20.34	16	6.78	7	2.97	....	.....	1	.42	236
North Carolina	3,185	1.10	1,228	.42	334	.12	164	.06	22	.01	288,548
South Carolina	4,030	1.05	1,251	.32	354	.09	167	.04	2,591	.68	384,984
Tennesssee	1,552	.65	520	.22	180	.08	78	.03	5	.....	239,459
Texas	193	.33	74	.13	24	.04	16	.03	25	.04	58,161
Virginia	6,292	1.33	2,154	.46	597	.13	271	.06	90	.02	472,528
Utah Territory	....	.....	....	.....	......	.....	....	.....	....	.....	26
Total	26,854	.84	9,118	.28	2,684	08	1,425	.05	3,692	.12	3,204,313

TABLE LXXXIII.—*Comparative Ages of Male and Female Slaves in* 1830, 1840 *and* 1850.

AGE.	1830.			Ratio per cent.	1840.			Ratio per cent.
	Males.	Females.	Total.		Males.	Females.	Total.	
Under 10 years of age	353,498	347,665	701,163	34.90	422,584	421,465	844,049	33.93
10 and under 24 " "	312,567	308,770	621,337	30.93	391,206	390,117	781,323	31.41
24 " 36 " "	185,585	185,786	371,371	18.48	235,386	239,825	475,211	19.11
36 " 55 " "	118,880	111,887	230,767	11.49	145,260	139,204	284,464	11.44
55 " 100 " "	41,545	41,436	82,981	4.13	51,331	49,746	101,077	4.06
100 and upwards	748	676	1,424	.07	750	581	1,331	.05
Total	1,012,823	996,220	2,009,043	100.00	1,246.517	1,240,938	2,487,455	100.00

TABLE LXXXIII—*Continued.*

AGE.	1850. Males.	Females.	Total.	Ratio per cent.
Under 5 years of age	267,088	273,406	540,494	16.87
5 and under 10 years of age	239,163	239,925	479,088	14.95
10 " 15 " "	221,480	214,712	436,192	13.61
15 " 20 " "	176,169	181,113	357,282	11.15
20 " 30 " "	289,595	282,615	572,210	17.86
30 " 40 " "	175,300	178,355	353,655	11.04
40 " 50 " "	109,152	110,780	219,932	6.86
50 " 60 " "	65,254	61,762	127,016	3.96
60 " 70 " "	38,102	36,569	74,671	2.33
70 " 80 " "	13,166	13,688	26,854	.84
80 " 90 " "	4,378	4,740	9,118	.28
90 " 100 " "	1,211	1,473	2,684	.08
100 and upwards	606	819	1,425	.05
Age unknown	1,581	1,533	3,114	.10
In Mississippi 578 slaves are returned without distinction of sex or age			578	.02
Total			3,204,313	100.00

TABLE LXXXIV.—*Ratio of Slaves,* 1830, 1840, 1850.

AGE.	1830. Number.	1830. Ratio.	1840. Number.	1840. Ratio.	1850. Number.	1850. Ratio.
Under 10 years of age	701,163	34.90	844,069	33.93	1,019,582	31.82
10 and under 24	621,337	30.93	781,206	31.41	2,180,192	68.04
24 " " 36	371,371	18.48	475,160	19.11		
36 " " 55	230,767	11.49	284,465	11.44		
55 " " 100	82,981	4.13	100,980	4.06		
100 and upwards	1,424	.07	1,333	.05	1,425	.04
Unknown	....	......	....	......	3,114	.10
Total	2,009,043	100.00	2,487,213	100.00	3,204,313	100.00

TABLE LXXXV.—*Proportion of Male Slaves to Female, for* 1850.

For every hundred Males there are in the different States, of the ages mentioned, the following number of Females:

STATES, &c.	INFANCY.	YOUTH.			MATURITY.			OLD AGE.					EXTREME OLD AGE.	
	Under 5.	5 and under 10.	10 and under 15.	15 and under 20.	20 and under 30.	30 and under 40.	40 and under 50.	50 and under 60.	60 and under 70.	70 and under 80.	80 and under 90.	90 and under 100.	100 and upwards.	Age unknown.
Alabama	101.1	99.7	95.9	104.6	98.5	99.3	103.0	94.6	91.4	89.7	100.0	95.8	93.8	....
Arkansas	104.1	101.9	93.8	100.7	95.0	103.3	104.2	88.7	89.6	117.3	80.0	54.5	55.5	.....
Columbia, Dis. of	115.3	137.9	142.6	154.1	177.8	192.9	200.0	232.7	159.0	241.6	200.0	300.0	......	.....
Delaware	98.9	79.8	94.6	68.9	114.6	125.3	138.7	110.0	137.5	116.6	......	......	100.0	.....
Florida	102.0	99.4	97.4	105.7	94.9	101.5	99.7	89.1	83.7	89.3	100.0	95.4	93.3	.....
Georgia	100.7	99.2	99.6	105.5	101.8	106.6	107.4	99.6	99.1	102.2	112.2	114.0	97.5	62.9
Kentucky	103.2	100.4	97.4	102.6	92.1	100.9	109.7	106.4	116.7	147.0	128.7	152.4	189 2	100.0
Louisiana	104.7	100.9	96.7	105.8	92.0	90.9	83.1	81.6	78.7	82.2	70.5	72.7	115.7	42.8
Maryland	99.0	97.2	91.9	96.8	91.9	105.4	99.2	96.0	98.9	92.9	103.1	180.4	129.1	200.0
Mississippi	103.3	99.4	95.8	102.8	100.3	102.2	99.3	90.4	90.7	88.1	84.3	100.0	155.3	97.6
Missouri	102.9	96.5	97.9	100.0	92.6	110.2	121.9	113.6	118.1	156.0	103.1	100.0	112.5	72.7
New Jersey	.....	200.0	100.0	40.0	10.0	......	450.0	180.9	155.5	182.3	77.7	250.0	......	.....
North Carolina	100.7	100.5	95.8	100.5	98.1	101.7	102.2	92.8	99.1	109.5	115.4	153.0	148.4	175.0
South Carolina	104.7	103.9	99.7	106.6	105.4	111.4	110.4	99.7	101.4	100.7	104.0	129.8	106.1	101.1
Tennessee	102.9	102.9	96.4	104.4	97.0	105.4	108.6	101.0	104.2	115.8	123.1	119.5	151.6	66.6
Texas	99.5	103.4	98.5	108.4	101.7	110.1	107.3	92.3	89.0	93.0	85.0	100.0	166.6	127.2
Virginia	101.9	98.7	95.4	96.3	92.4	95.3	95.1	89.3	91.6	107.7	124.8	127.0	211.4	83.6
Utah Territory	150.0	50.0	300.0	200.0	200.0	......	......	......	......	......	......	......	......	.....

[In infancy, and between 5 and 10, and 15 and 20, the females are generally in excess, the reverse of the case with the whites: for the two first periods between 10 and 15, the males are in excess of whites and slaves. To this there are some singular exceptions. For periods above 70, the females are generally in excess—strikingly so among the very aged. By another table the proportion of males and females at the different ages since 1820, is also shown. In 1850, the preponderance of aged females is worthy of note.]

TABLE LXXXVI.—*Ratio of Ages and Sex of the Slave Population.*

1. *Proportion of Slave Males and Females*, 1820 *and* 1830.

AGES.	1820.			AGES.	1830.		
	Males, per cent.	Females, per cent.	Proportion of males to females as 100 to		Males, per cent.	Females, per cent.	Proportion of males to females as 100 to
Under 14......	43.63	43.24	94.33	Under 10....	34.90	34.90	98.35
14 and under 26......	25.77	26.98	99.63	10 and under 24....	30.86	30.99	98.79
26 " 45......	20.78	20.36	93.26	24 " 36....	18.32	18.65	100.11
45 and upwards......	9.82	9.42	91.3	36 " 55....	11.74	11.23	94.12
				55 " 100....	4.10	4.16	99.76
				100 and upwards....	.08	.07	90.38
	100.00	100.00	95.18		100.00	100.00	98.4

2. *Proportion of Slave Males and Females*, 1840 *and* 1850.

AGES.	1840.			AGES.	1850.		
	Males, per cent.	Females, per cent.	Proportion of males to females as 100 to		Males, per cent.	Females, per cent.	Proportion of males to females as 100 to
Under 10.....	33.90	33.96	99.73	Under 5....	16.67	17.07	102.36
10 and under 24.....	31.39	31.44	99.72	5 and under 10....	14.92	14.98	100.32
24 " 36.....	18.88	19.33	101.88	10 " 15....	13.82	13.40	96.94
36 " 55.....	11.66	11.22	95.83	15 " 20....	10.99	11.31	102.8
55 " 100.....	4.11	4.00	96.91	20 " 30....	18.07	17.64	97.59
100 and upwards.....	.06	05	77.47	30 " 40....	10.94	11.14	101.74
				40 " 50....	6.81	6.92	101.49
				50 " 60....	4.07	3.86	94.65
				60 " 70....	2.38	2.28	95.98
				70 " 80....	.82	.85	103.96
				80 " 90....	.27	.30	108.27
				90 " 100....	.08	.09	121.63
				100 and upwards....	.04	.05	135.15
				Unknown	.12	.11	97.33
	100.00	100.00	99.55		100.00	100.00	99.95

5. *Births, Marriages and Deaths.*—The tables of Births in the Census, as previously explained, are nothing more than those of the several classes of population under one year of age. There are slave children of that age, in Alabama, 8,110; in Arkansas, 1,159; in the District of Columbia, 71; in Delaware, 59; in Florida, 914; in Georgia, 9,619; in Kentucky, 6,268; in Louisiana, 4,940; in Maryland, 2,446; in Mississippi, 7,399; in Missouri, 2,699; in North Carolina, 8,086; in South Carolina, 9,194; in Tennessee, 7,061; in Texas, 1,429; and in Virginia, 11,155.

The *Marriages* of slaves are not noted in the Census. They take place, upon the average, much earlier than those of the whites or free colored, and are probably more productive than either. But no exact information on an extended scale exists upon this point.

The number of deaths of slaves reported in 1849–1850, was 52,566, or 1.64 per cent. of the whole slave population. This number is certainly too small, though from the facility of reporting them, it approximates, perhaps, nearer to the truth than is the case with the free population.

TABLE LXXXVII.—*Mortality of the Slave Population.*

States, &c.	Deaths.	Ratio per cent. to whole slave population.	States, &c.	Deaths.	Ratio per cent. to whole slave population.
Alabama	4,692	1.369	Missouri	1,355	1.550
Arkansas	861	1.828	New Jersey	11	4.661
Columbia, District of	57	1.546	North Carolina	4,329	1.5
Delaware	21	.917	South Carolina	5,167	1.342
Florida	440	1.119	Tennessee	4,049	1.691
Georgia	5,331	1.397	Texas	877	1.508
Kentucky	4,193	1.987	Virginia	8,451	1.788
Louisiana	5,873	2.399			
Maryland	1,512	1.673			
Mississippi	5,347	1.726	Total	52,566	1.640

6. *Deaf and Dumb, Blind, Insane, and Idiotic.*—The slaves were not separated in these particulars from the free colored either in 1830 or 1840. In 1850 the statistics were as follows:

TABLE LXXXVIII.—*Deaf and Dumb, Blind, Insane, and Idiotic Slaves,* 1850.

States, &c.	Deaf and dumb.	Blind.	Insane.	Idiotic.	Total.	Ratio per cent. to whole slave population.	States, &c,	Deaf and dumb.	Blind.	Insane.	Idiotic.	Total.	Ratio per cent. to whole slave population.
Alabama	58	138	30	133	359	.105	Mississippi	27	93	24	84	228	.074
Arkansas	4	13	3	10	30	.064	Missouri	19	38	11	32	100	.114
Columbia, Dist. of	....	1	1	......	2	.054	North Carolina	75	155	33	151	414	.143
Delaware	2	......	....	4	6	.262	South Carolina	29	134	21	94	278	.072
Florida	11	14	2	8	35	.089	Tennessee	41	82	22	85	230	.096
Georgia	57	129	28	148	362	.095	Texas	10	11	....	11	32	.055
Kentucky	51	113	23	91	278	.132	Virginia	89	299	59	201	648	.137
Louisiana	32	122	45	62	261	.107							
Maryland	26	45	25	68	164	.181	Total	531	1,387	327	1,182	3,427	.107

TABLE LXXXIX.—*Deaf and Dumb, Blind, &c. Free Colored and Slave,* 1830, 1840 *and* 1850.

States, &c.	Deaf and Dumb.				Blind.				Insane.		Idiotic.		Insane and Idiotic.	
	Free Colored and Slave.			Slave.	Free Colored and Slave.			Slave.	1850.		1850.		Free Colored and Slave.	
	1830.	1840.	1850.	1850	1830.	1840.	1850.	1850.	Free Colored.	Slave.	Free Colored.	Slave.	1840.	1850.
Alabama	23	53	59	58	48	96	140	138	2	30	....	133	125	165
Arkansas	4	2	4	4	2	8	14	13	....	3	2	10	21	15
California	......	......	......	....	......	......	......	......	....	....	....	......	......	......
Columbia, District of	2	4	2	....	8	9	9	1	9	1	3	......	7	13
Connecticut	6	8	6	....	7	13	12	......	6	....	4	......	44	10
Delaware	9	8	6	2	11	18	14	......	20	....	14	4	28	38
Florida	6	2	11	11	16	10	15	14	....	2	....	8	12	10
Georgia	59	64	58	57	123	151	133	129	2	28	1	148	134	179
Illinois	......	24	2	....	4	10	5	......	2	....	2	......	79	4
Indiana	3	15	4	....	2	19	12	......	7	....	13	......	75	20
Iowa	......	4	......	....	......	3	......	......	....	....	....	......	4	......
Kentucky	46	77	56	51	83	141	133	113	2	23	20	91	180	136
Louisiana	21	17	35	32	77	36	142	122	11	45	6	62	45	124
Maine	5	13	1	....	1	10	......	......	5	....	2	......	94	7
Maryland	96	66	64	26	124	91	108	45	44	25	48	68	141	185
Massachusetts	9	17	2	....	5	22	6	......	19	....	5	......	63	24
Michigan	......	2	1	....	......	4	......	......	1	....	3	......	26	4
Mississippi	12	28	28	27	31	69	93	93	....	24	2	84	82	110
Missouri	8	27	19	19	10	42	41	38	2	11	....	32	68	45
New Hampshire	9	9	......	....	......	3	2	......	....	....	1	......	19	1
New Jersey	15	15	5	....	22	26	29	......	9	....	13	......	73	22
New York	43	68	7	....	82	91	44	......	34	....	21	......	194	55

TABLE LXXXIX.—*Continued.*

States, &c.	Deaf and Dumb.				Blind.				Insane.		Idiotic.		Insane and Idiotic.	
	Free Colored and Slave.			Slave.	Free Colored and Slave.			Slave.	1850.		1850.		Free Colored and Slave.	
	1830.	1840.	1850.	1850	1830.	1840.	1850.	1850.	Free Colored	Slave.	Free Colored	Slave.	1840.	1850.
North Carolina	83	74	82	75	161	167	182	155	10	33	28	151	221	222
Ohio	9	33	10	....	6	33	12	......	14	....	17	......	165	31
Pennsylvania	39	51	15	....	28	96	28	......	49	....	35	......	187	84
Rhode Island	4	3	3	....	8	1	6	......	7	....	4	......	13	11
South Carolina	69	78	31	29	136	156	148	134	4	21	5	94	137	124
Tennessee	28	67	43	41	37	99	91	82	5	22	5	85	152	117
Texas	......	......	10	10	......	......	12	11	....	....	....	11	......	11
Vermont	5	2	1	....	......	2	1	......	....	....	2	......	13	2
Virginia	130	150	102	89	438	466	384	299	47	59	90	201	384	397
Wisconsin	......	......	......	....	......	......	......	......	....	....	2	......	3	2
Total	743	981	667	531	1,470	1,892	1,816	1,387	311	327	348	1,182	2,789	2,168

7. *Nativities.*—It is almost impossible to distinguish between the native born and foreign born slaves, and no facts were collected upon this subject, except under the schedules of mortality. From these it appears that slaves, except to some extent Africans, were very generally considered of the nativity of the place of decease. As few slaves have been introduced into the country since 1808, and these chiefly into Florida, previously to 1819, under the Spanish rule, and into Louisiana, it will be necessary to look into the class over 60 years of age for the survivors of the original Africans. The whole number of slaves in 1850 over 60 years of age, was 114,752. Of these, no one familiar with the South would admit that more than 8,000 or 10,000 were Africans. In Louisiana, in 1849–1850, 110 African slaves are reported to have died, out of a total of 6,083 deaths of slaves of all ages. In Virginia, few or no African deaths are mentioned. The ages of deceased Africans on the schedules generally range higher than sixty, often more than seventy, and in South Carolina as high as eighty, ninety, one hundred, and one hundred and ten.

8. *Occupations.*—In no Census have the occupations of slaves been recorded. How many are employed as mechanics, how many as laborers, how many as house servants, cannot be known; nor, more than approximately, how many on the different agricultural crops of the South. Deducting the slaves who are known to be residents of towns, and approximating for those towns that are unknown, it might be safe to say that 400,000 slaves are urban, and 2,804,313 rural, and that of the latter class at least as many slaves will be employed as domestics as there are slave properties, which would leave about 2,500,000 slaves* to be directly employed in agriculture, including males and females, and persons of all ages. Slaves under ten and over sixty are seldom employed industrially.

The total number of families holding slaves, by thecensus of 1850, was 347,525.† On the average of 5.7 to a family there are about 2,000,000 persons in the relation of slave-owners, or about one-third of the whole white population of the slave States; in South Carolina, Alabama, Mississippi and Louisiana, excluding the largest cities, one half of the whole population.

* These are distributed between the several great staples of the South, in something like the following proportions as near as can be judged, after a careful consideration of the subject, bearing in mind that large quantities of bread stuffs are produced in additiou.

Hemp	60,000	2.4 per cent.
Rice,	125,000	5.0 " "
Sugar,	150,000	6.0 " "
Tobacco,	350,000	14.0 " "
Cotton, etc	1,815,000	72.6 " "
	2,500,000	100.

† The number includes slave-hirers, but is exclusive of those who are interested conjointly with others in slave property. The two will about balance each other, for the whole South, and leave the slave owners as stated.

TABLE XC.—*Classification of Slave Holders in the United States.*

States, &c.	Holders of 1 slave.	1 and under 5.	5 and under 10.	10 and under 20.	20 and under 50.	50 and under 100.	100 and under 200.	200 and under 300.	300 and under 500.	500 and under 1000.	1000 and over.	Aggregate holders of slaves.
Alabama	5,204	7,737	6,572	5,067	3,524	957	216	16	2	......	......	29,295
Arkansas	1,383	1,951	1,365	788	382	109	19	2	......	......	......	5,999
Columbia, District of	760	539	136	39	2	1	......	......	......	......	......	1,477
Delaware	320	352	117	20	......	......	......	......	......	......	......	809
Florida	699	991	759	588	349	104	29	.....	1	......	......	3,520
Georgia	6,554	11,716	7,701	6,490	5,056	764	147	22	4	2	......	38,456
Kentucky	9,244	13,284	9,579	5,022	1,198	53	5	......	......	......	......	38,385
Louisiana	4,797	6,072	4,327	2,652	1,774	728	274	36	6	4	......	20,670
Maryland	4,825	5,331	3,327	1,822	655	72	7	......	1	......	......	16,040
Mississippi	3,640	6,228	5,143	4,015	2,964	910	189	18	8	1	......	23,116
Missouri	5,762	6,878	4,370	1,810	345	19	......	1	......	......	......	19,185
North Carolina	1,204	9,668	8,129	5,898	2,828	485	76	12	3	......	......	28,303
South Carolina	3,492	6,164	6,311	4,955	3,200	990	382	69	29	2	2	25,596
Tennessee	7,616	10,582	8,314	4,852	2,202	276	19	2	1	......	......	33,864
Texas	1,935	2,640	1,585	1,121	374	82	9	1	......	......	......	7,747
Virginia	11,385	15,550	13,030	9,456	4,880	646	107	8	1	......	......	55,063
Total	68,820	105,683	80,765	54,595	29,733	6,196	1,479	187	56	9	2	347,525

Where the party owns slaves in different counties or in different States, he will be entered more than once. This will disturb the calculation very little, being only the case among the larger properties, and it will account for the fact that a smaller number of such properties are reported in some of the States than are known to exist, particularly in South Carolina, Virginia and Louisiana. By the table it would seem that one-fifth of the properties are in a single slave, and nearly one-half in less than five slaves.*

CHAPTER VI.

AGGREGATE POPULATION.

HAVING given in Chapter Second the Aggregate Population of the United States at all of the Census periods, the formation and relation of States and Territories, the density of population, &c., and, in subsequent Chapters, the White, Free Colored and Slave Population in detail, it will be in order now to include such remarks and tables as were not conveniently reducible under either of the several Chapters.

According to the ratio of increase from Census to Census, divided for the particular years so as to represent correctly the per centages for the lesser and greater population which is increasing, a table has been prepared showing the population of the United States at each year since 1790. The ratio of increase from 1840 to 1850 is assumed for the next decade.†

* The occupation and nativities of slave-holders were not taken off. An experiment in one southern town, gave accountants, barbers, bakers, blacksmiths, builders, butchers, carpenters, draymen, grocers, painters, plasterers, saddlers, tailors, tinners, etc., 32 out of a total of 250 holders, and 115 natives of free States (at home and abroad, 49 being foreign,) out of the same total of 250.

† For an explanation of the principle upon which such a table may be constructed, see Prof. Tucker, "*Progress of the United States,*" p. 107. By starting with the population of 1790 as a basis, which was 3,929,827, and adding three per cent. for every year, making 4,047,721 for 1791; 4,169,152 for 1792, and so on for every year until 1850, Mr. Darby, the well known geographer, arrived at results, which when compared with the particular census years, showed as follows:

Years.	Estimated.	Census.
1800	5,281,468	5,305,925
1810	7,095,964	7,239,814
1820	9,535,182	9,638,131
1830	12,811,118	12,866,020
1840	17,217,706	17,069,453
1850	23,138,004	23,191,876

TABLE XCI.—*Aggregate Population of the United States for each year from 1790 to 1860.*

Years.	Aggregate.	Years.	Aggregate.	Years.	Aggregate.	Years.	Aggregate.	Years.	Aggregate.	Years.	Aggregate.
1790	3,929,827	1802	5,646,176	1814	8,117,710	1826	11,462,088	1838	16,131,087	1850	23,191,876
1791	4,049,600	1803	5,824,398	1815	8,353,338	1827	11,798,013	1839	16,593,630	1851	23,873,717
1792	4,173,024	1804	6,008,246	1816	8,595,806	1828	12,143,783	1840	17,069,453	1852	24,575,604
1793	4,300,210	1805	6,197,897	1817	8,845,312	1829	12,499,687	1841	17,600,752	1853	25,298,126
1794	4.431,272	1806	6,393,534	1818	9,102,060	1830	12,866,020	1842	18,148,589	1854	26,041,890
1795	4,566,329	1807	6,595,346	1819	9,366,261	1831	13,234,931	1843	18,713,479	1855	26,807,521
1796	4,705,504	1808	6,803,528	1820	9,638,131	1832	13,614,420	1844	19,295,971	1856	27,595,662
1797	4,848,919	1809	7,018,282	1821	9,920,600	1833	14,004,789	1845	19,896,574	1857	28,406,974
1798	4,996,705	1810	7,239,814	1822	10,2[illegible]1,348	1834	14,406,350	1846	20,515,871	1858	29.242,139
1799	5,148,994	1811	7,449,960	1823	10,510,618	1835	14,819,425	1847	21,154,444	1859	30,101,857
1800	5,305,925	1812	7,666,206	1824	10,818,659	1836	15,244,344	1848	21,812,893	1860	30,986,851
1801	5,473,407	1813	7,888,729	1825	11,135,727	1837	15,681,447	1849	22,491,305		

A similar table was commenced for each of the States, but at too late an hour to be completed in this volume, involving, as it does, laborious calculations. As far as prepared it is given.

TABLE XCII.

States and Territories.	1795.	1805.	1815.	1825.	1835.	1842.	1845.	1848.	1852.	1854.
Alabama	....	....	....	198,975	427,611	623,169	675,153	731,474	813,960	858,020
Arkansas	....	....	....	21,816	54,449	113,729	143,109	180,077	244,646	285,148
Columbia, Dist. of	....	18,397	28,170	36,278	41,728	45,202	47,529	49,979	53,448	55,268
Connecticut	244,481	256,459	268,545	286,216	303,762	321,285	339,023	357,741	377,298	383,918
Delaware	59,096	68,321	72,709	74,721	77,414	80,605	84,540	88,666	92,703	93,889
Florida	....	....	....	....	43,496	59,884	68,992	79,357	96,082	105,574
Georgia	115,689	202,289	293,390	419,793	597,773	729,728	791,355	858,927	956,540	1,009,680
Illinois	....	....	....	93,232	273,811	534,958	636,839	757,773	956,404	1,074,271
Indiana	....	....	60,074	224,717	485,053	737,951	823,410	918,766	1,063,322	1,143,905
Iowa	....	....	....	....	....	58,136	91,035	142,552	259,196	349,520
Kentucky	127,070	299,658	478,963	623,059	732,435	816,690	875,273	938,056	1,028,839	1,077,468

TABLE XCIII.—*Increase of the whole Population of the United States at each Census, per cent.*

Divisions.	1800.	1810.	1820.	1830.	1840.	1850.
Present Slaveholding States	33.65	32.79	28.82	30.46	25.41	31.73
Present Non-Slaveholding States and Territories	36.38	40.02	37.11	36.13	38.73	38.98
Aggregate	35.02	36.45	33.13	33.49	32.67	35.87

The ratio of increase of the Slaveholding States has gained more largely upon the increase of 1840 than that of the non-slaveholding, and the increase of both together is larger than in any other decade except 1810.

The calculation in the note on the last page followed out to 1901, gave these results:

1851	23,832,144	1861	32,028,400	1871	41,836,239	1881	56,224,399	1891	75,573,639
1852	24,547,107	1862	32,989,252	1872	43,091,532	1882	57,911,130	1892	77,840,848
1853	25,283,520	1863	33,978,928	1873	44,384,064	1883	59,648,463	1893	80,176,063
1854	26,042,025	1864	34,998,825	1874	45,715,585	1884	61.447,916	1894	82,581,344
1855	26,823,285	1865	35,038,231	1875	47,087,052	1885	63,291,353	1895	85,058,784
1856	27,627,983	1866	36,089,377	1876	48,499,663	1886	65,190,192	1896	87,610,547
1857	28,456,822	1867	37,170,958	1877	49,954,652	1887	67,145,917	1897	90,228,863
1858	29,310,526	1868	38,286,086	1878	51,453,291	1888	69,160,294	1898	92,935,728
1859	30,189,841	1869	39,434,668	1879	52,996,889	1889	71,235,122	1899	95,723,799
1860	31,095,535	1870	40,617,708	1880	54,586,795	1890	73,382,185	1900	98,595,512
								1901	101,553,377

TABLE XCIV.—*Relative Rank of the States and Territories with reference to total Population.*

States and Territories.	1790.	1800.	1810.	1820.	1830.	1840.	1850.	States and Territories	1790.	1800.	1810.	1820.	1830.	1840.	1850.
Alabama	....	....	....	19	15	11	12	Missouri	....	....	22	23	21	16	13
Arkansas	....	....	....	26	28	25	26	New Hampshire	10	11	15	15	18	22	22
California	....	....	....	....	....	....	29	New Jersey	9	10	12	13	14	18	19
Columbia, District of.	....	18	21	25	25	28	33	New York	5	3	2	1	1	1	1
Connecticut	8	8	9	14	16	20	21	North Carolina	4	5	5	4	5	7	10
Delaware	15	16	18	22	24	26	30	Ohio	....	17	13	5	4	3	3
Florida	....	....	....	....	26	27	31	Pennsylvania	3	2	3	3	2	2	2
Georgia	12	12	11	11	10	9	9	Rhode Island	14	15	16	20	23	24	28
Illinois	....	....	23	24	20	14	11	South Carolina	7	6	6	8	9	12	14
Indiana	....	20	20	18	13	10	7	Tennessee	16	14	10	9	7	5	5
Iowa	....	....	....	....	....	29	27	Texas	....	....	....	....	....	....	25
Kentucky	13	9	7	6	6	6	8	Vermont	11	13	14	16	17	21	23
Louisiana	....	....	17	17	19	19	18	Virginia	1	1	1	2	3	4	4
Maine	....	....	....	12	12	13	16	Wisconsin	....	....	....	....	....	30	24
Maryland	6	7	8	10	11	15	17	Territories: Minnesota	....	....	....	....	....	....	36
Massachusetts	2	4	4	7	8	8	6	Territories: New Mexico	....	....	....	....	....	....	32
Michigan	....	....	24	27	27	23	20	Territories: Oregon	....	....	....	....	....	....	34
Mississsppi	....	19	19	21	22	17	15	Territories: Utah	....	....	....	....	....	....	35

Connecticut, which in 1790 was the eighth State in rank, is now the twenty-first; South Carolina has descended from the seventh to the fourteenth place; Virginia from the first to the fourth, whilst New York from the fifth place has in the last four decades maintained her rank at the head of the list.

TABLE XCV.—*Ratio of total Population of each State to total Population of the United States.*

States and Territories.	1790.	1800.	1810.	1820.	1830.	1840.	1850.
Alabama	....	....	....	1.33	2.41	3.47	3.33
Arkansas	....	....	....	.15	.24	.57	.90
California	....	....	....	....	....	....	.40
Columbia, District of	....	.27	.33	.34	.31	.26	.22
Connecticut	6.06	4.73	3.62	2.86	2.31	1.82	1.6
Delaware	1.5	1.21	1.0	.75	.6	.46	.39
Florida	....	....	....	....	.27	.32	.38
Georgia	2.1	3.06	3.49	3.54	4.02	4.06	3.91
Illinois	....	....	.17	.57	1.22	2.79	3.67
Indiana	....	.09	.34	1.53	2.67	4.03	4.26
Iowa	....	....	....	....	....	.25	.83
Kentucky	1.86	4.16	5.61	5.85	5.35	4.58	4.24
Louisiana	....	....	1.06	1.59	1.68	2.06	2.23
Maine	2.46	2.86	3.16	3.1	3.11	2.94	2.51
Maryland	8.14	6.44	5.26	4.23	3.48	2.75	2.51
Massachusetts	9.64	7.98	6.52	5.43	4.75	4.32	4.29
Michigan	....	....	.06	.09	.25	1.24	1.71
Mississippi	....	.17	.56	.78	1.06	2.21	2.61
Missouri	....	....	.29	.69	1.09	2.25	2.94
New Hampshire	3.61	3.46	2.96	2.53	2.09	1.67	1.37
New Jersey	4.69	4.00	3.39	2.88	2.49	2.19	2.11
New York	8.65	11.05	13.25	14.24	14.91	14.23	13.36
North Carolina	10.02	9.01	7.67	6.63	5.74	4.41	3.75
Ohio	....	.86	3.19	6.03	7.29	8.90	8.54
Pennsylvania	11.05	11.35	11.19	10.89	10.48	10.1	9.97
Rhode Island	1.76	1.3	1.07	.86	.76	.64	.64
South Carolina	6.34	6.51	5.73	5.22	4.52	3.48	2.88
Tennessee	.91	1.99	3.61	4.39	5.30	4.85	4.32
Texas	....	....	....	....	....	....	.92
Vermont	2.17	2.91	3.01	2.45	2.18	1.71	1.35
Virginia	19.04	16.59	13.46	11.05	9.42	7.26	6.13
Wisconsin	....	....	....	....	....	.18	1.32
Territories: Minnesota	....	....	....	....	....	....	.03
Territories: New Mexico	....	....	....	....	....	....	.27
Territories: Oregon	....	....	....	....	....	....	.06
Territories: Utah	....	....	....	....	....	....	.05

Thus New York has about one-eighth of the population of the Union, Pennsylvania about one-tenth, and Delaware one-two-hundred-and-sixty-third!

TABLE XCVI.—*Decennial Increase per cent. of the total Population of each State since* 1790.

STATES, &C.	1800.	1810.	1820.	1830.	1840.	1850.
Alabama	....	....	....	142.01	90.86	30.62
Arkansas	....	....	....	112.91	221.09	115.12
Columbia, District of	....	70.46	37.53	20.57	9.74	18.24
Connecticut	5.40	4.40	5.02	8.17	4.13	19 62
Delaware	8.76	13.07	.10	5.5	1.74	17.22
Florida	....	....	....	....	56.86	60.52
Georgia	96.37	55.73	35.08	51.57	33.78	31.07
Illinois	....	....	349.53	185.17	202.44	78.81
Indiana	....	402.97	500.24	133.07	99.94	44.11
Iowa	....	....	....	....	....	345.85
Kentucky	202.36	83.98	38.82	21.9	13.36	25.98
Louisiana	....	....	100.39	40.63	63.35	46.92
Maine	57.16	50.74	30.45	33.89	25.62	16.22
Maryland	6.82	11.42	7.04	9.74	5.14	24.04
Massachusetts	11.76	11.53	10.86	16.65	20.85	34.81
Michigan	....	....	86.81	255.65	570.9	87.34
Mississippi	....	355.95	86.97	81.08	174.96	61.46
Missouri	....	....	219.43	110.94	173.18	77.75
New Hampshire	29.50	16.65	13.90	10.31	5.66	11.74
New Jersey	15.10	15.86	13.04	15.58	16.36	31.14
New York	72.51	63.45	43.14	39.76	26.60	27.52
North Carolina	21.42	16.19	15.00	15.52	2.09	15.35
Ohio	....	408.67	151.96	61.31	62.01	30.33
Pennsylvania	38.67	34.49	29.55	28.47	27.87	34.09
Rhode Island	.02	11.44	7.83	17.02	11.97	35.57
South Carolina	38.75	20.12	21.11	15.6	2.27	12.47
Tennessee	195.05	147.84	61.55	61.28	21.6	20.92
Vermont	80.84	40.95	8.29	19.04	4.02	7.59
Virginia	17.63	10.73	9.31	13.71	2.34	14.67
Wisconsin	....	....	....	....	....	886.88

TABLE XCVII.—*Ratio of Increase of Population in the great Geographical Divisions.*

CENSUS PERIODS.	New England States.	Middle States.	Southern States.	South-western States.	North-western States.	California and Territories.	Aggregate.
1790—Population	1,009,823	1,337,456	1,473,680	35,791	73,077	....	3,929,827
1800—Population	1,233,315	1,820,984	1,865,995	114,452	271,195	....	5,305,925
" Per cent. of increase	22.13	36.15	26.62	219.78	271.11	....	35.02
1810—Population	1,471,891	2,491,938	2,197,670	378,635	699,680	....	7,239,814
" Per cent. of increase	19.34	36.85	17.77	230.82	158.00	....	36.45
1820—Population	1,659,808	3,212,983	2,547,936	793,842	1,423,622	....	9,638,131
" Per cent. of increase	12.77	28.94	15.94	109.66	103.47	....	33.13
1830—Population	1,954,717	4,151,286	3,082,130	1,374,179	2,298,390	....	12,866,020
" Per cent. of increase	17.77	29.20	20.96	73.10	61.45	....	33.49
1840—Population	2,234,822	5,118,076	3,333,483	2,245,602	4,131,370	....	17,069,453
" Per cent. of increase	14.33	23.29	8.16	63.41	79.75	....	32.67
1850—Population	2,728,116	6,624,988	3,952,837	3,321,117	6,379,923	184,895	23,191,876
" Per cent. of increase	22.07	29.44	18.58	47.89	54.43	....	35.87

From the following table it will be seen that whilst Vermont in the last ten years gained but 7.59 per cent., Wisconsin increased 886.88 per cent. Delaware in sixty years gained 54.89 per cent., whilst Tennessee, during the same period, gained 2,701.58 per cent.

TABLE XCVIII.—*Growth of States.*

EXHIBITING THE LEAST GROWTH IN 10 YEARS.					EXHIBITING THE MOST RAPID GROWTH IN 10 YEARS.				
States.	Population.		Increase.	Ratio per ct. for 10 years.	States.	Population.		Increase.	Ratio per ct. for 10 yeras.
	1840.	1850.				1840.	1850.		
Vermont	291,948	314,120	22,172	7.59	Illinois	476,183	851,470	375,287	78.81
New Hampshire	284,574	317,976	33,402	11.74	Michigan	212,267	397,654	185,387	87.34
North Carolina	753,419	869,039	115,620	15.35	Arkansas	97,574	209,897	112,323	115.12
South Carolina	594,398	668,507	74,109	12.47	Iowa	43,112	192,214	149,102	345.85
Virginia	1,239,797	1,421,661	181,864	14.67	Wisconsin	30,945	305,391	274,446	886.88

TABLE XCVIII.—*Continued.*

EXHIBITING THE LEAST GROWTH IN 60 YEARS.					EXHIBITING THE MOST RAPID GROWTH IN 60 YEARS.				
States.	Population.		Increase.	Ratio per ct. for 60 years.	States.	Population.		Increase.	Ratio per ct. for 60 years.
	1790.	1850.				1790.	1850.		
Delaware	59,096	91,532	32,436	54.89	Maine	96,540	583,169	486,629	504.07
Maryland	319,728	583,034	263,306	82.35	New York	340,120	3,097,394	2,757,274	810.68
Virginia	748,308	1,421,661	673,353	89.98	Georgia	82,548	906,185	823,637	997.77
Rhode Island	69,110	147,545	78,435	113.49	Tennessee	35,791	1,002,717	966,926	2,701.58
Connecticut	238,141	370,792	132,651	55.70	Kentucky	73,077	982,405	909,328	1,244.34

2. *Families and Dwellings.*—A *family* in the Census, is either one person living separately in a house or part of a house, and providing for him or herself, or several persons living together in a house upon one common means of support, and distinct from others in similar circumstances. A widow living alone, and separately providing for herself, or two hundred individuals living together and provided for by a common head, constitute a family. So of the inmates of a hotel, jail, hospital, &c. There were 3,598,195 such families among the white and free colored population in 1850.

A *Dwelling*, in the Census, embraces separate inhabited tenements, containing one or more families under one roof. Where several tenements are in one block, with walls either of brick or wood to divide them, they are considered as separate houses. Without such divisions they are one house. If the house be partly used for a store or shop, it is a dwelling, though not if so used wholly. Jails, hotels, penitentiaries, &c., are "Dwellings." The total number of Dwellings in the States is given below. (See Table XCIX.) The number of houses, including stores, shops, &c., untenanted or unfinished buildings cannot be stated, nor have the dwellings been ascertained for any earlier census, though the returns were sufficient for the purpose.

TABLE XCIX.—*Families, Dwellings, etc. of White and Free Colored Population.*

STATES AND TERRITORIES.	Dwellings of White and Free Colored.	Ratio of dwellings to 100 inhabitants.	Families—White and Free Colored.	Ratio of families to 100 inhabitants.	Ratio of families to 100 dwellings.	Ratio of deaths to 100 families.
Alabama	73,070	17.04	73,786	17.21	100.98	5.97
Arkansas	28,252	17.36	28,416	17.45	100.58	7.60
California	23,742	25.64	24,567	26.53	103.47	3.68
Columbia, District of	7,917	16.49	8,343	17.38	105.38	9.45
Connecticut	64,013	17.26	73,448	19.81	114.73	7.87
Delaware	15,290	17.13	15,439	17.30	100.97	7.69
Florida	9,022	18.74	9,107	18.92	100,94	5.39
Georgia	91,206	17.39	91,666	17.48	100.50	5.00
Illinois	146,544	17.21	149,153	17.52	101.77	7.78
Indiana	170,178	17.22	171,564	17.36	100.81	7.46
Iowa	32,962	17.15	33,517	17.44	101.68	6.09
Kentucky	130,769	16.95	132,920	17.23	101.64	8.15
Louisiana	49,101	17.99	54,112	19.82	110.20	11.24
Maine	95,802	16.43	103,333	17.72	107.86	7.33
Maryland	81,708	16.58	87,384	17.74	106.94	9.27
Massachusetts	152,835	15.37	192,675	19.37	126.06	10.07
Michigan	71,616	18.01	72,611	18.26	101.38	6.21
Mississippi	51,681	17.42	52,107	17.57	100.82	6.47
Missouri	96,849	16.29	100,890	16.97	104.17	12.01
New Hampshire	57,339	18.03	62,287	19.59	108.62	6.79
New Jersey	81,064	16.57	89,080	18.20	109.88	7.24
New York	473,936	15.30	566,869	18.30	119.60	8.04
North Carolina	104,996	18.09	105,451	18.16	100.43	5.71
Ohio	336,098	16.97	348,514	17.60	103.69	8.30
Pennsylvania	386,216	16.71	408,497	17.67	105.76	6.98
Rhode Island	22,379	15.17	28,216	19.12	126.08	7.94
South Carolina	52.642	18.57	52,937	18.67	100.56	5.43
Tennessee	129,419	16.96	130,004	17.03	100.45	6.01
Texas	27,988	18.12	28,377	18.37	101.38	7.81
Vermont	56,421	17.96	58,573	18.65	103.81	5.34
Virginia	165,815	17.47	167,530	17.65	101.03	6.34
Wisconsin	56,316	18.44	57,608	18.86	102.29	5.03
Territories. Minnesota	1,002	16.49	1,016	16.72	101.39	2.91
Territories. New Mexico	13,453	21.86	13,502	21.94	100.36	8.56
Territories. Oregon	2,374	17.86	2,374	17.86	100.00	1.97
Territories. Utah	2,322	20.45	2,322	20.45	100.00	10.29
Total	3,362,337	16.82	3,598,195	18.00	107.01	7.56

By reference to table XCIX, it will be perceived that there are eighteen families to every hundred white and free colored persons in the Union, or two families to every eleven, the ratio between the States varying from 17.21 families to a hundred persons in Alabama, to 26.5 in California. Comparing the different sections with each other, we have

TABLE C.—*Ratio of Dwellings to Families in the great Geographical Divisions, &c.*

Geographical Divisions.	Dwellings of white and free colored.	Ratio of dwellings to 100 families.	Families of white and free colored	Ratio of families to 100 inhabitants.	Ratio of families to 100 dwellings.	Ratio of deaths to 100 families.
New England	448,789	86.55	518,532	19.01	115.54	8.17
Middle States	1,046,131	88.98	1,175,612	18.01	112.38	7.71
Southern States	423,681	99.30	426,691	17.88	100.71	5.76
Southwestern States	359,511	98.00	366,802	17.65	102.04	7.11
Northwestern States	1,041,332	97.61	1,066,777	17.54	102.44	8.04
California and Territories	42,893	97.97	43,781	23.68	102.07	5.43
Total	3,362,337	93.44	3,598,195	18.00	107.01	7.56

Upon the average for the Union, there are 16.82 houses for every 100 white and free colored persons, or a little less than one house to every six persons, the ratio between the States varying from 15.17 dwellings to every 100 persons in Rhode Island to 25.6 in California. The proportion of families to dwellings in the Union is as 107.01 to 100. In Utah and Oregon there is one dwelling to every family; in Louisiana 100 to every 110; in Connecticut 100 to 114; in Massachusetts and Rhode Island 100 to 126, &c. &c.

There were 2,260,802 families in Great Britain exclusively of Ireland, in 1801, or 1 family to every 4.64 persons; in 1851 4,312,388, or 1 family to every 4.83 persons. In the interval 2,051,586 new families were started. The average number of persons to a family was as follows in the following countries.

TABLE CI.—*Ratio of Persons to Dwellings and Families in certain European States.*

Countries.	Number of persons to each dwelling.		Number of persons to each family.		Number of families to each dwelling.	
	1801.	1851.	1801.	1851.	1801.	1851.
Scotland	5.46	7.80	4.42	4.81	1.236	1.620
England and Wales	5.64	5.47	4.69	4.83	1.204	1.132
Great Britain	5.61	5.71	4.64	4.83	1.209	1.182
France	....	4.85	....	3.97	....	1.222
Austria	....	6.89	....	4.44	....	1.551
Prussia	....	8.13	....	5.13	....	1.585

The average number of persons to each dwelling in Ireland, in 1851, was 6.35; and in Belgium in 1846, 5.42.

The number of dwellings in Ireland in 1851 is stated at 1,047,735, making the total for the British empire, including the islands, 4,717,172. Adding the dwellings of the slave population, at least, on the average, as good as those of the operative classes of Europe, and estimating one dwelling for six slaves, the total dwellings in the United States will be 4,197,914. By comparison, one dwelling to every 5.82 persons in Great Britain, and one to every 5.52 persons in the United States.*

* In Boston, according to the State Census of 1845, there were 19,175 families to 10,812 houses. Of these, 3,361 were owned by the occupant, and 7,451 not owned by the occupant; 6,268 of these houses were occupied by one family each; 2,771 by two families; 902 by three; 419 by four; 174 by five; 105 by six, and the remainder by more than six families. The average for the city was one house to 1.77 families, and one family to 5.09 persons. The number of vacant houses at the same time, was 518, and the number building 559.

Paris, in 1835 contained 50,476 houses, and 1,106,891 persons, or 22 persons and four or five families to a house. In London, in 1851, there were 2,362,236 persons, and 305,933 houses, or 17 families to 10 houses.

In Liverpool in 1851 there were 47,271 families and 35,293 houses. In 1847, in the same city, 30,000 persons dwelt in cellars, but since that period police regulations have greatly reduced the number. In Manchester, in 1851, there were 44,621 families, and 36,701 houses. The "house" in England includes all dwellings isolated

3. *Sex.*—The number of males and females of the total population will be seen in Table CII, as well as their increase in each period of ten years.

TABLE CII.—*Ratio of Sex at each Census of the Total Population.**

Year.	Males.	Females.	Excess of males.	Aggregate number.	Increase in each 10 and in 60 years.	Increase per cent. in each 10, and also in 60 years.
1790	....	....	....	3,929,827	....	....
1800	....	....	....	5,305,925	1,376,098	35.0168
1810	....	....	....	7,239,814	1,933,889	36.4477
1820	4,898,127	4,740,004	158,123	9,638,131	2,398,317	33.1268
1830	6,529,696	6,336,324	193,372	12,866,020	3,227,889	33.4908
1840	8,688,532	8,380,921	307,611	17,069,453	4,203,433	32.6708
1850	11,837,661	11,354,215	483,446	23,191,876	6,122,423	35.8677
Total increase of all classes in 60 years	....	....	....	....	19,262,049	490.1500

4. *Age.*—The table on page 102 will exhibit the total number of persons of each age in the United States in 1850.

and separated by party walls, and in which the occupant has the exclusive use of the entrance hall and stairs. In Scotland, the flats containing as many habitations as stories, entered by common stairs, have generally, until 1851 been considered as separate houses. In that year the English rule was applied to them.

In Great Britain the family includes those who use the same kitchen and board together. A lodger who does not board in the house in which he lived, is considered a family. In 1851 "occupier" was substituted for "family," defined to be, 1st, a resident owner, or 2nd, a person who had paid rent, whether (3d) as a lodger for any distinct apartment, or floor, or the whole house. The rule, however, was not adhered to, and *family* in that census corresponds with the previous one.

Of 67,609 families in England in 1837, taken in order, 41,916 were under the head of "husband and wife," 10,854 under "widow or widower," 14,399 under "bachelor or spinster." Of 42,203 having at head "husband and wife," 11,947 had no children, 8,750 one child each, 7,376 two children, 5,611 three children, 4,027 four children, 2,348 five children, 1,276 six children, 573 seven children, 210 eight, 66 nine, 14 ten, 5 eleven, and 1 twelve children. In 2,017 public institutions or families, there were 295,856 persons, to wit: barracks, 53,933; workhouses, 131,582; prisons, males 24,593, females 6,366, total, 30,959; lunatic asylums, 21,004; hospitals, 11,647; asylums and other charitable institutions, 46,731.

* A writer in the American Journal of the Medical Sciences for July, 1854, remarks that nine months after the prevalence of cholera in Philadelphia there was a remarkable diminution in the proportion of male births, and that subsequent investigations lead to the conclusion that disease, exhausting labor, meagre diet, impure air, intemperance, and other social evils exert depressing influences upon the number of male births. He adds his belief that all measures tending to promote the health and welfare of a population, whilst serving immediately to increase its capacities for profitable labor, tend also to promote the multiplication of the male sex. Thus in England, the excess of male births, is but 5 per cent.; in France and Prussia, 6 per cent.; in Philadelphia, 7 per cent.; and in Kentucky, by its Registration report, 12 1-2 per cent.; in Massachusetts in the cities and towns, it is but 6 per cent., though reaching 9 per cent. among the agricultural population. Professor Tucker suggests as a query whether the preponderance of male births be an original provision, or whether the greater vitality of that sex is not the cause of a less number being still-born or perishing in delivery.

TABLE CIII.—*Aggregate Number in the United States of all Classes at each Age, 1850.*

STATES AND TERRITORIES.	Under 1 year.	1 and under 5.	5 and under 10.	10 and under 15.	15 and under 20.	20 and under 30.	30 and under 40.	40 and under 50.	50 and under 60.	60 and under 70.	70 and under 80.	80 and under 90.	90 and under 100.	100, and upwards.	Un-known.	Aggregate population
Alabama	20,375	110,668	119,389	104,955	88,865	135,326	85,289	53,102	30,207	15,643	5,478	1,671	392	163	100	771,623
Arkansas	6,642	31,514	33,480	29,749	23,626	38,125	22,673	13,457	6,502	2,950	876	209	39	24	31	209,897
California	273	1,628	2,100	1,978	5,532	46,770	22,714	8,103	2,247	463	85	23	8	....	673	92,597
Columbia, Dist.	1,319	5,428	6,731	6,119	5,606	9,965	6,944	4,526	2,844	1,433	531	186	30	7	18	51,687
Connecticut	7,646	32,808	39,190	38,715	38,771	71,836	50,413	36,848	25,787	16,694	8,602	2,889	323	10	260	370,792
Delaware	2,554	10,899	13,071	11,700	10,142	15,994	11,208	7,488	4,491	2,484	1,101	279	54	9	58	91,532
Florida	2,236	12,371	13,380	10,955	8,891	16,186	10,609	6,246	3,815	1,834	598	181	62	36	45	87,445
Georgia	24,858	129,939	141,835	126,715	103,837	157,429	93,479	61,532	34,321	20,950	7,684	2,547	595	221	243	906,185
Illinois	26,681	115,479	130,652	113,515	93,275	151,128	103,056	62,486	34,123	14,548	4,638	958	118	18	795	851,470
Indiana	32,296	135,416	157,714	134,275	111,925	169,018	108,419	67,994	42,602	19,531	6,872	1,699	289	32	334	988,416
Iowa	6,099	28,191	31,016	25,346	20,130	32,420	24,105	13,778	7,152	2,898	834	166	24	1	54	192,214
Kentucky	30,073	133,919	151,829	132,909	110,836	172,220	105,810	68,588	40,764	22,131	9,482	2,927	555	157	205	982,405
Louisiana	12,232	61,202	65,458	57,328	47,770	108,224	83,544	46,251	21,168	9,745	3,145	941	255	176	323	517,762
Maine	13,995	61,781	74,453	71,743	67,025	99,995	69,731	53,355	35,194	20,782	10,495	3,455	332	13	820	583,169
Maryland	16,482	69,162	78,269	72,376	61,748	106,125	74,531	48,693	29,581	16,455	6,959	2,057	447	131	18	583,034
Massachusetts	23,192	90,853	102,797	98,024	105,741	210,997	143,931	96,266	60,254	36,837	17,936	5,820	613	19	1,234	994,514
Michigan	10,898	49,143	59,576	49,786	42,663	69,201	51,552	34,443	18,186	8,631	2,816	560	67	9	123	397,654
Mississippi	16,086	88,975	94,355	81,780	65,784	110,890	70,927	40,159	20,717	11,121	3,406	994	238	140	954	606,525
Missouri	22,331	93,947	105,176	92,344	75,537	125,334	80,372	47,054	24,702	10,705	3,369	831	142	45	155	682,044
New Hampshire	6,111	26,952	34,264	34,314	35,781	57,265	39,847	32,334	23,722	15,369	8,480	3,067	406	12	52	317,976
New Jersey	13,556	54,828	63,761	58,049	52,424	89,475	62,096	42,578	27,291	15,874	6,982	2,189	252	25	175	489,555
New York	76,337	327,093	377,605	342,651	333,329	627,044	421,505	278,311	167,259	91,369	39,834	11,857	1,399	88	1,713	3,097,394
North Carolina	24,734	117,384	131,341	117,592	96,505	147,929	91,531	61,108	41,849	23,518	10,812	3,610	727	249	150	869,039
Ohio	56,884	253,442	291,286	254,921	221,060	351,931	230,597	152,213	89,974	51,393	20,222	5,116	606	58	626	1,980,329
Pennsylvania	64,331	281,066	318,226	277,912	246,628	426,633	284,383	192,069	117,531	65,572	27,711	7,651	823	75	1,175	2,311,786
Rhode Island	3,610	14,106	15,591	15,086	15,316	30,576	21,122	14,027	8,923	5,574	2,651	849	94	3	17	147.545
South Carolina	15,801	91,417	97,184	87,976	73,548	113,942	75,437	49,466	31,663	18,652	7,522	2,434	586	206	2,673	668,507
Tennessee	30,151	140,117	157,608	142,257	118,260	172,351	101,250	65,579	40,486	21,255	9,483	2,976	572	148	224	1,002,717
Texas	6,194	30,594	32,549	28,089	22,568	40,107	26,096	14,969	7,319	2,791	793	221	49	39	214	212,592
Vermont	6,594	31,055	38,153	36,168	34,326	53,253	39,117	31,142	21,129	13,383	7,093	2,460	259	10	38	314,120
Virginia	36,308	184,163	208,260	190,896	153,511	241,473	157,164	111,077	70,597	41,693	18,535	5,981	1,229	389	385	1,421,661
Wisconsin	10,424	40,948	42,279	34,008	28,793	58,425	44,856	24,816	13,229	5,550	1,543	307	19	2	192	305,391
Territories. Minnesota	168	751	721	568	462	1,732	979	425	182	62	20	5	2	....	....	6,077
Territories. N. Mexico	1,233	7,556	8,727	7,027	7,021	12,604	7,250	4,392	2,872	1,694	572	319	87	40	143	61,547
Territories. Oregon	310	1,778	1,873	1,429	1,223	3,230	1,918	866	428	148	21	3	2	....	65	13,294
Territories. Utah	432	1,744	1,369	1,374	1,333	2,165	1,364	919	429	194	53	4	....	....	....	11,380
Total	629,446	2,868,327	3,241,268	2,890,629	2,529,792	4,277,318	2,825,819	1,846,660	1,109,540	609,926	257,234	77,382	11,695	2,555	14,285	23,191,876

By Table CIII, the number in infancy, youth, maturity, old age, and extreme old age, will be seen. Those over 100 years of age being only one in about ten thousand of the total population.

TABLE CIV.—*Ages of the Whole Population.*

Age.	Number.	Ratio.	Age.	Number.	Ratio.
Under 1 year old	629,446	2.71	80 and under 100	89,077	.39
1 and under 5	*2,868,327	12.37	100 and over	2,555	.01
5 " 20	8,661,689	37.35	Age unknown	14,285	.06
20 " 50	8,949,797	38.59			
50 " 80	1,976,700	8.52	Aggregate population	23,191,876	100.00

Whilst the slaves have much more than their ratio of the dependent class of 15 and under, and more than their proportion of the whole supported class, including those below 15 and above 60, their ratio of the effective class is less than that either of the whites or free colored. The presumption here is that those in the several conditions under 15 who are industrially engaged, are about equal. The proportion is no doubt much larger among the slaves. The proportion of free colored above 60 is greater than that of the whites or slaves or total.

TABLE CV.

Age.	Whites.		Free Colored.		Slaves.		Aggregate.	
	Number.	Ratio per ct.	Number.	Ratio per ct.	Number.	Ratio per ct.	Number.	Ratio per ct.
15 years and under	8,002,715	40.93	171,181	39.40	1,455,774	45.43	9,629,670	41.52
Over 15 and under 60	10,720,175	54.83	238,859	54.97	1,630,095	50.87	12,589,129	54.28
60 and over	819,871	4.19	24,169	5.56	114,752	3.58	958,792	4.14
Unknown ages	10,307	.05	286	.07	3,692	.12	14,285	.06
Totals	19,553,068	100.00	434,495	100.00	3,204,313	100.00	23,191,876	100.00
80 and over	†74,585	0.381	3,820	0.887	13,227	0.413	91,032	0.395
100 and over	787	0.004	343	0.079	1,425	0.044	2,555	0.011

The average age of the different classes of population in 1850, and the age which divides the whole number of each about equally are given below. The results are sufficiently curious. In 1790 and 1800 the age of 16 nearly divided the whites. The average age of the slaves shows most favorably and that of the free colored least.

TABLE CVI.—*Average Age of Whites, Free Colored and Slaves,* 1850.

Classes.	Average age.	Age equally dividing population.
Whites	23.10	19.15
Free Colored	24.54	20.27
Slaves	21.35	17.02
Aggregate	22.89	18.87

* Under 10, 1830, 4,224,870; 32.84 per cent.; 1840, 5,440,470, 31.87 per cent.; 1850, 6,739,041, 29.06 per cent.; 100 and over, 1830, 2,618, .02 per cent.; 1840, 2,773, .02 per cent.; 1850, 2.555, .01 per cent.

† The number of persons living in the United States who were here when the Declaration of Independence was signed, cannot much exceed 20,000. It must consist of those now over 75 years of age, less the number of persons who have come into the country since 1775 and have now reached that age. By the tables of survivorship a nearer approximation may be obtained.

TABLE CVII.—*Specific Ages of the People of the United States.*

Age.	Ascertained exactly for 30,131.	Calculated for the whole.	Age.	Ascertained exactly for 30,131.	Calculated for the whole.	Age.	Ascertained exactly for 30,131.	Calculated for the whole.	Age.	Ascertained exactly for 30,131.	Calculated for the whole.
Under ¼	124	110,986	24....	544	431,164	51....	142	92,183	78.......	33	14,717
¼ " ½	193	172,681	25....	578	458,115	52....	179	116,186	79.......	28	12,495
½ " ¾	232	207,550	26....	490	388,383	53....	152	98,665	80.......	41	17,957
¾ " 1	155	138,701	27....	435	344,808	54....	131	85,042	81.......	39	17,087
1........	839	711,470	28....	503	398,682	55....	173	112,295	82.......	16	7,026
2........	876	742,851	29....	352	279,037	56....	183	118,778	83.......	15	6,588
3........	856	725,891	30....	630	487,053	57....	122	79,205	84.......	21	9,211
4........	812	688,588	31....	280	216,533	58....	122	79,205	85.......	14	6,158
5........	853	680,831	32....	392	303,095	59....	109	70,767	86.......	9	3,965
6........	816	650,833	33....	359	277,597	60....	237	135,893	87.......	13	5,719
7........	807	643,911	34....	313	242,039	61....	70	40,162	88.......	2	912
8........	849	677,755	35....	424	328,217	62....	98	56,207	89.......	7	3,109
9........	738	588,533	36....	310	240,110	63....	116	66,529	90.......	8	2,873
10........	826	662,676	37....	292	226,196	64....	102	58,507	91.......	2	743
11........	673	539,958	38....	359	277,984	65....	131	75,129	92.......	7	2,519
12........	742	595,299	39....	297	230,058	66....	75	43,032	93.......	5	1,805
13........	641	514,296	40....	497	362,122	67....	74	42,455	94.......	2	743
14........	722	579,264	41....	189	138,019	68....	87	49,908	95.......	3	1,098
15........	632	496,246	42....	250	182,400	69....	74	42,455	96.......	1	389
16........	680	533,915	43....	224	163,485	70....	122	54,330	97.......	2	743
17........	619	486,035	44....	206	150,387	71....	51	22,733	98.......	1	389
18........	691	542,549	45....	357	260,253	72....	70	31,186	99.......	2	743
19........	601	471,910	46....	215	156,933	73....	75	33,415	100 & over	......	2,555
20........	665	527,054	47....	185	135,103	74....	58	25,848			
21........	582	461,284	48....	202	147,479	75....	53	23,625	Total popu	lation.	*23,191,876
22........	609	482,683	49....	213	155,479	76....	45	20,064			
23........	640	507,242	50....	397	257,634	77....	43	19,171			

5. *Births, Marriages and Deaths.*—The ratio of Births, in the table on another page, shows 2.75 in the Union to every 100 free persons, or one birth to every thirty-six persons, or very nearly the same number that is given in the Massachusetts Registry reports for that State on the average of the years 1849–51, yet the Census shows for Massachusetts but one birth to every 42 persons in 1850. In Great Britain for the five years 1839–43, the average was one birth to 31 persons, in France one in 35, in Russia one in 36, in Prussia and Austria one in 26, in Boston one in 27.

Correcting the number of births by reference as explained before to the mortality tables, &c., the average for the United States would be about one birth to every 33 persons, a number intermediate between that of France and Great Britain, whilst without doubt it should be greater than either.

The ratio of Marriages is very nearly one person married to every two hundred persons, varying between the States from one to 316 as in Delaware, one to 150 as in New Mexico, or one to 192 as in Massachusetts, a sufficient proof of the incompleteness of the returns. The Massachusetts Registry for 1849–51 gives one in 102 for the State, and in Boston one in 64. In England there is one marriage to every 130 inhabitants, in France and Austria one in 123, in Prussia one in 110. The actual proportion in the United States cannot differ much from that of Massachusetts, and is no doubt larger. The number returned as married is twice the number of marriages, less those who have married and died, or removed in the year, not taken into account.

It will be seen by the table which follows, that there is but one death reported for every seventy-two persons in the Union, and that for the States the ratio varies from one in 283, as in Oregon, to one in 102, as in California, or one in 44, as in Louisiana. The Massachusetts reports show for 1849–50–51 one in fifty-three against one in fifty-one in the census—a near approximation.

* The ages which were returned in the census "unknown," are disposed of in something like the following manner. One-tenth to the class under 10 years; one-tenth to those between 10 and 20; one-tenth to those between 20 and 35; five and a half-tenths to those between 35 and 50, as in this class they are far more apt to occur; one-tenth between 50 and 80; one-twentieth to those between 80 and 100. In the 30,131 ascertained cases, there were 283 mulattoes, of whom only five exceeded 61 years of age, or 1 in 56. Out of 974 blacks, 34 exceeded that age, or 1 in 28. Of 28,874 whites, 1,475 or 1 in 19 exceeded the same age. No white exceeded 100, and only 23 exceeded 90. No mulatto exceeded 77, though two blacks were 78; four 80; two 85; one 88; one 91; one 120. The proportion of mulattoes and blacks under 10 was very nearly if not quite equal, being about 30 per cent., and the whites about 27 per cent. of the whole.

The preponderance of those at the ages 10, 15, 20, 25, 30, &c. is notable; evidencing that approximations assume round numbers, and that a disposition exists with persons also to assume them in returning their ages. The same will be found in the French Census of 1851, which gave a total of 35,783,170, of whom 29,634 were unknown. Under 1 year, 655,271; of 4 years, 642,381; 5 years, 653,830; 6 years, 673,748; 10 years, 661,359; 19 years, 578,956; 20 years, 618,230; 21, 555,893; 29, 495,711; 30, 690,638; 31, 467,219; 39, 420,327; 40, 665,939; 41, 401,550; 49, 356,354; 50, 591,861; 51, 357,216; 59, 237,137; 60, 403,655; 61, 219,118; 70, 219,954; 80, 62,794; 90, 5,257; 95, 1,228; 100, 180; over 100, 102.

TABLE CVIII.—*Total Deaths in each State and Ratio to Population.*

STATES AND TERRITORIES.	DEATHS.		STATES AND TERRITORIES.	DEATHS.	
	Number.	Ratio.		Number.	Ratio.
Alabama	9,103	1.18	New Hampshire	4,231	1.33
Arkansas	3,021	1.44	New Jersey	6,465	1.32
California	905	.98	New York	45,584	1.47
Columbia, District of	846	1.63	North Carolina	10,357	1.19
Connecticut	5,781	1.56	Ohio	28,949	1.46
Delaware	1,209	1.32	Pennsylvania	28,551	1.24
Florida	931	1.06	Rhode Island	2,241	1.52
Georgia	9,923	1.09	South Carolina	8,046	1.20
Illinois	11,619	1.36	Tennessee	11,874	1.18
Indiana	12,808	1.30	Texas	3,096	1.46
Iowa	2,044	1.06	Vermont	3,129	1.00
Kentucky	15,033	1.53	Virginia	19,059	1.34
Louisiana	11,956	2.31	Wisconsin	2,903	.95
Maine	7,582	1.30	Territ's. Minnesota	30	.49
Maryland	9,621	1.65	Territ's. New Mexico	1,157	1.88
Massachusetts	19,404	1.95	Territ's. Oregon	47	.35
Michigan	4,515	1.14	Territ's. Utah	239	2.10
Mississippi	8,721	1.44			
Missouri	12,292	1.80	Total	323,272	1.39

The true number of Deaths in the Union for 1850, considering it a sickly year, could not have fallen short of one in every fifty persons for all classes, which would swell the total deaths of the census from 323,272 to 463,839.

The Registration Reports of Massachusetts have been published annually for twelve years, and now assume this form :

Counties and towns.	Population.	Births.							Marriages.				Deaths.						
		Whole number.	Sex.			Parentage.			Whole number.	Nativity.			Whole number.	Sex.			Whole number.	Age.	
			M.	F.	U.	Amer.	For.	U.		Amer.	For.	U.		M.	F.	U.		Aggregate.	Average.

Other tables show the months of Births, Marriages and Deaths, distinguishing plural births and still-born, the native and the foreign, and whether the marriage was the first for both parties,—the first for one, the male,—the second or subsequent for the female, the second for the male, and the first for the female, the subsequent for both parties, &c. The deaths are shown by counties, male and female, and by months and also by ages and by sex.

Sex.	Months.													Diseases.	Whole number.				Ages.											
	January.	February.	March.	April.	May.	June.	July.	August.	September.	October.	November.	December.	Unknown.		Total.	Males.	Females.	Unknown.	Under 5.	5 to 10.	10 to 15.	15 to 20.	20 to 30.	30 to 40.	40 to 50.	50 to 60.	60 to 70.	70 to 80.	Over 80.	Unknown.
Males.																														
Females																														

In 1851 the still-born, not included in the detail, numbered 527. The deaths are published by counties in twelve classes, and the results for twelve years compared. The average ages of the different professions dying, are also classified; as for example, agriculturists, laborers, mechanics, merchants, paupers, professional men, public men, seamen, females, &c.

The English system of registration was established in 1836, and annual reports have been regularly published. They are considered to be so accurate that it is said "the marriage returns point out periods of prosperity little less distinctly than the funds measure the hopes and fears of the money market." In Massachusetts the system was organized in 1842, in New York in 1847, the first report being published in 1848 ; in New Jersey, 1848–51 ; in Connecticut in 1848, and three reports are published; in New Hampshire in 1849–51; in Pennsylvania and Kentucky in 1852. The reports of most of these States have been compared, and they resemble generally those of Massachusetts, which are especially admirable. It would be well if the tables for the several States followed one uniform standard. Those which are named are the only States, it is believed, that have registry systems in operation, although others are preparing to follow. In Louisiana an unsuccessful experiment was made. The matter is now before the legislature of South Carolina. The National Medical Convention has frequently and earnestly recommended registration systems to all of the States. In many of the large cities there are annual reports of diseases and deaths made up by the Boards of Health, which embody a vast amount of valuable statistical matter. Those for Charleston, Savannah, New Orleans, Mobile, Baltimore, Philadelphia and New York, have been collected in the office.*

Dr. E. H. Barton, of New Orleans, in a report to the American Medical Association in 1852, has analyzed with great care the mortality returns of the Census for the States of Louisiana, Mississippi, Arkansas and Texas, illustrating them with many most interesting sanitary charts and maps. He has subsequently been pursuing the subject, associated with Dr. Axson and others, with characteristic zeal, at the instance of the municipal authorities of the city. Dr. Barton admits the imperfections of the returns, but thinks them valuable, notwithstanding, for reference, and that they are much nearer correct in the country than in the cities. His totals of deaths differ slightly from those in the Census which were afterwards corrected.

TABLE CIX.—*Comparative Mortality.*

DISEASES.	For the city of N. Orleans for 1842.	City of Mexico for 1839.	City of Havana, 1842.	District of Jaruco, Cuba, 1842.	Average of the State of Louisiana, 1850.	Average of Arkansas, 1850.	Average of Mississippi, 1850.	Average of Texas, 1850.	Average of Maryland, 1850.
Population	81,347	180,000	188,198	3,208	517,739	209,651	592,853	187,403	583,034
Mortality per cent. to population	41.19	31.24	28.11	64.21	21.49	14.34	14.62	15.72	16.85
A. Zymotic	13.18	5.18	7.12	11.53	10.17	6.01	6.04	6.28	5.65
B. Sporadic	20.25	21.10	20.20	38.96	6.45	5.29	5.25	4.18	6.47
C. External	2.45	1.08	.76	1.37	1.68	.78	1.34	1.27	.74
I. Epidemic } II. Endemic }	11.82	4.67	6.62	11.53	7.33	4.96	4.80	5.96	4.19
III. Monoxysmal	1.97	.56	.49	......	.42	.85	.89	.43	1.40
IV. Variable	2.81	3.00	3.66	7.78	.92	.69	1.01	.76	9.53
V. Nervous	4.42	3.63	5.00	11.53	1.60	.80	.98	.95	1.55
VI. Respiratory	6.09	5.83	9.41	14.33	1.31	1.88	1.63	1.83	2.29
VII. Circulatory	.70	.27	.29	.31	.08	.02	.06	.05	.22
VIII. Digestive	3.49	7.11	6.64	4.39	.60	1.90	1.02	.75	.58
IX. Urinary	.07	.02	.07	.31	.01	.03	.02	.03	.04
X. Of males	.06	....	....	......	....	....	....	....	....
XI. Of females	.40	.56	.18	......	.16	.32	.20	.44	.18
XII. Locomotive	.14	.06	.02	......	.06	.08	.07	.08	.12
XIII. Integumentary	.01	.09	.12	......	.01	....	.03	.02	.01
XIV. Old age	.44	.24	.07	.31	.17	.17	.23	.17	.43
XV. Stillborn	1.58	.17	....	......	.06	.10	.05	.04	.04
XVI. Casualties	1.14	.22	.03	......	.57	.53	.93	.94	.58
XVII. Exopathic	.36	.66	.57	1.86	.05	.18	.31	.28	.05
XVIII. Esopathic	.93	.19	.13	......	.14	.08	.08	.03	.09
XIX. Treatment	.01	....	....	......	....	....	.01	....	....

* Mr. Shattuck who prepared the Report in 1850 of the Commissioners appointed by the legislature of Massachusetts, under a resolution relating to a sanitary survey of that State, introduces twelve considerations upon the subject of vital statistics, too valuable and instructive to be omitted in this place.

"The following principles may be considered as settled; though we have not space in this connection to illustrate them fully. They should govern all those who make sanitary surveys of different places or populations.

"1st. That a uniform law of mortality exists, which destroys more persons at one age than at another, in all other circumstances exactly similar, and that this is modified in its operation in a healthy and in an unhealthy locality, only by its being less stringently regarded in the one than in the other.

"2nd. That the generative power and ability to produce a healthy child at marriage, and the number of married persons living in the procreative ages, combined with other personal circumstances; and hence arises the sanitary importance of ascertaining in a census, as a characteristic of the population, the number of the married at different ages, and of recording each marriage and the age at marriage.

"3d. That when the number of births is great, the number of deaths is proportionally great, and the average age at death proportionally low; and that an excessive production of life is one of the causes, not consequences of great mortality; and hence the number of births is a necessary element in estimating the sanitary condition of a population.

"4th. That the average age at death, as well as the aggregate number of a population out of the whole of which one dies annually, though interesting as a characteristic of the population, is a fallacious test of its sanitary condition; and cannot be employed alone, for that purpose, without leading to serious errors. It can be applied as an accurate test only when the ages of the living inhabitants compared, are alike.

"5th. That selecting a class of the population, such as the professional men, the tradesmen, the laborers, the rich or the poor, and giving their average age, or the average number of years of life that either live, less than the others, or that either lose more than the others, as a test of the sanitary condition of the class, may mislead the inquirer, and cannot be relied upon as an accurate test.

"6th. That the information concerning the rate of mortality supposed to have prevailed in past ages, when the calculations have been made upon the erroneous basis mentioned in the last two conclusions, cannot be taken as an exact test for comparison with the present age, without some allowance of error. Few observations concerning the living or the dead were made with accuracy in the olden times.

"7th. That the only accurate tests of measurement for one place, are those founded on a joint comparison of the number of persons living at each age, with the number of deaths at the same age; or for different places,

TABLE CX.—*Comparison of South-Western States with Mexico, Havana, Four Rural Districts of Cuba, and Maryland, in relation to certain Classes of Disease.**

States, &c.	Total cholera in the State.	Proportion to entire mortality, per cent.	Phthisis.	Proportion to entire mortality.	All pulmonary diseases.	Proportion to entire mortality.	All fevers.	Proportion to entire mortality.	Diseases of the nervous system.	Proportion to entire mortality.	Total mortality.	Total population.
Louisiana	2,999	25.10	685	5.73	987	8.26	1,861	15.57	1,633	13.66	11,948	517,739
Mississippi	576	6.60	320	3.67	1,248	14.21	1,060	12.16	586	6.72	8,711	606,555
Arkansas	232	7.61	129	4.26	267	8.83	540	17.86	169	5.59	3,022	209,639
Texas	286	9.24	108	3.49	237	7.66	626	20.22	179	5.78	3,096	212,592
Mexico	......	......	296	5.26	757	13.46	826	14.68	659	11.71	5,624	180,000
Havana	......	......	1,357	28.61	415	7.83	1,076	20.46	942	17.82	5,297	188,198
Four Rural Districts of Cuba	......	......	238	12.14	174	8.88	130	6.63	475	24.28	1,959	78,195
Maryland	......	......	......	......	......	......	......	......	905	9.23	9,804	583,034
New Orleans in 1842	......	......	321	9.51	174	5.15	594	17.60	350	10.37	3,375	81,374

a comparison of the same facts regarding the population of the same ages in both places; or the same population in two places, supposing it to be removed from one place to the other.

"8th. That in estimating the effects of immigration on the sanitary condition of a population, the difference both between the ages of those who come in and those who go out, and the ages of the permanent population must always be considered. Other circumstances being equal, a difference in this respect will produce a different rate of the whole mortality.

"9th. The same joint comparison should be made separately of the ages of the living and the ages at death of all who die, by each disease; in each season of the year; of each sex; of each occupation; and of those characterized by other circumstances. The number as influenced by either of these circumstances, will be increased or diminished in proportion as more or less are found of one age more than of another. For this purpose a variety of tables might be constructed to exhibit the facts in condensed forms.

"10. That an accurate enumeration of the number, ages, &c., birth, every marriage, and every death, with all the information desired relating to each, are absolutely essential as the foundation of every estimation of the sanitary condition of a population; and a sanitary survey, where this is wanting, can be of little value.

"11th. That for all practical purposes, as means of comparison, the living and the dead may be divided as to the ages, into decennial periods, or periods of ten years each, for those over twenty; into quinquennial periods, or periods of five years each, for those under twenty, and into each year of life for those under five years. This admirable division has been adopted in England. For special purposes three divisions should be made: of those under 15, of those between 15 and 60, and of those over 60, as the dependent the productive, and the aged classes. The division sometimes made between those under 20, and over 20, as "boys and girls," and "men and women;" or as "children and adults," is indefinite, unmeaning, and useless; as are also the ages 4, 8, 14, 16, 21 and 45, which have been sometimes used as dividing points.

"12th. That to secure such uniformity at different places and at different times, in the abstracts of the facts concerning the living inhabitants, and the dead, that each may be accurately compared together, both should be made under the superintendence of one agency, and that agency should be the General Board of Health."

* *Table of Births, Marriages and Deaths in England and Wales.*

YEARS.	PERSONS.		MALES.		FEMALES.		Marriages.
	Births.	Deaths.	Births.	Deaths.	Births.	Deaths.	
1841	512,158	343,847	262,714	174,198	249,444	169,649	122,496
1842	517,739	349,519	265,204	176,594	252,535	172,925	118,825
1843	527,325	346,445	270,577	175,721	256,748	170,724	123,818
1844	540,763	356,933	277,436	181,126	263,327	175,807	132,249
1845	543,521	349,366	278,418	177,529	265,103	171,837	143,743
1846	572,625	390,315	293,146	198,325	279,479	191,990	145,664
1847	539,965	423,304	275,658	214,375	264,307	208,929	135,845
1848	563,059	399,833	288,346	202,949	274,713	196,851	138,230
1849	578,159	440,853	295,158	221,801	283,001	219,052	141,599
1850	593,422	368,986	302,834	186,459	290,588	182,527	....

Number and centesimal proportions of deaths at different ages that occurred in England in the seven years from 1838 to 1844.

Under 5 years, 964,807, 39.66 per cent.; 5 years and under 10 years, 121,562, 4.99 per cent.; 10 years and under 15 years, 63,690, 2.62 per cent.; 15 years and under 25 years, 179,985, 7.40 per cent.; 25 years and under 35 years, 169,670, 6.97 per cent.; 35 years and under 45 years, 154,524, 6.35 per cent.; 45 years and under 55 years, 147,727, 6.07 per cent.; 55 years and under 65 years, 171,814, 7.06 per cent.; 65 years and under 75 years, 210,565, 8.66 per cent.; 75 years and under 85 years, 182,941, 7.52 per cent.; 85 years and under 95 years, 60,664, 2.50 per cent.; 95 years and upwards, 4,839, 0.20 per cent.; ages unknown, 3,860. Total, 2,436,648, 100.00 per cent

The estimated proportions of deaths in the course of the preceding century, were: in 1700, one in 39 4-5; 1710, one in 36 1-10; 1720, one in 35½; 1730, one in 31 1-10; 1740, one in 35 1-5; 1750, one in 40 2-5; 1760, one in 41 4-5; 1770, one in 41 1-5; 1780, one in 41½; 1785, one in 41¾; 1790, one in 45 1-5; 1795, one in 47 1-5; 1800, one in 47¾.

The following exhibits the proportion of annual deaths to the whole population of certain European countries: Norway, one in 54; Sweden, one in 41½; Russia, one in 25 92-100; Denmark, one in 40; Mecklenburg, one

Should the mortality statistics of the Census be printed, (and they have been asked for by medical men, societies and associations in every part of the Union,) some very useful deductions could be made from them. The returns are sufficient to frame tables similar

in 46¼; Saxony, one in 34¼; Wurtemburg, one in 31½; North Holland, one in 30 6-10; Belgium, one in 43; France, one in 39 6-10; Azores, one in 48; Genoa, one in 28 4-7.

Number and centesimal proportions of deaths of different ages that occurred in Ireland during 10 years, between June 6th, 1831, and June 6th, 1841.

Births to 1 year, 269,199, 23.38 per cent.; 2 to 5 years, 165,918, 14.41 per cent.; 6 to 10 years, 58,272, 5.06 per cent.; 11 to 20 years, 83,259, 7.23 per cent.; 21 to 30 years, 101,518, 8.82 per cent.; 31 to 40 years, 86,585, 7.52 per cent.; 41 to 50 years, 82,537, 7.17 per cent.; 51 to 60 years, 108,518, 9.43 per cent.; 61 to 70 years, 89,507, 7.77 per cent.; 71 to 80 years, 69,997, 6.08 per cent.; 81 to 90 years, 27,579, 2.40 per cent.; 91 to 100 years, 8,365, 0.73 per cent.; ages not specified, 36,120. Total, 1,187,374, 100.00 per cent.

In connection with the mortality statistics of this report, and with a view to their comparison more fully with those prepared and published annually in the several large cities, the following statistics are appended.

In *Boston*, according to the report of the Sanitary Commission, the number of deaths of persons under five years of age during a period of nine years, was 11,705, being nine per cent. annually of the total population of that age; of persons aged from five to ten years, 1,312 or 1.28 per cent.; from ten to 15 years, 633, or 0.72 per cent.; from fifteen to twenty, 738, or 0.74 per cent.; from twenty to thirty, 3,303, or 1.24 per cent.; from thirty to forty, 2,917, or 1.62 per cent.; from forty to fifty, 1,948, or 2.15 per cent.; from fifty to sixty, 1,273, or 2.97 per cent.; from sixty to seventy, 1,057, or 4.75 per cent.; from seventy to eighty, 787, or 9.78 per cent.; from eighty to ninety, 379, or 19.04 per cent.; over ninety, 75, or 29.64 per cent.; those of all ages, 26,127, or 2.53 per cent.

In *New York*, according to the annual report of the City Inspector, there were in 1853, 22,702 deaths, of which 12,230 were males, and 10,472 females. Those of foreign birth were 7,104. Of the age of one year and under, there were 7,724 deaths; of one to two years, 2,942; of two to five, 2,297; of five to ten, 771; of ten to twenty, 854; of twenty to thirty, 2,441; of thirty to forty, 2,037; of forty to fifty, 1,413; of fifty to sixty, 866; of sixty to seventy, 671; of seventy to eighty, 439; of eighty to ninety, 140; of ninety to one hundred, 34; of one hundred and over, 2; ages unknown, 51.

Ratio of Deaths to the Total Mortality in each Decade of Life in New York.

AGE.	1847.	1848.	1849.	1850.	1851.	1852.	1853.
Birth to 10	1 to 1.60	1 to 1.45	1 to 1.57	1 to 1.55	1 to 1.67	1 to 1.86	1 to 1.65
10 " 20	" 24.43	" 24.54	" 22.04	" 27.00	" 25.50	" 26.93	" 26.58
20 " 30	" 8.10	" 8.16	" 8.16	" 9.59	" 8.70	" 9.89	" 9.30
30 " 40	" 8.61	" 8.60	" 7.79	" 10.61	" 10.50	" 10.78	" 11.14
40 " 50	" 12.34	" 12.00	" 10.96	" 15.43	" 16.54	" 15.79	" 16.07
50 " 60	" 21.16	" 19.32	" 19.15	" 22.64	" 23.70	" 24.54	" 25.62
60 " 70	" 26.72	" 28.20	" 25.89	" 31.41	" 35.00	" 34.34	" 33.83
70 " 80	" 45.23	" 37.12	" 48.02	" 56.59	" 60.00	" 55.38	" 51.71
80 " 90	" 103.18	" 74.65	" 105.19	" 94.30	" 123.25	" 120.05	" 162.16
90 " 100 and upwards	" 451.00	" 469.60	" 552.86	" 943.00	" 710.00	" 600.00	" 667.71
Unkown	" 74.16	" 111.25	" 74.00	" 99.25	" 203.75	" 175.61	" 445.13

In *Philadelphia*, according to the Report of the Board of Health for 1850, the total number of deaths during the year was 8,509, of whom 2,557 were under one year of age; 1,055 between one and two years; 930 between two and five; 419 between five and ten; 145 between ten and fifteen; 212 between fifteen and twenty; 1,649 males, and 1,542 females, of twenty and upwards; 460 over seventy.

In *Baltimore*, by the Report of the Board of Health, there were in 1850, 4,576 deaths, of which 411 were still-born; 995 of persons under one year of age; 500 between one and two years; 414 between two and five; 174 between five and ten; 93 between ten and fifteen; 144 between fifteen and twenty; 435 between twenty and thirty; 433 between thirty and forty; 336 between forty and fifty; 195 between fifty and sixty; 207 between sixty and seventy; 152 between seventy and eighty; 59 between eighty and ninety; twenty-one between ninety and one hundred, and 7 above one hundred.

In *Charleston*, according to the report of the Board of Health in 1850, there were 216 deaths of white males; of white females, 158; total white, 374; black males, 225; black females, 257; total black, 482; total deaths, 856. (This was a sickly year.) Of these, 702 were native born; 125 foreign; 29 were born in other States of the Union. The ages were as follows:

Ages of Persons Dying in Charleston, 1850.

AGE.	WHITES.		AGE.	BLACKS AND COLORED.	
	Males.	Females.		Males.	Females.
Under 1	20	23	Under 1	55	63
1 to 5	25	30	1 to 5	34	49
5 " 10	10	7	5 " 10	12	9
10 " 20	7	5	10 " 20	18	18
20 " 30	31	17	20 " 30	16	22
30 " 40	36	19	30 " 40	20	21
40 " 50	34	16	40 " 50	15	14
50 " 60	19	6	50 " 60	18	15
60 " 70	13	11	60 " 70	18	15
70 " 80	7	14	70 " 80	12	8
80 " 90	3	8	80 " 90	7	16
90 " 100	1	1	90 " 100	....	6
100 and over	....	1	100 and over	....	1
Total	....	374	Total	....	482

to those of Massachusetts, which assimilate to the English. The following arrangement has been adopted for a few of the States, being a combination of such as are in use in different countries. It is unfortunate that, upon the schedules, neither the nativities of the dead nor

Mobile.—The following table from Fenner's "Southern Medical Reports" gives the deaths in Mobile during the years 1844, 1845, 1846, 1847 and 1848.

Mortality of Mobile.

YEARS.	WHITE MALES.														WHITE FEMALES.													
	Unkown.	Under 1 yr.	1 under 10.	10 under 20.	20 under 30.	30 under 40.	40 under 50.	50 under 60.	60 under 70.	70 under 80.	80 under 90.	90 under 100.	Over 100.	Total white males.	Unknown.	Under 1 yr.	1 under 10.	10 under 20.	20 under 30.	30 under 40.	40 under 50.	50 under 60.	60 under 70.	70 under 80.	80 under 90.	90 under 100.	Over 100.	Total white females.
1844.....	43	15	17	8	44	27	25	8	7	..	..	..	..	194	....	....	....	3	13	10	2	2	..	..	..	..	..	30
1845.....	43	26	17	7	32	37	19	11	3	..	..	2	..	197	2	21	32	5	30	16	4	7	1	2	1	1	..	122
1846.....	13	39	22	13	46	41	33	7	4	3	..	2	2	225	....	20	18	6	14	10	5	3	2	1	1	1	..	81
1847.....	29	46	22	10	49	64	37	19	5	2	..	1	..	284	19	31	25	9	24	19	10	6	4	..	..	1	..	148
1848.....	26	58	72	25	70	85	37	14	6	2	..	2	..	397	3	49	60	14	14	18	3	3	2	2	..	..	..	168
Total..	154	194	150	63	241	254	151	59	25	7	..	7	2	1,297	24	121	135	37	95	73	24	21	9	5	2	3	..	549

YEARS.	BLACK MALES.														BLACK FEMALES.														Total of all classes.
	Unknown.	Under 1 yr.	1 under 10.	10 under 20.	20 under 30.	30 under 40.	40 under 50.	50 under 60.	60 under 70.	70 under 80.	80 under 90.	90 under 100.	Over 100.	Total black males.	Unknown.	Under 1 yr.	1 under 10.	10 under 20.	20 under 30.	35 under 40.	40 under 50.	50 under 60.	60 under 70.	70 under 80.	80 under 90.	90 under 100.	Over 100.	Total black females.	
1844.....	8	..	15	2	2	5	2	5	..	..	..	..	..	39	7	..	5	2	1	3	2	3	..	..	..	..	..	23	286
1845.....	3	26	6	2	12	10	3	2	1	3	..	3	..	71	1	14	7	5	9	6	1	3	1	..	..	2	..	49	439
1846.....	1	28	19	6	8	7	4	8	6	..	2	..	..	89	23	3	6	2	10	2	4	3	5	1	2	..	..	61	456
1847.....	12	17	18	8	9	9	11	6	5	4	1	2	..	102	1	26	11	7	3	4	6	2	2	2	..	..	..	64	598
1848.....	23	25	20	41	14	14	9	5	8	4	2	3	1	169	6	25	22	9	5	12	8	8	2	1	..	..	..	98	832
Total..	47	96	78	59	45	45	29	26	20	11	5	8	1	470	38	68	51	25	28	27	21	19	10	4	2	2	..	295	2,611

In New Orleans the Board of Health reported for the year preceding June, 1850, 7,265 deaths against 3,641 reported in the census. The following table will show the ages and color of those dying in 1849 and 1850 at New Orleans. Lafayette has since been incorporated with the city. The deaths in 1850 were regularly returned only in part. About 1,000 were mentioned by the marshal without any particulars, and were not therefore included in the mortality table.

Ages of Persons Dying in New Orlenas and Lafayette.

AGE.	1849.	1850.	1849 and 1850.				
	Total.	Total.	Total.	Whites.	Colored.	Males.	Females.
Under 1 month..	618	530	1,148	899	249	702	446
1 month and under 1 year	614	803	1,417	1,081	336	769	648
1 year " 5 years	903	917	1,820	1,427	393	954	866
5 years " 10 "	342	249	591	468	123	325	266
10 " " 15 "	530	126	935	723	212	547	388
15 " " 20 "		279					
20 " " 30 "	1,991	1,342	3,333	2,990	343	2,345	988
30 " " 40 "	1,603	1,192	2,795	2,529	266	2,035	760
40 " " 50 "	833	615	1,448	1,258	190	1,054	394
50 " " 60 "	382	321	703	561	142	462	241
60 " " 70 "	192	191	383	283	100	238	145
70 " " 80 "	101	100	201	135	66	91	110
80 " " 90 "	48	44	92	42	50	35	57
90 " " 100 "	20	19	39	9	30	8	31
Over 100........................	3	1	4	....	4	1	3
Specified	8,180	6,728	14,909	12,405	2,504	9,566	5,343
Age unknown—children & adults	*2,481	*1,358					
Total.........................	10,661	8,086					

* Including those of whom the sex and color is also unknown.

A large part of the mortality of New Orleans is among those who are born in other States or in foreign countries. This may be seen, in some measure, by the report of the Charity Hospital, which shows in 1850, the admission of only 264 Louisianians out of a total of 18,476 admissions! 395 were from New York, 110 from Massachusetts, and among the others, every State in the Union is represented. The total born in the United States was but 1,774; in foreign countries, 16,598. Of the foreigners, 11,132 were Irish; about 2,500

of the living population are separated into those born in the county or town of their residence or decease and those born in other parts of the State.

Proposed Tabular Form for Publishing the Mortality Statistics of the Census.

		Whites.									Free Colored		Slaves.		Married.		Place of Birth.	Occupation.	Period of Sickness.	Seasons
		Native divided as males and females.								Foreign.	Black	Mulatto.	Black	Mulatto.	White.	Free Col'd				
Disease or cause of death.	Total number of deaths.	Birth.	Under 1 year.	1 and under 5.	5 and under 20.	20 and under 50.	50 and under 100.	100 and upwards.	Total.	Same subdivisions of age and sex as native.	Same subdivisions as Whites.	Same subdivisions as Whites.	Same subdivisions as Whites.	Same subdivisions as Whites.	Subdivided by ages of under 20, 20 to 30, 30 to 40, 40 to 50, 50 to 70, and 70 and upwards.	Same subdivisions as Whites.	Subdivided by columns for State, for New England, Middle, Southern, S. W. and N. W. States, and for England, Ireland, Scotland, Germany and other foreign countries.	Subdivided by columns for Mechanical, Agricultural, Commercial, Laborious, Educational Pursuits, &c.; each divided into ages, as 15 to 20, 20 to 30, &c.	Subdivided by columns for under 1 week, 1 week to 1 month, 1 month to 3 months and over 3 months.	Subdivided by columns for Spring, Summer, Autumn and Winter.

The ages and other facts relating to the parents on both sides of the children born, distinguishing black from mulatto, the ages, &c. of persons married, male and female, the ages and sex, &c. of those who have died, are all very important considerations in the view of vital statisticians. Most of these could be ascertained with some labor, from the Census returns, but no attempt was made to do so when the population results were being aggregated in the

Germans, and 852 French. The reports of the hospital since 1839 show the following figures. It will be seen that in 1848, 11,650 out of 11,945, were persons who had not been three years in New Orleans. The table was prepared by Dr. Simonds.

Abstract of the Annual Reports of the Charity Hospital of New Orleans, for the years 1839 *to* 1850, *inclusive.*

YEARS.	Admitted.	Blacks.	Resident over three years in the State.	Discharged.	Died.	Total discharges and deaths.	Mortality, per cent.
1839	4,833	52	660	3,611	955	4,566	20.90
1840	5,041	......	1,231	4,370	619	4,989	12.40
1841	4,380	82	1,018	3,093	1,156	4,249	27.20
1842	4,404	70	791	3,516	761	4,277	17.80
1843	5,013	78	1,146	3,672	1,041	4,713	22.00
1844	5,846	54	966	5,059	713	5,772	12.30
1845	6,136	144	1,192	5,446	563	6,009	9.30
1846	8,044	110	2,034	7,074	855	7,929	10.80
1847	11,890	91	843	9,369	2,037	11,406	17.80
1848	11,945	15	295	10,010	1,897	11,907	15.90
1849	15,558	71	....	12,133	2,745	14,878	18.40
1850	18,476	53	....	15,989	1,884	17,873	9.98
12 years	101,566	......	....	83,342	15,226	98,568	15.44

Dr. Simonds makes the following calculation of the proportion of deaths to 100 persons. In Boston, for 39 years, from 1811 to 1849, 2.457 per cent.; in Lowell, for 13 years, from 1836 to 1848, 2.119 per cent.; in New York, for 33 years, from 1807 to 1840, 2.551 per cent.; in Baltimore, for 14 years, from 1836 to 1849, 2.491 per cent.; in Charleston, for 27 years, from 1822 to 1848, 2.482 per cent. for the whites, 2.645 per cent. for the blacks, and 2.579 for all classes; in Savannah, for 8 years, from 1840 to 1847, 4.161 per cent.; in New Orleans, for four and one-half years, from 1846 to 1850, 8.101 per cent.; in Massachusetts, in 1847 and 1848, 1.59 per cent.; in twelve counties of England, 1.93 per cent.; in twenty-six cities of England, 2.72 per cent.; in London the mean rate is 2.53 per cent.; in Liverpool the mean rate is 3.34 per cent., and in 1850 it was 2.73 per cent.; in Manchester, the mean rate is 3.48 per cent. The estimate for Savannah is calculated upon a small number of years, and must be too high. The same may be said of New Orleans, but deducting cholera, it would be 5.719.

Dr. Barton, in Fenner's "*Southern Medical Statistics*," Vol. I. p. 85, shows that the proportion dying from all pulmonary diseases is, in Philadelphia, 28.57 per cent.; in New York, 28.08 per cent.; in Havana, 25.07 per cent.; in Boston, 23.97 per cent.; in Baltimore, 23.33 per cent.; in Charleston, 22.73 per cent.; in the city of Mexico, 16.76 per cent.; in Norfolk, Va., 12.78 per cent.; and in New Orleans, 13.87 per cent.

Another calculation has lately been made of the mortality of the several cities named, from reports running back five to thirty years, showing the following results. The figures for New Orleans are too high, as they include years of large mortality. Exclusively of the transient and foreign population, New Orleans will compare favorably with any Western city. In Charleston, the deaths are estimated as one to 48; in Boston, as one to 46; in Philadelphia, one to 45; in Baltimore, one to 43; in Cincinnati, one to 35; in New York, one to 34; in New Orleans one to 19.

In Memphis in 1851, there were 717 deaths; in 1852, 705; in 1853, 412. The population in 1853 was 12,000.

early history of the office, and it would now be a work of great labor and expense. If the mortality tables are published hereafter, many results of this kind will be incorporated in them.

TABLE CXI.—*Births, Marriages and Deaths of the White and Free Colored, and their Ratios to the total Population in* 1850.

States, &c.	Births.	Ratio per cent.	Married.	Ratio per cent.	Deaths.	Ratio per cent.	States, &c.	Births.	Ratio per cent.	Married.	Ratio per cent.	Deaths.	Ratio per cent.
Alabama	12,265	2.86	3,940	0.92	4,411	1.03	New Jersey	13,556	2.77	3,719	0.76	6,454	1.32
Arkansas	5,483	3.36	2,112	1.30	2,160	1.33	New York	76,337	2.46	31,465	1.02	45.584	1.47
California	273	0.29	......	....	905	0.98	North Carolina	16,648	2.87	5,275	0.91	6,028	1.04
Columbia, Dist. of	1,248	2.60	373	0.78	789	1.64	Ohio	56,884	2.87	22,328	1.13	28,949	1.46
Connecticut	7,646	2.06	3,213	0.87	5,781	1.56	Pennsylvania	64,331	2.78	19,858	0.86	28,551	1.23
Delaware	2,495	2.80	564	0.63	1,188	1.33	Rhode Island	3,610	2.45	1,327	0.83	2,241	1.52
Florida	1,322	2.75	431	0.89	491	1.02	South Carolina	6,607	2.33	2,005	0.71	2,879	1.01
Georgia	15,239	2.90	4,977	0.95	4.592	0.88	Tennessee	23,090	3.02	7,872	1.03	7,825	1.03
Illinois	26,681	3.13	9,183	1.08	11,619	1.36	Texas	4,765	3.09	2,232	1.45	2,219	1.44
Indiana	32,296	3.27	12,423	1.26	12,808	1.29	Vermont	6,594	2.10	2,653	0.84	3,129	1.00
Iowa	6,099	3.17	1,824	0.95	2,044	1.06	Virginia	25,153	2.65	8,163	0.86	10,608	1.12
Kentucky	23,805	3.09	8,091	1.05	10,840	1.40	Wisconsin	10,424	3.41	3,015	0.99	2,903	0.95
Louisiana	7,292	2.67	2,890	1.06	6,083	2.23	Territories. Minnesota	168	2.77	39	0.64	30	0.49
Maine	13,995	2.40	4,886	0.84	7,582	1.30	Territories. N. Mexico	1,233	2.00	916	1.49	1,157	1.88
Maryland	14,036	2.85	3,703	0.75	8,109	1.65	Territories. Oregon	310	2.33	168	1.26	47	0.35
Massachusetts	23,192	2.33	10,347	1.04	19,404	1.95	Territories. Utah	432	3.80	404	3.56	239	2.11
Michigan	10,898	2.74	4,257	1.07	4,515	1.14							
Mississippi	8,687	2.93	2,774	0.93	3,374	1.14							
Missouri	19,632	3.30	6,989	1.17	10,937	1.60							
New Hampshire	6,111	1.92	2,613	0.82	4,231	1.33	Total	548,837	2.75	197,029	0.99	270,706	1.35

As an evidence of the extraordinary number of marriages of natives of different States, which are shown by the census, it may be stated that in one town in Mississippi, taken at random, out of 548 families the male and female of 225 were from different States, domestic or foreign, 61 were natives of non-slaveholding States intermarried with those of slaveholding, and 58 of natives with foreigners.

TABLE CXII.—*Marriages of White Persons—Ages and Nativity of the Parties.*

States.	Counties.	Under 20.				20 and under 30.				30 and under 40.				40 and under 60.				60 and upwards.				Totals.				Aggregate.
		Native. M.	Foreign. M.	Native. F.	Foreign. F.	Native. M.	Foreign. M.	Native. F.	Foreign. F.	Native. M.	Foreign. M.	Native. F	Foreign. F.	Native. M.	Foreign. M.	Native. F.	Foreign. F.	Native. M.	Foreign. M.	Native. F.	Foreign. F.	Native. M.	Foreign. M.	Native. F.	Foreign. F.	
Kentucky	Franklin	1	..	8	..	17	1	16	1	11	..	3	..	1	..	1	..	1	..	..	..	31	1	28	1	61
Louisiana	Pt. Coupee, Ouachita, Rapides, Plaquemine, E. Feliciana	4	1	19	1	24	13	17	2	14	1	6	..	10	4	3	1	..	..	..	..	52	19	45	4	120
Michigan	Allegan, Barry, Branch, Berrien	..	..	63	5	119	20	87	14	27	16	7	5	13	..	7	1	..	..	..	..	159	36	164	25	384
Ohio	Erie	1	..	29	4	53	19	41	25	12	11	2	..	50	2	1	1	..	..	..	2	116	32	73	32	253
Pennsylvania	Potter and Pike	3	..	29	..	51	3	28	3	6	1	6	..	2	..	1	..	..	..	..	..	62	4	64	3	133
Rhode Island	Kent, Bristol, & Washington	5	..	46	6	114	16	97	13	14	..	11	..	18	1	9	2	..	..	..	..	151	17	163	21	352
S. Carolina	Abbeville, Anderson, Barnwell, Beaufort, Charleston, Marion, Marlboro'	18	..	146	3	273	17	189	22	37	10	20	..	21	2	5	1	1	..	..	..	350	29	360	26	765

6. *Deaf and Dumb, Blind, Insane and Idiotic.*—The aggregate number of persons embraced within all of these classes, by the Census of 1850, was 50,994, being one for every 460 persons, or one deaf and dumb for every 2,365, and one blind for every 2,368. Some years ago, M. Quetelet computed the proportion of deaf and dumb for Belgium, at one in 2,226; in Great Britain, at one in 1,539; in Italy at one in 1,539; and in Europe generally at one in 1,474. For the blind, his proportions were, in Belgium, one in 998; in Prussia, one in 800; in France, one in 1,600; in Saxony, one in 1,666; and in Europe generally, one in 1,000.*

* In Belgium, in 1835, there were 1,746 deaf and dumb, of whom 963 were males, and 783 females. There were 3,892 Blind, of whom 2,462 were males, and 1,430 females. The proportion of Deaf and Dumb, to the total population was as 1 to 2,226. The proportion of Blind to the total population was as 1 to 998. Of the 1,746 Deaf and Dumb, 1,376 were afflicted from birth, and 370 by disease or accident; 373 were inhabitants of cities, and 1,373 of rural districts. Of the number of 3,892 Blind, 256 had been blind from birth, 908 were military men, afflicted with an opthalmia peculiar to their profession, and 2,728 blind from other causes. 1,196 were from cities, and 2,696 from rural districts.

TABLE CXIII.—*Aggregates of Deaf and Dumb, Blind, Insane and Idiotic,* 1850.*

STATES AND TERRITORIES.	Deaf and dumb.	Blind.	Insane.	Idiotic.	Aggregate.	STATES AND TERRITORIES.	Deaf and dumb.	Blind.	Insane.	Idiotic.	Aggregate.
Alabama	210	296	233	476	1,215	New Hampshire	162	134	378	351	1,025
Arkansas	84	92	63	115	354	New Jersey	189	207	379	419	1,194
California	7	1	2	7	17	New York	1,263	1,181	2,521	1,665	6,630
Columbia, District of	19	24	23	13	79	North Carolina	471	561	510	794	2,336
Connecticut	404	186	470	287	1,347	Ohio	915	642	1,317	1,361	4,235
Delaware	54	39	68	92	253	Pennsylvania	1,145	969	1,914	1,467	5,495
Florida	24	30	11	36	101	Rhode Island	65	67	217	114	463
Georgia	266	357	324	664	1,611	South Carolina	165	298	249	348	1,060
Illinois	356	264	238	363	1,221	Tennessee	377	474	407	846	2,104
Indiana	537	353	563	938	2,391	Texas	59	73	37	104	273
Iowa	59	50	42	94	245	Vermont	148	140	560	299	1,147
Kentucky	563	552	527	907	2,549	Virginia	642	881	970	1,182	3,675
Louisiana	117	214	200	174	705	Wisconsin	69	63	54	94	280
Maine	266	198	561	577	1,602	Territories: Minnesota	......	......	1	1	2
Maryland	261	323	546	391	1,521	Territories: New Mexico	34	98	11	44	187
Massachusetts	358	463	1,680	791	3,292	Territories: Oregon	......	......	5	4	9
Michigan	125	125	133	189	572	Territories: Utah	......	2	5	1	8
Mississippi	107	205	129	222	663						
Missouri	282	232	262	357	1,133	Total	9,803	9,794	15,610	15,787	50,994

By the annexed table, the nativities of the deaf and dumb will be seen, showing that the foreign born, who constitute less than an eighth of the white and free colored, furnish less than one-eleventh of the whole number. Such persons are not likely to be found among the immigrating class.

TABLE CXIV.—*Nativities of Deaf and Dumb, Blind, Insane and Idiotic White and Free Colored,* 1850.

States and Territories.	Deaf and Dumb.†			Blind.‡			Insane.				Idiotic.				Aggregate.
	Born in State.	Out of State and in U. S.	Foreign born.	Born in State.	Out of State and in U. S.	Foreign born.	Born in State.	Out of State and in U. S.	Foreign born.	Unknown.	Born in State.	Out of State and in U. S.	Foreign born.	Unknown.	
Alabama	79	69	4	35	119	....	56	132	6	9	161	169	6	7	856
Arkansas	25	54	....	12	63	3	11	45	1	3	30	72	....	3	324
California	2	3	2	1	......	....	1	1	......	....	5	1	1	....	17
Columbia, Dist. of	10	8	1	7	14	2	9	9	3	1	6	6	1	....	77
Connecticut	196	188	18	149	27	4	392	56	19	3	258	15	4	10	1,347
Delaware	46	3	3	39	......	....	51	8	3	6	72	2	4	10	247
Florida	7	6	....	1	12	3	2	7	......	....	13	13	2	....	66
Georgia	165	42	2	113	108	7	176	107	9	4	395	120	1	....	1,249
Illinois	115	142	19	42	161	39	34	169	29	6	129	208	23	3	1,221
Indiana	313	204	14	87	235	25	151	354	43	15	443	439	39	17	2,391
Iowa	9	44	5	4	38	8	......	37	5	....	10	77	7	....	245
Kentucky	395	113	4	181	242	14	345	127	30	2	640	168	4	4	2,271
Louisiana	62	15	8	53	18	20	59	28	61	7	55	35	21	1	444
Maine	253	6	6	158	28	11	473	52	26	10	535	26	12	4	1,602
Maryland	208	14	11	238	9	31	366	65	59	31	290	18	10	5	1,357
Massachusetts	279	47	28	361	58	43	1,147	149	321	63	704	47	32	8	3,292
Michigan	34	78	11	16	96	12	10	97	22	4	48	119	17	5	572
Mississippi	37	42	1	26	85	1	24	75	2	4	59	76	2	1	435
Missouri	127	107	23	43	118	29	44	160	44	3	129	177	17	2	1,033

* Dr. Peet, in the Report of the New York Deaf and Dumb Asylum, argues that the number returned by the census is short of the fact from the unwillingness often of families to confess. Idiots are frequently in popular use called dumb. Many reported deaf, he thinks, are also dumb, and such of them as are under 20 years of age, would in general be subjects for an asylum. The State Census of Alabama for 1850, gives 557 insane of the whites, showing that the idiotic are confounded with them. In fact the distinction in the United States Census between the two classes cannot be considered reliable, and it would be better to class them together as in 1840. The State Census of 1853 of Illinois, gives the names of 500 mutes.

† Of the Deaf and Dumb, there were returned as "nativity unknown," one person in each of the States of Arkansas, Iowa, Maine, South Carolina and Wisconsin; two persons in each of the States of Connecticut, Maryland, Michigan and Tennessee; four persons in Massachusetts; five persons in New York; six persons each in Indiana, Missouri and Ohio, and eighty persons in the State of Illinois.

‡ Of the Blind, the nativity was unknown of one person in each of the States of Arkansas, Louisiana, Maine, Massachusetts, Michigan, Pennsylvania, South Carolina, Texas, and Wisconsin; of two persons each in Kentucky, North Carolina and Virginia; of three persons in Vermont; of four persons each in Alabama, Missouri, Ohio and Tennessee; of six persons each in Connecticut and Indiana; of eight in New York and twenty-two in Illinois.

TABLE CXIV.—*Continued.*

States and Territories.	Deaf and Dumb.			Blind.			Insane.				Idiotic.				
	Born in State.	Out of State and in U. S.	Foreign born.	Born in State.	Out of State and in U. S.	Foreign born.	Born in State.	Out of State and in U. S.	Foreign born.	Unknown.	Born in State.	Out of State and in U. S.	Foreign born.	Unknown.	Aggregate.
New Hampshire..	134	26	2	108	19	7	324	42	11	1	332	18	1	....	1,025
New Jersey	170	12	7	167	24	16	322	23	32	2	382	24	13	....	1,194
New York........	1,002	120	136	666	296	211	1,388	390	642	101	1,328	164	161	12	6,630
North Carolina....	383	9	4	367	27	10	451	16	7	3	617	23	2	1	1,922
Ohio	587	263	59	222	344	72	489	568	218	42	853	407	84	17	4,235
Pennsylvania	946	111	88	667	160	141	1,317	227	355	15	1,288	84	91	4	5,495
Rhode Island	54	6	5	55	8	4	189	20	7	1	110	3	1	....	463
South Carolina ...	128	5	2	122	22	19	179	32	17	....	247	5	2	....	782
Tennessee........	264	69	1	168	217	3	219	154	2	10	559	196	2	4	1,874
Texas............	14	33	2	17	39	5	4	28	4	1	16	72	4	1	241
Vermont	114	27	7	81	45	11	271	260	28	1	246	46	5	2	1,147
Virginia	527	23	3	518	49	13	841	50	20	....	915	59	7	....	3,027
Wisconsin	7	40	21	4	30	28	2	30	21	1	3	69	22	....	280
Territ's. Minnesota....	......	......	....	......	......	....	......	1	......	....	1	......	....	....	2
Territ's. N. Mexico....	34	......	....	98	......	....	11	......	......	....	44	......	....	....	187
Territ's. Oregon	......	......	....	......	......	....	......	4	1	....	......	3	1	....	9
Territ's. Utah	......	......	....	......	2	....	......	4	1	....	......	......	1	....	8
Total	6,726	1,929	497	4,826	2,713	792	9,358	3,527	2,049	349	10,923	2,961	600	121	47,567

TABLE CXV.—*Ratio of White and Colored Deaf and Dumb, Blind, Idiotic and Insane to total White and Colored Population.*

States and Territories.	Ratio of White Deaf and Dumb and Blind to total White.			Ratio of Colored Deaf and Dumb and Blind to total Colored.			Ratio of white insane and idiotic to total white.		Ratio of colored insane and idiotic to total colored.		Mean of 1830, 1840 and 1850.	
	1830.	1840.	1850.	1830.	1840.	1850.	1840.	1850.	1840.	1850.	All classes white to tot'l white	All classes colored to total col'd
	as 1 to	as 1 to	as 1 to	as 1 to	as 1 to	as 1 to	as 1 to	as 1 to	as 1 to	as 1 to	as 1 to	as 1 to
Alabama	1,212	1,171	1,387	1,678	1,715	1,734	1,445	784	2,045	2,091	1,200	1,853
Arkansas	1,426	1,169	1,026	786	2,040	2,650	1,715	995	971	3,180	1,266	1,925
California	......	......	11,454	......	......	......	......	10,182	......	......	10,818	....
Columbia, District of..	1,198	2,190	1,186	1,227	1,004	1,250	2,189	1,649	1,865	1,057	1,682	1,281
Connecticut	600	667	635	620	388	427	606	486	185	767	599	477
Delaware	1,086	944	975	957	750	1,018	1,126	583	697	536	943	792
Florida	2,298	1,214	1,686	743	2,211	1,548	2,794	1,276	2,211	4,024	1,854	2,148
Georgia	1,006	1,239	1,207	1,319	1,319	2,014	1,387	645	2,117	2,149	1,097	1,760
Illinois	1,535	1,959	1,380	596	115	777	2,217	1,417	49	1,359	1,702	580
Indiana	1,501	1,571	1,118	726	210	704	1,394	659	96	563	1,249	460
Iowa................	......	3,301	1,760	......	27	......	6,132	1,410	47	......	3,151	37
Kentucky	1,097	928	822	1,319	869	1,169	742	588	1,053	1,625	835	1,207
Louisiana	1,052	2,005	1,659	1,288	3,659	1,482	2,881	1,022	4,310	2,115	1,723	2,571
Maine................	1,175	1,244	1,256	199	58	1,356	932	514	14	195	1,025	364
Maryland.............	1,032	928	1,014	708	965	959	822	555	1,077	892	869	920
Massachusetts	1,272	1,254	1,212	503	222	1,133	605	403	137	378	949	474
Michigan	1,567	3,777	1,586	......	117	2,583	5,425	1,242	27	646	2,720	843
Mississippi	1,304	1,673	1,304	1,539	2,026	2,568	1,544	1,227	2,397	2,825	1,459	2,271
Missouri	2,125	1,557	1,084	1,425	866	1,500	1,603	1,031	879	2,001	1,524	1,354
New Hampshire......	1,119	850	1,080	67	44	260	584	436	28	520	814	184
New Jersey	728	1,212	1,286	555	529	707	953	599	297	1,093	956	636
New York............	1,263	1,242	1,274	360	314	962	1,108	738	258	892	1,124	557
North Carolina	1,043	962	720	1,086	1,114	1,196	836	511	1,215	1,423	814	1,207
Ohio	1,410	1,613	1,274	638	262	1,149	1,257	738	105	815	1,259	594
Pennsylvania	1,062	1,268	1,090	572	326	1,247	860	685	256	638	993	608
Rhode Island	836	770	1,169	298	810	408	520	449	249	334	749	420
South Carolina........	934	949	967	1,577	1,433	2,200	689	580	2,447	3,177	824	2,167
Tennessee	1,539	1,173	1,056	2,248	1,136	1,835	916	666	1,241	2,102	1,070	1,713
Texas	......	......	1,400	......	......	2,662	......	1,185	......	5,324	1,292	3,993
Vermont	1,371	1,233	1,095	176	182	359	732	366	56	359	959	226
Virginia	897	842	863	910	809	1,084	706	509	1,299	1,327	763	1,085
Wisconsin	......	2,196	2,308	......	......	......	3,844	2,087	65	317	2,609	191
Territories. Minnesota......	......	......	......	......	......	......	......	3,019	......	......	3,019	....
Territories. N. Mexico......	......	......	466	......	......	......	......	1,118	......	......	792	....
Territories. Oregon.........	......	......	......	......	......	......	......	1,454	......	......	1,454	....
Territories. Utah	......	......	5,665	......	......	......	......	1,888	......	......	3,776	....
Non Slavehold'g States	1,149	1,300	1,208	452	287	919	982	672	163	709	1,062	506
Slaveholding States...	1,092	1,063	1,022	1,151	1,187	1,517	944	663	1,555	1,821	957	1,446

The proportions in the several States and Territories, have been calculated in table CXV. For all classes the mean of the last three Census' shows one affected person to every 957 whites in the slaveholding States, and one to 1,060 in the other States; one to every 1,444 colored in the slaveholding States, and one to 503 colored in the non-slaveholding.*

7. *Nativities.*—As before remarked, 2,240,535 white and 4,067 free colored persons are given by the census of 1850 as of foreign birth, and 17,279,875 whites and 428,424 free colored as of native birth. Of the native population, 13,103,650 still reside in, and 4,176,225 reside out of the States in which they were born. The English census is more complete, and separates even those residing in or out of their native *counties.* Connecticut, South Carolina and Vermont have more than half as many native born residing in other States, as remain at home. North Carolina, Kentucky, Tennessee and Virginia, have nearly one-half; Massachusetts, Maryland and New Jersey, about one-third. The largest proportion of foreigners is in Wisconsin and Minnesota being about one-third of the total population. The least proportion is in North Carolina, being one to 229 native born; in South Carolina one to 32; Arkansas one to 98; and in Mississippi, one to 62.

TABLE CXVI.—*Nativities of the White and Free Colored Population.*

States and Territories.	Born in the State and now residing in the State.	Born in the State and now residing out of the State.	Total number born in the State, now residing in the State and in other States.	Excess received from other States.	Excess given to other States.	Number born in other States now residing in the State.	Total native population.	Native and foreign.	Total, including unknown.
Alabama	237,542	83,388	320,930	99,102	....	182,490	420,032	427,670	428,779
Arkansas	63,206	10,916	74,122	86,223	....	97,139	160,345	161,973	162,797
California	6,602	96	6,698	62,912	....	63,008	69,610	91,968	92,597
Columbia, Dist of	24,967	7,269	32,236	10,720	....	17,989	42,956	47,923	48,000
Connecticut	292,653	154,891	447,544	....	115,019	39,872	332,525	369,998	370,792
Delaware	72,351	31,965	104,316	....	20,348	11,617	83,968	89,179	89,242
Florida	20,563	4,734	25,297	20,023	....	24,757	45,320	48,077	48,135
Georgia	402,666	122,954	525,620	....	7,541	115,413	518,079	523,986	524,503
Illinois	343,618	45,889	389,507	347,424	....	393,313	736,931	847,524	851,470
Indiana	541,079	92,038	633,117	298,275	....	390,313	931,392	985,818	988,416
Iowa	50,380	6,358	56,738	113,882	....	120,240	170,620	191,852	192,214
Kentucky	601,764	257,643	859,407	....	118,526	139,117	740,881	770,070	771,424
Louisiana	145,474	14,779	160,253	45,668	....	60,447	205,921	272,334	272,953
Maine	517,117	67,193	584,310	....	33,181	34,012	551,129	582,585	583,169
Maryland	400,594	127,799	528,393	....	89,477	38,322	438,916	492,204	492,666
Massachusetts	695,236	199,582	894,818	....	64,752	134,830	830,066	990,975	994,514
Michigan	140,648	12,409	153,057	188,534	....	200,943	341,591	396,443	397,654
Mississippi	140,885	31,588	172,473	118,641	....	150,229	291,114	296,072	296,648
Missouri	277,604	37,824	315,428	205,398	....	243,222	520,826	593,300	594,622
New Hampshire	261,591	109,878	371,469	....	67,242	42,636	304,227	317,798	317,976
New Jersey	385,429	133,381	518,810	....	88,369	45,012	430,441	488,805	489,319
New York	2,151,196	547,218	2,698,414	....	259,118	288,100	2,439,296	3,091,097	3,097,394
North Carolina	556,248	283,077	839,325	....	261,575	21,502	577,750	580,274	580,491
Ohio	1,219,432	295,453	1,514,885	242,671	....	538,124	1,757,556	1,976,068	1,980,329
Pennsylvania	1,844,672	422,055	2,266,727	....	252,108	169,947	2,014,619	2,309,490	2,311,786
Rhode Island	102,641	43,300	145,941	....	21,642	21,658	124,299	147,410	147,545
South Carolina	262,160	186,479	448,639	....	173,826	12,653	274,813	283,475	283,523
Tennessee	585,084	241,606	826,690	....	71,035	170,571	755,655	761,395	763,258
Texas	49,160	2,481	51,641	85,412	....	87,893	137,053	153,827	154,431
Vermont	232,086	145,655	377,741	....	96,775	48,880	280,966	313,797	314,120
Virginia	872,923	388,059	1,260,982	....	334,828	53,231	926,154	948,548	949,133
Wisconsin	63,015	3,775	66,790	131,122	....	134,897	197,912	304,607	305,391
Territories: Minnesota	1,334	949	65,260	19,355	......	2,673	4,007	6,055	6,077
Territories: N. Mexico	58,421					840	59,261	61,324	61,547
Territories: Oregon	3,175					8,817	11,992	13,151	13,294
Territories: Utah	1,381					7,974	9,355	11,345	11,354

The total number of those residing in the States of their birth is 13,624,897; of those residing out of the States of their birth 4,112,681, and the total of those born and resident in the United States is 17,737,578. The total native and foreign population is 19,948,417; the total unknown 39,146; and the total including unknown 19,987,563, excluding slaves.

Entering more into detail and giving the specific places of birth for each of the above classes of population, some most interesting facts will be obtained. The tables which are adopted, do not in this case separate the white and free colored, and they are the results of a first examination. If the ages of persons born in and those born out of the State of residence were ascertained, some useful facts bearing upon the value and probability of life would result.

* Of persons that are at the same time deaf, dumb and blind, there is one each in Massachusetts, Georgia, Florida and Tennessee; two in Ohio, and four in Virginia. Of those deaf and blind there is one each in South Carolina, Georgia and Tennessee; two each in Massachusetts, North Carolina and Florida, and six in Virginia. Of those deaf and idiotic there is one in Virginia and two in Maryland. Of those deaf, dumb and

TABLE CXVII.—*Ratio to Total Native Population of the United States.*

SECTIONS.	Living in the State where born.	Per cent.	Living in the Eastern Section.	Per cent.	Living in the Middle.	Per cent.	Living in the Southern.	Per cent.	Living in the South-Western.	Per cent.	Living in the North-Western and Territories.	Per cent.
Eastern	2,101,324	10.51	2,367,932	11.85	241,596	1.21	6,845	.03	9,376	.05	196,074	.98
Middle	4,879,209	24.41	48,781	.24	5,155,698	25.79	40,857	.20	27,146	.13	876,414	4.39
Southern	2,114,560	10.58	2,954	.02	31,101	.16	2,266,088	11.34	425,335	2.13	374,385	1.87
South-Western	1,221,351	6.11	718	.....	2,542	.01	19,086	.10	1,441,220	7.21	142,543	.71
North-Western and Territories	3,308,453	16.55	2,827	.01	19,259	.10	9,240	.05	67,043	.34	3,962,518	19.83

TABLE CXVIII.—*Nativities of the Population of Great Britain, Ireland and the Islands in the British Seas, according to the Census enumeration of* 1841.

NATIVITIES.	England.		Wales.		Scotland.		Ireland.		Islands. British
	Total population.	Proportion per cent.	Total population.	Proportion per cent.	Total population.	Proportion per cent.	Total population.	Proportion per cent.	Proportion per cent.
In the native counties	12,091,394	80.7	774,393	84.9	1,988,024	75.9	7,735,151	94.6	78.0
Out of native counties	2,370,556	15.9	126,328	13.9	451,245	17.2	405,365	5.0	.2
English and Welsh born	14,461,950	96.6	900,721	98.8	37,796	1.4	21,552	.2	14.5
Scottish born	102,065	.6	1,173	.1	2,439,269	93.2	8,585	.1	.9
Irish born	284,128	1.9	5,276	.6	126,321	4.8	8,140,516	99.6	2.9
Born in British Colonies.	1,076	......	12	......	272	......	....	......	......
Foreign's & British born abroad	38,628	.02	616	.1	2,776	.1	4,471	1.0	2.2
Not specified	107,291	.07	3,805	.4	13,750	.5	....	......	1.2
Total	14,995,138		911,603		2,620,184		8,175,124		

TABLE CXIX.—*Free Persons born in to those born out of each Section of the United States.*

SECTIONS.	Born and residing in	Ratio pr. cent.	Born in and residing out of	Ratio pr. cent.	Total born in
Eastern	2,367,932	83.91	453,891	16.09	2,821,823
Middle	5,155,698	83.85	993,198	16.15	6,148,896
Southern	2,266,088	73.10	833,775	26.90	3,099,863
Southwestern	1,441,220	89.73	164,889	10.27	1,606,109
Northwestern and Territories	3,962,518	97.58	98,369	2.42	4,060,887

Whilst more than one quarter of the free persons born in the Southern States have left those States for other sections, only one-sixth have left the Eastern or Middle States, only one tenth the Southwestern, and only one-fortieth the Northwestern and the Territories.

There are now 726,450 persons living in slaveholding States who are natives of non-slaveholding States, and 232,112 persons living in non-slaveholding States who are natives of slaveholding States. There are 1,866,397 persons of foreign birth in the non-slaveholding States and 378,205 in the slaveholding.

idiotic there is one each in North Carolina and South Carolina; two each in Massachusetts, Georgia and Wisconsin; three each in Tennessee, Illinois and Ohio, and seven in Virginia. There is one deaf, dumb, blind and insane person in Virginia. Of those deaf, dumb, blind and idiotic, there is one each in South Carolina and Virginia, and two in North Carolina. Of those deaf, dumb, blind, and insane there is one each in Massachusetts, Virginia, North Carolina, South Carolina, Illinois and Ohio, and two in Tennessee. Of those deaf and insane, there is one each in Georgia Tennessee and Illinois, and two in Virginia. Of those dumb and blind, there are four in Ohio; three in Virginia; two in Florida, and one in Tennessee. Of those dumb and idiotic, there are fourteen in Virginia; nine in Georgia; seven in North Carolina; five in Tennessee; four in Illinois; three in Ohio; two in Florida; and one each in Massachusetts and South Carolina. Of those dumb and insane, there are three in South Carolina; two each in Illinois and Ohio, and one each in Virginia and North Carolina. Of those blind and insane there are four in Virginia; three in Tennessee; two each in Massachusetts, Maryland, and Ohio, and one in North Carolina. Of those blind and idiotic, there are eight in Virginia; six in Tennessee; five each in Georgia and Ohio; two each in Massachusetts and Maryland, and one each in North Carolina, Florida and Illinois. There is one person in Ohio blind, deaf and insane. There are five persons in Massachusetts and one in Ohio, who are insane and idiotic. In Massachusetts there is one person idiotic, blind and dumb.

TABLE CXX.—*Place of Birth of the White and Free Colored Population of the United States*, 1850.

States and Territories.	Alabama.	Arkansas.	California.	Columbia, District of.	Connecticut.	Delaware.	Florida.	Georgia.	Illinois.	Indiana.	Iowa.	Kentucky.	Louisiana.	Maine.	Maryland.	Massachusetts	Michigan.	Mississippi.	Missouri.	N. Hampshire.	New Jersey.
Alabama	237,542	91	......	66	612	73	1,060	58,997	114	93	7	2,694	628	215	757	654	3	2,852	158	151	271
Arkansas	11,250	63,206	6	49	121	51	38	6,367	3,276	2,128	106	7,428	1,096	80	326	174	17	4,463	5,328	49	117
California	631	350	6,602	86	1,317	305	54	876	2,722	2,077	341	4,690	929	2,700	1,164	4,760	284	772	5,890	904	1,022
Columbia, Dis. of	45	4	......	24,967	135	99	26	67	24	29	1	90	58	87	9,245	331	28	55	28	84	163
Connecticut	74	......	......	50	292,653	58	46	217	80	47	18	41	64	670	265	11,366	89	23	28	795	1,174
Delaware	4	......	......	28	50	72,351	4	14	5	19	......	16	4	24	4,360	113	12	6	8	31	1,186
Florida	2,340	5	......	33	179	9	20,563	11,316	8	14	......	87	146	140	194	235	7	92	7	61	83
Georgia	3,154	25	......	72	712	117	1,103	402,666	41	50	1	458	42	178	703	594	3	184	60	122	331
Illinois	1,335	727	3	226	6,899	1,397	23	1,341	343,618	30,953	1,511	49,588	480	3,693	6,898	9,230	2,158	490	7,228	4,288	6,848
Indiana	395	151	......	227	2,485	2,737	21	761	4,173	541,079	407	68,651	321	976	10,177	2,678	1,817	287	1,006	886	7,837
Iowa......	180	163	3	70	1,090	439	51	119	7,247	19,925	50,380	8,994	133	713	1,888	1,251	521	138	3,807	580	1,199
Kentucky	792	271	......	176	448	507	30	892	1,649	5,898	59	601,764	671	227	6,470	665	59	657	1,467	225	1,249
Louisiana	7,346	803	1	156	469	117	372	5,917	401	414	28	2,968	145,474	816	1,440	1,620	68	10,913	909	247	498
Maine	6	6	2	28	460	36	24	24	38	5	1	14	21	517,117	113	16,535	19	16	11	13,509	134
Maryland.......	51	14	1	1,940	484	4,373	37	74	54	65	5	131	181	456	400,594	1,421	16	143	86	260	1,321
Massachusetts ..	71	10	7	196	15,602	90	32	237	165	60	12	75	179	29,507	744	695,236	122	34	58	39,592	778
Michigan	19	25	3	45	6,751	368	12	68	496	2,003	59	402	30	1,117	537	8,167	140,648	34	92	2,744	5,572
Mississippi	34,047	456	1	73	242	67	629	17,506	311	413	7	3,948	2,557	139	791	339	10	140,885	303	100	221
Missouri	2,067	2,120	4	238	742	518	67	1,254	10,917	12,752	1,366	69,694	746	311	4,253	1,103	295	638	277,604	304	885
New Hampshire	13	8	1	14	1,105	10	1	16	31	20	4	11	9	9,635	34	18,495	48	9	12	261,591	49
New Jersey.....	36	2	3	82	2,105	1,384	17	87	61	61	7	64	83	287	1,400	1,494	66	43	28	301	385,429
New York......	184	20	7	538	66,101	899	135	510	605	415	70	369	563	4,509	3,953	55,773	1,921	164	173	14,519	35,319
North Carolina..	131	1	......	28	272	96	54	844	23	67	3	141	14	68	635	261	2	57	33	26	174
Ohio	209	141	......	598	22,855	4,715	17	447	1,415	7,377	378	13,829	648	3,314	36,698	18,763	2,238	422	656	4,821	23,532
Pennsylvania ...	87	10	3	767	9,266	12,552	21	176	333	399	70	497	187	1,157	21,013	7,330	224	101	220	1,775	29,117
Rhode Island ...	13	......	......	64	3,976	50	22	68	15	11	9	19	21	768	365	11,888	22	8	13	716	193
South Carolina..	225	9	1	30	228	14	55	1,504	6	11	......	73	30	68	320	407	2	60	3	39	182
Tennessee	6,398	496	......	101	261	95	369	4,863	872	769	30	12,609	261	97	1,554	331	7	2,137	920	64	248
Texas..........	12,040	4,693	......	35	369	61	365	7,639	2,855	1,799	109	5,478	4,472	226	521	414	125	6,545	5,139	97	205
Vermont........	11	2	......	5	4,551	1	6	18	34	15	5	7	12	835	23	15,059	86	5	10	19,609	171
Virginia	92	150	4	1,184	556	542	26	193	126	288	37	2,029	93	271	10,328	1,193	33	78	223	239	11,447
Wisconsin	49	67	......	33	4,125	141	4	495	5,292	2,773	445	1,429	78	3,252	462	6,285	1,900	35	1,012	2,520	1,566
Territories. Minnesota	6	11	1	3	48	3	......	4	168	35	81	71	4	365	31	92	41	....	90	47	115
Territories. N. Mexico	5	17	6	12	10	6	5	9	24	11	3	62	4	12	37	24	8	....	93	6	9
Territories. Oregon ...	20	61	25	15	72	18	4	22	1,023	739	452	730	6	129	73	187	37	8	2,206	44	69
Territories. Utah	62	7	14	1	193	17	4	12	1,285	303	726	256	8	151	27	350	121	119	519	123	96
Total	320,930	74,122	6,698	32,236	447,544	104,316	25,297	525,620	389,507	633,117	56,738	859,407	160,253	584,310	528,393	894,818	153,057	172,473	315,428	371,469	518,810

TABLE CXX.—*Continued.*

States and Territories.	New York.	North Carolina.	Ohio.	Pennsylvania.	R. Island.	South Carolina.	Tennessee.	Texas.	Vermont.	Virginia.	Wisconsin.	Territories.	England.	Scotland.	Wales.	Ireland.	Total Great Britain and Ireland.	Prussia.	Rest of Germany.	Austria.	Holland.
Alabama	1,443	28,521	276	876	74	48,663	22,541	55	155	10,387	3	....	941	584	67	3,639	5,231	45	1,068	33	1
Arkansas	537	8,772	1,051	702	36	4,587	33,807	336	82	4,737	13	9	196	71	11	514	792	24	516	....	2
California	10,160	1,027	5,500	4,506	861	519	3,145	250	1,194	3,407	248	317	3,050	883	182	2,452	6,567	158	2,926	87	63
Columbia, Dis. of	817	100	123	1,164	23	100	58	7	43	4,950	2	3	682	142	20	2,373	3,217	11	1,404	3	4
Connecticut	14,416	95	400	1,055	6,890	116	13	20	1,508	228	23	3	5,091	1,916	111	26,689	33,807	42	1,671	20	19
Delaware	218	18	54	5,067	204	13	4	1	12	139	1	2	952	155	17	3,513	4,637	28	343	....	5
Florida	614	3,537	53	240	66	4,470	112	8	55	643	3	....	300	182	11	878	1,371	17	307	8	8
Georgia	1,203	37,522	46	642	138	52,154	8,211	28	186	7,331	2	....	679	367	13	3,202	4,261	25	947	13	11
Illinois	67,180	13,851	64,219	37,979	1,051	4,162	32,303	63	11,381	24,697	1,095	16	18,628	4,661	572	27,786	51,647	286	38,160	65	220
Indiana	24,310	33,175	120,193	44,245	438	4,069	12,734	44	3,183	41,819	99	11	5,550	1,341	169	12,787	19,847	740	28,584	17	43
Iowa	8,134	2,589	30,713	14,744	256	676	4,274	10	1,645	7,861	692	135	3,785	712	352	4,885	9,734	88	7,152	13	1,108
Kentucky	2,881	14,279	9,985	7,491	226	3,164	23,623	71	277	54,694	11	3	2,805	683	171	9,466	13,125	198	13,607	12	38
Louisiana	5,510	2,923	1,473	2,493	239	4,583	3,352	864	283	3,216	7	1	3,550	1,196	48	24,266	29,060	380	17,507	156	112
Maine	973	27	68	201	410	31	6	9	1,177	94	10	4	1,949	532	60	13,871	16,412	27	290	3	12
Maryland	2,646	225	535	16,076	209	158	39	24	262	7,030	4	1	3,467	1,093	260	19,557	24,377	188	26,936	16	106
Massachusetts	14,483	196	593	1,831	11,414	224	25	10	17,646	796	32	9	16,685	4,469	214	115,917	137,285	98	4,319	10	138
Michigan	133,756	312	14,677	9,452	1,031	81	101	4	11,113	1,504	332	36	10,620	2,361	127	13,430	26,538	190	10,070	21	2,542
Mississippi	952	21,487	594	981	62	27,908	27,439	139	141	8,357	4	5	593	317	10	1,928	2,848	71	1,064	16	8
Missouri	5,040	17,009	12,737	8,291	124	2,919	44,970	248	630	40,777	123	80	5,379	1,049	176	14,734	21,338	697	44,352	71	189
New Hampshire	1,171	10	66	148	364	21	3	2	11,266	48	10	2	1,469	467	11	8,811	10,758	2	147	1	1
New Jersey	20,561	98	372	15,014	264	141	21	6	280	628	15	1	11,377	2,263	166	31,092	44,898	57	10,686	20	357
New York	2,151,196	673	3,743	26,352	13,129	935	116	46	52,599	3,347	360	53	84,820	23,418	7,582	343,111	458,931	2,211	118,398	168	2,917
North Carolina	468	556,248	48	665	59	4,420	2,037	6	27	10,838	4	....	394	1,012	7	567	1,980	19	344	2	4
Ohio	83,979	4,807	1,219,432	200,634	1,959	1.468	1,873	29	14,320	85,762	196	24	25,660	5,232	5,849	51,562	88,303	765	111,257	29	348
Pennsylvania	58,835	409	7,729	1,844,672	1,946	559	158	17	4,532	10,410	45	2	38,048	7,292	8,920	151,723	205,983	413	78,592	49	257
Rhode Island	2,055	76	98	427	102,641	57	4	4	459	191	6	40	4,490	988	12	15,944	21,434	5	230	1	12
South Carolina	884	6,173	23	362	97	262,160	188	1	37	1,621	......	....	921	651	10	4,051	5,633	44	2,180	11	9
Tennessee	1,019	72,027	742	2,146	38	15,197	585,084	100	179	46,631	8	2	706	327	17	2,640	3,690	32	1,168	10	57
Texas	1,589	5,155	947	1,005	56	4,482	17,692	49,160	144	3,580	42	14	1,002	261	17	1,403	2,683	75	8,191	11	14
Vermont	7,218	7	165	158	801	5	6	1	232,086	21	32	1	1,546	1,045	57	15,377	18,025	6	218	....	2
Virginia	2,934	7,343	5,206	6,323	100	381	1,560	7	231	872,923	11	3	2,998	947	173	11,643	15,761	36	5,511	15	65
Wisconsin	68,595	322	11,402	9,571	690	107	449	4	10,157	1,611	63,015	26	18,952	3,527	4,319	21,043	47,841	3,545	34,519	61	1,157
Territ's. Minnesota	488	6	241	227	3	4	21	......	100	59	301	*7	84	39	2	271	396	5	141	1	16
Territ's. N. Mexico	101	13	34	97	1	18	25	46	8	77	1	*56	43	29	1	292	365	14	215	....	2
Territ's. Oregon	618	201	653	337	20	34	402	15	111	469	10	*7	207	106	9	196	518	1	155	....	1
Territ's. Utah	1,430	92	694	553	21	53	294	6	232	99	30	*76	1,056	232	125	106	1,519	6	50	3	......
Total	2,698,414	839,325	1,514,885	2,266,727	145,941	448,639	826,690	51,641	377,741	1,260,982	66,790	949	278,675	70,550	29,868	961,719	1,340,812	10,549	573,225	946	9,848

* These are the persons born out of the particular Territory in which they live, but in the other Territories. There were also in Minnesota 1,334 born in that Territory; in New Mexico 58,421 born in New Mexico; in Oregon 3,175 born in Oregon, and in Utah 1,381 born in Utah.

TABLE CXX.—*Continued.*

States and Territories.	Norway.	Denmark.	Sweden.	Belgium.	Switzerland.	Russia.	France.	Spain.	Portugal.	Italy.
Alabama	3	18	51	4	113	10	503	163	39	90
Arkansas	1	7	1	2	12	6	77	3	3	15
California	124	92	162	12	177	48	1,546	220	109	228
Columbia, Dis. of	......	6	5	14	36	2	80	20	6	74
Connecticut	1	16	13	2	55	5	321	12	74	16
Delaware	......	1	2	1	22	1	73	1	.....	.....
Florida	17	21	33	4	7	2	67	70	17	40
Georgia	6	24	11	41	38	8	177	13	5	33
Illinois	2,415	93	1,123	33	1,635	27	3,396	70	42	43
Indiana	18	10	16	86	724	6	2,279	3	6	6
Iowa	361	19	231	4	175	41	382	1	8	1
Kentucky	18	7	20	27	279	70	1,116	21	5	143
Louisiana	64	288	249	115	723	65	11,552	1,417	157	915
Maine	12	47	55	2	11	2	143	18	58	20
Maryland	10	35	57	5	68	23	507	18	29	82
Massachusetts	69	181	253	36	72	38	805	178	290	196
Michigan	110	13	16	112	118	25	945	10	2	12
Mississippi	8	24	14	3	41	9	440	49	2	121
Missouri	155	55	37	58	984	29	2,138	46	11	124
New Hampshire	2	3	12	.....	9	.....	69	8	8	.....
New Jersey	4	28	34	43	204	22	942	23	16	30
New York	392	429	753	401	1,850	617	12,515	461	194	833
North Carolina	......	6	9	1	3	8	43	4	12	4
Ohio	18	53	55	103	3,291	84	7,375	28	7	174
Pennsylvania	27	97	133	126	914	139	4,083	101	34	172
Rhode Island	25	15	17	2	8	1	80	14	58	25
South Carolina	7	24	29	.....	18	19	274	30	14	59
Tennessee	......	8	8	4	266	9	245	3	2	59
Texas	105	49	48	8	134	10	647	62	5	41
Vermont	8	.....	.....	.....	2	1	40	3	5	7
Virginia	5	15	16	7	83	8	321	29	51	65
Wisconsin	8,651	146	88	45	1,244	71	775	4	4	9
Territ's. Minnesota	7	1	4	1	22	2	29	1	.....	1
Territ's. New Mexico	2	2	1	.....	11	4	26	8	1	1
Territ's. Oregon	1	2	2	11	8	1	45	.....	.....	5
Territ's. Utah	32	2	1	.....	1	1	13	1	.....	1
Total	12,678	1,838	3,559	1,313	13,358	1,414	54,069	3,113	1,274	3,645

States and Territories.	Sardinia.	Greece.	Turkey.	China.	Rest of Asia.	Sandwich Islands.	Africa.	British America.	Mexico.	Central America.	South America.	West Indies.	Other Countries.
Alabama	..	7	1	....	....	3	18	49	39	3	2	28	116
Arkansas	..	..	....	....	....	....	1	41	68	....	....	7	50
California	1	9	....	660	117	319	65	834	6,454	39	877	64	400
Columbia, Dis. of	..	..	....	1	4	....	2	32	9	....	5	15	17
Connecticut	..	1	2	5	16	45	72	970	4	....	35	192	57
Delaware	..	..	....	....	....	....	10	21	3	....	3	25	35
Florida	..	..	....	....	3	....	23	97	6	....	3	599	37
Georgia	..	1	1	....	2	....	13	108	8	....	8	95	58
Illinois	..	4	....	1	2	9	11	10,699	30	....	12	75	495
Indiana	..	..	....	....	4	....	4	1,878	31	....	4	12	108
Iowa	..	1	....	....	2	....	....	1,756	16	....	1	14	124
Kentucky	1	1	....	....	3	....	4	275	42	1	2	41	133
Louisiana	9	23	48	33	17	1	90	499	405	3	15	1,337	1,173
Maine	..	..	4	3	5	1	5	14,181	2	....	31	61	51
Maryland	..	..	11	1	2	2	10	215	8	....	52	279	251
Massachusetts	1	23	14	2	31	89	27	15,862	32	7	84	303	466
Michigan	2	1	2	1	....	2	3	14,008	4	....	5	34	66
Mississippi	..	..	....	....	2	....	6	79	13	1	4	25	110
Missouri	1	..	7	....	3	1	7	1,053	94	....	20	50	954
New Hampshire	..	..	....	....	4	3	3	2,501	5	....	11	17	7
New Jersey	1	4	....	4	10	....	17	581	23	2	27	265	66
New York	..	..	12	34	66	40	80	47,200	83	29	179	1,067	1,941
North Carolina	..	..	....	2	....	....	2	30	2	4	3	37	5
Ohio	15	..	1	3	6	1	7	5,880	26	12	41	86	544
Pennsylvania	..	7	2	1	42	3	40	2,500	42	4	83	666	361
Rhode Island	..	..	1	....	1	8	9	1,024	7	21	4	57	52
South Carolina	..	1	....	1	4	....	9	57	4	....	8	177	50
Tennessee	2	2	....	....	3	....	5	76	12	....	.....	20	59
Texas	..	..	....	....	....	5	4	137	4,459	3	1	22	60
Vermont	..	..	....	....	7	4	....	14,470	......	....	3	6	23
Virginia	..	..	....	3	4	1	3	235	4	1	7	72	76
Wisconsin	1	1	....	....	17	1	1	8,277	9	11	6	20	191
Territ's. Minnesota	..	..	....	....	....	....	....	1,417	......	....	.....	.....	4
Territ's. New Mexico	..	..	....	....	....	....	....	38	1,365	....	1	2	5
Territ's. Oregon	..	..	....	2	....	50	....	293	1	....	6	.....	57
Territ's. Utah	..	..	....	1	....	....	....	338	7	....	.....	2	12
Total	34	86	106	758	377	586	551	147,711	13,317	141	1,543	5,772	8,214

States and Territories.	Total Native.	Total Foreign.	Unknown.	Total White and Free Colored Population.	Ratio per ct. of foreign born to total white and free colored population.
Alabama	420,032	7,638	1,109	428,779	1.78
Arkansas	160,345	1,628	824	162,797	1.00
California	69,610	22,358	629	92,597	24.15
Columbia, Dis. of	42,956	4,967	77	48,000	10.35
Connecticut	332,525	37,473	794	370,792	10.11
Delaware	83,968	5,211	63	89,242	5.84
Florida	45,320	2,757	58	48,135	5.73
Georgia	518,079	5,907	517	524,503	1.13
Illinois	736,931	110,593	3,946	851,470	12.99
Indiana	931,392	54,426	2,598	988,416	5.51
Iowa	170,620	21,232	362	192,214	11.05
Kentucky	740,881	29,189	1,354	771,424	3.78
Louisiana	205,921	66,413	619	272,953	24.33
Maine	551,129	31,456	584	583,169	5.39
Maryland	438,916	53,288	462	492,666	10.82
Massachusetts	830,066	160,909	3,539	994,514	16.18
Michigan	341,591	54,852	1,211	397,654	13.79
Mississippi	291,114	4,958	576	296,648	1.67
Missouri	520,826	72,474	1,322	594,622	12.19
New Hampshire	304,227	13,571	178	317,976	4.27
New Jersey	430,441	58,364	514	489,319	11.93
New York	2,439,296	651,801	6,297	3,097,394	21.04
North Carolina	577,750	2,524	217	580,491	.43
Ohio	1,757,556	218,512	4,261	1,980,329	11.03
Pennsylvania	2,014,619	294,871	2,296	2,311,786	12.75
Rhode Island	124,299	23,111	135	147,545	15.66
South Carolina	274,813	8,662	48	283,523	3.06
Tennessee	755,655	5,740	1,863	763,258	.75
Texas	137,053	16,774	604	154,431	10.86
Vermont	280,966	32,831	323	314,120	10.45
Virginia	926,154	22,394	585	949,133	2.36
Wisconsin	197,912	106,695	784	305,391	34.94
Territ's. Minnesota	4,007	2,048	22	6,077	33.70
Territ's. New Mexico	59,261	2,063	223	61,547	3.35
Territ's. Oregon	11,992	1,159	143	13,294	8.72
Territ's. Utah	9,355	1,990	9	11,354	17.53
Total	17,737,578	2,210,839	39,146	19,987,563	11.06

It appears there were in 1850 within the United States, 961,719 persons born in Ireland; 278,675, in England; 70,550 in Scotland; 29,868 in Wales, making a total for Great Britain and Ireland of 1,340,812, which is considerably more than half of the total foreign born residents of the country. If British America be added (147,711) there will be a total of 1,488,523, which is two-thirds of the total foreign born. From France there are 54,069; from Prussia, 10,549; from the rest of Germany, 573,225; from Austria, 946; from Switzerland, 13,358; from Norway, 12,678; from Holland, 9,848; from Sweden, 3,559; from Spain, 3,113; from Italy, 3,645; from the West Indies, 5,772; from Denmark, 1,838; from Belgium, 1,313; from Russia, 1,414; from Portugal, 1,274; from China, 758; from the Sandwich Islands, 588; from Mexico, 13,317; from South America, 1,543.

The tables of specific places of birth differ from those which were subsequently made out in the office for the whites and free colored separately, (embraced in those chapters, and intended to show the native and foreign born without distinction of State or country) after a careful examination. As both sets of tables are published in this volume, the discrepancy between them can be seen. In examining the names of many millions of persons, at distinct times, and by different persons, such discrepancies are to be expected.

It is probable that the number of foreign born inhabitants of the United States is slightly overrated in the census, and that young children of foreigners though born in the country, are to some extent included. Had the ages of foreigners been aggregated from the returns separately from the native, it would be easy to settle the question as well as to frame some other tables of great interest. When the census of 1850 was taken, there could not have been in the United States more than a certain number of foreign born children under 5 years of age. This number is ascertained by the returns of the State Department, giving the ages of the immigrants. Making deductions for mortality, it could be said approximately how many under 5 years of age survived in 1850, and any considerable difference on the returns would be evidence of error. A partial examination seems to indicate such a disproportion of very young children. Children of foreigners are apt to be regarded as of the nativities of the parents. Families consider themselves, or are considered entirely as German, Irish, &c., though embracing some children actually born in the country. A careless or hasty enumerator would stand in no small danger of committing errors, and even with the most careful, they could not on this account, be easily guarded against. When the statistics of mortality are examined an opportunity will be given of investigating the subject more fully. The returns show of foreign born families having native children the following: Franklin county, Kentucky, 25; Pike and Potter, Pennsylvania, 35; Bristol, Kent and Washington, R. Island, 57; Allegan, Barry, Berrian and Branch, of Michigan, 189; Abbeville, Anderson, Barnwell, Beaufort, Charleston, Marion and Marlborough, S. Carolina, 1,124; E. Feliciana, Ouachita, Point Coupee, Plaquemines, Rapides, Louisiana, 188; Erie, Pennsylvania, 475.

Estimating the survivors in 1850 of the foreigners who had arrived in the United States since the census of 1790 upon the principle of the English life tables, and making the necessary allowance for the less proportion of the old and very young among them, and for re-emigration, etc., their number is stated in the abstract of the census published in 1853, p. 15, at 2,460,000. From this, a deduction is then made of ten per cent., on account of the greater mortality of emigrants and their lower expectation of life, which brings the actual survivors very nearly to the figures of the census. The deduction of ten per cent. seems hardly sufficient, and does not accord with the deductions that are generally made in the reasonings of vital statisticians.* It would be safer to assume 15 per cent. than 10, which would reduce the survivors to a little more than 2,000,000. To this add 50 per cent. for the living descendants of foreigners who have come into the country since 1790, (observing that nearly four-fifths of the number have arrived since 1830, and could not have both children and grand children born in the country, and more than half have arrived since 1840, and must have had comparatively few native born children, it would not be safe to add any more,) and the number of foreigners and their descendants in 1853 is not likely to exceed 3,000,000 or 3,200,000.

Taking two States least affected by immigration, New Hampshire and North Carolina, Dr. Jarvis supposes for argument, that the descendants of the females there in 1800, surviving to 1850, would bear the same ratio to their numbers as the descendants of the foreign females who were there in 1800, &c., viz. that 1,000 females alive in those States in 1810, would have as many descendants alive in 1850 as 1,000 foreign females who were there in 1810, &c. Upon this basis he frames the following table.

* Dr. Jarvis thinks the deduction of 10 per cent. too small. Mr. Meech who made the calculation of 2,460,000, says in a note, January 20th, 1854. "I have lately re-computed the number of survivors of the emigration of 1790 and 1850, with some slight alterations since suggested, but the final number is substantially the same, or upwards of 2,400,000. It may seem too great, but there is certainly no mistake in the calculation, besides the reduction for extra deaths, there are others which would reduce it to the census number, such as returned, &c."

Tables of survivorship, or life tables, are calculated upon the following principle. From an extensive register of births and deaths, let a large number, as 10,000 infants be taken and traced through the whole course of their lives, determining how many are alive at the end of each year. Thus, according to the Carlisle Table of 10,000 infants born at the same epoch, only 8,461 would be living at the end of the first year, 7,779 at the end of the second year, and so on as exhibited in a column styled "number living." The series terminates at 105 years, the limiting age in this case. The column of "annual deaths" exhibits the difference of the numbers in the first column. Of 4,000 persons living at the age of 56, for example, 76 die in the ensuing year.

From the number living is deducted the expectation of life or its average duration after any given age, thus, at the age of 15 the average future life time is 45 years, &c. For purposes of reference the Carlisle Table is inserted entire. There is also a Swedish Table in use, and also one of British annuitants.

TABLE CXXI.—*Descendants living in* 1850 *of Immigrants to the United States since* 1790.

Arriving.	Number of Females.	Through years.	Ratio per cent. to original number of females.	Living in 1850.
1790—1810	49,800	40 and 50	264	131,472
1810—1820	47,310	30	177	83,738
1820—1830	84,651	20	114	96,502
1830—1840	316,383	10	59	186,665
1840—1850	631,577	5	30	189,473
Total	....	....	....	687,850

"In this calculation, no allowance is made for the time which the immigrants may have been here previous to the decennial year. Those who arrived between 1840 and 1850 averaged a residence of 3.9 years previous to the last date. Perhaps so much should be added to each of the above periods, except the last, which should be 3.9 instead of 5, and perhaps some allowance should be made for the greater proportion of immigrant females being of a marriageable and productive age, than the females of these States, (being 203 per 1,000 of all, while in New Hampshire and North Carolina they were 145 per 1,000 of all of both sexes.) On the other hand, allowance should be made for the great proportion of deaths among foreigners and their children, and also for the greater delay of their marriage in a new and strange country. The emigration *from* North Carolina and New Hampshire is balanced, in part, by the immigration *into* those States, and in part, by the foreigners that return or otherwise pass out of the country."

Professor Tucker, calculated, after a very laborious analysis, the number of foreigners and their descendants to be above one million in 1840. Dr. Chickering's estimate, 1847 or 1848, reaches as high as 3,943,673, and a statement calculated upon his principles but upon different data, was inserted in the Abstract, p. 133, making the total to 1850, 4,304,416. The objections to the course of reasoning by which these figures were obtained, are ably set forth in letters from Dr. Jarvis to the Census Office, from which some extracts are given in the notes, without the benefit however of his revision.*

The Carlisle Table.

Precise age. Years.	Number living.	Annual deaths.	Expectation of life.	Precise age. Years.	Number living.	Annual deaths.	Expectation of life.	Precise age. Years.	Number living.	Annual deaths.	Expectation of life.
0	10,000	1,539	38.72	35	5,362	55	31.00	70	2,401	124	9.18
1	8,461	682	44.68	36	5,307	56	30.32	71	2,277	134	8.65
2	7,779	505	47.55	37	5,251	57	29.64	72	2,143	146	8.16
3	7,274	276	49.82	38	5,194	58	28.96	73	1,997	156	7.72
4	6,998	201	50.76	39	5,136	61	28.28	74	1,841	166	7.33
5	6,797	121	51.25	40	5,075	66	27.61	75	1,675	160	7.01
6	6,676	82	51.17	41	5,009	69	26.97	76	1,515	156	6.69
7	6,594	58	50.80	42	4,940	71	26.34	77	1,359	146	6.40
8	6,536	43	50.24	43	4,869	71	25.71	78	1,213	132	6.12
9	6,493	33	49.57	44	4,798	71	25.09	79	1,081	128	5.80
10	6,460	29	48.82	45	4,727	70	24.46	80	953	116	5.51
11	6,431	31	48.04	46	4,657	69	23.82	81	837	112	5.21
12	6,400	32	47.27	47	4,588	67	23.17	82	725	102	4.93
13	6,368	33	46.51	48	4,521	63	22.50	83	623	94	4.65
14	6,335	35	45.75	49	4,458	61	21.81	84	529	84	4.39
15	6,300	39	45.00	50	4,397	59	21.11	85	445	78	4.12
16	6,261	42	44.27	51	4,338	62	20.39	86	367	71	3.90
17	6,219	43	43.57	52	4,276	65	19.68	87	296	64	3.71
18	6,176	43	42.87	53	4,211	68	18.97	88	232	51	3.59
19	6,133	43	42.17	54	4,143	70	18.28	89	181	39	3.47
20	6,090	43	41.46	55	4,073	73	17.58	90	142	37	3.28
21	6,047	42	40.75	56	4,000	76	16.89	91	105	30	3.26
22	6,005	42	40.04	57	3,924	82	16.21	92	75	21	3.37
23	5,963	42	39.31	58	3,842	93	15.55	93	54	14	3.48
24	5,921	42	38.59	59	3,749	106	14.92	94	40	10	3.53
25	5,879	43	37.86	60	3,643	122	14.34	95	30	7	3.53
26	5,836	43	37.14	61	3,521	126	13.82	96	23	5	3.46
27	5,793	45	36.41	62	3,395	127	13.31	97	18	4	3.28
28	5,748	50	35.69	63	3,268	125	12.81	98	14	3	3.07
29	5,698	56	35.00	64	3,143	125	12.30	99	11	2	2.77
30	5,642	57	34.34	65	3,018	124	11.79	100	9	2	2.28
31	5,585	57	33.68	66	2,894	123	11.27	101	7	2	1.79
32	5,528	56	33.03	67	2,771	123	10.75	102	5	2	1.30
33	5,472	55	32.36	68	2,648	123	10.23	103	3	2	83
34	5,417	55	31.68	69	2,525	124	9.70	104	1	1	

* "These tables pre-suppose two things which are errors: 1st. That all the immigrants who arrived from 1790 to 1850, were alive in 1850, for they are all included in the sum total. 2d. That all their children who

TABLE CXII.—*Proportion of Native to Foreign Born in different Sections of the United States—White and Free Colored.*

Sections.	Total free population—Native, including unknown.	Total foreign population.	Proportion of foreign to native, pr. cent.
Eastern	2,421,867	306,249	12.65
Middle	5,447,733	1,080,674	19.84
Southern	2,342,255	43,530	1.86
Southwestern	1,973,531	105,335	5.34
Northwestern and territories	5,557,529	708,860	12.75
Total	17,742,915	2,244,648	12.65

were born and survived to 1810, and to the decennial year next after their arrival survived to 1850, for these too are included in the total. On this supposition there had been no death of foreigners since their arrival in this country through 60 years up to 1850. And also if a child of a foreigner born between 1790 and 1810, survived to 1810, he lived 40 years longer. Those born between 1810 and 1820, alive in 1820, lived 30 years longer. Those born between 1820 and 1830, alive in 1830, lived 20 years longer, and if between 1830 and 1840 and alive in 1840, lived 10 years longer. The only chance given for a foreigner or his children to die, was between the time of his birth and the next decennial year. If he passed that he succeeded almost to immortality on earth, at least to a life lasting to the middle of this century.

"This matter of increase of foreigners by birth, is worth a little further examination. The production or natural increase must be in ratio of the number of the females of the productive age, and not to the whole number of the people. Foreigners generally intermarry with each other, so far as we have means of observation; there are comparatively few instances of natives and aliens uniting together, so few are these that they do not militate with the general rule. With the Irish especially, this rule is almost universal, and with all it will be safe to say that there are no more marriages of foreigners than there are foreign marriageable females, the exceptions are so rare as not to destroy any extensive calculation made in regard to it. Immigration brings a larger proportion of males. In 1847 the males were 139,491, and females 99,325, being in the ratio of 583 males, and 417 females per 1,000 of all. The females between 20 and 40 years old were 49 per cent. of their own sex, and 203 per 1,000 of both sexes. It is manifest that foreigners are not only subject to the same law of mortality with the natives, but they fall more readily beneath the diseases, and the wasting scourges of the land, than those who are born here. We well know that in New Orleans the mortality is in a far greater ratio among the foreigners than among our own people, from Yellow Fever, Cholera, &c. In the epidemic of 1841, the deaths were, foreign 1,355, natives 289. Another report which I find at this moment, states their nativity to have been, United States 288, foreign countries 1,055, unknown 298. In another epidemic there were 147 native and 452 foreign. In 1847 the deaths were, natives of the United States 240, other countries, 1,922. The deaths in 1849, natives of the United States, 491, foreign, 2,139, unknown, 2,086. I do not know the proportion of native and foreign population in New Orleans, but it cannot show a ratio like this, can it? (See mortality statistics of this volume.) In Boston, the mortality during the years 1849, '50, '51 and '52, was natives of the United States 7,072, foreigners and their children 10,265. The population was in 1850, native 75,322, foreigners and their children 63,446, to bring the ratio of mortality, the annual deaths were in 1,000 living, native 22, foreign and children 40.4; almost double. The deaths in the city of New York during the five years from 1848 to 1852, were natives 66,363, foreign 30,990; average per year, native 13,272, foreign 6,198. I have not the analysis of population of New York, but I think the foreign have a lower ratio of the living than of the deaths. The foreigners are generally—nearly universally, among the poor, who have a lower expectation of life, than the more comfortable classes. Almost all their circumstances operate to diminish their vital power, and thus they have less power of resistance to diseases, and consequently sink more readily under them than others.

"For these and other reasons, it may be safely assumed that the immigrants are subject to a larger decrement of life than the natives, and in estimating their present accumulated numbers, the law of mortality may be applied to them with a confidence that it will leave at least as many as, and probably more, than are in existence. * * * The only way to determine the number of foreigners and their descendants, is to first learn the number of immigrants from the Custom House records, certainly for one port, and by other observations approximately for the rest. Then ascertain their ages from the record, or from calculations divided into as short periods as your data will allow you. Ascertain from the tables of the law of mortality the proportion of those in each age who will survive to the various subsequent ages. Thus the proportion per cent. per 1,000 or 10,000 of those who are 0 to 5, 5 to 10, 10 to 15, 15 to 20, 20 to 25, etc., through all the ages discovered, or who will survive 5, 10, 15, 20, 25, &c., to 55 years. Applying their proportions to the numbers in each age, will show the number who will be alive at any future time as 1850, provided their expectation of life is as great as that of those upon whom the law of mortality was calculated. This will give you at least as many as were alive in 1850, and probably more. This method is an easy one, and the principle is plain, yet it will require considerable arithmetical labor, which however will be justified by the reliableness of the result. Knowing the number actually reported as having arrived through the custom houses, making such additions as will include those who came in otherwise, then calculating their survivorship in 1850, according to the plan herein stated, and even admitting the expectation of life of the foreign to be as good as that of the native, I think you will find a smaller number here than is reported in the returns of the marshals, and published in the Abstract, page 19, viz. 2,210,839.

"I have no doubt that many of the children of Irish parents, born in America, were reported to the marshals as natives of Ireland, and thus the number swelled from that to which you may arrive at by calculation to that which is stated. There are other foreigners who do not understand our language, and therefore mistake our inquiries and answer erroneously. Foreigners associate so exclusively together, and are socially so generally separated from the natives for a long time, that their feelings of alienship are inseparably connected with their families and their children as well as with themselves, and they do not always discriminate between locality of birth, parentage, blood, origin, even religion, and sometimes they merge all into one class, calling all Irish, &c., who are sons of Irish soil, because they have a common blood, origin, or religion. * * * * *

"I am aware that there is among the immigrants a larger proportion of females of the productive age than among the natives. Among those who came in 1847 there were 203 per 1000 of all, and among all the whites of the native in 1840, the females of this age were only 143 per 1000. This would give the foreigners an advantage of 41.9 per cent. in this respect. In Massachusetts and in Boston, where we have the means of making the comparison, there is a much larger proportion both of marriages and births to the population of each kind among the foreigners than among the natives within three or four years. The population of Massachusetts was in 1850, native 830,066, foreign 164,448; that of Boston was, native 75,322, foreigners and their children 63,466. The marriages were in Massachusetts during the year 1849, 1850, and 1851, Americans 18,286, or 220

The foreign born population, which is less than one-eighth of the native white and free colored in the Union, is less than one-fiftieth in the South; about one-twentieth in the South-west, and one-fifth in the Middle States. In the Eastern and North-western States the proportion is nearly the same as the average of the Union.

The number of foreigners who arrived in the United States since 1790 may be stated as follows; the arrivals from 1790 to 1820 are given on the authority of Professor Tucker; those subsequent to that period are obtained from the Custom House reports.*

TABLE CXXIII.—*Arrivals of Foreigners in the United States.*

Years.	Arrivals.	Years.	Arrivals.
1790 to 1800	50,000	1835–36	62,473
1800 to 1810	70,000	1836–37	78,083
1810 to 1820	114,000	1837–38	59,363
1820–21	5,993	1838–39	52,163
1821–22	7,329	1839–40	84,146
1822–23	6,749	1840–41	83,504
1823–24	7,088	1841–42	101,107
1824–25	8,532	1842–43	75,159
1825–26	10,151	1843–44	74,607
1826–27	12,418	1844–45	102,415
1827–28	26,114	1845–46	147,051
1828–29	24,459	1846–47	220,182
1829–30	27,153	1848, (15 months) to 30th September	296,387
1830–31	23,074	1849, 1 year to do.	296,938
1831–32	45,287	1850, " "	279,980
1832–33	56,547	1852, (15 months) to January 1	439,437
1833–34	65,335	1853, to 1st January	372,725
1834–35	52,899	1854, " "	368,643

TABLE CXXIV.—*Nativities of Passengers arriving in the United States.*

WHERE BORN.	Year ending Sept. 30, 1845.			Year ending Sept. 30, 1847.			Year ending Dec. 31, 1852.		
	Male.	Female.	Sex not stated.	Male.	Female.	Sex not stated.	Male.	Female.	Sex not stated.
United States	4,221	1,126	165	3,081	1,408	25	23,053	2,474	....
Ireland	3,858	3,961	822	15,966	13,359	215	85,715	71,808	25
Great Britain and Ireland	32,781	30,183	887	72,429	56,087	222	109,253	88,937	....
Germany	19,713	13,074	....	43,850	29,306	286	84,205	56,624	2,600
Prussia, Austria, Germany and Holland	21,148	14,010	....	45,921	30,705	286	86,695	58,342	2,600
All others†	11,038	3,971	419	17,735	11,125	456	15,434	8,704	2,953

in 10,000 of their own race; foreigners 7,414, or 450 in 10,000. This is 104.5 per cent. excess of foreign over native ratio. The females in Massachusetts between twenty and forty in 1840 were 163 per 1000 of all, and in the United States 143 per 1000. The productive ratio of the immigrants is 26.3 above that of the people of this State. The marriages in Boston in the three-and-a-half years from July, 1849, to December 31st, 1852, were, Americans 4,078, or 541 in 10,000 of their own race; foreign 5,073, or 799 in 10,000. This is 84.8 per cent. excess of foreign over native ratio. The births were in Massachusetts in the three years, 1849, '50, and '51, of American parents 47,982, or 578 in 10,000 of their own race; foreign 24,523, or 1491 in 10,000 of their own race. In Boston there were, American 7,278, or 966 in 10,000; foreign 13,032, or 2,053 in 10,000 in three years. These facts certainly show a much greater tendency to marriage and a more rapid production among the foreign than among the native population here. On the other hand, there is much more mortality, especially among the children of the foreign. A great mortality of young infants is usually attended with more frequent births. The latter is consecutive upon the former, and too often among the poor, the ill-housed, and ill fed, the ignorant, and those of low health, the former is consecutive upon the latter. Whether this excess of marriages and births among foreigners over those among natives will be followed by a similar excess of those in the coming generation, who shall arrive at the marriageable age, is extremely doubtful. From present appearances it seems that the proportion will then be reversed."

* The Custom House reports are known to give much less than the true number, though they are at present much more correct than formerly. Chickering from 1820 to 1846 supposes them to fall on the average fifty per cent. short of the truth for each year, and increases the total for that period from 1,354,305 to 2,031,472. Tucker, after making all deductions for persons going to and coming from Canada, makes the number 200,000 between 1820 and 1830, and 631,417 between 1840 and 1850, less 100,000 Americans who emigrated to Texas.

† The other countries specified are France, Spain, Portugal, Belgium, Turkey, Italy, Switzerland, Russia, Norway, Denmark, Sweden, Sardinia, Greece, China, Asia, Africa, British America, Mexico, Central America, South America, West Indies and the Sandwich Islands.

There were 118,674 Germans arriving in New York in 1852, of which not more than one-third came direct from German ports. The number arrived in New York between 1846 and 1852, was 347,614, whilst the whole number of Germans emigrating from European ports for all the world during the same period, according to Hubner, a distinguished German statistician, was but 751,072. The number arriving at all ports of the United States in 1852 was 147,637, and in 1853, 142,528. The New York State Census of 1845 gives 49,558 German residents, 277,890 from Great Britain, 10,619 from France, and 8,222 from all other foreign countries. The census of Boston taken by the State authorities in 1850, gave 52,923 Irish, 2,666 Germans, and from other foreign countries, 7,877; which totals include children of foreigners though native born, amounting as stated in another part of the report, to about 16,000. A late California authority estimates its population to consist of 215,000 Ameri-

TABLE CXXV.—*Arrivals of Passengers from abroad into the several States.**

STATES, &c.	Year ending Sept. 30, 1845.			Year ending Sept. 30, 1847.			Year ending Sept. 30, 1852.		
	Maies.	Fem's.	Total.	Males.	Fem's.	Total.	Males.	Fem's.	Total.
Maine	2,378	1,672	4,050	3,436	2,370	5,806	1,828	916	2,745
New Hampshire	9	9	18	4	3	7	30	9	39
Massachusetts	5,446	3,508	10,360	11,958	8,373	20,848	11,223	9,827	21,439
Rhode Island	80	75	155	133	74	207	40	14	54
Connecticut	8	2	10	43	31	74	....	....	....
New York	43,432	33,082	76,514	85,059	60,771	145,830	181,004	121,326	304,879
Pennsylvania	3,025	2,742	5,767	7,911	6,852	14,777	9,558	8,401	17,959
Delaware	14	24	38	....	....	....	....	....	....
Maryland	4,128	2,903	7,031	6,968	5,050	12,018	8,185	5,963	14,148
District of Columbia	6	6	12	....	....	....	1	7	8
Virginia	....	....	....	422	274	874	....	....	....
South Carolina	243	66	309	119	45	164	1,017	500	1,517
Georgia	....	....	....	4	7	11	219	153	397
Florida	65	18	83	102	86	188	34	36	70
Alabama	....	....	....	....	....	....	208	91	299
Louisiana	10,545	4,992	15,537	20,784	14,019	34,803	21,088	11,214	32,316
Texas	....	....	....	2,223	1,370	3,873	....	....	2,600
Total	69,188	49,290	119,884	139,166	99,325	239,480	234,435	158,457	398,470

cans, 25,000 Germans, 25,000 French, 17,000 Chinese, 20,000 Spaniards, 5,000 miscellaneous foreigners, 20,000 Indians and 2,500 Negroes. The whole number of foreigners in the United States, not naturalized, returned by the census of 1820, was 53,687; by that of 1840, 107,832. In the State of New York, by the State Census of 1845, 153,717.

Out of 9,763 foreign males in Boston in 1845, all over 21 years of age, only 1,623 were naturalized. In 1850, though the proportion of foreign born to native white in that city, was about one-half, they polled only one-eleventh as many votes.

The value of personal property brought by foreigners to the United States cannot be known. The emigrants registered in Berlin in 1851, 5,018 in number, took with them property to the aggregate amount of $323,250. (*Hubner's "Jahrbucher."*) On the average of $30 for all classes, there will be about $15,000,000; but how much has previously been sent back by other emigrants, it is not easy to say. The English Commissioners of Emigration have returned the following sums remitted from America, as having come under their own knowledge: in 1848, $2,226,400; in 1849, $2,613,600; in 1850, $4,719,000; in 1851, $4,825,480; making a total of $14,384,480 in four years. If the remittances have continued at the same rate during the last two years, $7,260,000 may be added to this sum, which would give a grand total of $21,644,480 for the six years.

That a large part of the foreign born population resides in cities† may be seen from the following:

1850.	In United States.	In large cities.	Ratio per ct. to whole.
Irish	961,719	382,402	39.76
Germans and Prussians	583,774	212,559	36.43

The following from Hubner's "*Jahrbucher*" for 1854, gives the destinations of natives of Germany embarking from the ports of Hamburg and Bremen:

Place of Destination.	1847.	1848.	1849.	1850.	1851.	1852.
United States	32,287	33,559	32,120	31,431	44,531	70,934
British America	7,352	1,322	315	593	647	4,948
All other places	1,671	1,651	1,814	1,244	4,594	4,585
Total to all places	41,310	36,532	34,249	33,268	49,772	80,467

*Among the arrivals as reported above in Massachusetts, in 1845, the sex of 1,406 is not stated. In 1847, the sex of 517 in Massachusetts, 14 in Pennsylvania, 178 in Virginia and 280 in Texas, is not stated. In 1852, the returns do not state the sex of 1 in Maine, 389 in Massachusetts, 2,549 in New York, 25 in Georgia, 14 in Louisiana and 2,600 in Texas. Arrivals 1853, males 236,596, females 164,181; males over 20, 162,178; females over 20, 96,659; citizens of the United States, males 28,572, females 3,562; from Ireland 162,481; arrived in New York 294,818, New Orleans 43,028, Charleston 1,069, Boston 25,929.

† The cities referred to are Albany, Baltimore, Boston, Charleston, Chicago, Cleveland, Cincinnati, Columbus, Detroit, Hartford, Little Rock, Louisville, Lowell, Manchester, Memphis, Milwaukie, Mobile, Nashville, Newark, New Haven, New Orleans, New York, Norfolk, Petersburg, Philadelphia, Portland, Me., Portsmouth, Providence, R. I., Richmond, San Augustin, Savannah, Springfield, Mass., St. Louis, Syracuse, N. Y., Troy, N. Y., Washington, D. C., Wilmington, Del., Wilmington, N. C.

TABLE CXXVI.—*Age and Sex of Passengers arriving in the United States.*

AGE.	Year ending Sept. 30, 1845.			Year ending Sept. 30, 1847.			Year ending Dec. 31, 1852.		
	Males.	Females.	Total including sex unknown.	Males.	Females.	Total including sex unknown.	Males.	Females.	Total including sex unknown.
Under 5 years of age.........	4,885	4,509	9,394	10,261	8,546	18,807	15,598	15,386	30,984
Of 5 and under 10 years.....	4,413	4,126	8,539	10,050	8,176	18,226	16,149	15,144	31,293
" 10 " 15 "	4,214	4,035	8,249	11,028	9,100	20,128	14,648	13,349	27,997
" 15 " 20 "	7,253	8,105	15,358	17,311	14,800	32,111	28,027	23,956	51,893
" 20 " 25 "	16,018	11,023	27,041	27,471	19,098	46,569	51,318	35,375	86,693
" 25 " 30 "	12,366	6,350	18,716	23,049	13,938	36,987	40,694	19,788	60,482
" 30 " 35 "	7,329	3,716	11,045	15,014	9,300	24,314	26,262	12,762	39,024
" 35 " 40 "	4,782	2,483	7,265	10,079	6,655	16,734	14,844	7,163	22,007
" 40 and upwards...........	7,458	4,600	12,058	12,465	8,335	20,800	26,468	16,925	43,393
Age and sex not stated.......	....	....	2,219	....	....	4,804	....	....	4,614
Total..................	68,718	48,947	119,884	136,728	97,948	239,480	234,008	159,848	398,470

TABLE CXXVII.—*Emigration from Great Britain.*

Years.	To North American Colonies.	To the United States.		To Australian colonies and New Zealand.	To all other places.	Total.
		Number.	Rate p. ct. to whole emigration.			
1825........................	8,741	5,551	37.28	485	114	14,891
1826........................	12,818	7,063	33.79	903	116	20,900
1827........................	12,648	14,526	51.87	715	114	28,003
1828........................	12,084	12,817	49.12	1,056	135	26,092
1829........................	13,307	15,678	50.25	2,016	197	31,198
1830........................	30,574	24,887	43.73	1,242	204	56,907
1831........................	58,067	23,418	28.16	1,561	114	83,160
1832........................	66,339	32,872	31.87	3,733	196	103,140
1833........................	28,808	29,109	46.55	4,093	517	62,527
1834........................	40,060	33,074	43.39	2,800	288	76,222
1835........................	15,573	26,720	60.07	1,860	325	44,478
1836........................	34,226	37,774	50.09	3,124	293	75,417
1837........................	29,884	36,770	51.05	5,054	326	72,034
1838........................	4,577	14,332	43.14	14,021	292	33,222
1839........................	12,658	33,536	53.91	15,786	227	62,207
1840........................	32,293	40,642	44.79	15,850	1,958	90,743
1841........................	38,164	45,017	37.96	32,625	2,786	118,592
1842........................	54,123	63,852	49.75	8,534	1,835	128,344
1843........................	23,518	28,335	49.53	3,478	1,881	57,212
1844........................	22,924	43,660	61.77	2,229	1,873	70,686
1845........................	31,803	58,538	62.61	830	2,330	93,501
1846........................	43,439	82,239	63.33	2,347	1,826	129,851
1847........................	109,680	142,154	55.04	4,949	1,487	258,270
1848........................	31,065	188,233	75.87	23,904	4,887	248,089
1849........................	41,367	219,450	73.27	32,191	6,490	299,498
1850........................	32,961	223,078	79.43	16,037	8,773	280,849
1851, to March 31st............	1,197	53,142	91.57	2,962	736	58,037
Total	842,898	1,536,467	58.55	204,385	40,320	2,624,070

Whether the foreign immigration can be kept up very long at its present high figure must be doubted. The wars in Europe which it was thought would check the tide have however had no effect as yet. The number arrived in New York for the quarter ending March 31st, 1854, was 29,023, against 29,657 in the corresponding quarter of 1853.*

* In regard to the number of immigrants who take the route to Canada through the United States, and those who come to the United States via Canada, Lord Elgin, the Governor General, was kind enough in answer to a request from the Census Office, to forward the following statement of the date 17th July, 1854, (56,214 persons in Canada are reported by the last census, as of United States origin.)

"Prior to 1852 the demand for labor was so much greater in the United States than in Canada, that no doubt large numbers of our emigrants were attracted thither by the high wages offered, but within the past two years this state of things has been reversed, and but few now proceed unless with the view of permanent settlement.

"During the season of 1853 large numbers of laborers came to Upper Canada in consequence of the temporary suspension of several of the Rail Road lines in the Western States, where they all readily found employment.

"In the reports of this Department, submitted annually to His Excellency, I have endeavored to give an approximate view of the distribution of the emigration received by the St. Lawrence ; this estimate is based upon the information collected on boarding the emigrant ships on their arrival.

8. *Occupations.*—In 1820, 1840 and 1850 efforts were made to ascertain by the Census the occupations of the people of the United States. In the first instance, the white, free colored and slaves, male and female, are classed together on the schedules as actually employed in commerce, agriculture, or in manufactures, and as individual producers; in the second, as employed in mining, agriculture, commerce, manufactures and trades, navigation of the ocean, navigation of canals, lakes and rivers, learned professions and engineers. In the last instance, the particular employment of each white and free colored male over fifteen years of age, is indicated, and where the person follows several occupations, the principal one.

TABLE CXXVIII.—*Occupations of the Free and Slave Population of the United States, of both sexes and of all ages, in* 1840.

STATES AND TERRITORIES.	Mining.	Agriculture.	Commerce.	Manufactures.	Navigating the ocean.	Internal navigation.	Learned professions.	Total.
Maine	36	101,630	2,921	21,879	10,091	539	1,889	
New Hampshire	13	77,949	1,379	17,826	452	198	1,640	
Vermont	77	73,150	1,303	13,174	41	146	1,563	
Massachusetts	499	87,837	8,063	85,176	27,153	372	3,804	
Rhode Island	35	16,617	1,348	21,271	1,717	228	457	
Connecticut	151	56,955	2,743	27,932	2,700	431	1,697	
New England States	811	414,138	17,757	187,258	42,154	1,914	11,050	675,082
New York	1,898	455,954	28,468	173,193	5,511	10,167	14,111	
New Jersey	266	56,701	2,283	27,004	1,143	1,625	1,627	
Pennsylvania	4,603	207,533	15,338	105,883	1,815	3,951	6,706	
Delaware	5	16,015	467	4,060	401	235	199	
Maryland	313	69,851	3,249	21,325	721	1,519	1,647	
District of Columbia	....	384	240	2,278	126	80	203	
Middle States	7,085	806,438	50,045	333,743	9,717	17,577	24,493	1,249,098
Virginia	1,995	318,771	6,361	54,147	582	2,952	3,866	
North Carolina	589	217,095	1,734	14,322	327	379	1,086	
South Carolina	51	198,363	1,958	10,325	381	348	1,481	
Georgia	574	209,383	2,428	7,984	262	352	1,250	
Florida	1	12,117	481	1,177	435	118	204	
Southern States	3,210	955,729	12,962	87,955	1,987	4,149	7,887	1,073,879
Alabama	96	177,439	2,212	7,195	256	758	1,514	
Mississippi	14	139,724	1,303	4,151	33	100	1,506	
Louisiana	....	79,289	8,549	7,565	1,322	662	1,018	
Arkansas	41	26,355	215	1,173	3	39	301	
Tennessee	103	227,739	2,217	17,815	55	302	2,042	
Southwestern States	254	650,546	14,496	37,899	1,669	1,861	6,381	713,106
Missouri	742	92,408	2,522	11,100	39	1,885	1,469	
Kentucky	331	197,738	3,448	23,217	44	968	2,487	
Ohio	704	272,579	9,201	66,265	212	3,323	5,663	
Indiana	233	148,806	3,076	20,590	89	627	2,257	
Illinois	782	105,337	2,506	13,185	63	310	2,021	
Michigan	40	56,521	728	6,890	24	166	904	
Wisconsin	794	7,047	479	1,814	14	209	259	
Iowa	217	10,469	355	1,629	13	78	365	
Northwestern States	3,843	890,905	22,315	144,690	498	7,566	15,425	1,085,242
Total	15,203	3,717,756	117,575	791,545	56,025	33,067	65,236	4,796,407

"On these reports, with the information obtained from the sub-agents and the different forwarding companies, the estimates of the emigration to the United States is based.

"The emigration to this Province, via the United States, is chiefly to Western Canada, and is estimated by Mr. Hawke at from 4 to 5,000 persons annually. Many of these parties are respectable farmers, who take the route of the United States, as owing to the facilities afforded by Rail Roads, &c., they are enabled to reach Western Canada frequently before the opening of the navigation by the route of the St. Lawrence.

"The following extract from the Annual Reports of this Department for the years 1851, 1852 and 1853, are submitted in further answer to the enquiry:

"Emigrants arrived via the St. Lawrence, 1851, 41,076; 1852, 31,176; 1853, 36,699. Estimated number who proceeded direct to the United States, 1851, 18,500; 1852, 13,300; 1853, 11,500. Estimated number arrived in Canada West via the United States as settlers, (this return does not include laborers who may have come in for temporary employment,) 1851, 5,000; 1852, 4,000; 1853; 5,000.

"Over three-fourths of the foreign emigration received by the St. Lawrence proceed direct to the western States. The numbers were in 1851, 876; 1852, 7,256; 1853, 7,456. To 15th July, 1854, direct, 6,805; for the same period, via Liverpool, 3,000, in all, 9, 805."

In 1850 the particular employments are embraced in the following list which is an aggregation of those upon the State sheets. It is unfortunate that no more reliable exposition of the occupations can be given, as any one at a glance will admit. States are returned with an aggregate of particular occupations greatly short of what are known to exist, by local registers and directories.* In the same manner occupations known to exist are omitted. Those which should prevail in about equal proportions in all of the States, are in great excess in some, and the ratio of persons employed in different States to the whole number in those States, varies without regard to, and in spite of, known rules. These difficulties result, first, from the number of persons who follow different occupations and whom the enumerators were instructed to designate under the leading one, a point about which there would be much difference of opinion and no uniformity of action, admitting the instructions to have been followed; secondly, from the want of distinction between employers and employees, persons actually engaged in a pursuit, or as mere laborers connected with it; thirdly, from the method pursued (explained in the Quarto Census) in condensing the figures from the returns under such heads as "mechanics not otherwise specified," "manufacturers not otherwise specified," "other occupations," &c. Under these heads were absorbed many employments which seemed to exist in such small numbers in particular States as to be unworthy of notice.

TABLE CXXIX.—*Occupation of the Male Population of the United States, over Fifteen Years of Age,* 1850—*White and Free Colored.*

OCCUPATIONS.	Number.	OCCUPATIONS.	Number.
Actors	722	Cattle dealers	182
Agents	6,264	Caulkers	1,915
Agricultural implement makers	1,313	Cement makers	29
Apothecaries and druggists	6,139	Chandlers	2,388
Apprentices	1,846	Charcoal burners	159
Architects	591	Chemists	465
Armorers	469	Chimney sweeps	59
Artificial flower makers	45	Chocolate manufacturers	29
Artists	2,093	City, county and town officers	12,579
Astronomical, mathematical and nautical instrument makers	390	Civil engineers	512
Auctioneers	890	Clerks	101,325
Authors	82	Clergymen	26,842
Bakers	14,256	Clock makers	1,181
Bankers	552	Clothiers	3,780
Bank and insurance officers	1,375	Cloth manufacturers	253
Barbers	6,013	Coach makers	14,049
Barkeepers	5,479	Collectors	1,493
Basket makers	1,841	Colliers	2,948
Bell and brass founders	1,353	Comb makers	1,786
Bell hangers and locksmiths	2,101	Cotton gin manufacturers	111
Bellow's makers	39	Confectioners	3,871
Blacking manufacturers	38	Contractors	1,999
Black and white smiths	99,703	Coopers	43,694
Block and pump makers	1,973	Coppersmiths	1,760
Boarding house keepers	2,554	Cordwainers	130,473
Boat builders	2,086	Cork cutters	103
Boatmen	32,454	Cotton manufacturers	522
Boiler makers	1,581	Cutlers	892
Boneblack makers	16	Daguerreotypists	938
Bookbinders	3,414	Dairy and milkmen	2,390
Booksellers and stationers	1,720	Dealers	4,604
Bottlers	366	Dentists	2,923
Box makers	940	Draughtsmen	189
Brass and composition workers	573	Drivers	10,968
Brewers and distillers	4,854	Drovers	1,964
Brick makers	11,514	Dyers and bleachers	3,241
Bridge and dock builders	270	Editors	1,372
Brokers	2,551	Engineers	11,626
Broom makers	1,244	Engravers	2,208
Brush makers	1,503	Enamellers	12
Builders	1,227	Factory hands	10,869
Butchers	17,733	Farmers	2,363,958
Button makers	433	Farriers	290
Cabinet and chair makers	37,359	Feather dressers	11
Cadets	221	File cutters	291
Calico printers	226	Fire engine makers	29
Card manufacturers	37	Firemen	195
Carpenters	184,671	Firework makers	115
Carpet makers	1,218	Fishermen	9,025
Carters	13,879	Flax dressers	147
Carvers and gilders	1,742	Frame makers	143
		Fringe makers	112

* Thus, the New England Directory gives the names of 63 booksellers and stationers in Maine, though the Census returns but 32; of 30 in New Hampshire, while the Census gives only 24. According to the Directory there are 7 card manufacturers in Massachusetts, 2 in Connecticut, etc., while the Census returns none for the whole of New England. The Directory returns of clockmakers in Rhode Island 19, the Census 6. According to the Directory, there are 13 starch manufacturers in Maine, 28 in New Hampshire, 76 in Vermont; the Census returns none in Maine, 6 in New Hampshire and 10 in Vermont. But the illustrations are innumerable. These deficiencies do not, however, affect the manufacturing statistics.

TABLE CXXIX.—*Continued.*

OCCUPATIONS.	Number.	OCCUPATIONS.	Number.
Fruiterers	667	Painters and glaziers	28,166
Furriers	341	Paper dealers	140
Gardeners and florists	8,144	Paper hangers and upholsterers	2,592
Gas fitters	564	Paper manufacturers	2,971
Gas makers	148	Paper rulers	22
Gate keepers	1,168	Paper stainers	598
Glass manufacturers	3,237	Patent leather manufacturers	157
Glass stainers	54	Patent medicine makers	59
Glovers	247	Pattern makers	1,374
Glue makers	144	Pavers	673
Gold beaters	229	Pawnbrokers	72
Gold pen makers	68	Pedlers	10,669
Gold and silver smiths	3,082	Pen makers	56
Grate makers	74	Pencil makers	157
Grindstone and millstone makers	45	Perfumers	132
Grocers	24,479	Philosophical instrument makers	663
Gunsmiths	3,843	Physicians	40,564
Hair workers	299	Piano forte and musical instrument makers	1,822
Hardware manufacturers	819	Pilots	2,015
Hat and cap manufacturers	11,024	Pin manufacturers	24
Hemp dressers	62	Pipe makers	73
Herdsmen, graziers and rancheros	472	Plane makers	377
Horse dealers	186	Planters	27,055
Hosiers	217	Plaster figure makers	82
Hunters, trappers and rangers	619	Platers	585
Ice dealers	219	Plumbers	1,304
India-rubber manufacturers	153	Pocket book manufacturers	193
Ink manufacturers	348	Porcelain manufacturers	13
Inn keepers	22,476	Porters and carriers	3,185
Iron founders	9,271	Pot and pearl ash manufacturers	164
Iron mongers	622	Polishers and finishers	654
Iron workers	5,008	Potters	4,155
Japanners	202	Powder manufacturers	220
Jewellers	5,111	Printers	14,740
Joiners	12,672	Produce and Provision dealers	1,579
Laborers	909,786	Professors	943
Lace manufacturers	192	Publishers	355
Lamp makers	636	Quarrymen	1,932
Lapidaries	28	Rag collectors	227
Last makers	383	Railroad men	4,831
Lathe makers	40	Razor makers	333
Lath makers	68	Razor strop makers	24
Lawyers	23,939	Refectory keepers	3,226
Lead workers	106	Refiners	352
Lightning rod makers	13	Reporters	138
Lime burners	1,013	Riggers	1,115
Linseed oil manufacturers	32	Roofers and slaters	429
Livery stable keepers	2,741	Rope and cord makers	2,200
Looking-glass makers	294	Saddle and harness makers	22,779
Lumbermen	10,070	Safe makers	92
Machinists	24,095	Sail makers	2,182
Manufacturers not otherwise specified	15,091	Salaeratus makers	62
Map makers	8	Salt makers	1,026
Mariners	70,603	Sash and blind makers	2,026
Market men	1,906	Saw makers	544
Masons and plasterers	63,392	Sawyers	11,974
Mast makers	233	Scale makers	188
Mat makers	61	Scourers	39
Match makers	250	Screw makers	29
Mechanics not otherwise specified	16,004	Sculptors	177
Merchants	100,752	Servants	22,243
Millers	27,795	Sextons	436
Millwrights	9,613	Shingle makers	1,285
Miners	77,410	Ship carpenters	14,585
Mineral water manufacturers	86	Shoe binders	412
Model makers	93	Shoe peg makers	49
Morocco dressers	1,923	Shot manufacturers	24
Moulders	7,237	Showmen	33
Mould makers	62	Silk manufacturers	103
Muleteers	431	Soldiers	5,149
Musicians	2,606	Spinners	5,692
Music sellers	78	Spoon manufacturers	132
Music teachers	944	Spring makers	158
Mustard makers	44	Starch manufacturers	162
Nail manufacturers	2,046	Stave makers	100
Needle makers	21	Steel manufacturers	42
Newsmen	209	Stencillers	4
Nurserymen	335	Stereotypists	124
Oculists	10	Stevedores	514
Oil cloth manufacturers	388	Stone and marble cutters	14,076
Oil makers	349	Store keepers	3,747
Opticians	154	Stove makers	907
Organ builders	242	Straw workers	182
Ostlers	4,029	Students	42,149
Overseers	18,859	Sugar manufacturers	307
Oystermen	2,244	Surgeons	191
Packers	622	Surgical instrument makers	207

TABLE CXXIX—*Continued.*

OCCUPATIONS.	Number.	OCCUPATIONS.	Number.
Surveyors	1,614	Warpers	303
Suspender makers	63	Watchmen	2,119
Tailors	52,069	Watchmakers	2,901
Tanners and curriers	14,988	Weavers	31,872
Teachers	29,587	Whalebone workers	30
Teamsters	14,469	Wheelwrights	30,693
Telegraph operators	544	Whip makers	633
Tinsmiths	11,747	Whitewashers	419
Tobacconists and segar makers	10,823	White lead manufacturers	39
Tool makers	1,191	Whiting manufacturers	13
Toymen	47	Wine makers	46
Traders	14,917	Wine and liquor dealers	719
Trimmers	1,238	Window shade makers	40
Trunk makers	1,161	Wire makers	174
Turners	3,823	Wire workers	452
Turpentine makers	507	Wood corders	206
Type cutters	213	Wood cutters	1,322
Type founders	211	Wood dealers	473
Umbrella manufacturers	722	Wooden ware manufacturers	556
Undertakers	495	Wool combers and carders	3,266
U. S. and State officers	10,268	Wool dealers	344
Varnish makers	326	Woolen manufacturers	1,007
Veterinarians	46	Other occupations	22,159
Vinegar makers	78		
Wagon makers	1,550	Total	5,371,876

TABLE CXXX.—*Employments of the Free Male Population of the United States over fifteen years of age*—1850.

States and Territories.	Commerce, trade, manufactures, mechanic arts, and mining.	Agriculture.	Labor, not agricultural.	Army.	Sea and river navigation.	Law, medicine, & divinity.	Other pursuits requiring education.	Government civil service.	Domestic servants.	Other occupations.	Total.
Alabama	16,630	68,635	7,683	......	807	2,610	3,638	325	42	97	100,467
Arkansas	4,296	28,942	5,684	33	106	911	676	110	......	27	40,785
California	69,007	2,059	3,771	140	617	876	198	130	710	123	77,631
Columbia, Dist. of.	6,128	421	2,535	91	186	330	436	559	507	16	11,209
Connecticut	38,653	31,881	16,813	......	4,801	1,614	2,162	189	220	677	97,010
Delaware	5,633	7,884	6,663	......	743	251	581	124	69	113	22,061
Florida	2,380	5,977	2,666	423	708	357	302	268	12	42	13,135
Georgia	20,715	83,362	11,505	18	282	2,815	3,942	416	15	173	123,243
Illinois	36,232	141,099	29,778	......	1,644	3,307	2,071	701	376	151	215,359
Indiana	45,318	163,229	29,854	......	1,725	4,229	3,031	677	184	449	248,696
Iowa	9,255	32,779	5,392	71	163	1,077	425	103	10	40	49,315
Kentucky	36,598	115,017	28,413	204	1,027	3,811	4,420	902	212	471	191,075
Louisiana	32,879	18,639	15,264	45	4,263	1,827	2,444	811	508	488	77,168
Maine	38,247	77,082	26,833	114	15,649	2,212	1,727	419	232	196	162,711
Maryland	47,616	28,588	32,102	67	9,740	2,059	2,442	963	1,021	278	124,876
Massachusetts	146,002	55,699	57,942	73	19,598	4,702	5,371	1,566	1,375	2,972	295,300
Michigan	22,375	65,815	15,662	143	1,220	2,007	1,092	337	220	167	108,978
Mississippi	12,053	50,284	6,067	......	292	2,329	3,380	377	69	231	75,082
Missouri	30,098	65,561	20,326	305	2,471	2,893	3,147	767	1,458	1,149	128,175
New Hampshire	27,905	47,440	14,953	38	778	1,642	1,425	305	47	31	94,564
New Jersey	46,544	32,834	38,383	......	4,351	1,731	2,457	373	404	1,663	128,740
New York	312,697	313,980	196,613	1,462	23,243	14,258	11,104	4,985	6,324	3,628	888,294
North Carolina	20,613	81,982	28,560	......	1,659	2,263	3,447	570	46	247	139,387
Ohio	142,687	270,362	92,766	......	4,109	9,001	8,263	1,218	1,167	1,219	530,792
Pennsylvania	266,927	207,495	163,628	101	9,064	9,954	10,830	3,719	4,431	4,495	680,644
Rhode Island	21,004	8,482	9,296	......	2,033	556	881	176	774	269	43,471
South Carolina	13,205	41,302	8,151	......	346	1,829	3,161	372	149	34	68,549
Tennessee	23,432	118,979	17,559	......	258	3,363	3,589	705	10	345	168,240
Texas	7,327	25,299	6,194	584	321	1,368	996	677	......	90	42,856
Vermont	17,063	48,327	22,997	......	159	1,827	1,563	129	34	127	92,226
Virginia	52,675	108,364	48,338	274	3,263	4,791	5,622	1,491	79	1,978	226,875
Wisconsin	20,526	40,980	13,196	77	561	1,477	800	185	191	146	78,139
Territories. Minnesota	656	563	751	163	4	68	37	59	15	20	2,336
Territories. New Mexico	1,054	7,956	6,209	655	2	45	58	206	1,292	1	17,478
Territories. Oregon	1,007	1,704	511	289	130	99	48	40	40	6	3,874
Territories. Utah	828	1,581	622	......	18	26	48	12	......	......	3,135
Total	1,596,265	2,400,583	993,620	5,370	116,341	94,515	95,814	24,966	22,243	22,159	5,371,876
Ratio p. ct. to total employed	29.72	44.69	18.50	.10	2.17	1.76	1.78	.46	.41	.41	....

The preceding table is an attempt to reduce the employments in the previous one under certain classes similar to those hitherto adopted in this country and in the English and Massachusetts returns. It must be considered very imperfect, but at the same time it is the best arrangement of the figures that could be devised, however arbitrary. The laborers are classed separately, and considered not to be agricultural, yet without doubt a large part of them are farm laborers, and many belong to the class of manufacturers, miners, &c. "Other occupations" should perhaps be added to "Trade Manufactures," &c., to which they mostly belong. The note will explain the rest of the method.*

TABLE CXXXI.—*Proportion of the leading Occupations in the Several Geographical Divisions to each thousand of the Population of the United States,* 1820, 1840, *and* 1850.

Geographical divisions.	Agriculture.			Commerce.		Commerce, Manufactures and Mining.			Navigation		Learned professions.		All Occupations.		
	1820.	1840.	1850.	1820.	1840.	1820.	1840.	1850.	1840.	1850.	1840.	1850.	1820.	1840.	1850.
New England.....	29.50	24.26	22.71	2.51	1.04	11.01	12.06	28.22	2.58	4.20	.64	1.22	40.57	39.55	75.19
Middle States.....	54.21	47.24	52.21	2.47	4.67	19.06	22.90	66.98	1.60	4.62	1.43	2.79	73.27	73.18	177.69
Southern States...	50.43	55.99	63.12	1.23	.76	6.88	6.10	10.70	.36	.61	.46	1.17	81.43	62.91	54.69
Southwest........	22.01	38.11	57.86	.83	.85	2.50	3.08	9.44	.21	.59	.37	1.21	24.51	41.77	48.31
Northwest........	34.50	52.19	84.29	.48	1.31	4.33	10.01	40.61	.47	1.34	.72	2.82	38.84	63.57	158.46
Free States.......	93.41	101.64	148.42	4.64	4.69	29.69	40.67	123.49	4.30	8.78	2.63	5.93	123.11	149.25	365.64
Slave States......	97.31	116.16	131.78	2.28	2.19	14.08	13.48	32.46	.92	2.58	1.18	3.30	135.51	131.74	148.72
Total...........	190.72	217.80	280.20	6.92	6.88	43.77	54.15	155.95	5.22	11.36	3.81	9.23	258.62	280.99	514.36

In 1820 and 1830 the occupations of both sexes and all classes, including slaves, were returned indiscriminately. Consequently the proportions given are for those years, to each thousand of the aggregate population. In 1850 they are given to each thousand of the free males, except for agriculture, where they are compared with the total free male and three-fifths of the slaves male. Had the proportion in 1850 been made to the total population, as before, the ratio of those employed in every thousand would not have been so much greater.

Though the employments profess to be of both males and females in 1820 and 1840, they were, of course, mainly of the males. The materials of the census are, however, insufficient for any very reliable comparison.

TABLE CXXXII.—*Persons employed in Manufacturing Establishments in each State in* 1820 *and* 1840, *and also in* 1850, *in those producing over* $500.

States and Territories.	1820.	1840.	1850.	States and Territories.	1820.	1840.	1850.
Alabama..................	1,412	7,195	4,936	New Hampshire.........	8,699	17,826	27,092
Arkansas..................	179	1,173	903	New Jersey.............	15,941	27,004	37,311
California................	....	....	3,964	New York............ ...	60,038	173,193	199,349
Columbia, District of.......	2,184	2,278	2,176	North Carolina...........	11,844	14,322	12,444
Connecticut..............	17,541	27,932	47,770	Ohio......................	18,956	66,265	51,489
Delaware.................	2,821	4,060	3,888	Pennsylvania.............	60,215	105,883	146,766
Florida....................	....	1,177	991	Rhode Island.............	6,091	21,271	20,881
Georgia...................	3,557	7,984	8,378	South Carolina...........	6,488	10,325	7,009
Illinois....................	1,007	13,185	12,065	Tennessee...............	7,860	17,815	12,032
Indiana...................	3,229	20,590	14,342	Texas.....................	....	....	1,066
Iowa......................	....	1,629	1,707	Vermont.................	8,484	13,174	8,445
Kentucky.................	11,779	23,217	24,385	Virginia..................	32,336	54,147	29,109
Louisiana.................	6,041	7,565	6,437	Wisconsin...............	....	1,814	6,089
Maine....................	7,643	21,879	28,078	Territories. Minnesota.........	....	....	63
Maryland.................	18,640	21,325	30,124	Territories. New Mexico.......	....	....	81
Massachusetts............	33,464	85,176	165,938	Territories. Oregon............	....	....	317
Michigan..................	196	6,890	9,290	Territories. Utah..............	....	....	51
Mississsppi................	650	4,151	3,173				
Missouri..................	1.952	11,100	16,850	Total.....................	349,247	791,545	944,991

* Farmers, gardeners, and florists, nurserymen and planters, hunters, trappers, herdsmen, &c., are put under the head of *Agriculture;* carriers, carters, chimney-sweeps, colliers, drivers, drovers, firemen, furnacemen, gate-keepers, laborers, lumbermen, ostlers, packers, porters, railroad men, sawyers, scavengers, stevedores, teamsters, wood-corders, wood-cutters, and muleteers, under *Labor not Agricultural;* cadets and soldiers under *Army;* baymen, boatmen, canalmen, fishermen, mariners, oystermen, pilots, sailing-masters, whalemen, under *Sea and River Navigation;* dentists, oculists, surgeons, and veterinarians, under *Medical Professions;* actors, architects, artists, authors, civil engineers, commissioners, teachers, draughtsmen, editors, engineers, musicians, music teachers, professions, reporters, sculptors, showmen, students, surveyors, &c., under *Pursuits Requiring Education;* city, county, and town officers, judges, watchmen, United States and State officers, under *Government Civil Service.* The other occupations, except those under that specific head, are all condensed under the head of *Commerce, Trade, Manufactures, and Mining;* it being difficult to separate them in any reliable and satisfactory manner.

The occupation tables of passengers arriving in the United States combine citizens with foreigners, and cannot be separated. It is difficult, therefore, to determine what improvements take place in the immigrant class. If certain employments be assumed as comprising mostly foreigners, there were, in 1845, of mantua-makers 96; in 1847, 183. In 1845 there were 28 miners; in 1847, 13; in 1852, 1,179. In 1845, 1,659 servants; in 1847, 3,198; in 1852, 942. In 1845, 18,656 laborers; in 1847, 37,571; in 1852, 82,571. In 1845, 10,154 mechanics; in 1847, 25,047; in 1852, 24,514. In 1845, 66 weavers; in 1847, 89; in 1852, 49. In 1845, 24,016 farmers; in 1847, 50,036; and in 1852, 63,628.

TABLE CXXXIII.—*Occupations of the Population of Great Britain in* 1841.

OCCUPATIONS.	MALES.		FEMALES.		TOTAL.	
	Total population.	Per cent.	Total population.	Per cent.	Total population.	Per cent.
Persons engaged in commerce, trade and manufactures	2,415,127	26.24	677,660	7.12	3,092,787	16.52
Agriculture	1,410,509	15.33	80,276	.84	1,490,785	7.96
Labor not agricultural	643,531	6.99	114,964	1.21	758,495	4.05
Army at home and abroad, including those on half pay and in the East India Company's service:						
At home	41,394	.45	....	.....	41,394	.22
Abroad and in Ireland	89,230	.97	....	.....	89,230	.48
Navy and merchant seamen afloat and ashore, including navy half-pay and marines, fishermen, watermen, &c.:						
At home	119,552	1.30	....	.....	119,552	.65
Afloat	96,799	1.05	....	.....	96,799	.52
Professions—clerical	23,406	.25	....	.....	23,406	.13
legal	17,340	.19	....	.....	17,340	.09
medical	20,585	.22	1,419	.02	22,004	.12
Other pursuits requiring education	107,684	1.17	34,293	.36	141,977	.76
Government civil service	16,231	.18	634	.....	16,865	.09
Municipal and parochial officers, &c	23,239	.25	1,971	.02	25,210	.13
Domestic servants	255,296	2.78	902,402	9.48	1,157,698	6.18
Persons of independent means	135,446	1.47	368,818	3.88	504,264	2.69
Alms people, pensioners, paupers, lunatics and prisoners	102,011	1.11	95,885	1.01	197,896	1.06
Total returned as occupied, &c	5,517,380	59.95	2,278,322	23.94	7,795,702	41.65
Remainder of population, including women and children	3,685,735	40.05	7,236,433	76.06	10,922,168	58.35
Total	9,203,115	.....	9,514,755	.....	*18,717,870	.....

Some reflections upon the future growth of the population of the Union, will not be improper in this place. The facts embraced in the volume show a regular diminution in the ratio of total as well as of natural increase from decade to decade, up to 1840, making corrections for the admission of new territory, and the shorter period than ten years included between the census of 1820 and 1830. From the declining per cent. of females and young children, Prof. Tucker argues that the natural increase of the population is inversely as its density in all of the States, and that the increase for the whole population, for the decades after 1840, would be 32; 31.3; 30.5; 29.6; 28.6; 27.5 per cent. Should emigration, however, remain as it was then, or be but slightly increased from year to year, the series, he supposed, would be 31.8; 30 9; 30; 29; 27.9; 26.8 per cent. The results upon either series will be here shown,† but upon both they fall greatly short of the fact for 1850. The ratio from 1840 to 1850 increased over three per cent., instead of declining as before from the previous decade, a result not to be accounted for by the admission of California, New Mexico, &c.

Years.	Population on first series.	Population on second series.
1850	22,400,000	22,000,000
1860	29,400,000	28,800,000
1870	38,300,000	36,500,000
1880	49,600,000	46,500,000
1890	63,000,000	59,800,000
1900	80,000,000	74,000,000

The following table has been carefully prepared upon eight distinct and more or less probable assumptions of future increase. The reader can choose between them. In 1950 the population of the United States would be, in round numbers, 50,000,000, if the increase were no greater than that of Delaware since 1790, which has increased by far the least of all the

* This does not include 1,016 persons, officers and prisoners on board convict hulks; nor 1,408 persons, passengers aboard Her Majesty's ships; together 2,424 persons; making the total population 18,720,394.

† The slave population in 1920, it is supposed by Prof. Tucker, cannot exceed 31,000,000. See his argument, page 115.

States. With the increase of the Union for the last ten years, excluding all the foreigners who arrived in that time, the number in 1950 would be 252,000,000. With its average increase since 1790, it would be 450,000,000, but with the increase from 1840 to 1850, nearly 500,000,000. All of these, however, are very improbable, if not to say impossible assumptions. The figures in column 6 will no doubt more nearly express the truth than any other for 1900, and for subsequent periods a mean between columns 7 and 8 would seem preferable.

TABLE CXXXIV.—*Future Progress of the United States.*

Years.	Increase of population from 1840 to 1850, 35.87 per cent.	Increase in each ten years from 1790 to 1850, 34.435 per cent.	Increase from 1840 to 1850, deducting the number of foreigners who arrived in that time, 26.95 per cent.	Average increase of Delaware from 1790 to 1850, 7.68 per cent.	Mean of the three ratios in columns 2, 3, and 4, 23.02 per cent.	Column 1 until 1890, and then the ratio of column 3, 26.95 per cent.	Column 3 till 1900, and then the ratio of column 4, 7.68 per cent.	Column 3 till 1900, and then a mean of 3 and 4, 17.31 per cent.
	1	2	3	4	5	6	7	8
1860...	31,510,802	31,178,998	29,442,086	24,973,012	28,530,645	31,510,802	29,442,086	....
1870...	42,813,726	41,915,486	37,376,728	26,890,939	35,098,400	42,813,726	....	....
1880...	58,171,009	56,349,083	47,449,756	28,956,163	43,178,052	58,171,009	....	....
1890...	79,036,950	75,752,890	60,237,465	31,279,996	53,117,640	79,036,950	....	....
1900...	107,387,504	101,838,397	76,471,462	33,681,300	65,345,320	100,337,408	64,863,702	70,667,582
1910...	145,907,400	136,906,449	97,080,521	36,268,024	80,387,813	127,378,339	69,845,234	82,903,673
1920...	198,244,384	184,050,184	123,243,721	39,053,408	98,893,088	161,706,801	75,209,347	97,258,443
1930...	269,354,644	247,427,865	156,457,904	42,052,710	121,658,277	205,286,783	80,985,424	114,098,742
1940...	365,972,154	332,629,650	198,623,309	45,282,358	149,664,012	260,611,571	87,205,104	133,854,939
1950...	497,246,365	447,159,670	252,152,290	48,760,043	184,116,667	330,846,389	93,902,456	157,031,921

Admitting these figures, and making an estimate for each great section of the Union for 1900 and 1950, the facts might stand as follows:

Geographical Divisions.	1900.	1950.
Atlantic slope	20,000,000	28,000,000
Mississippi valley	32,000,000	64,000,000
Pacific slope	11,000,000	21,000,000
Gulf slope	7,000,000	12,000,000
Total United States	70,000,000	125,000,000

These calculations are all based upon the assumption that the territories of the Union will not be increased during the period from any quarter, which, considering the past, may be taken with some hesitation. A few remarks upon the future growth of the great cities will have place under the appropriate head.

As compared with the other leading powers, the increase in the United States has been as follows:

TABLE CXXXIV.—*Comparative Progress of the Population of the United States and of certain European States.*

COUNTRIES.	Year.	Population.	Year.	Population.	Number of years.	Actual gain.	Ratio of increase pr. ct. pr annum.
United States	1790	3,929,827	1850	23,191,876	60	19,262,049	8.17
Prussia	1786	6,000,000	1849	16,331,187	63	10,331,187	2.73
Turkey (European)	1801	8,500,000	1844	15,500,000	43	7,000,000	1.92
Russia	1783	27,400,000	1850	62,088,000	67	34,688,000	1.89
Great Britain	1801	15,800,000	1851	27,475,271	50	11,675,271	1.48
Austria	1792	23,500,000	1851	36,514,397	59	13,014,397	.94
France	1762	21,769,000	1851	35,783,170	89	14,014,170	.72
Spain	1723	7,625,000	1834	12,232,194	111	5,607,194	.66

The annual increase of the United States has been nearly three times as great as that of Prussia, notwithstanding the large population that was added to her by the partition of Poland; more than four times as much as Russia; six times as much as Great Britain; nine times as much as Austria; ten times as much as France. Upon the basis of past increase the future of Great Britain and France may be thus estimated:

TABLE CXXXVI.—*Future Population of Great Britain and France, computed upon their past Ratios of increase.*

Years.	Great Britain.	Ratio of Increase.	France.	Ratio of Increase.
1801	15,800,000	73.89	27,349,003	30.84
1851	27,475,271		35,783,170	
1901	47,776,748	....	46,818,700	....
1951	83,078,987	....	61,257,587	....

PART III.

MORAL AND SOCIAL CONDITION.

THE subject so far as the materials of the Census admit, may be thus considered:

I. RELIGIOUS WORSHIP.
II. EDUCATION.
III. THE PRESS.
IV. LIBRARIES.
V. CHARITIES.
VI. WAGES OF LABOR.
VII. CRIME.

I. RELIGIOUS WORSHIP.—In the United States there is no established system, but freedom of religious faith and worship is guaranteed by the Constitution.

The statistics of the Census are as complete as they can be obtained from the schedules. It will be observed that they do not undertake, as they are often quoted, to give the number of members of each religious donomination, or even the number of actual attendants upon churches, but simply the capacity of the churches to accommodate. In an early publication of the office, places returned as churches, but without the extent of accommodation, or the value of church property, were not included in the tables, upon the ground that they were not probably exclusively set apart for religious worship. If the object were simply to ascertain the number of church buildings, their value, etc.; this would have answered, but as it is evident that conclusions will be drawn from the results favorable or adverse to the religious character of the several communities, it must be exceptionable. In the rural districts, thousands of buildings are used both for school houses, and for places of religious worship: rude sheds or log houses in which denominations meet with regularity, and in which prayer is as fervently offered as in the Cathedrals of the cities. There would be no propriety in excluding these. Where several sects worship in the same building, as the best that could be done, its accommodation and value are divided between them if named otherwise they are placed under the head of Free.

Under the head of "Minor Sects," such denominations in the States are included as were so few in number as to be deemed unworthy of special notice. Had they all been mentioned, the aggregate of the several denominations would have been somewhat increased. The minor sects will therefore be divided between the denominations mentioned by name, and the following, and perhaps a few others not specifically referred to in the tables.

Albright, Associate Reformed, Covenanters, Campbellites, Church of Brotherly Love, Church of God, Disciples, Dissenters, Emanuels, Evangelicals, New Jerusalem, Public Reformers, Second Advent, United Brethren, New Lights, Whitfield, Winebrenarian, Independent Welch, Grace, Central, Seceders, &c.

There are 38,183 buildings returned as used for purposes of religious worship in the United States in 1850, belonging to denominations having accommodations for 14,270,139 persons, and of a total value including other church possessions, of $87,446,371. The occupation sheets show 26,842 regular clergymen, to which if those performing occasional clerical duties be added, the number will be swelled to about 30,000.

TABLE CXXXVII.—*Number of Churches in the United States, 1850.*

States and Territories.	Baptist.	Christian.	Congregational.	Dutch Reformed.	Episcopal.	Free.	Friends.	German Reformed.	Jewish.	Lutheran.	Mennonite.	Methodist.	Moravian.	Orthodox Congregational.	Presbyterian.	Roman Catholic.	Swedenborgian.	Tunker.	Union.	Unitarian.	Universalist.	Minor sects.	Total.
Alabama	579	18			17	5				1		577			162	5			4	1	3	3	1,375
Arkansas	114				2	1						168			52	7			5			13	362
California	1				1							5			3	18							28
Columbia, District of	6				8		1			2		16			6	6				1			46
Connecticut	114	4	252		101	1	5		2			185			17	12			4	5	22	10	734
Delaware	12				21		9					106			26	3			1			2	180
Florida	56				10	1						87			16	5						2	177
Georgia	879	5	1		20	6	2			8		809	1		97	8			16		3	7	1,862
Illinois	282	69	46	2	27	2	6	3		42		405	2		206	59	2	4	30	4	7	25	1,223
Indiana	430	187	2	5	24	10	89	5		63		779	57		282	63		5	5	1	15	13	2,035
Iowa	23	11	14		5		5	4		5		76	3		38	18			3		1	1	207
Kentucky	798	120			19	34			1	5		530			224	48		1	30	1	7	31	1,849
Louisiana	77	3			15	3		1	1			125			18	55			6		1	2	307
Maine	326	12	180		9	22	26					199			7	12	2		73	15	60	2	945
Maryland	45				133	6	26	22		40		479			56	65						37	909
Massachusetts	266	30	448		54	7	40		1	1		262			16	41	6		6	163	123	13	1,477
Michigan	66	2	29	10	25	1	7			12		119	1		72	44			3		7	1	399
Mississippi	385	8			13	3						454			143	9			1				1,016
Missouri	304	57			11	13			2	24	1	263	3		128	68			11	2	1	21	909
New Hampshire	193	24	176		11	2	15					103			13	2			32	13	38	4	626
New Jersey	108	8	8	66	52	7	52			7		312			149	23		2	5	2	3	10	814
New York	781	65	215	233	279	15	133	1	14	81	4	1,231	3		700	176	2		75	22	114	25	4,169
North Carolina	604	29			51	54	31	16		49		786	7		151	4		1	4				1,787
Ohio	551	90	100	5	79	13	94	71	3	260	10	1,531	160		663	130	2	15	48	1	53	60	3,939
Pennsylvania	321	21		7	136	28	142	212	8	498	91	907	86	10	778	140	3	15	78	4	22	89	3,596
Rhode Island	106	8	21		26	2	18		1			23				7	2		4	4	4	5	231
South Carolina	413		1		72	5	1		3	41		484			136	14				1	3	8	1,182
Tennessee	648	63			17	30	4			12		867			363	4		1	15			3	2,027
Texas	70	5			5	7						173			47	13			2			6	328
Vermont	102	9	175		26	1	7					140			11	8			76	2	38	4	599
Virginia	650	16			173	108	15	9	1	50	6	1,025	8		241	17	1	8	52		1	5	2,386
Wisconsin	49	4	37	2	19	2				20		110			40	64			1		6	11	365
Territories. Minnesota												1			1	1							3
Territories. New Mexico																73							73
Territories. Oregon	1		1									1			1	5							9
Territories. Utah																						9	9
Total	9,360	868	1,706	330	1,461	389	728	344	37	1,221	112	13,338	331	10	4,863	1,227	20	52	590	242	532	422	38,183

TABLE CXXXVIII.—*Total Value of Church Property in the United States*, 1850.

States and Territories.	Baptist.	Christian.	Congregational.	Dutch Reformed.	Episcopal.	Free.	Friends.	German Reformed.	Jewish.	Lutheran.	Mennonite.
Alabama	$227,497	$6,165			$76,300	$2,300				$250	
Arkansas	21,870				4,250	200					
California	5,000										
Columbia, District of	29,300				57,500		$1,000			15,000	
Connecticut	406,634	5,200	$1,657,185		773,875	800	7,150				
Delaware	16,800				78,900		24,900				
Florida	25,640				37,800	400					
Georgia	390,801	12,050	2,700		109,910	2,650	400			34,850	
Illinois	204,095	42,950	89,250	$2,700	78,350	6,400	2,340	$310		40,120	
Indiana	212,735	89,790	8,000	1,800	74,000	5,700	60,355	3,500		37,425	
Iowa	19,550	6,300	21,550		5,000		6,300	800		6,950	
Kentucky	549,955	184,945			112,150	13,600			$13,000	21,300	
Louisiana	30,470	61,000			57,900	10,430		4,000	20,000		
Maine	436,732	14,626	529,970		52,600	28,150	15,680				
Maryland	130,710				610,877	6,100	114,050	197,800		247,950	
Massachusetts	1,460,350	84,450	3,279,089		697,250	12,650	108,600		1,200	11,193	
Michigan	84,050	1,000	59,550	6,250	82,800	3,000	4,850			12,625	
Mississippi	186,192	9,950			66,800	1,850					
Missouri	154,480	43,210			144,600	4,400			7,000	34,560	$420
New Hampshire	322,956	30,350	527,340		41,100	4,000	15,200				
New Jersey	334,600	10,400	37,700	460,430	525,409	7,500	207,100			28,512	
New York	2,253,050	79,650	779,304	3,542,850	4,110,824	28,700	309,380	15,000	211,000	252,200	2,050
North Carolina	205,090	10,575			112,340	16,860	8,075	17,500		29,525	
Ohio	621,730	56,155	207,880	2,600	367,425	9,550	82,175	71,860	29,000	259,975	1,925
Pennsylvania	811,395	24,400		79,500	1,483,700	15,450	662,287	648,110	45,700	1,642,656	82,400
Rhode Island	367,800	24,300	178,550		248,560	5,000	57,800		1,000		
South Carolina	293,863		70,000		616,950	1,700	500		83,700	109,500	
Tennessee	271,899	48,295			85,300	6,665	1,300			2,600	
Texas	23,090	150			15,100	7,100					
Vermont	159,475	12,350	454,667		81,500	300	5,500				
Virginia	688,818	7,595			529,450	61,900	18,825	16,200	4,000	52,445	5,550
Wisconsin	52,500	1,200	61,260	750	45,750	250				14,650	
Territories. Minnesota											
Territories. New Mexico											
Territories. Oregon	2,000		6,200								
Territories. Utah											
Total	11,001,127	867,056	7,970,195	4,096,880	11,384,210	263,605	1,713,767	975,080	415,600	2,854,286	92,345

TABLE CXXXVIII—*Continued.*

STATES AND TERRITORIES.	Methodist.	Moravian.	Orthodox Congregational.	Presbyterian.	Roman Catholic.	Swedenborgian.	Tunker.	Union.	Unitarian.	Universalist.	Minor Sects.	Total.
Alabama	$276,279			$222,775	$300,000			$1,650	$6,000	$400	$12,000	$1,131,616
Arkansas	27,070			28,275	6,650			1,000				89,315
California	18,300			11,000	233,500							267,800
Columbia, District of	71,900			73,000	105,300				10,000			363,000
Connecticut	351,550			88,700	97,500			28,400	42,000	90,200	6,000	3,555,194
Delaware	127,845			75,500	15,000			1,000			400	340,345
Florida	55,260			31,500	13,600						1,200	165,400
Georgia	393,943	$25		218,805	79,500			21,100		1,000	1,625	1,269,359
Illinois	327,640	350		395,130	220,400	$5,800	$2,250	30,550	8,700	13,300	11,550	1,482,185
Indiana	492,560	21,600		326,520	167,725		3,100	2,350	600	17,800	4,025	1,529,585
Iowa	43,475	2,200		28,350	28,250			7,100		1,600		177,425
Kentucky	460,755			491,303	336,910		200	17,000	15,000	11,650	24,150	2,251,918
Louisiana	236,500			149,300	1,045,650			8,220		100,000	59,000	1,782,470
Maine	268,716			32,000	20,700	8,000		93,670	103,000	121,601	400	1,725,845
Maryland	837,665			376,300	1,161,532						264,900	3,947,884
Massachusetts	934,380			82,500	477,500	66,000		9,550	2,320,147	643,875	17,450	10,206,184
Michigan	142,850	500		142,850	159,775			1,400		7,100	15,000	723,600
Mississippi	240,265			183,085	67,000			400				755,542
Missouri	281,745	20		299,270	497,575			6,200	70,000	500	43,430	1,587,410
New Hampshire	175,590			71,000	20,000			39,350	72,800	83,100	3,000	1,405,786
New Jersey	688,350			1,225,250	133,385		1,800	6,500	1,500	6,800	5,700	3,680,936
New York	2,886,043	36,000		4,356,606	1,569,875	1,400		110,300	292,075	327,400	55,500	21,219,207
North Carolina	292,608	34,000		172,530	5,900		100	650				905,753
Ohio	1,545,831	93,072		1,389,699	763,307	15,800	9,975	37,900	15,000	100,590	111,650	5,793,099
Pennsylvania	1,726,038	221,350	$17,250	2,585,250	1,084,204	11,700	11,700	77,925	28,000	86,800	240,500	11,586,315
Rhode Island	102,900				72,500	4,400		5,000	127,000	55,000	4,650	1,254,400
South Carolina	341,168			483,175	78,315				30,000	6,000	57,375	2,172,246
Tennessee	381,811			367,081	45,000		300	3,800			2,150	1,216,201
Texas	58,195			20,070	79,700			525			3,000	206,930
Vermont	227,783			17,500	42,200			107,950	32,000	74,100	800	1,216,125
Virginia	725,003	2,550		571,165	126,100	500	8,200	24,025		5,000	13,550	2,860,876
Wisconsin	64,130			35,800	66,685			800		3,000	7,125	353,900
Territories: Minnesota				800	100							900
Territories: New Mexico					94,100							94,100
Territories: Oregon	22,000			5,000	41,320							76,520
Territories: Utah											51,000	51,000
Total	14,826,148	411,667	17,250	14,557,089	9,256,758	113,600	37,625	644,315	3,173,822	1,756,816	1,017,130	87,446,371

Thus the Methodist and Baptist together have more than one-half of all the churches, and the Episcopal and Roman Catholic are about equal in number.

The Methodist and Presbyterian have a larger amount of church property than any other denomination, the two being very nearly equal in amount. The Baptist and Episcopal are next, and are also about equal. The Catholics, though they have but one-eleventh as many churches as the Methodists, have much more than half the church property.

TABLE CXXXIX.—*Church Accommodations of the United States in* 1850.

States and Territories.	Baptist.	Christian.	Congregational.	Dutch Reformed.	Episcopal.	Free.	Friends.	German Reformed.	Lutheran.
Alabama	189,980	4,350	....	....	6,920	1,800	....	....	200
Arkansas	18,600	....	....	....	350	200	....	....	....
California	400	....	....	....	....	....	....	....	....
Columbia, District of	3,460	....	....	....	6,400	....	200	....	1,000
Connecticut	44,434	950	127,320	....	45,150	325	1,025	....	....
Delaware	2,975	....	....	....	7,650	....	3,636	....	....
Florida	11,985	....	....	....	3,810	400	....	....	....
Georgia	321,668	1,710	250	....	9,325	1,730	500	....	2,825
Illinois	94,130	30,864	15,626	875	14,000	750	1,550	280	16,640
Indiana	138,783	65,341	1,400	1,275	7,300	2,750	44,915	1,150	19,050
Iowa	3,993	2,810	4,725	....	730	....	1,550	375	1,030
Kentucky	288,455	50,640	....	....	7,050	9,377	....	....	2,850
Louisiana	16,660	1,500	....	....	5,210	675	....	500	....
Maine	101,389	4,030	70,623	....	4,137	7,442	7,725	....	....
Maryland	15,950	....	....	....	60,105	1,350	7,760	14,800	24,700
Massachusetts	114,680	11,020	239,142	....	24,195	1,850	14,423	....	450
Michigan	17,865	350	10,500	1,975	8,425	700	1,400	....	3,205
Mississippi	113,675	2,350	....	....	4,550	700	....	....	....
Missouri	74,725	19,655	....	....	4,500	2,350	....	....	8,160
New Hampshire	64,671	7,240	80,831	....	4,425	750	4,700	....	....
New Jersey	43,425	2,835	3,500	39,146	19,647	2,400	25,545	....	2,900
New York	335,374	20,300	102,430	131,025	140,195	4,600	49,314	600	38,270
North Carolina	201,797	11,600	....	....	15,245	14,870	13,220	5,725	19,750
Ohio	185,673	30,190	41,920	1,150	31,975	5,100	30,866	26,315	90,448
Pennsylvania	128 458	6,900	....	4,640	67,574	7,950	61,274	105,793	261,502
Rhode Island	42,105	3,000	11,703	....	11,606	611	6,370	....	....
South Carolina	165,805	....	2,000	....	28,940	1,550	500	....	14,750
Tennessee	197,315	18,350	....	....	7,810	7,250	1,600	....	3,400
Texas	10,020	100	....	....	1,025	1,600	....	....	....
Vermont	35,627	2,770	78,302	....	10,525	100	2,550	....	....
Virginia	247,589	4,900	....	....	80,684	36,025	6,450	3,800	18,750
Wisconsin	16,814	875	11,063	550	5,140	275	....	....	5,300
Territ's. Minnesota	....	....	....	....	....	....	....	....	....
Territ's. New Mexico	....	....	....	....	....	....	....	....	....
Territ's. Oregon	100	....	500	....	....	....	....	....	....
Territ's. Utah	....	....	....	....	....	....	....	....	....
Total	3,248,580	304,630	801,835	180,636	644,598	115,480	287,073	159,338	535,180

TABLE CXXXIX—*Continued.*

States and Territories.	Methodist.	Moravian.	Presbyterian.	Roman Catholic.	Union.	Unitarian.	Universalists.	Minor Sects.	Total.
Alabama	169,025	....	58,805	5,200	1,125	1,000	750	1,000	440,155
Arkansas	25,745	....	10,731	1,600	1,800	....	....	1,200	60,226
California	1,600	....	700	7,500	....	....	....	....	10,200
Columbia, District of	10,460	....	5,000	7,100	....	500	....	....	34,120
Connecticut	57,775	....	7,500	9,015	1,850	1,750	8,905	1,300	307,299
Delaware	29,300	....	10,100	1,630	200	....	....	250	55,741
Florida	20,015	....	5,900	1,850	....	....	....	1,000	44,960
Georgia	240,638	75	40,596	4,250	7,250	....	900	1,275	632,992
Illinois	178,452	400	83,129	29,100	8,625	1,050	2,000	7,740	486,576
Indiana	266,372	18,250	105,582	25,115	1,250	250	5,050	2,822	709,655
Iowa	14,609	560	7,855	4,490	502	....	200	100	43,529
Kentucky	169,060	....	99,106	24,240	10,900	700	2,200	8,150	673,528
Louisiana	33,180	....	9,510	37,780	1,350	....	1,000	1,650	109,615
Maine	59,421	....	4,086	6,650	23,537	10,144	21,043	300	321,167
Maryland	181,715	....	22,635	31,100	....	....	....	19,350	379,465
Massachusetts	94,601	....	8,190	32,165	1,810	92,938	51,089	4,430	692,828
Michigan	33,885	200	22,530	16,122	800	....	1,360	800	120,117

TABLE CXXXIX—*Continued.*

States and Territories.	Methodist.	Moravian.	Presbyterian.	Roman Catholic.	Union.	Unitarian.	Universalist.	Minor Sects.	Total.
Mississippi	121,083	....	48,316	3,250	180	....	....	....	294,104
Missouri	62,844	12	45,570	33,950	2,350	2,100	250	7,850	264,979
New Hampshire	32,640	....	6,500	1,450	10,450	8,380	14,280	1,100	237,417
New Jersey	109,350	....	81,650	9,485	1,450	450	1,000	2,150	345,733
New York	481,270	1,500	370,189	126,288	27,529	10,225	55,570	9,350	1,915,179
North Carolina	222,687	3,000	64,230	1,400	1,200	....	....	....	574,924
Ohio	543,490	51,105	272,274	76,215	18,646	650	20,765	21,332	1,457,769
Pennsylvania	341,858	33,015	360,000	89,501	27,700	1,630	9,783	30,837	1,576,245
Rhode Island	9,310	....	....	7,300	2,450	2,950	2,230	1,780	102,040
South Carolina	165,740	....	67,765	6,030	....	700	950	3,320	460,450
Tennessee	249,853	....	135,517	1,400	3,900	....	....	1,600	628,495
Texas	34,085	....	8,520	6,760	350	....	....	1,695	64,155
Vermont	48,560	....	4,160	4,305	31,010	1,000	14,775	850	234,534
Virginia	323,708	1,500	104,125	7,930	13,250	....	200	1,825	858,086
Wisconsin	21,270	....	8,533	24,967	400	....	665	1,921	97,773
Territories. Minnesota	....	....	....	100	....	....	....	....	100
Territories. New Mexico	....	....	....	28,650	....	....	....	....	28,650
Territories. Oregon	500	....	200	1,833	....	....	....	....	3,133
Territories. Utah	....	....	....	....	....	....	....	4,200	4,200
Total	4,354,101	109,617	2,079,504	675,721	201,864	136,417	214,965	141,177	14,270,139

Jewish 19,588, included in aggregate, viz: Kentucky 600, Louisiana 600, Massachusetts 200, Missouri 463, New York 9,700, Ohio 1,300, Pennsylvania 3,425, Rhode Island 300, South Carolina 2,400, and Virginia 600.

Mennonite 28,860, included in aggregate, viz: Missouri 200, New York 1,000, Ohio 1,830, Pennsylvania 23,580, Virginia 2,250.

Orthodox Congregational 3,100, included in aggregate, viz: Pennsylvania 3,100.

Swedenborgian 5,475, included in aggregate, viz: Illinois 140, Maine 640, Massachusetts 1,645, New York 450, Ohio 700, Pennsylvania 1,475, Rhode Island 325, Virginia 100.

Tunkers 22,400, included in aggregate, viz: Illinois 1,225, Indiana 3,000, Kentucky 200, New Jersey 800, North Carolina 200, Ohio 5,825, Pennsylvania 6,250, Tennessee 500 and Virginia 4,400.

In capacity to accommodate worshippers at one time, the Methodists are placed highest upon the list; next in order are the Baptists, then the Presbyterians. The Catholics occupy the fourth place, though in point of fact, they have no doubt more actual worshippers than they can accommodate at one sitting in their churches.*

After filling out by averages, the blanks which were left by the marshals in the value and accommodation of many churches, the following figures result, which may be considered as expressing more nearly the facts. Three columns are added, showing the population and church accommodation and churches to the square mile. The average being about four churches to every 300 square miles, or one church to about seventy-five. In Massachusetts

* In Great Britain the churches are adequate to the accommodation of 57 per cent. of the population. There are 14,078 churches attached to the established religion, and among the dissenters the Catholics have 570 congregations, Congregationalists 3,244: Baptists 2,489; Friends 381; Unitarians 229; Methodists 11,007; Calvanistic Methodists, 800. Of the total population of Canada in 1851, 1,842,265 persons: 914,561 were of the Church of Rome; 268,592 Church of England. The remainder were of other creeds, including 42,261 unknown.

In *Prussia* there were in 1849, 8,164 parochial churches, and 837 houses of worship, with 10,016,798 Protestants; 5,320 churches and 2,008 chapels, with 6,079,613 Roman Catholics; 3 churches with 1,269 of the Greek Catholic faith; 30 houses of worship with 14,508 Mennonites and 901 Synagogues, with 218,998 Jews.

In *Switzerland* in 1850, there were 80,038 Catholics; 153,491 Protestants; and 599 Jews; total 234,128.

In *Austria* in 1851, there were 22,099,044 Roman Catholics, with 14,412 places of worship; 3,492,114 Greek Catholics, with 4,285 places of worship; 2,742,055 of the Independent Greek Church, with 3,198 places of worship, and 2,986,362 Protestants, with 3,175 places of worship. There were also 46,020 Unitarians, 835,196 Jews; other sects, 9,695.

From the annual publications of the several religious denominations in the United States, the following facts are condensed. Being made up from sources of information peculiar to each, they may be compared to advantage with the statistics of the census:

Congregationalists, 1854, 1,595 churches.

Reformed Protestant Dutch, 1853, 322 churches, 332 ministers.

Unitarian, 1850, 248 churches.

Lutheran, 1854, 3,000 congregations; 900 ministers, 25,000 communicants.

Catholics, 1,245 churches; 585 stations; 1,203 clergy; 28 institutions of Ecclesiastical education; 322 students; 223 educational institutions; 108 charitable institutions; 1,334,500 Catholic population.

Baptists, 1851, 578 associations; 10,441 churches; 7,464 clergy; 754,652 members.

Universalists, 1853, one general convention, one historical society, one reform convention, 20 State and Territorial conventions, 14 State societies for missionary, education, and other purposes, 83 ecclesiastical associations, 10 societies connected with associations for missionary and other purposes, 16 periodicals beside 3 annuals, 12 books published within the year, 10 schools of an academic character, 1,076 churches or societies, 821 meeting-houses, and 635 ministers.

there are nearly 19 churches to every 100 square miles, whilst in Texas the number is only about 1 in every 700, and in Arkansas 1 in 175 square miles.

TABLE CXL.—*Corrected Value and Accommodations of Churches, with their proportion to the area of the United States.*

States and Territories.	Value of Churches.	Accommodations of Churches.	Population to sq. mile.	Accommodations to square mile.	Churches to every 100 sq. ms.
Alabama	1,244,741	443,708	15.21	8.75	2.71
Arkansas	149,686	67,914	4.02	1.34	.69
California	288,400	10,984	.59	.07	.02
Columbia, District of	363,000	34,129	861.45	568.67	76.67
Connecticut	3,599,330	309,409	79.33	66.20	15.70
Delaware	340,345	55,741	43.18	26.25	8.49
Florida	192,600	44,960	1.48	.76	.30
Georgia	1,327,112	640,560	15.62	11.04	3.21
Illinois	1,532,305	488,172	15.37	8.81	2.21
Indiana	1,568,906	718,490	29.24	21.25	6.02
Iowa	235,412	44,604	3.78	.88	.41
Kentucky	2,295,353	676,456	26.07	17.95	4.91
Louisiana	1,940,495	111,063	12.55	2.69	.74
Maine	1,794,209	325,997	18.36	10.26	2.97
Maryland	3,974,116	379,465	52.41	34.11	8.17
Massachusetts	10,504,888	695,183	127.50	89.13	18.94
Michigan	793,180	128,838	7.07	2.29	.71
Mississippi	832,622	294,104	12.86	6.24	2.15
Missouri	1,730,135	270,028	10.12	4.01	1.35
New Hampshire	1,433,266	239,325	34.26	25.79	6.75
New Jersey	3,712,863	350,474	58.84	42.12	9.78
New York	21,539,561	1,917,479	65.90	40.80	8.87
North Carolina	907,785	577,185	17.14	11.38	3.52
Ohio	5,860,059	1,457,769	49.55	36.48	9.86
Pennsylvania	11,853,291	1,581,085	50.26	34.38	7.82
Rhode Island	1,293,600	103,384	112.97	79.16	17.69
South Carolina	2,181,476	460,450	22.75	15.67	4.02
Tennessee	1,246,951	632,551	21.99	13.87	4.45
Texas	408,944	74,325	.89	.31	.14
Vermont	1,251,655	237,544	30.76	23.26	5.87
Virginia	2,902,220	858,806	23.17	14.00	3.89
Wisconsin	512,552	97,773	5.66	1.81	.68
Territories. Minnesota	1,350	300	.04	....	....
Territories. New Mexico	94,100	28,650	.30	.14	.04
Territories. Oregon	76,520	3,133	.07	.02	....
Territories. Utah	....	....	.04	....	....
Total	89,983,028	14,360,038	7.90	4.89	1.30

The average value of churches in the United States, would therefore seem to be $2,357; their average capacity of accommodation 376 persons. There are about five churches to

Presbyterians, 1850, Synods 23; Presbyteries 127, 2,160 clergy, 2,595 churches, communicants 207,254; religious contributions for religious purposes, $390,630. These are the Old School. The census includes all Presbyterians, and irregular as well as regular churches, which may account for the difference.

A statement taken from the Baptist Almanac of 1850, with corrections for Cumberland Presbyterians, gives the following for all denominations.

Religious Denominations in the United States.

Names.	Churches.	Ministers.	Members.	Names.	Churches.	Ministers.	Members.
Methodist Episcopal	......	3,716	629,660	Presbyterians, Old School	2,512	1,860	200,830
Do. do. South	......	1,500	465,553	Do. New School	1,555	1,453	139,047
Do. Protestant	......	740	64,313	Do. Cumberland	1,250	900	100,000
Do. Wesleyan	......	500	20,000	Do. Associate, &c.	530	290	45,500
Baptists, (Regular)	8,406	5,142	686,807	Dutch Reformed	276	289	32,840
Do. Anti-Mission	2,035	907	67,845	German Reformed	261	273	69,750
Do. Seventh Day	52	43	6,243	Lutherans	1,604	663	163,000
Do. Six Principle	21	25	3,586	United Brethren	800	500	15,000
Do. Free Will	1,252	1,082	56,452	Evangelical, (German)	600	250	16,000
Do. Church of God	97	128	10,102	Moravians	22	24	6,000
Do. Campbellites	1,898	848	118,618	Mennonites	400	250	58,000
Do. Christian (Uni.)	607	498	33,040	Swedenborgians	42	30	3,000
Congregationalists (Orth.)	1,971	1,687	197,196	Universalists	918	700	60,000
Do. Unitarian	244	250	30,000	Mormons	......	100	20,000
Protestant Episcopal	1,192	1,497	67,550	Roman Catholic	812	864	1,173,700

The British Census of 1851, included religious statistics, but the returns are not yet published. In many European countries these statistics are carefully collected.

every 3,000 of the total population, and every 2,600 of the white and free colored. The average value of churches to each person, excluding slaves, is $4.50. Six hundred and nineteen persons in every 1,000 of the whole population of the United States, and 72 in every 100 of the whites and free colored, can be accommodated at one sitting in the churches. The Methodists have 1 church for every 1,739 of the total population, the Baptists 1 in 2,478, the Presbyterians 1 in 4,769, Episcopal 1 in 15,874, Catholic 1 in 18,901, other sects 1 in 2,923. For the several States the particulars of the table are curious and instructive.

TABLE CXLI.—*Ratio of Churches, Accommodations and Values.*

States and Territories.	Average value of Churches.	Average accommodation of churches.	Churches to every 1000 of the total population.	Churches to every 1000 white and free colored.	Church property to white and free colored.	Seats per 1000 of the whole population.	Accommodations to white & free col'd.	In the total population there is one church to the number of persons given.					
								Methodist.	Baptist.	Presbyterian.	Episcopal.	Catholic.	Other sects.
Alabama	$905	323	1.78	3.21	$2.90	575	1.03	1,337	1,333	4,763	45,390	154,325	22,046
Arkansas	413	188	1.72	2.22	.92	324	.42	1,249	1,841	4,036	104,948	29,985	11,047
California	10,300	392	.30	.30	3.11	119	.12	18,519	92,597	30,865	92,597	5,144	.....
Columbia, District of.	7,891	742	.89	.91	7.56	660	.71	3,230	8,614	8,614	6,461	8,614	12,922
Connecticut	4,904	422	1.98	1.98	9.71	834	.83	2,004	3,252	21,811	3,671	30,899	1,216
Delaware	1,891	310	1.97	2.02	3.81	609	.61	864	7,628	3,520	4,359	30,511	7,628
Florida	1,088	254	2.02	3.68	4.00	514	.93	1,005	1,562	5,465	8,744	17,489	29,148
Georgia	713	344	2.05	3.55	2.53	707	1.22	1,120	1,031	9,342	45,309	113,273	18,494
Illinois	1,253	399	1.44	1.44	1.80	573	.57	2,102	3,019	4,133	31,536	14,432	3,490
Indiana	771	353	2.06	2.06	1.59	727	.73	1,269	2,299	3,505	41,184	15,689	2,163
Iowa	1,137	215	1.08	1.08	1.22	232	.23	2,529	8,357	5,058	38,443	10,679	4,090
Kentucky	1,241	366	1.88	2.40	2.98	689	.88	1,854	1,231	4,386	51,706	20,467	4,271
Louisiana	6,321	362	59	1.12	7.19	214	.41	4,142	6,724	28,765	34,517	9,414	30,457
Maine	1,899	345	1.62	1.62	3.08	559	.56	2,930	1,789	83,310	64,797	48,597	1,488
Maryland	4,372	417	1.56	1.85	8.06	651	.77	1,217	12,956	10,411	4,384	8,970	4,451
Massachusetts	7,112	471	1.49	1.49	10.56	699	.70	3,796	3,739	62,157	18,417	24,256	1,187
Michigan	1,988	323	1.03	1.03	1.99	324	.32	3,342	6,025	5,523	15,906	9,038	5,447
Mississippi	820	289	1.68	3.42	2.81	485	.99	1,336	1,575	4,241	46,656	67,392	50,544
Missouri	1,903	297	1.33	1.53	2.91	396	.45	2,593	2,244	5,328	62,004	10,030	5.052
New Hampshire	2,290	382	1.97	1.97	4.51	753	.75	3,087	1,648	24,460	28,907	158,988	1,046
New Jersey	4,561	431	1.66	1.66	7.59	716	.72	1,569	4,533	3,286	9,415	21.285	2,880
New York	5,167	460	1.35	1.35	6.95	619	.62	2,516	3,966	4,425	11,102	17,599	3,091
North Carolina	508	323	2.06	3.08	1.56	664	.99	1,106	1,439	5,755	17,041	217,260	4,550
Ohio	1,488	370	1.99	1.99	2.96	736	.74	1,293	3,594	2,987	25,067	15,233	2,010
Pennsylvania	3,296	440	1.56	1.56	5.13	684	.08	2,549	7,202	2,971	16,998	16,513	1,759
Rhode Island	5,600	448	1.57	1.57	8.77	701	.70	6,415	1,392	......	5,675	21,078	2,138
South Carolina	1,846	390	1.77	4.17	7.69	689	1.62	1,381	1,619	4,915	9,285	47,750	10,611
Tennessee	615	312	2.02	2.66	1.63	631	.83	1,157	1,547	2,762	58,983	250,679	7,834
Texas	1,247	226	1.54	1.80	2.24	350	.41	1,229	3,037	4,523	42,518	16,353	10,630
Vermont	2,090	430	1.91	1.91	3.98	756	.76	2,244	3.080	28,556	12,082	39,265	2,120
Virginia	1,216	360	1.68	2.51	3.06	604	.90	1,387	2,187	5,899	8,218	83,627	5,077
Wisconsin	1,404	268	1.20	1.20	1.68	320	.32	2,776	6,242	7,635	16,073	4,772	3,680
Territories. Minnesota	450	100	.49	.49	.22	49	.05	6,077	......	6,077	....	6,077	......
Territories. New Mexico	1,289	392	1.19	1.19	1.53	466	.47	......	......	......	....	843	......
Territories. Oregon	8,502	348	.68	.68	5.76	236	.24	13,294	13,294	13,294	....	2,659	13,294
Territories. Utah	......	....	......	......	......	......	....	......	......	......	....	....	1,264
Total	2,357	376	1.65	1.91	4.50	619	.72	1,739	2,478	4,769	15,874	18,901	2,923

According to the returns of the marshals without correction in the office, the church statistics for the great sections of the Union, show that the New England and Middle States and the Territories and California, have nearly the same average value to their churches, which is nearly four times that of other sections. The average accommodation of churches differs much less. The South accommodates as much of its population as the Middle States, and only a little less than New England.

TABLE CXLII.—*Church Value and Accommodation for the several great Sections.*

Geographical Divisions.	Churches.	Church Property.	Average value.	Accommodation.	Average accommodation.	Ratio of accommodation.	Total population.
New England	4,612	$19,363,534	4,198	1,895,285	411	69.47	2,728,116
Middle States	9,714	41,137,687	4,235	4,306,483	443	65.00	6,624,988
Southern States	7,394	7,373,634	997	2,571,412	348	65.05	3,952,837
Southwestern States	5,415	5,182,074	957	1,596,750	295	48.08	3,321,117
Northwestern States	10,926	13,899,122	1,272	3,853,926	353	60.41	6,379,923
California and Territories	122	490,320	4,019	46,283	379	25.03	184,895

The annexed tables show the ratio of the whole church accommodation possessed by each of the leading denominations in the several sections. In New England the Congregational preponderates; in all others except the territories, the Methodist; in the Territories and California, the Catholic. The Baptists are second in rank every where except in the Middle States and California. The churches of Charleston accommodate a larger portion of the whole population than do those of Boston, and their average property and value to each person is about equal. If the slaves be excluded, the average value to each person is twice as large in Charleston as in Boston, &c.

Table CXLIII.—*Church Statistics of several large Cities.*

Cities.	States.	Churches.	Accommodation.	Church Property.	Ratio of accommodation.	Average accommodation.	Average population to each church.	Average value of property of each church.	Total population.	Total white and free colored population.	Average value to white and free colored.
Albany	New York....	29	35,800	$448,900	70.52	1,234	1,750	$15,479	50,763	50,763	$8.84
Baltimore	Maryland	99	80,455	2,410,300	47.59	813	1,708	24,346	169,054	166,108	14.51
Boston..........	Massachusetts	94	77,015	3,152,393	56.26	819	1,456	33,536	136,881	136,881	23.03
Charleston	S. Carolina ...	31	29,050	1,037,700	67.58	937	1,386	33,474	42,985	23,453	44.25
Chicago	Illinois	29	22,100	273,200	73.76	762	1,033	9,421	29,963	29,963	9.12
Cincinnati......	Ohio	73	53,837	1,427,200	46.63	737	1,581	19,551	115,435	115,435	12.36
Louisville	Kentucky	35	24,590	487,350	56.92	703	1,234	13,924	43,194	37,762	12.91
Mobile	Alabama	14	13,000	419,000	63.37	929	1,465	29,929	20,513	13,710	30.56
New Orleans....	Louisiana	30	27,350	1,153,500	23.50	912	3,879	38,450	116,375	99,364	11.61
New York......	New York....	214	219,098	9,098,700	41.53	1,023	2,409	42,517	515,547	515,547	17.65
Philadelphia	Pennsylvania .	246	186,814	4,779,050	45.70	759	1,662	19,427	408,762	408,762	11.69
St. Louis.......	Missouri......	50	34,425	1,043,900	42.74	689	1,557	20,878	77,860	75,204	13.88

Table CXLIV.—*Ratio of the Leading Sects to the Whole Church Accommodation.*

New England States.			Middle States.			Southern States.		
Denominaton.	Ratio pr. ct.	Seats.	Denomination.	Ratio pr. ct.	Seats.	Denomination.	Ratio pr. ct.	Seats.
Congregational....	32.07	607,921	Methodist	26.80	1,153,953	Methodist	37.79	971,788
Baptist	21.26	402,906	Presbyterian......	19.73	849,574	Baptist	36.51	948,844
Methodist	15.95	302,307	Baptist............	12.30	529,642	Presbyterian......	10.99	282,616
Unitarian.........	6.18	117,162	Lutheran..........	7.62	328,372	Episcopalian......	5.37	138,004
Universalist.......	5.92	112,322	Episcopalian......	7.00	301,571	Lutheran.........	2.18	56,075
Episcopalian......	5.28	100,038	Roman Catholic...	6.16	265,104	Free.............	2.12	54,575

South Western States.			North Western States.			California and Territories.		
Denomination.	Ratio pr. ct.	Seats.	Denomination.	Ratio pr. ct.	Seats.	Denomination.	Ratio pr. ct.	Seats.
Methodist	39.64	632,971	Methodist.........	33.50	1,290,982	Roman Catholic...	82.28	38,083
Baptist...........	34.21	546,250	Baptist...........	21.29	820,438	Methodist	4.54	2,100
Presbyterian......	17.00	271,399	Presbyterian......	16.73	644,579	Presbyterian......	1.94	900
Roman Catholic...	3.50	55,990	Roman Catholic...	6.08	234,199	Baptist...........	1.08	500
Christian..........	1.67	26,650	Christian..........	5.47	200,725	Congregational....	1.08	500
Episcopalian	1.62	25,865	Lutheran.........	3.80	146,683			

2. Education.—The objections that were taken to the statistics of Insanity in the Census of 1840, were also taken to those of Education, and were replied to in the report of the office, noticed under the chapter of Free Colored Population. Under Universities or Colleges in that census were included all institutions that were not academies, primary or common schools, and thus it was thought that their number was made too large. The distinction of "scholars at public charge," and not at public charge, was also objected to, since in some of the States common schools are supported by a public tax or by funds provided by the public *for the education of all the children*, and therefore none of them it was said could be considered as educated otherwise than at public charge. The distinction was no doubt one of difficult application, and by no means as satisfactory as that which was adopted in 1850, though at neither census was it true that *all* of the children at common schools in any of the States are educated at the public expense. Where a portion of the expense is voluntarily raised or contributed by parents, their children can hardly be considered as at public charge.

Instead of the distribution of institutions into "universities and colleges," "academies and grammar schools," and "primary schools," adopted in 1840, in 1850 they were classed as 1st. "Colleges," or institutions empowered to grant degrees, as well for male or female, including law, medical and theological institutions. 2d. "Academies and other schools," or all such as are not embraced under 3d, "Public schools," receiving their support in whole or in part from taxation or public funds. In framing the tables, however, it was found that female colleges, law institutions, etc., had been sometimes classed improperly with academies. In many of the States, particularly at the South, there is no general public school system, some counties, etc., supporting schools by taxes levied within their own limits, and in other cases the State contributing a proportion towards the support of private schools. Such schools are considered always as public in the census. Many academies also receive a limited support from public funds.

The marshals were instructed to specify whether the institution be a college, academy, female seminary, public school, military, theological, or other school, and state the number of teachers, and the average number of scholars in regular attendance. They were also instructed to give the annual revenue from any permanently invested fund or endowment—the amount received by each institution from taxes assessed for educational purposes, and if this cannot be ascertained, then the gross amount of taxes assessed in the district for school purposes—the amount received from State or district appropriations or public funds, exclusively of the taxes above mentioned—the amount otherwise received, including every other kind of revenue. There is no doubt that they did not always distinguish very carefully between the different sources of revenue and that the statistics upon the whole are imperfect, though the best that can be obtained.

TABLE CXLV.—*Educational Institutions—Scholars and Income*, 1850.

1. *Colleges.*

STATES AND TERRITORIES	Number.	Teachers.	Pupils.	Annual Income.				
				Endowment.	Taxation.	Public funds.	Other sources.	Total.
Alabama	5	55	567	$5,900	....	$305	$35,050	$41,255
Arkansas	3	14	150	....	....	....	3,100	3,100
California	.....	.....	.....	....	....	....	....	....
Columbia, Dist. of	2	36	218	1,200	....	....	22,800	24,000
Connecticut	4	56	738	24,060	....	....	29,579	53,639
Delaware	2	16	144	1,200	....	....	16,000	17,200
Florida	.....	.....	.....	....	....	....	....	....
Georgia	13	84	1,535	21,720	....	500	83,210	105,430
Illinois	6	35	442	4,500	....	700	8,100	13,300
Indiana	11	61	1,069	14,000	....	300	29,050	43,350
Iowa	2	4	100	200	....	....	1,800	2,000
Kentucky	15	100	1,773	45,608	$15,447	....	70,406	131,461
Louisiana	6	41	629	19,100	....	25,000	41,650	85,750
Maine	3	21	282	1,500	....	6,000	6,500	14,000
Maryland	13	98	1,127	....	....	1,700	112,014	113,714
Massachusetts	6	85	1,043	52,223	....	5,000	50,678	107,901
Michigan	3	22	308	....	....	....	14,000	14,000
Mississippi	11	45	862	10,600	....	....	31,800	42,400
Missouri	9	65	1,009	23,000	....	....	56,528	79,528
New Hampshire	1	18	273	4,000	....	....	7,000	11,000
New Jersey	4	49	470	6,000	....	....	73,700	79,700
New York	18	174	2,673	29,567	....	12,855	105,836	148,258
North Carolina	5	29	513	11,300	....	....	29,400	40,700
Ohio	26	180	3,621	25,136	....	....	100,656	125,792
Pennsylvania	22	134	3,520	97,900	38	7	188,860	286,805
Rhode Island	1	12	283	13,300	....	9,700	....	23,000
South Carolina	8	43	720	9,650	....	41,700	53,440	104,790
Tennessee	18	83	1,705	9,300	....	482	55,525	65,307
Texas	2	7	165	....	....	....	1,000	1,000
Vermont	5	30	464	4,700	....	....	16,858	21,558
Virginia	12	73	1,343	30,550	....	90,000	39,240	159,790
Wisconsin	2	8	75	400	....	....	4,300	4,700
Territories. Minnesota	.....	.....	.....	....	....	....	....	....
Territories. N. Mexico	.....	.....	.....	....	....	....	....	....
Territories. Oregon	.....	.....	.....	....	....	....	....	....
Territories. Utah	1	.....	.....	....	....	....	....	....
Total	239	1,678	27,821	466,614	15,485	194,249	1,288,080	1,964,428

Table CXLV.—*Continued.*

2. *Public Schools.*

States and Territories	Number.	Teachers.	Pupils.	Annual Income.				
				Endowment.	Taxation.	Public funds.	Other sources.	Total.
Alabama	1,152	1,195	28,380	$2,916	$800	$56,367	$255,519	$315,602
Arkansas	353	355	8,493	1,720	250	8,959	32,834	43,763
California	2	2	49	3,600	...	...	...	3,600
Columbia, District of	22	34	2,169	1,100	7,090	5,550	492	14,232
Connecticut	1,656	1,787	71,269	5,674	39,476	154,701	31,369	231,220
Delaware	194	214	8,970	...	14,422	27,753	1,686	43,861
Florida	69	73	1,878	...	...	250	22,136	22,386
Georgia	1,251	1,265	32,705	500	21,520	16,959	143,252	182,231
Illinois	4,052	4,248	125,725	20,526	100,694	129,906	98,586	349,712
Indiana	4,822	4,860	161,500	10,630	76,746	134,078	95,501	316,955
Iowa	740	828	29,556	...	16,549	19,078	15,865	51,492
Kentucky	2,234	2,306	71,429	...	41,276	46,376	124,200	211,852
Louisiana	664	822	25,046	3,200	194,984	93,428	58,067	349,679
Maine	4,042	5,540	192,815	2,695	269,603	31,110	12,028	315,436
Maryland	898	986	33,111	1,559	86,663	67,097	63,517	218,836
Massachusetts	3,679	4,443	176,475	16,906	935,141	37,341	17,407	1,006,795
Michigan	2,714	3,231	110,455	...	88,879	54,279	24,648	167,806
Mississippi	782	826	18,746	3,820	33,626	32,492	184,221	254,159
Missouri	1,570	1,620	51,754	7,178	3,024	74,807	75,761	160,770
New Hampshire	2,381	3,013	75,643	2,523	141,016	14,990	8,415	166,944
New Jersey	1,473	1,574	77,930	2,573	76,003	66,092	72,004	216,672
New York	11,580	13,965	675,221	20,426	756,693	564,104	131,434	1,472,657
North Carolina	2,657	2,730	104,095	1,535	42,936	97,378	16,715	158,564
Ohio	11,661	12,886	484,153	20,159	285,266	329,671	107,978	743,074
Pennsylvania	9,061	10,024	413,706	21,425	1,119,871	184,167	22,786	1,348,249
Rhode Island	416	518	23,130	660	62,296	31,434	6,091	100,481
South Carolina	724	739	17,838	3,000	1,200	35,973	160,427	200,600
Tennessee	2,680	2,819	104,117	8,912	4,500	98,548	86,558	198,518
Texas	349	360	7,946	...	...	...	44,088	44,088
Vermont	2,731	4,173	93,457	6,737	91,984	56,693	20,697	176,111
Virginia	2,930	2,997	67,353	12,235	43,470	60,828	198,092	314,625
Wisconsin	1,423	1,529	58,817	385	86,391	21,993	4,364	113,133
Territories. Minnesota	...	...	...	...	...	...	...	...
Territories. N. Mexico	...	...	...	...	...	...	...	...
Territories. Oregon	3	4	80	...	2,527	...	1,400	3,927
Territories. Utah	13	...	...	...	8,200	...	3,312	11,512
Total	80,978	91,966	3,354,011	182,594	4,653,096	2,552,402	2,141,450	9,529,542

3. *Academies and Private Schools and Total in all Schools, &c.*

States and Territories	Number.	Teachers.	Pupils.	Annual Income.					Schools, &c. to 100 sq. miles of the area.	Scholars in colleges, academies and public schools.
				Endowment.	Taxation.	Public funds.	Other sources.	Total.		
Alabama	166	380	8,290	$1,100	...	$4,949	$158,116	$164,165	2.61	37,237
Arkansas	90	126	2,407	...	...	...	27,937	27,937	.85	11,050
California	6	5	170	3,000	...	70	11,200	14,270	...	219
Columbia, District of	47	126	2,333	...	...	...	84,040	84,040	118.33	4,720
Connecticut	202	329	6,996	3,385	$1,729	25	140,828	145,967	39.84	79,003
Delaware	65	94	2,011	225	...	1	47,606	47,832	12.31	11,125
Florida	34	49	1,251	1,900	...	...	11,189	13,089	.17	3,129
Georgia	219	318	9,059	7,397	...	200	101,386	108,983	2.56	43,299
Illinois	83	160	4,244	1,985	...	806	37,697	40,488	7.47	130,411
Indiana	131	233	6,185	710	...	80	62,730	63,520	14.68	168,754
Iowa	33	46	1,111	2,500	...	...	5,480	7,980	1.52	30,767
Kentucky	330	600	12,712	5,445	...	5,534	241,638	252,617	6.84	85,914
Louisiana	143	354	5,328	52,200	...	2,985	137,892	193,077	1.97	31,003
Maine	131	232	6,648	8,376	120	6,986	35,705	51,187	13.15	199,745
Maryland	223	503	10,787	14,995	...	8,141	209,205	232,341	10.19	45,025
Massachusetts	403	521	13,436	19,470	100	48	290,559	310,177	52.41	190,924
Michigan	37	71	1,619	7,960	...	...	16,987	24,947	4.90	112,382
Mississippi	171	297	6,628	100	50	5,743	67,824	73,717	2.04	26,236
Missouri	204	368	8,829	...	...	870	142,301	143,171	2.65	61,592
New Hampshire	107	183	5,321	6,136	775	157	36,134	43,202	26.82	81,237
New Jersey	225	453	9,844	1,800	146	125	225,517	227,588	20.46	88,244
New York	887	3,136	49,328	23,185	4,812	46,465	735,870	810,332	26.56	727,222
North Carolina	272	403	7,822	15,987	...	...	171,661	187,648	5.79	112,430
Ohio	206	474	15,052	5,690	...	16,260	127,442	149,392	29.76	502,826
Pennsylvania	524	914	23,751	73,459	375	3,552	390,457	467,843	20.88	440,977

Table CXLV—*Continued.*

3. *Academies and Private Schools and Total in all Schools, &c.*

States and Territories	Number.	Teachers.	Pupils.	Annual Income. Endowment.	Taxation.	Public funds.	Other sources.	Total.	Schools, &c. to 100 sq. miles of the area.	Scholars in colleges, academies and public schools.
Rhode Island	46	75	1,601	$6,500	......	....	$26,248	$32,748	35.45	25,014
South Carolina	202	333	7,467	8,700	......	$226	196,563	205,489	3.18	26,025
Tennessee	264	404	9,928	6,183	$230	10,008	139,481	155,902	6.50	115,750
Texas	97	137	3,389	....	......	....	39,384	39,384	0.19	11,500
Vermont	118	257	6,864	3,727	5,865	1,989	37,354	48,935	27.95	100,785
Virginia	317	547	9,068	6,740	......	504	227,128	234,372	5.31	77,764
Wisconsin	58	86	2,723	....	......	....	18,796	18,796	2.75	61,615
Territories. Minnesota	1	1	12	....	......	....	140	140	......	12
New Mexico	1	1	40	....	......	....	....	....	......	40
Oregon	29	44	842	....	......	....	20,888	20,888	.02	922
Utah	13	......	....	....	......	....	2,050	2,050	.01	....
Total	6,085	12,260	263,096	288,855	14,202	115,724	4,225,433	4,644,214	2.97	3,644,928

Table CXLVI.—*Corrected and estimated Educational Income to each Pupil,* 1850.

States and Territories.	Colleges.	Academies.	To each academy scholar. Returned.	Estimated.	Public Schools.	To each P. S. scholar. Returned.	Estimated.	Total educational income.	White persons between 5 and 20.	To all bet. 5 & 20 white. Returned.	Estimated.
Alabama	$48,530	$224,279	$19.80	$27.05	$390,989	$11.12	$13.77	$663,798	176,657	2.95	3.75
Arkansas	3,100	34,308	11.60	14.25	68,411	5.15	8.05	105,819	67,545	1.10	1.50
California	....	20,392	83.94	119.95	14,700	73.47	300.00	35,092	9,484	1.88	3.70
Columbia, Dis. of	24,000	84,040	30.02	30.02	14,232	6.56	6.56	122,272	13,357	0.14	0.14
Connecticut	53,639	152,120	20.86	21.74	231,220	3.24	3.24	436,979	114,264	3.77	3.82
Delaware	17,200	53,498	23.78	26.60	43,861	4.89	4.89	114,559	26,609	4.09	4.30
Florida	....	22,742	10.46	18.17	31,777	11.92	16.92	54,519	18,097	1.96	3.01
Georgia	105,430	184,849	12.03	20.40	190,235	5.57	5.81	480,514	215,091	1.84	2.23
Illinois	15,389	47,678	9.54	11.23	356,416	2.78	2.83	419,483	335,463	1.23	1.25
Indiana	43,350	73,219	10.27	11.84	329,095	1.96	2.04	445,664	399,292	1.06	1.12
Iowa	2,000	11,180	7.18	10.06	52,620	1.74	1.78	65,800	76,363	.80	.86
Kentucky	131,461	306,507	19.87	24.11	215,068	2.96	3.01	653,036	302,899	1.96	2.15
Louisiana	85,750	283,003	36.24	53.12	362,412	13.96	14.96	731,165	84,283	7.45	8.67
Maine	17,784	64,966	7.69	9.79	318,597	1.63	1.65	401,347	212,782	1.78	1.88
Maryland	122,403	239,083	21.53	23.10	221,817	6.60	6.73	583,303	147,717	3.82	3.95
Massachusetts	121,929	354,521	23.08	26.38	1,010,346	5.70	5.72	1,486,796	303,920	4.68	4.89
Michigan	14,000	31,953	15.40	19.73	168,764	1.51	1.52	214,717	151,216	1.36	1.42
Mississippi	47,652	144,732	11.12	21.83	267,821	13.55	14.28	460,205	121,089	3.05	3.80
Missouri	88,277	183,403	16.21	20.77	168,961	3.10	3.26	440,641	234,773	1.63	1.87
New Hampshire	11,000	52,591	8.12	9.88	167,938	2.21	2.22	231,529	104,220	2.12	2.22
New Jersey	79,700	300,242	23.12	30.50	220,340	2.78	2.82	600,282	165,881	3.16	3.62
New York	217,267	1,015,249	16.02	20.58	1,486,423	2.18	2.20	2,718,939	1,038,407	2.34	2.61
North Carolina	40,700	222,695	23.99	28.47	158,564	1.52	1.52	421,959	215,454	1.79	1.95
Ohio	145,292	201,077	9.92	13.36	751,576	1.53	1.55	1,097,945	757,633	1.34	1.44
Pennsylvania	318,070	570,501	19.69	24.02	1,362,949	3.25	3.29	2,251,520	824,670	2.55	2.73
Rhode Island	23,000	37,423	20.45	23.37	100,481	4.34	4.34	160,904	44,943	3.47	3.58
South Carolina	104,790	205,489	27.52	27.52	200,600	11.24	11.24	510,879	107,813	4.73	4.73
Tennessee	67,689	175,926	15.70	17.72	200,253	1.90	1.92	443,868	214,120	1.96	2.07
Texas	4,125	79,732	11.62	23.52	94,554	5.54	11.89	178,411	59,335	1.42	3.01
Vermont	21,558	56,159	7.13	8.18	179,181	1.88	1.91	256,898	108,429	2.27	2.36
Virginia	162,574	351,007	25.84	38.70	341,279	4.67	5.06	854,860	345,265	2.05	2.47
Wisconsin	4,700	19,899	6.90	7.30	113,874	1.92	1.93	138,473	104,882	1.30	1.32
Territories. Minnesota	....	....	......	......	....	......	......	....	1,737	....	....
N. Mexico	....	....	......	......	....	......	......	....	22,774	....	....
Oregon	....	24,495	24.80	29.09	3,927	49.08	......	28,422	4,452	5.57	6.38
Utah	....	2,221	......	......	11,512	......	......	13,733	4,057	3.34	3.38
Slaveholding States	....	2,795,293	......	26.05	2,970,834	.....	5.09	6,819,808	2,350,104	....	2.90
Non-slaveholding do.	....	3,035,886	......	19.49	6,879,959	......	2.48	11,004,523	4,784,869	....	2.30
Total	....	5,831,179	......	22.16	9,850,793	......	2.94	17,824,331	7,134,973	....	2.50

The blanks which were left by the marshals in many of the returns of education are not supplied in table CXLV. Filling them up, however, with figures which are the average of the institutions returned in the same localities, the preceding table will result. The deficiencies were in the number of scholars, or amount of income, or both. The results for California must be considered questionable, growing out of a wrong classification of scholars, though the average to scholars in all schools may be nearer correct. It will be seen that the cost of academy and private school education to each pupil is a third larger at the south than at the north, and the average for the Union is $22.16. To each public school scholar the expense at the south is twice as great as at the north, and the average for the Union is $2.94. Whilst the south pays to its institutions of learning $2.90 for each person between the ages of five and twenty, the north pays but $2.30, and the average paid in the whole Union is $2.50.

The following table will show the number of persons returned by families at school in 1850. The number falls short of that returned by the institutions themselves, as will be seen on comparison. The families returned those at school at any time during the year excluding Sunday schools. The institutions returned the average at school during the year, which should be a smaller number, whereas, in fact, it is larger. Either, institutions have put their averages too high or families have been negligent in their returns. The latter is most probable, though the error may have occurred in both.

TABLE CXLVII.—*Attending School during the year as returned by Families.*

States and Territories.	WHITES.			FREE COLORED.			WHITE AND FREE COLORED.		
	Male.	Female.	Total.	Male.	Female.	Total.	Native.	Foreign.	Aggregate.
Alabama	34,125	28,653	62,778	33	35	68	62,738	108	62,846
Arkansas	12,918	10,432	23,350	6	5	11	23,343	18	23,361
California	800	192	992	1	....	1	976	17	993
Columbia, Dist. of	3,137	2,966	6,103	232	235	467	6,485	85	6,570
Connecticut	42,457	39,976	82,433	689	575	1,264	81,221	2,476	83,697
Delaware	7,632	6,584	14,216	92	95	187	14,077	326	14,403
Florida	2,545	2,201	4,746	29	37	66	4,704	108	4,812
Georgia	42,365	34,650	77,015	1	....	1	76,915	101	77,016
Illinois	97,245	84,724	181,969	162	161	323	173,403	8,889	182,292
Indiana	119,496	100,538	220,034	484	443	927	218,227	2,734	220,961
Iowa	18,677	16,779	35,456	12	5	17	34,383	1,090	35,473
Kentucky	69,783	61,134	130,917	128	160	288	129,955	1,250	131,205
Louisiana	16,903	15,935	32,838	629	590	1,219	30,795	3,262	34,057
Maine	97,443	88,498	185,941	144	137	281	183,051	3,171	186,222
Maryland	32,214	28,233	60,447	886	730	1,616	60,386	1,677	62,063
Massachusetts	112,210	108,571	220,781	726	713	1,439	211,293	10,927	222,220
Michigan	55,546	50,208	105,754	106	101	207	100,851	5,110	105,961
Mississippi	26,002	22,801	48,803	....	....	....	48,751	52	48,803
Missouri	51,146	44,099	95,245	23	17	40	92,031	3,254	95,285
New Hampshire	45,764	42,384	88,148	41	32	73	86,998	1,223	88,221
New Jersey	48,065	41,210	89,775	1,243	1,083	2,326	88,892	2,709	91,601
New York	356,602	331,272	687,874	2,840	2,607	5,447	644,087	49,234	693,321
North Carolina	54,727	45,864	100,591	113	104	217	100,258	550	100,808
Ohio	270,254	242,024	512,278	1,321	1,210	2,531	498,527	16,282	514,809
Pennsylvania	263,451	234,660	498,111	3,385	3,114	6,499	488,823	15,787	504,610
Rhode Island	14,782	13,577	28,359	304	247	551	27,712	1,198	28,910
South Carolina	21,738	18,555	40,293	54	26	80	40,073	300	40,373
Tennessee	78,943	67,187	146,130	40	30	70	146,033	167	146,200
Texas	10,570	8,799	19,369	11	9	20	18,788	601	19,389
Vermont	47,997	44,155	92,152	58	32	90	88,746	3,496	92,242
Virginia	59,204	50,507	109,711	37	27	64	109,564	211	109,775
Wisconsin	29,093	27,258	56,354	32	35	67	45,508	10,913	56,421
Territ's. Minnesota	105	102	207	....	2	2	202	7	209
Territ's. N. Mexico	361	105	466	....	....	....	464	2	466
Territ's. Oregon	1,016	859	1.875	2	....	2	1,852	25	1,877
Territ's. Utah	1,113	922	2,035	....	....	....	1,969	66	2,035
Total	2,146,432	1,916,614	4,063,046	13,864	12,597	26,461	3,942,081	147,426	4,089,597

The American Almanac for 1854 reports the names of 119 colleges and professional schools in the United States, 44 theological schools, 16 law schools, and 36 medical colleges; in all 215 such institutions. It will be seen that the number does not fall far short of the census, although the report of students is much less. The census gives the average of the whole year and should on that account exceed this statement, which has also many blanks unfilled.

TABLE CXLVIII.—*Colleges, Theological, Medical, and Law Schools.*

States, &c.	Colleges.				Theological Schools.				Medical Schools.			Law schools			Total.	
	Number.	Professors.	Students.	Volumes in library.	Number.	Professors.	Students.	Volumes in library.	Number.	Professors.	Students.	Number.	Professors.	Students.	Colleges.	Students.
Alabama	4	40	330	21,240	1	1	13	1,000	..	....	......	1	1	....	6	343
Columbia, District of	2	26	215	30,000	..	....	......	....	1	6	40	....	...	....	3	255
Connecticut	3	45	631	80,170	2	7	55	5,900	1	6	35	1	2	38	7	759
Delaware	1	6	45	7,500	..	....	......	....	..	....	......	....	...	....	1	45
Georgia	5	32	633	27,600	1	2	6	2,200	1	7	115	....	...	....	7	754
Illinois	4	29	223	13,560	1		not	given	1	6	70	....	...	....	6	293
Indiana	4	26	295	19,600	1	3	15	4,000	2	15	154	2	3	18	9	482
Kentucky	8	61	761	38,000	1	4	18	2,000	2	14	590	2	6	....	13	1,369
Louisiana	5	43	320	4,300	..	....	......	....	1	7	188	1	3	50	7	558
Maine	2	19	241	43,000	1	3	37	7,000	1	5	51	....	...	....	4	329
Maryland	5	66	433	33.292	..	....	......	....	2	12	125	....	...	....	7	558
Massachusetts	4	53	844	131,271	3	12	147	29,759	2	11	230	1	3	158	10	1,379
Michigan	2	21	94	9,400	..	....	......	....	1	5	95	....	...	....	3	189
Mississippi	3	14	220	8,750	..	....	......	....	..	....	......	....	...	....	3	220
Missouri	6	47	548	23,100	..	....	......	....	2	16	210	....	...	....	8	758
New Hampshire	1	10	237	25,000	3	8	99	8,300	1	6	45	....	...	....	5	381
New Jerssy	3	42	428	29,000	2	8	178	18,000	..	...	......	1	3	8	6	614
New York	8	82	834	78,000	7	21	256	49,450	4	31	692	1	3	50	20	1,832
North Carolina	3	20	427	23,700	..	....	......	....	..	....	......	1	1	10	4	437
Ohio	11	83	665	75,700	7	18	105	17,379	4	30	518	1	3	....	23	1,288
Pennsylvania	9	95	1,004	61,221	7	18	207	30,500	4	28	1,189	1	1	9	21	2,409
Rhode Island	1	10	243	31,000	..	....	......	....	..	....	......	....	...	....	1	243
South Carolina	2	14	190	23,800	3	10	72	7,400	1	8	158	....	...	....	6	420
Tennessee	8	39	570	29,737	1	2	24	6,000	1	11	152	1	3	75	11	821
Vermont	3	18	222	20,400	..	....	......	....	1	7	104	....	...	....	4	326
Virginia.	10	81	1,197	71,875	3	10	119	10,000	3	16	186	2	3	116	18	1,618
Wisconsin	2	10	53	3,500	..	....	......	....	..	....	......	....	...	....	2	53
Total	119	1,032	11,903	963,716	44	127	1,351	198,888	36	247	4,947	16	35	532	215	18,733

TABLE CXLIX.—*Persons in the United States over twenty years of age who cannot read and write.*

States and Territories.	WHITES.			FREE COLORED.			WHITE AND FREE COLORED.		
	Male.	Female.	Total.	Male.	Female.	Total.	Native.	Foreign.	Aggregate
Alabama	13,163	20,594	33,757	108	127	235	33,853	139	33,992
Arkansas	6,810	10,009	16,819	61	55	116	16,908	27	16,935
California	4,237	881	5,118	88	29	117	2,318	2,917	5,235
Columbia, District of	601	856	1,457	1,106	2,108	3,214	4,349	322	4,671
Connecticut	2,037	2,702	4,739	292	275	567	1,293	4,013	5,306
Delaware	2,012	2,524	4,536	2,724	2,921	5,645	9,777	404	10,181
Florida	1,736	2,123	3,859	116	154	270	3,834	295	4,129
Georgia	16,552	24,648	41,200	208	259	467	41,261	406	41,667
Illinois	16,633	23,421	40,054	605	624	1,229	35,336	5,947	41,283
Indiana	26,132	44,408	70,540	1,024	1,146	2,170	69,445	3,265	72,710
Iowa	2,928	5,192	8,120	15	18	33	7,076	1,077	8,153
Kentucky	27,754	38,933	66,687	1,431	1,588	3,019	67,359	2,347	69,706
Louisiana	9,842	11,379	21,221	1,038	2,351	3,389	18,339	6,271	24,610
Maine	3,259	2,888	6,147	77	58	135	2,134	4,148	6,282
Maryland	8,557	12,258	20,815	9,422	11,640	21,062	38,426	3,451	41,877
Massachusetts	11,578	15,961	27,539	375	431	806	1,861	26,484	28,345
Michigan	4,037	3,875	7,912	201	168	369	5,272	3,009	8,281
Mississippi	5,522	7,883	13,405	75	48	123	13,447	81	13,528
Missouri	14,458	21,823	36,281	271	226	497	34,917	1,861	36,778
New Hampshire	1,662	1,295	2,957	26	26	52	945	2,064	3,009
New Jersey	6,007	8,241	14,248	2,167	2,250	4,417	12,787	5,878	18,665
New York	39,178	52,115	91,293	3,387	4,042	7,429	30,670	68,052	98,722
North Carolina	26,239	47,327	73,566	3,099	3,758	6,857	80,083	340	80,423
Ohio	22,994	38,036	61,030	2,366	2,624	4,990	56,958	9,062	66,020
Pennsylvania	24,380	42,548	66,928	4,115	5,229	9,344	51,283	24,989	76,272
Rhode Island	1,330	2,010	3,340	130	137	267	1,248	2,359	3,607
South Carolina	5,897	9,787	15,684	421	459	880	16,460	104	16,564
Tennessee	28,469	49,053	77,522	506	591	1,097	78,114	505	78,619
Texas	4,988	5,537	10,525	34	24	58	8,095	2,488	10,583
Vermont	3,601	2,588	6,189	32	19	51	616	5,624	6,240
Virginia	30,244	46,761	77,005	5,141	6,374	11,515	87,383	1,137	88,520
Wisconsin	2,930	3,431	6,361	55	37	92	1,551	4,902	6,453
Territories. Minnesota	389	260	649	....	....	....	259	390	649
Territories. N. Mexico	13,334	11,751	25,085	2	2	4	24,429	660	25,089
Territories. Oregon	86	71	157	3	2	5	99	63	162
Territories. Utah	88	65	153	1	....	1	121	33	154
Total	389,664	573,234	962,898	40,722	49,800	90,522	858,306	195,114	1,053,420

"It has," says Chancellor Kent, "been uniformly a part of the land system of the United States to provide for public schools. The Articles of Confederation, 1787, the acts admitting into the Union Ohio, Indiana, Illinois, Missouri, Louisiana, Florida, Arkansas, &c., all provided for the appropriation of lands in each township for the use of public schools. The elevated policy of the federal government as one of our statesmen has observed, was a noble and beautiful idea of providing wise institutions for the unborn millions of the west, of anticipating their good by a sort of parental providence, and of associating together the social and the territorial development of the people, by incorporating these provisions with the land titles derived from the public domain."

TABLE CL.—*Whole amount of Lands appropriated by the Federal Government for Educational Purposes, to 1st of January,* 1854.

States and Territories.	For Schools.	For Universities.	States and Territories.	For Schools.	For Universities.
Ohio	704,488	23,040	Iowa	905,144	46,080
Indiana	650,317	23,040	Wisconsin	958,648	46,080
Illinois	978,755	23,040	California	6,719,324	46,080
Missouri	1,199,139	23,040	Tennessee	....	*3,553,824
Alabama	902,774	23,040	Territories. Minnesota	5,089,224	....
Mississippi	837,584	23,040	Territories. Oregon†	12,140,907	46,080
Louisiana	786,044	46,080	Territories. New Mexico	7,493,120	....
Michigan	1,067,397	46,080	Territories. Utah	6,681,707	....
Arkansas	886,460	46,080			
Florida	908,503	46,080	Total acres,	48,909,535	4,060,704

Some pains have been taken in the census office to collect the reports of the several States from year to year, from which the following in regard to common school education is condensed. The reader will compare the items with those of the census. The discrepancies may in part be explained by the faulty system of classification adopted, and by the distinction of average and regular scholars. The statistics which follow relate to the public schools of the several States and cities.‡ (See Note.)

* The vacant lands in Tennessee, amounting to 3,553,824 acres, were granted to the State provided $40,000 of the proceeds, if they amount to so much, be applied to establish and support a college.

† Donations not yet reported.

‡ *Alabama*—The Government of the United States has contributed in lands for Schools, about $2,000,000. *Louisiana*—Public expenditure for schools, New Orleans, 1853, $200,000; school funds paid out in the State same year under general system, $320,000; at school, 1853, $40,000. *Illinois*, 1852—schools 3,955; scholars taught 139,255. *Wisconsin*—Education funds of the State, if well administered, estimated at from 3 to 5 million dollars. *Ohio*—State common school fund apportioned among counties, $1,134,000; common schools, 1852, 12,664, scholars, 238,571 males, and 207,426 females; expended, 1851, $686,093 to teachers. *Pennsylvania*, 1852—9,699 schools, 11,713 teachers, scholars 480,778; paid out, including school houses, $1,116,918. *New Jersey*, 1850—children taught, 75,245; number of colored children taught, 1,607; received for school purposes, $152,578.62; expended, $99,560 13; 1853, amount appropriated, $325,219; number of teachers, 1,757. *New York*, 1850—794,500 children taught, of whom 9,679 were taught for 12 whole months; unincorporated and private schools, 1,697, and 70,606 pupils; number of colored pupils, 4,971; expended for school purposes, 1851, $2,249,814. *Rhode Island*, 1853—whole number of scholars, 26,200; average attendance, 18,722; cannot read and write, 2,744. *California*, 1853—3,314 scholars. *Indiana*—State Board reports to Legislature, State pays a quota out of fines and licenses, etc. *Iowa*, 1850—914 schools, 799 teachers, academies 14, colleges 4, other schools 44; public scholars 24,804. *Connecticut*, 1853—1,642 school districts; whole number of children between 4 and 16, 96,382; capital of school fund, $2,049,482; revenue from $143,693; town deposit fund, $763,661; society and local funds, $100,000; income from two last, $31,000; number of scholars, winter, 74,100 under 16, 1780 over 16; average attendance, 55,100; private schools, in winter 403, pupils 8,100, tuition $162,000; teachers, winter, 1,060 male, 730 female; summer, 670 male, 1,020 female. *Vermont*, 1850—2,594 districts; public moneys for same, $90,893, exclusive of district taxes; whole expense of schools, $217,402; paid to teachers, $127,671, board, $70,492, fuel, $19,837; average expense scholar, $2.20. *Rhode Island*—over 4 and under 15, 1852, 33,959; at school, 26,200; expended, $115,160 21. *New Hampshire*, 1852,—raised for schools, $189,925; average number at school, 55,770 in winter; summer, 44,564; number at school for two weeks, 84,900. *Maine*—2,853 male teachers in 1851, and 4,142 female; attendance in summer 129,000; winter, 157,000. *Massachusetts*, 1852—number of public schools 4,056—persons between 5 and 15, 202,880; scholars in summer, 185,752; in winter, 199,183: average attendance, 136,309; number under 5 years old at school, 18,260; over 15 at school, 21,695; teachers in summer, 369 males, and 3,973 females; in winter, 2,085 males, and 2,483 females; total 4,568; average length of public schools, 7 months and 15 days; average wages male teachers, including board, $37.26 per month—wages of female including board, $15.36; raised by taxes for the support of schools, including only the wages of teachers, board and fuel, $910,216.04; voluntary contributions of board, fuel and money, to maintain or prolong public schools, $39,778.87; appropriated to schools, as income of local funds, $37,174.63; received by the towns as their share of the income of the State school fund, $41,558.22; aggregate expended on public schools, for wages, fuel, and superintendence, $1,036,646.32; raised by taxes, (including income of surplus revenue,) for the education of each child in the State between 5 and 15, per child, $4.54; number of incorporated academies returned, 71; average number of scholars, 4,220; aggregate paid for tuition; $82,580.29; number of private schools, 749; estimated average attendance upon private schools, 16,131; estimated amount paid for tuition in private schools, $231,967.28; expended on public and private schools, and academies, exclusive of the cost of repairing and erecting school edifices, $1,351,193.89. In addition to this expenditure, the State appropriated, in 1852, to the State reform school, $20,000; education of the blind, $9,000; education of the deaf and dumb, at Hartford, $9,726; education of idiots, $3,750; American Institute of instruction, $300; county teachers' association, $550; agricultural societies, $10,000. *Georgia*—no public schools strictly, but schools receive a certain amount of aid from State funds. This is true for many Southern States. *Maryland* has appropriated $600,000 from government distribution fund as a school fund, yielding with other means, $65,631 per annum. *Indiana*—value of school fund $3,628,215; scholars, 1851, 225,318, schools, 5,899, children in State 400,000. *North Carolina*—annual common school

The proportion of scholars of every description in institutions of learning in all countries as compared with the United States will here be seen. The figures for foreign nations are taken from the note below, and from the table of population on page 42.

fund, $90,000. *Virginia*—school fund $1,606,802—32,072 scholars. *Arkansas*, 1850—though common schools are generally organized, their condition is not flourishing. *Texas*—primary and common schools are established in the chief towns and counties. *Delaware*, 1853—12,288 scholars, income of school fund, $27,507; contributions and taxes, $17,089; total, $44,596. *Mississippi*, 1850—762 public schools and 189 academies and other schools. *Kentucky*, 1851—school fund, $1,400,270; yields annually $75,000; scholars, 186,111; average scholars, 74,343; total expended for schools, $111,666. *Missouri*—State and school fund, $575,667; scholars, 160,000. *Tennessee*, 1851—common school fund, $114,468; academy fund, $18,000. *South Carolina*, 1852—appropriated for free schools, $36,188.34. *Florida*, 1851—payment from school fund, $39,000. *Michigan*—the present constitution of Michigan contains this liberal provision, which the State from her land and other funds has abundant means of carrying out.

"The legislature shall, within five years after the adoption of this constitution, provide for and establish a system of Primary Schools, whereby a school shall be kept without charge for tuition, at least three months in each year, in every school district in the State; and all instruction in said school shall be conducted in the English language. A school shall be maintained in each school district at least three months in each year. Any school district neglecting to maintain such schools, shall be deprived, for the ensuing year, of its proportion of the income of the primary school fund; and all funds arising from taxes for the support of schools."

Boston, 1850.—Number of public schools 220; scholars in summer, 21,723, winter, 21,942; average summer, 17,540, winter, 18,123; number under 5 years old, at school, 1,629; number over 15 at school, 519; number between 5 and 15 in the town, 24,722; average length of schools for the year, 10 months; amount raised by taxes for schools, including wages of teachers, board and fuel, $196,650; school funds, income of which for schools, $8,000; number of academies, and private schools 53; average scholars 1,549; paid for tuition, $94,800.

New York, 1850.—Average length of schools, 11 months; paid teachers $162,451; public money received, $230,585; number of volumes in district libraries, 9,240; number of children taught, 64,478, of whom 27,808 attended less than 4 months, and but 958 the whole 12 months; number of children between 5 and 16, 92,559; average number of pupils, 36,586; number of colored children at school, 2,610.

Philadelphia, 1850–51.—One high school, one normal, 53 grammar, 34 secondary—total schools 270; scholars, male, 24,508, female, 23,548; total 48,056. Expended for schools, 1851-52, $446,199; pupils, 49,635.

Baltimore, 1852.—Three high schools, 21 grammar and 26 primary schools, and 9,081 pupils, of whom in grammar schools and high schools, 5,280. Expended for school purposes, $72,308.

Charleston, 1850.—One college and one high school; 5 public schools, 394 scholars, $3,900 expended—average time of scholars at school, 5 years.

New Orleans, 1852.—Thirty-four schools, 8,761 pupils; estimated expenditure 1853, $200,000; receipts $65,000.

Cincinnati, 1853.—Number of pupils remaining in schools, 8,881, of which 15 were over 16 years old and none were under six.

The returns for the above cities are taken from official reports. A comparative statement for the several cities, was prepared for one of these reports, and is appended, with some omissions supplied, though the figures differ from those already given. This difference is perhaps to be attributed to the statistics being for different years.

Cities.	Population.	Schools.	Teachers.	Pupils.	Cost of Tuition.
Boston	135,000	200	331	21,000	*$241,860.00
New York	517,000	199	332	35,164	230,585.74
Philadelphia	409,000	256	727	45,383	336,979.54
Baltimore	169,012	34	119	7,093	45,352.84
Cincinnati	116,000	†17	124	6,006	*81,623.97
St. Louis	81,000	73	168	6,642	....
New Orleans‡	101,778	34	....	8,761	200,000.00

* Besides the amounts expended for tuition, there were paid for new buildings, in Boston, $56,000—and in Cincinnati, $10,004.08.

† The number of schools in Cincinnati, is taken from the several tabular statements in the report of 1850. From the number of teachers and amount of money expended, it seems to be too small.

‡ 1853—Whites.

Germany.—School laws adopted in Wirtemberg 1559, and modified in 1565, in Saxony in 1560, and improved in 1580, in Hesse in 1565, and in Brandenberg still earlier, substantially established the school system, which prevails at this day throughout Germany. Thus is recognized on the part of government the duty to co-operate with parents in the education of their children, and to provide against their neglect of doing so. This was secured in every state of Germany before the beginning of the present century.

Prussia.—The cardinal provisions of the school system are, that all children between the ages of 7 and 14 shall regularly attend school, and that their teachers shall be educated. As a proof of the workings of the system, in 1846 out of 122,897 men in the standing army, only 2 soldiers were found who could not both read and write. In 1846 there were 24,030 schools—average attendance of scholars, boys 1,235,448, girls 1,197,885 in elementary schools; in higher schools 43,516 boys and 48,302 girls; in town schools 15,624 scholars; in normal schools 2,186 pupils. Population 1848, 16,000,000; aggregate schools, primary 25,332 and 2,540,775 pupils; add 117 gymnasia for classical education, with 29,474 scholars and 1,664 professors; 7 universities, with 4,000 students and 471 professors; 382 infant schools, and 26,000 scholars, besides other special schools. In 1845 there were in the whole of Prussia only 2 young men in one hundred between the ages of 20 and 22, who could not read, write and cipher; 34,000 teachers had all been thoroughly educated in the studies they were to teach; 1843, number of children between 7 and 14, 2,992,124; at school 2,328,146; 1849 there were 24,201 elementary schools with 30,865 teachers, and 2,453,062 pupils; 890 academies, with 4,187 teachers, and 122,872 pupils; 117 gymnasia or colleges, with 1,664 teachers, and 29,474 pupils; and 7 universities with 255 professors and 4,306 students. The number of children between 6 and 14 years of age, and capable of receiving instruction, was 3,223,362, while the number of those who actually received it was 2,605,408.

Saxony.—Population 1846, 1,809,623—1 university, 85 professors and 835 students, 6 academies in arts and mining, 43 professors and 1,400 pupils; 11 gymnasia, 131 teachers, 1,590 pupils, 6 higher schools, 18 teachers and 270 pupils; 3 special, for commerce, &c., 240 pupils, 9 teachers, seminaries, 362 pupils, 17 schools of industry, &c., 779 pupils; 69 others, 6,966 pupils; 24 schools for lace making, 1,928 pupils; 2,155 common schools, 2,175 teachers, and 278,022 pupils, besides infant and private schools, &c.; 1849, 812 university students, 311,454 elementary scholars.

Baden, 1844.—Population 400,000—two universities, 4 lyceums, 6 gymnasiums, 6 pedagogiums, 14 latin schools, 8 female seminaries, 4 normal schools, 2 trade and military schools, 2,121 common schools.

TABLE CLI.—*Proportion of Scholars at Schools, to the whole Population.*

Countries.	1 scholar to every	Countries.	1 scholar to every
	Persons		Persons
Maine	3.1	Great Britain	8.5
Denmark	4.6	" actually at school	7.
United States	4.9	France	10.5
" including slaves	5.6	Austria	13.7
Sweden	5.6	Holland	14.3
Saxony	6.0	Ireland	14.5
Prussia	6.2	Greece	18.
Norway	7.0	Russia	50.
Belgium	8.3	Portugal	81.7

The comparisons in every instance are to the total population, and therefore will be somewhat affected by the greater or less predominance of persons at the school ages. With all

Wirtemberg—1 University—nine real schools, six gymnasia, five lycea, 87 latin schools, 2 religious, 1 polytechnic, 1 agricultural, 7 of art, 2 girl seminaries, 2,332 common schools, 6 teachers' seminaries. At the institute near Stutgard the course of agricultural education is as follows:—*Barnard.*

1st. *Agriculture.*—General principles of farming and horticulture, including the culture of the vine. The breeding of cattle, growing of wool, raising of horses, rearing of silkworms, arrangement and direction of farms, estimation of the value of farms, book-keeping.

2d. *Forestry.*—Encyclopedia of forestry, botany of forests, culture and superintendence of forests, guard of forests, hunting, taxation, uses of forests, technology. Laws and regulations, accounts, and technical correspondence relating to forests.

3d. *Accessory Branches.*—Veterinary art, agriculture technology, especially the manufacture of beet sugar, brewing, vinegar making and distilling. The construction of roads and hydraulic works. Besides these special branches, the following general courses are pursued. 1st. *The Natural Sciences.*—Geology, physiology of plants, botany as applied to agriculture and forestry. Natural history of animals, beneficial or noxious to plants and trees. General chemistry and its applications to agriculture. Physics and meteorology. 2d. *Mathematics.*—Theoretical and practical geometry, elements of trigonometry, arithmetic, elements of algebra.

Bavaria.—Population 4,250,000; 6,065 common schools, with 556,239 pupils, and 150 higher schools, universities, &c., with 99,512 scholars.

Austria, 1838.—Population 23,652,000; children from 5 to 13, 2,886,441; total at school 2,338,985, of which, boys 1,314,460, girls 1,024,525—superior institutions exclusive of Hungary, 222, with 1868 professors and 50,497 scholars, besides academies, &c.; 1849, 12,776 university students, 1,057,146 boys, 830,793 girls; total 1,887,939 elementary scholars, (exclusive of Hungary;) 1850, 549 colleges, with 72,286 students, 33,340 public schools, 43,381 teachers and 2,502,874 pupils, and 34,127 academy and other scholars.

Switzerland.—Nearly every boy and girl below the age of 17 can read and write.

France, 1843.—Whole number of communes 37,038; number provided with primary schools 34,578; total number of schools, primary and superior, for boys and girls 59,838; to which add night and Sunday schools for laborers, at which in 1843, 95,064 adults were taught. Of the total primary schools 56,812 are Catholic, 1,080 Protestant, 115 Jewish; 1,831, mixed; total scholars 1843, 3,164,297, of which 763,820 were gratuitously educated, and 2,400,447 who paid something. Normal schools 78, professors 495; secondary pupils in colleges and higher institutions, 69,341.

Belgium.—The system embraces primary schools, high schools, intermediate schools, normal, universities, industrial schools; 1850, 1,975 university students, 4,438 gymnasia students, 32,019 scholars in academies and higher schools, 268,186 boys, and 225,587 girls; total, 493,773 in elementary schools.

Holland.—382,370 scholars in primary schools, 1,300 in Latin schools, 1,800 in universities, total 385,470 in 1846, or one in every eight of the population; 1849, 3 universities and 1,037 students, 67 gymnasia with 1,776 scholars, 1,619 academies with 40,020 scholars, 2,448 elementary schools, with 166,889 scholars; total scholars, excluding students, 208,685.

Denmark.—4,700 primary schools and 300,000 pupils.

Ireland, 1847.—402,632 scholars; 1848, 507,469; 1849, 480,623.

Sweden, 1850.—Population 3,358,867, of which in various schools and educated at home, between 9 and 15 years of age, 448,205.

Portugal, 1850.—1,206 university scholars, 2,840 academy, 38,754 elementary scholars.

Norway.—In 1837 one-seventh of the population were being educated in the public schools.

Russia.—600,000 scholars educated by the government, and 597,000 estimated as receiving home education; total 1,200,000.

Greece.—47,000 pupils at all schools, 1853. In England and Wales the whole number of day scholars at school has risen from 674,883, or 1 in 17 of the population in 1818, to 2,108,473 in 1851, or 1 in 8¼ of the population. The day scholars having increased 212 per cent., and the population but 57 per cent. There were also in 1851, 2,407,409 children attending the Sunday schools.

Great Britain, 1851.

Pupils.	Public Day Schools.			Private Day Schools.		
	Males.	Females	Total.	Males.	Females	Total.
On the books	791,548	616,021	1,407,569	347,694	353,210	700,904
Attending school March 31st, 1851	635,107	480,130	....	317,388	322,351	639,739
Total public and private on books	1,139,242	969,231	2,108,473	....	....	....
Total at school 31st March, public and private	952,495	802,481	1,754,976	....	....	....

Proportion of scholars on books to total population, 11.76 per cent, or 1 in 8½. Number in attendance to those on books, 83½ per cent.

Estimating for the schools not properly returned, the whole number of day schools will be swelled to 46,114, of which 15,584 were public, and 30,530 were private, number of scholars to 2,144,377, of which 1,417,300 public, and 727,077 private. There were 955,865 scholars by one report in Church of England schools, 34,750 in Roman Catholic, 20,000, in ragged schools, etc.

corrections, the results are sufficiently remarkable. Maine has a larger proportion at school than any other State or country; Denmark exceeds the United States, and the United States exceeds all other countries, even if the slaves are not excluded from the calculation. Portugal is lowest in the list and is followed by Russia. The results cannot be considered as more than a fair approximation though founded upon official data. They do not take into account the greater or less time which each scholar is at school, or the greater or less amount of proficiency attained.

In the Southern States the number of children educated at home by private tutors in consequence of the population being scattered, is immensely greater in proportion to the whole than in other parts of the Union. Such children are therefore not reported in the table of institutions, and would perhaps be omitted in that of scholars by families, since the marshals were only required to ask what member of the family has been at school within the last year: "he is to insert a mark opposite the names of all those whether male or female who have been at educational institutions within that period." Again in the same States a large number of students are always abroad for education, and are returned with the schools, colleges, &c., of other States. An examination of Massachusetts shows, out of 2,357 "students" mentioned, 711 or one-third nearly, born out of the State, and 152, or one-fifteenth born in the South. On the other hand a southern town taken at random, furnished one out of three editors, four out of twelve teachers, two out of seven clergymen born in the non-slaveholding States.

The average annual time of attendance at school of each child is much larger in the Southern than in the Northern States, in consequence of white labor being less required in industrial pursuits. Thus three children at school for nine months may, for some purposes be compared with nine children at school for three months, &c. It would require perhaps ten times the number of school houses and teachers in Virginia, to educate the same number of persons as in Massachusetts. "The social intercourse of the South compensates to some extent for its want of schools. The people are taught to think and to converse, and the reunions which are so frequent are the occasions of interchanging opinions and of diffusing intelligence.*

The statistics for this note are made up from official sources, and in some cases where these have not been accessible, from other data. In addition there are in Europe 345 schools of agriculture, with lectures in 16 universities on the same subject.

In the whole of England and Wales, among 367,894 couples married in 3 years, 122,458 men and 181,378 women could neither read nor write. In 1842, 38,031 men and 56,965 women, out of a total of 118,825 couples, affixed their marks instead of signatures; in 1844, 42,912 men and 65,073 women out of a total of 132,249 couples. In 1846 in London, 11.6 per cent. of the men, and 22.6 of the women affixed their mark. Throughout all England and Wales, 32.6 per cent. of the men and 48.1 of the women marrying, affixed their mark. In the French army in 1851, of 311,218 conscripts, 34 in a hundred could neither read nor write, 3½ could read only, 59½ in a hundred could read and write, 3 in 100 unknown. It has already been stated that in the Prussian army of 122,897 only 2 persons could not read and write.

* Professor Tucker remarks as follows upon the statistics of education for 1840, at the North and the South:

"These diversities are attributable to several causes, but principally to the difference in density of numbers, and in the proportion of town population. In a thinly peopled country, it is very difficult for a poor man to obtain schooling for his children, either by his own means, or by any means that the State is likely to provide, but where the population is dense, and especially in towns, it is quite practicable to give to every child the rudiments of education, without onerously taxing the community. This is almost literally true in all the New England States and New York, and is said to be the case in the Kingdom of Prussia. It is true that, in the North-western States, and particularly those which are exempt from slaves, the number of their elementary schools is much greater than that of the Southern or South-western States, although their population is not much more dense; but, besides that, the settlers of those States, who were mostly from New England or New York, brought with them a deep sense of the value and importance of the schools for the people, they were better able to provide such schools, in consequence of their making their settlement, as had been done in their parent States, in townships and villages. We thus see that Michigan, which has but a thin population even in the settled parts of the State, has schools for nearly one-seventh of its population. The wise policy pursued, first in New England, and since by the States settled principally by their emigrants, of laying off their territory into townships, and of selling all the lands of a portion before those of other townships are brought into market, has afforded their first settlers the benefits of social intercourse and of co-operation. In this way they were at once provided with places of worship, and with schools adapted to their circumstances."

Mr. Porter, in his Progress of Great Britain, remarks upon the deficiency of actual information which often exists among those who are capable of reading and writing:

"The reports of the statistical societies of Manchester and London have shown how unworthy of the name of education, is the result of what is attempted in the majority of schools frequented by children of the working classes, and which are frequently kept by persons whose only qualification for this employment seems to be their unfitness for every other.

"A lamentable proof of the correctness of this remark is offered in the following extract from the report for 1839, of the chaplain of the Juvenile Prison at Parkhurst:—One point has forcibly struck my attention, and that is, the comparatively large amount of acquirement in the mechanical elements of instruction (the art of reading and repetition from memory,) contrasted with the lamentably small degree of actual knowledge possessed, either of moral duty or religious principle.

"This appears mainly to have arisen from the meaning of the words read, or sounds repeated, having rarely been made the subjects of inquiry or reflection. The following digest will in some degree illustrate this position. Your Lordship will perceive that although fifty-eight prisoners can in some degree read, eighty-three repeat some or all of the church catechism, and forty-three possess some knowledge of Holy Scripture, only twenty-nine (exactly half the number of readers) can give even a *little* account of the meaning of words read, or sounds in use; and of these it appears very often to be the strength of the intellect exercised *at the moment*, and not the result of *prior* reflection, that leads them to the meaning of a word.

"Another feature of the moral condition of the Parkhurst prisoners cannot but arrest the attention strongly, and that is, the very large proportion that have received instruction for a considerable period of time in the various schools with which our country abounds. A digest of this portion of the general table will show, that out of 102 lads, 94 have attended schools; 69 of whom have been day scholars for terms longer than a year, eight only having never been at school.

"Read tolerable 20; read indifferently 38; read scarcely at all 14; read not at all 30—total 102. Of those there attended school from 8 to 12 years, 2; from 5 to 8, 5; from 3 to 5, 21; from 1 to 3, 44; under 1 year, 22; never at school, 8—total 102."

In the table which follows, the proportion of whites at school, as returned by families, to the total whites, and to the whites between the ages of 5 and 15, native and foreign, is given. The foreign whites of those ages were obtained by taking 14 per cent. of the whole foreign, as is explained in the note.*

TABLE CLII.—*Native and Foreign Whites, and the proportion of those at School*—1850.

States and Territories.	Native whites.	Foreign whites.	Whites, including unknown nativity.	Native whites between 5 and 15.	Foreign whites between 5 and 15.	Native whites at school.	Per cent. of whites at school.	Per cent. of native whites at school.	Per cent. of foreign at school.	Per cent. of native whites at school to those of 5 and under 15.	Foreign whites at school to those of 5 and under 15.
Alabama	418,015	7,498	426,514	125,845	1,049	62,670	14.72	15.01	1.44	49.80	10.29
Arkansas	159,946	1,468	162,189	49,291	205	23,332	14.39	13.33	1.22	47.33	8.78
California	69,562	21,629	91,635	1,010	3,028	975	1.08	1.40	.08	96.53	.56
Columbia, Dist. of.	32,995	4,913	37,941	8,620	688	6,018	16.08	18.24	1.73	69.81	12.35
Connecticut	324,095	38,374	363,099	70,879	5,372	79,957	22.70	21.58	6.45	112.81	46.09
Delaware	65,917	5,243	71,169	18,107	734	13,890	19.97	21.07	6.22	76.71	44.41
Florida	44,452	2,740	47,203	12,964	383	4,638	10.05	10.43	3.93	35.77	28.19
Georgia	514,566	6,452	521,572	155,606	903	76,914	14.76	14.95	1.56	49.43	11.18
Illinois	730,822	111,860	846,034	227,105	15,660	173,080	21.51	23.68	7.94	76.21	56.76
Indiana	919,278	55,537	977,154	280,844	7,775	217,300	22.52	23.64	4.95	77.23	35.16
Iowa	170,553	21,014	191,881	53,326	2,942	34,366	18.48	20.15	5.20	64.44	37.13
Kentucky	728,711	31,401	761,413	213,587	4,396	129,667	17.19	17.79	3.98	60.71	28.43
Louisiana	187,558	67,308	255,491	51,742	9,423	29,576	12.85	15.76	4.85	57.16	34.63
Maine	549,674	31,695	581,813	141,454	4,437	182,770	31.96	33.25	10.00	129.21	71.57
Maryland	366,650	51,011	417,943	97,348	7,141	58,770	14.46	16.03	3.28	60.37	23.48
Massachusetts	819,044	163,598	985,450	176,104	22,904	209,854	22.40	25.62	6.68	119.16	47.70
Michigan	339,223	54,593	395,071	101,119	7,643	100,644	26.77	26.72	9.36	99.53	66.86
Mississippi	290,447	4,782	295,718	88,416	669	48,751	16.50	16.78	1.09	55.14	7.47
Missouri	514,527	76,570	592,004	159,504	10,720	91,991	16.09	17.88	4.25	57.61	3.12
New Hampshire	303,057	14,257	317,456	66,483	1,996	86,925	27.76	25.05	8.58	130.72	61.27
New Jersey	405,402	59,804	465,509	107,449	8,372	86,566	18.75	21.33	4.53	80.56	32.36
New York	2,388,830	655,224	3,048,325	617,933	91,731	638,640	22.56	26.73	7.51	103.35	53.67
North Carolina	550,267	2,565	553,028	153,140	359	100,041	18.19	18.18	21.44	65.32	153.63
Ohio	1,732,698	218,099	1,955,050	508,884	30,534	495,996	26.20	28.62	7.46	97.46	53.33
Pennsylvania	1,953,276	303,105	2,258,160	540,972	42,442	482,324	22.05	24.69	5.21	89.16	37.20
Rhode Island	119,975	23,832	143,875	26,607	3,336	27,161	19.71	22.64	5.01	102.08	35.91
South Carolina	266,000	8,508	274,563	76,360	1,191	39,993	14.67	15.03	3.53	52,37	25.19
Tennessee	749,661	5,638	756,836	224,367	789	145,963	19.30	19.47	2.78	65.05	21.22
Texas	135,938	17,620	154,034	40,960	2,466	18,768	12.57	13.81	3.41	45.82	24.37
Vermont	279,383	33,688	313,402	69,455	4,716	88,656	29.40	31.73	10.38	127.48	74.13
Virginia	871,393	22,953	894,800	244,399	3,213	109,500	12.26	12.56	.92	44.80	6.53
Wisconsin	193,478	110,471	304,756	60,677	15,466	45,441	18.49	23.48	9.88	74.90	70.56
Territories. Minnesota	4,058	1,977	6,038	1,004	277	200	3.43	4.93	.35	19.92	2.53
Territories. New Mexico	59,165	2,151	61,525	15,453	301	464	.75	.78	.09	3.00	.66
Territories. Oregon	11,937	959	13,087	3,116	134	1,850	14.33	10.72	2.61	59.37	18.65
Territories. Utah	9,276	2,044	11,330	2,446	286	1,969	17.96	21.12	3.23	80.50	23.07
Total	17,279,829	2,240,581	19,553,068	4,792,576	313,681	3,915,620	20.78	20.00	6.58	80.81	51.73

The following table will show the educational results of the Census of 1840. Under the instructions, white and free colored scholars would be included.

TABLE CLIII.—*Education Statistics of* 1840.

STATES.	Universities and colleges.	Students.	Academies and grammar schools.	Scholars.	Primary schools.	Scholars.	Scholars at public charge.	White illiterate over 20 years old.
Maine	4	266	86	8,477	3,385	164,477	60,212	3,241
New Hampshire	2	433	68	5,799	2,127	83,632	7,715	942
Vermont	3	233	46	4,113	2,402	82,817	14,701	2,270
Massachusetts	4	769	251	16,746	3,362	160,257	158,351	4,448
Rhode Island	2	324	52	3,664	434	17,355	10,749	1,614
Connecticut	4	832	127	4,865	1,619	65,739	10,912	526
New England States	19	2,857	630	43,664	13,329	574,277	262,640	13,041

* The foreign born children between five and fifteen years of age in four counties of Iowa, four of Michigan, three of Tennessee, three of Rhode Island, five of Louisiana, and one ward of New York, were exactly ascertained from the returns, and constituted 13.5 per cent. of the whole foreign born there. The proportion of those who arrived in the country between five and fifteen years of age in 1845, '47, and '52, was about 15 per cent. A mean between the two was taken, or 14 per cent. The foreign born over twenty years of age were obtained from the returns of immigration for the same years, which showed an average of about 60 per cent.

TABLE CLIII.—*Continued.*

STATES.	Universities and colleges.	Students.	Academies and grammar schools.	Scholars.	Primary schools.	Scholars.	Scholars at public charge.	White illiterate over 20 years old.
New York	12	1,285	505	34,715	10,593	502,367	27,075	44,452
New Jersey	3	443	66	3,027	1,207	52,583	7,128	6,385
Pennsylvania	20	2,034	290	15,970	4,968	179,989	73,908	33,940
Delaware	1	23	20	764	152	6,924	1,571	4,832
Maryland	12	813	127	4,178	567	16,982	6,565	11,605
District of Columbia	2	224	26	1,389	29	851	482	1,033
Middle States	50	4,822	1,034	60,043	17,516	759,696	116,729	102,247
Virginia	13	1,097	382	11,083	1,561	35,331	9,791	58,787
North Carolina	2	158	141	4,398	632	14,937	124	56,609
South Carolina	1	168	117	4,326	566	12,520	3,524	20,615
Georgia	11	622	176	7,878	601	15,561	1,333	30,717
Florida	......	....	18	732	51	925	14	1,303
Southern States	27	2,045	834	28,417	3,411	79,274	14,786	168,031
Alabama	2	152	114	5,018	639	16,243	3,213	22,592
Mississippi	7	454	71	2,553	382	8,236	107	8,360
Louisiana	12	989	52	1,995	179	3,573	1,190	4,861
Arkansas	......	....	8	300	113	2,614	....	6,567
Tennessee	8	492	152	5,539	983	25,090	6,907	58,531
Southwestern States	29	2,087	397	15,405	2,296	55,756	11,417	100,911
Missouri	6	495	47	1,926	642	16,788	526	19,457
Kentucky	10	1,419	116	4,906	952	24,641	429	40,018
Ohio	18	1,717	73	4,310	5,186	218,609	51,812	35,394
Indiana	4	322	54	2,946	1,521	48,189	6,929	38,100
Illinois	5	311	42	1,967	1,241	34,876	1,683	27,502
Michigan	5	158	12	485	975	29,701	998	2,173
Wisconsin	......	....	2	65	77	1,937	315	1,701
Iowa	.....	....	1	25	63	1,500	....	1,118
Northwestern States	48	4,422	347	16,630	10,657	376,241	62,692	165,463
Total	173	16,233	3,242	164,159	47,209	1,845,244	468,264	549,693

TABLE CLIV.—*Age of Population for purposes of Educational Comparison*, 1850.

States and Territories.	Under 20 Whites.	TWENTY YEARS AND OVER.					
		Whites.	free colored.	white and free colored.	white foreign.	foreign white and free col'd.	native white and free col'd.
Alabama	248,097	178,417	1,083	179,500	4,498	4,505	174,995
Arkansas	97,402	64,787	310	65,097	880	882	64,215
California	11,378	80,257	829	81,086	12,937	13,081	68,005
Columbia, District of	18,400	19,541	5,277	24.818	2,977	2,950	21,868
Connecticut	153,862	209,237	4,425	213,662	23,024	23,110	185.552
Delaware	36,873	34,296	8,112	42,408	3,145	3,151	39,277
Florida	25,898	21,305	442	21,747	1,644	1,661	20,086
Georgia	303,798	217,774	1,390	219,164	3,871	3,892	215,272
Illinois	476,823	369,213	2,657	371,868	67,116	67,135	304,733
Indiana	565,179	411,975	4,815	416,790	33,322	33,343	383,447
Iowa	110,608	81,273	159	81,432	12,608	12,609	68,823
Kentucky	429,043	332,370	5,478	337,848	18,840	18,852	318,996
Louisiana	121,458	134,033	9,052	143,085	40,385	40,939	102,146
Maine	288,396	293,417	755	294,172	19,017	19,095	275,077
Maryland	208,084	209,859	37,194	247,053	30,606	30,725	216,328
Massachusetts	416,917	568,533	5,374	573,907	98,158	98,414	475,493
Michigan	210,831	184,240	1,348	185,588	32,755	32,821	152,767
Mississippi	172,496	123,222	489	123,711	2,869	2,872	120,839
Missouri	334,936	257,068	1,602	258,670	45,942	45,955	212,715
New Hampshire	137,224	180,232	322	180,554	8,554	8,559	171,995
New Jersey	230,849	234,660	12,055	246,715	35,882	35,968	210,747
New York	1,436,113	1,612,212	28,167	1,640,379	393,134	393,557	1,246,822
North Carolina	301,106	251,922	12,050	263,972	1,539	1,548	262,424
Ohio	1,064,212	890,838	11,898	902,736	130,860	130,915	771,821
Pennsylvania	1,162,874	1,095,286	28,337	1,123,623	181,863	182,050	941,573
Rhode Island	62,270	81,605	2,231	83,836	14,300	14,341	69,495
South Carolina	149,322	125,241	4,109	129,350	5,105	5,224	124,126
Tennessee	440,627	316,209	2,912	319,121	3,382	3,391	315,730
Texas	85,869	68,165	193	68,358	10,572	10,608	57,750
Vermont	145,989	167,413	411	167,824	20,212	20,229	147,595
Virginia	481,372	413,428	25,538	438,966	13,772	13,791	425,175
Wisconsin	156,175	148,581	358	148,939	66,282	66,286	82,653
Territories. Minnesota	2,656	3,382	25	3,407	1,186	1,186	2,221
Territories. New Mexico	31,572	29,953	20	29,973	1,291	1,291	28,682
Territories. Oregon	6,499	6,588	93	6,681	575	613	6,068
Territories. Utah	6,223	5,107	10	5,117	1,226	1,226	3,891

The annexed table will show the ratio of whites and colored, native and foreign, who cannot read and write, over 20 years of age, when compared with the whole number of cach of these classes, and also when compared with the actual number of and over 20 years of age. The population at 20 was necessarily included, the ages being only classified in periods of 5 and 10 years. As to foreigners over 20 see note on page 150.

TABLE CLV.—*Foreign and Native Illiterate.*

States and Territories.	Per cent. of white illiterate to total white.	Per cent. of free colored illiterate to total free colored.	Per cent. of native white and free colored illiterate to total native white and free colored.	Per cent. of foreign white and free colored illiterate to total foreign white and free colored.	Per cent. of native illiterate white and free colored to total of both native over 20 years of age.	Per cent. of foreign illiterate white and free colored to the total of both foreign over 20 years of age.	Foreign illiterate over 20 years of age.	Per cent. of foreign illiterate to total foreign over 20 years of age, supposing the illiterate to be all white
Alabama	7.91	10.37	8.06	1.85	18.85	3.08	139	3.09
Arkansas	10.37	19.08	10.53	1.84	24.44	3.13	27	3.97
California	5.58	12.16	3.30	13.38	2.86	22.30	2,917	22.54
Columbia, District of	3.84	31.95	10.11	6.55	17.52	11.14	322	10.92
Connecticut	1.30	7.37	.39	10.42	.62	17.36	4,013	17.43
Delaware	6.37	31.23	11.64	7.69	23.03	12.91	404	12.52
Florida	8.17	28.97	8.45	10.73	9.18	17.76	295	17.94
Georgia	8.99	15.93	7.97	6.26	18.82	10.43	406	10.49
Illinois	4.85	22.61	4.80	5.31	9.47	8.86	5,947	8.86
Indiana	7.22	19.26	7.46	5.88	9.46	9.79	3,265	9.80
Iowa	4.23	9.99	4.14	5.13	8.69	8.54	1,077	8.56
Kentucky	8.74	30.15	9.12	7.47	19.93	12.43	2,347	12.45
Louisiana	8.30	19.40	8.99	9.19	12.89	15.32	6,271	15.28
Maine	1.05	9.95	.39	13.03	.73	21.72	4,148	21.81
Maryland	4.98	28.18	8.71	6.74	11.10	11.23	3,451	11.27
Massachusetts	2.79	8.89	.22	16.15	.32	26.91	26,484	26.98
Michigan	2.00	10.41	1.54	5.50	2.84	9.17	3,009	9.19
Mississippi	4.53	13.22	4.62	1.69	10.87	2.82	81	2.82
Missouri	6.12	15.16	6.75	2.43	13.49	4.05	1,861	4.05
New Hampshire	.93	10.00	.31	14.47	.52	24.11	2,064	24.13
New Jersey	3.06	18.76	2.98	9.81	5.10	16.33	5,878	13.59
New York	2.99	15.14	1.26	10.37	1.87	17.29	68,052	17.31
North Carolina	13.30	21.32	13.86	13.17	30.34	2.19	340	22.03
Ohio	3.12	19.74	3.24	4.15	6.31	6.92	9,062	6.92
Pennsylvania	2.50	17.42	2.56	8.24	4.56	13.72	24,989	13.74
Rhode Island	2.32	7.27	1.01	9.87	1.49	16.45	2,359	16.49
South Carolina	5.71	9.82	5.99	1.19	12.73	1.99	104	2.04
Tennessee	10.21	17.08	10.33	8.92	18.64	14.89	505	14.90
Texas	6.18	14.60	5.94	14.07	11.84	23.45	2,488	23.53
Vermont	1.97	7.10	.22	16.68	.37	27.80	5,624	22.33
Virginia	8.60	21.19	9.44	4.95	19.90	8.24	1,137	8.25
Wisconsin	2.08	14.49	.80	4.44	1.04	7.39	4,902	7.39
Territories. Minnesota	10.74	....	6.32	19.73	7.60	3.29	390	32.80
Territories. New Mexico	40.77	18.18	41.27	30.68	61.11	51.12	660	51.15
Territories. Oregon	1.38	24.15	.82	6.16	1.48	10.27	63	10.95
Territories. Utah	.25	4.17	1.30	1.61	2.36	2.69	33	2.69
Total	4.92	20.83	4.85	8.24	10.35	14.48	195,114	14.51

TABLE CLVI.—*Ratio of Pupils and Illiterate in the great Sections*—1840-50.

Geographical Divisions.	1840. Whites.*	1840. Free Colored.	1840. Pupils.	1840. Illiterate.	Pupils to white population per cent., 1840.	Pupils to white and free colored population pr. ct., 1840.	Pupils to white population per cent., 1850.	Pupils to white and free colored population pr. ct., 1850.	Illiterate to white population per ct., 1840.	White illiterate to white population per cent., 1850.
New England States	2,212,165	22,634	620,798	13,041	28.06	27.78	25.90	25.71	.59	1.88
Middle States	4,814,015	206,283	824,561	102,247	17.13	16.42	21.79	21.02	2.12	3.16
Southern States	1,920,450	84,430	109,736	168,031	5.71	5.47	14.52	13.92	8.75	9.22
Southwestern States	1,390,517	34,896	73,248	100,911	5.27	5.14	16.32	16.10	7.26	8.45
Northwestern & Territories.	3,852,448	38,060	397,293	165,463	10.31	10.21	21.72	21.51	4.30	5.03
Slaveholding States	4,634,519	215,575	265,307	345,887	5.72	5.47	15.70	15.12	7.46	8.27
Non-slaveholding States	9,561,176	170,728	1,760,329	203,806	18.41	18.09	23.35	23.01	2.13	3.36
Total	14,195,695	386,303	2,025,636	549,693	12.27	13.89	14.27	20.46	3.87	4.92

* The population of the several sections is exclusive of 6,100 sailors, except in the Slaveholding and Non-Slaveholding States.

By the preceding table it seems that the proportion of pupils to the whole population has increased largely in the several sections, but most considerably in the South and Southwest. The figures for 1850 are those which were returned by families. The proportion for the Union has increased from 13.89 to 20.14 per cent. On the other hand, in consequence of the large influx of foreigners, those over twenty years of age of the whole white population who cannot read and write has increased in every section, and in the United States from 3.77 per cent. to 5.03. By another table which follows, the proportion of the illiterate native and foreign white and free colored, will be seen. The proportion of foreign illiterate in the Union is twice that of the native, whilst the proportion of foreign illiterate to the whole number of foreign over 20 is only a little less than twice as great as for the native.

TABLE CLVII.—*Ratio of Illiterate Persons, Foreign, Native, and Free Colored in* 1850.

Geographical Divisions.	Whites.										Free Colored	
	Native including unknown.	Illiterate.	Ratio per cent.	Native over 20 years old.	Ratio.	Foreign.	Illiterate.	Ratio per cent.	Foreign over 20 years old.	Ratio of illiterate per cent.	Illiterate.	Ratio per cent.
New England.	2,399,651	6,219	.26	1,495,437	.42	305,444	44,692	14.63	183,266	24.39	1,878	8.45
Middle States.	5,219,747	96,181	1.84	3,205,854	3.00	1,079,300	103,096	9.55	647,580	15.92	51,111	22.42
Southern "	2,247,948	209,032	9.30	1,029,570	20.30	43,218	2,282	5.28	25,930	8.80	19,989	21.20
Southwestern.	1,946,468	163,738	8.41	984,833	16.63	104,314	9,511	9.12	62,588	15.20	5,018	18.54
Northwest....	5,343,818	265,515	4.97	2,675,557	9.92	679,499	31,470	4.63	407,699	7.72	12,399	21.44
California and Territories ..	154,855	27,099	17.50	125,287	21.63	28,806	4,063	14.13	17,283	23.51	127	12.47
Slave States..	5,905,748	494,161	8.37	2,867,537	17.23	316,670	20,178	6.37	190,002	10.62	58,444	24.75
Free States...	11,406,759	273,623	2.40	6,649,001	4.12	1,923,911	174,936	9.09	1,154,344	15.15	32,078	16.55
Total	17,312,487	787,784	4.55	9,516,538	8.28	2,240,581	195,114	8.71	1,344,346	14.51	90,522	21.03

In New England, so admirable is the school system and so deserving of all imitation, that only one person over twenty years of age is incapable of reading and writing, in every four hundred of the number of native whites. In the south and southwest the number is one in about twelve; and in the territories one in about six; in the slaveholding states one in twelve; in the non-slaveholding one in forty; in the whole Union one in about twenty-two. In this calculation the unknown nativities are given to the natives, and the free colored illiterate are supposed to be native, as they have not been separated. If all the foreign illiterate be assumed to be white, it would seem they are in excess in the southern States over the northern, in proportion to the whole number, and that for the Union they are nearly twice as numerous as the native, being about one illiterate to every twelve foreign born persons. Comparing, however, with the total foreign over twenty, assuming sixty per cent. to be of that age, as is explained in another place, it appears that one in every seven in the United States cannot read and write, whilst for the native one in twelve. The proportion of colored natives who cannot read and write is about 21.03; the same at the south and in the north west; sixteen per cent. in the non-slaveholding States and twenty-four per cent. in the slaveholding States, assuming all the illiterate colored to be native. The assumptions do not affect the result in any appreciable manner, though necessary to the calculation.

TABLE CLVIII.

Geographical Divisions.	Native whites at school to those of 5 & under 15, per ct.	Foreign whites at school to those of 5 & under 15, per ct.
New England States	122.57	52.60
Southern States	51.53	21.00
Northwest	80.28	52.05
Slaveholding States........	56.09	27.23
Non-slaveholding States........	96.90	50.25
Total........	82.25	47.00

The actual ages of persons attending school is given in the table for the county of Franklin, in Kentucky; for East Feliciana, Plaquemines, Point Coupee, Rapides and Ouachita, Louisiana; Allegan, Barry, Berrien and Branch, Michigan; Erie, Ohio; Pike and Potter, Pennsylvania; Bristol, Kent and Washington, Rhode Island; Abbeville, Anderson, Barnwell, Beaufort, Charleston, Marion and Marlboro', South Carolina. In the same counties there was but one foreign colored at school, and 219 native colored, of whom six were under 5, three above 20, and thirty-one between 15 and 20, of the whole population of these counties.

TABLE CLIX.—*Classification of the Age and Nativity of Whites attending School.*

For several counties in the States of	Uuder 5.				5 and under 15.				15 and under 20.				20 and upwards.				Total.				Aggregate classified.
	Male		Female.		Male.		Female.		Male.		Female.		Male.		Fem		Male.		Female.		
	Native.	Foreign.	Native.	Foreign.	Native.	Foreign.	Native.	Foreign.	Native.	Foreign.	Native.	Foreign.	Native.	Foreign.	Native.	Foreign.	Native.	Foreign.	Native.	Foreign.	
Kentucky.....	5	..	1	..	510	2	526	2	140	....	79	..	15	..	8	..	670	2	614	2	1,288
Louisiana.....	8	..	4	1	912	4	858	3	228	3	139	1	46	..	24	..	1,194	7	1,025	5	2,231
Michigan......	140	4	121	..	3,359	82	3,285	80	922	27	694	11	128	5	53	11	4,549	118	4,153	102	8,922
Ohio	78	..	85	..	1,696	105	1,653	94	512	31	381	26	54	7	25	4	2,340	143	2,144	124	4,751
Pennsylvania..	83	3	77	2	1,122	25	1,088	17	199	4	170	2	15	1	10	..	1,419	33	1,345	21	2,818
Rhode Island..	196	7	149	8	3,229	93	3,118	93	775	5	546	3	92	..	74	..	4,292	105	3,887	104	8,388
South Carolina	34	1	23	..	6,034	110	5,711	77	1,561	7	1,001	10	230	..	49	..	7,859	118	6,784	87	14,848

TABLE CLX.—*Education—Free Colored—Mulatto and Black.*

States and Cities.	Attending School.			Illiterate.		
	Blacks.	Mulattoes	Total.	Blacks.	Mulattoes	Total.
Connecticut..................................	945	319	1,264	416	151	567
Louisiana.....................................	127	1,092	1,219	1,157	2,232	3,389
New York....................................	963	455	1,418	1,263	404	1,667
New Orleans................................	118	890	1,008	1,031	1,248	2,279

3. THE PRESS.—Another important branch of social statistics is supplied by the periodical press. In every country the Press must be regarded a great educational agency. Professor Tucker well remarks: "In attending to the vast it does not overlook the minute. We meet with the speculations of wisdom and science, the effusions of sentiment, the sallies of wit. The most secluded hermit, if he only takes a newspaper, sees as in a telescope, and often as in a mirror, every thing that is transacted in the most distant regions; nor can any thing memorable happen, that it is not forthwith communicated with the speed of steam to the whole civilized world." Freedom of speech and of the press are the inalienable birth right of every American citizen, and constitute the ægis of his liberties.

The origin of newspapers may be traced to Italy in the sixteenth century. The first in England appeared under Queen Elizabeth, at the time of the Spanish Armada. The earliest newspaper was entitled the English Mercurie, imprinted at London, by her Highness' printer, 1588. *Periodical* papers were first used during the civil wars of the commonwealth.* The earliest newspaper in North America was the Boston News-Letter, issued April 24, 1704. In 1720, there were but seven newspapers in the American Colonies. In 1775 thirty-five, to wit: 7 in Massachusetts, 1 each in New Hampshire, and Georgia, 2 each in Rhode Island, Maryland, Virginia and North Carolina, 3 in South Carolina, 4 each in Connecticut and New York, and 9 in Pennsylvania.

The newspaper and periodical statistics of 1850 fall short of, rather than exceed, the reality. An effort was made to obtain at least one copy of every journal published in the United States in that year, and the assistant marshals were entrusted with the matter. It has been attended to but partially, and the papers obtained fall very far short of the actual number returned by name. This is to be regretted, as such a file, complete in every respect, properly bound and placed away in the Library of Congress, would be a great national curiosity, and have great interest with the future antiquarian. As far as the papers are received, proper care will be taken in their preservation. In the whole list, between forty and fifty are published in German; about a dozen in French; several in Spanish, Italian, etc.

* In 1827, there appeared in Great Britain, 483 different newspapers and other periodicals to 23,400,000 inhabitants. In 1842: papers in London 125, circulation 32,166,474; England, exclusive of London, 221 papers, 17,508,381 circulation; Wales 12 papers, 445,930 circulation; Scotland 76 papers, 5,388,079; Ireland 87, 5,986,639. Total papers 521, circulation 61,495,503. In Sweden and Norway, 82 journals to 3,866,000 inhabitants; in the States of the Church, 6 newspapers to 2,598,000 inhabitants, (Stockholm, with 78,000 inhabitants, has 30 journals; Rome, with 154,000 only 3;) Denmark, to 1,950,000 inhabitants, has 80 journals, of which 71 are in the Danish language; 23 are devoted to politics; 25 to the sciences. Prussia has 12,416,000 inhabitants, and 288 journals and periodicals. (Berlin has 221,000 inhabitants, and 53 periodical works; Copenhagen has 109,000 inhabitants, and 57 journals.) The Netherlands have 3,000,000 inhabitants, and 150 journals. In the German Confederation, (excluding Austria and Prussia,) there are 13,300,000 inhabitants, and 305 journals; in Saxony, to 1,400,000 inhabitants, 54 newspapers; in Hanover, to 1,550,000 inhabitants, 16 newspapers; in Ba-

TABLE CLXI.—*Newspaper and Periodical Statistics,* 1810, 1828 *and* 1840.†

STATES, &c.	1810.		1828.	1840.				
	Papers.	Circulation.	Papers.	Daily.	Weekly.	Semi and Tri-weekly.	Periodicals.	Total.
Alabama	......	....	10	3	24	1	......	28
Arkansas	......	....	2	......	6	3	......	9
California	......	....	......	......	......	......	......	......
Columbia, District of	6	686,400	9	3	5	6	3	17
Connecticut	11	657,800	33	2	27	4	11	44
Delaware	2	166,400	4	......	3	3	2	8
Florida	......	....	2	......	10	......	......	10
Georgia	13	707,200	18	5	24	5	6	40
Illinois	......	....	4	3	38	2	9	52
Indiana	1	15,600	17	......	69	4	3	76
Iowa	......	....	......	......	4	......	......	4
Kentucky	17	618,800	23	5	26	7	8	46
Louisiana	11	‡763,900	9	11	21	2	3	37
Maine	......	....	29	3	30	3	5	41
Maryland	21	1,903,200	37	7	28	7	7	49
Massachusetts	32	2,873,000	78	10	67	14	14	105
Michigan	......	....	2	6	26	......	1	33
Mississippi	4	83,200	6	2	28	1	......	31
Missouri	......	....	5	6	24	5	......	35
New Hampshire	12	624,000	17	......	27	......	6	33
New Jersey	8	332,800	22	4	31	1	4	40
New York	66	4,139,200	161	34	198	13	57	302
North Carolina	10	416,000	20	......	26	1	2	29
Ohio	14	473,200	66	9	107	7	20	143
Pennsylvania	71	4,542,200	185	12	165	10	42	229
Rhode Island	7	332,800	14	2	10	4	2	18
South Carolina	10	842,400	16	3	12	2	4	21
Tennessee	6	171,600	8	2	38	6	10	56
Texas	......	....	......	......	......	......	......	......
Vermont	14	682,400	21	2	26	2	3	33
Virginia	23	1,289,600	34	4	35	12	5	56
Wisconsin	......	....	......	......	6	......	......	6
Total	359	22,321,700	852	138	1,141	125	227	1,631

TABLE CLXII.—*Newspapers and Periodicals published in the United States,* 1850.

STATES AND TERRITORIES.	Daily.		Tri-weekly.		Semi-weekly.		Weekly.	
	Number.	Number of copies printed annually.	Number.	Number of copies printed annually.	Number.	Number of copies printed annually.	Number.	Number of copies printed annually.
Alabama	6	869,201	5	*266,500	......	....	48	1,509,040
Arkansas	......	....	......	....	......	....	9	377,000
California	4	626,000	......	....	......	....	3	135,200
Columbia, District of	5	6,149,198	5	*1,208,610	......	....	8	3,769,428
Connecticut	7	1,752,800	4	374,400	......	....	30	2,117,232
Delaware	......	....	......	....	3	62,400	7	358,800
Florida	......	....	1	*31,200	......	....	9	288,600
Georgia	5	1,086,110	3	*146,380	......	....	37	2,609,776
Illinois	8	1,120,540	4	*214,500	......	....	84	3,575,936
Indiana	9	1,153,092	2	*195,000	......	....	95	2,920,736
Iowa	......	....	2	*577,200	......	....	25	923,000
Kentucky	9	2,243,584	7	*1,125,280	......	....	38	3,053,024
Louisiana	11	9,947,140	6	*676,000	......	....	37	1,646,684
Maine	4	964,040	5	*302,900	......	....	39	2,906,124
Maryland	6	15,806,500	4	499,700	......	....	54	3,166,124
Massachusetts	22	40,498,444	4	351,000	11	2,070,016	126	20,371,104
Michigan	3	1,252,000	2	*52,000	......	....	47	1,685,736

varia, to 3,960,000 inhabitants, 48 newspapers. France, with a population of 32,000,000 has 490 periodical works, (660 printing establishments, 1,500 presses;) in Paris, 81 printing establishments, or 850 presses. In Paris alone, containing 890,000 inhabitants, there are 176 periodical works. This note has reference to the population at the periods when the newspaper statistics were collected.

† The figures for 1810 and 1828 of the above table are taken from the American Almanac, 1830, and from an early issue of the National Intelligencer.

‡ Including Louisiana and Orleans Territories.

* Papers "tri-weekly and semi-weekly" arranged under the head of "tri-weekly;" those "semi-monthly and monthly" under the head of "semi-monthly."

TABLE CLXII.—*Continued.*

STATES AND TERRITORIES.	Daily.		Tri-weekly.		Semi-weekly.		Weekly.	
	Number.	Number of copies printed annually.	Number.	Number of copies printed annually.	Number.	Number of copies printed annually.	Number.	Number of copies printed annually.
Mississippi	......	....	4	*245,440	......	....	46	1,507,064
Missouri	5	3,380,400	4	*273,000	......	....	45	2,406,560
New Hampshire	......	....	......	....	......	....	35	3,538,152
New Jersey	6	2,175,350	......	....	......	....	43	1,900,288
New York	51	63,928,685	8	776,100	13	3,116,360	308	39,205,920
North Carolina	......	....	5	*414,310	......	....	40	1,530,204
Ohio	26	14,285,633	10	*1,047,930	......	....	201	13,334,204
Pennsylvania	24	50,416,788	2	78,000	1	62,400	261	27,359,384
Rhode Island	5	1,768,450	......	....	2	25,200	12	963,300
South Carolina	7	5,070,600	5	*549,250	......	....	27	1,413,880
Tennessee	8	4,407,666	2	*266,240	......	....	36	2,139,644
Texas	......	....	5	*525,400	......	....	29	771,524
Vermont	2	172,150	......	....	1	228,800	30	2,142,712
Virginia	15	4,992,350	12	*1,416,550	......	....	55	2,518,568
Wisconsin	6	1,053,245	4	*198,250	......	....	35	1,395,992
Territories. Minnesota	......	....	......	....	......	....	......	....
Territories. New Mexico	......	....	......	....	......	....	1	20,800
Territories. Oregon	......	....	......	....	......	....	2	58,968
Territories. Utah	......	....	......	....	......	....	......	....
Total	254	235,119,966	115	11,811,140	31	5,565,176	1,902	153,120,708

STATES AND TERRITORIES.	Semi-monthly.		Monthly.		Quarterly.		Aggregate.	
	Number.	Number of copies printed annually.	Number.	Number of copies printed annually.	Number.	Number of copies printed annually.	Number.	Number of copies printed annually.
Alabama	1	18,000	......	....	......	....	60	2,662,741
Arkansas	......	....	......	....	......	....	9	377,000
California	......	....	......	....	......	....	7	761,200
Columbia, District of	......	....	......	....	......	....	18	11,127,236
Connecticut	......	....	1	6,000	2	8,800	46	4,267,932
Delaware	......	....	......	....	......	....	10	421,200
Florida	......	....	......	....	......	....	10	319,800
Georgia	6	*228,600	......	....	......	....	51	4,070,866
Illinois	3	43,200	7	147,200	1	900	107	5,102,276
Indiana	1	48,000	......	....	......	....	107	4,316,828
Iowa	......	....	2	12,600	......	....	29	1,512,800
Kentucky	8	*160,950	......	....	......	....	62	6,582,838
Louisiana	......	....	1	146,400	......	....	55	12,416,224
Maine	......	....	1	30,000	......	....	49	4,203,064
Maryland	1	48,000	3	92,400	......	....	68	19,612,724
Massachusetts	3	61,800	29	1,357,200	7	24,000	209	64,820,564
Michigan	3	134,400	3	123,600	......	....	58	3,247,736
Mississippi	......	....	......	....	......	....	50	1,752,504
Missouri	......	....	7	135,600	......	....	61	6,195,560
New Hampshire	1	15,600	2	13,800	......	....	38	3,067,552
New Jersey	2	23,040	......	....	......	....	51	4,098,678
New York	9	1,704,000	36	6,629,808	3	24,600	428	115,385,473
North Carolina	6	*76,050	......	....	......	....	51	2,020,564
Ohio	23	*1,781,640	......	....	1	24,000	261	30,473,407
Pennsylvania	19	6,972,000	......	....	2	7,600	310	84,898,672
Rhode Island	......	....	......	....	......	....	19	2,756,950
South Carolina	5	*102,600	......	....	2	9,600	46	7,145,930
Tennessee	......	....	4	127,200	......	....	50	6,940,750
Texas	......	....	......	....	......	....	34	1,296,924
Vermont	......	....	2	24,000	......	....	35	2,567,662
Virginia	3	267,600	1	24,000	1	4,000	87	9,223,068
Wisconsin	......	....	1	18,000	......	....	46	2,665,487
Territories. Minnesota	......	....	......	....	......	....	......	....
Territories. New Mexico	1	18,000	......	....	......	....	2	38,800
Territories. Oregon	......	....	......	....	......	....	2	58,968
Territories. Utah	......	....	......	....	......	....	......	....
Total	95	11,703,480	100	8,887,808	19	103,500	2,526	426,409,978

* Papers "tri-weekly and semi-weekly," arranged under the head of "tri-weekly;" those "semi-monthly and monthly" under the head of "semi-monthly."

The following journals, though included in the aggregates of the States, are not classified under any of the heads: Massachusetts, four bi-monthly, 42,000 circulation per annum; three annuals, aggregate circulation of 45,000. Connecticut, one bi-monthly, circulation 7,200 per annum; one published three times a year, 1,500 annual circulation. Pennsylvania, one annual, 2,500 circulation.

TABLE CLXIII.—*Character of the Newspaper and Periodical Press.*

1. *Number of Copies Printed Annually.*

States and Territories.	Literary and Miscellaneous	Neutral and Independent.	Political.	Religious.	Scientific.	Aggregate.
Alabama	265,200	313,000	1,889,169	158,400	36,972	2,662,741
Arkansas	171,600	...	205,400	...	...	377,000
California	135,200	626,000	...	...	...	761,200
Columbia, Dist. of	81,900	54,600	10,990,736	...	...	11,127,236
Connecticut	489,900	...	3,422,432	223,200	7,200	*4,267,932
Delaware	46,800	...	374,400	...	...	421,200
Florida	...	...	202,800	117,000	...	319,800
Georgia	1,411,976	747,340	1,491,350	239,200	181,000	4,070,866
Illinois	721,700	403,770	3,384,162	499,044	93,600	5,102,276
Indiana	647,504	...	3,569,324	100,000	...	4,316,828
Iowa	36,000	187,200	1,281,800	7,800	...	1,512,800
Kentucky	650,800	250,400	5,245,888	429,450	6,300	6,582,838
Louisiana	657,300	3,335,100	8,356,224	52,000	15,600	12,416,224
Maine	987,216	...	2,501,680	438,568	275,600	4,203,064
Maryland	14,654,000	8,400	4,196,924	669,400	84,000	19,612,724
Massachusetts	11,794,304	13,591,000	32,996,800	4,405,200	2,033,260	64,820,564
Michigan	456,500	26,000	2,556,836	134,400	74,000	3,247,736
Mississippi	233,480	...	1,519,024	...	...	1,752,504
Missouri	608,800	...	5,496,280	90,480	...	6,195,560
New Hampshire	579,480	...	1,673,672	778,000	36,400	3,067,552
New Jersey	181,640	93,900	3,823,138	...	...	4,098,678
New York	18,449,016	37,317,010	45,463,015	12,438,432	1,718,000	115,385,473
North Carolina	266,200	113,750	1,457,664	182,950	...	2,020,564
Ohio	3,865,880	4,220,805	18,865,282	3,334,240	187,200	30,473,407
Pennsylvania	18,515,028	21,908,548	37,808,960	6,588,136	78,000	84,898,672
Rhode Island	280,800	782,500	1,693,650	...	...	2,756,950
South Carolina	474,800	2,140,400	4,310,930	195,000	24,800	7,145,930
Tennessee	206,200	503,930	5,138,580	1,092,040	...	6,940,750
Texas	350,324	148,400	660,400	137,800	...	1,296,924
Vermont	208,600	...	2,025,430	333,632	...	2,567,662
Virginia	247,880	1,251,900	6,698,176	1,001,112	24,000	9,223,068
Wisconsin	130,000	...	2,517,487	...	18,000	2,665,487
Territories. Minnesota	...	...	...	...	...	...
Territories. New Mexico	38,800	...	...	...	...	38,800
Territories. Oregon	32,448	...	26,520	...	...	58,968
Territories. Utah	...	...	...	...	...	...
Total	77,877,276	88,023,953	221,844,133	33,645,484	4,893,932	426,409,978

2. *Number of Papers and the Circulation of each Class.*

States and Territories	Literary and Miscellaneous.		Neutral and Independent.		Political.		Religious.		Scientific.		Aggregate.	
	Number.	Circulation.	Number.	Circulation.	Number.	Circulation.	Number.	Circulation.	Number.	Circulation.	Number.	Circulation.
Alabama	11	5,100	1	1,000	45	24,336	2	3,450	1	711	60	34,597
Arkansas	3	3,300	..	...	6	3,950	...	...	..	...	9	7,250
California	3	2,600	4	2,000	...	...	...	...	..	...	7	4,600
Columbia, Dist. of	2	1,575	1	350	15	99,437	...	...	..	...	18	101,362
Connecticut	12	11,200	..	...	28	34,916	4	5,400	1	1,200	46	53,116
Delaware	2	900	..	...	8	6,600	...	...	..	...	10	7,500
Florida	...	...	..	...	7	3,500	3	2,250	..	...	10	5,750
Georgia	18	29,638	6	3,046	20	20,900	3	4,600	4	9,300	51	67,484
Illinois	22	17,725	1	1,290	73	51,111	8	12,097	3	6,400	107	88,623
Indiana	21	12,452	..	...	84	47,900	2	3,000	..	...	107	63,352
Iowa	2	1,000	1	1,200	25	20,150	1	650	..	...	29	23,000
Kentucky	12	14,900	2	800	42	55,936	5	12,525	1	525	62	84,686
Louisiana	13	22,025	6	12,000	34	45,522	1	1,000	1	300	55	80,847
Maine	15	20,458	..	...	29	29,695	4	8,434	1	5,300	49	63,887
Maryland	20	71,000	1	700	39	31,637	6	13,950	2	7,000	68	124,287
Massachusetts	80	283,027	9	50,700	82	171,387	24	117,650	14	94,205	209	716,969
Michigan	13	13,625	1	200	39	28,793	3	5,600	2	4,500	58	52,718
Mississsppi	10	4,490	..	...	40	26,380	...	...	..	...	50	30,870
Missouri	17	19,400	..	...	42	48,340	2	2,740	..	...	61	70,480
New Hampshire	10	11,790	..	...	22	32,186	5	15,500	1	700	38	60,176
New Jersey	6	4,010	1	300	44	40,144	...	...	..	...	51	44,454
New York	101	528,908	15	127,370	263	399,755	37	507,246	12	59,500	428	1,622,779
North Carolina	8	5,675	2	875	35	24,564	6	5,725	..	...	51	36,839

* Including one paper—character not defined—400 circulation and 125,000 printed annually.

TABLE CLXIII—*Continued.*

States and Territories	Literary and Miscellaneous.		Neutral and Independent.		Political.		Religious.		Scientific.		Aggregate.	
	Number.	Circulation.	Number.	Circulation.	Number.	Circulation.	Number.	Circulation.	Number.	Circulation.	Number.	Circulation.
Ohio	37	111,790	6	13,485	192	189,304	21	90,130	5	10,400	261	415,109
Pennsylvania	71	445,364	12	70,396	198	267,940	28	198,018	1	1,500	310	983,218
Rhode Island	6	5,400	1	2,500	12	18,075	....	....	..	....	19	25,975
South Carolina	10	12,700	5	8,300	24	28,115	5	4,600	2	2,000	46	55,715
Tennessee	5	10,350	2	1,610	36	33,147	7	22,770	..	....	50	67,877
Texas	17	6,737	1	1,400	14	8,350	2	2,650	..	....	34	19,137
Vermont	5	5,550	..	....	27	33,990	3	6,416	..	....	35	45,956
Virginia	10	5,690	5	4,200	62	51,988	9	25,256	1	2,000	87	89,134
Wisconsin	3	2,500	..	....	42	29,236	....	....	1	1,500	46	33,236
Territories. Minnesota	....	....	..	....	.....	....	....	....	..	....	.....	....
Territories. New Mexico	2	900	..	....	.....	....	....	....	..	....	2	900
Territories. Oregon	1	624	..	....	1	510	....	....	..	....	2	1,134
Territories. Utah	....	....	..	....	.....	....	....	....	..	....	.....	....
Total	568	1,692,403	83	303,722	1,630	1,907,794	191	1,071,657	53	207,041	2,526	5,183,017

TABLE CLXIV.—*Circulation of Newspapers &c., to White Population.*

Years.	Total white Population.	Number of Papers.	Proportion to every 100,000 persons.	Annual circulation.	Number to each person.
1810	5,862,004	359	6.1	22,321,700	3.81
1828	*11,500,000	852	7.4	*68,117,796	5.92
1840	14,195,695	1,631	11.5	*195,838,673	13.80
1850	19,553,068	2,526	12.9	426,409,978	21.81

TABLE CLXV.—*Annual Circulation of Papers to White Population*—1850.

Geographical Divisions.	Literary.		Political.		Religious.	
	Number.	Ratio to each person.	Number.	Ratio to each person.	Number.	Ratio to each person.
New England	14,340,300	5.30	44,313,664	16.38	6,178,600	2.28
Middle States	51,928,384	8.24	102,657,173	16.30	19,695,968	3.13
Southern States	2,400,856	1.05	14,160,920	6.18	1,735,262	.76
Southwestern	1,884,104	.92	17,768,797	8.66	1,440,240	.70
Northwestern and Territories	7,323,632	1.18	42,943,579	6.92	4,595,414	.74
Total	77,877,276	3.98	221,844,133	11.35	33,645,484	1.72

TABLE CLXVI.—*Publications and their Circulation in the Principal Cities*—1850.

Cities.	States.	Publications	Annual circulation.	Average circulation.	Annual Circulation to each white inhabitant.
Albany	New York	8	16,050,460	2,006,307	321
Baltimore	Maryland	31	20,711,100	668,100	147
Boston	Massachusetts	113	54,482,644	482,147	404
Charleston	South Carolina	†12	5,675,800	472,983	284
Chicago	Illinois	‡17	1,886,952	110,997	64
Cincinnati	Ohio	39	8,753,200	224,441	78
Louisville	Kentucky	23	3,186,638	138,550	88
Mobile	Alabama	4	1,002,000	250,500	77
New Orleans	Louisiana	18	11,260,860	625,603	‖126
New York	New York	104	78,747,600	757,188	157
Saint Louis	Missouri	18	4,890,030	271,668	66
Philadelphia	Pennsylvania	51	48,457,240	950,142	125

* Estimated. † The weekly and tri-weekly issues not returned for Charleston as in other cities, and one paper (weekly) has a circulation of 10,000 instead of 1,000 as returned.

‡ In addition to seventeen entered there are three weekly and one daily left blank, circulation uncertain.

‖ New Orleans Price Current circulation returned uncertain.

Averaging the subscription of each newspaper and periodical published in the United States, the daily at two cents, tri-weekly, &c., at three, weekly at five, semi-monthly at seven, monthly at twelve, and quarterly at fifty cents, there would be a total of $15,000,000 expended upon that department of the press, if actually collected. The whole issue for one year, estimateed upon the basis of an ordinary country paper, would cover a surface of one hundred square miles, or constitute a belt of thirty feet wide around the earth, and weigh nearly 70,000,000 pounds. The very heavy circulation of the Northern cities is accounted for from the fact that these cities supply every section of the country, and more especially the Southern and South-western States, which show such a small proportion of native papers. Unless the proper deductions are made, the newspaper statistics will not be a fair criterion in judging of the several sections, but no data exists in the office for such corrections.

4. Public Libraries.—Great attention is bestowed in every part of the United States in the establishment of libraries for the use of institutions and the public. The number of such libraries and their statistics, as returned by the census of 1850, are given in the table. Private libraries containing over 1000 volumes were also returned, but not generally, and they will not therefore be published.

Table CLXVII.—*Libraries, other than private, in the United States.*

States, &c.	Public.		School.		Sunday School.		College.		Church.		Total.	
	Number.	Volumes.	Number.	Volumes.	Number.	Volumes.	Number.	Volumes.	Number.	Volumes.	Number.	Volumes.
Alabama	4	3,848	32	3,500	15	5,775	5	7,500	....	......	56	20,623
Arkansas	1	250	.....	....	2	170	....	....	....	......	3	420
California*	.....	....	.....	....	.....	....	....	....	....	......	.....	....
Columbia, Dis. of	7	66,100	.....	....	.....	....	2	32,500	....	......	9	98,600
Connecticut	42	38,609	4	5,039	107	38,445	8	82,600	3	625	164	165,318
Delaware	4	10,250	.....	....	12	2,700	1	5,000	....	......	17	17,950
Florida	1	1,000	2	800	4	860	....	....	....	......	7	2,660
Georgia	3	6,500	11	1,800	15	1,988	9	21,500	....	......	38	31,788
Illinois	33	35,982	29	5,875	86	12,829	4	7,800	....	......	152	62,486
Indiana	58	46,238	3	1,800	85	11,265	4	8,700	1	400	151	68,403
Iowa	4	2,650	4	160	24	2,980	....	....	....	......	32	5,790
Kentucky	47	40,424	.....	....	18	4,617	11	33,225	4	1,200	80	79,466
Louisiana	5	9,800	2	12,000	.....	....	3	5,000	....	......	10	26,800
Maine	77	51,439	11	2,225	131	26,988	8	39,625	9	1,692	236	121,969
Maryland	17	54,750	8	6,335	84	28,315	10	33,792	5	1,850	124	125,042
Massachusetts	177	257,737	792	104,645	433	165,476	18	141,400	42	14,757	1,462	684,015
Michigan	280	65,116	119	31,427	15	3,500	3	7,900	....	......	417	107,943
Mississippi	4	7,264	103	3,650	6	730	4	10,093	....	......	117	21,737
Missouri	13	23,106	13	17,150	66	14,500	4	19,700	1	600	97	75,056
New Hampshire	47	42,017	3	1,200	70	20,117	3	19,975	6	2,450	129	85,759
New Jersey	77	43,903	10	4,080	35	8,564	4	24,000	2	338	128	80,885
New York	43	197,229	10,802	1,388,729	137	33,294	25	138,870	6	2,698	11,013	1,760,820
North Carolina	4	2,500	1	1,500	19	2,352	5	21,593	9	1,647	38	29,592
Ohio	65	65,703	13	9,665	248	53,910	22	56,573	4	975	352	186,826
Pennsylvania	90	184,666	30	17,161	226	58,071	21	77,050	26	26,452	393	363,400
Rhode Island	26	42,007	12	5,814	50	23,765	1	31,000	7	1,756	96	104,342
South Carolina	16	73,758	3	2,750	.....	....	7	30,964	....	......	26	107,472
Tennessee	9	5,373	2	5,100	18	2,498	5	9,925	....	......	34	22,896
Texas	3	2,100	3	430	5	1,600	1	100	....	......	12	4,230
Vermont	30	21,061	16	9,700	38	10,020	9	23,280	3	580	96	64,641
Virginia	21	32,595	6	2,706	11	1,975	14	50,856	2	330	54	88,462
Wisconsin	9	12,040	33	2,163	28	5,017	2	1,800	....	......	72	21,020
Total	1,217	1,446,015	12,067	1,647,404	1,988	542,321	213	942,321	130	58,350	15,615	4,636,411

In a volume on Public Libraries, published by the Smithsonian Institution, and prepared by Professor Jewett, the following statistics appear, obtained for a large part from replies to circulars, and therefore less full than those of the Census.

Libraries.	No.	Volumes.
State Libraries	39	288,937
Social Libraries	126	611,334
College Libraries	126	586,912
Students' Libraries	142	254,639
Seminaries and Professional Libraries	227	320,909
Scientific and Historical Societies, do.	34	138,901

* None returned.

Whole number of libraries exclusive of Public School; libraries having 1,000 volumes and upwards, 423; having 1,000 and less than 5,000, 198; having 5,000 and less than 10,000, 175; having 10,000 and less than 20,000, 43; having 20,000 and less than 50,000, 11; having 50,000 and over, 5, viz: Harvard University 84,200, Philadelphia Library 60,000; Yale College 50,481; Library of Congress 50,000; Boston Athenæum 50,000. The number of volumes in the libraries of cities will be found in the appropriate chapter. The following statistics of European libraries are taken from the work of Edward Edwards, published in London, in 1849.

TABLE CLXVIII.—*The chief University Libraries of Europe in* 1848 *ranked as follows.*

Libraries.	Vols.	Libraries.	Vols.	Libraries.	Vols.
* † Göttingen University	360,000	† Cambridge, Public	166,724	* † Turin University	110,000
Breslau University	250,000	Bologna University	150,000	Louvain do.	105,000
† Oxford, Bodleian	220,000	* † Prague do.	130,000	† Dublin, Trinity College	104,239
Tubingen University	200,000	Vienna do.	115,000	* Upsal University	100,000
Munich do.	200,000	Leipsic do.	112,000	Erlangen do.	100,000
Heidelberg do.	200,000	Copenhagen do.	110,000	Edinburgh do.	90,854

The date of the foundation of some of the libraries is as follows: Turin 1436, Cambridge 1484, Leipsic 1544, Edinburgh 1582, the Bodleian 1597. The library of the University of Salamanca (24,000 volumes) is said to have been founded in 1215.

TABLE CLXIX.—*Whole number of Printed Volumes in the Public Libraries of some of the principal Cities of Europe in* 1848.

Libraries.	Volumes.	Libraries.	Volumes.	Libraries.	Volumes.	Libraries.	Volumes.
Aberdeen	46,000	Cologne	109,300	Leipsic	192,000	Paris	1,474,000
Amsterdam	16,000	Copenhagen	557,000	Lisbon	98,000	Prague	198,000
Antwerp	15,000	Dresden	340,500	London	490,500	Rome	465,000
Barcelona	45,000	Dublin	143,654	Lyons	82,000	Seville	58,000
Berlin	460,000	Edinburgh	288,854	Milan	250,000	Stockholm	82,000
Bologna	233,000	Florence	299,000	Moscow	66,000	St. Petersburg	595,900
Bremen	36,000	Genoa	120,000	Munich	800,000	Stutgard	197,000
Breslau	370,000	Glasgow	80,096	Naples	290,000	Venice	137,000
Brussels	143,500	Göttingen	350,000	Oxford	273,000	Vienna	453,000
Buda-Pesth	68,000	Halle	121,000	Padua	177,000	Weimar	110,000
Cambridge	261,724	Hamburg	200,367				

TABLE CLXX.—*Libraries of Europe*, 1848.

States.	Libraries.	Volumes of printed books.	Volumes of manuscript.	States.	Libraries.	Volumes of printed books.	Volumes of manuscript.
Anhalt	2	25,700	....	Mecklenburg-Strelitz	1	50,000	....
Austrian States	49	2,408,000	41,103	Modena	1	90,000	3,000
Baden	5	404,300	3,170	Naples and Sicily	8	413,000	3,000
Bavaria	18	1,268,500	30,156	Nassau	1	50,000	....
Belgium	14	509,100	20,728	Oldenburg	1	60,000	....
Bremen	2	36,000	....	Papal States	16	957,000	33,495
Brunswick	6	223,000	4,580	Parma	3	146,000	....
Cracow	2	52,000	2,210	Portugal	7	276,000	7,587
Denmark	5	647,000	3,200	Prussian States	53	2,040,450	15,417
France	186	5,510,295	119,119	Reuss	1	5,000	....
Frankfort-on-the-Maine	1	62,000	550	Rudolstadt	1	46,000	....
Great Britain and Ireland	34	1,771,493	62,149	Russian Empire	12	852,090	21,604
Hamburg‡	6	200,367	5,000	Sardinia and Piedmont	11	297,000	4,500
Hanover	5	492,000	5,743	Saxe-Coburg-Gotha	5	247,000	5,000
Hesse	5	273,200	400	Saxe-Meininger	1	32,000	....
Hesse-Darmstadt	3	282,600	5,268	Saxe-Weimar	2	180,000	2,000
Hildburghausen	1	12,000	....	Saxony‡	9	570,500	7,950
Holland	7	228,310	12,000	Spain	27	711,050	8,262
Lippe-Detmold	1	21,500	100	Sweden and Norway	8	353,000	9,300
Lubec	2	52,000	400	Switzerland	13	480,300	12,73
Lucca	1	25,000	....	Tuscany	10	401,000	30,000
Luxemburg	1	19,600	162	Waldeck Pyrmont	1	30,000	....
Mecklenburg	3	85,400	....	Wurtemburg	6	433,000	5,200

* These are leading libraries. † These are legally entitled to copies of all works published in the states to which they respectively belong.

‡ In these States the enumeration embraces libraries of less extent than 10,000 volumes.

TABLE CLXXI.—*Great Libraries of Europe in* 1848.

Libraries.	Vols.	Libraries.	Vols.	Libraries.	Vols.
* Paris National	824,000	Madrid National	200,000	* Naples Royal	150,000
* Munich Royal	600,000	Wolfenbuttel Ducal	200,000	* Brussels Royal	133,500
Petersburg Imperial	446,000	Stutgard Royal	187,000	Rome Casanate	120,000
* London British Museum	435,000	Paris Arsenal	180,000	* Hague Royal	100,000
* Copenhagen Royal	412,000	* Milan Breza	170,000	Paris Mazarin	100,000
* Berlin Royal	410,000	Paris St. Genevieve	150,000	Rome Vatican	100,000
* Vienna Imperial	313,000	Darmstadt Grand Ducal	150,000	* Parma Ducal	100,000
* Dresden Royal	300,000	*Florence Magliabecchian	150,000		

These marked thus (*) are entitled by law to a copy of every book published within the States to which they respectively belong.

5. CHARITIES.—Pauperism being one of the evils of old and densely settled communities, could not prevail in the United States to any considerable extent, even were the system of government and laws prevailing not an additional guarantee against its existence. An examination of the returns of public hospitals, poor houses, &c., will show that the foreign immigrants furnish a large part of their material. It is also found as in other countries, that in communities purely agricultural pauperism is much less recognized than in those that are commercial and manufacturing*.

The census returns the number of paupers supported in each county in the United States, in whole or in part at public expense within the year preceding, and the actual number on the 1st June, 1850, native and foreign, with other particulars. As no account is taken in it of those supported or relieved by individual charities, the statistics, it has been thought, would not represent the whole of the facts, and if absolutely relied upon as a test of condition would be unjust towards those sections in which nearly the whole of the relief is public. Perceiving the weight of the objection the superintendent issued a circular in March, 1854, to the proper officers of several States in different sections, in order, if possible, to make some estimates of the *private* charities, benevolent associations, etc., but although many interesting returns were received, they were not as numerous as were desired. The following, however, from Massachusetts and Rhode Island, New Jersey, Georgia and South Carolina will show that private relief by societies and associations, is administered to a large extent in States where the poor laws are most perfect, and reasoning for the whole from a part taken from sections indiscriminately, it may not be unfair to assume that the proportion relieved by other than public means does not differ much in the several States.†

TABLE CLXXII.—*Charities.*‡

Town.	County.	State.	Population.	Number relieved. Wholly.	Number relieved. In part.	Amount annually expended.	Remarks.
Patterson	Passaic	N. J.	22,569	30	12	......	
Chalmond		Mass.	1,000	15	10	$500	Estimated. Report says, "From 10 to 15 paupers supported wholly or in part."
Bristol	Bristol	R. I.	4,616	....	73	410	
Worthington	Hampshire	Mass.	1,134	....	20	500	
Brewster	Barnstable	"	1,525	....	55	490	
Northborough	Worcester	"	1,535	....	1	25	
Truro	Barnstable	"	2,051	....	16	300	
Sudbury	Middlesex	"	1,578	55	......	500	Estimated—being the income from legacies.
Northampton	Hampshire	"	5,278	38	16	633	Of the 38 wholly relieved, 17 were by the Masons and Odd-Fellows.
Harwich	Barnstable	"	3,258	....	20	52	Relieved by Congregational, Baptist, and Methodist sewing circles.
Colerain	Franklin	"	1,785	....	10	25	One Odd-Fellows' Lodge in the town.
Bangor	Penobscot	Me.	14,432	12	218	1,638	By Fuel Society, City Mission, Female Orphan Society, and Old Ladies' Society.
Tisbury	Dukes	Mass.	1,800	....	......	......	No charitable societies; poor supported by private charity.
Falmouth	Barnstable	"	2,621	....	24	80	Ladies' Sewing, Widows and Orphans', and the church, individuals.
Roxbury	Norfolk	"	18,364	....	800	5,500	Thirteen charitable societies.

* Mr. Porter in his "Progress of the Nation," page 98, however states that the burthen of the poor rate in proportion to population in England, was found to press generally greatest in the most agricultural counties.

‡ The northern population and returns are of the towns which are named, and the southern of the counties, including slaves, except in the case of Macon, which is for the town only, and the aggregates of each are nearly equal; yet the north expends one-third more and relieves more than four times the number of persons. Compared with the white population, she would still relieve as much or more.

† The annual sum expended in relief by the several societies in Charleston, is estimated in its census at about $25,000, which is exclusive of clothing, food, medicine, &c., and private relief. Of 410 persons admitted to the poor house of Charleston in 1848, only 63 were born in the city, and 258 were foreigners. In the five

TABLE CLXXII—*Continued.*

Town.	County.	State.	Population.	Number relieved. Wholly.	Number relieved. In part.	Amount annually expended.	Remarks.
Rockport......	Essex......	Mass.	3,274	....	13	168	I. O. O. F. $8, Rechabites $75, Masons $25, and Sons of Temperance $60.
Gloucester....	"	"	7,786	....	150	680	Religious Societies $120, Fem. Char. Ass. $114, I. O. O. F. $233, Sons of T. $55, and Daughters of T. $158.
Medfield......	Norfolk....	"	966	....	9	80	Four charitable societies.
West Boylston.	Worcester..	"	1,749	....	25	151	Five charitable societies in the town.
New Shoreham	Newport....	R. I..	1,262	8	4	400	A charitable society.
Wellfleet......	Barnstable..	Mass.	2,411	....	21	577	Marine Benevolent So. $177, Sons of T. $400.
Marblehead...	Essex......	"	6,167	3	67	1,666	Six charitable associations.
Franklin......	Norfolk....	"	1,818	....	2	20	Ladies' sewing circle.
West Norbury.	Essex......	"	1,746	....	22	80	Hill Fund.
Total northern.	....	......	110,725	161	1,588	14,475	
....	Scriven....	Geo..	6,847	....	......	250	Assessed by Superior Court.
Lincolnton....	Lincoln....	"	5,998	....	......	106	....
Palmyra.......	Lee........	"	6,660	....	15	150	....
Bennetsville...	Marlboro'..	S. C..	10,789	27	......	253	Sons of Temperance.
Watterboro'...	Colleton....	"	39,505	....	1	20	Masonic Lodge, in addition to $40 sent away.
....	Walton....	Geo..	....	22	......	311	....
Lancaster.....	Lancaster..	S. C..	376	....	7	70	Four societies, Masons $30, and S. of T. $40.
Cassville......	Cass.......	Geo..	13,300	....	4	150	Three Masonic Lodges, two I. O. O. F., and two Knights of Jericho.
Franklin......	Heard......	"	6,923	....	20	100	Four Masonic Lodges.
Spring Place...	Murray.....	"	14,433	....	25	100	Estimated. One Masonic Lodge, one Republicans, one S. T., and one Knights of Jericho.
Macon........	Bibb.......	"	5,720	5	259	9,249	County court, $2,200, Hibernian Society, $15, Masonic Lodge $44, Presbyterian church $165, Methodist $154, Baptist $63, Episcopal $60, Ladies' Benevolent Society $474, Odd-Fellows' Lodges $603, Annual Conference of the Methodist Church South in Dec., 1853, for indigent preachers, &c., $5,470.
Total southern.	....	.....	110,551	54	331	10,759	

The following table will show the number of public paupers and the amount expended in their support during the year preceding June 1, 1850, as returned in the schedules of social statistics. These schedules did not separate the color of either criminals or paupers as indicated in the act of Congress. For such distinction the schedules of population must be consulted. The number of paupers on the 1st of June the marshals were required to obtain from the population returns and the other facts from parish or county records.

years ending 1848, the cost of pauperism in Charleston averaged less than $7,000 per annum, of which the city, deducting the value of labor, did not pay much more than $1,000. In a pamphlet upon the charities of Boston, published in the North American Review, the donations by individuals for charitable institutions and charitable purposes in that city in 30 years, are given, and average about $40,000 per annum. A more complete statement in the Boston census gives the total contributions up to 1845, to institutions for charitable purposes, $2,272,990. An average of 2,076 paupers, by the same volume, received out door support in the years 1841 to 1845, 1,402, in door, 3,478 total. In the year 1837–'40 of 8,671 paupers of Massachusetts, 2,567 only were American. In 1845 the cost of pauperism in Boston was paid by the city, $23,944, and by the State, $26,894. The local report of New York shows number admitted to Blackwell Island alms house, last six months of 1849, 1,672, of whom 411 were natives, and 1,006 Irish. At Belleview 3,114 admitted, 618 being native and 2,052 Irish. Colored in the Colored Home of New York, 1849, 713. New York city, January to July 1849, 1st District sent to State Prison 28 white and 4 colored; to Blackwell Island 783 white, 94 colored; remaining in prison, 253 white and 27 colored; 2d District, whole year 1849, committed 1,908 whites, 21 colored. As the amount of mortality has much to do with the physical well being of a people, and will be dependent in some measure upon pauperism, some remarks may be appended here which were too late for the sections of mortality. According to Dr. Emerson, the proportion of black deaths to the total black population, in Philadelphia, for the ten years from 1821 to 1830, was about one in every 21; in the ten years ending in 1840, 1 in every 31; the ratio for the whites in the latter period being 1 in every 43. In the report of the Prison Discipline Association at Philadelphia in 1845, it is said, out of 1,000 of each color residing in the city, 196 blacks die for every 100 whites, and in the Penitentiary 316 blacks for every 100 whites. In the Wethersfield (Conn.) Penitentiary, the average rate of deaths from 1841 to 1844 was, white 2.82; colored 10.96. In the Eastern Penitentiary of Pennsylvania, during the three years ending with 1843, the average rate of deaths was 1.85 white deaths and 6.63 black. In the Philadelphia Prison during a period of ten years the proportion of deaths among the whites was one in 46, among the blacks, one in 12. The admissions into the Eastern Penitentiary of Pennsylvania from October 29th, 1845 until December 1845, were 2,054 whites, 692 blacks. The city inspector of New York, in his report for 1853, says that the deaths among the colored population averaged 604 each year from 1847 to 1853, and that "while the general population is rapidly swelling, and the deaths bearing their proportional increase, the colored mortal record exhibits its significant declination.

Public expenditure in England and Wales for the poor—1840, £4,576,965, population 15,710,270; 1843, £5,208,027, population 16,314,671; 1848, £6,180,764, population 17,521,956. The average from 1825 to 1835 was much larger to a smaller population.

Number relieved in England and Wales—1840, in door 169,232, out door 1,030,297, total 1,199,529; 1843, in door 238,560, out door 1,300,930: total 1,539,490; 1848, in door 265,140, out door 1,361,061: total 1,626,201.

Before completing the tables of charities, the following statistics of the Order of Odd Fellows which has been doing so much in this field, may be properly inserted. They are aggregated for ten years, from 1843 to

TABLE CLXXIII.—*Pauperism in the United States,* 1850.

States.	Whole number of Paupers supported in whole or part within the year ending June 1.			Whole number of Paupers on June 1.			Annual cost of support.
	Native.	Foreign.	Total.	Native.	Foreign.	Total.	
Alabama	352	11	363	306	9	315	$17,559
Arkansas	97	8	105	67	....	67	6,888
California	....	....	....	....	....	....	....
Connecticut	1,872	465	2,337	1,463	281	1,744	95,624
Delaware	569	128	697	240	33	273	17,730
Florida	64	12	76	58	4	62	937
Georgia	978	58	1,036	825	29	854	27,820
Illinois	386	411	797	279	155	434	45,213
Indiana	860	322	1,182	446	137	583	57,560
Iowa	100	35	135	27	17	44	5,358
Kentucky	971	155	1,126	690	87	777	57,543
Louisiana	133	290	423	76	30	106	39,806
Maine	4,553	950	5,503	3,209	326	3,535	151,664
Maryland	2,591	1,903	4,494	1,681	320	2,001	71,668
Massachusetts	6,530	9,247	15,777	4,059	1,490	5,549	392,715
Michigan	649	541	1,190	248	181	429	27,556
Mississippi	248	12	260	245	12	257	18,132
Missouri	1,248	1,729	2,977	251	254	505	53,243
New Hampshire	2,853	747	3,600	1,998	186	2,184	157,351
New Jersey	1,816	576	2,392	1,339	239	1,578	93,110
New York	19,275	40,580	59,855	5,755	7,078	12,833	817,336
North Carolina	1,913	18	1,931	1,567	13	1,580	60,085
Ohio	1,904	609	2,513	1,254	419	1,673	95,250
Pennsylvania	5,898	5,653	11,551	2,654	1,157	3,811	232,138
Rhode Island	1,115	1,445	2,560	492	204	696	45,837
South Carolina	1,313	329	1,642	1,113	180	1,293	48,337
Tennessee	994	11	1,005	577	14	591	30,981
Texas	7	....	7	4	....	4	438
Vermont	2,043	1,611	3,654	1,565	314	1,879	120,462
Virginia	4,933	185	5,118	4,356	102	4,458	151,722
Wisconsin	169	497	666	72	166	238	14,743
Total	66,434	68,538	134,972	36,916	13,437	50,353	2,954,806

1853, and extending as they do over the whole Union, furnish interesting material for comparison with the returns of the census relating to sickness and death. The ratios between the States are striking.

State Grand Lodges.	Total paid sick.	Amount paid each.	Annual cost per member.	Number deaths.	Ratio deaths.	Total paid for mortality	Am't each.	Annual cost per member.	Total relief.	Annual cost per member.
Alabama	$12,048	16.34	$1.61	119	62	7,652	$64	106	$19,685	2.63
Columbia, Dist. of	25,779	10.48	2.48	77	135	7,358	95	70	32,844	3.15
Connecticut	83,533	14.28	2.2[illegible]	273	138	12,454	46	33	98,080	2.60
Delaware	11,272	11.16	1.52	61	120	3,005	49	40	14,739	1.99
Georgia	19,187	13.67	1.63	134	87	9,200	68	98	28,647	2.43
Illinois	16,782	10.40	1.21	162	85	7,015	43	50	25,391	1.77
Indiana	38,551	13.77	2.14	203	88	12,625	62	70	53,352	2.96
Iowa	2,772	6.65	96	36	78	1,466	40	51	5,586	1.97
Kentucky	35,239	16.03	2.00	243	72	17,895	73	101	60,711	3.45
Louisiana	29,732	26.78	2.80	211	45	17,664	83	185	49,287	5.03
Maine	55,047	15.53	1.66	271	122	9,672	35	29	68,282	2.00
Maryland	135,939	10.43	2.30	641	92	133,891	208	226	277,439	4.69
Massachusetts	188,647	19.07	2.39	659	118	48,439	73	61	246,884	3.13
Michigan	22,265	10.71	1.62	111	129	5,322	48	37	26,862	1.87
Mississippi	11,852	14.52	1.43	89	92	6,980	78	84	20,188	2.44
Missouri	23,290	16.10	2.18	187	53	22,037	117	221	45,146	4.10
New Hampshire	33,830	18.66	2.27	120	120	5,810	48	40	34,721	2.40
New Jersey	90,324	12.92	2.11	322	132	20,215	62	47	115,643	2.71
New York, South	483,452	16.77	2.98	1,733	93	136,061	78	84	621,102	3.84
New York, North	188,367	12.84	2.02	653	145	34,551	53	37	222,397	2.38
North Carolina	6,758	10.16	1.06	59	107	3,695	62	58	10,372	1.66
Ohio	142,495	14.29	2.38	639	93	31,979	50	53	168,423	2.82
Pennsylvania	443,563	11.93	2.16	1,829	111	125,174	68	62	568,195	2.77
Rhode Island	23,782	15.40	2.47	78	122	5,957	76	61	30,071	3.12
South Carolina	37,798	18.32	2.01	128	107	21,053	172	151	48,302	3.49
Tennessee	16,527	19.21	1.44	93	123	5,959	64	52	23,063	1.93
Texas	2,136	16.37	1.86	34	33	1,752	51	152	2,943	2.56
Vermont	6,603	13.48	1.63	27	149	1,297	48	32	8,669	2.14
Virginia	51,192	10.61	1.64	336	92	33,934	100	109	84,953	2.73
Wisconsin	9,172	13.05	1.23	58	106	2,367	40	31	11,246	1.82
Total 10 years	2,247,934	14.03	2.22	9,586	103	752,479	78	74	3,023,223	3.02

Table CLXXIV.—*Paupers in Poor Houses 1st June, 1850.*

States.	Whites.			Free Colored						Aggregate.	Age.			Nativities.					
				Black.			Mulatto.												
	M.	F.	Total.	M	F	Total.	M	F	Total.		Under 14 years.	14 and under 24.	24 and over.	Born in the State.	Born out of State and in U. States.	Born in Ireland.	Born in Germany.	Born in other foreign countries.	Unknown.
Massachusetts..	1,947	1,676	3,623	32	38	70	11	8	19	3,712	800	365	2,547	2,488	218	803	13	173	17
Maryland......	432	397	829	69	83	152	2	5	7	988	123	75	790	661	69	128	88	27	15
Virginia.......	546	807	1,353	63	60	123	28	35	63	1,539	377	111	1,051	1,438	52	30	5	5	9
Mississippi.....	11	3	14	..	1	1	1	..	1	16	1	2	13	2	9	1	....	3	1
Missouri.......	165	110	275	1	..	1	..	..	..	276	74	35	167	62	61	77	43	31	2
Indiana	209	203	412	5	9	14	..	1	1	427	72	64	291	144	177	49	16	18	23
North Carolina..	315	482	797	12	17	29	30	17	47	873	164	87	622	816	43	2	2	4	6

The above table was compiled in the office from the population schedules, and gives the number in poor houses. Time did not admit of an examination of other States. The table differs from the previous one which includes paupers in or out of poor houses, but receiving public support on the same day.

6. Wages.—The marshals were instructed to report the rates of wages prevailing in the several sections, from which the following was aggregated.

Table CLXXV.—*Average Wages, 1850.*

States and Territories.	Monthly to a farm hand with board.	To a day laborer with board.	To a day laborer without board.	Day wages to a carpenter without board.	Weekly to a female domestic with board.	Weekly board to laboring men.
Alabama	$ 9.62	$ 49	$ 70	$ 1.76	$ 1.41	$1.89
Arkansas.......	10.63	54	75	1.77	1.67	1.61
California	60.00	4.00	5.00	7.60	13.00	11.00
Columbia, Dis. of	10.00	63	98	1.50	1.31	2.37
Connecticut	12.72	76	98	1.30	1.36	1.95
Delaware.......	8.79	51	78	1.23	84	1.83
Florida	10.00	68	1.03	2.15	1.83	2.64
Georgia	9.03	50	72	1.66	1.52	1.82
Illinois	12.55	62	85	1.47	1.14	1.47
Indiana.........	10.50	55	78	1.30	90	1.43
Iowa	11.80	61	83	1.50	1.07	1.58
Kentucky	10.00	50	69	1.34	1.09	1.41
Louisiana.	12.80	73	1.04	2.36	2.57	2.70
Maine	13.12	76	1.00	1.40	1.09	1.72
Maryland	7.88	49	69	1.25	89	1.75
Massachusetts ..	13.55	84	1.09	1.45	1.48	2.12
Michigan........	12.00	66	88	1.40	1.10	1.59
Mississippi......	11.00	69	95	1.94	1.52	2.00
Missouri	$11.81	$ 55	$ 75	$1.48	$1.17	$1.31
New Hampshire	12.12	63	89	1.31	1.27	1.63
New Jersey.....	10.18	65	88	1.28	97	1.89
New York.......	11.50	67	90	1.38	1.05	1.78
North Carolina .	7.21	42	54	1.22	87	1.33
Ohio.	11.10	56	78	1.27	96	1.45
Pennsylvania ...	10.82	51	80	1.23	80	1.72
Rhode Island ...	13.52	72	95	1.23	1.42	2.06
South Carolina.	7.72	49	66	1.40	1.42	1.73
Tennessee......	8.67	43	58	1.38	1.00	1.32
Texas	12.00	75	1.00	2.00	2.00	2.00
Vermont	13.00	72	97	1.44	1.19	1.95
Virginia	8.43	47	65	1.22	96	1.49
Wisconsin......	12.69	71	1.00	1.54	1.27	1.88
Territories: Minnesota	17.00	86	1.37	2.25	2.25	3.50
Territories: N. Nexico	6.00	33	53	5.18	78	2.00
Territories: Oregon ...	75.00	4.00	5.00	10.00	10.00	7.00
Territories: Utah	22.00	1.32	2.00	3.14	1.46	4.14

The Commissioner of Patents in 1848 sent out a circular to all of the States, in order to ascertain the rates of wages paid by the agricultural interest. Answers were received from most of the States, which showed a remarkable uniformity. The average wages to field laborers with board, ranged from 10 to 15 dollars for the whites, and from 5 to 12 for the slaves, the average for female domestics with board, ranged from 4 to 6 dollars for the whites and 3 to 5 for slaves. The average wages of mechanics from 75 cents to $1.50 per day, reaching in Texas as high as $3. Upon the whole the rates seemed to be lowest in the Northwest, and highest in the Southwest for white labor—the South and the North differing very little.† The money

Since the preparation of table CLXXII, Glynn county, Georgia, reports no persons relieved by private societies, but that all of its schools are free schools supported from a county fund. Quincy, Mass., 112 persons relieved, cost $159.55; Newburyport 280 relieved, cost $2,496; Salem 195 relieved wholly, 1,302 in part, cost $11,675.29; Florida, Alachua county, 69 in part, 28 wholly, cost $131.00.

† The weekly net earnings of factory hands at Manchester, England, in full employment, in 1849:—Card Room, males 12*s*.; females 8*s*. 6*d*.; spinners 12*s*.; Power Loom Weavers 9*s*. 5*d*.; helpers 4*s*. 8*d*.; Mechanics 19*s*. 3*d*. The wages of other workmen were as follows: Colliers at iron works in Staffordshire, average weekly, 16*s*. 3*d*.; miners 13*s*. 11*d*.; masons, smiths and carpenters, 10*s*. 6*d*.

From the replies addressed by British Consuls to the home government in 1833, it appears that wages ranged upon the continent for agricultural laborers, viz: Ploughmen in France 100 to 160 shillings per annum with board, laborers in France, 5 to 15*d*. per day, in the latter case without board or dwelling furnished; in Germany 4½*d*. to 7*d*., with lodging, but without board; in the Netherlands 3*d*. to 4*d*. with board and lodging, 5*d*. to 16*d*. without either; in Italy at Genoa, 60 shillings to 100 shillings per annum; in Tuscany 40 shilling per annum, in both cases with board and lodging. These are for farm servants. Farm laborers are returned at 6*d*. per day, without board or lodging. The replies to the Poor Law Commissioners gave for 6 or 800 parishes in England an average earning to a family consisting of man, wife and four children, ages 14, 11, 8 and 5, the eldest a boy, £41 17*s*. 8d. In 71 parishes this amount was stated to be insufficient for support without relief, and in 337 barely sufficient or sufficient without meat.

price of wages unless the prices of other articles be known, gives but an unsatisfactory idea of the condition of the laboring population at different periods and in different countries.

7. Crime.—Upon this subject the material of the Census is very full.

Table CLXXVI.—*Statistics of Criminals.*

States and Territories.	Whole number of criminals convicted within the year.			In prison on June 1, 1850.			States and Territories.	Whole number of criminals convicted within the year.			In prison on June 1, 1850.		
	Native.	Foreign.	Total.	Native.	Foreign.	Total.		Native.	Foreign.	Total.	Native.	Foreign.	Total.
Alabama	117	5	122	69	1	70	New Hampshire	66	24	90	28	5	33
Arkansas	24	1	25	17	.....	17	New Jersey	346	257	603	198	92	290
California	1	......	1	35	27	62	New York	3,962	6,317	10,279	649	639	1,288
Columbia, Dist.	......	......	132	.....	.....	46	North Carolina	634	13	647	43	1	44
Connecticut	545	305	850	244	66	310	Ohio	689	154	843	102	31	133
Delaware	22	......	22	14	.....	14	Pennsylvania	564	293	857	296	115	411
Florida	33	6	39	9	2	11	Rhode Island	309	287	596	58	45	103
Georgia	72	8	80	36	7	43	South Carolina	32	14	46	21	15	36
Illinois	127	189	316	164	88	252	Tennessee	73	8	81	276	12	288
Indiana	150	25	175	41	18	59	Texas	15	4	19	5	10	15
Iowa	2	1	3	5	.....	5	Vermont	34	45	79	64	41	105
Kentucky	126	34	160	41	11	52	Virginia	98	9	107	291	22	313
Louisiana	197	100	297	240	183	423	Wisconsin	105	162	267	26	35	61
Maine	284	460	744	66	34	100	Territ's. Minnesota	1	1	2	.....	1	1
Maryland	183	24	207	325	72	397	Territ's. New Mexico	104	4	108	37	1	38
Massachusetts	3,366	3,884	7,250	653	583	1,236	Territ's. Oregon	5	......	5	5	.....	5
Michigan	273	386	659	139	102	241	Territ's. Utah	6	3	9	6	3	9
Mississippi	49	2	51	45	1	46							
Missouri	242	666	908	55	125	180	Total	......	......	......	.....	.....	.....

The following tables were made up in the office from the population returns, whilst the preceding is from the schedules of social statistics returned by the marshals. Time admitted only of the examination of a few States.

Table CLXXVII.—*Convicts in Penitentiaries,* 1850.

States.	Whites.			Free Colored.						Aggregate.	Ages.			Nativities.					
				Black.			Mulatto.												
	M.	F.	Total.	M.	F.	Total.	M.	F.	Total.		Under 14.	14 and under 24.	24 and over.	Born in the State.	Born out of State and in U. States.	Born in Ireland.	Born in Germany.	Born in other foreign countries.	Unknown.
Massachusetts	389	..	389	34	....	34	8	..	8	431	..	165	266	170	130	74	3	53	1
Maryland	110	5	115	77	19	96	22	2	24	235	2	102	131	163	37	5	25	5	.
Virginia	130	2	132	44	4	48	23	..	23	203	2	21	180	160	32	5	3	3	..
Mississippi	85	..	85	1	....	1	....	..	....	86	..	18	68	5	76	3	...	2	.
Missouri	164	..	164	1	....	1	1	..	1	166	..	55	111	4	103	29	12	17	1
Indiana	146	..	146	....	....	....	....	..	....	146	..	40	106	16	105	8	8	9	

Table CLXXVIII.—*Persons in Jails and Houses of Correction.*

States.	Whites.			Free Colored.						Aggregate.	Ages.			Nativities.					
				Black.			Mulatto.												
	M.	F.	Total.	M.	F.	Total.	M.	F.	Total.		Under 14.	14 and under 24.	24 and over.	Born in the State.	Born out of State and in U. States.	Born in Ireland.	Born in Germany.	Born in other foreign countries.	Unknown.
Massachusetts	906	212	1,118	60	17	77	12	8	20	1,215	140	458	617	410	222	443	7	104	29
Maryland	86	3	89	16	1	17	9	6	15	121	2	42	77	67	21	14	5	......	14
Virginia	84	11	95	9	7	16	5	3	8	119	6	29	84	96	15	....	2	1	5
Mississippi	20	3	23	1	....	1	1	..	1	25	1	7	17	....	24	....	....	......	1
Missouri	243	13	256	6	4	10	3	1	4	270	....	17	253	2	188	35	29	15	1
Indiana	45	....	45	2	....	2	....	..	..	47	....	6	41	5	31	4	1	1	5
North Carolina	31	....	31	1	....	1	2	..	2	34	....	6	28	26	2	....	....	1	5

TABLE CLXXIX.—*State Prisons and Penitentiaries*, 1850.

States, &c.	Place where located.	Whites.					Colored, including slaves.				Total white and colored.	In every 10,000 native whites.	In every 10,000 foreign whites.	In every 10,000 native and foreign white.	In every 10,000 colored.
		Male.	Female.	Total.	Native.	Foreign.	Male.	Female.	Total.	Foreign.					
Alabama	Wetumpka	116	1	117	21	96	2	..	2	..	119	.502	128.034	2.743	.057
Arkansas	Little Rock	37	...	37	37	.....	1	..	1	..	38	2.312	......	2.281	.209
Columbia, Dist. of.	Washington	25	2	27	17	10	18	10	28	..	55	5.152	20.354	7.116	20.363
Connecticut	Wethersfield	136	10	146	117	29	27	3	30	2	176	3.610	7.554	4.020	38.996
Delaware	County jails	1	...	1	1	.....	4	1	5	..	6	.151	......	.140	2.455
Florida	County jails	12	...	12	12	.....	....	..	....	..	12	2.699	......	2.754	.....
Georgia	Milledgeville	88	1	89	85	4	....	..	....	..	89	1.651	6.199	1.514	.....
Illinois	Alton	127	...	127	85	42	8	1	9	..	136	1.162	3.754	1.382	16.556
Indiana	Jeffersonville	131	...	131	106	25	15	..	15	..	146	1.044	4.501	1,340	13.319
Iowa	County jails	2	...	2	2	.....	....	..	....	..	2	.117	......	.104	.....
Kentucky	Frankfort	147	...	147	126	21	15	..	15	..	162	1.729	6.687	1.930	.678
Louisiana	Baton Rouge	191	4	195	89	106	59	12	71	..	266	4.745	15.633	7.632	2.707
Maine	Thomaston	79	...	79	62	17	....	..	....	..	79	1.127	5.363	1.357	.....
Maryland	Baltimore	110	5	115	81	34	99	21	120	1	235	2.209	6.665	2.751	7.268
Massachusetts	Charlestown	389	...	389	264	125	42	..	42	5	431	3.223	7.640	3.947	46.337
Michigan	Jackson	111	...	111	73	38	16	..	16	2	127	2.151	6.960	2.809	61.943
Mississippi	Jackson	85	...	85	80	5	1	..	1	..	86	2.754	10.455	2.874	.032
Missouri	Jefferson City.	165	...	165	107	58	1	..	1	..	166	2.079	7.574	2.785	.111
New Hampshire	Concord	89	2	91	77	14	....	..	....	..	91	2.540	9.819	2.866	.....
New York	Auburn	609	...	609	438	171	69	..	69	2	678	.....	.....	.....	.....
	Sing Sing	583	70	653	315	338	155	21	176	4	829	.....	.....	.....	.....
	Clinton county	118	...	118	82	36	6	..	6	..	124	.....	.....	.....	.....
	Total	1,310	70	1,380	835	545	230	21	251	6	1,631	3.495	8.192	4.527	51.130
New Jersey	Trenton	117	6	123	86	37	48	1	49	..	172	2.121	6.186	2.642	20.377
North Carolina	County jails	11	1	12	12	.....	2	..	2	..	14	.238	......	.216	.063
Ohio	Columbus	359	3	362	291	71	41	3	44	..	406	1.679	3.255	1.851	17.405
Pennsylvania	Philadelphia	227	5	232	153	79	77	8	85	4	317	.....	.....	.....	.....
	Allegheny city	95	1	96	52	44	17	1	18	2	114	.....	.....	.....	.....
	Total	322	6	328	205	123	94	9	103	6	431	1.049	4.057	1.452	19.207
Rhode Island	Providence	35	...	35	21	14	3	..	3	..	38	1.750	5.874	2.432	8.174
South Carolina	District jails	31	1	32	19	13	....	..	....	..	32	.714	15.279	1.165	.....
Tennessee	Nashville	188	1	189	180	9	6	1	7	..	196	2.401	15.962	2.497	.284
Texas	County jails	5	...	5	2	3	1	..	1	..	6	.147	1.702	.324	.170
Virginia	Richmond	128	2	130	119	11	65	4	69	..	199	1.365	4.792	1.452	1.309
Vermont	Windsor	69	...	69	39	30	....	..	....	..	69	1.395	8.905	2.201	.....
Wisconsin	County jails	27	...	27	8	19	3	..	3	..	30	.413	1.719	.885	47.245
Slaveholding States		1,340	18	1,358	988	370	274	49	323	1	1,681	1.673	11.684	2.182	* .938
Non-Slaveholding States		3,303	97	3,400	2,271	1,129	527	38	565	21	3,965	1.991	5.868	2.551	28.743
Total		4,643	115	4,758	3,259	1,499	801	87	888	22	5,646	1.882	6.690	2.433	2.440

The above table includes the statistics of the institutions named in the several States as they are reported in the schedules of population, and also the proportion of white and colored, native and foreign, in each of the States, at the South and at the North.

TABLE CLXXX.—*Statistics of* 20 *Penitentiaries.* [*From Prison Society Report.*]

Penitentiaries, 1850.	Number at the first of the year.	Number at the close of the year.	Average in the year.	Increase.	Diminution.	Received in the year.	Discharged.	Pardoned.	Died.	Earnings.	Expenses.	Deficit.
Maine	67	86	76	19	....	19	16	3	......	3,462	8,562	5,100
New Hampshire	77	82	80	5	....	17	9	2	1	4,735	5,631	895
Vermont	52	62	57	10	....	34	13	6	4	6,713	3,652	3,060
Massachusetts	281	349	315	68	....	190	104	16	3	34,972	36,400	1,428
Rhode Island	20	28	24	8	....	16	4	4	2	1,192	3,613	2,421
Connecticut	157	175	166	18	....	61	35	4	4	14,148	12,315	....
Auburn, N. Y.	473	645	559	172	....	312	116	15	7	54,762	49,316	....
Sing Sing, (Male)	611	672	641	61	....	246	133	11	19	81,850	66,376	....
Sing Sing, (Female)	83	78	80	....	5	29	32	2	......	2,373	10,411	8,038
Clinton County, N. Y.	163	124	148	....	39	65	33	4	4	9,210	50,127	40,917
New Jersey	176	185	180	9	....	108	79	17	3	16,798	10,557	....
Philadelphia	293	299	296	6	....	128	81	34	6	11,990	16,632	4,864
Pittsburg, Pa.	115	123	119	8	....	84	54	15	7	9,184	8,560	....
Baltimore, Md	258	229	243	....	29	78	75	11	21	15,381	32,504	16,123
District of Columbia	40	46	43	6	....	25	15	4	......	1,772	1,482	....
Virginia	200	199	200	....	1	56	32	11	14	11,442	10,521	....
Georgia	98	91	95	....	7	32	......	34	3	....	....	....
Kentucky	161	141	151	....	20	52	42	23	4	....	....	....
Ohio	425	336	381	....	89	156	58	62	121	37,883	29,616	....
Michigan	128	110	119	....	18	31	30	16	1	8,148	20,835	12,687
Total	3,878	4,060	3,973	390	208	1,739	961	294	224	326,015	377,110	95,533

* Excluding slaves about 13 in ten thousand.

The tables below are taken from a report made in 1845 by the Secretary of State upon the census, now in manuscript in the office. The facts were obtained from answers to a special circular.

TABLE CLXXX.—*Proportion of Convicts, Persons in Jails, Houses of Correction and Refuge, and Almshouses, to the Total Population.*

Cities and Counties.	Colored.	White.
Boston (Suffolk county) ... as one to	16.17	34.27
New York (county)	24.3	45.8
Philadelphia (county)	29.8	78.
Richmond, (county) including lowest class of misdemeanors	45.9	112.6
Charleston (district) for four years	63.48	48.

TABLE CLXXXI.—*Number of Convicts, Male and Female, White and Colored, in the States named, for the year* 1840.

Prisons in each of the States named.	Convicts in 1840.				Proportion of white convicts to the whole white population.	Proportion of colored convicts to the whole colored population.
	Whites.		Colored.			
	Males.	Females	Males.	Females		
Maine	63	1	4	0	1 to 7,819	1 to 338
New Hampshire	77	0	1	0	1 to 3,688	1 to 538
Massachusetts*	289	0	33	0	1 to 2,522	1 to 262
Rhode Island	13	0	4	1	1 to 8,122	1 to 648
Connecticut	122	3	40	4	1 to 2,414	1 to 185
Vermont	84	0	2	1	1 to 3,466	1 to 243
New York	1,122	35	319	32	1 to 2,056	1 to 142
New Jersey	97	2	49	4	1 to 3,551	1 to 409
Pennsylvania	376	19	157	27	1 to 4,243	1 to 260
Maryland	180	6	116	27	1 to 1,708	1 to 1,059
Virginia †	134	1	38	5	1 to 5,570	1 to 11,600
Kentucky	149	1	11	1	1 to 3,930	1 to 15,797
Tennessee	115	0	4	0	1 to 4,242	1 to 47,145
Georgia	153	2	0	0	1 to 2,664	none.
Louisiana	141	1	25	7	1 to 1,115	1 to 6,061

The figures below were prepared for a report to the legislature of Virginia by a citizen of that State.

TABLE CLXXXII.—*Ratio of Imprisonment.*

States.	Whites.	Free Colored.	Ratio of white to col'd as 1 to
Virginia—Ratio for 10 years ending 1850 of convicts in penitentiaries to the average population as 1 to	23,003	3,001	7.18
Massachusetts—in the same period	7,587	727	9.58
Do. year ending 30th September, 1852, according to the population of 1850	6,527	488	13.37
Maryland, according to the population of 1850	9,285	1,452	6.39
Pennsylvania, two penitentiaries, year ending 31st December, 1852	11,406	2,158	5.28
New York, three penitentiaries, year ending 1st December, 1851	5,304	722	8.86
Ratio of Convicts remaining in Prison.			7.71
Virginia penitentiary, 1st February 1853	5,813	625	9.30
Massachusetts do. 30th September, 1851	2,335	175	13.00
Maryland do. 30th November, 1852	2,584	500	5.16
Pennsylvania, two penitentiaries, 31st December, 1852	7,811	750	10.41
New York, three penitentiaries, 1st December, 1851	1,713	225	7.62
Average of the five States	......	....	7.49
New Jersey penitentiary, 1st January, 1850	3,554	453	7.84
Connecticut do. do. do.	2,838	159	17.85
Indiana........ do. 30th September, 1849	8,427	719	11.72
‡ Average	....	....	12.47
Average for eight States	....	....	9.11

* Female felons, of whom there are a large number, are not sent to the State prison of Massachusetts.

† In the tabular statement for 1840, made by the superintendent of the Penitentiary at Richmond, the precise numbers of the different conditions of convicts do not appear. The numbers set down are the just proportional average for forty-four years.

‡ The following is condensed from the several State reports:

The *Alabama* Penitentiary for 1850, embraced only four colored persons—total confined 129. *Ohio*—convicts in Penitentiary during 1853, 237; permanent number Nov., 1852, 508. *Pennsylvania*—prisoners from July 1826 to January 1853, in Western Penitentiary, 1387 whites and 261 colored; Eastern, 241 whites and 52 colored on the 1st January, 1853. House of Refuge, admitted since 1828, 3,238 whites and 329 colored; remaining 31st December, 1851, 198 whites and 124 colored. Owing to the crowded state of the colored department, the Board declined to receive any longer males of 14 years and over. *Rhode Island*, committed 1852, 307 whites and 10 colored to State prison. *Connecticut*—convicts in State prison, 31st March, 1853, 142 whites and 39 colored. *Massachusetts*—the report of the keeper of jails 1852, shows, whole number of prisoners in the State, 7,281, of which 273 colored, in *Boston* alone, 4,779 whites and 186 colored; in the House of Correction, Boston, 50 colored and 1,006 whites; of the whites 738 foreign; in the State, whole whites 3,028, whole colored 159, of which, foreigners 1,942. Out of a total of 9,353 criminal offences, for which persons were imprisoned, 3,941 were for intemperance, and 1,363 for debt. In 1852 the whole number of paupers supported or relieved in the State was 27,737, of whom 11,321 were foreigners: 12,337 were relieved in alms houses—the average in such houses being 5,010; total expense of paupers $476,674. In *Boston* alone, 9,464 paupers, of whom 5,913 were foreign. Average in alms houses 1,295; 3,098 children under 14 supported at public expense. The average of 5 years, 1841 to 1845, shows 2,653 commitments to jail, 2,855 cases in police courts, 708 in city court, 426 convictions, 33 sent to State prison, and 637 to house of correction—40 per cent. in the house of correction were females, 8.63 per cent. were colored, 25 per cent. were citizens of Massachusetts, and 51.98 per cent. foreigners.

England and Wales.

Year.	Committals.			Convictions.
	Males.	Females.	Total.	
1840	21,975	5,212	27,187	19,927
1843	24,521	5,340	29,591	21,092
1849	22,415	5,401	27,816	21,001

Mr. Porter, in review of the above result finds nothing whatever, he says, to support the assertion so often hazarded, that vice and crime are fostered by bringing men together in large masses, while innocence is preserved by rural pursuits. For each million of inhabitants there were charged with offences in 20 more agricultural counties in 1841, 1,723, and in 20 less agricultural, 1,842. He adds—if we class together those who can neither read nor write, and those who have acquired only an imperfect acquaintance with those elementary branches of knowledge, in 13 years, out of a total of 335,429 persons committed, and whose degree of instruction was ascertained, the great proportion of 304,772, or more than 90 in 100, were uninstructed, while only 1,333 persons had enjoyed the benefit of instruction beyond the elementary degree, and only 29,324 had mastered without advancing beyond the art of reading and writing.

In England and Wales in 1841, the commitments were 1 in every 573 persons, and in Scotland 1 in 738.

Ireland.

Year.	Committals.			Convictions.
	Males.	Females.	Total.	
1840	17,835	5,998	23,833	11,197
1843	15,250	4,876	20,126	8,620
1849	31,340	10,649	41,989	21,202

The total number of persons confined in the various State prisons in France on the 31st December, 1852, was 19,720 of which 15,873 were males and 3,847 females. The following interesting statistics are given in the official report for that year:

Description of Convicts.	Males	Fem's
From rural districts	5,801	1,317
From towns	10,072	2,530
Unmarried or widowed without children.	10,285	1,942
Married, with children	3,887	846
Married, without children	1,125	354
Widowed, with children	549	423
Having recognised natural children	27	282
Ages—from 16 to 20	1,579	257
20 to 30	5,610	1,434
30 to 40	4,138	1,049
40 to 50	2,670	666
50 to 60	1,286	327
60 and upwards	590	114
Catholics	15,165	3,774
Protestants	547	51
Israelites	118	12
Mahometans	44	9
Farm laborers and servants	3,635	622
Artificers in wood, iron, &c	3,255	267
Bakers, butchers, and provision venders.	655	9
Tailors, shoemakers, barbers, &c	1,265	677
Engaged in commerce	1,082	214
Engaged in transportation	2,259	580
Innkeepers, boarding-house keepers, and city servants	606	697
Liberal professions and of independent means	662	80
Without any occupation	2,454	701
Confined for offences against the person.	3,331	1,181
Do. do. do. property	12,356	2,662
Do. political offences	204	4

Description of Convicts.	Males	Fem's
Condemned to hard labor for 5 to 10 years	488	Both sexes.
Do. do. do. 10 to 20 "	560	
Do. do. do. life	327	
Condemned to solitary confinement for 5 to 7 years	3,017	
Ditto, from 7 to 10 years	1,551	
Condemned to correctional imprisonment for 1 to 2 years	5,277	
Ditto, for 2 to 3 years	2,962	
3 to 4 "	1,970	
4 to 5 "	1,738	
5 to 10 "	1,830	
Condemned after having before suffered punishment from hard labor	478	
Ditto, after solitary confinement	937	
Ditto, after correctional imprisonment	4,656	
Having before imprisonment an education superior to that of primary schools	523	36
Ditto, knowing how to read and write	6,028	736
Ditto, knowing how to read and not write.	1,680	718
Ditto, entirely illiterate	7,642	2,357
After imprisonment, having learned to read	2,667	535
After do., having learned to read and write	4,654	576
After do., having received primary instruction	1,219	176
Deaths by disease	1,005	227
Total product of manual labor 1,497,349 francs; average daily labor per hand, (centimes)	42	28

PART IV.

INDUSTRY.

1. AGRICULTURE.—The following table will show the relative number of farms, and quantity of acres in each in the several States and Territories, as well as the value of farms and implements. The unimproved land embraces such as is in occupancy and necessary to the enjoyment of the improved, though not itself reclaimed. Meadow lands in all of the States are therefore regarded improved. The returns do not, however, distinguish always very clearly the improved from the unimproved.

TABLE CLXXXIII.—*Farming Lands and Improvements,* 1850.

States and Territories.	Farms, Plantations, &c.	Acres of improved land.	Acres of unimproved land.	Average number of acres to each farm.	Cash value of farms.	Value of farming implements and machinery.	Average value of farms.	Average value of farming implements and machinery.	Average value of farms, implements and machinery.
Alabama	41,964	4,435,614	7,702,067	289	$64,323,224	$5,125,663	$1.533	$122	$1.655
Arkansas	17,758	781,530	1,816,684	146	15,265,245	1,601,296	860	90	950
California	872	32,454	3,861,531	4,466	3,874,041	103,483	4,443	118	4,561
Columbia, Dis. of	267	16,267	11,187	103	1,730,460	40,220	6,481	151	6,632
Connecticut	22,445	1,768,178	615,701	106	72,726,422	1,892,541	3,240	84	3,324
Delaware	6,063	580,862	375,282	158	18,880,031	510,279	3,114	84	3,198
Florida	4,304	349,049	1,246,240	371	6,323,109	658,795	1,469	153	1,622
Georgia	51,759	6,378,479	16,442,900	441	95,753,445	5,894,150	1,850	114	1,964
Illinois	76,208	5,039,545	6,997,867	158	96,133,290	6,405,561	1,261	84	1,345
Indiana	93,896	5,046,543	7,746,879	136	136,385,173	6,704,444	1,453	71	1,524
Iowa	14,805	824,682	1,911,382	185	16,657,567	1,172,869	1,125	79	1,204
Kentucky	74,777	5,968,270	10,981,478	227	155,021,262	5,169,037	2,073	69	2,142
Louisiana	13,422	1,590,025	3,399,018	372	75,814,398	11,576,938	5,648	863	6,511
Maine	46,760	2,039,596	2,515,797	97	54,861,748	2,284,557	1,173	49	1,222
Maryland	21,860	2,797,905	1,836,445	212	87,178,545	2,463,443	3,988	113	4,101
Massachusetts	34,069	2,133,436	1,222,576	99	109,076,347	3,209,584	3,202	94	3,296
Michigan	34,089	1,929,110	2,454,780	129	51,872,446	2,891,371	1.521	85	1,606
Mississippi	33,960	3,444,358	7,046,061	309	54,738,634	5,762,927	1,612	170	1,782
Missouri	54,458	2,938,425	6,794,245	179	63,225,543	3,981,525	1,161	73	1,234
New Hampshire	29,229	2,251,488	1,140,926	116	55,245,997	2,314,125	1,890	79	1,969
New Jersey	23,905	1,767,991	984,955	115	120,237,511	4,425,503	5,030	185	5,215
New York	170,621	12,408,964	6,710,120	113	554,546,642	22,084,926	3,250	129	3,379
North Carolina	56,963	5,453,975	15,543,008	369	67,891,766	3,931,532	1,192	69	1,261
Ohio	143,807	9,851,493	8,146,000	125	358,758,603	12,750,585	2,495	88	2,583
Pennsylvania	127,577	8,623,619	6,294,728	117	407,876,099	14,722,541	3,197	115	3,312
Rhode Island	5,385	356,487	197,451	103	17,070,802	497,201	3,170	92	3,262
South Carolina	29,967	4,072,551	12,145,049	541	82,431,684	4,136,354	2,751	138	2,889
Tennessee	72,735	5,175,173	13,808,849	261	97,851,212	5,360,210	1,345	74	1,419
Texas	12,198	643,976	10,852,363	942	16,550,008	2,151,704	1,357	176	1,533
Vermont	29,763	2,601,409	1,524,413	139	63,367,227	2,739,282	2,129	92	2,221
Virginia	77,013	10,360,135	15,792,176	340	216,401,543	7,021,772	2,810	91	2,901
Wisconsin	20,177	1,045,499	1,931,159	148	28,528,563	1,641,568	1,414	81	1,495
Territories. Minnesota	157	5,035	23,846	184	161,948	15,981	1,031	102	1,133
Territories. N. Mexico	3,750	166,201	124,370	77	1,653,922	77,960	441	21	462
Territories. Oregon	1,164	132,857	299,951	372	2,849,170	183,423	2,448	157	2,605
Territories. Utah	926	16,333	30,516	51	311,799	84,288	337	91	428
Total	1,449,075	113,032,614	180,528,000	203	3,271,575,426	151,587,638	2,258	105	2,362

The average number of acres embraced in each farm in the United States is 203, valued at $2,258, and upon each farm there is an average of $105 in implements and machinery. In Louisiana, so complicated is the sugar process, the average machinery is $863 to the farm.

By another table prepared by sections, it would seem that only about one-thirteenth of the whole area of the organized States and Territories is improved, and about one-eighth more is occupied and not improved. In New England about 26 acres in the 100 are improved, in the South 16 acres, in the Northwest 12, and in the Southwest 5. In the South the number of acres to the farm is largest, but the value per acre is most in the Middle States. The average value per acre for the Union, improved and unimproved, is $11.14. The whole number of acres occupied is 293,560,614, or nearly one-sixth part of the national domain.

TABLE CLXXXIV.—*Agricultural Ratio Tables of the States*, 1850.

Sections.	Whole area in acres.	Land in use. Improved.	Land in use. Unimproved.	Proportion of land in use to area. Improved, per cent.	Proportion of land in use to area. Unimproved per cent.	Number of Farms.	Average value of agricultural implements to each farm.	Average number of acres to each farm.	Average value per acre.
New England	41,624,320	11,150,594	7,216,864	26.79	17.34	167,651	77.17	109.55	20.27
Middle States	73,359,360	26,200,608	16,212,717	35.72	22.10	350,293	126.31	121.08	28.07
Southern States	165,573,760	26,614,289	61,169,373	16.07	36.94	220,008	98.37	399.09	5.34
Southwestern States*	151,635,840	15,426,730	33,772,679	10.17	22.27	179,839	163.63	273.57	6.26
Northwestern States	253,004,160	32,643,567	46,963,790	12.90	18.56	512,217	79.49	155.41	11.39
California & organized territories	629,255,680	352,880	4,340,214	.06	.69	6,869	67.71	683.23	1.89
Texas	152,002,560	643,946	10,852,363	.42	7.14	12,198	176.40	942.47	1.44
Total	1,466,455,680	113,032,614	180,528,000	7.71	12.31	1,449,075	104.61	202.59	11.14

The annexed table embraces the returns of agricultural products and live stock by the Census of 1840 and 1850. The quantity of wheat in 1850 is believed to be understated, and the crop was also short. Rough rice is returned for 1850, and clean rice for 1840. Corrections have been made in the cotton and sugar returns since the publication of the Quarto Census, pounds having been intended by the enumerators in many cases, where they returned bales or hogsheads. It is impossible to reconcile the hemp and flax returns of 1840 and 1850. No doubt in both cases tons and pounds have often been confounded. In a few of the States, such as Indiana and Illinois, the returns of 1850 were rejected altogether for insufficiency. Letters from Kentucky entitled to high credit, state the water-rotted hemp for that year to be not a third as much as the census gives, and the dew-rotted to be about 22,000 tons. In this case the whole hemp crop of 1850 may have reached 35 or 40,000 tons, and that of 1840, 25 to 30,000 tons.†

TABLE CLXXXV.—*Live Stock upon Farms and Agricultural Productions of the States and Territories*, 1840 *and* 1850.

States and Territories.	1850. Horses.	1850. Asses and mules.	1850. Horses, asses and mules.	Horses and mules. 1840.	1850. Milch cows.	1850. Working oxen.	1850. Other cattle.	1850. Total neat cattle.	Neat cattle. 1840.	Sheep. 1850.	Sheep. 1840.
Alabama	128,001	59,895	187,896	143,147	227,791	66,961	433,263	728,015	668.018	371,880	163,243
Arkansas	60,197	11,559	71,756	51,472	93,151	34,239	165,320	292,710	188,786	91,256	42,151
California	21,719	1,666	23,385	....	4,280	4,780	253,599	262,659	....	17,574	....
Columbia, Dis. o.	824	57	881	2,145	813	104	123	1,040	3,274	150	706
Connecticut	26,879	49	26,928	34,650	85,461	46,988	80,226	212,675	238,650	174,181	403,462
Delaware	13,852	791	14,643	14,421	19,248	9,797	24,166	53,211	53,883	27,503	39,247
Florida	10,848	5,002	15,850	12,043	72,876	5,794	182,415	261,085	118,081	23,311	7,198
Georgia	151,331	57,379	208,710	157,540	334,223	73,286	690,019	1,097,528	884,414	560,435	267,107
Illinois	267,653	10,573	278,226	199,235	294,671	76,156	541,209	912,036	626,274	894,043	395,672
Indiana	314,299	6,599	320,898	241,036	284,554	40,221	389,891	714,666	619,980	1,122,493	675,982
Iowa	38,536	754	39,290	10,794	45,704	21,892	69,025	136,621	38,049	149,960	15,354
Kentucky	315,682	65,609	381,291	395,853	247,475	62,274	442,763	752,512	787,098	1,102,091	1,008,240
Louisiana	89,514	44,849	134,363	99,888	105,576	54,968	414,798	575,342	381,248	110,333	98,072
Maine	41,721	55	41,776	59,208	133,556	83,893	125,890	343,339	327,255	451,577	649,264
Maryland	75,684	5,644	81,328	92,220	86,856	34,135	98,595	219,586	225,714	177,902	257,922
Massachusetts	42,216	34	42,250	61,484	130,099	46,611	83,284	259,994	282,574	188,651	378,226
Michigan	58,506	70	58,576	30,144	99,676	55,350	119,471	274,497	185,190	746,435	99,618
Mississippi	115,460	54,547	170,007	109,227	214,231	83,485	436,254	733,970	623,197	304,929	128,367
Missouri	225,319	41,667	266,986	196,032	230,169	112,168	449,173	791,510	433,875	762,511	348,018
New Hampshire	34,233	19	34,252	43,892	94,277	59,027	114,606	267,910	275,562	384,756	617,390
New Jersey	63,955	4,089	68,044	70,502	118,736	12,070	80,455	211,261	220,202	160,488	219,285
New York	447,014	963	447,977	474,543	931,324	178,909	767,406	1,877,639	1,911,244	3,453,241	5,118,777
North Carolina	148,693	25,259	173,952	166,608	221,799	37,309	434,402	693,510	617,371	595,249	538,279
Ohio	463,397	3,423	466,820	430,527	544,499	65,381	749,067	1,358,947	1,217,874	3,942,929	2,028,401
Pennsylvania	350,398	2,259	352,657	365,129	530,224	61,527	562,195	1,153,946	1,172,665	1,822,357	1,767,620
Rhode Island	6,168	1	6,169	8,024	18,698	8,139	9,375	36,262	36,891	44,296	90,146
South Carolina	97,171	37,483	134,654	129,921	193,244	20,507	563,935	777,686	572,608	285,551	232,981
Tennessee	270,636	75,303	345,939	341,409	250,456	86,255	414,051	750,762	822,851	811,591	741,593
Texas	76,760	12,463	89,223	....	217,811	51,285	661,018	930,114	....	100,530	....
Vermont	61,057	218	61,275	62,402	146,128	48,577	154,143	348,848	384,341	1,014,122	1,681,819
Virginia	272,403	21,483	293,886	326,438	317,619	89,513	669,137	1,076,269	1,024,148	1,310,004	1,293,772
Wisconsin	30,179	156	30,335	5,735	64,339	42,801	76,293	183,433	30,269	124,896	3,462
Territories. Minnesota	860	14	874	....	607	655	740	2,002	....	80	....
Territories. N. Mexico	5,079	8,654	13,733	....	10,635	12,257	10,085	32,977	....	377,271	....
Territories. Oregon	8,046	420	8,466	....	9,427	8,114	24,188	41,729	....	15,382	....
Territories. Utah	2,429	325	2,754	....	4,861	5,266	2,489	12,616	....	3,262	....

* Exclusive of Texas and California.

† By the manufacturing schedules it appears that 18,276 tons hemp were consumed by the manufacturers of Kentucky and Missouri, and by the receipts at the cities of St. Louis, Cincinnati and New Orleans, with proper deductions, that 14 or 15 thousand tons hemp were exported in the rough to other States.

TABLE CLXXXV—*Continued.*

States and Territories.	Swine.		Value of live stock.	Value of animals slaught'd.	Wheat, bushels.		Rye, bushels.		Oats, bushels.
	1850.	1840.	1850.	1850.	1850.	1840.	1850.	1840.	1850.
Alabama	1,904,540	1,423,873	$21,690,112	$4,823,485	294,044	838,052	17,261	51,008	2,965.696
Arkansas	836,727	393,058	6,647,969	1,163,313	199,639	105,878	8,047	6,219	656,183
California	2,776	....	3,351,058	107,173	17,228	....	....	....	....
Columbia, Dis. of	1,635	4,673	71,643	9,038	17,370	12,147	5,509	5,081	8,134
Connecticut	76,472	131,961	7,467,490	2,202,266	41,762	87,009	600,893	737,424	1,258,738
Delaware	56,261	74,228	1,849,281	373,665	482,511	315,165	8,066	33,546	604,518
Florida	209,453	92,680	2,880,058	514,685	1,027	412	1,152	305	66.586
Georgia	2,168,617	1,457,755	25,728,416	6,339,762	1,088,534	1,801,830	53,750	60,693	3,820,044
Illinois	1,915,907	1,495,254	24,209,258	4,972,286	9,414,575	3,335,393	83.364	88.197	10,087,241
Indiana	2,263,776	1,623,608	22,478,555	6,567,935	6,214,458	4,049,375	78,792	129,621	5,655,014
Iowa	323,247	104,899	3,689,275	821,164	1,530,581	154,693	19,916	3,792	1,524,345
Kentucky	2,891,163	2,310,533	29,661,436	6,462,598	2,142,822	4,803,152	415,073	1,321,373	8,201.311
Louisiana	597,301	323,220	11,152,275	1,458,990	417	60	475	1,812	89,637
Maine	54,598	117,386	9,705,726	1,646,773	296,259	848,166	102,916	137,941	2,181,037
Maryland	352,911	416,943	7,997,634	1,954,800	4,494,680	3,345,783	226,014	723,577	2,242,151
Massachusetts	81,119	143,221	9,647,710	2,500,924	31,211	157,923	481,021	536,014	1,165,146
Michigan	205,847	295,890	8,008,734	1,328,327	4,925,889	2,157,108	105,871	34,236	2,866,056
Mississippi	1,582,734	1,001,209	19,403,662	3,636,582	137,990	196,626	9,606	11,444	1,503,288
Missouri	1,702,625	1,271,161	19,887,580	3,367,106	2,981,652	1,037,386	44,268	68,608	5,278,079
New Hampshire	63,487	121,671	8,871,901	1,522,873	185,658	422,124	183,117	308,148	973,381
New Jersey	250,370	261,443	10,679,291	2,638,552	1,601,190	774,203	1,255,578	1,665,820	3,378,063
New York	1,018,252	1,900,065	73,570,499	13,573,883	13,121,498	12,286,418	4,148,182	2,979,323	26,552,814
North Carolina	1,812,813	1,649,716	17,717,647	5,767,866	2,130,102	1,960,855	229,563	213,971	4,052,078
Ohio	1,964,770	2,099,746	44,121,741	7,439,243	14,487,351	16,571,661	425,918	814,205	13,472,742
Pennsylvania	1,040,366	1,503,964	41,500,053	8,219,848	15,367,691	13,213,077	4,805,160	6,613,873	21,538,156
Rhode Island	19,509	30,659	1,532,637	667,486	49	3,098	26,409	34,521	215,232
South Carolina	1,065,503	878,532	15,060,015	3,502,637	1,066,277	968,354	43,790	44,738	2,322,155
Tennessee	3,104,800	2,926,607	29,978,016	6,401,765	1,619,386	4,569,692	89,137	304,320	7,703,086
Texas	692,022	....	10,412,927	1,116,137	41,729	....	3,108	....	199,017
Vermont	66,296	203,800	12,643,228	1,861,336	535,955	495,800	176,233	230,993	2,307,734
Virginia	1,829,843	1,992,155	33,656,659	7,502,986	11,212,616	10,109,716	458,930	1,482,799	10,179,144
Wisconsin	159,276	51,383	4,897,385	920,178	4,286,131	212,116	81,253	1,965	3,414,672
Territ's. Minnesota	734	....	92,859	2,840	1,401	....	125	....	30,582
Territ's. N. Mexico	7,314	....	1,494,629	82,125	196,516	....	....	....	5
Territ's. Oregon	30,235	....	1,876,189	164,530	211,943	....	106	....	61,214
Territ's. Utah	914	....	546,968	67,985	107,702	....	210	....	10,900

States and Territories.	Oats, bushels.	Indian corn, bushels.		Irish and sweet potatoes, bushels.				Barley, bushels.
				1850.			1840.	
	1840.	1850.	1840.	Irish.	Sweet.	Total.	Irish and sweet.	1850.
Alabama	1,406,353	28,754,048	20,947,004	246,001	5,475,204	5,721,205	1,708,356	3,958
Arkansas	189,553	8,893,939	4,846,632	193,832	788,149	981,981	293,608	177
California	....	12,236	....	9,292	1,000	10,292	....	9,712
Columbia, Dis. of	15,751	65,230	39,485	28,292	3,497	31,789	12,035	75
Connecticut	1,453,262	1,935,043	1,500,441	2,689,725	80	2,689,805	3,414,238	19,099
Delaware	927,405	3,145,542	2,099,359	240,542	65,443	305,985	200,712	56
Florida	13,829	1,996,809	898,974	7,828	757,226	765,054	264,617	....
Georgia	1,610,030	30,080,099	20,905,122	227,379	6,986,428	7,213,807	1,291,366	11,501
Illinois	4,988,008	57,646,984	22,634,211	2,514,861	157,433	2,672,294	2,025,520	110,795
Indiana	5,981,605	52,964,363	28,155,887	2,083,337	201,711	2,285,048	1,525,794	45,483
Iowa	216,385	8,656,799	1,406,241	276,120	6,243	282,363	234,063	25,093
Kentucky	7,155,974	58,672,591	39,847,120	1,492,487	998,179	2,490,666	1,055,085	95,343
Louisiana	107,353	10,266,373	5,952,912	95,632	1,428,453	1,524,085	834,341	....
Maine	1,076,409	1,750,056	950,528	3,436,040	....	3,436,040	10,392,280	151,731
Maryland	3,534,211	10,749,858	8,233,086	764,939	208,993	973,932	1,036,433	745
Massachusetts	1,319,680	2,345,490	1,809,192	3,585,384	....	3,585,384	5,385,652	112,385
Michigan	2,114,051	5,641,420	2,277,039	2,359,897	1,177	2,361,074	2,109,205	75,249
Mississippi	668,624	22,446,552	13,161,237	261,482	4,741,795	5,003,277	1,630,100	228
Missouri	2,234,947	36,214,537	17,332,524	939,006	335,505	1,274,511	783,768	9 631
New Hampshire	1,296,114	1,573,670	1,162,572	4,304,919	....	4,304,919	6,206,606	70,256
New Jersey	3,083,524	8,759,704	4,361,975	3,207,236	508,015	3,715,251	2,072,069	6,492
New York	20,675,847	17,858,400	10,972,286	15,398,368	5.629	15,403,997	30.123,614	3,585,059
North Carolina	3,193,941	27,941,051	23,893,763	620,318	5,095,709	5,716,027	2,609,239	2,735
Ohio	14,393,103	59,078,695	33,668,144	5,057,769	187,991	5,245,760	5,805,021	354,358
Pennsylvania	20,641,819	19,835,214	14,240,022	5,980,732	52,172	6,032,904	9,535,663	165,584
Rhode Island	171,517	539,201	450,498	651,029	....	651,029	911,973	18,875
South Carolina	1,486,208	16,271,454	14,722,805	136,494	4,337,469	4,473,960	2,698,313	4,583
Tennessee	7,035,678	52,276,223	44,986,188	1,067,844	2,777,716	3,845,560	1,904,370	2,737
Texas	....	6,028,876	....	94,645	1,332,158	1,426,803	....	4,776
Vermont	2,222,584	2,032,396	1,119,678	4,951,014	....	4,951,014	8,869,751	42,150
Virginia	13,451,062	35,254,319	34,577,591	1,316,933	1,813,634	3,130,567	2,944,660	25,437
Wisconsin	406,514	1,988,979	379,359	1,402,077	879	1,402,956	419,608	209,692
Territ's. Minnesota	....	16,725	....	21,145	200	21,345	....	1,216
Territ's. N. Mexico	....	365,411	....	3	....	3	....	5
Territ's. Oregon	....	2,918	....	91,326	....	91,326	....	....
Territ's. Utah	....	9,899	....	43,968	60	44,028	....	1.799

TABLE CLXXXV—*Continued.*

States and Territories.	Barley, bushels.	Buckwheat, bushels.		Hay, tons.		Hops, pounds.		Clover seed.	Other grass seeds.
	1840.	1850.	1840.	1850.	1840.	1850.	1840.	1850.	1850.
Alabama	7,692	348	58	32,685	12,718	276	825	138	547
Arkansas	760	175	88	3,976	586	157	....	90	436
California	....	....	....	2,038	....	....	....	....	....
Columbia, Dis. of	294	378	272	2,279	1,331	15	28	3	....
Connecticut	33,759	229,297	303,043	516,131	426,704	554	4,573	13,841	16,628
Delaware	5,260	8,615	11,299	30,159	22,483	348	746	2,525	1,403
Florida	30	55	....	2,510	1,197	14	....	....	2
Georgia	12,979	250	141	23,449	16,970	261	773	132	428
Illinois	82,251	184,504	57,884	601,952	164,932	3,551	17,742	3,427	14,380
Indiana	28,015	149,740	49,019	403,230	178,029	92,796	38,591	18,320	11,951
Iowa	728	52,516	6,212	89,055	17,953	8,242	83	342	2,096
Kentucky	17,491	16,097	8,169	113,747	88,306	4,309	742	3,230	21,481
Louisiana	....	3	....	25,752	24,651	125	115	2	97
Maine	355,161	104,523	51,543	755,889	691,358	40,120	36,940	9,097	9,214
Maryland	3,594	103,671	73,606	157,956	106,687	1,870	2,357	15,217	2,561
Massachusetts	165,319	105,895	87,000	651,807	569,395	121,595	254,795	1,002	5,085
Michigan	127,802	472,917	113,592	404,934	130,805	10,663	11,381	16,989	9,285
Mississippi	1,654	1,121	61	12,504	171	473	154	84	533
Missouri	9,801	23,641	15,318	116,925	49,083	4,130	789	619	4,346
New Hampshire	121,899	65,265	105,103	598,854	496,107	257,174	243,425	829	8,071
New Jersey	12,501	878,934	856,117	435,950	334,861	2,133	4,531	28,280	63,051
New York	2,520,068	3,183,955	2,287,885	3,728,797	3,127,047	2,536,299	447,250	88,222	96,493
North Carolina	3,574	16,704	15,391	145,653	101,369	9,246	1,063	576	1,275
Ohio	212,440	638,060	633,139	1,443,142	1,022,037	63,731	62,195	103,197	37,310
Pennsylvania	209,893	2,193,692	2,113,742	1,842,970	1,311,643	22,088	49,481	125,030	53,913
Rhode Island	66,490	1,245	2,979	74,418	63,449	277	113	1,328	3,708
South Carolina	3,967	283	72	20,925	24,618	26	93	376	30
Tennessee	4,809	19,427	17,118	74,091	31,233	1,032	850	5,096	9,118
Texas	....	59	....	8,354	....	7	....	10	....
Vermont	54,781	209,819	228,416	866,153	836,739	288,023	48,137	760	14,936
Virginia	87,430	214,898	243,822	369,098	364,708	11,506	10,597	29,727	23,428
Wisconsin	11,062	79,878	10,654	275,662	30,938	15,930	133	483	5,003
Territ's. Minnesota	....	515	....	2,019	....	....	....	....	....
N. Mexico	....	100	....	....	....	....	....	....	....
Oregon	....	....	....	373	....	8	....	4	22
Utah	....	332	....	4,805	....	50	....	2	....

States and Territories.	Butter and Cheese, lbs. 1850.			Dairy products.	Peas and Beans.	Produce of market gardens.	Value of market products	Value of nursery products	Value of orchard products.
	Butter.	Cheese.	Total.	1840.	1850.	1850.	1840.	1840.	1850.
Alabama	4,008,811	31,412	4,040,223	$265,200	892,701	$84,821	$31,978	$370	$15,408
Arkansas	1,854,239	30,088	1,884,327	59,205	285,738	17,150	2,736	415	40,141
California	705	150	855	....	2,292	75,275	....	....	17,700
Columbia, Dis. of	14,872	1,500	16,372	5,566	7,754	67,222	52,895	850	14,843
Connecticut	6,498,119	5,363,277	11,861,396	1,376,534	19,090	196,874	61,936	18,114	175,118
Delaware	1,055,308	3,187	1,058,495	113,828	4,120	12,714	4,035	1,120	46,574
Florida	371,498	18,015	389,513	23,094	135,359	8,721	11,758	10	1,280
Georgia	4,640,559	46,976	4,687,535	605,172	1,142,011	76,500	19,346	1,853	92,776
Illinois	12,526,543	1,278,225	13,804,768	428,175	82,814	127,494	71,911	22,990	446,049
Indiana	12,881,535	624,564	13,506,099	742,269	35,773	72,864	61,212	17,231	324,940
Iowa	2,171,188	209,840	2,381,028	23,609	4,775	8,848	2,170	4,200	8,434
Kentucky	9,947,523	213,954	10,161,477	931,363	202,574	303,120	125,071	6,226	106,230
Louisiana	683,069	1,957	685,026	153,069	161,732	148,329	240,042	32,415	22,359
Maine	9,243,811	2,434,454	11,678,265	1,496,902	205,541	122,387	51,579	460	342,865
Maryland	3,806,160	3,975	3,810,135	457,466	12,816	200,869	133,197	10,591	164,051
Massachusetts	8,071,370	7,088,142	15,159,512	2,373,299	43,709	600,020	283,904	111,814	463,995
Michigan	7,065,878	1,011,492	8,077,370	301,052	74,254	14,738	4,051	6,307	132,650
Mississippi	4,346,234	21,191	4,367,425	359,585	1,072,757	46,250	42,896	499	50,405
Missouri	7,834,359	203,572	8,037,931	100,432	46,017	99,454	37,181	6,205	514,711
New Hampshire	6,977,056	3,196,563	10,173,619	1,638,543	70,856	56,810	18,085	35	248,563
New Jersey	9,487,210	365,756	9,852,966	1,328,032	14,174	475,242	249,613	26,167	607,268
New York	79,766,094	49,741,413	129,507,507	10,496,021	741,546	912,047	499,126	75,980	1,761,950
North Carolina	4,146,290	95,921	4,242,211	674,349	1,584,252	39,462	28,475	48,581	34,348
Ohio	34,449,379	20,819,542	55,268,921	1,848,869	60,168	214,004	97,606	19,707	695,921
Pennsylvania	39,878,418	2,505,034	42,383,452	3,187,292	55,231	688,714	232,912	50,127	723,389
Rhode Island	995,670	316,508	1,312,178	223,229	6,846	98,298	67,741	12,604	63,994
South Carolina	2,981,850	4,970	2,986,820	577,810	1,026,900	47,286	38,187	2,139	35,108
Tennessee	8,139,585	177,681	8,317,266	472,141	369,321	97,183	19,812	71,100	52,894
Texas	2,344,900	95,299	2,440,199	....	179,350	12,354	....	....	12,505
Vermont	12,137,980	8,720,834	20,858,814	2,008,737	104,649	18,853	16,276	5,600	315,255
Virginia	11,089,359	436,292	11,525,651	1,480,488	521,579	183,047	92,359	38,799	177,137
Wisconsin	3,633,750	400,283	4,034,033	35,677	20,657	32,142	3,106	1,025	4,823
Territ's. Minnesota	1,100	....	1,100	....	10,002	150	....	....	....
N. Mexico	111	5,848	5,959	....	15,688	6,679	....	....	8,231
Oregon	211,464	36,980	248,444	....	6,566	90,241	....	....	1,271
Utah	83,309	30,998	114,307	....	289	23,868	....	....	....

TABLE CLXXXV—*Continued.*

States and Territories	Value of orchard products. 1840.	Beeswax and Honey lbs. of 1850.	Wax lbs. of 1840.	Value of poultry. 1840.	Home made manufact's. 1850.	Cords of wood sold. 1840.	Flaxseed bush. of 1850.	Flax lbs. of 1850.	Dew rotted hemp, tons. 1850.	Water rotted hemp, tons. 1850.
Alabama	$55,240	897,021	25,226	$404,994	$1,934,120	60,955	69	3,921	......	......
Arkansas	10,680	192,338	7,079	109,468	638,217	78,606	321	12,291	......	15
California	....	....	......	....	7,000	....	......	....	......	......
Columbia, Dist. of	3,507	550	44	3,092	2,075	1,287	......	....	......	......
Connecticut	296,232	93,304	3,897	176,629	192,252	159,062	703	17,928	......	......
Delaware	28,211	41,248	1,088	47,265	38,121	67,864	904	11,174	......	......
Florida	1,035	18,971	75	61,007	75,582	9,943	......	50	......	......
Georgia	156,122	732,514	19,799	449,623	1,838,968	57,459	622	5,387	......	......
Illinois	126,756	869,444	29,173	309,204	1,155,902	134,549	10,787	160,063	......	......
Indiana	110,055	935,329	30,647	357,594	1,631,039	183,712	36,888	584,469	......	......
Iowa	50	321,711	2,132	16,529	221,292	7,304	1,959	62,660	......	......
Kentucky	434,935	1,158,019	38,445	536,439	2,459,128	264,222	75,801	2,100,116	16,432	1,355
Louisiana	11,769	96,701	1,012	283,559	139,232	202,867	......	....	......	......
Maine	149,384	189,618	3,723	123,171	513,599	205,011	580	17,081	......	......
Maryland	105,740	74,802	3,674	218,765	111,828	178,181	2,446	35,686	63	....
Massachusetts	389,177	59,508	1,196	178,157	205,333	278,069	72	1,162	......	......
Michigan	16,075	359,232	4,533	82,730	340,947	54,498	519	7,152	......	......
Mississippi	14,458	397,460	6,835	369,482	1,164,020	118,423	26	665	7	......
Missouri	90,878	1,328,972	56,461	270,647	1,674,705	81,981	13,696	627,160	15,968	60
New Hampshire	239,979	117,140	1,345	107,092	393,455	116,266	189	7,652	......	......
New Jersey	464,006	156,694	10,061	336,953	112,781	340,602	16,525	182,965	......	......
New York	1,701,935	1,755,830	52,795	1,153,413	1,280,333	1,058,923	57,963	940,577	1	3
North Carolina	386,006	512,289	118,923	544,125	2,086,522	40,034	38,196	593,796	36	3
Ohio	475,271	804,275	38,950	551,193	1,712,196	272,527	188,880	446,932	100	50
Pennsylvania	618,179	839.509	33,107	685,801	749,132	269,516	41,728	530,307	44	......
Rhode Island	32,098	6,347	165	61,702	26,495	48,666	......	85	......	......
South Carolina	52,275	216,281	15,857	396,364	909,525	171,451	55	333	......	......
Tennessee	367,105	1,036,572	50,907	606,969	3,137,790	104,014	18,904	368,131	454	141
Texas	....	380,825	......	....	266,984	....	26	1,048	......	......
Vermont	213,944	249,422	4,660	131,578	267,710	96,399	939	20,852	......	......
Virginia	705,765	880,767	65,020	754,698	2,156,312	403,590	52,318	1,000,450	88	51
Wisconsin	37	131,005	1,474	16,167	43,624	22,910	1,191	68,393	......	......
Territ's. Minnesota	....	80	......	....	....	....	......	....	......	......
Territ's. New Mexico	....	2	......	....	6,033	....	......	....	......	......
Territ's. Oregon	....	....	......	....	....	....	......	640	......	......
Territ's. Utah	....	10	......	....	1,392	....	5	550	......	......

States and Territories	Dew and water rt'd hemp, t'ns 1850.	Hemp and Flax, tons. 1840.	Maple sugar, lbs. 1850.	Canesugar hhds. of 1000 lbs. 1850.	Molasses galls. of 1850.	Sugar, lbs. made. 1840.	Gin'd cotton, bales of 400 lbs. 1850.	Cotton gathered, lbs. of 1840.	Rough Rice, lbs. 1850.
Alabama	......	5	643	87	83,428	10,143	564,429	117,138,823	2,312,252
Arkansas	15	1,039½	9,330	....	18	1,542	65,344	6,028,642	63,179
California	......	....	....	....	....	....	......	....	....
Columbia, Dist. of	......	....	....	....	....	....	......	....	....
Connecticut	......	41¾	50,796	....	665	51,764	......	....	....
Delaware	......	52¾	....	....	50	....	......	334	....
Florida	......	2	....	2,750	352,893	275,317	45,131	12,110,533	1,075,090
Georgia	......	10¾	50	846	216,245	329,744	499,091	163,392,396	38,950,691
Illinois	......	1,976¼	248,904	....	8,354	399,813	......	200,947	....
Indiana	......	8,605½	2,921,192	....	180,325	3,727,795	14	180	....
Iowa	......	313¼	78,407	....	3,162	41,450	......	....	....
Kentucky	17,787	9,992¼	437,405	10	30,079	1,377,835	758	691,456	5,688
Louisiana	......	....	255	226,001	10,931,177	119,947,720	178,737	152,555,368	4.425,349
Maine	......	38	93,542	....	3,167	257,464	......	....	....
Maryland	63	488	47,740	....	1,430	36,266	......	5,673	....
Massachusetts	......	2¼	795,525	....	4,693	579,227	......	....	....
Michigan	......	755¼	2,439,794	....	19,823	1,329,784	......	....	....
Mississippi	7	16	....	8	18,318	77	484,292	193,401,577	2,719,856
Missouri	16,028	18,010¾	178,910	....	5,636	274,853	......	121,122	700
New Hampshire	......	26½	1,298,863	....	9,811	1,162,368	......	....	....
New Jersey	......	2,165¾	2,197	....	954	56	......	....	....
New York	4	1,130⅝	10,357,484	....	56,539	10,048,109	......	....	....
North Carolina	39	9,879⅓	27,932	....	704	7,163	50,545	51,926,190	5,465,868
Ohio	150	9,080¼	4,588,209	....	197,308	6,363,386	......	....	....
Pennsylvania	44	2,649¾	2,326,525	....	50,652	2,265,755	......	....	....
Rhode Island	......	¼	28	....	4	50	......	....	....
South Carolina	......	....	200	77	15,904	30,000	300,901	61,710,274	159,930,613
Tennessee	595	3,344½	158,557	3	7,223	258,073	194,532	27,701,277	258,854
Texas	......	....	....	7,351	441,918	....	58,072	....	88,203
Vermont	......	29½	6,349,357	....	5,997	4,647,934	......	....	....
Virginia	139	25,594¼	1,227,665	....	40,322	1,541,833	3,947	3,494,483	17,154
Wisconsin	......	2	610,976	....	9,874	135,288	......	....	....
Territ's. Minnesota	......	....	2,950	....	....	....	......	....	....
Territ's. New Mexico	......	....	....	....	4,236	....	......	....	....
Territ's. Oregon	......	....	....	....	24	....	......	....	....
Territ's. Utah	......	....	....	....	58	....	......	....	....

TABLE CLXXXV—*Continued.*

States and Territories.	Rice, lbs.	Tobacco, pounds.		Wool, pounds.		Silk cocoons, pounds.		Wine, galls.		Value of family goods.
	1840.	1850.	1840.	1850.	1840.	1850.	1840.	1850.	1840.	1840.
										Dollars.
Alabama........	149,019	164,990	273,202	657,118	220,353	167	1,592¼	220	177	1,656,119
Arkansas.......	5,454	218,936	148,439	182,595	64,943	38	95	35	......	489,750
California.......	....	1,000	....	5,520	....	......	....	58,055	......	....
Columbia, Dis. of	....	7,800	55,550	525	707	......	651	863	25	1,500
Connecticut	....	1,267,624	471,657	497,454	889,870	328	17,538	4,269	2,666	226,162
Delaware.......	....	....	272	57,768	64,404	......	1,458¾	145	322	62,116
Florida	481,420	998,614	75,274	23,247	7,285	6	124¾	10	......	20,205
Georgia.........	12,384,732	423,924	162,894	990,019	371,303	813	2,992¼	796	8,647	1,467,630
Illinois	460	841,394	564,326	2,150,113	650,007	47	1,150	2,997	474	993,567
Indiana.........	....	1,044,620	1,820,306	2,610,287	1,237,919	387	379	14,055	10,265	1,289,802
Iowa...........	....	6,041	8,076	373,898	23,039	246	....	420	......	25,966
Kentucky.......	16,376	55,501,196	53,436,909	2,297,433	1,786,847	1,281	737	8,093	2,209	2,622,462
Louisiana.......	3,604,534	26,878	119,824	109,897	49,283	29	317	15	2,884	65,190
Maine..........	....	....	30	1,364,034	1,465,551	252	211	724	2,236	804,397
Maryland.......	....	21,407,497	24,816,012	477,438	488,201	39	2,290½	1,431	7,585	176,050
Massachusetts ..	....	138,246	64,955	585,136	941,906	7	1,741	4,688	193	231,942
Michigan........	....	1,245	1,602	2,043,283	153,375	108	266	1,654	......	113,955
Mississippi......	777,195	49,960	83,471	559,619	175,196	2	91	407	12	682,945
Missouri........	50	17,113,784	9,067,913	1,627,164	562,265	186	70	10,563	22	1,149,544
New Hampshire.	....	50	115	1,108,476	1,260,517	191	419⅞	344	94	538,303
New Jersey.....	....	310	1,922	375,396	397,207	23	1,966	1,811	9,416	201,625
New York......	....	83,189	744	10,071,301	9,845,295	1,774	1,735¾	9,172	6,799	4,636,547
North Carolina..	2,820,388	11,984,786	16,772,359	970,738	625,044	229	3,014	11,058	28,752	1,413,242
Ohio	....	10,454,449	5,942,275	10,196,371	3,685,315	1,552	4,317½	48,207	11,524	1,853,937
Pennsylvania ...	....	912,651	325,018	4,481,570	3,048,564	285	7,262½	25,590	14,328	1,303,093
Rhode Island ...	....	....	317	129,692	183,830	......	458	1,013	803	51,180
South Carolina .	60,590,861	74,285	51,519	487,233	299,170	123	2,080	5,880	643	930,703
Tennessee......	7,977	20,148,932	29,550,432	1,364,378	1,060,332	1,923	1,217	92	653	2,886,661
Texas	....	66,897	....	131,917	....	22	....	99	......	....
Vermont........	....	....	585	3,400,717	3,699,235	268	4,286	659	94	674,548
Virginia	2,956	56,803,227	75,347,106	2,860,765	2,538,374	517	3,191	5,408	13,911	2,441,672
Wisconsin......	....	1,268	115	253,963	6,777	......	½	113	......	12,567
Territ's. Minnesota..	....	....	....	85	....	......	....	......	......	....
Territ's. N. Mexico..	....	8,467	....	32,901	....	......	....	2,363	......	....
Territ's. Oregon	....	325	....	29,686	....	......	....	......	......	....
Territ's. Utah	....	70	....	9,222	....	......	....	......	......	....

TABLE CLXXXVI.—*Agricultural Products of the United States*—1850 *and* 1840.

Agricultural Products.	1850.	1840.	Agricultural Products.	1850.	1840.
Horses......................	4,336,719	4,335,669	Butter, pounds............	313,345,306	....
Mules and asses............	559,331	horses and	Cheese, "	105,535,893	....
Horses, asses and mules....	4,896,050	mules.	Butter and cheese.........	418,881,199	*$33,787,008
Milch cows	6,385,094	....	Peas and beans, bushels	9,219,901	....
Working oxen	1,700,744	....	Market gardens	$5,280,030	$2,601,196
Other cattle................	10,293,069	....	Nursery products..........	....	$593,534
Total neat cattle	18,378,907	14,971,586	Orchard "	$7,723,186	$7,256,904
Sheep	21,723,220	19,311,374	Beeswax and honey, pounds	14,853,790	wax 628,303
Swine......................	30,354,213	26,301,293	Poultry	....	9,344,410
Value of live stock..........	$544,180,516	....	Family goods..............	$27.493,644	$29,023,380
Value of animals slaughtered	$111,703,142	....	Cords of wood............	....	5,088,891
Wheat, bushels	100,485,944	84,823,272	Flax seed, bushels.........	562,312	95,251 tons
Rye, "	14,188,813	18,645,567	Flax, pounds..............	7,709,676	hemp and
Oats, "	146,584.179	123,071,341	Dew rotted hemp, tons.....	33,193	flax.
Indian corn, bushels.......	592,071,104	377,531,875	Water " " "	1,678	
Irish potatoes, "	65,797,896	....	Maple sugar, pounds........	34,253,436	155,100,809
Sweet potatoes, "	38,268,148	....	Sugar, cane, hogsheads.....	237,133	pounds.
Total, "	104,066,044	108,298,060	Molasses, gallons..........	12,700,991	....
Barley, "	5,167,015	4,161,504	Cotton, bales..............	2,445,793	1,976,198
Buckwheat, "	8,956,912	7,291,743	Rice, pounds..............	215.313,497	80,841,422
Hay, tons..................	13,838,642	10,248,108	Tobacco, "	199,752,655	219,163,319
Hops, pounds	3,497,029	1,238,502	Wool, "	52,516,959	35,802,114
Clover seed, bushels........	468,978	....	Silk cocoons, pounds.......	10,843	61,652
Other grass seeds, bushels..	416,831	....	Wine, gallons..............	221,249	†124,734

* Dairy products.

† Amounts produced by individuals less than a bale, hogshead or ton of any agricultural product, where these measures are adopted, are not aggregated or reported. Hence a large production of such articles escaped enumeration. This is important to be observed in reading the county tables.

TABLE CLXXXVII.—*Ratio of Farm Land to Area and Crops to Population in the several sections of the United States*—1850 *and* 1840.

Geographical Divisions.	Proportion of improved land to the whole in each section.	Proportion of occupied land to the whole.	Average value of occupied land per acre.	Average value of implements and machinery per acre.	Horses, asses, and mules to each person.	Cows, working oxen and other cattle to each person.	Sheep and swine to each person.	Bush. wheat, rye, barley and buckwheat to each person.	Bushels of corn to each person.	Bushels of Irish and sweet potatoes to each person.	Bushels of peas and beans to each person.	Value of home manufacture to each person.
New England	26.79	44.13	20.27	.70	.08	.54	.96	1.39	3.73	7.19	.17	.59
Middle States	35.72	57.82	28.07	1.04	.15	.53	1.26	8.40	9.12	4.00	.13	.35
Southern States	16.07	53.02	5.34	.25	.29	.99	2.49	4.19	28.22	5.39	1.12	1.79
Southwestern States *	10.17	32.44	6.26	.60	.29	.99	3.13	.77	39.45	5.49	.89	2.26
Northwestern States	12.90	31.47	11.39	.51	.29	.80	3.18	7.80	44.02	2.82	.08	1.45
California and Territories	.06	.75	1.89	.10	.27	1.90	2.46	2.97	2.20	.90	.19	.08
Non-slaveholding States	14.72	28.56	19.00	.77	.17	.64	1.80	7.31	18.06	4.39	.11	1.39
Slaveholding States	10.09	33.17	6.09	.36	.27	.95	2.84	3.11	36.12	4.64	.79	1.93
United States, 1850.†	7.71	20.02	11.14	.51	.21	.77	2.25	5.55	25.53	4.49	.40	1.19
United States, 1840	......	.....	......	......	.25	.88	2.67	6.73	22.12	6.34	.....	1.70

TABLE CLXXXVIII.—*Proportion of certain Crops to each Person*—1850.

Divisions.	Rice, pounds.	Tobacco, pounds.	Cotton, pounds.	Wool, pounds.	Hemp, pounds.	Cane Sugar, pounds.
Non-Slaveholding States	....	1.10	.00	3.07	.00	.00
Slaveholding "	22.28	19.14	101.23	1.16	7.17	25.62

There would have been little difficulty in framing a table like the following for all of the States, had time admitted, with other similar ones for cotton, sugar, rice, &c., showing the producers of under five bales, hogsheads, &c., between 5 and 10, 10 and 100, 100 and 500. The counties here selected have been taken at random, and represent New England, the South and the West, to wit: Franklin in Kentucky; Point Coupee, Ouachita, Rapides, Plaquemines and East Feliciana in Louisiana; Allegan, Barry, Branch and Berrien, in Michigan; Erie in Ohio; Potter and Pike in Pennsylvania; Bristol, Kent and Washington in Rhode Island; Abbeville, Anderson, Barnwell, Beaufort, Charleston, Marlboro', and Marion, in South Carolina.

TABLE CLXXXIX.—*Landholders occupying in certain Counties.*

Counties in the States of	Less than 5 acres.	5 and less than 10.	10 and less than 50.	50 and less than 100.	100 and less than 500.	500 and less than 1,000.	1,000 and less than 10,000.	10,000 and upwards.	No. of farms classified.
Kentucky	70	40	230	205	365	29	4	....	943
Louisiana	64	6	214	185	622	260	206	1	1,558
Michigan	9	7	526	1,250	1,359	21	9	....	3,181
Ohio	....	....	164	381	491	16	3	....	1,055
Pennsylvania	....	....	58	344	625	10	7	....	1,044
Rhode Island	43	41	400	574	1,176	16	....	....	2,250
South Carolina	60	106	1,392	773	4,351	1,472	1,230	16	9,400

Of the cultivators embraced, one in 9 in Kentucky, one in 22 in Louisiana, one in 27 in Rhode Island, one in 56 in South Carolina, and one in 198 in Michigan, cultivate less than ten acres. Of the larger cultivators, South Carolina and Louisiana show an excess.

The latest returns of agriculture are for the crop of 1849. Consulting the Prices Current at the points of production and consumption, and forming the mean, a table of valuation has been prepared. The approximation is as near as can be arrived at.

* Exclusive of Texas—area 237,504 miles; improved land 643,976 acres; unimproved 10,852,363 acres; value of farms $16,550,008; implements and machinery $2,151,704.

† Exclusive of unorganized Territories.

TABLE CXC.—*Value of the Agricultural Products of the United States*, 1850

Products.	Value.	Products.	Value.
Indian Corn	$296,035,552	Live stock, over 1 year old—annual product	$175,000,000
Wheat	100,485,944	Animals slaughtered	55,000,000
Cotton	98,603,720	Poultry on the basis of 1840	13,000,000
Hay	96,870,494	Feathers	2,000,000
Oats	43,975,253	Milk, (not included in butter and cheese)	7,000,000
Butter	50,135,248	Eggs	5,000,000
Home made manufactures	27,493,644	Cord wood on the basis of 1840	20,000,000
Potatoes—Irish	26,319,158	Home made manufactures—one-half for agricultural part.—*Tucker*	13,746,822
Potatoes—sweet	19,134,074	Small crops—basis of Rhode Island for onions, carrots, &c	5,000,000
Wool	15,755,087	Residuum of crops, not consumed by stock, corn fodder, cotton, seed, straw, rice flour, and manure, (Patent Reports.)	100,000,000
Tobacco	13,982,686	Cattle, sheep and pigs, under one year old	50,000,000
Cane sugar	12,378,850		1,311,691,326
Rye	7,803,847	Add for orchard and garden products of cities, not included in above—milk, butter, poultry, horses, cows, &c., in cities and towns.	15,000,000
Orchard products	7,723,186	Total agricultural products—1849–50	*$1,326,691,326
Buckwheat	6,969,838	To which add for increase since 1850, and for the greater value of agricultural products would give total for 1854	1,600,000,000
Peas and Beans	5,762,436		
Market garden products	5,280,030		
Cheese	5,276,795		
Hemp	5,247,430		
Rice	4,000,000		
Barley	3,616,910		
Molasses	2,540,179		
Beeswax and Honey	2,376,606		
Clover seed	2,344,890		
Maple sugar	1,712,671		
Hops	1,223,960		
Flaxseed	843,468		
Grass seeds (other than clover)	833,662		
Flax	770,967		
Wine	442,498		
Silk cocoons	5,421		

By a special resolution of the Senate, the Census office was requested to furnish a statement showing the quantity of land cultivated in each of the agricultural staples of the country. The time was not sufficient for the collection of material necessary to prepare such a statement fully for the present volume, as an extensive correspondence would be required. By an examination of the marshals' returns, showing the average product to the acre in every county for a good crop, and the actual product in the year of the census, approximate data were obtained from which the following table was compiled. It is the best that can be offered, and is the only table of the kind ever published.

TABLE CXCI.—*Land actually cultivated in the several Crops of the United States*, 1849—50.

Products.	Acres.	Products.	Acres.
Indian Corn	31,000,000	Tobacco	400,000
Meadow or pasture lands—that proportion which is regarded improved, and exclusive of Hay crop	20,000,000	Sugar	400,000
Hay	13,000,000	Barley	300,000
Wheat	11,000,000	Rice	175,000
Oats	7,500,000	Hemp	110,000
Cotton	5,000,000	Flax	100,000
Rye	1,200,000	Orchards	500,000
Peas and Beans	1,000,000	Gardens	500,000
Irish Potatoes	1,000,000	Vineyards	250,000
Sweet Potatoes	750,000	Other products	1,000,000
Buckwheat	600,000	Improved but not in actual cultivation	17,247,614
		Total improved lands	113,032,614

It would thus appear that the actual crops do not account for 17,247,614 acres, which are returned as being improved. It is possible the total reported as improved is exaggerated by a part of this difference, say 9,000,000 acres, which would leave about 8,000,000 for waste, yet improved lands.†

* Professor Tucker estimated the crop of 1840 at $654,387,597. It was no doubt nearer $800,000,000.

† The New York State census of 1845 reports 11,757,276 acres improved land, a near approximation to the United States census of 1850. Of this amount only 3,851,594 were cultivated in barley, peas, beans, buckwheat, turnips, potatoes, flax, wheat, corn, rye and oats, leaving nearly eight millions for meadows, hay, gardens, orchards, etc., and unaccounted for. The State reports of Ohio for 1851 show 1,677,253 acres in wheat, and 1,664,429 acres in corn. If the occupied land sustained the same relation to the whole population in 1840

TABLE CXCII.—*Ratio per cent. of Population and certain Products in the States to the total of the United States.*

STATES AND TERRITORIES.	Population.	Wheat.	Indian corn.	Rice.	Tobacco.	Cotton.	Wool.	Hemp.	Sugar.
Alabama	3.33	.29	4.86	1.07	.08	23.08	1.25	....	.04
Arkansas	.91	.20	1.50	.03	.11	2.67	.35	.04	....
California	.4	.02	....	....	....	....	.01	....	....
Columbia, District of	.22	.02	.01	....	....	....	....	....	....
Connecticut	1.6	.04	.33	....	.63	....	.95	....	....
Delaware	.39	.48	.53	....	....	....	.11	....	....
Florida	.38	....	.34	.5	.5	1.85	.4	....	1.16
Georgia	3.48	1.08	5.08	18.09	.21	20.41	1.88	....	.36
Illinois	3.07	9.37	9.73	....	.42	....	4.10	....	....
Indiana	4.26	6.18	8.95	....	.52	....	4.97	....	....
Iowa	.83	1.52	1.46	....	....	....	.71	....	....
Kentucky	4.24	2.13	9.91	....	27.78	.03	4.37	51.01	....
Louisiana	2.23	....	1.73	2.05	.01	7.31	.21	....	95.31
Maine	2.51	.29	.3	....	....	....	2.6	....	....
Maryland	2.9	4.47	1.82	....	10.72	....	.91	.18	....
Massachusetts	4.29	.03	.40	....	.07	....	1.11	....	....
Michigan	1.71	4.90	.95	....	....	....	3.91	....	....
Mississippi	2.92	0.14	3.79	1.26	0.02	19.80	1.07	0.02	....
Missouri	2.94	2.97	6.12	....	8.57	....	3.10	45.96	....
New Hampshire	1.37	0.18	0.27	....	....	....	2.11	....	....
New Jersey	2.11	1.60	1.48	....	....	....	0.71	....	....
New York	13.36	13.06	3.02	....	0.04	....	19.18	0.01	....
North Carolina	3.75	2.12	4.72	2.54	6.0	2.07	1.85	0.11	....
Ohio	8.54	14.42	9.97	....	5.23	....	19.41	0.43	....
Pennsylvania	9.97	15.29	3.35	....	0.46	....	8.53	0.13	....
Rhode Island	0.64	....	0.09	....	....	....	0.25	....	....
South Carolina	2.88	1.06	2.75	74.28	0.04	12.30	0.93	....	.03
Tennessee	4.32	1.61	8.83	0.12	10.09	7.95	2.60	1.7	....
Texas	0.92	0.04	1.02	0.04	0.03	2.37	0.25	....	3.10
Vermont	1.35	0.53	0.34	....	....	....	6.47	....	....
Virginia	6.13	11.16	5 95	....	28.44	0.16	5.45	*0.4	....
Wisconsin	1.32	4.26	0.34	....	....	....	0.48	....	....
Territ's. Minnesota	0.03	....	....	....	....	....	....	....	....
Territ's. New Mexico	0.27	0.19	0.06	....	....	....	0.06	....	....
Territ's. Oregon	0.06	0.21	....	....	....	....	0.05	....	....
Territ's. Utah	0.05	0.10	....	....	....	....	0.02	....	....

The table which follows is very incomplete, but nothing better can be framed from the returns, which in general were very carelessly made or entirely neglected.

and 1800 as in 1850, it would seem that 77,000,000 acres have been taken up or brought into use in the last ten years, and 226,000,000 acres in the last fifty years. In the same period 4,129,777 acres were brought into use in England.

The following table was prepared for the English House of Commons in 1827 in statute acres.

Divisions.	Cultivated.	Uncultivated.	Unprofitable.	Summary.
England	25,632,000	3,454,000	3,256,400	32,342,400
Wales	3,117,000	530,000	1,105,000	4,752,000
Scotland	5,265,000	5,950,000	8,523,930	19,738,930
Ireland	12,125,280	4,900,000	2,416,664	19,441,944
British Islands	383,690	166,000	569,469	1,119,159
Total	46,522,970	15,000,000	15,871,463	77,394,333

Of this total, 19,135,990 acres were in arable lands and gardens, 27,386,980 in meadows, pastures and marshes, 15,000,000 wastes, capable of improvement, 15,871,463 wastes, incapable of improvement. In France there are 82,790,702 acres improved land, in Prussia 39,478,704, in Austria 138,808,366. Unimproved in France, 38,238,616, in Austria 25,812,517, in Prussia 28,741,156. By the census of 1849–50 for Austria and Prussia, it appears that the former had 3,229,884 horses, 112,820 asses and mules, 5,910,886 milch cows, 3,239,365 working oxen, 13,583,254, other cattle, and the latter, 1,575,417 horses, 7,475 asses and mules, 3,078,126 cows, 676,395 oxen 1,617,123 other cattle, 16,296,928 sheep, 2,466,316 swine, and produced 15,998,450 bushels corn, 96,803,080 of rye, 114,503,300 of oats, 21,583,320 lbs. tobacco, 21,581,890 lbs. wool, 423,555,000 bushels Irish potatoes, 29,143,000 bushels barley, and 6,670,670 gallons wine.

* Crop underrated. In 1852, Virginia reports gave 3,450 tons dew-rotted hemp and 1,149 tons water-rotted.

TABLE CXCIII.—*Actual Crops per acre on the average as returned by the Marshals for* 1849-50.

States.	Wheat, bushels.	Rye, bush.	Indian corn, bushels.	Oats, bush.	Rice, lbs.	Tobacco, lbs.	Seed cotton, lbs.	Peas and beans, bush.	Irish potatoes, bush.	Sweet potatoes, bush.	Barley, bush.	Buckwheat, bushels.	Hay, tons.	Hops, lbs.	Hemp, dew rotted.	Cane sugar, pounds.
Alabama	5	....	15	12	....	....	525	12	60	200	....	....	....	....	....	....
Arkansas	10	....	22	18	....	....	700	....	....	100	....	....	....	....	....	....
Connecticut	....	....	40	21	....	....	....	....	85	....	....	20	....	....	....	....
Delaware	11	....	20	20	....	....	....	....	....	....	....	10	....	....	....	....
Florida	15	....	....	....	1,850	....	250	....	175	....	....	....	....	....	....	750
Georgia	5	7	16	18	....	....	500	5	125	400	....	....	....	....	....	....
Illinois	11	14	33	29	....	....	....	....	115	....	40	15	$1\frac{1}{2}$	....	....	....
Indiana	12	18	33	20	....	....	....	....	100	....	25	25	1	....	....	....
Iowa	14	....	32	36	....	....	....	....	100	....	....	....	....	....	....	....
Kentucky	8	11	24	18	....	575	....	....	130	65	....	....	$1\frac{1}{2}$	....	650	....
Louisiana	....	....	16	....	1,400	....	550	....	....	175	....	....	....	....	....	1,000
Maine	10	11	27	20	....	....	....	....	120	....	20	....	$\frac{7}{8}$	....	....	....
Maryland	13	18	23	21	....	650	....	....	75	....	....	....	1	....	....	....
Massachusetts	16	13	31	26	....	....	....	....	170	....	21	....	1	....	....	....
Michigan	10	....	32	26	....	....	....	....	140	....	....	14	....	....	....	....
Mississippi	9	....	18	12	....	....	650	12	105	....	....	....	....	....	....	....
Missouri	11	....	34	26	....	775	....	....	110	....	....	....	$1\frac{1}{4}$	....	775	....
New Hampshire	11	14	30	30	....	....	....	....	220	....	22	....	1	....	....	....
New Jersey	11	8	33	26	....	....	....	....	75	....	18	16	....	....	....	....
New York	12	17	27	25	....	....	....	....	100	....	25	22	$1\frac{1}{8}$	950	....	....
North Carolina	7	15	17	10	....	....	....	....	65	....	....	....	....	....	....	....
Ohio	12	25	36	21	....	730	....	....	75	....	30	20	$1\frac{5}{8}$	....	....	....
Pennsylvania	15	14	20	22	....	....	....	....	75	....	....	....	$1\frac{3}{4}$	....	....	....
Rhode Island	....	16	....	30	....	....	....	....	100	....	18	....	....	....	....	....
South Carolina	8	....	11	12	1,750	....	320	18	70	....	....	....	....	....	....	....
Tennessee	7	7	21	19	....	750	300	....	120	....	....	....	....	....	....	....
Texas	15	....	20	....	....	....	750	....	250	45	....	....	....	....	....	....
Vermont	13	20	32	26	....	....	....	20	178	....	....	25	1	....	....	....
Virginia	7	5	18	13	....	660	....	....	75	....	....	7	1	....	....	....
Wisconsin	14	....	30	35	....	....	....	....	125	....	18	....	....	....	....	....

TABLE CXCIV.—*Number of Cotton, Sugar, Rice, Tobacco and Hemp Plantations.*

STATES.	Number of cotton plantations raising 5 bales and over.	Number of sugar planters.	Number of rice plantations each raising 20,000 lbs. and over	No. of tobacco plantations each raising 3,000 lbs. and over.	Number of hemp planters.
Alabama	16,100	.....	.....	.....	.....
Arkansas	2,175	.....	.....	.....	.....
Florida	990	958	.....	.....	.....
Georgia	14,578	.....	80	.....	.....
Kentucky	21	.....	.....	5,987	3,520
Louisiana	4,205	1,558	.....	.....	.....
Maryland	.....	.....	.....	1,726	.....
Mississippi	15,110	.....	.....	.....	.....
Missouri	.....	.....	.....	.....	4,807
North Carolina	2,827	.....	25	.....	.....
South Carolina	11,522	.....	446	.....	.....
Tennessee	4,043	.....	.....	2,215	.....
Texas	2,262	165	.....	.....	.....
Virginia	198	.....	.....	5,817	.....
Total	74,031	2,681	551	15,745	8,327

There are in the Southern States 74,031 cotton plantations, including all producers of more than five bales, 2,681 sugar planters including the smallest; 551 estates making more than 20,000 pounds of rough rice each; 15,745 tobacco estates of 3,000 pounds each and over in Kentucky, Tennessee and Virginia; 8,327 hemp planters in Kentucky and Missouri. Only such States are taken as are considered crop States.

2. MANUFACTURES.—The complete statistics of manufactures in the United States are being now aggregated from the returns of the census of 1850. They are no doubt quite as full and reliable as those of the census of 1810, 1820 or 1840, and perhaps more complete.* It will be very long before any country can expect entire accuracy in such reports, although by their means close and valuable approximations may be made. The heavy expense at which these statistics were obtained and the extensive ground which they cover entitle them to publication, and all chances of material error can be guarded against by appending to them notes of comparison with the local reports of the several States, cities, associations, etc.

* For example, in 1840, 6 or 8 importing merchants were given to Abbeville, S. C. where there was not in fact one, and in Boston $2,442,309 was given as the capital invested and $4,016,573 the product, though the State census of manufactures in 1839 reported $5,830,572 capital and $11,071,576 product in the same articles. The whole manufacturing product of the United States in 1810 was estimated at $172,000,000 and in 1840 about $500,000,000.

The following tables have undergone a few revisions since their first preparation and are proper to be placed in the present volume. There are 121,855 establishments of every description reported, producing each of any kind of manufactured article the amount annually of five hundred dollars. The capital invested in real and personal estate is $527,209,193; the value of raw material used, including fuel, $554,655,038; the amount paid for labor, $229,736,377, and the gross annual value produced $1,013,336,463, making 43 per cent. profit upon the whole investment. The ratio of profits in the several States is also given, presenting some anomalies which cannot at present be reconciled. Those who will examine the manufacturing returns of 1840 and 1820 will find still greater ones. The figures giving the number of hands employed and the value of annual product are no doubt entirely correct, the chances of error being mainly in the returns of the cost of raw material and the amount of capital invested. An average profit of 43 per cent. would not be too high for the whole industrial operations of the country. The number of hands employed of all ages was 719,479 males and 225,512 females; total, 944,991. The County tables of this volume will show the amount of capital invested, the hands employed and the total product of every county in the United States. The motive power, as steam, horse, water, etc. was ascertained for each establishment requiring such, but has not been prepared in tabular form. As the examination of the Industrial schedules progresses it is probable many of the figures in the tables will be modified and corrected.

TABLE CXCV.—*Product of Manufactures, Mining and the Mechanic Arts,* 1850.

States and Territories.	Individuals and establishment.	Capital.	Raw material used.	Hands employed.		Annual wages.	Annual product.*	Per cent. profit.
				Male.	Female.			
Alabama	1,026	$3,450,606	$2,224,960	4,399	539	$1,106,112	$4,528,878	34.71
Arkansas	272	324,065	268,564	873	30	169,356	607,436	52.31
California	1,003	1,006,197	1,201,154	3,964	....	3,485,820	12,862,522	812.52
Columbia, District of	395	888,965	1,339,146	1,678	498	616,152	2,493,008	60.49
Connecticut	3,482	23,890,348	23,589,397	31,287	16,483	11,695,236	45,110,102	41.13
Delaware	531	2,978,945	2,864,607	3,237	651	936,924	4,649,296	28.46
Florida	103	547,060	220,611	876	115	199,452	668,335	45.38
Georgia	1,527	5,460,483	3,404,917	6,660	1,718	1,712,304	7,086,525	36.06
Illinois	3,164	6,385,387	8,915,173	11,632	433	3,286,249	17,236,073	78.85
Indiana	4,288	7,941,602	10,214,337	13,677	665	2,809,116	18,922,651	74.28
Iowa	522	1,292,875	2,356,881	1,687	20	473,016	3,551,783	55.83
Kentucky	3,609	12,350,734	12,170,225	22,445	1,940	4,764,096	24,588,483	61.97
Louisiana	1,017	5,318,074	2,958,988	5,581	850	2,086,212	7,320,948	42.79
Maine	3,977	14,700,452	13,555,806	21,856	6,222	7,502,916	24,664,135	24.52
Maryland	3,708	14,753,143	17,326,734	22,641	7,483	7,374,672	32,477,702	52.71
Massachusetts	8,259	83,357,642	85,856,771	96,261	69,677	39,784,116	151,137,145	30.59
Michigan	1,963	6,534,250	6,105,561	8,930	360	2,387,928	10,976,894	38.01
Mississippi	877	1,833,420	1,290,271	3,065	108	775,128	2,972,038	49.45
Missouri	3,029	9,079,695	12,446,738	15,977	873	3,184,764	23,749,265	89.41
New Hampshire	3,211	18,242,114	12,745,466	14,103	12,989	6,123,876	23,164,503	23.55
New Jersey	4,108	22,184,730	21,992,186	28,549	8,762	9,202,788	39,713,586	38.40
New York	23,553	99,904,405	134,655,674	147,737	51,612	49,131,000	237,597,249	53.86
North Carolina	2,604	7,252,225	4,805,463	10,693	1,751	1,796,748	9,111,245	34.60
Ohio	10,622	29,019,538	34,677,937	47,054	4,435	13,467,660	62,647,259	49.97
Pennsylvania	21,605	94,473,810	87,206,377	124,688	22,078	37,163,232	155,044,910	32.47
Rhode Island	853	12,923,176	13,183,889	12,837	8,044	5,008,656	22,093,258	30.18
South Carolina	1,431	6,056,865	2,809,534	5,935	1,074	1,128,432	7,063,513	51.60
Tennessee	2,861	6,975,279	4,900,952	11,154	878	2,277,228	9,728,438	36.56
Texas	309	539,290	394,642	1,042	24	322,368	1,165,538	83.17
Vermont	1,849	5,001,377	4,172,552	6,894	1,551	2,202,348	8,570,920	43.91
Virginia	4,741	18,109,993	18,103,433	25,789	3,320	5,413,764	29,705,387	34.17
Wisconsin	1,262	3,382,148	5,414,931	5,798	291	1,712,496	9,293,068	64.00
Territories. Minnesota	5	94,000	24,000	63	....	21,420	57,500	12.85
Territories. New Mexico	23	68,300	110,220	81	....	20,772	249,010	172.79
Territories. Oregon	52	843,600	809,560	285	32	388,620	2,236,640	123.10
Territories. Utah	14	44,400	337,381	51	....	5,400	291,220	†
Total	121,855	527,209,193	554,655,038	719,479	225,512	229,736,377	1,013,336,463	43.43
New England States	21,631	158,115,109	153,103,881	183,238	114,966	72,317,148	274,740,063	31.19
Middle "	53,900	235,183,998	265,384,724	328,530	91,084	104,424,768	471,975,751	43.44
Southern "	10,406	37,426,626	29,343,958	49,953	7,978	10,250,700	53,635,005	37.51
Southwest "	6,362	18,440,734	12,038,377	26,114	2,435	6,736,404	26,323,276	40.93
Northwest "	29,556	78,042,726	94,784,098	131,644	9,049	36,007,357	186,662,368	71.59
Non-slavehold'g "	93,815	431,290,351	467,125,253	577,434	203,654	195,872,665	845,430,428	51.57
Slaveholding "	28,040	95,918,842	87,529,785	142,045	21,858	33,863,712	167,906,035	48.49

* Exclusive of those in families.

† A loss of 116.13 per cent.

Table CXCVI.—*Cotton Manufactures*, 1850.*

States, &c.	Establishments.	Capital.	Raw Material used.			Hands employed.		Average wages per month.		Products.†
			Bales of cotton.	Tons of coal.	Value of raw material.	Male.	Female.	Male.	Female.	
Alabama	12	$ 651,900	5,208	....	$ 237,081	346	369	$ 11.71	$ 7.98	$ 382,260
Arkansas	3	16,500	170	....	8,975	13	18	14.61	5.88	16,637
Columbia, Dis. of	1	85,000	960	....	67,000	41	103	14.02	8.00	100,000
Connecticut	128	4,219,100	39,483	2,866	2,500,062	2,708	3,478	19.08	11.80	4,257,522
Delaware	12	460,100	4,730	1,920	312,068	413	425	15.31	11.58	538,439
Florida	......	80,000	600	....	30,000	28	67	32.14	5.00	49,920
Georgia	35	1,736,156	20,230	1,000	900,419	873	1,399	14.57	7.39	2,135,044
Indiana	2	43,900	675	300	28,220	38	57	13.02	6.77	44,200
Kentucky	8	239,000	3,760	720	180,907	181	221	14.95	9.36	273,439
Maine	12	3,329,700	31,531	2,921	1,573,110	780	2,959	29.35	12.15	2,596,356
Maryland	24	2,236,000	23,325	2,212	1,165,579	1,008	2,014	15.42	9.48	2,120,504
Massachusetts	213	28,455,630	223,607	46,545	11,289,309	9,293	19,437	22.90	13.60	19,712,461
Mississippi	2	38,000	430	....	21,500	19	17	14.21	5.94	30,500
Missouri	2	102,000	2,160	1,658	86,446	75	80	10.93	10.00	142,900
New Hampshire	44	10,950,500	83,026	7,679	4,839,429	2,911	9,211	26.00	13.47	8,830,619
New Jersey	21	1,483,500	14,437	4,467	666,645	616	1,096	17.98	9.56	1,109,524
New York	86	4,176,920	37,778	1,539	1,985,973	2,632	3,688	18.32	9.68	3,591,989
North Carolina	28	1,058,800	13,617	....	531,903	442	1,177	11.65	6.13	831,342
Ohio	8	297,000	4,270	2,152	237,060	132	269	16.59	9.42	394,700
Pennsylvania	208	4,528,925	44,162	24,189	3,152,530	3,564	4,099	17.85	9.91	5,322,262
Rhode Island	158	6,675,000	50,713	13,116	3,484,579	4,959	5,916	18.60	12.95	6,447,120
South Carolina	18	857,200	9,929	....	295,971	399	620	13.94	8.30	748,338
Tennessee	33	669,600	6,411	3,010	297,500	310	581	10.94	6.42	510,624
Vermont	9	202,500	2,243	....	114,415	94	147	15.53	12.65	196,100
Virginia	27	1,908,900	17,785	4,805	828,375	1,275	1,688	10.18	6.98	1,486,384
Total	1,094	74,500,931	641,240	121,099	34,835,056	33,150	59,136	....	....	61,869,184

Table CXCVII.—*Woollen Manufactures*, 1850.

States &c.	Establishments.	Capital.	Raw material used.			Hands employed.		Average wages per month.		Products.‡
			Pounds of wool.	Tons of Coal.	Value of raw material.	Male.	Fem.	Male.	Fem.	
Columbia, Dist. of	1	$700	5,000	......	$1,630	2	......	30.00	......	$2,400
Connecticut	149	3,773,950	9,414,100	7,912	3,325,709	2,907	2,581	24.12	12.86	6,465,216
Delaware	8	148,500	393,000	45	204,172	122	18	18.79	17.33	251,000
Georgia	3	68,000	153,816	......	30,392	40	38	27.47	14.10	88,750
Illinois	16	154,500	396,964	987	115,367	124	54	22.00	12.52	206,572
Indiana	33	171,545	413,350	90	120,486	189	57	21.81	11.05	205,802
Iowa	1	10,000	14,500	......	3,500	7	......	11.14	......	13,000
Kentucky	25	249,820	673,900	......	205,287	256	62	15.30	11.11	318,819
Maine	36	467,600	1,438,434	......	495,940	310	314	22.57	11.77	753,300
Maryland	38	244,000	430,300	100	165,568	262	100	18.60	11.89	295,140
Massachusetts	119	9,089,342	22,229,952	15,400	8,671,671	6,167	4,963	22.95	14.22	12,770,565
Michigan	15	94,000	162,250	......	43,402	78	51	21.65	11.47	90,242
Missouri	1	20,000	80,000	1,071	16,000	15	10	32.00	6.50	56,000
New Hampshire	61	2,437,700	3,604,103	3,600	1,267,329	926	1,201	22.86	14.53	2,127,745
New Jersey	41	494,274	1,510,289	1,889	548,367	411	487	25.22	8.60	1,164,446
New York	249	4,459,370	12,538,786	......	3,838,292	4,262	2,412	19.97	11.76	7,030,604
North Carolina	1	18,000	30,000	......	13,950	15	15	18.00	7.00	23,750
Ohio	130	870,220	1,657,726	2,110	578,423	903	298	20.14	10.90	1,111,027
Pennsylvania	380	3,005,064	7,560,379	10,777	3,282,718	3,490	2,236	19.23	10.41	5,321,866
Rhode Island	45	1,013,000	4,103,370	2,032	1,463,900	987	771	20.70	15.18	2,381,825
Tennessee	4	10,900	6,200	......	1,675	15	2	17.66	6.00	6,310
Texas	1	8,000	30,000	......	10,000	4	4	20.00	20.00	15,000
Vermont	72	886,300	2,328,100	......	830,684	683	710	24.46	11.81	1,579,161
Virginia	121	392,640	1,554,110	357	488,899	478	190	18.17	9.91	841,013
Wisconsin	9	31,225	134,200	......	32,630	25	......	22.48	......	87,992
Total	1,559	28,118,650	70,862,829	46,370	25,755,991	22,678	16,574	......	......	43,207,545

* In these tables, the States which report no product will be omitted.
† 763,678,407 yards sheeting, &c., were produced, and nearly 30,000,000 lbs. yarn and batting.
‡ 82,206,652 yards cloth were manufactured, 4,294,336 lbs. of yarn, besides blankets and hats.

Table CXCVIII.—*Manufactures of Pig Iron*, 1850.

States.	Establishments	Capital.	Raw material used.		Hands employed.		Average wages per month.		Annual product.		Total value.
			Tons of ore.	Value.	M.	F.	M.	F.	Tons of pig iron.	Other products	
Alabama	3	$11,000	1,838	$6,770	40	....	$17.60	....	522	$5,000	$22,500
Connecticut	13	225,600	35,450	289,225	148	....	26.80	....	13,420	20,000	415,600
Georgia	3	26,000	5,189	25,840	135	3	17.44	5.00	900	28,000	57,300
Illinois	2	65,000	5,500	15,500	150	....	22.03	....	2,700	....	70,200
Indiana	2	72,000	5,200	24,400	88	....	26.00	....	1,850	....	58,000
Kentucky	21	924,700	72,010	260,152	1,845	10	20.23	4.70	24,245	10,000	604,037
Maine	1	214,000	2,907	14,939	71	....	22.00	....	1,484	....	36,616
Maryland	18	1,420,000	99,866	560,725	1,370	....	20.14	....	43,641	96,000	1,056,400
Massachusetts	6	469,000	27,909	185,741	263	....	27.52	....	12,287	....	295,123
Michigan	1	15,000	2,700	14,000	25	....	35.00	....	660	6,000	21,000
Missouri	5	619,000	37,000	97,367	334	....	24.28	....	19,250	....	314,600
New Hampshire	1	2,000	500	4,900	10	....	18.00	....	200	....	6,000
New Jersey	10	967,000	51,266	332,707	600	....	21.20	....	24,031	....	560,544
New York	18	605,000	46,385	321,027	505	....	25.00	....	23,022	12,800	597,920
North Carolina	2	25,000	900	27,900	26	5	8.00	4.40	400	....	12,500
Ohio	35	1,503,000	140,610	630,037	2,415	....	24.48	...	52,658	....	1,255,850
Pennsylvania	180	8,570,425	877,283	3,732,427	9,285	9	21.65	5.11	*285,702	40,000	6,071,513
Tennessee	23	1,021,400	88,810	254,900	1,713	109	12.81	5.11	30,420	41,900	676,100
Vermont	3	62,500	7,676	40,175	100	....	22.08	....	3,200	....	68,000
Virginia	29	513,800	67,319	158,307	1,115	14	12.76	6.86	22,163	....	521,924
Wisconsin	1	15,000	3,000	8,250	60	....	30.00	....	1,000	....	27,000
Total	377	17,346,425	1,579,318	†7.005,289	20,298	150	......	....	563,755	259,700	12,748,727

Table CXCIX.—*Manufactures of Iron Casting*, 1850.

States, &c.	Establishments	Capital.	Raw material used.				Hands employed.		Average wages per month.		Products.
			Tons pig Iron.	Tons old metal.	Tons ore.	Value of raw material, fuel, &c.	Male.	Fem.	Male.	Fem.	
Alabama	10	$216,625	2,348	......	......	$102,085	212	......	$30.05	......	$271,126
California	1	5,000	75	......	......	8,530	3	......	23.33	......	20,740
Columbia, Dist. of	2	14,000	545	......	......	18,100	27	......	27.05	......	41,696
Connecticut	60	580,800	11,396	337	......	351,369	942	7	27.02	$8.00	981,400
Delaware	13	373,500	4,440	......	......	153,852	250	......	23.36	......	267,462
Georgia	4	35,000	440	......	......	11,950	39	......	27.43	......	46,200
Illinois	29	260,400	4,818	50	......	172,330	332	......	28.50	......	441,185
Indiana	14	82,900	1,968	5	.....	66,918	143	......	25.74	......	149,430
Iowa	3	5,500	81	......	......	2,524	17	......	32.35	......	8,500
Kentucky	20	502,200	9,731	......	......	295,533	558	20	24.89	4.15	744,316
Louisiana	8	255,000	1,660	......	.....	75,300	347	......	35.60	......	312,500
Maine	25	150,100	3,591	245	......	112,570	243	1	29.00	5.00	265,000
Maryland	16	359,100	7,220	......	......	259,190	761	......	27.50	......	685,000
Massachusetts	68	1,499,050	31,134	3,361	......	1,057,904	1,596	......	30.90	......	2,235,635
Michigan	63	195,450	2,494	......	......	91,865	337	......	28.68	......	279,697
Mississippi	8	100,000	1,197	......	......	50,370	112	......	37.91	......	117,400
Missouri	6	187,000	5,100	200	......	133,114	297	......	19.63	......	336,495
New Hampshire	26	232,700	5,673	500	......	177,060	374	......	33.05	......	371,710
New Jersey	45	593,250	10,666	350	......	301,048	803	......	24.00	......	686,430
New York	323	4,622,482	108,945	3,212	......	2,393,768	5,925	......	27.49	......	5,921,980
North Carolina	5	11,500	192	......	......	8,341	15	......	23.46	......	12,867
Ohio	183	2,063,650	37,555	1,843	2,000	1,199,700	2,758	......	27.32	......	3,069,350
Pennsylvania	320	3,422,924	69,501	819	......	2,372,467	4,782	1	27.55	6.00	5,354,881
Rhode Island	20	428,800	8,918	......	.....	258,267	800	......	29.63	......	728,705
South Carolina	6	185,700	169	......	2,800	29,128	153	2	13.59	4.00	87,683
Tennessee	16	139,500	1,682	......	5,050	90,035	261	8	17.96	4.50	264,325
Texas	2	16,000	250	......	......	8,400	35	......	43.43	......	55,000
Vermont	26	290,720	5,279	274	......	160,603	381	......	28.27	......	460,831
Virginia	54	471,160	7,114	205	......	297,014	810	9	19.91	9.44	674,416
Wisconsin	15	116,350	1,371	15	......	86,930	228	......	26.73	......	216,195
Total	1,391	17,416,361	345,553	11,416	9,850	‡10,346,265	23,541	48	......	......	25,108,155

* The production of pig or cast iron in Pennsylvania was estimated by the local reports in 1850 at 564,575 tons. The product of Great Britain is about 2,700,000 tons of iron annually; of France, 600,000; of Russia, 150,000; Belgium, 230,000; Sweden, 157,000.

† 645,242 tons of mineral coal used and 54,165,236 bushels charcoal.

‡ Tons of mineral coal used, 190,891; bushels coke and charcoal, 2,413,750; tons of casting made, 322,745.

TABLE CC.—*Manufactures of Wrought Iron*, 1850.

States.	Establishments.	Capital.	Value of raw material.	Hands employed.		Average wages per month.		Annual product.
				Male.	Fem.	Male.	Fem.	
Alabama	3	$ 7,000	$ 3,355	34	.....	$15.29	.....	$ 7,500
Connecticut	20	601,000	517,554	394	.....	31.59	.....	847,196
Delaware	3	75,000	35,410	47	.....	25.53	.....	38,200
Georgia	3	9,200	4,136	26	1	11.35	5.00	12,384
Indiana	4	17,000	4,425	22	2	27.45	4.00	11,760
Kentucky	4	176,000	180,800	183	.....	32.06	.....	299,700
Maryland	17	412,050	386,216	468	.....	24.31	.....	771,431
Massachusetts	58	2,561,100	2,430,533	2,472	52	29.46	12.79	*3,908,952
Missouri	2	42,100	24,509	101	.....	30.00	.....	68,700
New Hampshire	3	7,000	11,575	9	.....	31.34	.....	20,400
New Jersey	64	1,300,393	566,865	932	3	27.31	13.34	1,079,576
New York	81	1,871,650	2,305,441	2,130	.....	28.91	.....	3,758,547
North Carolina	30	170,609	50,089	262	18	10.43	4.78	331,914
Ohio	6	164,800	193,148	276	.....	29.58	.....	127,849
Pennsylvania	162	7,828,916	5,698,563	6,591	7	28.31	6.57	9,224,256
Rhode Island	2	209,400	112,123	222	.....	57.85	.....	223,650
Tennessee	42	755,050	385,616	731	55	15.20	5.00	670,618
Vermont	10	77,200	83,094	79	.....	32.08	.....	127,886
Virginia	38	747,811	531,325	1,131	.....	25.41	.....	1,098,252
Total	552	17,033,279	13,524,777	16,110	138	.....	.....	22,629,271

TABLE CCI.—*Distilleries and Breweries*, 1850.

States and Territories.	Establishments.	Capital.	Raw Material Used.			Hands employed.	Quantities Produced.		
			Bushels of barley.	Bushels of corn.	Bushels of rye.		Barrels of ale, &c.	Gallons of whiskey & high wines	Gallons of rum.
Alabama	1	$ 500	....	....	....	2	....	....	3,000
California	1	4,000	....	....	....	2	800	....	....
Columbia, Dist. of	1	12,000	5,000	....	....	5	1,350	....	....
Connecticut	8	19,600	....	20,000	20,000	27	....	130,000	1,200
Georgia	8	9,230	....	20,150	2,500	27	....	60,450	....
Illinois	52	303,400	98,000	703,500	48,700	274	27,925	2,315,000	....
Indiana	59	359,450	118,150	1,417,900	48,700	333	11,114	4,472,074	....
Iowa	4	13,500	....	51,150	7,200	16	....	37,600	....
Kentucky	81	201,335	65,650	551,350	30,520	320	25,000	1,366,895	....
Louisiana	3	47,000	10,000	....	....	22	2,500	45,000	....
Maine	2	17,400	....	....	....	7	400	....	220,000
Maryland	34	247,100	76,900	166,100	54,300	131	26,380	787,400	....
Massachusetts	27	584,700	80,000	19,400	26,600	166	25,800	120,000	3,786,000
Michigan	29	126,625	32,030	212,300	19,150	98	2,382	873,920	....
Missouri	22	298,900	124,440	309,200	24,900	179	48,350	939,400	....
New Jersey	68	409,655	103,700	254,000	58,400	265	34,750	1,250,530	....
New York	189	2,585,900	2,062,250	1,647,266	909,067	1,676	644,700	9,231,700	2,488,800
North Carolina	47	21,930	....	64,650	4,700	72	....	153,030	....
Ohio	58	1,262,974	330,950	3,588,140	281,750	1,033	96,943	11,865,150	....
Pennsylvania	371	1,719,960	550,105	1,483,555	517,180	1,092	189,581	6,548,810	1,500
Rhode Island	2	17,000	12,500	....	....	10	3,900	....	....
South Carolina	18	3,475	....	18,100	....	35	....	43,900	....
Tennessee	30	25,025	3,000	258,400	5,480	79	....	174,935	....
Vermont	1	7,000	2,500	....	....	2	500	....	....
Virginia	60	100,915	20,000	250,700	62,680	131	5,500	879,440	....
Wisconsin	33	98,700	91,020	29,900	9,200	112	31,320	127,000	....
Ter. { N. Nexico	7	7,300	....	2,000	12,900	21	....	42,000	....
Ter. { Utah	1	3,000	1,000	....	....	3	300	....	....
Total	1,217	8,507,574	3,787,195	11,067,761	†2,143,927	6,140	1,179,495	41,364,224	6,500,500

* Nail factories, spike and tack included.
† Also 56,607 bushels of oats, 526,840 bushels of apples, 1,294 tons of hops and 61,675 hogshead of molasses.

TABLE CCII.—*Fisheries of the United States.*

States.	Fisheries.	Capital.	Value of raw material.	Hands employed.		Entire wages per month.		Annual product.
				Male.	Female.	Male.	Female.	
Connecticut	252	1,986,300	$19,574	2,961	....	$61,729	....	$1,734,483
Florida	15	13,975	1,280	93	5	1,635	$42	18,676
Maine	263	496,910	19,137	2,783	....	53,210	....	569,876
Massachusetts	593	5,582,650	....	11,523	....	180,885	....	6,606,849
Michigan	69	30,806	....	244	....	5,474	....	72,775
New Hampshire	36	43,700	6,836	300	....	3,000	....	59,281
New York	26	482,100	....	583	....	11,862	....	484,345
North Carolina	76	235,115	....	1,843	424	44,578	4,993	250,025
Ohio	16	11,184	4,979	85	....	1,621	....	27,565
Rhode Island	11	32,500	12,096	109	....	3,708	....	64,430
Virginia	15	40,564	32,944	133	....	2,887	....	95,002
Wisconsin	12	10,240	2,835	47	....	1,010	....	16,875
Total	1,384	8,966,044	99,681	20,704	429	371,599	5,035	10,000,182

Sundries.—Connecticut—36,946,000 white fish, 243,448 shad, 825 barrels other fish, 70,357 barrels whale oil, 3,240 barrels sperm oil, 271 tons bone. Florida—2,000 quintals fish, 85,000 pounds turtle, 483 barrels mullet fish. Maine—173,094 quintals codfish, 29,685 boxes herring, 12,681 barrels mackerel, 2,156 barrels oil. Massachusetts—215,170 quintals codfish, 236,468 barrels mackerel, 1,250 barrels herring, 187,157 barrels oil and bone. Michigan—15,451 barrels white fish. New Hampshire—2,471,056 pounds dry codfish, 1,096 barrels mackerel, 8,958 gallons oil. New York—25,283,000 fish, 16,475 barrels oil, 169,570 pounds bone. North Carolina—56,482 barrels shad and herring. Ohio—389,150 pounds fish, 3,630 barrels fish. Rhode Island—187,000 barrels meuhadeu fish, 1,000 barrels sperm oil. Virginia—177,930 bushels oysters, 75 barrels fish. Wisconsin—3,365 barrels white fish. Vessels employed, 547.

TABLE CCIII.—*Statistics of the Salt Manufactures in the United States for the year ending June* 1, 1850.

States.	Number.	Capital.	Raw material.	Hands employed.		Average yearly wages paid.		Annual product, bushels.	Value.
				Male.	Female.	Male.	Female.		
Connecticut	1	$4,000	$4,000	1	1	360	144	40,000	$5,600
Florida	1	19,000	....	6	2	1,440	288	....	6,000
Illinois	1	2,500	2,000	3	....	720	....	20,000	6,000
Kentucky	12	121,450	17,050	153	9	16,896	432	246,500	57,825
Maine	3	3,100	7,225	4	....	1,080	....	....	9,700
Massachusetts	9	40,400	60,000	28	7	8,088	1,092	....	93,850
New York	192	819,950	631,955	873	....	299,376	....	4,500,000	998,315
Ohio	32	188,750	35,633	167	....	42,036	....	550,350	132,293
Pennsylvania	47	168,360	57,189	219	....	55,020	....	919,100	206,796
Texas	2	3,475	1,750	15	1	2,280	72	8,000	5,900
Virginia	40	1,269,900	234,623	1,230	67	317,136	7,764	3,479,890	700,466
Total	340	2,640,885	1,051,425	2,699	87	744,432	9,792	9,763,840	2,222,745

3. COMMERCE.—The statistics of the various branches of commerce in the several States, though ascertained by the census of 1840, were omitted among the items of that of 1850, except as to the number of persons employed and the nature of the business employing them. There were in 1850 100,752 merchants proper, and 14,917 traders, if reliance can be placed on the figures, which is doubtful. Prof. Tucker from the returns, estimated the annual product from commerce in 1840 at $97,721,086 ; $40,680,081, or more than half being for the Middle States, $13,528,740 for the New England, $11,967,281 for the South, $14,255,964 for the South-west, and $17,289,020 for the North-west. Without doubt the figures are low. It would be fair to estimate the home and foreign commerce of the United States in 1850 at $1,500,000,000,* paying a profit of 20 per cent, or $300,000,000, or more than the profits of manufactures. However these are but mere hypotheses.

The following statistics are presented as a proper and necessary appendage to the Industrial Report of the census. They have been carefully collected in the office from official sources, or such as are regarded official, as Seybert, Pitkins, Hazard, &c., and will give in a condensed form all that can be desired here in relation to the early and growing commerce of the Colonies, States,

* The Western River commerce has been estimated at $339,502,744: Lake and River commerce together, $653,976,202. (*Corwin's Report on Steam Marine of the Interior.*) If half the agricultural products and all of the manufacturing were subjects of commerce, the whole commercial movement might be estimated at between $1,500,000,000 and $2,000,000,000. Mr. Walker, in his Treasury Report of 1847, estimated the whole products of the country at $3,000,000,000 annually. $300,000,000 profit in commerce would be less than $3,000 to each of the 100,752 merchants reported in 1850

and Union, the countries with which the commerce was conducted, the nature of the commodities bartered, the extent of revenues, expenditures, debt, tonnage, with instructive ratio tables. A digest has never before been published of these matters, so complete.

TABLE CCIV.—*Commerce of Principal Colonies prior to the Revolution*, 1700-76

Years.	New England.		New York.		Pennsylvania.		Virginia and Maryland.		Carolina.		Georgia.	
	Exports	Imports.	Exports	Imports.	Exports	Imports.	Exports	Imports.	Exports	Imports	Exports	Imports
							£	£				
1700	£41,486	£91,918	£17,567	£49,410	£4,608	£18,529	317,302	173,481	£14,058	£11,003	....	....
1701	32,656	86,322	18,547	31,910	5,220	12,003	235,738	199,683	16,973	13,908	....	....
1702	37,026	64,625	7,965	29,991	4,145	9,342	274,782	72,391	11,870	10,460	....	....
1703	33,539	59,608	7,471	17,562	5,160	9,899	144,928	196,713	13,197	12,428	....	....
1704	30,823	74,896	10,540	22,294	2,430	11,819	264,112	60,458	14,067	6,621	....	....
1705	22,793	62,504	7,393	27,902	1,309	7,206	116,768	174,322	2,698	19,788	....	....
1706	22,210	57,050	2,849	31,588	4,210	11,037	149,152	58,015	8,652	4,001	....	....
1707	38,793	120,631	14,283	29,855	786	14,365	207,625	237,901	23,311	10,492	....	....
1708	49,635	115,505	10,847	26,899	2,120	6,723	213,493	79,061	10,340	11,996	....	....
1709	29,559	120,349	12,259	34,577	617	5,881	261,668	80,268	20,431	28,521	....	....
1710	31,112	106,338	8,203	31,475	1,277	8,594	188,429	127,639	20,793	19,613	....	....
1711	26,415	137,421	12,193	28,856	38	19,408	273,181	91,535	12,871	20,406	....	....
1712	24,699	128,105	12,466	18,524	1,471	8,464	297,941	134,583	29,394	20,015	....	....
1713	49,904	120,778	14,428	46,470	178	17,037	206,263	76,304	32,449	23,967	....	....
1714	51,541	121,288	29,810	44,643	2,663	14,927	280,470	128,873	31,290	23,712	....	....
1715	66,555	164,650	21,316	54,629	5,461	17,182	174,756	199,274	29,158	16,631	....	....
1716	69,595	121,156	21,971	52,173	5,193	21,842	281,343	179,595	46,287	27,272	....	....
1717	58,898	132,001	24,534	44,140	4,499	22,505	296,884	215,962	41,275	25,058	....	....
1718	61,591	131,885	27,331	62,966	5,588	22,716	316,576	191,925	46,385	15,841	....	....
1719	54,452	125,317	19,596	56,355	6,564	27,068	332,069	164,630	50,373	19,630	....	....
1720	49,206	128,769	16,836	37,397	7,928	24,531	331,482	110,717	62,736	18,290	....	....
1721	50,483	114,524	15,681	50,754	8,037	21,548	357,812	127,376	61,858	17,703	....	....
1722	47,955	133,722	20,118	57,478	6,882	26,397	283,091	172,754	79,650	34,374	....	....
1723	59,339	176,486	27,992	53,013	8,332	15,992	287,997	123,833	78,103	42,246	....	....
1724	69,585	168,507	21,191	63,020	4,057	30,324	277,344	161,894	90,504	37,839	....	....
1725	72,021	201,768	24,976	70,650	11,981	42,209	214,730	195,884	91,942	39,182	....	....
1726	63,816	200,882	38,307	84,866	5,960	57,634	324,767	185,981	93,453	43,934	....	....
1727	75,052	187,277	31,617	67,452	12,823	31,979	421,588	192,965	96,055	23,254	....	....
1728	64,680	194,590	21,142	81,634	15,230	37,478	413,089	171,092	91,175	33,067	....	....
1729	52,512	161,102	15,833	64,760	7,434	29,799	386,174	108,931	113,329	58,366	....	....
1730	54,701	208,196	8,740	64,356	10,582	48,592	346,823	150,931	151,739	64,785	....	....
1731	49,048	183,467	20,756	66,116	12,786	44,260	408,502	171,278	159,771	71,145	....	....
1732	64,095	216,600	9,411	65,540	8,524	41,698	310,799	148,289	126,207	58,298	....	£ 828
1733	61,983	184,570	11,626	65,417	14,776	40,565	403,198	186,177	177,845	70,466	£ 203	1,695
1734	82,252	146,460	15,307	81,758	20,217	54,392	373,090	172,086	120,466	99,658	18	1,921
1735	72,899	189,125	14,155	80,405	21,919	48,804	394,995	220,381	145,348	117,837	3,010	12,112
1736	66,788	222,158	17,944	86,000	20,786	61,513	380,163	204,794	214,083	101,147	....	2,012
1737	63,347	223,923	16,833	125,833	15,198	56,690	492,246	211,301	187,758	58,986	....	5,701
1738	59,116	203,233	16,228	133,438	11,918	61,450	391,814	258,860	141,119	87,793	17	6,496
1739	46,604	220,378	18,459	106,070	8,134	54,452	444,654	217,200	236,192	94,445	233	3,324
1740	72,389	171,081	21,498	118,777	15,048	56,751	341,997	281,428	265,560	181,821	924	3,524
1741	60,052	198,147	21,142	140,430	17,158	91,010	577,109	248,582	236,830	224,270	....	2,553
1742	53,166	148,899	13,536	167,591	8,527	75,295	427,769	264,186	154,607	127,063	1,622	17,018
1743	63,185	172,461	15,067	134,487	9,596	79,340	557,821	328,195	235,136	111,499	2	2,291
1744	50,248	143,982	14,527	119,920	7,446	62,214	402,709	234,855	192,594	79,141	....	769
1745	38,948	140,463	14,083	54,957	10,130	54,280	399,423	196,799	91,847	86,815	....	939
1746	38,612	209,177	8,841	86,712	15,779	73,699	419,371	282,545	76,897	102,809	....	984
1747	41,771	210,640	14,992	137,984	2,832	82,404	492,619	200,088	107,500	95,529	....	24
1748	29,748	197,682	12,358	143,311	12,363	75,330	494,852	252,624	167,305	160,172	....	1,314
1749	39,999	238,286	23,413	265,773	14,944	238,637	434,618	323,600	120,499	164,085	51	5
1750	48,455	343,659	35,632	267,130	28,191	217,713	508,939	349,419	191,607	134,037	1,942	2,125
1751	63,287	305,974	42,363	248,941	23,870	190,917	460,085	247,027	245,491	138,244	355	2,065
1752	74,313	273,340	40,648	194,030	29,978	201,666	569,453	325,151	288,264	150,777	1,526	3,163
1753	83,395	345,523	40,553	277,864	38,527	245,644	632,575	356,776	164,634	213,009	3,057	14,128
1754	66,538	329,433	26,663	127,497	30,649	244,647	573,435	323 513	397,238	149,215	3,236	1,974
1755	59,533	341,796	28,055	151,071	32,336	144,456	489,668	285,157	325,525	189,887	4,437	2,630
1756	47,359	384,371	24,073	250,425	20,091	200,169	337,759	334,897	222,915	181,780	7,155	536
1757	27,556	363,404	19,168	353,311	14,190	168,426	418,881	426,687	130,889	213,949	....	2,571
1758	30,204	465,694	14,260	356,555	21,383	260,953	454,362	438,471	150,511	181,002	....	10,212
1759	25,985	527,067	21,684	630,785	22,404	498,161	357,228	459,007	206,534	215,255	6,074	15,178
1760	37,802	599,647	21,125	480,106	22,754	707,998	504,451	605,882	162,769	218,131	12,198	....
1761	46,225	334,225	48,648	289,570	39,170	204,067	455,083	545,350	253,002	254,587	5,764	24,279
1762	41,733	247,385	58,882	288,046	38,091	200,199	415,709	418,599	181,595	194,170	6,522	23,761
1763	74,815	258,854	52,998	238,560	38,228	284,152	642,294	555,391	282,366	250,132	14,469	44,908
1764	88,157	459,765	53,697	515,416	36,258	436,191	559,508	515,192	341,727	305,808	31,325	18,338
1765	145,819	451,299	54,959	382,349	25,148	363,368	505,671	383,224	385,918	334,709	34,183	29,165
1766	141,733	409,642	67,020	330,829	26,851	327,314	461,693	372,548	293,587	296,732	53,074	67,268
1767	128,207	406,081	61,422	417,957	37,641	371,830	437,926	437,628	395,027	244,093	35,856	23,334
1768	148,375	419,797	87,115	482,930	59,404	432,107	406,048	475,984	508,108	289,868	42,402	56,562
1769	129,353	207,992	73,466	74,918	26,111	199,906	361,892	488,362	587,114	306,600	82,270	58,340
1770	148,011	394,451	69,882	475,991	28,109	134,881	435,094	717,782	278,907	146,273	55,532	56,193
1771	150,381	1,420,119	95,875	653,621	31,615	728,744	577,848	920,326	420,311	409,169	63,810	70,493
1772	126,265	824,830	82,707	343,970	29,133	507,909	528,404	793,910	425,923	449,610	66,083	92,406
1773	124,624	527,055	76,246	289,214	36,652	426,448	589,803	328,904	456,513	344,859	85,391	62,932
1774	112,248	562,476	80,008	437,937	69,611	625,652	612,030	528,738	432,302	378,116	67,647	57,518
1775	116,588	71,625	187,018	1,228	175,962	1,366	758,356	1,921	579,349	6,245	103,477	113,777
1776	762	55,050	2,318	....	1,421	365	73,226	....	13,668	....	12,569	....

TABLE CCV.—*Commerce, Tonnage, Debt, Revenues, etc., of the United States, 1789–1853.**

Years.	Tonnage.	Imports.	Exports.	Debt.	Revenue.	Expenditures.	Population.
1789–91	502,146	$29,200,000	$19,012,041	$75,463,476	†$4,418,913	†$1,718,129	4,049,600
1792	564,437	31,500,000	20,753,098	77,227,924	3,661,932	1,766,077	4,173,024
1793	491,780	31,100,000	26,109,572	80,352,634	4,614,423	1,707,348	4,300,210
1794	628,817	34,600,000	33,026,233	78,427,405	5,128,432	3,500,348	4,431,272
1795	747,964	69,756,268	47,989,472	80,747,587	5,954,534	4,350,596	4,566,329
1796	831,900	81,436,164	67,064,097	83,762,172	7,137,529	2,531,930	4,705,504
1797	876,913	75,379,406	56,850,206	82,064,479	8,303,560	2,833,590	4,848,919
1798	898,328	68,551,700	61,527,097	79,228,529	7,820,575	4,623,223	4,906,705
1799	946,408	79,069,148	78,665,522	78,408,670	7,475,773	6,480,166	5,148,994
1800	972,492	91,252,768	70,971,780	82,976,294	10,777,709	7,411,369	5,305,925
1801	1,033,219	111,363,511	94,115,925	83,038,051	12,846,530	4,981,669	5,473,407
1802	892,101	76,333,333	72,483,160	80,712,632	13,668,233	3,737,079	5,646,176
1803	949,147	64,666,666	55,800,033	77,054,686	11,064,097	4,002,824	5,824,398
1804	1,042,404	85,000,000	77,699,074	86,427,121	11,826,307	4,452,858	6,008,246
1805	1,140,369	120,600,000	95,566,021	82,312,150	13,560,693	6,357,234	6,197,897
1806	1,208,735	129,410,000	101,536,963	75,723,271	15,559,931	6,080,209	6,393,534
1807	1,268,548	138,500,000	108,343,150	69,218,399	16,398,019	4,984,572	6,595,346
1808	1,242,595	56,990,000	22,430,960	65,196,318	17,060,661	6,504,338	6,803,528
1809	1,350,281	59,400,000	52,203,233	57,023,192	7,773,473	7,414,672	7,018,282
1810	1,424,783	85,400,000	66,757,970	53,173,217	9,384,214	5,311,082	7,239,814
1811	1,232,502	53,400,000	61,316,833	48,005,588	14,423,529	5,592,604	7,449,960
1812	1,269,997	77,030,000	38,527,236	45,209,738	9,801,132	17,829,498	7,666,206
1813	1,666,628	22,005,000	27,855,997	55,962,828	14,340,409	28,082,396	7,888,729
1814	1,159,209	12,965,000	6,927,441	81,487,846	11,181,625	30,127,686	8,117,710
1815	1,368,127	113,041,274	52,557,753	99,833,660	15,411,634	26,953,571	8,353,338
1816	1,372,218	147,103,000	81,920,452	127,334,934	47,403,204	23,373,432	8,595,806
1817	1,399,912	99,250,000	87,671,569	123,491,965	32,786,862	15,454,610	8,845,312
1818	1,225,184	121,750,000	93,281,133	103,466,634	21,002,563	13,808,674	9,102,060
1819	1,260,751	87,125,000	70,142,521	95,529,648	23,871,276	16,300,273	9,366,261
1820	1,280,166	74,450,000	69,691,669	91,015,566	16,779,331	13,134,530	9,638,131
1821	1,298,958	62,585,724	64,974,382	89,987,428	14,315,790	10,723,479	9,920,600
1822	1,324,969	83,241,511	72,160,281	93,546,677	19,481,961	9,827,642	10,211,348
1823	1,336,566	77,579,267	74,699,030	90,875,877	20,049,536	9,784,155	10,510,618
1824	1,389,163	80,549,007	75,986,657	90,269,778	18,903,609	15,330,145	10,818,659
1825	1,423,112	96,340,075	99,535,388	83,788,433	21,342,906	11,490,459	11,135,727
1826	1,534,191	84,974,477	77,595,322	81,054,060	24,763,345	13,062,316	11,462,088
1827	1,620,608	79,484,068	82,324,827	73,987,357	21,230,641	12,254,397	11,798,013
1828	1,741,392	88,509,824	72,264,686	67,475,044	24,243,504	12,506,041	12,143,783
1829	1,260,798	74,492,527	72,358,671	58,421,414	24,224,979	12,651,489	12,499,687
1830	1,191,776	70,876,920	73,849,508	48,565,406	24,280,888	13,220,534	12,866,020
1831	1,267,847	103,191,124	81,310,583	39,123,192	27,452,697	13,863,768	13,234,931
1832	1,439,450	101,029,266	87,176,943	24,322,235	31,107,040	16,514,088	13,614,420
1833	1,606,151	108,118,311	90,140,433	7,001,699	33,003,344	22,049,298	14,004,789
1834	1,758,907	126,521,332	104,336,973	4,760,082	21,076,774	18,420,466	14,406,350
1835	1,824,940	149,895,742	121,693,577	37,733	34,163,635	17,005,419	14,819,425
1836	1,882,103	189,980,035	128,663,040	37,513	48,288,219	29,655,244	15,244,344
1837	1,896,686	140,989,217	117,419,376	1,878,224	18,032,846	31,793,587	15,681,447
1838	1,994,640	113,717,404	108,486,616	4,857,660	19,372,984	31,578,785	16,131,087
1839	2,096,380	162,092,132	121,028,416	11,983,738	30,399,043	25,488,547	16,593,630
1840	2,180,764	107,141,519	132,085,946	5,125,078	16,993,858	23,327,772	17,069,453
1841	2,130,744	127,946,177	121,851,803	6,737,398	15,957,512	26 196,840	17,600,752
1842	2,092,391	100,162,087	104,691,534	15,028,486	19,643,967	24,361,337	18,148,589
1843	2,158,603	‡64,753,799	‡84,346,480	26,898,953	‡8,065,326	‖10,698,391	18,713,479
1844	2,280,095	108,435,035	111,200,046	26,143,996	28,504,519	19,960,055	19,295,971
1845	2,417,002	117,254,564	114,646,606	16,801,647	29,769,134	21,370,049	19,896,574
1846	2,562,085	121,691,797	113,488,516	24,256,495	29,499,247	26,813,290	20,515,871
1847	2,839,046	146,545,638	158,648,622	45,659,659	26,346,790	55,929,093	21,154,444
1848	3,154,042	154,998,928	154,032,131	65,804,450	35,436,750	42,811,970	21,812,893
1849	3,334,015	147,857,439	145,755,820	64,704,693	31,074,347	57,631,667	22,491,305
1850	3,535,454	178,138,318	151,898,720	64,228,238	43,375,798	43,002,168	23,191,876
1851	3,772,439	220,779,355	218,388,011	62,560,395	52,312,979	48,005,879	23,873,717
1852	4,138,441	212,613,282	209,641,625	65,131,692	49,728,386	46,007,896	24,575,604
1853	4,407,010	267,978,647	230,452,250	56,336,157	61,337,574	54,026,818	25,298,126

* "During the war of the Revolution, our commerce was suspended; after the peace in 1783, our trade continued to languish; it had to contend with domestic and foreign obstacles; foreign nations entertained a jealousy concerning these States; at home a rivalship was prevalent amongst the several members of the confederacy, and checked the prosperity of the nation. Each of the thirteen independent sovereignties contemplated its own immediate interests; some of the States declared the commercial intercourse with them to be equally free to all nations, and they cautiously avoided to lay duties on such merchandize as was subject to them, when imported into other States."

From the records of the English custom house: Exports from America to Great Braitain 1784, £749,345; imports to America from Great Britain, £3,679,467; 1785, exports £893,594, imports £2,308,023; 1786, exports £443,119, imports £1,603,465; 1787, exports £893,637, imports £2,009,111; 1788, exports £1,023,784, imports £1,886,142; 1789, exports £1,050,198, imports £2,525,298; 1790, exports £1,191,071, imports £3,431,778.

† From March 4, 1789, to Dec. 31, 1791. ‡ 9 months of 1843. ‖ 6 months of 1843.

TABLE CCVI.—*Comparative employment of American and Foreign Tonnage, as shown in the imports of the United States, in* 1821, '31, '41 *and* '51.

States, &c.	1821.*		1831.		1841.		1851.	
	In American vessels.	In Foreign vessels.	In American vessels.	In Foreign vessels.	In American vessels.	In Foreign vessels.	In American vessels.	In Foreign vessels.
Alabama	....	....	143,320	81,115	410,358	120,461	43,736	369,710
California	....	....	....	....	....	....	4,462,700	....
Columbia, District of	398,984	....	180,573	12,982	53,863	23,400	80,527	286
Connecticut	312,090	....	405,066	....	293,221	2,768	320,858	22,136
Delaware	80,997	....	21,656	....	1,188	2,088	....	....
Florida	11,830	1,440	110,196	5,514	116,712	28,469	38,875	56,122
Georgia	757,622	245,062	236,298	163,642	299,977	149,030	404,477	317,070
Illinois	....	....	....	....	....	....	3,609	1,048
Indiana	....	....	....	....	....	....	1,754	....
Kentucky	....	....	....	....	....	....	213,576	....
Louisiana	2,697,049	682,668	5,969,622	3,797,071	8,141,088	2,115,262	10,134,465	2,393,995
Maine	972,795	7,499	832,303	109,104	574,664	126,297	968,061	208,529
Maryland	3,982,914	87,928	4,513,897	312,680	5,348,866	752,447	5,662,066	988,579
Massachusetts	14,647,778	178,954	13,982,768	286,288	18,835,492	1,482,511	23,117,834	9,597,493
Michigan	15,132	13,944	27,299	....	137,608	192	182,146	....
Mississippi	....	....	....	....	....	....	845	....
Missouri	....	....	....	....	33,875	....	622,039	....
New Hampshire	350,021	....	146,205	....	61,585	12,116	44,682	13.346
New Jersey	17,606	....	....	....	1,919	396	....	1,111
New York	21,926,635	1,702,611	53,617,033	3,460,384	66,688,750	9,024,676	106,568,635	34,977,903
North Carolina	200,673	....	186,802	9,554	214,731	5,629	125,978	80,953
Ohio	12	....	153	464	9,563	1,755	586,460	99,871
Pennsylvania	7,873,092	285,830	11,623,584	500,499	9,840,354	506,344	11,541,212	2,627,549
Rhode Island	1,030,195	2,773	562,161	....	333,929	5,663	295,209	15,421
South Carolina	1,787,590	1,219,523	853,171	384,992	1,217,955	339,476	1,646,915	434,397
Tennessee	....	....	....	....	7,523	....	64,761	....
Texas	....	....	....	....	....	....	62,745	31,970
Vermont	15,987	....	166,206	....	246,739	....	691,268	....
Virginia	946,904	131,586	383,797	104,725	351,917	25,320	227,339	325,594
Oregon Territory	....	....	....	....	....	....	103,500	....
Total	58,025,906	4,559,818	93,962,110	9,229,014	113,221,877	14,724,300	168,216,272	52,563,083

TABLE CCVIII.—*Commerce of the principal States from* 1821 *to* 1853.—*Imports.*†

Years	Massachusetts.	New York.	Pennsylvania.	Maryland.	Virginia.	South Carolina.	Georgia.	Alabama.	Louisiana.
1821	14,826,732	23,629,246	8,158,922	4,070,842	1,078,490	3,007,113	1,002,684	....	3,379,717
1822	18,337,320	35,445,628	11,874,170	4,792,486	864,162	2,283,586	989,591	36,421	3,817,238
1823	17,607,160	29,421,349	13,696,770	4,946,179	681,810	2,419,101	670,705	125,770	4,283,125
1824	15,378,758	36,113,723	11,865,531	4,551,442	639,787	2,166,185	551,888	91,604	4,539,769
1825	15,848,141	49,639,174	15,041,797	4,751,815	553,562	1,892,297	343,356	113,411	4,290,034
1826	17,063,482	38,115,630	13,551,779	4,928,569	635,438	1,534,483	330,998	179,554	4,167,521
1827	13,370,564	38,719,644	11,212,935	4,405,708	431,765	1,434,106	312,609	201,909	4,531,645
1828	15,070,444	41,927,792	12,884,408	5,629,694	375,238	1,242,048	308,669	171,909	6,217,881
1829	12,520,744	34,743,307	10,100,152	4,804,135	395,352	1,139,618	380,293	233,720	6,857,209
1830	10,453,544	35,624,070	8,702,122	4,523,866	405,739	1,054,619	282,346	144,823	7,599,083
1831	14,269,056	57,077,417	12,124,083	4,826,577	488,522	1,238,163	399,940	224,435	9,766,693
1832	18,118,900	53,214,402	10,678,358	4,629,303	553,639	1,213,725	253,417	107,787	8,871,653
1833	19,940,911	55,918,449	10,451,250	5,437,057	690,391	1,517,705	318,990	265,918	9,590,505
1834	17,672,129	73,188,594	10,479,268	4,647,483	837,325	1,787,267	546,802	395,361	13,781,809
1835	19,800,373	88,191,305	12,389,937	5,647,153	691,255	1,891,805	393,049	525,955	17,519,814
1836	25,681,462	118,253,416	15,068,233	7,131,867	1,106,814	2,801,361	573,222	651,618	15,117,549
1837	19,975,667	79,301,722	11,680,111	7,857,033	813,823	2,510,860	774,349	609,385	14,020,012
1838	13,300,925	68,453,206	9,360,371	5,701,869	577,142	2,318,791	776,068	524,548	9,496,808
1839	19,385,223	99,882,438	15,050,715	6,995,285	913,462	3,086,077	413,987	895,201	12,064,942
1840	16,513,858	60,440,750	8,469,882	4,910,746	545,085	2,058,870	491,428	574,651	10,673,690
1841	20,318,003	75,713,426	10,346,698	6,101,313	377,237	1,557,431	449,007	530,819	10,256,350
1842	17,986,433	55,875,604	7,385,758	4,417,078	316,705	1,359,465	341,764	363,871	8,033,590
1843	16,789,452	31,356,540	2,760,630	2,479,132	187,062	1,294,769	207,432	360,655	8,170,015
1844	20,296,087	65,079,510	7,217,267	3,917,750	267,654	1,131,515	305,634	442,818	7,826,789
1845	22,781,024	70,909,085	8,159,227	3,741,804	230,470	1,143,158	206,301	473,491	9,354,397
1846	24,190,963	74,254,283	7,989,396	4,042,915	209,004	902,536	205,495	259,607	7,223,090
1847	34,477,008	84,167,352	9,587,516	4,432,314	386,127	2,580,658	207,180	390,161	9,222,969
1848	28,647,707	94,525,141	12,147,584	5,343,643	215,081	1,485,299	217,114	419,396	9,380,439
1849	24,745,917	92,567,369	10,645,500	4,976,731	241,935	1,475,695	371,024	657,147	10,050,697
1850	30,374,684	111,123,524	12,066,154	6,124,201	426,599	1,933,785	636,964	865,362	10,760,499
1851	32,715,327	141,546,538	14,168,761	6,650,645	552,933	2,081,312	721,547	413,446	12,528,460
1852	33,504,789	132,329,306	14,785,917	6,719,986	735,858	2,175,614	474,925	588,382	12,057,724
1853	41,367,956	178,270,999	18,834,410	6,330,078	399,004	1,808,517	508,261	809,562	13,630,686

* Previous to 1821 the value of Merchandise imported was not required in the returns made to the Treasury.

† Cannot be seperated for earlier periods.

TABLE CCVIII.—*Commerce of the principal Commercial States from* 1791 *to* 1853.
Exports.

Years.	Massachusetts.	New York	Pennsylvania.	Maryland.	Virginia.	South Carolina.	Georgia.	Alabama.	Louisiana.
1791	$2,519,651	$2,505,465	$3,436,093	$2,239,691	$3,130,865	$2,693,268	$491,250	....	....
1792	2,888,104	2,535,790	3,820,662	2,623,808	3,552,825	2,428,250	459,106	....	....
1793	3,755,347	2,932,370	6,958,836	3,665,056	2,987,098	3,191,867	520,955	....	....
1794	5,292,441	5,442,183	6,643,092	5,686,191	3,321,636	3,867,908	263,832	....	....
1795	7,117,907	10,304,581	11,518,260	5,811,380	3,490,041	5,998,492	695,986	....	....
1796	9,949,345	12,208,027	17,513,866	9,201,315	5,268,665	7,620,049	950,158	....	....
1797	7,502,047	13,308,064	11,446,291	9,811,799	4,908,713	6,505,118	644,307	....	....
1798	8,639,252	14,300,892	8,915,463	12,746,190	6,113,451	6,994,179	961,848	....	....
1799	11,421,591	18,719,527	12,431,967	16,299,609	6,292,986	8,729,015	1,396,759	....	....
1800	11,326,876	14,045,079	11,949,679	12,264,331	4,430,689	10,663,510	2,174,268	....	....
1801	14,870,556	19,851,136	17,438,193	12,767,530	5,655,574	14,304,045	1,755,939	....	....
1802	13,492,632	13,792,276	12,677,475	7,914,225	3,978,363	10,639,365	1,854,951	....	....
1803	8,768,566	10,818,387	7,525,710	5,078,062	6,100,708	7,811,108	2,370,875	....	....
1804	16,894,378	16,081,281	11,030,157	9,151,939	5,790,001	7,451,616	2,077,572	....	1,600,362
1805	19,435,657	23,482,943	13,762,252	10,859,480	5,606,620	9,066,625	2,394,846	....	3,371,545
1806	21,199,243	21,762,845	17,574,702	14,580,905	5,055,396	9,743,782	82,764	....	3,887,323
1807	20,112,125	26,357,963	16,864,744	14,298,984	4,761,234	10,912,564	3,744,845	....	4,320,555
1808	5,128,322	5,606,058	4,013,330	2,721,106	526,473	1,664,445	24,626	....	1,261,101
1809	12,142,293	12,581,562	9,049,241	6,627,326	2,894,125	3,247,341	1,082,108	....	541,924
1810	13,013,048	17,242,330	10,993,398	6,489,018	4,822,611	5,290,614	2,238,686	....	1,890,592
1811	11,235,465	12,266,215	9,560,117	6,833,987	4,822,307	4,861,279	2,568,866	....	2,650,050
1812	6,583,338	8,961,922	5,973,750	5,885,979	3,011,112	2,036,195	1,066,703	....	1,060,471
1813	1,807,923	8,185,494	3,577,117	3,787,865	1,819,722	2,968,484	1,094,595	....	1,045,153
1814	1,133,799	209,670	....	248,434	17,581	737,899	2,183,121	....	387,191
1815	5,280,083	10,675,373	4,593,919	5,036,601	6,676,976	6,675,129	4,172,319	....	5,102,610
1816	10,136,439	19,690,031	7,196,246	7,338,767	8,212,860	10,849,409	7,511,929	....	5,602,948
1817	11,927,997	18,707,433	8,735,592	8,933,930	5,621,422	10,372,613	8,790,714	....	9,024,812
1818	11,998,156	17,872,261	8,759,402	7,570,734	7,016,246	11,440,962	11,132,096	96,857	12,924,309
1819	11,399,913	13,587,378	6,293,788	5,926,216	4,392,391	8,250,790	6,310,434	50,906	9,768,753
1820	11,008,922	13,163,244	5,743,549	6,609,364	4,557,957	8,882,940	6,594,623	96,636	7,596,157
1821	12,484,691	13,162,917	7,391,767	3,850,394	3,079,209	7,200,511	6,014,310	108,960	2,272,172
1822	12,598,525	17,100,482	9,047,802	4,536,796	3,217,389	7,260,320	5,484,870	209,748	7,978,645
1823	13,683,239	19,038,990	9,617,192	5,030,228	4,006,788	6,898,814	4,293,666	200,387	7,779,072
1824	10,434,328	22,897,134	9,364,893	4,863,233	3,277,564	8,034,082	4,623,982	460,727	7,928,820
1825	11,432,987	35,259,261	11,269,981	4,501,304	4,129,520	11,056,742	4,222,833	692,635	12,582,924
1826	10,098,862	21,947,791	8,331,722	4,010,748	4,596,732	7,554,036	4,368,504	1,527,112	10,284,380
1827	10,424,383	23,834,137	7,575,833	4,516,406	4,657,938	8,322,561	4,261,555	1,376,364	11,728,997
1828	9,025,785	22,777,649	6,051,480	4,334,422	3,340,185	6,550,712	3,104,425	1,182,559	11,947,400
1829	8,254,937	20,119,011	4,089,935	4,804,465	3,787,431	8,175,586	4,981,376	1,693,958	12,386,060
1830	7,213,194	19,697,983	4,291,793	3,791,482	4,791,644	7,627,031	5,336,626	2,294,594	15,488,692
1831	7,733,763	25,535,144	5,513,713	4,308,647	4,150,475	6,575,201	3,959,813	2,413,894	16,761,989
1832	11,993,768	26,000,945	3,516,066	4,499,918	4,510,650	7,752,731	5,515,883	2,736,387	16,530,930
1833	9,683,122	25,395,117	4,078,951	4,062,467	4,467,587	8,434,325	6,270,040	4,527,961	18,941,373
1834	10,148,820	25,512,014	3,989,746	4,168,245	5,483,098	11,207,778	7,567,327	5,670,797	26,557,524
1835	10,043,790	30,345,264	3,739,275	3,925,234	6,064,063	11,338,016	8,890,674	7,574,692	36,270,823
1836	10,384,346	28,920,438	3,971,555	3,675,475	6,192,040	13,684,376	10,722,200	11,184,166	37,179,828
1837	9,728,190	27,338,419	3,841,599	3,789,917	3,702,714	11,220,161	8,935,041	9,671,401	35,328,697
1838	9,104,862	23,008,471	3,477,151	4,524,575	3,986,228	11,042,070	8,803,839	9,688,244	31,502,248
1839	9,276,085	33,268,099	5,255,415	4,756,561	5,187,196	10,385,426	5,970,443	10,338,159	33,181,167
1840	10,186,261	34,264,080	6,820,145	5,768,768	4,778,220	10,036,769	6,862,956	12,854,690	34,236,936
1841	11,487,343	33,139,833	5,152,501	4,947,166	5,630,286	8,043,289	3,696,513	10,981,271	34,387,483
1842	9,807,116	27,576,778	3,776,727	4,904,766	3,750,386	7,525,723	4,300,257	9,965,675	28,404,149
1843	4,431,681	13,443,234	2,071,945	2,820,214	1,954,510	7,754,152	4,522,401	1,115,460	26,653,927
1844	9,096,286	32,861,540	3,535,256	5,133,169	2,942,279	7,433,282	4,283,805	9,907,654	30,498,307
1845	10,351,030	36,175,298	3,574,363	5,221,977	2,104,581	8,890,648	4,557,435	10,538,228	27,157,495
1846	10,313,118	36,935,413	4,751,005	6,869,055	3,529,299	6,848,477	2,708,003	5,260,317	31,275,704
1847	11,248,462	49,844,368	8,544,391	9,762,244	5,658,374	10,431,517	5,712,149	9,054,580	42,051,633
1848	13,419,699	53,351,157	5,732,333	7,129,782	3,681,412	8,081,917	3,670,415	11,927,749	40,971,361
1849	10,264,862	45,963,100	5,343,421	8,000,660	3,373,738	9,701,176	6,857,806	12,823,725	37,611,667
1850	10,681,763	52,712,789	4,501,606	6,967,353	3,415,646	11,447,800	7,551,943	10,544,858	38,105,350
1851	12,352,682	86,007,019	5,356,036	5,635,786	3,090,068	15,316,578	9,159,989	18,528,824	54,413,963
1852	16,546,499	87,484,456	5,828,571	6,667,861	2,724,657	11,670,021	4,999,090	17,385,704	49,058,885
1853	16,895,304	66,030,355	6,255,229	7,768,224	3,302,561	15,400,408	7,371,883	16,786,913	67,768,724

TABLE CCIX.—*Imports of several leading articles into the U. States,* 1821-1853.

Years.	Cotton manufactures.	Woolens.	Linen manufactures.	Silk manufactures.	Coffee.	Sugar.	Tea.	Specie and bullion.	Iron and steel manufactures.
1821	$7,589,711	$7,437,737	$2,564,159	$4,486,924	$4,489,970	$3,553,895	$1,322,636	$8,064,890	$1,868,529
1825	12,509,516	11,392,264	3,887,787	10,299,743	5,250,828	4,232,662	3,728,935	6,150,765	3,706,416
1830	7,862,326	5,766,396	3,011,280	5,932,242	4,227,021	4,630,922	2,425,018	8,155,964	3,655,848
1835	15,367,585	17,834,424	6,472,021	16,677,547	10,715,466	6,806,425	4,522,806	13,131,447	5,351,616
1840	6,504,484	9,071,184	4,614,466	9,835,757	8,546,222	5,581,428	5,427,010	8,882,813	3,184,900
1845	13,863,282	10,666,176	4,923,109	9,928,411	6,243,532	4,780,720	5,761,788	4,070,242	5,077,788
1850	20,108,719	17,151,509	8,134,674	19,596,858	11,234,835	7,558,554	4,719,232	4,628,972	7,078,603
1851	22,164,442	19,507,309	8,795,742	28,026,268	12,851,070	13,845,940	4,798,005	5,453,592	8,182,438
1852	19,689,496	17,573,694	8,515,709	23,609,279	14,474,900	14,718,359	7,285,817	5,505,044	8,048,618
1853	27,731,313	27,621,911	10,236,037	33,048,542	15,564,590	14,993,003	8,224,853	4,201,382	7,838,791

TABLE CCX.—*Exports of certain leading articles from the U. States,* 1821-1853.

Years.	Cotton.	Tobacco.	Specie.	Rice.	Flour.	Fish.	Manufactures.	Lumber.	Beef and pork, cattle & hogs.
1821.....	$20,157,484	$5,648,962	$10,478,059	$1,494,307	$4,298,043	$973,591	$2,584,916	$1,822,077	$2,052,439
1825.....	36,846,649	6,115,623	8,797,055	1,925,245	4,212,127	1,078,773	5,417,978	1,988,220	2,763,144
1830.....	29,674,883	5,586,365	2,178,773	1,986,824	6,085,953	756,677	5,320,980	2,056,289	2,032,928
1835.....	64,961,302	8,250,577	6,477,775	2,210,331	4,394,777	1,008,534	7,294,073	3,402,934	2,415,493
1840.....	63,870,307	9,883,957	8,417,014	1,942,076	10,143,615	720,164	9,873,462	2,926,846	2,518,267
1845.....	51,739,643	7,469,819	8,606,495	2,160,456	5,398,593	1,012,007	10,329,701	3,099,455	4,918,093
1850.....	71,984,616	9,951,023	7,522,994	2,631,557	7,098,570	456,794	9,992,444	4,493,658	9,155,895
1851.....	112,315,317	9,219,251	29,472,752	2,170,927	10,524,331	481,661	21,296,498	4,630,206	6,057,973
1852.....	87,965,732	10,031,283	42,674,135	2,470,029	11 869,143	453,010	19,978,430	4,991,184	5,265,899
1853.....	109,456,404	11,319,319	27,486,875	1,657,658	14,783,394	461,016	22,721,660	4,996,014	8,416,878

TABLE CCXI.—*Commerce of the U. States with several Foreign Nations,* 1790–1853.

Years.	Great Britain and dependencies.		France and dependencies.		West Indies generally.		Netherlands and dependencies.		Hanse Towns.	
	Imports.	Exports.	Imports.	Exports.	Imps.	Exports.	Imports.	Exports.	Imports.	Exports.
1790..	....	9,246,562	....	4,668,902	.....	....	....	47,240	....	478,050
1795..	30,972,215	9,218,540	20,288,017	12,653,635	85,186	1,543,348	3,699,615	2,884,817	1,663,433	9,655,524
1800..	42,577,590	27,310,289	9,644,323	5,163,833	26,937	115,631	7,132,627	5,669,016	4,998,975	8,012,846
1805..	....	25,047,386	....	21,072,747	.....	3,496,947	....	17,835,216	....	3,232,508
1810..	....	16,555,488	....	137,630	.....	360,931	....	174,078	....	1,126,382
1821..	29,277,938	26,522,272	5,900,581	6,474,718	3,727	560,513	2,934,272	7,688,336	990,165	2,591,275
1830..	26,804,984	31,647,881	8,240,885	11,806,238	7,386	247,121	1,356,765	4,562,437	1,873,278	2,274,880
1840..	39,130,921	70,420,846	17,908,127	22,349,154	.....	....	2,326,896	4,546,085	2,521,493	4,198,159
1850..	85,117,477	88,388,675	27,636,265	20,183,094	9,417	67,934	2,732,560	3,571,607	8,787,874	5,206,522
1853..	143,219,260	145,553,624	33,525,999	27,044,479	.....	98,125	2,549,619	2,979,332	13,843,455	8,020,053

Years.	Russia.		China.		Spain and dependencies.		Mexico.		Colombia, C. America, Brazil, Argentine Conf. and Chili.	
	Imports.	Exports.	Imports.	Exports.	Imports.	Exports.	Imports.	Exports.	Imports.	Exports.
1790..	....	....	....	....	....	1,989,421	....	....	....	....
1795..	1,168,715	66,221	1,144,103	1,023,242	3,942,445	4,714,864	....	....	....	....
1800..	1,524,995	....	4,613,463	1,047,385	16,071,918	15,660,606	....	....	....	....
1805..	....	71,372	....	322,075	....	12,672,768	....	....	....	....
1810..	....	3,975,698	....	319,479	....	14,941,942	....	....	....	....
1821..	1,852,199	628,894	3,111,951	4,290,560	9,653,728	7,218,265	....	....	....	....
1830..	1,621,899	416,575	3,878,141	742,193	8,373,681	6,049,051	5,235,241	4,837,458	5,528,856	4,756,347
1840..	2,572,427	1,169,481	6,640,829	1,009,966	14,019,647	7,617,347	4,175,001	2,515,341	9,093,688	5,891,478
1850..	1,511,572	864,941	6,593,462	1,605,217	15,864,748	9,931,240	2,135,366	2,012,827	16,553,499	8,125,825
1853..	1,278,501	2,456,653	10,573,710	3,736,992	26,030,320	11,847,101	2,167,985	3,558,824	23,280,079	8,577,131

TABLE CCXII.—*Ratio of Commerce, Debt, Revenues, Expenditures, etc., to the Population of the United States,* 1790–1853.

Years.	Retained of imports for home consumption.	Exports.		Proportion of retained imports to each person.	Prop'n of exports of domestic goods to each person.	Proportion of debt to each person.	Proportion of revenue to each person.	Proportion of expenditure to each person.	Proportion of tonnage to 100 persons.	Ratio per ct. of imports in American vessels.	Ratio per ct. of exports in American vessels.
		Domestic.	Foreign.								
1790.........	$22,460,844	$19,660,000	$539,156	$5.72	$5.00	$19.21	$0.71	$0.38	$12.78	......	......
1795.........	61,266,796	39,500,000	8,489,472	13.42	8.65	17.68	1.29	0.95	16.38	......	......
1800.........	52,121,891	31,840,903	39,130,877	9.82	6.00	15.64	2.00	1.39	18.33	......	......
1805.........	67,420,981	42,387,002	53,179,019	10.87	6.84	13.28	2.18	1.03	18.40	......	......
1810.........	61,008,705	42,366,679	24,391,295	8.43	5.84	7.34	1.30	0.73	19.68	......	......
1820.........	56,441,971	51,683,640	18,008,029	5.86	5.36	9.44	1.74	1.36	13.28	......	......
1830.........	56,489,441	59,462,029	14,387,479	4.39	4.62	3.77	1.89	1.03	9.26	......	......
1840.........	88,951,207	113,895,634	18,190,312	5.21	6.67	0.30	1.00	1.37	12.77	......	......
1850.........	163,186,510	134,900,233	14,951,808	7.04	5.82	2.77	1.87	1.85	15.24	$78.40	......
1853.........	250,944,094	213,417,697	17,034,553	9.92	8.44	2.23	2.43	2.13	17.42	71.53	67.04

4. INTERNAL IMPROVEMENTS.—The following will show the number of miles of rail roads existing in the United States in each year since the period of their first introduction: In 1828, 3 miles, 1829. 28; 1830, 41; 1831, 54; 1832, 131; 1833, 576; 1834, 762; 1835, 918; 1836, 1,102; 1837, 1,421: 1838, 1,843; 1839, 1,920; 1840, 2,167; 1841, 3,319; 1842, 3,877; 1843, 4,174; 1844, 4,311; 1845, 4,511; 1846, 4,870; 1847, 5,336; 1848, 5,682; 1849, 6,350; 1850, 7,355; 1851, 9,090 1852, 11,631; 1853, 13,379; 1854, 17,317.

The following will show the present results of rail roads and canals in the United States. The funded debt of rail roads, in 1853 was $130,000,000, and their gross earnings $38,356,632. A report of 2,356 miles of canals, shows a total cost of $54,676,936. There were in 1853, 89 telegraphic lines having 23,261 miles of wire. At present the miles of wire may be estimated at over 30,000.

TABLE CCXIII.—*Rail Roads and Canals*, 1854.

States.	Canals, miles.	RAIL ROADS.				States.	Canals, miles.	RAIL ROADS.			
		Number.	Miles in operation.	Miles in construc-tion.	Cost.			Number.	Miles in operation.	Miles in construc-tion.	Cost.
Alabama	51	6	221	659	$3,636,208	New Hampshire	11	15	512	24	16,185,254
Connecticut	61	15	669	83	20,857,357	New Jersey	147	11	408	29	11,536,505
Delaware	14	2	16	43	600,000	New York......	989	32	2,345	564	94,523,785
Florida.........	....	2	54	......	250,000	North Carolina .	13	3	249	223	4,106,000
Georgia	28	15	884	445	16,084,872	Ohio	921	46	2,367	1,578	44,927,058
Illinois.........	100	25	1,262	1,945	25,420,000	Pennsylvania...	936	64	1,464	987	58,494,675
Indiana	367	18	1,127	748	22,400,000	Rhode Island ...	.. ...	1	50	......	2,614,484
Iowa...........	....	2	......	480	....	South Carolina..	50	9	575	374	11,287,093
Kentucky	486	9	233	452	4,909,990	Tennessee	......	9	388	695	7,800,000
Louisiana	101	7	117	119	1,131,000	Texas..........	......	1	......	72	....
Maine..........	50	11	417	90	12,662,645	Vermont	......	8	422	59	14,116,195
Maryland.......	184	3	597	30	26,024,620	Virginia	189	21	673	1,180	12,720,421
Massachusetts ..	100	43	1,283	48	55,602,687	Wisconsin	.. ...	4	178	200	3,800,000
Michigan	....	4	601	......	13,842,279						
Mississippi	....	4	155	436	3,070,000	Total.........	4,798	396	17,317	12,526	489,603,128
Missouri	....	6	50	963	1,000,000						

In Great Britain 7,686 miles of railway in 1853 were open to traffic, and charters existed for 2,164 miles more; in 1850, 625 miles were opened, in 1853, 350 miles. Total capital invested 1852, £264,165,680. Total passengers conveyed, 102,286,660. Total receipts from all sources, £18,635,879. In France, 1853, there were 4,070 kilometres (5/8 of a mile, 1,093 yards) of railroad in operation, 1890 under construction, and 3,665 proposed. Dr. Lardner estimated the railroads opened in the world in 1845, 18,656, and in construction 7,829, with a total capital of about £500,000,000. A late French authority, 1854, states the miles of railroad in Europe to be 52,011 kilom. of which 45,589 were opened. The relation of the governments to each other with regard to railroads and in proportion to territory, is expressed in the figures. France 0.77, Prussia 1.06, smaller German States 1.30, Belgium 3.06, Great Britain 3.91.

The number of miles of railway now in operation upon the surface of the globe is 35,480, of which 16,890 are in the Eastern Hemisphere, and 18,590 are in the Western; and which are distributed as follows:

In the United States 17,317 miles, British Provinces 823, Island of Cuba 359, Panama 31, South America 60, Great Britain 7,686, Germany 5,340, France 2,480, Belgium 532, Russia 422, Sweden 75, Italy 170, Spain 60, Africa 25, India 100.

PART V.

PROPERTY, REVENUE, TAXATION, &c.

THE value of real and personal estate in the United States in 1850 was $7,066,562,966. Supposing this to be correct, and estimating the increase since that time to have averaged as much as in Kentucky, which in 1853 was $366,957,487, the total in 1854 would be upwards of $7,500,000,000 for the official and $9,000,000,000 for the real. This is but an approximation, as the taxable property is only included, which in all of the States is greatly less than the whole. The real estate in farms alone, as was seen in another place, amounted in value to $3,271,575,426 in 1850. From the official report of States and cities, collected independently of the census: Taxable property of Texas, 1850, $51,814,615; 1853, $99,155,114; Pennsylvania, 1852, $531,370,454; California, 1852, $64,388,175; Ohio, 1850, $430,839,885; Virginia, 1850, $274,680,226 for lands alone; Arkansas, 1852, $43,569,458; Illinois, 1851, real $86,512,537, real and personal $119,868,336; Iowa, 1852, $38,427,370; Louisiana, 1850, $220,165,172; 1851, $270,000,000; New York, 1852, real $946,467,907, personal $221,802,950; Tennessee, 1850, $159,558,183; Maryland, 1851, $191,888,088; Georgia, 1853, lands $116,437,117, city property included $19,314,347; Mississippi, taxable land valued at $76,201,031; Indiana, 1853, assessed value of property $266,097,614; Baltimore, real and personal, 1850, $80,237,960; Mobile, 1850, $11,985,960; 1851, $17,670,295; New York city, real $227,015,855, real and personal $320,110,866; 1853, 413,686,932; Savannah, 1848, $3,600,000 real estate; New Orleans, 1853, $66,350,260 for real, and for real and personal $83,588,055; Boston, 1850, real $105,093,400, personal $74,907,100, total $180,000,000; Charleston, 1852, $11,942,886; 1854, $23,000,000 by a new assessment of real estate.

The total debt of the United States July 1, 1854, as reported by the Secretary of the Treasury, was $47,180,506.05; the amount of bonds and stocks outstanding on June 30, 1853, of the General and State governments, cities, counties, rail roads, banks, insurance companies is estimated by the Secretary at $1,178,567,882, of which those held by foreigners are between $184,184,714 and $222,225,315 or between one-fifth and one-sixth. The property owned by State governments exclusively of lots, buildings, &c. devoted to government uses he estimates at $171,889,889.

Receipts into the Treasury, 1852: revenues from customs $47,339,326, for public lands $2,043,239, total receipts $49,728,386. Expenditure: civil list $3,422,939, foreign intercourse $4,132,671, including $3,180,000 to Mexico, miscellaneous $5,198,828, War Department $8,225,246, navy $8,928,236, public debt $6,275,815, total expenditure $46,007,896. Revenue of Great Britain, 1853, £50,468,193, of which £21,622,493 from imposts. Relative annual expenditure of Britain $256,000,000, debt $3,822.000,000; of France $285,600,000; debt $943,000 000; of Russia, $77,650,000, debt $550,000,000; of Spain $51,000,000, debt $700,000,000.

TABLE CCXIV.—*Real and Personal Estate*, 1850—*Taxation and Debt*, 1852.

States and Territories.	Real estate.	Personal estate.	Total.	True valuation.	Revenue.	Expenditure.	Debt.
Alabama,‡‡ *a*......	$78,870,718	$162,463,705	$241,334,423	$228,204,332	$658,976	$513,559	*$3,983,616
Arkansas,†	17,372,524	19,056,151	36,428,675	39,841,025	68,412	74,076	1,506,562
California,‡........	16,347,442	5,575,731	21,923,173	22,161,872	366,825	925,625	2,159,403
Columbia, Dist. of..	14,409,413	1,774,342	16,183,755	16,723,619	....	....	....
Connecticut, *a*.....	96,412,947	22,675,725	119,088,672	155,707,980	150,189	137,326	8,000
Delaware, *a*	14,486,595	1,410,275	15,896,870	18,855,863	....	....	30,000
Florida, *a*	7,924,588	15,274,146	23,198,734	23,198,734	60,619	55,234	2,800
Georgia, *a*.........	121,619,739	213,490,486	335,110,225	335,425,714	1,142,405	597,882	2,801,972
Illinois, *a*..........	81,524,835	33,257,810	114,782,645	156,265,006	736,030	192,940	17,500,000
Indiana, *a*	112,947,740	39,922,659	152,870,399	202,650,264	1,283,064	1,061,605	6,712,880
Iowa, *a*	15,672,332	6,018,310	21,690,642	23,714,638	139,681	131,631	81,795
Kentucky,‖*a*	177,013,407	114,374,147	291,387,554	301,628,456	779,293	674,697	5,726,307
Louisiana,§........	176,623,654	49,832,464	226,456,118	233,998,764	1,146,568	1,098,911	11,492,566
Maine, *a*....	64,336,119	32,463,434	96,799,553	122,777,571	744,879	624,101	471,500
Maryland,.........	139,026,610	69,536,956	208,563,566	219,217,364	1,279,953	1,360,458	15,260,667
Massachusetts,¶*a*..	349,129,932	201,976,892	551,106,824	573,342,286	598,170	674,622	6,259,930
Michigan, *a*........	25,580,371	5,296,852	30,877,223	59,787,255	548,326	431,918	2,307,850
Mississippi	65,171,438	143,250,729	208,422,167	228,951,130	221,200	223,637	7,271,707
Missouri, *a*........	66,802,223	31,793,240	98,595,463	137,247,707	326,579	207,656	857,000
New Hampshire, *a*.	67,839,108	27,412,488	95,251,596	103,652,835	141,686	149,890	74,399
New Jersey, *a*.....	153,151,619	not returned.	153,151,619	153,151,619	139,166	180,614	71,346
New York.........	564,649,649	150,719,379	715,369,028	1,080,309,216	2,698,310	2,520,932	22,623,838
North Carolina	71,702,740	140,368,673	212,071,413	226,800,472	219,000	228,173	977,000
Ohio, *a*............	337,521,075	96,351,557	433,872,632	504,726,120	3,016,403	2,736,060	15,520,768
Pennsylvania, *a*....	427,865,660	72,410,191	500,275,851	729,144,998	7,716,552	6,876,480	41,524,875
Rhode Island,***a* ..	54,358,231	23,400,743	77,758,974	80,508,794	124,944	115,835	....
South Carolina,††..	105,737,492	178,130,217	283,867,709	288,257,694	532,152	463,021	3,144,931
Tennessee, *a*	107,981,793	87,299,565	195,281,358	207,454,704	502,126	623,625	3,776,856
Texas, *a*..........	28,149,671	25,414,000	53,563,671	55,362,340	140,688	156,622	5,725,671
Vermont, *a*........	57,320,369	15,660,114	72,980,483	92,205,049	185,830	183,058	48,436
Virginia, *a*.........	252,105,824	130,198,429	382,304,253	391,646,438	1,265,744	1,272,382	13,573,355
Wisconsin	22,458,442	4,257,083	26,715,525	42,056,595	135,155	136,096	12,892
Territories. Minnesota....	97,363	164,725	262,088	262,088	....	....	....
Territories. New Mexico.	2,679,486	2,494,985	5,174,471	5,274,867	....	....	....
Territories. Oregon......	3,997,332	1,066,142	5,063,474	5,063,474	....	....	....
Territories. Utah	337,866	648,217	986,083	986,083	....	....	....
Total	3,899,226,347	2,125,440,562	6,024,666,909	7,066,562,966	27,068,925	24,628,666	191,508,922

An attempt was made by the Census to ascertain the amount paid for Taxes in the U. States, but the returns are very incomplete. The following is the best that can be digested from the returns and embraces but a part of the States. The total of taxation in these States appears to be $25,055,129. Estimating the same proportion in the other States, the total would be swelled to about $43,000,000, or including federal taxes about $83,000,000, an average of $4.24 to each white person or $3.58 to each inhabitant. In 1832 the Secretary of State collected material upon this subject, which was embodied not long after in a full report. Upon averaging a few States fully returned, he estimated the amonnt paid by each individual for clergy, road building, militia, poor rates, town expenses, schools, county, state and federal expenses together at $2.55; excluding clergy, road and militia, $2.15.

TABLE CCXV.—*Annual Taxes.*

States.	Annual Taxes.						
	State.	County.	School.	Poor.	Road.	All others.	Total.
Alabama..................	$ 428,690	$ 202,960	$ 7,519	$ 2,904	$ 3,000	$ 12,029	$ 663,446
Connecticut..............	67,947	1,101	48,669	80,444	80,117	288,065	566,343
Florida..................	58,616	23,690	105	....	....	2,876	85,287
Georgia..................	292,707	156,061	15,728	14,027	1,388	42,571	522,482
Indiana	552,463	449,616	96,736	54,838	171,554	58,153	1,383,360
Maine	381,911	141,705	234,842	102,747	563,887	327,945	1,753,037
Mississippi	779,163	436,993	31,106	7,461	4,698	80,979	1,340,400
New Hampshire............	77,313	84,854	144,178	150,745	250,913	200,993	908,996
New Jersey...............	....	190,685	62,706	54,591	119,614	171,808	599,404
New York	....	....	....	....	....	....	7,160,255
North Carolina...........	114,086	144,189	42,340	66,162	660	87,906	455,343
Pennsylvania.............	1,536,662	1,689,212	840,066	358,757	816,867	847,891	6,089,455
Rhode Island	16,951	....	56,937	45,587	29,077	198,559	347,111
South Carolina	373,421	....	....	49,143	20,817	188,781	632,162
Texas....................	74,936	35,055	....	....	....	21,332	131,313
Vermont..................	138,533	3,578	88,930	90,809	247,801	149,763	719,414
Virginia.................	368,649	229,285	45,697	110,077	20,309	352,835	1,126,852
Wisconsin	93,982	151,835	75,980	9,194	72,103	167,375	570,469
Total....................	....	....	....	....	....	....	$25,055,129

* Including bonds to banks, &c. $8,500,000. † Average of two years. ‡ 1853. ‖ Exclusive of sinking fund account, the revenue from which $373,537 in 1852 and expenditures from same for same year $341,011. § But a small part of this is the State debt proper, viz. $2,154,319. ¶ Including bonds to rail road companies. ** No debt except what has been used of the United States revenue fund—exact amount not stated. †† The valuation used for purposes of taxation is explained on page 26. ‡‡ 1851.

NOTE.—The amount of $30,000 set down as the debt of Delaware was a sum borrowed from the Farmers' Bank to meet extraordinary expenses of the Commonwealth for 1852; it is only a temporary loan, being principal and interest.

Of a grand total of bonds outstanding June 30, 1853, by the States, amounting to $190,718,221, $110,972,108 is estimated by the Secretary of the Treasury as held by foreigners.

For all marked thus (*a*) the revenue, expenditure and debt are taken from official replies to inquiries—all others are from the American Almanac, 1853. In several States the personal property is estimated from partial returns.

The total number of real estate holders in the U. States, upon a rough estimate from the returns of two or three States which were examined, cannot fall short of 1,500,000, or one to 3.19 of the free males over 21 years of age.

In the counties of the following States, which are named upon page 153, the real estate holders are thus classified: In Connecticut $215,535 in real estate were owned by free blacks, and $88,000 by mulattoes, total $303,535; in Louisiana $311,465 by free blacks, and $3,958,830 by free mulattoes, total $4,270,295; New York city, owned by mulattoes $44,000, by blacks $65,310; New Orleans, including Lafayette, mulattoes $1,991,050, blacks $222,970; in Barnwell, Beaufort, and Charleston, S. C., 58 free colored owned under $1,000 each in real estate, 10 between $1,000 and $5,000 each, 2 between $5,000 and $10,000, etc.

Counties in the States of	Persons owning under $1,000.		Between 1,000 and 5,000.		5,000 and 10,000.		10,000 & 50,000.		50,000 & 100,000.		100,000 and 500,000.		500,000 and 1,000,000		Aggregate.		Aggregate in the counties classified.
	Nat.	For.	Nat.	For.	Nat.	For.	Nat.	For.	Nat.	For.	Nat.	For.	Nat.	For.	Native	For'gn.	
Kentucky	394	19	333	9	85	....	64	....	2	....	1	....	....	....	879	28	907
Michigan	3,139	460	1,634	147	82	8	28	....	1	....	....	....	....	....	4,884	615	5,499
Pennsylvania	798	91	645	27	65	18	18	....	....	....	....	....	....	....	1,526	136	1,662
Rhode Island	1,017	8	1,523	19	216	....	49	....	1	....	....	....	....	....	2,757	76	2,833
South Carolina	3,006	44	3,438	148	802	76	759	96	69	8	17	3	1	....	8,092	375	8,467
Louisiana	426	103	626	96	290	20	348	20	73	5	21	2	....	....	1,784	246	2,030
Ohio	463	363	821	119	102	13	43	3	....	....	....	....	....	....	1,429	498	1,927

INDIANS.—The number of Indians within the territory of the United States was stated by General Knox, Secretary of War, to be 76,000 in 1789. In consequence of annexation of new territory, notwithstanding the extinction of tribes, the whole number in 1825 reported by the Indian Department, was 129,366, exclusive of those in the Missouri valley, &c. In 1853 the present commissioner of Indian Affairs estimated the total number at 400,764, of which 271,930 were in California, Oregon, Texas, &c., and therefore not embraced in 1828. This would show a decline of 532 upon the number then existing. The names of tribes and past and present locations will be seen on page 94, quarto census. The following are the numbers of some of the largest tribes in 1853: Creeks of Indian country, 25,000; Cherokees of Indian country, 19,130; Choctaws of Indian country, 17,000; Sioux of Minnesota, 8,000; Chippewas of Minnesota, 8,000; California Indians, 100,000; Oregon and Washington Indians, 23,000; Utah Indians, 11,500; New Mexico Indians, 45,000; Texas Indians, 29,000; Missouri Valley Indians, 43,430; Arkansas River Indians, 20,000.

MISCELLANEOUS.—1850, 855 Whig and 742 Democratic papers published in the United States as shown by the returns. In 1800, exclusive of the army and navy, there were 3,806 persons in the employment of the federal government; in 1854 the number is 35,456, a nine-fold increase, the population having increased about five-fold.

The coinage of the United States Mint and branches was in 1800, $317,760 gold, $224,296 silver, $29,279 copper, total $571,335; in 1820, $1,319,030 gold, $501,680 silver, $44,075 copper, total $1,864,786; 1852, $56,205,638 gold, $847,310 silver, $51,620 copper, total $57,104,569.

The steam marine of the United States, by report of the Secretary of the Treasury in 1852, consisted of ocean steamers 96, ordinary 382, propellers 67, ferry boats 80; total 625 of 212,500 tonnage. High pressure 213, low pressure 412, officers and crew 11,700, passengers 33,342,846, of which 24,009,550 were on ferry boats. The inland steam marine consists of 767 steamers of 204,723 tonnage, carrying 5,860,950 passengers, of which 2,481,915 by ferry boats. That of Great Britain was but 1,184 boats of 142,080 tonnage.

The following will show the number of vessels built in the United States: In 1815 136 ships, 224 brigs, 680 schooners, 274 sloops and canal boats, total 1,314, tons 154,624. In 1829 44 ships, 68 brigs, 485 schooners, 145 sloops and canal boats, 43 steamers, total 785, tons 77,098. In 1852 255 ships, 79 brigs, 584 schooners, 267 sloops and canal boats, 259 steamers, 1,444 total, 351,493 tons.

The amount of tonnage at several periods will here be seen: In 1820 619,047 registered, 661,118 enrolled, total 1,280,166, in whale fishery 35,391, coasting trade 539,080. In 1840 899,704 registered, 1,280,999 enrolled, total 2,180,764, in whale fishery, 136,929, coasting trade, 1176,694. In 1852 1,899,448 registered, 2,238,992 enrolled, total 4,138,440, in whale fishing 193,797, incoasting trade 2,008,021. Tonnage entered 1851, Great Britain, native 4,388,245, foreign 2,599,088; France, native 866,145, foreign 1,312,411; U.States, native 3,054,349, foreign 1,939,091.

The commerce of the Lakes in 1852 was thus estimated: Owned steam, 77,061 tons, owned sail, 138,914 tons; American entered steam, 1,434,779, American entered sail, 464,822 tons; foreign entered steam, 397,587, foreign sail, 174,619 tons; American cleared steam, 1,482,548, American cleared sail, 438,862 tons; foreign cleared steam, 898,702, foreign cleared sail, 166,010 tons. Exports, $132,017,470 coasting; imports, $182,455,988 coasting; exports, $8,207,750, imports, $3,912,147 Canadian and foreign; value coasting trade $314,473,458; value foreign trade, $12,119,877. *Andrew's Report.*

Revenues collected at ports in the U. States for the year ending 30th June, 1853: New York, $38,289,341.58, Boston $7,203,048.52, Philadelphia $4,537,046.16, Baltimore $836,437.99, New Orleans $2,628,421.32, San Francisco $1,794,140.68, Charleston $432,299.19, Portland $350,349.22, Savannah $125,755.86, St. Louis $294,790.78, Cincinnati $251,649.90, New Haven $125,173.40, Mobile $102,981.47, Louisville, $48,307.67, Oswego $128,667.27, Richmond $73,992.98, Norfolk $31,255.51, all other districts $1,678,206.04. New Orleans.—Receipts by river, 1854, $115,836,798; 1850, $106,924,083; 1853, $134,233,735; received at the Hudson River by canals, 1852, $66,839,102; 1853, $74,443,06.

Public Domain.—Lands sold from opening of land office to 30th June, 1852, 102,113,861 acres, granted for schools &c., 40,588,978 deaf and dumb asylums, 44,971, for internal improvements, 10,007,677; military service, 18,709,219; reserved for Indians, 3,400,725; swamp-lands granted to States, 28,156,670; lands unsold, 1,387,534,001 acres.

Patent Office.—In 1841, 847 applications, 312 caveats, 495 patents issued; 1847, 1531 applications, 533 caveats, 572 patents issued; 1852, 2,639 applications, 996 caveats, 1,020 patents issued.

Upon the subject of agriculture the following notes are given in regard to sugar and cotton. Similar ones upon other crops are excluded for want of space, but will be found admirably digested in the report of the Patent Office for the present year.

Sugar crop of Louisiana, 1823, 30,000 hhds., 1839–40 119,947, 1844–5 204,913 hhds., 1846, planters producing over 1,000 hhds. 8, 900 3, 800 8, 700 20, 600 20, 500 48, 400 45, 300 99, 200 104, under 200 407, or 160 planters produced half of the crop. The largest crops to a planter were 2,035 and 2,324 hhds. 1852, sugar-houses in Louisiana 1,474, of which by steam power 914, horse 560, product 236,922 hhds.; product of molasses 70 gallons to the hogshead. Product 1854 449,324 hhds., 3,100,000 gals. molasses. The whole consumption of sugar in the United States in 1851 is estimated at 568,406,575 lbs; now largely increased.

Cotton crop 1790 1,500,000 lbs. 1800 35,000,000, 1810 85,000,000, 1820 160,000,000, 1827 757,000 bales, 1833 1,070,000, 1838 1,801,000, 1840 2,178,000, 1843 2,379,000, 1847 1,779,000, 1849 2,727,000, 1851 2,355,000, 1852 3,015,029, 1853 3,262,882, 1854 2,930,027. American Consumption north of Virginia, 1844 407,000 bales, 1848 623,000, 1850 597,000, 1854 610,571, to which add about 100,000 bales in the south and west. Continental consumption, 1846 452,000, 1848 623,000, 1851 504,000, 1852 603,029. Great Britain, 1852, all kinds consumed, 1,650,000 bales. France, American cotton, 300,000. The receipts of cotton in England other than from the United States in 1852 was 450,000 bales.

Average prices of cotton, 1821 16.2, 1825 20.9, 1835, 16.8, 1836 16.8, 1840 8.6, 1841, 10.2, 1842 8.1, 1843 6, 1844 8.1, 1845 6, 1846 7.9, 1847 10.1, 1848 7.6, 1849 6.5. Average price from 1825 to 1830 12.8, 1830 to 1835 10.9, 1835 to 1840 14.4, 1840 to 1845 8.1, 1845 to 1850 7.3 cents.

PART VI.

CITIES, TOWNS, COUNTIES, &c.

The Census does not furnish material for separating the urban and rural population of the United States, so as to admit of a statement showing the extent of either. Such a table to each of the States would be very valuable, and it is much to be regretted that it can be deduced from none of the census publications.

So imperfect is the Census of 1850 in this respect that hundreds of important towns and cities in all parts of the country, and especially in the South and West, are not even distinguished on the returns from the body of the counties in which they are situated, and therefore their population cannot be ascertained at all. Again, slaves are often included in the towns, simply because their owners reside there. But what is of more importance and the greatest cause of embarrassment is the fact that in New England and the Northern States, what are returned as cities, and towns, often include whole rural districts. If the information in regard to town and city population is ever to be correctly ascertained, there must be explicit instructions to separate upon the returns, distinctly, all places having an aggregation of over fifty or a hundred persons, with a store, tavern, blacksmith shop or school house and post office, or some or all of these, and to include within such village, town or city, no person not resident within its limits proper. It would not be difficult to frame suitable instructions upon this point.

Table CCXVI.—*Comparative Population of the largest Cities of the U. States.*

Cities.	State.	Settled.	Years.	1790.	1800.	1810.	1820.	1830.	1840.	1845.	1850.
Portland	Me.				3,677	7,169	8,581	12,601	15,218		20,815
Portsmouth	N. H.			4,720	5,339	6,934	7,327	8,082	7,887		9,738
Manchester	N. H.								3,235		13,932
Boston	Mass.		1722..10,567 1765..15,520	18,038	24,937	33,250	43,298	61,392	‡93,383	114,366	136,881
Lowell	Mass.							6,474	20,796	28,841	33,383
Springfield	Mass.					2,767	3,914	6,784	10,985		11,766
Salem	Mass.		1637.. 900 1765.. 4,427	7,921	9,457	12,613	12,731	13,895	15,082	16,762	20,264
Providence	R. I.	1635		6,380	7,614	10,071	11,767	16,832	23,171		41,513
New Haven	Conn.	1638			4,049	5,772	7,147	10,180	12,960		20,345
Hartford	Conn.	1635				3,955	4,726	7,076	9,468		13,555
New York	N. Y.	1612	1656.. 1,000 1731.. 8,628 1773..21,876	33,131	60,489	96,373	123,706	202,589	312,710	371,223	515,547
Brooklyn	N. Y.				3,298	4,402	7,175	15,396	36,233	59,566	96,838
Albany	N. Y.			3,498	5,289	9,356	12,630	24,238	33,721	41,139	50,763
Buffalo	N. Y.					1,508	2,095	8,653	18,213	29,773	42,261
Rochester	N. Y.		1812.. 15				1,502	9,269	20,191	25,265	36,403
Syracuse	N. Y.								6,500		22,271
Troy	N. Y.					3,895	5,264	11,405	19,334	21,709	28,785
Utica	N. Y.						2,972	8,323	12,782		17,565
Newark	N. J.						6,507	10,953	17,290	34,140	38,894
Philadelphia	Penn.	1682	1683.. 600 1731..12,000	42,520	69,403	91,874	112,772	161,410	220,423		340,045
Pittsburg	Penn.				1,565	4,768	7,248	12,568	21,115		46,601
Baltimore	Md.	1729		13,503	26,114	35,583	62,738	80,625	102,313		169,054
Washington	D. C.				3,210	8,208	13,247	18,827	23,364		40,001
Richmond	Va.	1742		3,761	5,737	9,735	12,067	16,060	20,153		27,570
Norfolk	Va.	1705					8,478	9,814	10,920		14,326
Petersburg	Va.				3,521	5,668	6,690	8,322	11,136		14,010
Wilmington	N. C.							3,000	4,744		7,264
Charleston	S. C.	1672		16,359	20,473	24,711	24,780	30,289	29,261		42,985
Savannah	Ga.	1732			5,166	5,215	7,523	7,776	11,214		15,312
Mobile	Ala.		1785.. *746 1788..*1,468				1,500	3,194	12,672		20,515
Nashville	Tenn.							5,566	6,929		10,478
Louisville	Ky.		1788.. 30		359	1,357	4,012	10,341	21,210		43,194
Cincinnati	Ohio				750	2,540	9,642	24,831	46,338		115,436
Columbus	Ohio	1812							6,048		17,882
Cleveland	Ohio	1796							6,071		17,034
Detroit	Mich.							2,222	9,102		21,019
Chicago	Ill.	1831							4,853		29,963
St. Louis	Mo.	1764	1769.. *891 1785.. *897 1788..*1,197			1,600	4,598	5,852	16,469	63,491	77,860
New Orleans	La.	1717	1769.. 3,190 1785.. 4,980 1788.. 5,331 1797.. 8,056			17,242	27,176	46,310	‡102,193		116,375
San Francisco	Cal.										†34,776
Milwaukie	Wis.		1846.. 9,655						1,700		20,061

Note.—The year 1845 and the periods earlier than 1790 are taken from State enumerations, and from other sources of information.

* Population of the settlement. † State census of 1852.

‡ Errors were made in Boston and New Orleans in 1840, underestimating the population in the first city, as proved by Mr. Shattuck, to the extent of about 8,000; and overestimating it in New Orleans, as proved by Dr. Barton, by at least 10 or 15,000.

TABLE CCXVII.—*Comparative Population of other large Cities*, 1840 *and* 1850.

City or Town.	State.	1840.	1850.	City or Town.	State.	1840.	1850.
Augusta	Maine	5,314	8,225	West Troy	New York	5,000	7,564
Bangor	do	8,627	14,432	Whitestown	do	5,156	6,810
Bath	do	5,141	8,020	Kingston	do	5,824	10,232
Gardiner	do	5,042	6,486	Paterson	New Jersey	7.596	11,334
Thomaston	do	*6,227	2,723	Harrisburg	Pennsylvania	5,986	7,834
Dover	N. Hampshire	6,458	8,196	Lancaster	do	8,417	12,369
Nashua	do	*6,054	5,820	Reading	do	8,410	15,743
Burlington	Vermont	4,271	6,110	Allegheny City	do	10,089	21,261
Andover	Massachusetts	5,207	6,945	Wilmington	Delaware	8,367	13,979
Cambridge	do	8,409	15,215	Fredericktown	Maryland	5,182	6,028
Danvers	do	5,020	8,109	Georgetown	D. of Columbia	7,312	8,366
Fall River	do	6,738	11,524	Alexandria	Virginia	8,459	8,734
Gloucester	do	6,350	7,786	Lynchburg	do	6,395	8,071
Lynn	do	9,367	14,257	Portsmouth	do	6,477	8,122
Marblehead	do	5,575	6,167	Wheeling	do	7,885	11,435
Middleborough	do	5,085	5,336	Newbern	North Carolina	3,690	4,681
Nantucket	do	9,012	8,452	Fayetteville	do	4,285	4,646
Newburyport	do	7,161	9,572	Raleigh	do	2,244	4,518
Plymouth	do	5,281	6,024	Columbia	South Carolina	4,340	6,060
Roxbury	do	9,089	18,364	Augusta	Georgia	6,403	†11,753
Taunton	do	7,645	10,441	Columbus	do	3,114	5,942
Worcester	do	7,497	17,049	Vicksburg	Mississippi	....	3,678
Newport	Rhode Island	8,333	9,563	Natchez	do	....	4,434
Smithfield	do	9,534	11,500	Galveston	Texas	....	4,177
New London	Connecticut	5,519	8,991	Memphis	Tennessee	....	8,839
Auburn	New York	5,626	9,548	Lexington	Kentucky	6,997	‡9,180
Canandaigua	do	5,652	6,143	Chilicothe	Ohio	3,977	7,100
Hudson	do	5,672	6,286	Steubenville	do	5,203	6,140
Ithaca	do	5,650	6,909	Dayton	do	6,067	10,977
Johnstown	do	5,409	6,131	Zanesville	do	....	10,355
Poughkeepsie	do	10,006	13,944	Ann Arbor	Michigan	....	4,868
Schenectady	do	6,784	8,921	Indianapolis	Indiana	2,692	8,034
Newburgh	do	6,000	11,415	Burlington	Iowa	....	4,082
Lockport	do	6,500	12,323				

In Richmond the number of persons to a dwelling in 1850 averaged 5.2, Charleston 5.6, Mobile 5.8, New Orleans 6.5, Philadelphia 6.6, Baltimore 6.9, St. Louis 7.7, Cincinnati 8.2, Boston 8.9, New York 13.6. In the whole embraced within the corporate limits of Mobile there are 1.6 persons to the acre, in Washington 7.2, St. Louis 26.3, Cincinnati 30.0, New York, 42.2, Boston 53.9; in the portions of these cities actually and fully settled, the number to the acre was as follows: Mobile 13.8, New Orleans 45.4, Cincinnati 45.0, St. Louis 47.4, Philadelphia 80.0, Boston 82.7, New York 135.6. In 30 years Charleston in 1850 had increased 73 per cent., Savannah 103, Baltimore 169, Philadelphia 198, Boston 221, Providence 252, New York 316, New Orleans 328, Louisville 976, Cincinnati 1097; in 20 years the increase of Richmond was 71, Nashville 82, Mobile 542, Chicago 570, Milwaukie 1071, St. Louis 1464. In an average period of about 30 years the increase of European cities in 1852 had been as follows: Amsterdam 15 per cent., Copenhagen 22, Naples 23, St. Petersburg 42, Madrid 43, Paris 47, Brussels 69, Vienna and London 91, Berlin 134.

The population of 17,150 places was ascertained by the British census of 1851—10,929 by the U. S. census 1850. 815 towns in Great Britain contained 10,556,228 persons, or one-half nearly of the whole population. In the United States it may be assumed that the village, town and city population includes about one-fourth of the whole. There were, in 1850, 2,500,000 persons resident of cities exceeding 20,000 each, and the aggregate of tables CCXVI and CCXVII is about 3,000,000. The rural population might be ascertained by multiplying the number of farms into the average persons existing upon each. Other statistics of cities will be found in previous chapters and in the appendix.

NOTES ON THE COUNTY TABLES WHICH FOLLOW.

The table of counties which follows will show for 1850 the whites, free colored and slave, and the total in 1840, (the male and female of the colored can be ascertained by deducting those of the whites from the total males and females there given,) the nativities of the white and free colored born out of the State and in the United States or in foreign countries, the dwellings and the families of the free population, the pupils, white and colored, and income of public schools and of all other schools and colleges as returned by institutions, and also of whites as returned by families, the whites between 5 and 20 years of age, the whites over 20 unable to read and write, the number of persons for whom there are church accommodation, the number of farms, the quantity and value of lands and implements, the stock and agricultural products, the manufactures produced in families, with the capital, hands employed and annual product of establishments as contradistinguished from families, including all mechanical pursuits, &c. in shops where the annual value of product at the place of manufacture exceeds $500.

The blanks indicate that nothing has been returned by the marshals, whether from its non-existence, from the impossibility of ascertaining the facts, or from neglect or oversight.

The remarks upon counties denote such changes as have taken place between 1840 and 1850 in their organization or boundaries, so as to estimate the true increase.

The aggregates of the columns will be found in the tables by States in the former part of the volume, and could not be inserted here without widening the columns, and increasing unnecessarily the extent of the work.

Out of 1,626 counties in the United States in 1850, 480 had been created or altered in the previous ten years—in 54 the females greatly preponderated, 155 the slaves and in 7 the foreign born. In 441 counties there were few or no foreigners; in 20 counties the native and foreign were about equal. In 1,023 counties there were slaves; in 192 there were no free colored.

* Population of township, since sub-divided. † Population in 1852. ‡ Estimated population in 1852.

	COUNTIES.	POPULATION.								
		Whites.			Colored.		All classes.		Total population.	
		Male.	Female.	Total.	Free.	Slave.	Male.	Female.	1850.	1840.
1	Autauga	3,231	3,043	6,274	19	8,730	7,590	7,433	15,023	14,342
2	Baldwin	1,161	939	2,100	96	2,218	2,419	1,995	4,414	2,951
3	Barbour	6,603	6,239	12,842	10	10,780	11,872	11,760	23,632	12,024
4	Benton	6,834	6,563	13,397	3	3,763	8,710	8,453	17,163	14,260
5	Bibb	3,642	3,455	7,097	11	2,861	5,095	4,874	9,969	8,284
6	Blount	3,520	3,421	6,941	....	426	3,719	3,648	7,367	5,570
7	Butler	3,606	3,556	7,162	35	3,639	5,424	5,412	10,836	8,685
8	Chambers	6,569	6,215	12,784	18	11,158	12,173	11,787	23,960	17,333
9	Cherokee	6,180	5,990	12,170	23	1,691	7,007	6,877	13,884	8,773
10	Choctaw	2,451	2,169	4,620	....	3,769	4,407	3,982	8,389	....
11	Clarke	2,565	2,336	4,901	9	4,876	5,021	4,765	9,786	8,640
12	Coffee	2,787	2,593	5,380	3	557	3,046	2,894	5,940	....
13	Conecuh	2,481	2,444	4,925	3	4,394	4,630	4,692	9,322	8,197
14	Coosa	5,358	5,056	10,414	9	4,120	7,389	7,154	14,543	6,995
15	Covington	1,511	1,566	3,077	88	480	1,781	1,864	3,645	2,435
16	Dale	2,927	2,695	5,622	3	757	3,301	3,081	6,382	7,397
17	Dallas	3,845	3,616	7,461	8	22,258	15,098	14,629	29,727	25,199
18	DeKalb	3,871	3,859	7,730	9	506	4,118	4,127	8,245	5,929
19	Fayette	4,359	4,092	8,451	9	1,221	4,954	4,727	9,681	6,942
20	Franklin	5,874	5,524	11,398	15	8,197	10,051	9,559	19,610	14,270
21	Greene	4,740	4,525	9,265	49	22,127	15,960	15,481	31,441	24,024
22	Hancock	739	741	1,480	....	62	774	768	1,542	....
23	Henry	3,549	3,227	6,776	1	2,242	4,707	4,312	9,019	5,787
24	Jackson	5,931	5,823	11,754	42	2,292	7,106	6,982	14,088	15,715
25	Jefferson	3,452	3,262	6,714	8	2,267	4,531	4,458	8,989	7,131
26	Lauderdale	5,618	5,479	11,097	60	6,015	8,689	8,483	17,172	14,485
27	Lawrence	4,290	4,052	8,342	64	6,852	7,580	7,678	15,258	13,313
28	Limestone	4,208	4,191	8,399	21	8,063	8,201	8,282	16,483	14,374
29	Lowndes	3,814	3,444	7,258	8	14,649	11,177	10,738	21,915	19,539
30	Macon	5,913	5,373	11,286	16	15,596	13,657	13,241	26,898	11,247
31	Madison	6,061	5,876	11,937	164	14,326	13,245	13,182	26,427	25,706
32	Marengo	3,829	3,272	7,101	37	20,693	14,537	13,294	27,831	17,264
33	Marion	3,510	3,412	6,922	3	908	3,954	3,879	7,833	5,847
34	Marshall	4,018	3,934	7,952	26	868	4,453	4,393	8,846	7,553
35	Mobile	9,479	7,824	17,303	941	9,356	14,494	13,106	27,600	18,741
36	Monroe	2,934	2,714	5,648	40	6,325	6,074	5,939	12,013	10,680
37	Montgomery	5,448	4,721	10,169	115	19,427	15,312	14,399	29,711	24,574
38	Morgan	3,319	3,318	6,637	51	3,437	5,071	5,054	10,125	9,841
39	Perry	4,260	4,082	8,342	26	13,917	11,388	10,897	22,285	19,086
40	Pickens	5,634	5,338	10,972	6	10,534	10,961	10,551	21,512	17,118
41	Pike	6,181	5,921	12,102	24	3,794	8,075	7,845	15,920	10,108
42	Randolph	5,447	5,169	10,616	29	936	5,905	5,676	11,581	4,973
43	Russell	4,424	3,981	8,405	32	11,111	10,015	9,533	19,548	13,513
44	St. Clair	2,829	2,672	5,501	7	1,321	3,486	3,343	6,829	5,638
45	Shelby	3,681	3,472	7,153	7	2,376	4,870	4,666	9,536	6,112
46	Sumter	3,890	3,479	7,369	50	14,831	11,402	10,848	22,250	29,937
47	Talladega	5,901	5,716	11,617	36	6,971	9,291	9,333	18,624	12,587
48	Tallapoosa	5,864	5,647	11,511	....	4,073	7,862	7,722	15,584	6,444
49	Tuscaloosa	5,164	5,407	10,571	8	7,477	8,924	9,132	18,056	16,583
50	Walker	2,490	2,367	4,857	1	266	2,622	2,502	5,124	4,032
51	Washington	616	579	1,195	22	1,496	1,399	1,314	2,713	5,300
52	Wilcox	2,875	2,642	5,517	....	11,835	8,816	8,536	17,352	15,278

STATISTICS OF

1	Arkansas	918	776	1,694	13	1,538	1,752	1,493	3,245	1,346
2	Ashley	781	628	1,409	5	644	1,105	953	2,058	....
3	Benton	1,777	1,731	3,508	1	201	1,882	1,828	3,710	2,228
4	Bradley	1,393	1,208	2,601	2	1,226	1,999	1,830	3,829	....
5	Carroll	1,269	2,122	4,391	10	213	2,375	2,239	4,614	2,844
6	Chicot	630	492	1,122	9	3,984	2,636	2,479	5,115	3,806
7	Clark	1,663	1,450	3,113	7	950	2,132	1,938	4,070	2,309
8	Conway	1,728	1,611	3,339	4	240	1,842	1,741	3,583	2,892
9	Crawford	3,607	3,328	6,935	92	933	4,093	3,867	7,960	4,266
10	Crittenden	1,017	825	1,842	5	801	1,451	1,197	2,648	1,561
11	Dallas	2,349	1,984	4,333	2	2,542	3,682	3,195	6,877	....
12	Desha	952	733	1,685	57	1,169	1,593	1,318	2,911	1,598
13	Drew	1,271	1,090	2,361	....	915	1,717	1,559	3,276	....
14	Franklin	1,805	1,692	3,497	3	472	2,037	1,935	3,972	2,665
15	Fulton	913	855	1,768	1	50	939	880	1,819	....
16	Greene	1,346	1,184	2,530	10	53	1,375	1,218	2,593	1,586
17	Hempstead	2,781	2,399	5,180	32	2,460	4,007	3,665	7,672	4,921
18	Hot Springs	1,775	1.462	3,237	11	361	1,954	1,655	3,609	1,907
19	Independence	3,556	3,371	6,927	12	828	3,974	3,793	7,767	3,669

NATIVITIES, DWELLINGS, &c.				EDUCATION AND RELIGION.									
Born out of State.				Colleges, academies and private schools.		Public Schools.							
United States.	Foreign countries.	Dwellings.	Families.	Pupils.	Annual income.	Pupils.	Annual income.	Total educational income.	White scholars during year.	Whites 5 and under 20 years old.	Whites over 20 unable to read & write.	Accommodation of churches—persons.	
2,245	57	1,114	1,133	61	$......	649	$15,564	$15,564	1,112	2,578	504	12,150	1
532	124	397	397	11	200	88	1,675	1,875	261	747	100	590	2
7,195	120	2,306	2,379	240	5,850	435	4,783	10,633	1,221	5,252	629	9,900	3
7,798	36	2,188	2,192	206	167	1,633	9,865	10,032	1,768	5,773	660	10,400	4
2,138	30	1,153	1,153	......	....	400	816	816	1,127	3,037	1,157	13,200	5
2,095	5	1,127	1,132	......	....	435	3,852	3,852	712	2,996	1,257	1,575	6
2,152	26	1,210	1,210	144	2,658	91	1,075	3,733	916	3,019	663	1,600	7
8,263	63	2,138	2,138	521	7,000	1,045	19,003	26,003	2,088	5,483	737	16,350	8
7,523	28	2,039	2,039	30	200	1,292	2,878	3,078	2,304	5,148	1,213	3,150	9
1,611	37	760	760	......	....	420	142	142	501	1,916	389	6,000	10
1,250	49	873	873	100	1,500	566	5,349	6,849	682	1,985	598	4,995	11
2,503	9	893	893	......	....	290	3,480	3,480	712	2,312	665	4,375	12
1,381	31	847	847	80	1,700	400	6,701	8,401	810	2,104	296	6,120	13
5,469	87	1,725	1,725	150	3,200	381	4,742	7,942	1,696	4,337	766	12,625	14
1,121	7	503	503	......	....	144	875	875	298	1,314	610	1,450	15
2,959	6	928	928	......	....	190	....	....	762	2,386	1,092	9,800	16
2,847	63	1,375	1,375	724	23,000	1,039	39,049	62,049	1,603	2,953	97	17,175	17
4,088	6	1,251	1,251	55	650	510	3,240	3,890	1,347	3,422	1,273	4,050	18
3,266	18	1,408	1,408	......	....	689	8,832	8,832	1,266	3,681	1,100	5,720	19
4,106	77	1,955	1,955	340	10,950	716	9,014	19,964	1,194	4,823	772	10,200	20
3,600	139	1,730	1,730	312	10,630	715	12,710	23,340	1,923	3,663	518	12,575	21
351	....	251	251	......	....	74	....	....	155	677	276	....	22
3,234	10	1,142	1,162	115	....	411	3,280	3,280	788	2,934	854	4,675	23
4,114	10	2,000	2,000	40	500	453	2,725	3,225	1,649	5,034	2,030	8,250	24
2,174	22	1,140	1,141	......	....	350	1,089	1,089	1,043	2,996	741	6,750	25
4,542	106	1,868	1,892	283	....	909	562	562	1,739	4,650	798	11,455	26
2,671	26	1,469	1,471	41	....	728	7,747	7,747	1,271	3,550	824	10,220	27
3,235	10	1,429	1,429	290	5,870	665	5,589	11,459	1,474	3,516	573	6,600	28
2,989	52	1,354	1,354	150	....	466	2,850	2,850	1,012	2,980	120	11,335	29
6,756	41	1,849	1,857	784	....	568	14,914	14,914	1,698	4,967	57	11,910	30
3,932	90	2,046	2,047	130	....	800	26,270	26,270	2,261	4,898	1,097	22,300	31
2,711	132	1,353	1,353	212	4,000	376	16,000	20,000	1,110	2,816	40	12,820	32
2,706	6	1,108	1,130	......	....	63	315	315	940	2,985	948	....	33
3,192	24	1,301	1,336	......	....	429	3,358	3,358	1,322	3,422	955	1,600	34
5,444	4,935	3,027	3,318	893	59,750	1,774	19,593	79,343	2,247	5,435	17	14,900	35
1,596	54	1,005	1,005	90	1,400	167	4,777	6,177	827	2,250	266	8,400	36
4,567	367	1,881	1,934	264	9,260	366	7,765	17,025	1,648	3,877	608	7,100	37
2,238	23	1,103	1,104	30	320	172	574	894	710	2,920	176	4,000	38
3,064	104	1,332	1,352	663	30,015	714	7,900	37,915	1,542	3,422	229	8,700	39
4,737	94	1,896	1,949	336	6,655	718	8,706	15,361	2,024	4,596	699	13,570	40
5,525	32	1,973	1,973	195	4,390	498	5,746	10,136	1,831	5,170	1,674	25,475	41
6,576	19	1,904	1,904	......	....	1,829	....	....	1,794	4,624	762	8,000	42
5,163	24	1,411	1,411	163	....	600	2,349	2,349	828	3,608	75	3,870	43
2,148	2	944	944	......	....	120	3,172	3,172	686	2,349	897	5,850	44
2,271	6	1,170	1,173	......	....	992	795	795	1,093	3,123	377	....	45
3,026	95	1,342	1,373	160	....	433	3,968	3,968	1,179	2,967	151	8,500	46
5,836	47	1,861	1,907	370	7,605	715	6,819	14,424	2,081	5,016	592	14,650	47
7,684	9	2,037	2,037	135	950	140	1,200	2,150	1,210	4,323	1,441	10,000	48
3,807	100	1,914	1,914	240	7,000	404	3,894	10,894	1,506	3,967	1,133	29,500	49
1,409	1	799	799	......	....	45	....	....	222	2,070	134	2,175	50
407	1	258	262	......	....	120	....	....	85	468	114	1,100	51
1,666	49	983	983	299	....	153	....	....	500	2,118	3	2,450	52

ARKANSAS.

United States.	Foreign countries.	Dwellings.	Families.	Pupils.	Annual income.	Pupils.	Annual income.	Total educational income.	White scholars during year.	Whites 5 and under 20 years old.	Whites over 20 unable to read & write.	Accommodation of churches—persons.	
847	26	328	328	......	....	95	1,914	1,914	185	692	168	685	1
1,121	8	269	269	......	....	150	2,500	2,500	158	562	46	1,500	2
2,077	20	572	572	55	....	146	....	....	651	1,558	55	400	3
1,932	12	440	440	......	....	140	176	176	268	1,001	254	1,700	4
2,567	2	686	686	......	....	460	100	100	883	1,973	470	....	5
750	44	226	226	......	....	75	1,400	1,400	166	387	59	200	6
1,740	15	537	537	196	872	......	....	872	283	1,242	184	700	7
1,835	25	595	595	......	....	......	....	....	134	1,424	281	....	8
3,953	289	1,247	1,248	360	3,410	75	1,150	4,560	1,232	2,860	1,018	1,850	9
1,161	17	360	360	......	....	55	600	600	109	710	89	550	10
3,434	7	740	740	124	....	194	....	....	351	1,810	306	2,650	11
1,031	55	350	350	......	....	40	1,007	1,007	81	591	114	....	12
1,806	12	430	430	45	800	145	1,813	2,613	284	973	230	1,420	13
1,957	43	617	617	......	....	180	950	950	560	1,488	437	1,750	14
1,106	3	288	288	......	....	......	....	....	279	740	321	....	15
1,528	4	436	468	......	....	120	925	925	307	1,088	516	280	16
2,974	10	855	855	130	4,650	166	2,580	7,230	442	2,133	373	2,000	17
2,116	8	579	608	273	2,000	36	161	2,161	691	1,319	526	2,386	18
3,302	15	1,159	1,163	85	....	310	....	....	938	2,892	785	4,100	19

	Counties.	Land occupied or improved.				Live stock.			
		Farms.	Acres improved.	Acres unimproved.	Value with improvements and implements.	Horses, asses, and mules.	Neat cattle.	Sheep.	Swine.
1	Autauga	711	108,172	173,604	$1,477,805	3,578	14,020	5,047	30,444
2	Baldwin	121	6,093	40,254	132,039	944	13,900	4,196	5,98[illegible]
3	Barbour	1,325	147,124	229,149	2,110,347	4,769	20,301	9,280	54,950
4	Benton	1,227	74,991	131,603	1,416,900	3,728	12,085	7,560	34,559
5	Bibb	654	53,411	129,744	678,741	2,633	11,977	6,730	25,566
6	Blount	753	27,915	43,255	272,768	1,687	6,987	4,792	24,784
7	Butler	553	46,551	102,731	446,514	1,986	16,454	6,913	27,543
8	Chambers	1,342	171,290	225,261	2,444,420	5,740	17,459	12,954	50,509
9	Cherokee	1,126	55,158	126,277	1,263,508	3,574	11,441	6,635	35,413
10	Choctaw	445	43,367	128,318	703,147	2,106	12,867	3,793	23,890
11	Clarke	456	47,927	163,126	745,319	2,653	16,823	5,961	32,352
12	Coffee	604	24,820	36,433	262,043	1,166	16,664	2,744	20,266
13	Conecuh	498	55,076	94,615	482,746	1,993	17,865	5,815	23,853
14	Coosa	1,130	67,081	161,822	900,710	2,898	15,325	8,101	31,301
15	Covington	138	9,201	17,901	109,597	824	10,617	1,306	18,272
16	Dale	697	33,565	68,344	339,062	1,447	10,181	3,057	26,320
17	Dallas	749	205,616	371,973	4,272,524	7,889	18,374	12,024	64,660
18	DeKalb	616	31,972	47,034	495,912	2,331	8,588	3,750	24,910
19	Fayette	1,065	46,641	99,789	470,354	2,385	12,480	7,068	9,790
20	Franklin	913	105,461	296,370	2,354,617	5,184	14,825	10,176	50,075
21	Greene	1,310	239,367	287,360	3,975,699	8,383	22,014	12,962	65,111
22	Hancock	144	6,829	5,258	44,884	426	2,065	949	8,159
23	Henry	671	52,919	85,004	677,789	2,047	14,420	5,699	34,776
24	Jackson	856	73,333	158,696	1,021,281	4,537	15,204	10,483	54,788
25	Jefferson	752	51,921	85,438	636,329	2,429	10,475	4,414	2[illegible],265
26	Lauderdale	1,180	98,646	141,602	1,741,823	4,973	10,886	11,849	43,405
27	Lawrence	930	125,525	153,286	1,728,117	5,172	11,376	8,247	46,778
28	Limestone	649	103,001	127,215	2,125,177	4,641	10,031	8,625	48,590
29	Lowndes	874	157,560	244,447	1,961,658	6,083	20,949	10,210	60,497
30	Macon	1,203	186,014	292,729	2,659,645	6,072	25,291	10,222	56,743
31	Madison	1,080	165,024	163,982	3,429,792	7,082	15,984	11,463	63,080
32	Marengo	818	174,097	246,556	3,782,963	6,837	17,183	7,752	59,741
33	Marion	573	30,018	84,149	304,131	2,120	10,471	4,424	24,304
34	Marshall	586	27,826	34,389	454,928	1,860	6,792	2,919	22,462
35	Mobile	249	5,152	3[illegible],544	519,190	1,263	9,389	976	5,141
36	Monroe	692	67,188	191,523	920,195	2,805	16,662	7,988	35,290
37	Montgomery	962	203,045	284,804	3,076,817	7,030	12,578	12,203	69,948
38	Morgan	584	64,123	102,821	957,771	3,330	10,951	5,964	31,839
39	Perry	1,006	159,822	207,448	2,818,178	5,910	14,641	9,014	46,022
40	Pickens	1,438	147,014	235,883	1,936,000	5,606	19,090	12,439	50,478
41	Pike	1,533	93,431	165,234	1,079,353	3,760	17,716	7,245	50,657
42	Randolph	969	41,477	111,572	659,850	2,491	12,923	7,078	33,380
43	Russell	1,049	148,947	223,857	1,876,472	4,555	21,813	7,174	43,109
44	St. Clair	573	31,841	71,879	422,081	2,089	7,184	4,556	23,854
45	Shelby	693	51,402	107,147	713,574	2,878	11,318	5,188	31,323
46	Sumter	668	154,785	187,816	1,917,577	5,366	18,430	9,497	49,506
47	Talladega	998	96,999	182,645	1,720,964	4,125	15,427	9,445	42,496
48	Tallapoosa	1,270	76,207	194,950	1,103,993	3,380	14,886	9,367	35,298
49	Tuscaloosa	1,115	97,833	241,605	1,223,769	4,246	17,418	10,225	38,842
50	Walker	609	19,831	44,905	270,063	1,257	6,191	3,351	23,126
51	Washington	141	12,001	45,110	191,577	898	13,174	2,214	11,247
52	Wilcox	666	111,004	265,610	2,118,174	4,730	15,850	9,836	49,846

STATISTICS OF

	Counties.	Farms.	Acres improved.	Acres unimproved.	Value with improvements and implements.	Horses, asses, and mules.	Neat cattle.	Sheep.	Swine.
1	Arkansas	153	12,193	38,416	580,117	925	7,640	365	14,042
2	Ashley	173	7,526	13,613	172,481	536	1,225	227	9,204
3	Benton	295	12,267	22,372	231,792	1,427	3,739	2,533	9,371
4	Bradley	303	15,157	35,237	324,569	936	4,764	971	16,504
5	Carroll	541	13,387	12,849	198,668	2,059	6,574	3,910	17,174
6	Chicot	142	29,886	103,362	1,403,284	1,854	7,747	2,007	14,915
7	Clark	362	14,351	33,745	312,805	1,138	5,974	1,151	23,037
8	Conway	387	11,885	33,216	166,459	1,365	7,455	2,175	17,196
9	Crawford	499	18,273	34,363	425,206	2,422	9,025	2,924	28,328
10	Crittenden	192	8,475	78,775	506,050	793	7,078	287	10,437
11	Dallas	399	24,065	64,625	573,969	1,514	5,913	714	17,812
12	Desha	118	9,207	33,659	415,053	634	4,656	234	10,121
13	Drew	277	11,854	23,770	170,417	942	4,506	728	14,277
14	Franklin	454	15,502	26,526	232,876	1,755	6,158	2,575	23,196
15	Fulton	222	6,055	5,578	81,995	999	3,842	1,306	7,261
16	Greene	345	9,118	4,039	84,102	1,066	4,451	3,111	13,501
17	Hempstead	550	32,618	56,904	673,496	2,372	9,058	3,157	35,975
18	Hot Springs	320	9,408	19,679	212,454	1,085	4,650	592	12,017
19	Independence	694	23,602	60,062	557,898	2,848	8,119	3,443	25,334

AGRICULTURAL PRODUCTS.												
Wheat, bushels.	Rye & oats, bushels.	Indian corn, bushels.	Irish and sweet potatoes, bushels.	Peas and beans, bushels.	Barley, bushels.	Buckwheat, bushels.	Butter and cheese, pounds.	Hay, tons.	Hops, pounds.	Clover & other grass seeds, bushels.	Flaxseed, bushels.	
3,101	56,615	492,381	137,592	41,892	23	......	101,712	2,440	......	......	......	1
6	543	74,301	25,076	813	......	......	14,280	1,755	......	......	......	2
9,820	81,391	742,132	224,257	57,065	......	......	61,225	....	......	......	......	3
11,168	69,516	580,356	98,830	14,873	81	28	110,255	28	7	56	3	4
219	19,708	343,455	80,690	3,296	5	3	50,788	1	3	......	......	5
4,473	21,213	267,025	31,591	3,193	8	......	41,650	....	......	......	......	6
5,085	17,146	305,272	84,911	910	15	......	1,602	....	......	......	......	7
20,281	119,201	876,038	168,387	24,780	156	......	111,712	....	4	36	......	8
15,708	68,870	546,986	88,191	14,204	10	21	114,321	48	13	65	40	9
470	15,385	269,560	108,697	21,281	......	......	23,967	....	......	......	......	10
159	21,043	329,061	109,121	9,872	......	......	52,921	9	......	......	......	11
1,731	6,036	136,610	51,447	9,251	20	......	25,459	....	......	......	......	12
2,031	26,408	300,210	91,772	13,721	......	......	36,995	....	......	......	......	13
1,700	38,824	418,991	126,593	18,062	......	......	113,190	2,160	......	......	......	14
178	1,920	80,205	38,842	2,982	......	......	18,495	....	......	......	......	15
3,917	12,205	182,396	70,112	17,416	1	......	26,874	....	......	......	......	16
5,127	107,370	1,267,011	236,970	63,847	80	......	112,368	6,467	......	......	......	17
3,830	75,698	363,225	40,439	5,487	......	1	74,485	45	......	39	15	18
2,473	24,930	326,844	67,405	8,990	......	......	87,472	753	......	......	......	19
6,130	96,253	892,891	79,897	54,813	1,465	......	33,487	....	......	......	......	20
17,815	122,897	1,336,144	279,298	40,755	79	4	137,967	186	73	131	......	21
260	1,938	39,624	8,060	258	2	......	12,433	....	......	......	......	22
2,087	36,763	277,356	93,340	10,137	......	......	47,395	....	......	......	......	23
2,335	72,129	796,201	57,065	8,335	......	......	106,273	16	......	25	......	24
2,040	22,960	342,743	46,176	3,085	15	......	78,362	1	......	......	......	25
16,301	82,260	785,145	69,293	15,462	52	165	105,495	1,474	......	13	......	26
4,820	89,004	815,114	82,070	34,923	660	......	169,011	1,734	......	2	......	27
3,243	86,275	861,664	73,214	26,092	52	21	96,513	3,324	97	52	......	28
3,880	96,107	933,287	168,835	10,525	13	......	74,777	....	5	......	......	29
13,009	187,722	998,867	298,563	15,136	......	......	145,533	....	......	......	......	30
7,723	163,655	1,195,037	101,331	36,355	442	27	140,645	4,942	45	234	10	31
215	94,605	1,242,460	261,080	1,410	......	......	131,460	1	......	......	......	32
3,761	20,567	01,405	40,642	2,280	......	......	59,476	....	......	......	......	33
961	30,404	357,201	38,322	3,387	......	......	50,665	7	......	30	......	34
....	2,260	34,500	58,229	2,457	......	......	28,475	606	7	......	......	35
1,753	20,511	409,506	143,380	14,141	5	......	50,214	35	22	......	......	36
1,795	192,490	1,265,645	300,884	39,622	......	......	130,546	11	......	......	......	37
1,533	60,961	464,440	47,762	13,511	231	60	76,409	470	......	2	......	38
7,375	68,211	934,116	185,214	28,202	205	......	108,454	3,908	......	......	......	39
10,613	54,212	868,705	159,232	12,012	......	......	118,807	53	......	......	......	40
5,986	41,443	531,192	153,841	13,408	......	......	63,733	....	......	......	......	41
18,212	35,473	319,183	64,916	5,682	98	3	107,939	20	......	......	1	42
16,425	98,008	683,164	185,680	49,128	28	10	73,306	....	......	......	......	43
4,424	22,920	283,377	41,021	8,500	8	......	64,675	....	......	......	......	44
12,944	52,197	384,389	73,300	18,998	23	5	131,968	2	......	......	......	45
7,162	62,896	926,826	186,894	6,723	6	......	98,675	278	......	......	......	46
7,277	114,685	715,584	119,922	2[illegible],783	5	......	117,472	....	......	......	......	47
17,800	60,615	462,276	106,411	22,738	154	......	94,099	....	......	......	......	48
3,270	50,553	626,452	117,095	27,729	16	......	84,739	1,902	......	......	......	49
831	7,073	202,476	28,567	5,887	......	......	48,875	....	......	......	......	50
52	937	101,483	36,673	3,077	......	......	14,539	9	......	......	......	51
535	49,951	673,446	134,075	2,205	......	......	52,035	....	......	......	......	52

ARKANSAS.

Wheat, bushels.	Rye & oats, bushels.	Indian corn, bushels.	Irish and sweet potatoes, bushels.	Peas and beans, bushels.	Barley, bushels.	Buckwheat, bushels.	Butter and cheese, pounds.	Hay, tons.	Hops, pounds.	Clover & other grass seeds, bushels.	Flaxseed, bushels.	
40	724	116,535	12,163	4,204	......	......	15,022	136	......	......	......	1
535	1,097	65,[illegible]87	16,936	2,487	......	......	13,330	....	......	2	......	2
12,405	26,773	144,385	5,782	....	......	......	34,101	276	......	......	......	3
155	7,784	145,865	38,973	12,615	3	......	19,099	....	......	......	5	4
11,825	18,304	264,060	18,191	156	......	35	208	16	......	1	13	5
50	1,990	222,595	34,410	12,868	......	......	39,910	210	43	......	......	6
1,204	3,985	122,860	19,929	2,154	......	......	16,052	16	......	......	......	7
3,464	5,276	164,192	11,617	248	......	......	24,585	....	......	......	......	8
3,718	41,046	240,567	17,407	25	......	15	78,121	86	......	......	......	9
....	1,050	163,970	11,643	10	......	......	26,843	62	......	5	......	10
713	2,460	209,940	48,057	28,797	......	......	33,879	....	......	......	......	11
....	....	95,355	8,678	495	......	......	....	60	......	......	......	12
107	1,576	120,731	34,129	6,937	3	......	23,251	....	......	1	2	13
2,357	23,936	213,980	12,127	2,064	......	2	102,470	141	......	......	......	14
3,128	7,758	111,523	7,200	441	......	1	22,819	4	......	1	28	15
3,809	9,623	106,560	8,271	1,107	......	......	41,770	7	......	2	......	16
4,284	23,951	278,818	42,233	28,407	......	......	71,001	121	6	......	......	17
1,708	5,723	127,565	15,946	4,411	......	......	26,827	5	12	......	......	18
10,114	29,368	388,395	24,827	1,591	......	......	65,720	78	......	75	3	19

	COUNTIES.	AGRICULTURAL PRODUCTS.									
		Flax, pounds.	Hemp, dew and water-rotted, tons.	Maple sugar, pounds.	Cane sugar, hhds. of 1,000 pounds.	Molasses, gallons.	Rice, pounds.	Tobacco, pounds.	Ginned cotton, bales of 400 pounds.	Wool, pounds.	Silk cocoons, pounds.
1	Autauga						75,647	1,160	12,016	12,792	
2	Baldwin						52,075		628	2,944	
3	Barbour				5	11,168	315,080		21,573	18,843	
4	Benton	120					17,802	17,008	5,995	13,295	
5	Bibb						1,184	312	4,643	11,762	
6	Blount						330	4,271	248	8,784	
7	Butler					42	30,930		4,094	10,851	
8	Chambers					45	31,043	193	17,442	20,037	
9	Cherokee	837		160		2	8,296	23,582	2,717	10,523	
10	Choctaw						78,555		4,433	7,904	
11	Clarke				35	2,000	31,117	801	4,881	8,954	
12	Coffee				3	6,953	65,863	785	1,408	4,120	
13	Conecuh				1	397	75,970		4,628	11,137	150
14	Coosa						137	30	5,524	13,131	
15	Covington					859	37,798	170	416	2,540	
16	Dale					9,986	68,950	505	2,158	6,512	
17	Dallas					2,520	123,750		35,275	21,493	
18	DeKalb	2,141		10		1	1,524	6,457	260	7,182	
19	Fayette				2	284	16,001	5,120	2,920	15,539	
20	Franklin						357	765	15,045	20,809	
21	Greene				18	1,170	34,803	770	25,680	26,937	
22	Hancock			70			13	2,391	26	1,594	
23	Henry				1	36,133	63,191		5,235	9,438	
24	Jackson			330			436	13,555	2,382	20,769	
25	Jefferson						2,640	1,355	2,451	10,319	
26	Lauderdale	300					1,024	6,849	10,606	19,538	
27	Lawrence						3,630	3,866	13,427	17,630	
28	Limestone	108					2,199	15,514	14,809	15,900	3
29	Lowndes						161,155	1,450	23,872	17,798	
30	Macon						191,140	20	29,089	15,411	
31	Madison	200		53			7,710	17,548	20,888	21,018	3
32	Marengo					175	14,550		32,295	15,908	
33	Marion					15	7,825	2,821	1,552	9,222	
34	Marshall	100		20			2,681	8,462	1,966	5,818	
35	Mobile						90,402			864	
36	Monroe				2	1,880	100,031	1,670	6,977	12,115	
37	Montgomery				20	161	156,539		25,326	26,043	
38	Morgan						1,960	3,252	4,777	9,679	
39	Perry					200	160		24,524	17,994	
40	Pickens						32,614	642	12,305	21,398	
41	Pike					830	72,310	271	8,679	11,803	
42	Randolph	75				3	7,185	3,609	1,986	11,223	10
43	Russell						119,150	5	21,088	10,912	
44	St. Clair						5,796	7,374	1,434	8,096	
45	Shelby						638	3,633	3,737	10,837	
46	Sumter	40					13,340	100	14,066	14,741	
47	Talladega						3,316	878	8,509	16,755	
48	Tallapoosa						32,001	1,775	6,589	15,352	
49	Tuscaloosa						18,748	1,080	73,561	16,329	
50	Walker					8,604	711	4,745	592	6,124	1
51	Washington						44,300	193	988	3,158	
52	Wilcox						87,645		18,709	7,243	

STATISTICS OF

	Counties	Flax, pounds.	Hemp, dew and water-rotted, tons.	Maple sugar, pounds.	Cane sugar, hhds. of 1,000 pounds.	Molasses, gallons.	Rice, pounds.	Tobacco, pounds.	Ginned cotton, bales of 400 pounds.	Wool, pounds.	Silk cocoons, pounds.
1	Arkansas						180	750	3,769	785	
2	Ashley						3,580	42,130	689	526	
3	Benton									4,154	
4	Bradley	100					4,370	80	1,425	1,916	1
5	Carroll	1,618		820			70	7,839		8,711	5
6	Chicot						1,700		12,192	5,391	
7	Clark						104	1,713	826	1,975	
8	Conway								499	4,294	
9	Crawford	40						200	986	4,711	
10	Crittenden								698	530	
11	Dallas						1,450	582	1,556	1,306	
12	Desha							230	2,672	635	
13	Drew	50					67	1,436	1,516	1,608	
14	Franklin			25			55	2,585	801	4,909	
15	Fulton	205				8	182	9,247	27	2,397	
16	Greene	20		405		10		5,123	15	3,526	
17	Hempstead						111	1,152	2,552	7,633	
18	Hot Springs	5					375	1,079	130	1,005	3
19	Independence	840						14,330	274	6,466	

AGRICULTURAL PRODUCTS.					MANUFACTURES.				REMARKS.	
					Establishments.					
Beeswax and honey, pounds.	Value of animals slaughtered.	Value of produce of market gardens.	Value of orchard produce.	Wine, gallons.	Capital.	Hands employed.	Annual product.	Produced in families.		
18,685	$ 101,928	$ 496	$ 748	......	$ 239,025	330	$ 298,652	$ 98,348	....	1
1,355	23,030	3,325	....	......	567,236	366	1[illegible]7,540	1,744	....	2
34,295	134,907	....	330	......	30,720	123	122,750	31,839	....	3
17,971	107,011	107	6	......	60,600	118	88,251	65,308	....	4
17,273	54,897	....	....	......	129,400	120	73,968	22,431	....	5
9,802	32,539	....	25	......	11,700	23	17,075	21,480	....	6
25	57,035	....	....	......	37,800	52	21,650	16,855	....	7
51,865	162,962	....	250	......	59,335	136	172,079	40,714	....	8
12,487	94,818	1,141	....	......	35,110	45	31,755	76,111	....	9
6,752	62,418	....	....	......	....	......	....	13,461	Formed in 1848 from	10
37,112	66,391	....	....	......	38,870	84	42,858	28,301	Sumter & Washingt'n	11
19,394	49,083	....	4,165	70	10,970	18	8,268	26,406	Formed in 1842 from	12
14,356	70,070	....	....	......	22,175	43	23,620	21,281	Dale.	13
29,657	79,256	....	....	......	51,900	83	34,700	98,118	....	14
7,449	28,111	....	....	......	5,700	30	9,050	14,890	....	15
19,187	65,771	....	....	......	....	......	....	26,045	Divided in 1842 to form	16
18,634	195,746	10	20	......	154,780	159	194,420	24,799	Coffee.	17
7,606	42,470	....	20	......	4,250	21	10,470	27,573	....	18
27,030	64,691	....	....	......	13,800	49	37,840	80,687	....	19
910	122,561	....	470	......	66,900	111	105,200	42,333	....	20
40,559	240,289	100	615	7	146,185	199	137,715	66,016	....	21
1,815	9,689	....	25	......	....	......	....	9,032	Formed in 1850 from	22
12,947	90,051	....	....	......	....	......	....	43,178	Walker.	23
16,059	83,018	10	....	......	7,010	30	18,140	42,600	....	24
22,346	56,849	....	7	......	6,000	38	9,728	37,692	....	25
9,972	97,393	20	....	......	195,175	277	224,050	47,844	....	26
13,729	106,185	....	....	......	22,580	61	41,859	58,970	....	27
12,457	94,774	....	....	......	35,175	98	61,105	44,905	....	28
27,074	126,154	....	....	......	28,000	25	32,700	20,041	....	29
35,990	176,180	....	50	......	89,300	130	106,090	35,962	....	30
12,139	124,125	836	553	......	239,350	372	307,925	43,449	....	31
1,420	167,105	100	50	......	6,700	26	17,706	25,115	....	32
11,729	52,391	....	121	......	4,600	21	16,800	38,084	....	33
10,022	36,930	....	140	......	15,250	41	23,680	22,655	....	34
620	181,322	67,579	3,360	85	522,800	540	1,261,450	240	....	35
31,516	96,903	20	42	......	37,425	70	33,550	48,513	....	36
37,592	197,008	8,620	297	1	111,100	121	157,200	31,869	....	37
4,759	56,085	80	237	......	3,035	25	15,550	28,569	....	38
19,379	116,353	....	20	......	33,750	96	43,530	20,211	....	39
11,761	144,107	....	....	......	40,700	100	62,230	51,743	....	40
49,465	135,131	....	....	......	8,250	13	12,360	52,300	....	41
18,299	97,834	....	552	7	7,350	83	30,339	61,225	....	42
....	....	450	580	50	7,400	14	9,000	25,000	....	43
18,991	50,482	....	....	......	....	......	....	48,651	....	44
28,184	85,726	....	10	......	19,000	32	29,800	63,091	....	45
17,634	156,400	....	....	......	26,325	51	39,500	24,524	Divided in 1848 to form	46
7,663	120,766	....	....	......	37,290	92	75,039	42,489	Choctaw.	47
41,007	93,401	450	35	......	66,850	143	73,925	46,739	....	48
19,453	96,449	30	....	......	176,550	264	183,810	23,947	[Hancock.	49
5,087	35,977	1,447	2,680	......	9,135	43	22,799	27,532	Divided in 1850 to form	50
3,451	7,726	....	....	......	....	......	....	3,208	Divided in 1848 to form	51
2,057	74,987	....	....	......	8,050	22	11,150	20,002	Choctaw.	52

ARKANSAS.

Beeswax and honey, pounds.	Value of animals slaughtered.	Value of produce of market gardens.	Value of orchard produce.	Wine, gallons.	Capital.	Hands employed.	Annual product.	Produced in families.	Remarks.	
8,457	16,656	....	710	......	....	......	....	395	[Drew.	1
526	20,942	....	20	......	....	......	....	2,428	Formed in 1848 from	2
100	11,243	....	3,242	......	8,700	21	11,200	9,608	[Dallas.	3
787	28,770	....	77	......	1,200	3	1,600	6,632	Divided in 1844 to form	4
1,775	16,992	20	867	......	500	1	1,000	19,983	Divided in 1842 to form	5
4,395	30,978	815	125	......	....	......	....	230	Newton.	6
8,446	28,132	70	1,294	......	1,200	3	2,400	12,253	Divided in 1844 to form	7
....	19,294	....	....	......	3,000	16	4,000	20,361	Dallas.	8
3,467	32,558	755	2,020	......	16,040	36	38,123	19,885	....	9
1,240	13,275	....	250	......	....	......	....	130	....	10
210	32,124	4,969	135	......	4,025	23	11,000	5,980	Formed in 1844 from	11
942	15,760	....	70	......	2,200	4	1,860	30	Clark and Bradley.	12
1,592	21,477	28	2,698	......	2,480	15	4,900	5,243	Formed '46 from Chicot;	13
10,352	27,603	....	76	......	1,350	9	6,105	16,848	div. '48 to form Ashley.	14
1,571	8,011	321	503	......	....	......	....	8,332	Formed in 1842 from	15
13,468	21,389	....	....	......	....	......	....	41,515	Izard.	16
9,467	51,596	40	84	25	19,500	34	16 114	17,972	....	17
870	21,187	938	45	......	5,700	16	9,450	7,198	Divided in 1842 to form	18
1,432	43,297	....	315	......	9,900	26	20,100	25,729	Montgomery.	19

	COUNTIES.	POPULATION.								
		Whites.			Colored.		All classes.		Total population.	
		Male.	Female.	Total.	Free.	Slave.	Male.	Female.	1850.	1840.
20	Izard	1,548	1,469	3,017	....	196	1,650	1,563	3,213	2,240
21	Jackson............	1,356	1,161	2,517	6	563	1,636	1,450	3,086	1,540
22	Jefferson	1,694	1,503	3,197	16	2,621	3,047	2,787	5,834	2,566
23	Johnson.......	2,387	2,102	4,489	7	731	2,741	2,486	5,227	3,433
24	Lafayette	1,011	889	1,900	....	3,320	2,760	2,460	5,220	2,200
25	Lawrence..........	2,575	2,307	4,882	4	388	2,763	2,511	5,274	2,835
26	Madison	2,395	2,264	4,659	....	164	2,473	2,350	4,823	2,775
27	Marion	1,074	979	2,053	129	126	1,212	1,096	2,308	1,325
28	Mississippi.........	824	672	1,496	7	865	1,261	1,107	2,368	1,410
29	Monroe.............	851	800	1,651	3	395	1,047	1,002	2,049	936
30	Montgomery	984	907	1,891	1	66	1,016	942	1,958	....
31	Newton.............	871	833	1,704	7	47	896	862	1,758	....
32	Ouachita	3,331	2,954	6,285	2	3,304	5,018	4,573	9,591	....
33	Perry	501	456	957	6	15	509	469	978	....
34	Phillips	2,374	1,967	4,341	3	2,591	3,681	3,254	6,935	3,547
35	Pike	925	826	1,751	....	110	973	888	1,861	969
36	Poinsett............	1,086	940	2,02	3	279	1,231	1,077	2,308	1,320
37	Polk	626	570	1,196	....	67	659	604	1,263	....
38	Pope...............	2,22	2,009	4,231	....	479	2,464	2,246	4,710	2,850
39	Prairie..............	974	838	1,812	12	273	1,109	988	2,097	....
40	Pulaski.............	2,404	2,102	4,506	32	1,119	2,938	2,719	5,657	5,350
41	Randolph	1,596	1,433	3,029	3	243	1,710	1,565	3,275	2,196
42	St. Francis..........	2,042	1,728	3,770	2	707	2,403	2,076	4,479	2,499
43	Saline..............	1,833	1,561	3,394	6	503	2,089	1,814	3,903	2,061
44	Scott	1,543	1,378	2,921	16	146	1,621	1,462	3,083	1,694
45	Searcy.............	1,027	923	1,950	....	29	1,039	940	1,979	936
46	Sevier	1,518	1,319	2,837	31	1,372	2,208	2,032	4,240	2,810
47	Union	2,970	2,556	5,526	5	4,767	5,387	4,911	10,298	2,889
48	Van Buren	1,460	1,301	2,761	....	103	1,500	1,364	2,864	1,518
49	Washington.........	4,552	4,205	8,757	14	1,199	5,119	4,851	9,970	7,148
50	White	1,211	1,098	2,309	2	308	1,349	1,270	2,619	929
51	Yell	1,578	1,324	2,902	15	424	1,792	1,549	3,341	....

STATISTICS OF

1	Butte...............	3,441	100	3,541	33	....	3,473	101	3,574	....
2	Calaveras...........	16,537	265	16,802	82	....	16,617	267	16,884	....
3	Colusi	77	38	115	....	....	77	38	115	....
4	Contra Costa........	....	....	....	....	....	....	....	....	....
5	El Dorado...........	19,231	677	19,908	149	....	19,373	684	20,057	....
6	Los Angeles	2,006	1,512	3,518	12	....	2,011	1,519	3,530	....
7	Marin	232	89	321	2	....	234	89	323	....
8	Mariposa	4,104	80	4,184	195	....	4,271	108	4,379	....
9	Mendocino	40	15	55	....	....	40	15	55	....
10	Monterey............	1,121	733	1,854	18	....	1,135	737	1,872	....
11	Napa	242	163	405	....	....	242	163	405	....
12	Sacramento.........	8,277	598	8,875	212	....	8,472	615	9,087	....
13	Santa Barbara.......	617	564	1,181	4	....	620	565	1,185	....
14	Santa Clara.........	....	....	....	....	....	....	....	....	....
15	Santa Cruz..........	411	232	643	....	....	411	232	643	....
16	San Diego	552	238	790	8	....	558	240	798	....
17	San Francisco.......	....	....	....	....	....	....	....	....	....
18	San Joaquin	3,402	214	3,616	31	....	3,429	218	3,647	....
19	San Luis Obispo....	193	142	335	1	....	194	142	336	....
20	Shasta	371	7	378	....	....	371	7	378	....
21	Solano..............	449	94	543	37	....	482	98	580	....
22	Sonoma.............	355	204	559	1	....	356	204	560	....
23	Sutter	3,300	124	3,424	20	....	3,320	124	3,444	....
24	Trinity	1,534	83	1,617	18	....	1,552	83	1,635	....
25	Tuolumne	7,871	417	8,288	63	....	7,930	421	8,351	....
26	Yolo................	953	123	1,076	10	....	960	126	1,086	....
27	Yuba	9,392	215	9,607	66	....	9,452	221	9,673	....

STATISTICS OF

1	Washington	18,494	19,447	37,941	10,059	3,687	24,164	27,523	51,687	33,745

NATIVITIES, DWELLINGS, &c.				EDUCATION AND RELIGION.									
Born out of State.				Colleges, academies, and private schools.		Public Schools.							
United States.	Foreign countries.	Dwellings.	Families.	Pupils.	Annual income.	Pupils.	Annual income.	Total educational income.	White scholars during the year.	Whites 5 and under 20 years old.	Whites over 20 unable to read & write.	Accommodation of churches—persons.	
1,768	5	496	498	....	....	195	$1,900	$1,900	611	1,322	448	2,500	20
1,800	8	447	447	....	....	125	1,200	1,200	112	1,042	214	....	21
2,127	35	595	605	25	$550	234	4,345	4,895	415	1,264	311	2,525	22
2,661	11	777	796	280	1,320	....	....	1,320	684	1,900	548	500	23
1,368	4	349	349	....	....	125	2,500	2,500	207	706	214	1,050	24
2,773	12	800	800	....	....	366	716	716	782	2,140	759	....	25
2,610	2	843	843	....	....	410	3,478	3,478	637	2,026	606	3,550	26
1,179	4	361	362	....	....	150	1,490	1,490	154	870	356	....	27
1,073	13	284	284	....	....	55	189	189	157	538	148	....	28
1,093	13	310	323	....	....	....	150	150	225	669	231	150	29
1,132	4	319	322	....	....	100	600	600	260	805	264	950	30
972	....	288	288	....	....	130	....	....	91	751	373	700	31
4,628	20	1,122	1,122	90	....	90	2,436	2,436	859	2,586	76	....	32
475	17	154	158	....	....	45	210	210	69	413	149	....	33
2,951	98	809	809	95	85	....	....	85	462	1,639	367	1,250	34
1,015	....	306	306	....	....	214	....	....	201	718	95	550	35
1,314	5	350	350	....	....	220	....	....	223	866	39	950	36
670	5	189	189	28	....	89	200	200	205	512	220	....	37
2,558	13	695	695	....	....	326	3,892	3,892	1,104	1,790	538	2,195	38
1,160	63	328	328	20	....	100	....	....	166	745	143	635	39
2,523	337	808	817	195	4,600	247	1,581	6,181	626	1,709	477	1,500	40
1,738	18	538	538	....	....	157	....	....	475	1,286	557	375	41
2,490	16	643	643	45	....	305	200	200	460	1,633	381	775	42
2,203	7	621	640	....	....	500	....	....	1,057	1,453	80	6,200	43
1,363	12	514	514	....	....	250	250	250	501	1,260	456	1,000	44
1,090	1	322	330	....	....	120	450	450	247	767	354	150	45
1,439	33	500	500	....	....	264	700	700	265	1,227	111	1,550	46
4,234	29	964	964	275	8,700	....	....	8,700	891	2,202	282	4,200	47
1,776	4	448	448	....	....	174	....	....	414	1,201	539	....	48
4,508	37	1,430	1,430	236	4,050	915	....	4,050	1,991	3,890	713	3,700	49
1,604	17	455	465	....	....	....	....	....	250	937	222	....	50
1,625	13	473	473	....	....	200	2,000	2,000	547	1,235	316	1,100	51

CALIFORNIA.*

United States.	Foreign countries.	Dwellings.	Families.	Pupils.	Annual income.	Pupils.	Annual income.	Total educational income.	White scholars during the year.	Whites 5 and under 20 years old.	Whites over 20 unable to read & write.	Accommodation of churches—persons.	
2,673	662	850	850	....	....	....	....	....	....	235	....	....	1
10,857	5,855	5,588	5,588	....	....	....	....	....	67	905	1,839	....	2
90	13	21	22	....	....	....	....	....	....	17	....	....	3
....	....	....	....	....	....	....	....	....	....	....	....	....	4
16,007	3,683	6,207	6,913	....	....	....	....	....	554	1,857	985	300	5
308	807	518	518	....	....	....	....	....	9	1,392	1,096	1,500	6
133	67	55	58	....	....	....	....	....	3	88	22	300	7
3,732	633	885	885	....	....	....	....	....	....	183	....	....	8
45	3	9	10	....	....	....	....	....	....	16	1	....	9
201	394	311	322	....	....	....	....	....	110	624	238	600	10
335	15	159	159	75	4,000	....	....	4,000	53	145	....	....	11
7,296	1,466	2,418	2,487	45	6,000	....	....	6,000	21	749	44	2,400	12
19	92	149	171	....	1,470	12	3,600	5,070	71	536	299	3,800	13
....	....	....	....	....	....	....	....	....	....	....	....	....	14
232	60	101	101	....	....	....	....	....	81	194	59	200	15
297	172	115	115	....	....	....	....	....	....	216	108	....	16
....	....	....	....	....	....	....	....	....	....	....	....	....	17
2,086	1,360	868	868	35	2,800	....	....	2,800	....	353	....	600	18
22	92	53	60	....	....	....	....	....	13	139	....	....	19
243	48	104	104	....	....	....	....	....	....	19	....	....	20
390	95	178	178	15	....	....	....	....	5	86	12	....	21
347	83	119	119	....	....	37	....	....	5	192	1	500	22
2,331	557	1,150	1,150	....	....	....	....	....	....	214	....	....	23
1,160	430	558	563	....	....	....	....	....	....	117	....	....	24
3,925	4,340	1,456	1,456	....	....	....	....	....	....	664	408	....	25
938	120	317	317	....	....	....	....	....	....	165	6	....	26
8,908	755	1,553	1,553	....	....	....	....	....	....	378	....	....	27

THE DISTRICT OF COLUMBIA.

United States.	Foreign countries.	Dwellings.	Families.	Pupils.	Annual income.	Pupils.	Annual income.	Total educational income.	White scholars during the year.	Whites 5 and under 20 years old.	Whites over 20 unable to read & write.	Accommodation of churches—persons.	
18,661	4,918	7,917	8,343	2,551	108,040	2,169	14,232	122,272	6,103	13,357	1,457	34,120	1

* For the results of the State census for the year 1852, see the end of the volume.

	COUNTIES.	LAND OCCUPIED OR IMPROVED.				LIVE STOCK UPON FARMS.			
		Farms.	Acres improved.	Acres unimproved.	Value with improvements and implements.	Horses, asses, and mules.	Neat cattle.	Sheep.	Swine.
20	Izard	332	9,467	9,115	$158,221	1,373	5,530	2,327	13,339
21	Jackson	232	10,319	23,328	264,812	1,020	4,973	384	14,224
22	Jefferson	317	22,245	62,167	882,259	2,009	8,816	1,391	16,075
23	Johnson	526	17,742	36,017	346,826	1,880	7,347	3,283	20,765
24	Lafayette	177	27,476	56,802	512,434	1,392	5,515	498	14,919
25	Lawrence	601	20,188	34,623	296,227	2,718	7,463	3,678	22,030
26	Madison	660	19,319	27,029	285,718	2,353	8,241	5,851	21,787
27	Marion	255	7,776	17,477	151,510	1,492	4,531	1,773	9,582
28	Mississippi	170	8,111	50,544	344,556	739	3,693	100	8,622
29	Monroe	183	4,501	28,725	103,952	583	2,766	341	13,753
30	Montgomery	215	6,659	3,239	112,586	740	4,381	970	10,601
31	Newton	230	5,555	7,814	70,845	833	2,823	1,601	9,143
32	Ouachita	697	43,908	71,150	350,806	2,362	7,407	1,494	30,242
33	Perry	75	2,095	2,851	28,151	312	2,216	382	4,563
34	Phillips	409	26,427	92,236	1,086,775	1,974	8,084	686	24,047
35	Pike	207	5,531	8,337	91,803	492	2,710	866	7,357
36	Poinsett	264	8,046	51,354	116,242	730	3,619	678	16,283
37	Polk	155	4,237	1,652	57,852	441	2,384	726	5,524
38	Pope	534	15,502	22,260	291,338	1,622	7,593	2,717	19,129
39	Prairie	155	6,615	52,194	196,995	680	3,318	504	7,508
40	Pulaski	306	12,939	49,299	457,363	1,348	7,064	1,152	13,784
41	Randolph	396	14,377	23,240	189,367	1,561	5,376	2,47[illegible]	14,977
42	St. Francis	348	14,442	50,219	301,655	1,380	5,663	845	18,822
43	Saline	405	17,871	28,710	253,076	1,338	5,749	1,329	15,112
44	Scott	365	10,104	7,685	115,048	1,393	4,424	1,691	15,995
45	Searcy	246	7,440	1,812	96,276	805	3,072	1,927	12,887
46	Sevier	326	18,221	37,567	263,544	1,377	8,976	2,045	25,579
47	Union	679	56,841	97,435	758,872	2,383	8,976	2,161	36,234
48	Van Buren	380	11,092	9,403	145,644	1,154	4,829	1,849	11,557
49	Washington	850	38,847	108,130	807,873	4,531	12,822	10,916	33,257
50	White	307	8,515	25,584	172,021	782	3,718	698	9,967
51	Yell	330	11,693	17,896	232,203	1,289	6,057	1,510	19,361

STATISTICS OF

1	Butte								
2	Calaveras	80		14,820	91,553	1,275	1,981	18	19
3	Colusi	3	128	34,420	60,100	65	306	96	42
4	Contra Costa								
5	El Dorado								
6	Los Angeles	134	2,648	1,034,550	685,450	5,838	89,977	6,541	172
7	Marin	39	8	93,380	125,650	862	7,079	500	262
8	Mariposa								
9	Mendocino	16		13,320	6,250	66	161		111
10	Monterey	115	13,713	690,610	900,399	912	37,348	1,780	73
11	Napa	51	1,140	23,570	184,440	783	12,008		212
12	Sacramento	19	2,044	78,992	229,050	811	6,944	1,510	5[illegible]
13	Santa Barbara	76	9,234	1,265,568	755,037	5,247	62,694	4,807	142
14	Santa Clara								
15	Santa Cruz	130	2,045	287,500	417,800	794	15,901	725	62
16	San Diego								
17	San Francisco								
18	San Joaquin								
19	San Luis Obispo								
20	Shasta								
21	Solano	23	68	74,563	132,265	498	3,312	26	450
22	Sonoma	90	897	243,766	225,760	3,596	17,777	1,071	274
23	Sutter	41	200	1,000	110,000	1,285	1,865	500	90
24	Trinity								
25	Tuolumne								
26	Yolo	55	279	5,463	53,770	1,353	5,306		287
27	Yuba								

STATISTICS OF

1	Washington	264	16,267	11,187	1,770,680	881	1,040	15	1,635

AGRICULTURAL PRODUCTS.

Wheat, bushels.	Rye & oats, bushels.	Indian corn, bushels.	Irish and sweet potatoes, bushels.	Peas and beans, bushels.	Barley, bushels.	Buckwheat, bushels.	Butter and cheese, pounds.	Hay, tons.	Hops, pounds.	Clover & other grass seeds, bushels.	Flaxseed, bushels.	
7,054	12,273	173,479	8,589	1,872	110	......	47,799	....	......	......	......	20
415	1,635	108,615	12,024	8	......	......	41,450	....	......	......	......	21
81	1,494	191,829	21,531	7,944	25	......	26,378	224	......	6	......	22
6,812	35,257	251,070	20,023	1,353	......	......	49,252	24	......	12	......	23
86	3,995	160,090	24,609	19,576	......	......	22,270	16	......	......	......	24
11,802	23,172	283,457	17,750	653	......	......	71,981	15	1	6	10	25
23,422	36,628	342,764	16,980	341	......	7	77,119	188	......	2	255	26
5,358	12,741	144,302	8,345	108	......	......	41,215	10	......	......	......	27
....	50	200,250	6,785	390	......	......	21,273	340	......	268	......	28
225	2,455	70,321	8,063	433	......	......	15,681	28	......	......	......	29
5,287	3,585	85,280	8,439	1,518	......	3	41,875	2	......	......	......	30
2,835	6,584	94,125	6,458	1,345	......	......	12,006	2	......	......	......	31
1,194	9,299	290,696	81,327	56,988	......	......	42,223	....	......	......	......	32
259	1,530	31,770	3,980	....	......	......	6,833	4	......	......	......	33
....	1,839	281,889	23,684	....	......	40	20,340	17	......	......	......	34
1,474	2,942	58,826	5,600	541	......	......	7,330	....	......	......	2	35
2,079	4,990	98,746	9,246	479	......	......	23,294	3	......	......	......	36
1,892	4,163	43,405	6,273	635	......	2	7,967	14	......	16	......	37
4,596	19,770	202,830	18,918	505	......	16	162,393	15	30	7	......	38
474	2,820	54,905	7,269	340	......	......	18,962	108	......	......	......	39
543	6,643	191,085	21,118	347	......	10	50,137	385	60	11	1	40
6,792	17,976	176,669	10,998	943	......	5	37,802	4	5	2	......	41
336	5,516	181,442	23,225	2,019	4	......	30,483	....	......	......	......	42
3,922	9,015	186,305	17,658	2,361	......	......	29,635	486	......	21	2	43
1,756	18,297	128,460	14,094	756	......	17	34,520	....	......	......	......	44
4,878	14,801	123,618	5,572	78	......	......	2,283	2	......	5	......	45
1,637	8,078	142,030	23,494	5,806	......	......	49,655	1	......	......	......	46
662	15,753	341,406	99,305	65,208	......	......	33,861	....	......	......	......	47
3,181	12,758	154,565	7,263	290	......	2	13,661	....	......	......	......	48
34,472	136,833	557,757	35,725	431	12	......	105,941	847	......	83	......	49
1,291	5,676	110,935	6,305	593	20	......	14,335	....	......	......	......	50
5,208	13,238	127,335	12,812	1,860	......	20	69,365	23	......	......	......	51

CALIFORNIA.

Wheat, bushels.	Rye & oats, bushels.	Indian corn, bushels.	Irish and sweet potatoes, bushels.	Peas and beans, bushels.	Barley, bushels.	Buckwheat, bushels.	Butter and cheese, pounds.	Hay, tons.	Hops, pounds.	Clover & other grass seeds, bushels.	Flaxseed, bushels.	
....	....	....	....	......	......	......	....	....	......	......	......	1
....	....	....	....	......	......	......	....	....	......	......	......	2
1,100	....	250	....	......	......	......	....	....	......	......	......	3
....	....	....	....	......	......	......	....	....	......	......	......	4
....	....	....	....	......	......	......	....	....	......	......	......	5
5,926	....	8,391	380	944	3,440	......	....	....	......	......	......	6
....	....	....	1,000	......	......	......	....	....	......	......	......	7
....	....	....	....	......	......	......	....	....	......	......	......	8
....	....	200	....	......	......	......	....	....	......	......	......	9
....	....	....	....	......	......	......	....	....	......	......	......	10
....	....	....	651	440	890	......	....	258	......	......	......	11
7,500	....	....	900	......	3,050	......	....	1,780	......	......	......	12
2,602	....	3,065	454	858	1,432	......	805	....	......	......	......	13
....	....	....	....	......	......	......	....	....	......	......	......	14
....	....	....	....	......	......	......	....	....	......	......	......	15
....	....	....	....	......	......	......	....	....	......	......	......	16
....	....	....	....	......	......	......	....	....	......	......	......	17
....	....	....	....	......	......	......	....	....	......	......	......	18
....	....	....	....	......	......	......	....	....	......	......	......	19
....	....	....	....	......	......	......	....	....	......	......	......	20
....	....	....	....	......	......	......	....	....	......	......	......	21
....	....	80	5,707	......	900	......	50	....	......	......	......	22
200	....	250	1,200	50	......	......	....	....	......	......	......	23
....	....	....	....	......	......	......	....	....	......	......	......	24
....	....	....	....	......	......	......	....	....	......	......	......	25
....	....	....	....	......	......	......	....	....	......	......	......	26
....	....	....	....	......	......	......	....	....	......	......	......	27

THE DISTRICT OF COLUMBIA.

Wheat, bushels.	Rye & oats, bushels.	Indian corn, bushels.	Irish and sweet potatoes, bushels.	Peas and beans, bushels.	Barley, bushels.	Buckwheat, bushels.	Butter and cheese, pounds.	Hay, tons.	Hops, pounds.	Clover & other grass seeds, bushels.	Flaxseed, bushels.	
17,370	13,643	65,230	31,789	7,754	75	378	16,372	2,279	15	3	......	1

	COUNTIES.	AGRICULTURAL PRODUCTS.									
		Flax, pounds.	Hemp, dew and water-rotted, tons.	Maple sugar, pounds.	Cane sugar, hhds. of 1,000 pounds.	Molasses, gallons.	Rice, pounds.	Tobacco, pounds.	Ginned cotton, bales of 400 pounds.	Wool, pounds.	Silk cocoons, pounds.
20	Izard	520					215	8,205	78	4,756	
21	Jackson							100	870	162	
22	Jefferson						375	1,150	4,273	3,116	
23	Johnson	60					280	6,947	813	6,392	
24	Lafayette						1,650		1,977	1,316	
25	Lawrence	257					20	16,366	65	8,991	6
26	Madison	5,112		7,550				5,845	3	11,045	
27	Marion	25						5,071	1,100	2,777	
28	Mississippi								455	247	
29	Monroe							375	587	873	
30	Montgomery	140						1,650	39	2,652	
31	Newton	280		317			50	4,856		2,974	
32	Ouachita						42,350	910	3,302	2,732	
33	Perry							1,100		766	
34	Phillips							4,500	5,165	861	
35	Pike	200					558	1,385	301	1,603	
36	Poinsett							2,380	270	1,435	
37	Polk	55					920	1,910	22	1,562	
38	Pope			25			12	3,780	1,056	5,580	
39	Prairie								246	643	
40	Pulaski	5					50	590	478	2,624	
41	Randolph	470					1,202	22,732	1	4,844	
42	St. Francis						313	1,380	1,540	1,894	
43	Saline	704	15				10	2,240	1,287	2,300	
44	Scott						1,441	2,522	368	3,430	
45	Searcy			80				7,839		5,308	
46	Sevier						12	745	2,254	7,275	
47	Union						1,377		7,037	2,713	
48	Van Buren			108			100	3,975	112	4,477	1
49	Washington	1,585						19,987	1	20,613	22
50	White							1,920	262	727	
51	Yell								755	3,429	

STATISTICS OF

1	Butte										
2	Calaveras										
3	Colusi										
4	Contra Costa										
5	El Dorado										
6	Los Angeles							1,000		730	
7	Marin										
8	Mariposa										
9	Mendocino										
10	Monterey										
11	Napa										
12	Sacramento										
13	Santa Barbara									4,790	
14	Santa Clara										
15	Santa Cruz										
16	San Diego										
17	San Francisco										
18	San Joaquin										
19	San Luis Obispo										
20	Shasta										
21	Solano										
22	Sonoma										
23	Sutter										
24	Trinity										
25	Tuolumne										
26	Yolo										
27	Yuba										

STATISTICS OF

1	Washington							7,800		525	

AGRICULTURAL PRODUCTS.					MANUFACTURES.					
					Establishments.					
Beeswax and honey, pounds.	Value of animals slaughtered.	Value of produce of market gardens.	Value of orchard produce.	Wine, gallons.	Capital.	Hands employed.	Annual product.	Produced in families.	REMARKS.	
2,997	$16,155	....	....	......	$9,500	35	8,670	$24,281	Divided in 1842 to form	20
1,669	15,886	....	....	......	8,440	15	14,730	3,717	Fulton.	21
....	24,173	25	....	......	11,500	35	15,688	....	....	22
7,741	25,184	....	382	......	26,715	79	39,096	15,278	....	23
8,991	25,555	....	....	......	600	3	1,700	10,810	....	24
4,417	24,052	13	638	......	....	......	....	50,291	....	25
9,980	34,545	3,597	5,193	10	18,100	30	35,500	28,041	....	26
405	11,654	....	1,340	......	450	4	1,500	9,824	....	27
8,305	18,125	80	595	......	400	5	2,250	1,384	['44 to form Polk.	28
3,592	15,635	15	26	......	....	......	....	1,982	[Springs, divided in	29
1,143	11,639	30	340	......	6,600	21	20,150	7,117	Formed in '42 from Hot	30
1,825	12,477	348	571	......	....	......	....	12,972	Formed '42 f'm Carroll.	31
3,398	51,230	....	....	......	3,500	10	5,400	15,697	Formed '42 f'm Union.	32
270	5,305	....	285	......	3,500	6	1,680	2,014	....	33
2,040	37,631	265	1,010	......	17,100	42	36,150	4,168	....	34
2,041	9,652	....	114	......	4,200	6	2,900	4,820	....	35
11,286	16,758	....	....	......	1,000	2	1,100	8,695	....	36
2,685	6,433	....	....	......	600	2	3,700	7,515	Formed in '44 from Se-	37
1,347	20,729	312	714	......	32,600	93	36,900	14,352	vier and Montgomery	39
....	10,333	2,210	....	......	....	......	....	3,540	Formed '46 f'm Pulaski.	39
3,866	19,401	2,229	3,368	......	27,450	99	53,500	5,614	Divided in 1846 to form	40
591	19,583	....	....	......	12,000	13	11,400	14,133	Prairie.	41
7,015	30,895	70	646	......	....	......	....	5,916	....	42
397	25,339	....	1,244	......	6,500	22	12,250	12,705	....	43
361	20,913	....	782	......	18,900	30	31,060	12,426	....	44
2,373	9,750	....	182	......	....	......	....	22,330	[Polk.	45
9,276	23,465	....	756	......	1,600	9	5.200	14,463	Divided in 1844 to form	46
....	66,057	....	....	......	....	......	....	15,456	Divided in 1842 to form	47
1,485	28,422	....	125	......	....	......	....	18,024	Ouachita.	48
16,487	46,708	....	9,299	......	26,350	81	86,610	52,411	....	49
2,608	14,081	....	....	......	1,550	5	2,800	5,684	....	50
4.650	4,264	....	....	......	9,115	49	49,650	11,805	....	51

CALIFORNIA.

Beeswax and honey, pounds.	Value of animals slaughtered.	Value of produce of market gardens.	Value of orchard produce.	Wine, gallons.	Capital.	Hands employed.	Annual product.	Produced in families.	REMARKS.	
....	....	....	....	......	....	......	....	....	All the present counties	1
....	....	....	....	......	....	......	....	....	except Trinity were	2
....	....	....	....	......	....	......	....	....	formed Feb. 18, 1850.	3
....	....	....	....	......	....	......	....	....	Returns lost on their	4
....	....	....	....	......	117,865	274	884,184	....	way to this office.	5
....	42,101	6,550	1,840	57,355	1,000	2	8,560	7,000	....	6
....	....	....	1,200	......	10,000	18	69,885	....	....	7
....	....	....	....	......	730,182	3,343	8,894,160	....	....	8
....	....	....	....	......	....	......	....	....	....	9
....	....	....	....	......	....	......	....	....	....	10
....	....	....	....	......	....	......	....	....	....	11
....	....	41,000	....	......	112,950	274	2,869,735	....	....	12
....	53,622	....	1,660	700	....	......	....	....	....	13
....	....	....	....	......	....	......	....	....	Returns lost on their	14
....	....	....	....	......	27,000	36	100,000	....	way to this office.	15
....	....	....	....	......	....	......	....	....	....	16
....	....	....	....	......	....	......	....	....	Returns destroyed by	17
....	....	....	....	......	....	......	....	....	fire.	18
....	....	....	....	......	....	......	....	....	....	19
....	....	....	....	......	....	......	....	....	....	20
....	....	....	....	......	....	......	....	....	....	21
....	11,450	27,725	13,000	......	7,200	17	36,000	....	....	22
....	....	....	....	......	....	......	....	....	....	23
....	....	....	....	......	....	......	....	....	Formed May 25, 1850.	24
....	....	....	....	......	....	......	....	....	....	25
....	....	....	....	......	....	......	....	....	....	26
....	....	....	....	......	....	......	....	....	....	27

THE DISTRICT OF COLUMBIA.

Beeswax and honey, pounds.	Value of animals slaughtered.	Value of produce of market gardens.	Value of orchard produce.	Wine, gallons.	Capital.	Hands employed.	Annual product.	Produced in families.	REMARKS.	
550	9,038	67,222	14,843	863	888,965	2,17[illegible]	2,493,008	2,07[illegible]	....	1

	COUNTIES.	POPULATION.								
		Whites.			Colored.		All classes.		Total population.	
		Male.	Female.	Total.	Free.	Slave.	Male.	Female.	1850.	1840.
1	Fairfield	28,185	30,134	58,319	1,456	....	28,888	30,887	59,775	49,917
2	Hartford	33,882	34,825	68,707	1,260	....	34,478	35,489	69,967	55,629
3	Litchfield	22,270	21,952	44,222	1,031	....	22,821	22,432	45,253	40,448
4	Middlesex	13,322	13,605	26,927	289	....	13,469	13,747	27,216	24,879
5	New Haven	31,881	32,278	64,159	1,429	....	32,552	33,036	65,588	48,619
6	New London	25,373	24,940	50,313	1,508	....	26,181	25,640	51,821	44,463
7	Tolland	9,887	10,059	19,946	145	....	9,962	10,129	20,091	17,980
8	Windham	15,084	15,422	30,506	575	....	15,353	15,728	31,081	28,080

STATISTICS OF

1	Kent	8,202	7,882	16,084	6,385	347	11,593	11,223	22,816	19,872
2	New Castle	17,248	17,517	34,765	7,621	394	21,263	21,517	42,780	33,120
3	Sussex	10,296	10,024	20,320	4,067	1,549	13,099	12,837	25,936	25,093

STATISTICS OF

1	Alachua	888	729	1,617	1	906	1,343	1,181	2,524	2,282
2	Benton	360	244	604	....	322	526	400	926	....
3	Calhoun	486	400	886	38	453	741	636	1,377	1,142
4	Columbia	1,886	1,655	3,541	1	1,266	2,536	2,272	4,808	2,102
5	Dade	118	29	147	1	11	123	36	159	446
6	Duval	1,227	1,111	2,338	95	2,106	2,339	2,200	4,539	4,156
7	Escambia	1,538	1,106	2,644	375	1,332	2,358	1,993	4,351	3,993
8	Franklin	711	473	1,184	....	377	913	648	1,561	1,030
9	Gadsden	2,027	1,870	3,897	7	4,880	4,400	4,384	8,784	5,992
10	Hamilton	962	855	1,817	9	685	1,294	1,217	2,511	1,4 4
11	Hillsborough	1,114	592	1,706	11	660	1,491	886	2,377	452
12	Holmes	536	501	1,037	5	163	615	590	1,205	....
13	Jackson	1,627	1,448	3,075	30	3,534	3,437	3,202	6,639	4,681
14	Jefferson	1,419	1,356	2,775	5	4,938	3,875	3,843	7,718	5,713
15	Leon	1,695	1,488	3,183	56	8,203	5,830	5,612	11,442	10,713
16	Levy	150	170	320	....	145	221	244	465	....
17	Madison	1,482	1,320	2,802	....	2,688	2,922	2,568	5,490	2,644
18	Marion	1,147	921	2,068	1	1,269	1,781	1,557	3,338	....
19	Monroe	1,351	737	2,088	126	431	1,644	1,001	2,645	688
20	Nassau	524	537	1,061	26	1,077	1,059	1,105	2,164	1,892
21	Orange	139	99	238	2	226	260	206	466	73
22	Putnam	271	202	473	10	204	391	296	687	....
23	St. Johns	678	739	1,417	115	993	1,175	1,350	2,525	2,694
24	St. Lucie	90	21	111	1	27	107	32	139	....
25	Santa Rosa	1,131	964	2,095	4	784	1,585	1,298	2,883	....
26	Wakulla	616	548	1,164	1	790	1,008	947	1,955	....
27	Walton	774	707	1,481	....	336	946	871	1,817	1,461
28	Washington	758	676	1,434	12	504	1,007	943	1,950	859

STATISTICS OF

1	Appling	1,271	1,249	2,520	25	404	1,491	1,458	2,949	2,052
2	Baker	2,310	2,041	4,351	4	3,765	4,214	3,906	8,120	4,226
3	Baldwin	1,885	1,634	3,519	27	4,602	4,180	3,968	8,148	7,250
4	Bibb	3,619	3,390	7,009	53	5,637	6,271	6,428	12,699	9,802
5	Bryan	604	560	1,164	15	2,245	1,702	1,722	3,424	3,182
6	Bullock	1,435	1,405	2,840	....	1,460	2,163	2,137	4,300	3,102
7	Burke	2,759	2,359	5,118	150	10,832	8,350	7,750	16,100	13,176
8	Butts	1,888	1,792	3,680	3	2,805	3,282	3,206	6,488	5,308
9	Camden	1,028	1,041	2,069	4	4,246	3,030	3,289	6,319	6,075
10	Campbell	2,893	2,825	5,718	7	1,507	3,622	3,610	7,232	5,370
11	Carroll	4,174	4,078	8,252	4	1,101	4,711	4,646	9,357	5,252
12	Cass	5,333	4,938	10,271	21	3,008	6,868	6,432	13,300	9,390
13	Chatham	4,794	4,358	9,152	731	14,018	11,726	12,175	23,901	18,801
14	Chattooga	2,628	2,503	5,131	4	1,680	3,461	3,354	6,815	3,438
15	Cherokee	5,921	5,709	11,630	13	1,157	6,470	6,330	12,800	5,895
16	Clark	2,710	2,803	5,513	17	5,589	5,478	5,641	11,119	10,522
17	Clinch	282	224	506	2	129	344	293	637	....
18	Cobb	5,872	5,696	11,568	3	2,272	6,952	6,891	13,843	7,539
19	Columbia	1,838	1,779	3,617	72	8,272	6,018	5,943	11,961	11,356

NATIVITIES, DWELLINGS, &C.				EDUCATION AND RELIGION.									
Born out of State.				Colleges, academies, and private schools.		Public Schools.							
United States.	Foreign countries.	Dwellings.	Families.	Pupils.	Annual income.	Pupils.	Annual income.	Total educational income.	White scholars during year.	Whites 5 and under 20 years old.	Whites over 20 unable to read & write.	Accommodation of churches—persons.	
6,561	5,499	10,817	12,114	1,614	$47,321	9,051	$39,101	$86,422	13,073	18,943	992	52,630	1
7,594	10,072	11,318	13,284	1,529	28,924	15,392	49,773	78,697	15,846	21,307	1,013	55,990	2
4,968	3,244	8,721	9,247	611	11,516	8,828	24,678	36,194	10,417	13,961	405	34,665	3
782	2,995	4,726	5,324	725	15,700	5,916	16,328	32,028	5,979	8,309	39	27,800	4
6,577	9,288	10,860	13,167	1,582	76,352	10,781	42,662	119,014	13,122	19,766	864	54,265	5
6,709	4,774	8,336	10,079	1,215	14,915	10,073	30,953	45,868	11,610	15,766	970	40,126	6
2,456	982	3,741	4,081	35	113	4,381	11,642	11,755	4,839	6,328	150	15,975	7
5,929	1,664	5,494	6,152	423	4,765	6,847	16,083	20,848	7,547	9,884	306	25,848	8

DELAWARE.

United States.	Foreign countries.	Dwellings.	Families.	Pupils.	Annual income.	Pupils.	Annual income.	Total educational income.	White scholars during year.	Whites 5 and under 20 years old.	Whites over 20 unable to read & write.	Accommodation of churches—persons.	
1,623	184	3,873	3,883	175	1,551	2,403	11,395	12,946	3,726	6,267	1,546	12,500	1
8,800	5,031	7,098	7,234	1,900	62,321	3,227	20,456	82,777	6,870	12,440	907	29,616	2
1,032	38	4,319	4,322	80	1,160	3,340	12,010	13,170	3,620	7,902	2,083	13,625	3

FLORIDA.

United States.	Foreign countries.	Dwellings.	Families.	Pupils.	Annual income.	Pupils.	Annual income.	Total educational income.	White scholars during year.	Whites 5 and under 20 years old.	Whites over 20 unable to read & write.	Accommodation of churches—persons.	
854	9	274	274	......	....	30	....	....	79	642	272	635	1
325	10	113	117	......	....	60	960	960	93	223	65	875	2
598	12	165	165	......	....	44	....	....	105	377	95	200	3
1,830	8	569	569	......	....	162	2,356	2,356	278	1,471	363	2,700	4
36	85	23	23	......	....	......	....	....	....	31	15	....	5
936	69	451	455	......	....	64	....	....	159	850	165	3,050	6
1,337	469	563	563	25	$420	269	5,280	5,700	415	873	197	2,500	7
528	273	261	261	100	2,900	30	350	3,250	152	315	100	1,500	8
2,153	25	684	684	180	3,600	300	3,600	7,200	454	1,588	49	7,300	9
1,021	....	301	302	......	....	......	....	....	97	763	201	1,350	10
801	283	253	257	60	1,000	120	1,400	2,400	250	485	132	660	11
684	2	185	187	......	....	20	....	....	53	442	168	230	12
2,177	18	560	577	40	1,000	......	....	1,000	221	1,233	437	950	13
1,562	39	520	520	47	....	172	4,300	4,300	426	1,173	280	3,900	14
1,828	78	737	737	349	....	54	....	....	400	1,195	166	4,850	15
146	10	64	64	......	....	......	....	....	2	127	15	....	16
1,902	11	498	498	100	....	140	....	....	185	1,153	29	6,200	17
1,358	16	394	394	......	....	60	600	600	128	810	59	1,800	18
479	1,082	420	443	73	1,300	85	1,150	2,450	241	592	154	1,200	19
387	9	188	188	......	....	......	....	....	104	421	133	....	20
63	6	55	55	......	....	33	300	300	53	99	20	....	21
379	7	108	108	......	....	......	....	....	25	186	95	....	22
184	63	321	346	160	1,450	50	100	1,550	375	552	100	1,700	23
49	50	22	22	......	....	......	....	....	5	17	2	....	24
1,347	56	526	527	60	1,000	100	1,750	2,750	239	815	178	1,600	25
724	23	227	229	22	419	20	240	659	86	450	114	1,250	26
827	37	267	267	35	....	20	....	....	50	639	69	275	27
913	20	273	275	......	....	45	....	....	71	575	186	235	28

GEORGIA.

United States.	Foreign countries.	Dwellings.	Families.	Pupils.	Annual income.	Pupils.	Annual income.	Total educational income.	White scholars during year.	Whites 5 and under 20 years old.	Whites over 20 unable to read & write.	Accommodation of churches—persons.	
396	3	410	410	......	....	222	806	806	218	1,066	379	2,550	1
970	35	755	755	100	....	250	413	413	489	1,724	608	19,000	2
326	139	647	647	189	8,150	85	3,794	11,944	310	1,340	8	2,500	3
1,503	373	1,234	1,280	425	18,300	390	4,780	23,080	1,191	2,657	161	5,690	4
48	3	212	212	......	....	100	300	300	155	487	39	1,450	5
123	19	477	487	......	....	253	3,150	3,150	347	1,201	250	2,150	6
367	210	1,017	1,017	127	3,200	150	3,866	7,066	654	1,846	684	7,250	7
655	17	642	642	85	....	211	374	374	546	1,506	132	4,897	8
283	42	400	400	45	450	70	1,150	1,600	188	830	95	8,870	9
1,320	49	920	920	......	....	450	276	276	1,214	2,494	138	5,010	10
1,924	12	1,379	1,379	140	....	700	700	700	1,383	3,565	1,135	550	11
4,971	115	1,712	1,750	80	....	620	375	375	1,245	4,371	912	7,900	12
1,856	2,276	1,915	1,979	191	5,700	340	6,954	12,654	1,180	2,712	227	9,025	13
2,028	3	869	869	20	400	330	260	660	782	2,098	359	5,300	14
4,855	25	1,970	1,994	93	1,600	650	775	2,375	1,703	4,894	1,826	8,850	15
860	66	1,024	1,024	357	19,700	482	5,003	24,703	605	2,276	294	7,500	16
76	1	76	76	......	....	......	....	....	13	243	66	....	17
3,246	56	1,918	1,918	130	....	210	....	....	1,275	5,088	397	5,500	18
212	38	751	751	230	3,600	260	3,600	7,200	474	1,400	23	10,000	19

	COUNTIES.	LAND OCCUPIED OR IMPROVED.				LIVE STOCK UPON FARMS.			
		Farms.	Acres improved.	Acres unimproved.	Value with improvements and implements.	Horses, asses, and mules.	Neat cattle.	Sheep.	Swine.
1	Fairfield	3,155	206,525	58,367	$13,252,292	3,921	31,245	12,055	12,886
2	Hartford	3,850	280,317	84,845	14,004,683	5,280	30,687	22,487	12,175
3	Litchfield	3,621	346,697	119,288	12,828,479	4,973	46,869	47,900	15,470
4	Middlesex	2,018	130,494	32,667	4,724,958	1,483	14,881	10,323	3,869
5	New Haven	2,794	206,325	75,378	10,413,662	3,476	25,429	15,327	8,763
6	New London	2,619	221,997	103,168	8,506,985	2,691	24,635	29,402	9,659
7	Tolland	1,943	163,677	55,478	3,895,150	2,321	16,123	18,935	4,623
8	Windham	2,445	212,146	86,510	6,992,754	2,783	22,806	17,752	9,027

STATISTICS OF

1	Kent	1,655	174,784	107,945	4,099,945	4,282	14,808	7,793	16,092
2	New Castle	1,662	168,076	50,872	11,748,815	6,036	20,229	5,908	10,918
3	Sussex	2,746	238,002	216,465	3,541,550	4,325	18,174	13,802	29,251

STATISTICS OF

1	Alachua	233	9,270	46,234	189,412	718	17,627	502	11,710
2	Benton	82	2,657	10,996	85,839	215	10,083	38	2,636
3	Calhoun	63	2,282	10,373	162,401	164	2,852	329	3,216
4	Columbia	475	18,467	28,012	274,585	1,128	29,090	955	24,651
5	Dade	6	51	36	2,300	1	....	....	13
6	Duval	167	12,056	73,568	316,508	667	13,778	539	8,154
7	Escambia	34	1,172	6,431	35,485	134	5,074	366	2,043
8	Franklin	......	....	472,000	no returns.	66	791	....	893
9	Gadsden	482	50,574	107,454	1,004,946	1,794	17,571	3,171	19,570
10	Hamilton	205	10,733	16,251	136,252	519	8,762	457	8,994
11	Hillsborough	120	3,984	19,215	247,657	278	19,710	114	5,141
12	Holmes	103	3,833	821	22,879	218	5,397	506	5,356
13	Jackson	287	33,287	55,515	442,433	1,303	13,251	1,380	17,402
14	Jefferson	377	49,403	104,956	597,065	1,947	11,889	[illegible]	18,554
15	Leon	356	80,952	97,625	1,840,537	2,739	14,398	6,742	23,341
16	Levy	......	1,069	4,802	34,015	118	4,342	....	1,842
17	Madison	262	25,580	42,955	548,595	1,206	19,881	[illegible]	13,482
18	Marion	329	11,451	44,168	378,580	695	21,251	346	12,007
19	Monroe	6	39	155	4,453	2	15	....	13
20	Nassau	137	8,370	28,776	108,706	382	8,763	735	6,825
21	Orange	19	963	4,083	74,095	70	3,058	....	799
22	Putnam	20	693	2,755	35,245	77	2,570	....	[illegible]
23	St. Johns	34	2,486	12,050	174,295	194	2,637	65	717
24	St. Lucie	......	....	....	....	......	....	....	....
25	Santa Rosa	91	1,815	37,971	63,414	264	8,715	611	4,901
26	Wakulla	100	7,018	5,932	70,800	305	3,624	175	5,016
27	Walton	161	4,446	5,485	47,582	302	9,273	1,143	4,796
28	Washington	155	6,378	7,621	83,825	344	6,683	431	5,972

STATISTICS OF

1	Appling	313	9,957	343,701	152,536	671	17,736	2,328	20,835
2	Baker	444	56,954	215,043	1,607,214	2,096	28,481	3,985	28,365
3	Baldwin	240	71,449	157,999	695,557	1,785	8,156	4,398	15,049
4	Bibb	308	44,919	90,321	958,472	1,481	6,804	2,630	15,470
5	Bryan	209	21,577	148,823	326,514	590	9,816	1,721	7,573
6	Bullock	412	26,760	473,233	364,965	1,309	16,528	6,844	18,677
7	Burke	712	190,910	334,028	2,416,997	4,879	15,040	7,778	40,536
8	Butts	391	50,369	63,505	710,140	1,650	[illegible]	3,064	15,238
9	Camden	235	25,222	181,675	932,058	712	16,524	1,649	8,767
10	Campbell	694	40,118	104,300	907,367	1,854	5,355	3,532	18,544
11	Carroll	782	38,522	178,649	723,818	2,202	10,778	4,812	25,827
12	Cass	601	52,575	15,591	1,569,446	2,470	8,158	5,873	24,149
13	Chatham	132	31,888	110,403	2,217,491	811	5,707	2,807	3,067
14	Chattooga	419	29,325	78,186	826,318	1,790	6,582	4,242	18,789
15	Cherokee	1,000	50,535	128,501	969,231	2,054	8,460	8,932	27,273
16	Clark	400	91,148	107,105	1,124,465	2,062	7,564	4,693	17,074
17	Clinch	58	3,118	42,893	60,668	191	5,570	293	3,409
18	Cobb	931	52,697	155,557	800,170	2,669	9,254	8,015	26,965
19	Columbia	489	147,684	152,693	1,606,232	3,176	[illegible]	7,632	29,619

AGRICULTURAL PRODUCTS.												
Wheat, bushels.	Rye & oats, bushels.	Indian corn, bushels.	Irish and sweet potatoes, bushels.	Peas and beans, bushels.	Barley, bushels.	Buckwheat, bushels.	Butter and cheese, pounds.	Hay, tons.	Hops, pounds.	Clover & other grass seeds, bushels.	Flaxseed, bushels.	
21,962	373,640	350,603	381,158	81	420	38,238	1,210,088	72,010	2	441	323	1
5,260	360,985	381,744	490,413	2,303	1,533	37,888	1,440,084	80,817	125	316	2	2
6,364	390,707	279,136	293,511	980	2,386	66,447	4,077,051	109,238	48	1,084	362	3
4,591	79,059	95,118	223,733	162	1,348	4,864	533,418	38,579	10	87	......	4
2,819	220,586	225,881	445,125	1,157	4,842	25,326	1,401,736	67,176	153	142	9	5
189	128,317	234,412	354,397	5,645	3,359	11,197	1,137,079	53,181	53	1,065	......	6
429	117,033	127,873	204,353	2,768	1,882	17,247	303,690	38,992	58	1,828	......	7
148	189,394	240,276	297,115	5,994	3,329	28,090	1,416,077	56,138	105	25,506	7	8

DELAWARE.

Wheat, bushels.	Rye & oats, bushels.	Indian corn, bushels.	Irish and sweet potatoes, bushels.	Peas and beans, bushels.	Barley, bushels.	Buckwheat, bushels.	Butter and cheese, pounds.	Hay, tons.	Hops, pounds.	Clover & other grass seeds, bushels.	Flaxseed, bushels.	
119,774	111,403	899,079	89,225	1,503	15	3,599	180,091	4,109	143	......	616	1
319,012	484,594	1,066,377	125,954	681	21	4,947	769,915	24,417	205	3,926	14	2
43,725	16,587	1,180,086	90,806	1,936	20	69	108,489	1,633	......	2	274	3

FLORIDA.

Wheat, bushels.	Rye & oats, bushels.	Indian corn, bushels.	Irish and sweet potatoes, bushels.	Peas and beans, bushels.	Barley, bushels.	Buckwheat, bushels.	Butter and cheese, pounds.	Hay, tons.	Hops, pounds.	Clover & other grass seeds, bushels.	Flaxseed, bushels.	
77	465	64,724	28,115	2,668	......	......	25,962	16	......	......	......	1
....	42	23,515	12,295	1,614	......	......	12,176	35	......	......	......	2
....	300	29,495	10,589	251	......	......	1,310	....	......	......	......	3
169	3,112	112,090	52,657	12,806	......	......	31,610	628	......	......	......	4
....	....	....	1,100	10	......	......	....	....	......	......	......	5
....	....	51,788	28,504	1,645	......	......	175	53	......	......	......	6
....	160	4,950	4,457	190	......	......	2,520	....	......	......	......	7
....	....	....	....	....	......	......	....	....	......	......	......	8
106	13,822	292,850	143,000	21,295	......	......	60,561	....	......	......	......	9
151	883	56,705	22,298	7,460	......	......	8,259	....	......	......	......	10
30	50	16,263	26,746	2,235	......	......	21,860	147	......	......	......	11
....	560	23,880	7,776	431	......	......	2,007	....	......	......	......	12
....	2,118	227,582	43,770	3,221	......	......	2,038	....	......	......	......	13
9	14,597	275,477	76,167	17,861	......	......	24,535	1,123	14	2	......	14
10	14,709	407,976	120,563	28,174	......	......	21,127	63	......	......	......	15
....	....	6,310	7,425	....	......	......	5,260	....	......	......	......	16
469	16,015	119,640	43,181	27,181	......	......	114,274	86	......	......	......	17
....	100	96,192	41,550	....	......	......	24,120	....	......	......	......	18
....	....	....	1,150	40	......	......	....	....	......	......	......	19
....	....	29,812	22,343	2,523	......	......	10,259	299	......	......	......	20
....	....	4,865	2,980	443	......	......	2,850	....	......	......	......	21
....	....	4,610	4,365	890	......	......	2,879	....	......	......	......	22
....	....	14,390	6,714	1,356	......	......	2,995	56	......	......	......	23
....	....	....	....	....	......	......	....	....	......	......	......	24
....	245	10,328	13,945	303	......	55	2,315	....	......	......	......	25
6	560	40,216	14,482	1,491	......	......	7,651	4	......	......	......	26
....	....	28,920	12,375	110	......	......	525	....	......	......	......	27
....	....	54,231	16,507	1,161	......	......	2,245	....	......	......	......	28

GEORGIA.

Wheat, bushels.	Rye & oats, bushels.	Indian corn, bushels.	Irish and sweet potatoes, bushels.	Peas and beans, bushels.	Barley, bushels.	Buckwheat, bushels.	Butter and cheese, pounds.	Hay, tons.	Hops, pounds.	Clover & other grass seeds, bushels.	Flaxseed, bushels.	
800	2,055	53,794	35,282	3,750	......	......	24,283	....	......	......	......	1
862	11,923	284,595	81,034	28,151	2,780	......	46,968	5	......	......	......	2
7,496	21,483	255,910	47,795	2,459	203	......	24,484	1,376	......	......	......	3
3,581	30,403	255,275	82,303	11,002	57	12	34,985	4	......	......	......	4
10	1,778	54,927	38,163	9,519	......	......	13,686	1,000	......	......	......	5
766	2,262	98,612	60,710	6,805	......	......	24,398	7	......	......	......	6
3,471	29,149	643,608	113,024	36,075	......	......	49,736	115	......	......	......	7
7,216	24,768	224,930	52,539	4,457	52	2	31,649	....	......	......	......	8
....	126	63,478	52,925	7,677	......	......	14,726	27	......	......	......	9
11,485	27,268	271,500	45,857	7,730	6	......	47,606	....	......	20	......	10
21,071	40,878	316,871	79,795	5,811	......	......	95,125	....	......	......	......	11
29,153	55.573	497,769	70,091	6,483	......	......	60,134	7	......	......	......	12
....	4,650	57,427	40,940	9,415	......	......	10,158	1	......	......	......	13
15,891	36,481	301,180	55,948	7,808	1	3	54,471	52	......	41	20	14
32,921	62,225	444,984	82,320	3,330	100	......	66,168	....	......	......	......	15
14,229	66,177	289,575	53,124	25,172	210	6	91,209	44	20	......	1	16
11	200	17,350	5,385	3,446	......	......	2,165	....	......	......	......	17
34.936	52,890	318,738	59,437	8,699	1,005	9	86,980	747	......	......	......	18
15,326	94,641	434,777	80,493	25,724	......	......	87,899	....	......	......	......	19

	Counties.	Agricultural products.									
		Flax, pounds.	Hemp, dew and water-rotted, tons.	Maple sugar, pounds.	Cane sugar, hhds. of 1,000 pounds.	Molasses, gallons.	Rice, pounds.	Tobacco, pounds.	Ginned cotton, bales of 400 pounds.	Wool, pounds.	Silk cocoons, pounds.
1	Fairfield	9,816		4						30,027	
2	Hartford	4,565		3,168		136		1,132,114		65,503	
3	Litchfield	2,713		44,477		347		13,800		143,518	10
4	Middlesex	70						22,400		2[illegible],409	
5	New Haven	590		220		3				45,986	
6	New London	52		20						80,110	
7	Tolland	12		531		52		99,31		53,30[illegible]	97
8	Windham	110		2,37[illegible]		127				55,593	221

STATISTICS OF

	Counties.	Flax, pounds.	Hemp, dew and water-rotted, tons.	Maple sugar, pounds.	Cane sugar, hhds. of 1,000 pounds.	Molasses, gallons.	Rice, pounds.	Tobacco, pounds.	Ginned cotton, bales of 400 pounds.	Wool, pounds.	Silk cocoons, pounds.
1	Kent	7,732				50				19,582	
2	New Castle	160								14,372	
3	Sussex	3,282								23,814	

STATISTICS OF

	Counties.	Flax, pounds.	Hemp, dew and water-rotted, tons.	Maple sugar, pounds.	Cane sugar, hhds. of 1,000 pounds.	Molasses, gallons.	Rice, pounds.	Tobacco, pounds.	Ginned cotton, bales of 400 pounds.	Wool, pounds.	Silk cocoons, pounds.
1	Alachua				68	5,558	17,935	140	561	590	
2	Benton				86	3,910	5,150	8,620	8	4	
3	Calhoun				9	12,340	20,570	30,252	137	532	
4	Columbia				179	5,162	138,180	383	802	1,809	
5	Dade										
6	Duval				391	21,531	27,040		216	440	
7	Escambia						10,150			175	
8	Franklin										
9	Gadsden				120	65,403	108,370	776,177	5,609	4,320	
10	Hamilton				47	2,763	14,455	40	560	614	
11	Hillsborough				6	24,250	5,575	100	18	36	
12	Holmes				9	1,050	7,070	130	114	611	
13	Jackson				23	36,309	50,490	14,202	4,744	1,030	
14	Jefferson				116	22,682	56,205	3,000	9,468	5,408	6
15	Leon				178	31,792	83,232	37,780	16,107	2,725	
16	Levy				63	3,250			59		
17	Madison				226	46,320	63,630	100	5,024	3,194	
18	Marion				508	31,625	21,425	109,000	701		
19	Monroe										
20	Nassau				44	4,964	404,305		279	1,232	
21	Orange				279	12,690	100	3,500	34		
22	Putnam				74	7,030		500	32		
23	St. Johns				290	6,325	426				
24	St. Lucie										
25	Santa Rosa	50					4,676		11	75	
26	Wakulla				2[illegible]	3,171	18,686	10,890	480	307	
27	Walton				8	2,438	600		60	120	
28	Washington				6	2,330	16,820	3,800	107	25	

STATISTICS OF

	Counties.	Flax, pounds.	Hemp, dew and water-rotted, tons.	Maple sugar, pounds.	Cane sugar, hhds. of 1,000 pounds.	Molasses, gallons.	Rice, pounds.	Tobacco, pounds.	Ginned cotton, bales of 400 pounds.	Wool, pounds.	Silk cocoons, pounds.
1	Appling				17	4,505	30,800	240	63	3,925	
2	Baker				73	10,417	15,225	100	8,820	9,633	
3	Baldwin						100		4,483	7,160	
4	Bibb								3,394	4,116	100
5	Bryan				4	2,996	2,409,387	150	536	2,773	
6	Bullock				30	1,122	112,475		594	12,687	
7	Burke					3,105	36,380	280	19,175	18,238	
8	Butts						1,540	265	4,110	4,761	
9	Camden				45	7,502	6,400,940		858	2,680	
10	Campbell						4,975	2,489	3,040	6,769	
11	Carroll						430	7,201	1,243	9,550	
12	Cass							5,735	2,385	7,165	
13	Chatham					246	19,453,750		580	2,799	
14	Chattooga						43	7,360	1,668	6,963	5
15	Cherokee						142	27,050	272	13,489	
16	Clark						2,475	1,772	4, 72	7,576	
17	Clinch				10				108	584	
18	Cobb						29,531	2,176	2,401	12,793	
19	Columbia								11,336	18,710	

AGRICULTURAL PRODUCTS.					MANUFACTURES.				REMARKS.	
Beeswax and honey, pounds.	Value of animals slaughtered.	Value of produce of market gardens.	Value of orchard produce.	Wine, gallons.	Establishments. Capital.	Hands employed.	Annual product.	Produced in families.		
4,048	$298,327	$21,018	$12,571	426	$2,222,785	7,770	$5,667,320	$984	......	1
19,609	393,276	123,535	58,295	281	6,126,260	11,716	10,888,780	25,156	......	2
24,613	389,028	644	9,438	132	2,434,855	3,475	4,068,228	18,819	......	3
1,587	139,875	18,046	6,294	......	1,406,950	2,646	2,109,560	54,152	......	4
6,541	344,495	20,364	43,483	2,474	5,076,331	9,933	11,283,816	73,439	......	5
5,107	224,553	5,632	6,686	25	2,667,900	5,379	5,624,978	1,780	......	6
9,059	144,767	1,186	10,036	195	1,357,225	2,476	2,697,042	5,200	......	7
22,740	267,945	6,449	28,315	736	2,598,042	4,405	2,770,378	12,722	......	8

DELAWARE.

10,545	100,878	3,961	9,897	35	184,840	424	424,906	8,443	......	1
2,303	124,965	8,753	29,659	50	2,593,830	3,235	3,945,399	50	......	2
28,397	147,822	......	7,018	60	200,275	229	278,991	29,628	......	3

FLORIDA.

......	25,875	......	......	......	......	......	......	5,198	Div. several times since '40	1
......	9,966	564	130	......	......	......	......	244	Formed '43 from Alachua.	2
384	6,412	38	20	......	6,500	8	1,860	1,253	In '45 part of Jackson ad-	3
2,481	51,617	56	143	......	4,000	8	8,400	9,624	ded.	4
......	......	1,375	......	......	6,000	29	28,800	......	......	5
2	19,954	100	......	......	49,000	64	114,500	7,995	......	6
100	2,905	......	565	......	59,500	84	32,400	595	Divided in 1845 to form	7
......	500	......	......	......	......	......	......	......	St. Rosa.	8
......	67,390	......	......	......	......	......	......	......	......	9
1,475	21,711	......	158	......	......	......	......	4,483	[Levy.	10
......	13,355	1,242	144	......	4,000	9	5,400	......	Divided in 1845 to form	11
105	8,914	......	......	......	......	......	......	1,947	'47 fm Walton & Calhoun.	12
......	39,421	20	......	......	......	......	......	2,125	In 1845 part added to Cal-	13
5,634	38,887	......	70	......	13,800	16	14,775	10,652	houn.	14
3,123	65,683	285	......	10	40,950	113	62,129	3,995	Div. '43 to form Wakulla.	15
......	4,145	......	......	......	......	......	......	795	Formed in 1845 from Ala-	16
......	53,331	......	......	......	9,750	16	18,000	9,405	chua and Hillsboro'.	17
......	28,687	......	......	......	......	......	......	2,699	Formed in 1844 from Ala-	18
......	......	2,300	50	......	20,000	10	6,700	......	chua, Hillsboro', and	19
......	10,751	......	......	......	68,100	76	36,780	6,071	Mosquito.	20
......	1,475	......	......	......	......	......	......	138	Formed in '45 fm Mosquito	21
......	2,155	......	......	......	......	......	......	115	In '48 fm Orange, Alachua,	22
......	3,175	2,311	......	......	6,310	26	16,450	......	Marion, and St. Johns.	23
......	......	......	......	......	......	......	......	......	Formed '44 from Mosquito.	24
......	9,180	130	......	......	236,950	489	290,720	1,217	Formed '42 frm Escambia.	25
3,860	2,644	300	......	......	2,800	7	8,121	1,735	Formed 1843 from Leon.	26
......	12,060	......	......	......	......	......	......	2,998	[ton and Jackson.	27
1,807	14,492	......	......	......	19,400	36	23,300	2,298	Formed 1846 from Wal-	28

GEORGIA.

4,878	29,902	......	345	......	......	......	......	10,785	......	1
2,578	69,737	......	533	......	30,350	43	24,239	14,051	......	2
195	43,117	......	211	......	92,200	132	85,422	947	......	3
7,930	51,402	4,812	432	......	138,920	453	533,200	7,456	......	4
431	16,875	......	45	......	......	......	......	3,811	......	5
180	36,530	......	4,616	......	1,150	7	2,500	8,441	......	6
10,391	111,100	......	......	......	62,033	128	60,651	5,673	......	7
13,301	43,130	......	30	......	87,145	100	84,040	9,715	......	8
1,645	22,319	......	101	......	70,000	102	43,000	......	......	9
12,968	53,596	......	150	......	66,595	107	78,442	16,570	......	10
......	57,137	......	......	......	54,300	101	49,045	27,316	......	11
4,389	68,846	12	......	......	32,800	168	82,205	19,070	Divided in 1849 to form	12
......	2,703	16,295	40	......	130,550	215	256,250	1,217	Gordon.	13
3,769	47,950	......	5	3	30,025	70	47,670	17,872	......	14
13,315	63,366	......	......	......	18,300	42	22,050	20,120	......	15
6,550	67,291	480	658	73	320,350	498	345,220	13,621	......	16
300	6,063	......	......	......	......	......	......	1,412	In '49 fr. Lowndes & Ware;	17
3,891	106,664	4,194	11,147	50	154,900	211	187,700	55,438	part taken fr. Lowndes	18
......	80,241	......	......	......	89,300	115	94,500	11,293	only returned separately.	19

	COUNTIES.	POPULATION.								
		Whites.			Colored.		All classes.		Total population.	
		Male.	Female.	Total.	Free.	Slave.	Male.	Female.	1850.	1840.
20	Coweta	4,223	3,979	8,202	18	5,415	6,887	6,748	13,635	10,364
21	Crawford	2,253	2,089	4,342	13	4,629	4,662	4,322	8,984	7,981
22	Dade	1,246	1,286	2,532	....	148	1,313	1,367	2,680	1,364
23	Decatur	2,391	2,227	4,618	5	3,639	4,220	4,042	8,262	5,872
24	DeKalb	5,702	5,670	11,372	32	2,924	7,093	7,235	14,328	10,467
25	Dooly	2,844	2,736	5,580	6	2,775	4,165	4,196	8,361	4,427
26	Early	1,909	1,807	3,716	1	3,529	3,622	3,624	7,246	5,444
27	Effingham	1,027	980	2,007	9	1,848	2,026	1,838	3,864	3,075
28	Elbert	3,374	3,302	6,676	16	6,267	6,545	6,414	12 959	11,125
29	Emanuel	1,846	1,745	3,591	24	962	2,325	2,252	4,577	3,129
30	Fayette	3,451	3,290	6,741	3	1,965	4,427	4,282	8,709	6.191
31	Floyd	2,781	2,421	5,202	4	2,999	4,232	3,973	8,205	4,441
32	Forsyth	3,950	3,862	7,812	11	1,027	4,476	4,374	8,850	5,619
33	Franklin	4,519	4,557	9,076	55	2,382	5,689	5,824	11,513	9,886
34	Gilmer	4,242	3,994	8,236	4	200	4,339	4,101	8,440	2,536
35	Glynn	355	341	696	5	4,232	2,336	2,597	4,933	5,302
36	Gordon	2,646	2,510	5,156	....	828	3,050	2,934	5,984	....
37	Greene	2,420	2,324	4,744	58	8,266	6,636	6,432	13,068	11,690
38	Gwinnett	4,498	4,454	8,952	11	2,294	5,644	5,613	11,257	10,804
39	Habersham	3,962	3,713	7,675	2	1,218	4,565	4,330	8,895	7,961
40	Hall	3,639	3,731	7,370	7	1,336	4,313	4,400	8,713	7,875
41	Hancock	2,133	2,077	4,210	62	7,306	5,908	5,670	11,578	9,659
42	Harris	3,391	3,318	6,709	30	7,982	7,414	7,307	14,721	13,933
43	Heard	2,295	2,225	4,520	3	2,400	3,457	3,466	6,923	5,329
44	Henry	4,978	4,764	9,742	15	4,969	7,354	7,372	14,726	11,756
45	Houston	3,358	3,152	6,510	16	9,924	8,332	8,118	16,450	9,711
46	Irwin	1,479	1,404	2,883	1	450	1,699	1,635	3,334	2,038
47	Jackson	3,372	3,436	6,808	19	2,941	4,777	4,991	9,768	8,522
48	Jasper	2,229	2,092	4,321	31	7,134	5,836	5,650	11,486	11,111
49	Jefferson	1,885	1,832	3,717	47	5,367	4,612	4,519	9,131	7,254
50	Jones	1,972	1,927	3,899	46	6,279	5,108	5,116	10,224	10,065
51	Laurens	1,740	1,719	3,459	9	2,974	3,318	3,124	6,442	5,585
52	Lee	1,577	1,448	3,025	8	3,627	3,398	3,262	6,660	4,520
53	Liberty	1,021	981	2,002	16	5,908	3,902	4,024	7,926	7,241
54	Lincoln	1,109	1,078	2,187	31	3,780	3,045	2,953	5,998	5,895
55	Lowndes	2,716	2,623	5,339	20	2,355	3,882	3,832	7,714	5,574
56	Lumpkin	3,973	4,022	7,995	21	939	4,477	4,478	8,955	5,671
57	Macon	2,091	1,997	4,088	3	2,961	3,502	3.550	7,052	5,045
58	Madison	1,846	1,917	3,763	7	1,933	2,779	2,924	5,703	4,510
59	McIntosh	690	636	1,326	72	4,629	3,062	2,965	6,027	5,360
60	Marion	3,369	3,298	6,667	9	3,604	5,160	5,120	10,280	4,812
61	Meriwether	4,269	4,212	8,481	2	7,993	8,258	8,218	16,476	14,132
62	Monroe	3,472	3,338	6,810	5	10,170	8,536	8,449	16,985	16,275
63	Montgomery	819	722	1,541	....	613	1,105	1,049	2,154	1,616
64	Morgan	1,861	1,773	3,634	16	7,094	5,424	5,320	10,744	9,121
65	Murray	6,604	5,888	12,492	11	1,930	7,570	6,863	14,433	4,695
66	Muscogee	5,277	5,078	10,355	67	8,156	9,244	9,334	18,578	11,699
67	Newton	4,110	3,967	8,077	32	5,187	6,742	6,554	13,296	11,628
68	Oglethorpe	2,228	2,154	4.382	3	7,874	5,973	6,286	12,259	10,868
69	Paulding	2,873	2,687	5,560	2	1,477	3,592	3,447	7,039	2,556
70	Pike	4,477	4,209	8,686	62	5,558	7,205	7,101	14,306	9,176
71	Pulaski	1,896	1,888	3,784	39	2,804	3,323	3,304	6,627	5,389
72	Putnam	1,681	1,619	3,3 0	26	7,468	5,518	5,276	10,794	10,260
73	Rabun	1,210	1,128	2,338	....	110	1,263	1,185	2,448	1,912
74	Randolph	4,067	3,790	7,857	3	5,008	6,502	6,366	12,868	8,276
75	Richmond	4,140	4,013	8,153	281	7,812	8,053	8,193	16,246	11,932
76	Scriven	1,625	1,548	3,173	1	3,673	3,532	3,315	6,847	4,794
77	Stewart	4,480	4,169	8,649	5	7,373	8,126	7,901	16,027	12,933
78	Sumter	3,346	3,123	6,469	18	3,835	5,278	5,044	10,322	5,759
79	Talbot	4,023	3,770	7,793	18	8,723	8,353	8,181	16,534	15,627
80	Taliaferro	1,082	969	2,051	51	3,044	2,638	2,508	5,146	5,190
81	Tatnall	1,221	1,157	2,378	18	831	1,660	1,567	3,227	2,724
82	Telfair	1,069	1,027	2,096	....	930	1,539	1,487	3,026	2,763
83	Thomas	2,576	2,367	4,943	4	5,156	5,030	5,073	10,103	6,766
84	Troup	3,890	3,901	7,791	40	9,048	8,297	8,582	16,879	15,733
85	Twiggs	1,795	1,722	3,517	42	4,620	4,212	3,967	8,179	8,422
86	Union	3,536	3,419	6,955	1	278	3,677	3,557	7,234	3,152
87	Upson	2,347	2,373	4,720	....	4,704	4,769	4,655	9,424	9,408
88	Walker	5,803	5,605	11,408	37	1,664	6,616	6,493	13,109	6,572
89	Walton	3,531	3,364	6,895	17	3,909	5,441	5,380	10,821	10,209
90	Ware	1,824	1,773	3,597	3	288	1,962	1,926	3,888	2,323
91	Warren	3,066	3,092	6,158	159	6,108	6,244	6,181	12,425	9,789
92	Washington	3,008	2,983	5,991	37	5,738	5,992	5,774	11,766	10,565
93	Wayne	549	539	1,088	5	406	740	759	1,499	1,258
94	Wilkes	1,883	1,922	3,805	21	8,281	5,958	6,149	12,107	10,148
95	Wilkinson	2,849	2,702	5,551	....	2,745	4,173	4,123	8,296	6,842

NATIVITIES, DWELLINGS, &c.				EDUCATION AND RELIGION.									
Born out of State.				Colleges, academies, and private schools.		Public Schools.							
United States.	Foreign countries.	Dwellings.	Families.	Pupils.	Annual income.	Pupils.	Annual income.	Total educational income.	White scholars during year.	Whites 5 and under 20 years old.	Whites over 20 unable to read & write.	Accommodation of churches—persons.	
1,935	73	1,382	1,382	454	$6,755	346	$3,965	$10,720	1,580	3,410	805	12,350	20
744	16	754	754	......	....	367	413	413	788	1,809	220	6,000	21
1,596	4	421	421	60	....	250	....	....	355	1,057	375	1,160	22
971	30	898	898	100	....	150	5,638	5,638	351	1,851	322	2,430	23
2,854	169	1,987	1,989	140	1,370	728	7,829	9,199	1,646	4,650	697	11,390	24
1,008	20	962	962	......	....	225	1,523	1,523	822	2,337	861	5,950	25
824	24	656	656	85	2,500	109	....	2,500	280	1,416	292	3,600	26
63	9	355	355	50	1,200	158	2,501	3,701	288	784	38	5,050	27
797	27	1,177	1,177	......	....	1,202	890	890	1,255	2,706	841	9,000	28
209	3	605	605	......	....	202	606	606	299	1,524	735	2,725	29
1,210	20	1,196	1,206	47	503	253	2,006	2,509	924	2,854	313	4,645	30
1,782	75	866	866	392	....	17	....	....	442	2,214	85	3,525	31
2,477	7	1,334	1,334	35	....	370	1,912	1,912	1,468	3,309	1,451	8,300	32
2,178	8	1,546	1,546	200	2,560	500	4,099	6,659	1,668	3,746	182	7,825	33
4,551	7	1,396	1,396	30	....	205	617	617	1,309	3,519	1,510	2,025	34
228	28	145	145	147	3,534	29	400	3,934	151	244	32	1,090	35
2,109	16	861	868	......	....	300	130	130	684	2,207	330	....	36
618	79	854	854	250	11,000	333	726	11,726	1,078	1,969	381	13,000	37
2,176	24	1,610	1,610	85	2,700	800	556	3,256	1,186	3,645	869	10,050	38
2,218	17	1,338	1,338	......	....	20	550	550	1,022	3,144	458	15,700	39
1,921	23	1,300	1,300	67	700	209	752	1,452	1,252	2,978	1,457	6,160	40
588	18	761	785	132	....	207	623	623	673	1,629	114	6,100	41
886	11	1,175	1,242	193	3,925	206	2,907	6,832	1,282	2,920	232	13,800	42
948	1	724	741	......	....	403	240	240	565	1,997	341	7,700	43
1,949	39	1,680	1,680	80	....	350	500	500	1,898	4,266	662	15,100	44
1,338	24	1,138	1,138	160	4,253	456	5,532	9,785	1,257	2,710	807	11,800	45
337	12	448	448	......	....	176	192	192	326	1,285	508	2,250	46
1,075	12	1,200	1,200	50	700	217	2,267	2,967	695	2,751	561	4,800	47
542	4	812	812	210	....	213	370	370	667	1,690	272	10,000	48
224	24	765	765	35	700	196	3,080	3,780	446	1,443	142	6,500	49
582	17	739	739	63	....	350	1,244	1,244	700	1,556	508	6,100	50
318	6	634	634	120	....	200	472	472	402	1,405	710	....	51
554	20	550	550	23	350	136	1,967	2,317	469	1,192	345	2,550	52
201	7	360	362	95	300	151	77	377	321	706	160	12,276	53
231	6	378	378	75	....	78	2,138	2,138	330	879	177	5,550	54
1,034	25	856	856	......	....	509	3,129	3,129	375	2,334	456	5,640	55
3,051	11	1,381	1,381	75	500	1,170	635	1,135	1,153	3,416	1,033	7,100	56
931	10	679	679	......	....	350	848	848	384	1,686	79	2,325	57
429	1	692	692	40	125	191	182	307	381	1,468	245	2,600	58
157	27	283	283	38	1,000	82	686	1,686	198	487	82	3,350	59
1,364	8	1,101	1,101	130	....	466	316	316	975	2,876	776	6,700	60
1,580	22	1,428	1,428	132	....	360	....	....	1,306	3,643	375	7,450	61
1,006	45	1,194	1,194	215	1,000	750	737	1,737	1,147	2,834	109	16,600	62
257	19	236	236	......	....	200	360	360	213	646	123	1,605	63
423	33	621	621	752	29,820	......	....	29,820	643	1,503	44	9,500	64
6,304	217	2,047	2,047	......	....	400	1,100	1,100	1,088	5,068	850	8,650	65
2,296	293	1,884	1,981	255	463	......	....	463	1,491	4,232	251	13,000	66
1,608	42	1,374	1,374	291	8,598	393	4,213	12,811	1,353	3,394	337	10,810	67
397	23	819	820	212	5,500	350	561	6,061	807	1,779	85	13,250	68
1,350	8	1,059	1,059	......	....	324	350	350	948	2,384	803	5,050	69
1,375	28	1,474	1,474	184	....	354	966	966	1,699	3,736	315	11,750	70
725	8	701	701	......	....	127	331	331	259	1,585	729	3,440	71
616	47	609	609	134	....	197	600	600	698	1,352	300	5,850	72
611	2	385	385	65	....	644	377	377	699	995	64	1,850	73
1,626	20	1,408	1,408	80	1,000	635	7,937	8,937	924	3,290	724	9,150	74
2,451	801	1,556	1,556	565	22,100	720	7,056	29,156	1,322	2,913	166	10,500	75
370	23	567	567	60	....	280	132	132	281	1,319	69	2,900	76
1,381	31	1,432	1,445	138	1,750	660	7,883	9,633	1,399	3,686	549	11,375	77
1,203	16	1,109	1,109	30	....	265	581	581	890	2,580	557	5,850	78
1,174	36	1,324	1,324	195	....	492	250	250	1,451	3,252	387	10,000	79
232	54	408	408	30	....	180	220	220	368	787	214	2,758	80
288	3	434	434	......	....	130	1,220	1,220	102	945	198	2,425	81
355	17	340	340	16	....	243	150	150	231	870	136	1,400	82
597	12	838	838	160	....	266	....	....	836	2,145	148	5,750	83
1,306	17	1,295	1,333	548	36,320	1,440	15,055	51,375	1,777	3,472	129	12,050	84
449	12	696	696	......	....	210	450	450	309	1,429	15	4,800	85
3,966	3	1,141	1,141	......	....	275	2,700	2,700	1,102	2,947	1,225	6,300	86
635	14	795	795	125	....	650	575	575	552	2,011	268	10,000	87
5,499	25	1,867	1,867	......	....	984	9,840	9,840	1,700	4,817	692	6,705	88
737	11	1,191	1,191	160	167	680	315	482	1,466	2,812	271	11,325	89
428	13	561	561	......	....	95	247	247	135	1,615	785	1,500	90
470	41	1,135	1,135	121	1,920	470	6,737	8,657	1,058	2,437	662	10,220	91
698	16	1,077	1,077	115	....	450	663	663	836	2,379	811	7,750	92
156	2	182	182	13	....	42	....	....	64	471	92	821	93
295	23	709	709	125	....	326	8,407	8,407	556	1,567	40	7,400	94
480	67	983	983	......	....	460	3,124	3,124	988	2,239	471	5,000	95

	COUNTIES.	LAND OCCUPIED OR IMPROVED.				LIVE STOCK UPON FARMS.			
		Farms.	Acres improved.	Acres unimproved.	Value with improvements and implements.	Horses, asses, and mules.	Neat cattle.	Sheep.	Swine.
20	Coweta	911	88,088	160,500	$1,951,348	3,263	9,024	6,265	29,878
21	Crawford	444	72,857	134,073	1,181,994	2,156	8,294	5,552	22,822
22	Dade	235	11,245	36,614	246,663	757	2,496	1,478	9,036
23	Decatur	441	45,478	199,971	781,124	2,041	24,751	7,377	25,639
24	De Kalb	1,019	67,992	153,739	1,184,550	2,896	7,819	5,468	24,449
25	Dooly	663	59,859	308,583	498,316	2,116	28,034	6,621	28,283
26	Early	367	44,742	135,632	759,092	1,596	26,168	5,198	29,252
27	Effingham	308	21,784	210,972	327,171	905	11,122	6,779	12,660
28	Elbert	804	84,069	229,375	1,656,762	3,285	10,724	7,452	25,092
29	Emanuel	511	35,092	502,609	600,304	1,515	21,351	8,872	22,635
30	Fayette	818	56,104	156,094	1,037,516	2,391	8,100	5,088	21,941
31	Floyd	397	32,358	96,195	1,125,962	1,637	5,427	5,165	19,258
32	Forsyth	765	43,140	107,379	758,772	1,880	5,583	6,213	19,848
33	Franklin	1,305	69,416	330,811	1,152,405	3,210	11,045	11,472	24,924
34	Gilmer	577	23,900	121,876	508,366	1,231	5,561	5,062	18,949
35	Glynn	92	20,472	85,777	793,402	1,227	6,102	826	2,597
36	Gordon	419	25,915	83,512	611,605	1,641	4,807	4,098	15,529
37	Greene	512	104,658	148,985	1,845,442	3,367	10,696	9,041	30,323
38	Gwinnett	1,036	85,881	197,210	1,030,570	3,014	9,475	6,829	26,494
39	Habersham	732	44,798	275,541	496,709	2,120	8,522	8,019	19,410
40	Hall	697	38,824	201,558	630,410	1,930	5,770	6,502	18,419
41	Hancock	444	125,691	162,644	1,405,638	3,204	12,976	8,433	30,919
42	Harris	873	135,292	150,911	1,732,573	3,804	12,343	6,999	36,958
43	Heard	512	42,691	96,409	772,640	1,776	6,253	4,042	18,101
44	Henry	1,003	104,199	215,952	1,835,415	3,730	9,811	7,902	24,812
45	Houston	750	145,386	184,000	2,842,679	3,899	14,151	9,516	40,969
46	Irwin	414	14,325	320,433	107,247	955	22,859	3,315	26,496
47	Jackson	547	70,741	128,608	785,001	1,919	6,301	4,571	16,773
48	Jasper	588	139,948	89,875	1,533,684	3,508	8,424	6,493	31,289
49	Jefferson	538	79,715	217,600	1,450,623	2,780	10,123	8,958	28,386
50	Jones	405	138,972	99,617	1,310,319	2,680	9,586	8,490	26,634
51	Laurens	328	62,249	282,158	439,929	1,767	19,852	8,027	24,038
52	Lee	387	56,074	112,242	1,103,881	1,914	13,716	4,715	23,542
53	Liberty	244	38,563	303,518	809,518	1,100	15,450	4,609	10,006
54	Lincoln	273	48,320	101,668	676,077	1,662	6,491	4,245	14,260
55	Lowndes	591	40,897	429,462	892,823	2,042	38,988	11,2[illegible]	35,000
56	Lumpkin	598	31,962	94,899	650,114	1,732	6,190	6,485	23,657
57	Macon	419	51,588	134,548	1,127,344	1,726	9,467	5,311	21,493
58	Madison	404	45,708	100,901	613,803	1,551	5,086	4,459	12,257
59	McIntosh	117	19,482	83,090	792,654	425	8,444	1,554	4,761
60	Marion	563	61,938	119,311	1,215,044	2,070	9,821	5,743	21,212
61	Meriwether	824	122,838	180,223	2,179,142	3,933	9,694	7,784	38,912
62	Monroe	746	157,797	158,338	2,576,933	4,439	13,556	9,610	9,880
63	Montgomery	168	10,022	177,244	126,827	667	13,806	4,241	12,464
64	Morgan	336	138,163	78,969	1,436,056	2,999	8,996	5,070	27,638
65	Murray	1,034	51,102	163,470	1,680,905	3,152	10,930	6,910	29,864
66	Muscogee	581	78,015	131,361	1,714,322	2,779	11,849	4,430	26,881
67	Newton	812	91,993	125,993	1,288,267	3,117	7,903	6,189	25,116
68	Oglethorpe	555	219,712	78,553	1,966,011	3,327	12,193	8,998	27,275
69	Paulding	422	28,295	62,685	764,455	1,686	6,827	3,055	20,801
70	Pike	807	82,563	154,268	1,746,288	2,807	9,361	5,[illegible]	26,898
71	Pulaski	371	98,964	138,657	760,172	1,639	14,573	5,974	21,819
72	Putnam	351	134,829	72,669	1,182,240	2,727	9,010	5,558	25,280
73	Rabun	282	12,741	120,634	167,334	643	3,325	2,498	9,090
74	Randolph	930	93,211	239,605	1,417,181	3,148	16,141	9,445	36,548
75	Richmond	272	37,644	111,592	1,216,397	1,623	6,065	2,291	15,004
76	Scriven	498	56,008	454,748	652,517	2,070	27,758	11,311	23,915
77	Stewart	990	145,821	233,130	2,353,997	4,397	15,902	8,105	43,560
78	Sumter	768	68,165	157,748	1,324,577	1,853	10,198	6,452	29,422
79	Talbot	928	136,933	159,251	2,216,851	4,096	14,730	8,336	40,086
80	Taliaferro	294	39,184	89,823	651,512	1,473	5,853	3,151	13,331
81	Tatnall	327	14,244	379,369	243,284	810	16,463	5,298	15,496
82	Telfair	280	15,360	183,235	180,426	742	18,649	6,627	19,237
83	Thomas	534	63,931	383,453	1,212,281	2,493	23,255	11,851	20,410
84	Troup	789	128,190	130,900	2,112,758	4,519	10,576	7,032	41,620
85	Twiggs	367	101,619	142,171	817,499	2,275	7,937	4,133	23,656
86	Union	911	31,316	147,967	501,806	1,844	6,878	8,202	23,410
87	Upson	436	73,512	89,792	1,057,795	2,123	6,631	4,768	23,305
88	Walker	600	36,191	72,917	883,315	2,189	6,976	6,249	24,503
89	Walton	864	101,490	126,883	1,085,224	3,099	8,559	5,888	25,598
90	Ware	339	11,316	265,315	181,961	781	20,993	919	26,054
91	Warren	605	135,115	236,236	1,773,227	3,320	10,912	8,764	30,710
92	Washington	632	117,433	308,418	1,424,978	3,276	16,110	11,388	41,40[illegible]
93	Wayne	172	5,356	69,727	96,117	271	9,526	616	7,156
94	Wilkes	468	97,545	190,547	1,428,336	3,167	12,323	7,227	28,197
95	Wilkinson	645	75,721	239,951	981,456	2,349	12,484	6,633	30,070

AGRICULTURAL PRODUCTS.												
Wheat, bushels.	Rye & oats, bushels.	Indian corn, bushels.	Irish and sweet potatoes, bushels.	Peas and beans, bushels.	Barley, bushels.	Buckwheat, bushels.	Butter and cheese, pounds.	Hay, tons.	Hops, pounds.	Clover & other grass seeds, bushels.	Flaxseed, bushels.	
11,402	93,196	516,910	95,182	2,407	12	......	96,820	....	......	......	......	20
12,089	35,481	339,426	94,359	6,161	132	1	49,064	....	13	......	......	21
2,098	18,180	147,849	15,533	575	......	......	27,882	2	36	42	2	22
131	8,827	275,497	106,736	8,784	......	......	28,451	....	......	......	......	23
22,118	86,153	432,435	74,244	3,999	47	......	60,779	....	......	......	......	24
6,018	9,366	289,378	94,795	13,611	20	......	22,101	....	......	......	400	25
2,360	28,020	223,037	76,377	13,285	......	......	18,460	....	......	......	......	26
391	294	87,794	37,584	11,046	......	......	13,478	21	2	......	......	27
31,070	66,479	614,966	70,706	32,589	36	5	122,946	....	......	......	......	28
2,982	2,403	121,874	49,588	8,425	......	......	28,725	....	......	......	......	29
13,430	34,509	318,113	57,363	6,726	......	......	51,772	....	......	......	1	30
16,179	15,439	254,722	39,582	3,854	815	......	47,324	41	......	......	......	31
23,206	73,246	339,954	85,698	8,843	3	7	70,819	1	......	......	......	32
34,800	104,997	447,050	122,757	19,686	......	......	145,484	....	......	......	......	33
3,805	28,256	214,193	24,551	584	......	44	54,743	5	5	......	57	34
....	1,480	49,739	55,401	7,290	......	......	9,959	....	15	......	......	35
19,161	20,908	285,360	32,690	921	1	......	39,379	....	10	......	......	36
13,882	97,356	480,326	89,331	38,456	1,662	......	68,487	2,913	......	......	......	37
29,296	102,155	436,227	80,590	2,983	7	......	94,821	3	......	......	1	38
10,082	52,190	268,695	63,567	2,758	......	......	64,219	310	12	16	2	39
19,910	68,336	295,759	53,954	7,656	1	......	71,126	2	......	8	30	40
12,160	73,441	440,699	123,172	39,411	223	......	75,026	2,134	7	......	......	41
24,130	82,780	554,895	114,248	20,412	56	......	72,576	....	......	11	1	42
12,047	35,151	265,242	41,434	182	10	......	42,108	....	......	......	......	43
36,489	89,178	514,796	110,742	13,411	10	......	77,021	1	......	......	......	44
15,106	47,167	662,600	191,280	5,340	......	......	44,655	....	......	......	......	45
1,199	4,025	89,000	51,658	8,221	......	......	17,427	2	......	......	......	46
23,072	63,827	309,272	51,878	8,438	32	......	74,598	....	23	......	......	47
18,730	63,202	460,680	81,985	15,524	270	......	57,108	....	......	......	......	48
6,282	5,352	354,836	61,990	4,870	......	......	36,267	....	......	......	......	49
13,859	54,720	402,360	87,473	23,750	287	......	48,404	4	......	......	......	50
8,902	7,826	211,958	83,113	6,648	11	20	19,028	....	......	......	......	51
2,116	21,432	207,614	72,318	26,470	......	......	40,225	....	......	......	......	52
100	2,127	114,310	115,132	22,929	......	......	20,910	759	......	......	......	53
9,546	64,585	204,594	33,783	1,433	34	......	35,142	....	......	......	......	54
837	11,461	233,569	80,806	25,486	......	......	29,295	....	......	......	......	55
6,630	43,205	242,717	48,266	1,385	100	2	51,908	....	......	......	......	56
6,162	28,948	258,364	96,325	22,478	151	10	27,566	....	......	......	......	57
16,525	28,859	195,421	32,261	2,315	10	......	61,801	....	......	......	1	58
12	158	34,715	53,192	4,895	......	......	7,150	509	......	......	......	59
9,857	16,128	333,904	81,395	641	......	......	31,045	....	......	......	......	60
25,014	98,981	594,601	121,702	19,155	20	......	64,737	3	......	......	......	61
40,003	109,428	724,670	175,420	18,962	280	......	86,697	....	......	......	......	62
1,241	1,605	55,365	28,770	2,551	......	......	13,166	....	......	......	......	63
19,145	87,129	411,857	69,474	3,022	490	......	63,048	....	......	......	......	64
19,596	56,750	518,745	79,467	1,538	......	6	76,264	340	......	113	......	65
9,547	34,860	399,113	83,425	27,774	14	......	48,460	....	......	......	......	66
16,224	60,416	463,130	104,560	1,180	31	......	40,327	2,167	1	......	......	67
14,257	100,482	445,575	79,628	12,201	77	......	133,362	4,519	......	......	......	68
8,634	24,107	256,019	46,771	5,798	5	25	42,219	772	3	......	......	69
12,204	46,677	418,990	86,457	8,674	22	......	67,709	....	......	......	......	70
2,058	6,087	229,815	61,310	14,495	......	......	20,967	....	......	......	......	71
17,785	45,618	392,821	65,139	4,307	421	......	49,634	....	......	......	......	72
256	12,966	64,699	13,957	3,232	5	65	29,769	104	24	228	45	73
3,713	57,483	454,533	151,360	40,084	......	......	82,023	....	......	......	......	74
4,064	28,463	297,780	53,278	19,693	260	2	33,511	1,599	......	40	......	75
3,560	7,113	264,860	141,420	9,473	......	......	93,235	....	90	34	......	76
12,152	70,947	684,499	173,687	33,596	453	......	70,729	....	......	......	......	77
7,258	34,208	354,842	122.894	22,477	11	10	46,100	....	......	......	......	78
28,349	89,354	655,802	163,251	18,477	444	......	73,968	....	......	......	......	79
8,879	28,752	193,327	29,939	2,825	163	1	30,669	....	......	......	......	80
1,132	3,781	71,740	46,232	2,924	......	......	16,005	....	......	......	......	81
1,047	4,965	77,805	44,251	6,376	......	......	6,902	....	......	......	......	82
249	16,598	353,920	146,022	....	......	......	24,001	....	......	......	......	83
17.644	120,640	687,205	145,613	18,819	151	......	79,697	3,441	......	......	6	84
5,892	9,323	379.537	77,283	11,447	2	......	22,110	....	......	......	......	85
2,176	53,470	274,345	35,285	82	......	20	54,657	102	......	......	53	86
19,701	48,420	343,017	71,128	11,768	68	......	38,702	....	......	......	......	87
11,913	52,227	371,760	44,131	586	......	......	17,927	53	......	7	2	88
21,494	92,873	426,516	106,529	18,851	48	......	78,473	3	......	......	......	89
388	2,854	68,270	44,530	4,033	5	......	14,732	....	......	......	......	90
19,155	45,021	428,364	126,981	61,429	88	......	80,244	....	......	......	......	91
11,550	13,156	446,730	113,005	18,067	17	......	41,534	....	......	......	......	92
60	82	21,545	24,433	457	......	......	10,540	5	......	......	......	93
12,649	133,376	418,176	59,640	7,929	64	......	71,381	....	......	......	......	94
12,149	19,809	323.976	106,631	41,337	18	......	41,107	....	......	......	......	95

	COUNTIES.	AGRICULTURAL PRODUCTS.									
		Flax, pounds.	Hemp, dew and water-rotted, tons.	Maple sugar, pounds.	Cane sugar, hhds. of 1,000 pounds.	Molasses, gallons.	Rice, pounds.	Tobacco, pounds.	Ginned cotton, bales of 400 pounds.	Wool, pounds.	Silk cocoons, pounds.
20	Coweta	....	....	....	....	....	6,365	605	10,369	11,527	....
21	Crawford	....	....	....	....	1,457	21,020	157	7,477	7,578	4
22	Dade	70	....	....	....	....	63	4,773	15	2,826	....
23	Decatur	....	....	....	65	30,701	55,303	157,937	5,308	14,385	35
24	De Kalb	....	....	....	....	....	1,275	1,930	2,397	8,820	....
25	Dooly	100	....	....	8	12,265	10,825	25	5,962	16,988	1
26	Early	....	....	....	16	10,158	48,790	....	4,354	9,995	....
27	Effingham	....	....	....	22	3,580	257,901	....	15	15,639	....
28	Elbert	....	....	....	....	....	2,509	3,858	8,565	12,981	....
29	Emanuel	....	....	....	21	5,564	8,824	746	559	25,787	5
30	Fayette	....	....	....	....	....	420	545	4,253	7,494	....
31	Floyd	....	....	....	....	....	53	450	1,976	4,429	....
32	Forsyth	....	....	....	....	....	5,135	59,548	472	11,196	14
33	Franklin	....	....	....	....	....	16,288	18,207	2,653	19,740	....
34	Gilmer	1,973	....	....	....	....	5,805	14,752	....	8,609	....
35	Glynn	....	....	....	71	5,766	3,829,875	....	1,036	1,554	....
36	Gordon	....	....	....	....	....	100	1,130	184	6,837	....
37	Greene	....	....	....	....	....	....	....	12,600	13,940	....
38	Gwinnett	120	....	....	....	....	108	5,901	2,531	10,858	....
39	Habersham	85	....	....	....	....	443	12,508	36	16,438	....
40	Hall	7	....	....	....	....	19,366	22,767	205	11,207	....
41	Hancock	....	....	....	....	....	....	70	11,374	12,171	....
42	Harris	....	....	....	....	....	8,103	350	11,935	11,767	11
43	Heard	....	....	....	....	....	30	....	3,384	5,442	....
44	Henry	50	....	....	....	....	88	100	9,352	12,857	....
45	Houston	....	....	....	....	8,167	71,720	....	19,362	14,728	....
46	Irwin	....	....	....	37	7,521	25,126	489	112	7,652	....
47	Jackson	10	....	....	....	....	738	3,395	1,202	8,427	14
48	Jasper	....	....	....	....	....	3,420	467	9,899	10,421	....
49	Jefferson	....	....	....	....	200	826	....	10,441	17,251	....
50	Jones	....	....	....	....	....	100	....	9,000	12,592	....
51	Laurens	....	....	....	1	5,205	8,885	245	3,883	14,849	....
52	Lee	....	....	....	....	9,190	11,010	60	9,342	9,821	....
53	Liberty	....	....	....	24	11,640	1,892,462	....	1,883	8,865	....
54	Lincoln	....	....	....	....	....	25	....	5,447	7,925	....
55	Lowndes	....	....	....	198	9,397	66,300	....	2,912	22,420	....
56	Lumpkin	....	....	....	....	....	16,037	5,401	14	11,843	....
57	Macon	....	....	....	....	2,180	24,890	....	5,773	9,768	....
58	Madison	50	....	....	....	....	1,220	4,006	2,219	8,000	505
59	McIntosh	....	....	....	3	7,217	3,122,919	....	520	300	....
60	Marion	....	....	....	6	3,547	....	....	7,149	7,509	....
61	Meriwether	....	....	....	....	....	3,934	375	12,862	11,326	21
62	Monroe	....	....	....	....	240	352	115	15,012	16,624	....
63	Montgomery	....	....	....	9	5,202	5,770	557	292	10,923	....
64	Morgan	....	....	....	....	....	....	....	11,541	9,111	....
65	Murray	....	....	....	....	....	5,200	1,391	159	11,779	....
66	Muscogee	....	....	....	....	100	15,556	....	8,508	2,224	....
67	Newton	....	....	....	....	....	44	100	6,938	7,490	20
68	Oglethorpe	....	....	....	....	....	....	950	12,249	12,622	....
69	Paulding	....	....	....	....	....	1,065	8,742	1,439	5,362	....
70	Pike	20	....	....	....	....	2,620	815	8,002	8,862	....
71	Pulaski	....	....	....	....	1,700	5	....	5,501	10,264	....
72	Putnam	....	....	....	....	....	....	....	8,621	8,395	....
73	Rabun	1,268	....	....	....	2	....	6,787	....	6,603	....
74	Randolph	....	....	....	4	7,493	7,425	75	10,533	15,085	....
75	Richmond	....	....	....	....	....	9,413	....	1,087	5,578	....
76	Scriven	....	....	....	....	4,585	510,550	....	3,936	37,760	....
77	Stewart	....	....	....	....	65	16,390	70	19,165	11,190	5
78	Sumter	....	....	50	....	13,332	....	....	7,535	9,241	....
79	Talbot	....	....	....	....	90	13,368	410	13,732	11,360	50
80	Taliaferro	....	....	....	....	....	43	360	5,170	4,743	....
81	Tatnall	....	....	....	20	1,426	47,800	....	321	9,933	....
82	Telfair	....	....	....	43	5,319	41,670	....	572	11,585	....
83	Thomas	....	....	....	109	9,312	102,480	2,204	7,667	26,990	....
84	Troup	400	....	....	....	170	3,952	1,190	14,481	11,441	10
85	Twiggs	....	....	....	....	....	....	20	9,689	6,403	....
86	Union	1,174	....	....	....	....	....	11,827	....	16,829	....
87	Upson	....	....	....	....	....	17	....	7,443	7,494	....
88	Walker	60	....	....	....	....	4,903	9,795	359	9,585	....
89	Walton	....	....	....	....	....	7,280	2,100	5,599	8,980	....
90	Ware	....	....	....	....	2,792	40,895	....	394	1,727	....
91	Warren	....	....	....	....	94	5,210	664	9,994	12,964	13
92	Washington	....	....	....	....	85	4,395	37	7,445	20,968	....
93	Wayne	....	....	....	10	540	41,180	....	87	1,133	....
94	Wilkes	....	....	....	....	....	....	20	12,024	12,061	....
95	Wilkinson	....	....	....	....	50	16,614	80	4,920	10,077	....

AGRICULTURAL PRODUCTS.					MANUFACTURES.					
					Establishments.				REMARKS.	
Beeswax and honey, pounds.	Value of animals slaughtered.	Value of produce of market gardens.	Value of orchard produce.	Wine, gallons.	Capital.	Hands employed.	Annual product.	Produced in families.		
21,141	$98,588	....	....	......	$79,190	127	$157,372	$25,477	....	20
16,554	83,641	....	$5	6	11,255	20	12,880	19,729	....	21
4,510	16,231	$4	5	......	10,100	15	15,425	14,761	....	22
1,445	63,045	....	202	......	19,425	19	18,075	13,720	....	23
10,013	72,170	....	270	......	68,895	182	126,592	32,284	....	24
1,318	76,985	....	55	......	13,725	26	14,195	33,502	....	25
9,370	48,175	....	....	......	19,000	39	33,575	....	....	26
808	26,462	....	....	......	....	.....	....	3,553	....	27
15,128	83,075	....	19,403	......	63,850	102	67,900	27,062	....	28
925	48,570	....	566	......	....	.....	....	21,436	....	29
15,353	81,236	....	....	......	3,100	9	7,275	30,367	....	30
317	42,601	....	154	......	12,800	56	28,925	8,093	Divided in 1849 to form	31
10,113	60,121	197	65	......	14,300	25	13,000	57,162	Gordon.	32
20,259	99,634	18,082	65	......	11,762	8	4,927	105,066	....	33
3,641	40,677	39	....	......	3,400	12	7,520	19,997	....	34
1,804	11,189	....	....	25	50,550	74	22,000	1,032	....	35
2,705	45,019	150	20	......	....	.....	....	16,452	Formed in 1849 from	36
8,060	91,925	....	....	......	160,699	298	183,897	15,712	Cass and Floyd.	37
8,373	75,852	100	592	......	47,200	82	113,350	27,374	....	38
1,769	55,617	10	1,314	......	15,100	29	9,790	31,275	....	39
10,536	49,301	10	16,089	......	....	.....	....	31,556	....	40
7,832	96,004	....	600	80	126,185	115	76,064	17,809	....	41
36,627	135,999	....	5,073	......	86,965	194	175,925	25,901	....	42
150	50,319	....	....	......	19,500	23	19,980	34,734	....	43
29,585	105,265	....	....	......	16,800	24	22,150	70,944	....	44
11,289	148,740	....	25	......	108,200	114	78,403	23,439	....	45
1,475	37,010	30	....	......	....	.....	....	12,134	....	46
8,104	52,009	23	120	......	20,550	23	60,054	27,145	....	47
13,899	89,427	....	7,102	20	25,925	31	42,045	17,322	....	48
159	66,665	....	....	......	86,800	91	116,450	12,782	....	49
9,561	86,398	....	731	155	55,625	95	109,664	16,455	....	50
434	50,877	....	100	......	22,750	25	30,414	12,168	....	51
540	71,421	....	....	......	25,500	30	22,790	32,962	....	52
3,048	28,557	....	....	......	4,950	24	7,042	4,737	....	53
6,642	47,496	....	....	......	19,625	36	22,423	8,064	....	54
....	66,703	....	....	......	2,800	4	1,550	21,721	Divided in 1849 to form	55
2,026	65,446	292	356	......	....	.....	....	21,050	Clinch.	56
8,212	63,085	....	....	......	....	.....	....	25,210	....	57
4,107	43,011	....	....	......	2,850	7	2,700	21,276	....	58
125	13,928	....	....	......	140,150	156	172,268	....	....	59
10	68,193	....	....	......	1,660	6	7,080	13,637	....	60
30,105	114,756	....	....	......	....	.....	....	26,571	....	61
35,999	139,516	....	378	......	36,200	46	27,000	35,556	....	62
....	18,282	....	....	6	....	.....	....	6,293	....	63
340	93,655	....	....	......	120,106	198	169,075	5,625	....	64
....	90,400	....	50	......	38,900	81	52,400	47,556	....	65
20	66,641	....	54	......	713,217	719	738,580	9,441	....	66
8,778	71,626	....	40	......	86,050	138	70,866	15,615	....	67
1,466	95,444	....	25	......	31,100	67	58,700	18,963	....	68
3,517	43,084	155	....	......	7,750	16	10,400	16,247	....	69
18,692	86,268	....	....	......	66,525	120	97,200	41,934	....	70
556	65,140	....	16	......	4,500	4	2,318	7,263	....	71
274	77,551	....	1,006	......	121,010	182	129,978	9,469	....	72
10,355	18,060	3,479	10,818	......	....	.....	....	19,363	....	73
34,676	139,523	....	....	40	71,350	97	55,600	31,270	....	74
2,474	81,573	21,587	6,875	320	775,600	995	1,020,651	2,351	....	75
....	107,583	....	....	......	....	.....	....	12,762	....	76
46,396	111,249	....	....	......	44,175	113	83,887	15,247	....	77
11,671	84,798	26	250	10	41,180	81	43,094	20,855	....	78
26,028	122,385	....	105	......	71,545	125	147,745	29,698	....	79
3,688	36,480	....	45	......	16,560	29	15,864	7,819	....	80
165	29,106	....	....	......	9,300	13	21,070	6,283	....	81
....	31,502	....	....	......	....	.....	....	7,800	....	82
....	75,576	....	....	......	23,400	24	26,332	23,561	....	83
30,545	128,774	....	25	......	84,910	92	62,340	23,702	....	84
766	86,731	....	....	......	....	.....	....	15,256	....	85
1,949	46,366	6,483	20	......	2,700	6	3,544	24,665	....	86
12,278	63,416	70	195	5	174,200	268	194,195	10,477	....	87
573	49,310	....	....	......	3,000	25	10,000	11,513	....	88
15,620	84,635	....	150	3	45,735	124	124,002	59,812	....	89
9,680	31,107	....	1,499	......	....	.....	....	9,526	Divided by act of 1849 to	90
11,473	113,481	....	....	......	67,236	109	57,280	3,818	form Clinch, but the	91
6,647	106,249	....	....	......	13,605	21	13,770	24,116	returns have not been	92
1,320	11,472	....	....	......	....	.....	....	2,336	separated.	93
23	78,216	....	....	......	28,025	55	39,800	16,422	....	94
11,762	105,171	....	....	......	12,500	17	11,000	19,875	....	95

	COUNTIES.	POPULATION.								
		Whites.			Colored.		All classes.		Total population.	
		Male.	Female.	Total.	Free.	Slave.	Male.	Female.	1850.	1840.
1	Adams	13,679	12,690	26,369	139	....	13,734	12,774	26,508	14,476
2	Alexander	1,330	1,134	2,464	20	....	1,339	1,145	2,484	3,313
3	Bond	3,215	2,921	6,136	8	....	3,220	2,924	6,144	5,060
4	Boone	4,002	3,616	7,618	6	....	4,005	3,619	7,624	1,705
5	Brown	3,802	3,380	7,182	16	....	3,807	3,391	7,198	4,183
6	Bureau	4,663	4,168	8,831	10	....	4,667	4,174	8,841	3,067
7	Calhoun	1,834	1,396	3,230	1	....	1,835	1,396	3,231	1,741
8	Carroll	2,496	2,087	4,583	3	....	2,496	2,090	4,586	1,023
9	Cass	3,865	3,383	7,248	5	....	3,870	3,383	7,253	2,981
10	Champaign	1,396	1,251	2,647	2	....	1,398	1,251	2,649	1,475
11	Christian	1,669	1,534	3,203	....	....	1,669	1,534	3,203	1,878
12	Clark	4,873	4,621	9,494	38	....	4,892	4,640	9,532	7,453
13	Clay	2,265	2,003	4,268	21	....	2,276	2,013	4,289	3,228
14	Clinton	2,703	2,299	5,002	137	....	2,778	2,361	5,139	3,718
15	Coles	4,752	4,547	9,299	36	....	4,771	4,564	9,335	9,616
16	Cook	23,485	19,522	43,007	378	....	23,694	19,691	43,385	10,201
17	Crawford	3,660	3,458	7,118	17	....	3,670	3,465	7,135	4,422
18	Cumberland	1,899	1,819	3,718	....	....	1,899	1,819	3,718	....
19	De Kalb	3,958	3,581	7,539	1	....	3,959	3,581	7,540	1,697
20	De Witt	2,554	2,447	5,001	1	....	2,554	2,448	5,002	3,247
21	Du Page	4,940	4,347	9,287	3	....	4,943	4,347	9,290	3,535
22	Edgar	5,504	5,136	10,640	52	....	5,534	5,158	10,692	8,225
23	Edwards	1,842	1,648	3,490	34	....	1,858	1,666	3,524	3,070
24	Effingham	1,978	1,814	3,792	7	....	1,981	1,818	3,799	1,675
25	Fayette	4,109	3,918	8,027	48	....	4,132	3,943	8,075	6,328
26	Franklin	2,906	2,740	5,646	35	....	2,922	2,759	5,681	3,682
27	Fulton	11,592	10,900	22,492	16	....	11,601	10,907	22,508	13,142
28	Gallatin	2,618	2,477	5,095	353	....	2,771	2,677	5,448	10,760
29	Greene	6,492	5,877	12,369	60	....	6,526	5,903	12,429	11,951
30	Grundy	1,645	1,376	3,021	2	....	1,647	1,376	3,023	....
31	Hamilton	3,271	3,039	6,310	52	....	3,303	3,059	6,362	3,945
32	Hancock	7,723	6,910	14,633	19	....	7,734	6,918	14,652	9,946
33	Hardin	1,441	1,367	2,808	79	....	1,478	1,409	2,887	1,378
34	Henderson	2,452	2,158	4,610	2	....	2,454	2,158	4,612	....
35	Henry	1,934	1,873	3,807	....	....	1,934	1,873	3,807	1,260
36	Iroquois	2,152	1,918	4,070	79	....	2,193	1,956	4,149	1,695
37	Jackson	3,037	2,792	5,829	33	....	3,054	2,808	5,862	3,566
38	Jasper	1,725	1,481	3,206	14	....	1,732	1,488	3,220	1,472
39	Jefferson	4,151	3,932	8,083	26	....	4,162	3,947	8,109	5,762
40	Jersey	3,941	3,359	7,300	54	....	3,970	3,384	7,354	4,535
41	Joe Daviess	9,905	8,481	18,386	218	....	10,026	8,578	18,604	6,180
42	Johnson	2,107	1,990	4,097	17	....	2,116	1,998	4,114	3,626
43	Kane	8,658	8,039	16,697	6	....	8,662	8,041	16,703	6,501
44	Kendall	4,116	3,608	7,724	6	....	4,120	3,610	7,730	....
45	Knox	6,874	6,323	13,197	82	....	6,909	6,370	13,279	7,060
46	Lake	7,533	6,654	14,187	39	....	7,553	6,673	14,226	2,634
47	Lasalle	9,512	8,287	17,799	16	....	9,522	8,293	17,815	9,348
48	Lawrence	3,005	2,838	5,843	278	....	3,149	2,972	6,121	7,092
49	Lee	2,804	2,484	5,288	4	....	2,806	2,486	5,292	2,035
50	Livingston	827	725	1,552	....	....	827	725	1,552	759
51	Logan	2,709	2,419	5,128	....	....	2,709	2,419	5,128	2,333
52	McDonough	4,047	3,564	7,611	5	....	4,049	3,567	7,616	5,308
53	McHenry	7,927	7,048	14,975	3	....	7,927	7,051	14,978	2,578
54	McLean	5,252	4,869	10,121	42	....	5,276	4,887	10,163	6,565
55	Macon	2,089	1,896	3,985	3	....	2,091	1,897	3,988	3,039
56	Macoupin	6,433	5,839	12,272	83	....	6,479	5,876	12,355	7,826
57	Madison	10,947	9,045	19,992	449	....	11,166	9,275	20,441	14,433
58	Marion	3,467	3,249	6,716	4	....	3,469	3,251	6,720	4,742
59	Marshall	2,717	2,461	5,178	2	....	2,718	2,462	5,180	1,849
60	Mason	3,161	2,737	5,898	23	....	3,167	2,754	5,921	....
61	Massac	2,113	1,957	4,070	22	....	2,129	1,963	4,092	....
62	Menard	3,297	3,031	6,328	21	....	3,310	3,039	6,349	4,431
63	Mercer	2,796	2,448	5,244	2	....	2,797	2,449	5,246	2,352
64	Monroe	4,166	3,467	7,633	46	....	4,191	3,488	7,679	4,481
65	Montgomery	3,180	3,078	6,258	19	....	3,190	3,087	6,277	4,490
66	Morgan	8,337	7,602	15,939	125	....	8,404	7,660	16,064	19,547
67	Moultrie	1,680	1,545	3,225	9	....	1,687	1,547	3,234	....
68	Ogle	5,360	4,630	9,990	30	....	5,379	4,641	10,020	3,479
69	Peoria	9,360	8,101	17,461	86	....	9,409	8,138	17,547	6,153
70	Perry	2,813	2,454	5,267	11	....	2,819	2,459	5,278	3,222
71	Piatt	863	743	1,606	....	....	863	743	1,606	....
72	Pike	9,670	9,106	18,776	43	....	9,692	9,127	18,819	11,728
73	Pope	2,049	1,822	3,871	104	....	2,102	1,873	3,975	4,094
74	Pulaski	1,181	1,076	2,257	8	....	1,185	1,080	2,265	....
75	Putnam	2,063	1,857	3,920	4	....	2,065	1,859	3,924	2,131
76	Randolph	5,709	4,987	10,696	383	....	5,901	5,178	11,079	7,944

NATIVITIES, DWELLINGS, &c.				EDUCATION AND RELIGION.									
Born out of State.				Colleges, academies, and private schools.		Public Schools.							
United States.	Foreign countries.	Dwellings.	Families.	Pupils.	Annual income.	Pupils.	Annual income.	Total educational income.	White scholars during the year.	Whites 5 and under 20 years old.	Whites over 20 unable to read & write.	Accommodation of churches—persons.	
12,373	4,294	4,459	4,731	250	$4,360	4,000	$7,353	$11,713	5,440	10,176	790	8,285	1
1,280	96	455	455	......	......	228	843	843	328	954	469	550	2
2,613	167	1,076	1,100	60	720	1,500	13 715	14,435	1,531	2,645	34	5,050	3
4,617	1,402	1,352	1,405	90	......	1,843	2,504	2,504	2,034	2,905	75	1,900	4
3,655	340	1,353	1,356	......	......	1,662	1,756	1,756	1,640	2,997	748	2,220	5
5,177	903	1,464	1,566	......	......	1,473	3,687	3,687	2,272	3,400	87	3,726	6
1,352	425	600	602	......	......	196	......	......	292	1,200	456	350	7
2,988	437	814	835	......	......	1,135	1,954	1,954	1,116	1,725	44	250	8
2,560	1,161	1,169	1,245	......	......	1,000	......	......	1,650	2,884	150	3,725	9
1,607	49	480	480	......	......	......	......	......	820	1,088	25	1,000	10
1,609	51	555	568	......	......	592	7,200	7,200	686	1,300	290	3,200	11
5,113	282	1,621	1,621	......	......	2,816	5,098	5,098	2,158	4,099	141	1,765	12
2,441	27	715	720	......	......	480	375	375	862	1,819	661	1,200	13
1,493	948	947	954	......	......	375	1,400	1,400	743	1,921	361	6,200	14
5,205	70	1,571	1,592	50	......	1,290	1,390	1,390	1,456	4,027	443	3,750	15
11,872	21,863	7,674	7,755	477	4,000	3,910	16,396	20,396	5,228	13,993	681	25,975	16
2,490	34	1,192	1,192	......	......	620	776	776	1,691	2,992	938	2,950	17
2,250	26	634	634	......	......	425	250	250	786	1,598	209	450	18
4,986	822	1,303	1,356	100	......	1,865	2,497	2,497	2,096	2,925	237	600	19
2,758	47	881	886	......	......	941	787	787	1,433	2,065	56	2,514	20
4,286	2,664	1,568	1,598	130	1,535	850	3,646	5,181	2,468	3,412	251	3,540	21
5,762	140	1,702	1,713	165	1,667	690	5,950	7,617	2,910	4,399	1,025	11,150	22
906	622	595	602	......	......	1,054	915	915	736	1,555	204	3,600	23
1,670	601	712	713	......	......	526	188	188	491	1,458	140	1,180	24
3,788	159	1,431	1,443	......	......	900	2,170	2,170	1,277	3,423	171	1,300	25
2,236	23	971	1,003	60	610	350	2,650	3,260	1,065	2,441	589	3,000	26
13,229	766	3,811	3,978	95	612	3,525	5,324	5,936	6,388	9,172	454	9,575	27
2,073	227	1,000	1,001	......	......	555	2,835	2,835	896	2,041	563	2,050	28
5,103	461	2,024	2,037	......	......	1,700	2,750	2,750	2,301	5,199	289	5,800	29
1,593	775	543	547	......	......	350	450	450	608	1,073	216	150	30
2,605	145	1,058	1,058	......	......	1,468	3,205	3,205	1,046	2,672	1,079	2,700	31
8,169	1,386	2,585	2,594	......	......	2,630	5,448	5,448	3,745	5,908	173	4,950	32
1,277	13	485	485	......	......	375	1,775	1,775	253	1,167	98	2,400	33
2,969	210	805	820	......	......	......	2,243	2,243	1,146	1,816	68	1,950	34
1,841	811	772	772	......	......	728	2,431	2,431	882	1,480	......	......	35
2,783	231	718	718	......	......	......	362	362	1,145	1,727	301	200	36
2,150	164	1,038	1,060	......	......	1,050	1,138	1,138	1,203	2,461	1,032	3,170	37
2,010	261	588	588	......	......	180	200	200	177	1,318	194	1,500	38
3,638	32	1,368	1,368	......	......	2,274	3,405	3,405	1,702	3,475	1,260	27,800	39
3,236	439	1,222	1,226	......	......	963	2,362	2,362	1,823	2,839	388	2,060	40
6,080	6,389	3,431	3,436	246	2,904	2,480	55,362	58,266	3,287	6,586	603	3,880	41
2,194	7	718	718	......	......	524	591	591	661	1,700	656	2,200	42
9,160	3,629	2,828	3,087	225	1,175	3,965	6,579	7,754	3,961	6,285	323	4,535	43
4,515	1,334	1,258	1,258	......	......	3,556	2,082	2,082	2,019	3,004	54	3,800	44
8,065	689	2,193	2,244	337	4,000	2,508	7,148	11,148	4,177	5,534	217	4,800	45
7,239	3,587	2,455	2,500	60	......	2,450	2,552	2,552	4,166	5,234	497	1,850	46
8,214	4,835	3,074	3,163	85	......	1,405	3,671	3,671	3,798	6,528	566	8,300	47
2,859	150	1,057	1,057	......	......	1,000	1,441	1,441	1,396	2,426	264	4,300	48
3,173	863	905	920	40	300	1,518	653	953	1,220	2,066	243	2,900	49
967	59	261	267	......	......	200	83	83	189	614	15	300	50
2,491	246	835	844	......	......	......	......	......	1,393	2,169	167	......	51
4,181	206	1,262	1,263	......	......	1,879	671	671	1,903	3,291	57	3,645	52
9,112	2,445	2,650	2,689	......	......	5,936	5,782	5,782	4,245	5,785	238	2,500	53
5,641	216	1,851	1,890	100	2,100	800	1,795	3,895	2,406	4,090	100	21,800	54
2,219	......	693	693	......	......	600	800	800	1,010	1,692	159	1,500	55
5,652	725	2,037	2,072	45	......	1,958	6,034	6,034	3,356	5,054	627	5,575	56
6,678	5,155	3,490	3,498	254	1,100	3,654	6,282	7,382	3,975	7,516	836	24,200	57
3,124	23	1,132	1,663	......	......	668	2,336	2,336	1,838	2,838	936	2,800	58
2,976	506	910	910	......	......	800	......	......	656	2,024	212	3,800	59
2,991	456	1,041	1,041	......	......	440	1,800	1,800	660	2,311	423	400	60
2,642	74	704	704	......	......	143	164	164	618	1,654	563	410	61
2,732	249	1,035	1,046	65	......	655	1,300	1,300	1,689	2,700	120	3,100	62
3,224	333	892	892	......	......	196	1,045	1,045	1,061	2,166	81	1,750	63
1,631	2,707	1,421	1,444	......	......	759	172	172	1,307	2,953	726	2,830	64
2,806	44	1,051	1,078	60	......	1,663	2,803	2,803	1,472	2,682	153	4,900	65
6,745	1,477	2,661	2,724	381	10,500	1,613	32,060	42,560	3,503	6,401	102	13,250	66
1,589	85	554	554	......	......	380	1,254	1,254	755	1,383	264	2,100	67
6,458	1,237	1,678	1,725	70	1,200	2,065	2,552	3,752	2,507	3,845	80	2,025	68
9,610	2,633	3,036	3,118	30	2,400	3,260	5,304	7,704	3,627	6,531	337	4,795	69
2,143	256	967	973	......	......	340	695	695	808	2,188	102	750	70
1,049	29	157	163	......	......	300	250	250	377	633	69	900	71
10,036	798	3,152	3,219	30	245	3,241	11,449	11,694	4,683	7,663	412	4,640	72
1,912	59	747	747	......	......	570	2,825	2,825	216	1,593	55	10,600	73
1,002	53	418	425	......	......	149	481	481	324	929	347	2,178	74
2,177	398	636	713	......	......	880	2,427	2,427	1,098	1,469	62	3,830	75
3,132	1,987	2,046	2,056	......	......	1,414	215	215	1,474	4,214	336	28,400	76

	COUNTIES.	LAND OCCUPIED OR IMPROVED.				LIVE STOCK UPON FARMS.			
		Farms.	Acres improved.	Acres unimproved.	Value with improvements and implements.	Horses, asses, and mules.	Neat cattle.	Sheep.	Swine.
1	Adams	2,294	147,273	168,872	$ 3,363,950	7,580	23,821	25,329	65,712
2	Alexander	202	5,333	16,882	101,483	558	1,752	570	11,106
3	Bond	665	48,038	85,214	610,539	3,200	10,400	9,156	18,610
4	Boone	897	50,763	76,711	1,129,243	1,775	8,032	9,005	6,001
5	Brown	818	34,846	73,458	921,534	2,374	6,454	8,785	19,389
6	Bureau	741	62,470	74,325	1,345,442	3,392	10,095	9,232	12,367
7	Calhoun	205	7,295	29,076	194,385	745	2,923	688	6,580
8	Carroll	482	32,776	54,760	652,733	1,404	5,270	4,311	6,786
9	Cass	606	54,578	46,732	1,281,418	2,834	10,375	7,233	27,885
10	Champaign	273	22,873	35,300	477,850	1,174	4,752	3,625	8,687
11	Christian	434	27,654	43,412	530,212	1,682	6,208	3,650	17,968
12	Clark	636	35,899	67,120	615,384	1,884	5,672	7,984	18,262
13	Clay	237	18,354	29,996	257,762	821	3,608	3,331	11,086
14	Clinton	628	40,410	66,532	554,386	2,456	8,432	4,321	18,684
15	Coles	996	77,544	123,669	1,322,326	4,059	16,097	14,637	28,707
16	Cook	1,857	154,090	109,844	2,694,523	3,586	22,072	13,496	9,398
17	Crawford	542	34,697	65,041	569,932	2,164	5,034	6,752	20,738
18	Cumberland	326	16,001	49,602	304,434	999	3,739	3,070	6,953
19	De Kalb	812	63,749	81,293	993,218	1,999	7,093	5,666	7,593
20	De Witt	482	36,945	48,402	831,287	1,835	6,290	7,402	10,364
21	Du Page	960	86,200	59,231	1,800,078	2,266	10,020	12,617	5,080
22	Edgar	1,175	91,532	106,503	1,782,425	5,812	16,759	20,103	37,448
23	Edwards	329	20,216	37,212	283,860	1,339	3,597	5,650	13,548
24	Effingham	391	14,457	43,259	257,902	1,066	5,117	3,441	12,171
25	Fayette	826	38,258	100,529	693,039	3,319	10,792	9,066	26,829
26	Franklin	577	29,003	50,304	299,059	2,193	6,231	5,228	21,299
27	Fulton	1,942	124,817	148,203	3,007,713	6,465	18,818	32,919	52,724
28	Gallatin	570	19,956	52,026	347,788	1,760	3,366	2,074	22,514
29	Greene	1,155	87,257	113,574	1,872,492	5,770	17,415	20,923	48,236
30	Grundy	327	15,916	35,738	380,954	803	3,501	1,194	2,776
31	Hamilton	417	19,102	37,475	379,385	1,483	3,955	4,543	14,948
32	Hancock	1,167	80,163	93,769	1,480,884	3,478	13,258	10,557	28,547
33	Hardin	326	10,531	34,283	209,298	839	2,704	2,337	9,579
34	Henderson	420	35,796	48,879	804,578	1,539	6,513	4,489	11,823
35	Henry	281	22,983	24,276	331,498	1,370	5,484	3,465	7,104
36	Iroquois	387	30,118	36,812	555,640	1,475	5,711	10,313	10,455
37	Jackson	604	22,778	40,657	315,061	2,502	6,606	3,746	22,002
38	Jasper	283	10,948	38,774	208,686	765	2,477	2,339	5,831
39	Jefferson	470	29,660	19,727	284,791	2,370	7,834	6,998	15,670
40	Jersey	645	56,491	66,858	1,655,565	3,214	8,758	4,792	22,543
41	Joe Daviess	1,370	60,311	137,839	1,430,488	2,768	10,918	5,217	13,912
42	Johnson	301	9,658	18,261	119,088	849	1,855	1,424	9,254
43	Kane	1,015	83,738	102,256	2,039,036	2,567	11,139	18,079	6,610
44	Kendall	659	79,257	70,885	1,430,486	3,372	10,293	7,079	12,570
45	Knox	619	103,267	77,248	1,872,416	5,592	15,271	22,773	40,414
46	Lake	1,595	88,929	127,914	2,035,954	2,234	16,226	18,580	7,178
47	Lasalle	1,336	93,008	118,546	1,917,641	4,521	15,323	11,646	13,698
48	Lawrence	636	34,684	56,968	646,437	2,570	5,800	5,045	21,556
49	Lee	478	38,678	46,484	730,114	1,408	5,055	4,386	5,679
50	Livingston	185	13,334	18,499	181,125	676	2,602	2,637	4,812
51	Logan	476	46,694	67,925	981,192	2,236	8,047	8,973	15,689
52	McDonough	843	51,541	82,072	1,175,019	3,224	11,635	11,945	25,985
53	McHenry	1,950	125,010	159,204	2,246,413	3,808	18,193	21,652	12,885
54	McLean	916	92,540	91,730	1,665,436	4,482	20,511	19,676	29,863
55	Macon	487	33,330	69,901	836,505	2,117	7,696	7,536	16,981
56	Macoupin	1,183	97,897	113,892	1,792,242	5,962	17,229	13,397	44,953
57	Madison	1,367	93,251	165,067	2,577,611	7,062	21,210	9,085	40,233
58	Marion	827	43,916	65,250	464,614	2,888	9,227	10,409	19,938
59	Marshall	464	36,301	58,192	870,721	2,119	6,290	6,021	9,878
60	Mason	727	46,223	42,201	773,759	2,018	6,218	4,216	9,855
61	Massac	385	10,571	31,691	188,273	979	2,327	1,732	13,750
62	Menard	706	55,785	55,704	1,181,991	3,520	10,678	12,160	25,194
63	Mercer	517	34,929	47,434	625,353	2,068	5,871	6,576	14,393
64	Monroe	874	39,687	74,186	780,148	2,860	8,213	1,488	16,078
65	Montgomery	811	49,206	86,829	714,675	3,912	9,681	8,465	21,184
66	Morgan	1,574	142,272	97,662	3,018,828	6,796	23,581	20,032	61,372
67	Moultrie	304	23,132	41,839	383,115	1,354	4,357	6,748	9,096
68	Ogle	1,058	77,208	146,848	1,877,532	3,269	10,855	12,925	15,513
69	Peoria	1,191	83,718	100,790	2,213,933	4,305	12,255	16,837	23,252
70	Perry	638	32,333	58,544	412,639	3,295	8,560	7,509	15,582
71	Piatt	163	23,502	22,892	290,010	813	3,778	2,167	8,373
72	Pike	1,382	87,957	105,455	1,563,336	5,342	14,505	16,516	41,871
73	Pope	504	15,629	30,898	208,033	1,214	3,073	2,594	12,301
74	Pulaski	266	7,332	22,809	140,394	757	1,565	763	7,834
75	Putnam	317	28,105	27,965	697,495	1,644	3,665	3,576	7,064
76	Randolph	1,100	50,655	108,246	972,539	4,037	14,325	7,808	22,587

AGRICULTURAL PRODUCTS.												
Wheat, bushels.	Rye & oats, bushels.	Indian corn, bushels.	Irish and sweet potatoes, bushels.	Peas and beans, bushels.	Barley, bushels.	Buckwheat, bushels.	Butter aud cheese, pounds.	Hay, tons.	Hops, pounds.	Clover & other grass seeds, bushels.	Flaxseed, bushels.	
502,034	277,760	2,092,713	40,489	79	797	6,745	360,380	10,878	100	411	48	1
1,698	3,435	92,920	4,356	88	......	......	19,810	44	......	......	......	2
7,655	86,556	460,985	9,091	2,292	20	715	122,938	3,529	......	5	......	3
248,107	143,227	159,114	40,641	836	1,190	6,681	202,321	12,676	32	108	119	4
76,658	51,816	513,118	16,826	131	20	1,119	73,150	3,000	1	55	482	5
171,402	119,278	542,823	49,462	309	656	2,228	172,471	9,428	18	205	4	6
3,370	9,125	146,205	5,626	20	......	......	20,027	163	......	4	......	7
136,301	74,803	218,061	24,608	158	3,277	1,947	113,268	6,625	5	109	......	8
131,136	151,533	1,417,750	9,871	5	25	438	99,102	3,385	......	49	......	9
7,023	38,890	441,060	3,688	......	10	96	54,440	1,406	......	8	15	10
17,295	51,080	594,475	7,162	996	......	673	67,879	1,008	......	65	493	11
18,350	81,296	431,490	17,789	529	126	4,123	89,295	1,720	80	327	318	12
2,244	38,681	245,755	3,841	181	......	298	28,190	320	111	77	95	13
19,682	72,038	414,898	9,814	143	106	467	99,577	930	......	......	......	14
21,338	136,716	1,012,735	16,302	3	......	1,715	169,523	4,125	......	133	142	15
238,952	406,098	429,513	205,039	531	6,068	14,565	734,752	48,449	10	60	375	16
16,943	61,853	453,955	15,871	1,128	......	3,144	110,509	1,411	13	138	391	17
5,122	34,411	217,015	8,620	10	......	3,353	52,421	863	......	85	91	18
221,796	138,903	215,733	41,531	259	685	3,969	160,390	21,193	......	121	19	19
22,401	46,357	704,600	8,420	19	15	1,136	65,650	2,083	......	12	253	20
259,283	230,512	198,363	53,068	245	5,745	3,282	217,975	23,617	......	187	162	21
49,424	139,981	1,250,278	22,481	1,002	810	2,173	189,068	6,153	74	449	382	22
4,001	37,682	227,035	8,690	547	100	138	24,727	1,502	205	397	72	23
5,169	36,699	227,025	9,626	154	......	2,167	43,044	341	......	42	133	24
18,277	89,523	398,765	15,883	606	......	1,624	148,031	1,657	50	81	130	25
3,008	24,902	268,690	9,811	7,298	5	19	49,567	383	......	52	73	26
274,479	179,660	1,430,717	42,278	851	4,077	6,316	325,478	9,931	3	1,538	......	27
1,777	26,177	436,125	12,603	212	......	......	47,017	286	6	6	......	28
168,822	105,468	1,346,973	23,984	1,217	137	1,669	220,786	5,611	......	319	......	29
46,875	32,851	143,778	16,147	103	332	806	64,925	7,329	......	75	......	30
2,948	28,841	242,955	10 421	1,732	43	10	48,921	264	......	74	359	31
189,436	139,166	689,110	22,375	302	2,511	2,575	226,278	6,076	226	254	60	32
613	6,420	164,400	14,694	721	......	42	6,664	9	......	75	2	33
121,775	53,416	352,840	10,278	80	45	353	98,899	2,813	50	36	......	34
61,108	44,574	203,820	3,226	50	1,915	587	76,055	15	......	......	......	35
27,125	70,035	311,115	14,730	379	180	2,131	78,198	1,496	......	37	109	36
22,354	30,155	273.050	14,712	836	15	956	45,974	240	28	21	34	37
3,540	19,691	132,585	3,033	8	......	554	35,635	379	......	3	150	38
3,965	38,883	302,944	7,459	2,742	......	46	74,457	647	200	44	39	39
154,127	97,316	759,530	31,182	155	50	1,531	115,530	2,883	......	28	......	40
207,288	251,044	220.615	78,731	610	2,408	3,232	196,839	20,029	329	176	4	41
6,887	10,709	133,295	8,358	303	......	10	19,066	34	37	47	31	42
316,493	206,364	337,593	63,472	152	7,162	10,992	274,411	23,244	21	681	72	43
213,660	139,098	410,986	38,428	1,079	4,751	5,512	207,492	14,700	50	2,004	......	44
201,481	229,391	1,570,361	29,538	214	801	1,343	251,704	13,164	10	1,372	267	45
320,071	250,897	168,915	89,619	905	4,761	5,888	482,440	35,506	74	425	19	46
253,598	200,145	637,483	61,579	359	627	3,939	180,651	25,179	7	303	......	47
15,582	59,727	427,850	15,966	576	......	1,530	95,876	1,926	......	165	571	48
97,538	99,631	232,010	31,001	454	2,021	4,749	102,632	8,661	......	147	13	49
15,517	25,409	129,785	4,361	......	90	100	15,329	298	......	71	......	50
26,598	36,650	839,638	8,197	58	65	551	61,723	2,093	......	88	42	51
100,107	76,789	550,768	6,643	262	......	377	131,014	3,286	6	156	111	52
562,269	270,560	301.248	89,706	744	10,022	7,949	390,343	27,678	11	417	......	53
63,893	126,199	1,226,533	16,871	25	148	1,510	220,661	5,450	......	23	1,204	54
22,226	91,460	698,220	12,569	204	25	284	101,585	1,451	......	52	......	55
77,022	258,130	1,598,829	24,637	2,955	......	1,550	407,752	3,411	22	139	13	56
88,893	202,670	1,153,183	276,936	1,669	220	839	265,960	6,499	56	85	49	57
5,813	72,082	413,335	12,974	239	2	254	114,662	1,553	......	95	184	58
104,469	47,390	392,317	21,833	29	30	255	73,681	4,967	......	64	......	59
142,474	70,580	555,610	1[illegible],441	......	......	30	66,377	1,825	......	......	......	60
4,179	12,608	146,700	31,473	151	20	1	30,760	30	1	14	192	61
69,106	129,107	1,280,206	8,745	2	......	389	129,974	3,447	......	102	4	62
103,479	60,544	430,991	10,034	18	76	1,407	87,685	1,029	12	121	4	63
89,856	58,561	399,250	26,581	68	942	74	73,657	267	......	1	......	64
21,455	98,700	452,885	14,273	3,878	45	1,536	96,452	3,048	......	64	90	65
91,453	171,107	2,693,021	26,259	21	1,556	676	396,640	9,723	......	49	3	66
6,148	60,318	373,630	4,419	3	......	190	44,806	995	......	25	9	67
289,323	199,992	480,758	49,476	292	2,248	4,025	226,108	13,019	16	307	3	68
185,157	138,800	1,013,289	39,013	291	886	2,537	110,391	12,553	2	298	20	69
6,605	66,363	363,300	8,389	11,439	20	396	133,979	157	......	15	73	70
5,769	29,115	430,655	2,813	......	......	460	39,080	158	......	2	......	71
194,051	130,989	1,375,045	28,290	3	370	5,771	126,025	4,491	13	441	......	72
2,352	10,958	223,592	14,908	477	......	......	13,932	14	......	......	......	73
4,305	16,326	87,145	11,192	644	......	20	25,695	118	22	9	52	74
88,771	29.671	279,260	25,656	30	390	506	56,185	3,732	......	27	......	75
60,914	125,205	443,491	29,194	127	163	649	105,138	1,296	......	126	309	76

	COUNTIES.	AGRICULTURAL PRODUCTS.									
		Flax, pounds.	Hemp, dew and water-rotted, tons.	Maple sugar, pounds.	Cane sugar, hhds. of 1,000 pounds.	Molasses, gallons.	Rice, pounds.	Tobacco, pounds.	Ginned cotton, bales of 400 pounds.	Wool, pounds.	Silk cocoons, pounds.
1	Adams	1,290		3,750		24		270		59,541	
2	Alexander	50								711	
3	Bond			270		27				18,098	6
4	Boone	360		3,160		43		150		26,282	
5	Brown	1,312		7,183		307				21,649	
6	Bureau	230				5				25,698	
7	Calhoun									1,662	
8	Carroll	92						20		9,900	
9	Cass	120								19,651	
10	Champaign	87		1,875		17				9,098	
11	Christian	320		380		30		2,000		9,948	
12	Clark	7,384		21,070		801				17,598	2
13	Clay	3,570		2,053		78		1,580		8,289	
14	Clinton	100								10,006	
15	Coles	3,102		5,122		121		100		34,087	
16	Cook	100		1,750						27,954	
17	Crawford	34,545		7,601		263		16,350		13,789	
18	Cumberland	6,412		10,990		214				6,186	
19	De Kalb	239		4,905		151				14,200	
20	De Witt	2,415						4,950		18,833	
21	Du Page	481		1,665				590		34,034	
22	Edgar	6,610		24,616		1,241		3,870		43,739	
23	Edwards	2,175		290		9		1,175		12,898	
24	Effingham	5,073		4,070				2,699		7,105	
25	Fayette	5,179		9,509		9		14,720		2,035	
26	Franklin	1,773						18,565		9,506	
27	Fulton	2,457		3,335		85				83,791	
28	Gallatin	1,120		150				200		4,567	
29	Greene	25				12				43,682	
30	Grundy									3,280	
31	Hamilton	1,833		10		10		7,242		8,295	6
32	Hancock	750		12,285		262		142		26,742	
33	Hardin	200		30				5,560		2,718	
34	Henderson	250		25				360		12,572	
35	Henry									10,762	
36	Iroquois	2,540		3,166		162				18,763	10
37	Jackson	1,656		5,685		124		580		7,371	13
38	Jasper	2,501		4,010		6				4,369	
39	Jefferson	1,136		1,368		28		3,120		14,027	
40	Jersey									11,631	
41	Joe Daviess	935						120		12,060	
42	Johnson	300		3,360		113		15,966		2,913	1
43	Kane	75		660		308		2,000		43,803	
44	Kendall			560		3		212		15,738	
45	Knox	986		3,568		150		110		67,849	5
46	Lake	469								45,895	
47	Lasalle									33,0[illegible]3	
48	Lawrence	10,528		2,370		79		7,297		12,617	3
49	Lee	75		1,000		10		180		12,125	
50	Livingston									6,815	
51	Logan	1,180		135				160		23,527	
52	McDonough	283		540		24		25		28,481	
53	McHenry	320						77		45,094	
54	McLean			4,135		3				49,883	
55	Macon									18,883	
56	Macoupin	560						200		32,851	
57	Madison	110						100		19,878	
58	Marion	1,060		3,625				8,488		22,116	
59	Marshall			60						18,586	
60	Mason									10,284	
61	Massac	135						16,520		2,904	
62	Menard	1,315		500				250		31,752	
63	Mercer	470		200						19,493	
64	Monroe			500		600		250		4,043	
65	Montgomery	375								18,858	
66	Morgan	40		28				2,600		54,643	
67	Moultrie	2,190								15,368	
68	Ogle	600		1,245		16				34,194	
69	Peoria	126		750		90				40,225	
70	Perry	40								15,988	
71	Piatt									5,769	
72	Pike	82						1,960		38,450	
73	Pope	60		100				4,290		2,937	
74	Pulaski	381		225		19		695		1,474	
75	Putnam			1,325		42				10,774	
76	Randolph	70								17,751	

AGRICULTURAL PRODUCTS.					MANUFACTURES.				REMARKS.	
					Establishments.					
Beeswax and honey, pounds.	Value of animals slaughtered.	Value of produce of market gardens.	Value of orchard produce	Wine, gallons.	Capital.	Hands employed.	Annual product.	Produced in families.		
21,717	$257,247	$1,896	$19,775	150	$260,200	632	$981,787	$34,749	......	1
269	11,655	......	......	......	19,250	34	34,681	1,614	Divided in 1842 to form	2
1,255	53,489	......	3,224	......	19,600	34	34,400	11,169	Pulaski.	3
4,090	35,427	796	1,070	......	42,175	55	136,350	6,691	......	4
9,235	65,238	580	16,566	......	85,655	160	156,216	28,198	......	5
11,847	63,098	333	3,405	4	29,200	48	99,758	4,259	......	6
4,440	15,359	......	2,500	......	......	......	......	934	......	7
2,952	27,120	4,343	918	5	73,350	50	171,601	3,194	......	8
987	68,928	295	5,802	......	84,800	263	370,937	6,068	......	9
1,418	20,638	20	2,080	......	......	......	......	3,439	......	10
5,850	19,596	......	2,365	......	17,800	37	37,600	8,407	......	11
11,424	38,426	3,204	2,401	10	10,565	35	62,405	13,050	......	12
10,903	24,364	......	916	......	4,950	14	9,000	7,794	Divided in 1844 to form	13
13,316	30,988	50	4,230	......	10,550	22	20,215	4,509	Richland.	14
20,780	70,338	......	8,143	......	......	......	......	28,558	Divided in 1841 to form	15
19,138	42,550	3,080	5,230	35	1,068,025	2,081	2,562,583	4,131	Cumberland.	16
16,387	42,851	25	1,383	......	......	......	......	17,406	......	17
10,777	14,872	......	170	......	......	......	......	9,655	Formed '41 from Coles.	18
4,873	33,259	76	559	......	5,000	9	8,717	2,683	......	19
9,128	17,441	......	4,340	......	17,700	45	19,462	12,956	Divided in 1841 to form	20
5,030	41,442	3	755	......	30,780	45	58,070	2,568	Piatt.	21
10,998	108,713	195	11,176	277	53,310	123	88,010	28,217	......	22
6,144	23,713	......	......	35	17,020	27	16,078	7,549	......	23
7,131	16,529	427	943	......	......	......	......	6,311	......	24
15,419	41,477	477	1,634	2	7,150	20	9,470	22,164	......	25
13,789	27,945	......	131	......	......	......	......	20,288	......	26
51,016	152,100	333	17,015	......	255,915	349	790,976	35,587	......	27
1,659	38,064	......	4,645	......	32,300	60	60,150	6,398	Divided in 1847 to form	28
1,949	51,101	108	17,378	......	38,270	78	80,918	21,163	Saline.	29
4,222	19,920	1,342	510	......	7,200	28	11,300	185	Formed in 1841 from	30
5,854	29,454	120	830	16	......	......	......	18,080	La Salle.	31
18,869	79,425	680	10,420	60	43,993	119	143,372	16,451	......	32
175	8,756	10	155	......	111,050	187	96,150	5,044	......	33
6,188	43,395	170	3,468	......	49,560	75	57,800	13,597	Formed in 1841 from	34
......	......	......	110	......	......	......	......	......	Warren.	35
13,474	17,000	......	1,665	......	......	......	......	3,686	......	36
2,889	26,569	1,404	3,186	5	21,450	65	48,851	11,537	......	37
5,342	10,391	......	711	......	......	......	......	6,656	......	38
12,885	21,146	10	561	......	4,570	7	17,530	18,648	......	39
745	92,238	30	7,501	115	23,925	71	58,010	5,450	......	40
13,885	44,957	31,690	4,305	......	287,636	669	1,897,464	4,542	[Massac.	41
1,877	17,801	566	357	......	4,900	14	4,925	9,996	Divided in 1842 to form	42
1,661	58,486	1,113	1,354	......	252,993	325	684,025	4,180	Div. '41 to form Kendall.	43
3,358	63,679	4,431	3,171	10	......	......	......	3,019	Formed in 1841 from	44
12,799	166,560	9,994	8,749	29	75,175	141	185,560	18,745	La Salle and Kane.	45
5,772	50,254	344	792	......	76,515	206	145,673	3,383	[Grundy and Kendall.	46
6,515	95,587	1,243	3,104	104	160,950	220	293,057	1,792	Divided in 1841 to form	47
12,356	53,787	......	261	......	35,175	71	108,855	12,274	Divided in 1844 to form	48
6,086	28,162	341	487	7	24,350	23	56,035	2,785	Richland.	49
5,196	6,688	......	12	......	......	......	......	200	Divided in 1841 to form	50
9,397	21,961	......	4,670	......	17,300	37	12,224	11,372	Woodford.	51
4,837	76,333	......	5,310	......	34,610	64	73,700	25,279	......	52
10,248	71,783	100	107	......	74,350	42	153,160	5,741	[Woodford.	53
58,055	45,454	160	8,073	10	27,000	44	85,037	15,363	Divided in 1841 to form	54
5,110	17,827	148	2,397	......	10,200	43	24,360	9,914	Divided in '41 and '42 to	55
12,193	65,951	4,565	10,143	......	29,175	76	48,811	57,665	form Piatt and Moul-	56
11,006	115,680	2,269	17,411	923	332,045	931	1,418,371	28,960	trie.	57
29,776	34,448	6,141	880	10	10,275	20	45,990	17,636	......	58
1,217	50,209	158	4,324	......	9,800	41	26,800	732	[Menard & Tazewell.	59
......	29,147	......	......	......	4,600	8	27,000	3,086	Formed in 1841 from	60
1,991	17,378	......	......	5	6,100	29	19,893	4,681	In '42 f. Pope & Johns'n	61
4,818	43,383	200	9,608	......	53,961	132	176,196	15,758	Divided in 1841 to form	62
4,927	46,105	20	1,895	65	......	......	......	7,723	Mason.	63
2,110	28,908	170	2,236	50	65,288	119	222,924	1,595	......	64
2,765	47,899	......	2,490	......	11,400	37	16,600	10,868	......	65
894	136,692	210	16,306	1	98,450	380	313,230	30,155	......	66
8,290	20,464	......	2,504	......	1,200	39	11,300	8,601	Formed in 1842 from	67
7,632	61,747	5,136	1,953	40	67,500	99	167,080	6,856	Macon and Shelby.	68
6,823	103,911	1,029	9,241	25	419,730	577	722,957	8,603	......	69
7,800	41,025	......	92	......	6,050	11	10,150	16,878	......	70
13,870	7,356	......	1,393	......	......	......	......	3,352	Formed in 1841 from	71
4,666	155,892	168	11,194	5	86,013	146	137,385	18,748	Macon and De Witt.	72
5	14,936	......	72	......	......	......	......	6,409	Div. '42 to form Massac.	73
2,723	12,450	569	1,273	......	11,095	42	20,649	3,308	Formed in 1842 from	74
8,057	30,961	149	3,442	6	17,380	44	39,364	2,083	Alexander.	75
364	37,095	......	5,809	......	105,250	148	237,143	1,167	......	76

	COUNTIES.	POPULATION.								
		Whites.			Colored.		All classes.		Total population.	
		Male.	Female.	Total.	Free.	Slave.	Male.	Female.	1850.	1840.
77	Richland	2,095	1,907	4,002	10	....	2,101	1,911	4,012	....
78	Rock Island	3,706	3,229	6,935	2	....	3,707	3,230	6,937	2,610
79	St. Clair	10,480	9,119	19,599	581	....	10,786	9,394	20,180	13,631
80	Saline	2,811	2,684	5,495	93	....	2,861	2,727	5,588	....
81	Sangamon	9,911	9,064	18,975	253	....	10,023	9,205	19,228	14,716
82	Schuyler	5,514	5,033	10,547	26	....	5,526	5,047	10,573	6,972
83	Scott	4,044	3,858	7,902	12	....	4,048	3,866	7,914	6,215
84	Shelby	4,025	3,737	7,762	45	....	4,051	3,756	7,807	6,659
85	Stark	1,940	1,770	3,710	....	....	1,940	1,770	3,710	1,573
86	Stephenson	6,267	5,391	11,658	8	....	6,271	5,395	11,666	2,800
87	Tazewell	6,381	5,635	12,016	36	....	6,394	5,658	12,052	7,221
88	Union	3,852	3,718	7,570	45	....	3,873	3,742	7,615	5,524
89	Vermillion	5,904	5,577	11,481	11	....	5,909	5,583	11,492	9,303
90	Wabash	2,338	2,302	4,640	50	....	2,362	2,328	4,690	4,240
91	Warren	4,339	3,823	8,162	14	....	4,346	3,830	8,176	6,739
92	Washington	3,611	3,318	6,929	24	....	3,623	3,330	6,953	4,810
93	Wayne	3,473	3,349	6,822	3	....	3,475	3,350	6,825	5,133
94	White	4,578	4,238	8,816	109	....	4,336	4,289	8,925	7,919
95	Whitesides	2,861	2,498	5,359	2	....	2,863	2,498	5,361	2,514
96	Will	8,850	7,820	16,670	33	....	8,871	7,832	16,703	10,167
97	Williamson	3,668	3,481	7,149	67	....	3,704	3,512	7,216	4,457
98	Winnebago	6,329	5,432	11,761	12	....	6,338	5,435	11,773	4,609
99	Woodford	2,287	2,128	4,415	....	....	2,287	2,128	4,415	....

STATISTICS OF

1	Adams	3,040	2,749	5,789	8	....	3,044	2,753	5,797	2,264
2	Allen	8,836	7,981	16,817	102	....	8,884	8,035	16,919	5,942
3	Bartholomew	6,445	5,901	12,346	82	....	6,483	5,945	12,428	10,042
4	Benton	620	524	1,144	....	....	620	524	1,144	....
5	Blackford	1,463	1,386	2,849	11	....	1,468	1,392	2,860	1,226
6	Boone	5,897	5,714	11,611	20	....	5,905	5,726	11,631	8,121
7	Brown	2,498	2,329	4,827	19	....	2,510	2,336	4,846	2,364
8	Carroll	5,672	5,310	10,982	33	....	5,687	5,328	11,015	7,819
9	Cass	5,790	5,170	10,960	61	....	5,815	5,206	11,021	5,480
10	Clark	7,856	7,390	15,246	582	....	8,143	7,685	15,828	14,595
11	Clay	4,094	3,832	7,926	18	....	4,102	3,842	7,944	5,567
12	Clinton	6,065	5,780	11,845	24	....	6,075	5,794	11,869	7,508
13	Crawford	3,366	3,157	6,523	1	....	3,367	3,157	6,524	5,282
14	Daviess	5,504	4,804	10,308	44	....	5,527	4,825	10,352	6,720
15	Dearborn	10,491	9,528	20,019	147	....	10,571	9,595	20,166	19,327
16	Decatur	7,514	7,437	14,951	156	....	7,588	7,519	15,107	12,171
17	De Kalb	4,342	3,899	8,241	10	....	4,346	3,905	8,251	1,968
18	Delaware	5,555	5,284	10,839	4	....	5,557	5,286	10,843	8,843
19	Dubois	3,234	3,066	6,300	21	....	3,244	3,077	6,321	3,632
20	Elkhart	6,615	6,059	12,674	16	....	6,622	6,068	12,690	6,660
21	Fayette	5,162	4,983	10,145	72	....	5,197	5,020	10,217	9,837
22	Floyd	7,445	6,856	14,301	574	....	7,716	7,159	14,875	9,454
23	Fountain	6,975	6,226	13,201	52	....	7,000	6,253	13,253	11,218
24	Franklin	9,093	8,666	17,759	209	....	9,197	8,771	17,968	13,349
25	Fulton	3,152	2,828	5,980	2	....	3,153	2,829	5,982	1,993
26	Gibson	5,480	5,074	10,554	217	....	5,582	5,189	10,771	8,977
27	Grant	5,724	5,221	10,945	147	....	5,799	5,293	11,092	4,875
28	Greene	6,302	5,936	12,238	75	....	6,338	5,975	12,313	8,321
29	Hamilton	6,381	6,121	12,502	182	....	6,474	6,210	12,684	9,855
30	Hancock	4,871	4,723	9,594	104	....	4,925	4,773	9,698	7,535
31	Harrison	7,701	7,494	15,195	91	....	7,748	7,538	15,286	12,459
32	Hendricks	7,263	6,784	14,047	36	....	7,282	6,801	14,083	11,264
33	Henry	8,722	8,596	17,318	287	....	8,870	8,735	17,605	15,128
34	Howard	3,490	3,062	6,552	105	....	3,558	3,099	6,657	....
35	Huntington	4,166	3,681	7,847	3	....	4,168	3,682	7,850	1,579
36	Jackson	5,533	5,300	10,833	214	....	5,649	5,398	11,047	8,961
37	Jasper	1,871	1,668	3,539	1	....	1,872	1,668	3,540	1,267
38	Jay	3,602	3,415	7,017	30	....	3,618	3,429	7,047	3,863
39	Jefferson	12,195	11,153	23,348	568	....	12,468	11,448	23,916	16,614
40	Jennings	6,181	5,592	11,773	323	....	6,332	5,764	12,096	8,829
41	Johnson	6,245	5,841	12,086	15	....	6,252	5,849	12,101	9,352
42	Knox	5,483	5,071	10,554	530	....	5,753	5,331	11,084	10,657
43	Kosciusko	5,342	4,900	10,242	1	....	5,342	4,901	10,243	4,170
44	La Grange	4,374	3,995	8,369	18	....	4,384	4,003	8,387	3,664
45	Lake	2,227	1,763	3,990	1	....	2,227	1,764	3,991	1,468
46	Laporte	6,338	5,729	12,067	78	....	6,377	5,768	12,145	8,184
47	Lawrence	6,252	5,751	12,003	94	....	6,301	5,796	12,097	11,782

NATIVITIES, DWELLINGS, &c.				EDUCATION AND RELIGION.									
Born out of State.				Colleges, academies, and private schools.		Public Schools.							
United States.	Foreign countries.	Dwellings.	Families.	Pupils.	Annual income.	Pupils.	Annual income.	Total educational income.	White scholars during year.	Whites 5 and under 20 years old.	Whites over 20 unable to read & write.	Accommodation of churches—persons.	
1,963	191	704	705	......	....	360	$337	$337	927	1,657	568	1,800	77
3,974	925	1,246	1,246	165	$1,900	180	984	2,884	1,378	2,642	54	1,050	78
3,604	7,170	3,727	3,728	79	3,100	......	....	3,100	2,666	7,529	686	11,200	79
2,255	24	961	961	......	....	410	2,210	2,210	942	2,364	735	1,750	80
9,120	1,243	3,173	3,196	80	2,400	3,220	2,250	4,650	4,172	7,504	1,966	28,150	81
5,253	423	1,783	1,855	100	1,300	......	....	1,300	2,273	4,377	808	4,000	82
3,279	531	1,300	1,335	67	760	1,844	4,264	5,024	1,848	3,175	771	5,100	83
3,725	82	1,411	1,411	......	....	869	1,710	1,710	1,182	3,381	969	12,600	84
2,298	242	594	621	......	....	483	1,668	1,668	1,293	1,521	77	300	85
7,009	1,782	1,950	2,052	100	1,000	1,800	6,023	7,023	2,774	4,517	302	900	86
6,414	1,379	1,991	1,991	......	....	2,941	5,091	5,091	2,114	4,695	72	5,100	87
3,286	67	1,289	1,289	......	....	1,300	1,929	1,929	1,306	3,236	1,318	10,388	88
6,305	174	1,985	1,985	280	500	70	1,000	1,500	3,230	4,791	372	7,700	89
1,655	323	808	816	......	....	750	1,268	1,268	1,233	1,935	8	7,400	90
4,868	241	1,401	1,401	......	....	409	2,864	2,864	2,552	3,338	115	4,650	91
2,302	999	1,288	1,288	......	....	1,000	500	500	1,424	2,841	814	3,660	92
2,664	86	1,209	1,226	......	....	......	561	561	850	2,910	863	4,200	93
2,977	209	1,537	1,537	......	....	1,000	10,000	10,000	1,536	3,811	847	5,050	94
3,344	436	923	923	......	....	1,364	3,147	3,147	1,314	1,985	13	1,300	95
6,621	4,957	2,796	2,833	200	2,150	3,742	10,400	12,550	3,664	6,477	1,173	6,100	96
3,470	52	1,195	1,208	60	....	360	906	906	1,101	3,106	1,115	5,200	97
6,776	2,273	1,979	2,126	......	....	2,385	2,639	2,639	2,705	4,350	9	3,800	98
2,052	660	747	749	50	1,250	750	1,875	3,125	1,126	1,821	7	1,850	99

INDIANA.

United States.	Foreign countries.	Dwellings.	Families.	Pupils.	Annual income.	Pupils.	Annual income.	Total educational income.	White scholars during year.	Whites 5 and under 20 years old.	Whites over 20 unable to read & write.	Accommodation of churches—persons.	
3,206	847	1,002	1,002	......	....	555	2,117	2,117	1,119	2,345	157	950	1
7,581	3,753	3,097	3,109	580	8,800	2,500	5,434	14,234	3,838	6,436	616	5,850	2
5,400	405	2,149	2,160	95	730	2,558	3,108	3,898	3,008	5,214	1,153	7,400	3
521	57	180	180	......	....	180	272	272	326	451	95	....	4
1,699	62	514	514	......	....	20	510	510	594	1,171	166	1,600	5
4,943	50	1,914	1,936	75	....	2,708	2,009	2,009	2,613	5,064	954	11,630	6
1,995	57	790	805	......	....	......	....	....	834	2,065	825	800	7
5,611	266	1,909	1,909	......	....	1,250	3,447	3,447	2,860	4,415	978	6,000	8
5,678	532	1,863	1,881	100	....	1,795	2,788	2,788	2,284	4,468	172	3,800	9
5,016	1,029	2,757	2,807	259	4,762	1,700	8,500	13,262	2,934	6,082	795	16,980	10
3,130	140	1,326	1,326	......	....	......	....	....	1,114	3,467	532	1,500	11
5,562	125	2,001	2,001	......	....	4,710	4,750	4,750	2,581	5,140	1,057	5,000	12
1,865	49	1,027	1,027	100	350	1,418	2,744	3,094	1,250	2,862	945	2,400	13
2,987	962	1,803	1,803	......	....	1,124	1,680	1,680	1,157	4,170	1,214	7,600	14
5,648	4,077	3,549	3,602	195	2,500	7,461	5,762	8,262	4,993	7,569	697	16,300	15
5,889	339	2,662	2,683	65	367	3,721	1,204	1,571	3,988	6,006	1,301	13,850	16
5,903	222	1,421	1,424	......	....	......	2,362	2,362	1,915	3,336	614	750	17
5,051	129	1,874	1,874	......	....	1,894	1,625	1,625	2,887	4,611	1,089	5,000	18
1,141	1,618	1,146	1,146	135	350	138	537	887	515	2,544	430	3,500	19
7,775	484	2,254	2,316	20	....	1,800	3,201	3,201	3,175	5,175	1,055	5,100	20
3,753	306	1,818	1,835	200	200	2,346	7,456	7,656	2,881	3,915	626	11,030	21
4,532	2,384	2,448	2,677	184	8,000	2,011	11,267	19,267	2,597	5,415	902	10,750	22
5,786	346	2,251	2,301	40	100	3,622	6,537	6,637	3,865	5,289	1,444	9,200	23
5,967	2,152	3,286	3,286	60	700	2,315	8,841	9,541	4,333	7,065	646	17,891	24
3,249	197	1,085	1,085	......	....	1,200	866	866	1,402	2,430	482	2,975	25
3,145	530	1,833	1,834	......	....	2,060	6,277	6,277	2,538	4,335	1,128	5,700	26
5,780	88	1,884	1,901	......	....	1,250	3,535	3,535	2,991	4,620	1,069	6,975	27
4,473	448	2,089	2,094	......	....	2,346	2,367	2,367	2,332	5,224	1,503	6,350	28
5,302	189	2,159	2,161	......	....	456	1,428	1,428	2,718	5,303	1,272	3,600	29
3,815	244	1,685	1,685	40	200	605	946	1,146	2,413	4,089	624	3,850	30
3,900	1,178	2,645	2,645	......	....	2,322	1,917	1,917	1,951	6,375	89	16,300	31
5,937	377	2,390	2,412	60	300	3,176	16,500	16,800	3,365	5,903	1,302	14,220	32
7,652	147	3,064	3,066	130	1,143	3,846	4,963	6,106	4,655	7,237	918	14,335	33
2,905	42	1,190	1,190	......	....	......	1,273	1,273	1,158	2,640	143	2,600	34
4,623	458	1,356	1,356	......	....	1,500	1,194	1,194	1,254	3,040	571	2,200	35
2,898	699	1,956	1,965	......	....	1,154	2,820	2,820	2,073	4,523	1,368	9,450	36
1,793	73	592	592	......	....	238	....	....	964	1,492	202	110	37
4,404	134	1,179	1,185	80	400	810	1,876	2,276	2,026	2,959	410	1,425	38
8,234	3,113	4,092	4,204	201	5,000	4,055	11,413	16,413	5,577	9,140	1,432	31,029	39
3,995	991	2,064	2,064	......	....	1,857	2,750	2,750	2,587	4,854	437	12,850	40
4,923	129	2,067	2,067	134	2,000	4,708	6,636	8,636	2,725	5,163	470	22,646	41
2,459	877	1,969	1,969	135	4,100	1,600	4,000	8,100	2,151	4,259	670	8,100	42
6,371	278	1,783	1,795	......	....	2,451	2,098	2,098	2,428	4,332	1,092	2,450	43
5,790	327	1,479	1,486	97	1,000	2,234	1,590	2,590	2,133	3,408	103	1,150	44
1,954	863	715	715	40	375	375	380	755	1,063	1,572	131	1,500	45
6,743	770	2,124	2,150	105	8,875	5,700	4,036	12,911	3,760	4,788	593	8,050	46
3,673	347	2,012	2,012	......	....	4,974	1,680	1,680	1,441	4,973	1,104	9,750	47

	COUNTIES.	LAND OCCUPIED OR IMPROVED.				LIVE STOCK UPON FARMS.			
		Farms.	Acres improved.	Acres unimproved.	Value with improvements and implements.	Horses, asses, and mules.	Neat cattle.	Sheep.	Swine.
77	Richland	204	13,255	25,460	194,296	723	2,660	1,792	7,499
78	Rock Island	585	24,803	47,512	568,599	1,288	5,632	3,374	7,489
79	St. Clair	1,961	113,101	161,001	2,773,545	6,916	19,447	8,752	33 309
80	Saline	678	19,568	39,138	223,293	1,861	3,809	3,856	25,187
81	Sangamon	1,578	176,895	146,377	3,490,364	9,090	27,267	46,900	64,839
82	Schuyler	624	37,776	60,313	868,266	2,262	6,461	9,111	16,060
83	Scott	712	48,216	54,216	1,180,379	3,327	9,642	10,135	26,213
84	Shelby	834	51,454	109,520	1,065,403	3,369	11,752	11,676	29,403
85	Stark	343	24,552	28,480	492,049	1,710	4,315	5,643	10,227
86	Stephenson	1,179	76,343	122,319	1,997,170	2,729	9,115	7,734	15,275
87	Tazewell	1,110	72,882	92,077	1,686,925	4,556	10,912	8,651	21,203
88	Union	810	30,448	65,505	380,620	2,416	6,426	4,869	21,315
89	Vermillion	1,269	11,759	135,623	2,210,652	6,064	22,263	23,586	30,835
90	Wabash	533	24,369	39,648	443,290	1,863	4,281	4,427	16,915
91	Warren	956	75,334	61,267	1,277,538	4,359	13,003	16,017	33,452
92	Washington	829	47,557	68,276	555,717	3,947	12,262	8,775	21,672
93	Wayne	492	23,938	45,957	308,202	1,774	5,607	5,765	21,850
94	White	1,101	48,548	88,996	571,282	3,314	6,825	7,523	42,069
95	Whitesides	404	35,992	55,184	767,552	1,460	6,791	5,372	3,642
96	Will	1,200	102,578	82,789	2,053,750	3,490	16,667	21,703	8,650
97	Williamson	752	27,149	31,586	284,901	2,116	5,552	7,525	37,084
98	Winnebago	919	64,929	94,325	1,638,015	2,623	9,337	12,330	9,570
99	Woodford	506	36,651	57,842	749,715	1,982	6,948	5,818	10,809

STATISTICS OF

	COUNTIES.	Farms.	Acres improved.	Acres unimproved.	Value with improvements and implements.	Horses, asses, and mules.	Neat cattle.	Sheep.	Swine.
1	Adams	574	22,760	50,850	639,154	1,779	4,716	3,882	9,417
2	Allen	1,300	50,481	103,624	1,722,980	2,497	10,508	5,905	13,291
3	Bartholomew	1,249	70,203	96,534	2,403,755	4,314	9,336	14,531	44,869
4	Benton	149	12,100	21,092	288,928	644	3,132	1,524	3,991
5	Blackford	308	11,740	38,647	373,946	1,200	2,717	2,305	5,170
6	Boone	1,393	54,593	109,841	1,560,981	5,093	8,067	16,456	27,760
7	Brown	535	16,984	48,586	362,308	1,347	2,755	5,260	9,977
8	Carroll	1,129	54,876	104,830	2,181,795	4,049	7,977	10,701	23,995
9	Cass	1,134	44,990	107,321	1,711,262	3,563	7,569	7,087	17,720
10	Clark	1,048	65,631	84,356	2,195,843	3,996	7,777	11,005	32,730
11	Clay	829	38,811	71 213	744,179	2,439	6,254	10,176	19,942
12	Clinton	1,411	66,553	99,204	1,516,123	4,761	8,488	15,198	28,350
13	Crawford	540	24,918	55,775	463,584	1,767	3,768	6,299	14,082
14	Daviess	1,221	54,593	93,706	876,042	3,531	7,885	13,293	33,508
15	Dearborn	1,520	85,335	69,209	3,748,735	5,060	8,440	9,765	29,454
16	Decatur	1,377	86,449	90,895	2,584,364	5,160	11,532	21,084	44,600
17	De Kalb	831	31,981	85,327	1,019,370	1,439	7,382	6,066	8,041
18	Delaware	1,084	51,757	99,559	1,663,227	3,277	7,157	15,895	24,241
19	Dubois	794	27,543	52,123	357,608	1,875	4,701	5,709	22,026
20	Elkhart	1,226	67,557	93,782	1,951,353	3,156	9,532	16,601	12,792
21	Fayette	956	71,516	60,075	3,151,399	4,333	8,491	13,521	32,400
22	Floyd	428	24,742	33,174	992,973	2,035	3,364	4,020	7,414
23	Fountain	1,357	72,347	109,952	1,976,029	5,980	10,652	17,810	29,310
24	Franklin	1,739	90,073	142,866	4,320,838	5,713	9,915	13,129	37,685
25	Fulton	777	31,843	101,454	823,716	1,959	5,623	6,474	9,509
26	Gibson	1,220	63,343	103,873	1,371,798	4,545	8,391	11,095	56,054
27	Grant	900	37,942	69,752	1,254,246	2,460	5,489	8,502	12,989
28	Greene	1,227	56,254	131,371	1,095,024	4,305	9,350	14,939	35,287
29	Hamilton	1,261	54,250	95,954	1,716,856	4,330	7,809	14,929	27,354
30	Hancock	1,176	48,600	87,469	1,483,745	3,594	6,606	12.456	33,782
31	Harrison	1,650	90,278	163,667	1,800,900	5,454	11,390	17,966	36,465
32	Hendricks	1,444	93,072	131,042	2,770,324	6,844	13,789	26,813	41,150
33	Henry	1,666	89,232	107,244	3,116,917	5,452	10,355	24,716	39,387
34	Howard	746	15,551	68,734	778,356	1,503	3,095	3,052	10,718
35	Huntington	782	26,703	66,507	956,682	1,969	4,769	4,316	11,289
36	Jackson	1,173	59,503	108,582	1,047,660	4,254	8,565	11,519	42,106
37	Jasper	343	24,161	44,077	428,838	1,155	5,682	4,261	8,099
38	Jay	876	29,576	74,972	847,701	2,623	4,945	6,529	12,971
39	Jefferson	1,396	76,449	94,558	2,163,497	5,389	10,060	16,741	21,411
40	Jennings	1,208	55,220	103,644	1,155,747	3,552	9,962	14,490	23,667
41	Johnson	1,153	71,230	94,026	2,025,808	4,605	8,848	19,335	36,055
42	Knox	961	50,434	89,609	875,027	3,931	9,107	11,089	33,693
43	Kosciusko	1,127	46,679	110,040	1,360,923	3,216	9,781	10,458	16,322
44	La Grange	1,062	53,003	85,415	1,358,444	2,253	8,436	13,284	8,015
45	Lake	423	25,171	34,148	424,808	1,151	6,007	4,534	5,671
46	Laporte	1,116	75,259	58,647	1,889,003	3,910	12,075	18,306	13,275
47	Lawrence	1,031	116,228	98,318	1,728,039	4,271	10,074	18,258	47,389

AGRICULTURAL PRODUCTS.												
Wheat, bushels.	Rye & oats, bushels.	Indian corn, bushels.	Irish and sweet potatoes, bushels.	Peas and beans, bushels.	Barley, bushels.	Buckwheat, bushels.	Butter and cheese, pounds.	Hay, tons.	Hops, pounds.	Clover & other grass seeds, bushels.	Flaxseed, bushels.	
5,836	26,455	113,205	4,936	197	......	362	23,895	809	10	85	119	77
83,076	31,380	215 255	14,265	636	2,692	1,009	81.735	7,443	16	30	......	78
224,049	264,903	1,102,563	81,801	106	21,222	947	248,915	3,596	75	40	......	79
4,799	23,966	341,900	15,558	3,125	10	......	29,696	185	......	24	75	80
104,126	346,347	3,318,304	31,040	675	753	2,367	400,660	9,200	30	635	1,572	81
79,930	56,590	398,160	11,524	56	......	1,177	142,593	3,307	......	75	......	82
84,232	45,313	762,950	11,859	....	300	700	116,669	3,823	......	15	......	83
21,998	97,404	757,382	12,001	21	8	574	126,521	2,646	......	40	110	84
54,327	50,703	312,475	11,627	126	223	1,981	81,300	5,630	......	50	4	85
228,267	228,817	303,285	43,063	379	4,444	3.911	321,847	16,023	1,230	831	19	86
144,241	147,322	1,114,640	20,547	20	1,350	761	199,642	9,986	12	98	55	87
31,902	42,287	314,705	21,083	132	......	17	34,258	209	8	12	51	88
46,301	169,403	1,475,195	17,409	178	60	2,413	187,040	5,545	25	518	29	89
12,438	45,225	320,000	10,646	2,492	16	934	61,474	2,222	149	290	130	90
122,645	176,566	1,021,542	19,872	67	624	404	219,920	8,293	5	138	......	91
12,080	133,394	467,690	16,591	11,998	......	580	159,615	1,69[illegible]	......	15	171	92
6,342	29,085	301,935	10,496	1,072	16	453	64,460	458	......	7	319	93
15,293	56,247	708,815	21,839	2,319	6	331	147,234	747	25	233	143	94
149,661	70,654	211,027	35,464	635	[illegible],265	1,685	158,917	8,950	61	206	17	95
230,885	334,490	527,903	64,782	1,109	1,795	8,136	374,789	32,043	4	488	30	96
6,376	33,333	235,729	18,936	2,193	......	6	59,361	242	......	19	51	97
316,586	190,134	281,452	40,495	27	657	5,477	168,086	14,444	......	27	3	98
76,770	51,590	404,244	14,157	13	5,545	347	86,114	4,553	......	130	......	99

INDIANA.

Wheat, bushels.	Rye & oats, bushels.	Indian corn, bushels.	Irish and sweet potatoes, bushels.	Peas and beans, bushels.	Barley, bushels.	Buckwheat, bushels.	Butter and cheese, pounds.	Hay, tons.	Hops, pounds.	Clover & other grass seeds, bushels.	Flaxseed, bushels.	
52,292	23,220	101,688	14,635	424	41	1,088	92,035	3,338	34	243	89	1
189,509	59,038	281,339	48,360	119	363	5,981	137,856	5,919	30	337	159	2
102,591	60,038	1,173,902	20,722	641	1,410	603	181,937	3,558	750	219	102	3
2,612	14,554	160,400	1,295	51	187	460	14,581	948	5	3	4	4
18,262	9,705	67,060	5,783	364	......	462	58,533	1,254	111	143	51	5
76,289	46,352	583,045	19,215	2,336	6	1,008	195,673	4,259	841	194	362	6
14,154	19,019	179,304	7,514	17	......	140	49,343	642	......	66	534	7
133,371	53,249	549,882	20,548	280	616	1,380	194,094	4,397	253	1,078	324	8
107,078	40,118	397,915	23,307	64	464	1,240	190,579	3,092	39	85	418	9
62,067	120,837	567,964	53,229	43	26	226	193,695	4,600	80	68	87	10
33,039	39,588	357,832	15,354	780	......	893	75,097	2,003	......	164	219	11
95,839	34,207	710,973	13,619	17	1,974	1,965	194,815	5,068	5	533	213	12
20,009	37,614	183,930	12,439	737	......	17	36,304	918	169	83	578	13
30,200	63,487	643,685	35,313	190	......	563	123,290	3,938	20	87	1,296	14
70,506	98,032	938 491	59,662	955	5,543	4,272	280,230	13,889	19,962	717	339	15
88,493	49,000	1,050,217	20,155	315	322	1,847	205,511	5,537	1,400	323	365	16
75,995	34,812	139,986	28,044	579	184	3,022	134,784	4,660	8	712	38	17
55,078	42 667	429,209	14,039	111	359	1,024	145,736	4,957	40	337	402	18
15,213	40,648	287,905	16,989	....	78	30	58,449	1,242	35	8	74	19
174,716	106,539	370,973	53,544	66	265	6,697	200,009	8,287	......	505	202	20
93,469	45,060	945,614	18,836	144	55	1,394	184,215	4,691	72	1,006	113	21
30,706	61,397	131,261	43,875	10	8	6	73,750	3,241	......	48	4	22
60,031	53,975	927,278	17,341	214	90	2,008	191,808	7,554	27	233	87	23
124,289	103,814	1,002,149	39,019	724	1,578	6,015	329,287	6,392	17,578	871	24	24
70,757	33,264	221,761	20,567	34	513	3,820	85,063	4,637	27	239	169	25
43.888	77,833	947,590	20,007	120	205	566	152,536	1,693	28	258	108	26
90,961	40,973	361,318	11,813	322	11	785	100,274	3,273	......	336	120	27
32,091	64,871	615,050	21,786	430	27	1,159	122,129	2,306	40	125	1,650	28
64,872	59,697	663,903	17,870	98	20	752	155,526	5,131	40	231	191	29
58,267	49,854	664,715	13,826	134	191	1,743	165,125	3,851	367	631	317	30
108.819	155,515	549,276	63,893	371	299	109	152,759	2,450	......	90	891	31
80,814	75,338	775,539	20,815	231	......	468	223.033	4,934	97	1,757	449	32
129,303	91,481	940,042	12,765	107	545	1,078	201,949	7,334	101	946	1,994	33
27,930	6,157	238,853	12,151	564	347	219	57,458	569	44	35	179	34
76,750	27,597	216,173	21,934	781	57	655	69,638	2,707	100	298	101	35
38,464	76,289	949,174	15,963	359	......	6	101,781	2,458	......	42	299	36
9,051	27,731	250,895	8,108	16	18	1,592	78,670	3,822	20	7	6	37
47,290	40,287	170,455	15,756	319	......	570	144,903	4,266	254	680	922	38
58,659	99,152	549,471	60,752	422	1,189	323	253,328	8,944	916	211	120	39
62,843	78,415	516,053	33,224	80	......	805	239,380	5,701	600	87	93	40
99,038	34,802	993,375	15,496	909	75	774	140,668	3,082	174	541	228	41
27,187	52,023	720,725	15,204	94	103	99	102,288	2,783	......	36	53	42
117,918	79,656	341,556	33,619	420	57	3,705	186,186	4,338	193	370	205	43
127,905	76,191	321,211	61,514	678	2,759	6.977	161,539	7,203	......	560	32	44
46,389	92,529	138,040	23,694	574	77	9,725	102,898	8,949	......	102	2	45
206,016	177,623	663,949	58.260	1,764	8,981	10,250	220,552	21,322	139	922	3	46
43,953	150,046	838,238	14,390	138	......	20	132,791	2,746	......	......	870	47

	Counties.	Agricultural products.									
		Flax, pounds.	Hemp, dew and water-rotted, tons.	Maple sugar, pounds.	Cane sugar, hhds. of 1,000 pounds.	Molasses, gallons.	Rice, pounds.	Tobacco, pounds.	Ginned cotton, bales of 400 pounds.	Wool, pounds.	Silk cocoons, pounds.
77	Richland	2,915	.....	4,408	.....	305	.....	810	.....	4,658	.....
78	Rock Island	150	.....	500	.....	.....	.....	.....	.....	8,865	.....
79	St. Clair	.....	.....	.....	.....	.....	.....	.....	.....	20,895	.....
80	Saline	4,475	.....	1,412	.....	.....	.....	113,650	.....	7,558	.....
81	Sangamon	112	.....	120	.....	.....	.....	2,000	.....	120,868	.....
82	Schuyler	1,283	.....	4,316	.....	135	.....	1,050	.....	22,295	.....
83	Scott	.....	.....	.....	.....	.....	.....	.....	.....	24,897	.....
84	Shelby	902	.....	3,551	.....	.....	.....	200	.....	27,208	.....
85	Stark	130	.....	60	.....	2	.....	.....	.....	16,047	.....
86	Stephenson	1,537	.....	19,984	.....	123	.....	1,000	.....	18,404	.....
87	Tazewell	.....	.....	657	.....	74	.....	.....	.....	20,813	.....
88	Union	825	.....	6,241	.....	578	.....	2,228	.....	8,820	.....
89	Vermillion	2,396	.....	23,990	.....	656	.....	100	.....	59,938	.....
90	Wabash	4,687	.....	2,250	.....	191	.....	4,900	.....	10,230	.....
91	Warren	.....	.....	3,480	.....	60	.....	.....	.....	51,277	.....
92	Washington	.....	.....	.....	.....	.....	.....	.....	.....	19,563	.....
93	Wayne	4,734	.....	100	.....	.....	.....	2,051	.....	11,347	.....
94	White	12,762	.....	780	.....	59	.....	28,129	.....	19,364	1
95	Whitesides	750	.....	1,980	.....	510	.....	505	.....	14,445	.....
96	Will	574	.....	9,617	.....	167	.....	2,760	.....	50,237	.....
97	Williamson	1,359	.....	299	.....	8	.....	536,268	.....	14,030	.....
98	Winnebago	160	.....	.....	.....	.....	.....	.....	.....	30,170	.....
99	Woodford	60	.....	.....	.....	.....	.....	.....	.....	16,033	.....

STATISTICS OF

1	Adams	1,516	.....	17,317	.....	748	.....	.....	.....	9,532	.....
2	Allen	510	.....	24,256	.....	331	.....	.....	.....	14,240	.....
3	Bartholomew	2,484	.....	6,653	.....	309	.....	4,800	.....	32,014	30
4	Benton	70	.....	250	.....	5	.....	.....	.....	4,846	.....
5	Blackford	1,898	.....	22,095	.....	1,077	.....	.....	.....	5,865	.....
6	Boone	9,026	.....	87,661	.....	6,214	.....	6,010	.....	39,380	.....
7	Brown	11,807	.....	22,412	.....	1,092	.....	9,504	.....	10,029	.....
8	Carroll	11,852	.....	53,470	.....	3,371	.....	558	.....	27,487	.....
9	Cass	1,639	.....	40,779	.....	4,411	.....	.....	.....	17,510	11
10	Clark	2,850	.....	6,987	.....	978	.....	235	.....	22,772	1
11	Clay	5,591	.....	12,908	.....	379	.....	1,280	.....	18,584	.....
12	Clinton	1,381	.....	48,374	.....	1,765	.....	4,400	.....	33,722	.....
13	Crawford	30,507	.....	4,776	.....	400	.....	10,530	.....	11,686	2
14	Daviess	71,165	.....	6,185	.....	25	.....	19,900	.....	28,495	69
15	Dearborn	2,557	.....	1,598	.....	557	.....	1,102	.....	27,380	12
16	Decatur	13,872	.....	19,621	.....	2,022	.....	700	.....	47,029	.....
17	De Kalb	1,468	.....	115,230	.....	2,975	.....	.....	.....	15,790	.....
18	Delaware	3,642	.....	39,033	.....	1,518	.....	22	.....	36,797	.....
19	Dubois	6,141	.....	3,501	.....	102	.....	2,654	.....	12,269	.....
20	Elkhart	.....	.....	155,671	.....	5,100	.....	.....	.....	41,112	.....
21	Fayette	741	.....	17,074	.....	2,828	.....	500	.....	34,689	.....
22	Floyd	635	.....	21	.....	71	.....	1,500	.....	7,581	.....
23	Fountain	4,163	.....	53,817	.....	3,608	.....	2,670	.....	49,203	.....
24	Franklin	1,445	.....	2,467	.....	1,193	.....	.....	.....	34,587	150
25	Fulton	1,205	.....	34,278	.....	1,393	.....	190	.....	11,795	.....
26	Gibson	6,341	.....	3,960	.....	367	.....	14,825	.....	25,434	.....
27	Grant	2,735	.....	50,070	.....	2,166	.....	4,428	.....	22,842	.....
28	Greene	26,777	.....	16,887	.....	591	.....	190,476	.....	31,502	.....
29	Hamilton	1,475	.....	62,490	.....	4,603	.....	.....	.....	38,864	.....
30	Hancock	4,926	.....	38,213	.....	2,2[illegible]	.....	6,040	.....	30,704	3
31	Harrison	10,864	.....	90	.....	.....	.....	24	.....	32,956	.....
32	Hendricks	5,344	.....	67,302	.....	4,981	.....	1,292	.....	64,117	.....
33	Henry	1,005	.....	58,671	.....	4,153	.....	1,800	.....	57,336	.....
34	Howard	4,085	.....	59,279	.....	3,269	.....	6,653	.....	6,896	.....
35	Huntington	2,072	.....	43,931	.....	2,289	.....	78	.....	9,675	.....
36	Jackson	3,844	.....	6,648	.....	445	.....	2,442	.....	24,323	.....
37	Jasper	.....	.....	.....	.....	.....	.....	5	.....	10,811	.....
38	Jay	2,686	.....	45,917	.....	2,339	.....	50	.....	16,925	14
39	Jefferson	3,200	.....	2,184	.....	379	.....	5,540	.....	38,160	5
40	Jennings	11,070	.....	8,013	.....	396	.....	710	.....	28,874	.....
41	Johnson	5,139	.....	25,705	.....	1,659	.....	11,538	.....	41,602	.....
42	Knox	952	.....	6,285	.....	137	.....	2,122	.....	21,941	.....
43	Kosciusko	4,062	.....	93,521	.....	3,436	.....	355	.....	28,540	.....
44	La Grange	240	.....	84,287	.....	2,471	.....	.....	.....	36,346	.....
45	Lake	160	.....	.....	.....	.....	.....	126	.....	11,526	.....
46	Laporte	65	.....	40,893	.....	1,451	.....	2,236	.....	57,891	33
47	Lawrence	8,023	.....	21,350	.....	1,720	.....	7,800	.....	36,697	.....

AGRICULTURAL PRODUCTS.					MANUFACTURES.				REMARKS.	
					Establishments.					
Beeswax and honey, pounds.	Value of animals slaughtered.	Value of produce of market gardens.	Value of orchard produce.	Wine, gallons.	Capital.	Hands employed.	Annual product.	Produced in families.		
8,911	$12,245	....	$485	......	$3,200	8	$13,200	$4,576	Formed in 1844 from Law-	77
8,915	27,956	$141	1,982	......	45,365	128	126,390	3,999	rence and Clay.	78
17,260	95,445	3,360	25,509	425	231,890	288	678,318	10,242	....	79
2,710	43,372	....	5,058	......	9,800	23	16,470	14,752	Formed in 1847 from Gal-	80
3,507	79,662	23,110	28,819	325	196,750	429	511,767	33,143	latin.	81
6,430	56,172	55	6,994	......	28,480	155	103,443	8,346	....	82
4,887	92,775	75	9,731	......	78,340	138	209,226	16,829	....	83
1,476	44,705	....	1,531	135	14,480	26	18,435	25,827	Divided in 1842 to form	84
5,220	39,487	....	1,140	8	21.505	28	42,465	5,249	Moultrie.	85
24,193	72,807	2,005	2,402	......	115,700	207	296,600	6,313	....	86
586	84,413	....	8,693	10	120,625	228	351,525	6,561	Divided in 1841 to form	87
....	26,783	....	1,615	......	20,100	47	43,345	12,698	Mason and Woodward.	88
21,439	81,358	30	19,428	10	36,680	61	50,313	21,461	....	89
8,148	33,655	....	910	......	33.900	37	47,885	8,590	....	90
4,030	111,536	....	4,220	30	37,400	52	139,002	23,278	Divided in 1841 to form	91
33,412	33,585	....	199	......	7,375	14	16,100	14,234	Henderson.	92
19,019	19,571	79	1,405	......	11,600	14	6,700	18,318	....	93
6,867	76,355	6,675	3,826	25	27,800	56	55,860	26,558	....	94
9,256	27,614	....	1,035	......	119,020	77	114,829	4,715	....	95
15,175	62,576	718	4,437	10	213,200	271	460,718	4,742	....	96
2,778	31,805	....	145	......	8,383	24	14,900	31,563	....	97
4,333	51,733	....	981	15	109,005	164	236,527	3,651	[Tazewell and McLean.	98
7,255	43,458	325	2,218	......	32,010	34	63,740	7,765	F'd 1841 from Livingston,	99

INDIANA.

Beeswax and honey, pounds.	Value of animals slaughtered.	Value of produce of market gardens.	Value of orchard produce.	Wine, gallons.	Capital.	Hands employed.	Annual product.	Produced in families.	Remarks.	
5,270	15,356	....	182	......	3,586	19	12,900	5,628	....	1
18,986	41,025	527	5,293	155	298,850	491	701,300	6,341	....	2
6,244	104,663	35	1,284	......	116,780	168	244,083	28,675	....	3
2,010	9,783	....	517	......	....	......	....	1,959	Formed in 1840 from Jas-	4
7,41	8,748	20	376	......	6,100	8	4,900	4,675	per.	5
20,280	46,505	134	9,249	14	43,200	75	97,514	30,566	....	6
2,946	17,269	....	153	......	11,482	18	14,500	7,993	....	7
15,230	68,032	265	16,030	229	112,500	209	234,135	18,848	....	8
12,431	48,426	853	3,056	400	149,220	323	466,846	11,433	....	9
5,513	110,255	4,560	208	5,611	195,125	335	566,208	14,713	....	10
6,784	42,267	25	1,136	......	13,200	22	24,500	15,239	....	11
5,050	64,735	115	885	4	33,800	43	76,484	19,446	....	12
1,134	20,668	....	2,488	......	17,431	75	55,813	9,251	....	13
6,943	79,854	....	850	15	6,398	33	15,100	30,274	....	14
3,514	96,071	520	3,848	2,931	342,670	538	1,432.501	13,605	Divided in 1844 to form	15
18,311	50,823	135	1,145	......	41,775	115	126,225	32,076	Ohio.	16
5,789	21,387	....	877	......	17,150	24	41,505	7,942	....	17
2,986	30,732	36	8,349	14	64,950	82	99,108	20,291	....	18
401	35,907	....	75	16	10,100	19	7,750	7,125	....	19
165	44,205	....	2,338	......	132,800	161	297,543	12,563	....	20
7,898	169,432	1,669	1,856	75	280,510	355	366,052	10,428	....	21
1,660	18,811	14,005	1,530	780	465,550	793	922,911	4,178	....	22
17,301	141,395	418	14,150	24	118,971	245	283,838	25,450	....	23
4,555	116,464	262	3,434	674	261,448	343	533,317	17,540	....	24
19,497	27,465	687	4,303	......	22,200	31	21,080	7,764	....	25
5,829	126,232	1,041	1,275	5	35,850	79	52,438	24,039	....	26
7,609	33,962	....	3,300	......	60,980	89	133,509	16,105	....	27
14,065	59,852	178	697	......	51,638	91	73,941	30,725	....	28
14,894	43,004	17	14,069	34	34,075	40	57,155	16,734	....	29
11,297	39,596	44	4,538	15	31,145	75	66.341	18,586	....	30
249	63,903	....	....	40	45,500	49	76,950	23,375	....	31
8,294	66,128	60	11,775	......	77,306	193	259,400	45,695	....	32
15,506	99,053	41	1,160	5	167,175	280	385,194	28,905	....	33
9,180	19,637	136	67	......	41,725	48	54,270	6,044	Formed in 1844 from Mi-	34
9,331	30,147	3,796	373	......	57,215	90	80,660	6,562	ami Reservation.	35
7,211	95,289	20	335	110	21,400	30	61,450	13,389	....	36
13,404	12,983	....	1,682	......	7,600	10	7,537	5,891	Divided in 1840 to form	37
9,569	30,432	1,848	5,272	100	9,350	22	11,900	16,529	Benton.	38
8,409	1,028,384	9,412	4,010	130	544,539	1,072	1,930,976	20,590	....	39
17,459	66,375	....	245	166	77,350	215	195,592	26,078	....	40
5,054	77,080	....	5,745	50	56,756	83	137,604	29,824	....	41
2,481	74,045	17	139	......	137,400	116	173,546	8,048	....	42
22,401	34,184	5	7,807	......	53,425	55	51,360	14,186	....	43
11,491	44,155	....	2,732	......	95,325	112	120,554	10,252	....	44
7,878	18,290	129	746	......	19,300	12	40,550	1,450	....	45
16.300	60,062	922	10,028	35	191,380	331	343,505	11,796	....	46
6,590	120,642	450	849	......	42,170	67	95,599	25,975	....	47

	COUNTIES.	POPULATION.								
		Whites.			Colored.		All classes.		Total population.	
		Male.	Female.	Total.	Free.	Slave.	Male.	Female.	1850.	1840.
48	Madison	6,414	5,947	12,361	14	....	6,421	5,954	12,375	8,874
49	Marion	12,123	11,330	23,453	650	....	12,439	11,664	24,103	16,080
50	Marshall	2,783	2,563	5,346	2	....	2,784	2,564	5,348	1,651
51	Martin	2,984	2,861	5,845	96	....	3,039	2,902	5,941	3,875
52	Miami	5,823	5,470	11,293	11	....	5,828	5,476	11,304	3,048
53	Monroe	5,745	5,514	11,259	27	....	5,761	5,525	11,286	10,143
54	Montgomery	9,248	8,693	17,941	143	....	9,323	8,761	18,084	14,438
55	Morgan	7,496	7,005	14,501	75	....	7,532	7,044	14,576	10,741
56	Noble	4,131	3,809	7,940	6	....	4,135	3,811	7,946	2,702
57	Ohio	2,704	2,567	5,271	37	....	2,722	2,586	5,308	....
58	Orange	5,359	5,199	10,558	251	....	5,492	5,317	10,809	9,602
59	Owen	6,050	5,900	11,950	156	....	6,132	5,974	12,106	8,359
60	Parke	7,607	7,133	14,740	228	....	7,713	7,255	14,968	13,499
61	Perry	3,738	3,521	7,259	9	....	3,743	3,525	7,268	4,655
62	Pike	4,272	3,438	7,710	10	....	4,277	3,443	7,720	4,769
63	Porter	2,782	2,447	5,229	5	....	2,786	2,448	5,234	2,162
64	Posey	6,436	6,015	12,451	98	....	6,485	6,064	12,549	9,683
65	Pulaski	1,385	1,210	2,595	....	....	1,385	1,210	2,595	561
66	Putnam	9,520	9,061	18,581	34	....	9,537	9,078	18,615	16,843
67	Randolph	7,200	6,863	14,063	662	....	7,571	7,154	14,725	10,684
68	Ripley	7,540	7,184	14,724	96	....	7,583	7,237	14,820	10,392
69	Rush	8,201	7,817	16,018	427	....	8,401	8,044	16,445	16,456
70	St. Joseph	5,652	5,273	10,925	29	....	5,668	5,286	10,954	6,425
71	Scott	3,033	2,837	5,870	15	....	3,039	2,846	5,885	4,242
72	Shelby	7,975	7,508	15,483	19	....	7,988	7,514	15,502	12,005
73	Spencer	4,469	4,133	8,602	14	....	4,477	4,139	8,616	6,305
74	Stark	298	259	557	....	....	298	259	557	149
75	Steuben	3,145	2,957	6,102	2	....	3,146	2,958	6,104	2,578
76	Sullivan	5,249	4,854	10,103	38	....	5,271	4,870	10,141	8,315
77	Switzerland	6,675	6,191	12,866	66	....	6,709	6,223	12,932	9,920
78	Tippecanoe	10,349	8,867	19,216	161	....	10,439	8,938	19,377	13,724
79	Tipton	1,821	1,704	3,525	7	....	1,823	1,709	3,532	....
80	Union	3,516	3,390	6,906	38	....	3,534	3,410	6,944	8,017
81	Vanderburg	5,864	5,323	11,187	227	....	5,989	5,425	11,414	6,250
82	Vermillion	4,431	4,212	8,643	18	....	4,438	4,223	8,661	8,274
83	Vigo	7,517	7,024	14,541	748	....	7,903	7,386	15,289	12,076
84	Wabash	6,380	5,744	12,124	14	....	6,387	5,751	12,138	2,756
85	Warren	3,926	3,452	7,378	9	....	3,929	3,458	7,387	5,656
86	Warrick	4,518	4,264	8,782	29	....	4,529	4,282	8,811	6,321
87	Washington	8,643	8,145	16,788	252	....	8,769	8,271	17,040	15.269
88	Wayne	12,363	11,921	24,284	1,036	....	12,921	12,399	25,320	23,290
89	Wells	3,185	2,956	6,141	11	....	3,189	2,963	6,152	1,822
90	White	2,482	2,270	4,752	9	....	2,487	2,274	4,761	1,832
91	Whitley	2,679	2,416	5,095	95	....	2,731	2,459	5,190	1,237

STATISTICS OF

1	Allamakee	421	356	777	....	....	421	356	777	....
2	Appanoose	1,655	1,469	3,124	7	....	1,659	1,472	3,131	....
3	Benton	345	327	672	....	....	345	327	672	....
4	Black Hawk	75	60	135	....	....	75	60	135	....
5	Boone	422	313	735	....	....	422	313	735	....
6	Buchanan	266	251	517	....	....	266	251	517	....
7	Cedar	2,140	1,799	3,939	2	....	2,141	1,800	3,941	1,253
8	Clark	41	38	79	....	....	41	38	79	....
9	Clayton	2,147	1,724	3,871	2	....	2,148	1,725	3,873	1,101
10	Clinton	1,474	1,328	2,802	20	....	1,484	1,338	2,822	821
11	Dallas	473	381	854	....	....	473	381	854	....
12	Davis	3,817	3,440	7,257	7	....	3,819	3,445	7,264	....
13	Decatur	526	438	964	1	....	527	438	965	....
14	Delaware	938	821	1,759	....	....	938	821	1,759	168
15	Des Moines	6,925	6,038	12,963	25	....	6,938	6,050	12,988	5,577
16	Du Buque	5,782	5,031	10,813	28	....	5,799	5,042	10,841	3,059
17	Fayette	450	375	825	....	....	450	375	825	....
18	Fremont	657	587	1,244	....	....	657	587	1,244	....
19	Henry	4,545	4,150	8,695	12	....	4,550	4,157	8,707	3,772
20	Iowa	409	412	821	1	....	409	413	822	....
21	Jackson	3,855	3,346	7,201	9	....	3,857	3,353	7,210	1,411
22	Jasper	659	621	1,280	....	....	659	621	1,280	....
23	Jefferson	4,984	4,919	9,903	1	....	4,985	4,919	9,904	2,773
24	Johnson	2,249	2,201	4,450	22	....	2,259	2,213	4,472	1,491
25	Jones	1,627	1,379	3,006	1	....	1,627	1,380	3,007	471
26	Keokuk	2,502	2,320	4,822	....	....	2,502	2,320	4,822	....

NATIVITIES, DWELLINGS, &c.				EDUCATION AND RELIGION.									
Born out of State.				Colleges, academies, and private schools.		Public Schools.							
United States.	Foreign countries.	Dwellings.	Families.	Pupils.	Annual income.	Pupils.	Annual income.	Total educational income.	White scholars during the year.	Whites 5 and under 20 years old.	Whites over 20 unable to read and write.	Accommodation of churches—persons.	
5,175	118	2,159	2,160	......	....	2,752	$936	$936	2,754	5,219	815	5,600	48
9,444	1,927	3,984	4,003	581	$8,005	5,156	14,850	22,855	4,405	9,451	850	35,625	49
2,777	268	928	928	......	....	360	1,324	1,324	1,025	2,321	468	800	50
1,802	70	1,025	1,027	......	....	320	1,760	1,760	1,665	2,430	1,564	1,050	51
6,530	263	1,944	1,975	170	425	2,500	3,196	3,621	2,620	4,548	1,073	2,400	52
4,148	154	1,892	1,892	285	5,650	2,439	2,464	8,114	2,493	4,856	1,035	10,500	53
8,314	207	2,971	3,009	250	4,075	1,770	6,589	10,664	5,155	7,589	1,137	20,450	54
5,450	270	2,401	2,401	118	....	1,972	2,700	2,700	3,399	6,122	902	19,710	55
5,458	228	1,395	1,402	......	....	1,844	1,688	1,688	1,893	3,284	365	2,460	56
1,732	305	946	962	100	....	2,022	1,800	1,800	979	2,044	37	5,000	57
3,037	50	1,841	1,846	40	....	1,300	1,200	1,200	2,046	4,377	1,396	7,000	58
4,709	148	2,000	2,002	......	....	1,153	1,450	1,450	2,648	5,165	1,117	7,200	59
6,039	138	2,468	2,472	45	....	1,650	3,300	3,300	1,943	6,122	316	6,300	60
2,292	632	1,231	1,250	......	....	476	1,335	1,335	969	2,852	1,108	1,700	61
2,012	755	1,261	1,261	......	....	375	458	458	900	2,961	1,083	3,600	62
3,041	393	885	885	......	....	1,418	775	775	1,424	2,133	259	1,000	63
3,608	1,193	2,260	2,278	50	600	1,000	3,300	3,900	2,835	4,847	1,496	7,500	64
1,516	110	454	454	......	....	161	310	310	444	1,052	172	40	65
7,464	318	3,088	3,094	200	3,500	4,311	3,449	6,949	4,928	8,037	2,021	23,275	66
6,911	162	2,513	2,539	......	....	......	....	....	3,556	6,009	1,030	8,200	67
4,818	1,916	2,667	2,689	40	300	3,572	5,155	5,455	3,396	5,874	1,029	11,500	68
6,486	154	2,824	2,839	153	1,700	1,355	1,618	3,318	4,568	6,616	1,514	22,300	69
5,729	817	1,885	1,885	60	7,000	1,353	3,788	10,788	3,002	4,267	245	4,175	70
1,799	127	1,040	1,047	......	....	1,665	854	854	1,562	2,446	898	4,550	71
5,832	414	2,721	2,764	60	158	538	3,897	4,055	3,916	6,356	1,641	8,864	72
2,923	969	1,485	1,488	280	600	980	2,341	2,941	1,464	3,526	945	3,550	73
349	8	100	101	......	....	15	30	30	48	238	81	....	74
4,449	225	1,109	1,109	60	480	1,600	1,638	2,118	1,639	2,515	61	800	75
2,862	62	1,675	1,678	......	....	2,047	1,500	1,500	1,238	4,337	743	7,450	76
3,973	509	2,254	2,254	......	....	......	....	....	3,540	5,152	112	10,360	77
8,754	1,786	3,227	3,227	429	5,190	2,102	4,133	9,323	4,375	7,339	1,549	10,750	78
1,483	21	627	627	......	....	334	427	427	577	1,416	480	200	79
2,594	154	1,220	1,229	130	1,300	1,678	3,568	4,868	1,824	2,709	87	8,800	80
2,369	4,059	2,059	2,104	220	4,400	980	7,068	11,468	1,728	4,214	97	4,950	81
3,594	93	1,509	1,522	......	....	550	4,450	4,450	2,163	3,535	690	5,100	82
6,125	743	2,645	2,725	308	4,780	1,256	3,660	8,440	3,365	5,732	1,431	11,800	83
6,857	420	2,079	2,121	......	....	1,916	2,355	2,355	3,076	4,867	816	2,625	84
3,747	93	1,273	1,295	......	....	1,700	3,060	3,060	2,055	3,102	328	5,500	85
2,972	394	1,513	1,513	40	50	985	2,339	2,389	2,081	3,718	371	6,200	86
4,602	449	2,897	2,954	90	....	2,575	25,150	25,150	3,220	6,882	1,222	14,800	87
10,478	960	4,515	4,529	415	8,405	3,467	5,524	13,929	5,608	9,554	1,091	35,545	88
3,893	295	1,021	1,021	......	....	1,510	1,349	1,349	1,491	2,509	562	3,800	89
2,560	64	821	825	......	....	1,600	515	515	1,179	1,994	401	2,550	90
3,362	241	913	941	......	....	......	12,895	12,895	1,472	2,040	326	1,580	91

IOWA.

508	140	152	158	......	....	......	....	....	18	267	26	....	1
2,535	28	521	521	......	....	329	333	333	271	1,303	334	....	2
526	18	121	121	......	....	60	106	106	74	259	39	....	3
114	3	26	26	......	....	......	....	....	4	51	9	....	4
565	68	119	121	......	....	......	....	....	51	265	92	....	5
434	20	74	74	......	....	40	45	45	117	223	18	....	6
2,754	274	686	686	......	....	509	604	604	991	1,552	266	875	7
58	4	14	14	......	....	......	....	....	....	30	......	....	8
2,388	834	728	728	......	....	......	....	....	474	1,320	99	....	9
1,795	525	499	508	......	....	893	1,797	1,797	735	1,088	154	335	10
746	12	156	157	......	....	......	....	....	12	343	96	....	11
5,726	71	1,180	1,186	......	....	1,159	2,110	2,110	1,350	3,093	773	250	12
787	31	145	145	95	145	......	....	145	107	429	88	....	13
1,221	200	338	343	......	....	304	521	521	262	669	17	1,700	14
7,781	1,955	1,919	2,061	......	....	562	1,114	1,114	2,895	4,965	345	2,425	15
3,933	4,301	1,952	2,002	30	2,500	1,547	3,355	5,855	1,500	4,030	469	3,900	16
600	46	153	154	......	....	......	....	....	29	306	1	....	17
1,022	45	222	222	......	....	......	....	....	214	516	97	....	18
6,156	347	1,545	1,545	130	1,240	3,540	1,941	3,181	2,075	3,645	26	4,900	19
592	67	143	143	......	....	45	165	165	100	311	85	97	20
4,253	1,304	1,277	1,277	50	600	1,185	5,965	6,565	1,366	2,765	343	1,260	21
1,044	25	214	214	......	....	......	....	....	109	499	114	....	22
5,983	526	1,649	1,684	100	1,000	4,154	3,559	4,559	1,842	4,120	651	2,100	23
2,893	522	799	799	......	....	534	890	890	814	1,729	157	2,252	24
1,964	342	559	559	......	....	576	587	587	599	1,198	216	....	25
3,564	189	820	857	60	....	955	2,640	2,640	949	2,025	474	2,249	26

	Counties.	Land occupied or improved.				Live stock upon farms.			
		Farms.	Acres improved.	Acres unimproved.	Value with improvements and implements.	Horses, asses, and mules.	Neat Cattle.	Sheep.	Swine.
48	Madison	1,494	61,925	116,833	$ 1,952,147	4,943	8,926	17,107	39,999
49	Marion	1,581	82,525	108,648	3,576,254	5,669	10,470	22,748	38,606
50	Marshall	570	20,070	65,018	601,011	1,268	5,161	3,751	7,766
51	Martin	633	23,982	47,337	379,991	1,615	3,540	7,851	15,986
52	Miami	1,184	43,403	106,286	2,115,179	3,024	7,853	7,807	19,256
53	Monroe	1,230	81,976	94,139	1,454,665	4,818	8,415	17,248	37,478
54	Montgomery	1,880	130,657	122,290	3,567,387	8,399	17,445	34,069	48,948
55	Morgan	1,392	83,196	119,945	1,495,499	4,715	9,378	19,732	50,461
56	Noble	772	32,206	74,754	1,060,945	1,837	7,552	9,071	11,807
57	Ohio	386	24,056	27,159	1,237,706	1,206	2,145	3,172	6,682
58	Orange	1,118	69,133	97,089	1,063,826	4,000	6,662	16,097	34,094
59	Owen	1,142	63,072	127,120	1,462,843	4,069	8,697	20,494	41,980
60	Parke	1,390	85,288	137,181	2,431,581	6,206	11,532	26,588	53,317
61	Perry	540	19,748	43,350	452,922	1,470	3,244	5,333	13,963
62	Pike	909	33,663	57,634	421,675	2,584	6,367	8,727	27,190
63	Porter	467	36,882	45,855	599,169	1,486	5,288	8,068	6,900
64	Posey	1,270	52,889	74,729	1,133,774	3,758	6,872	8,258	35,294
65	Pulaski	286	14,620	34,271	317,288	723	2,666	1,650	4,421
66	Putnam	1,696	111,934	138,579	3,156,911	6,396	15,023	36,367	58,118
67	Randolph	1,477	67,037	104,984	2,037,585	4,820	9,429	18,250	25,521
68	Ripley	1,495	65,792	100,854	1,669,394	4,339	9,091	14,072	20,038
69	Rush	1,809	126,449	115,576	4,474,637	7,782	13,280	27,200	64,294
70	St. Joseph	847	56,081	87,474	1,546,574	2,915	8,027	11,747	12,646
71	Scott	719	32,083	56,849	694,764	2,434	4,891	8,506	15,367
72	Shelby	1,620	86,101	121,587	2,799,023	6,507	10,386	20,440	54,887
73	Spencer	988	38,310	74,164	853,671	2,850	5,170	7,377	29,135
74	Stark	53	2,092	6,929	36,769	99	530	237	956
75	Steuben	586	32,125	63,189	772,514	1,112	5,815	8,575	4,442
76	Sullivan	1,215	57,471	87,617	794,371	4,701	11,057	15,725	33,744
77	Switzerland	1,270	64,356	83,120	1,920,631	3,520	6,084	20,178	15,081
78	Tippecanoe	1,377	136,856	132,144	4,035,327	6,173	19,106	20,779	31,789
79	Tipton	339	10,588	57,044	429,021	1,095	2,456	2,380	9,058
80	Union	606	52,820	40,522	2,012,816	2,722	5,999	8,237	26,577
81	Vanderburg	743	27,754	54,923	937,546	2,114	4,595	3,261	15,342
82	Vermillion	733	54,294	72,535	1,397,447	3,200	8,269	14,046	18,237
83	Vigo	1,113	67,759	110,962	2,136,649	6,098	9,721	14,510	38,185
84	Wabash	1,068	44,252	111,124	2,051,001	3,208	7,478	6,675	17,932
85	Warren	782	87,007	65,670	1,529,609	3,921	14,163	12,316	18,374
86	Warrick	994	39,463	84,239	850,782	2,724	5,165	9,224	23,423
87	Washington	1,718	117,450	138,070	2,039,016	5,806	11,672	23,551	41,922
88	Wayne	1,934	135,352	122,115	6,039,002	8,312	16,838	27,468	55,442
89	Wells	640	23,901	68,545	904,221	1,692	4,083	2,736	8,651
90	White	458	41,058	52,697	754,152	1,491	7,653	5,723	7,298
91	Whitley	522	20,353	50,085	611,487	1,344	4,149	3,858	7,746

STATISTICS OF

1	Allamakee	2	210	420	4,58[illegible]	4	33	....	39
2	Appanoose	153	4,724	1[illegible],346	83,305	257	870	747	1,609
3	Benton	67	2,967	9,237	48,434	128	495	402	835
4	Black Hawk	9	289	2,015	5,555	15	108	40	182
5	Boone	......	......	......	......	......	......	......	......
6	Buchanan	45	1,888	6,893	38,080	66	314	282	462
7	Cedar	358	24,241	46,830	496,611	1,232	3,486	3,860	8,260
8	Clark	......	......	......	......	......	......	......	......
9	Clayton	200	10,934	36,716	258,680	481	1,559	884	2,711
10	Clinton	306	19,008	28,934	275,680	779	3,459	1,795	3,505
11	Dallas	......	......	......	......	......	......	......	......
12	Davis	613	31,224	90,171	564,354	1,939	4,717	6,691	19,226
13	Decatur	46	2,131	7,980	19,077	158	660	521	2,098
14	Delaware	141	7,866	21,234	164,973	376	1,664	1,289	2,048
15	Des Moines	883	56,254	95,359	1,423,679	2,646	9,622	10,838	25,768
16	Du Buque	755	37,625	122,899	858,412	1,561	6,233	2,856	7,417
17	Fayette	8	585	984	10,940	18	76	60	109
18	Fremont	105	4,436	1,949	47,648	288	2,055	1,145	2,942
19	Henry	947	50,241	80,651	1,195,001	2,342	8,275	9,529	20,533
20	Iowa	70	3,494	6,163	130,693	93	351	279	1,379
21	Jackson	703	34,857	115,158	763,396	1,616	6,925	4,812	10,939
22	Jasper	150	6,173	24,347	132,583	397	1,057	939	3,715
23	Jefferson	1,067	54,499	106,577	1,162,830	2,505	8,915	13,851	25,332
24	Johnson	377	25,356	55,179	500,504	988	3,5[illegible]	4,247	7,464
25	Jones	225	13,739	25,700	259,818	524	1,810	2,238	3,653
26	Keokuk	226	21,075	62,263	494,335	1,044	3,463	4,428	11,730

AGRICULTURAL PRODUCTS.												
Wheat, bushels.	Rye & oats, bushels.	Indian corn, bushels.	Irish and sweet potatoes, bushels.	Peas and beans, bushels.	Barley, bushels.	Buckwheat, bushels.	Butter and cheese, pounds.	Hay, tons.	Hops, pounds.	Clover & other grass seeds, bushels.	Flaxseed, bushels.	
107,483	48,327	895,817	19,473	245	76	......	147,178	4,353	......	59	270	48
110,334	89,757	1,123,860	23,756	867	720	1,431	241,047	7,485	63	656	238	49
51,435	30,454	168,080	22,391	416	5	1,886	84,095	3,998	51	120	105	50
8,423	33,959	251,700	8,662	951	......	213	57,524	839	......	20	870	51
114,454	29,569	548,338	21,392	8	233	770	260,374	3,701	......	74	170	52
61,416	93,882	710,463	17,648	402	15	162	154,984	3,073	111	570	1,502	53
121,988	99,130	1,392,404	29,411	13	1,420	2,934	300,293	10,714	19	1,318	447	54
93,850	93,199	1,213,153	24,196	566	......	482	159,844	2,689	71	556	752	55
69,802	57,027	206,295	35,201	80	896	4,704	154,535	2,487	......	160	7	56
45,479	10,099	269,085	57,256	78	1,055	43	61,806	2,023	......	75	3	57
46,941	96,849	484,165	13,998	314	15	24	134,661	2,298	62	58	741	58
60,327	60,958	764,029	21,091	812	78	553	147,097	2,176	317	298	1,575	59
101,720	81,154	1,195,656	26,531	485	511	188	191,340	5,548	5	240	382	60
3,848	33,539	232,835	12,526	184	......	45	58,897	999	......	......	329	61
15,128	27,668	407,231	8,452	120	......	15	52,896	733	......	38	64	62
70,252	76,330	205,655	20,983	590	345	6,337	79,842	5,896	30	167	55	63
21,245	30,280	895,794	16,270	26	509	332	104,176	846	......	251	......	64
27,593	15,165	95,915	10,739	6	......	2,111	37,109	2,276	......	1	57	65
82,965	84,773	1,313,209	24,714	192	5	310	247,416	5,115	84	1,509	383	66
67,048	75,486	526,197	15,414	189	3	1,561	217,906	7,362	60	749	3,560	67
39,587	94,569	464,904	34,688	1,657	768	1,770	217,537	10,306	44,011	107	372	68
133,473	66,188	1,685,994	10,334	26	300	518	240,500	6,520	......	469	159	69
161,956	110,969	346,841	48,164	396	85	5,061	221,902	5,904	65	383	12	70
20,417	66,059	251,375	15,866	517	25	339	186,379	2,452	1,068	97	423	71
118,820	54,965	1,231,884	23,891	335	606	2,000	220,122	3,892	21	566	396	72
19,777	37,494	598,135	40,380	1,588	191	271	85,544	1,697	128	36	295	73
3,153	1,509	11,170	2,903	2	......	572	7,460	698	......	6	......	74
73,141	40,087	101,190	31,666	492	292	4,390	77,437	5,389	22	166	19	75
56,725	80,048	742,136	29,267	671	3	948	196,592	3,751	10	326	2,049	76
78,169	45,163	401,884	145,195	17	745	1,182	166,894	9,769	2	241	63	77
68,259	95,178	1,833,311	24,665	404	1,556	5,531	228,858	6,872	48	159	......	78
8,487	7,775	151,961	4,467	75	......	227	44,059	913	0	34	101	79
58,862	53,687	631,515	9,622	33	925	1,303	204,269	3,665	......	438	495	80
19,079	36,863	408,075	20,678	23	1,513	384	51,818	2,337	......	57	......	81
45,144	91,145	701,770	10,537	54	282	1,189	93,817	2,829	850	70	35	82
58,598	92,862	996,481	38,884	740	644	1,895	199,533	3,978	27	382	146	83
117,803	28,392	434,962	30,727	115	70	699	170,102	4,107	730	294	136	84
21,068	95,551	1,024,386	9,368	167	25	1,948	117,605	5,900	......	2	105	85
38,479	40,342	415,061	19,683	1,080	5	50	88,374	2,074	7	175	133	86
103,262	216,548	756,001	26,785	1,891	17	125	278,727	6,131	2	841	863	87
163,667	208,112	1,398,455	39,165	179	2,069	2,128	387,438	11,377	156	1,252	4,103	88
50,287	21,083	148,565	16,060	213	......	749	96,025	2,757	.....	251	107	89
32,930	36,408	373,013	11,803	92	169	2,638	70,828	3,917	25	91	180	90
46,669	20,910	126,049	13,902	316	264	1,181	69,174	2,5[illegible]	143	342	100	91

IOWA.

Wheat, bushels.	Rye & oats, bushels.	Indian corn, bushels.	Irish and sweet potatoes, bushels.	Peas and beans, bushels.	Barley, bushels.	Buckwheat, bushels.	Butter and cheese, pounds.	Hay, tons.	Hops, pounds.	Clover & other grass seeds, bushels.	Flaxseed, bushels.	
650	1,100	600	220	....	......	......	800	60	......	15	......	1
1,221	7,913	80,930	1,025	127	......	400	16,196	32	2	3	69	2
8,013	2,483	19,370	653	55	351	183	10,350	678	......	2	5	3
160	100	2,150	348	3	......	75	1,840	235	......	......	4	4
....	....	....	....	....	......	......	....	....	......	......	......	5
4,604	5,196	13,720	1,253	13	30	34	6,135	546	2	8	8	6
81,876	31,821	223,370	8,420	112	1,882	1,608	64,275	3,926	3	46	18	7
....	....	....	....	....	......	......	....	....	......	......	......	8
36,860	25,773	42,604	12,473	373	710	313	37,557	3,202	......	60	......	9
61,945	31,329	94,100	11,168	39	1,056	1,210	73,443	5,144	24	64	......	10
....	....	....	....	....	......	......	....	....	......	......	......	11
34,939	61,594	431,207	5,119	185	200	1,491	82,620	706	5	49	151	12
1,067	4,130	33,420	626	29	......	349	8,596	14	......	2	12	13
22,150	14,085	48,515	6,978	17	199	159	25,440	2,504	5,000	42	......	14
11,635	126,290	579,332	2,693	7	163	2,437	175,592	2,693	......	......	......	15
102,038	87,647	164,045	64,014	95	2,694	1,274	115,004	11,123	3,004	81	......	16
485	485	5,000	222	8	......	115	1,510	183	......	2	......	17
10,589	3,450	47,240	1,267	7	......	276	13,739	584	2	......	......	18
81,675	136,311	642,910	7,558	6	1,438	2,515	149,898	3,312	......	31	......	19
5,535	1,755	31,145	963	3	......	276	7,549	680	......	......	......	20
132,024	65,952	202,791	26,082	692	2,190	2,777	108,684	7,594	......	28	......	21
4,494	4,414	62,635	2,179	146	......	234	15,904	541	......	2	36	22
59,539	134,154	705,296	8,647	108	809	4,050	134,791	2,796	5	273	422	23
54,081	33,943	225,105	9,392	4	411	1,218	80,225	4,615	......	......	16	24
38,523	22,025	99,070	5,403	70	291	677	38,990	3,371	5	33	14	25
24,990	58,891	346,650	4,657	683	10	1,206	58,777	509	......	86	168	26

	Counties.	Agricultural products.									
		Flax, pounds.	Hemp, dew and water-rotted, tons.	Maple sugar, pounds.	Cane sugar, hhds. of 1,000 pounds.	Molasses, gallons.	Rice, pounds.	Tobacco, pounds.	Ginned cotton, bales of 400 pounds.	Wool, pounds.	Silk cocoons, pounds.
48	Madison	4,361		80,194		3,305				37,775	
49	Marion	1,691		28,644		2,846		650		51,193	
50	Marshall	2,089		39,415		1,413				9,504	2
51	Martin	12,268		13,088		595		36,700		14,569	
52	Miami	2,017		78,803		3,787		300		17,511	
53	Monroe	21,609		46,210		3,705		13,719		40,371	
54	Montgomery	11,743		108,522		8,106		3,760		85,233	
55	Morgan	12,731		35,400		3,376		2,175		44,595	
56	Noble	470		85,910		1,526		100		21,625	
57	Ohio	100		100		63				5,801	
58	Orange	11,187		6,928		199		26,635		33,761	
59	Owen	48,142		64,533		4,583		49,810		39,541	
60	Parke	5,441		52,905		3,742		800		60,743	
61	Perry	5,806		5,355				35,535		10,581	
62	Pike	3,147		4,778		143		5,575	10	16,991	
63	Porter	230		11,083				100		20,842	
64	Posey									17,667	
65	Pulaski	90								3,839	
66	Putnam	11,705		100,942		7,362		4,550		85,837	11
67	Randolph	1,430		80,697		5,400		170		50,125	
68	Ripley	5,273		13,573		1,263		11,855		34,322	
69	Rush	1,672		59,011		5,587		1,070		69,531	
70	St. Joseph	55		65,491		1,322		63		31,167	
71	Scott	6,572		3,010		327		7,335		17,407	
72	Shelby	3,681		18,209		1,792		12,740		48,333	2
73	Spencer	20,215		561		14		84,192	4	16,638	
74	Stark	20								616	
75	Steuben	41		40,863		254				19,530	
76	Sullivan	40,749		59,301		634		1,040		31,452	
77	Switzerland	880		550						22,913	6
78	Tippecanoe	155		7,501		1,969				54,458	
79	Tipton	3,876		24,601		18,034		910		7,838	
80	Union	165		9,046		1,657				22,882	10
81	Vanderburg	75						7,200		5,719	
82	Vermillion	3,430		12,328		320				32,776	
83	Vigo	2,685		18,557		722		1,050		32,707	
84	Wabash	2,725		79,868		4,574				17,137	
85	Warren	233		3,630		168				33,384	
86	Warrick	16,666		360		17		309,099		20,077	3
87	Washington	20,334		7,646		1,162		100,907		48,454	
88	Wayne	1,794		44,393		4,843		1,030		71,659	4
89	Wells	2,315		38,152		1,998				7,601	
90	White	108		300		15		290		16,957	1
91	Whitley	1,273		38,604		1,915		165		10,269	

STATISTICS OF

	Counties	Flax, pounds.	Hemp, dew and water-rotted, tons.	Maple sugar, pounds.	Cane sugar, hhds. of 1,000 pounds.	Molasses, gallons.	Rice, pounds.	Tobacco, pounds.	Ginned cotton, bales of 400 pounds.	Wool, pounds.	Silk cocoons, pounds.
1	Allamakee										
2	Appanoose	1,562		1,68[illegible]		39				2,337	
3	Benton	385		785		6		440		1,068	
4	Black Hawk	30		3,36[illegible]						120	
5	Boone										
6	Buchanan	107		500		16				705	
7	Cedar	1,623		810		6				11,141	
8	Clark										
9	Clayton	221		5,729		293		130		2,057	
10	Clinton	650						500		5,082	
11	Dallas										
12	Davis	7,877		430		8				17,445	
13	Decatur	1,620								1,415	
14	Delaware			1,132		427				2,769	
15	Des Moines	500								26,210	
16	Du Buque	200		2,525		58				6,118	
17	Fayette			1,950		39		300		192	
18	Fremont	50		5		4		650		2,489	
19	Henry	30		1,190						27,165	
20	Iowa			60						1,039	
21	Jackson	1,100		20,661		939				9,939	
22	Jasper	1,682		370		14		989		2,077	
23	Jefferson	3,703								33,726	
24	Johnson	1,050		200						11,361	
25	Jones	540		3,095		25				5,771	
26	Keokuk	13,130		110		5				11,923	

Agricultural products.					Manufactures.				Remarks.	
					Establishments.					
Beeswax and honey, pounds.	Value of animals slaughtered.	Value of produce of market gardens.	Value of orchard produce.	Wine, gallons.	Capital.	Hands employed.	Annual product.	Produced in families.		
13,257	$46,687	$37	$555	......	$61,825	111	$114,360	$29,573	......	48
13,272	110,650	5,725	15,247	20	320,410	1,961	892,133	22,060	......	49
15,208	16,605	2,760	1,948	......	15,100	30	37,555	8,400	......	50
2,308	35,780	13	24	......	15,700	37	37,000	13,221	......	51
10,342	58,525	......	2,127	......	57,850	101	147,991	13,482	......	52
8,717	62,523	10	2,360	165	60,600	196	169,425	46,379	......	53
21,959	102,500	151	16,637	71	124,890	239	345,655	43,378	......	54
28,017	78,602	30	7,227	600	34,577	33	88,029	34,565	......	55
10,096	25,617	......	1,969	30	22,750	42	48,530	11,563	......	56
40	30,719	250	240	......	67,050	109	232,101	4,875	Formed in 1844 from Dear-	57
3,248	74,264	......	569	......	6,270	25	15,167	25,540	born.	58
7,888	130,170	190	3,766	80	25,003	70	80,466	32,523	......	59
10,297	147,569	360	20,319	......	123,100	170	217,755	29,858	......	60
1,983	26,167	......	270	......	27,800	81	44,350	4,880	......	61
24	38,442	94	56	......	3,500	11	8,500	12,952	......	62
578	20,258	200	1,142	......	6,825	27	15,500	6,652	......	63
284	75,884	5	734	......	41,000	93	136,301	12,605	......	64
5,861	9,932	18	992	......	......	......	......	2,102	......	65
18,218	57,984	141	15,751	100	55,600	116	80,445	46,740	......	66
12,173	57,347	2,973	6,117	12	9,435	34	26,935	23,013	......	67
10,376	56,129	60	1,049	304	65,750	127	110,459	26,706	......	68
7,571	64,288	......	287	......	103,530	170	175,554	31,215	......	69
10,962	49,502	80	970	36	223,575	258	331,182	9,884	......	70
5,729	41,127	12	572	......	14,080	45	27,600	27,504	......	71
14,897	63,247	......	3,362	24	85,260	156	142,151	24,246	......	72
9,591	48,136	110	1,185	......	25,153	56	40,896	47,931	......	73
2,265	1,340	313	53	......	......	......	......	371	......	74
6,713	16,633	40	1,789	......	37,480	61	85,284	5,161	......	75
2,675	74,399	1,412	1,311	......	25,675	94	62,200	27,454	......	76
3,138	55,420	47	1,073	438	52,775	171	139,380	22,112	......	77
12,575	114,941	3,046	10,012	......	355,205	759	1,216,246	12,273	......	78
6,056	11,898	17	695	29	......	......	......	5,492	Formed in 1844 from Mi-	79
3,220	45,954	28	335	5	......	......	......	15,549	ami Reservation.	80
59	32,205	1,052	227	69	162,920	341	362,481	2,986	......	81
2,347	70,915	......	5,313	5	60,380	119	150,160	15,926	......	82
7,509	349,893	7,044	4,915	55	194,075	462	824,404	16,498	......	83
20,023	46,390	5	2,879	5	84,675	111	204,100	10,572	......	84
7,910	67,366	......	4,914	......	28,725	46	40,800	15,317	......	85
6,037	65,916	808	846	95	26,025	58	116,512	20,347	......	86
9,678	110,623	30	1,051	......	119,625	249	236,180	52,384	......	87
12,266	232,435	3,394	9,362	160	415,969	688	739,773	30,490	......	88
147,788	25,619	12	1,474	......	30,200	58	45,450	8,653	......	89
11,247	27,543	......	2,476	108	11,170	24	54,905	6,868	......	90
8,118	16,078	15	1,553	12	16,430	19	22,592	5,958	......	91

IOWA.

Beeswax and honey, pounds.	Value of animals slaughtered.	Value of produce of market gardens.	Value of orchard produce.	Wine, gallons.	Capital.	Hands employed.	Annual product.	Produced in families.	Remarks.	
290	146	......	......	......	......	......	......	......	Org. '49 fr. Clayt'n & Fay.	1
4,229	5,333	562	......	......	3,000	6	18,950	1,602	" '49.	2
26	1,583	......	......	......	......	......	......	1,195	" '45.	3
640	250	......	......	......	5,000	4	2,000	76	Est. '43, not organized '50.	4
......	......	......	......	......	......	......	......	......	" 1846, organized 1850.	5
2,274	1,390	......	5	......	5,000	6	17,500	371	" before 1840, org. 1846.	6
6,619	27,791	199	89	......	9,500	12	62,730	5,768	......	7
......	......	......	......	......	......	......	......	......	Est. '46, not organized '50.	8
9,788	10,406	......	8	......	56,575	28	39,646	414	Divided in '49 to form Alla-	9
4,860	14,681	381	70	......	23,300	21	30,075	4,734	makee and Winneshiek.	10
					8,475	27	34,912	......	Est. 1846, organized 1847.	11
23,132	31,615	198	117	......	......	......	......	16,162	" '43, " '44.	12
5,381	2,182	269	......	......	......	......	......	1,207	" '46, " '50.	13
2,372	9,169	7	......	......	5,700	7	32,300	1,371	......	14
8,346	57,378	931	1,475	350	63,500	86	350,900	7,098	......	15
4,690	33,205	292	281	60	180,695	170	337,850	2,178	[lamakee & Winneshiek.	16
1,238	240	......	......	......	......	......	......	48	Org. '49; div. '49 to form Al	17
4,905	5,410	......	......	......	......	......	......	1,585	Est. 1846, organized 1849.	18
......	69,031	36	631	......	70,500	71	171,150	14,978	......	19
3,620	4,563	20	......	......	1,000	2	1,500	1,108	Est. 1843, organized 1845.	20
15,957	41,206	117	5	......	63,650	46	105,600	4,942	......	21
6,772	6,323	......	161	......	......	......	......	1,900	Est. 1846, organized 1846.	22
11,754	47,349	......	143	......	35,070	107	183,745	22,263	......	23
10,407	27,974	360	......	......	24,200	48	44,459	5,762	......	24
4,657	12,954	......	......	......	17,000	17	53,210	2,783	......	25
16,598	12,811	65	304	......	18,200	28	78,690	9,221	Est. 1843, organized 1844.	26

	COUNTIES.	POPULATION.								
		Whites.			Colored.		All classes.		Total population.	
		Male.	Female.	Total.	Free.	Slave.	Male.	Female.	1850.	1840.
27	Lee	9,889	8,920	18,809	52	....	9,911	8,950	18,861	6,093
28	Linn	2,912	2,529	5,441	3	....	2,914	2,530	5,444	1,373
29	Louisa	2,617	2,306	4,923	16	....	2,624	2,315	4,939	1,927
30	Lucas	258	213	471	....	....	258	213	471	....
31	Madison	620	559	1,179	....	....	620	559	1,179	....
32	Mahaska	3,154	2,834	5,988	1	....	3,154	2,835	5,989	....
33	Marion	2,860	2,593	5,453	29	....	2,875	2,607	5,482	....
34	Marshall	174	164	338	....	....	174	164	338	....
35	Monroe	1,502	1,382	2,884	....	....	1,502	1,382	2,884	....
36	Muscatine	3,032	2,630	5,662	69	....	3,068	2,663	5,731	1,942
37	Page	290	261	551	....	....	290	261	551	....
38	Polk	2,430	2,083	4,513	....	....	2,430	2,083	4,513	....
39	Pottawatomie	3,933	3,895	7,828	....	....	3,933	3,895	7,828	....
40	Poweshiek	316	299	615	....	....	316	299	615	....
41	Scott	3,159	2,813	5,972	14	....	3,169	2,817	5,986	2,140
42	Tama	5	3	8	....	....	5	3	8	....
43	Taylor	106	98	204	....	....	106	98	204	....
44	Van Buren	6,287	5,978	12,265	5	....	6,289	5,981	12,270	6,146
45	Wapello	4,393	4,073	8,466	5	....	4,396	4,075	8,471	....
46	Warren	505	456	961	....	....	505	456	961	....
47	Washington	2,567	2,390	4,957	....	....	2,567	2,390	4,957	1,594
48	Wayne	194	145	339	1	....	195	145	340	....
49	Winneshiek	300	246	546	....	....	300	246	546	....

STATISTICS OF

	COUNTIES.	White Male.	White Female.	White Total.	Colored Free.	Colored Slave.	All classes Male.	All classes Female.	Total 1850.	Total 1840.
1	Adair	4,090	3,993	8,083	108	1,707	4,963	4,935	9,898	8,466
2	Allen	3,741	3,644	7,385	43	1,314	4,406	4,332	8,742	7,329
3	Anderson	2,533	2,415	4,948	30	1,282	3,203	3,057	6,260	5,452
4	Ballard	2,434	2,194	4,628	26	842	2,856	2,640	5,496	....
5	Barren	7,855	7,688	15,543	113	4,584	10,182	10,058	20,240	17,288
6	Bath	4,809	4,655	9,464	116	2,535	6,082	6,033	12,115	9,763
7	Boone	4,774	4,270	9,044	37	2,104	5,819	5,366	11,185	10,034
8	Bourbon	3,760	3,395	7,155	245	7,066	7,501	6,965	14,466	14,478
9	Boyle	2,777	2,598	5,375	317	3,424	4,663	4,453	9,116	....
10	Bracken	4,155	3,794	7,949	114	840	4,628	4,275	8,903	7,053
11	Breathitt	1,880	1,723	3,603	12	170	1,971	1,814	3,785	2,195
12	Breckenridge	4,462	4,154	8,616	11	1,966	5,424	5,169	10,593	8,944
13	Bullitt	2,857	2,535	5,392	27	1,355	3,555	3,219	6,774	6,334
14	Butler	2,573	2,482	5,055	19	681	2,922	2,833	5,755	3,898
15	Caldwell	5,032	4,770	9,802	139	3,107	6,855	6,193	13,048	10,365
16	Callaway	3,568	3,520	7,088	16	992	4,053	4,043	8,096	9,794
17	Campbell	6,797	6,074	12,871	79	177	6,896	6,231	13,127	5,214
18	Carroll	2,364	2,185	4,549	28	949	2,847	2,679	5,526	3,966
19	Carter	3,122	2,838	5,960	24	257	3,264	2,977	6,241	2,905
20	Casey	2,952	2,911	5,863	59	634	3,287	3,269	6,556	4,939
21	Christian	5,898	5,392	11,290	150	8,140	9,959	9,621	19,580	15,587
22	Clark	3,986	3,723	7,709	134	4,840	6,476	6,207	12,683	10,802
23	Clay	2,410	2,324	4,734	172	515	2,788	2,633	5,421	4,607
24	Clinton	2,379	2,210	4,589	38	262	2,513	2,376	4,889	3,863
25	Crittenden	2,766	2,707	5,473	30	848	3,225	3,126	6,351	....
26	Cumberland	2,778	2,698	5,476	44	1,485	3,534	3,471	7,005	6,090
27	Daviess	4,952	4,467	9,419	54	2,889	6,368	5,994	12,362	8,331
28	Edmonson	1,898	1,850	3,748	15	325	2,059	2,029	4,088	2,914
29	Estill	2,909	2,659	5,568	6	411	3,108	2,877	5,985	5,535
30	Fayette	5,747	5,431	11,178	668	10,889	11,786	10,949	22,735	22,194
31	Fleming	5,916	5,701	11,617	158	2,139	7,011	6,903	13,914	13,268
32	Floyd	2,826	2,677	5,503	62	149	2,930	2,784	5,714	6,302
33	Franklin	4,770	3,970	8,740	357	3,365	6,538	5,924	12,462	9,420
34	Fulton	1,806	1,693	3,499	4	943	2,281	2,165	4,446	....
35	Gallatin	2,333	2,066	4,399	34	704	2,685	2,452	5,137	4,003
36	Garrard	3,607	3,422	7,029	32	3,176	5,242	4,995	10,237	10,480
37	Grant	3,086	2,907	5,993	6	532	3,344	3,187	6,531	4,192
38	Graves	5,063	4,887	9,950	8	1,439	5,745	5,652	11,397	7,465
39	Grayson	3,267	3,240	6,507	10	320	3,440	3,397	6,837	4,461
40	Greene	3,223	3,112	6,335	117	2,608	4,583	4,477	9,060	14,212
41	Greenup	4,762	4,230	8,992	56	606	5,083	4,571	9,654	6,297
42	Hancock	1,675	1,541	3,216	15	622	1,988	1,865	3,853	2,581
43	Hardin	6,074	5,949	12,023	43	2,459	7,235	7,290	14,525	16,357
44	Harlan	2,006	2,102	4,108	37	123	2,085	2,183	4,268	3,015
45	Harrison	4,914	4,819	9,733	146	3,185	6,608	6,456	13,064	12,472
46	Hart	3,938	3,801	7,739	53	1,301	4,622	4,471	9,093	7,031
47	Henderson	3,981	3,670	7,651	123	4,397	6,299	5,872	12,171	9,548

NATIVITIES, DWELLINGS, &c.				EDUCATION AND RELIGION.									
Born out of State.				Colleges, academies, and private schools.		Public Schools.		Total educational income.	White scholars during the year.	Whites 5 and under 20 years old.	Whites over 20 unable to read & write.	Accommodation of churches—persons.	
United States.	Foreign countries.	Dwellings.	Families.	Pupils.	Annual income.	Pupils.	Annual income.						
11,458	2,287	3,252	3,258	266	$2,570	2,308	$3,150	$5,720	4,042	7,367	611	5,275	27
3,877	250	991	1,011	80	....	612	1,893	1,893	2,070	2,110	5	5,100	28
3,430	251	842	850	......	....	674	1,747	1,747	1,200	1,938	69	1,550	29
415	8	92	92	......	....	......	....	....	8	178	12	....	30
1,034	6	180	192	25	25	56	76	101	64	522	56	....	31
4,754	103	981	1,012	......	....	805	1,827	1,827	1,144	2,498	89	400	32
3,541	1,003	930	1,000	240	....	792	1,495	1,495	745	2,151	220	350	33
274	....	62	62	......	....	......	....	....	3	140	35	....	34
2,374	61	515	515	......	....	296	884	884	382	1,175	75	700	35
3,862	868	999	1,009	......	....	590	1,400	1,400	1,192	2,173	47	1,515	36
467	3	94	94	......	....	......	....	....	74	215	72	....	37
3,774	114	756	782	......	....	346	1,194	1,194	542	1,838	477	150	38
5,089	1,522	1,475	1,475	......	....	......	....	....	983	3,109	26	....	39
523	4	102	102	......	....	......	....	....	8	244	27	....	40
3,167	1,520	991	1,045	135	1,900	2,041	2,401	4,301	963	2,253	92	2,950	41
7	....	1	1	......	....	......	....	....	....	4	......	....	42
147	1	38	38	......	....	......	....	....	12	78	43	....	43
9,227	555	2,069	2,079	......	....	2,000	4,237	4,237	2,519	5,099	661	1,550	44
6,746	216	1,416	1,416	......	....	1,567	2,293	2,293	1,655	3,505	166	400	45
832	4	152	166	......	....	115	268	268	26	377	45	....	46
3,939	191	856	856	......	....	962	2,895	2,895	842	2,061	243	1,246	47
266	3	57	57	......	....	......	....	....	24	138	38	....	48
383	148	100	100	......	....	......	....	....	....	189	22	....	49

KENTUCKY.

United States.	Foreign countries.	Dwellings.	Families.	Pupils.	Annual income.	Pupils.	Annual income.	Total educational income.	White scholars during the year.	Whites 5 and under 20 years old.	Whites over 20 unable to read & write.	Accommodation of churches—persons.	
1,292	6	1,513	1,513	20	100	2,774	1,618	1,718	1,989	3,379	804	11,300	1
1,826	9	1,249	1,261	......	....	931	1,421	1,421	1,867	3,078	1,281	7,550	2
518	15	883	883	50	750	332	1,359	2,109	983	1,986	400	10,250	3
1,317	14	775	775	......	....	480	463	463	1,138	1,971	574	2,600	4
3,102	24	2,667	2,735	225	1,790	1,067	4,011	5,801	2,862	6,303	807	14,250	5
1,030	29	1,595	1,595	160	....	898	2,274	2,274	2,121	3,805	1,001	5,800	6
2,039	267	1,615	1,615	70	150	650	1,600	1,750	1,824	3,528	472	9,650	7
789	343	1,348	1,355	175	8,500	281	4,960	13,460	1,230	2,618	193	19,600	8
696	73	927	988	399	17,662	658	878	18,540	1,244	2,150	146	6,625	9
1,201	158	1,437	1,437	......	....	500	1,042	1,042	853	3,170	206	5,000	10
556	3	625	625	......	....	80	300	300	79	1,538	85	750	11
1,176	63	1,452	1,453	70	....	600	1,359	1,359	1,307	3,558	499	6,650	12
457	69	970	970	150	....	......	....	....	507	2,095	580	1,100	13
1,206	14	897	897	......	....	818	1,245	1,245	1,068	2,041	735	3,646	14
2,493	91	1,746	1,746	240	3,406	670	2,508	5,914	1,337	3,894	988	8,810	15
2,968	17	1,191	1,194	40	500	880	2,275	2,775	1,629	2,947	543	8,300	16
4,019	3,414	2,319	3,355	35	280	725	8,023	8,303	1,800	4,595	628	7,250	17
747	104	766	791	22	264	500	2,840	3,104	792	1,765	140	3,310	18
1,487	40	944	944	......	....	696	1,734	1,734	642	2,514	944	1,580	19
747	3	1,005	1,005	......	....	1,156	1,442	1,442	1,485	2,493	814	6,400	20
3,591	77	1,965	2,101	779	9,510	650	6,400	15,910	2,043	4,457	801	13,375	21
711	78	1,364	1,365	62	1,800	833	1,850	3,650	1,507	3,218	437	8,550	22
1,175	8	782	782	......	....	300	60	60	301	2,015	1,180	2,000	23
1,119	4	774	774	......	....	1,563	1,169	1,169	1,175	1,895	891	1,900	24
1,751	98	978	978	40	600	600	3,362	3,962	1,200	2,148	736	5,900	25
1,097	5	942	942	......	....	1,552	2,036	2,036	925	2,238	605	3,152	26
1,338	143	1,631	1,666	215	....	......	728	728	1,660	3,641	568	10,200	27
390	2	651	652	......	....	210	530	530	481	1,544	556	2,200	28
592	9	934	934	......	....	215	206	206	855	2,386	928	2,150	29
1,730	574	2,089	2,114	1,031	11,698	794	1,996	13,694	2,054	4,001	513	15,540	30
1,355	196	1,983	2,031	424	4,500	1,062	7,817	12,317	1,710	4,497	1,276	9,055	31
947	31	862	862	......	....	302	411	411	188	2,374	971	240	32
1,026	708	1,453	1,460	215	17,575	556	6,389	23,964	1,283	3,221	942	9,820	33
1,604	14	586	588	153	2,160	125	1,145	3,305	729	1,455	508	2,600	34
629	80	747	747	30	....	380	258	258	793	1,803	481	2,200	35
550	22	1,285	1,373	115	....	......	....	....	1,095	2,808	133	5,500	36
729	83	1,031	1,032	......	....	450	305	305	872	2,289	590	6,800	37
3,984	58	1,694	1,694	......	....	1,150	4,855	4,855	2,850	4,195	914	9,945	38
768	12	1,065	1,065	......	....	522	1,199	1,199	913	2,726	964	1,900	39
866	6	1,105	1,105	190	1,540	649	635	2,175	1,014	2,660	298	3,900	40
3,555	313	1,529	1,540	40	480	554	2,635	3,115	1,105	3,596	1,009	3,790	41
579	29	551	569	......	....	275	305	305	594	1,246	406	2,300	42
1,284	84	2,005	2,005	386	9,100	2,024	1,749	10,849	2,631	5,063	796	9,500	43
1,047	....	687	687	......	....	330	505	505	565	1,746	814	450	44
1,093	43	1,753	1,759	120	....	1,201	4,750	4,750	1,525	3,791	360	8,700	45
1,111	8	1,212	1,250	23	....	630	385	385	1,372	3,252	1,198	4,500	46
1,860	164	1,337	1,350	125	....	511	885	885	1,269	3,185	444	4,350	47

	COUNTIES.	LAND OCCUPIED OR IMPROVED.				LIVE STOCK UPON FARMS.			
		Farms.	Acres improved.	Acres unimproved.	Value with improvements and implements.	Horses, asses, and mules.	Neat cattle.	Sheep.	Swine.
27	Lee	1,350	87,186	148,328	$ 1,714,093	3,334	12,801	13,095	25,059
28	Linn	526	37,216	74,549	765,748	1,644	4,264	5,138	11,960
29	Louisa	388	29,490	51,098	506,566	1,100	4,463	3,918	9,519
30	Lucas	32	1,079	5,750	22,705	66	287	214	568
31	Madison	53	1,980	11,919	44,908	159	432	584	1,638
32	Mahaska	480	25,046	74,512	617,387	1,346	4,177	6,150	12,697
33	Marion	342	13,619	59,942	321,109	778	3,135	2,748	11,296
34	Marshall	34	953	2,420	18,252	65	293	291	1,146
35	Monroe	337	13,399	43,066	287,481	670	2,382	2,855	5,925
36	Muscatine	460	25,201	49,388	596,048	1,432	5,503	3,215	10,226
37	Page	61	1,864	....	20,505	159	871	960	1,958
38	Polk	321	15,958	60,223	429,492	784	2,806	3,442	7,637
39	Pottawatomie	82	2,835	....	25,360	108	932	313	795
40	Poweshiek	71	2,906	12,120	65,454	183	508	476	1,706
41	Scott	384	19,993	50,404	563,700	1,009	3,637	2,621	5,183
42	Tama	....	....	....	....	....	....	....	....
43	Taylor	27	631	....	5,207	37	285	364	644
44	Van Buren	998	60,185	128,682	1,481,292	2,843	9,273	16,765	19,506
45	Wapello	828	43,513	98,699	841,389	2,717	5,610	9,486	20,258
46	Warren	47	1,815	11,684	49,546	106	490	196	1,335
47	Washington	428	24,871	59,260	505,354	1,209	4,545	5,190	11,516
48	Wayne	....	1,126	3,333	9,672	84	212	206	719
49	Winneshiek	....	....	....	....	....	....	....	....

STATISTICS OF

1	Adair	1,010	63,746	145,395	700,937	4,161	9,082	15,968	41,886
2	Allen	740	46,188	105,913	611,973	3,414	6,151	10,633	29,823
3	Anderson	420	43,208	35,333	883,973	2,904	3,395	9,026	17,070
4	Ballard	483	20,876	87,976	392,991	1,836	4,491	2,015	20,439
5	Barren	1,833	117,604	204,564	1,412,195	7,883	14,500	23,923	65,710
6	Bath	1,018	108,170	54,783	2,801,051	6,108	10,333	16,928	35,058
7	Boone	982	92,910	65,369	4,132,512	4,751	9,865	15,294	49,446
8	Bourbon	734	168,891	1,111	7,901,450	11,902	17,396	25,288	39,492
9	Boyle	443	53,717	43,151	2,410,229	5,864	8,558	13,552	22,499
10	Bracken	728	41,196	48,436	1,134,938	2,642	3,571	6,265	15,969
11	Breathitt	433	13,517	274,043	279,674	885	4,452	5,565	12,657
12	Breckenridge	889	67,822	181,745	935,739	3,588	7,556	14,526	34,583
13	Bullitt	562	50,144	111,734	1,096,569	2,876	4,917	6,619	27,341
14	Butler	629	26,272	112,896	359,485	2,236	5,670	4,357	23,797
15	Caldwell	889	69,713	182,549	1,110,001	5,356	9,173	10,767	48,868
16	Callaway	933	48,164	184,409	573,521	3,458	6,349	7,924	21,814
17	Campbell	730	27,009	33,111	1,599,036	1,776	2,758	3,241	10,588
18	Carroll	376	30,663	36,601	1,023,027	1,707	4,140	6,352	13,628
19	Carter	654	28,234	218,630	461,696	1,776	4,824	7,918	11,754
20	Casey	758	49,594	140,339	723,365	2,845	5,476	12,215	29,588
21	Christian	1,190	105,670	171,260	2,543,768	7,060	11,793	19,584	61,961
22	Clark	792	153,096	17,056	4,563,412	8,287	16,170	19,760	30,494
23	Clay	511	19,186	137,006	320,102	1,485	6,617	8,015	13,413
24	Clinton	499	29,771	55,767	318,266	1,619	4,719	5,887	18,495
25	Crittenden	662	34,016	103,958	474,082	2,355	5,301	6,485	25,406
26	Cumberland	607	40,066	108,351	661,479	2,646	7,067	9,861	29,730
27	Daviess	1,057	67,408	312,489	1,965,057	4,474	9,603	11,620	45,138
28	Edmonson	507	20,027	75,294	290,555	1,494	3,902	4,955	17,907
29	Estill	604	26,839	84,619	493,554	1,741	4,417	7,447	12,968
30	Fayette	799	173,818	1,404	9,698,184	11,906	18,416	20,855	42,790
31	Fleming	1,211	102,879	100,906	2,687,486	5,919	10,648	17,818	32,142
32	Floyd	365	16,700	94,897	301,877	1,153	5,221	5,421	8,105
33	Franklin	850	61,895	52,969	1,804,288	3,981	5,811	8,685	25,424
34	Fulton	361	17,672	44,948	408,463	1,400	3,526	2,700	13,113
35	Gallatin	414	25,976	32,497	832,012	1,606	3,515	4,602	14,782
36	Garrard	666	92,140	47,989	2,502,599	6,479	10,158	14,843	36,265
37	Grant	730	40,544	74,839	1,241,498	2,441	3,880	6,285	20,432
38	Graves	1,279	56,868	228,342	834,596	4,724	10,804	10,319	32,363
39	Grayson	824	36,612	115,857	351,280	2,324	6,269	7,678	24,784
40	Greene	791	61,323	114,576	832,095	3,529	7,941	12,825	29,571
41	Greenup	453	30,008	111,396	765,206	1,538	4,351	5,466	10,921
42	Hancock	319	17,775	44,274	483,833	1,185	3,451	4,892	13,371
43	Hardin	1,406	108,282	257,081	1,680,684	6,257	12,718	20,588	55,691
44	Harlan	535	19,052	288,717	303,404	1,371	6,539	5,368	13,510
45	Harrison	1,130	137,883	63,238	3,530,611	8,925	11,519	22,390	40,343
46	Hart	829	47,659	135,584	668,458	3,026	7,928	10,807	27,127
47	Henderson	1,037	70,432	160,711	2,091,022	4,938	10,003	9,235	46,734

AGRICULTURAL PRODUCTS.												
Wheat, bushels.	Rye & oats, bushels.	Indian corn, bushels.	Irish and sweet potatoes, bushels.	Peas and beans, bushels.	Barley, bushels.	Buckwheat, bushels.	Butter and cheese, pounds.	Hay, tons.	Hops, pounds.	Clover & other grass seeds, bushels.	Flaxseed, bushels.	
149,414	168,554	754,138	14,169	758	2,727	4,895	247,132	2,601	74	898	146	27
85,633	37,187	306,390	11,218	80	90	1,066	77,314	6,144	......	27	8	28
49,713	40,171	379,449	3,253	53	251	1,188	93,121	873	12	42	63	29
505	300	11,925	151	16	......	32	2,781	100	......	......	......	30
842	387	26,250	726	....	......	257	6,005	211	......	......	......	31
40,092	30,826	341,150	6,332	110	140	549	41,491	1,170	......	131	17	32
17,094	13,003	219,565	8,562	32	379	1,621	54,583	1,780	10	......	26	33
213	210	12,410	319	52	......	38	4,230	185	......	......	......	34
17,792	20,708	200,463	2,584	73	75	192	55,209	236	5	23	34	35
68,246	42,615	341,465	13,679	296	2,975	3,129	39,785	5,433	......	65	......	36
1,998	1,936	28,270	593	....	......	......	6,861	197	......	......	......	37
13,455	11,274	211,677	7,514	176	......	1,888	42,351	2,091	68	36	64	38
9,117	360	31,955	938	50	......	511	10,160	....	......	......	......	39
3,011	1,875	26,455	448	20	20	119	7,072	595	......	......	3	40
120,034	26,341	153,915	13,037	....	3,734	1,495	88,579	6,034	......	23	......	41
....	....	....	....	....	......	......	....	....	......	......	......	42
437	785	10,100	55	....	......	......	4,215	97	......	......	......	43
88,591	172,121	595,082	6,280	....	2,128	9,972	186,447	4,168	7	194	187	44
53,169	73,302	589,395	6,238	179	140	1,973	117,748	1,245	14	160	488	45
633	540	23,920	463	....	......	269	5,630	300	......	......	......	46
30,767	37,774	277,205	4,217	87	......	427	59,359	530	......	12	......	47
732	3,151	14,415	227	11	......	18	3,040	17	......	......	......	48
....	....	....	....	....	......	......	....	....	......	......	......	49

KENTUCKY.

Wheat, bushels.	Rye & oats, bushels.	Indian corn, bushels.	Irish and sweet potatoes, bushels.	Peas and beans, bushels.	Barley, bushels.	Buckwheat, bushels.	Butter and cheese, pounds.	Hay, tons.	Hops, pounds.	Clover & other grass seeds, bushels.	Flaxseed, bushels.	
15,938	80,958	537,945	42,803	2,191	......	......	168,189	607	......	39	2,200	1
9,563	65,412	411,655	23,444	333	......	4	74,426	115	2	28	383	2
13,258	72,233	338,595	7,619	840	300	160	56,024	724	25	180	503	3
9,141	25,470	272,550	18,565	1,120	......	......	43,368	72	70	2	133	4
37,097	210,244	1,007,560	58,243	1,119	......	13	200,279	761	......	......	2,075	5
22,043	100,049	1,033,990	21,211	4,582	88	51	119,409	1,606	16	24	577	6
71,749	77,071	1,056,650	33,405	2,840	578	247	170,240	2,943	24	81	271	7
78,133	190,497	1,705,599	25,465	3,675	540	58	200,091	2,905	136	231	406	8
23,907	114,190	689,780	20,404	2,801	133	1,173	90,257	2,062	30	225	593	9
27,410	59,259	370,025	12,102	6	746	273	102,186	1,420	......	16	187	10
32	2,083	155,840	8,239	3,683	10	......	37,535	38	......	......	65	11
12,387	139,612	521,766	16,657	1,668	......	99	80,734	1,309	8	4	1,803	12
16,974	82,769	418,530	11,689	36	170	25	53,295	1,822	35	23	448	13
4,058	40,905	289,774	16,432	1,637	......	......	63,203	354	33	4	1,201	14
8,574	89,762	767,725	34.517	559	......	3	108,717	502	14	52	50	15
8,414	64,664	405,785	28,542	962	100	39	85,247	97	25	35	263	16
9,988	39,606	301,125	45,074	9	515	22	72,415	1,179	......	9	10	17
13,253	20,774	354,510	23,877	874	170	93	59,042	1,920	45	248	62	18
2,416	36,867	279,777	13,588	4,927	......	45	77,586	1,062	41	17	701	19
9,041	36,427	511,416	29,942	6,145	......	252	95,610	911	10	379	2,838	20
45,678	332,020	1,235,290	64,773	6,446	......	66	190,560	672	454	147	720	21
25,162	84,682	1,213,007	22,820	3,408	27	154	157,065	1,634	63	118	656	22
952	15,744	214,659	11,877	2,348	27	39	944	298	......	......	28	23
7,910	29,124	239,601	15,748	319	......	......	46,433	24	......	28	518	24
5,759	45,898	386,705	23,632	2,715	......	13	68,448	76	89	42	206	25
7,850	30,503	434,340	33,855	4,975	......	27	88,612	358	23	154	225	26
21,953	82,521	739,860	17,776	663	......	......	52,769	1,872	48	37	378	27
4,322	34,578	193,095	16,033	130	......	......	63,204	159	......	......	......	28
1,786	18,679	291,728	12,630	174	......	......	43,043	388	......	10	147	29
73,074	197,351	1,579,598	63,047	8,500	30	1,888	262,349	3,894	589	13,937	273	30
52,283	111,182	926,708	25,011	2,411	7,998	1,386	203,442	3,233	6	295	547	31
1,795	17,636	208,325	10,353	724	......	86	23,325	451	......	......	30	32
25,335	101,727	549,723	32,847	1,046	227	135	157,455	1,415	97	206	117	33
4,879	25,743	236,315	20,442	333	......	1	45,313	364	16	63	519	34
27,388	18,727	402,150	12,033	427	10	90	40,345	796	2	70	713	35
34,920	180,295	973,875	27,913	414	180	84	159,930	1,705	2	202	1,178	36
13,415	34,8[illegible]6	542,955	9,349	848	......	66	76,343	1,188	2	196	163	37
15,036	116,327	653,838	48,391	2,657	2	36	160,277	77	15	91	169	38
8,089	78,755	314,260	14,742	2,158	......	57	79,220	700	5	244	2,416	39
19,870	114,611	505,757	29,904	2,276	......	2	97,341	814	50	10	1,669	40
5,513	39,841	323,488	11,394	528	......	48	51,338	1,849	42	8	32	41
4,599	18,464	210,730	10,419	685	......	47	44,212	1,128	24	15	272	42
46,596	261,018	835,520	32,128	3,809	6	75	191,786	2,726	42	103	3,920	43
948	21,223	181,013	15,933	2,118	......	29	50,838	46	......	2	135	44
44,330	134,910	1,400,281	23,719	1,784	942	169	203,187	3,208	2	216	543	45
14,763	90,631	434,613	24,345	1,181	......	......	84,361	275	......	......	......	46
10,571	73,650	926,865	45,675	1,582	......	55	102,910	1,620	......	......	34	47

	Counties.	Flax, pounds.	Hemp, dew and water-rotted, tons.	Maple sugar, pounds.	Cane sugar, hhds. of 1,000 pounds.	Molasses, gallons.	Rice, pounds.	Tobacco, pounds.	Ginned cotton, bales of 400 pounds.	Wool, pounds.	Silk cocoons, pounds.
		AGRICULTURAL PRODUCTS.									
27	Lee	1,122	.....	3,440	.....	61	....	500	.....	29,885	240
28	Linn	1,117	.....	4,375	.....	.....	....	....	.....	13,881	.....
29	Louisa	395	.....	1,360	.....	22	....	....	.....	11,681	.....
30	Lucas	....	.....	....	.....	.....	....	200	.....	442	.....
31	Madison	117	.....	7,855	.....	273	....	....	.....	1,410	.....
32	Mahaska	15	.....	....	.....	.....	....	....	.....	12,006	.....
33	Marion	1,124	.....	80	.....	3	....	1,982	.....	6,064	.....
34	Marshall	300	.....	990	.....	5	....	30	.....	601	.....
35	Monroe	4,295	.....	....	.....	.....	....	....	.....	7,394	.....
36	Muscatine	2,090	.....	....	.....	.....	....	300	.....	7,078	.....
37	Page	....	.....	....	.....	.....	....	....	.....	2,190	.....
38	Polk	5,067	.....	11,173	.....	527	....	....	.....	9,054	.....
39	Pottawatomie	....	.....	....	.....	.....	....	....	.....	435	.....
40	Poweshiek	340	.....	50	.....	.....	....	20	.....	1,253	.....
41	Scott	....	.....	....	.....	.....	....	....	.....	7,365	.....
42	Tama	....	.....	....	.....	.....	....	....	.....	....	.....
43	Taylor	....	.....	....	.....	.....	....	....	.....	1,008	.....
44	Van Buren	5,558	.....	4,008	.....	366	....	....	.....	40,858	6
45	Wapello	4,214	.....	350	.....	14	....	....	.....	24,388	.....
46	Warren	796	.....	130	.....	12	....	....	.....	1,242	.....
47	Washington	....	.....	....	.....	.....	....	....	.....	12,977	.....
48	Wayne	50	.....	....	.....	.....	....	....	.....	537	.....
49	Winneshiek	....	.....	....	.....	.....	....	....	.....	....	.....

STATISTICS OF

	Counties.	Flax, pounds.	Hemp, dew and water-rotted, tons.	Maple sugar, pounds.	Cane sugar, hhds. of 1,000 pounds.	Molasses, gallons.	Rice, pounds.	Tobacco, pounds.	Ginned cotton, bales of 400 pounds.	Wool, pounds.	Silk cocoons, pounds.
1	Adair	28,069	.....	7,756	.....	341	....	509,003	163	24,307	.....
2	Allen	8,974	.....	6,304	.....	214	451	760,806	.....	14,945	12
3	Anderson	13,798	55	1,600	.....	567	....	14,875	.....	18,864	.....
4	Ballard	7,351	.....	....	.....	.....	....	152,700	.....	3,680	.....
5	Barren	40,936	.....	8,795	4	410	....	2,155,551	.....	40,626	24
6	Bath	11,830	142	7,824	.....	722	....	9,003	.....	39,574	.....
7	Boone	19,074	2	898	.....	314	....	298,152	.....	35,027	.....
8	Bourbon	7,148	1,202	200	.....	72	....	....	.....	78,621	2
9	Boyle	17,341	307	2,560	.....	489	....	1,600	.....	29,931	38
10	Bracken	1,675	5	547	.....	20	....	2,129,370	.....	13,550	40
11	Breathitt	1,536	.....	5,923	.....	17	....	....	.....	8,916	.....
12	Breckenridge	20,813	3	3,775	.....	306	....	2,288,334	.....	24,280	14
13	Bullitt	7,605	.....	3,848	.....	785	....	2,990	.....	13,146	.....
14	Butler	10,811	.....	6,761	.....	969	....	207,819	.....	7,375	.....
15	Caldwell	5,322	.....	1,880	.....	25	30	1,435,479	1	20,649	2
16	Callaway	6,082	.....	475	.....	5	520	957,381	2	13,637	3
17	Campbell	170	.....	....	.....	.....	....	23,108	.....	6,571	.....
18	Carroll	3,256	.....	1,138	.....	275	....	232,612	.....	12,753	.....
19	Carter	37,957	.....	12,197	.....	666	....	9,320	.....	15,674	.....
20	Casey	27,197	3	8,242	.....	334	....	74,600	.....	24,422	134
21	Christian	24,661	.....	5,577	.....	215	....	6,312,076	.....	37,822	.....
22	Clark	18,663	409	5,960	5	634	....	66,335	.....	53,164	10
23	Clay	8,624	.....	4,516	.....	5	2	....	.....	10,419	.....
24	Clinton	12,210	.....	2,526	.....	65	70	32,509	.....	11,012	.....
25	Crittenden	7,232	.....	3,440	.....	164	....	505,637	.....	12,545	4
26	Cumberland	8,880	.....	1,161	.....	22	1,087	1,238,802	.....	14,140	6
27	Daviess	14,217	26	285	.....	37	....	3,426,633	.....	20,319	.....
28	Edmonson	12,891	.....	5,882	.....	.....	....	86,980	.....	7,940	.....
29	Estill	5,731	.....	9,335	.....	463	....	24,150	.....	13,098	.....
30	Fayette	6,947	2,967	2,458	.....	1,207	....	....	.....	75,062	.....
31	Fleming	10,207	461	14,630	.....	1,780	....	81,175	.....	45,001	5
32	Floyd	13,541	.....	2,644	.....	25	....	900	.....	9,422	.....
33	Franklin	6,814	270	2,175	.....	343	....	37,125	.....	23,598	.....
34	Fulton	6,390	.....	....	.....	5	....	222,482	.....	4,209	6
35	Gallatin	1,143	351	560	.....	.....	....	198,095	.....	10,755	45
36	Garrard	12,660	84	2,067	.....	312	....	50,150	.....	30,255	.....
37	Grant	4,493	2	4,948	.....	281	....	104,303	.....	16,031	17
38	Graves	10,982	15	35	.....	4	1,602	1,090,545	.....	17,657	.....
39	Grayson	53,225	930	25,752	.....	541	....	248,227	.....	15,096	.....
40	Greene	118,132	.....	2,470	.....	77	....	1,267,971	.....	20,934	83
41	Greenup	1,509	.....	1,745	.....	133	....	540	.....	10,491	10
42	Hancock	20,172	1	619	.....	31	....	398,843	.....	8,768	.....
43	Hardin	134,188	.....	2,055	.....	67	1,035	285,028	56	39,512	34
44	Harlan	7,989	.....	6,356	.....	2	10	3,136	.....	9,051	.....
45	Harrison	14,170	247	27,926	.....	1,534	....	93,927	.....	48,028	.....
46	Hart	14,301	20	835	.....	.....	....	814,444	.....	19,692	.....
47	Henderson	2,875	.....	....	.....	.....	....	4,292,960	.....	16,259	.....

AGRICULTURAL PRODUCTS.					MANUFACTURES.				REMARKS.	
					Establishments.					
Beeswax and honey, pounds.	Value of animals slaughtered.	Value of produce of market gardens.	Value of orchard produce.	Wine, gallons.	Capital.	Hands employed.	Annual product.	Produced in families.		
9,554	$74,417	$855	$1,632	...	$252,360	426	$417,065	$12,941	...	27
15,912	26,625	...	...	...	36,800	51	85,030	8,618	...	28
16,831	45,677	100	1,148	...	11,180	53	28,780	6,720	...	29
125	455	...	...	...	...	...	...	302	Organized in 1849.	30
2,251	1,805	...	...	...	...	...	...	1,055	" " 1850.	31
6,964	22,614	100	...	...	35,450	57	48,300	7,818	" " 1844.	32
16,089	13,772	15	...	...	18,970	53	38,355	5,252	" " 1845.	33
480	563	...	...	...	...	...	...	419	" " 1850.	34
8,833	12,913	...	...	...	...	...	...	6,062	" " 1845.	35
2,111	25,599	1,099	772	...	87,250	114	436,425	3,400	...	36
4,252	2,465	...	...	...	...	...	...	1,181	Est. '47, not organized '50.	37
19,717	17,885	510	...	...	19,100	46	190,000	4,994	Organized in 1846.	38
3,010	2,088	...	...	...	8,700	17	23,100	444	" " 1848.	39
2,575	1,856	...	...	...	...	...	...	943	" " 1848.	40
3,264	18,723	2,616	608	...	73,000	82	283,130	1,417	...	41
...	...	...	...	...	...	...	...	...	Est. '43, not organized '50.	42
2,122	880	...	...	...	...	...	...	932	" '47, " " '50.	43
32,897	49,798	...	927	10	142,100	97	402,875	23,589	...	44
22,064	43,019	28	58	...	16,400	21	28,327	19,519	Organized in 1844.	45
2,435	1,692	...	...	...	...	...	...	849	" " 1849.	46
361	34,407	...	...	...	1,200	4	5,179	7,676	...	47
1,309	921	88	...	...	...	...	...	395	Est. '46, not organized '50.	48
...	...	...	...	...	...	...	...	...	" '47 fr. Clayton & Fayette, not org. in 1850.	49

KENTUCKY.

Beeswax and honey, pounds.	Value of animals slaughtered.	Value of produce of market gardens.	Value of orchard produce.	Wine, gallons.	Capital.	Hands employed.	Annual product.	Produced in families.	Remarks.	
6,070	44,844	...	...	...	12,425	51	17,650	26,844	...	1
10,950	43,855	9	91	...	20,695	36	25,830	33,432	...	2
10,108	38,876	170	90	36	68,745	127	73,981	12,879	...	3
7,061	31,100	...	25	...	11,200	22	16,200	8,510	Formed in 1842 from Hick-	4
17,036	91,786	...	65	...	49,835	97	46,315	56,349	man and McCracken.	5
18,398	67,523	2,355	761	...	38,530	109	90,584	34,565	...	6
15,760	72,994	726	12,894	221	47,300	78	132,000	22,855	...	7
26,328	105,300	618	...	...	104,725	173	188,272	27,597	...	8
17,346	62,558	1,650	27	22	88,645	206	179,260	22,449	Formed in 1842 from Mer-	9
1,357	55,339	...	309	685	79,000	88	87,060	14,711	cer and Lincoln.	10
74,305	24,261	1,182	1,500	...	10,350	52	16,772	9,176	Divided in 1843 to form	11
3,566	64,123	...	538	5	82,250	83	164,730	20,786	Owsley.	12
3,035	54,849	...	94	...	101,800	125	162,950	7,120	...	13
6,090	23,059	...	...	...	12,680	16	13,645	28,890	...	14
5,670	89,723	20	20	...	523,240	728	510,180	25,029	...	15
6,798	45,738	9	10	...	7,415	24	14,812	29,633	Divided in 1842 to form	16
685	30,594	12,910	1,192	2,471	212,150	224	403,815	1,560	Marshall.	17
6,582	36,605	148	1,663	...	48,690	82	133,663	8,504	...	18
8,235	37,459	1,438	742	...	118,000	211	60,127	19,933	...	19
27,641	61,923	7,699	17,153	...	13,800	24	22,750	45,069	...	20
6,039	182,850	295	5,906	...	127,987	289	318,099	51,412	...	21
24,581	80,843	10	600	...	39,100	86	50,114	28,440	...	22
1,770	28,734	150	...	...	156,650	146	65,125	10,492	Divided in 1843 to form	23
7,288	21,779	...	20	...	6,400	6	3,170	16,440	Owsley.	24
5,140	44,277	26	165	...	64,850	189	66,635	30,265	Formed in 1842 from Liv-	25
11,805	50,023	...	75	5	8,900	27	13,285	37,640	ingston.	26
7,674	83,390	97	95	2	221,400	112	130,800	14,350	...	27
5,084	19,547	...	...	...	1,300	8	6,775	15,084	...	28
8,653	30,663	55	...	...	150,000	131	78,500	13,153	Divided in 1843 to form	29
28,308	204,413	41,119	2,202	44	888,404	1,414	1,338,216	38,296	Owsley.	30
21,460	95,171	8	262	...	119,210	229	296,488	30,454	...	31
1,754	20,474	287	1,525	...	17,700	31	11,700	10,317	Divided in 1843 to form	32
10,851	60,869	5,083	285	...	110,920	495	423,025	17,958	Johnson.	33
9,185	27,074	1,355	254	...	56,950	64	69,505	8,197	Formed in 1845 from Hick-	34
5,059	54,111	20	1,135	30	19,200	40	43,500	7,805	man.	35
17,643	49,542	...	...	...	38,450	80	74,305	30,611	...	36
6,972	59,569	15	140	...	15,450	25	19,476	13,770	...	37
16,549	83,215	429	256	62	23,500	89	51,961	59,824	...	38
5,013	32,841	...	125	...	38,700	38	29,820	30,560	...	39
12,371	62,231	70	1,380	62	20,596	50	61,612	26,985	Divided in 1848 to form	40
4,146	40,857	329	805	...	459,730	958	299,992	6,232	Taylor.	41
3,994	27,564	100	635	...	17,500	49	47,380	9,644	[La Rue.	42
6,791	139,626	25	18	6	95,745	153	169,385	47,463	Divided in 1843 to form	43
9,574	18,187	10	91	...	...	...	...	12,846	Divided in 1842 to form	44
16,618	84,703	5	84	...	82,9[illegible]0	164	134,810	33,680	Letcher.	45
9,148	60,809	...	...	...	13,900	64	24,750	21,656	...	46
13,555	92,805	680	3,880	...	63,550	174	85,400	19,930	...	47

	COUNTIES.	POPULATION.								
		Whites.			Colored.		All classes.		Total population.	
		Male.	Female.	Total.	Free.	Slave.	Male.	Female.	1850.	1840.
48	Henry	4,371	4,004	8,375	54	3,013	5,887	5,555	11,442	10,015
49	Hickman	2,024	1,908	3,932	18	841	2,450	2,341	4,791	8,968
50	Hopkins	5,262	4,937	10,199	50	2,192	6,332	6,109	12,441	9,171
51	Jefferson	25,328	21,955	47,283	1,637	10,911	31,426	28,405	59,831	36,346
52	Jessamine	3,214	3,042	6,256	168	3,825	5,286	4,963	10,249	9,396
53	Johnson	1,945	1,898	3,843	....	30	1,959	1,914	3,873	....
54	Kenton	8,263	7,854	16,117	91	830	8,664	8,374	17,038	7,816
55	Knox	3,157	3,081	6,238	200	612	3,554	3,496	7,050	5,722
56	La Rue	2,598	2,579	5,177	10	672	2,953	2,906	5,859	....
57	Laurel	2,062	1,885	3,947	6	192	2,139	2,006	4,145	3,079
58	Lawrence	3,158	2,984	6,142	2	137	3,217	3,064	6,281	4,730
59	Letcher	1,218	1,222	2,440	10	62	1,251	1,261	2,512	....
60	Lewis	3,626	3,246	6,872	8	322	3,774	3,428	7,202	6,306
61	Lincoln	3,386	3,248	6,634	104	3,355	5,140	4,953	10,093	10,187
62	Livingston	2,883	2,518	5,401	59	1,118	3,504	3,074	6,578	9,025
63	Logan	5,405	5,345	10,750	364	5,467	8,212	8,369	16,581	13,615
64	McCracken	2,810	2,427	5,237	22	808	3,193	2,874	6,067	4,745
65	Madison	5,194	5,075	10,269	65	5,393	7,862	7,865	15,727	16,355
66	Marion	4,264	4,334	8,598	81	3,086	5,826	5,939	11,765	11,032
67	Marshall	2,555	2,445	5,000	20	249	2,672	2,597	5,269	....
68	Mason	7,090	6,584	13,674	386	4,284	9,304	9,040	18,344	15,719
69	Meade	3,008	2,791	5,799	21	1,573	3,804	3,589	7,393	5,780
70	Mercer	5,363	5,108	10,471	336	3,260	7,161	6,906	14,067	18,720
71	Monroe	3,421	3,481	6,902	23	831	3,829	3,927	7,756	6,526
72	Montgomery	3,421	3,245	6,666	164	3,073	5,034	4,869	9,903	9,332
73	Morgan	3,857	3,538	7,395	38	187	3,976	3,644	7,620	4,603
74	Muhlenburg	4,264	3,986	8,250	37	1,522	5,000	4,809	9,809	6,964
75	Nelson	4,830	4,713	9,543	116	5,130	7,359	7,430	14,789	13,637
76	Nicholas	4,524	4,158	8,682	166	1,513	5,291	5,070	10,361	8,745
77	Ohio	4,399	4,169	8,568	49	1,132	5,007	4,742	9,749	6,592
78	Oldham	2,770	2,386	5,156	49	2,424	4,000	3,629	7,629	7,380
79	Owen	4,636	4,246	8,882	48	1,514	5,431	5,013	10,444	8,232
80	Owsley	1,946	1,670	3,616	22	136	2,041	1,733	3,774	....
81	Pendleton	3,228	3,002	6,230	35	509	3,494	3,280	6,774	4,455
82	Perry	1,578	1,394	2,972	3	117	1,635	1,457	3,092	3,089
83	Pike	2,706	2,544	5,250	17	98	2,763	2,602	5,365	3,567
84	Pulaski	6,523	6,338	12,861	27	1,307	7,210	6,985	14,195	9,620
85	Rock Castle	2,187	2,102	4,289	33	375	2,377	2,320	4,697	3,409
86	Russell	2,500	2,401	4,901	13	435	2,701	2,648	5,349	4,238
87	Scott	4,654	4,237	8,891	219	5,836	7,666	7,280	14,946	13,668
88	Shelby	5,337	4,952	10,289	189	6,617	8,865	8,230	17,095	17,768
89	Simpson	2,893	2,863	5,756	42	1,935	3,833	3,900	7,733	6,537
90	Spencer	2,422	2,237	4,659	32	2,151	3,515	3,327	6,842	6,581
91	Taylor	2,713	2,749	5,462	148	1,640	3,565	3,685	7,250	....
92	Todd	3,718	3,643	7,361	97	4,810	6,165	6,103	12,268	9,991
93	Trigg	3,761	3,491	7,252	80	2,797	5,218	4,911	10,129	7,716
94	Trimble	2,587	2,406	4,993	29	941	3,049	2,914	5,963	4,480
95	Union	3,451	3,253	6,704	16	2,292	4,589	4,423	9,012	6,673
96	Warren	5,438	5,159	10,597	209	4,317	7,715	7,408	15,123	15,446
97	Washington	4,633	4,453	9,086	63	3,045	6,162	6,032	12,194	10,596
98	Wayne	3,914	3,941	7,855	7	830	4,329	4,363	8,692	7,399
99	Whitley	3,800	3,422	7,222	24	201	3,901	3,546	7,447	4,673
100	Woodford	3,004	2,874	5,878	169	6,376	6,528	5,895	12,423	11,740

STATISTICS OF

1	Ascension	1,725	1,615	3,340	146	7,266	5,513	5,239	10,752	6,951
2	Assumption	2,698	2,472	5,170	27	5,341	5,704	4,834	10,538	7,141
3	Avoyelles	2,158	1,901	4,059	106	5,161	4,847	4,479	9,326	6,616
4	Baton Rouge, E	2,916	2,431	5,347	279	6,351	6,320	5,657	11,977	8,138
5	Baton Rouge, W	979	836	1,815	105	4,350	3,340	2,930	6,270	4,638
6	Bienville	1,961	1,662	3,623	21	1,895	2,905	2,634	5,539	....
7	Bossier	1,395	1,112	2,507	....	4,455	3,665	3,297	6,962	....
8	Caddo	2,084	1,550	3,634	42	5,208	4,749	4,135	8,884	5,282
9	Calcasieu	1,426	1,292	2,718	239	957	2,009	1,905	3,914	2,057
10	Caldwell	843	741	1,584	....	1,231	1,426	1,389	2,815	2,017
11	Carroll	1,311	1,025	2,336	10	6,443	4,622	4,167	8,789	4,237
12	Catahoula	1,929	1,656	3,585	19	3,528	3,765	3,367	7,132	4,955
13	Claiborne	2,660	2,289	4,949	....	2,522	3,880	3,591	7,471	6,185
14	Concordia	479	344	823	1	6,934	4,051	3,707	7,758	9,414
15	De Soto	1,990	1,559	3,549	24	4,450	4,280	3,743	8,023	....
16	Feliciana, E	2,196	1,864	4,060	24	9,514	6,837	6,761	13,598	11,893
17	Feliciana, W	1,382	1,091	2,473	106	10,666	6,639	6,606	13,245	10,910

NATIVITIES, DWELLINGS, &c.				EDUCATION AND RELIGION.									
Born out of State.				Colleges, academies, and private schools.		Public Schools.							
United States.	Foreign countries.	Dwellings.	Families.	Pupils.	Annual income.	Pupils.	Annual income.	Total educational income.	White scholars during year.	Whites 5 and under 20 years old.	Whites over 20 unable to read & write.	Accommodation of churches—persons.	
722	100	1,438	1,442	120	$3,560	885	$1,890	$5,450	1,602	3,396	332	11,275	48
1,412	37	656	682	165	....	410	397	397	896	1,636	492	3,000	49
2,343	38	1,738	1,738	......	....	2,310	3,326	3,326	1,360	4,191	1,007	7,300	50
14,392	15,782	7,690	8,821	2,055	94,039	2,789	10,294	104,333	7,603	15,530	2,010	35,390	51
658	30	1,093	1,093	85	1,760	601	6,420	8,180	1,194	2,436	487	7,800	52
1,005	2	608	608	......	....	305	627	627	583	1,640	484	....	53
4,376	3,364	2,854	2,888	310	8,000	1,418	12,319	20,319	2,394	5,745	932	10,900	54
1,755	7	1,060	1,087	......	....	975	1,390	1,390	1,304	2,557	1,303	3,550	55
578	30	845	845	70	....	500	734	734	1,104	2,038	576	4,500	56
956	15	671	671	......	....	180	425	425	756	1,741	146	700	57
1,817	52	989	1,008	......	....	687	1,597	1.597	1,109	2,628	1,067	1,875	58
567	....	416	416	......	....	298	451	451	351	1,026	599	2,150	59
1,414	111	1,223	1,227	......	....	513	245	245	938	2,772	712	4,700	60
922	22	1,145	1,145	175	2,300	600	960	3,260	775	2,610	116	5,500	61
1,587	198	915	915	40	560	447	213	773	640	2,141	433	4,600	62
3,032	51	1,917	1,923	99	1,950	746	1,447	3,397	1,814	4,343	61	13,455	63
2,132	380	835	867	187	750	458	1,939	2,689	1,109	2,095	518	4,800	64
886	51	1,847	1,852	195	4,125	1,762	1,160	5,285	1,775	4,036	1,268	20,200	65
837	71	1,428	1,428	173	15,050	1,400	5,000	20,050	1,173	3,545	1,003	7,350	66
1,726	11	865	869	......	....	720	943	943	1,257	2,092	874	4,550	67
2,504	1,034	2,423	2,450	417	14,350	542	5,563	19,913	2,548	5,028	646	14,870	68
1,019	57	947	949	......	....	......	....	....	391	2,461	333	3,250	69
1,147	96	1,762	1,762	377	10,770	1,523	2,773	13,543	1,802	4,136	637	12,250	70
2,206	2	1,190	1,241	......	....	879	919	919	1,481	2,736	891	5,200	71
933	67	1,103	1,103	150	1,800	1,020	12,298	14,098	1,512	2,681	372	7,300	72
1,598	1	1,201	1,201	......	....	558	1,146	1,146	741	3,106	679	2,380	73
1,615	40	1 451	1,451	117	1,109	......	....	1,109	1,471	3,252	801	10,600	74
1,222	196	1,613	1,613	522	52,100	118	791	52,891	1,718	3,841	844	6,550	75
912	131	1,497	1,501	160	....	1,068	504	504	1,690	3,470	764	4,300	76
1,224	24	1,425	1,425	......	....	899	2,009	2,009	1,806	3,523	622	7,200	77
751	158	856	889	97	3,000	380	5,095	8,095	591	2,035	16	7,250	78
735	79	1,623	1,623	390	....	585	266	266	1,558	3,705	870	5,900	79
779	17	588	588	200	....	......	....	....	269	1,471	771	1,050	80
1,011	212	1,057	1,057	70	100	380	205	305	865	2,510	80	5,500	81
508	....	471	500	......	....	......	....	....	132	1,314	687	1,800	82
1,475	5	905	905	......	....	180	138	138	276	2,207	1,351	1,995	83
2,020	39	2,263	2,263	......	....	1,220	2,340	2,340	2,646	5,321	435	12,550	84
623	....	746	746	......	....	425	640	640	504	1,770	453	2,800	85
690	4	840	840	......	....	863	1,208	1,208	1,154	2,009	976	3,250	86
899	186	1,566	1,566	915	18,105	30	360	18,465	1,865	3,533	691	10,470	87
1,367	307	1,803	1,823	529	28,700	813	8,336	37,036	1,438	4,084	454	17.180	88
1,587	16	963	964	98	1,470	833	1,772	3,242	1,156	2,381	419	5,850	89
443	48	810	810	107	....	437	....	....	686	1,878	219	5,200	90
807	3	971	975	65	1,000	461	835	1.835	975	2,203	719	6,400	91
2,225	26	1,316	1.322	115	2,700	409	899	3,599	1,237	2,980	351	9,700	92
2,447	17	1,281	1,282	135	....	631	....	....	1,272	2,922	651	6,325	93
993	94	865	865	......	....	320	272	272	760	1,984	176	5,450	94
1,222	167	1,140	1,140	71	4.050	1,284	8,036	12,086	1,148	2,730	475	4,300	95
1,984	55	1,798	1,798	140	2.220	1,100	1,613	3.833	2,201	4,357	789	7,650	96
850	84	1,517	1,517	170	9,200	1,325	400	9.600	1,832	3,671	1,183	6,900	97
1,515	13	1,359	1,369	......	....	1,484	1,676	1,676	1,300	3,202	1,242	3,925	98
1,580	3	1,214	1,214	......	....	1,197	2,089	2,089	1,642	3,170	1,353	15,650	99
719	273	1,053	1,081	362	8,945	327	3,975	12,920	1,048	2,152	158	9,000	100

LOUISIANA.

253	375	755	755	43	5,000	300	7,800	12,800	629	1,250	83	3,000	1
106	210	926	926	10	....	693	7,036	7,036	695	2,098	1,396	1,000	2
380	128	792	792	100	3,331	566	4,198	7,529	421	1,639	705	2,100	3
1,243	699	1,044	1,044	20	600	500	3,600	4,200	744	1,834	268	1,370	4
149	140	392	438	50	1,500	250	2,500	4,000	354	703	155	700	5
2,389	12	571	571	85	1,443	756	2,452	3,895	683	1,562	307	2,675	6
1,715	27	478	478	......	....	460	2,210	2,210	489	1,040	72	750	7
2,543	214	742	747	......	....	......	....	....	528	1,263	75	1,500	8
233	35	548	626	......	....	150	520	520	389	1,145	413	....	9
797	16	300	300	......	....	426	1,801	1,801	266	676	116	1,250	10
1,413	132	582	582	......	....	360	2,000	2,000	281	778	49	950	11
1,539	70	655	679	40	1,500	508	4,442	5,942	445	1,447	29	1,400	12
3,208	120	842	842	70	460	1,250	4,070	4,530	913	2,080	367	2,400	13
478	35	219	221	......	....	150	5,791	5,791	18	244	......	300	14
2,269	57	685	692	190	....	260	2,500	2,500	676	1,377	82	3,200	15
1,161	293	712	712	335	16,500	160	5,760	22,260	804	1,565	26	1,700	16
785	261	599	617	130	....	170	3,440	3,440	475	816	85	2,400	17

	Counties.	Land occupied or improved.				Live stock upon farms.			
		Farms.	Acres improved.	Acres unimproved.	Value with improvements and implements.	Horses, asses, and mules.	Neat cattle.	Sheep.	Swine.
48	Henry	1,029	118,714	44,496	$ 2,763,052	4,993	9,609	18,309	42,132
49	Hickman	546	21,874	62,939	401,110	1,789	4,312	3,194	16,288
50	Hopkins	1,354	70,065	204,441	1,031,262	3,722	10,017	16,131	53,314
51	Jefferson	877	90,720	65,928	5,522,543	5,250	7,987	10,798	39,573
52	Jessamine	651	65,485	42,304	3,356,476	6,218	8,139	12,941	24,994
53	Johnson	504	15,094	110,382	261,284	944	3,800	5,961	12,259
54	Kenton	656	41,616	36,915	2,468,370	2,088	3,928	5,914	17,149
55	Knox	657	32,595	127,548	439,739	1,771	5,978	7,640	19,315
56	La Rue	420	32,961	75,335	546,668	2,273	4,203	7,883	19,031
57	Laurel	284	22,759	152,864	277,569	1,256	4,088	7,372	11,941
58	Lawrence	655	26,665	173,411	458,811	1,543	6,292	8,740	17,397
59	Letcher	343	11,261	89,328	158,188	808	3,483	4,093	8,538
60	Lewis	651	34,662	86,054	859,251	2,176	4,676	7,279	13,843
61	Lincoln	614	90,094	77,288	2,334,941	5,469	14,623	17,211	30,013
62	Livingston	485	26,902	96,758	515,535	2,018	4,880	4,208	19,730
63	Logan	1,130	105,036	167,760	1,971,767	6,938	10,744	19,353	55,858
64	McCracken	348	16,477	46,399	331,222	1,253	2,954	1,825	10,461
65	Madison	1,185	149,164	102,331	4,785,130	8,635	18,456	28,015	57,495
66	Marion	963	86,959	125,741	2,629,279	6,966	9,176	17,490	49,032
67	Marshall	415	18,521	67,930	219,960	1,405	3,437	3,093	11,115
68	Mason	888	93,559	56,884	4,919,502	6,027	9,960	14,584	27,584
69	Meade	489	40,366	80,573	672,080	2,191	4,775	6,831	18,179
70	Mercer	881	97,281	48,454	3,113,262	7,105	8,246	19,757	40,252
71	Monroe	746	43,662	91,922	480,670	3,035	5,214	8,248	30,567
72	Montgomery	856	99,296	121,970	3,059,514	6,977	12,642	15,908	29,457
73	Morgan	615	31,742	260,193	539,774	1,675	5,992	8,700	13,467
74	Muhlenburg	921	50,935	202,285	765,077	3,448	7,864	11,630	37,862
75	Nelson	844	112,574	96,702	2,979,035	5,524	10,292	17,810	54,100
76	Nicholas	711	57,092	49,908	2,171,987	5,223	6,591	13,478	25,949
77	Ohio	1,122	55,196	165,500	879,204	3,598	10,058	12,094	44,292
78	Oldham	414	59,490	30,406	1,632,961	2,750	5,065	8,209	24,666
79	Owen	917	64,755	95,840	1,801,676	3,661	6,181	13,556	31,420
80	Owsley	484	14,887	226,241	369,148	967	3,944	4,849	9,825
81	Pendleton	696	39,977	86,779	1,044,975	2,475	4,840	9,866	18,105
82	Perry	396	14,145	279,673	233,263	900	5,316	5,536	12,519
83	Pike	448	18,474	178,006	378,783	1,114	6,319	7,025	14,003
84	Pulaski	1,528	75,529	247,002	1,148,712	4,415	12,922	22,092	44,021
85	Rock Castle	441	25,938	73,463	292,554	1,422	3,002	6,032	9,733
86	Russell	665	42,342	87,997	376,040	1,913	4,420	5,669	24,560
87	Scott	758	126,756	27,684	4,978,575	7,547	10,420	15,728	30,043
88	Shelby	1,202	147,170	76,556	6,094,014	8,727	16,819	23,829	76,393
89	Simpson	686	45,296	72,419	754,749	3,767	5,283	8,668	26,521
90	Spencer	578	77,496	39,319	1,986,668	3,455	4,804	10,362	40,887
91	Taylor	648	45,888	70,833	558,138	2,685	5,707	8,887	23,653
92	Todd	930	78,511	108,805	1,496,140	4,941	8,385	14,596	44,569
93	Trigg	843	50,143	14,816	744,594	3,627	6,275	7,755	31,303
94	Trimble	469	37,287	38,002	996,046	1,922	3,675	6,561	13,454
95	Union	681	52,453	141,403	1,204,589	4,144	9,306	8,914	38,177
96	Warren	1,145	91,507	155,325	1,844,251	6,836	14,114	18,842	54,135
97	Washington	867	102,441	83,802	2,252,914	7,104	7,665	18,615	46,513
98	Wayne	929	69,532	190,897	920,515	3,759	12,316	14,043	42,450
99	Whitley	980	38,863	214,207	531,473	2,394	10,045	8,034	41,886
100	Woodford	580	108,828	7,347	4,445,026	6,587	8,529	15,166	26,150

STATISTICS OF

1	Ascension	157	28,346	65,138	7,121,695	2,346	4,077	1,627	5,649
2	Assumption	520	31,361	91,525	6,000,325	3,197	4,968	990	5,242
3	Avoyelles	393	33,898	99,449	1,409,239	2,777	11,884	4,090	18,910
4	Baton Rouge, E.	287	37,535	115,247	2,458,886	2,595	13,406	3,874	25,045
5	Baton Rouge, W.	138	25,775	41,988	2,291,125	2,016	2,688	1,034	1,257
6	Bienville	271	18,015	42,559	301,238	995	4,619	523	14,749
7	Bossier	333	40,284	114,086	808,483	1,890	8,026	1,006	19,788
8	Caddo	305	44,174	136,621	1,009,921	2,029	15,198	1,383	17,055
9	Calcasieu	239	18,542	20,943	157,323	8,512	83,387	2,126	8,969
10	Caldwell	185	12,081	16,736	252,586	745	4,195	1,127	12,098
11	Carroll	238	47,701	98,943	2,919,629	2,870	10,960	1,687	18,318
12	Catahoula	358	26,077	83,265	832,776	1,943	13,516	2,089	30,765
13	Claiborne	554	31,971	85,039	460,573	1,820	8,827	1,913	28,510
14	Concordia	148	50,059	109,854	2,790,830	2,692	5,379	1,919	9,054
15	De Soto	427	37,520	110,566	773,770	1,888	8,622	847	23,679
16	Feliciana, E.	361	82,936	125,057	1,727,798	3,221	13,126	6,800	23,004
17	Feliciana, W.	234	76,311	109,060	3,420,665	3,897	12,553	5,051	11,005

AGRICULTURAL PRODUCTS.

Wheat, bushels.	Rye & oats, bushels.	Indian corn, bushels.	Irish and sweet potatoes, bushels.	Peas and beans, bushels.	Barley, bushels.	Buckwheat, bushels.	Butter and cheese, pounds.	Hay, tons.	Hops, pounds.	Clover & other grass seeds, bushels.	Flaxseed, bushels.	
38,844	117,688	964,372	24,884	581	120	46	138,119	2,082	......	18	377	48
14,471	32,339	317,691	24,230	1,620	30	......	46,386	72	......	1	628	49
14,325	61,928	741,032	29,291	2,375	......	......	138,144	436	......	3	29	50
92,809	130,822	983,429	114,861	2,327	6,110	110	194,264	4,944	11	211	83	51
35,880	149,981	725,891	21,063	532	......	215	123,050	1,131	30	21	429	52
1,736	22,174	185,120	12,819	544	......	80	43,523	587	......	26	463	53
28,208	39,324	473,545	20,403	11	5	312	123,935	2,044	......	......	5	54
2,526	48,916	290,965	22,867	6,150	......	111	69,[illegible]08	761	95	31	701	55
18,578	74,408	335,275	12,505	1,143	......	70	100,105	536	13	617	926	56
1,156	17,788	54,927	2,714	603	1	165	5,812	525	10	5	270	57
939	30,933	278,317	18,910	1,311	30	276	38,324	645	15	16	720	58
2,054	8,225	86,718	9,174	3,296	......	228	40,461	133	......	1	426	59
7,213	54,693	398,686	12,785	1,190	1,538	80	85,686	1,698	11	104	290	60
23,686	95,263	740,499	17,606	258	2	112	116,122	1,333	3	......	3,282	61
2,308	25,841	331,436	22,888	384	......	10	43,798	212	20	3	30	62
50,316	243,043	1,103,186	45,395	1,864	3	67	164,824	1,027	111	175	644	63
5,536	18,524	174,976	19,180	172	......	......	30,060	21	......	......	3	64
32,962	193,387	1,424,856	39,264	8,865	......	19	270,426	2,265	71	463	2,973	65
22,930	228,561	1,001,919	32,422	498	......	129	155,969	1,670	40	806	2,878	66
2,991	27,686	192,835	12,666	143	......	......	44,199	38	......	24	6	67
52,486	63,448	978,470	29,506	2,638	71,667	503	214,721	3,904	406	72	83	68
11,216	126,321	373,145	12,010	730	93	......	51,337	659	......	2	433	69
68,690	185,234	1,098,395	30,169	5,366	26	1,742	202,213	3,904	110	671	1,170	70
12,443	77,532	384,705	29,249	4,125	......	110	65,636	164	10	5	1,940	71
18,673	111,651	914,863	21,012	496	......	84	150,867	1,848	......	125	550	72
2,427	29,179	267,275	15,664	2,240	......	101	68,548	1,082	......	......	906	73
13,916	74,125	495,328	23,078	1,840	......	67	84,453	1,070	1	80	2,526	74
63,864	235,276	1,070,066	32,828	212	......	151	167,111	2,791	2	297	2,693	75
31,286	74,370	733,750	11,403	401	1,170	47	112,098	949	11	113	113	76
10,607	18,930	521,128	22,361	2,418	......	......	120,725	1,720	......	10	1,691	77
45,067	75,512	510,960	22,261	75	......	46	84,317	1,548	......	731	430	78
22,794	49,284	632,870	15,136	677	......	77	2,902	8	3	89	233	79
796	8,910	164,021	13,549	373	5	21	25,010	28	......	5	105	80
12,262	51,747	429,855	13,040	3,747	140	1,039	74,168	1,113	60	191	136	81
786	4,788	124,296	9,290	3,321	......	7	43,445	39	......	6	146	82
2,454	18,569	198,764	16,714	2,389	......	196	66,246	480	15	33	277	83
13,385	126,099	558,862	52,382	8,805	48	171	206,374	526	......	141	3,460	84
3,715	28,981	177,974	8,365	375	......	11	41,297	169	......	136	276	85
4,707	51,699	316,165	21,769	2,180	16	3	78,621	117	12	24	718	86
49,677	161,928	1,089,109	27,136	2,342	160	768	150,290	2,952	......	10	57	87
83,931	210,005	1,731,740	35,216	2,166	8	521	211,310	4,056	198	458	1,519	88
19,914	146,178	516,158	30,572	892	......	35	75,909	208	22	54	473	89
55,614	118,754	775,878	12,837	1,331	190	142	120,775	1,369	......	48	1,260	90
10,087	91,829	365,085	22,512	3,326	......	38	77,289	258	......	6	1,594	91
40,485	203,627	803,941	48,988	31	......	......	125,773	279	......	6	31	92
11,149	87,144	604,515	32,105	1,318	......	30	81,115	776	......	8	41	93
19,516	33,328	286,795	12,856	325	15	54	72,975	858	4	183	2,294	94
11,994	51,577	680,640	23,387	613	15	81	92,370	1,001	5	12	99	95
33,473	199,704	1,031,545	44,898	3,772	......	72	184,530	668	855	98	783	96
28,653	138,567	824,925	14,908	169	146	343	37,060	1,479	......	451	2,033	97
14,276	104,977	495,409	38,908	6,416	......	14	131,875	131	......	66	1,005	98
3,609	53,214	312,918	36,120	8,027	......	179	136,940	448	......	210	871	99
51,250	122,845	812,490	25,903	899	1,006	304	126,359	1,606	80	54	165	100

LOUISIANA.

....	....	368,500	10,671	1,325	......	......	250	25	75	......	......	1
....	....	564,302	25,561	....	......	......	7,538	2,443	......	......	......	2
....	260	310,985	33,265	5,339	......	......	22,639	580	......	......	......	3
....	30	226,942	33,896	3,851	......	......	....	1,392	......	......	......	4
....	....	151,750	13,676	1,327	......	......	....	1,051	......	......	......	5
84	3,364	122,530	35,817	15,624	......	......	16,896	....	......	......	......	6
6	2,650	225,122	34,572	9,698	......	......	23,470	....	......	......	......	7
....	22,095	265,945	71,565	19,249	......	......	27,851	....	......	......	......	8
....	....	44,360	32,117	....	......	......	....	41	......	......	......	9
....	693	71,418	14,258	1,415	......	......	8,691	44	......	......	......	10
....	630	237,364	36,872	850	......	......	41,957	367	......	54	......	11
54	115	183,736	33,055	2,136	......	3	16,376	15	10	......	......	12
108	2,230	234,470	59,420	6,231	......	......	23,899	....	......	......	......	13
....	25	239,670	21,909	7,479	......	......	25,755	242	......	......	......	14
....	5,253	240,080	69,446	5,589	......	......	45,572	....	......	......	......	15
....	15,375	391,789	111,187	5,583	......	......	53,464	263	......	2	......	16
....	4,825	360,585	58,362	6,157	......	......	61,254	486	14	......	......	17

	Counties.	Agricultural products.									
		Flax, pounds.	Hemp, dew and water-rotted, tons.	Maple sugar, pounds.	Cane sugar, hhds. of 1,000 pounds.	Molasses, gallons.	Rice, pounds.	Tobacco, pounds.	Ginned cotton, bales of 400 pounds.	Wool, pounds.	Silk cocoons, pounds.
48	Henry	17,933	4					1,057,273		39,963	
49	Hickman	18 838						378,580		6,339	
50	Hopkins	42,011		180			5	2,180,699		23,654	
51	Jefferson	2,976	120	1,025		92		9,500		21,540	
52	Jessamine	24,005	1,563	328		472		4,800		37,153	
53	Johnson	6,380		4,737		184		9,250		11,173	2
54	Kenton	50						125,440		13,561	
55	Knox	9,334		7,416		190	213	16,869	1	18,776	2
56	La Rue	17,682		4,018		241		131,950		13,348	
57	Laurel	12,546		145		12	28	2,122	10	11,688	
58	Lawrence	8,193	30	7,108		279		8,891		15,561	1
59	Letcher	8,856		7,982		259	20	3,122		8,370	60
60	Lewis	7,515	1	5,675		1,360		36,820		14,604	119
61	Lincoln	38,718	4	603		51		2,000		40,655	
62	Livingston	415		135		145	20	41,200		5,888	
63	Logan	20,452	3	6,374		159	64	2,684,767		38,001	42
64	McCracken	330						84,196	4	2,743	
65	Madison	130,173	6	12,742		1,626		60,511		55,409	1
66	Marion	195,857		12.291		1,079	50	16,450		38,568	
67	Marshall	1,748		1,554			80	122,883		6,519	6
68	Mason	1,763	1,853	45		139		2,492,622		47,140	
69	Meade	8,954	3	136				210,427		13,095	
70	Mercer	64,440	470	7,831		938		12,420		47,850	60
71	Monroe	15,231		6,576		341	111	392,762		15,118	4
72	Montgomery	9,094	106	9,045		823		4,410		35,302	
73	Morgan	10,811								16,988	
74	Muhlenburg	29,294	1	3,997		189	172	685,050		20,250	20
75	Nelson	38,721	54	17,306		1,477				37,328	110
76	Nicholas	5,468	161	4,025		190		100,280		32,263	
77	Ohio	37,878		3,435		105		1,543,692		22,545	
78	Oldham	6,214	75			107		36,620		18,905	
79	Owen	11,449	2	5,524		542	50	746,871		28,373	150
80	Owsley	5,504		5,145		209	45	3,130		8,002	
81	Pendleton	10,735	5	7,419		630		253,827		20,166	
82	Perry	6,222		4,333	1	50		2,669		11,288	
83	Pike	7,964	1	3,438		16		4,401		12,058	
84	Pulaski	44,461		9,005		494	23	6,883		34,876	125
85	Rock Castle	6,003		6,058		346		5,543		10,226	
86	Russell	9,915		3,448		32		40,757		12,133	3
87	Scott	7,559	1,612	5,064		732		200		44,539	
88	Shelby	40,827	1,022	1,373		316		221,122		60,176	13
89	Simpson	67,430		303		18		1,221,314	521	14,883	3
90	Spencer	30,547	17	7,011		605		15,660		22,326	
91	Taylor	34,278		4,651		143		592,106		15,960	
92	Todd	10,396		8,440		32		3,739,685		27,750	
93	Trigg	7,047		1,519		104		1,653,485		15,309	
94	Trimble	9,350		1,184		188		454,722		13,331	61
95	Union	8,466		108				494.784		17,864	
96	Warren	61,542	2	1,567		104		1,401,751		32,336	10
97	Washington	25,935	212	5,893		161		12,500		34,639	
98	Wayne	19,535		10,065		385		14,230		24,501	
99	Whitley	48,889		4,309				11,674		13,916	
100	Woodford	4,400	2,958	150		36		2,600		45,586	

STATISTICS OF

1	Ascension				13,438	554,975	33,500		406	150	
2	Assumption				17,160	930,185	99,770		130		
3	Avoyelles				4,481	248,720	291,350	1,085	3,538	4,363	
4	Baton Rouge, E.				7,074	407,358	4,009		1,346	5,551	
5	Baton Rouge, W				7,920	518,870	900		262	270	
6	Bienville						6,688	10	1,648	1,362	
7	Bossier						145		4,181	1,285	
8	Caddo						10		4,819	2,652	
9	Calcasieu				460	18,160	1,176		122		
10	Caldwell						2,820		1,570	2,061	
11	Carroll								15,544	3,490	
12	Catahoula					36	903	40	6,648	2,027	
13	Claiborne						60		2,483	3,240	
14	Concordia				33	41	100		18,297	2,737	
15	De Soto				2	580	33,400	200	2,995	565	
16	Feliciana, E.				1,105	71,200	42,675	800	9,967	13,366	
17	Feliciana, W.				4,767	395,612	8,000		18,291	10,993	

AGRICULTURAL PRODUCTS.					MANUFACTURES.					
					Establishments.				REMARKS.	
Beeswax and honey, pounds.	Value of animals slaughtered.	Value of produce of market gardens.	Value of orchard produce.	Wine, gallons.	Capital.	Hands employed.	Annual product.	Produced in families.		
900	$86,250	$25	....	140	$54,500	173	$135,292	$19,608	....	48
12,295	26,829	....	$6,316	......	9,800	52	29,090	17,462	Divided in 1842 to form	49
12	81,770	50	30	......	9,500	31	14,635	35,822	Ballard, and in 1845 to	50
3,362	107,052	63,236	604	2,109	4,115,582	8,865	11,002,103	8,806	form Fulton.	51
15,581	95,101	170	....	......	109,900	421	251,570	24,188	....	52
6,316	24,286	170	143	......	4,025	9	7,053	15,310	Formed in 1843 from Floyd,	53
4,425	80,277	5,939	8,883	968	464,850	752	866,961	11,025	Lawrence and Morgan.	54
20,822	38,652	....	10	......	8,630	15	10,015	20,676	....	55
2,374	44,975	....	....	......	13,150	30	16,225	12,750	Formed in 1843 from Har-	56
14,292	28,098	25	5,891	30	24,465	22	8,200	10,892	din.	57
5,323	31,421	4,225	110	......	27,400	73	49,700	15,004	Div. '43 to form Johnson.	58
8,847	19,251	16	61	......	....	......	....	15,812	Formed in 1842 from Perry	59
7,425	44,029	285	820	......	50,450	91	99,880	12,255	and Harlan.	60
423	70,654	210	....	......	149,098	149	247,605	22,987	Divided '42 to form Boyle.	61
2,179	37,688	6,437	235	......	129,300	131	83,995	10,962	Divided in 1842 to form	62
5,958	140,448	11,314	....	......	46,700	120	97,363	35,646	Crittenden.	63
2,694	23,365	2,115	50	10	73,750	290	652,740	5,618	Divided in 1842 to form	64
28,393	97,638	609	1,079	76	64,565	133	104,077	44,672	Ballard.	65
35,241	173,126	....	5	......	85,075	143	96,445	46,981	....	66
3,823	24,372	171	1,452	......	6,150	23	7,660	24,623	Formed in 1842 from Cal-	67
11,279	135,673	3,428	1,170	80	623,300	1,280	1,061,746	24,973	laway.	68
2,631	47,661	....	195	5	67,000	99	519,400	8,405	....	69
28,396	82,433	4,995	8,339	7	151,700	356	348,583	51,852	Divided in 1842 to form	70
6,121	36,797	....	156	......	6,000	17	8,680	27,522	Boyle.	71
19,557	61,796	70	150	4	63,550	132	70,205	33,145	....	72
11,435	30,416	....	....	......	....	......	....	18,792	Divided in 1843 to form	73
6,201	56,662	184	85	......	54,725	120	56,286	23,640	Johnson.	74
10,817	114,310	85	3,623	......	77,270	223	207,813	31,735	....	75
19,993	49,016	54	3	......	31,650	85	44,470	22,468	....	76
9,608	51,751	....	25	......	26,155	60	40,933	41,937	....	77
9,025	50,890	....	80	......	19,100	25	57,600	8,180	....	78
14,751	67,092	107,211	96	40	38,600	49	35,004	31,086	....	70
4,555	24,758	57	80	......	29,000	114	45,150	11,132	Formed in 1843 from Clay,	80
4,493	46,151	5,890	3,215	58	17,200	30	20,190	18,711	Estill and Breathitt.	81
5,290	24,104	....	145	......	....	......	....	17,164	Divided in 1842 to form	82
24,692	26,338	....	3,229	......	15,700	17	8,355	16,539	Letcher.	83
14,901	99,110	557	1,046	10	32,100	68	57,300	50,912	....	84
5,533	22,079	....	48	......	14,500	20	18,000	11,910	....	85
11,238	27,627	29	38	......	9,725	30	13,568	30,898	....	86
32,535	91,610	845	....	3	153,270	228	248,717	20,044	....	87
31,011	132,212	1,571	....	191	190,675	487	381,578	42,092	....	88
3,203	46,084	....	....	......	22,225	104	36,218	33,468	....	99
12,663	67,118	....	....	......	54,340	67	44,681	19,775	....	90
9,881	39,643	....	156	20	13,875	47	60,524	30,621	Formed 1848 from Greene.	91
1,460	94,810	....	10	......	11,300	75	36,300	30,489	....	92
5,631	68,698	....	....	......	178,295	356	175,893	28,233	....	93
5,315	241,455	355	455	350	43,700	73	199,770	11,622	....	94
19,530	80,765	364	917	7	59,800	147	62,970	22,212	....	95
13,462	159,997	109	....	......	65,727	128	80,625	107,276	....	96
24,715	82,640	162	....	334	34,400	58	24,000	27,319	....	97
15,053	53,591	1,805	141	......	21,110	48	17,357	38,766	....	98
20,802	43,512	....	....	......	....	......	....	40,081	....	99
11,511	82,841	1,250	27	......	267,345	643	551,534	15,637	....	100

LOUISIANA.

17,500	3,680	12,500	....	......	....	......	....	19,300	....	1
....	17,009	....	....	......	....	......	....	5,318	....	2
34,565	39,418	....	....	......	25,500	37	19,300	8,522	....	3
40	27,481	....	....	......	....	......	....	......	....	4
1,180	6,475	2,840	100	......	17,300	50	32,650	337	....	5
2,966	23,965	....	....	......	3,220	5	2,500	2,738	Formed '48 fr. Claiborne.	6
325	32,723	500	....	......	....	......	....	345	Formed '43 fr. Claiborne.	7
50	40,536	....	1,735	......	....	......	....	1,113	Div. '43 to form De Soto.	8
....	26,930	....	150	......	....	......	....	4,943	....	9
2,708	12,911	....	....	......	1,000	3	1,080	2,103	....	10
2,217	23,461	500	....	......	44,815	59	28,600	125	....	11
360	29,206	....	40	......	18,000	18	19,000	25	Div. '43 to form Franklin.	12
720	41,487	....	....	......	7,200	16	13,500	3,416	Divided. See Nos. 6, 7 & 20	13
....	14,040	....	625	......	....	......	....	......	Divided '43 to form Tensas.	14
2,985	48,477	....	....	......	9,320	39	23,095	1,120	Formed in 1843 from Nat-	15
1,584	47,395	450	....	15	68,850	142	86,845	5,343	chitoches and Caddo.	16
343	32,013	1,058	30	......	419,715	804	780,082	995	....	17

	COUNTIES.*	POPULATION.								
		Whites.			Colored.		All classes.		Total population.	
		Male.	Female.	Total.	Free.	Slave.	Male.	Female.	1850.	1840.
18	Franklin...........	899	765	1,664	14	1,573	1,655	1,596	3,251	....
19	Iberville	1,998	1,570	3,568	104	8,606	6,671	5,607	12,278	8,495
20	Jackson	1,789	1,617	3,406	2	2,158	2,829	2,737	5,566	....
21	Jefferson...........	9,533	8,513	18,046	851	6,196	13,347	11,746	25,093	10,470
22	Lafayette...........	1,774	1,616	3,390	160	3,170	3,486	3,234	6,720	7,841
23	Lafourche...........	2,702	2,440	5,142	22	4,368	5,122	4,410	9,532	7,303
24	Livingston..........	1,391	1,133	2,524	19	842	1,836	1,549	3,385	2,315
25	Madison	826	590	1,416	4	7,353	4,650	4,123	8,773	5,142
26	Morehouse..........	1,065	812	1,877	30	2,006	2,034	1,879	3,913	....
27	Natchitoches........	2,965	2,501	5,466	881	7,881	7,349	6,879	14,228	14,350
28	Orleans.............	52,878	38,553	91,431	9,961	18,068	64,229	55,231	119,460	102,193
29	Ouachita	1,231	1,061	2,292	8	2,708	2,543	2,465	5,008	4,640
30	Plaquemines........	1,328	893	2,221	390	4,779	4,097	3,293	7,390	5,060
31	Point Coupee........	1,657	1,311	2,968	560	7,811	6,038	5,301	11,339	7,898
32	Rapides.............	2,809	2,228	5,037	184	11,340	8,763	7,798	16,561	14,132
33	Sabine..............	1,809	1,538	3,347	....	1,168	2,392	2,123	4,515	....
34	St. Bernard..........	814	592	1,406	73	2,323	2,418	1,384	3,802	3,237
35	St. Charles..........	463	404	867	121	4,132	2,919	2,201	5,120	4,700
36	St. Helena..........	1,237	1,117	2,354	11	2,196	2,313	2,248	4,561	3,525
37	St. James...........	1,696	1,589	3,285	62	7,751	6,100	4,998	11,098	8,548
38	St. John Baptist.....	1,302	1,284	2,586	191	4,540	3,991	3,326	7,317	5,776
39	St. Landry...........	5,222	4,918	10,140	1,242	10,871	11,423	10,830	22,253	15,233
40	St. Martin's..........	2,577	2,166	4,743	529	6,489	6,221	5,540	11,761	8,674
41	St. Mary's...........	1,930	1,493	3,423	424	9,850	7,583	6,114	13,697	8,950
42	St. Tammany........	1,940	1,702	3,642	359	2,363	3,430	2,934	6,364	4,598
43	Tensas..............	528	372	900	2	8,138	4,712	4,328	9,040	....
44	Terre Bonne........	1,840	1,465	3,305	91	4,328	4,336	3,388	7,724	4,410
45	Union...............	2,482	2,296	4,778	....	3,425	4,082	4,121	8,203	1,838
46	Vermillion..........	1,200	1,128	2,328	14	1,067	1,744	1,665	3,409	....
47	Washington.........	1,226	1,141	2,367	4	1,037	1,731	1,677	3,408	2,649

STATISTICS OF

1	Aroostook	6,725	5,798	12,523	6	....	6,728	5,801	12,529	9,413
2	Cumberland.........	39,207	39,732	78,939	599	....	39,152	40,026	79,538	68,658
3	Franklin............	10,231	9,777	20,008	19	....	10,243	9,784	20,027	20,801
4	Hancock	17,773	16,570	34,343	29	....	17,789	16,583	34,372	28,605
5	Kennebeck	31,378	31,004	62,382	139	....	31,455	31,066	62,521	55,823
6	Lincoln.............	38,540	36,063	74,603	272	....	38,686	36,189	74,875	63,517
7	Oxford.............	20,544	19,214	39,758	5	....	20,547	19,216	39,763	38,351
8	Penobscot	32,862	30,160	63,022	67	....	32,901	30,188	63,089	45,705
9	Piscataquis	7,798	6,934	14,732	3	....	7,800	6,935	14,735	13,138
10	Somerset	18,471	17,096	35,567	14	....	18,479	17,102	35,581	33,912
11	Waldo	24,147	23,044	47,191	39	....	24,170	23,060	47,230	41,509
12	Washington.........	19,912	18,771	38,683	128	....	19,984	18,827	38,811	28,327
13	York................	29,157	30,905	60,062	36	....	29,177	30,921	60,098	54,034

STATISTICS OF

1	Alleghany...........	11,545	10,088	21,633	412	724	12,042	10,727	22,769	15,690
2	Anne Arundel.......	8,314	8,228	16,542	4,602	11,249	16,591	15,802	32,393	29,532
3	Baltimore	88,112	86,741	174,853	29,075	6,718	103,609	107,037	210,646	134,379
4	Calvert.............	1,867	1,763	3,630	1,530	4,486	4,837	4,809	9,646	9,229
5	Caroline............	3,027	3,069	6,096	2,788	808	4,821	4,871	6,692	7,806
6	Carroll.............	9,434	9,233	18,667	974	975	10,409	10,207	20,616	17,241
7	Cecil...............	7,951	7,521	15,472	2,623	844	9,736	9,203	18,939	17,232
8	Charles.............	2,829	2,836	5,665	913	9,584	8,293	7,869	16,162	16,023
9	Dorchester..........	5,433	5,314	10,747	3,848	4,282	9,461	9,416	18,877	18,843
10	Frederick...........	16,529	16,785	33,314	3,760	3,913	20,336	20,651	40,987	36,405
11	Harford.............	7,384	7,029	14,413	2,777	2,166	9,871	9,485	19,356	17,120
12	Kent	2,930	2,686	5,616	3,143	2,627	5,914	5,472	11,386	10,842
13	Montgomery.........	4,758	4,677	9,435	1,311	5,114	8,022	7,838	15,860	15,456
14	Prince George.......	4,457	4,444	8,901	1,138	11,510	10,940	10,609	21,549	19,539
15	Queen Anne........	3,579	3,357	6,936	3,278	4,270	7,406	7,078	14,484	12,633
16	St. Mary's..........	3,100	3,123	6,223	1,633	5,842	6,899	6,799	13,698	13,224
17	Somerset	6,655	6,730	13,385	3,483	5,588	11,326	11,130	22,456	19,508
18	Talbot	3,577	3,507	7,084	2,593	4,134	7,000	6,811	13,811	12,090
19	Washington........	13,468	13,462	26,930	1,828	2,090	15,289	15,559	30,848	28,850
20	Worcester..........	6,238	6,163	12,401	3,014	3,444	9,521	9,338	18,859	18,377

* In Louisiana—*Parishes.*

NATIVITIES, DWELLINGS, &c.				EDUCATION AND RELIGION.									
Born out of State.				Colleges, academies, and private schools.		Public Schools.							
United States.	Foreign countries.	Dwellings.	Families.	Pupils.	Annual income.	Pupils.	Annual income.	Total educational income.	White scholars during the year.	Whites 5 and under 20 years old.	Whites over 20 unable to read and write.	Accommodation of churches—persons.	
754	16	346	346	......	....	140	$2,054	$2,054	230	592	178	200	18
410	443	638	640	63	....	168	9,577	9,577	257	1,148	152	2,465	19
2,414	5	622	632	......	....	560	4,446	4,446	377	1,325	90	2,900	20
2,446	9,216	3,825	3,961	324	....	2,049	33,574	33,574	2,733	5,592	937	9,540	21
78	126	630	630	43	....	242	10,333	10,333	216	1,428	749	300	22
232	250	938	938	156	$600	520	5,362	5,962	419	2,220	528	4,500	23
567	118	480	480	46	276	400	2,461	2,737	377	949	317	560	24
985	32	448	448	25	600	98	1,400	2,000	174	453	42	500	25
1,319	22	372	393	97	3,575	103	1,612	5,187	333	719	75	300	26
1,705	275	1,432	1,432	......	....	35	320	320	705	2,035	1,180	2,925	27
17,298	51,227	15,621	19,765	3,138	181,802	5,946	103,084	284,886	10,606	22,394	5,462	27,350	28
1,114	54	442	449	15	....	604	2,485	2,485	302	855	184	300	29
371	562	615	615	83	2,310	280	6,265	8,575	160	689	271	500	30
449	248	760	760	84	1,600	160	6,029	7,629	229	1,041	333	450	31
1,474	267	1,032	1,032	70	....	980	14,500	14,500	519	1,870	96	3,500	32
1,412	25	632	636	......	....	1,051	7,172	7,172	783	1,377	506	2,550	33
44	330	283	283	......	....	150	2,400	2,400	182	463	314	90	34
31	31	191	191	......	....	55	3,865	3,865	162	336	1	1,000	35
621	66	390	390	......	....	355	3,280	3,280	553	936	311	3,770	36
79	250	591	591	148	20,000	238	6,800	26,800	403	1,205	304	1,000	37
17	89	530	530	......	....	452	4,700	4,700	297	1,009	6	2,000	38
442	321	2,421	2,910	254	35,930	900	8,600	44,530	1,308	4,141	1,692	2,400	39
129	219	940	952	28	....	350	5,517	5,517	576	1,876	828	800	40
562	326	746	752	15	....	98	9,545	9,545	174	1,210	254	2,800	41
883	643	786	786	170	....	500	2,222	2,222	456	1,332	426	5,520	42
597	24	244	244	......	....	55	6,237	6,237	100	246	12	1,200	43
196	88	550	550	......	....	270	7,100	7,100	252	1,449	648	700	44
662	31	942	942	125	1,800	514	8,126	9,926	652	1,918	199	1,800	45
134	72	406	406	......	....	314	5,493	5,493	138	981	582	100	46
[illegible]	33	406	406	......	....	500	5,000	5,000	355	977	316	900	47

MAINE.

United States.	Foreign countries.	Dwellings.	Families.	Pupils.	Annual income.	Pupils.	Annual income.	Total educational income.	White scholars during the year.	Whites 5 and under 20 years old.	Whites over 20 unable to read and write.	Accommodation of churches—persons.	
376	4,075	2,042	2,049	129	969	2,021	8,294	9,263	2,223	4,947	775	5,600	1
4,848	5,020	12,762	14,683	1,384	21,684	22,426	42,678	64,362	23,296	26,656	1,228	50,783	2
1,959	123	3,487	3,690	125	360	6,789	9,798	10,158	7,624	7,577	64	12,455	3
1,063	1,078	5,550	5,850	100	1,150	12,258	17,066	18,216	11,209	13,494	165	14,565	4
4,715	2,167	10,162	11,226	1,000	12,055	20,648	33,287	45,342	19,611	22,161	620	47,266	5
2,735	3,222	12,175	13,220	508	4,427	25,757	37,088	41,515	22,329	26,257	756	41,652	6
4,154	935	6,713	7,148	928	4,953	13,051	18,937	23,890	13,696	14,468	313	18,417	7
4,849	4,498	10,374	10,850	646	10,611	21,107	41,109	51,720	19,923	23,540	770	28,727	8
1,014	321	2,590	2,635	303	900	4,061	5,426	6,326	5,541	5,741	34	5,938	9
1,956	735	5,917	6,209	522	3,635	12,086	18,062	21,697	13,393	13,657	218	10,997	10
2,148	704	7,631	8,272	214	1,300	19,922	24,995	26,295	17,263	18,284	184	20,242	11
1,282	7,699	5,835	6,404	466	2,160	12,590	22,698	24,858	12,208	15,005	574	17,525	12
4,196	1,248	10,564	11,097	605	983	20,099	35,998	36,981	17,625	20,995	446	47,000	13

MARYLAND.

United States.	Foreign countries.	Dwellings.	Families.	Pupils.	Annual income.	Pupils.	Annual income.	Total educational income.	White scholars during the year.	Whites 5 and under 20 years old.	Whites over 20 unable to read and write.	Accommodation of churches—persons.	
3,273	5,095	3,850	3,902	105	2,050	2,480	6,480	8,530	1,657	7,677	1,039	13,900	1
644	837	3,712	3,745	295	11,250	1,283	10,016	21,266	2,473	6,343	570	41,875	2
21,969	39,503	30,065	34,925	7,661	178,695	9,096	69,696	248,391	23,519	57,272	6,486	96,740	3
22	19	1,006	1,006	42	518	375	4,312	4,830	580	1,399	358	7,400	4
435	10	1,526	1,526	......	....	518	6,074	6,074	887	2,396	403	8,870	5
1,609	765	3,476	3,593	1,020	13,305	......	....	13,305	2,700	6,805	129	20,300	6
2,990	702	3,056	3,114	182	2,372	1,331	12,760	15,132	2,555	5,686	157	10,020	7
92	21	1,335	1,335	50	200	784	4,173	4,373	825	2,153	399	5,850	8
221	19	2,705	2,709	180	2,070	758	10,566	12,636	1,631	4,128	1,665	13,075	9
2,174	1,370	6,397	6,614	1,076	90,811	5,182	16,090	106,901	6,583	12,569	1,504	36,600	10
1,243	991	2,977	2,985	135	650	657	4,150	4,800	2,213	5,128	207	9,550	11
667	85	1,584	1,584	200	4,600	700	5,553	10,153	1,042	2,123	204	9,300	12
715	273	1,923	1,960	99	5,190	811	9,542	14,732	1,266	3,393	1,152	8,450	13
427	265	1,875	1,875	149	1,000	815	10,450	11,450	1,343	3,373	404	8,750	14
261	47	1,864	1,864	......	....	729	8,423	8,423	1,045	2,682	731	4,900	15
127	42	1,512	1,646	170	2,200	494	2,372	4,572	1,782	2,509	1,855	5,850	16
434	11	3,158	3,158	65	800	1,026	4,799	5,599	904	4,994	673	24,015	17
245	73	1,751	1,776	78	7,200	985	11,429	18,629	1,114	2,496	309	11,720	18
3,207	1,074	5,052	5,182	207	20,264	3,522	16,790	37,054	4,258	10,092	892	28,200	19
957	7	2,884	2,885	200	2,880	1,565	5,161	8,041	2,070	4,499	1,678	14,100	20

	COUNTIES.	LAND OCCUPIED OR IMPROVED.				LIVE STOCK UPON FARMS.			
		Farms.	Acres improved.	Acres unimproved.	Value with improvements and implements.	Horses, asses, and mules.	Neat cattle.	Sheep.	Swine.
18	Franklin	283	14,473	41,817	$ 375,992	1,114	6,901	1,059	21,460
19	Iberville	219	46,050	84,755	5,128,400	3,417	6,563	4,221	2,468
20	Jackson	290	18,621	47,381	336,361	1,028	4,824	648	16,856
21	Jefferson	81	22,430	35,003	1,821,928	2,369	2,938	845	309
22	Lafayette	441	24,448	57,676	413,430	11,501	36,199	7,028	5,895
23	Lafourche	235	40,268	40,031	2,479,374	2,024	1,709	114	1,841
24	Livingston	219	9,163	64,699	246,808	834	8,934	1,292	21,171
25	Madison	218	56,619	126,032	2,924,599	2,743	7,989	1,708	14,368
26	Morehouse	260	15,895	26,108	368,705	1,015	6,102	1,105	14,541
27	Natchitoches	842	70,784	144,939	1,689,635	4,456	15,928	4,094	33,103
28	Orleans	51	4,844	3,435	579,200	3,142	1,630	60	193
29	Ouachita	242	20,373	38,539	695,285	1,250	5,672	1,376	14,274
30	Plaquemines	205	39,774	96,259	5,669,150	2,226	6,252	1,261	834
31	Point Coupee	248	43,010	124,962	2,547,777	2,827	5,576	3,720	3,395
32	Rapides	187	69,653	124,767	3,202,235	4,068	13,182	6,548	18,739
33	Sabine	522	18,254	62,429	262,923	1,287	9,475	1,043	30,372
34	St. Bernard	34	11,435	12,273	1,211,043	730	1,140	36	....
35	St. Charles	70	20,596	66,746	2,362,000	1,858	2,546	841	529
36	St. Helena	273	21,913	130,180	310,769	1,287	7,586	3,598	17,854
37	St. James	145	41,905	49,164	3,096,155	3,053	3,452	911	785
38	St. John Baptist	162	22,285	33,412	2,367,300	1,980	2,710	797	913
39	St. Landry	775	87,584	193,622	2,184,748	12,755	96,687	12,457	27,935
40	St. Martin's	420	35,971	150,119	1,635,127	4,857	20,167	6,936	5,625
41	St. Mary's	198	43,051	166,780	4,710,920	4,882	11,937	1,448	3,125
42	St. Tammany	90	5,824	73,076	157,889	593	9,689	1,370	5,195
43	Tensas	165	59,391	158,539	2,683,517	3,430	6,742	2,856	12,406
44	Terre Bonne	224	18,706	101,937	2,397,939	1,671	2,623	1,078	2,116
45	Union	717	45,135	73,544	522,312	2,152	8,730	535	32,059
46	Vermillion	198	5,913	56,195	144,978	3,554	26,087	1,672	3,439
47	Washington	260	13,071	88,523	127,975	827	9,941	1,590	12,404

STATISTICS OF

	County	Farms.	Acres improved.	Acres unimproved.	Value with improvements and implements.	Horses, asses, and mules.	Neat cattle.	Sheep.	Swine.
1	Aroostook	1,228	55,097	140,523	861,343	1,275	8,593	11,411	2,086
2	Cumberland	5,352	250,607	202,676	8,562,568	4,993	36,680	33,693	6,845
3	Franklin	2,521	154,568	143,944	2,445,332	2,751	23,400	48,018	3,174
4	Hancock	2,271	74,046	140,232	1,944,177	986	13,946	25,420	1,846
5	Kennebeck	5,256	248,637	201,511	7,409,823	5,756	39,622	48,448	6,146
6	Lincoln	4,975	188,466	224,712	6,558,937	3,782	34,637	41,525	5,113
7	Oxford	4,288	216,081	290,458	4,687,522	4,441	41,316	49,755	6,764
8	Penobscot	3,983	158,611	250,575	4,201,150	3,438	22,649	27,228	4,581
9	Piscataquis	1,779	75,191	126,872	1,401,290	1,536	11,303	17,856	2,254
10	Somerset	3,813	163,438	235,754	3,972,349	4,138	33,162	60,024	3,646
11	Waldo	4,415	178,264	193,688	4,692,257	3,453	29,080	44,522	3,802
12	Washington	1,875	63,590	141,367	1,821,914	1,041	10,345	13,642	1,444
13	York	5,004	213,000	223,485	8,587,643	4,186	38,606	30,035	6,897

STATISTICS OF

	County	Farms.	Acres improved.	Acres unimproved.	Value with improvements and implements.	Horses, asses, and mules.	Neat cattle.	Sheep.	Swine.
1	Alleghany	892	2,577	144,695	2,580,226	2,911	10,553	12,439	7,877
2	Anne Arundel	1,295	222,228	126,955	6,936,358	6,479	14,037	14,075	29,989
3	Baltimore	1,655	173,106	119,551	10,558,231	6,380	12,976	9,922	21,677
4	Calvert	434	65,980	45,611	1,568,988	1,947	5,365	5,297	9,350
5	Caroline	730	117,300	54,801	1,138,227	2,061	5,874	3,570	9,218
6	Carroll	1,387	153,519	65,252	5,540,580	5,061	9,585	6,557	19,227
7	Cecil	1,208	115,866	63,821	5,331,740	3,334	10,645	4,705	9,767
8	Charles	709	126,232	115,120	2,530,064	3,442	11,782	10,116	16,815
9	Dorchester	1,049	112,521	113,650	2,767,439	2,452	12,946	7,498	16,442
10	Frederick	1,983	252,129	94,379	10,905,735	9,008	18,488	12,483	38,606
11	Harford	1,278	123,094	86,509	4,333,161	3,886	10,631	8,424	14,342
12	Kent	667	125,310	41,103	3,140,011	3,191	7,355	6,826	11,756
13	Montgomery	1,051	162,815	111,122	3,218,540	4,211	8,766	9,780	16,332
14	Prince George	885	191,553	92,178	5,691,407	4,812	11,101	11.650	20,193
15	Queen Anne	936	156,926	48,603	2,897,258	4,048	9,187	8,168	11,619
16	St. Mary's	813	100,216	107,652	2,352,461	2,901	9,973	7,399	14,690
17	Somerset	1,485	127,626	146,434	3,205,693	2,705	14,715	10,477	25,204
18	Talbot	793	114,109	55,312	3,857,946	3,517	9,563	7,869	15,551
19	Washington	1,292	159,851	60,878	8,601,942	6,170	13,071	9,736	24,345
20	Worcester	1,318	124,947	142,819	2,485,981	2,812	12,973	10,911	19,911

AGRICULTURAL PRODUCTS.

Wheat, bushels.	Rye & oats, bushels.	Indian corn, bushels.	Irish and sweet potatoes, bushels.	Peas and beans, bushels.	Barley, bushels.	Buckwheat, bushels.	Butter and cheese, pounds.	Hay, tons.	Hops, pounds.	Clover & other grass seeds, bushels.	Flaxseed, bushels.	
......	647	103,795	18,747	4,487	......	......	10,436	13	......	3	......	18
......	......	371,065	13,890	......	......	......	4,800	......	......	......	......	19
61	932	136,404	30,846	14,362	......	......	15,344	......	......	......	......	20
......	......	197,849	34,064	......	......	......	......	3,662	......	......	......	21
......	......	288,358	29,829	75	......	......	200	......	......	......	......	22
......	......	227,015	5,789	230	......	......	......	......	......	......	......	23
......	1,130	47,506	26,114	545	......	......	7,026	4	......	......	......	24
......	680	214,365	28,486	4,474	......	......	42,380	780	......	......	......	25
104	1,427	119,235	27,989	2,137	......	......	27,185	6	6	......	......	16
......	3,225	394,011	40,793	11,565	......	......	30,459	......	......	......	......	27
......	......	32,180	200	300	......	......	385	......	......	......	......	28
......	695	128,000	20,324	1,538	......	......	19,914	12	20	......	......	29
......	......	149,090	19,456	3,920	......	......	19,205	2,242	......	40	......	30
......	2,000	199,790	43,743	......	......	......	......	......	......	......	......	31
......	5,730	357,480	37,035	3,660	......	......	35,175	50	......	......	......	32
......	3,460	89,514	46,128	11,670	......	......	22,584	......	......	......	......	33
......	......	12,756	16,032	359	......	......	......	1,783	......	......	......	34
......	680	178,980	1,787	......	......	......	......	1,302	......	......	......	35
......	6,085	109,751	45,251	2,745	......	......	1,570	......	......	......	......	36
......	......	334,480	2,060	......	......	......	......	5,044	......	......	......	37
......	......	188,390	1,781	......	......	......	......	1,886	......	......	......	38
......	......	372,180	69,361	......	......	......	......	1,691	......	......	......	39
......	......	517,401	6,943	699	......	......	920	......	......	......	......	40
......	......	305,290	50,545	......	......	......	......	......	......	......	......	41
......	701	17,849	22,652	450	......	......	2,570	178	......	......	......	42
......	250	338,725	36,606	3,191	......	......	28,635	147	......	......	......	43
......	......	187,420	17,914	200	......	......	......	......	......	......	......	44
......	......	292,095	105,820	......	......	......	39,926	......	......	......	......	45
......	......	46,061	4,641	......	......	......	......	......	......	......	......	46
......	4,925	69,790	23,610	3,272	......	......	700	3	......	......	......	47

MAINE.

Wheat, bushels.	Rye & oats, bushels.	Indian corn, bushels.	Irish and sweet potatoes, bushels.	Peas and beans, bushels.	Barley, bushels.	Buckwheat, bushels.	Butter and cheese, pounds.	Hay, tons.	Hops, pounds.	Clover & other grass seeds, bushels.	Flaxseed, bushels.	
10,675	209,016	13,746	191,541	10,932	13,645	86,529	207,955	17,314	62	1,741	62	1
8,880	144,507	233,870	266,586	10,283	2,501	306	1,384,552	94,535	41	121	26	2
47,860	124,793	84,879	210,942	11,281	5,676	194	673,954	49,717	2,805	6,ó43	33	3
3,934	49,378	24,749	75,163	7,448	15,824	55	488,965	31,523	......	......	......	4
31,462	306,049	296,108	380,014	27,415	18,214	2,429	1,563,977	97,946	3,164	502	89	5
7,815	92,217	154,452	239,492	18,853	21,497	915	1,054,036	86,805	38	36	1	6
40,225	175,631	227,439	488,168	15,573	1,765	8,367	1,282,616	69,309	31,417	1,620	167	7
28,819	316,788	119,584	221,248	24,680	14,457	974	900,683	51,758	800	4,327	26	8
14,646	172,578	48,925	147,034	11,892	8,599	557	419,870	21,746	762	1,361	13	9
56,595	335,775	183,780	327,556	24,046	13,000	1,236	972,779	66,183	......	1,789	158	10
38,191	250,029	130,899	232,340	22,471	20,205	540	1,048,500	69,552	960	118	......	11
1,461	36,777	4,579	144,183	4,151	12,070	2,153	404,818	20,942	49	......	......	12
5,696	70,415	227,046	511,773	16,516	4,278	268	1,275,560	78,559	22	53	5	13

MARYLAND.

Wheat, bushels.	Rye & oats, bushels.	Indian corn, bushels.	Irish and sweet potatoes, bushels.	Peas and beans, bushels.	Barley, bushels.	Buckwheat, bushels.	Butter and cheese, pounds.	Hay, tons.	Hops, pounds.	Clover & other grass seeds, bushels.	Flaxseed, bushels.	
73,525	193,130	101,773	21,920	67	100	19,887	231,918	10,896	......	7	5	1
360,923	158,702	925,448	52,128	1,202	......	4,498	170,677	5,580	376	826	32	2
234,187	295,524	755,224	141,119	825	205	12,299	355,710	21,810	......	773	......	3
67,489	26,136	351,890	4,398	130	......	......	26,787	112	......	......	......	4
42,879	31,130	355,520	17,864	......	......	......	41,864	50	......	......	......	5
265,007	250,557	343,008	48,436	176	......	5,765	445,909	20,771	6	2,721	394	6
168,112	208,612	410,060	46,239	83	6	15,673	280,303	9,288	39	2,977	11	7
149,533	29,991	458,348	15,383	868	50	13	43,215	235	3	5	......	8
137,470	10,796	597,252	38,261	766	......	46	84,816	40	10	38	88	9
731,684	230,800	782,603	53,933	573	40	1,169	723,564	23,838	609	3,476	125	10
186,421	222,022	516,537	56,515	118	76	34,180	236,825	12,837	20	2,717	15	11
194,860	136,406	556,731	46,473	620	......	695	46,122	856	25	332	......	12
164,108	173,397	396,947	49,520	589	56	6,083	245,297	8,588	170	1,085	701	13
231,687	85,777	693,020	51,503	1,004	43	1,646	101,100	5,557	25	70	......	14
173,003	69,499	697,159	24,741	540	77	646	97,183	652	134	21	61	15
156,369	34,076	378,461	26,837	450	......	79	71,950	441	255	......	76	16
58,248	72,116	718,073	145,433	2,380	......	......	99,473	7,082	......	......	38	17
272,963	15,829	621,980	48,917	835	10	717	97,585	663	169	63	1	18
809,093	135,809	368,056	22,508	......	82	239	341,798	14,860	29	2,667	3	19
17,119	87,856	721,768	61,804	1,590	......	36	68,039	13,800	......	......	896	20

	COUNTIES.	AGRICULTURAL PRODUCTS.									
		Flax, pounds.	Hemp, dew and water-rotted, tons.	Maple sugar, pounds.	Cane sugar, hhds. of 1,000 pounds.	Molasses, gallons.	Rice, pounds.	Tobacco, pounds.	Ginned cotton, bales of 400 pounds.	Wool, pounds.	Silk cocoons, pounds.
18	Franklin						76		3,044	1,759	
19	Iberville				23,208	1,310,750			64	250	29
20	Jackson						5,070		1,394	682	
21	Jefferson				8,897	430,580	122,000				
22	Lafayette				2,629	95,164	2,168	262	2,560		
23	Lafourche			5	10,055	345,126	231,980				
24	Livingston				120	10,800	83,480	524	265	1,411	
25	Madison						8,150		12,771	5,434	
26	Morehouse						17,255		3,303	2,302	
27	Natchitoches			250	4	1,650	14,375	4,467	15,574	5,382	
28	Orleans				1,495	52,505	40,000				
29	Ouachita						420	7,200	3,486	2,986	
30	Plaquemines				16,835	589,130	1,536,740	500	60		
31	Point Coupee				8,560	321,546	16,840		1,622	130	
32	Rapides				4,613	438,170	4,500		4,222	14,190	
33	Sabine				1	531	21,130	1,170	1,107	1,594	
34	St. Bernard				4,367	173,000					
35	St. Charles				10,206	531,300	619,000				
36	St. Helena						54,868		1,284	6,408	
37	St. James				21,670	926,438	68,500	9,370			
38	St. John Baptist				11,935	638,230	314,200				
39	St. Landry				5,951	317,970	6,144	1,200	3,920		
40	St. Martin's				4,188	237,160	3,700		4,073		
41	St. Mary's				24,765	897,660	140		84		
42	St. Tammany				20	600	97,793		41	1,458	
43	Tensas						3,000	50	21,665	6,210	
44	Terre Bonne				9,171	435 290	466,900				
45	Union								5,213	1,125	
46	Vermillion				871	31,720	1,664		45	2,330	
47	Washington					120	159,750		693	2,134	

STATISTICS OF

	Counties	Flax	Hemp	Maple sugar	Cane sugar	Molasses	Rice	Tobacco	Ginned cotton	Wool	Silk cocoons
1	Aroostook	70		25,737		43				30,317	
2	Cumberland	362		820		85				97,399	1
3	Franklin	1,178		17,481		1,636				163,609	15
4	Hancock			61						64,968	
5	Kennebeck	9,600		2,573		440				149,617	102
6	Lincoln	338		413						115,410	
7	Oxford	790		23,238		16				156,353	124
8	Penobscot	342		3,182		91				105,977	5
9	Piscataquis	657		4,883		396				54,334	
10	Somerset	2,888		8,750		399				180,307	5
11	Waldo	330		2,963		61				134,920	
12	Washington	55		340						35,252	
13	York	471		3,101						75,571	

STATISTICS OF

	Counties	Flax	Hemp	Maple sugar	Cane sugar	Molasses	Rice	Tobacco	Ginned cotton	Wool	Silk cocoons
1	Alleghany	1,517		47,740		1,430				25,244	
2	Anne Arundel	635						4,523,340		22,685	
3	Baltimore							20		19,745	
4	Calvert							3,109,258		14,773	
5	Caroline	45								9,297	
6	Carroll	3,696	30					165,332		14,711	1
7	Cecil	155	3							17,373	2
8	Charles							2,862,300		20,928	
9	Dorchester	2,110						125		20,113	
10	Frederick	2,673						175,394		32,232	2
11	Harford	262								21,072	
12	Kent	6	5							21,312	
13	Montgomery	5,510						426,995		28,961	21
14	Prince George							8,380,851		43,409	
15	Queen Anne	610								28,730	11
16	St. Mary's	1,849						1,763,882		19,774	
17	Somerset	790	25							28,928	
18	Talbot	140								27,416	
19	Washington									35,601	
20	Worcester	15,688								25,134	2

AGRICULTURAL PRODUCTS.					MANUFACTURES.				REMARKS.	
					Establishments.					
Beeswax and honey, pounds.	Value of animals slaughtered.	Value of produce of market gardens.	Value of orchard produce.	Wine, gallons.	Capital.	Hands employed.	Annual product.	Produced in families.		
889	$18,835	......	$25	......	......	......	......	$366	Formed '43 fr. Catahoula,	18
......	......	......	......	......	$9,700	40	$35,450	......	Ouachita and Madison.	19
......	24,460	......	......	......	4,780	14	5,113	13,148	Formed '45 from Ouachita,	20
......	337,000	$81,200	3,100	......	796,900	707	1,014,620	......	Union and Claiborne.	21
160	53,277	......	......	......	......	......	......	12,586	Div. '44 to form Vermillion.	22
......	......	......	......	......	22,500	19	27,625	......	......	23
218	16,764	......	......	......	79,495	121	41,762	954	......	24
3,803	36,665	2,051	40	......	116,350	124	78,069	554	Div. '43 to form Franklin.	25
545	28,265	......	......	......	8,800	17	16,300	4,020	Formed '44 from Ouachita.	26
7,799	51,218	950	640	......	17,200	59	21,800	6,089	Divided since 1840 to form	27
......	......	37,050	1,000	......	2,969,660	3,134	4,470,454	......	De Soto and Sabine.	28
3,399	19,552	......	......	......	11,750	8	10,872	5,505	Divided since 1840 to form	29
570	42,605	1,030	14,120	......	......	......	......	50	Franklin, Jackson and	30
1,170	39,635	350	......	......	......	......	......	1,950	Morehouse.	31
......	41,730	1,800	......	......	42,000	51	41,500	6,795	......	32
10,160	29,183	......	754	......	5,800	11	9,500	4,380	Formed 1843 from Natchi-	33
......	......	5,550	......	......	......	......	......	......	toches.	34
......	......	......	......	......	5,000	21	15,875	......	......	35
......	19,140	......	......	......	17,575	27	95,819	5,335	......	36
......	8,700	......	......	......	57,900	57	37,400	......	......	37
......	......	......	......	......	31,200	96	77,450	......	......	38
......	90,725	500	......	......	54,500	71	80,252	11,280	......	39
......	700	......	......	......	......	......	......	......	......	40
......	17,160	......	......	......	......	......	......	......	......	41
......	6,654	......	......	......	429,944	637	210,035	229	......	42
20	30,203	......	......	......	14,100	26	12,200	933	Formed in 1843 from Con-	43
......	5,748	......	......	......	7,000	22	10,200	......	cordia.	44
25	63,024	......	......	......	1,000	2	2,000	5,794	Div. '45 to form Jackson.	45
......	8,800	......	......	......	......	......	......	3,521	Formed '44 from Lafayette.	46
400	1,740	......	......	......	......	......	......	......	......	47

MAINE.

Beeswax and honey, pounds.	Value of animals slaughtered.	Value of produce of market gardens.	Value of orchard produce.	Wine, gallons.	Capital.	Hands employed.	Annual product.	Produced in families.	Remarks.	
956	55,840	7,736	981	......	282,650	849	430,895	21,734	......	1
8,373	189,284	5,954	17,346	......	1,896,365	5,064	4,243,978	52,222	......	2
22,786	88,155	392	23,450	10	133,898	282	281,586	51,205	......	3
3,042	50,515	7,227	3,742	......	634,912	1,705	1,185,241	18,780	......	4
43,968	194,847	18,572	71,224	37	1,637,158	3,075	2,967,729	37,907	......	5
10,204	181,862	16,938	37,139	11	1,760,848	3,295	3,057,133	50,843	......	6
25,151	153,725	2,955	35,345	......	343,782	583	601,292	31,037	......	7
13,399	130,236	7,570	26,379	5	1,385,625	3,535	4,075,310	36,991	......	8
8,421	63,605	3,071	15,174	......	357,940	227	205,248	16,335	......	9
28,945	153,319	3,543	31,034	125	304,710	643	784,688	64,276	......	10
22,978	149,107	19,860	39,463	75	697,718	1,947	1,432,635	75,042	......	11
157	71,705	18,584	1,639	306	1,085,611	2,167	1,621,105	31,287	......	12
1,238	164,573	9,985	39,949	155	4,179,235	4,706	3,777,295	25,940	......	13

MARYLAND.

Beeswax and honey, pounds.	Value of animals slaughtered.	Value of produce of market gardens.	Value of orchard produce.	Wine, gallons.	Capital.	Hands employed.	Annual product.	Produced in families.	Remarks.	
6,451	57,587	475	6,714	65	750,100	403	491,391	9,397	......	1
5,379	62,266	57,774	32,437	465	402,570	968	937,260	2,885	......	2
2,555	108,808	115,690	8,045	56	9,929,332	23,863	24,540,014	10	......	3
......	46,864	......	922	......	......	......	......	5,941	......	4
......	40,367	......	580	......	......	......	......	593	......	5
1,900	186,246	......	11,166	99	246,800	357	352,369	3,303	......	6
1,113	77,868	125	5,837	......	529,990	893	776,857	634	......	7
1,243	71,481	1,202	591	......	......	......	......	13,408	......	8
81	84,878	513	6,341	......	7,250	46	24,500	3,287	......	9
4,315	239,594	4,202	17,062	198	815,581	880	1,600,967	2,384	......	10
4,286	100,560	336	9,507	56	428,655	324	545,676	5,051	......	11
1,495	60,118	1,240	20,715	......	45,700	82	111,750	400	......	12
4,334	99,393	4,470	8,513	75	137,810	242	331,167	9,802	......	13
250	103,351	13,281	8,202	10	428,370	708	414,859	3,331	......	14
4,765	75,909	197	3,428	20	42,060	128	122,226	1,820	......	15
3,994	86,107	50	6,262	39	38,500	31	68,312	14,095	......	16
16,533	112,490	634	1,713	......	109,600	200	155,350	11,115	......	17
6,448	97,956	555	4,922	343	54,600	180	119,050	2,154	......	18
244	141,736	100	8,217	5	726,375	730	1,859,993	......	......	19
9,416	101,221	25	2,877	......	69,850	89	65,961	22,218	......	20

	COUNTIES.	POPULATION.								
		Whites.			Colored.		All classes.		Total population.	
		Male.	Female.	Total.	Free.	Slave.	Male.	Female.	1850.	1840.
1	Barnstable..........	17,803	17,350	35,153	123	....	17,868	17,408	35,276	32,548
2	Berkshire..........	23,958	24,300	48,258	1,333	....	24,629	24,962	49,591	41,745
3	Bristol..............	36,641	38,018	74,659	1,533	....	37,342	38,850	76,192	60,164
4	Dukes..............	2,306	2,181	4,487	53	....	2,328	2,212	4,540	3,958
5	Essex	63,862	66,820	130,682	618	....	64,148	67,152	131,300	94,987
6	Franklin	15,407	15,372	30,779	91	....	15,455	15,415	30,870	28,812
7	Hampden......	24,943	25,837	50,780	503	....	25,171	26,112	51,283	37,366
8	Hampshire..........	17,392	18,011	35,403	329	....	17,550	18,182	35,732	30,897
9	Middlesex	76,918	83,758	160,676	707	....	77,286	84,097	161,383	106,611
10	Nantucket....	4,119	3,939	8,058	394	....	4,391	4,061	8,452	9,012
11	Norfolk.............	38,562	40,081	78,643	249	....	38,679	40,213	78,892	53,140
12	Plymouth...........	27,720	27,521	55,241	456	....	27,948	27,749	55,697	47,373
13	Suffolk	68,622	73,857	142,479	2,038	....	69,557	74,960	144,517	95,773
14	Worcester...	65,840	64,312	130,152	637	....	66,165	64,624	130,789	95,313

STATISTICS OF

1	Allegan..............	2,734	2,386	5,120	5	....	2,735	2,390	5,125	1,783
2	Barry...............	2,742	2,291	5,033	39	....	2,777	2,295	5,072	1,078
3	Berrien............	5,872	5,306	11,178	239	....	5,991	5,426	11,417	5,011
4	Branch.............	6,484	5,972	12,456	16	....	6,492	5,980	12,472	5,715
5	Calhoun............	9,833	9,122	18,955	207	....	9,945	9,217	19,162	10,599
6	Cass...............	5,494	5,024	10,518	389	....	5,712	5,195	10,907	5,710
7	Chippewa..........	509	381	890	8	....	514	384	898	534
8	Clinton............	2,701	2,399	5,100	2	....	2,703	2,399	5,102	1,614
9	Eaton..............	3,671	3,384	7,055	3	....	3,673	3,385	7,058	2,379
10	Genesee	6,331	5,672	12,003	28	....	6,342	5,689	12,031	4,268
11	Hillsdale...........	8,545	7,608	16,153	6	....	8,548	7,611	16,159	7,240
12	Houghton..........	515	192	707	1	....	516	192	708	....
13	Huron.............	132	78	210	....	....	132	78	210	....
14	Ingham............	4,539	4,067	8,606	25	....	4,551	4,080	8,631	2,498
15	Ionia..............	4,007	3,582	7,589	8	....	4,012	3,585	7,597	1,923
16	Jackson	10,164	9,182	19,346	85	....	10,212	9,219	19,431	13,130
17	Kalamazoo.........	6,890	6,190	13,080	99	....	6,942	6,237	13,179	7,380
18	Kent	6,351	5,631	11,982	34	....	6,371	5,645	12,016	2,587
19	Lapeer	3,688	3,319	7,007	22	....	3,697	3,332	7,029	4,265
20	Lenawee...........	13,585	12,695	26,280	92	....	13,636	12,736	26,372	17,889
21	Livingston.........	7,122	6,359	13,481	4	....	7,126	6,359	13,485	7,430
22	Macomb............	8,080	7,421	15,501	29	....	8,098	7,432	15,530	9,716
23	Marquette..........	105	31	136	....	....	105	31	136	....
24	Mason..............	74	19	93	....	....	74	19	93	....
25	Michillimackinac, and 21 unorganized counties..........	2,265	1,296	3,561	37	....	2,287	1,311	3,598	923
26	Midland	36	28	64	1	....	37	28	65	....
27	Monroe.............	7,571	7,071	14,642	56	....	7,599	7,099	14,698	9,922
28	Montcalm..........	479	412	891	....	....	479	412	891	....
29	Newago.............	325	184	509	1	....	325	185	510	....
30	Oakland............	16,285	14,921	31,206	64	....	16,327	14,943	31,270	23,646
31	Oceana.............	195	86	281	19	....	207	93	300	496
32	Ontonogon..........	302	81	383	6	....	306	83	389	....
33	Ottowa.............	3,196	2,352	5,548	39	....	3,225	2,362	5,587	208
34	Saginaw............	1,466	1,143	2,609	....	....	1,466	1,143	2,609	892
35	St. Clair...........	5,539	4,857	10,396	24	....	5,550	4,870	10,420	4,606
36	St. Joseph..........	6,709	5,990	12,699	26	....	6,725	6,000	12,725	7,068
37	Sanilac............	1,175	937	2,112	....	....	1,175	937	2,112	....
38	Schoolcraft.........	11	5	16	....	....	11	5	16	....
39	Shiawassee.........	2,805	2,425	5,230	....	....	2,805	2,425	5,230	2,103
40	Tuscola	168	123	291	....	....	168	123	291	....
41	Van Buren..........	3,061	2,725	5,786	14	....	3,069	2,731	5,800	1,910
42	Washtenaw.........	14,781	13,555	28,336	231	....	14,908	13,659	28,567	23,571
43	Wayne	21,928	20,104	42,032	724	....	22,323	20,433	42,756	24,173

NATIVITIES, DWELLINGS, &c.				EDUCATION AND RELIGION.									
Born out of State.				Colleges, academies, and private schools.		Public Schools.							
United States.	Foreign countries.	Dwellings.	Families.	Pupils.	Annual income.	Pupils.	Annual income.	Total educational income.	White scholars during the year.	Whites 5 and under 20 years old.	Whites over 20 unable to read & write.	Accommodation of churches—persons.	
496	953	6,532	7,255	1,082	$10,435	7,682	$24,876	$35,311	10,049	12,014	59	26,802	1
10,583	5,819	8,638	9,460	881	26,028	7,523	23,795	49,823	10,513	15,699	949	40,705	2
9,278	10,401	12,134	15,240	1,118	7,750	13,378	73,540	81,290	16,818	23,893	2,718	55,765	3
302	89	771	908	......	....	897	2,636	2,636	1,104	1,361	7	3,820	4
18,440	16,684	18,878	26,945	2,634	54,658	25,158	122,923	177,581	29,582	40,633	2,320	92,489	5
3,088	1,397	5,832	6,230	269	3,310	7,360	21,963	25,273	8,734	9,909	237	24,850	6
10,406	8,034	9,083	9,750	560	7,783	8,666	39,986	47,769	11,916	15,723	1,311	36,065	7
3,859	3,286	5,905	6,694	791	27,721	7,677	26,660	54,381	9,205	11,533	391	30,935	8
32,252	31,122	23,450	30,241	1,978	97,246	26,728	183,390	280,636	34,525	48,906	5,318	105,891	9
766	465	1,285	1,670	356	3,836	1,232	9,278	13,114	1,792	2,446	74	5,021	10
8,346	15,650	12,545	15,690	1,350	23,070	14,086	87,149	110,219	16,922	23,460	3,101	51,125	11
2,935	3,243	9,506	11,557	468	10,692	10,781	50,170	60,862	13,722	17,342	439	43,075	12
23,162	49,632	16,567	25,416	1,800	133,000	17,230	248,356	381,356	24,304	40,945	7,443	78,025	13
18 193	17,249	21,709	25,619	1,192	12,549	28,077	92,073	104,622	31,595	40,056	3,172	98,260	14

MICHIGAN

2,573	947	997	1,047	......	....	1,196	4,431	4,431	1,489	1,846	133	1,180	1
3,345	248	1,037	1,056	......	....	1,189	3,816	3,816	1,226	1,881	98	....	2
6,937	952	2,126	2,156	30	2,500	4,032	5,972	8,472	3,038	4,333	49	4,850	3
8,201	525	2,300	2,367	......	....	4,123	7,367	7,367	3,216	4,842	129	1,400	4
12,059	1,187	3,433	3,510	345	8,550	5,864	13,586	22,136	5,524	7,115	102	5,700	5
6,836	324	1,914	1,932	......	....	3,396	2,900	2,900	2,854	4,149	217	2,850	6
206	343	187	187	......	....	......	....	....	127	281	177	....	7
2,833	363	946	950	......	....	1,017	2,373	2,373	1,461	2,004	93	400	8
4,464	289	1,328	1,355	......	....	2,297	2,716	2,716	2,258	2,790	158	750	9
6,989	997	2,257	2,271	......	....	3,876	5,087	5,087	3,710	4,671	104	1,500	10
10,188	1,298	2,965	3,030	......	....	5,628	4,828	4,828	5,093	6,119	298	600	11
93	502	116	116	......	....	......	....	....	36	124	126	....	12
86	72	52	52	......	....	......	....	....	5	60	8	....	13
4,911	508	1,583	1,592	25	....	2,936	2,602	2,602	2,782	3,389	160	600	14
4,347	750	1,367	1,386	......	....	2,610	3,552	3,552	2,331	2,930	106	1,100	15
11,795	1,102	3,540	3,578	95	1,600	4,276	10,562	12,162	6,144	7,524	161	5,140	16
8,021	1,025	2,387	2,402	235	3,173	4,184	5,343	8,516	1,322	5,065	10	3,300	17
6,135	2,303	2,251	2,251	60	....	3,513	6,370	6,370	2,920	4,389	88	2,575	18
3,963	568	1,286	1,295	90	....	2,315	2,205	2,205	2,163	2,746	217	2,565	19
15,173	1,879	4,892	4,909	......	....	8,059	6,675	6,675	8,885	10,184	357	12,540	20
7,262	1,389	2,368	2,372	......	....	4,465	2,186	2,186	4,222	5,319	229	3,550	21
6,440	2,058	2,666	2,717	......	....	4,427	5,334	5,334	3,740	6,151	387	5,650	22
70	37	18	18	......	....	......	....	....	2	27	16	....	23
57	31	12	12	......	....	......	....	....	4	14	......	....	24
1,187	1,199	584	602	180	1,300	378	7,854	9,154	327	1,070	529	2,990	25
38	....	10	10	......	....	......	....	....	20	24	9	....	26
4,839	2,438	2,544	2,562	264	5,794	3,317	6,882	12,676	3,835	6,016	1,182	4,000	27
542	54	164	166	......	....	......	....	....	229	334	6	....	28
237	116	92	92	......	....	......	....	....	76	155	3	....	29
16,063	2,977	5,699	5,768	50	....	10,451	6,701	6,701	9,025	12,567	169	8,610	30
131	115	58	58	......	....	......	....	....	7	79	5	....	31
104	248	46	46	......	....	......	....	....	8	45	49	....	32
1,858	2,637	1,129	1,129	......	....	515	2,686	2,686	667	1,799	74	400	33
1,332	407	473	488	......	....	......	....	....	431	869	45	550	34
3,188	3,258	1,816	1,816	95	450	3,062	9,495	9,945	2,425	3,812	98	2,850	35
7,700	725	2,301	2,315	......	....	4,338	6,041	6,041	3,610	4,907	131	4,550	36
600	1,009	372	372	......	....	414	710	710	289	801	28	300	37
14	2	5	5	......	....	......	....	....	4	4	......	....	38
3,047	302	972	972	......	....	1,562	3,100	3,100	1,703	2,050	14	350	39
177	28	65	65	......	....	63	....	....	63	105	......	....	40
3,814	261	1,053	1,075	......	....	1,567	2,007	2,007	1,300	2,150	4	700	41
12,850	4,723	5,142	5,142	378	14,500	8,302	9,208	23,708	7,765	11,100	225	16,405	42
12,524	14,507	7,063	7,367	80	1,080	7,083	15,217	16,297	9,418	15,376	1,918	22,162	43

	COUNTIES.	LAND OCCUPIED OR IMPROVED.				LIVE STOCK UPON FARMS.			
		Farms.	Acres improved.	Acres unimproved.	Value with improvements and implements.	Horses, asses, and mules.	Neat cattle.	Sheep.	Swine.
1	Barnstable..........	789	27,786	40,556	$1,278,828	934	3,836	1,566	1,283
2	Berkshire	2,897	272,489	174,956	9,577,926	5,310	32,608	79,333	7,587
3	Bristol	2,547	105,522	98,140	7,101,582	2,546	13,090	5,717	6,451
4	Dukes...............	265	21,92	11,794	686,620	233	1,739	9,643	750
5	Essex	2,708	145,921	54,204	9,582,992	2,768	17,823	2,103	6,761
6	Franklin............	2,537	197,232	93,753	6,333,281	3,372	23,464	23,829	4,731
7	Hampden............	2,615	198,153	96,843	7,420,723	3,709	21,755	14,973	6,403
8	Hampshire..........	2,955	211,219	86,983	7,554,456	3,986	22,748	32,835	6,725
9	Middlesex	4,293	220,203	128,111	19,417,796	5,237	30,380	1,844	10,765
10	Nantucket..........	58	3,792	4,265	149,605	89	597	977	153
11	Norfolk.............	2,637	107,884	67,444	13,748,505	3,311	12,656	580	8,209
12	Plymouth...........	2,447	101,135	114,254	6,048,442	2,458	11,855	5,384	4,574
13	Suffolk	76	3,542	190	671,245	96	470	2	218
14	Worcester..........	7,245	516,632	251,083	22,713,930	8,201	66,373	9,865	16,509

STATISTICS OF

	Counties	Farms	Acres improved	Acres unimproved	Value	Horses, asses, and mules	Neat cattle	Sheep	Swine
1	Allegan.............	270	12,380	24,965	428,500	320	2,391	4,445	1,500
2	Barry...............	733	25,024	64,388	667,157	598	4,822	8,644	4,298
3	Berrien	690	34,606	58,100	1,108,324	1,612	5,126	11,279	7,239
4	Branch..............	1,442	65,324	89,119	1,714,181	1,738	9,767	22,441	7,001
5	Calhoun.............	1,724	118,963	139,722	3,162,180	3,343	16,590	49,579	11,728
6	Cass	950	59,786	80,217	1,602,081	2,013	6,670	18,932	9,008
7	Chippewa	17	....	....	....	....	....	....	....
8	Clinton.............	614	22,015	50,441	590,160	532	4,321	5,079	4,782
9	Eaton	746	27,538	55,032	762,924	713	5,627	8,757	4,194
10	Genesee.............	1,255	58,223	95,754	1,676,665	1,699	10,641	25,895	6,299
11	Hillsdale	1,411	78,582	85,618	2,168,954	2,090	10,885	28,818	7,306
12	Houghton	18	....	....	....	....	....	....	....
13	Huron...............	18	....	....	....	....	....	....	....
14	Ingham..............	991	39,110	78,879	1,041,453	811	6,878	10,545	4,132
15	Ionia	601	30,120	48,261	754,127	711	5,226	8,598	3,371
16	Jackson	2,250	147,859	167,322	3,679,401	3,480	16,851	48,694	11,702
17	Kalamazoo...........	1,098	73,200	81,782	2,198,474	2,389	9,301	38,331	9,267
18	Kent	849	35,560	72,456	1,080,322	803	6,376	7,945	4,910
19	Lapeer..............	628	34,510	39,153	794,405	940	5,420	14,723	3,660
20	Lenawee.............	2,470	138,499	137,262	4,366,430	4,865	20,606	66,198	12,261
21	Livingston..........	1,644	104,189	124,604	2,414,161	2,235	11,776	32,256	8,185
22	Macomb..............	1,277	74,905	87,694	2,317,805	2,543	11,362	34,147	7,748
23	Marquette...........	....	....	....	....	....	....	....	....
24	Mason	....	....	....	....	....	....	....	....
25	Michillimackinac, and 21 unorganized counties	13	1,518	14,125	80,624	117	353	11	166
26	Midland.............	4	207	1,281	14,100	9	41	37	40
27	Monroe..............	1,277	55,993	81,207	1,700,817	2,839	11,222	20,125	11,133
28	Montcalm............	26	1,711	3,414	36,520	49	201	469	158
29	Newago	....	746	699	8,925	7	80	3	130
30	Oakland.............	3,446	234,005	208,275	6,845,928	6,584	28,662	106,247	17,736
31	Oceana	....	....	....	....	....	....	....	....
32	Ontonogan...........	....	....	....	....	....	....	....	....
33	Ottawa..............	278	4,904	19,054	200,843	90	1,702	439	1,357
34	Saginaw	72	2,930	7,881	109,740	145	821	783	478
35	St. Clair...........	492	21,273	49,816	689,728	821	4,551	6,569	1,562
36	St. Joseph	1,379	102,214	110,457	2,440,901	2,974	10,531	24,542	10,882
37	Sanilac.............	61	3,932	10,454	113,933	85	797	884	442
38	Schoolcraft.........	....	....	....	....	....	....	....	....
39	Shiawassee..........	640	30,233	56,124	779,292	663	5,101	7,169	3,281
40	Tuscola.............	18	....	....	....	....	....	....	....
41	Van Buren...........	459	21,013	36,172	551,191	549	3,461	6,305	3,337
42	Washtenaw...........	2,543	182,510	161,948	5,390,020	5,670	22,338	94,105	16,911
43	Wayne...............	1,685	85,528	113,104	3,273,551	4,539	13,990	33,441	9,643

AGRICULTURAL PRODUCTS.												
Wheat, bushels.	Rye & oats, bushels.	Indian corn, bushels.	Irish and sweet potatoes, bushels.	Peas and beans, bushels.	Barley, bushels.	Buckwheat, bushels.	Butter and cheese, pounds.	Hay, tons.	Hops, pounds.	Clover & other grass seeds, bushels.	Flaxseed, bushels.	
546	22,561	52,639	34,756	2,529	2,714	63	113,083	9,142	......	24	......	1
7,802	386,655	240,899	369,642	4,127	12,746	43,347	3,635,952	92,460	1,121	486	53	2
189	73,505	164,064	250,488	2,492	4,130	313	420,312	28,552	......	2,072	......	3
45	5,608	12,395	9,899	35	774	......	27,677	2,015	......	......	......	4
1,435	59,261	158,264	339,423	5,212	12,222	463	717,346	57,968	63	268	......	5
3,948	145,450	223,359	185,114	1,485	8,189	5,485	1,218,685	52,766	13,090	207	11	6
3,076	215,986	252,213	305,637	3,350	1,082	30,649	1,226,756	48,749	172	738	7	7
4,867	177,595	272,370	292,734	1,419	5,782	11,287	1,334,541	59,064	1,743	139	1	8
1,098	125,987	269,908	586,804	9,646	9,735	3,836	1,033,588	81,992	65,636	686	......	9
55	1,278	3,206	5,997	47	928	......	21,271	1,439	5	......	......	10
356	32,362	112,132	253,158	3,952	5,462	454	437,249	41,588	81	381	......	11
251	43,952	105,243	208,402	871	3,267	239	505,294	28,532	12	152	......	12
....	1,383	2,691	10,069	297	505	......	1,690	2,446	......	6	......	13
7,543	354,584	476,107	733,261	8,247	44,849	9,759	4,466,068	145,094	39,672	928	......	14

MICHIGAN.

Wheat, bushels.	Rye & oats, bushels.	Indian corn, bushels.	Irish and sweet potatoes, bushels.	Peas and beans, bushels.	Barley, bushels.	Buckwheat, bushels.	Butter and cheese, pounds.	Hay, tons.	Hops, pounds.	Clover & other grass seeds, bushels.	Flaxseed, bushels.	
25,121	18,342	52,155	43,741	541	1,006	2,031	70,955	3,312	......	301	......	1
79,999	42,700	108,242	53,612	563	1,593	3,018	124,304	6,541	20	309	......	2
88,239	73,668	224,306	59,519	289	360	3,239	140,986	6,165	......	193	......	3
161,284	124,632	266,818	113,892	1,457	2,257	16,299	295,032	11,013	846	880	150	4
385,959	170,777	327,544	154,310	836	13,764	21,594	400,177	18,779	451	1,219	......	5
160,592	120,412	418,360	68,020	23	1,145	4,947	213,790	3,902	20	410	......	6
....	....	....	....	......	......	......	....	......	......	......	......	7
53,554	39,354	61,255	40,612	578	161	8,350	140,111	5,100	25	245	1	8
50,860	44,929	73,212	49,811	1,350	1,160	6,089	162,948	7,207	13	601	2	9
134,021	85,636	128,326	52,117	2,381	1,631	15,637	326,021	16,964	555	1,522	......	10
216,126	137,694	247,520	108,110	2,529	1,780	20,889	405,929	12,557	72	1,182	7	11
....	....	....	....	......	......	......	....	......	......	......	......	12
....	....	....	....	......	......	......	....	......	......	......	......	13
88,577	63,854	94,721	60,652	1,032	277	13,937	155,281	8,837	296	569	4	14
77,833	45,900	76,035	53,555	905	1,213	7,376	136,817	5,598	......	266	1	15
486,616	183,570	270,112	168,521	935	4,077	26,980	298,588	28,464	26	790	6	16
225,855	100,101	366,578	106,923	1,167	6,054	6,344	222,642	11,736	2,200	595	2	17
69,275	66,565	96,584	77,964	965	2,165	11,953	195,170	8,770	141	447	1	18
84,521	55,035	66,967	44,532	1,205	456	7,886	192,816	6,875	41	271	7	19
315,210	179,980	399,676	126,482	2,018	2,143	38,323	651,304	25,643	1,437	3,366	27	20
304,588	103,128	174,022	101,292	1,799	2,022	45,380	341,585	22,183	......	1,156	27	21
129,803	160,393	107,596	61,897	4,058	2,210	21,025	309,499	18,582	500	566	6	22
....	....	....	....	......	......	......	....	......	......	......	......	23
....	....	....	....	......	......	......	....	......	......	......	......	24
....	1,910	230	19,760	35	......	20	1,200	814	......	......	......	25
300	200	1,650	750	......	......	......	600	50	......	......	......	26
114,600	112,300	198,818	78,248	1,575	2,753	20,801	322,194	18,191	1,225	428	120	27
3,681	3,005	4,570	3,590	13	......	1,075	5,560	199	......	......	......	28
327	380	7,200	2,230	52	......	883	1,825	122	......	......	......	29
586,346	308,996	488,813	207,527	32,908	7,165	71,097	1,045,212	53,206	108	3,897	88	30
....	....	....	....	......	......	......	....	......	......	......	......	31
....	....	....	....	......	......	......	....	......	......	......	......	32
3,814	5,361	23,995	25,152	100	55	571	32,415	1,502	......	96	......	33
4,420	4,331	13,935	6,635	546	30	1,101	16,335	1,084	......	......	......	34
20,391	62,800	42,742	26,143	5,091	1,067	5,014	137,105	8,068	3	12	30	35
265,011	118,989	431,337	99,550	767	3,271	16,440	297,056	12,678	185	915	1	36
7,627	7,926	6,369	5,286	1,823	25	523	19,735	1,214	3	66	1	37
....	....	....	....	......	......	......	....	......	......	......	......	38
71,337	33,837	57,065	26,917	884	290	6,515	130,525	7,422	11	368	7	39
....	....	....	....	......	......	......	....	......	......	......	......	40
75,083	35,824	131,890	49,991	241	1,069	2,317	88,904	3,582	1,100	......	......	41
528,042	218,106	389,218	133,227	3,348	7,070	42,478	696,285	40,387	1,370	5,061	25	42
106,876	241,292	283,559	130,506	2,240	6,980	22,785	497,864	28,187	15	543	6	43

	Counties.	Flax, pounds.	Hemp, dew and water-rotted, tons.	Maple sugar, pounds.	Cane sugar, hhds. of 1,000 pounds.	Molasses, gallons.	Rice, pounds.	Tobacco, pounds.	Ginned cotton, bales of 400 pounds.	Wool, pounds.	Silk cocoons, pounds.
		Agricultural products.									
1	Barnstable									4,124	
2	Berkshire	520		316,288		958				256,289	
3	Bristol									14,390	
4	Dukes									22,430	
5	Essex									5,956	
6	Franklin	420		268,607		2,392		14,590		78,690	
7	Hampden	190		52,626		91		68,156		41,529	7
8	Hampshire	15		152,777		911		55,300		108,540	
9	Middlesex	17						200		5,475	
10	Nantucket									2,970	
11	Norfolk									879	
12	Plymouth									13,643	
13	Suffolk									9	
14	Worcester			5,227		341				30,212	

STATISTICS OF

	Counties.	Flax, pounds.	Hemp, dew and water-rotted, tons.	Maple sugar, pounds.	Cane sugar, hhds. of 1,000 pounds.	Molasses, gallons.	Rice, pounds.	Tobacco, pounds.	Ginned cotton, bales of 400 pounds.	Wool, pounds.	Silk cocoons, pounds.
1	Allegan			92,610						13,188	
2	Barry			94,588		315		200		22,103	
3	Berrien	30		51,250		1,196				28,834	
4	Branch	468		212,429		2,788				57,007	
5	Calhoun			40,444		1,593				126,991	
6	Cass			107,400						50,197	
7	Chippewa										
8	Clinton	200		124,479		32				14,724	
9	Eaton	556		210,167		2,990				23,769	
10	Genesee			139,418		372				73,804	
11	Hillsdale	241		169,556		1,807				82,095	
12	Houghton										
13	Huron										
14	Ingham	380		166,304		1,991				28,447	
15	Ionia	178		115,578		2,225				22,963	
16	Jackson	140		400						143,876	
17	Kalamazoo	40		80,980		300				94,750	
18	Kent	18		93,145		30				21,972	
19	Lapeer	179		63,343		231				33,798	
20	Lenawee	547		152,939		723		30		187,570	
21	Livingston	880		15,690						89,991	
22	Macomb	397		65,159		50				101,034	
23	Marquette										
24	Mason										
25	Michillimackinac, and 21 unorganized counties			23,050							
26	Midland									128	
27	Monroe	160		28,095		166				56,613	
28	Montcalm	40								940	
29	Newago									9	
30	Oakland	426		63,982		189				293,981	8
31	Oceana										
32	Ontonogon										
33	Ottawa	15		43,667		492				1,164	
34	Saginaw			9,465						2,406	
35	St. Clair	100		1,100						17,597	
36	St. Joseph	180		21,085		337				68,137	
37	Sanilac	50		10,515		32				2,483	
38	Schoolcraft										
39	Shiawassee	610		65,966		656				20,967	
40	Tuscola										
41	Van Buren			63,855		285				15,912	100
42	Washtenaw	712		61,007		689				250,775	
43	Wayne	605		55,128		334		1,015		95,058	

AGRICULTURAL PRODUCTS.					MANUFACTURES.				REMARKS.	
					Establishments.					
Beeswax and honey, pounds.	Value of animals slaughtered.	Value of produce of market gardens.	Value of orchard produce.	Wine, gallons.	Capital.	Hands employed.	Annual product.	Produced in families.		
....	$52,322	$5,037	$8,241	51	$587,390	765	$817,031	$3,682	....	1
17,761	208,635	4,966	10,604	......	3,177,795	3,872	4,267,706	8,557	....	2
3,722	193,201	27,263	18,678	15	6,854,615	9,536	12,595,695	6,990	....	3
....	16,470	....	1,286	......	56,700	38	305,070	853	....	4
2,114	174,468	132,431	65,727	251	12,895,647	35,267	22,906,805	14,580	....	5
7,662	164,676	740	23,696	......	896,752	1,949	1,662,584	56,929	....	6
5,283	180,242	16,994	13,137	547	6,555,590	7,836	6,653,548	11,482	....	7
5,961	205,845	2,631	19,094	10	2,004,748	3,453	3,410,745	26,697	....	8
3,529	310,917	220,982	134,640	2,623	20,473,880	29,356	26,548,932	17,908	....	9
30	5,492	2,994	160	......	617,900	156	1,077,448	....	....	10
1,047	229,809	136,796	55,458	91	5,433,300	15,628	13,223,595	25,702	....	11
3,352	176,102	13,502	19,205	21	2,397,305	8,024	6,713,906	953	....	12
136	4,856	10,020	2,473	20	10,887,690	25,296	32,013,869	....	....	13
8,911	577,889	25,664	91,596	1,059	10,518,330	24,762	18,940,211	31,000	....	14

MICHIGAN.

Beeswax and honey, pounds.	Value of animals slaughtered.	Value of produce of market gardens.	Value of orchard produce.	Wine, gallons.	Capital.	Hands employed.	Annual product.	Produced in families.	REMARKS.	
5,472	16,773	250	2,582	......	113,900	131	156,980	2,515	....	1
9,503	23,025	310	474	......	37,075	63	57,700	5,634	....	2
10,561	31,516	150	6,512	......	145,500	190	326,200	5,235	....	3
16,816	42,948	2,512	4,373	......	143,590	141	248,030	14,818	....	4
15,683	56,826	....	5,186	5	313,350	289	479,075	7,471	....	5
1,495	49,379	....	5,485	110	41,100	43	68,765	7,492	....	6
....	....	....	....	......	....	.....	....	....	....	7
4,359	22,627	....	372	......	21,200	28	55,135	7,718	....	8
4,204	20,490	....	1,570	......	57,450	84	115,589	7,357	....	9
3,175	44,676	30	2,783	......	112,825	137	184,772	9,404	....	10
21,688	56,288	....	6,457	174	122,720	120	190,825	17,645	[Peninsula.	11
....	....	....	....	......	....	.....	....	....	Formed in 1848 from Upper	12
....	....	....	....	......	12,025	13	12,660	....	Formed since 1840 from	13
16,964	28,680	1,073	332	.....	53,200	52	64,895	9,626	Saginaw.	14
11	24,747	40	841	......	27,300	60	55,830	7,216	Divided in 1850 to form	15
11,882	78,268	50	2,377	8	251,375	383	527,750	19,278	Montcalm.	16
6,130	52,313	350	4,070	415	176,600	221	362,014	4,534	....	17
7,613	36,231	64	837	......	149,350	346	272,325	8,637	Divided since 1840 to form	18
6,700	22,457	....	1,413	......	101,450	113	151,695	11,503	Newago.	19
21,027	95,642	353	6,533	72	473,650	577	814,685	23,547	....	20
26,623	52,478	165	2,145	......	90,850	96	193,935	21,677	....	21
12,129	56,937	300	9,257	105	163,235	249	447,155	35,487	[Upper Peninsula.	22
....	....	....	....	......	....	.....	....	....	Formed since 1840 from	23
....	....	....	....	......	15,000	20	17,400	....	Formed since 1840 from Ottawa.	24
....	1,957	....	300	......	855,345	1,240	621,485	....	....	25
....	307	....	....	......	....	.....	....	....	Formed since 1840 from	26
14,519	48,326	2,260	8,199	10	151,600	146	201,295	9,915	Saginaw.	27
....	1,326	....	....	......	27,000	80	35,000	253	Formed in 1850 from Ionia.	28
....	1,245	....	....	......	24,100	67	32,750	20	Formed since 1840 from	29
37,065	141,806	311	24,426	646	325,015	339	747,294	30,988	Kent.	30
....	....	....	....	......	11,600	38	15,500	....	....	31
....	....	....	....	......	....	.....	....	....	Not organized in 1840.	32
964	6,884	45	219	......	150,300	387	326,350	1,256	Div. since '40 to fm Mason	33
500	5,407	....	93	......	75,665	113	75,250	418	Div.'40 frm Hur. & Midl'nd	34
3,372	20,139	1,631	2,113	......	316,950	517	465,000	1,286	Div. '50 to form Sanilac.	35
6,443	58,383	....	3,712	......	270,655	291	447,892	9,568	[divided to form Tuscola.	36
350	4,709	70	....	......	59,750	102	63,075	1,050	For. since '40 fm St. Clair,	37
....	....	....	....	......	....	.....	....	....	Formed since 1840 from	38
44,885	20,982	....	1,249	......	69,525	79	119,435	9,144	Upper Peninsula.	39
....	....	....	....	......	12,025	13	12,660	....	Formed since 1840 from	40
5,000	18,497	18	2,950	......	43,500	85	70,700	8,950	Sanilac.	41
26,266	115,482	488	14,746	71	452,220	570	988,810	25,960	....	42
17,833	70,576	4,268	11,044	38	1,066,255	1,975	1,950,983	15,345	....	43

	COUNTIES.	POPULATION.								
		Whites.			Colored.		All classes.		Total population.	
		Male.	Female.	Total.	Free.	Slave.	Male.	Female.	1850.	1840.
1	Adams	1,986	1,962	3,948	258	14,395	9,341	9,260	18,601	19,434
2	Amité	1,848	1,793	3,641	3	6,050	4,933	4,761	9,694	9,511
3	Attala	4,031	3,540	7,571	8	3,412	5,723	5,268	10,991	4,303
4	Bolivar	234	161	395	2	2,180	1,377	1,200	2,577	1,356
5	Carroll	4,568	4,085	8,653	26	9,812	9,479	9,012	18,491	10,481
6	Chickasaw	5,252	4,635	9,887	2	6,480	8,530	7,839	16,369	2,955
7	Choctaw	4,430	3,990	8,420	4	2,978	5,856	5,546	11,402	6,010
8	Claiborne	1,906	1,543	3,449	42	11,450	7,738	7,203	14,941	13,078
9	Clark	2,039	1,784	3,823	6	1,648	2,832	2,645	5,477	2,986
10	Coahoma	787	600	1,387	2	1,391	1,526	1,254	2,780	1,290
11	Copiah	3,324	2,979	6,303	11	5,480	5,984	5,810	11,794	8,954
12	Covington	1,199	1,023	2,222	2	1,114	1,748	1,590	3,338	2,717
13	De Soto	5,083	4,404	9,487	2	9,553	9,982	9,060	19,042	7,002
14	Franklin	1,383	1,157	2,540	14	3,350	3,030	2,874	5,904	4,775
15	Greene	751	628	1,379	1	638	1,054	964	2,018	1,636
16	Hancock	1,289	1,155	2,444	12	1,216	1,934	1,738	3,672	3,367
17	Harrison	1,903	1,475	3,378	56	1,441	2,715	2,160	4,875	....
18	Hinds	4,767	3,923	8,690	25	16,625	13,313	12,027	25,340	19,098
19	Holmes	2,931	2,616	5,547	4	8,377	7,161	6,767	13,928	9,452
20	Issaquena	219	147	366	7	4,105	2,360	2,118	4,478	....
21	Itawamba	5,879	5,516	11,395	6	2,127	6,851	6,677	13,528	5,375
22	Jackson	1,235	1,031	2,266	105	825	1,726	1,470	3,196	1,965
23	Jasper	2,271	2,022	4,293	4	1,887	3,156	3,028	6,184	3,958
24	Jefferson	1,409	1,225	2,634	66	10,493	6,689	6,504	13,193	11,650
25	Jones	961	926	1,887	3	274	1,091	1,073	2,164	1,258
26	Kemper	3,731	3,407	7,138	1	5,378	6,390	6,127	12,517	7,663
27	Lafayette	4,466	3,880	8,346	4	5,719	7,293	6,776	14,069	6,531
28	Lauderdale	3,101	2,951	6,052	4	2,661	4,343	4,374	8,717	5,358
29	Lawrence	1,888	1,661	3,549	....	2,929	3,340	3,138	6,478	5,920
30	Leake	2,051	1,931	3,982	2	1,549	2,800	2,733	5,533	2,162
31	Lowndes	3,436	3,087	6,523	28	12,993	9,981	9,563	19,544	14,513
32	Madison	2,351	1,977	4,328	2	13,843	9,222	8,951	18,173	15,530
33	Marion	1,178	1,037	2,215	....	2,195	2,344	2,066	4,410	3,830
34	Marshall	7,573	6,698	14,271	1	15,417	15,328	14,361	29,689	17,526
35	Monroe	4,958	4,460	9,418	37	11,717	10,861	10,311	21,172	9,250
36	Neshoba	1,768	1,625	3,393	....	1,335	2,397	2,331	4,728	2,437
37	Newton	1,810	1,622	3,432	1	1,032	2,289	2,176	4,465	2,527
38	Noxubee	2,571	2,405	4,976	....	11,323	8,417	7,882	16,299	9,975
39	Oktibbeha	2,303	2,006	4,309	18	4,844	4,690	4,481	9,171	4,276
40	Panola	2,697	2,324	5,021	3	6,420	5,893	5,551	11,444	4,657
41	Perry	861	818	1,679	10	749	1,250	1,188	2,438	1,889
42	Pike	2,191	2,034	4,225	33	3,102	3,747	3,613	7,360	6,151
43	Pontotoc	6,369	5,767	12,133	8	4,968	8,869	8,243	17,112	4,491
44	Rankin	2,072	1,868	3,940	11	3,276	3,662	3,565	7,227	4,631
45	Scott	1,436	1,342	2,778	1	1,182	1,993	1,968	3,961	1,653
46	Simpson	1,668	1,522	3,190	3	1,541	2,422	2,312	4,734	3,380
47	Smith	1,580	1,493	3,073	....	998	2,052	2,019	4,071	1,961
48	Sunflower	206	142	348	....	754	599	503	1,102	....
49	Tallahatchee	1,122	974	2,096	....	2,547	2,421	2,222	4,643	2,985
50	Tippah	8,143	7,664	15,807	6	4,928	10,553	10,188	20,741	9,444
51	Tishemingo	7,031	6,497	13,528	1	1,961	7,943	7,547	15,490	6,681
52	Tunica	241	155	396	1	917	754	560	1,314	821
53	Warren	3,288	2,708	5,996	28	12,096	9,221	8,899	18,120	15,820
54	Washington	339	207	546	7	7,836	4,402	3,987	8,389	7,287
55	Wayne	767	732	1,499	....	1,393	1,437	1,455	2,892	2,120
56	Wilkinson	1,923	1,701	3,624	30	13,260	8,440	8,474	16,914	14,193
57	Winston	2,656	2,522	5,178	10	2,768	4,018	3,938	7,956	4,650
58	Yalobusha	4,527	4,125	8,652	9	8,597	8,764	8,494	17,258	12,248
59	Yazoo	2,300	1,769	4,069	....	10,349	7,461	6,957	14,418	10,480

STATISTICS OF

1	Adair	1,191	1,092	2,283	8	51	1,216	1,126	2,342	....
2	Andrew	4,489	4,268	8,757	14	662	4,800	4,633	9,433	....
3	Atchison	887	754	1,641	7	30	903	775	1,678	....
4	Audrian	1,580	1,468	3,048	1	457	1,813	1,693	3,506	1,949
5	Barry	1,741	1,576	3,317	....	150	1,805	1,662	3,467	4,795
6	Bates	1,832	1,688	3,520	8	141	1,919	1,750	3,669	....
7	Benton	2,281	2,266	4,547	8	460	2,501	2,514	5,015	4,205
8	Boone	5,809	5,491	11,300	13	3,666	7,660	7,319	14,979	13,561
9	Buchanan	6,427	5,645	12,072	1	902	6,853	6,122	12,975	6,337
10	Butler	812	751	1,563	....	53	835	781	1,616	....
11	Caldwell	1,112	1,064	2,176	4	133	1,182	1,134	2,316	1,458

NATIVITIES, DWELLINGS, &c.				EDUCATION AND RELIGION.									
Born out of State.				Colleges, academies, and private schools.		Public Schools.							
United States.	Foreign countries.	Dwellings.	Families.	Pupils.	Annual income.	Pupils.	Annual income.	Total educational income.	White scholars during year.	Whites 5 and under 20 years old.	Whites over 20 unable to read & write.	Accommodation of churches—persons.	
1,235	627	900	900	195	....	820	$9,500	$9,500	808	1,367	2	7,700	1
857	34	660	660	30	....	685	1,134	1,134	693	1,505	44	5,000	2
3,849	31	1,431	1,463	150	$1,653	440	2,160	3,813	1,439	3,230	441	2,400	3
205	6	95	95	......	....	......	....	....	32	133	6	450	4
4,239	60	1,441	1,530	365	300	623	1,335	1,635	1,761	3,571	304	10,245	5
6,837	36	1,647	1,647	115	....	477	6,082	6,082	1,389	4,087	632	7,386	6
4,839	41	1,405	1,406	......	....	406	4,730	4,730	1,490	3,534	890	4,685	7
983	156	659	659	239	10,284	365	11,400	21,684	452	1,198	68	6,900	8
1,731	21	631	633	30	....	145	1,540	1,540	425	1,561	79	1,600	9
891	11	260	260	......	....	97	875	875	186	481	164	770	10
1,663	38	1,148	1,151	30	600	436	7,970	8,570	1,077	2,515	293	11,700	11
646	24	348	348	45	1,500	81	....	1,500	469	932	237	1,950	12
6,714	44	1,644	1,644	30	800	416	22,114	22,914	1,800	3,844	120	15,550	13
520	41	447	447	......	....	132	2,940	2,940	408	979	213	3,850	14
366	13	217	217	130	2,000	57	....	2,000	179	581	142	1,450	15
764	283	492	503	27	925	197	3,173	4,098	344	935	204	1,050	16
1,184	715	727	727	......	....	100	2,550	2,550	599	1,207	165	1,100	17
3,547	300	1,656	1,656	545	3,000	767	5,400	8,400	1,873	3,300	159	10,350	18
2,441	65	995	995	215	5,000	736	3,494	8,494	1,069	2,252	109	1,650	19
193	6	110	110	......	....	......	....	....	31	114	6	....	20
6,883	19	1,855	1,862	......	....	661	2,085	2,085	1,768	4,927	409	12,425	21
707	109	440	440	......	....	114	703	703	408	468	154	1,670	22
1,671	38	674	705	115	1,600	339	3,917	5,517	752	1,770	308	3,375	23
664	104	514	514	......	....	181	4,085	4,085	394	903	35	5,150	24
545	4	319	319	......	....	76	246	246	153	800	292	1,465	25
4,455	41	1,249	1,249	......	....	297	5,902	5,902	581	3,247	171	7,400	26
5,292	31	1,382	1,382	218	15,775	469	9,340	25,115	1,838	3,519	239	8,915	27
3,380	34	1,008	1,024	......	....	521	6,585	6,585	722	2,611	494	5,665	28
896	35	613	613	160	....	200	500	500	474	1,405	241	4,300	29
2,112	13	635	700	40	600	342	3,100	3,700	748	1,714	351	5,350	30
3,757	83	1,168	1,168	607	....	503	7,639	7,639	1,500	2,650	94	2,250	31
2,181	32	767	784	183	5,460	413	10,634	16,094	1,037	1,718	46	5,800	32
476	18	377	382	......	....	132	....	....	249	898	240	2,900	33
9,792	24	2,306	2,306	470	28,264	304	2,180	30,444	3,139	5,865	659	11,230	34
5,560	87	1,576	1,611	453	9,170	600	5,434	14,604	1,695	3,876	616	7,165	35
2,118	44	545	575	73	2,100	109	2,225	4,325	322	1,438	69	2,550	36
1,332	67	586	586	......	....	180	....	....	493	1,440	227	2,900	37
3,206	26	957	957	594	10,000	894	13,280	23,280	1,333	2,023	51	6,650	38
2,831	37	744	744	......	....	511	6,584	6,584	719	1,808	76	5,680	39
3,367	25	891	891	......	....	439	9,702	9,702	665	2,081	181	5,350	40
444	11	265	265	......	....	......	....	....	64	708	64	1,300	41
875	23	698	699	......	....	458	6,910	6,910	671	1,719	354	6,600	42
8,580	46	2,001	2,001	90	....	578	17,528	17,528	1,114	5,135	49	14,035	43
1,505	51	698	698	414	....	......	....	....	594	1,647	57	1,500	44
1,138	13	422	422	25	....	157	2,000	2,000	373	1,193	121	3,125	45
909	14	526	526	60	532	220	3,468	4,000	527	1,304	369	3,300	46
1,194	13	515	515	75	750	174	1,920	2,670	418	1,320	320	2,000	47
167	5	75	75	......	....	......	....	....	....	109	10	....	48
1,199	16	368	368	......	....	200	700	700	421	817	120	1,050	49
10,597	35	2,655	2,655	257	6,964	202	2,424	9,388	2,925	6,761	960	10,100	50
9,449	36	2,201	2,201	......	....	490	6,831	6,831	1,315	5,913	806	13,618	51
279	7	73	73	......	....	41	....	....	45	146	28	100	52
2,394	711	1,230	1,262	65	3,500	708	8,623	12,123	956	1,991	127	3,750	53
368	21	126	126	......	....	......	....	....	53	131	1	300	54
568	8	281	281	......	....	......	....	....	193	627	170	1,300	55
824	142	736	741	169	....	400	12,227	12,227	621	1,345	110	3,750	56
3,087	27	866	875	55	3,820	310	3,165	6,985	973	2,205	292	4,300	57
5,150	32	1,491	1,491	1,137	....	......	....	....	1,390	3,646	96	9,150	58
1,615	151	935	970	84	1,520	543	7,825	9,345	636	1,485	60	3,750	59

MISSOURI.

1,211	18	383	383	......	....	260	2,120	2,120	302	924	229	....	1
5,222	190	1,377	1,377	......	....	1,600	2,335	2,335	2,106	3,719	933	2,950	2
841	124	291	293	......	....	175	840	840	370	630	250	....	3
1,367	18	498	523	60	650	400	1,556	2,206	495	1,272	221	1,570	4
2,135	9	544	546	......	....	148	....	....	657	1,390	489	450	5
1,772	31	626	626	......	....	285	209	209	493	1,518	230	1,350	6
2,155	297	789	789	......	....	......	....	....	557	1,923	152	1,150	7
4,509	97	1,924	1,924	100	14,800	2,460	27,000	41,800	2,003	4,836	579	14,075	8
6,717	823	2,030	2,045	......	....	625	1,641	1,641	1,795	4,818	637	1,450	9
896	....	265	271	......	....	91	206	206	215	677	296	460	10
1,252	45	358	358	......	....	115	1,350	1,350	485	941	101	....	11

	COUNTIES.	LAND OCCUPIED OR IMPROVED.				LIVE STOCK UPON FARMS.			
		Farms.	Acres improved.	Acres unimproved.	Value with improvements and implements.	Horses, asses, and mules.	Neat Cattle.	Sheep.	Swine.
1	Adams	136	77,675	93,766	$ 2,427,212	4,155	10,547	7,929	10,274
2	Amité	510	63,585	149,544	500,452	2,821	13,717	7,706	32,426
3	Attala	1,336	62,796	159,136	885,005	3,252	17,409	7,810	39,741
4	Bolivar	57	16,973	31,117	808,526	741	3,894	903	3,911
5	Carroll	986	105,886	206,111	1,725,588	4,660	17,261	7,672	43,844
6	Chickasaw	1,167	89,550	223,615	1,462,048	4,937	15,995	5,499	47,847
7	Choctaw	1,132	58,006	167,104	584,757	3,156	13,623	6,434	34,198
8	Claiborne	310	96,896	152,398	2,225,146	4,786	17,981	11,692	27,843
9	Clark	500	22,919	51,092	346,662	1,331	13,253	3,939	18,891
10	Coahoma	161	11,478	32,415	419,059	856	4,358	192	9,315
11	Copiah	951	69,943	180,205	986,050	3,512	16,610	9,753	39,899
12	Covington	272	16,765	27,011	156,029	956	6,900	2,496	13,163
13	De Soto	1,257	116,044	168,291	2,072,394	5,567	18,788	7,690	50,548
14	Franklin	330	39,944	77,013	552,691	1,632	8,102	2,677	18,357
15	Greene	93	5,316	33,272	61,645	498	9,275	982	8,280
16	Hancock	77	3,646	33,629	92,415	303	7,772	656	4,967
17	Harrison	84	1,890	5,437	81,865	206	7,079	1,582	3,623
18	Hinds	852	164,457	276,966	2,416,416	6,636	23,805	12,283	58,471
19	Holmes	640	89,395	159,434	1,447,136	3,954	14,955	4,734	38,146
20	Issaquena	76	27,631	66,559	1,072,088	1,408	4,683	620	6,249
21	Itawamba	1,499	67,980	281,979	970,385	4,011	16,074	8,866	40,636
22	Jackson	212	4,047	69,257	277,792	652	13,728	2,595	9,659
23	Jasper	540	31,103	66,878	298,583	1,805	11,050	4,988	23,811
24	Jefferson	239	93,817	135,868	1,827,048	5,090	16,799	9,606	26,660
25	Jones	274	8,867	11,171	62,763	650	7,261	1,694	12,686
26	Kemper	730	77,385	135,175	796,137	3,337	19,048	4,257	33,852
27	Lafayette	1,044	83,326	191,626	1,343,336	3,913	13,613	6,157	57,097
28	Lauderdale	922	51,386	86,714	426,689	2,498	13,114	6,191	28,481
29	Lawrence	458	37,017	88,392	439,180	1,949	10,125	5,066	23,105
30	Leake	437	24,428	106,841	239,219	1,350	8,475	2,358	15,281
31	Lowndes	725	126,998	166,312	2,348,960	5,093	13,084	5,878	40,100
32	Madison	552	164,121	225,111	2,058,193	5,575	17,759	10,740	43,249
33	Marion	322	20,393	57,461	241,139	1,237	13,853	2,790	18,977
34	Marshall	1,611	180,980	269,581	3,694,393	8,316	22,332	12,630	62,797
35	Monroe	848	123,353	210,366	2,607,689	5,660	15,814	8,223	47,241
36	Neshoba	426	21,637	113,587	277,405	1,296	10,347	3,296	14,672
37	Newton	350	20,987	66,218	234,555	1,331	9,466	3,859	20,325
38	Noxubee	676	123,394	176,741	1,816,236	5,215	17,045	6,338	49,255
39	Oktibbeha	560	58,453	88,548	762,027	3,057	10,341	2,733	27,205
40	Panola	618	73,713	124,221	1,312,725	3,661	12,075	4,831	28,778
41	Perry	131	6,768	32,690	95,236	946	13,468	1,808	14,052
42	Pike	558	43,286	70,650	448,714	2,326	11,730	6,084	25,810
43	Pontotoc	1,248	77,078	163,484	1,226,064	4,346	15,199	4,783	44,337
44	Rankin	420	37,199	101,305	619,323	1,916	11,034	4,162	23,054
45	Scott	257	14,656	32,855	165,348	804	4,663	2,293	11,064
46	Simpson	451	23,152	52,147	261,315	1,454	7,652	3,405	18,123
47	Smith	425	13,348	36,105	137,284	1,262	8,865	2,925	19,317
48	Sunflower	43	5,966	22,322	215,099	335	1,764	41	5,106
49	Tallahatchee	282	27,372	48,462	514,589	1,292	6,277	968	13,550
50	Tippah	1,890	102,770	282,543	1,522,735	5,730	19,854	11,020	53,448
51	Tishemingo	1,247	59,450	263,274	915,468	4,011	13,669	8,730	38,367
52	Tunica	41	6,015	24,374	282,767	429	2,505	126	3,247
53	Warren	435	78,472	134,825	2,242,047	4,552	17,522	6,136	23,712
54	Washington	109	59,126	97,780	3,593,705	2,809	9,744	2,957	12,451
55	Wayne	162	12,359	30,898	142,734	632	7,295	1,427	7,948
56	Wilkinson	404	96,630	149,611	1,902,992	4,792	16,902	10,552	22,990
57	Winston	551	40,627	120,045	503,824	2,222	10,936	4,842	22,768
58	Yalobusha	872	98,606	248,669	1,376,948	4,600	19,598	8,670	56,435
59	Yazoo	464	107,298	167,860	1,977,731	4,486	17,883	7,655	33,095

STATISTICS OF

1	Adair	326	12,273	31,808	150,931	983	3,602	3,747	11,762
2	Andrew	873	40,447	114,951	1,398,332	2,717	9,314	12,080	20,461
3	Atchison	188	6,477	30,204	176,811	628	3,366	1,694	8,159
4	Audrian	417	31,731	52,767	370,704	2,143	6,708	7,180	11,367
5	Barry	389	11,563	14,910	172,997	1,345	4,462	3,368	5,930
6	Bates	472	20,828	27,660	202,584	1,990	11,095	4,135	16,500
7	Benton	510	18,940	54,823	276,950	2,589	8,344	7,313	9,905
8	Boone	1,376	104,163	182,459	1,834,701	8,893	17,703	24,416	32,159
9	Buchanan	1,258	56,897	133,359	2,606,581	4,022	14,667	15,054	30,323
10	Butler	143	4,950	12,094	44,765	674	1,608	594	5,905
11	Caldwell	232	14,707	36,837	253,076	1,190	4,006	4,931	8,149

AGRICULTURAL PRODUCTS.												
Wheat, bushels.	Rye & oats, bushels.	Indian corn, bushels.	Irish and sweet potatoes, bushels.	Peas and beans, bushels.	Barley, bushels.	Buckwheat, bushels.	Butter and cheese, pounds.	Hay, tons.	Hops, pounds.	Clover & other grass seeds, bushels.	Flaxseed, bushels.	
....	6,660	334,353	39,600	12,847	......	......	22,75[illegible]	500	......	3	......	1
....	15,326	380,917	111,335	24,485	......	......	42,607	170	......	......	......	2
1,109	15,307	522,503	118,442	2,190	15	......	89,993	895	2	3	1	3
....	60	107,075	31,108	806	......	......	15,732	....	......	......	......	4
744	82,430	727,340	182,753	65,315	......	......	139,965	2,836	5	43	......	5
7,802	25,805	771,452	115,611	12,789	......	......	140,042	....	......	......	......	6
8,082	36,953	404,244	90,069	18,479	3	......	94,836	....	......	......	......	7
....	13,924	488,003	94,190	65,217	......	......	83,013	1,170	......	......	......	8
215	2,710	174,235	78,955	485	......	......	50,476	....	......	......	......	9
....	255	134,815	25,458	2,430	......	......	35,150	3	33	......	......	10
....	42,179	436,485	127,864	52,208	......	......	73,728	130	30	......	......	11
104	9,503	108,920	52,892	14,897	15	......	23,642	399	......	......	......	12
4,482	68,385	741,519	154,016	38,231	......	......	191,165	27	7	66	......	13
....	4,995	189,195	45,247	18,999	......	......	23,197	123	......	......	......	14
....	115	41,275	17,236	780	......	......	10,710	....	......	......	......	15
....	305	22,825	34,255	1,070	......	......	3,405	20	......	......	......	16
....	....	9,524	19,830	735	......	......	205	....	......	......	......	17
....	61,779	853,305	259,146	79,001	......	......	114,327	2,336	......	......	......	18
1,814	48,788	543,155	135,211	53,856	......	8	131,968	5	......	......	......	19
....	1,045	143,130	20,424	2,240	......	......	23,535	33	......	......	......	20
4,430	26,711	533,507	108,824	20,166	......	3	161,376	....	......	......	......	21
....	....	29,848	30,549	2,389	......	......	10,517	....	......	......	......	22
194	14,988	209,691	79,470	1,821	15	......	18,680	43	......	......	......	23
....	14,035	417,745	87,764	46,079	......	......	85.874	230	......	......	......	24
11	3,416	60,988	32,699	4,660	......	......	7,895	....	......	......	......	25
238	40,555	504,685	175,960	4,444	......	......	187,175	....	......	......	......	26
14,749	58,817	562,530	113,320	31,566	34	2	180,430	2,006	15	27	......	27
2,808	21,880	324,459	115,209	15,411	20	150	69,922	10	20	5	12	28
2,820	14,302	229,129	67,552	12,413	......	6	34,463	2	......	......	......	29
321	9,429	180,637	47,843	3,957	......	......	33,373	1	......	......	......	30
1,166	41,120	871,864	99,432	6,439	......	......	145,347	2	......	1	2	31
331	77,582	785,485	185,036	45,957	10	887	111,381	502	8	40	......	32
10	5,836	130,504	62,465	22,340	......	......	16,705	....	......	......	......	33
19,326	149,443	1,236,006	238,153	52,458	21	65	278,540	153	152	338	3	34
7,485	63,310	901,136	175,341	48,896	30	......	117.500	63	......	10	......	35
1,703	9,455	153,235	56,730	1,185	2	......	42,050	16	......	26	......	36
305	12,866	165,186	58,241	2,292	......	......	55,518	....	......	......	......	37
1,853	52,765	895,713	101,273	4,345	......	......	171,500	117	29	32	......	38
2,094	24,224	389,796	68,752	5,214	......	......	66.658	18	15	5	......	39
4,809	45,421	451,909	81,516	29,108	......	......	95,283	14	......	8	......	40
....	1,714	58,360	45,250	6,428	......	......	16,000	....	......	......	......	41
....	27,417	245,751	64,166	6,841	......	......	48,664	39	......	......	......	42
8,339	30,659	667,012	118,668	3,546	6	......	130,020	....	......	......	......	43
....	11,626	217,673	69,673	8,000	......	......	54,034	67	......	......	......	44
....	3.865	95,500	34,402	808	......	......	14,008	1	......	......	......	45
113	6,201	165,099	40,952	21,589	5	......	26,143	1	......	......	......	46
212	8,354	128,641	47,110	3,527	......	......	25,620	3	12	......	......	47
....	....	33,390	9,410	....	......	......	5,655	....	......	......	......	48
203	10,974	190,930	41,888	9,703	4	......	29,16[illegible]	[illegible]	39	2	......	49
22,011	83,915	865,131	133,590	9,484	......	......	216,464	3	......	......	5	50
8,559	51,06[illegible]	526,769	83,556	8,578	48	......	132,900	13	......	8	3	51
....	730	94,735	10,038	368	......	......	8,855	23	......	......	......	52
....	7,790	451,875	92.004	23,319	......	......	88,664	320	81	......	......	53
....	1,400	424,600	32,375	13,433	......	......	17,710	15	25	......	......	54
....	580	84,280	37,60[illegible]	....	......	......	7,510	....	......	......	......	55
....	19,450	504,795	34.460	13,06[illegible]	......	......	10,965	150	......	......	......	56
6,235	34,490	326,408	89.386	8,90[illegible]	......	......	100,86[illegible]	....	......	......	......	57
3,313	59,6[illegible]	640,775	140,687	65.8[illegible]	......	......	173,901	....	......	......	......	58
....	30,30[illegible]	556,50[illegible]	138,28[illegible]	41,140	......	......	59,63[illegible]	42	......	......	......	59

MISSOURI.

Wheat, bushels.	Rye & oats, bushels.	Indian corn, bushels.	Irish and sweet potatoes, bushels.	Peas and beans, bushels.	Barley, bushels.	Buckwheat, bushels.	Butter and cheese, pounds.	Hay, tons.	Hops, pounds.	Clover & other grass seeds, bushels.	Flaxseed, bushels.	
5,801	11,687	141,370	3,815	13	......	548	33,425	231	......	......	6	1
109,547	59,683	518,795	15,286	25	1,742	250	121,930	2,478	......	115	104	2
15,577	10,097	149,387	1,594	....	......	45	350	24	......	......	5	3
11,448	76,022	285,186	11,141	....	......		61,044	1,092	......	......	......	4
13,166	23.483	194,525	9,683	317	......	......	28,896	154	......	4	9	5
8,614	49,051	120,340	8,219	346	17	60	50,257	859	......	3	72	6
11,072	39,415	154,965	6,444	69	14	247	69,843	597	......	43	53	7
70,163	85,484	1,001,983	21,863	1,676	67	477	154,178	4,812	17	419	643	8
121,682	56,849	1,935,713	16,717	407	35	245	183,461	1,075	......	106	......	9
2,337	3,068	55,800	2,373	87	......	......	10,563	7	......	......	11	10
12,734	45,740	16,13[illegible]	3,569	16	......	155	17,365	1,015	......	......	110	11

	COUNTIES.	AGRICULTURAL PRODUCTS.									
		Flax, pounds.	Hemp, dew and water-rotted, tons.	Maple sugar, pounds.	Cane sugar, hhds. of 1,000 pounds.	Molasses, gallons.	Rice, pounds.	Tobacco, pounds.	Ginned cotton, bales of 400 pounds.	Wool, pounds.	Silk cocoons, pounds.
1	Adams	......	......	......	......	480	......	......	17,473	11,627	......
2	Amité	......	......	......	......	......	151,603	550	7,847	14,993	......
3	Attala	50	......	......	......	12	27,015	450	5,631	1,439	......
4	Bolivar	......	......	......	......	......	......	......	4,723	1,948	......
5	Carroll	......	......	......	......	......	39,070	945	17,989	13,427	......
6	Chickasaw	......	......	......	......	......	7,540	2,897	9,644	11,752	......
7	Choctaw	......	......	......	......	......	23,259	1,377	4,458	13,276	......
8	Claiborne	......	......	......	......	......	20	......	20,795	26,336	......
9	Clark	......	......	......	......	......	6,690	......	1,817	2,352	......
10	Coahoma	......	......	......	......	......	6,727	500	2,430	510	......
11	Copiah	......	......	......	1	1,110	241,685	100	9,318	19,884	......
12	Covington	......	......	......	......	115	41,235	......	1,164	6,226	......
13	De Soto	......	......	......	......	......	10,275	1,330	20,278	14,836	......
14	Franklin	......	......	......	......	......	83,220	......	4,347	5,618	......
15	Greene	......	......	......	......	......	30,810	......	81	2,928	......
16	Hancock	......	......	......	......	750	129,420	......	70	1,913	......
17	Harrison	......	......	......	......	......	81,380	......	......	2,371	......
18	Hinds	......	......	......	1	1,680	105,650	350	19,829	26,962	......
19	Holmes	......	......	......	......	......	72,550	......	12,635	8,491	......
20	Issaquena	......	......	......	......	......	......	600	8,461	1,495	......
21	Itawamba	......	......	......	......	......	473	375	5,519	13,965	......
22	Jackson	......	......	......	......	......	113,975	......	......	4,818	......
23	Jasper	......	......	......	......	......	39,110	......	1,422	6,186	......
24	Jefferson	......	......	......	......	......	......	......	16,193	21,160	......
25	Jones	......	......	......	......	......	74,555	90	250	2,971	......
26	Kemper	......	......	......	......	......	......	......	5,115	11,009	......
27	Lafayette	......	......	......	......	......	45,985	10,548	10,387	11,813	......
28	Lauderdale	200	......	......	......	......	102,203	1,529	4,195	10,590	......
29	Lawrence	......	......	......	2	5,999	76,103	1,253	3,304	11,235	......
30	Leake	......	......	......	......	140	70,040	331	1,644	4,306	......
31	Lowndes	200	......	......	......	......	5,850	100	15,127	7,953	......
32	Madison	......	......	......	......	......	54,821	1,301	14,863	21,386	......
33	Marion	......	......	......	4	5,945	134,540	......	1,411	4,492	......
34	Marshall	20	......	......	......	......	82,683	5,368	32,775	20,979	......
35	Monroe	......	......	......	......	......	4,436	1,218	17,814	14,171	......
36	Neshoba	......	......	......	......	......	14,050	......	1,422	5,243	2
37	Newton	......	......	......	......	......	32,330	......	1,474	7,424	......
38	Noxubee	......	2	......	......	......	123	470	12,555	10,773	......
39	Oktibbeha	......	......	......	......	......	7,189	485	5,479	6,024	......
40	Panola	......	......	......	......	......	15,889	1,550	8,918	8,874	......
41	Perry	......	......	......	......	230	88,000	100	388	2,799	......
42	Pike	......	......	......	......	914	290,550	183	4,128	12,440	......
43	Pontotoc	......	......	......	......	......	32,131	2,761	9,017	9,702	......
44	Rankin	......	......	......	......	......	66,105	......	2,676	3,390	......
45	Scott	......	......	......	......	......	57,590	......	881	4,470	......
46	Simpson	......	......	......	......	235	83,207	373	1,851	6,228	......
47	Smith	......	......	......	......	508	36,195	596	1,111	4,898	......
48	Sunflower	......	......	......	......	......	......	1,300	1,900	......	......
49	Tallahatchee	......	......	......	......	......	282	520	4,977	1,526	......
50	Tippah	100	......	......	......	......	32,333	7,593	12,098	21,113	......
51	Tishemingo	95	5	......	......	......	10,600	820	3,945	15,534	......
52	Tunica	......	......	......	......	......	50	......	717	410	......
53	Warren	......	......	......	......	......	580	900	18,513	18,385	......
54	Washington	......	......	......	......	......	......	500	26,178	9,664	......
55	Wayne	......	......	......	......	......	6,300	......	1,217	......	......
56	Wilkinson	......	......	......	......	......	17,690	......	26,381	15,596	......
57	Winston	......	......	......	......	......	44,394	598	3,091	10,305	......
58	Yalobusha	......	......	......	......	200	5,135	......	14,314	16,131	......
59	Yazoo	......	......	......	......	......	16,210	......	22,052	13,272	......

STATISTICS OF

	COUNTIES.	Flax, pounds.	Hemp, dew and water-rotted, tons.	Maple sugar, pounds.	Cane sugar, hhds. of 1,000 pounds.	Molasses, gallons.	Rice, pounds.	Tobacco, pounds.	Ginned cotton, bales of 400 pounds.	Wool, pounds.	Silk cocoons, pounds.
1	Adair	2,238	......	7,303	......	126	......	......	......	7,287	......
2	Andrew	9,432	475	4,762	......	240	......	9,443	......	25,969	40
3	Atchison	862	5	......	......	......	......	......	......	4,424	......
4	Audrian	13,250	......	......	......	......	......	144,380	......	14,084	......
5	Barry	2,323	......	1,019	......	......	......	500	......	7,263	......
6	Bates	2,800	......	100	......	......	......	4,590	......	12,836	......
7	Benton	2,554	......	477	......	90	......	7,850	......	12,502	......
8	Boone	21,695	51	20,020	......	914	......	584,949	......	55,725	11
9	Buchanan	620	1,894	385	......	......	60	300	......	30,073	......
10	Butler	440	......	1,820	......	15	......	1,050	......	1,558	......
11	Caldwell	2,000	20	......	......	......	......	760	......	13,691	2

Agricultural products.					Manufactures.					
					Establishments.					
Beeswax and honey, pounds.	Value of animals slaughtered.	Value of produce of market gardens.	Value of orchard produce.	Wine, gallons.	Capital.	Hands employed.	Annual product.	Produced in families.	Remarks.	
886	$8,054	$4,050	$1,590	4	$97,550	131	$207,850	$6,945	....	
215	51,991	....	....	......	500	2	5,200	10,588	....	
11,040	107,201	....	20	......	99,175	129	121,043	28,802	....	3
690	12,064	200	100	......	....	......	....	150	Divided since 1840 to form	4
21,076	130,479	....	660	......	67,230	156	114,686	22,558	Sunflower.	5
9,758	113,450	....	....	......	14,770	63	37,471	37,892	....	6
17,062	79,628	....	....	......	58,455	84	81,900	44,546	....	7
1,973	60,723	....	200	......	36,400	74	66,919	13,030	....	8
300	39,535	....	....	......	7,850	19	6,900	18,720	....	9
5,156	21,346	....	26	......	....	......	....	8,676	....	10
1,983	100,234	....	550	......	29,650	47	28,120	32,768	....	11
3,769	29,921	....	621	......	5,900	12	11,137	29,124	....	12
32,907	128,713	....	692	......	41,165	102	100,060	35,496	....	13
1,715	31,779	....	....	......	14,000	16	11,445	6,696	....	14
....	14,460	....	....	......	....	......	....	1,581	....	15
100	7,359	350	560	......	106,000	118	97,688	1,441	....	16
107	3,685	1,215	1,862	100	170,050	286	181,800	370	Formed since 1840.	17
16,682	122,812	9,115	4,100	30	3,000	6	8,000	14,018	....	18
21,440	101,339	5	248	......	27,525	78	60,900	11,949	....	19
1,480	15,105	....	....	......	....	......	....	102	Formed since 1840 from	20
6,074	87,380	....	....	......	17,283	35	34,090	48,424	Washington.	21
9,025	15,807	1,788	2,326	......	37,000	69	46,100	2,474	....	22
3,885	38,847	....	....	......	10,865	22	20,110	20,382	....	23
616	59,312	225	400	225	20,300	30	46,910	5,589	....	24
560	18,472	....	....	......	....	......	....	8,903	....	25
....	93,086	....	....	......	5,500	11	18,700	41,648	....	26
22,288	102,270	80	13,085	......	81,550	124	125,365	129,944	....	27
20,344	69,933	....	5	......	24,900	59	82,246	28,234	....	28
2,416	45,814	50	1,147	......	15,700	33	41,785	21,217	....	29
3,471	34,528	....	....	......	4,915	11	4,540	10,976	....	30
3,442	120,736	....	....	......	110,685	268	208,797	28,342	....	31
15,274	137,751	830	24	......	23,450	32	23,569	11,560	....	32
....	31,704	....	....	......	5,500	15	5,500	10,402	....	33
19,775	170,606	639	3,115	10	69,286	169	183,542	42,435	....	34
2,584	140,201	5	350	......	36,300	51	40,370	31,329	....	35
8,735	27,583	....	....	......	....	......	....	10,631	....	36
770	37,467	....	....	......	....	......	....	20,686	....	37
8,699	117,065	35	....	......	66,235	87	43,050	16,958	....	38
6,944	58,386	....	300	......	21,300	38	21,438	14,254	....	39
447	86,273	....	....	......	....	......	....	80	....	40
12,110	24,423	....	....	......	....	......	....	16,595	....	41
5,567	58,868	....	....	......	39,700	45	91,580	21,375	....	42
8,484	72,126	....	....	......	27,215	79	61,205	32,362	....	43
12,893	50,528	....	....	......	23,150	19	18,100	14,742	....	44
3,555	20,071	....	....	......	....	......	....	7,988	....	45
6,563	39,119	....	400	......	37,650	29	40,515	38,063	....	46
10,618	29,693	....	25	30	11,386	21	11,880	21,637	....	47
....	12,443	....	....	......	....	......	....	......	Formed since 1840 from	48
4,528	30,523	325	1,945	......	....	......	....	4,637	Bolivar.	49
2,793	111,736	....	....	......	29,500	81	85,497	53,648	....	50
7,504	76,018	....	....	......	20,200	61	67,250	39,703	....	51
950	9,835	....	....	......	....	......	....	1,055	....	52
10,665	55,288	25,778	13,289	......	193,700	184	260,550	2,787	....	53
....	41,634	....	....	......	....	......	....	......	Divided since 1840 to form	54
....	16,950	....	....	......	....	......	....	......	Issaquena.	55
425	41,374	50	50	......	12,300	48	33,600	1,081	....	56
18,249	54,273	....	....	......	14,260	50	32,000	21,698	....	57
3,320	131,337	....	985	8	27,670	93	65,750	49,966	....	58
5,548	87,244	1,510	1,730	......	66,700	86	96,880	6,763	....	59

MISSOURI.

11,879	9,131	....	30	1	7,200	12	7,365	9,120	Formed in 1841.	1
29,893	50,635	942	1,436	......	49,269	98	417,752	27,439	Formed in 1841.	2
5,652	12,930	....	....	......	7,370	7	26,955	3,428	Formed in 1845.	3
....	22,675	....	1,945	......	6,100	16	16,400	12,924	....	4
2,939	13,664	15	1,150	10	1,400	3	1,300	11,447	....	5
16,863	20,937	282	1,184	10	....	......	....	14,080	Formed in 1841.	6
6,522	22,310	....	....	......	11,200	26	18,828	12,259	....	7
11,599	99,147	710	18,585	170	20,235	83	107,950	36,788	....	8
32,300	75,212	2,012	165	......	126,810	256	748,237	38,923	....	9
406	5,458	3	457	......	....	......	....	4,862	Formed in 1849.	10
9,886	17,307	....	....	......	6,600	16	20,850	6,890	....	11

	Counties.	Population.								
		Whites.			Colored.		All classes.		Total population.	
		Male.	Female.	Total.	Free.	Slave.	Male.	Female.	1850.	1840.
12	Callaway	5,148	4,747	9,895	25	3,907	7,057	6,770	13,827	11,765
13	Camden	1,130	1,078	2,208	....	130	1,193	1,145	2,338	....
14	Cape Girardeau	6,212	5,991	12,203	35	1,674	7,059	6,853	13,912	9,359
15	Carroll	2,578	2,234	4,812	8	621	2,894	2,547	5,441	2,423
16	Cass	2,933	2,677	5,610	2	478	3,166	2,924	6,090	4,693
17	Cedar	1,677	1,601	3,278	1	82	1,714	1,647	3,361	....
18	Chariton	2,940	2,745	5,685	51	1,778	3,864	3,650	7,514	4,746
19	Clark	2,677	2,336	5,013	10	504	2,943	2,584	5,527	2,846
20	Clay	4,048	3,537	7,585	5	2,742	5,469	4,863	10,332	8,282
21	Clinton	1,747	1,599	3,346	1	439	1,971	1,815	3,786	2,724
22	Cole	3,050	2,649	5,699	18	979	3,544	3,152	6,696	9,286
23	Cooper	5,065	4,772	9,837	22	3,091	6,539	6,411	12,950	10,484
24	Crawford	3,189	2,923	6,112	....	285	3,333	3,064	6,397	3,561
25	Dade	2,086	1,885	3,971	6	269	2,206	2,040	4,246	....
26	Dallas	1,830	1,722	3,552	8	88	1,877	1,771	3,648	....
27	Daviess	2,706	2,350	5,056	1	241	2,811	2,487	5,298	2,736
28	De Kalb	1,036	974	2,010	....	65	1,071	1,004	2,075	....
29	Dodge	195	178	373	....	2	195	180	375	....
30	Dunklin	600	605	1,205	11	13	611	618	1,229	....
31	Franklin	4,949	4,593	9,542	20	1,459	5,717	5,304	11,021	7,515
32	Gasconade	2,596	2,288	4,884	....	112	2,648	2,348	4,996	5,330
33	Gentry	2,131	2,064	4,195	3	50	2,156	2,092	4,248	....
34	Greene	5,844	5,704	11,548	7	1,230	6,454	6,331	12,785	5,372
35	Grundy	1,485	1,371	2,856	1	149	1,559	1,447	3,006	....
36	Harrison	1,265	1,169	2,434	....	13	1,274	1,173	2,447	....
37	Henry	1,710	1,667	3,377	3	672	2,035	2,017	4,052	4,726
38	Hickory	1,130	1,013	2,143	1	185	1,220	1,109	2,329	....
39	Holt	2,011	1,816	3,827	3	127	2,071	1,886	3,957	....
40	Howard	4,539	4,500	9,039	40	4,890	7,123	6,846	13,969	13,108
41	Jackson	5,797	5,193	10,990	41	2,969	7,280	6,720	14,000	7,612
42	Jasper	2,088	1,921	4,009	1	213	2,184	2,039	4,223	....
43	Jefferson	3,389	3,018	6,407	9	512	3,659	3,269	6,928	4,296
44	Johnson	3,397	3,176	6,573	12	879	3,828	3,636	7,464	4,471
45	Knox	1,371	1,255	2,626	2	266	1,520	1,374	2,894	....
46	Laclede	1,231	1,126	2,357	1	140	1,302	1,196	2,498	....
47	Lafayette	4,732	4,273	9,005	70	4,615	7,172	6,518	13,690	6,815
48	Lawrence	2,323	2,285	4,608	3	248	2,446	2,413	4,859	....
49	Lewis	3,665	2,692	5,357	15	1,206	3,226	3,352	6,578	6,040
50	Lincoln	3,782	3,607	7,389	5	2,027	4,822	4,599	9,421	7,449
51	Linn	1,913	1,766	3,679	2	377	2,092	1,966	4,058	2,245
52	Livingston	2,012	1,921	3,933	6	308	2,151	2,096	4,247	4,325
53	McDonald	1,109	1,023	2,132	21	83	1,151	1,085	2,236	....
54	Macon	3,224	3,038	6,262	....	303	3,359	3,206	6,565	6,034
55	Madison	2,802	2,476	5,278	29	696	3,174	2,829	6,003	3,395
56	Marion	4,866	4,456	9,322	76	2,832	6,251	5,979	12,230	9,623
57	Mercer	1,355	1,316	2,671	6	14	1,367	1,324	2,691	....
58	Miller	1,913	1,732	3,645	....	189	1,996	1,838	3,834	2,282
59	Mississippi	1,278	1,095	2,373	4	746	1,670	1,453	3,123	....
60	Moniteau	2,779	2,655	5,434	4	566	3,060	2,944	6,004	....
61	Monroe	4,377	4,084	8,461	32	2,048	5,403	5,138	10,541	9,505
62	Montgomery	2,261	2,188	4,449	3	1,037	2,764	2,725	5,489	4,371
63	Morgan	2,156	2,036	4,192	5	453	2,368	2,282	4,650	4,407
64	New Madrid	2,217	1,836	4,053	7	1,481	2,991	2,550	5,541	4,554
65	Newton	2,092	1,920	4,012	15	241	2,209	2,059	4,268	3,790
66	Nodaway	1,048	1,000	2,048	....	70	1,081	1,037	2,118	....
67	Oregon	710	682	1,392	22	18	732	700	1,432	....
68	Osage	3,371	3,063	6,434	....	270	3,478	3,226	6,704	....
69	Ozark	1,173	1,106	2,279	....	15	1,179	1,115	2,294	....
70	Perry	3,375	3,020	6,395	26	794	3,781	3,434	7,215	5,760
71	Pettis	2,223	2,038	4,261	5	884	2,642	2,508	5,150	2,930
72	Pike	5,300	4,999	10,299	35	3,275	6,936	6,673	13,609	10,646
73	Platte	7,496	6,500	13,996	51	2,798	8,919	7,926	16,845	8,913
74	Polk	2,928	2,876	5,804	13	369	3,102	3,084	6,186	8,449
75	Pulaski	2,012	1,873	3,885	....	113	2,061	1,937	3,998	6,529
76	Putnam	830	787	1,617	....	19	835	801	1,636	....
77	Ralls	2,454	2,321	4,775	8	1,368	3,146	3,005	6,151	5,670
78	Randolph	3,746	3,516	7,262	21	2,156	4,814	4,625	9,439	7,198
79	Ray	4,606	4,227	8,833	26	1,514	5,364	5,009	10,373	6,553
80	Reynolds	908	916	1,824	....	25	920	929	1,849	....
81	Ripley	1,418	1,313	2,731	13	86	1,464	1,366	2,830	2,856
82	St. Charles	5,073	4,419	9,492	13	1,949	6,084	5,370	11,454	7,911
83	St. Clair	1,626	1,481	3,107	1	448	1,840	1,716	3,556	....
84	St. François	2,167	2,066	4,233	51	680	2,567	2,397	4,964	3,211
85	St. Genevieve	2,483	2,153	4,636	61	616	2,805	2,508	5,313	3,148
86	St. Louis	56,022	41,519	97,541	1,470	5,967	59,769	45,209	104,978	35,979
87	Saline	3,179	2,926	6,105	19	2,719	4,562	4,281	8,843	5,258

NATIVITIES, DWELLINGS, &c.				EDUCATION AND RELIGION.									
Born out of State.				Colleges, academies, and private schools.		Public Schools.							
United States.	Foreign countries.	Dwellings.	Families.	Pupils.	Annual income.	Pupils.	Annual income.	Total educational income.	White scholars during year.	Whites 5 and under 20 years old.	Whites over 20 unable to read & write.	Accommodation of churches—persons.	
4,287	100	1,612	1,612	......	....	1,717	$5,320	$5,320	1,847	4,228	331	9,450	12
1,154	5	360	360	......	....	......	....	....	230	921	266	....	13
3,720	1,357	2,108	2,110	260	$19,800	54	310	20,110	1,794	5,043	1,046	2,950	14
2,390	118	770	770	43	....	321	695	695	751	2,003	484	1,850	15
2,855	29	933	943	180	900	748	1,992	2,892	1,109	2,496	273	3,600	16
1,650	7	561	561	......	....	320	280	280	654	1,442	269	880	17
2,461	202	1,096	1,096	500	....	1,000	936	936	714	2,250	158	3,250	18
3,148	243	805	834	......	....	1,246	1,635	1,635	1,250	2,043	188	1,750	19
3,566	185	1,352	1,352	170	....	780	2,043	2,043	1,848	3,163	169	1,450	20
1,761	11	560	560	......	....	......	....	....	774	1,382	214	....	21
1,884	1,185	984	996	......	....	725	2,542	2,542	756	2,205	116	4,900	22
3,861	635	1,717	1,717	268	3,830	460	2,777	6,607	2,085	4,090	318	2,550	23
2,871	35	994	994	40	....	280	791	791	941	2,723	390	1,400	24
2,381	1	659	670	......	....	223	1,966	1,966	674	1,681	287	501	25
2,102	3	597	603	......	....	375	....	....	520	1,412	572	....	26
2,823	30	784	792	......	....	420	2,310	2,310	812	2,184	414	350	27
1,014	5	338	338	......	....	......	....	....	267	838	204	....	28
236	2	57	61	......	....	40	48	48	34	159	20	....	29
749	10	215	215	......	....	80	86	86	115	514	230	150	30
2,488	2,152	1,925	1,925	75	....	461	1,160	1,160	871	3,583	338	3,750	31
1,052	1,877	950	951	72	1,980	73	219	2,199	632	1,830	236	1,800	32
2,412	24	708	708	......	....	......	....	....	561	1,818	577	....	33
7,408	16	2,046	2,046	182	57	352	334	391	2,274	5,012	524	3,700	34
1,655	15	477	477	......	....	325	761	761	594	1,218	273	....	35
1,443	6	387	415	297	....	81	156	156	373	1,037	333	175	36
1,503	29	561	571	......	....	332	1,400	1,400	661	1,479	90	300	37
1,096	4	364	365	......	....	186	766	766	376	889	157	800	38
1,828	120	614	614	......	....	330	775	775	575	1,637	85	245	39
3,462	150	1,635	1,637	......	....	2,058	2,074	2,074	2,050	3,761	107	7,400	40
5,649	360	1,719	1,719	216	....	1,195	708	708	2,268	4,582	258	3,280	41
2,243	16	664	664	......	....	369	2,371	2,371	602	1,669	501	2,260	42
1,468	737	1,119	1,124	......	....	281	2,510	2,510	935	2,008	405	800	43
3,207	43	1,030	1,039	205	790	1,151	2,115	2,905	1,763	2,838	623	2,600	44
1,481	68	427	429	......	....	124	276	276	597	1,114	153	200	45
1,468	8	385	385	......	....	......	....	....	315	974	454	....	46
4,841	536	1,459	1,459	513	3,500	962	2,247	5,747	2,018	3,513	145	2,500	47
2,775	7	743	748	75	200	600	1,200	1,400	331	1,986	211	3,000	48
2,995	157	905	907	45	225	1,178	3,349	3,574	1,200	2,232	44	3,500	49
3,129	161	1,239	1,239	40	500	1,564	2,064	2,564	1,652	3,038	170	2,450	50
1,714	22	625	625	......	....	100	588	588	411	1,556	260	....	51
2,104	29	658	658	30	400	205	983	1,383	580	1,694	187	950	52
1,306	1	371	371	218	1,828	......	....	1,828	374	839	63	850	53
3,046	11	1,079	1,091	......	....	588	1,491	1,491	1,224	2,675	614	1,290	54
1,896	206	878	878	120	12,000	......	....	12,000	927	2,186	714	850	55
4,751	464	1,595	1,646	277	4,650	1,436	5,291	9,941	2,490	3,821	211	10,750	56
1,559	3	412	412	......	....	100	370	370	232	1,101	273	800	57
1,810	4	592	592	......	....	......	....	....	633	1,543	446	....	58
1,454	40	443	443	......	....	190	....	....	299	959	130	1,040	59
2,059	245	901	901	......	....	780	970	970	698	2,408	602	2,500	60
4,180	42	1,296	1,296	......	....	1,954	5,219	5,219	2,386	3,676	514	15,100	61
1,879	200	754	754	51	459	597	1,656	2,115	981	1,844	185	2,370	62
1,813	285	754	754	......	....	280	300	300	772	1,715	398	1,950	63
1,790	56	752	752	160	....	332	....	....	484	1,596	393	2,900	64
2,452	6	653	653	......	....	278	1,204	1,204	689	1,686	236	619	65
1,174	18	325	333	......	....	......	....	....	295	909	272	100	66
725	....	252	252	......	....	86	292	292	172	563	266	1,100	67
2,181	1,167	1,082	1,082	......	....	208	666	666	547	2,728	666	1,250	68
1,257	1	361	361	......	....	......	....	....	157	1,005	525	....	69
1,406	1,177	1,111	1,111	95	5,800	360	1,618	7,418	1,146	2,600	218	4,600	70
1,850	158	714	714	......	....	700	2,600	2,600	808	1,770	47	950	71
4,476	133	1,671	1,700	110	2,500	2,730	4,490	6,990	2,655	4,211	422	11,800	72
7,432	616	2,490	2,490	200	3,000	1,784	2,500	5,500	2,777	5,657	185	7,820	73
3,398	3	907	907	......	....	864	1,366	1,366	1,221	2,507	719	2,800	74
1,998	4	640	642	......	....	75	50	50	337	1,685	758	....	75
810	2	265	277	......	....	200	252	252	244	713	136	....	76
2,208	38	777	782	......	....	1,428	4,123	4,123	259	2,077	119	3,750	77
3,383	19	1,157	1,157	24	250	607	3,562	3,812	1,481	3,181	192	5,050	78
4,323	102	1,457	1,457	123	1,317	500	6,000	7,317	2,031	3,766	1,034	1,650	79
929	....	293	293	......	....	465	270	270	283	794	412	200	80
1,807	6	445	449	75	92	20	60	152	249	1,159	521	101	81
1,969	2,972	1,633	1,720	261	3,000	788	2,996	5,996	1,723	3,660	284	6,800	82
1,668	25	531	531	80	800	120	2,025	2,825	450	1,361	193	800	83
1,819	135	704	717	......	....	277	469	469	604	1,693	533	1,800	84
1,077	667	814	833	145	4,610	260	1,550	6,160	536	1,854	623	1,450	85
18,648	52,969	13,430	16,959	4,243	129,561	3,607	14,334	143,895	8,593	28,381	1,708	52,093	86
2,853	150	950	955	60	2,500	1,057	4,064	6,564	1,480	2,453	142	3,525	87

	COUNTIES.	LAND OCCUPIED OR IMPROVED.				LIVE STOCK UPON FARMS.			
		Farms.	Acres improved.	Acres unimproved.	Value with improvements and implements.	Horses, asses, and mules.	Neat cattle.	Sheep.	Swine.
12	Callaway	1,169	92,616	220,494	$ 1,655,294	7,951	19,726	27,963	33,018
13	Camden	214	20,305	34,440	265,666	2,962	10,066	9,549	17,804
14	Cape Girardeau	1,019	53,356	119,222	952,430	4,779	10,827	10,300	34,463
15	Carroll	383	22,437	68,299	461,223	1,995	8,186	5,551	18,952
16	Cass	729	34,800	85,898	557,804	3,234	9,895	7,964	14,006
17	Cedar	347	13,176	22,563	178,858	1,443	5,844	5,054	8,911
18	Chariton	659	34,651	94,054	749,834	3,037	6,106	6,952	31,266
19	Clark	425	30,450	78,135	765,940	1,852	5,925	6,878	15,370
20	Clay	944	71,905	142,661	2,034,259	5,648	14,701	17,688	25,532
21	Clinton	334	26,244	85,217	834,808	2,066	7,461	6,424	13,419
22	Cole	638	26,450	70,204	547,469	2,887	6,817	8,557	14,139
23	Cooper	1,064	73,880	153,888	1,521,071	7,646	17,309	21,358	37,770
24	Crawford	715	26,912	39,564	316,667	3,261	10,051	8,368	21,231
25	Dade	567	21,463	36,850	252,094	2,084	7,259	6,104	11,825
26	Dallas	361	16,414	17,589	171,726	1,354	5,069	4,250	5,691
27	Daviess	342	17,919	64,422	346,666	1,771	5,842	5,378	12,120
28	De Kalb	229	8,852	36,042	210,706	974	3,294	3,155	6,613
29	Dodge	49	4,106	22,547	74,665	485	1,384	2,196	7,358
30	Dunklin	76	3,062	3,975	44,455	519	2,883	528	7,801
31	Franklin	1,096	42,674	171,269	1,074,030	4,113	13,799	10,077	31,959
32	Gasconade	533	14,114	37,013	230,423	1,617	5,780	3,892	12,044
33	Gentry	444	14,246	35,354	229,277	968	4,316	4,366	7,525
34	Greene	1,283	61,124	109,613	812,517	6,916	22,160	20,698	38,987
35	Grundy	255	13,639	46,295	200,258	1,135	3,981	5,300	10,413
36	Harrison	141	6,447	16,999	106,560	497	1,780	2,234	5,156
37	Henry	385	24,657	67,739	323,969	1,882	8,750	6,645	10,266
38	Hickory	190	6,827	21,030	111,341	925	3,253	3,086	4,013
39	Holt	305	16,640	65,693	238,554	1,321	7,129	5,187	9,373
40	Howard	1,105	110,880	305,810	3,669,923	8,747	18,441	23,757	42,210
41	Jackson	986	49,619	129,688	1,808,980	5,913	14,670	14,784	28,312
42	Jasper	408	22,612	43,838	325,234	2,333	8,693	5,205	13,272
43	Jefferson	704	24,160	94,924	603,437	2,640	8,701	4,523	18,712
44	Johnson	750	41,000	105,915	805,995	4,832	11,649	13,281	19,806
45	Knox	303	18,845	55,118	381,429	1,349	6,785	4,283	15,387
46	Laclede	233	10,312	12,927	155,098	1,319	4,026	3,561	9,295
47	Lafayette	895	77,504	177,241	2,654,282	5,459	12,331	14,773	27,373
48	Lawrence	410	18,239	33,072	224,079	2,245	6,737	6,250	9,409
49	Lewis	448	37,071	73,483	777,384	2,220	7,445	8,307	18,350
50	Lincoln	849	48,444	142,854	1,011,904	4,890	11,814	15,175	28,254
51	Linn	429	18,851	66,705	275,762	1,929	7,165	5,758	16,411
52	Livingston	457	23,488	63,054	368,449	1,924	6,313	6,111	15,889
53	McDonald	326	9,711	23,234	145,944	883	3,165	1,912	4,208
54	Macon	711	33,329	79,287	397,411	2,789	8,679	9,732	31,773
55	Madison	515	19,955	35,089	399,454	2,197	5,581	4,933	17,703
56	Marion	810	62,145	122,248	1,741,833	4,318	12,793	17,883	32,547
57	Mercer	272	10,141	18,873	132,056	772	3,125	3,528	9,740
58	Miller	369	13,434	26,308	183,641	1,865	6,074	6,202	10,582
59	Mississippi	271	14,817	37,724	256,067	1,457	3,845	666	18,303
60	Moniteau	761	33,866	86,187	492,825	3,390	11,023	12,912	16,787
61	Monroe	926	74,792	159,247	1,236,424	5,116	15,626	19,277	23,290
62	Montgomery	607	28,390	97,869	236,614	2,965	8,357	9,181	15,382
63	Morgan	455	22,622	54,799	319,891	2,854	9,383	9,693	11,751
64	New Madrid	407	28,246	57,977	580,973	2,422	6,581	1,190	22,370
65	Newton	293	14,355	19,460	188,389	1,537	4,682	2,949	7,890
66	Nodaway	241	9,576	35,639	246,528	700	3,056	3,194	6,775
67	Oregon	130	3,905	1,522	43,261	510	1,609	952	4,465
68	Osage	711	23,324	50,232	354,286	3,258	8,817	7,010	16,286
69	Ozark	253	7,191	1,284	82,328	1,093	4,033	1,690	7,340
70	Perry	743	32,896	92,910	520,280	2,887	6,848	5,718	18,851
71	Pettis	500	49,112	91,545	731,930	3,043	8,934	11,710	16,915
72	Pike	989	72,672	139,549	1,483,664	6,448	14,791	21,417	29,369
73	Platte	1,651	94,446	124,752	3,927,507	7,248	20,408	20,234	45,133
74	Polk	543	28,565	59,367	384,662	3,430	9,021	8,099	12,251
75	Pulaski	471	15,500	18,928	226,676	2,305	6,574	5,034	15,030
76	Putnam	202	2,005	8,724	27,794	199	784	1,054	2,925
77	Ralls	541	40,420	83,947	783,885	2,987	8,628	13,275	21,173
78	Randolph	993	62,420	134,212	1,055,201	5,048	11,767	17,087	29,639
79	Ray	833	46,704	127,398	1,156,413	3,955	12,646	12,876	28,482
80	Reynolds	145	4,916	3,440	78,804	888	2,188	2,130	8,139
81	Ripley	258	8,310	2,785	91,336	1,154	3,450	1,496	10,519
82	St. Charles	1,035	56,371	122,558	1,709,316	4,772	14,914	10,425	30,957
83	St. Clair	327	15,791	51,047	202,188	1,633	7,610	4,977	8,015
84	St. Francois	437	19,188	50,779	399,203	2,166	4,915	4,153	14,872
85	St. Genevieve	425	18,428	59,020	311,504	1,692	5,099	1,893	11,521
86	St. Louis	1,294	70,983	120,774	6,143,241	5,200	14,279	6,309	28,839
87	Saline	587	47,033	139,916	1,234,344	4,026	15,504	10,414	25,838

AGRICULTURAL PRODUCTS.												
Wheat, bushels.	Rye & oats, bushels.	Indian corn, bushels.	Irish and sweet potatoes, bushels.	Peas and beans, bushels.	Barley, bushels.	Buckwheat, bushels.	Butter and cheese, pounds.	Hay, tons.	Hops, pounds.	Clover & other grass seeds, bushels.	Flaxseed, bushels.	
50,178	185,208	811,855	25,596	260	......	191	179,484	4,943	15	31	760	12
22,241	45,411	256,054	12,146	44	......	51	75,969	219	......	6	26	13
52,640	65,843	510,730	25,356	642	44	265	123,322	608	10	18	54	14
26,452	34,225	311,675	8,173	86	......	100	83,449	231	......	15	33	15
13,524	65,142	300,976	9,450	318	......	......	62,645	1,610	1	53	59	16
9,067	45,784	147,225	8,446	49	42	16	58,876	202	20	......	140	17
14,592	34,447	377,397	12,671	696	75	139	78,149	730	3	58	37	18
48,936	53,235	320,970	7,042	14	221	1,401	109,011	2,023	8	194	102	19
50,890	114,045	834,830	26,874	2,714	10	49	122,172	2,959	......	48	381	20
22,363	48,703	299,070	7,274	43	......	52	54,686	1,585	......	31	50	21
31,252	43,951	220,173	14,671	55	620	694	78,600	1,314	......	6	32	22
92,666	124,000	997,870	25,351	632	62	171	173,496	3,800	960	437	325	23
26,482	48,842	297,133	15,501	812	23	250	70,643	597	......	10	67	24
11,371	105,588	325,958	13,576	345	......	87	71,206	588	64	30	99	25
8,858	65,866	187,580	8,716	68	......	......	47,013	155	......	16	63	26
19,168	46,096	212,536	4,516	223	30	76	2,652	742	......	31	27	27
11,731	13,547	103,865	3,380	10	18	162	32,168	108	......	......	25	28
1,770	5,742	75,208	1,692	21	......	32	16,638	87	......	1	16	29
215	2,796	77,360	5,586	240	......	......	27,845	......	......	......	......	30
51,960	72,103	521,382	25,014	187	31	1,099	68,103	1,067	......	15	154	31
20,427	26,693	190,913	12,473	......	924	293	58,244	334	2	......	58	32
17,045	23,924	160,523	4,435	......	10	98	57,386	1,191	4	41	57	33
61,306	289,545	1,010,987	44,986	6,467	231	23	316,472	900	10	......	142	34
10,902	28,257	152,770	2,836	75	......	......	19,900	201	......	......	......	35
4,120	16,264	80,980	1,981	39	......	37	17,057	464	......	11	27	36
5,684	53,437	184,650	5,329	......	......	145	3,326	892	......	......	74	37
4,278	28,212	79,212	3,567	101	......	......	27,165	542	......	......	16	38
48,355	11,538	240,327	3,203	12	......	43	46,935	870	......	66	2	39
114,196	99,580	939,048	55,719	7,405	317	204	233,115	5,401	59	309	1,403	40
55,856	124,378	938,309	24,575	323	85	90	141,507	798	......	80	276	41
16,909	63,360	275,116	7,140	59	135	......	56,921	201	......	26	154	42
17,322	35,682	289,116	17,645	351	167	201	42,449	751	315	14	30	43
22,930	89,780	445,895	11,392	29	......	200	103,780	1,247	......	62	27	44
20,906	27,445	216,027	5,815	397	314	1,065	47,704	1,378	......	41	69	45
9,601	18,701	136,829	8,475	204	......	......	31,612	53	......	7	37	46
83,037	94,946	788,675	25,676	121	207	412	155,973	2,358	......	141	597	47
19,488	68,821	293,564	11,188	1,031	......	......	30,463	30	......	......	......	48
68,527	67,264	336,730	7,762	20	45	1,025	95,811	2,224	6	75	35	49
64,552	70,980	567,472	12,874	74	4	162	121,027	1,200	......	......	9	50
15,570	24,457	219,500	7,017	341	......	46	48,827	873	52	9	96	51
32,233	39,989	270,270	6,117	......	......	4	44,571	972	......	61	6	52
7,839	7,870	145,659	3,581	40	......	......	27,180	25	......	......	9	53
19,131	77,961	420,023	14,600	2,222	20	537	102,761	954	8	95	216	54
11,439	39,656	266,690	14,716	1,304	......	5	46,101	540	......	11	185	55
105,841	65,916	668,653	15,288	532	30	1,263	146,423	4,585	127	141	355	56
7,311	26,543	149,555	3,651	104	6	34	34,254	375	......	12	10	57
14,724	34,759	144,994	7,764	43	......	51	43,265	182	......	13	26	58
3,727	5,013	354,700	5,614	99	......	......	23,216	95	......	......	......	59
24,540	68,615	343,914	11,114	126	20	120	63,830	630	......	1	124	60
43,669	131,658	793,145	18,208	144	43	403	136,654	4,298	47	164	583	61
21,170	75,578	344,721	12,084	449	......	735	114,170	1,009	87	20	220	62
11,933	54,432	234,015	9,280	31	......	777	70,543	572	......	8	384	63
195	13,260	586,260	24,098	140	......	......	13,265	......	......	......	......	64
18,416	31,347	196,210	7,807	130	50	9	44,451	66	......	1	16	65
10,208	17,250	167,113	3,001	......	......	27	34,013	64	......	2	19	66
2,257	5,644	69,201	4,652	106	......	5	13,747	16	......	5	9	67
26,229	43,688	301,383	11,486	......	113	665	80,549	558	16	2	1	68
5,090	6,488	115,670	5,944	424	......	......	29,167	......	......	......	36	69
65,395	42,956	349,280	19,235	141	25	16	73,845	230	......	......	18	70
20,000	90,070	519,434	11,483	64	......	72	63,025	1,244	......	46	74	71
106,241	86,231	748,540	19,557	66	......	572	139,005	3,695	20	134	320	72
129,067	129,847	1,844,287	52,806	200	135	419	960,838	3,551	......	51	......	73
14,360	105,045	308,000	12,179	395	......	12	63,103	308	......	......	793	74
11,352	33,098	246,430	8,821	138	......	10	56,744	143	......	......	28	75
680	2,265	40,940	985	20	......	19	10,089	35	......	4	24	76
61,427	49,603	495,435	9,081	10	......	464	80,225	2,291	......	149	200	77
35,483	111,925	668,195	19,906	1,440	20	404	142,443	2,578	81	96	464	78
48,003	138,711	655,020	14,831	3,400	......	177	188,216	1,226	......	45	9	79
2,882	7,704	75,925	4,141	105	20	12	10,900	54	......	......	24	80
2,808	8,685	115,241	5,695	253	......	......	24,889	2	......	......	1	81
122,902	115,054	658,001	31,977	393	1,031	352	155,382	2,369	92	97	52	82
13,208	56,338	126,615	5,387	140	......	392	59,527	638	......	15	96	83
14,741	32,243	226,759	13,679	324	......	10	47,543	1,114	......	25	102	84
30,183	34,667	195,214	12,832	343	330	54	35,578	453	28	44	26	85
98,430	141,342	668,210	80,741	764	1,488	715	205,677	14,169	25	897	58	86
42,146	65,447	539,030	14,620	129	......	10	100,450	2,595	1	42	8	87

	COUNTIES.	AGRICULTURAL PRODUCTS.									
		Flax, pounds.	Hemp, dew and water rotted, tons.	Maple sugar, pounds.	Cane sugar, hhds. of 1,000 pounds.	Molasses, gallons.	Rice, pounds.	Tobacco, pounds.	Ginned cotton, bales of 400 pounds.	Wool, pounds.	Silk cocoons, pounds.
12	Callaway	25,035	45	9,215		456		886,800		56,019	
13	Camden	6,980	3	245				11,800		17,253	
14	Cape Girardeau	1,693		11,027		254		32,055		20,001	
15	Carroll	1,779	300				80	289,869		13,668	30
16	Cass	2,048	1					5,353		18,475	
17	Cedar	4,277						3,080		9,456	
18	Chariton	3,213	170					2,667,908		15,779	
19	Clark	5,903	29	955		26		700		15,839	26
20	Clay,	8,497	1,288	3,900		119		20,050		41,461	4
21	Clinton	6,276	193	930		40		6,850		14,672	5
22	Cole	5,129	11					43,150		14,126	
23	Cooper	9,835	39	300				127,800		42,292	
24	Crawford	3,165	2	2,492		250		44,847		15.212	
25	Dade	22,862	125	100				10,607		12,335	
26	Dallas	12,340		435			560	2,050		8,903	
27	Daviess	2,962	12					1,775		14,015	
28	De Kalb	1,204	13					1,000		9,178	
29	Dodge	1,343		7,880		92		1,388		4,092	
30	Dunklin									917	
31	Franklin	7,249		530		5		656,821		19,514	
32	Gasconade	1,710		60				2,000		5,081	
33	Gentry	5,866	6	50				8,117		11,582	
34	Greene	6,385		300				63,830		39,216	
35	Grundy	435		1,330		88		26,935		11,828	
36	Harrison	2,896		5,510		80		900		5,466	
37	Henry	6,981						30		13,689	
38	Hickory	7,385								6,048	
39	Holt		94					2,100		11,607	
40	Howard	16,948	904	6,230		287		3,188,122		48,590	24
41	Jackson	1,443	361					38,920		30,027	
42	Jasper	5,373		258				6,163		11,775	
43	Jefferson	1,185		1,519		50		800		7,503	
44	Johnson	7,670	65					900		31,589	
45	Knox	4,317	7					200		11,076	
46	Laclede	1,192		60				7,391		6,420	
47	Lafayette	6,807	2,462	50				75,035		32,925	
48	Lawrence							1,040		11,169	
49	Lewis	13,535	20	670				15,350		19,983	
50	Lincoln	1,495	5	5,987		391		695,758		29,434	
51	Linn	5,621	14	55				344,665		14,634	
52	Livingston	70	3	9[illegible]				52,900		13,558	
53	McDonald	125		[illegible]				8,187		4,841	5
54	Macon	33,162	2					845,110		20,976	
55	Madison	7,673	10	9,030		315		2,740		10,102	
56	Marion	18,855	500	4,662		172		86,190		39,088	
57	Mercer	5,069		2,925		100		18,400		8,575	
58	Miller	5,600	3	160				12,900		11.304	
59	Mississippi									1,050	
60	Moniteau	7,621	11	2,965				39,550		21,674	
61	Monroe	23,570	10	5,659		195		629,412		41,102	
62	Montgomery	7,721	8	5,018				353,865		20,696	
63	Morgan	6,099		350				850		18,343	
64	New Madrrd									2,419	
65	Newton	2,650		524				14,690		7,062	
66	Nodaway	1,612	5					2,200		7,487	
67	Oregon	250						5,220		2,019	
68	Osage	1,755	16					99,535		13,244	
69	Ozark	849		595				6,151		4,218	
70	Perry	16		1,905				3,700		11,731	
71	Pettis	2,784	52					1,300		25,516	
72	Pike	10,032	145	4,950				848,830		44,405	
73	Platte	420	4,355	250				66,000		59,786	
74	Polk	3,688		240				1,087		17,173	
75	Pulaski	7,545		535		23		4,780		11,894	
76	Putnam	865		4,261		86		2,750		2,203	
77	Ralls	3,370	66	3,195		47		18,350		29,388	
78	Randolph	17,368	23	4,171		136		2,262,796		38,309	1
79	Ray	6,802	431	7,640		35		516,906		27,277	1
80	Reynolds	1,305		200				1,100		2,793	
81	Ripley	10		833				4,870		3,000	
82	St. Charles	2,518	34	40		15		210,712		21,028	
83	St. Clair	4,031	1	300		5		8,700		9,139	
84	St. François	4,380	4	2,020		145		6,613		8,953	
85	St. Genevieve	2,525		200		204		43,600		4,333	
86	St. Louis	1,690	116	100		20		10,300		13,245	1
87	Saline	160	1,559					287,533		20,583	

AGRICULTURAL PRODUCTS.					MANUFACTURES.				REMARKS.	
					Establishments.					
Beeswax and honey, pounds.	Value of animals slaughtered.	Value of produce of market gardens.	Value of orchard produce.	Wine, gallons.	Capital.	Hands employed.	Annual product.	Produced in families.		
6,623	$71,152	$65	$14,625	15	$20,030	121	$47,221	$39,758	....	12
1,650	26,490	....	2,639	......	....	......	....	18,025	Formed in 1841.	13
3,554	66,509	457	6,120	5	76,900	120	131,775	29,582	....	14
20,821	53,537	34	2,144	......	54,500	49	145,006	21,262	....	15
22,024	34,249	603	1,962	......	22,825	51	51,124	19,450	Formerly Van Buren.	16
10,028	13,523	14	807	9	6,950	14	6,250	19,962	Formed in 1845.	17
27,000	43,638	201	2,111	44	223,850	264	359,922	11,290	....	18
23,018	35,120	122	1,779	......	18,575	42	64,758	13,429	....	19
11,891	94,580	50	19,355	......	63,845	138	126,125	31,947	....	20
9,303	25,985	....	2,333	......	15,030	32	27,900	19,366	....	21
470	28,681	225	5,298	2,020	64,850	203	134,437	10,479	....	22
12,153	80,569	1,225	5,997	10	101,855	273	252,290	19,938	....	23
2,740	32,349	87	1,255	......	58,900	145	112,027	18,346	....	24
16,339	23,402	....	3,583	6	7,661	47	20,350	27,294	Formed in 1841.	25
3,848	13,239	....	474	......	5,300	6	6,294	10,635	Formed in 1841.	26
27,246	17,968	....	676	......	1,800	5	2,800	8,919	....	27
15,335	11,213	....	326		800	3	1,500	8,799	Formed in 1845.	28
14,111	7,059	414	30	......	....	......	....	4,600	Formed in 1849.	29
22,235	4,888	....	30	......	850	3	1,460	3,209	Formed in 1845.	30
1,030	58,050	401	1,060	25	95,050	185	218,569	12,342	....	31
134	12,595	....	788	5,228	12,015	31	40,715	6,764	....	32
24,845	21,546	....	....	......	....	......	....	11,074	Formed in 1845.	33
134,802	85,621	....	6,901	500	48,350	142	83,550	108,797	....	34
22,212	8,665	....	....	......	9,000	16	12,115	7,353	Formed in 1841.	35
16,586	6,200	....	125	......	....	......	....	5,038	Formed in 1845.	36
25,106	18,729	....	1,425	80	10,550	30	29,600	14,195	Formerly Rives.	37
4,959	8,166	....	527	......	5,025	19	10,013	4,959	Formed in 1845.	38
6,873	18,982	....	....	......	9,700	9	27,020	6,825	Formed in 1841.	39
7,379	116,276	270	119,716	329	208,582	310	318,356	100,088	....	40
4,253	84,456	....	2,575	83	107,903	270	270,553	21,869	....	41
18,332	22,690	....	1,816	......	7,000	18	14,000	16,528	Formed in 1841.	42
471	34,384	....	1,189	......	275,300	82	66,807	5,131	....	43
30,765	45,535	25	936	8	20,050	57	57,908	21,369	....	44
12,661	18,495	....	395	......	10,550	16	20,175	6,832	Formed in 1845.	45
2,931	12,886	....	287	......	2,700	5	5,200	8,879	Formed in 1849.	46
19,445	70,450	1,227	10,555	3	83,770	421	387,460	25,429	....	47
5,343	18,145	250	343	......	5,500	16	6,600	19,500	Formed in 1845.	48
13,340	39,700	120	3,515	8	17,745	42	73,054	14,578	....	49
791	56,539	....	1,579	......	12,680	57	42,853	14,775	....	50
36,872	20,419	....	336	......	....	......	....	9,399	....	51
32,513	25,861	....	1,967	......	6,000	5	7,000	13,659	....	52
10,742	14,042	....	1,105	......	59,368	63	154,253	16,561	Formed in 1849.	53
24,726	31,798	189	2,362	3	11,900	26	9,185	17,156	....	54
494	30,286	....	2,760	......	275,050	160	146,600	11,744	....	55
14,830	60,656	12,343	19,400	82	365,070	368	371,253	29,516	....	56
40,533	8,605	57	70	......	2,200	8	3,420	9,958	Formed in 1845.	57
1,160	17,589	....	2,184	......	....	......	....	11,689	....	58
5,160	15,968	....	10	......	....	......	....	1,697	Formed in 1845.	59
2,910	34,308	....	4,503	50	10,575	42	23,546	22,903	Formed in 1845.	60
10,281	50,760	6,393	8,889	5	19,400	50	67,805	33,287	....	61
2,432	27,806	....	2,672	......	11,450	40	22,505	16,236	....	62
9,659	26,851	....	1,975	......	15,875	26	12,055	17,958	....	63
3,471	27,900	....	1,765	......	44,576	90	57,941	......	....	64
3,331	16,485	....	894	......	7,200	27	17,300	10,956	....	65
12,490	10,233	2,335	....	35	4,070	8	13,585	6,741	Formed in 1845.	66
1,722	5,040	....	1,237	......	2,200	10	4,100	4,490	Formed in 1845.	67
332	27,327	....	883	25	9,395	25	25,767	9,890	Formed in 1841.	68
2,748	8,488	90	2,266	......	4,550	14	3,400	7,091	Formed in 1841.	69
5	33,678	45	5,540	......	45,400	131	82,800	12,147	....	70
14,557	31,992	....	2,197	......	13,050	32	36,737	14,623	....	71
10,635	67,975	100	22,718	......	76,170	201	225,411	38,122	....	72
136,213	150,979	221	6,358	......	207,215	249	789,484	54,179	....	73
5,980	30,682	....	1,479	......	7,900	12	14,280	21,852	....	74
2,881	25,139	5	1,563	......	3,800	4	9,753	11,459	....	75
5,539	2,595	....	....	......	....	......	....	2,363	Formed in 1845.	76
3,908	52,224	....	9,384	......	12,560	30	22,623	16,846	....	77
20,907	57,500	5,147	10,046	27	61,050	186	146,760	39,176	....	78
29,376	88,939	120	7,546	25	37,150	92	94,390	30,159	....	79
....	5,493	....	67	......	....	......	....	4,576	Formed in 1845.	80
470	11,499	....	421	......	13,000	19	6,406	16,733	....	81
7,428	94,969	1,110	19,005	482	59,800	155	147,580	8,443	....	82
15,525	13,932	40	65	......	4,800	18	10,500	13,929	Formed in 1841.	83
321	26,471	....	3,589	......	275,550	139	127,150	10,187	....	84
996	20,598	....	1,515	765	43,965	53	34,292	3,714	....	85
5,953	86,234	59,404	92,827	500	5,215,716	10,239	16,046,521	6,898	....	86
12,818	48,152	175	4,879	......	16,075	27	43,000	14,854	....	87

No.	Counties.	Population. Whites. Male.	Whites. Female.	Whites. Total.	Colored. Free.	Colored. Slave.	All classes. Male.	All classes. Female.	Total population. 1850.	Total population. 1840.
88	Schuyler	1,654	1,576	3,230	2	55	1,678	1,609	3,287	....
89	Scotland	1,895	1,736	3,631	....	151	1,974	1,808	3,782	....
90	Scott	1,446	1,327	2,773	16	393	1,675	1,507	3,182	5,974
91	Shannon	630	560	1,190	....	9	635	564	1,199	....
92	Shelby	1,949	1,795	3,744	11	498	2,209	2,044	4,253	3,056
93	Stoddard	2,140	2,081	4,221	6	50	2,163	2,114	4,277	3,153
94	Sullivan	1,478	1,417	2,895	....	88	1,521	1,462	2,983	....
95	Taney	2,210	2,064	4,274	....	99	2,259	2,114	4,373	3,264
96	Texas	1,230	1,040	2,270	....	42	1,253	1,059	2,312	....
97	Warren	2,606	2,315	4,921	4	935	3,093	2,767	5,860	4,253
98	Washington	4,036	3,677	7,713	23	1,075	4,607	4,204	8,811	7,213
99	Wayne	2,113	2,039	4,152	6	360	2,285	2,233	4,518	3,403
100	Wright	1,655	1,650	3,305	....	82	1,693	1,694	3,387	....

STATISTICS OF

No.	Counties.	Whites. Male.	Whites. Female.	Whites. Total.	Colored. Free.	Colored. Slave.	All classes. Male.	All classes. Female.	Total population. 1850.	Total population. 1840.
1	Belknap	8,671	9,021	17,692	29	....	8,686	9,035	17,721	....
2	Carroll	10,140	10,015	20,155	2	....	10,140	10,017	20,157	....
3	Cheshire	15,732	14,384	30,116	28	....	15,744	14,400	30,144	26,429
4	Coos	6,212	5,637	11,849	4	....	6,214	5,639	11,853	9,849
5	Grafton	21,537	20,779	42,316	27	....	21,553	20,790	42,343	42,311
6	Hillsborough	26,643	30,716	57,359	119	....	26,712	30,766	57,478	42,494
7	Merrimac	19,834	20,410	40,244	93	....	19,884	20,453	40,337	36,253
8	Rockingham	24,246	24,821	49,067	127	....	24,301	24,893	49,194	45,771
9	Strafford	13,366	15,958	29,324	50	....	13,386	15,988	29,374	61,127
10	Sullivan	9,579	9,755	19,334	41	....	9,600	9,775	19,375	20,340

STATISTICS OF

No.	Counties.	Whites. Male.	Whites. Female.	Whites. Total.	Colored. Free.	Colored. Slave.	All classes. Male.	All classes. Female.	Total population. 1850.	Total population. 1840.
1	Atlantic	4,587	4,156	8,743	217	1	4,699	4,262	8,961	8,726
2	Bergen	6,656	6,404	13,060	1,624	41	7,518	7,207	14,725	13,223
3	Burlington	20,645	20,449	41,094	2,109	....	21,693	21,510	43,203	32,831
4	Camden	11,500	11,692	23,192	2,230	....	12,580	12,842	25,422	....
5	Cape May	3,089	3,097	6,186	247	....	3,207	3,226	6,433	5,324
6	Cumberland	8,142	7,917	16,059	1,130	....	8,723	8,466	17,189	14,374
7	Essex	35,157	36,459	71,616	2,328	6	36,238	37,712	73,950	44,621
8	Gloucester	7,312	6,723	14,035	620	....	7,629	7,026	14,655	25,438
9	Hudson	10,482	10,837	21,319	500	3	10,723	11,099	21,822	9,483
10	Hunterdon	14,094	14,079	28,173	808	9	14,508	14,482	28,990	24,789
11	Mercer	12,975	12,975	25,950	2,036	6	13,960	14,032	27,992	21,502
12	Middlesex	13,458	13,797	27,255	1,369	11	14,098	14,537	28,635	21,893
13	Moumouth	14,175	13,740	27,915	2,323	75	15,362	14,951	30,313	32,909
14	Morris	14,664	14,467	29,131	1,008	19	15,171	14,987	30,158	25,844
15	Ocean	5,069	4,823	9,892	140	....	5,141	4,891	10,032	....
16	Passaic	10,928	10,995	21,923	615	31	11,226	11,343	22,569	16,734
17	Salem	8,851	8,541	17,392	2,075	....	9,938	9,529	19,467	16,024
18	Somerset	8,971	8,979	17,950	1,711	31	9,864	9,828	19,692	17,455
19	Sussex	11,486	11,162	22,648	340	1	11,660	11,329	22,989	21,770
20	Warren	11,211	10,765	21,976	380	2	11,408	10,950	22,358	20,366

STATISTICS OF

No.	Counties.	Whites. Male.	Whites. Female.	Whites. Total.	Colored. Free.	Colored. Slave.	All classes. Male.	All classes. Female.	Total population. 1850.	Total population. 1840.
1	Albany	45,523	46,562	92,085	1,194	....	46,072	47,207	93,279	68,593
2	Alleghany	19,401	18,279	37,680	128	....	19,471	18,337	37,808	40,975
3	Broome	15,539	14,690	30,229	431	....	15,775	14,905	30,660	22,338
4	Cattaraugus	20,940	17,908	38,848	102	....	20,986	17,964	38,950	28,872
5	Cayuga	28,121	26,794	54,915	543	....	28,409	27,049	55,458	50,338
6	Chautauque	25,821	24,532	50,353	140	....	25,891	24,602	50,493	47,975
7	Chemung	14,604	13,931	28,535	286	....	14,753	14,068	28,821	20,732
8	Chenango	19,960	20,087	40,047	264	....	20,083	20,22[illegible]	40,311	40,785
9	Clinton	20,547	19,388	39,935	112	....	20,614	19,433	40,047	28,157
10	Columbia	20,946	20,815	41,761	1,312	....	21,556	21,517	43,073	43,252
11	Cortlandt	12,680	12,418	25,098	42	....	12,704	12,436	25,140	24,607
12	Delaware	20,293	19,340	39,633	201	....	20,398	19,436	39,834	35,396
13	Dutchess	28,210	28,812	57,022	1,970	....	29,147	29,845	58,992	52,398
14	Erie	51,583	48,585	100,168	825	....	52,005	48,988	100,993	62,465
15	Essex	16,183	14,915	31,098	50	....	16,218	14,930	31,148	23,634

NATIVITIES, DWELLINGS, &c.				EDUCATION AND RELIGION.									
Born out of State.				Colleges, academies, and private schools.		Public Schools.							
United States.	Foreign countries.	Dwellings.	Families.	Pupils.	Annual income.	Pupils.	Annual income.	Total educational income.	White scholars during the year.	Whites 5 and under 20 years old.	Whites over 20 unable to read & write.	Accommodation of churches—persons.	
1,658	81	539	539	......	....	240	$400	$400	504	1,347	318	675	88
2,221	41	588	588	......	....	247	407	407	782	1,523	343	....	89
1,124	262	500	500	225	$2,700	......	....	2,700	356	1,178	251	950	90
538	1	204	204	......	....	......	....	....	68	496	216	....	91
1,908	272	632	654	......	....	1,051	1,786	1,786	1,070	1,590	45	3,200	92
2,026	5	719	734	......	....	......	....	....	415	1,830	843	700	93
1,681	18	457	457	......	....	......	....	....	629	1,239	293	450	94
2,372	3	680	680	......	....	......	....	....	341	1,914	644	....	95
1,155	15	394	395	......	....	20	29	29	206	936	367	500	96
1,290	1,302	899	899	......	....	......	....	....	582	1,938	31	4,100	97
2,320	291	1,291	1,291	......	....	400	860	860	925	3,288	685	5,400	98
2,017	21	699	719	......	....	250	450	450	368	1,745	729	1,650	99
2,064	3	541	541	......	....	......	....	....	470	1,420	565	500	100

NEW HAMPSHIRE.

United States.	Foreign countries.	Dwellings.	Families.	Colleges, &c. Pupils.	Colleges, &c. Annual income.	Public Schools Pupils.	Public Schools Annual income.	Total educational income.	White scholars during the year.	Whites 5 and under 20 years old.	Whites over 20 unable to read & write.	Accommodation of churches—persons.	
880	190	3,436	3,791	290	1,950	4,152	7,063	9,013	5,175	5,627	70	11,840	1
2,255	84	3,724	3,909	260	1,020	5,709	7,808	8,828	6,389	7,035	67	16,900	2
5,695	2,343	5,302	5,968	520	2,697	8,065	17,772	20,469	8,615	9,403	233	23,910	3
2,112	560	2,114	2,222	165	550	3,594	4,613	5,163	4,058	4,377	113	5,650	4
5,507	1,093	7,898	8,175	649	12,287	10,836	21,859	34,146	13,478	14,413	228	33,575	5
10,395	3,913	9,939	10,731	666	4,258	12,583	33,832	38,090	14,514	18,647	549	42,593	6
4,209	1,371	7,400	7,741	1,271	11,640	9,303	16,169	27,809	11,011	12,923	545	31,085	7
5,233	2,454	9,113	10,333	1,037	13,960	10,905	32,303	46,263	12,110	15,518	392	36,955	8
5,440	1,807	4,764	5,400	320	1,920	5,724	15,152	17,072	6,813	9,836	704	16,919	9
3,376	450	3,649	4,017	416	3,920	4,772	10,373	14,293	5,985	6,441	56	17,990	10

NEW JERSEY.

United States.	Foreign countries.	Dwellings.	Families.	Colleges, &c. Pupils.	Colleges, &c. Annual income.	Public Schools Pupils.	Public Schools Annual income.	Total educational income.	White scholars during the year.	Whites 5 and under 20 years old.	Whites over 20 unable to read & write.	Accommodation of churches—persons.	
287	291	1,584	1,608	......	....	665	5,293	5,293	1,773	3,419	967	4,900	1
1,470	1,691	2,606	2,776	......	....	2,730	6,357	6,357	1,879	4,539	247	10,038	2
4,196	3,226	7,356	7,650	1,122	128,006	7,282	39,955	167,961	8,277	14,941	1,434	34,745	3
5,633	2,283	4,690	4,253	336	150	3,779	15,370	15,520	3,568	8,198	324	13,575	4
188	98	1,218	1,226	......	....	1,360	4,312	4,312	1,353	2,304	200	4,600	5
663	297	3,281	3,486	50	....	4,215	11,029	11,029	3,863	5,967	75	11,250	6
9,732	20,263	10,964	13,893	3,600	76,959	7,138	16,365	93,324	13,053	23,800	2,289	49,275	7
1,274	994	2,600	2,690	......	....	3,746	3,324	3,324	3,342	5,238	235	7,750	8
4,723	7,858	2,861	4,047	765	3,580	1,641	10,931	14,511	3,394	6,843	1,422	9,967	9
1,161	915	5,167	5,386	75	76	4,616	8,851	8,927	5,480	10,131	455	27,996	10
3,363	3,265	4,624	4 993	1,333	53,522	3,586	9,792	63,314	4,245	8,819	508	18,600	11
2,415	4,062	4,657	4,945	467	7,200	3,221	10,072	17,272	4,392	9,608	277	19,782	12
1,874	1,885	5,155	5,402	384	16,595	5,819	15,766	32,361	5,781	10,390	1,041	23,760	13
1,533	3,210	5,076	5,545	280	7,050	5,729	10,674	17,724	6,222	10,369	427	19,985	14
248	249	1,758	1,791	......	....	2,289	3,050	3,050	1,746	3,875	705	5,450	15
2,667	5,971	3,369	4,293	960	8,290	1,157	6,145	14,435	3,335	7,793	2,082	13,405	16
1,320	600	3,545	3,620	135	1,000	3,263	9,054	10,054	3,437	6,423	197	17,200	17
921	1,595	3,448	3,576	70	560	4,203	15,459	16,019	3,498	6,253	45	17,330	18
1,682	686	3,851	3,922	110	2,700	7,196	8,574	11,274	5,979	8,764	944	16,625	19
1,470	509	3,854	3,978	627	400	4,295	7,499	7,899	4,658	8,207	374	19,900	20

NEW YORK.

United States.	Foreign countries.	Dwellings.	Families.	Colleges, &c. Pupils.	Colleges, &c. Annual income.	Public Schools Pupils.	Public Schools Annual income.	Total educational income.	White scholars during the year.	Whites 5 and under 20 years old.	Whites over 20 unable to read & write.	Accommodation of churches—persons.	
4,227	27,444	12,747	17,311	1,501	26,155	17,469	50,590	76,745	18,105	31,383	3,053	69,960	1
6,328	2,332	6,968	7,297	384	4,467	6,301	10,349	14,816	11,759	13,924	504	14,025	2
4,489	1,580	5,651	5,840	555	10,493	8,828	11,723	22,216	6,710	10,678	298	22,400	3
6,120	4,639	6,750	6,898	262	110	12,743	13,557	13,667	11,388	13,883	1,877	12,580	4
5,726	5,953	9,259	9,978	606	11,144	14,586	20,395	31,539	13,414	18,614	937	35,855	5
8,899	3,622	9,074	9,328	413	870	18,235	30,920	31,790	14,531	18,568	734	30,420	6
5,570	1,779	5,095	5,206	189	1,722	[illegible],195	12,169	13,891	7,313	10,263	249	13,365	7
6,030	970	7,572	7,775	299	348	19,257	21,219	21,567	11,862	14,012	289	40,460	8
5,305	13,204	6,713	7,051	443	4,890	5,085	19,708	24,598	9,758	15,227	6,436	14,214	9
2,228	3,573	7,029	7,686	379	6,276	8,972	17,321	23,597	8,604	14,227	1,715	27,175	10
3,508	1,049	4,580	4,773	490	4,818	9,213	12,499	17,317	7,708	9,169	60	20,675	11
2,633	3,236	7,105	7,252	742	4,293	12,597	24,867	29,160	11,451	14,219	225	23,050	12
2,290	7,387	9,562	10,959	899	26,420	13,423	43,283	69,703	9,920	19,239	1,986	45,872	13
10,907	37,473	17,104	18,975	2,330	13,328	20,002	45,934	59,262	23,731	34,121	3,867	68,870	14
3,934	2,912	5,321	5,535	512	1,219	8,482	17,606	18,825	6,881	11,389	1,145	15,300	15

	Counties.	Land occupied or improved. Farms.	Acres improved.	Acres unimproved.	Value with improvements and implements.	Live stock upon farms. Horses, asses, and mules.	Neat cattle.	Sheep.	Swine.
88	Schuyler	446	16,121	35,828	$ 217,819	1,118	3,439	4,954	12,399
89	Scotland	384	23,461	57,969	402,315	1,782	5,517	5,869	19,604
90	Scott	208	9,977	33,200	211,891	1,114	2,975	1,119	10,715
91	Shannon	152	3,613	167	39,113	610	1,548	1,369	4,569
92	Shelby	397	22,522	63,414	469,501	1,598	6,045	6,181	17,931
93	Stoddard	418	13,124	8,829	140,166	1,489	3,882	1,078	20,172
94	Sullivan	317	14,108	45,968	274,643	1,196	4,407	4,788	13,876
95	Taney	509	13,544	22,534	224,690	2,309	8,226	5,272	17,407
96	Texas	232	6,991	7,576	98,793	980	3,546	1,933	6,608
97	Warren	744	32,176	85,515	656,450	2,526	8,030	7,565	18,706
98	Washington	713	36,139	86,606	755,502	3,621	9,759	7,607	25,539
99	Wayne	478	16,822	33,457	241,218	1,924	5,386	3,020	17,606
100	Wright	371	10,991	10,982	150,142	1,716	4,723	4,619	11,515

STATISTICS OF

	Counties.	Farms.	Acres improved.	Acres unimproved.	Value with improvements and implements.	Horses, asses, and mules.	Neat cattle.	Sheep.	Swine.
1	Belknap	2,438	143,524	67,408	3,874,710	2,000	18,802	17,516	4,226
2	Carroll	2,805	152,631	142,843	3,675,068	2,701	23,418	16,069	5,856
3	Cheshire	2,805	278,697	94,993	6,013,724	3,765	28,245	49,667	6,064
4	Coos	1,439	90,339	113,224	1,728,531	1,799	14,812	18,877	3,679
5	Grafton	5,063	401,145	263,690	8,313,565	5,832	46,180	107,571	7,465
6	Hillsborough	3,675	317,294	111,482	8,289,752	4,707	35,370	22,706	8,995
7	Merrimac	3,220	288,109	123,429	7,704,892	4,343	34,950	54,475	9,403
8	Rockingham	3,811	236,069	102,986	9,469,777	3,941	27,860	15,856	8,274
9	Strafford	1,844	136,226	48,629	4,448,962	1,996	15,813	10,519	4,664
10	Sullivan	2,129	207,454	72,242	4,041,141	3,168	22,460	71,500	4,861

STATISTICS OF

	Counties.	Farms.	Acres improved.	Acres unimproved.	Value with improvements and implements.	Horses, asses, and mules.	Neat cattle.	Sheep.	Swine.
1	Atlantic	327	15,006	34,585	712,811	686	3,608	1,549	2,169
2	Bergen	1,128	80,494	28,234	6,517,276	2,465	6,968	1,711	4,886
3	Burlington	1,638	132,017	40,670	11,982,767	5,616	21,121	20,981	35,376
4	Camden	731	53,968	77,416	4,804,670	2,301	5,056	2,133	9,107
5	Cape May	285	14,310	37,653	846,821	519	3,563	3,849	1,905
6	Cumberland	884	48,469	71,646	2,878,361	2,219	8,335	5,846	6,627
7	Essex	1,745	76,949	23,407	7,219,566	3,058	11,207	2,344	5,539
8	Gloucester	954	68,810	52,897	4,739,500	2,678	6,043	2,758	11,423
9	Hudson	254	9,223	7,729	3,019,855	524	1,844	179	1,157
10	Hunterdon	2,486	196,342	49,322	11,987,484	7,975	18,401	24,541	24,613
11	Mercer	1,051	95,380	21,587	6,592,071	3,609	8,564	7,457	12,603
12	Middlesex	1,523	115,938	42,106	6,980,288	4,217	10,930	3,970	10,154
13	Monmouth	2,014	145,739	82,440	11,948,828	6,191	15,919	13,696	26,426
14	Morris	1,843	136,543	99,542	8,285,195	4,622	17,569	14,919	11,836
15	Ocean	379	26,466	28,387	1,145,603	933	3,804	3,029	4,745
16	Passaic	610	34,152	62,203	3,302,051	1,181	5,825	1,954	3,173
17	Salem	1,313	105,956	38,942	6,935,870	4,405	11,358	9,316	12,916
18	Somerset	1,550	137,700	27,212	8,187,825	4,765	13,355	14,869	10,181
19	Sussex	1,653	149,582	94,895	8,603,645	4,423	25,549	8,309	30,115
20	Warren	1,537	124,947	64,082	7,972,527	5,657	12,242	17,078	25,419

STATISTICS OF

	Counties.	Farms.	Acres improved.	Acres unimproved.	Value with improvements and implements.	Horses, asses, and mules.	Neat cattle.	Sheep.	Swine.
1	Albany	2,903	228,505	68,877	11,810,634	8,591	22,374	37,558	25,285
2	Alleghany	3,173	191,969	186,320	5,902,047	7,087	37,707	103,219	11,453
3	Broome	2,497	158,392	131,070	5,783,343	4,237	27,048	30,650	8,393
4	Cattaraugus	3,655	206,850	261,859	6,576,326	7,390	51,352	71,638	12,585
5	Cayuga	4,228	298,633	99,863	15,628,092	12,512	41,446	122,446	28,769
6	Chautauque	5,163	310,733	281,581	11,211,385	10,283	72,520	137,453	17,633
7	Chemung	2,170	124,715	108,557	6,604,229	4,869	19,846	22,597	12,051
8	Chenango	4,406	332,909	169,082	9,992,453	8,761	58,098	88,811	16,282
9	Clinton	2,095	133,578	102,504	4,454,289	5,721	14,885	31,725	9,179
10	Columbia	2,511	297,483	62,066	16,176,984	7,911	27,795	103,532	38,278
11	Cortlandt	2,465	165,447	95,312	5,757,028	5,728	36,682	38,660	10,211
12	Delaware	4,747	352,941	291,963	9,023,307	8,231	63,455	65,196	17,302
13	Dutchess	3,208	378,506	96,621	25,840,197	8,877	42,772	96,330	49,757
14	Erie	4,880	270,874	191,832	12,957,048	11,926	47,182	66,318	20,240
15	Essex	1,872	166,951	136,610	3,575,831	4,377	17,640	50,206	5,796

AGRICULTURAL PRODUCTS.												
Wheat, bushels.	Rye & oats, bushels.	Indian corn, bushels.	Irish and sweet potatoes, bushels.	Peas and beans, bushels.	Barley, bushels.	Buckwheat, bushels.	Butter and cheese, pounds.	Hay, tons.	Hops, pounds.	Clover & other grass seeds, bushels.	Flaxseed, bushels.	
7,395	23,083	221,780	5,585	162	60	843	39,178	415	20	18	893	88
14,461	41,870	236,370	4,782	415	20	534	67,770	778	......	3	47	89
3,700	9,435	169,100	8,912	23	35	48	25,590	62	......	......	......	90
2,248	4,677	56,713	2,801	76	......	31	10,746	1	......	......	15	91
22,477	35,917	278,435	10,359	91	600	2,277	69,324	2,335	......	13	149	92
5,972	17,286	151,094	8,126	228	......	....	33,408	63	5	33	15	93
11,482	16,399	176,789	4,014	138	......	281	36,129	1,201	......	54	83	94
11,557	39,006	301,116	13,561	1,089	10	....	81,215	229	......	4	678	95
2,848	5,995	112,042	6,611	81	......	....	32,672	6	......	......	5	96
35,732	53,480	365,496	15,971	186	75	270	66,819	730	2,027	13	262	97
30,299	79,432	334,348	16,932	825	10	73	71,945	1,330	......	64	225	98
10,072	21,682	253,138	12,237	3	......	33	26,793	221	......	2	9	99
8,631	32,770	194,695	11,830	1,017	......	....	67,570	98	......	8	247	100

NEW HAMPSHIRE.

Wheat	Rye & oats	Indian corn	Potatoes	Peas and beans	Barley	Buckwheat	Butter and cheese	Hay	Hops	Clover & grass seeds	Flaxseed	
14,028	47,561	118,007	335,092	5,218	2,638	947	744,932	38,445	20	57	1	1
13,104	60,991	147,715	340,278	8,930	314	860	702,974	34,675	7,380	87	10	2
6,897	144,848	177,301	364,501	5,722	28,071	2,594	1,195,862	67,129	5,105	1,153	2	3
22,197	103,265	40,376	256,928	4,608	4,038	38,721	564,634	30,795	3,182	4,326	36	4
64,359	264,379	228,799	1,006,237	13,388	2,110	10,278	1,852,941	103,001	18,962	1,438	102	5
12,038	164,229	205,634	340,719	7,140	14,377	3,345	1,350,098	76,350	135,562	674	......	6
22,126	145,557	231,610	500,051	8,249	3,925	3,098	1,270,385	82,003	47,342	345	3	7
4,115	82,008	201,359	668,395	7,538	5,398	565	1,025,788	72,185	2	197	......	8
2,732	30,871	100,260	309,998	4,981	3,830	27	609,555	40,233	21,500	29	......	9
24,062	112,789	122,609	182,720	5,082	5,555	4,830	856,450	54,038	18,119	594	35	10

NEW JERSEY.

Wheat	Rye & oats	Indian corn	Potatoes	Peas and beans	Barley	Buckwheat	Butter and cheese	Hay	Hops	Clover & grass seeds	Flaxseed	
7,382	12,024	68,868	21,645	464	......	673	38,942	9,569	342	212	......	1
9,350	134,431	150,709	166,368	264	115	48,724	328,779	16,582	......	146	4	2
152,369	278,318	883,011	412,143	2,048	10	29,744	927,808	41,783	......	697	......	3
66,440	44,277	259,684	373,060	27	......	10,620	320,738	12,946	297	28	......	4
16,334	12,429	84,915	18,548	5	......	61	46,269	9,972	......	4	......	5
78,000	89,272	370,267	137,313	529	......	21,835	179,142	21,795	302	2,309	......	6
34,637	175,418	297,076	159,282	1,134	373	24,611	378,918	29,287	......	650	17	7
59,037	43,702	380,221	508,834	....	......	12,111	269,317	14,152	4	125	......	8
3,663	15,720	37,155	32,885	....	135	3,998	49,893	4,161	81	3	......	9
188,828	813,201	954,788	78,734	1,211	892	103,271	976,379	32,247	137	13,672	9,563	10
124,735	398,758	468,670	96,322	1,334	114	38,593	460,818	20,481	25	2,971	1,728	11
78,022	251,443	438,668	127,024	417	225	52,678	501,698	22,267	......	622	21	12
152,904	241,379	841,072	813,849	498	1,044	35,647	664,787	29,120	365	1,492	......	13
61,326	352,952	524,366	135,518	1,577	1,671	103,262	780,175	39,092	......	1,466	439	14
12,063	30,234	108,447	40,371	31	30	2,889	89,559	6,679	81	......	......	15
8,096	82,955	140,213	79,169	1,609	343	31,309	240,402	11,025	129	131	......	16
173,871	241,345	825,622	248,315	1,633	80	25,299	424,050	27,822	188	53,875	......	17
109,367	579,835	685,673	63,573	1,241	1,309	37,425	565,093	26,631	108	7,767	3,416	18
66,006	380,806	459,254	110,020	125	28	178,188	1,816,940	37,711	69	1,342	94	19
198,760	455,142	781,025	92,278	27	123	117,996	793,259	22,628	5	3,819	1,243	20

NEW YORK.

Wheat	Rye & oats	Indian corn	Potatoes	Peas and beans	Barley	Buckwheat	Butter and cheese	Hay	Hops	Clover & grass seeds	Flaxseed	
18,471	899,641	244,411	408,269	22,230	80,793	212,977	1,028,946	71,804	123	2,061	753	1
183,631	507,566	133,700	258,950	29,552	23,152	39,882	2,286,553	73,212	218	3,300	883	2
60,201	449,343	159,616	190,262	1,810	1,924	63,321	1,239,889	52,637	38,787	438	103	3
104,715	723,238	183,978	350,873	17,303	12,246	23,732	2,905,612	79,526	40	2,431	435	4
468,730	765,136	704,954	281,719	5,691	303953	46,784	1,890,728	72,590	1,442	4,223	1,324	5
185,734	616 512	513,827	319,051	11,311	24,207	10,287	4,978,502	125,947	5,735	2,003	1,333	6
223,340	371,009	166,804	108,067	2,288	28,602	57,222	864,250	40,106	50	1,329	21	7
51,479	719,146	278,113	280,837	4,084	28,668	43,473	4,138,752	124,453	26,674	1,582	461	8
75,415	274,005	129,782	352,167	23,487	6,033	48,097	733,497	36,584	708	641	18	9
17,839	1,498,465	560,079	409,497	2,287	14,653	148,241	1,704,787	74,478	425	328	169	10
45,662	436,290	201,988	186,629	8,518	58,002	31,961	3,060,898	73,871	10,327	2,451	1,978	11
20,295	731,076	119,334	373,317	2,946	3,339	147,541	3,869,623	120,964	5,538	36,035	195	12
69,760	1,387,219	782,605	385,951	1,774	6,863	89,107	1,865,170	97,832	289	1,251	342	13
242,221	777,149	443,160	375,249	18,537	70,820	36,885	5,838,150	90,984	894	5,456	259	14
66,510	208,417	120,425	307,549	14,602	505	14,372	541,160	37,868	......	297	2	15

	COUNTIES.	AGRICULTURAL PRODUCTS.									
		Flax, pounds.	Hemp, dew and water-rotted, tons.	Maple sugar, pounds.	Cane sugar, hhds. of 1,000 pounds.	Molasses, gallons.	Rice, pounds.	Tobacco, pounds.	Ginned cotton, bales of 400 pounds.	Wool, pounds.	Silk cocoons, pounds.
88	Schuyler	5,903	4	2,775		38		28,900		12,584	15
89	Scotland	2,047	12	10				7,400		14,669	
90	Scott							7,000		2,177	
91	Shannon	891		1,045		41		2,303		2,937	
92	Shelby	7,528	25					36,790		14,446	
93	Stoddard	661	5	868		94		11,118		2,961	
94	Sullivan	4,925		1,049		30		33,675		11,420	
95	Taney	4,560		4,715		78		16,100		10,657	18
96	Texas	1,670						3,490		3,495	
97	Warren	3,221	14	1,390		24		431,000		17,090	
98	Washington	5,761		3,071		310		100		13,244	3
99	Wayne	2,114		5,193				1,700		6,199	
100	Wright	8,441						10,400		8,510	

STATISTICS OF

	COUNTIES.	Flax, pounds.	Hemp, dew and water-rotted, tons.	Maple sugar, pounds.	Cane sugar, hhds. of 1,000 pounds.	Molasses, gallons.	Rice, pounds.	Tobacco, pounds.	Ginned cotton, bales of 400 pounds.	Wool, pounds.	Silk cocoons, pounds.
1	Belknap	221		30,448						53,681	
2	Carroll	985		98,017		55				45,140	130
3	Cheshire	238		226,153		3,896				152,190	
4	Coos	893		157,057		300				48,143	1
5	Grafton	3,229		397,754		2,421		50		280,859	60
6	Hillsborough	94		21,694		29				67,331	
7	Merrimac	286		40,657		807				156,221	
8	Rockingham	77		1,857		167				44,475	
9	Strafford	319		4,820		154				28,739	
10	Sullivan	1,310		320,406		1,982				231,697	

STATISTICS OF

	COUNTIES.	Flax, pounds.	Hemp, dew and water-rotted, tons.	Maple sugar, pounds.	Cane sugar, hhds. of 1,000 pounds.	Molasses, gallons.	Rice, pounds.	Tobacco, pounds.	Ginned cotton, bales of 400 pounds.	Wool, pounds.	Silk cocoons, pounds.
1	Atlantic							20		3,518	
2	Bergen	65		232				290		3,418	
3	Burlington									43,781	
4	Camden					30				2,777	
5	Cape May									10,149	
6	Cumberland					25				13,8[illegible]0	
7	Essex	350								6,466	
8	Gloucester									3,079	
9	Hudson									132	
10	Hunterdon	122,153				580				60,489	
11	Mercer	28,702								17,793	17
12	Middlesex	935				310				5,587	
13	Monmouth									31,543	
14	Morris	3,483		5						41,213	2
15	Ocean									6,385	
16	Passaic	310		280						5,320	
17	Salem									18,822	
18	Somerset	19,916		5						27,466	
19	Sussex	1,566		1,360		9				24,874	4
20	Warren	5,485		315						48,754	

STATISTICS OF

	COUNTIES.	Flax, pounds.	Hemp, dew and water-rotted, tons.	Maple sugar, pounds.	Cane sugar, hhds. of 1,000 pounds.	Molasses, gallons.	Rice, pounds.	Tobacco, pounds.	Ginned cotton, bales of 400 pounds.	Wool, pounds.	Silk cocoons, pounds.
1	Albany	7,203		13,032		490				99,295	54
2	Alleghany	7,861		585,550		3,458				270,212	
3	Broome	3,109		113,026		330		20		77,296	
4	Cattaraugus	9,839		788,631		991				176,796	
5	Cayuga	10,761		109,048		410				367,085	
6	Chautauque	15,177		787,408		581				369,997	511
7	Chemung	1,042		34,123		682				70,953	
8	Chenango	12,606		547,382		1,106				266,026	200
9	Clinton	615		147,643		830				144,190	
10	Columbia	2,950		840		32				278,772	12
11	Cortlandt	42,916		521,053		2,946				119,060	22
12	Delaware	1,508	1	469,517		663				165,221	
13	Dutchess	7,182		1,799		20		65		277,404	5
14	Erie	6,553		307,001		1,697				184,489	
15	Essex	285		60,554		6				150,258	

	AGRICULTURAL PRODUCTS.				MANUFACTURES.					
					Establishments.					
Beeswax and honey, pounds.	Value of animals slaughtered.	Value of produce of market gardens.	Value of orchard produce.	Wine, gallons.	Capital.	Hands employed.	Annual product.	Produced in families.	REMARKS.	
19,973	$19,434	....	$273	......	$2,625	10	$4,025	$9,459	Formed in 1845.	88
14,001	24,242	....	278	......	6,700	25	17,750	8,474	Formed in 1841.	89
....	8,555	....	45	......	6,600	44	16,050	2,930	....	90
1,098	6,387	$5	464	......	....	....	....	4,234	Formed in 1841.	91
12,576	20,779	....	1,241	......	6,850	44	28,754	13,670	....	92
12,756	18,637	1,694	2,070	......	1,500	8	4,500	11,285	....	93
21,248	20,915	....	61	......	1,490	10	2,500	16,399	Formed in 1845.	94
7,085	21,919	....	7,044	......	10,300	19	13,500	20,880	....	95
195	5,509	....	475	......	64,000	176	72,100	8,403	Formed in 1845..........	96
613	47,302	10	2,419	......	15,725	79	38,100	11,311	....	97
84	43,063	187	3,748	......	116,700	110	211,550	19,986	....	98
1,097	14,001	30	985	......	900	2	1,300	14,103	....	99
17,742	15,223	....	903	......	5,000	6	2,500	15,605	Formed in 1841.	100

NEW HAMPSHIRE.

Beeswax and honey, pounds.	Value of animals slaughtered.	Value of produce of market gardens.	Value of orchard produce.	Wine, gallons.	Capital.	Hands employed.	Annual product.	Produced in families.	REMARKS.	
6,405	96,752	8,003	10,446	......	330,525	656	630,297	17,650	Formed in '40 fr. Strafford.	1
5,313	123,436	117	20,008	60	162,000	395	481,675	34,775	Formed in 1840 from Straf-	2
13,820	180,807	4,178	28,310	......	896,195	1,991	1,933,018	56,630	ford.	3
5,740	64,910	....	6,732	5	146,480	127	113,823	36,772	....	4
38,952	271,285	16,987	47,053	20	726,920	1,291	1,429,891	139,305	....	5
15,262	196,327	9,975	29,277	63	7,483,335	8,986	7,506,877	5,356	....	6
9,969	180,172	7,373	31,098	6	1,257,261	2,276	1,944,542	30,012	....	7
10,735	194,717	6,666	43,448	187	2,228,443	4,528	3,883,268	36,330	....	8
2,917	102,532	3,306	18,637	3	4,461,755	5,872	4,455,799	9,157	Divided in 1840 to form	9
8,027	111,935	205	13,554	......	549,200	970	785,313	27,468	Belknap and Carroll.	10

NEW JERSEY.

Beeswax and honey, pounds.	Value of animals slaughtered.	Value of produce of market gardens.	Value of orchard produce.	Wine, gallons.	Capital.	Hands employed.	Annual product.	Produced in families.	REMARKS.	
1,677	22,307	5,523	2,657	......	287,395	424	346,765	9,411	....	1
6,648	84,081	88,691	46,528	83	402,880	493	1,012,165	213	....	2
3,050	394,380	51,639	53,433	255	1,329,867	2,050	2,091,256	433	....	3
2,554	72,382	42,301	20,805	......	1,533,216	1,497	1,514,055	216	Formed in 1844 from Glou	4
....	20,580	70	2,188	......	1,200	4	2,400	1,425	cester.	5
8,497	78,301	7,919	11,252	2	616,895	965	916,732	3,172	....	6
4,556	118,481	31,932	34,819	234	6,076,092	16,706	16,293,198	864	....	7
....	112,324	44,329	22,995	782	518,100	588	605,877	624	Divided in 1844 to form	8
1,135	16,830	91,619	4,367	60	1,082,300	1,254	2,305,696	....	Camden.	9
14,171	220,714	540	27,476	......	413,215	517	753,605	5,428	....	10
7,595	132,062	6,765	61,968	77	1,133,445	1,296	1,786,081	471	....	11
9,343	124,439	14,054	88,518	......	1,139,450	1,593	2,162,980	763	....	12
9,572	280,947	56,139	93,853	38	478,620	961	775,867	17,375	Divided in 1850 to form	13
16,005	183,900	12,753	25,101	24	1,151,137	1,133	1,210,680	16,302	Ocean.	14
770	21,572	....	1,811	......	288,350	332	188,677	1,860	Formed in 1850 from Mon-	15
9,125	47,576	14,807	9,648	161	2,993,850	4,583	4,213,699	1,116	mouth.	16
3,583	190,357	5,245	37,730	......	346,790	456	637,742	427	....	17
19,999	138,583	365	47,571	70	426,113	631	641,727	29,860	....	18
21,035	229,011	141	3,307	......	787,320	580	603,519	9,647	....	19
17,379	149,725	410	11,241	25	1,178,495	1,248	1,650,865	13,174	....	20

NEW YORK.

Beeswax and honey, pounds.	Value of animals slaughtered.	Value of produce of market gardens.	Value of orchard produce.	Wine, gallons.	Capital.	Hands employed.	Annual product.	Produced in families.	REMARKS.	
35,851	239,076	59,084	35,824	118	4,000,748	5,650	7,177,107	22,112	....	1
41,048	154,113	11,792	44,436	1,037	664,350	844	894,838	64,9[illegible]4	Divided in 1846, and por-	2
14,756	123,146	100	5,557	......	427,355	605	887,778	17,947	tions annexed to Living-	3
50,3[illegible]2	158,089	10,986	23,747	6	362,290	655	775,180	48,455	ston and Wyoming.	4
34,678	350,676	4,454	60,937	......	1,845,527	2,969	3,227,470	23,117	....	5
36,170	275,298	1,500	26,616	190	726,850	1,209	1,335,100	45,962	....	6
31,746	126,253	2,337	6,365	......	609,211	1,331	1,451,612	11,120	....	7
29,666	210,117	195	19,081	......	682,245	1,326	1,143,110	30,798	....	8
28,458	127,902	36,731	6,355	64	1,899,685	2,701	3,132,833	36,978	....	9
39,420	235,496	9,177	15,970	411	1,474,077	1,837	2,144,243	17,054	....	10
24,360	150,562	508	21,168	20	286,905	521	562,414	21,173	....	11
62,469	199,248	1,884	24,613	......	617,395	900	1,077,329	46,671	....	12
48,572	482,029	6,339	15,886	47	2,305,330	4,193	4,477,110	8,183	....	13
35,886	276,063	18,950	45,234	121	3,095,983	5,372	6,295,741	44,776	....	14
20,039	106,422	2,937	21,586	......	1,200,325	1,300	1,355,542	5,396	....	15

	COUNTIES.	POPULATION.								
		Whites.			Colored.		All classes.		Total population.	
		Male.	Female.	Total.	Free.	Slave.	Male.	Female.	1850.	1840.
16	Franklin	13,193	11,847	25,040	62	....	13,226	11,876	25,102	16,518
17	Fulton	10,081	9,988	20,069	102	....	10,124	10,047	20,171	18,049
18	Genesee	14,399	14,012	28,411	77	....	14,436	14,052	28.488	59,587
19	Greene	16,487	15,744	32,231	895	....	16,928	16,198	33,126	30,446
20	Hamilton	1,208	978	2,186	2	....	1,208	980	2,188	1,907
21	Herkimer	19,544	18,497	38,041	203	....	19,649	18,595	38,244	37,477
22	Jefferson	34,742	33,220	67,962	191	....	34,836	33,317	68,153	60,984
23	Kings	65,406	69,411	134,817	4,065	....	67,364	71,518	138,882	47,613
24	Lewis	12,540	11,982	24,522	42	....	12,564	12,000	24,564	17,830
25	Livingston	20,892	19,774	40,666	209	....	21,003	19,872	40,875	35,140
26	Madison	21,564	21,210	42,774	298	....	21,706	21,366	43,072	40,008
27	Monroe	44,427	42,524	86,951	699	....	44,764	42,886	87,650	64,902
28	Montgomery	16,275	15,243	31,518	474	....	16,521	15,471	31,992	35,818
29	New York	248,008	253,724	501,732	13,815	....	254,106	261,441	515,547	312,710
30	Niagara	21,586	20,373	41,959	317	....	21,757	20,519	42,276	31,132
31	Oneida	50,083	48,811	98,894	672	....	50,422	49,144	99,566	85,310
32	Onondaga	44,610	40,667	85,277	613	....	44,915	40,975	85,890	67,911
33	Ontario	22,054	21,265	43,319	610	....	22,340	21,589	43,929	43,501
34	Orange	27,374	27,307	54,681	2,464	....	28,606	28,539	57,145	50,739
35	Orleans	14,623	13,770	28,393	108	....	14,671	13,830	28,501	25,127
36	Oswego	32,153	29,830	61,983	215	....	32,260	29,938	62,198	43,619
37	Otsego	24,065	24,398	48,463	175	....	24,144	24,494	48,638	49,638
38	Putnam	7,089	6,911	14,000	138	....	7,163	6,975	14,138	12,825
39	Queens	16,810	16,572	33,382	3,451	....	18,507	18,326	36,833	30,324
40	Rensselaer	35,782	36,562	72,344	1,019	....	36,261	37,102	73,363	60,259
41	Richmond	7,325	7,146	14,471	590	....	7,634	7,427	15,061	10,965
42	Rockland	8,700	7,666	16,366	596	....	8,992	7,970	16,962	11,975
43	St. Lawrence	34,996	33,582	68,578	39	....	35,015	33,602	68,617	56,706
44	Saratoga	22,527	22,501	45,028	618	....	22,809	22,837	45,646	40,553
45	Schenectady	10,168	9,498	19,666	388	....	10,342	9,712	20,054	17,387
46	Schoharie	16,694	16,376	33,070	478	....	16,946	16,602	33,548	32,358
47	Seneca	12,793	12,467	25,260	181	....	12,879	12,562	25,441	24,874
48	Steuben	33,090	30,310	63,400	371	....	33,268	30,503	63,771	46,138
49	Suffolk	17,396	17,409	34,805	2,117	....	18,457	18,465	36,922	32,469
50	Sullivan	13,281	11,707	24,988	100	....	13,337	11,751	25,088	15,629
51	Tioga	12,742	11,941	24,683	197	....	12,846	12,034	24,880	20,527
52	Tompkins	19,344	19,077	38,421	325	....	19,520	19,226	38,746	37,948
53	Ulster	30,090	27,709	57,799	1,585	....	30,827	28,557	59,384	45,822
54	Warren	8,863	8,290	17,153	46	....	8,879	8,320	17,199	13,422
55	Washington	22,638	21,762	44,400	350	....	22,808	21,942	44,750	41,080
56	Wayne	22,863	21,822	44,685	268	....	22,983	21,970	44,953	42,057
57	Westchester	29,014	27,174	56,188	2,075	....	30,115	28,148	58,263	48,686
58	Wyoming	16,196	15,721	31,917	64	....	16,233	15,748	31,981	....
59	Yates	10,423	10,002	20,425	165	....	10,508	10,082	20,590	20,444

STATISTICS OF

1	Alamance	3,805	4,116	7,921	327	3,196	5,567	5,877	11,444	....
2	Alexander	2,274	2,379	4,653	24	543	3,60[illegible]	3,596	5,22[illegible]	....
3	Anson	3,298	3,256	6,554	103	6,832	5,627	5,882	13,489	15,077
4	Ashe	4,102	3,994	8,096	86	595	4,441	4,336	8,777	7,467
5	Beaufort	3,764	3,900	7,664	903	5,249	6,932	6,884	13,816	12,225
6	Bertie	2,558	2,777	5,335	322	7,194	6,288	6,563	12,851	12,175
7	Bladen	2,534	2,515	5,049	360	4,358	4,916	4,851	9,767	8,022
8	Brunswick	1,816	1,835	3,651	319	3,302	3,839	3,433	7,272	5,265
9	Buncombe	5,914	5,687	11,601	107	1,717	6,818	6,607	13,425	10,084
10	Burke	2,669	2,808	5,477	163	2,132	3,859	3,913	7,772	15,799
11	Cabarras	3,500	3,442	6,942	120	2,685	4,932	4,815	9,747	9,259
12	Caldwell	2,455	2,550	5,005	109	1,203	3,068	3,249	6,317	....
13	Camden	1,775	1,790	3,565	297	2,187	3,089	2,960	6,049	5,663
14	Carteret	2,546	2,620	5,166	150	1,623	3,377	3,562	6,939	6,591
15	Caswell	3,421	3,655	7,076	423	7,770	7,566	7,703	15,269	14,693
16	Catawba	3,585	3,690	7,275	18	1,569	4,348	4,514	8,862	....
17	Chatham	5,987	6,174	12,161	303	5,985	9,117	9,332	18,449	16,242
18	Cherokee	3,340	3,153	6,493	8	337	3,502	3,336	6,838	3,427
19	Chowan	1,377	1,562	2,939	109	3,673	3,305	3,416	6,721	6,690
20	Cleveland	4,326	4,265	8,591	58	1,747	5,216	5,180	10,396	....
21	Columbus	2,138	2,117	4,255	151	1,503	2,949	2,960	5,909	3,941
22	Craven	3,579	3,641	7,220	1,538	5,951	7,087	7,622	14,709	13,438
23	Cumberland	6,134	6,313	12,447	946	7,217	10,222	10,388	20,610	15,284
24	Currituck	2,231	2,368	4,599	190	2,447	3,578	3,658	7,236	6,703
25	Davidson	5,978	6,159	12,137	191	2,992	7,585	7,735	15,320	14,606
26	Davie	2,804	2,808	5,612	83	2,171	3,892	3,974	7,866	7,574

Nativities, dwellings, &c. — Born out of State: United States.	Born out of State: Foreign countries.	Dwellings.	Families.	Education and religion. — Colleges, academies, and private schools: Pupils.	Colleges, academies, and private schools: Annual income.	Public Schools: Pupils.	Public Schools: Annual income.	Total educational income.	White scholars during year.	Whites 5 and under 20 years old.	Whites over 20 unable to read & write.	Accommodation of churches—persons.	
4,426	7,965	4,233	4,313	173	$649	6,585	$8,027	$8,676	5,371	9,506	2,329	8,050	16
978	1,421	3,730	3,794	194	1,316	5,814	3,818	5,134	4,942	7,054	1,023	11,550	17
4,793	2,874	5,014	5,363	741	3,191	8,760	24,147	27,338	8,422	9,800	250	23,950	18
1,061	2,049	5,745	5,989	325	1,500	8,216	15,709	17,209	8,011	11,606	651	25,956	19
202	184	407	418	......	....	493	754	754	490	811	128	590	20
2,452	3,614	6,664	6,976	335	2,554	9,635	17,513	20,067	9,864	13,163	1,346	26,125	21
6,882	4,556	11,926	12,235	574	1,285	21,584	32,485	33,770	18,575	24,930	1,560	43,342	22
15,073	56,201	15,809	25,049	4,551	88,727	11,636	92,997	181,724	21,807	42,722	8,456	59,255	23
1,849	4,358	4,624	4,688	140	100	6,416	8,680	8,780	5,944	8,947	473	16,850	24
5,805	5,128	7,172	7,353	556	7,263	11,841	23,173	30,436	10,450	14,407	846	30,040	25
5,706	2,801	8,198	8,438	1,037	13,958	11,827	18,330	32,288	11,303	14,535	1,081	35,235	26
9,340	26,077	15,027	15,954	1,803	7,446	21,790	36,386	43,832	18,925	29,749	1,792	50,128	27
839	3,116	5,358	5,711	292	1,912	7,250	19,218	21,130	7,437	11,283	494	29,560	28
42,867	240,989	37,677	93,608	11,164	385,353	45,509	225,595	610,948	75,267	147,220	17,140	219,098	29
4,971	9,000	7,435	7,562	123	396	11,961	20,412	20,808	10,696	15,487	1,418	21,650	30
8,929	22,711	16,751	17,587	2,015	26,681	23,318	32,251	58,932	23,842	34,185	2,626	64,642	31
7,540	16,829	15,335	15,879	1,483	12,453	20,847	57,389	69,842	19,769	29,347	3,188	45,650	32
5,517	4,888	7,868	8,039	950	15,656	12,482	21,765	37,421	11,855	14,981	778	42,778	33
1,796	7,715	9,686	10,372	1,315	8,449	9,370	16,409	24,858	9,190	19,138	532	39,890	34
4,164	2,349	5,273	5,319	517	11,619	7,817	17,763	29,382	8,002	10,429	191	16,750	35
6,615	9,276	11,064	11,352	1,078	6,428	14,710	23,164	29,592	17,309	22,482	2,040	27,795	36
5,076	1,807	9,087	9,526	406	4,653	14,515	21,502	26,155	13,673	16,692	731	43,365	37
408	1,507	2,425	2,762	180	1,400	3,017	7,960	9,360	3,288	4,765	836	9,100	38
883	6,261	6,230	6,809	383	4,068	5,064	17,250	21,318	4,966	11,051	1,059	22,425	39
5,334	14,498	10,972	13,565	2,428	26,360	13,267	32,806	59,166	15,183	24,132	2,597	28,200	40
1,438	3,063	2,334	2,481	510	23,825	1,401	6,267	30,092	2,229	4,953	241	12,500	41
1,260	3,569	3,011	3,297	207	1,000	2,745	8,405	9,405	2,143	5,302	917	10,900	42
11,358	13,713	11,704	11,914	972	5,842	23,050	25,016	30,858	19,233	26,123	1,975	45,270	43
3,319	4,914	7,894	8,501	1,013	11,744	10,060	23,758	35,502	10,689	15,258	971	44,350	44
393	2,985	3,195	3,421	490	23,081	3,609	8,992	32,073	4,109	6,769	34	16,300	45
705	963	5,878	5,986	......	....	8,370	12,268	12,268	8,312	12,241	516	34,500	46
3,801	2,109	4,541	4,728	420	2,308	6,728	18,324	20,632	6,645	9,081	179	20,470	47
7,342	4,822	11,210	11,426	400	1,598	18,232	31,642	33,240	18,558	23,554	1,751	32,800	48
1,394	2,095	6,745	7,414	570	2,441	8,115	19,042	21,483	9,010	12,168	417	30,385	49
1,467	4,263	4,355	4,491	160	1,001	6,266	13,590	14,591	5,539	8,892	255	12,920	50
2,891	973	4,442	4,529	248	4,431	8,647	12,796	17,227	6,886	9,198	730	14,460	51
4,228	1,427	7,103	7,251	460	5,197	13,103	23,378	28,575	10,825	13,540	257	35,856	52
1,089	8,431	9,735	10,781	409	726	8,389	21,448	22,174	11,452	19,833	2,117	37,288	53
2,230	1,356	2,976	3,190	384	2,437	5,178	6,534	8,971	4,547	6,150	156	8,450	54
5,338	6,004	8,043	8,317	700	7,614	12,733	22,605	30,219	10,736	14,901	813	37,210	55
4,361	4,063	8,074	8,291	467	2,912	13,801	23,315	26,227	13,599	16,072	834	28,960	56
14,469	11,225	8,754	10,377	1,378	110,061	9,055	27,615	137,676	10,015	18,336	1,465	36,005	57
6,211	3,822	5,918	6,013	396	2,402	11,027	11,379	13,781	9,787	11,527	532	39,670	58
2,124	831	3,784	3,936	50	....	6,600	8,640	8,640	5,844	7,171	193	20,690	59

NORTH CAROLINA.

76	6	1,516	1,516	44	1,750	2,275	2,272	4,022	1,653	2,948	253	6,900	1
36	8	827	827	45	400	900	828	1,228	1,246	1,890	398	4,000	2
195	29	1,166	1,166	40	....	882	2,000	2,000	1,459	2,621	450	10,200	3
494	23	1,407	1,407	......	....	1,205	1,548	1,548	1,476	3,330	617	7,900	4
167	77	1,663	1,673	250	....	1,572	2,303	2,303	1,267	2,814	1,355	5,100	5
54	7	1,070	1,070	110	....	1,280	2,731	2,731	728	1,940	1,038	6,400	6
32	32	1,005	1,007	......	....	691	2,377	2,377	676	1,913	584	7,325	7
145	13	771	771	58	1,050	469	1,772	2,822	404	1,351	374	4,205	8
1,196	165	1,942	1,942	125	2,750	4,682	1,716	4,466	2,856	4,850	1,705	10,690	9
160	8	983	984	65	1,300	960	966	2,266	933	2,138	1,110	5,400	10
122	30	1,296	1,296	58	1,160	2,619	1,939	3,099	1,714	2,648	835	9,750	11
180	6	926	927	89	817	680	782	1,599	774	1,950	1,093	13,200	12
102	12	770	770	......	....	1,350	1,378	1,378	639	1,356	893	6,900	13
19	6	972	972	95	1,150	1,035	1,368	2,518	1,045	2,001	742	3,725	14
1,138	12	815	817	242	5,939	616	2,632	8,571	1,087	2,669	993	7,120	15
122	7	1,237	1,237	......	....	1,680	2,864	2,864	1,545	2,854	362	2,600	16
104	13	2,210	2,211	169	3,482	1,750	2,443	5,925	2,403	4,795	718	25,275	17
1,004	5	1,020	1,020	80	....	1,050	531	531	1,147	2,766	448	450	18
78	20	613	613	85	2,500	1,040	1,117	3,617	426	1,130	417	3,325	19
537	10	1,526	1,526	20	200	2,500	1,399	1,599	1,117	3,518	1,243	5,875	20
176	5	777	782	......	....	462	746	746	779	1,658	645	5,400	21
124	89	1,842	1,842	147	6,500	758	2,834	9,334	1,090	2,531	1,385	8,820	22
357	369	2,531	2,545	316	4,440	1,471	3,982	8,422	1,809	4,514	1,560	14,850	23
135	3	925	926	......	....	305	1,471	1,471	414	1,752	933	7,900	24
151	27	2,308	2,338	77	1,815	2,963	2,695	4,510	2,859	4,741	1,420	14,750	25
225	1	1,027	1,027	60	....	700	1,508	1,508	1,100	2,218	858	8,550	26

	COUNTIES.	LAND OCCUPIED OR IMPROVED.				LIVE STOCK UPON FARMS.			
		Farms.	Acres improved.	Acres unimproved.	Value with improvements and implements.	Horses asses, and mules.	Nea cattle.	Sheep.	Swine.
16	Franklin	1,647	103,203	64,146	$2,458,490	3,654	17,795	27,436	5,222
17	Fulton	1,361	117,413	47,122	3,664,384	3,724	14,343	13,484	8,239
18	Genesee	2,574	203,871	69,708	10,938,862	9,690	21,922	116,829	18,710
19	Greene	2,672	207,523	106,895	8,287,622	5,850	25,938	22,280	16,515
20	Hamilton	261	13,845	23,687	235,391	289	2,037	1,647	316
21	Herkimer	2,723	245,648	94,534	10,905,914	7,650	48,031	15,794	15,073
22	Jefferson	5,490	418,540	179,799	14,666,116	15,407	77,992	60,330	27,873
23	Kings	363	17,419	3,443	4,221,160	3,161	3,506	20	5,366
24	Lewis	2,374	137,822	95,229	5,646,941	4,309	32,308	15,368	9,041
25	Livingston	2,503	229,762	86,938	14,379,316	9,957	24,906	146,846	18,825
26	Madison	3,845	363,392	93,203	11,218,078	9,904	42,618	95,308	16,527
27	Monroe	4,113	302,102	84,394	20,400,179	13,577	32,369	112,297	31,207
28	Montgomery	1,883	192,260	46,868	9,047,796	7,206	24,468	13,379	13,128
29	New York	168	2,428	245	4,976,131	7,779	2,374	11	3,802
30	Niagara	3,143	178,664	102,128	7,110,831	9,510	24,191	59,093	20,504
31	Oneida	6,292	476,669	189,572	16,457,705	14,695	76,553	70,341	26,793
32	Onondaga	4,595	317,280	113,291	17,859,344	13,987	46,361	112,990	31,018
33	Ontario	3,058	274,381	90,996	15,633,426	10,319	28,201	149,544	20,147
34	Orange	3,426	315,795	107,903	18,037,216	8,277	64,511	23,562	42,051
35	Orleans	2,271	163,823	53,631	9,285,215	7,530	16,798	58,791	11,135
36	Oswego	4,497	193,220	170,060	8,461,041	8,760	40,992	35,370	16,621
37	Otsego	4,764	376,868	171,294	13,158,005	12,240	58,348	108,244	26,184
38	Putnam	989	85,501	35,344	4,962,474	1,601	13,041	4,503	10,304
39	Queens	2,303	123,360	46,286	12,798,263	5,943	13,752	12,474	18,160
40	Rensselaer	2,930	274,543	75,203	14,105,990	8,504	29,383	85,578	27,739
41	Richmond	212	10,311	4,863	1,666,840	452	1,750	71	1,327
42	Rockland	682	43,080	34,323	3,337,732	1,685	4,565	999	3,010
43	St. Lawrence	6,124	377,086	262,627	9,900,053	13,811	74,361	89,910	18,423
44	Saratoga	3,465	281,427	131,562	13,718,082	9,642	33,624	56,769	28,198
45	Schenectady	1,040	76,939	28,892	4,014,373	3,227	10,008	12,295	5,560
46	Schoharie	2,439	205,745	105,444	7,684,802	6,995	29,887	31,340	17,820
47	Seneca	1,555	127,937	39,541	8,817,755	5,754	13,687	34,599	11,201
48	Steuben	5,797	336,981	338,415	14,258,060	12,748	55,490	156,776	23,939
49	Suffolk	2,323	143,612	210,292	7,406,947	5,889	21,006	31,449	14,545
50	Sullivan	1,889	94,425	141,830	3,710,110	2,676	17,745	10,829	6,455
51	Tioga	2,026	118,240	103,111	5,026,872	3,863	20,475	26,895	8,111
52	Tompkins	3,193	223,213	104,284	10,786,294	8,930	33,301	89,631	14,535
53	Ulster	3,539	233,059	207,938	12,930,611	8,587	33,939	25,387	36,292
54	Warren	1,505	95,481	126,359	2,070,594	2,724	13,438	18,403	5,264
55	Washington	3,037	299,802	102,242	12,472,751	9,394	37,257	152,337	28,375
56	Wayne	3,957	233,603	97,857	12,410,598	12,134	32,778	81,279	20,702
57	Westchester	2,587	196,701	55,228	19,968,790	5,197	28,595	11,001	23,355
58	Wyoming	3,360	223,533	126,747	8,466,488	8,729	37,083	133,116	15,634
59	Yates	1,673	133,971	52,529	7,774,733	5,516	15,110	62,297	11,762

STATISTICS OF

1	Alamance	923	98,260	114,846	999,332	3,369	8,09	8,058	22,475
2	Alexander	633	27,379	103,924	278,614	1,380	3,599	5,121	10,056
3	Anson	675	93,965	215,167	1,345,590	3,012	11,452	8,171	23,320
4	Ashe	1,253	64,805	302,885	505,165	2,713	14,675	18,250	25,267
5	Beaufort	594	30,760	180,981	631,314	1,123	13,499	8,169	18,279
6	Bertie	542	92,699	203,803	1,244,044	2,397	10,882	6,295	33,081
7	Bladen	486	47,678	393,677	863,079	1,558	12,011	6,654	23,735
8	Brunswick	385	18,419	247,622	549,530	653	8,386	3,457	12,227
9	Buncombe	1,105	75,360	506,216	1,328,424	3,708	16,349	14,000	28,608
10	Burke	373	29,195	108,175	597,559	1,547	5,137	3,858	10,664
11	Cabarras	875	64,895	125,700	934,705	3,251	7,414	5,027	19,877
12	Caldwell	366	26,568	97,759	450,071	1,236	4,554	4,221	11,101
13	Camden	579	38,521	36,950	1,008,120	1,130	4,205	2,276	10,702
14	Carteret	208	9,941	49,313	159,536	481	3,303	1,883	5,107
15	Caswell	707	123,975	115,887	1,462,108	2,838	7,106	7,554	21,311
16	Catawba	957	64,439	157,214	930,650	2,918	6,163	6,280	19,891
17	Chatham	1,633	139,563	309,631	1,543,391	5,165	14,892	14,765	41,165
18	Cherokee	459	23,952	73,172	405,869	1,321	6,585	5,074	12,477
19	Chowan	344	40,617	52,041	833,010	1,126	4,634	2,240	13,976
20	Cleveland	961	62,620	186,818	581,858	2,531	7,249	7,829	16,311
21	Columbus	399	26,764	262,395	313,131	738	10,089	7,445	20,188
22	Craven	388	45,197	298,167	798,921	956	10,632	8,032	17,330
23	Cumberland	959	77,260	557,473	1,354,229	3,068	15,006	14,321	35,281
24	Currituck	501	37,405	75,016	758,401	1,085	7,199	5,939	15,113
25	Davidson	1,231	95,243	195,114	1,214,252	3,797	8,545	9,157	29,702
26	Davie	404	45,770	79,504	515,241	1,723	3,947	4,029	15,286

AGRICULTURAL PRODUCTS.												
Wheat, bushels.	Rye & oats, bushels.	Indian corn, bushels.	Irish and sweet potatoes, bushels.	Peas and beans, bushels.	Barley, bushels.	Buckwheat, bushels.	Butter and cheese, pounds.	Hay, tons.	Hops, pounds.	Clover & other grass seeds, bushels.	Flaxseed, bushels.	
71,883	158,068	87,100	164,764	9,759	3,495	14,657	729,160	32,348	50,436	1,015	87	16
9,750	330,535	130,361	160,974	15,656	24,883	48,761	1,260,688	32,146	....	556	687	17
734,051	317,848	390,424	181,364	6,996	42,254	23,717	1,080,619	47,739	1,091	2,575	299	18
10,883	477,104	189,325	219,708	2,204	6,589	118,490	1,277,239	72,271	13	344	55	19
233	10,958	5,434	23,310	106	118	3,884	69,858	4,004	....	68	2	20
43,223	619,956	209,292	273,227	23,338	68,894	35,395	10,945,930	95,520	163,408	3,239	2,780	21
276,137	501,733	367,731	77,417	76,244	227,416	15,182	7,777,095	131,949	....	6,158	644	22
29,926	35,200	91,949	208,452	17,085	230	1,966	635	6,804	....	655	......	23
73,584	198,515	83,027	287,717	14,817	23,813	10,117	4,722,545	67,280	11,322	2,439	1,171	24
1,111,986	331,167	366,557	181,474	6,296	122,271	21,846	996,582	44,274	7,018	3,262	225	25
113,257	612,269	339,906	268,786	20,029	295,067	18,533	4,034,671	93,565	529,070	2,070	544	26
1,441,653	457,298	767,021	561,745	8,215	106,049	26,306	1,545,388	62,603	58,023	4,786	76	27
49,421	1,066,731	219,648	189,825	47,087	125,204	128,127	2,674,385	50,063	34,955	4,585	4,030	28
115	400	4,698	13,321	78	....	....	3,195	948	....	......	......	29
917,739	322,761	345,257	162,082	13,823	76,510	20,069	862,476	35,724	20	5,079	317	30
76,805	855,927	645,359	540,255	15,034	141,939	53,452	9,182,126	167,047	294,944	10,090	24	31
427,535	936,426	782,220	437,566	24,081	440,293	33,673	3,152,396	82,004	5,523	3,640	1,703	32
929,342	429,450	520,917	231,684	8,404	170,300	21,513	1,303,066	62,478	16,171	4,408	266	33
46,527	683,760	491,074	146,341	843	1,495	90,749	3,769,654	96,593	36	1,145	39	34
854,676	190,081	421,126	141,157	3,836	28,958	20,101	810,459	26,875	....	2,641	153	35
41,739	371,203	396,605	320,185	10,424	16,769	37,620	3,372,119	60,930	8,761	1,264	324	36
76,652	1,008,650	290,608	500,402	22,362	80,574	105,353	4,547,544	113,209	1,132,052	7,277	1,475	37
3,869	110,605	132,376	99,821	585	....	34,063	793,193	25,140	19	67	6	38
124,494	338,711	403,705	307,561	15,468	3,340	58,605	563,927	48,027	20	767	......	39
14,562	1,000,860	469,877	602,595	8,021	14,055	98,814	2,025,137	84,642	....	663	11,061	40
15,388	28,048	46,195	30,282	13	1,880	2,052	34,792	5,642	....	......	......	41
6,439	74,060	73,628	46,570	12	....	31,842	219,283	11,712	50	15	10	42
289,956	380,757	244,690	476,934	56,319	16,520	19,227	4,473,368	122,688	101,855	2,806	149	43
21,907	960,254	438,413	596,614	8,533	25,626	109,900	1,642,182	67,538	4,324	1,536	489	44
12,695	407,413	116,413	138,285	6,904	60,181	66,618	603,690	24,269	25	792	1,454	45
63,241	693,372	116,831	215,318	32,872	110,543	161,027	1,702,438	52,759	10,587	9,640	2,601	46
527,097	318,849	200,271	79,347	1,009	81,703	18,976	533,459	29,763	19	10,039	1,561	47
653,484	929,981	297,717	360,971	45,202	153,056	115,390	2,129,354	111,869	424	5,865	1,270	48
128,237	292,791	377,985	178,955	3,342	15,014	37,359	463,023	33,080	109	1,296	20	49
1,720	203,301	94,529	122,980	510	102	87,754	737,226	22,001	72	1,237	19	50
121,891	296,934	145,171	137,344	2,686	6,053	45,414	924,117	39,524	....	622	103	51
421,302	712,135	340,612	183,248	5,225	81,689	109,785	1,707,178	67,981	18	4,061	2,355	52
27,489	1,133,587	333,057	234,384	647	394	150,418	1,213,050	67,407	177	1,399	1,705	53
7,990	99,638	95,410	150,176	940	....	16,993	550,673	22,353	5	76	22	54
34,026	722,171	510,205	526,303	12,182	14,819	40,401	2,192,543	89,752	410	965	9,247	55
614,041	562,288	660,739	278,256	4,191	107,453	27,486	1,541,797	54,034	1,033	4,234	467	56
45,152	372,232	445,333	439,959	1,479	2,796	37,616	1,548,574	79,646	139	843	......	57
331,639	547,677	189,192	226,405	20,477	48,186	27,878	2,207,656	75,067	11,870	4,156	1,265	58
483,159	235,080	177,636	91,546	1,733	174,768	22,944	636,500	34,673	1,050	2,514	982	59

NORTH CAROLINA.

82,877	110,935	419,130	39,133	5,031	20	14	80,675	3,783	5	......	1,407	1
10,501	36,734	165,805	24,600	2,899	72	95	31,436	673	....	......	1,140	2
35,796	66,234	389,828	102,804	23,971	....	....	74,706	104	....	3	......	3
6,164	181,803	210,533	3,890	2,820	331	7,148	114,471	9,702	9	84	1,281	4
7,499	10,935	198,542	131,325	19,580	....	12	28,409	38	....	......	687	5
3,684	35,143	762,563	105,608	84,212	....	....	21,632	3,566	5	......	227	6
247	7,757	217,415	103,957	15,526	....	40	24,929	347	4	......	......	7
6	722	63,229	102,121	4,533	....	....	11,109	77	....	......	......	8
27,548	143,095	487,014	29,342	1,252	....	1,020	132,430	3,244	5	117	589	9
16,013	39,820	232,237	18,256	3,523	5	84	52,821	1,200	102	22	602	10
76,946	65,167	418,320	22,274	3,847	154	46	74,323	3,668	175	58	51	11
9,467	36,719	192,470	13,710	1,647	17	177	41,404	774	10	85	663	12
4,380	5,953	363,000	39,456	7,635	....	15	23,050	66	109	19	1,453	13
2,211	1,064	40,225	55,588	1,320	....	....	2,860	272	....	......	......	14
75,243	111,391	417,509	44,098	6,005	....	11	97,117	280	28	......	753	15
52,190	70,937	355,185	31,821	2,624	201	33	74,478	2,925	131	30	899	16
126,178	99,871	625,828	88,151	16,902	....	10	121,095	4,893	4	15	555	17
1,214	46,785	204,827	28,532	385	28	90	44,456	219	....	55	63	18
29.358	10,404	295,227	90,394	34,026	....	....	14,551	1,773	....	3	1,694	19
36,952	65,429	335,572	49,773	4,884	....	....	92,533	273	2	......	83	20
187	1,036	106,842	119,309	5,011	....	....	16,743	1	....	......	......	21
1,456	4,685	174,366	99,029	17,834	....	....	20,324	1,658	....	......	14	22
4,914	30,356	376,843	149,965	40,602	13	....	54,162	2,060	4	......	3	23
1,561	2,860	292,593	74,199	10,378	....	....	20,382	....	....	......	1,054	24
82,424	176,310	507,961	40,004	5,764	77	216	102,683	7,888	68	41	311	25
29,076	82,339	301,010	17,467	3,901	....	....	37,511	3,217	....	......	368	26

	COUNTIES.	Agricultural products.									
		Flax, pounds.	Hemp, dew and water-rotted, tons.	Maple sugar, pounds.	Cane sugar, hhds. of 1,000 pounds.	Molasses, gallons.	Rice, pounds.	Tobacco, pounds.	Ginned cotton, bales of 400 pounds.	Wool, pounds.	Silk cocoons, pounds.
16	Franklin	1,291		252,279		1,605		100		81,101	3
17	Fulton	10,621		43,240		1,495				45,468	
18	Genesee	1,553	1	192,399		2,801				369,957	
19	Greene	634		68,946		1,929				49,923	
20	Hamilton	40		14,683						5,486	
21	Herkimer	63,246		105,361		3,440				44,189	
22	Jefferson	2,954		818,394		1,705				192,168	
23	Kings										
24	Lewis	31,905		436,378		1,393		958		44,137	
25	Livingston	1,786		47,556		455				410,447	3
26	Madison	4,421		125,480		1,822		7,970		194,292	87
27	Monroe	1,457		37,468		592				365,084	5
28	Montgomery	20,034		45,196		1,095				68,025	
29	New York										
30	Niaga*a	435		13,258		145				168,330	1
31	Oneida	1,684		177,351		2,792				283.122	
32	Onondaga	20,064		128,785		582		73,731		345,880	60
33	Ontario	595		128,599		925		100		462,955	
34	Orange	996	2	1,681				75		47,438	
35	Orleans	451		34,460		1,140				199,228	50
36	Oswego	5,960		197,825		1,774				102,968	60
37	Otsego	22,066		384,996		2,990				325,598	5
38	Putnam	100		1,925				20		13,388	
39	Queens					225				25,830	
40	Rensselaer	268,091		30,180		63				256,509	
41	Richmond										
42	Rockland									1,876	
43	St. Lawrence	3,045		1,236,504		80		100		287,900	
44	Saratoga	6,621		16,895		826				158,736	
45	Schenectady	32,120								31,407	
46	Schoharie	10,497		111,344		2,065		50		95,185	6
47	Seneca	367		11,999		935				123,358	
48	Steuben	16,241		294,897		3,547				399.543	2
49	Suffolk	496								77,350	107
50	Sullivan	600		11,276		21				28,832	
51	Tioga	2,008		43,213		1,166				60,044	
52	Tompkins	16,578		102,099		1,296				242,004	
53	Ulster	14,724		51,399		1,463				68,322	
54	Warren	414		34,253		24				52,247	
55	Washington	230,698		13,781		145				457,093	55
56	Wayne	2,665		45,497		322				255,289	194
57	Westchester			50						28,775	
58	Wyoming	12,417		572,593		989				380,472	26
59	Yates	1,095		38,637		450				204,291	306

STATISTICS OF

	Counties	Flax	Hemp	Maple sugar	Cane sugar	Molasses	Rice	Tobacco	Ginned cotton	Wool	Silk cocoons
1	Alamance	79,955						14,650	121	14,009	54
2	Alexander	11,408					515	6,028		7,940	11
3	Anson						161		10,864	15,740	
4	Ashe	27,244		10,815		235		4,904		32,406	10
5	Beaufort	6,372					184,925	70	31	13,938	13
6	Bertie	2,501					15.588	300	1,310	14,291	
7	Bladen	74	10				73.530	255	9	10,904	3
8	Brunswick						2,687,415	50	7	4,766	
9	Buncombe	11,485						18,999		24,957	
10	Burke	4,344				50	10,892	7,288	3	7,708	
11	Cabarras	721						408	2,344	10,107	4
12	Caldwell	6,958					6,610	3,377	42	7,476	
13	Camden	36,204					195		2	4,468	
14	Carteret	75					3,940			3,346	
15	Caswell	7,780		20				2,282,939	76	12,768	
16	Catawba	6,776	8			71	2,664	6.086	815	10,524	5
17	Chatham	9,486						13,757	960	15,025	
18	Cherokee	3,478					705	7,934		9,909	
19	Chowan	2,123					6,477		129	5.191	
20	Cleveland	1,637					2.710	6.369	321	14,035	4
21	Columbus					85	195,850	3,145	26	15.479	
22	Craven	446					70,238		15	15,711	
23	Cumberland	452					95,645	2,062	156	23,538	
24	Currituck	30,950								12.284	
25	Davidson	13,615						45,839	932	16.957	
26	Davie	6,727						41,430	154	6,746	

Agricultural products.					Manufactures.					
					Establishments.					
Beeswax and honey, pounds.	Value of animals slaughtered.	Value of produce of market gardens.	Value of orchard produce.	Wine, gallons.	Capital.	Hands employed.	Annual product.	Produced in families.	Remarks.	
7,993	$81,722	$50	$12,458	......	$313,060	464	$510,301	$18,781	....	16
20,247	90,590	....	17,499	......	341,930	1,500	1,063,258	6,811	....	17
24,039	196,860	11,137	13,371	63	468,150	741	932,394	17,749	Divided in 1841 to form	18
70,331	172,133	19,150	21,159	......	1,042,025	2,194	1,985,167	8,525	Wyoming.	19
2,376	7,890	5	889	......	53,975	61	60,200	6,969	....	20
36,566	165,505	25	47,025	......	973,210	1,399	1,424,684	16,417	....	21
26,186	323,360	2,056	43,227	54	1,553,002	2,485	2,657,983	80,110	....	22
....	31,212	88,080	1,798	......	4,771,096	7,184	14,681,093	......	....	23
17,968	100,768	....	13,116	75	143,980	189	396,355	15,971	....	24
26,596	191,201	880	19,989	857	646,419	1,295	1,888,819	14,158	....	25
27,846	223,187	1,157	37,792	......	1,069,995	1,553	1,963,423	25,013	....	26
17,335	347,236	35,262	67,192	667	3,180,885	6,013	8,488,314	15,764	....	27
33,660	150,374	1,461	30,087	228	451,155	669	846,670	17,841	....	28
250	1,618,753	121,535	4,435	......	29,407,754	80,302	90,382,015	......	....	29
13,035	180,145	4,786	32,349	15	1,106,340	1,799	2,257,167	25,234	....	30
31,586	498,290	11,092	88,322	921	4,447,145	7,834	8,058,366	37,696	....	31
39,766	474,235	15,577	66,635	182	3,342,375	6,294	6,907,220	24,430	....	32
30,330	334,664	7,973	49,382	105	719,865	967	1,883,180	13,013	....	33
35,232	372,042	3,797	15,921	908	1,607,900	2,467	2,865,896	3,901	....	34
12,745	140,889	601	33,531	14	571,075	859	1,669,432	13,234	....	35
35,629	238,4[illegible]8	2,669	70,605	15	2,002,495	2,680	6,785,335	50,132	....	36
45,472	260,131	220	44,257	1	676,285	1,244	1,110,014	32,271	....	37
10,975	118,084	274	14,934	83	365,445	1,254	1,008,031	2,064	....	38
5,299	319,441	308,957	63,675	136	304,000	370	669,480	767	....	39
42,702	303,863	11,928	56,759	228	4,060,905	9,196	10,005,962	9,458	....	40
....	14,529	14,412	2,880	75	261,100	536	848,180	......	....	41
5,025	54,623	6,669	5,241	78	1,081,000	2,048	2,080,216	204	....	42
23,013	284,571	4,468	29,955	10	1,141,370	1,516	1,783,617	82,812	....	43
63,241	320,118	5,512	33,439	129	1,450,085	1,996	2,438,330	20,721	....	44
11,294	78,464	3,709	14,563	25	603,970	1,407	1,109,803	1,971	....	45
31,481	187,472	486	32,827	271	394,405	729	1,030,105	26,093	....	46
18,547	17,042	222	26,990	......	921,465	1,131	1,818,508	3,904	....	47
94,991	296,798	3,740	30,565	285	1,238,355	1,722	2,106,636	76,287	....	48
3,454	232,297	2,608	11,335	112	683,062	1,161	782,140	5,677	....	49
28,061	108,660	....	8,557	6	1,024,265	1,110	2,003,786	10,546	....	50
10,225	91,032	32	4,996	......	605,151	690	898,074	13,158	....	51
73,003	193,315	455	23,930	100	913,585	1,452	1,846,138	20,942	....	52
55,846	324,236	472	28,875	5	1,687,820	2,854	3,583,441	21,689	....	53
19,230	70,309	400	8,712	300	405,050	515	779,933	10,330	....	54
52,231	314,281	3,705	65,159	97	651,900	1,083	1,177,389	9,870	....	55
29,948	263,728	5,092	83,451	430	623,925	1,039	1,295,836	31,287	....	56
6,528	311,482	43,936	67,587	259	1,604,310	4,427	3,734,513	8,555	....	57
37,571	155,091	458	21,575	339	479,430	882	964,208	29,029	Formed '41 from Genesee.	58
24,526	100,292	25	21,531	85	315,415	624	878,230	6,283	....	59

NORTH CAROLINA.

Beeswax and honey, pounds.	Value of animals slaughtered.	Value of produce of market gardens.	Value of orchard produce.	Wine, gallons.	Capital.	Hands employed.	Annual product.	Produced in families.	Remarks.	
12,397	67,390	....	38	......	238,800	237	220,907	30,081	Formed in '49 from Orange.	1
12,331	30,744	147	357	3	3,600	7	5,200	12,791	'47 f'm Ired., Cald., Wilkes	2
7,187	90,140	....	....	......	54,075	96	93,760	45,787	Div. '42 to form Union.	3
23,196	57,595	....	2,330	......	4,000	22	5,780	58,302	Divided in '49 to form Wa-	4
3,499	68,071	428	546	381	308,302	354	210,000	18,351	tauga.	5
2,709	123,645	....	....	......	42,800	320	125,308	15,880	....	6
1,077	65,360	104	20	1,269	362,719	309	87,552	45,123	....	7
500	29,873	135	29	......	129,177	503	404,665	12,920	....	8
14,350	89,491	5	1,002	......	23,100	80	48,012	93,312	....	9
12,385	35,364	237	305	5	53,900	142	51,695	14,591	Divided in 1842 to form	10
3,790	63,772	....	58	175	141,150	251	240,602	14,698	McDowell.	11
10,506	29,880	539	855	......	10,150	17	18,636	13,370	Divided '47 and '49 to form	12
7,887	45,569	....	152	......	11,400	19	16,358	10,586	Alexander and Watauga.	13
759	17,446	42	95	......	44,400	76	35,772	4,159	....	14
12,732	86,298	....	....	......	186,000	397	325,212	39,849	....	15
11,292	62,366	31	262	......	3,459	19	7,944	29,358	Formed '42 from Lincoln.	16
2,185	142,835	....	55	......	86,480	108	174,203	48,425	....	17
6,437	26,584	4,461	288	......	7,500	18	10,200	18,306	....	18
1,637	59,781	50	1,315	......	56,525	138	41,700	7,884	....	19
9,336	49,451	198	....	......	18,450	56	41,263	29,059	Formed since 1840 from	20
200	49,723	....	....	156	4,000	13	4,400	11,365	Rutherford and Lincoln.	21
7,974	43,077	371	196	228	267,125	291	191,949	8,986	....	22
1,000	104,642	106	25	230	581,712	970	505,762	31,671	....	23
1,695	47,879	....	....	......	....	......	....	13,630	....	24
5,633	89,636	....	306	......	512,650	72	87,264	53,804	....	25
2,150	51,977	....	....	......	31,750	89	46,165	24,348	....	26

	COUNTIES.	POPULATION.								
		Whites.			Colored.		All classes.		Total population.	
		Male.	Female.	Total.	Free.	Slave.	Male.	Female.	1850.	1840.
27	Duplin	3,527	3,635	7,162	345	6,007	6,696	6,818	13,514	11,182
28	Edgecomb	4,085	4,274	8,359	283	8,547	8,545	8,644	17,189	15,708
29	Forsyth	4,665	4,996	9,661	154	1,353	5,430	5,738	11,168	....
30	Franklin	2,717	2,926	5,643	563	5,507	5,744	5,969	11,713	10,980
31	Gaston	2,951	2,984	5,935	26	2,112	4,044	4,029	8,073	....
32	Gates	2,015	2,144	4,159	396	3,871	4,101	4,325	8,426	8,161
33	Granville	5,093	5,201	10,294	1,090	9,865	10,515	10,734	21,249	18,817
34	Green	1,537	1,722	3,259	116	3,244	3,193	3,426	6,619	6,595
35	Guilford	7,869	8,005	15,874	694	3,186	9,765	9,989	19,754	19,175
36	Halifax	2,838	2,927	5,765	1,870	8,954	8,149	8,440	16,589	16,865
37	Haywood	3,341	3,300	6,641	15	418	3,551	3,523	7,074	4,975
38	Henderson	3,013	2,879	5,892	37	924	3,516	3,337	6,853	5,129
39	Hertford	1,702	1,851	3,553	873	3,716	4,024	4,118	8,142	7,484
40	Hyde	2,399	2,357	4,756	253	2,627	3,910	3,726	7,636	6,458
41	Iredell	5,108	5,439	10,547	30	4,142	7,182	7,537	14,719	15,685
42	Johnson	4,401	4,478	8,879	184	4,663	6,902	6,824	13,726	10,599
43	Jones	1,049	1,090	2,139	142	2,757	2,500	2,538	5,038	4,945
44	Lenoir	1,775	1,792	3,567	145	4,116	3,921	3,907	7,828	7,605
45	Lincoln	2,730	2,925	5,655	36	2,055	3,832	3,914	7,746	25,160
46	McDowell	2,368	2,403	4,771	213	1,262	3,087	3,159	6,246	....
47	Macon	2,896	2,838	5,734	106	549	3,214	3,175	6,389	4,869
48	Martin	2,355	2,262	4,617	323	3,367	4,265	4,042	8,307	7,637
49	Mecklenburgh	4,148	4,137	8,285	156	5,473	6,894	7,020	13,914	18,273
50	Montgomery	2,514	2,541	5,055	44	1,773	3,380	3,492	6,872	10,780
51	Moore	3,476	3,720	7,196	170	1,976	4,513	4,829	9,342	7,988
52	Nash	2,908	3,064	5,972	629	4,056	5,204	5,453	10,651	9,047
53	New Hanover	4,099	4,102	8,201	886	8,581	8,927	8,741	17,668	13,312
54	Northampton	2,875	3,119	5,994	830	6,511	6,665	6,670	13,335	13,369
55	Onslow	2,427	2,576	5,003	172	3,108	4,048	4,235	8,283	7,527
56	Orange	5,639	5,691	11,330	481	5,244	8,401	8,654	17,055	24,356
57	Pasquotank	2,315	2,295	4,610	1,235	3,105	4,573	4,377	8,950	8,514
58	Perquimans	1,831	1,799	3,630	450	3,252	3,747	3,585	7,332	7,346
59	Person	2,723	2,870	5,593	295	4,893	5,319	5,462	10,781	9,790
60	Pitt	3,255	3,409	6,664	100	6,633	6,604	6,793	13,397	11,806
61	Randolph	6,864	6,923	13,787	405	1,640	7,877	7,955	15,832	12,875
62	Richmond	2,405	2,484	4,889	225	4,704	4,873	4,945	9,818	8,909
63	Robeson	3,610	3,621	7,231	1,230	4,365	6,329	6,497	12,826	10,370
64	Rockingham	4,245	4,502	8,747	419	5,329	7,074	7,421	14,495	13,442
65	Rowan	4,843	5,057	9,900	116	3,854	6,801	7,069	13,870	12,109
66	Rutherford	5,151	5,274	10,425	220	2,905	6,733	6,817	13,550	19,202
67	Sampson	4,175	4,248	8,423	477	5,685	7,299	7,286	14,585	12,157
68	Stanley	2,708	2,729	5,437	49	1,436	3,491	3,431	6,922	....
69	Stokes	3,575	3,689	7,264	149	1,793	4,491	4,715	9,206	16,265
70	Surry	7,925	8,234	16,159	284	2,000	9,008	9,435	18,443	15,079
71	Tyrrel	1,636	1,665	3,301	130	1,702	2,584	2,549	5,133	4,657
72	Union	3,997	4,021	8,018	51	1,982	4,998	5,053	10,051	....
73	Wake	6,796	7,377	14,173	1,306	9,409	11,994	12,894	24,888	21,118
74	Warren	2,235	2,366	4,601	444	8,867	6,929	6,983	13,912	12,919
75	Washington	1,584	1,625	3,209	240	2,215	2,836	2,828	5,664	4,525
76	Watauga	1,684	1,558	3,242	29	129	1,764	1,636	3,400	....
77	Wayne	3,817	3,984	7,801	665	5,020	6,694	6,792	13,486	10,891
78	Wilkes	5,256	5,477	10,733	224	1,142	5,911	6,188	12,099	12,577
79	Yancey	3,935	3,844	7,809	50	346	4,133	4,072	8,205	5,962

STATISTICS OF

1	Adams	9,666	9,162	18,828	55	....	9,695	9,188	18,883	13,183
2	Allen	6,237	5,845	12,082	27	....	6,254	5,855	12,109	9,097
3	Ashland	12,071	11,739	23,810	3	....	12,072	11,741	23,813	....
4	Ashtabula	14,597	14,127	28,724	43	....	14,622	14,145	28,767	23,724
5	Athens	9,235	8,874	18,109	106	....	9,295	8,920	18,215	19,109
6	Auglaize	5,868	5,383	11,251	87	....	5,916	5,422	11,338	....
7	Belmont	17,154	16,668	33,822	778	....	17,553	17,047	34,600	30,901
8	Brown	13,413	13,056	26,469	863	....	13,826	13,506	27,332	22,715
9	Butler	15,874	14,548	30,422	367	....	16,051	14,738	30,789	28,173
10	Carroll	8,835	8,79	17,633	52	....	8,862	8,823	17,685	18,108
11	Champaign	9,955	9,333	19,288	494	....	10,209	9,573	19,782	16,721
12	Clark	11,369	10,486	21,855	323	....	11,525	10,653	22,178	16,882
13	Clermont	15,365	14,678	30,043	412	....	15,571	14,884	30,455	23,106
14	Clinton	9,435	8,805	18,240	598	....	9,742	9,096	18,838	15,719
15	Columbiana	16,999	16,440	33,439	182	....	17,097	16,524	33,621	40,378
16	Coshocton	12,921	12,709	25,630	44	....	12,933	12,741	25,674	21,590
17	Crawford	9,302	8,865	18,167	10	....	9,307	8,870	18,177	13,152

NATIVITIES, DWELLINGS, &c.				EDUCATION AND RELIGION.									
Born out of State.				Colleges, academies, and private schools.		Public Schools.							
United States.	Foreign countries.	Dwellings.	Families.	Pupils.	Annual income.	Pupils.	Annual income.	Total educational income.	White scholars during the year.	Whites 5 and under 20 years old.	Whites over 20 unable to read and write.	Accommodation of churches—persons.	
42	20	1,419	1,419	130	$2,000	906	$2,888	$4,888	1,412	2,568	1,330	3,625	27
107	17	1,649	1,649	160	3,000	1,290	3,200	6,200	1,467	3,216	1,935	7,700	28
381	53	1,739	1,765	150	20,000	2,071	2,069	22,069	2,232	3,748	952	6,300	29
114	6	1,115	1,115	255	4,740	800	1,755	6,495	1,087	2,293	865	6,950	30
89	20	1,072	1,072	......	....	1,520	391	391	1,572	2,400	1,308	5,800	31
318	3	880	880	210	3,052	520	1,108	4,160	580	1,563	956	5,550	32
807	51	2,093	2,093	113	3,150	1,535	4,334	7,484	1,936	4,012	1,946	5,825	33
7	....	684	684	60	850	420	736	1,586	434	1,201	309	3,750	34
548	38	3,048	3,048	280	11,255	3,927	3,442	14,697	3,806	6,091	1,639	12,900	35
235	22	1,759	1,792	15	40	750	2,530	2,570	793	2,119	276	2,825	36
399	3	1,110	1,137	75	195	824	762	957	1,236	2,721	1,147	5,975	37
69	21	931	931	......	....	1,680	1,239	1,239	723	2,473	2	4,550	38
59	....	831	831	155	13,910	378	1,170	15,080	574	1,310	535	7,400	39
13	2	923	923	78	630	691	1,227	1,857	772	1,808	686	1,925	40
384	52	1,834	1,846	60	700	2,399	2,476	3,176	2,735	4,182	477	14,916	41
91	21	1,704	1,704	90	....	1,086	2,160	2,160	1,049	3,513	1,447	7,360	42
22	4	440	440	......	....	240	1,082	1,082	324	789	297	2,900	43
18	10	702	702	35	....	200	1,768	1,768	489	1,365	611	9,000	44
110	16	1,022	1,038	12	....	68	537	537	1,032	2,142	171	8,450	45
200	6	860	860	175	700	600	635	1,335	795	1,892	680	3,550	46
653	10	963	978	100	550	1,250	643	1,193	973	2,378	944	3,000	47
9	6	923	923	100	2,400	900	1,415	3,815	681	1,705	140	2,700	48
238	90	1,632	1,645	226	8,670	1,354	6,934	15,604	1,503	3,221	125	15,000	49
77	23	902	904	68	1,200	1,022	1,011	2,211	1,170	2,016	541	3,600	50
41	174	1,286	1,286	84	1,200	1,400	958	2,158	1,431	2,780	990	7,400	51
83	14	1,248	1,258	260	2,500	726	1,029	3,529	788	2,312	1,308	5,906	52
537	246	1,888	1,888	323	7,068	1,170	1,398	8,466	1,461	2,869	456	3,900	53
591	5	1,341	1,341	173	....	343	2,184	2,184	842	2,234	1,364	5,957	54
19	20	962	962	45	1,000	565	1,592	2,592	556	1,981	1,005	7,600	55
167	3	2,186	2,186	510	35,040	4,220	4,594	39,634	1,903	4,499	1,276	12,200	56
89	26	1,150	1,150	185	3,450	640	2,065	5,515	717	1,715	240	6,600	57
87	2	818	818	105	3,250	375	1,291	4,541	467	1,270	656	4,725	58
371	2	1,070	1,078	......	....	......	618	618	809	2,154	606	7,050	59
41	7	1,315	1,318	56	....	1,035	2,170	2,170	1,153	2,491	1,135	3,975	60
126	18	2,512	2,523	48	830	1,550	2,624	3,454	2,935	5,502	1,854	19,100	61
264	152	949	950	25	500	903	4,321	4,821	807	1,839	659	3,675	62
310	153	1,513	1,513	130	3,300	1,415	5,292	8,592	1,523	2,759	658	8,660	63
1,136	30	1,693	1,703	45	745	1,015	2,594	3,339	1,226	3,373	1,200	5,700	64
170	46	1,242	1,268	40	800	2,362	3,825	4,625	2,346	3,797	1,258	14,425	65
878	25	1,856	1,901	75	....	4,800	2,307	2,307	2,419	4,132	1,281	15,100	66
77	13	1,582	1,582	70	2,100	3,317	3,900	6,000	990	3,305	1,474	10,250	67
45	9	946	951	60	775	660	1,140	1,915	1,176	2,303	987	6,825	68
1,024	1	1,268	1,311	......	....	1,035	1,800	1,800	866	2,992	1,684	3,400	69
805	20	2,797	2,806	140	2,480	2,098	2,264	4,744	2,513	6,536	3,163	6,455	70
34	6	636	636	......	....	400	850	850	415	1,186	595	2,100	71
445	16	1,422	1,422	50	190	1,038	1,110	1,300	1,337	3,365	1,012	3,885	72
478	55	2,844	2,844	558	23,900	2,001	7,153	31,053	2,986	5,559	2,393	17,600	73
405	25	905	905	261	19,475	1,486	2,244	21,719	1,011	1,780	430	7,750	74
46	14	670	670	139	3,650	1,178	1,790	5,440	942	1,200	197	2,600	75
136	....	569	573	5	900	520	360	1,260	544	1,351	516	1,450	76
98	34	1,576	1,576	226	2,900	1,498	1,088	3,988	1,149	2,938	1,462	7,000	77
252	6	2,050	2,050	......	....	2,419	1,502	1,502	1,771	4,381	967	11,575	78
518	2	1,322	1,391	......	....	1,600	787	787	1,487	3,238	992	3,900	79

OHIO.

United States.	Foreign countries.	Dwellings.	Families.	Pupils.	Annual income.	Pupils.	Annual income.	Total educational income.	White scholars during the year.	Whites 5 and under 20 years old.	Whites over 20 unable to read and write.	Accommodation of churches—persons.	
4,044	592	3,205	3,205	......	....	4,500	6,700	6,700	3,803	7,664	607	19,595	1
2,309	631	2,070	2,070	......	....	4,500	1,737	1,737	3,214	5,080	360	5,584	2
8,441	1,129	4,123	4,161	170	2,600	4,295	9,940	12,540	6,806	9,534	211	13,850	3
12,698	1,119	5,306	5,631	230	4,580	4,688	10,417	14,997	9,174	10,563	162	19,280	4
5,041	460	3,121	3,151	145	5,433	3,936	5,145	10,578	5,019	7,245	506	9,150	5
1,643	2,685	2,020	2,020	......	....	580	560	560	2,475	4,633	145	6,650	6
8,347	1,639	5,823	5,927	200	670	4,008	14,267	14,937	7,936	13,444	1,178	27,445	7
5,628	1,498	4,838	4,872	115	5,000	......	5,886	10,886	6,230	10,699	1,375	26,320	8
6,854	3,795	5,315	5,456	555	11,640	5,467	19,334	30,974	8,238	11,442	1,354	28,040	9
3,964	1,399	3,068	3,076	40	500	3,330	4,328	4,828	4,945	7,239	1,404	20,400	10
5,998	462	3,437	3,469	......	....	5,300	14,775	14,775	4,971	7,677	214	12,570	11
6,812	1,956	3,753	3,820	443	5,428	3,560	12,115	17,543	5,370	8,264	357	22,750	12
6,921	1,668	5,437	5,460	280	4,463	6,913	16,598	21,061	8,543	11,715	2,468	34,255	13
4,903	262	3,245	3,245	320	1,440	3,920	8,877	10,317	5,187	7,292	1,109	16,805	14
8,435	3,041	5,834	5,947	326	2,370	12,296	12,423	14,793	9,332	12,837	875	28,680	15
5,802	1,868	4,325	4,328	87	....	6,233	7,731	7,731	7,732	10,275	1,991	17,805	16
5,259	2,696	3,070	3,089	......	....	4,740	6,937	6,937	5,134	7,497	18	14,300	17

	Counties.	Land occupied or improved.				Live stock upo i farms.			
		Farms.	Acres improved.	Acres unimproved.	Value with improvements and implements.	Horses, asses, and mules.	Neat cattle.	Sheep.	Swine.
27	Duplin	923	93,018	334,030	$1,460,926	2,222	12,819	10,521	35,192
28	Edgecomb	737	145,321	226,672	2,087,034	3,697	11,297	9,754	53,106
29	Forsyth	936	51,873	120,029	650,271	2,059	5,142	4,661	18,770
30	Franklin	588	103,084	169,734	876,823	2,294	9,839	7,605	30,587
31	Gaston	724	57,519	156,583	719,815	2,299	7,029	6,097	15,497
32	Gates	490	48,267	91,114	731,346	1,200	6,237	3,437	21,438
33	Granville	1,074	173,332	242,131	1,482,723	4,279	13,657	13,464	39,325
34	Green	372	57,161	80,173	783,972	1,459	4,102	3,536	21,781
35	Guilford	1,668	190,309	183,437	1,563,098	4,900	12,747	13,210	36,308
36	Halifax	868	141,698	248,006	1,599,316	3,169	14,380	8,234	44,107
37	Haywood	653	35,006	357,042	489,643	2,070	7,749	8,166	18,410
38	Henderson	413	26,251	126,767	396,746	1,769	7,530	6,389	11,079
39	Hertford	378	55,222	104,536	640,295	1,176	5,363	4,790	20,838
40	Hyde	293	24,324	322,911	1,159,166	991	7,562	3,414	10,232
41	Iredell	1,096	92,053	192,740	1,221,302	3,644	9,639	10,769	26,321
42	Johnson	1,002	113,374	392,906	1,079,766	3,144	15,848	12,006	43,376
43	Jones	240	55,641	128,798	484,214	979	4,863	3,792	15,970
44	Lenoir	362	72,712	147,892	1,215,130	1,474	5,545	4,190	23,887
45	Lincoln	711	51,478	137,815	757,738	2,122	6,164	5,336	12,898
46	McDowell	508	29,636	119,657	583,349	1,564	6,121	4,031	13,908
47	Macon	631	32,436	110,083	401,397	2,213	8,584	7,059	17,614
48	Martin	510	54,763	149,506	762,485	1,414	7,448	6,945	21,680
49	Mecklenburgh	1,030	92,183	176,313	1,261,389	3,926	11,083	7,964	25,343
50	Montgomery	541	43,001	167,400	402,364	1,648	5,331	4,246	12,777
51	Moore	718	45,602	254,677	499,211	2,114	8,351	8,724	18,276
52	Nash	728	82,626	220,623	667,562	2,118	7,855	7,425	28,649
53	New Hanover	559	49,694	365,244	1,035,874	1,396	12,969	8,777	23,026
54	Northampton	644	107,025	157,664	1,099,457	2,379	8,373	4,711	33,460
55	Onslow	349	52,999	167,045	559,277	1,127	8,065	4,855	17,380
56	Orange	1,082	140,587	183,065	1,200,816	3,703	11,471	11,535	29,507
57	Pasquotank	530	50,002	50,215	1,263,948	1,505	5,727	2,372	13,275
58	Perquimans	505	46,660	76,022	1,066,450	1,448	6,444	4,632	14,356
59	Person	684	83,611	133,502	872,480	2,190	6,594	8,455	13,686
60	Pitt	816	86,382	216,142	1,155,651	2,343	10,700	7,622	35,431
61	Randolph	1,092	96,908	262,964	1,120,569	3,645	10,291	13,232	22,996
62	Richmond	496	62,508	213,016	656,410	1,763	8,409	6,164	14,857
63	Robeson	1,112	91,463	459,029	1,188,819	2,716	16,058	16,237	47,100
64	Rockingham	717	70,757	187,476	1,040,663	2,355	6,840	6,133	21,480
65	Rowan	1,070	104,157	145,157	1,156,432	4,069	8,541	6,926	29,317
66	Rutherford	959	67,645	213,421	1,035,022	2,866	9,599	8,251	23,898
67	Sampson	948	112,987	358,148	1,867,574	2,712	12,948	10,388	40,179
68	Stanley	515	33,632	152,240	371,640	1,616	4,384	3,501	11,646
69	Stokes	591	33,027	132,785	476,857	1,281	4,154	4,071	10,638
70	Surry	1,503	104,119	302,795	1,040,670	3,179	10,261	11,702	34,519
71	Tyrrel	210	15,188	37,268	335,542	553	3,595	1,847	6,455
72	Union	873	56,093	248,063	782,484	2,820	9,285	11,635	15,646
73	Wake	1,410	161,091	352,178	1,680,660	4,776	17,151	13,787	50,056
74	Warren	543	100,247	182,495	1,320,233	2,305	10,078	8,019	26,827
75	Washington	444	23,990	75,907	405,659	876	6,774	2,791	11,364
76	Watauga	442	17,113	121,761	365,559	948	5,220	4,949	10,239
77	Wayne	668	112,938	212,930	1,665,111	2,801	9,588	7,250	46,522
78	Wilkes	1,097	65,322	270,556	845,809	1,481	11,720	11,476	30,922
79	Yancey	970	38,690	254,895	630,413	331	10,379	20,061	28,132

STATISTICS OF

1	Adams	1,509	104,797	117,107	2,903,514	4,847	12,605	19,894	28,836
2	Allen	1,146	50,766	87,259	1,716,038	3,341	9,063	11,357	14,653
3	Ashland	2,235	144,786	98,662	5,344,391	7,093	17,432	74,034	25,510
4	Ashtabula	2,243	174,355	88,841	5,279,612	4,743	26,781	44,237	6,846
5	Athens	1,372	82,168	103,109	2,218,250	3,345	11,893	35,945	15,675
6	Auglaize	1,373	48,285	93,179	1,420,180	3,322	9,413	9,286	14,369
7	Belmont	2,552	179,697	130,296	7,459,581	9,744	20,753	135,814	36,687
8	Brown	1,843	129,006	110,021	5,354,139	6,382	13,564	18,010	39,144
9	Butler	2,262	172,345	102,004	10,906,250	9,156	15,072	12,322	58,086
10	Carroll	1,926	140,988	92,950	4,093,897	6,221	14,167	72,472	15,387
11	Champaign	1,677	147,267	108,564	5,415,559	8,228	19,583	52,050	31,337
12	Clark	1,398	142,708	80,038	6,129,052	5,871	19,025	52,984	21,993
13	Clermont	2,098	132,002	90,673	5,762,155	7,449	11,843	17,144	47,258
14	Clinton	1,366	112,589	96,517	4,764,774	5,560	16,129	43,439	42,194
15	Columbiana	2,338	173,181	115,161	6.421,498	7,930	20,339	124,716	20,822
16	Coshocton	2,736	184,460	152,386	5.241,675	8,752	22,396	67,208	35,453
17	Crawford	1,210	82,836	63,120	2,562,476	3,885	12,153	43,359	13,133

AGRICULTURAL PRODUCTS.												
Wheat, bushels.	Rye & oats, bushels.	Indian corn, bushels.	Irish and sweet potatoes, bushels.	Peas and beans, bushels.	Barley, bushels.	Buckwheat, bushels.	Butter and cheese, pounds.	Hay, tons.	Hops, pounds.	Clover & other grass seeds, bushels.	Flaxseed, bushels.	
3,037	8,691	372,530	258,807	49,746	......	2	44,460	781	4	......	3	27
12,722	33,122	759,373	195,817	103,646	......	......	22,895	4,046	......	......	29	28
40,735	102,508	349,320	27,679	1,151	......	41	90,449	5,369	40	......	1,289	29
21,898	57,289	398,031	90,255	25,030	......	......	42,867	2,560	......	......	......	30
51,762	56,645	329,377	28,909	7,674	1,112	......	104,153	5,625	......	......	22	31
4,204	6,344	310,138	125,160	47,588	......	......	14,836	1,562	......	......	161	32
84,613	162,245	551,365	79,703	9,381	......	19	101,139	2,716	97	201	448	33
7,042	11,073	268,370	78,418	49,387	......	......	11,185	......	......	......	......	34
121,379	219,041	884,286	40,081	499	40	......	126,675	6,217	......	......	681	35
15,051	41,688	879,040	108,388	64,774	......	......	47,915	1,117	......	......	......	36
12,704	46,956	278,221	13,819	1,657	......	1,190	55,520	558	......	170	387	37
559	42,716	163,186	16,586	94	......	24	50,478	426	......	104	20	38
2,481	7,606	288,805	106,322	37,022	......	......	14,891	1,083	......	......	37	39
14,867	12,879	332,525	27,738	4,856	......	......	7,735	2	......	......	82	40
53,111	138,747	506,491	46,797	8,274	267	34	92,453	4,933	......	5	942	41
5,354	42,818	451,528	201,946	58,698	......	......	49,874	3,179	15	......	137	42
2,101	10,954	235,362	67,629	19,208	......	......	13,288	1,183	......	......	......	43
6,718	9,860	322,584	96,389	47,637	......	......	21,693	......	......	......	50	44
36,256	52,370	274,331	25,680	2,802	52	30	66,751	4,623	130	3	217	45
5,600	36,940	255,262	24,877	2,710	......	23	48,078	232	2	10	467	46
3,687	74,826	225,397	23,014	39	......	106	71,175	721	......	......	......	47
2,860	4,215	267,477	125,529	38,307	......	......	12,067	......	......	......	......	48
56,375	91,792	549,162	34,017	10,149	115	10	116,967	2,145	......	5	10	49
22,336	25,892	192,191	29,326	3,695	......	......	33,723	194	2	30	150	50
27,828	34,137	223,476	49,806	8,765	......	......	41,593	63	......	......	131	51
9,028	30,525	324,146	119,579	26,224	......	......	30,807	2,515	27	......	55	52
37	2,135	215,488	166,045	54,140	......	......	1,730	22	8,000	......	......	53
19,294	23,910	657,951	97,379	67,167	......	......	33,221	......	......	......	......	54
523	4,969	233,283	139,870	40,503	......	......	14,226	1,263	5	......	......	55
83,338	108,101	459,088	44,423	5,094	......	......	106,883	1,845	80	......	1,245	56
19,436	22,946	624,575	41,511	6,752	......	......	23,957	......	......	230	5,035	57
45,943	12,388	418,355	46,734	10,965	......	......	23,437	1,565	......	34	517	58
49,802	84,979	259,072	30,401	1,851	30	......	63,593	25	29	444	290	59
9,697	12,188	458,478	174,096	80,477	......	......	28,375	37	10	......	33	60
83,634	88,806	440,086	42,189	2,110	42	26	85,865	3,971	2	10	1,081	61
14,808	16,511	225,017	59,715	27,658	......	......	29,136	1,006	......	......	......	62
1,562	7,870	327,257	140,748	32,805	......	......	42,388	8	......	......	......	63
44,156	105,262	377,604	31,103	1,082	......	......	78,122	380	......	......	682	64
86,613	142,365	540,637	29,063	9,535	138	78	92,586	6,837	10	......	239	65
29,384	81,310	472,335	62,366	7,568	8	2	94,168	5,058	3	......	172	66
2,167	8,467	426,805	242,796	53,693	......	......	38,418	2	......	......	......	67
31,267	23,582	203,281	23,636	5,366	......	......	28,388	1,245	16	25	182	68
16,004	48,642	223,000	27,416	4,249	......	49	47,242	800	......	......	897	69
25,412	163,516	552,454	62,612	1,088	13	640	117,355	1,869	4	3	3,659	70
7,952	1,829	149,385	24,430	12,718	......	......	7,977	1	21	......	261	71
59,856	34,511	39,875	41,860	5,645	......	......	65,444	538	......	......	......	72
54,126	80,133	681,390	180,960	49,436	......	......	109,142	5,096	5	......	106	73
34,474	89,000	349,502	54,086	8,563	......	......	50,304	2,245	13	......	......	74
15,352	2,703	218,468	55,337	31,027	......	......	23,746	1,103	70	......	347	75
1,427	59,427	69,211	2,904	1,044	......	3,327	56,709	2,774	......	21	591	76
13,498	25,733	480,240	162,722	93,045	......	......	32,348	1,628	......	......	17	77
14,440	85,194	408,150	51,620	11,268	......	178	113,652	593	......	......	2,806	78
7,500	128,801	284,016	12,928	4,008	......	1,914	89,842	1,191	......	24	821	79

OHIO.

128,904	115,812	767,798	22,783	165	15,050	467	225,033	3,495	8	1,144	85	1
140,580	62,668	288,450	40,273	329	340	1,377	201,861	8,636	320	1,906	248	2
338,718	279,155	446,818	65,310	585	428	11,876	390,794	23,826	1,649	5,469	1,332	3
40,167	195,741	267,209	131,271	1,858	1,326	6,325	6,195,868	56,618	5,978	869	361	4
72,146	74,650	443,546	36,775	662	10	7,095	315,472	12,188	3	604	348	5
77,501	72,118	289,544	28,255	471	1,271	1,959	196,668	8,669	141	857	122	6
359,399	365,359	854,771	57,881	321	15,991	9,917	637,487	16,397	8,398	2,508	347	7
192,065	183,656	1,209,485	44,413	1,686	27,309	2,245	351,647	7,220	168	462	371	8
291,782	348,930	2,737,734	92,845	620	57,896	4,771	750,552	10,494	51	874	825	9
263,755	238,823	220,931	44,161	....	13	18,440	312,545	11,571	......	1,301	759	10
225,808	173,250	964,607	35,535	194	1,047	3,067	432,548	17,870	1,732	1,422	4,382	11
195,514	124,175	839,576	40,582	541	1,457	2,251	403,604	19,097	3,907	561	3,725	12
188,169	261,858	1,292,511	119,402	2,138	2,257	5,831	493,801	13,171	64	947	93	13
110,561	130,475	1,224,517	29,667	385	30	3,487	462,524	12,945	3	799	755	14
311,507	358,549	393,804	95,375	286	5,911	22,256	689,638	30,249	592	4,172	1,440	15
416,918	205,074	897,016	69,605	628	2,673	17,495	598,302	14,240	172	1,651	665	16
132,153	135,492	275,653	26,242	180	5,078	5,668	278,965	16,000	15	5,003	169	17

	COUNTIES.	AGRICULTURAL PRODUCTS.									
		Flax, pounds.	Hemp, dew and water-rotted, tons.	Maple sugar, pounds.	Cane sugar, hhds. of 1,000 pounds.	Molasses, gallons.	Rice, pounds.	Tobacco, pounds.	Ginned cotton, bales of 400 pounds.	Wool, pounds.	Silk cocoons, pounds.
27	Duplin	150	12	.....	.....	50	101,302	332	461	16,854	.....
28	Edgecomb	865	.....	.....	.....	.....	10,265	404	3,097	16,392	.....
29	Forsyth	14,715	.....	.....	.....	.....	.....	49,880	.....	9,596	.....
30	Franklin	.....	.....	.....	.....	.....	.....	300,268	880	7,774	.....
31	Gaston	378	.....	.....	.....	.....	7	95	535	11,238	.....
32	Gates	3,179	.....	.....	.....	.....	610	.....	28	5,847	.....
33	Granville	10,795	.....	.....	.....	.....	193	3,420,884	76	22,134	20
34	Green	530	.....	.....	.....	.....	12,580	.....	178	4,831	.....
35	Guilford	16,798	.....	.....	.....	.....	.....	1,900	600	25,138	.....
36	Halifax	.....	.....	.....	.....	.....	1,113	34,885	1,740	16,186	.....
37	Haywood	5,944	.....	10	.....	1	.....	8,550	.....	14,324	.....
38	Henderson	588	.....	.....	.....	.....	15	450	.....	11,304	.....
39	Hertford	1,487	.....	.....	.....	.....	427	.....	270	10,251	.....
40	Hyde	1,463	.....	.....	.....	.....	46,145	.....	3	4,802	.....
41	Iredell	24,942	.....	.....	.....	.....	240	34,875	1,112	17,047	.....
42	Johnson	1,194	.....	.....	.....	.....	9,000	125	753	15,786	3
43	Jones	20	.....	.....	.....	.....	92,470	70	98	8,355	.....
44	Lenoir	40	.....	.....	.....	.....	94,130	.....	185	7,383	.....
45	Lincoln	2,589	2	.....	.....	.....	248	1,103	506	8,079	.....
46	McDowell	7,103	.....	.....	.....	.....	1,801	4,977	1	8,105	.....
47	Macon	875	.....	.....	.....	.....	.....	34,710	.....	11,944	.....
48	Martin	.....	.....	.....	.....	.....	2,365	.....	89	10,647	.....
49	Mecklenburgh	1,520	5	.....	.....	.....	.....	.....	4,219	13,213	.....
50	Montgomery	3,670	.....	.....	.....	.....	175	6,990	1,456	6,854	.....
51	Moore	1,857	.....	.....	.....	.....	6,303	3,500	555	15,474	.....
52	Nash	1,399	.....	.....	.....	.....	4,181	5,338	345	12,865	.....
53	New Hanover	.....	.....	.....	.....	.....	1,413,525	.....	3	2,402	.....
54	Northampton	.....	.....	.....	.....	.....	450	27,100	1,378	8,717	.....
55	Onslow	175	.....	.....	.....	.....	22,505	.....	53	8,980	.....
56	Orange	14,541	.....	.....	.....	.....	.....	194,275	305	14,906	.....
57	Pasquotank	35,174	.....	.....	.....	.....	.....	.....	.....	5,952	51
58	Perquimans	23,402	.....	.....	.....	.....	.....	.....	2	10,089	.....
59	Person	4,018	.....	.....	.....	.....	18	1,562,119	18	11,776	1
60	Pitt	845	.....	.....	.....	.....	71,431	102	171	11,497	.....
61	Randolph	13,903	.....	.....	.....	.....	400	1,915	38	19,609	.....
62	Richmond	.....	.....	.....	.....	.....	10,857	500	3,816	10,809	.....
63	Robeson	.....	.....	.....	.....	.....	68,280	.....	2,299	17,705	.....
64	Rockingham	7,461	.....	.....	.....	.....	.....	908,729	.....	10,241	.....
65	Rowan	1,893	.....	.....	.....	.....	.....	40	854	10,731	4
66	Rutherford	2,612	2	.....	.....	.....	4,298	8,162	188	15,371	.....
67	Sampson	.....	.....	.....	.....	.....	68,300	100	313	16,263	.....
68	Stanley	2,624	.....	.....	.....	.....	250	4,609	701	5,541	20
69	Stokes	7,779	.....	.....	.....	.....	.....	393,106	.....	6,364	.....
70	Surry	32,212	.....	.....	.....	.....	.....	43,953	53	21,940	.....
71	Tyrrel	4,333	.....	.....	.....	.....	9,056	.....	.....	3,445	.....
72	Union	.....	.....	.....	.....	.....	1,780	641	2,264	18,005	.....
73	Wake	2,625	.....	.....	.....	.....	6,890	14,820	2,059	18,343	26
74	Warren	365	.....	.....	.....	.....	10	2,430,730	165	12,273	.....
75	Washington	6,019	.....	.....	.....	.....	9,408	.....	15	5,423	.....
76	Watauga	10,327	.....	10,446	.....	22	.....	1,044	.....	10,197	.....
77	Wayne	600	.....	.....	.....	.....	36,780	110	335	12,076	.....
78	Wilkes	38,772	.....	.....	.....	.....	.....	5,210	1	19,608	.....
79	Yancey	11,204	.....	6,641	.....	190	.....	12,245	.....	19,829	.....

STATISTICS OF

1	Adams	1,784	.....	11,996	.....	817	.....	29,500	.....	45,546	2
2	Allen	845	.....	43,860	.....	2,193	.....	.....	.....	32,827	3
3	Ashland	5,062	.....	163,472	.....	4,779	.....	.....	.....	205,566	67
4	Ashtabula	3,492	.....	260,517	.....	645	.....	31,910	.....	135,203	12
5	Athens	7,618	4	28,665	.....	2,052	.....	58,356	.....	92,990	.....
6	Auglaize	456	17	36,746	.....	1,559	.....	.....	.....	26,127	41
7	Belmont	9,234	.....	10,506	.....	1,445	.....	1,652,598	.....	187,666	3
8	Brown	3,412	22	6,280	.....	933	.....	1,279,510	.....	45,796	.....
9	Butler	405	25	7,592	.....	4,035	.....	2,500	.....	34,689	.....
10	Carroll	13,560	.....	1,283	.....	8	.....	.....	.....	198,558	.....
11	Champaign	515	.....	42,566	.....	3,704	.....	135	.....	126,206	47
12	Clark	70	.....	3,712	.....	603	.....	.....	.....	154,838	.....
13	Clermont	1,869	3	1,082	.....	1,326	.....	184,508	.....	47,142	.....
14	Clinton	665	.....	69,551	.....	4,906	.....	1,460	.....	112,897	3
15	Columbiana	18,898	.....	49,567	.....	4,324	.....	.....	.....	322,965	6
16	Coshocton	7,857	.....	32,898	.....	2,269	.....	.....	.....	174,919	.....
17	Crawford	2,089	.....	41,623	.....	1,916	.....	.....	.....	108,874	2

AGRICULTURAL PRODUCTS.					MANUFACTURES.				REMARKS.	
					Establishments.					
Beeswax and honey, pounds.	Value of animals slaughtered.	Value of produce of market gardens.	Value of orchard produce.	Wine, gallons.	Capital.	Hands employed.	Annual product.	Produced in families.		
1,593	138,397	....	5	......	163,980	169	79,193	36,435	....	27
4,109	179,038	....	321	113	88,425	122	168,810	25,495	....	28
10,019	59,693	....	290	......	271,400	308	253,871	21,710	Formed '49 from Stokes.	29
....	95,235	....	30	......	40,440	62	71,838	17,839	....	30
1,455	77,767	....	120	......	194,300	208	135,796	27,989	Formed '46 from Lincoln.	31
539	87,928	....	87	......	24,400	116	35,990	12,045	....	32
9,504	121,201	....	102	18	56,727	138	129,668	28,213	....	33
5,518	63,729	....	4	......	11,000	101	29,625	14,361	....	34
65	134,851	363	110	......	89,625	159	154,127	53,594	....	35
720	131,601	....	....	......	15,000	26	6,270	18,206	....	36
2,248	37,953	....	730	......	....	......	....	30,027	....	37
30	32,018	....	....	......	7,000	11	2,300	17,941	....	38
2,589	63,445	....	5,040	......	25,100	68	41,055	17,678	....	39
5,381	32,776	....	194	......	4,775	49	12,575	3,734	....	40
9,817	91,661	70	151	......	53,875	116	58,020	55,435	Div. '47 to form Alexander.	41
105	128,602	....	....	......	87,955	290	598,380	61,465	....	42
3,040	44,918	5	30	......	29,285	42	12,825	8,058	....	43
1,072	68,443	....	825	......	8,500	60	31,232	14,979	[tawba and Gaston.	44
5,033	45,629	20	155	44	231,180	327	177,547	18,062	Div. '42 and '46 to form Ca-	45
9,804	41,870	....	574	5	88,275	184	37,792	15,476	Formed in '42 from Burke	46
....	46,474	250	270	......	8,710	45	19,120	33,187	and Rutherford.	47
3,528	79,665	....	....	10	26,450	103	41,125	14,005	....	48
7,316	82,022	....	47	857	45,950	121	80,750	17,624	Div. '42 to form Union.	49
5,835	33,854	53	23	......	49,250	134	59,025	15,741	Divided since 1840 to form	50
2,195	48,970	....	....	100	4,750	9	12,795	20,956	Stanley.	51
1,086	87,579	14,100	....	......	17,075	57	87,112	30,244	....	52
1,000	62,273	1,335	....	......	593,250	922	1,409,568	137	....	53
5,569	114,762	....	....	......	1,900	51	9,448	14,183	....	54
6,681	71,557	100	10	45	166,400	186	238,750	11,264	....	55
2,084	86,467	....	20	......	37,400	51	63,645	44,202	Div. '49 to form Alamance.	56
2,023	52,640	....	35	......	41,500	96	64,900	10,715	....	57
635	56,308	....	....	......	15,835	29	19,650	12,617	....	58
3,423	61,490	5	124	......	43,355	74	53,040	24,309	....	59
6,621	109,164	150	87	613	46,755	125	64,563	33,454	....	60
7,226	83,584	62	32	......	279,395	382	274,576	27,366	....	61
2,766	63,408	....	....	108	60,000	60	37,000	16,048	....	62
1,450	101,505	....	....	40	14,800	117	32,523	37,348	....	63
336	64,598	....	....	......	120,663	407	194,569	23,224	....	64
595	83,277	57	210	8	190,535	496	339,349	37,658	....	65
15,083	78,318	5	6,113	......	65,000	121	63,044	33,486	Div. '42 to form McDowell.	66
205	138,790	....	....	10	89,300	163	52,980	26,925	[Montgomery.	67
13,549	32,897	44	....	......	26,227	26	13,079	21,510	Formed since 1840 from	68
25,607	44,213	....	....	......	56,310	168	60,520	16,226	Div. '49 to form Forsyth.	69
31,356	91,668	3,585	70	......	123,455	168	99,979	40,037	....	70
16,613	24,526	....	12	480	34,900	266	68,915	6,381	....	71
1,918	69,165	....	139	......	19,470	74	33,073	29,075	Formed '42 from Mecklen-	72
231	163,803	272	55	......	161,350	265	202,903	57,218	burgh and Anson.	73
5,244	90,562	....	....	......	55,229	86	108,299	27,925	....	74
12,641	51,220	50	1,992	6,110	83,295	200	78,630	21,129	[Yancey and Caldwell.	75
13,031	22,078	....	2,408	......	10,000	16	4,500	17,392	For. '49 from Ashe, Wilkes,	76
4,380	148,183	20	106	50	75,300	234	168,629	26,893	[exander and Watauga.	77
48,837	73,564	7	85	......	3,150	12	8,515	69,148	Div. '47 and '49 to form Al-	78
15,740	48,938	12,055	5,508	......	5,800	20	9,455	64,279	Div. '49 to form Watauga.	79

OHIO.

7,039	94,262	40	582	......	55,104	118	132,532	30,097	....	1
4,032	36,356	91	2,266	38	56,430	115	152,135	14,703	Div. 1848 to form Auglaize.	2
6,034	93,804	146	8,565	76	68,600	194	198,300	23,974	Formed '46 from Richland,	3
31,076	110,669	122	11,341	4	314,575	619	622,587	22,784	Wayne, Huron & Lorain.	4
9,983	75,551	5,029	6,199	......	185,350	214	170,617	28,325	Div. 1850 to form Vinton.	5
1,258	45,417	10	1,459	31	82,650	73	352,220	8,977	Formed '48 from Allen and	6
21,949	179,445	7,612	14,452	210	250,726	543	714,510	25,482	Mercer.	7
6,558	176,627	2,018	3,318	1,420	188,045	283	394,469	28,531	....	8
4,795	30,255	3,866	16,070	2,689	484,690	928	1,057,780	15,320	....	9
5,315	69,874	....	4,975	......	52,650	97	95,950	12,441	....	10
1,578	106,102	350	7,251	8	240,950	294	397,834	12,192	....	11
2,372	88,062	1,509	11,141	55	371,033	577	810,714	7,781	....	12
10,393	197,654	983	13,228	3,298	359,178	735	1,012,869	22,300	....	13
15,241	180,699	65	10,013	60	130,220	233	210,167	20,913	....	14
8,518	121,693	3,672	16,021	74	412,739	693	1,059,772	14,914	Div '46 to form Mahoning.	15
22,495	110,799	280	16,840	65	233,835	392	844,909	43,251	....	16
8,265	45,721	....	3,239	2	12,900	19	16,700	16,187	Div. '45 to form Wyandott.	17

	COUNTIES.	POPULATION.								
		Whites.			Colored.		All classes.		Total population.	
		Male.	Female.	Total.	Free.	Slave.	Male.	Female.	1850.	1840.
18	Cuyahoga	24,358	23,382	47,740	359	....	24,538	23,561	48,099	26,506
19	Darke	10,310	9,718	20,028	248	....	10,440	9,836	20,276	13,282
20	Defiance	3,629	3,318	6,947	19	....	3,640	3,326	6,966	....
21	Delaware	11,163	10,519	21,682	135	....	11,232	10,585	21,817	22,060
22	Erie	9,573	8,793	18,366	202	....	9,687	8,881	18,568	12,599
23	Fairfield	15,254	14,730	29,984	280	....	15,387	14,877	30,264	31,924
24	Fayette	6,388	6,047	12,435	291	....	6,536	6,190	12,726	10,984
25	Franklin	21,860	19,442	41,302	1,607	....	22,671	20,238	42,909	25,049
26	Fulton	4,103	3,677	7,780	1	....	4,104	3,677	7,781	....
27	Gallia	8.155	7,710	15,865	1,198	....	8,786	8,277	17,063	13,444
28	Geauga	9,040	8,780	17,820	7	....	9,044	8,783	17,827	16,297
29	Greene	10,873	10,419	21,292	654	....	11,194	10,752	21,946	17,528
30	Guernsey	15.248	15,022	30,270	168	....	15,325	15,113	30,438	27,748
31	Hamilton	80,912	72,332	153,244	3,600	....	82,643	74,201	156,844	80,145
32	Hancock	8,549	8,176	16,725	26	....	8,564	8,187	16,751	9,986
33	Hardin	4,303	3,934	8,237	14	....	4,311	3,940	8,251	4,598
34	Harrison	10,114	9,756	19,870	287	....	10,264	9,893	20,157	20,099
35	Henry	1,867	1,567	3,434	....	....	1,867	1,567	3,434	2,503
36	Highland	12,605	12,280	24,885	896	....	13,063	12,718	25,781	22,269
37	Hocking	7,121	6,881	14,002	117	....	7,192	6,927	14,119	9,741
38	Holmes	10,420	10,027	20,447	5	....	10,424	10,028	20,452	18,088
39	Huron	13.638	12,526	26,164	39	....	13,660	12,543	26,203	23,933
40	Jackson	6,322	6,006	12,328	391	....	6,515	6,204	12,719	9,744
41	Jefferson	14,212	14.256	28,468	665	....	14,525	14,608	29,133	25,030
42	Knox	14,727	14,083	28,810	62	....	14,759	14,113	28,872	29,579
43	Lake	7,414	7,203	14,616	38	....	7,439	7,215	14,654	13,719
44	Lawrence	7,805	7,115	14,920	326	....	7,961	7,285	15,246	9,738
45	Licking	19,621	19,097	38,718	128	....	19,691	19,155	38,846	35,096
46	Logan	9,711	8,915	18,626	536	....	9,983	9,179	19,162	14,015
47	Lorain	13,508	12,314	25,822	264	....	13,641	12,445	26,086	18,467
48	Lucas	6,497	5.727	12,224	139	....	6,578	5,785	12,363	9,382
49	Madison	5,087	4,850	9,937	78	....	5,128	4,887	10,015	9,025
50	Mahoning	12,051	11,594	23,645	90	....	12,105	11,630	23,735	....
51	Marion	6,396	6,201	12,597	21	....	6,409	6,209	12,618	14,765
52	Medina	12.607	11,799	24,406	35	....	12,625	11,816	24,441	18,352
53	Meigs	9,104	8,815	17,919	52	....	9,131	8,840	17,971	11,452
54	Mercer	3,807	3,506	7,313	399	....	4,014	3,698	7,712	8,277
55	Miami	12,481	11,916	24,397	602	....	12,795	12,204	24,999	19,688
56	Monroe	14,393	13,889	28,282	69	....	14,433	13,918	28,351	18,521
57	Montgomery	19,458	18,511	37,969	249	....	19,564	18,654	38,218	31,938
58	Morgan	14,571	13,924	28,495	90	....	14,615	13,970	28,585	20,852
59	Morrow	10,278	9,984	20,262	18	....	10,286	9,994	20,280	....
60	Muskingum	22,058	22,360	44,418	631	....	22,363	22,686	45,049	38,749
61	Ottawa	1,803	1,504	3,307	1	....	1,804	1,504	3,308	2,248
62	Paulding	961	804	1,765	1	....	962	804	1,766	1,034
63	Perry	10,375	10,371	20,746	29	....	10,392	10,383	20,775	19,344
64	Pickaway	10,521	10,073	20,594	412	....	10,736	10,270	21,006	19.725
65	Pike	5,338	4,997	10,335	618	....	5,672	5,281	10,953	7,626
66	Portage	12,426	11,935	24,361	58	....	12,459	11,960	24,419	22,965
67	Preble	11,094	10,565	21,659	77	....	11,136	10,600	21,736	19,482
68	Putnam	3,810	3.400	7,210	11	....	3,817	3,404	7,221	5,189
69	Richland	15,740	15,072	30,812	67	....	15,773	15,106	30,879	44,532
70	Ross	15,263	14,905	30,168	1,906	....	16,202	15,872	32,074	27,460
71	Sandusky	7,413	6,845	14,258	47	....	7,440	6,865	14,305	10,182
72	Scioto	9.627	8,590	18,217	211	....	9,737	8,691	18.428	11,192
73	Seneca	14,005	12,948	26,953	151	....	14,068	13,036	27,104	18,128
74	Shelby	7,029	6,522	13.551	407	....	7,248	6,710	13,958	12,154
75	Stark	20.334	19,385	39,719	159	....	20,402	19,476	39,878	34,603
76	Summit	14,117	13,247	27,364	121	....	14,171	13,314	27,485	22,560
77	Trumbull	15.381	15,044	30,425	65	....	15,414	15,076	30,490	38,107
78	Tuscarawas	16,205	15,467	31,672	89	....	16,256	15,505	31,761	25,631
79	Union	6,222	5,854	12,076	128	....	6,283	5,921	12,204	8,422
80	Van Wert	2,456	2,290	4,746	47	....	2,481	2,312	4,793	1,577
81	Vinton	4,730	4,516	9,246	107	....	4,778	4,575	9,353	....
82	Warren	12,796	12,162	24,954	602	....	13,082	12,478	25,560	23,141
83	Washington	14,931	14,219	29,150	390	....	15,124	14,416	29,540	20,823
84	Wayne	16,873	16,080	32,953	28	....	16,890	16,091	32,981	35,808
85	Williams	4,287	3,731	8,018	....	....	4,287	3,731	8,018	4,465
86	Wood	4,737	4,402	9,139	18	....	4,748	4,409	9,157	5,357
87	Wyandott	5,756	5,389	11,145	49	....	5,784	5,410	11,194	....

NATIVITIES, DWELLINGS, &c.				EDUCATION AND RELIGION.									
Born out of State.				Colleges, academies, and private schools.		Public Schools.							
United States.	Foreign countries.	Dwellings.	Families.	Pupils.	Annual income.	Pupils.	Annual income.	Total educational income.	White scholars during year.	Whites 5 and under 20 years old.	Whites over 20 unable to read & write.	Accommodation of churches—persons.	
14,380	14,495	8,289	8,802	1,086	$42,400	5,850	$15,005	$57,405	11,541	16,756	694	22,640	18
5,027	1,028	3,476	3,550	......	....	7,585	5,835	5,835	5,411	8,332	910	8,500	19
2,027	681	1,237	1,237	......	....	1,220	2,148	2,148	1,737	2,764	266	1,900	20
6,310	1,087	3,754	3,783	257	1,000	8,261	20,103	21,103	5,771	8,958	348	15,560	21
6,459	4,052	3,362	3,393	110	1,200	4,976	22,010	23,210	4,741	6,517	320	6,604	22
6,915	1,859	5,207	5,310	......	....	6,140	14,167	14,167	9,169	11,683	1,932	38,440	23
2,885	119	2,155	2,155	......	....	2,090	3,373	3,373	3,074	4,979	728	7,600	24
11,712	6,786	6,701	7,291	397	19,933	14,287	15,303	35,236	9,497	15,210	640	29,710	25
3,142	686	1,355	1,361	......	....	......	....	....	2,820	3,194	224	1,300	26
4,982	886	2,975	2,986	......	....	2,819	3,078	3,078	3,355	6,420	590	6,950	27
7,576	579	3,240	3,410	225	12,000	4,336	5,048	17,048	4,904	6,656	3	13,075	28
6,108	974	3,760	3,820	176	200	2,215	13,275	13,475	5,715	8,233	799	18,620	29
7,539	850	5,079	5,117	60	700	8,135	7,329	8,029	8,140	12,375	1,369	26,450	30
30,799	65,459	21,021	28,224	5,599	58,240	15,949	45,462	103,702	24,041	48,831	3,154	82,952	31
4,227	847	2,824	2,839	......	....	5,873	5,234	5,234	4,930	7,090	491	8,758	32
1,807	735	1,402	1,402	......	....	754	1,269	1,269	1,369	3,376	126	1,950	33
4,738	822	3,526	3,578	165	1,916	2,634	8,461	10,377	5,105	7,604	1,507	21,445	34
1,034	473	610	618	......	....	1,564	1,273	1,273	751	1,352	36	635	35
6,238	552	4,477	4,482	202	....	6,376	9,964	9,964	5,636	10,013	399	25,400	36
2,784	810	2,367	2,390	......	....	2,031	2,833	2,833	3,615	5,986	850	8,025	37
5,001	1,532	3,436	3,507	......	....	3,690	5,493	5,493	6,089	8,470	319	11,850	38
11,222	1,750	4,619	4,728	158	1,863	7,380	11,173	13,036	8,801	9,972	326	13,400	39
2,939	1,379	2,120	2,129	......	....	4,082	3,149	3,149	3,005	5,208	601	4,098	40
7,716	1,963	5,191	5,397	411	17,000	4,828	10,996	27,996	7,732	11,128	286	30,600	41
8,772	1,143	4,853	4,938	387	8,800	6,315	6,278	15,078	8,192	11,577	391	28,800	42
5,863	993	2,700	2,744	510	8,000	3,517	4,556	12,556	4,697	5,452	16	30,400	43
3,911	1,327	2,553	2,602	......	....	6,205	2,513	2,513	1,714	5,996	1,855	2,900	44
11,635	2,113	6,639	6,869	215	10,950	16,989	12,078	23,028	11,294	14,659	359	32,345	45
5,127	625	3,243	3,251	35	1,000	7,965	9,982	10,982	5,678	7,551	215	6,650	46
10,879	3,619	4,674	4,857	649	....	8,027	8,276	8,276	7,831	9,664	242	16,000	47
4,462	3,210	2,225	2,251	......	....	5,122	5,326	5,326	2,601	4,443	392	5,020	48
2,471	289	1,742	1,742	......	....	3,833	5,734	5,734	2,572	3,975	628	8,625	49
6,604	2,033	4,298	4,316	194	1,480	6,476	5,602	7,082	7,216	9,064	384	24,390	50
2,856	1,257	2,158	2,170	......	....	2,300	3,474	3,474	3,637	5,280	308	5,150	51
10,297	2,041	4,430	4,458	25	75	9,915	6,408	6,483	8,371	9,500	211	13,400	52
4,703	1,766	3,136	3,170	160	....	5,366	6,675	6,675	4,965	7,144	585	8,200	53
1,529	1,048	1,312	1,324	......	....	1,335	2,094	2,094	1,491	3,059	373	3,600	54
7,006	1,234	4,391	4,445	......	....	10,579	17,020	17,020	7,083	9,753	539	19,350	55
6,325	2,505	4,892	4,893	30	200	5,409	6,642	6,842	6,776	11,731	1,837	19,841	56
11,059	4,449	6,527	6,569	......	....	13,828	16,343	16,343	8,509	14,335	208	27,735	57
6,737	845	4,886	4,913	60	800	5,905	7,332	8,132	7,934	11,694	1,002	21,250	58
6,877	825	3,652	3,726	40	400	1,268	4,098	4,498	7,057	8,218	913	17,305	59
12,158	3,743	7,757	7,819	648	7,466	15,800	17,912	25,378	10,881	17,310	1,496	43,006	60
899	519	613	613	......	....	1,296	1,165	1,165	940	1,283	272	1,350	61
571	112	307	307	......	....	......	....	....	337	678	62	....	62
5,933	1,303	3,587	3,602	111	200	......	....	200	5,806	8,314	1,088	22,600	63
5,180	697	3,600	3,656	......	....	8,625	8,601	8,601	5,711	8,217	1,343	18,972	64
2,114	1,098	1,935	1,935	......	....	1,478	2,892	2,892	2,237	3,983	1,324	11,255	65
8,500	1,832	4,512	4,633	106	890	11,024	12,047	12,937	7,717	9,118	174	24,425	66
6,308	643	3,749	3,756	......	....	3,120	11,239	11,239	6,480	8,631	376	16,380	67
1,339	1,083	1,246	1,249	......	....	3,063	3,221	3,221	2,205	2,976	520	4,300	68
10,701	2,315	5,205	5,232	......	....	15,397	9,032	9,032	9,361	12,217	175	21,775	69
7,193	2,584	5,575	5,585	365	4,419	7,324	12,769	17,188	6,732	11,504	2,379	29,918	70
4,381	1,680	2,437	2,481	150	....	3,531	3,452	3,452	4,271	6,008	754	4,350	71
4,537	2,058	3,086	3,086	......	....	1,650	2,674	2,674	3,771	7,001	79	5,820	72
8,629	3,517	4,645	4,670	100	....	6,451	8,408	8,408	7,984	10,839	360	16,705	73
2,757	1,110	2,405	2,413	154	700	2,597	5,101	5,801	3,053	5,562	673	11,200	74
10,404	5,997	6,778	6,959	243	4,880	13,290	17,679	22,559	10,123	15,664	728	35,036	75
10,395	2,740	4,885	4,933	370	7,500	9,614	10,945	18,445	8,699	10,486	744	19,400	76
10,081	1,761	5,429	5,583	186	1,470	14,904	33,184	34,654	9,461	11,624	224	27,710	77
6,236	4,640	5,441	5,546	824	....	6,927	10,875	10,875	7,310	12,592	1,682	31,550	78
3,038	376	2,059	2,094	32	353	3,279	4,094	4,447	4,093	5,052	666	7,400	79
1,163	392	786	805	......	....	1,762	6,623	6,623	1,146	1,887	116	1,700	80
2,147	189	1,569	1,578	......	....	2,358	2,534	2,534	2,422	3,901	989	7,325	81
6,671	1,029	4,494	4,495	625	4,700	4,117	6,632	11,332	7,422	9,291	681	22,295	82
6,894	2,726	4,906	5,049	457	8,125	6,008	10,738	18,863	7,321	11,658	1,199	17,545	83
11,160	3,135	5,712	5,822	240	2,200	13,927	14,918	17,118	9,706	13,042	723	32,000	84
2,597	493	1,390	1,401	......	....	2,040	3,015	3,015	2,257	3,271	176	1,125	85
2,804	1,137	1,542	1,559	......	....	2,876	3,142	3,142	2,871	3,823	17	1,725	86
3,301	658	1,964	1,979	......	....	......	....	....	3,285	4,399	300	....	87

	Counties.	Land occupied or improved.				Live stock upon farms.			
		Farms.	Acres improved.	Acres unimproved.	Value with improvements and implements.	Horses, asses, and mules.	Neat Cattle.	Sheep.	Swine.
18	Cuyahoga	2,228	130,534	78,153	$5,215,997	4,989	22,541	83,493	10,133
19	Darke	2,151	102,977	140,154	3,744,794	7,198	17,284	23,840	40,224
20	Defiance	296	18,524	27,166	514,488	729	3,060	1,844	4,627
21	Delaware	1,855	109,458	111,538	3,652,492	6,524	16,745	52,525	26,598
22	Erie	1,021	85,773	39,442	3,132,631	3,443	11,399	62,003	8,758
23	Fairfield	2,383	191,146	113,155	7,051,430	9,267	22,842	45,201	37,734
24	Fayette	1,007	123,255	84,905	3,671,374	4,828	20,797	36,715	31,891
25	Franklin	2,666	153,648	105,206	6,557,111	9,971	20,458	33,391	63,256
26	Fulton	826	38,077	57,762	1,143,320	1,410	7,402	8,932	7,670
27	Gallia	1,190	82,706	132,831	1,962,157	3,198	9,033	18,756	12,688
28	Geauga	1,906	132,387	69,666	3,449,064	4,371	26,165	68,980	5,571
29	Greene	1,626	131,316	108,589	6,248,593	7,171	17,444	47,898	36,994
30	Guernsey	2,209	170,632	143,121	4,721,548	8,151	19,149	74,379	26,650
31	Hamilton	2,602	137,517	72,883	17,694,328	7,492	11,730	7,696	34,997
32	Hancock	1,636	80,995	113,475	2,520,182	4,671	12,127	20,196	19,028
33	Hardin	783	33,353	64,588	1,142,250	2,199	6,346	6,833	13,768
34	Harrison	1,6[illegible]	134,298	90,102	4,937,620	5,892	13,366	114,262	23,450
35	Henry	307	10,131	38,158	407,198	592	2,651	1,252	3,894
36	Highland	2,323	169,513	136,290	5,961,959	8,507	17,682	33,365	53,289
37	Hocking	1,180	59,709	82,626	1,398,829	3,055	8,273	16,328	11,058
38	Holmes	2,171	143,604	107,567	4,381,019	6,702	17,609	54,234	22,135
39	Huron	2,414	148,392	99,734	5,568,102	6,741	23,462	83,707	20,912
40	Jackson	1,164	72,073	93,903	1,470,446	2,273	9,684	18,138	13,432
41	Jefferson	1,838	140,986	91,448	7,391,930	6,183	15,237	120,526	25,203
42	Knox	2,268	166,981	131,094	5,790,742	8,205	18,574	88,224	24,750
43	Lake	1,449	88,334	45,969	3,279,731	3,439	16,594	54,952	5,928
44	Lawrence	254	17,279	31,638	524,843	721	1,987	3,622	4,306
45	Licking	3,313	233,761	167,984	8,017,822	10,333	29,248	128,179	30,114
46	Logan	1,626	97,672	119,036	3,589,025	6,826	15,304	65,600	24,919
47	Lorain	2,430	127,165	90,262	4,295,232	5,811	26,555	91,835	13,102
48	Lucas	683	30,115	42,646	1,038,438	1,379	5,649	8,009	5,861
49	Madison	774	157,813	96,605	3,750,817	5,193	27,333	55,279	25,896
50	Mahoning	2,052	143,098	86,746	5,772,161	6,601	22,278	96,068	13,887
51	Marion	919	109,444	67,635	2,290,126	4,260	16,894	60,705	19,586
52	Medina	2,461	144,661	76,617	4,943,225	5,943	25,119	107,182	15,535
53	Meigs	1,149	58,139	87,445	1,716,720	2,357	7,962	19,893	7,938
54	Mercer	675	26,176	48,258	720,039	1,835	4,599	4,565	8,655
55	Miami	1,882	115,063	94,907	5,518,019	6,948	12,678	26,813	25,907
56	Monroe	2,637	124,100	164,349	3,101,515	7,235	16,878	31,212	30,911
57	Montgomery	2,068	151,306	109,233	7,957,456	7,798	14,631	18,683	32,399
58	Morgan	2,126	133,657	137,183	4,417,336	6,660	15,827	53,016	23,010
59	Morrow	1,552	95,976	83,951	3,003,341	5,558	14,289	50,433	14,777
60	Muskingum	2,680	212,795	157,796	8,303,636	9,554	24,873	76,758	33,825
61	Ottawa	227	13,158	16,513	331,340	719	2,673	6,712	3,399
62	Paulding	77	4,221	5,566	132,140	219	821	337	1,233
63	Perry	1,314	103,668	78,707	3,284,783	4,842	12,246	41,083	19,477
64	Pickaway	1,261	160,288	113,300	6,319,958	7,399	27,054	29,832	52,284
65	Pike	731	68,185	75,386	1,760,384	2,873	6,162	9,668	15,748
66	Portage	2,264	162,659	88,273	5,632,629	5,117	33,543	108,084	9,296
67	Preble	1,799	130,101	114,065	6,213,332	7,381	15,355	25,288	51,417
68	Putnam	603	26,399	49,467	812,841	1,678	4,723	5,053	9,013
69	Richland	2,522	162,545	119,402	6,493,200	8,235	20,910	71,778	26,991
70	Ross	1,435	179,002	130,557	7,186,009	6,866	22,056	23,227	56,104
71	Sandusky	1,391	72,806	77,885	2,412,386	3,673	10,863	23,106	15,796
72	Scioto	751	51,150	75,235	2,338,509	2,855	7,828	11,485	16,169
73	Seneca	2,582	152,554	131,822	5,972,907	7,703	20,718	73,791	31,431
74	Shelby	1,363	62,651	86,791	2,153,419	4,004	10,215	19,724	19,271
75	Stark	3,177	206,116	124,173	8,816,570	9,273	26,452	100,219	34,674
76	Summit	2,329	158,901	77,400	5,895,020	5,792	23,646	97,591	17,066
77	Trumbull	2,753	210,525	125,026	7,022,708	6,962	44,521	70,669	12,800
78	Tuscarawas	2,250	155,359	120,340	4,576,475	7,228	19,813	65,349	24,883
79	Union	1,255	77,678	92,215	2,096,768	4,714	12,774	23,574	19,729
80	Van Wert	317	14,850	30,229	364,608	810	3,407	2,312	6,277
81	Vinton	806	53,282	77,981	1,200,728	2,064	9,240	15,005	9,580
82	Warren	1,985	143,582	99,777	8,997,807	8,251	16,631	26,694	49,943
83	Washington	1,776	96,545	151,685	2,942,459	3,779	14,684	39,570	13,667
84	Wayne	2,904	204,129	130,906	9,731,192	10,379	25,859	92,924	35,935
85	Williams	651	28,670	55,906	908,183	1,211	5,434	4,521	7,769
86	Wood	704	36,796	58,428	1,032,477	1,989	7,003	6,514	7,217
87	Wyandott	928	78,898	67,262	1,918,229	2,922	12,347	39,026	14,952

AGRICULTURAL PRODUCTS.												
Wheat, bushels.	Rye & oats, bushels.	Indian corn, bushels.	Irish and sweet potatoes, bushels.	Peas and beans, bushels.	Barley, bushels.	Buckwheat, bushels.	Butter and cheese, pounds.	Hay, tons.	Hops, pounds.	Clover & other grass seeds, bushels.	Flaxseed, bushels.	
65,487	198,062	362,102	122,768	917	2,818	4,326	1,373,145	37,560	1,109	323	36	13
132,594	129,339	590.077	37,780	160	1,121	5,028	393.203	11,519	39	1,183	16,622	19
47,806	26,841	90,691	19,754	365	......	1,135	50,918	2,372	19	207	36	20
44,525	144,817	774,289	57,085	265	2,228	11,949	480,319	22,021	2,319	367	1,223	21
180,521	117,643	374,988	80,064	400	2,294	9,876	353,793	17,204	3	668	......	22
274,903	204,852	1,574,971	64,348	146	2,191	6,138	588,732	22,188	519	3,664	482	23
46,958	42,732	1,177,815	13,255	355	......	1,434	193,902	14,283	36	254	111	24
97,993	178,965	2,521,988	114,628	1,096	1,332	10,721	985,015	19,644	107	811	111	25
81,847	54,789	136,310	44,914	527	95	7,658	174,834	10,490	6	905	27	26
62,095	97,163	377,365	37,920	1,825	35	2,128	203,127	7,908	80	150	242	27
37,096	176,030	258,430	85,464	139	4,433	8,663	2,722,310	38,211	......	324	367	28
241,794	123,772	1,219,944	48,029	349	1,373	2,733	524,129	15,704	2	910	9,445	29
217,275	306,124	682,757	20,324	156	834	12,319	618,965	16,260	80	1,649	1,031	30
112,632	249,306	1,593,618	416,682	4,402	61,140	4,949	757,854	19,992	20	157	......	31
197,003	97,523	451,391	57,169	40	384	3.533	266.391	10,728	215	1,806	184	32
34,463	34,735	248,320	23,047	177	103	3,546	268,125	6,527	......	423	291	33
235,152	272,792	503,771	32,514	598	1,423	9,199	400,487	15,270	1,004	3,204	533	34
19,250	15,496	76,415	17,744	186	31	963	47,549	1,498	51	43	15	35
191,556	171,102	1,578,967	34,977	222	112	3,057	494,028	11,426	37	2,285	153	36
85,195	79,766	334,342	23,070	601	......	5,341	157,672	5,352	......	1,032	1,033	37
294,677	218,477	358,360	70,926	528	467	19,656	470,506	16,357	88	4,057	1,241	38
301,892	244,885	666,416	135,285	1,726	2,347	7,543	841,157	31,433	870	3,078	239	39
38,180	74,884	316,337	16,534	1,864	205	2,696	140,690	7,184	61	203	395	40
411,905	374,360	582,844	59,701	453	14,678	10,222	595,131	15,495	509	2,122	108	41
239,177	217,828	723,729	72,269	582	1,165	25,059	525,086	20,588	2,032	2,002	1,377	42
51,744	159,936	336,312	120,502	2,205	10,335	5,647	844,392	25,582	......	766	211	43
9,395	37,255	188,418	28,394	68	......	312	46,594	1,082	......	16	......	44
336,317	246,965	1,433,345	86,147	710	1,950	19,035	1,005,887	33,754	99	1,667	78	45
166,811	100,637	665,606	27,691	130	296	3,781	364,962	14,555	28	1,122	2,092	46
142,881	174,722	385,837	96,205	2,212	349	4,491	1,169,152	37,500	716	734	108	47
51,914	38,198	118,947	47,762	2,788	225	9,702	134,481	9,045	5	194	273	48
23,540	53,775	726,451	14,463	732	151	3,444	378,698	19,308	319	442	15	49
151,110	299,130	281,019	76,476	491	13,400	14,863	800,060	40,930	62	3,423	7,697	50
32,806	101,212	559,794	22,688	120	1,203	4,376	259,006	17,434	261	2,115	173	51
132,446	217,998	418,027	82,858	2,491	3,880	6,750	850,073	37,571	19,751	5,965	1,148	52
113,091	71,329	267,404	66,273	506	200	9,144	226,390	8,871	......	262	298	53
51,661	35,774	149,506	15,730	88	183	831	145,412	4,128	......	164	283	54
222,122	180,106	1,129,456	48,232	177	2,978	2,776	526,364	11,057	2	1,973	24,764	55
148,351	228,353	617,667	30,508	1,151	651	13,579	364,229	6,793	3,480	857	788	56
315,769	215,240	1,273,932	71,777	1,388	12,541	2,009	373,519	12,301	6	2,382	36.093	57
266,236	163,259	570,846	29,858	487	71	7,919	595,663	13,825	600	1,890	420	58
81,925	174,906	366,679	52,020	911	831	17,966	372,966	19,428	12	3,356	2,549	59
415,847	285,748	1,144,855	85,962	349	1,683	12,024	819,492	20,997	18	2,421	304	60
23,288	13,118	55.584	8,345	270	351	2,932	35,544	4.445	......	192	5	61
10,704	4,546	41,699	4,232	......	......	134	400	362	......	......	2	62
160,043	104,879	428,913	25,486	94	118	8.542	266,470	9.887	82	1,616	991	63
144,377	60,494	2,672,303	133,230	108	166	2,400	311,889	7,616	22	1,509	44	64
16,725	68,936	797,655	15,260	418	70	864	124,945	2,598	100	97	155	65
137,147	174,410	264,171	130,065	1,502	2,934	9,363	3,534,417	46,189	342	1,629	3,469	66
228,435	188,576	1,175,391	31,617	58	8,022	1,935	490,886	10,221	119	1,747	30,532	67
68,853	32,537	189,165	23,987	150	32	908	92,420	4,478	......	376	13	68
347,487	314,510	495,253	81,723	630	3,049	19,557	598,393	2,779	147	6,580	1,311	69
141,131	85,202	2,840,443	34,502	148	2,691	2,148	354,673	8,383	74	672	46	70
160,393	99,476	312,689	63,182	204	338	8,830	258,502	14,794	36	1,092	13	71
19,398	84,314	921,811	46,690	178	12	1,334	105,003	5,123	......	56	19	72
474,737	238,176	632,879	102,480	518	1,430	3,194	596,322	25,580	158	6,471	337	73
89,109	111,284	439,798	20,536	24	555	2,253	265,669	7,205	......	670	6,065	74
590,594	430,283	578,171	124,452	215	13,061	10,279	1,221,893	41,746	589	5,293	2,107	75
325,642	237,533	365,762	100,393	2,846	3,013	10,136	1,927,351	37,793	265	2,812	1,628	76
121,068	241,553	302,906	137,995	549	280	24,960	5,563,055	64,116	221	913	7,873	77
350;773	295,178	402,761	27,502	21	2,044	15,552	507,948	18,523	405	3,259	1,464	78
26,563	92,106	624,898	30,936	437	467	8,260	457,747	16,969	1,700	269	162	79
31,900	16,130	67,175	9,433	4	25	686	83,406	2,371	......	330	51	80
27,097	45,440	249,899	17,347	729	......	2,926	114,703	6,357	49	152	361	81
251,606	261,812	1,886,836	73,153	946	23,415	6,100	622,614	14,201	121	1,279	1,322	82
79,615	133,559	474,464	119,550	2,901	107	14,238	392,167	12,045	47	752	377	83
571,377	439,916	627,460	110,590	238	1,887	15,442	1,040,398	41,722	1,320	8,801	1,732	84
84,322	37,782	105,922	15,882	276	38	1,559	91,443	4,431	32	350	4	85
36,933	56,971	171,285	37,786	133	67	13,677	160,962	8,982	......	205	......	86
75,447	67,328	349,094	29,234	439	363	6,803	207,984	10,165	136	1,260	174	87

	Counties.	Agricultural products.									
		Flax, pounds.	Hemp, dew and water rotted, tons.	Maple sugar, pounds.	Cane sugar, hhds. of 1,000 pounds.	Molasses, gallons.	Rice, pounds.	Tobacco, pounds.	Ginned cotton, bales of 400 pounds.	Wool, pounds.	Silk cocoons, pounds.
18	Cuyahoga	370	.....	70,116	.....	2,396	.....	.....	.....	222,915	1
19	Darke	489	.....	47,756	.....	4,791	.....	7,132	.....	61,132	20
20	Defiance	429	.....	14,658	.....	583	.....	.....	.....	5,311	.....
21	Delaware	180	.....	106,062	.....	2,320	.....	.....	.....	124,064	.....
22	Erie	190	.....	7,067	.....	122	.....	.....	.....	156,536	.....
23	Fairfield	5,009	.....	41,557	.....	3,220	.....	118,328	.....	113,596	.....
24	Fayette	1,004	.....	657	.....	93	.....	225	.....	98,328	.....
25	Franklin	1,329	16	26,763	.....	1,208	.....	.....	.....	90,587	.....
26	Fulton	315	.....	41,531	.....	705	.....	.....	.....	27,578	.....
27	Gallia	6,060	.....	6,853	.....	334	.....	.....	.....	40,576	50
28	Geauga	330	.....	349,314	.....	2,090	.....	200	.....	184,719	.....
29	Greene	178	.....	53,622	.....	3,245	.....	.....	.....	112,063	.....
30	Guernsey	20,775	20	8,279	.....	1,187	.....	1,738,131	.....	178,267	2
31	Hamilton	.....	.....	1,015	.....	604	.....	.....	.....	18,619	.....
32	Hancock	4,374	.....	106,433	.....	5,373	.....	.....	.....	53,404	.....
33	Hardin	1,809	.....	64,404	.....	3,733	.....	.....	.....	19,726	.....
34	Harrison	10,764	.....	14,550	.....	2,369	.....	.....	.....	306,161	.....
35	Henry	484	.....	20,537	.....	748	.....	.....	.....	2,769	.....
36	Highland	3,108	20	27,608	.....	2,458	.....	1,130	.....	83,920	5
37	Hocking	6,222	.....	17,310	.....	1,588	.....	222,887	.....	37,828	.....
38	Holmes	8,555	5	48,502	.....	2,240	.....	.....	.....	138,633	17
39	Huron	2,628	2	104,659	.....	459	.....	137	.....	255,134	.....
40	Jackson	3,681	.....	6,226	.....	266	.....	640	.....	40,416	.....
41	Jefferson	4,650	.....	5,016	.....	1,206	.....	.....	.....	334,030	.....
42	Knox	3,410	.....	117,058	.....	4,738	.....	65,200	.....	231,318	210
43	Lake	884	.....	79,345	.....	1,491	.....	.....	.....	142,779	.....
44	Lawrence	303	.....	250	.....	18	.....	.....	.....	7,405	.....
45	Licking	3,546	.....	64,726	.....	2,246	.....	.....	.....	338,245	1
46	Logan	176	.....	162,929	.....	6,643	.....	.....	.....	88,258	.....
47	Lorain	558	1	142,899	.....	889	.....	.....	.....	262,500	.....
48	Lucas	40	.....	5,375	.....	24	.....	.....	.....	20,321	.....
49	Madison	370	.....	3,615	.....	320	.....	96	.....	120,696	.....
50	Mahoning	42,551	.....	72,709	.....	5,958	.....	.....	.....	288,010	.....
51	Marion	1,845	.....	37,166	.....	2,037	.....	.....	.....	126,595	14
52	Medina	32,150	5	238,641	.....	2,156	.....	.....	.....	306,602	.....
53	Meigs	5,880	.....	11,464	.....	405	.....	190	.....	44,142	3
54	Mercer	288	.....	12,684	.....	729	.....	.....	.....	11,656	.....
55	Miami	2,268	.....	34,806	.....	6,033	.....	22,500	.....	71,430	215
56	Monroe	19,593	.....	24,682	.....	1,660	.....	3,681,705	.....	70,696	.....
57	Montgomery	112	.....	67,234	.....	8,450	.....	196,971	.....	53,813	.....
58	Morgan	5,303	.....	12,976	.....	903	.....	421,144	.....	135,387	104
59	Morrow	1,611	.....	111,501	.....	3,339	.....	.....	.....	134,995	.....
60	Muskingum	6,535	.....	5,661	.....	1,214	.....	5,000	.....	194,866	5
61	Ottawa	100	.....	5,040	.....	115	.....	.....	.....	19,326	.....
62	Paulding	50	.....	5,360	.....	.....	.....	.....	.....	721	.....
63	Perry	7,430	.....	38,747	.....	3,225	.....	116,010	.....	104,526	.....
64	Pickaway	690	.....	15,673	.....	492	.....	.....	.....	73,983	.....
65	Pike	5,768	.....	14,593	.....	501	.....	.....	.....	23,475	.....
66	Portage	5,883	.....	176,033	.....	4,290	.....	1,550	.....	295,069	.....
67	Preble	989	.....	23,558	.....	3,286	.....	50	.....	72,151	165
68	Putnam	785	.....	31,198	.....	1,046	.....	.....	.....	15,123	.....
69	Richland	4,197	.....	132,239	.....	6,869	.....	.....	.....	194,573	8
70	Ross	960	.....	35,701	.....	4,945	.....	.....	.....	61,964	15
71	Sandusky	212	.....	38,609	.....	1,016	.....	.....	.....	67,061	.....
72	Scioto	2,500	.....	1,930	.....	80	.....	.....	.....	23,516	.....
73	Seneca	904	4	68,317	.....	2,197	.....	.....	.....	202,181	.....
74	Shelby	453	.....	10,781	.....	387	.....	.....	.....	47,534	72
75	Stark	10,890	.....	52,323	.....	3,447	.....	300	.....	275,664	.....
76	Summit	65,173	.....	58,647	.....	1,775	.....	900	.....	268,971	.....
77	Trumbull	17,746	6	145,955	.....	4,873	.....	33	.....	208,055	13
78	Tuscarawas	8,500	.....	30,614	.....	2,144	.....	68,096	.....	176,200	47
79	Union	1,275	.....	193,842	.....	11,189	.....	.....	.....	62,233	.....
80	Van Wert	1,435	.....	10,093	.....	344	.....	.....	.....	5,609	.....
81	Vinton	6,242	.....	23,296	.....	1,052	.....	1,500	.....	33,788	.....
82	Warren	310	.....	81,068	.....	7,233	.....	2,600	.....	78,365	120
83	Washington	9,609	.....	19,072	.....	597	.....	540,392	.....	95,066	2
84	Wayne	5,240	.....	59,431	.....	3,016	.....	925	.....	255,511	277
85	Williams	283	.....	44,077	.....	606	.....	.....	.....	12,154	.....
86	Wood	.....	.....	31,380	.....	375	.....	.....	.....	18,544	.....
87	Wyandott	1,121	.....	32,500	.....	2,103	.....	.....	.....	96,173	.....

AGRICULTURAL PRODUCTS.					MANUFACTURES.				REMARKS.	
					Establishments.					
Beeswax and honey, pounds.	Value of animals slaughtered.	Value of produce of market gardens.	Value of orchard produce.	Wine, gallons.	Capital.	Hands employed.	Annual product.	Produced in families.		
9,219	$ 141,209	$ 23,967	$ 12,473	346	$ 542,960	876	$ 883,924	$12,279	....	18
10,035	86,385	155	4,000	233	....	......	....	42,577	[liams, Henry & Paulding.	19
4,860	15,026	42	2,047	49	55,405	79	102,154	2,305	Formed in 1845 from Wil-	20
3,732	72,954	156	1,376	......	231,550	311	233,285	21,895	Divided in 1848 to form	21
10,174	66,997	2,420	9,334	500	327,390	393	550,540	4,600	Morrow.	22
11,069	114,879	661	10,257	......	293,075	458	714,667	30,352	....	23
11,122	52,071	135	3,052	......	34,950	80	63,790	18,594	....	24
6,002	145,151	6,928	10,726	96	985,470	1,886	1,739,774	28,943	[Henry and Williams.	25
15,648	28,164	....	3,585	......	38,765	61	60,305	9,133	Formed in '50 from Lucas,	26
23,694	54,833	12	232	32	166,500	159	158,000	19,512	Divided in 1850 to form	27
9,737	62,815	....	3,177	5	49,175	95	87,322	9,556	Vinton.	28
9,420	121,352	669	25,314	15	418,693	501	769,606	10,973	....	29
17,530	101,029	53	22,024	6	98,687	187	251,175	37,659	....	30
5,943	194,642	91,186	26,245	35,284	7,426,716	15,638	20,790,743	30,994	[Wyandott.	31
8,679	55,457	10	4,088	5	58,875	91	144,847	28,970	Divided in 1845 to form	32
15,202	32,379	....	7,710	......	42,250	84	67,900	10,815	Divided in 1845 to form	33
16,728	85,188	....	18,204	......	88,660	181	156,712	20,223	Wyandott.	34
3,950	13,088	64	706	......	28,885	53	42,535	2,209	Div. '45, '48, '50 to form De-	35
12,935	106,301	....	3,722	......	174,161	362	370,642	33,726	fiance, Morrow & Fulton.	36
1,930	41,468	....	2,923	......	27,505	45	31,555	22,717	Div. 1850 to form Vinton.	37
9,522	84,690	445	9,258	113	102,895	254	218,794	35,359	....	38
24,431	104,149	418	10,928	104	472,025	805	1,011,561	28,864	Div. '46 to form Ashland.	39
2,038	38,037	101	837	40	201,400	394	230,549	20,289	Div. 1850 to form Vinton.	40
15,828	143,279	6,255	16,867	51	704,120	1,525	1,996,704	16,693	....	41
8,727	90,567	270	8,115	3	451,150	553	793,126	15,151	....	42
14,845	78,517	5,853	7,313	60	367,535	701	603,074	35,648	....	43
2,015	17,996	....	650	......	835,900	1,251	716,288	4,786	....	44
7,459	155,567	4,466	5,285	266	458,982	1,158	981,665	35,659	....	45
4,382	91,654	82	4,449	20	156,950	194	399,700	25,990	....	46
17,409	92,231	37	8,614	2	129,300	199	225,086	11,764	Div. '46 to form Ashland.	47
10,213	25,432	802	2,610	36	271,700	497	771,175	2,715	Div. 1850 to form Fulton.	48
10,213	41,278	5	4,507	......	31,256	113	65,225	12,171	[and Columbiana.	49
4,392	109,705	5	3,872	......	379,040	579	536,400	19,587	Formed '46 from Trumbull	50
13,821	37,127	30	4,165	84	24,750	63	46,855	10,869	Divided in '45 & '48 to form	51
15,144	93,699	37	14,284	6	108,382	270	247,936	26,699	Wyandott and Morrow.	52
5,026	49,966	280	12,259	......	222,540	567	446,770	21,046	....	53
2,549	25,300	140	813	......	13,850	19	20,220	4,620	Divided in 1848 to form	54
4,627	113,464	2,158	6,773	5	708,865	643	934,446	15,934	Auglaize.	55
20,391	80,978	20	6,637	283	49,867	86	93,611	33,759	....	56
2,308	127,836	4,482	10,813	665	1,049,139	1,477	2,002,076	2,146	....	57
16,626	82,775	207	10,487	......	352,349	350	618,002	36,838	....	58
7,485	52,275	10	1,769	......	80,830	108	141,290	21,690	Formed in 1848 from Ma-	59
21,815	143,489	9,983	29,483	......	976,652	1,826	1,887,386	49,229	rion, Delaware, Henry	60
4,630	10,951	50	183	......	28,200	58	42,175	2,611	and Richland.	61
10	4,652	25	363	......	8,500	14	7,850	596	Divided in 1845 to form	62
8,325	51,091	6	4,919	3	44,625	53	111,205	22,771	Defiance.	63
5,693	83,515	10	6,673	......	102,215	304	272,352	18,568	....	64
4,191	37,109	323	2,751	94	77,000	130	247,488	14,824	....	65
15,046	82,873	249	15,679	......	208,925	376	470,350	15,101	....	66
5,003	204,588	50	11,679	......	221,150	298	465,173	26,983	....	67
1,445	22,870	....	974	......	17,875	38	43,450	8,602	[Ashland and Morrow.	68
9,012	104,262	888	8,700	9	255,642	384	418,540	29,221	Divided '46 and '48 to form	69
19,236	89,892	4,841	6,229	300	814,317	759	1,211,769	22,994	Divided in 1850 to form	70
7,098	56,241	2,874	1,865	60	90,580	150	158,785	15,866	Vinton.	71
4,445	49,365	5,011	1,470	170	728,800	1,117	907,858	15,424	....	72
5,504	130,461	3,605	7,861	9	250,520	630	703,461	41,711	....	73
....	60,529	....	2,478	181	55,975	91	80,200	3,741	....	74
5,833	156,805	465	14,703	25	401,859	1,010	1,207,914	13,107	....	75
14,943	111,663	1,586	17,548	48	839,896	1,239	1,833,206	15,977	....	76
12,448	142,839	284	8,558	10	257,153	535	489,766	23,669	Divided in 1846 to form	77
12,163	88,617	111	10,312	646	559,108	522	740,152	26,910	Mahoning.	78
5,359	37,360	....	2,886	......	26,385	47	44,405	20,378	....	79
1,940	9,773	....	38	......	21,250	30	52,300	2,928	....	80
3,429	26,712	25	1,226	......	34,945	49	62,308	19,969	Formed in '50 from Athens,	81
7,455	301,160	3,810	18,587	165	508,930	671	1,044,812	33,415	Gallia, Hocking, Jackson	82
9,260	85,522	1,309	6,258	93	236,688	483	492,368	34,960	and Ross.	83
5,219	158,291	108	37,707	44	384,670	994	906,434	25,025	Div. '46 to form Ashland.	84
559	25,551	....	278	8	46,635	68	78,708	7,226	Div. '45 and '50 to form	85
9,355	33,885	5	4,560	3	11,900	49	24,820	5,779	Defiance and Fulton.	86
10,898	38,267	32	2,193	......	46,965	82	77,930	10,130	For. '45 from Crawford, Ma-	87
									rion, Hardin & Hancock.	

	COUNTIES.	POPULATION.								
		Whites.			Colored.		All classes.		Total population.	
		Male.	Female.	Total.	Free.	Slave.	Male.	Female.	1850.	1840.
1	Adams..............	12,581	12,845	25,426	555	....	12,841	13,140	25,981	23,044
2	Allegheny	68,986	65,873	134,859	3,431	....	70,637	67,653	138,290	81,235
3	Armstrong...........	15,117	14,314	29,431	129	....	15,180	14,380	29,560	28,365
4	Beaver	13,383	13,061	26,444	245	....	13,505	13,184	26,689	29,368
5	Bedford.............	11,617	11,020	22,637	415	....	11,825	11,227	23,052	29,335
6	Berks...............	38,425	38,154	76,579	550	....	38,716	38,413	77,129	64,569
7	Blair	11,059	10,458	21,517	260	....	11,181	10,596	21,777	....
8	Bradford............	22,140	20,494	42,634	197	....	22,242	20,589	42,831	32,769
9	Bucks	27,559	26,810	54,369	1,722	....	28,400	27,691	56,091	48,107
10	Butler..............	15,429	14.833	30,262	84	....	15,476	14,870	30,346	22,378
11	Cambria.............	9,286	8,359	17,645	128	....	9,348	8,425	17,773	11,256
12	Carbon	8,669	6,987	15.656	30	....	8,684	7,002	15,686	....
13	Centre	11,784	11,328	23,112	243	....	11,906	11,449	23,355	20,492
14	Chester.............	30,763	30,452	61,215	5,223	....	33,414	33,024	66,438	57,515
15	Clarion.............	12,255	11,193	23,448	117	....	12,314	11,251	23,565	....
16	Clearfield	6,709	5,773	12,482	104	....	6,758	5,828	12,586	7,834
17	Clinton.............	5,740	5,315	11,055	152	....	5,825	5,382	11,207	8,323
18	Columbia............	8,977	8,630	17,607	103	....	9,026	8,684	17,710	24,267
19	Crawford............	19,353	18.397	37,750	99	....	19,403	18,446	37,849	31,724
20	Cumberland..........	16,502	16,868	33,370	957	....	16,966	17,361	34,327	30,953
21	Dauphin.............	17,473	17,003	34,476	1,278	....	18,077	17,677	35,754	30,118
22	Delaware............	11,548	11,574	23,122	1,557	....	12,328	12,351	24,679	19,791
23	Elk.................	1,888	1,641	3,529	2	....	1,890	1,641	3,531	....
24	Erie	19,693	18,900	38,593	149	....	19,773	18,969	38,742	31,344
25	Fayette.............	18,722	18,721	37,443	1,669	....	19,560	19,552	39,112	33,574
26	Franklin............	18,876	19,080	37,956	1,948	....	19,800	20,104	39,904	37,793
27	Fulton..............	3,839	3,635	7,474	93	....	3,874	3,693	7,567	....
28	Greene..............	11,028	10,632	21,660	476	....	11,270	10,866	22,136	19,147
29	Huntingdon..........	12,685	11,766	24,451	335	....	12,857	11,929	24,786	35,484
30	Indiana	13,467	13,449	26,916	254	....	13,607	13,563	27,170	20,782
31	Jefferson...........	7,029	6,395	13,424	94	....	7,079	6,439	13,518	7,253
32	Juniata.............	6,472	6,426	12,898	131	....	6,537	6,492	13,029	11,080
33	Lancaster...........	47,859	47,471	95,330	3,614	....	49,700	49,244	98,944	84,203
34	Lawrence	10,667	10,280	20,947	132	....	10,749	10,330	21,079	....
35	Lebanon.............	13,118	12,867	25,985	86	....	13,165	12,906	26,071	21,872
36	Lehigh	16,468	15,963	32,431	48	....	16,499	15,980	32,479	25,787
37	Luzerne.............	29,465	26,234	55,699	373	....	29,669	26,403	56,072	44,006
38	Lycoming............	13,154	12,736	25,890	367	....	13,338	12,919	26,257	22,649
39	McKean..............	2,772	2,446	5,218	36	....	2,789	2,465	5,254	2,975
40	Mercer..............	16,719	16,162	32,881	291	....	16,875	16,297	33,172	32,873
41	Mifflin.............	7,425	7,145	14,570	410	....	7,632	7,348	14,980	13,092
42	Monroe..............	6,888	6,282	13,170	100	....	6,950	6.320	13,270	9,879
43	Montgomery..........	29.286	28,148	57,434	857	....	29,703	28,588	58,291	47,241
44	Montour.............	6,689	6,466	13,155	84	....	6,727	6,512	13,239	....
45	Northampton	20,361	19,738	40,099	136	....	20,428	19,807	40,235	40,996
46	Northumberland......	11,499	11,681	23.180	92	....	11,549	11,723	23,272	20,027
47	Perry	10,169	9,784	19,953	135	....	10,247	9,841	20,088	17,096
48	Philadelphia........	187,956	201,045	389,001	19,761	....	196,391	212,371	408,762	258,037
49	Pike	3.098	2,594	5,692	189	....	3,192	2,689	5,881	3,832
50	Potter	3,175	2,867	6,042	6	....	3,179	2,869	6,048	3,371
51	Schuylkill	31,351	28,954	60,305	408	....	31,560	29,153	60,713	29,053
52	Somerset............	12,313	12.004	24.317	99	....	12,372	12,044	24,416	19,650
53	Sullivan............	1.881	1,802	3,683	11	....	1,884	1,810	3,694	....
54	Susquehanna.........	14,764	13,764	28,528	160	....	14,848	13,840	28,688	21,195
55	Tioga...............	12,443	11,446	23.889	98	....	12,494	11,493	23,987	15,498
56	Union...............	13,078	12,904	25,982	101	....	13,131	12.952	26,083	22,787
57	Venango.............	9,506	8,764	18,270	40	....	9,526	8,784	18,310	17,900
58	Warren..............	7,178	6,415	13.593	78	....	7,223	6,448	13,671	9,278
59	Washington..........	21,746	21,634	43,380	1,559	....	22,520	22,419	44,939	41,279
60	Wayne...............	11,758	10,083	21,841	49	....	11,787	10,103	21,890	11,848
61	Westmoreland........	26,867	24,413	51,280	446	....	27,099	24,627	51,726	42,699
62	Wyoming.............	5,648	5,002	10,650	5	....	5,653	5,002	10,655	....
63	York................	28,379	27,946	56,325	1,125	....	28,925	28,525	57,450	47,010

STATISTICS OF

1	Bristol.............	4,086	4,117	8,203	311	....	4,257	4,257	8,514	6,476
2	Kent................	7,222	7,617	14,839	229	....	7,327	7,741	15,068	13,083
3	Newport.............	9,309	9,916	19,225	782	....	9,697	10.310	20,007	16,874
4	Providence	41,811	43,897	85,708	1,818	....	42,631	44,895	87.526	58,073
5	Washington..........	7,912	7,988	15,900	530	....	8,166	8,264	16,430	14,324

NATIVITIES, DWELLINGS, &c.				EDUCATION AND RELIGION.									
Born out of State.				Colleges, academies, and private schools.		Public Schools.							
United States.	Foreign countries.	Dwellings.	Families.	Pupils.	Annual income.	Pupils.	Annual income.	Total educational income.	White scholars during the year.	Whites 5 and under 20 years old.	Whites over 20 unable to read & write.	Accommodation of churches—persons.	
1,170	731	4,386	4,600	249	$10,000	6,429	$13,658	$23,658	6,027	9,712	1,066	18,850	1
7,493	43,414	22,551	24,278	3,623	40,749	19,664	105,841	146,590	24,042	46,971	3,824	97,822	2
488	3,002	5,052	5,124	135	920	6,477	13,586	14,506	6,379	11,375	974	21,541	3
1,965	3,106	4,564	4,687	320	3,798	5,992	13,783	17,581	7,084	9,954	343	23,618	4
717	589	3,896	3,987	52	500	5,227	10,414	10,914	5,332	8,936	565	15,025	5
566	2,911	12,931	13,912	1,275	4,574	13,686	42,825	47,399	15,423	28,692	1,279	57,823	6
617	1,734	3,718	3,846	190	2,500	6,249	12,684	15,184	4,877	8,322	1,057	20,800	7
12,819	2,800	7,391	7,516	250	2,310	11,333	13,078	15,388	11,437	16,300	928	17,750	8
2,648	3,291	9,757	10,299	383	4,502	9,278	36,542	41,044	12,998	19,026	984	44,820	9
419	3,820	5,254	5,323	113	....	6,395	13,572	13,572	7,851	11,865	606	28,742	10
426	3,264	2,898	3,073	30	67	4,070	10,403	10,470	3,695	6,718	2,034	13,900	11
403	4,514	2,544	2,650	150	750	2,200	8,987	9,737	2,498	5,154	1,121	14,195	12
250	797	3,936	4,000	57	365	3,353	9,808	10,173	5,800	9,194	1,173	20,800	13
3,279	4,100	11,580	11,859	1,324	82,047	11,360	45,768	127,815	15,647	21,998	1,453	58,045	14
414	1,827	4,008	4,082	......	....	3,267	4,650	4,650	5,505	8,951	594	18,022	15
427	1,002	2,157	2,160	50	630	2,810	6,371	7,001	2,059	4,769	98	8,180	16
427	566	1,930	1,936	......	....	1,724	7,492	7,492	2,425	4,307	205	4,700	17
491	739	2,924	3,091	60	960	4,558	7,743	8,703	4,816	6,889	1,601	13,725	18
9,491	2,186	6,592	6,682	707	11,991	9,796	15,700	27,691	10,023	14,858	27	26,495	19
665	878	6,021	6,239	264	10,640	8,888	21,612	32,252	8,597	12,383	1,242	28,710	20
754	1,830	6,033	6,463	76	7,200	6,223	22,088	29,288	8,483	12,854	1,638	36,325	21
1,820	4,384	4,118	4,205	303	25,555	2,995	17,640	43,195	5,142	8,320	768	18,776	22
400	1,277	643	652	......	....	415	1,584	1,584	634	1,195	195	700	23
12,952	4,652	6,825	7,078	375	3,357	9,393	21,586	24,943	11,435	14,613	716	24,750	24
3,792	1,230	6,597	6,629	168	18,950	8,741	19,239	38,189	8,574	14,581	1,169	34,610	25
2,261	1,558	6,690	6,989	232	5,374	8,579	19,764	25,138	9,206	14,311	989	32,215	26
403	271	1,333	1,374	......	....	560	2,708	2,708	1,867	2,870	163	5,000	27
1,745	180	3,777	3,782	148	1,923	4,257	10,710	12,633	5,079	8,596	1,102	15,250	28
905	975	4,298	4,386	136	1,860	5,925	14,247	16,107	5,276	9,131	572	20,650	29
437	1,435	4,644	4,656	57	300	5,271	11,265	11,565	5,975	10,612	426	25,300	30
969	996	2,253	2,307	80	300	2,837	8,616	8,916	2,735	5,234	373	7,600	31
64	108	2,168	2,198	60	3,000	2,000	4,100	7,100	3,708	5,170	130	15,500	32
2,333	6,164	17,138	18,057	968	26,095	16,511	64,240	90,335	21,106	34,764	1,810	75,475	33
1,471	1,583	3,687	3,701	......	....	3,640	10,791	10,791	5,932	8,159	169	16,503	34
109	581	4,452	4,719	174	1,640	5,738	18,070	19,710	6,524	9,690	365	22,025	35
155	1,196	5,589	5,964	151	530	7,888	17,630	18,160	7,651	11,812	288	31,065	36
6,987	12,567	9,587	9,672	445	1,240	6,815	10,264	11,504	11,156	19,911	2,228	13,300	37
747	1,507	4,586	4,608	130	1,550	5,179	13,765	15,315	4,940	10,094	125	15,815	38
2,618	265	953	953	52	500	20	4,000	4,500	1,490	1,906	95	1,500	39
3,478	2,798	5,402	5,548	75	910	8,615	12,168	13,078	10,485	12,939	242	24,475	40
214	684	2,591	2,670	......	....	60	10,961	10,961	4,072	5,593	176	10,500	41
538	431	2,155	2,155	80	960	3,199	5,784	6,744	3,211	5,263	659	7,175	42
1,052	5,198	10,022	10,366	1,159	27,930	9,166	32,135	60,065	12,626	20,261	715	43,071	43
410	1,079	2,289	2,352	60	933	3,715	8,064	8,997	3,492	4,959	779	15,300	44
1,388	2,377	6,836	7,530	1,442	30,145	7,339	17,648	47,793	8,008	14,773	1,134	28,502	45
264	454	4,062	4,074	927	3,806	3,900	8,268	12,074	5,472	9,125	1,414	17,910	46
410	432	3,412	3,550	25	300	6,373	10,542	10,842	5,884	7,957	531	17,356	47
43,264	117,891	61,278	72,392	7,375	372,981	40,896	341,478	714,459	62,950	125,656	11,688	186,814	48
1,276	968	964	983	......	....	955	1,909	1,909	1,142	2,016	399	3,300	49
3,053	223	1,135	1,137	2	2,435	1,020	4,814	7,249	1,674	2,303	35	450	50
592	18,377	10,671	10,927	701	4,519	8,993	40,616	45,135	10,979	22,031	5,833	44,995	51
711	1,073	3,969	4,128	105	250	3,345	11,176	11,426	5,696	9,738	2,636	23,850	52
250	640	660	660	......	....	899	1,082	1,082	882	1,406	291	900	53
8,352	2,562	5,203	5,337	310	1,000	8,901	10,224	11,224	8,186	10,727	377	16,450	54
10,539	1,389	4,222	4,332	218	760	5,749	8,684	9,444	7,077	9,125	827	7,750	55
188	204	4,455	4,556	397	11,100	7,469	12,917	24,017	6,291	10,311	1,346	17,800	56
1,452	851	3,065	3,107	......	....	4,643	6,505	6,505	4,647	7,460	267	12,050	57
5,005	1,201	2,489	2,491	40	240	4,008	5,682	5,922	3,637	5,040	225	6,100	58
3,632	2,307	8,045	8,120	694	11,600	9,181	28,319	39,919	10,546	16,219	572	37,620	59
5,157	5,833	3,719	3,865	378	4,802	3,709	7,214	12,016	4,502	7,522	473	13,150	60
837	4,713	8,350	8,429	181	1,200	13,112	22,169	23,369	12,337	18,728	301	31,430	61
1,352	914	1,834	1,890	......	....	2,440	3,343	3,343	2,392	4,037	194	2,150	62
1,618	2,788	9,927	10,161	315	2,100	10,282	29,723	31,823	12,495	21,284	1,319	41,225	63

RHODE ISLAND.

1,529	1,097	1,167	1,586	456	3,436	1,057	6,193	9,629	1,709	2,481	134	6,420	1
984	1,306	2,625	2,903	258	....	2,475	5,537	5,537	2,658	4,956	265	13,039	2
2,826	2,434	2,936	3,589	58	....	2,951	12,159	12,159	4,327	6,056	524	15,956	3
15,569	18 476	12,760	16,959	1,112	52,312	13,370	68,125	120,437	15,645	26,212	2,160	52,370	4
1,396	589	2,891	3,179	......	....	3,277	8,467	8,467	4,020	5,238	257	14,255	5

	COUNTIES.	LAND OCCUPIED OR IMPROVED.				LIVE STOCK UPON FARMS.			
		Farms.	Acres improved.	Acres unimproved.	Value with improvements and implements.	Horses, asses, and mules.	Neat cattle.	Sheep.	Swine.
1	Adams	1,902	183,009	72,106	$ 6,618,811	6,432	15,370	7,723	20,571
2	Allegheny	3,729	236,292	147,709	18,309,368	11,006	25,756	82,133	35,175
3	Armstrong	1,612	138,601	191,196	3,832,430	7,982	20,582	41,231	19,361
4	Beaver	1,841	124,743	97,251	5,508,531	5,510	13,131	81,911	18,560
5	Bedford	1,875	148,299	199,262	4,130,267	6,333	15,335	19,027	16,153
6	Berks	4,780	320,190	92,211	22,163,500	14,417	37,927	9,524	43,311
7	Blair	826	80,033	55,150	3,989,983	3,601	9,665	10,227	9,712
8	Bradford	5,096	234,029	278,250	8,685,909	7,244	43,706	60,403	17,739
9	Bucks	4,707	293,631	34,810	19,413,985	13,254	35,488	14,579	29,104
10	Butler	2,945	179,642	188,322	5,314,757	7,961	30,473	82,695	25,467
11	Cambria	1,089	51,021	107,749	1,429,079	3,108	10,583	13,267	5,946
12	Carbon	246	14,439	23,578	517,151	600	1,547	841	2,041
13	Centre	1,043	114,215	113,510	5,189,737	5,132	17,006	16,763	20,174
14	Chester	4,835	333,572	89,713	26,235,320	11,906	55,076	13,364	36,591
15	Clarion	1,726	107,317	111,504	2,940,191	4,173	14,448	26,860	13,150
16	Clearfield	2,317	61,115	117,468	1,813,158	2,633	8,245	12,232	7,265
17	Clinton	638	44,982	38,229	2,102,165	1,797	5,708	6,116	5,877
18	Columbia	1,179	90,185	61,293	3,329,762	3,603	6,760	8,392	12,783
19	Crawford	4,070	187,481	205,609	5,328,090	7,489	45,763	86,705	18,199
20	Cumberland	1,842	187,934	51,067	9,051,109	7,388	18,322	10,238	27,155
21	Dauphin	1,956	150,492	71,285	7,391,213	6,217	15,744	5,682	21,602
22	Delaware	1,376	88,796	16,773	9,067,082	3,723	17,630	7,424	11,287
23	Elk	254	9,730	37,870	300,863	333	1,891	1,536	676
24	Erie	3,334	179,089	146,790	6,077,584	7,032	41,940	66,705	15,417
25	Fayette	2,139	178,397	153,143	7,618,919	8,108	23,495	38,278	22,912
26	Franklin	2,247	248,557	98,583	12,267,012	8,875	21,626	13,375	34,532
27	Fulton	531	50,613	63,267	1,192,685	1,487	4,962	4,896	5,613
28	Greene	1,789	161,612	143,862	4,573,713	6,112	17,783	54,978	21,376
29	Huntingdon	1,445	146,863	156,226	5,313,854	5,390	15,596	19,636	15,262
30	Indiana	2,496	157,655	189,246	3,314,652	8,289	25,116	46,345	19,315
31	Jefferson	1,170	56,850	122,900	1,390,881	2,278	9,695	13,999	7,208
32	Juniata	832	73,412	42,790	2,707,270	3,054	9,135	6,309	10,152
33	Lancaster	5,629	402,480	116,053	36,393,678	19,075	55,035	19,876	57,535
34	Lawrence	1,606	108,836	68,899	4,093,555	5,004	15,239	76,654	15,504
35	Lebanon	1,449	119,846	46,258	7,283,415	5,873	14,991	2,974	14,875
36	Lehigh	2,074	141,935	37,099	10,318,256	6,580	15,029	5,297	18,318
37	Luzerne	1,936	134,580	147,889	6,336,358	4,966	18,797	18,496	16,364
38	Lycoming	1,561	113,264	90,997	4,274,845	4,070	11,443	14,230	14,197
39	McKean	246	9,217	21,167	294,672	301	2,433	3,726	390
40	Mercer	2,989	171,792	162,399	5,041,177	8,050	31,951	80,652	23,580
41	Mifflin	787	79,109	47,725	4,300,099	3,362	7,541	7,471	11,332
42	Monroe	904	60,355	75,397	2,080,875	2,198	6,677	5,995	7,913
43	Montgomery	4,456	239,251	42,315	21,054,257	11,509	36,134	10,982	24,678
44	Montour	738	67,132	38,002	2,737,157	2,361	5,273	6,233	9,239
45	Northampton	2,102	30,059	7,123	2,617,942	1,643	3,400	1,501	5,483
46	Northumberland	1,748	135,086	62,682	6,009,210	5,026	10,587	9,980	17,748
47	Perry	1,456	111,292	104,969	3,447,968	4,133	11,174	10,154	13,515
48	Philadelphia	1,530	60,706	4,970	13,937,929	4,488	10,506	989	9,278
49	Pike	370	19,079	47,503	990,736	564	3,144	1,560	2,261
50	Potter	668	23,732	56,281	777,295	671	5,316	8,394	1,512
51	Schuylkill	1,247	81,599	82,909	3,267,272	3,189	8,730	5,872	10,877
52	Somerset	1,613	165,824	210,442	4,056,208	6,854	26,972	28,306	11,365
53	Sullivan	425	17,044	47,465	336,600	511	4,105	4,713	2,953
54	Susquehanna	3,909	195,798	183,287	5,613,545	5,257	36,456	42,971	11,345
55	Tioga	2,183	106,799	147,939	3,575,029	3,250	20,812	32,750	7,757
56	Union	1,597	132,049	74,881	5,984,805	5,295	11,889	9,931	15,911
57	Venango	1,730	98,362	187,191	2,330,819	3,851	16,757	41,639	13,616
58	Warren	1,207	49,258	92,780	1,684,079	1,733	11,740	22,026	3,189
59	Washington	3,572	344,046	170,165	15,284,954	12,077	26,162	370,944	44,470
60	Wayne	1,335	59,569	90,369	2,291,212	1,605	12,578	10,963	3,535
61	Westmoreland	4,013	364,203	145,524	13,128,696	14,249	39,998	61,344	42,233
62	Wyoming	895	46,709	54,386	1,694,670	1,394	8,254	8,809	5,104
63	York	3,734	306,812	110,940	14,242,296	11,051	29,319	13,531	34,603

STATISTICS OF

1	Bristol	200	10,999	2,110	771,115	316	1,287	1,548	1,116
2	Kent	688	51,974	31,095	1,951,111	731	4,459	3,184	2,429
3	Newport	1,027	57,833	12,423	3,941,664	1,145	7,226	16,148	5,019
4	Providence	2,162	115,837	97,474	7,660,356	2,585	12,957	4,189	6,918
5	Washington	1,308	119,844	54,349	3,243,757	1,392	10,333	19,227	4,027

AGRICULTURAL PRODUCTS.												
Wheat, bushels.	Rye & oats, bushels.	Indian corn, bushels.	Irish and sweet potatoes, bushels.	Peas and beans, bushels.	Barley, bushels.	Buckwheat, bushels.	Butter and cheese, pounds.	Hay, tons.	Hops, pounds.	Clover & other grass seeds, bushels.	Flaxseed, bushels.	
318,842	312,976	293,979	39,140	5	30	2,412	621,204	36,639	33	5,255	690	1
526,856	963,519	438,966	264,400	1,460	10,525	22,302	975,078	35,836	403	783	55	2
197,697	557,176	195,501	55,520	451	3,044	56,189	490,442	16,047	76	999	1,436	3
244,112	365,810	226,253	77,408	376	5,082	35,231	501,532	17,915	2,636	2,168	499	4
248,302	329,085	206,344	34,695	......	1,204	18,400	347,597	18,094	6	779	2	5
577,668	1,320,309	811,947	246,477	1,113	944	32,372	1,877,221	83,257	1,153	6,330	2,192	6
267,349	223,842	145,851	25,196	......	3,636	5,226	204,846	13,637	80	1,437	71	7
301,675	565,025	371,143	322,341	4,476	3,975	128,031	1,698,667	74,028	22	1,979	463	8
403,909	1,398,359	1,157,781	246,781	2,850	440	55,429	2,342,525	95,842	2,587	19,881	6,290	9
231,595	707,465	237,339	124,287	439	5,034	133,806	723,602	31,695	1,157	2,660	1,950	10
42,898	212,029	58,947	20,784	230	3,622	21,653	293,078	10,326	......	290	226	11
7,325	44,520	21,852	20,808	29	......	10,511	31,390	3,041	63	138	54	12
433,612	295,255	316,112	55,568	34	11,263	6,919	415,065	18,530	......	6,119	......	13
547,498	1,198,129	1,339,466	175,910	372	1,913	12,558	2,125,031	96,315	2,364	17,897	131	14
165,060	391,297	111,534	42,936	106	1,017	56,575	422,309	17,086	703	1,606	167	15
80,588	189,910	55,943	25,925	490	180	35,159	169,715	10,556	18	486	7	16
191,065	102,794	115,760	35,707	20	814	10,960	140,581	6,696	232	1,311	54	17
153,760	262,567	199,530	86,580	83	......	38,956	368,055	12,884	79	2,140	905	18
142,414	461,546	387,556	165,662	731	1,175	92,339	2,078,020	70,784	54	544	810	19
487,182	512,083	361,166	48,821	45	7,620	2,129	785,104	31,788	833	3,054	288	20
308,879	487,633	340,755	118,643	1,801	339	9,216	575,782	27,814	91	3,299	311	21
121,096	171,663	294,209	108,539	188	170	593	1,349,453	27,932	161	1,600	5	22
4,789	30,305	10,776	16,708	199	117	5,653	32,065	26,661	......	113	1	23
147,825	443,968	433,692	172,025	3,141	42,352	27,272	1,007,295	69,422	1,260	2,973	860	24
304,102	526,342	696,092	49,299	52	142	21,668	573,105	22,096	108	2,308	363	25
837,062	470,549	539,976	52,088	1,637	2,568	3,800	675,037	33,591	247	9,962	221	26
83,758	76,855	50,835	8,876	......	......	6,416	100,420	4,752	......	724	70	27
189,149	306,286	556,684	18,350	10	18	19,450	479,955	15,086	4	1,056	704	28
365,278	309,542	221,392	41,581	170	2,033	21,015	334,724	17,842	524	2,967	448	29
209,763	591,947	213,636	49,304	591	316	67,238	474,535	18,189	27	1,631	2,928	30
76,999	186,571	53,877	28,746	374	308	30,897	150,166	9,116	40	496	181	31
187,187	134,931	138,633	23,728	40	1,395	8,167	262,035	12,233	......	2,320	14	32
1,365,111	1,729,388	1,803,312	222,117	459	7,377	6,684	1,921,186	96,134	470	13,466	564	33
168,246	325,033	205,620	61,177	556	7,589	64,171	433,475	22,025	403	1,222	1,644	34
274,095	447,664	241,939	45,773	......	360	371	417,174	25,602	8	2,190	169	35
261,301	617,174	397,048	181,482	60	1,516	28,265	838,816	30,332	91	3,573	2,340	36
165,328	413,401	290,122	183,047	831	291	116,173	649,781	31,601	114	1,234	292	37
285,925	261,582	262,456	86,318	5	1,309	52,609	300,521	15,035	27	1,307	196	38
1,962	30,559	10,172	17,604	676	92	3,689	74,056	5,356	......	44	7	39
206,729	436,871	263,710	101,916	365	1,885	114,425	840,503	41,579	860	1,258	2,310	40
305,994	217,688	218,896	34,330	11	2,057	4,406	267,180	13,196	5	3,832	3	41
14,620	170,829	101,829	67,471	190	20	77,366	174,204	10,253	293	627	251	42
309,255	963,116	878,244	238,873	604	1,785	15,641	3,058,751	98,701	484	8,860	3,014	43
126,217	154,186	138,279	47,224	107	42	16,379	277,031	10,429	222	2,489	447	44
105,147	117,526	136,668	47,330	......	660	1,194	205,839	7,126	......	375	256	45
289,522	315,030	282,087	121,706	8	82	34,427	501,626	20,310	279	4,170	757	46
190,697	235,240	155,271	49,122	201	51	19,872	302,576	16,690	470	2,623	398	47
121,204	135,992	294,891	385,402	994	848	7,205	671,694	28,288	73	1,055	......	48
3,546	56,739	38,608	52,059	......	......	29,615	100,387	4,479	......	......	22	49
13,359	81,198	18,562	43,780	2,817	348	15,997	181,931	8,717	......	391	42	50
64,928	243,557	165,556	136,380	70	......	42,334	324,173	16,644	160	1,134	342	51
92,136	565,238	31,166	34,387	28	93	33,618	777,445	29,620	83	737	1,456	52
11,959	38,155	21,437	27,349	350	......	17,802	90,735	4,719	21	168	12	53
83,783	399,591	237,343	171,088	1,977	447	80,377	1,141,597	50,105	......	877	48	54
141,896	306,629	147,140	163,415	16,140	6,383	50,954	781,671	37,614	90	1,311	193	55
353,095	310,636	180,563	73,701	2	260	12,782	377,190	20,811	53	2,466	440	56
98,189	304,331	109,042	48,603	31	70	100,378	323,878	15,663	28	784	183	57
33,756	162,094	83,398	97,237	2,080	1,893	23,868	365,275	20,990	10	315	35	58
558,182	882,817	804,540	51,225	262	14,368	12,682	881,368	41,269	974	3,566	328	59
6,177	123,379	50,577	135,672	3,446	140	60,786	414,720	25,380	66	104	......	60
668,476	1,244,011	839,711	104,547	1,246	2,824	47,295	1,744,069	48,024	1,535	6,205	2,392	61
62,734	128,871	116,349	65,821	78	150	52,803	232,355	9,788	4	239	32	62
578,828	774,503	707,151	133,915	124	1,368	50,982	1,086,611	50,760	304	7,016	1,159	63

RHODE ISLAND.

....	13,063	25,451	24,898	109	1,392	8	36,172	3,062	......	733	......	1
....	9,795	57,401	85,052	1,388	525	40	149,525	8,734	24	409	......	2
15	138,211	156,698	78,688	976	9,695	70	308,691	13,776	......	1,379	......	3
24	19,095	157,070	308,379	2,881	4,204	975	565,297	33,205	243	1,443	......	4
10	61,477	142,581	154,012	1,492	3,059	152	252,493	16,041	10	1,072	......	5

	COUNTIES.	AGRICULTURAL PRODUCTS.									
		Flax, pounds.	Hemp, dew and water-rotted, tons.	Maple sugar, pounds.	Cane sugar, hhds. of 1,000 pounds.	Molasses, gallons.	Rice, pounds.	Tobacco, pounds.	Ginned cotton, bales of 400 pounds.	Wool, pounds.	Silk cocoons, pounds.
1	Adams	7,556								23,697	
2	Allegheny	1,305		1,587		511		72		215,302	
3	Armstrong	11,446		3,103		208				90,973	
4	Beaver	9,917		3,390		429		1,680		211,878	10
5	Bedford			12,969		221				37,791	
6	Berks	15,373	2			100		200		19,576	1
7	Blair	395		2,550		40				26,278	
8	Bradford	10,100		193,391		271				154,924	
9	Bucks	104,235		78						33,280	
10	Butler	29,723	4	7,354		560				187,280	82
11	Cambria	2,547		39,055		4,508				29,609	
12	Carbon	534								1,761	
13	Centre			100						36,528	
14	Chester	2,974	3							22,738	
15	Clarion	2,719	3	1,524		230				67,730	
16	Clearfield	100		5,577		527				31,498	
17	Clinton	2,635		1,030		134				15,589	
18	Columbia	15,127		14,310		517				23,394	
19	Crawford	9,210		219,992		2,016				208,058	30
20	Cumberland	3,086	10					200		26,363	5
21	Dauphin	4,461						50,200		14,932	1
22	Delaware	228								3,406	
23	Elk	50		9,394		446				4,514	
24	Erie	13,729		333,748		1,875		8,000		179,103	
25	Fayette	7,651		86,630		3,967				102,604	
26	Franklin	1,224	7	798		17				44,192	
27	Fulton	1,078								13,094	
28	Greene	18,400		67,431		2,888		2,250		135,565	
29	Huntingdon	2,844		6,356		783		7,000		51,384	
30	Indiana	36,305		16,293		1,180				105,436	
31	Jefferson	3,139		33,570		2,265				33,327	
32	Juniata	60								14,686	
33	Lancaster	7,313								29,043	6
34	Lawrence	16,546		20,731		1,554		378,050		196,145	2
35	Lebanon	2,281								6,713	22
36	Lehigh	13,312								21,920	
37	Luzerne	4,748	2	19,758		143		1,000		49,372	10
38	Lycoming	2,858		1,430						35,220	
39	McKean	350		45,674						9,657	
40	Mercer	41,501	2	64,242		3,856				213,359	1
41	Mifflin	177		80						21,068	
42	Monroe	4,548	5	879		15		20		14,616	
43	Montgomery	29,160				150		100		14,807	40
44	Montour	5,367		25						14,899	
45	Northampton	3,453								2,756	
46	Northumberland	8,708	2	230		62		23,552		26,670	7
47	Perry	3,181		1,518		6				24,469	2
48	Philadelphia							3,500		1,579	
49	Pike	450								3,519	
50	Potter	1,313		134,887		2,106				22,048	
51	Schuylkill	3,183								15,255	
52	Somerset	13,580	2	373,798		7,667				66,503	
53	Sullivan	225		55,000		1,589				12,066	21
54	Susquehanna	2,648		157,181		472				91,450	
55	Tioga	2,656		202,851		299				86,212	
56	Union	3,133		2,065		528				25,149	
57	Venango	1,144		14,678		436		300		80,114	9
58	Warren	1,003		83,705		456		2		54,493	
59	Washington	5,530	2	25,963		3,540				933,167	2
60	Wayne	4		27,398		819				28,928	
61	Westmoreland	23,420		31,242		3,261		17,970		161,351	5
62	Wyoming	2,092		2,960						19,339	
63	York	8,272						418,555		33,193	29

STATISTICS OF

1	Bristol									8,997	
2	Kent	15								6,059	
3	Newport									48,565	
4	Providence	70		28		4				18,700	
5	Washington									47,371	

AGRICULTURAL PRODUCTS.					MANUFACTURES.				REMARKS.	
					Establishments.					
Beeswax and honey, pounds.	Value of animals slaughtered.	Value of produce of market gardens.	Value of orchard produce.	Wine, gallons.	Capital.	Hands employed.	Annual product.	Produced in families.		
2,708	$118,487	$4	$5,347	......	$432,176	348	$609,360	$3,068	....	1
12,580	165,941	48,307	38,130	480	10,855,894	14,653	16,686,032	11,514	....	2
12,544	79,485	5,279	3,829	......	837,310	1,117	905,879	15,520	Div. in '40 to form Clarion.	3
19,102	90,550	1,695	13,952	2,571	525,976	752	838,964	14,517	Div. '49 to form Lawrence.	4
....	76,976	55	1,036	......	212,500	427	561,339	5,621	Div. in'46 and '50 to form	5
6,462	427,676	17,116	71,452	16,325	2,639,178	3,920	4,139,980	21,175	Blair and Fulton.	6
289	73,615	....	1,276	2	1,065,730	1,383	1,385,526	1,686	Formed '46 from Hunting-	7
62,924	230,794	315	5,779	70	669,500	1,037	1,185,169	39,858	don and Bedford.	8
15,944	394,126	2,464	69,309	875	911,877	1,649	2,005,076	14,862	....	9
49,295	113,822	5,902	7,843	6	313,028	769	487,575	31,166	....	10
4,189	43,913	....	....	......	356,512	736	347,455	9,970	....	11
1,865	18,767	40	92	4	674,255	2,234	1,275,411	137	Formed in '43 from North-	12
10	105,288	75	4,990	......	915,749	899	1,034,864	5,472	ampton and Monroe.	13
10,815	495,190	3,457	39,689	389	2,867,159	3,949	4,409,199	4,013	[strong and Venango.	14
77,981	99,741	83	259	......	1,207,703	1,860	1,239,755	16,673	Formed in '40 from Arm-	15
5,201	60,954	....	4	......	189,200	230	297,091	7,017	Divided '43 to form Elk.	16
4,804	44,417	....	4,633	3	275,602	356	405,905	693	....	17
20,428	97,620	1,636	7,817	6	820,850	1,010	1,055,396	14,202	Div. '50 to form Montour.	18
43,567	128,137	71	28,575	......	322,710	678	822,518	32,802	....	19
1,295	155,414	4,330	18,559	51	1,021,385	1,013	1,274,901	5,416	....	20
1,153	157,838	9,966	17,457	5	1,813,505	1,247	1,302,213	3,793	....	21
1,621	280,755	4,350	13,717	28	2,165,225	3,319	3,347,668	2,226	....	22
561	7,749	40	288	......	130,600	219	112,845	10,621	Formed '43 from Jefferson,	23
23,239	157,571	8,833	17,327	129	665,725	1,167	1,064,951	28,581	Clearfield, and McKean.	24
13,952	150,807	4,692	3,927	......	789,205	1,433	1,415,845	24,374	....	25
1,310	196,765	2,616	34,319	30	1,119,719	1,505	2,113,116	4,245	....	26
1,560	30,235	....	515	......	126,775	94	164,590	3,558	Formed '50 from Bedford.	27
15,327	74,307	4,804	2,602	......	126,340	200	216,692	27,340	....	28
12,534	129,563	7,386	9,159	......	1,335,525	1,218	1,029,860	10,582	Div. in '46 to form Blair.	29
25,873	103,812	154	1,137	......	130,385	220	241,232	31,182	....	30
2,885	45,003	30	1,047	......	299,992	625	444,068	5,126	Div. in 1843 to form Elk.	31
70	73,250	40	6,401	......	309,300	182	467,550	....	....	32
7,466	517,879	14,035	30,151	1,047	3,927,349	4,782	5,633,656	14,056	....	33
23,120	61,371	273	7,185	90	396,515	667	699,681	2,502	Formed in '49 from Beaver	34
294	135,887	....	2,477	520	946,725	895	867,134	3,267	and Mercer.	35
3,926	162,999	1,456	9,155	995	1,284,925	1,278	1,616,387	9,316	....	36
25,521	139,236	8,192	8,335	......	2,078,900	2,087	1,699,746	17,883	Div. '42 to form Wyoming.	37
7,803	97,531	5,481	5,586	25	717,450	803	975,244	2,260	Div. '47 to form Sullivan.	38
3,094	11,469	....	1,059	......	134,300	98	107,550	1,759	Div '43 to form Elk.	39
24,125	118,164	461	6,787	20	429,090	803	764,915	19,712	Div. '49 to form Lawrence.	40
2,390	73,323	....	1,907	11	129,235	300	310,452	742	....	41
8,274	54,380	....	1,186	......	190,000	187	492,526	6,057	Div. in '43 to form Carbon.	42
7,175	472,336	13,162	19,100	1,083	3,178,662	3,886	4,737,419	8,360	....	43
5,678	63,334	4,379	6,700	20	789,924	877	918,063	8,107	Formed '50 from Columbia	44
....	42,180	1,200	3,532	......	1,730,490	2,141	3,118,867	252	Div. in '43 to form Carbon.	45
14,237	107,602	1,472	7,829	27	314,146	501	840,211	8,280	....	46
2,396	79,879	1,603	12,227	5	336,992	609	845,360	11,518	....	47
1,229	201,853	436,813	13,432	292	31,406,404	57,903	61,869,871	156	....	48
1,167	23,786	....	....	......	94,200	128	115,609	175	....	49
13,056	27,181	....	1,467	......	240,628	181	134,513	9,829	....	50
9,984	96,459	14,317	20,084	40	3,588,745	9,329	5,494,808	2,976	....	51
4,778	72,531	89	109	69	272,100	365	422,946	26,887	....	52
10,369	16,392	....	832	......	31,750	52	42,432	5,754	Formed '47 f'm Lycoming.	53
22,998	116,360	170	6,029	......	508,100	703	1,082,972	39,084	....	54
38,458	103,535	16	3,645	5	964,565	682	907,214	13,462	....	55
3,440	94,193	23	8,045	......	553,684	595	633,353	4,362	....	56
27,449	79,193	400	629	......	443,680	483	408,797	14,045	Div. 1840 to form Clarion.	57
12,917	45,326	50	5,926	......	521,225	651	501,232	10,758	....	58
38,679	169,312	17,318	59,377	......	467,170	952	1,107,786	24,724	....	59
12,272	72,372	3,519	3,059	58	458,116	802	1,097,865	10,051	....	60
22,967	250,896	29,460	15,706	129	898,852	1,540	1,810,209	51,616	....	61
7,855	54,005	....	1,533	......	79,625	108	189,970	6,025	Formed '42 from Luzerne.	62
24,394	230,316	1,085	29,833	180	1,233,673	1,929	2,710,097	7,463	....	63

RHODE ISLAND.

35	25,898	27,354	1,938	......	729,437	1,031	852,498	56	....	1
405	58,488	5,716	4,959	845	1,695,075	2,520	2,620,788	2,465	....	2
545	123,635	13,553	13,425	132	638,975	1,212	1,630,060	5,100	....	3
3,996	348,166	46,452	38,861	35	8,870,089	14,463	15,219,326	12,245	....	4
1,366	111,299	5,223	4,811	1	989,600	1,655	1,770,586	6,629	....	5

	Counties.*	Population.								
		Whites.			Colored.		All classes.		Total population.	
		Male.	Female.	Total.	Free.	Slave.	Male.	Female.	1850.	1840.
1	Abbeville	6,384	6,315	12,699	357	19,262	15,968	16,350	32,318	29,351
2	Anderson	6,782	7,085	13,867	94	7,514	10,422	11,053	21,475	18,493
3	Barnwell	6,201	6,088	12,289	311	14,008	13,322	13,286	26,608	21,471
4	Beaufort	3,012	2,935	5,947	579	32,279	18,946	19,859	38,805	35,794
5	Charleston	12,925	12,283	25,208	3,861	54,775	40,158	43,686	83,844	82,661
6	Chester	3,997	4,006	8,003	148	9,887	8,940	9,098	18,038	17,747
7	Chesterfield	3,317	3,361	6,678	218	3,894	5,380	5,410	10,790	8,574
8	Colleton	3,470	3,305	6,775	319	21,372	13,877	14,589	28,466	25,548
9	Darlington	3,531	3,216	6,747	42	10,041	8,524	8,306	16,830	14,822
10	Edgefield	8,121	8,131	16,252	285	22,725	19,617	19,645	39,262	32,852
11	Fairfield	3,679	3,389	7,068	90	14,246	10,792	10,612	21,404	20,165
12	Georgetown	1,158	1,035	2,193	201	18,253	9,998	10,649	20,647	18,274
13	Greenville	6,648	6,722	13,370	95	6,691	9,934	10,222	20,156	17,839
14	Horry	2,807	2,715	5,522	49	2,075	3,880	3,766	7,646	5,755
15	Kershaw	2,321	2,360	4,681	214	9,578	7,225	7,248	14,473	12,281
16	Lancaster	2,888	2,969	5,857	117	5,014	5,463	5,525	10,988	9,907
17	Laurens	5,563	5,807	11,370	84	11,953	11,615	11,792	23,407	21,584
18	Lexington	3,658	3,692	7,350	23	5,557	6,395	6,535	12,930	12,111
19	Marion	4,829	4,952	9,781	106	7,520	8,474	8,933	17,407	13,932
20	Marlborough	2,504	2,529	5,033	156	5,600	5,351	5,438	10,789	8,408
21	Newberry	3,630	3,612	7,242	213	12,688	10,013	10,130	20,143	18,350
22	Orangeburgh	4,080	4,040	8,120	78	15,384	11,607	11,975	23,582	18,519
23	Pickens	6,495	6,610	13,105	120	3,679	8,333	8,571	16,904	14,356
24	Richland	3,541	3,223	6,764	501	12,978	10,205	10,038	20,243	16,397
25	Spartanburgh	9,118	9,193	18,311	50	8,039	13,160	13,240	26,400	23,669
26	Sumter	4,883	4,930	9,813	342	23,065	16,395	16,825	33,220	27,892
27	Union	4,630	4,687	9,317	143	10,392	9,759	10,093	19,852	18,936
28	Williamsburgh	1,982	1,920	3,902	37	8,508	6,158	6,289	12,447	10,327
29	York	5,593	5,706	11,299	127	8,007	9,723	9,710	19,433	18,383

STATISTICS OF

1	Anderson	3,147	3,244	6,391	41	506	3,404	3,534	6,938	5,658
2	Bedford	7,920	8,017	15,937	72	5,502	10,645	10,866	21,511	20,546
3	Benton	2,953	2,978	5,931	21	363	3,135	3,180	6,315	4,772
4	Bledsoe	2,450	2,586	5,036	96	827	2,941	3,018	5,959	5,676
5	Blount	5,556	5,657	11,213	127	1,084	6,142	6,282	12,424	11,745
6	Bradley	5,865	5,613	11,478	37	744	6,243	6,016	12,259	7,385
7	Campbell	2,850	2,801	5,651	99	318	3,049	3,019	6,068	6,149
8	Cannon	4,053	4,062	8,115	24	843	4,455	4,527	8,982	7,193
9	Carroll	6,500	6,315	12,815	17	3,135	7,995	7,972	15,967	12,362
10	Carter	2,987	2,924	5,911	32	353	3,166	3,130	6,296	3,372
11	Claiborne	4,349	4,261	8,610	99	660	4,739	4,630	9,369	9,474
12	Cocke	3,712	3,789	7,501	80	719	4,128	4,172	8,300	6,992
13	Coffee	3,592	3,482	7,074	10	1,267	4,208	4,143	8,351	8,184
14	Davidson	12,643	11,210	23,853	854	14,175	20,276	18,606	38,882	30,509
15	Decatur	2,597	2,666	5,263	17	723	2,983	3,020	6,003	....
16	De Kalb	3,694	3,637	7,331	17	668	4,009	4,007	8,016	5,868
17	Dickson	3,115	3,170	6,285	1	2,118	4,242	4,162	8,404	7,074
18	Dyer	2,568	2,316	4,884	9	1,468	3,304	3,057	6,361	4,484
19	Fayette	5,969	5,447	11,416	39	15,264	13,570	13,149	26,719	21,501
20	Fentress	2,205	2,100	4,305	1	148	2,280	2,174	4,454	3,550
21	Franklin	5,168	4,917	10,085	60	3,623	7,033	6,735	13,768	12,033
22	Gibson	7,718	7,568	15,286	68	4,194	9,746	9,802	19,548	13,689
23	Giles	8,390	8,128	16,518	73	9,358	12,980	12,969	25,949	21,494
24	Grainger	5,531	5,639	11,170	165	1,035	6,161	6,209	12,370	10,572
25	Greene	8,204	8,322	16,526	205	1,093	8,847	8,977	17,824	16,076
26	Grundy	1,325	1,197	2,522	15	236	1,448	1,325	2,773	....
27	Hamilton	4,647	4,569	9,216	187	672	5,055	5,020	10,075	8,175
28	Hancock	2,727	2,720	5,447	11	202	2,842	2,818	5,660	....
29	Hardeman	5,352	4,956	10,308	40	7,108	8,930	8,526	17,456	14,563
30	Hardin	4,579	4,461	9,040	31	1,257	5,233	5,095	10,328	8,245
31	Hawkins	5,780	5,787	11,567	113	1,690	6,654	6,716	13,370	15,035
32	Haywood	4,518	4,193	8,711	50	8,498	8,802	8,457	17,259	13,870
33	Henderson	5,336	5,234	10,570	2	2,592	6,580	6,584	13,164	11,875
34	Henry	6,844	6,543	13,387	25	4,821	9,202	9,031	18,233	14,906
35	Hickman	3,701	3,858	7,559	22	1,816	4,645	4,752	9,397	8,618
36	Humphreys	2,610	2,694	5,304	21	1,097	3,132	3,290	6,422	5,195
37	Jackson	7,037	6,963	14,000	115	1,558	7,916	7,757	15,673	12,872
38	Jefferson	5,726	5,732	11,458	118	1,628	6,562	6,642	13,204	12,076
39	Johnson	1,739	1,746	3,485	14	206	1,853	1,852	3,705	2,658
40	Knox	8,081	8,304	16,385	229	2,193	9,285	9,522	18,807	15,485
41	Lauderdale	1,740	1,657	3,397	6	1,766	2,621	2,548	5,169	3,435

* In South Carolina—*Districts.*

NATIVITIES, DWELLINGS, &c.				EDUCATION AND RELIGION.									
Born out of State.				Colleges, academies, and private schools.		Public Schools.							
United States.	Foreign countries.	Dwellings.	Families.	Pupils.	Annual income.	Pupils.	Annual income.	Total educational income.	White scholars during year.	Whites 5 and under 20 years old.	Whites over 20 unable to read & write.	Accommodation of churches—persons.	
540	261	2,391	2,391	599	$18,105	1,179	$16,245	$34,350	2,917	5,075	109	27,500	1
768	79	2,440	2,445	395	8,746	826	6,480	15,226	2,550	5,629	979	22,885	2
60	64	2,460	2,460	......	....	450	5,160	5,160	1,530	4,965	701	19,450	3
190	122	1,385	1,385	302	9,320	598	1,800	11,120	1,270	2,301	206	18,640	4
1,890	5,954	5,350	5,541	3,082	139,875	1,196	19,549	159,424	4,342	8,578	184	40,770	5
332	216	1,541	1,541	139	1,588	413	4,512	6,100	1,248	3,033	214	8,250	6
734	85	1,263	1,263	36	1,500	355	4,540	6,040	789	2,653	1,181	8,975	7
40	55	1,378	1,378	230	7,696	64	760	8,456	930	2,714	727	10,920	8
351	28	1,313	1,313	46	1,380	620	7,320	8,700	854	2,740	267	9,000	9
720	216	3,019	3,027	283	7,484	1,093	13,398	20,882	2,453	6,546	536	26,400	10
210	235	1,282	1,283	417	16,650	700	13,200	29,850	1,059	2,663	154	10,075	11
130	21	575	575	281	7,000	170	1,800	8,800	455	772	12	9,900	12
838	108	2,351	2,351	150	6,000	960	9,800	15,800	1,960	5,501	1,821	15,100	13
405	9	980	980	......	....	488	1,675	1,675	473	2,294	189	8,250	14
196	82	928	928	75	2,672	340	5,800	8,472	417	1,859	98	9,050	15
67	35	1,096	1,096	......	....	569	3,520	3,520	905	2,375	305	10,860	16
191	82	2,132	2,132	225	3,066	863	8,630	11,696	1,438	4,500	426	28,000	17
68	69	1,312	1,312	93	2,160	700	8,400	10,560	971	2,923	633	10,800	18
180	5	1,856	1,863	50	2,000	350	3,700	5,700	1,331	4,034	774	11,050	19
562	39	929	929	......	....	524	6,634	6,634	923	1,990	748	9,850	20
93	54	1,494	1,494	......	....	1,181	14,172	14,172	1,148	2,777	2	16,825	21
81	35	1,513	1,515	......	....	1,120	8,833	8,833	982	3,293	575	16,440	22
1,116	52	2,332	2,383	......	....	370	2,883	2,883	2,051	5,415	2,161	23,970	23
644	463	1,588	1,618	895	54,650	185	1,600	56,250	874	2,396	33	9,270	24
331	39	3,185	3,185	175	7,200	1,000	11,500	18,700	1,353	7,532	35	26,550	25
354	74	1,908	1,908	304	7,660	504	9,311	16,971	1,364	3,811	942	24,250	26
387	60	1,734	1,734	159	3,402	474	4,817	8,219	1,689	3,598	876	14,490	27
100	15	717	717	......	....	378	3,150	3,150	570	1,530	279	5,100	28
1,137	150	2,190	2,190	260	2,125	168	1,411	3,536	1,447	4,316	509	7,830	29

TENNESSEE.

United States.	Foreign countries.	Dwellings.	Families.	Pupils.	Annual income.	Pupils.	Annual income.	Total educational income.	White scholars during year.	Whites 5 and under 20 years old.	Whites over 20 unable to read & write.	Accommodation of churches—persons.	
825	3	1,091	1,099	105	825	1,347	1,459	2,284	1,477	2,624	1,203	2,950	1
3,429	52	2,754	2,754	210	4,130	2,056	9,543	13,673	2,633	6,654	855	13,740	2
1,166	8	984	984	60	240	600	950	1,190	1,238	2,559	881	5,650	3
1,026	3	854	854	40	552	650	1,250	1,802	895	2,093	861	5,550	4
1,442	65	1,992	1,992	80	428	1,253	1,587	2,015	1,488	4,604	370	6,600	5
1,606	19	1,955	1,955	......	....	......	2,486	2,486	1,276	4,817	215	8,605	6
931	3	916	916	25	420	650	1,100	1,520	1,207	2,471	1,208	5,700	7
1,343	5	1,326	1,326	245	1,255	990	1,092	2,347	2,375	3,437	771	6,900	8
4,274	28	2,105	2,105	96	3,000	671	2,233	5,233	2,786	5,432	966	12,700	9
1,030	13	1,002	1,002	55	556	720	1,062	1,618	1,201	2,398	1,007	11,600	10
1,790	26	1,425	1,425	75	1,025	815	1,240	2,265	1,507	3,718	1,424	4,800	11
1,575	17	1,295	1,295	55	475	1,294	1,174	1,649	1,375	3,139	1,605	7,000	12
1,378	42	1,179	1,195	60	390	900	1,308	1,698	1,564	3,003	1,066	5,400	13
6,332	1,384	4,257	4,391	1,337	36,690	1,208	9,412	42,167	4,070	9,161	1,584	31,525	14
1,220	9	941	941	70	360	1,058	2,164	2,524	1,037	2,194	884	1,500	15
1,352	1	1,247	1,247	70	1,700	1,912	1,078	2,778	1,872	2,954	1,451	3,750	16
1,097	22	1,080	1,080	40	240	1,755	934	1,174	1,083	2,544	1,013	5,150	17
1,508	3	824	824	......	....	700	656	656	1,139	2,039	638	2,400	18
4,671	47	1,951	1,951	505	7,665	816	3,827	11,492	2,275	4,820	113	12,900	19
756	3	707	707	174	586	480	516	1,102	524	1,834	556	2,950	20
2,154	197	1,638	1,638	235	2,800	3,340	1,760	4,560	2,178	4,220	36	9,500	21
3,910	10	2,529	2,529	47	240	1,150	1,500	1,740	2,380	6,437	1,500	12,700	22
3,846	21	2,830	2,830	197	....	1,123	3,000	3,000	3,650	6,955	1,253	20,319	23
1,793	6	1,894	1,979	73	668	1,636	2,801	3,469	2,633	4,867	2,429	10,190	24
2,715	46	2,938	2,938	104	5,065	516	2,010	7,075	3,320	6,636	2,974	13,980	25
451	....	435	439	25	246	400	390	636	576	1,053	547	1,460	26
1,656	29	1,590	1,590	35	441	1,355	2,931	3,372	1,252	3,908	501	2,200	27
1,186	3	939	939	......	....	1,462	857	857	1,072	2,295	1,205	7,600	28
3,814	40	1,735	1,736	264	3,872	961	9,655	13,527	2,756	4,368	624	11,950	29
2,427	34	1,503	1,513	30	320	1,410	1,442	1,762	1,526	3,779	1,514	1,200	30
1,370	10	2,019	2,019	140	....	4,442	1,812	1,812	790	4,835	442	8,300	31
3,145	52	1,454	1,454	195	4,363	270	4,900	9,263	1,596	3,659	430	6,700	32
3,083	18	1,798	1,798	125	240	800	1,692	1,932	1,792	4,440	950	2,250	33
4,238	25	2,245	2,271	190	260	1,500	2,048	2,308	2,942	5,647	414	20,900	34
1,425	17	1,296	1,296	30	540	......	1,255	1,795	1,915	3,216	822	5,250	35
837	18	919	919	60	717	1,922	2,035	2,752	1,073	2,177	882	6,000	36
2,590	4	2,324	2,324	100	350	6,377	3,462	3,812	2,345	5,973	1,864	9,200	37
1,879	17	1,975	2,040	396	662	3,000	3,606	4,268	2,298	4,760	1,469	9,900	38
1,063	2	565	588	40	230	600	514	744	673	1,401	758	1,850	39
2,985	206	2,804	2,823	355	7,500	2,500	2,472	9,972	3,258	6,665	2,408	12,581	40
1,238	11	568	568	80	1,391	180	1,108	2,499	578	1,427	81	3,350	41

	COUNTIES.	LAND OCCUPIED OR IMPROVED.				LIVE STOCK UPON FARMS.			
		Farms.	Acres improved.	Acres unimproved.	Value with improvements and implements.	Horses, asses, and mules.	Neat cattle.	Sheep.	Swine.
1	Abbeville	1,814	212,628	425,031	$5,006,610	8,918	25,959	16,364	66,548
2	Anderson	1,986	178,455	282,495	2,559,483	5,796	19,215	13,135	43,242
3	Barnwell	1,558	197,676	957,393	2,877,754	6,528	34,678	13,106	68,303
4	Beaufort	842	239,289	687,469	5,601,350	5,026	48,338	16,892	37,855
5	Charleston	682	183,236	636,495	5,903,220	5,023	41,903	13,415	30,247
6	Chester	844	192,801	143,138	3,171,782	5,139	13,566	7,514	29,579
7	Chesterfield	548	52,511	241,317	903,477	1,890	9,508	4,628	21,167
8	Colleton	888	121,475	632,458	3,627,534	4,221	43,312	15,150	37,062
9	Darlington	857	123,162	540,408	2,935,880	3,980	13,717	6,191	36,650
10	Edgefield	2,030	263,379	688,042	5,654,033	10,255	38,001	18,538	73,742
11	Fairfield	675	121,593	237,268	3,289,563	4,678	13,797	7,123	23,080
12	Georgetown	550	49,609	318,514	5,704,920	1,403	12,908	4,336	9,311
13	Greenville	1,068	130,727	239,730	2,102,038	4,312	14,047	9,255	36,555
14	Horry	731	33,664	472,971	385,840	907	14,814	10,298	29,830
15	Kershaw	383	61,102	296,960	1,443,868	2,674	11,690	6,182	21,024
16	Lancaster	580	100,728	196,937	1,568,576	2,945	10,955	6,630	20,997
17	Laurens	1,603	182,525	282,957	4,060,899	7,286	22,848	11,583	55,288
18	Lexington	837	70,730	437,841	1,075,318	3,353	14,609	5,961	25,182
19	Marion	1,374	124,306	652,342	2,680,544	3,642	22,617	11,442	46,620
20	Marlborough	621	85,395	204,505	1,987,613	2,483	8,750	4,419	22,260
21	Newberry	1,045	182,952	169,703	3,703,458	5,942	18,952	8,838	38,033
22	Orangeburgh	1,206	181,393	732,681	3,176,806	4,931	26,315	12,797	41,680
23	Pickens	1,231	93,206	474,756	1,708,636	4,134	16,056	6,124	37,786
24	Richland	543	89,426	235,695	2,075,052	2,991	11,575	4,603	19,163
25	Spartanburgh	1,555	207,666	354,281	2,792,626	7,353	23,840	14,026	51,921
26	Sumter	1,343	226,274	651,935	3,749,065	6,154	198,949	13,931	50,742
27	Union	869	162,787	235,363	3,161,665	5,364	13,277	7,360	31,262
28	Williamsburgh	454	70,360	432,440	861,538	1,974	18,337	4,397	24,577
29	York	1,252	133,596	283,924	2,798,890	5,352	15,153	11,313	35,797

STATISTICS OF

1	Anderson	698	40,291	129,879	504,621	2,292	5,164	5,360	21,259
2	Bedford	986	101,650	123,312	2,369,660	8,161	13,224	21,651	62,607
3	Benton	706	33,796	201,151	367,163	1,917	5,099	5,199	22,587
4	Bledsoe	325	35,076	92,218	568,906	2,209	8,212	4,542	26,375
5	Blount	976	90,987	761,786	1,205,065	4,514	10,054	10,653	31,203
6	Bradley	886	57,824	109,881	1,069,521	2,843	6,254	7,657	25,546
7	Campbell	521	29,420	141,506	402,198	1,823	6,343	4,812	18,990
8	Cannon	877	40,328	117,291	707,367	3,859	7,526	11,797	26,762
9	Carroll	1,404	76,341	202,875	1,039,832	5,012	10,543	10,397	47,560
10	Carter	565	23,645	74,533	439,290	1,724	4,492	5,857	12,914
11	Claiborne	944	56,170	167,640	718,850	2,608	8,397	9,467	28,021
12	Cocke	836	48,554	119,293	755,917	2,430	6,188	6,722	24,516
13	Coffee	485	37,368	89,445	566,997	2,638	5,653	6,450	24,371
14	Davidson	1,348	117,029	214,276	6,619,199	10,853	16,683	21,342	79,209
15	Decatur	443	22,367	109,218	320,804	1,716	3,831	3,631	14,846
16	De Kalb	717	29,220	111,381	503,894	2,369	4,782	7,935	29,089
17	Dickson	467	31,029	162,249	463,399	2,361	5,419	5,422	20,184
18	Dyer	515	23,120	156,365	718,245	2,280	6,375	2,621	32,713
19	Fayette	1,172	159,430	197,793	3,509,502	6,285	18,564	8,382	52,108
20	Fentress	499	21,561	100,654	230,989	1,215	5,368	4,364	17,259
21	Franklin	1,015	70,606	165,122	1,461,322	5,000	12,453	10,904	53,787
22	Gibson	2,160	88,861	229,892	2,222,522	7,230	16,840	11,505	69,881
23	Giles	2,075	150,905	234,737	4,604,153	10,684	20,028	22,201	116,834
24	Grainger	723	58,251	125,628	844,104	3,054	5,827	7,611	28,900
25	Greene	1,346	124,445	186,560	1,707,302	6,388	11,986	20,167	42,679
26	Grundy	263	13,939	131,775	189,137	1,074	2,393	1,748	13,487
27	Hamilton	633	38,611	142,028	952,216	2,861	8,110	5,492	28,568
28	Hancock	787	34,892	98,769	437,170	1,702	5,955	7,618	19,670
29	Hardeman	1,027	107,022	298,178	1,791,708	5,159	15,130	9,819	45,823
30	Hardin	690	34,466	164,432	586,153	2,439	6,911	6,663	24,618
31	Hawkins	735	93,023	220,086	1,400,797	4,859	11,065	16,997	42,030
32	Haywood	967	93,619	197,997	1,817,871	4,541	12,928	6,574	44,509
33	Henderson	973	65,559	197,708	761,548	3,695	11,247	9,103	33,666
34	Henry	1,478	91,188	181,675	1,260,383	5,727	11,816	13,352	49,715
35	Hickman	778	44,667	197,376	804,968	4,169	7,870	8,144	34,234
36	Humphreys	679	28,076	144,336	396,675	2,533	5,765	6,226	25,082
37	Jackson	1,211	66,653	239,448	881,522	4,575	11,870	16,602	62,638
38	Jefferson	904	80,196	140,698	1,384,594	4,008	6,743	10,074	32,881
39	Johnson	325	16,578	80,881	333,285	917	3,432	4,617	7,266
40	Knox	1,403	107,598	213,552	1,977,168	5,822	9,593	12,219	38,005
41	Lauderdale	287	17,971	64,991	473,020	1,307	5,002	1,705	18,511

Wheat, bushels.	Rye & oats, bushels.	Indian corn, bushels.	Irish and sweet potatoes, bushels.	Peas and beans, bushels.	Barley, bushels.	Buckwheat, bushels.	Butter and cheese, pounds.	Hay, tons.	Hops, pounds.	Clover & other grass seeds, bushels.	Flaxseed, bushels.	
AGRICULTURAL PRODUCTS.												
99,101	282,278	1,054,233	130,843	15,014	1,173	......	269,646	6,509	6	......	......	1
120,382	209,695	820,549	146,061	25,414	173	20	240,277	2,326	......	......	10	2
10,866	15,533	839,629	169,869	98,038	......	......	26,425	5	......	......	......	3
2,465	29,913	492,671	485,219	76,353	......	25	88,421	17	......	......	......	4
235	40,664	417,627	669,350	77,813	......	200	83,101	2,440	2	376	......	5
55,864	74,476	573,070	43,342	3,743	50	......	128,420	483	......	......	......	6
12,954	41,706	257,651	59,484	21,588	......	......	48,210	2,286	5	......	......	7
2,443	34,671	382,044	241,269	69,819	......	......	120,198	59	......	......	......	8
12,092	73,955	471,357	119,458	92,135	......	......	37,114	......	......	......	......	9
62,810	287,088	1,155,489	180,115	60,558	281	......	226,325	16	......	......	......	10
30,233	48,914	529,461	72,546	9,537	60	......	115,940	387	......	......	......	11
245	21,891	136,312	209,800	7,210	......	......	12,845	......	......	......	......	12
60,682	111,074	637,784	88,516	19,863	15	......	116,903	22	......	......	......	13
494	481	127,100	138,013	8,155	......	......	21,755	563	......	......	......	14
6,621	23,982	362,165	55,205	25,688	......	......	36,170	66	......	......	......	15
21,644	66,337	352,218	40,605	13,403	......	......	90,828	163	......	......	......	16
129,694	193,721	895,291	112,004	11,428	1,315	......	165,286	2	......	......	......	17
36,942	34,530	382,518	62,042	19,625	......	25	41,834	234	3	......	......	18
2,986	26,281	476,718	153,657	43,842	......	......	50,888	6	......	......	......	19
11,038	59,922	351,670	96,586	27,219	......	......	39,224	......	......	......	......	20
79,515	100,494	664,058	85,690	24,643	1,081	......	105,075	8	......	......	......	21
13,465	8,225	614,418	195,320	76,611	......	......	39,016	47	......	......	......	22
42,052	127,821	634,011	113,077	14,760	5	13	172,893	460	......	......	5	23
6,538	34,688	433,998	95,328	49,098	......	......	50,841	2,469	......	......	......	24
102,993	154,509	873,654	92,880	16,654	......	......	211,055	55	......	......	39	25
7,410	45,334	750,520	376,815	87,984	......	......	65,897	575	10	......	......	26
68,286	100,441	655,078	49,354	2,582	231	......	135,012	162	......	30	......	27
1,472	7,630	239,713	143,314	22,035	......	......	27,450	......	......	......	1	28
64,755	109,691	690,447	48,201	6,088	199	......	219,771	1,565	......	......	......	29

TENNESSEE.

Wheat, bushels.	Rye & oats, bushels.	Indian corn, bushels.	Irish and sweet potatoes, bushels.	Peas and beans, bushels.	Barley, bushels.	Buckwheat, bushels.	Butter and cheese, pounds.	Hay, tons.	Hops, pounds.	Clover & other grass seeds, bushels.	Flaxseed, bushels.	
8,919	53,041	317,724	23,780	457	......	22	62,947	714	58	86	502	1
18,054	279,194	1,521,867	62,342	757	......	1	148,865	539	11	100	14	2
4,287	23,540	305,490	26,179	720	......	......	50,057	......	......	......	......	3
2,020	84,261	407,025	22,902	1,013	......	29	44,572	264	16	179	112	4
33,107	175,500	621,981	36,230	5,235	4	84	77,896	2,068	......	446	511	5
34,662	151,511	574,698	39,121	1,800	......	30	82,438	325	......	87	48	6
5,973	44,385	277,395	19,433	386	1	56	49,408	210	10	102	429	7
17,881	67,515	554,497	35,832	6,311	27	......	70,452	152	......	207	194	8
25,038	108,254	801,175	57,354	4,080	20	......	109,003	421	10	34	18	9
19,307	94,759	178,541	10,284	1,105	4	3,793	78,181	1,129	......	131	560	10
10,414	90,111	441,061	26,610	163	......	178	17,844	337	......	56	400	11
15,168	129,517	544,516	30,083	550	......	84	83,205	604	......	7	435	12
5,112	72,558	433,215	26,908	826	......	7	47,327	75	1	46	54	13
17,522	164,660	1,598,463	168,125	5,918	385	10	262,746	7,845	15	1,365	1	14
3,539	43,555	261,790	22,159	1,291	......	25	52,271	439	......	4	......	15
6,603	22,604	417,251	27,614	297	......	7	50,752	18	2	88	23	16
3,789	61,231	388,731	21,327	634	......	......	57,807	417	......	......	......	17
11,420	23,013	413,020	31,458	702	......	......	59,760	203	15	15	8	18
18,940	113,834	963,945	123,519	34,746	......	......	143,814	130	......	27	......	19
3,243	26,475	180,089	20,001	847	61	23	37,218	56	......	......	324	20
8,492	140,803	788,380	62,202	16,401	35	33	143,261	135	......	39	5	21
47,097	93,843	1,107,730	97,303	3,607	......	......	247,433	185	8	......	150	22
31,537	189,048	1,857,647	115,329	20,229	403	2	324,008	5,730	45	58	23	23
29,452	143,025	488,968	30,447	684	......	104	67,243	472	......	197	1,035	24
99,970	244,897	784,381	48,915	132	......	2,995	209,363	4,306	14	640	2,113	25
1,359	21,139	158,000	12,113	769	......	......	17,404	31	......	8	28	26
11,389	69,606	520,542	47,742	386	......	20	64,750	113	......	61	18	27
7,425	49,580	280,070	16,273	137	......	167	79,172	241	......	66	448	28
18,015	114,170	798,545	109,568	50,039	......	......	124,417	213	92	79	......	29
7,488	40,303	449,328	27,172	248	......	......	62,429	132	......	80	......	30
43,381	141,488	550,136	30,668	461	......	492	132,766	2,432	16	579	1,973	31
20,967	68,514	754,510	79,823	7,962	......	......	121,475	23	50	50	......	32
19,453	70,711	562,280	52,003	5,005	35	......	67,245	28	22	17	50	33
45,606	141,202	893,328	69,444	954	......	15	125,816	516	......	73	......	34
5,336	82,606	635,265	41,870	11,291	......	......	94,930	410	......	132	8	35
4,643	30,289	419,387	31,963	3,018	......	......	91,328	14	......	199	......	36
13,429	58,409	805,737	58,436	2,922	......	33	179,400	653	......	......	168	37
40,426	192,892	659,187	32,188	790	30	28	108,854	2,432	......	438	346	38
6,925	59,139	87,801	3,624	402	......	2,171	45,879	1,138	......	89	365	39
39,611	257,502	861,703	45,330	4,888	95	423	185,256	2,943	27	596	827	40
4,915	13,580	216,896	23,351	1,152	......	83	31,264	106	199	211	1	41

	COUNTIES.	AGRICULTURAL PRODUCTS.									
		Flax, pounds.	Hemp, dew and water-rotted, tons.	Maple sugar, pounds.	Cane sugar, hhds. of 1,000 pounds.	Molasses, gallons.	Rice, pounds.	Tobacco, pounds.	Ginned cotton, bales of 400 pounds.	Wool, pounds.	Silk cocoons, pounds.
1	Abbeville	.....	.....	.....	.....	.....	7,180	4,455	27,192	28,615	.....
2	Anderson	100	.....	.....	.....	.....	956,940	18,540	6,670	22,372	100
3	Barnwell	.....	.....	200	21	55	7,440	.....	10,138	15,996	.....
4	Beaufort	.....	.....	.....	20	6,621	47,230,082	.....	12,672	24,730	.....
5	Charleston	.....	.....	.....	.....	.....	16,906,273	12	7,807	18,634	.....
6	Chester	.....	.....	.....	.....	.....	1,110	800	17,810	8,705	.....
7	Chesterfield	.....	.....	.....	.....	.....	42,748	100	3,194	8,269	.....
8	Colleton	.....	.....	.....	33	8,520	44,102,990	.....	3,006	25,789	.....
9	Darlington	.....	.....	.....	.....	.....	96,510	.....	13,005	9,748	.....
10	Edgefield	.....	.....	.....	.....	25	12,304	1,190	25,880	34,735	.....
11	Fairfield	.....	.....	.....	.....	.....	4,316	.....	18,122	8,562	.....
12	Georgetown	.....	.....	.....	2	.....	46,765,040	.....	81	22,171	.....
13	Greenville	.....	.....	.....	.....	.....	15,782	12,505	2,452	15,760	.....
14	Horry	.....	.....	.....	1	483	484,970	2,379	15	16,672	.....
15	Kershaw	.....	.....	.....	.....	.....	74,675	.....	9,015	7,102	.....
16	Lancaster	.....	.....	.....	.....	.....	27,900	.....	8,661	10,536	.....
17	Laurens	.....	.....	.....	.....	.....	128	1,519	15,842	19,699	.....
18	Lexington	.....	.....	.....	.....	180	50,829	25	4,608	9,133	.....
19	Marion	.....	.....	.....	.....	20	513,825	817	8,680	18,401	.....
20	Marlborough	.....	.....	.....	.....	.....	20,854	.....	9,501	9,439	.....
21	Newberry	.....	.....	.....	.....	.....	1,460	200	19,894	14,411	.....
22	Orangeburgh	.....	.....	.....	.....	.....	1,299,379	.....	10,024	22,332	.....
23	Pickens	186	.....	.....	.....	.....	28,044	29,967	1,357	19,427	.....
24	Richland	.....	.....	.....	.....	.....	87,970	.....	11,365	6,868	.....
25	Spartanburgh	15	.....	.....	.....	.....	3,601	1,526	6,671	22,348	3
26	Sumter	.....	.....	.....	.....	.....	833,651	.....	18,799	24,809	.....
27	Union	.....	.....	.....	.....	.....	.....	.....	14,156	12,497	.....
28	Williamsburgh	20	.....	.....	.....	.....	354,543	100	4,298	8,928	20
29	York	12	.....	.....	.....	.....	69	150	9,986	20,545	.....

STATISTICS OF

	COUNTIES.	Flax, pounds.	Hemp, dew and water-rotted, tons.	Maple sugar, pounds.	Cane sugar, hhds. of 1,000 pounds.	Molasses, gallons.	Rice, pounds.	Tobacco, pounds.	Ginned cotton, bales of 400 pounds.	Wool, pounds.	Silk cocoons, pounds.
1	Anderson	15,248	.....	5,442	2	.....	40	8,196	.....	10,191	.....
2	Bedford	165	59	330	.....	.....	1,815	57,240	404	36,872	.....
3	Benton	.....	.....	.....	.....	.....	3,310	144,508	14	8,770	.....
4	Bledsoe	3,101	.....	1,029	.....	45	75	10,147	.....	7,868	5
5	Blount	4,197	15	25	.....	46	236	7,572	6	16,549	21
6	Bradley	13,982	.....	.....	.....	.....	5,771	9,755	1,600	10,653	1
7	Campbell	8,702	.....	5,563	.....	16	336	9,573	1	8,167	7
8	Cannon	5,944	1	4,599	.....	150	440	21,301	7	20,099	.....
9	Carroll	500	.....	6	.....	.....	4	817,145	2,362	14,850	.....
10	Carter	11,158	.....	8,616	.....	387	.....	2,718	.....	17,141	.....
11	Claiborne	18,542	.....	7,925	.....	45	1,615	12,270	.....	9,595	4
12	Cocke	7,381	.....	4,072	.....	41	1,175	.....	3	9,957	.....
13	Coffee	1,699	14	718	.....	18	388	8,620	44	12,120	.....
14	Davidson	20	3	227	.....	90	.....	102,700	1,277	38,322	.....
15	Decatur	490	.....	.....	.....	.....	100	66,180	123	5,955	.....
16	De Kalb	1,798	.....	2,390	.....	14	120	57,361	.....	14,507	.....
17	Dickson	.....	.....	.....	.....	.....	60	25,350	19	10,148	.....
18	Dyer	205	.....	42	.....	.....	1,681	548,815	386	4,618	.....
19	Fayette	.....	.....	.....	.....	.....	5,300	300	28,302	14,893	.....
20	Fentress	17,975	.....	3,268	.....	4	.....	6,349	1	7,097	1,208
21	Franklin	1,486	.....	267	.....	35	2,724	30,895	637	18,519	36
22	Gibson	339	.....	.....	.....	.....	6,615	466,390	4,918	18,80[illegible]	.....
23	Giles	435	.....	600	.....	14	1,860	10,693	10,301	35,963	10
24	Grainger	8,508	5	10,704	.....	164	.....	15,196	1	13,810	.....
25	Greene	26,289	.....	17,764	.....	548	.....	2,071	.....	33,315	22
26	Grundy	782	.....	1,683	.....	15	297	3,178	24	3,787	25
27	Hamilton	496	.....	.....	.....	.....	.....	.....	2	10,251	.....
28	Hancock	34,601	.....	6,917	.....	516	270	4,722	2	11,832	10
29	Hardeman	4	.....	.....	.....	.....	51,335	12,683	15,065	16,811	.....
30	Hardin	50	30	55	.....	.....	1,330	6,098	686	12,836	.....
31	Hawkins	21,700	.....	2,545	.....	78	.....	3,021	.....	21,826	.....
32	Haywood	.....	.....	.....	.....	.....	6,230	2,800	15,967	10,079	.....
33	Henderson	869	.....	.....	.....	.....	5,650	65,720	5,212	14,297	.....
34	Henry	1,515	.....	.....	.....	.....	.....	2,029,132	685	28,256	.....
35	Hickman	638	.....	542	.....	280	.....	34,136	261	17,202	.....
36	Humphreys	420	.....	3,852	.....	.....	1,870	11,045	2	12,088	.....
37	Jackson	4,119	3	2,466	.....	16	76	432,114	.....	28,421	.....
38	Jefferson	5,704	.....	3,911	.....	15	10	4,745	.....	18,509	48
39	Johnson	6,280	.....	6,679	.....	228	.....	1,801	.....	9,675	5
40	Knox	14,912	.....	4,430	.....	1,126	1,188	20,231	.....	22,223	11
41	Lauderdale	300	.....	70	.....	.....	8,830	157,440	1,604	2,624	5

AGRICULTURAL PRODUCTS.					MANUFACTURES.				REMARKS.	
					Establishments.					
Beeswax and honey, pounds.	Value of animals slaughtered.	Value of produce of market gardens.	Value of orchard produce.	Wine, gallons.	Capital.	Hands employed.	Annual product.	Produced in families.		
36,042	$267,864	....	....	......	$268,920	403	$257,183	$71,774	....	1
20,842	163,485	....	$66	3,000	134,445	233	289,105	86,795	....	2
280	148,717	....	....	......	179,900	348	226,250	14,643	....	3
7,975	121,317	$200	2,185	300	63,800	75	50,030	10,690	....	4
1,034	78,086	26,940	4,751	......	1,487,800	1,413	2,749,961	17,799	....	5
6,770	119,304	....	7,847	20	104,370	162	101,360	22,405	....	6
4,790	67,910	25	495	......	65,775	213	83,434	45,080	....	7
5,166	117,157	135	....	......	35,700	58	17,150	19,240	....	8
....	125,739	705	....	......	76,400	126	71,670	12,070	....	9
32,015	306,325	1,115	2,196	......	724,435	1,064	635,096	94,468	....	10
736	122,360	17,073	15,029	350	19,400	70	44,200	16,360	....	11
....	21,425	90	....	......	43,500	74	68,519	....	....	12
5,724	104,677	20	220	......	176,850	290	213,510	28,625	....	13
....	75,545	....	....	......	59,200	109	130,129	24,555	....	14
1,120	44,698	340	170	......	100,200	185	127,825	7,686	....	15
246	74,092	....	475	......	36,400	35	46,100	19,590	....	16
15,890	174,337	....	568	10	184,475	250	419,715	54,670	....	17
11,420	72,379	....	....	......	249,663	321	176,343	17,458	....	18
....	148,404	....	....	......	....	.....	....	40,624	....	19
480	78,810	....	....	......	56,405	79	68,600	32,674	....	20
4,872	149,701	....	100	......	71,810	116	151,145	35,343	....	21
....	130,446	....	....	......	58,450	96	67,130	27,597	....	22
17,769	123,070	43	46	......	27,923	59	41,192	68,599	....	23
1,636	32,082	600	750	2,200	157,920	324	349,954	4,442	....	24
6,644	158,706	....	....	......	265,350	363	173,820	39,078	....	25
....	176,807	....	210	......	104,650	180	227,394	24,248	....	26
15,023	135,432	....	....	......	286,518	227	194,793	41,897	....	27
46	62,818	....	....	......	....	.....	....	12,825	....	28
19,761	100,944	....	....	......	1,016,606	136	81,905	18,290	....	29

TENNESSEE.

Beeswax and honey, pounds.	Value of animals slaughtered.	Value of produce of market gardens.	Value of orchard produce.	Wine, gallons.	Capital.	Hands employed.	Annual product.	Produced in families.	REMARKS.	
13,471	39,605	....	480	......	11,350	26	25,520	24,285	Divided '49 to form Scott.	1
20,492	98,516	50	....	......	19,821	66	33,990	59,070	....	2
7,510	32,169	....	10	......	1,800	11	3,000	16,964	....	3
6,431	25,373	34	89	......	1,000	3	2,000	18,508	....	4
5,504	83,504	....	260	......	59,477	122	93,375	38,416	....	5
214	76,599	30	....	......	23,605	59	84,765	27,309	....	6
10,078	50,822	521	324	......	16,450	64	83,981	20,637	Divided '49 to form Scott.	7
35,924	72,047	....	201	......	8,150	15	15,300	51,516	....	8
10,417	90,374	....	....	......	22,868	61	38,349	76,756	....	9
28,536	33,922	23,324	19,320	......	47,015	108	74,750	53,350	....	10
13,526	57,103	....	106	......	25,830	69	34,101	28,692	Divided in 1844 to form	11
7,754	45,543	150	37	......	27,257	128	116,077	28,120	Hancock.	12
7,173	31,047	100	....	......	13,700	46	23,122	21,529	Divided in 1844 to form	13
6,143	628,036	36,719	2,603	......	855,015	1,219	1,075,287	40,695	Grundy.	14
4,822	26,246	....	....	......	71,850	151	98,475	18,616	Formed in 1845 from Perry.	15
19,911	32,180	54	203	......	16,344	60	29,686	31,214	....	16
4,242	37,219	....	....	......	157,987	318	212,750	19,098	....	17
5,110	62,568	....	24	......	19,000	31	34,400	13,563	....	18
10,340	125,829	70	510	......	30,175	101	67,190	35,785	....	19
5,683	20,889	....	65	......	3,050	10	5,733	14,073	Divided '49 to form Scott.	20
9,637	81,612	138	89	......	98,116	301	201,526	45,009	....	21
11,661	132,306	15	65	2	104,935	155	86,075	113,345	....	22
55,353	201,216	520	38	......	164,425	342	200,321	77,977	....	23
18,702	63,574	100	....	......	51,710	74	88,104	32,310	....	24
27,055	96,637	....	5	......	32,835	106	56,857	60,035	....	25
4,456	15,562	65	103	......	912	5	1,200	11,296	Formed in 1844 from War-	26
1,583	60,344	....	....	......	13,100	37	12,975	21,964	ren and Coffee.	27
15,570	33,684	....	303	......	10,450	30	30,466	32,968	Formed in 1844 from Clai-	28
1,440	107,119	799	8	......	135,475	204	126,062	36,023	borne and Hawkins.	29
15,068	51,628	....	1,772	......	66,740	165	63,625	27,037	....	30
5,175	59,083	....	35	10	72,700	90	77,820	35,603	Divided in 1844 to form	31
13,690	97,690	....	95	......	13,100	53	32,200	26,565	Hancock.	32
10,084	81,366	....	967	......	17,090	50	29,629	63,186	....	33
5,097	99,972	50	52	......	125,310	238	505,400	36,347	....	34
8,994	54,073	....	....	......	53,775	166	209,745	57,233	Divided in 1843 to form	35
8,724	43,475	....	....	......	15,535	51	35,324	31,976	Lewis.	36
38,851	58,364	....	1	......	4,000	10	10,300	98,012	....	37
8,916	67,003	....	80	......	65,397	135	98,626	31,825	....	38
6,978	19,392	....	1,202	......	40,720	100	59,219	15,814	....	39
17,963	103,325	198	1,635	30	168,980	275	182,772	58,203	....	40
5,431	32,013	....	790	......	9,460	4	6,768	15,233	....	41

	COUNTIES.	POPULATION.								
		Whites.			Colored.		All classes.		Total population.	
		Male.	Female.	Total.	Free.	Slave.	Male.	Female.	1850.	1840.
42	Lawrence	4,114	3,980	8,094	24	1,162	4,701	4,579	9,280	7,121
43	Lewis..............	1,804	1,890	3,694	8	736	2,144	2,294	4,438	....
44	Lincoln	8,863	8,939	17,802	69	5,621	11,660	11,832	23,492	21,493
45	McMinn............	6,200	6,086	12,286	52	1,568	6,949	6,957	13,906	12,719
46	McNairy...........	5,840	5,607	11,447	24	1,393	6,518	6,346	12,864	9,385
47	Macon..............	3,025	3,097	6,122	60	766	3,416	3,532	6,948	....
48	Madison............	6,634	6,223	12,857	61	8,552	10,819	10,651	21,470	16,530
49	Marion..............	2,893	2,825	5,718	45	551	3,194	3,120	6,314	6,070
50	Marshall............	5,929	5,986	11,915	67	3,634	7,716	7,900	15,616	14,555
51	Maury...............	8,505	8,254	16,759	91	12,670	14,730	14,790	29,520	28,186
52	Meigs...............	2,282	2,198	4,480	4	395	2,474	2,405	4,879	4,794
53	Monroe.............	5,217	5,406	10,623	63	1,188	5,819	6,055	11,874	12,056
54	Montgomery.........	6,151	5,749	11,900	74	9,071	10,923	10,122	21,045	16,927
55	Morgan..............	1,708	1,593	3,301	28	101	1,772	1,658	3,430	2,660
56	Obion	3,394	3,178	6,572	4	1,057	3,918	3,715	7,633	4,814
57	Overton	4,946	5,142	10,088	58	1,065	5,478	5,733	11,211	9,279
58	Perry........	2,747	2,756	5,503	5	313	2,898	2,923	5,821	7,419
59	Polk................	2,995	2,889	5,884	54	400	3,214	3,124	6,338	3,570
60	Rhea................	2,006	1,945	3,951	28	436	2,226	2,189	4,415	3,985
61	Roane..............	5,206	5,319	10,525	116	1,544	6,029	6,156	12,185	10,948
62	Robertson..........	5,808	5,695	11,503	26	4,616	8,097	8,048	16,145	13,801
63	Rutherford..........	8,599	8,311	16,910	234	11,978	14,548	14,574	29,122	24,280
64	Scott	983	885	1,868	....	37	1,000	905	1,905	....
65	Sevier..............	3,172	3,278	6,450	67	403	3,389	3,531	6,920	6,442
66	Shelby..............	8,867	7,712	16,579	218	14,360	16,177	14,980	31,157	14,721
67	Smith	6,933	6,776	13,709	186	4,517	9,274	9,138	18,412	21,179
68	Stewart.............	3,568	3,449	7,017	127	2,575	5,197	4,522	9,719	8,587
69	Sullivan............	5,243	5,360	10,603	135	1,004	5,828	5,914	11,742	10,736
70	Sumner.............	7,359	7,128	14,487	224	8,006	11,440	11,277	22,717	22,445
71	Tipton..............	2,417	2,256	4,673	22	4,192	4,551	4,336	8,887	6,800
72	Van Buren..........	1,253	1,228	2,481	18	175	1,348	1,326	2,674	....
73	Warren..............	4,216	4,170	8,386	83	1,710	5,087	5,092	10,179	10,803
74	Washington.........	6,247	6,424	12,671	260	930	6,833	7,028	13,861	11,751
75	Wayne...............	3,572	3,660	7,232	8	930	4,057	4,113	8,170	7,705
76	Weakly	5,929	5,596	11,525	13	3,070	7,448	7,160	14,608	9,870
77	White...............	5,005	5,096	10,101	129	1,214	5,653	5,701	11,444	10,747
78	Williamson	7,166	7,100	14,266	71	12,864	13,554	13,647	27,201	27,006
79	Wilson..............	9,961	9,952	19,913	403	7,127	13,612	13,831	27,443	24,460

STATISTICS OF

1	Anderson...........	1,174	1,110	2,284	....	600	1,462	1,422	2,884	....
2	Angelina............	490	455	945	24	196	600	565	1,165	....
3	Austin	1,286	1,000	2,286	6	1,549	2,092	1,749	3,841	....
4	Bastrop.............	1,211	969	2,180	....	919	1,653	1,446	3,099	....
5	Bexar	3,413	2,220	5,633	30	389	3,608	2,444	6,052	....
6	Bowie...............	715	556	1,271	....	1,641	1,503	1,409	2,912	....
7	Brazoria............	822	507	1,329	5	3,507	2,611	2,230	4,841	....
8	Brazos..............	253	213	466	....	148	325	289	614	....
9	Burleson............	662	551	1,213	....	500	925	788	1,713	....
10	Caldwell............	621	433	1,054	1	274	751	578	1,329	....
11	Calhoun	469	398	867	9	234	596	514	1,110	....
12	Cameron, includ.Star	5,013	3,456	8,469	19	53	5,045	3,496	8,541	....
13	Cass.....[and Webb.	1,715	1,374	3,089	....	1,902	2,670	2,321	4,991	....
14	Cherokee...........	2,933	2,456	5,389	1	1,283	3,532	3,141	6,673	....
15	Collin	978	838	1,816	....	134	1,044	906	1,950	....
16	Colorado............	854	680	1,534	....	723	1,203	1,054	2,257	....
17	Comal...............	925	737	1,662	....	61	957	766	1,723	....
18	Cook	116	103	219	....	1	117	103	220	....
19	Dallas..............	1,357	1,179	2,536	....	207	1,450	1,293	2,743	....
20	Denton..............	332	299	631	....	10	337	304	641	....
21	De Witt	636	512	1,148	....	568	918	798	1,716	....
22	Ellis................	477	425	902	10	77	522	467	989	....
23	Fannin..............	1,783	1,477	3,260	....	528	2,032	1,756	3,788	....
24	Fayette.............	1,507	1,233	2,740	....	1,016	1,991	1,765	3,756	....
25	Fort Bend	564	410	974	5	1,554	1,343	1,190	2,533	....
26	Galveston...........	2,000	1,785	3,785	30	714	2,342	2,187	4,529	....
27	Gaudalupe..........	650	521	1,171	5	335	823	688	1,511	....
28	Gillespie............	725	510	1,235	....	5	727	513	1,240	....
29	Goliad..............	276	159	435	....	213	385	263	648	....
30	Gonzales	490	401	891	....	601	777	715	1,492	....
31	Grayson	986	836	1,822	....	186	1,078	930	2,008	....
32	Grimes	1,274	1,052	2,326	2	1,680	2,128	1,880	4,008	....

NATIVITIES, DWELLINGS, &c.				EDUCATION AND RELIGION.									
Born out of State.				Colleges, academies, and private schools.		Public Schools.							
United States.	Foreign countries.	Dwellings.	Families.	Pupils.	Annual income.	Pupils.	Annual income.	Total educational income.	White scholars during the year.	Whites 5 and under 20 years old.	Whites over 20 unable to read and write.	Accommodation of churches—persons.	
1,925	43	1,364	1,364	70	$230	1,200	$2,546	$2,776	1,893	3,475	567	4,790	42
726	2	599	599	80	228	1,400	580	808	939	1,599	575	3,550	43
4,221	39	3,010	3,010	125	3,615	1,914	4,727	8,342	4,051	7,411	1,834	8,940	44
2,880	13	2,040	2,041	145	1,881	3,851	3,020	4,901	2,845	5,074	1,532	6,140	45
3,664	18	1,895	1,899	......	....	2,500	2,913	2,913	2,915	4,632	1,489	11,250	46
1,140	4	1,044	1,045	20	333	680	875	1,208	890	2,474	910	5,650	47
4,454	58	2,282	2,282	274	18,730	1,308	17,199	35,929	2,704	5,228	346	19,360	48
972	19	957	958	60	201	1,060	1,270	1,471	65	2,483	409	4,625	49
2,894	10	2,061	2,061	251	1,325	2,971	2,735	4,060	2,999	4,804	1,121	11,375	50
4,012	84	2,961	2,961	1,443	55,010	930	1,197	56,207	4,328	6,953	959	16,520	51
681	3	819	819	......	....	2,145	968	968	916	1,885	950	5,700	52
2,445	20	1,816	1,816	90	115	2,029	2,556	2,671	2,701	4,473	1,956	9,300	53
3,279	95	2,086	2,086	378	6,325	90	193	6,518	586	4,808	50	8,495	54
630	317	581	581	30	250	650	1,233	1,483	660	1,371	267	500	55
1,901	49	1,131	1,131	129	1,576	50	405	1,981	896	2,785	863	1,350	56
1,927	6	1,673	1,674	......	....	1,723	2,112	2,112	1,962	4,227	1,553	6,295	57
811	156	927	927	......	....	685	869	869	1,232	2,406	943	4,200	58
2,016	30	1,012	1,021	65	480	700	2,108	2,588	1,027	2,473	677	5,300	59
726	2	681	681	90	974	40	900	1,874	442	1,600	404	1,800	60
1,762	98	1,812	1,872	60	1,286	4,182	4,500	5,786	2,305	4,367	2,128	7,450	61
2,344	28	1,995	1,995	......	....	......	....	....	2,248	4,738	1,174	....	62
3,612	68	2,895	2,895	629	7,896	1,673	5,130	13,026	3,287	6,990	1,163	16,730	63
266	....	296	298	......	....	......	....	....	....	819	14	900	64
639	13	1,071	1,071	60	233	1,000	1,065	1,298	1,416	2,693	1,005	2,550	65
7,448	1,629	2,926	2,965	......	....	1,810	6,386	6,386	3,048	6,006	586	13,495	66
2,909	16	2,422	2,422	80	866	1,718	4,508	5,374	3,025	5,675	1,819	14,855	67
734	35	1,225	1,225	20	232	248	1,017	1,249	1,036	2,827	324	7,000	68
1,504	16	1,826	1,826	24	458	825	2,716	3,174	1,357	4,277	771	12,100	69
2,276	56	2,555	2,555	......	....	1,542	400	400	2,155	6,063	89	11,350	70
1,771	44	813	813	......	....	295	6,930	6,930	738	1,959	170	4,900	71
342	5	404	404	108	1,798	505	703	2,501	732	1,083	271	1,300	72
1,634	9	1,387	1,387	238	6,320	780	1,554	7,874	1,998	3,432	1,457	4,880	73
2,075	14	2,155	2,202	280	4,870	1,025	11,050	16,520	2,493	5,100	1,703	10,450	74
1,368	8	1,216	1,243	65	240	825	1,300	1,540	1,276	3,172	892	3,820	75
3,628	11	1,948	1,948	40	470	83	318	788	1,805	4,966	1,677	4,600	76
2,150	26	1,706	1,708	58	240	2,500	1,550	1,790	2,664	4,199	1,599	5,525	77
1,264	32	2,534	2,534	475	4,360	309	1,870	6,230	2,745	5,938	875	18,900	78
3,998	38	3,411	3,411	223	10,225	3,452	2,194	12,419	4,126	8,379	626	17,800	79

TEXAS.

United States.	Foreign countries.	Dwellings.	Families.	Pupils.	Annual income.	Pupils.	Annual income.	Total educational income.	White scholars during the year.	Whites 5 and under 20 years old.	Whites over 20 unable to read and write.	Accommodation of churches—persons.	
1,591	3	375	375	38	....	58	....	....	280	931	172	....	1
595	8	166	166	......	....	62	675	675	86	392	144	190	2
865	810	432	432	20	....	122	3,600	3,600	208	787	50	800	3
1,412	188	377	397	......	....	......	....	....	384	842	62	1,150	4
1,270	2,086	1,204	1,204	98	2,130	16	180	2,310	402	1,727	1,172	1,000	5
850	17	250	250	......	....	......	....	....	183	527	52	....	6
773	173	296	296	......	....	......	....	....	118	380	15	....	7
251	26	81	81	......	....	75	1,115	1,115	98	201	38	....	8
768	19	224	224	......	....	115	1,853	1,853	192	509	98	1,050	9
733	30	174	174	......	....	164	....	....	190	422	68	....	10
345	342	182	182	......	....	126	....	....	34	304	1	....	11
642	3,100	1,554	1,776	296	....	119	....	....	908	2,951	2,528	900	12
2,386	43	558	576	340	....	500	....	....	611	1,224	58	....	13
4,309	24	891	891	......	....	340	2,149	2,149	983	2,166	331	6,000	14
1,415	4	311	311	......	....	273	....	....	260	756	171	....	15
549	585	283	295	......	....	165	....	....	160	583	......	1,100	16
93	1,230	367	367	......	....	130	550	550	257	532	13	900	17
175	5	38	39	......	....	40	....	....	40	94	18	60	18
2,017	21	435	450	......	....	170	....	....	438	1,032	285	350	19
541	17	109	110	......	....	104	....	....	70	286	47	1,200	20
566	228	231	231	......	....	......	....	....	73	458	......	....	21
See Na	varro.	155	155	......	....	......	....	....	113	389	38	....	22
2,500	17	548	548	......	....	573	....	....	561	1,347	291	2,915	23
1,452	465	494	494	150	....	120	....	....	323	1,023	42	3,150	24
524	50	199	199	40	....	120	....	....	263	331	6	1,500	25
1,178	1,729	727	741	398	8,200	45	900	9,100	468	1,219	22	6,200	26
437	419	216	216	......	....	......	....	....	80	386	39	1,500	27
154	913	274	274	......	....	137	210	210	216	390	......	1,550	28
291	54	88	88	......	....	28	....	....	16	126	2	....	29
556	17	188	188	70	1,800	75	1,500	3,300	83	309	6	900	30
1,466	11	295	295	......	....	247	....	....	242	808	200	1,520	31
1,356	143	405	431	67	....	123	4,000	4,000	380	884	164	390	32

	Counties.	Land occupied or improved.				Live stock upon farms.			
		Farms.	Acres improved.	Acres unimproved.	Value with improvements and implements.	Horses, asses, and mules.	Neat cattle.	Sheep.	Swine.
42	Lawrence	993	36,725	200,989	$ 702,549	2,863	6,947	7,166	29,658
43	Lewis	394	19,526	63,367	414,553	1,789	3,093	6,639	15,653
44	Lincoln	1,926	134,768	194,113	3,476,592	10,996	18,961	16,118	101,875
45	McMinn	1,688	97,306	203,419	1,366,882	5,027	10,619	10,326	47,640
46	McNairy	1,379	64,173	285,474	822,832	4,456	15,094	10,317	37,335
47	Macon	782	30,771	109,854	438,297	2,183	4,688	6,475	16,919
48	Madison	1,408	115,872	199,405	2,332,262	9,120	17,213	14,564	56,981
49	Marion	724	39,985	202,533	680,600	2,509	9,102	3,969	31,496
50	Marshall	1,032	79,951	119,734	2,096,281	8,419	12,978	19,531	71,133
51	Maury	1,501	143,730	144,434	4,358,771	13,634	20,507	25,883	103,538
52	Meigs	598	38,211	136,558	134,766	1,789	4,899	4,432	20,225
53	Monroe	918	83,610	257,125	1,343,956	4,147	7,149	8,502	33,459
54	Montgomery	1,227	101,225	203,252	1,359,836	7,258	13,958	16,732	68,306
55	Morgan	430	14,807	521,283	333,970	995	4,112	2,278	13,338
56	Obion	653	26,027	114,222	667,437	2,481	6,280	3,079	35,878
57	Overton	929	60,537	246,179	711,340	4,127	12,704	13,988	53,297
58	Perry	458	22,157	174,428	433,962	1,974	6,047	5,975	26,564
59	Polk	561	29,568	145,235	606,298	1,422	3,637	4,447	14,984
60	Rhea	305	21,694	56,712	379,467	1,241	4,439	3,209	13,043
61	Roane	842	66,440	174,443	1,061,936	3,622	10,060	10,346	35,917
62	Robertson	1,063	98,700	167,676	1,392,692	5,772	9,434	13,817	50,785
63	Rutherford	1,507	149,563	170,994	4,522,394	12,222	18,321	25,604	88,794
64	Scott	290	8,587	126,845	100,691	672	2,195	3,108	14,881
65	Sevier	531	39,830	167,936	501,539	2,561	6,083	6,663	20,433
66	Shelby	1,115	121,889	184,792	3,423,456	5,894	15,427	6,269	56,233
67	Smith	1,310	90,548	144,908	1,280,423	7,195	14,566	22,040	73,216
68	Stewart	936	39,118	184,722	374,789	3,745	9,715	10,477	32,913
69	Sullivan	816	95,034	121,371	1,403,556	4,098	9,562	15,998	22,285
70	Sumner	1,335	118,391	155,017	2,833,346	9,149	16,071	25,785	76,001
71	Tipton	631	48,176	132,622	1,108,049	2,837	9,670	3,222	31,014
72	Van Buren	217	12,115	164,851	148,123	869	2,796	2,268	10,716
73	Warren	645	52,100	131,547	731,629	2,806	7,310	8,974	26,519
74	Washington	922	86,794	116,150	1,801,927	4,981	9,394	14,606	27,312
75	Wayne	689	33,230	284,772	564,900	3,066	8,404	7,639	32,394
76	Weakly	1,467	61,933	192,445	872,167	4,389	11,423	8,826	42,928
77	White	1,341	79,174	219,678	796,079	4,559	11,733	12,283	44,150
78	Williamson	1,355	169,792	164,840	5,382,713	12,536	17,462	24,326	92,133
79	Wilson	1,988	140,784	186,299	2,881,325	11,683	17,574	32,109	83,951

STATISTICS OF

	Counties.	Farms.	Acres improved.	Acres unimproved.	Value with improvements and implements.	Horses, asses, and mules.	Neat cattle.	Sheep.	Swine.
1	Anderson	206	9,844	103,264	236,891	943	7,621	720	14,925
2	Angelina	88	3,004	33,375	143,265	558	6,371	95	4,812
3	Austin	230	12,381	107,922	433,268	2,715	22,55	2,104	12,871
4	Bastrop	219	9,672	78,991	316,257	1,912	18,610	883	11,699
5	Bexar	117	5,062	135,182	224,328	704	9,289	7,007	2,715
6	Bowie	157	19,045	335,398	210,801	1,349	8,184	592	12,108
7	Brazoria	134	22,251	1,023,706	1,117,469	2,454	50,192	235	13,940
8	Brazos	47	1,928	174,210	68,986	448	6,309	444	6,872
9	Burleson	115	5,182	316,531	156,585	973	12,766	376	13,607
10	Caldwell	51	1,991	18,131	71,582	218	4,042	306	3,434
11	Calhoun	22	1,085	38,570	76,529	410	8,278	480	845
12	Cameron, includ. Star	11	574	215,230	104,730	942	4,319	9,670	110
13	Cass.....[and Webb.	365	24,062	263,295	534,140	1,340	8,157	772	16,732
14	Cherokee	454	19,133	169,750	584,500	1,618	9,583	971	17,970
15	Collin	218	6,697	130,141	175,362	977	4,813	630	4,858
16	Colorado	116	13,744	285,654	199,589	3,107	22,261	4,720	12,297
17	Comal	55	1,704	8,768	81,165	119	1,283	356	418
18	Cook	25	433	34,922	6,395	68	503	96	1,463
19	Dallas	178	7,305	96,232	175,502	756	3,643	567	6,089
20	Denton	81	2,131	60,027	21,493	249	1,754	215	2,929
21	De Witt	100	5,493	93,884	196,943	2,635	17,954	391	8,097
22	Ellis	75	2,600	57,048	65,223	327	2,858	259	2,858
23	Fannin	331	14,118	127,462	300,107	1,877	10,192	2,607	12,362
24	Fayette	209	9,023	78,852	312,639	1,722	14,085	1,921	8,390
25	Fort Bend	109	10,892	92,260	366,009	1,835	29,223	521	9,792
26	Galveston	33	478	19,659	35,200	391	13,328	175	836
27	Gaudalupe	101	4,433	89,449	211,754	1,389	11,563	2,120	4,420
28	Gillespie	40	2,217	8,407	26,388	86	788	85	703
29	Goliad	30	1,470	27,680	55,623	432	7,731	2,555	1,749
30	Gonzales	123	6,504	362,193	524,558	2,319	29,726	565	14,328
31	Grayson	171	5,891	99,252	173,795	873	5,111	670	5,890
32	Grimes	217	15,627	108,667	293,932	1,570	22,324	4,101	13,643

AGRICULTURAL PRODUCTS.													
Wheat, bushels.	Rye & oats, bushels.	Indian corn, bushels.	Irish and sweet potatoes, busnels.	Peas and beans, bushels.	Barley, bushels.	Buckwheat, bushels.	Butter and cheese, pounds.	Hay, tons.	Hops, pounds.	Clover & other grass seeds, bushels.	Flaxseed, bushels.	
4,626	50,670	34,123	36,944	1,957	......	......	83,146	1,824	3	79	1	42
4,119	19,143	293,610	17,161	2,251	15	5	39,834	729	13	230	11	43
18,612	241,947	1,873,321	88,274	2,222	......	146	263,490	2,088	10	156	354	44
32,132	216,154	939,116	80,060	13,385	......	35	114,928	1,637	40	271	273	45
21,577	55,511	571,080	53,475	2,846	......	......	141,168	174	......	17	......	46
8,798	44,651	302,505	23,538	1,221	......	2	49,234	38	......	24	301	47
32,707	2,914	1,045,424	105,871	21,329	......	......	187,089	55	......	57	......	48
3,019	57,147	468,294	38,567	2,670	50	......	79,507	95	......	12	193	49
28,324	165,042	1,291,675	66,691	6,283	......	6	151,988	468	25	305	93	50
33,140	196,782	2,016,600	114,833	5,654	38	15	242,690	2,507	80	2,163	37	51
6,502	72,471	432,875	25,931	929	......	......	60,629	135	......	39	108	52
42,499	177,921	671,167	49,647	2,487	......	63	73,696	1,518	......	85	36	53
43,807	153,942	1,077,304	72,013	2,784	......	50	155,809	816	30	304	6	54
651	19,425	103,522	19,658	1,682	......	92	35,288	634	......	......	110	55
9,413	15,829	445,420	28,187	615	......	......	54,429	258	......	159	12	56
16,656	64,946	622,485	55,756	950	7	149	106,320	109	4	66	1,008	57
2,650	23,503	395,535	24,979	4,718	......	......	41,948	......	......	......	......	58
14,727	52,210	299,917	27,601	2,489	......	56	47,586	37	15	62	35	59
3,129	42,072	231,124	18,224	1,273	......	......	36,482	683	4	161	63	60
20,026	138,459	595,296	53,486	2,744	......	58	138,356	2,090	......	160	349	61
36,837	116,556	858,615	47,799	957	33	......	112,383	135	8	79	539	62
28,684	182,696	1,667,320	106,835	2,258	10	2	186,011	408	13	54	3	63
1,298	7,317	66,421	7,634	3,355	748	134	29,768	367	11	372	403	64
11,845	64,549	375,940	32,421	1,987	......	365	64,741	803	......	402	225	65
5,452	76,198	837,837	128,693	24,541	......	......	163,042	3,905	50	3	......	66
27,210	99,785	1,066,410	64,422	6,754	......	......	125,583	1,159	10	59	41	67
3,880	43,427	584,050	35,297	3,229	112	50	94,290	119	......	......	70	68
69,937	164,249	373,698	19,027	451	43	2,834	106,330	3,560	1	466	1,421	69
38,874	211,664	1,375,590	66,682	2,390	25	15	201,535	509	......	265	12	70
17,308	35,476	439,785	52,896	17,718	......	......	84,756	492	......	......	......	71
1,752	12,456	131,890	12,781	71	......	......	24,786	4	......	......	6	72
11,908	90,277	474,705	34,188	1,324	......	......	81,432	441	......	16	......	73
96,967	202,603	395,742	19,384	88	......	4,160	161,174	4,265	67	566	1,329	74
3,386	41,239	458,148	32,702	945	60	......	48,548	11	......	......	1	75
27,713	77,575	736,930	59,560	1,853	......	50	85,594	204	2	144	34	76
14,679	62,652	599,015	56,103	2,857	5	220	122,691	363	35	163	583	77
43,854	229,104	1,697,570	109,954	16,093	291	3	157,035	2,127	......	401	52	78
55,774	211,397	1,543,869	91,261	2,646	200	2	253,694	1,125	......	282	4	79

TEXAS.

907	1,397	87,506	19,167	296	......	......	39,574	......	......	......	......	1
6	1,117	22,005	11,116	448	......	......	14,113	20	......	......	......	2
120	1,474	149,230	40,852	929	......	......	98,412	355	......	......	......	3
215	6,577	148,360	22,313	2,520	......	4	96,573	98	......	......	......	4
120	2,365	82,975	2,162	262	......	5	19,626	740	......	......	......	5
568	6,598	93,110	56,477	545	4,300	......	40,282	......	......	......	......	6
......	100	213,225	88,250	2,226	......	......	56,455	394	5	......	......	7
21	392	15,934	810	156	......	......	8,246	......	......	......	......	8
54	533	70,000	4,169	169	......	......	18,270	76	......	......	......	9
199	......	29,885	5,245	1,760	......	......	13,380	4	1	......	......	10
199	......	7,660	2,300	......	......	......	......	......	......	......	......	11
......	......	8,700	200	......	......	......	......	......	......	......	......	12
360	13,417	167,250	48,061	21,855	......	......	55,382	548	......	......	......	13
466	5,677	226,660	55,477	43,562	......	......	124,106	17	......	......	......	14
2,433	3,794	88,195	4,878	55	......	......	61,440	465	......	......	1	15
......	......	92,865	19,780	......	......	......	9,645	......	......	......	......	16
210	70	37,575	1,740	119	......	......	12,321	414	......	......	......	17
......	100	5,170	439	44	......	......	5,429	27	......	......	......	18
2,983	3,993	94,870	5,969	228	......	11	40,182	366	......	......	3	19
176	983	14,171	963	24	......	......	19,103	32	......	......	3	20
50	......	66,545	1,050	......	......	......	......	......	......	......	......	21
945	1,360	28,744	2,617	923	30	......	17,220	57	......	......	......	22
4,849	8,045	124,634	11,906	321	5	5	101,858	624	......	......	12	23
30	1,630	116,030	21,916	1,859	......	......	36,805	36	......	......	......	24
......	......	135,205	55,666	1,555	......	......	14,414	......	......	......	......	25
......	......	5,720	5,450	......	......	......	7,750	30	......	......	......	26
294	635	80,330	3,554	91	......	......	36,480	179	......	......	......	27
80	......	15,240	729	169	......	......	5,140	117	......	......	......	28
......	......	21,735	......	......	......	......	......	......	......	......	......	29
25	975	37,375	10,518	......	......	......	78,425	......	......	......	......	30
1,485	1,786	59,015	5,795	123	......	2	57,127	321	......	......	......	31
48	2,674	138,405	32,011	1,940	......	......	57,840	47	......	......	......	32

	Counties.	Agricultural products.									
		Flax, pounds.	Hemp, dew and water-rotted, tons.	Maple sugar, pounds.	Cane sugar, hhds. of 1,000 pounds.	Molasses, gallons.	Rice, pounds.	Tobacco, pounds.	Ginned cotton, bales of 400 pounds.	Wool, pounds.	Silk cocoons, pounds.
42	Lawrence	434		432			3,054	16,765	125	11,486	3
43	Lewis	198		222			587	8,260	155	8,421	5
44	Lincoln	5,121	3	566		24	1,928	13,285	2,576	47,492	
45	McMinn	6,033	21	440		16	300	10,720		15,876	124
46	McNairy						4,330	9,180	2,821	14,437	
47	Macon	5,917		2,811	1	48		941,268		10,677	
48	Madison						66,955	34,340	15,823	20,058	
49	Marion	2,263	20	306			2,657	6,538	24,413	7,368	
50	Marshall	2,163	2	1,419		16	887	60,757	1,054	34,544	
51	Maury	1,153	282	961			44,862	167,517	9,972	47,437	
52	Meigs	881	1	65		2	1,704	17,667		8,874	10
53	Monroe	5,263					4,640	14,064		15,661	113
54	Montgomery	650	30				160	3,454,745		30,114	
55	Morgan	2,560		123				6,735		5,072	
56	Obion	1,953		330				139,305	55	3,547	
57	Overton	14,657		9,904		309	465	63,752		24,436	70
58	Perry			430		100		940	53	9,691	
59	Polk	1,106		5			2,439	29,266	29	8,072	
60	Rhea	4,408		76			245	3,755		5,572	
61	Roane	7,468	2	466		6	3,235	15,121	121	17,257	
62	Robertson	867		717		37	80	1,445,670	7	26,299	88
63	Rutherford	1,401		400		173	490	169,047	14,070	39,064	
64	Scott	4,796	39	2,425		193	646	5,492		4,735	86
65	Sevier	6,519		4,927		627	4,417	8,324		10,655	
66	Shelby								20,741	9,933	
67	Smith	1,655		1,602		25	468	2,377,394	22	30,881	1
68	Stewart	696		520		87	265	290,320	40	14,534	
69	Sullivan	15,403		10,398		460	450	2,610		16,122	
70	Sumner	780	2	550				809,517	153	44,934	
71	Tipton						310		6,611	5,609	
72	Van Buren	1,700		1,655		24			2	4,634	
73	Warren			929				200		16,454	
74	Washington	16,833		4,208		989	300	3,238		24,046	
75	Wayne	231		99				3,646	303	11,649	
76	Weakly	572					900	2,228,990	93	13,489	
77	White	13,092		4,734		181	1,126	20,779		23,537	3
78	Williamson	704	63	100		15	203	1,302,209	5,314	30,399	2
79	Wilson	100						1,237,305	63	51,813	

STATISTICS OF

	Counties.	Flax, pounds.	Hemp, dew and water-rotted, tons.	Maple sugar, pounds.	Cane sugar, hhds. of 1,000 pounds.	Molasses, gallons.	Rice, pounds.	Tobacco, pounds.	Ginned cotton, bales of 400 pounds.	Wool, pounds.	Silk cocoons, pounds.
1	Anderson								734	1,681	
2	Angelina				2	390	3,975	1,190	174	171	
3	Austin				60	4,195		9,663	3,205	2,317	
4	Bastrop								1,478	1,626	
5	Bexar							230		5,225	5
6	Bowie								1,113		
7	Brazoria				4,811	314,164		3,200	3,531	870	
8	Brazos						9	20	142	1,000	
9	Burleson				10	300	50	784	1,010	559	
10	Caldwell								122	624	
11	Calhoun								109		
12	Cameron, includ. Starr									2,000	
13	Cass.....[and Webb.						55	335	1,573	1,938	
14	Cherokee						4,250	1,295	1,083	2,492	
15	Collin	20						200	1	1,920	
16	Colorado							13,500	4,771	10,660	
17	Comal							1,595	10	621	4
18	Cook							130		349	
19	Dallas	105						50	44	2,144	
20	Denton	135								457	
21	De Witt								547	520	
22	Ellis	30					287	200		783	
23	Fannin	570						193	374	7,813	
24	Fayette							4,830	1,194	820	
25	Fort Bend				100	420		20	2,465	3,000	
26	Galveston										
27	Gaudalupe	8						1,540	182	4,281	
28	Gillespie							20		120	
29	Goliad										
30	Gonzales								1,271	720	
31	Grayson	5						75	5	1,532	
32	Grimes				14	700		370	2,282	5,404	

AGRICULTURAL PRODUCTS.					MANUFACTURES.				REMARKS.	
					Establishments.					
Beeswax and honey, pounds.	Value of animals slaughtered.	Value of produce of market gardens.	Value of orchard produce.	Wine, gallons.	Capital.	Hands employed.	Annual product.	Produced in families.		
6,733	$53,237	$67	....	......	$156,635	218	$136,155	$36,473	Div. in '43 to form Lewis.	42
6,993	20,687	26	$25	......	43,140	80	47,681	13,761	Formed in '43 from Hick-	43
61,455	196,256	....	....	......	78,190	212	156,843	111,174	man, Lawrence, Maury	44
1,756	141,756	6,517	562	......	120,290	219	219,860	50,906	and Wayne.	45
14,206	77,784	....	....	......	23,800	63	35,900	49,821	....	46
15,633	29,833	....	13	......	4,700	8	3,714	16,261	Divided in 1842 from Sum-	47
6,986	126,730	....	....	......	53,525	137	95,250	41,727	ner and Smith.	48
11,817	41,532	....	....	......	5,250	17	9,600	496	....	49
54,051	122,895	121	6,579	......	34,075	93	63,024	74,549	....	50
31,639	185,386	700	25	......	133,595	433	242,560	69,982	Divided in 1843 to form	51
1,326	40,741	662	400	......	25,000	21	10,080	23,343	Lewis.	52
814	72,866	81	20	......	102,840	184	134,599	36,437	....	53
2,215	158,588	395	15	......	1,072,000	1,368	1,376,300	49,299	....	54
5,256	16,828	....	256	......	3,210	14	2,762	10,826	Divided in 1849 to form	55
8,800	47,375	....	1,442	......	14,250	26	33,500	13,999	Scott.	56
18,455	51,890	....	3,981	......	5,350	24	10,900	41,733	....	57
5,762	44,083	....	....	......	48,137	128	42,737	28,014	Divided in 1845 to form	58
2,339	43,521	2	25	......	16,000	26	31,166	23,456	Decatur.	59
6,954	20,878	....	35	......	200	1	1,200	12,791	....	60
9,923	98,588	28	365	......	154,650	133	55,106	48,259	....	61
320	97,853	....	....	......	39,375	161	100,405	69,592	....	62
12,857	173,026	....	1,000	......	35,015	115	61,035	75,257	....	63
10,485	22,094	2,070	3,568	......	....	......	....	13,192	Formed in 1849 from An-	64
8,221	28,487	....	148	......	....	......	....	43,806	derson, Campbell, Mor-	65
25,007	110,759	19,375	2,185	......	424,130	789	840,789	24,503	gan and Fentress.	66
51,827	108,394	....	57	......	74,158	86	90,385	63,646	Div. in '42 to form Macon.	67
7,898	66,208	112	....	......	695,650	771	481,705	30,711	....	68
20,855	54,616	....	15	......	45,050	109	43,058	36,537	....	69
9,155	167,706	....	....	......	167,900	286	331,150	83,130	Div. in '42 to form Macon.	70
12,030	54,438	....	....	......	19,100	44	24,900	18,252	[and Warren.	71
3,920	9,115	....	....	......	2,500	14	4,905	12,669	Formed in '40 from White	72
4,483	47,081	....	....	......	20,850	32	24,880	27,998	Div. in '40 and '44 to form	73
27,698	86,823	3,422	435	......	132,800	216	243,832	56,792	Van Buren and Grundy.	74
2,966	48,735	....	....	......	116,945	122	69,050	28,902	Div. in '43 to form Lewis.	75
7,914	81,313	....	....	......	34,800	39	68,600	31,273	....	76
18,213	83,591	173	135	......	100,840	65	40,046	42,734	Divided in 1840 to form	77
12,280	190,945	495	145	50	103,270	238	159,280	81,831	Van Buren.	78
13,621	150,098	....	....	......	171,550	281	168,616	77,501	....	79

TEXAS.

5,364	14,263	....	35	......	....	......	....	4,340	Formed in 1846.	1
1,366	6,925	....	212	......	....	......	....	1,930	Formed in 1846.	2
10,005	21,667	....	....	......	....	......	....	710	Exist'g prior to annexation	3
16,272	25,258	....	....	......	56,900	67	82,100	812	" " "	4
4,085	9,551	910	10	5	24,600	57	95,830	....	" " "	5
....	23,443	....	....	......	3,600	14	12,100	....	" " "	6
....	63,101	1,380	3,120	7	....	......	....	....	" " "	7
1,340	3,675	....	1,360	......	....	......	....	100	" " "	8
637	10,373	....	3,317	......	....	......	....	427	Formed in 1846.	9
1,342	4,773	120	10	......	....	......	....	29,534	Formed in 1848.	10
....	325	....	....	......	....	......	....	....	Formed in 1846.	11
....	....	....	....	......	....	......	....	....	Formed in 1848.	12
649	27,705	....	....	......	5,500	24	13,860	20,099	Formed in 1846.	13
....	29,157	....	....	3	10,000	23	32,050	12,936	Formed in 1846.	14
22,682	8,578	....	....	......	....	......	....	6,516	Formed in 1846.	15
....	25,070	....	....	......	5,750	9	8,960	....	Exist'g prior to annexation	16
520	4,615	....	....	......	12,900	28	46,800	379	Formed in 1846.	17
700	946	....	....	......	....	......	....	854	Formed in 1848.	18
8,096	12,112	....	....	......	200	1	1,000	3,058	Formed in 1846.	19
1,599	3,375	....	....	......	....	......	....	2,493	Formed in 1846.	20
....	6,702	....	....	......	1,300	7	3,300	100	Formed in 1846.	21
3,974	4,028	92	50	......	....	......	....	1,711	Formed in 1849.	22
49,786	15,254	....	....	......	7 500	8	3,800	11,464	Exist'g prior to annexation	23
4,960	17,761	....	....	......	7,150	18	9,775	2,516	" " "	24
240	23,786	....	....	......	....	......	....	....	" " "	25
....	1,356	7,975	....	......	46,450	131	207,100	....	" " "	26
665	9,179	....	25	......	2,300	8	7,800	110	Formed in 1846.	27
100	1,459	....	....	......	5,075	13	17,326	30	Formed in 1848.	28
....	2,122	....	....	......	....	......	....	....	Exist'g prior to annexation	29
....	15,645	....	....	......	....	......	....	10,553	" " "	30
20,599	8,640	....	....	......	....	......	....	5,260	Formed in 1846.	31
11,890	25,255	....	....	......	....	......	....	5,848	Formed in 1846.	32

	COUNTIES.	POPULATION.								
		Whites.			Colored.		All classes.		Total population.	
		Male.	Female.	Total.	Free.	Slave.	Male.	Female.	1850.	1840.
33	Harris	2,051	1,705	3,756	7	905	2,454	2,214	4,668	....
34	Harrison	3,045	2,559	5,604	5	6,213	6,039	5,783	11,822	....
35	Hays	148	111	259	....	128	209	178	387	....
36	Henderson	628	527	1,155	1	81	671	566	1,237	....
37	Hopkins	1,306	1,163	2,469	....	154	1,370	1,253	2,623	....
38	Houston	1,082	954	2,036	12	673	1,419	1,302	2,721	....
39	Hunt	782	695	1,477	2	41	802	718	1,520	....
40	Jackson	356	271	627	30	339	551	445	996	....
41	Jasper	661	565	1,226	....	541	929	838	1,767	....
42	Jefferson	821	683	1,504	63	269	988	848	1,836	....
43	Kaufman	525	457	982	....	65	557	490	1,047	....
44	Lamar	1,516	1,377	2,893	....	1,085	2,065	1,913	3,978	....
45	Lavacca	620	519	1,139	....	432	821	750	1,571	....
46	Leon	730	595	1,325	....	621	1,055	891	1,946	....
47	Liberty	884	739	1,623	7	892	1,326	1,196	2,522	....
48	Limestone	1,108	882	1,990	....	618	1,393	1,215	2,608	....
49	Matagorda	499	414	913	3	1,208	1,154	970	2,124	....
50	Medina	580	301	881	....	28	597	312	909	....
51	Milam	1,428	1,041	2,469	2	436	1,640	1,267	2,907	....
52	Montgomery	786	653	1,439	....	945	1,272	1,112	2,384	....
53	Nacogdoches	2,036	1,722	3,758	31	1,404	2,733	2,460	5,193	....
54	Navarro	1,112	831	1,943	1	246	1,237	953	2,190	....
55	Newton	663	592	1,255	8	426	879	810	1,689	....
56	Nueces	430	220	650	1	47	449	249	698	....
57	Panola	1,428	1,248	2,676	2	1,193	2,009	1,862	3,871	....
58	Polk	843	699	1,542	1	805	1,206	1,142	2,348	....
59	Red River	1,292	1,201	2,493	7	1,406	1,999	1,907	3,906	....
60	Refugio	143	126	269	....	19	149	139	288	....
61	Robertson	366	304	670	....	264	502	432	934	....
62	Rusk	3,352	2,660	6,012	....	2,136	4,454	3,694	8,148	....
63	Sabine	793	763	1,556	....	942	1,273	1,225	2,498	....
64	San Augustine	1,146	941	2,087	....	1,561	1,907	1,741	3,648	....
65	San Patricio	112	85	197	....	3	113	87	200	....
66	Shelby	1,741	1,537	3,278	....	961	2,204	2,035	4,239	....
67	Smith	1,940	1,635	3,575	....	717	2,275	2,017	4,292	....
68	Star, (see Cameron.)	....	....	....	....	....	....	....	....	....
69	Tarrant	355	244	599	....	65	391	273	664	....
70	Titus	1,645	1,523	3,168	1	467	1,872	1,764	3,636	....
71	Travis	1,309	1,027	2,336	11	791	1,718	1,420	3,138	....
72	Tyler	784	692	1,476	....	418	980	914	1,894	....
73	Upshur	1,439	1,273	2,712	....	682	1,769	1,625	3,394	....
74	Van Zandt	685	623	1,308	....	40	704	644	1,348	....
75	Victoria	756	640	1,396	52	571	1,103	916	2,019	....
76	Walker	1,445	1,218	2,663	....	1,301	2,089	1,875	3,964	....
77	Washington	1,736	1,430	3,166	....	2,817	3,152	2,831	5,983	....
78	Webb (see Cameron)	....	....	....	....	....	....	....	....	....
79	Wharton	293	217	510	....	1,242	925	827	1,752	....
80	Williamson	762	648	1,410	3	155	829	739	1,568	....

STATISTICS OF

1	Addison	13,398	13,043	26,441	108	....	13,452	13,097	26,549	23,583
2	Bennington	9,434	9,077	18,511	78	....	9,478	9,111	18,589	16,872
3	Caledonia	12,344	11,240	23,584	11	....	12,350	11,245	23,595	21,891
4	Chittenden	14,620	14,307	28,927	109	....	14,679	14,357	29,036	22,977
5	Essex	2,401	2,246	4,647	3	....	2,403	2,247	4,650	4,226
6	Franklin	14,596	13,904	28,500	86	....	14,641	13,945	28,586	24,531
7	Grand Isle	2,176	1,966	4,142	3	....	2,176	1,969	4,145	3,883
8	Lamoille	5,583	5,286	10,869	3	....	5,585	5,287	10,872	10,475
9	Orange	13,617	13,660	27,277	19	....	13,624	13,672	27,296	27,873
10	Orleans	7,999	7,695	15,694	13	....	8,006	7,701	15,707	13,634
11	Rutland	16,957	15,981	32,938	121	....	17,024	16,035	33,059	30,699
12	Washington	12,462	12,178	24,640	14	....	12,467	12,187	24,654	23,506
13	Windham	14,818	14,207	29,025	37	....	14,838	14,224	29,062	27,442
14	Windsor	19,253	18,954	38,207	113	....	19,310	19,010	38,320	40,356

NATIVITIES, DWELLINGS, &c. — Born out of State — United States.	NATIVITIES, DWELLINGS, &c. — Born out of State — Foreign countries.	Dwellings.	Families.	EDUCATION AND RELIGION. — Colleges, academies, and private schools — Pupils.	Colleges, academies, and private schools — Annual income.	Public Schools — Pupils.	Public Schools — Annual income.	Total educational income.	White scholars during year.	Whites 5 and under 20 years old.	Whites over 20 unable to read & write.	Accommodation of churches—persons.	
1,403	1,209	834	834	276	$5,838	......	....	$5,838	379	1,300	124	1,900	33
4,550	91	972	977	69	....	496	$1,040	1,040	867	2,262	132	3,500	34
167	10	41	41	......	....	40	480	480	89	111	16	200	35
916	38	192	193	......	....	121	....	....	168	524	109	....	36
1,870	5	435	435	......	....	......	....	....	....	1,027	......	....	37
1,257	20	357	357	50	....	......	....	....	87	802	220	....	38
1,164	5	268	282	30	....	20	....	....	265	631	177	....	39
349	83	114	114	......	....	20	400	400	135	212	2	....	40
756	15	192	193	......	....	140	2,082	2,082	246	523	85	100	41
930	64	259	259	......	....	90	....	....	177	594	113	....	42
813	5	170	170	......	....	129	....	....	204	414	115	....	43
1,984	12	497	497	......	....	180	....	....	382	1,249	11	....	44
672	49	203	203	12	216	......	....	216	272	446	70	160	45
871	21	231	231	......	....	93	1,500	1,500	180	490	55	....	46
879	109	312	312	......	....	100	1,000	1,000	103	605	27	150	47
1,422	24	380	380	30	500	75	1,500	2,000	174	741	80	550	48
450	186	176	177	80	1,820	......	....	1,820	155	295	14	800	49
123	622	177	177	......	....	37	225	225	46	272	39	500	50
1,691	115	414	421	41	400	134	1,467	1,867	164	962	215	180	51
870	59	260	276	75	....	......	....	....	194	553	63	200	52
2,433	75	631	631	69	1,700	260	2,346	4,046	506	1,491	416	7,885	53
*2,650	*166	336	336	......	....	211	3,130	3,130	323	757	231	....	54
863	5	219	220	......	....	83	1,436	1,436	247	531	122	620	55
229	358	151	151	......	....	......	....	....	17	168	149	....	56
1,923	10	456	456	......	....	79	....	....	275	1,027	62	....	57
1,022	25	292	292	30	....	30	....	....	206	626	112	....	58
2,009	42	420	420	257	12,530	......	....	12,530	405	1,068	157	1,000	59
79	104	56	56	......	....	18	....	....	....	104	......	500	60
446	23	132	132	40	400	45	800	1,200	48	260	2	950	61
4,877	37	1,045	1,045	80	1,200	117	1,170	2,370	671	2,419	45	1,400	62
954	21	288	288	......	....	92	....	....	149	606	37	1,000	63
1,225	25	350	350	60	1,500	198	3,960	5,400	300	848	59	1,350	64
41	106	38	38	......	....	30	....	....	26	68	24	....	65
2,166	33	560	560	30	450	181	2,615	3,065	338	1,318	126	1,425	66
3,072	10	603	605	25	400	105	1,175	1,575	450	1,460	208	2,400	67
....	....	......	......	......	....	......	....	....	....	....	......	....	68
See	Navarro	85	85	......	....	......	....	....	103	221	55	....	69
2,422	12	548	548	128	1,300	50	300	1,600	204	1,399	49	525	70
1,570	163	423	423	83	....	183	....	....	444	883	84	200	71
1,005	27	267	267	25	....	35	....	....	72	575	......	....	72
2,094	6	484	484	......	....	131	....	....	267	1,088	233	315	73
1,018	60	246	246	......	....	......	....	....	95	536	197	610	74
511	641	327	327	71	....	......	....	....	64	506	15	....	75
1,678	60	478	478	91	....	181	....	....	451	1,055	171	500	76
1,987	117	600	600	365	....	115	....	....	501	1,238	1	1,000	77
....	....	......	......	......	....	......	....	....	....	....	......	....	78
319	15	112	112	......	....	......	....	....	10	176	......	....	79
1,038	21	230	242	......	....	80	730	730	190	578	170	....	80

VERMONT.

United States.	Foreign countries.	Dwellings.	Families.	Colleges — Pupils.	Colleges — Annual income.	Public Schools — Pupils.	Public Schools — Annual income.	Total educational income.	White scholars during year.	Whites 5 and under 20 years old.	Whites over 20 unable to read & write.	Accommodation of churches—persons.	
3,676	3,794	4,679	4,830	501	6,355	7,884	14,353	20,708	6,838	9,034	664	21,022	1
3,415	1,103	3,404	3,541	205	1,600	5,946	12,318	13,918	5,071	6,471	146	11,900	2
4,523	2,118	4,325	4,467	638	6,683	7,361	11,987	18,670	7,471	8,254	391	18,475	3
3,218	6,726	4,805	5,099	896	11,373	7,177	16,918	28,291	6,495	9,972	1 306	16,355	4
1,264	277	846	846	74	173	1,666	3,376	3,549	1,701	1,682	16	2,850	5
2,438	6,318	4,827	4,977	279	1,125	7,537	9,520	10,645	7,683	10,367	1,511	19,405	6
348	1,043	691	692	33	1,200	1,364	2,640	3,840	888	1,516	382	2,600	7
1,898	462	2,022	2,101	933	3,305	3,269	5,120	8,425	3,572	3,906	30	8,100	8
5,170	861	5,192	5,380	806	5,461	9,212	18,661	24,122	9,042	9,334	153	25,025	9
2,923	1,864	2,780	2,811	195	1,939	4,722	8,267	10,206	5,255	5,919	154	7,019	10
4,747	4,394	5,661	6,155	1,190	16,433	9,395	15,886	32,319	9,658	10,997	720	24,908	11
3,756	1,823	4,442	4,452	281	1,500	7,456	12,566	14,066	8,586	8,689	176	18,725	12
5,603	1,880	5,374	5,636	666	3,776	8,773	16,250	20,026	8,654	9,531	410	24,480	13
8,135	1,052	7,373	7,586	631	9,570	11,695	28,249	37,819	11,238	12,757	130	33,670	14

* Includes Ellis and Tarrant.

	COUNTIES.	LAND OCCUPIED OR IMPROVED.				LIVE STOCK UPON FARMS.			
		Farms.	Acres improved.	Acres unimproved.	Value with improvements and implements.	Horses, asses, and mules.	Neat Cattle.	Sheep.	Swine.
33	Harris	197	4,512	53,411	$ 137,937	1,718	29,123	930	6,685
34	Harrison	521	56,277	220,498	1,123,528	2,940	12,530	2,742	24,762
35	Hays	22	725	17,498	58,748	216	1,733	998	1,332
36	Henderson	106	2,468	357	64,214	264	3,392	222	9,343
37	Hopkins	221	5,447	99,503	114,340	850	8,963	2,463	13,784
38	Houston	192	9,402	81,617	185,893	1,028	13,016	483	15,664
39	Hunt	93	2,131	33,306	39,201	361	3,480	772	6,463
40	Jackson	73	3,034	121,926	176,473	1,074	20,792	864	4,002
41	Jasper	123	5,676	330,823	320,341	437	5,800	215	7,081
42	Jefferson	91	1,832	42,690	52,916	1,927	29,159	562	4,384
43	Kaufman	94	2,702	323	88,072	303	2,865	647	6,585
44	Lamar	407	16,031	237,313	504,488	1,988	14,483	3,174	24,008
45	Lavacca	139	4,859	93,143	169,134	1,456	12,590	1,431	8,418
46	Leon	151	6,485	109,592	206,972	1,202	14,089	600	12,746
47	Liberty	149	7,084	118,574	249,290	2,451	45,670	954	9,478
48	Limestone	279	8,638	326,374	125,858	1,248	13,294	585	14,155
49	Matagorda	39	8,475	50,412	503,015	1,078	35,009	2,119	6,022
50	Medino	40	1,424	8,371	21,602	90	797	17	346
51	Milam	152	3,146	80,923	175,920	1,151	10,630	397	5,060
52	Montgomery	180	8,642	58,198	204,449	1,016	11,777	934	6,926
53	Nacogdoches	287	16,546	114,866	296,818	1,486	9,879	1,287	16,994
54	Navarro	178	5,904	55,271	131,326	896	9,265	844	9,586
55	Newton	141	4,749	154,365	170,459	331	4,940	126	7,092
56	Nueces	8	995	93,988	110,393	677	10,075	5,600	15
57	Panola	209	13,110	103,212	225,506	1,116	6,719	885	11,334
58	Polk	172	7,856	456,182	505,618	1,058	15,436	504	9,972
59	Red River	166	14,711	211,790	347,756	1,343	9,182	2,255	13,590
60	Refugio	21	458	22,780	20,515	407	10,124	190	323
61	Robertson	18	4,249	241,519	61,190	710	11,634	1,040	9,086
62	Rusk	567	27,500	204,717	689,096	2,480	12,423	1,859	20,221
63	Sabine	171	12,759	419,704	417,439	784	7,293	461	12,044
64	San Augustine	158	17,903	91,810	258,535	1,048	9,063	1,189	11,645
65	San Patricio	10	210	40,255	24,233	47	1,692	150	220
66	Shelby	380	19,4[illegible]0	251,055	446,823	1,353	10,985	1,296	21,280
67	Smith	248	8,9[illegible]6	82,434	287,177	980	6,133	706	11,699
68	Star, (see Cameron.)	......	......	......	......	......	......	......	......
69	Tarrant	51	1,726	2,680	22,755	159	1,549	23	2,279
70	Titus	269	9,743	89,919	182,348	953	6,838	1,014	12,315
71	Travis	146	6,941	66,380	310,923	1,511	11,953	2,346	5,874
72	Tyler	137	5,244	97,705	145,553	547	4,938	172	9,469
73	Upshur	240	9,564	120,082	266,089	996	5,473	1,005	11,537
74	Van Zandt	138	3,127	45,463	78,945	623	4,097	641	10,429
75	Victoria	84	4,072	130,545	213,735	1,838	13,288	190	2,832
76	Walker	234	11,976	433,885	443,422	1,818	23,923	916	15,267
77	Washington	306	19,535	244,382	692,961	2,552	21,873	4,052	15,671
78	Webb (see Cameron)	......	......	......	......	......	......	......	......
79	Wharton	55	7,242	76,305	319,990	1,173	15,668	524	6,596
80	Williamson	107	4,506	122,105	278,708	2,223	21,060	2,937	13,646

STATISTICS OF

1	Addison	2,292	243,312	115,287	8,055,527	5,922	26,754	188,154	5,822
2	Bennington	1,397	138,065	85,760	3,469,950	3,344	16,052	71,294	5,162
3	Caledonia	2,830	210,474	151,607	5,071,168	5,716	28,845	30,252	2,864
4	Chittenden	1,908	177,707	104,454	5,841,782	4,914	24,973	57,184	6,49[illegible]
5	Essex	602	42,993	52,310	828,281	1,025	7,252	7,519	82[illegible]
6	Franklin	2,172	180,843	127,002	4,499,488	5,490	34,414	58,509	5,413
7	Grand Isle	339	33,171	15,113	1,228,675	1,300	3,059	18,949	93[illegible]
8	Lamoille	1,082	76,083	76,070	1,958,976	2,071	13,860	15,193	2,476
9	Orange	2,677	226,257	120,142	5,087,429	5,585	29,479	71,551	7,337
10	Orleans	2,055	119,377	127,520	2,642,204	3,730	21,324	27,422	3,825
11	Rutland	2,668	290,392	154,524	8,227,420	6,151	33,414	186,319	5,634
12	Washington	2,104	165,654	120,239	4,130,564	4,155	26,619	32,355	5,507
13	Windham	3,363	319,558	99,674	6,550,374	5,055	37,804	58,553	6,005
14	Windsor	4,274	377,523	174,711	8,514,671	6,817	44,999	190,868	8,600

AGRICULTURAL PRODUCTS.

Wheat, bushels.	Rye & oats, bushels.	Indian corn, bushels.	Irish and sweet potatoes, bushels.	Peas and beans, bushels.	Barley, bushels.	Buckwheat, bushels.	Butter and cheese, pounds.	Hay, tons.	Hops, pounds.	Clover & other grass seeds, bushels.	Flaxseed bushels.	
......	160	49,664	21,306	......	......	......	30,880	......	......	......	......	33
166	8,996	376,620	135,474	15,512	......	......	47,261	......	......	......	......	34
75	800	19,000	525	100	......	20	9,450	138	......	......	......	35
1,463	890	31,350	4,453	......	......	......	......	......	......	......	......	36
1,708	3,215	48,453	8,556	281	......	5	41,574	......	......	......	......	37
50	1,324	71,495	21,707	1,967	......	......	48,004	......	......	......	......	38
1,725	572	19,520	4,128	35	......	......	10,370	60	......	......	......	39
40	68	30,590	9,660	......	......	......	27,040	43	......	......	......	40
......	2,040	44,498	16,364	1,495	......	......	6,550	......	......	......	......	41
......	72	16,545	9,874	458	......	......	8,554	19	1	......	......	42
4,024	2,239	30,685	2,954	......	......	......	......	......	......	......	......	43
4,824	23,166	116,594	16,465	2,482	......	......	104,601	1,343	......	3	6	44
......	300	50,286	10,300	13	......	......	37,500	71	......	......	......	45
209	3,483	66,545	19,715	5,760	......	......	37,595	41	......	......	......	46
......	56	54,310	21,021	25	......	......	16,590	132	......	......	......	47
1,053	1,550	99,800	9,995	2,786	200	......	35,047	24	......	......	......	48
......	......	103,360	41,270	300	......	......	22,930	......	......	......	......	49
......	......	26,106	274	63	......	......	2,931	129	......	......	......	50
515	330	38,539	8,070	60	......	......	28,588	295	......	......	......	51
350	1,888	80,441	19,058	295	......	......	40,500	207	......	......	......	52
124	9,079	139,110	39,743	1,050	......	......	45,400	12	......	......	......	53
657	1,629	73,040	12,366	1,049	......	1	54,304	29	......	......	1	54
16	586	34,135	20,108	3,459	......	......	10,548	......	......	......	......	55
......	......	7,150	......	......	......	......	......	......	......	......	......	56
12	667	108,870	35,625	7,197	......	......	24,369	......	......	......	......	57
......	1,075	60,065	14,806	450	......	......	......	......	......	......	......	58
3,028	16,090	95,510	9,298	5	......	......	57,550	62	......	6	......	59
......	......	6,240	......	......	......	......	......	......	......	......	......	60
99	1,725	41,395	7,381	576	......	......	19,690	......	......	......	......	61
390	9,449	280,353	68,128	21,183	28	......	77,028	......	......	......	......	62
200	2,510	61,619	21,225	3,287	8	......	18,029	......	......	......	......	63
265	12,587	115,284	33,737	6,338	......	......	20,556	209	......	......	......	64
......	......	4,350	......	......	......	......	......	......	......	......	......	65
92	9,840	99,518	40,784	160	......	......	64,240	......	......	......	......	66
665	3,326	125,565	31,344	7,076	5	1	30,600	15	......	......	......	67
......	......	......	......	......	......	......	......	......	......	......	......	68
384	405	17,520	2,193	297	......	......	11,600	71	......	......	......	69
1,099	8,170	66,000	17,336	4,747	......	......	39,675	......	......	......	......	70
656	2,156	149,365	19,290	1,068	......	......	43,442	339	......	......	......	71
4	388	35,099	12,539	833	......	......	5,058	......	......	......	......	72
91	1,457	90,000	22,883	4,782	200	5	28,139	8	......	......	......	73
92	620	30,920	8,683	1,672	......	......	17,393	......	......	......	......	74
......	......	54,110	1,050	......	......	......	......	......	......	......	......	75
......	2,565	102,475	17,610	2	......	......	1,985	8	......	......	......	76
57	840	161,743	29,161	223	......	......	101,300	111	......	1	......	77
......	......	......	......	......	......	......	......	......	......	......	......	78
......	......	103,700	35,865	5	......	......	2,235	......	......	......	......	79
753	120	57,015	2,899	80	......	......	65,495	21	......	......	......	80

VERMONT.

Wheat, bushels.	Rye & oats, bushels.	Indian corn, bushels.	Irish and sweet potatoes, bushels.	Peas and beans, bushels.	Barley, bushels.	Buckwheat, bushels.	Butter and cheese, pounds.	Hay, tons.	Hops, pounds.	Clover & other grass seeds, bushels.	Flaxseed bushels.	
103,434	231,481	175,478	318,421	26,355	149	15,659	1,693,920	88,793	5,962	1,594	51	1
6,973	194,781	150,920	200,013	3,150	3,003	22,797	1,061,280	54,600	193	622	132	2
62,551	220,825	93,389	565,341	6,419	3,658	14,380	1,327,874	59,449	1,422	3,170	113	3
36,491	210,318	198,598	383,113	10,390	682	10,003	2,501,937	57,407	......	621	26	4
8,826	46,957	21,931	94,124	2,506	1,221	15,400	414,936	14,972	28,250	961	11	5
55,488	154,978	137,896	258,757	10,255	815	10,095	2,596,115	78,619	1,610	1,050	33	6
31,324	85,013	23,245	31,793	10,469	739	12,142	120,018	6,980	......	301	8	7
14,466	97,097	66,017	278,252	4,351	629	10,373	650,145	26,973	15,657	596	41	8
52,822	215,197	176,586	599,925	5,658	1,861	28,942	1,297,918	70,549	23,827	815	158	9
58,515	174,440	70,306	407,132	3,723	8,974	15,305	713,252	45,288	77,605	1,837	140	10
25,874	204,304	258,831	416,000	4,220	627	12,051	3,050,861	103,950	162	774	22	11
30,580	219,121	133,477	446,551	4,954	865	10,135	1,407,844	54,959	12,125	804	31	12
8,749	178,695	210,141	338,295	2,279	14,124	7,531	1,614,381	84,749	41,510	468	10	13
39,862	250,760	312,581	613,297	9,920	4,803	25,006	2,408,333	118,865	79,700	2,083	163	14

	COUNTIES.	AGRICULTURAL PRODUCTS.									
		Flax, pounds.	Hemp, dew and water-rotted, tons.	Maple sugar, pounds.	Cane sugar, hhds. of 1,000 pounds.	Molasses, gallons.	Rice, pounds.	Tobacco. pounds.	Ginned cotton, bales of 400 pounds.	Wool, pounds.	Silk cocoons, pounds.
33	Harris	...	...	...	6	...	...	2,300	11	1,048	...
34	Harrison	...	...	...	...	...	196	...	4,581	830	...
35	Hays	...	...	...	...	...	...	50	2	1,091	...
36	Henderson	...	...	...	...	...	...	5,000	31	...	...
37	Hopkins	...	...	...	...	...	...	190	8	6,769	...
38	Houston	...	...	...	82	340	...	...	750	1,471	...
39	Hunt	20	...	...	...	...	...	378	5	1,050	...
40	Jackson	...	...	...	31	3,040	...	...	290	525	...
41	Jasper	...	...	...	27	2,242	3,565	3,750	359	350	10
42	Jefferson	...	...	...	41	1,514	18,900	...	2	1,100	...
43	Kaufman	...	...	...	...	...	...	213	6	...	...
44	Lamar	105	...	...	...	...	161	3,988	1,055	9,084	...
45	Lavacca	...	...	...	...	280	...	...	526	543	...
46	Leon	...	...	...	...	70	...	1,380	913	1,320	...
47	Liberty	...	...	...	115	4,820	6,541	...	253	...	...
48	Limestone	...	...	...	...	...	...	1,787	603	816	...
49	Matagorda	...	...	...	1,394	73,000	60	...	1,613	3,170	...
50	Medina	...	...	...	...	...	...	...	...	...	...
51	Milam	...	...	...	...	...	...	...	...	675	...
52	Montgomery	...	...	...	2	1,430	1,510	560	1,109	835	...
53	Nacogdoches	...	...	...	...	...	285	1,109	835	2,544	...
54	Navarro	50	...	...	...	...	...	266	2	1,982	...
55	Newton	...	...	...	14	2,920	23,570	300	152	662	...
56	Nueces	...	...	...	...	...	...	...	...	...	...
57	Panola	...	...	...	...	...	...	...	887	1,145	...
58	Polk	...	...	...	20	2,164	...	...	582	...	...
59	Red River	...	...	...	...	...	...	...	579	1,889	...
60	Refugio	...	...	...	...	...	...	...	...	250	...
61	Robertson	...	...	...	...	...	...	535	429	3,061	...
62	Rusk	...	...	...	101	1,090	400	1,715	2,659	4,632	...
63	Sabine	...	...	...	13	4,178	11,815	...	702	1,057	...
64	San Augustine	...	...	...	23	2,460	6,780	475	1,020	2,785	...
65	San Patricio	...	...	...	...	...	...	...	...	...	...
66	Shelby	...	...	...	...	500	...	...	790	1,770	...
67	Smith	...	...	...	...	100	450	555	415	1,495	3
68	Star, (see Cameron.)	...	...	...	...	...	...	...	...	...	...
69	Tarrant	...	...	...	...	...	...	50	...	86	...
70	Titus	...	...	...	...	...	...	250	292	3,505	...
71	Travis	...	...	...	...	...	...	...	234	4,499	...
72	Tyler	...	...	...	33	2,871	5,260	560	184	221	...
73	Upshur	...	...	...	...	...	15	1,061	673	1,245	...
74	Van Zandt	...	...	...	...	...	69	785	57	1,646	...
75	Victoria	...	...	...	120	6,700	...	...	270	420	...
76	Walker	...	...	...	6	540	...	...	873	95	...
77	Washington	...	...	...	9	...	...	200	4,008	1,045	...
78	Webb (see Cameron)	...	...	...	...	...	...	...	...	...	...
79	Wharton	...	...	...	317	11,490	...	...	2,892	60	...
80	Williamson	...	...	...	...	...	...	...	...	3,499	...

STATISTICS OF

1	Addison	1,282	...	205,263	...	650	...	...	...	622,594	76
2	Bennington	2,522	...	220,009	...	165	...	...	...	221,679	...
3	Caledonia	2,365	...	854,820	...	364	...	...	...	136,790	...
4	Chittenden	968	...	242,842	...	70	...	...	...	185,215	4
5	Essex	855	...	145,041	...	129	...	...	...	29,614	...
6	Franklin	1,052	...	684,511	...	36	...	...	...	209,350	...
7	Grand Isle	331	...	32,665	...	...	...	...	...	70,291	30
8	Lamoille	1,293	...	427,918	...	23	...	...	...	49,053	...
9	Orange	3,752	...	532,156	...	674	...	...	...	248,715	15
10	Orleans	660	...	656,883	...	...	...	...	...	81,947	...
11	Rutland	986	...	492,664	...	...	...	...	...	623,199	...
12	Washington	2,730	...	765,429	...	407	...	...	...	153,843	...
13	Windham	518	...	470,934	...	1,360	...	...	...	179,122	1
14	Windsor	1,538	...	618,222	...	2,119	...	...	...	589,305	142

AGRICULTURAL PRODUCTS.					MANUFACTURES.				REMARKS.	
					Establishments.					
Beeswax and honey, pounds.	Value of animals slaughtered.	Value of produce of market gardens.	Value of orchard produce.	Wine, gallons.	Capital.	Hands employed.	Annual product.	Produced in families.		
....	$11,065	$1,135	....	......	$56,100	136	$204,200	....	Exist'g prior to annexation.	33
....	57,658	100	....	......	59,700	90	61,200	$2,610	" " "	34
1,150	4,245	....	....	......	4,450	7	17,100	240	Formed in 1848.	35
....	8,543	....	....	......	....	......	....	9,788	Formed in 1846.	36
1,800	17,101	....	....	......	....	......	....	6,774	Formed in 1846.	37
4,269	11,857	....	....	......	....	......	....	1,717	Exist'g prior to annexation.	38
1,620	5,266	....	....	......	....	......	....	2,485	Formed in 1846.	39
....	13,286	....	....	......	....	......	....	3,635	Exist'g prior to annexation.	40
2,794	10,635	....	....	......	16,600	23	8,250	2,241	" " "	41
639	9,975	6	$65	......	13,810	25	28,552	1,984	" " "	42
....	4,930	....	....	......	....	......	....	7,622	Formed in 1848.	43
114,860	23,895	175	50	......	9,600	17	22,700	21,698	Exist'g prior to annexation.	44
143	10,049	....	....	......	....	......	....	11,260	Formed in 1846.	45
7,445	13,148	50	....	......	4,775	8	5,150	940	Formed in 1846.	46
4,705	17,279	....	265	......	500	2	1,600	40	Exist'g prior to annexation.	47
4,558	12,360	20	....	......	....	......	....	1,714	Formed in 1846.	48
1,300	18,211	....	....	......	....	......	....	....	Exist'g prior to annexation.	49
305	1,494	....	....	......	....	......	....	....	Formed in 1848.	50
3,070	9,975	....	....	......	400	2	1,150	698	Exist'g prior to annexation.	51
6,485	13,640	10	1,785	8	6.550	21	11,400	1,130	" " "	52
5,338	26,324	....	125	......	27,515	22	31,390	6,194	" " "	53
4,949	11,072	....	....	......	8,300	30	26,000	3,211	Formed in 1846.	54
1,750	9,525	....	....	16	14,000	19	7,000	2,730	Formed in 1846.	55
....	....	....	....	......	200	2	1,050	....	Formed in 1846.	56
970	20,413	....	640	......	....	......	....	6,096	Formed in 1846.	57
....	8,921	....	....	......	....	......	....	....	Formed in 1846.	58
15	13,714	....	20	......	34,800	38	28,300	6,566	Exist'g prior to annexalion.	59
....	805	....	....	......	....	......	....	....	" " "	60
2,952	7,504	....	....	......	....	......	....	387	" " "	61
3,377	36,212	....	....	......	24,650	56	74,020	7,643	" " "	62
1,519	18,746	....	....	......	10,400	31	20,380	2,646	" " "	63
1,480	23,105	....	70	......	13,895	35	21,275	3,061	" " "	64
....	212	....	....	......	....	......	....	....	" " "	65
85	27,677	....	....	......	10,765	12	6,350	7,929	" " "	66
4,589	13,548	....	305	......	1,000	8	4,500	4,112	Formed in 1846.	67
....	....	....	....	......	....	......	....	....	Formed in 1848.	68
690	2,756	....	....	......	....	......	....	1,112	Formed in 1849.	69
3,480	17,894	....	....	......	900	8	3,500	6,507	Formed in 1846.	70
20	19,574	....	....	......	4,000	1	3,000	140	Exist'g prior to annexation.	71
978	10,695	25	....	......	8,775	15	5,770	1,046	Formed in 1846.	72
4,962	16,871	356	1,041	......	3,700	14	4,800	2,840	Formed in 1846.	73
102	8,946	....	....	......	9,950	18	5,700	2,872	Formed In 1848.	74
....	4,608	....	....	......	4,230	16	17,900	....	Exist'g prior to annexation.	75
1,020	15,672	....	....	......	....	......	....	....	Formed in 1846.	76
8,445	60,007	....	....	......	....	......	....	150	Exist'g prior to annexation.	77
....	....	....	....	......	....	......	....	....	Formed in 1848.	78
406	17,808	....	....	60	....	......	....	200	Formed in 1846.	79
11,690	22,757	....	....	......	500	2	1,500	3,186	Formed in 1848.	80

VERMONT.

40,654	176,856	....	41,696	114	289,375	597	659,838	9,648	....	1
14,814	86,123	1,558	16,629	7	468,050	769	880,216	6,450	....	2
22,863	135,537	355	26,094	47	444,180	816	799,053	40,343	....	3
18,319	134,536	10,913	33,841	303	771,610	1,216	1,320,730	13,359	....	4
3,855	37,020	....	4,523	......	31,250	55	48,794	22,044	....	5
20,536	141,682	107	19,429	......	147,710	394	285,697	26,247	....	6
4,866	19,967	12	11,223	......	13,100	47	15,600	3,449	....	7
11,501	80,296	....	9,095	94	110,300	146	175,861	6,584	....	8
12,438	160,430	270	23,980	......	171,045	253	219.165	27,346	....	9
6,461	86,672	....	5,920	......	64,450	125	119,036	16,422	....	10
37,370	184,251	537	38,457	19	828,975	1,379	1,284,756	12,620	....	11
17,299	155,477	1,475	20,620	......	231,337	449	525,236	17,269	....	12
7,255	189,095	581	19,139	15	476,720	922	831,209	13,321	....	13
31,191	273,394	3,045	44,609	60	953,275	1,277	1,405,729	52,608	....	14

	COUNTIES.	POPULATION.								
		Whites.			Colored.		All classes.		Total population.	
		Male.	Female.	Total.	Free.	Slave.	Male.	Female.	1850.	1840.
1	Accomac	4,775	4,833	9,608	3,295	4,987	8,842	9,048	17,890	17,096
2	Albemarle	6,206	5,669	11,875	587	13,338	13,416	12,384	25,800	22,924
3	Alexandria	3,397	3,820	7,217	1,409	1,382	4,545	5,463	10,008	....
4	Alleghany	1,383	1,380	2,763	58	694	1,792	1,723	3,515	2,749
5	Amelia	1,375	1,410	2,785	166	6,819	4,912	4,858	9,770	10,320
6	Amherst	3,256	3,096	6,352	394	5,953	6,438	6,261	12,699	12,576
7	Appomattox	2,089	2,120	4,209	185	4,799	4,601	4,592	9,193	....
8	Augusta	9,678	9,305	18,983	574	5,053	12,631	11,979	24,610	19,628
9	Barbour	4,380	4,290	8,670	222	113	4,550	4,455	9,005	....
10	Bath	1,254	1,180	2,434	45	947	1,785	1,641	3,426	4,300
11	Bedford	7,003	6,553	13,556	463	10,061	12,522	11,558	24,080	20,203
12	Berkeley	4,974	4,592	9,566	249	1,956	6,075	5,696	11,771	10,972
13	Boone	1,603	1,451	3,054	....	183	1,702	1,535	3,237	....
14	Botetourt	5,587	5,159	10,746	426	3,736	7,827	7,081	14,908	11,679
15	Braxton	2,111	2,012	4,123	....	89	2,152	2,060	4,212	2,575
16	Brooke	2,490	2,433	4,923	100	31	2,556	2,498	5,054	7,948
17	Brunswick	2,387	2,498	4,885	553	8,456	6,908	6,986	13,894	14,346
18	Buckingham	2,684	2,742	5,426	250	8,161	6,962	6,875	13,837	18,786
19	Cabell	2,974	2,928	5,902	8	389	3,171	3,128	6,299	8,163
20	Campbell	6,012	5,521	11,533	846	10,866	12,022	11,223	23,245	21,030
21	Caroline	3,311	3,580	6,891	904	10,661	8,775	9,681	18,456	17,813
22	Carroll	2,874	2,852	5,726	29	154	2,954	2,955	5,909	....
23	Charles City	840	824	1,664	772	2,764	2,712	2,488	5,200	4,774
24	Charlotte	2,231	2,384	4,615	352	8,988	7,014	6,941	13,955	14,595
25	Chesterfield	4,218	4,188	8,406	467	8,616	9,137	8,352	17,489	17,148
26	Clarke	1,856	1,758	3,614	124	3,614	3,809	3,543	7,352	6,353
27	Culpeper	2,457	2,655	5,112	487	6,683	6,143	6,139	12,282	11,393
28	Cumberland	1,538	1,544	3,082	340	6,329	4,985	4,766	9,751	10,399
29	Dinwiddie	5,299	5,643	10,942	3,296	10,880	12,366	12,752	25,118	22,558
30	Doddridge	1,396	1,322	2,718	1	31	1,414	1,336	2,750	....
31	Elizabeth City	1,183	1,158	2,341	97	2,148	2,306	2,280	4,586	3,706
32	Essex	1,457	1,578	3,035	409	6,762	5,147	5,059	10,206	11,309
33	Fairfax	3,531	3,304	6,835	597	3,250	5,440	5,242	10,682	9,370
34	Fauquier	4,863	5,012	9,875	643	10,350	10,287	10,581	20,868	21,897
35	Fayette	1,923	1,857	3,780	19	156	2,007	1,948	3,955	3,924
36	Floyd	2,955	3,046	6,001	14	443	3,166	3,292	6,458	4,453
37	Fluvanna	2,259	2,280	4,539	211	4,737	4,833	4,654	9,487	8,812
38	Franklin	5,821	5,817	11,638	66	5,726	8,604	8,826	17,430	15,832
39	Frederick	6,384	6,385	12,769	912	2,294	7,920	8,055	15,975	14,242
40	Giles	2,934	2,924	5,858	55	657	3,289	3,281	6,570	5,307
41	Gilmer	1,776	1,627	3,403	....	72	1,815	1,660	3,475	....
42	Gloucester	2,173	2,117	4,290	680	5,557	5,302	5,225	10,527	10,715
43	Goochland	1,849	2,014	3,863	644	5,845	5,253	5,099	10,352	9,760
44	Grayson	3,066	3,076	6,142	36	499	3,337	3,340	6,677	9,087
45	Greenbrier	4,315	4,234	8,549	156	1,317	5,037	4,985	10,022	8,695
46	Greene	1,319	1,348	2,667	34	1,699	2,164	2,236	4,400	4,232
47	Greenville	874	857	1,731	123	3,785	2,837	2,802	5,639	6,366
48	Halifax	5,427	5,549	10,976	534	14,452	13,111	12,851	25,962	25,936
49	Hampshire	6,521	5,858	12,379	224	1,433	7,347	6,689	14,036	12,295
50	Hancock	2,124	1,916	4,040	7	3	2,127	1,923	4,050	....
51	Hanover	3,168	3,371	6,539	221	8,393	7,518	7,635	15,153	14,968
52	Hardy	4,085	3,842	7,927	356	1,260	4,918	4,625	9,543	7,622
53	Harrison	5,674	5,539	11,213	27	488	5,916	5,812	11,728	17,669
54	Henrico	12,015	11,811	23,826	3,637	16,109	22,183	21,389	43,572	33,076
55	Henry	2,639	2,685	5,324	208	3,340	4,370	4,502	8,872	7,335
56	Highland	1,960	1,877	3,837	26	364	2,163	2,064	4,227	....
57	Isle of Wight	2,274	2,436	4,710	1,248	3,395	4,581	4,772	9,353	9,972
58	Jackson	3,405	3,075	6,480	11	53	3,433	3,111	6,544	4,890
59	James City	786	703	1,489	663	1,868	2,016	2,004	4,020	3,779
60	Jefferson	5,453	5,023	10,476	540	4,341	7,942	7,415	15,357	14,082
61	Kanawha	6,278	5,723	12,001	212	3,140	8,298	7,055	15,353	13,567
62	King and Queen	1,947	2,147	4,094	461	5,764	4,941	5,378	10,319	10,862
63	King George	1,105	1,196	2,301	267	3,403	2,981	2,990	5,971	5,927
64	King William	1,324	1,377	2,701	347	5,731	4,266	4,513	8,779	9,258
65	Lancaster	907	895	1,802	266	2,640	2,300	2,408	4,708	4,628
66	Lee	4,690	4,750	9,440	40	787	5,086	5,181	10,267	8,441
67	Lewis	4,852	4,768	9,620	43	368	5,050	4,981	10,031	8,151
68	Logan	1,866	1,667	3,533	....	87	1,911	1,709	3,620	4,309
69	Loudon	7,477	7,604	15,081	1,357	5,641	10,932	11,147	22,079	20,431
70	Louisa	3,226	3,197	6,423	404	9,864	8,307	8,384	16,691	15,433
71	Lunenburg	2,141	2,173	4,314	191	7,187	5,831	5,861	11,692	11,055
72	Madison	2,197	2,259	4,456	151	4,724	4,660	4,671	9,331	8,107
73	Marion	5,200	5,239	10,439	19	94	5,249	5,303	10,552	....
74	Marshall	5,087	4,963	10,050	39	49	5,133	5,005	10,138	6,937
75	Mason	3,562	3,279	6,841	51	647	3,900	3,639	7,539	6,777
76	Matthews	1,691	1,951	3,642	149	2,923	3,209	3,505	6,714	7,442

NATIVITIES, DWELLINGS, &c. — Born out of State. — United States.	Born out of State. — Foreign countries.	Dwellings.	Families.	EDUCATION AND RELIGION. — Colleges, academies, and private schools. — Pupils.	Colleges, academies, and private schools. — Annual income.	Public Schools. — Pupils.	Public Schools. — Annual income.	Total educational income.	White scholars during year.	Whites 5 and under 20 years old.	Whites over 20 unable to read & write.	Accommodation of churches—persons.	
337	8	2,540	2,540	40	$4,000	1,260	$3,676	$7,676	1,267	3,454	1,310	6,400	1
213	363	2,022	2,022	465	34,500	550	12,000	46,500	1,110	4,545	722	14,100	2
1,581	477	1,484	1,540	304	....	619	1,624	1,624	1,364	2,584	689	8,050	3
61	25	464	465	30	....	153	....	....	414	1,123	227	2,345	4
30	51	568	568	45	1,900	161	2,565	4,465	358	988	142	4,000	5
35	101	1,127	1,130	......	....	380	1,000	1,000	129	2,493	217	5,825	6
22	10	785	785	22	450	339	4,550	5,000	665	1,660	332	6,575	7
429	529	3,207	3,208	226	210	745	1,423	1,633	939	7,126	505	14,150	8
215	14	1,467	1,467	......	....	546	570	570	1,441	3,717	1,172	5,400	9
14	35	410	410	85	1,020	70	969	1,989	286	970	4	1,250	10
105	493	2,396	2,477	72	800	638	2,540	3,340	1,614	5,108	1,266	8,075	11
1,214	650	1,668	1,703	102	7,364	550	827	8,191	1,040	3,387	380	7,595	12
99	13	495	495	......	....	171	586	586	184	1,284	551	855	13
355	454	1,803	1,803	62	830	428	3,685	4,515	1,073	4,080	825	7,975	14
50	35	679	679	......	....	......	....	....	348	1,734	316	600	15
1,615	332	839	839	203	8,470	60	....	8,470	1,056	1,854	216	3,350	16
59	12	1,051	1,051	86	1,066	186	436	1,502	595	1,915	167	8,175	17
42	29	1,062	1,062	96	16,100	194	2,029	18,129	853	2,095	495	9,400	18
524	140	976	976	20	300	374	2,020	2,320	810	2,427	643	3,750	19
228	556	2,203	2,207	......	....	994	6,198	6,198	1,366	4,178	316	13,640	20
45	43	1,451	1,453	115	16,820	516	6,366	23,186	721	2,646	493	12,350	21
672	3	996	996	......	....	900	2,600	2,600	785	2,351	952	2,350	22
54	48	486	486	92	1,400	......	....	1,400	118	593	189	3,675	23
46	14	903	903	......	....	436	6,108	6,108	480	1,767	245	11,000	24
112	576	1,757	1,792	......	....	567	2,753	2,753	643	3,095	1,008	15,175	25
152	95	636	636	77	2,262	98	1,273	3,535	598	1,335	117	4,300	26
107	31	1,034	1,034	105	1,950	488	3,829	5,779	739	1,777	328	8,450	27
13	20	640	640	30	....	275	....	....	505	1,164	77	4,600	28
412	327	2,745	2,955	547	18,147	535	6,928	25,075	1,285	3,955	1,189	13,926	29
250	39	525	553	......	....	115	160	160	350	1,107	299	200	30
211	156	456	462	110	2,100	139	185	2,285	406	818	207	4,000	31
26	7	725	725	115	....	101	....	....	430	1,107	376	5,750	32
1,329	274	1,380	1,380	195	15,880	60	418	16,298	727	2,465	387	7,400	33
212	73	1,839	1,842	350	7,626	554	6,853	14,479	1,462	3,643	526	12,850	34
56	15	593	593	......	....	96	569	569	226	1,568	369	1,700	35
56	3	987	987	102	....	832	356	356	961	2,458	1,086	2,600	36
38	74	678	881	63	....	355	445	445	673	1,684	323	4,600	37
28	....	2,024	2,024	......	....	700	950	950	896	4,852	806	7,550	38
726	186	2,325	2,357	305	260	360	1,200	1,460	1,431	4,758	134	8,750	39
228	61	919	925	......	....	820	459	459	775	2,321	618	5,400	40
127	41	571	571	......	....	159	954	954	430	1,355	327	1,200	41
75	10	1,000	1,006	95	1,975	253	1,790	3,765	517	1,634	833	5,700	42
33	23	876	878	......	....	320	4,146	4,146	576	1,402	321	4,950	43
349	7	1,001	1,001	......	....	217	425	425	482	2,646	131	3,030	44
114	71	1,419	1,419	30	600	900	729	1,329	910	3,283	859	8,800	45
4	....	494	494	......	....	152	1,244	1,244	362	982	492	2,075	46
84	4	385	385	30	1,000	95	1,130	2,130	246	628	184	2,225	47
35	29	2,152	2,155	......	....	288	3,445	3,445	620	4,275	561	27,700	48
896	696	2,035	2,035	145	3,230	1,500	5,500	8,730	1,507	4,696	1,191	10,800	49
1,503	200	690	690	25	400	360	1,000	1,400	865	1,655	183	2,800	50
40	46	1,327	1,327	63	1,240	345	4,020	5,260	588	2,409	439	8,100	51
303	200	1,327	1,340	57	38	622	550	588	1,070	3,025	1,010	4,400	52
819	78	1,866	1,866	60	900	330	820	1,720	576	4,569	306	4,600	53
1,628	2,536	5,317	5,701	1,233	39,668	901	9,539	49,207	2,907	8,113	1,175	30,510	54
212	14	936	936	......	....	1,391	4,085	4,085	920	2,175	812	4,050	55
15	14	651	651	......	....	135	428	428	680	1,513	53	2,125	56
23	9	1,200	1,200	56	1,225	149	1,086	2,311	479	1,713	914	6,650	57
1,108	123	1,034	1,040	......	....	1,350	250	250	924	2,716	857	800	58
47	18	396	396	150	7,045	165	....	7,045	197	540	52	6,900	59
1,574	598	1,960	2,000	165	....	1,000	7,628	7,628	1,535	3,756	444	10,650	60
630	225	2,110	2,160	162	3,823	1,500	3,933	7,756	1,269	4,854	1,592	10,450	61
16	6	892	896	110	2,800	281	2,250	5,050	507	1,592	408	10,500	62
33	13	526	527	......	....	200	2,412	2,412	288	941	245	3,100	63
14	1	625	625	......	....	238	....	....	402	1,044	207	4,400	64
34	5	426	427	46	800	282	2,880	3,680	302	723	131	3,500	65
1,199	10	1,536	1,572	......	....	550	4,884	4,884	1,193	4,119	1,758	8,650	66
374	203	1,533	1,533	......	....	1,602	500	500	1,587	3,937	1,083	6,300	67
120	12	572	572	......	....	175	640	640	204	1,503	677	1,700	68
667	180	2,834	2,834	85	....	1,703	....	....	2,353	5,588	580	14,750	69
59	61	1,254	1,254	......	....	452	605	605	900	2,386	461	9,850	70
14	14	820	820	......	....	450	413	413	460	1,674	145	8,400	71
60	11	827	827	......	....	386	4,763	4,763	646	1,652	284	12,500	72
1,037	72	1,786	1,791	......	....	720	740	740	1,503	4,292	1,175	8,500	73
2,612	317	1,668	1,678	60	1,080	700	1,180	2,260	2,073	4,137	1,031	4,850	74
1,216	86	1,151	1,173	......	....	1,150	527	527	1,123	2,820	994	3,600	75
87	1	711	716	......	....	400	4,000	4,000	390	1,384	426	4,400	76

	Counties.	Land occupied or improved.				Live stock upon farms.			
		Farms.	Acres improved.	Acres unimproved.	Value with improvements and implements.	Horses, asses, and mules.	Neat cattle.	Sheep	Swine.
1	Accomac	1,007	112,942	110,791	$ 3,846,270	2,803	13,266	8,582	25,365
2	Albemarle	935	220,467	169,154	5,490,031	5,002	14,067	20,523	34,662
3	Alexandria	94	6,092	6,021	425,665	265	614	17	896
4	Alleghany	216	20,184	68,464	535,389	741	11,560	4,108	4,216
5	Amelia	354	109,109	83,878	1,465,823	1,729	6,395	9,216	12,119
6	Amherst	728	110,150	116,486	1,890,838	2,429	8,627	6,165	19,255
7	Appomattox	502	198,016	79,775	1,051,773	1,829	5,473	6,603	10,012
8	Augusta	1,264	178,695	155,981	7,263,407	7,513	19,875	16,316	25,975
9	Barbour	1,075	57,731	138,469	1,788,833	3,477	11,054	17,881	11,805
10	Bath	261	28,879	105,615	712,852	1,189	5,810	5,629	3,540
11	Bedford	1,364	219,172	219,666	3,333,753	5,170	15,748	14,370	33,846
12	Berkeley	570	96,594	44,587	3,715,615	3,568	7,849	11,246	15,174
13	Boone	361	11,673	127,822	263,323	723	4,123	3,808	7,116
14	Botetourt	712	83,443	121,559	1,875,218	3,176	10,508	10,064	18,305
15	Braxton	408	16,111	904,332	1,315,312	1,130	5,005	7,357	12,162
16	Brooke	284	33,811	18,630	1,316,591	1,278	2,789	59,426	5,984
17	Brunswick	655	177,196	117,772	1,097,948	2,609	11,798	9,751	25,546
18	Buckingham	616	141,536	166,342	2,063,151	2,575	8,144	11,395	15,146
19	Cabell	498	27,326	83,312	764,501	1,234	5,613	6,806	11,007
20	Campbell	758	122,912	158,227	2,452,604	2,722	9,303	10,574	17,201
21	Caroline	715	187,647	127,547	2,786,447	2,750	9,163	8,436	15,712
22	Carroll	615	39,161	135,292	515,761	1,343	7,170	9,666	12,423
23	Charles City	199	33,124	49,796	914,676	827	2,316	1,518	5,034
24	Charlotte	563	155,613	142,248	2,551,788	3,035	10,284	15,039	18,710
25	Chesterfield	564	87,180	103,933	1,562,286	2,441	5,655	6,020	14,812
26	Clarke	271	60,275	23,946	3,191,934	2.505	5.767	10,920	10,772
27	Culpeper	504	135,366	78,374	3,001,497	3,078	11,548	16,308	17,744
28	Cumberland	398	94,153	83,630	1,556,528	1,882	5,916	9,374	9,611
29	Dinwiddie	703	102,517	192,529	1,505,059	2,363	9,194	7,096	18,161
30	Doddridge	240	10,343	60,606	281,613	608	2,392	3,678	2,794
31	Elizabeth City	173	16,909	15,067	676,824	558	2,562	883	4,661
32	Essex	328	93,223	59,797	1,941,868	1,341	5,621	4,731	8,237
33	Fairfax	610	82,694	96,650	2,345,319	2,288	7,635	8,637	11,588
34	Fauquier	889	247,297	130,206	6,148,795	5,733	25,247	20,741	23,969
35	Fayette	428	19,912	116,293	505,990	1,004	4,560	6,529	7,269
36	Floyd	444	34,398	94,494	605,207	1,251	5,428	7,248	9,500
37	Fluvanna	454	61,304	80,223	1,431,056	1,645	4,852	5,366	8,991
38	Franklin	1,299	126,269	225,598	1,705,258	3,649	13,538	9,411	26,805
39	Frederick	1,055	126,972	111,965	3,903,207	4,976	8,911	12,372	15,716
40	Giles	539	45,935	167,842	882,018	2,134	8,147	10,762	11,589
41	Gilmer	325	10,746	75,440	309,889	771	3,160	4,333	7,380
42	Gloucester	573	64,515	60,111	1,579.394	1,257	7,027	4,109	14,213
43	Goochland	405	76,971	83,747	2,094,871	1,850	6,198	4,897	10,029
44	Grayson	604	42,200	136,301	604,527	2,150	9,287	13,322	12,843
45	Greenbrier	603	97,917	250,631	2,401,454	4,198	15,713	20.971	13,161
46	Greene	301	37,998	39,385	719,894	931	2,579	2,806	7,217
47	Greenville	242	74,906	82,066	427,173	1,079	4,481	3,713	14,862
48	Halifax	1,309	242,758	201,291	3.420.990	5,000	16,790	20.506	42,480
49	Hampshire	1,063	136,288	294,871	3,099,663	4,360	15,818	20,731	14,866
50	Hancock	306	26,877	22,862	1,181,512	1,019	2,495	24,858	2,695
51	Hanover	603	188,064	99,998	2.090,429	2,449	5,948	7,939	14,845
52	Hardy	723	100,861	245,588	2,628,460	3,277	12,102	12,368	11,184
53	Harrison	1,093	87,533	143,613	2,237,941	3,313	17,096	16,203	10,798
54	Henrico	454	53,617	53.804	2,673,988	2,047	3,607	1,778	7,735
55	Henry	528	61.539	96,409	820.070	1,560	4,812	4,330	12,897
56	Highland	389	43,699	163,473	1,257,138	1,951	10,998	12,592	4,483
57	Isle of Wight	629	65,925	92,901	982,739	1,234	5,780	4,484	23,928
58	Jackson	602	28,384	255,539	866,257	1,708	5,967	11,062	17,905
59	James City	129	21,251	44,132	561,931	534	2.365	1,217	4,009
60	Jefferson	447	81,087	29,716	5,392,671	3,512	5,969	11,086	16,940
61	Kanawha	777	32,771	266,317	1,069,927	1,897	7,941	9,180	18,689
62	King and Queen	502	93,589	89,917	1,319,593	1,340	6,664	4,442	11,045
63	King George	279	59,385	39,927	1,117,196	1,210	3,933	3,401	3,762
64	King William	388	84,639	66,803	1,497,835	1,555	5,231	3,481	9,077
65	Lancaster	299	30,037	31,436	701,999	660	3,446	1,780	5,926
66	Lee	595	54,844	206,030	1,133,428	2,900	10,611	12,181	25,114
67	Lewis	878	48,152	126,827	1,166,743	2,744	10,616	13.393	14,977
68	Logan	469	12,887	112,853	282,965	983	8,631	4,793	11,186
69	Loudon	1,256	208,454	86.221	8.545,165	6,779	22,388	20,727	25,697
70	Louisa	838	185,649	108,645	2,628,630	3,128	8,638	9,545	17,844
71	Lunenburg	548	114,862	123,778	1,062.586	1,901	7,375	9,270	14,343
72	Madison	513	111,138	110,870	2,170,838	2,305	8,128	8,057	18,180
73	Marion	904	60,641	88,265	1,646,779	2,753	9,532	17,459	8,429
74	Marshall	847	53,478	79,711	1,695,383	2,730	6,395	17,524	2,314
75	Mason	563	40,055	118,803	1,311,061	1,992	6,684	10,428	15,373
76	Matthews	293	24,521	18,573	638,726	550	3,182	1,909	5,981

AGRICULTURAL PRODUCTS.

Wheat, bushels.	Rye & oats, bushels.	Indian corn, bushels.	Irish and sweet potatoes, bushels.	Peas and beans, bushels.	Barley, bushels.	Buckwheat, bushels.	Butter and cheese, pounds.	Hay, tons.	Hops, pounds.	Clover & other grass seeds, bushels.	Flaxseed, bushels.	
13,267	449,535	761,636	164,843	8,081	119	6	94,268	......	2,659	1	876	
278,575	192,074	798,354	35,332	3,788	......	......	164,882	4,328	......	51	797	
6,238	8,050	28,380	10,130	20	75	111	13,770	912	......	......	......	3
16,937	44,714	88,426	3,891	344	4	1,139	30,564	1,211	121	82	199	4
109,960	70,074	250,251	16,932	3,810	......	......	56,790	182	1,006	618	7	5
122,088	97,151	358,183	16,733	2,103	33	486	85,018	724	17	93	109	6
76,345	92,148	186,855	20,236	1,532	......	129	83,299	824	......	55	731	7
419,006	278,130	505,800	24,389	171	1,396	2,461	287,577	15,285	142	5,388	781	8
38,110	54,951	209,673	9,723	5,237	49	3,965	156,293	9,916	2	29	1,549	9
17,502	47,588	73,671	4,745	......	......	1,591	36,460	3,853	......	6	271	10
178,990	297,190	602,262	57,325	12,656	57	796	241,384	3,950	264	931	1,575	11
356,234	53,825	171,686	5,235	......	60	......	160,151	6,667	......	953	......	12
3,215	19,356	134,040	11,818	2,863	......	119	34,056	110	......	......	596	13
121,694	159,870	368,141	16,115	69	10	1,913	145,247	5,531	......	1,972	650	14
9,062	28,334	137,120	7,862	2,222	1	509	74,059	796	53	61	967	15
65,516	52,227	150,571	9,898	......	2,546	20	91,394	4,755	......	198	......	16
79,287	98,841	394,200	44,952	4,099	......	......	80,089	2,889	13	15	......	17
133,819	117,341	304,711	30,533	4,143	......	332	83,480	525	122	88	592	18
11,559	45,036	281,826	15,403	1,802	......	172	45,616	912	26	32	197	19
100,500	167,709	339,267	40,744	7,915	......	30	94,552	2,168	5	980	......	20
173,353	44,037	629,994	35,181	7,548	......	52	71,270	231	90	16	......	21
11,578	89,278	132,189	4,470	408	399	4,973	61,707	2,715	28	95	1,221	22
81,229	26,536	178,940	5,522	1,164	......	20	24,065	1,045	45	......	......	23
85,653	171,872	372,867	39,366	5,831	......	10	69,671	1,043	143	2,743	520	24
95,875	116,965	333,938	22,113	3,646	50	81	73,044	2,892	96	608	......	25
306,210	37,415	166,897	7,523	61	450	35	77,609	2,236	71	667	......	26
191,395	64,931	359,670	15,874	1,690	......	226	96,804	3,472	44	346	917	27
118,616	69,870	220,535	21,611	5,421	......	......	60,884	67	......	26	8	28
60,275	97,517	304,556	37,892	4,233	......	253	80,941	576	304	5	......	29
2,757	13,722	59,423	3,295	667	......	970	36,189	1,860	166	89	138	30
22,188	17,784	87,295	45,601	1,732	......	1	18,971	704	7	13	......	31
104,840	8,960	391,895	12,210	11,777	......	......	57,747	782	10	42	......	32
56,155	82,658	207,531	28,181	503	442	5,153	144,873	4,420	21	181	......	33
386,324	127,509	562,959	27,580	1,087	......	1,110	300,570	8,523	326	244	573	34
8,414	57,755	111,064	4,044	22	......	1,417	56,669	950	......	272	648	35
23,992	101,170	104,630	3,694	1,219	......	7,963	64,483	3,326	430	78	1,131	36
92,657	62,137	200,174	14,556	251	......	15	45,229	420	5	211	136	37
76,831	192,079	431,408	35,733	1,893	33	865	126,643	1,260	150	339	2,667	38
311,060	55,958	199,242	13,642	168	179	2,025	198,876	6,433	117	1,202	109	39
38,565	76,269	204,720	4,908	238	......	4,883	88,744	1,960	55	561	1,277	40
5,652	22,535	117,990	4,318	515	......	1,034	34,107	1,023	32	117	295	41
65,551	37,126	336,063	30,663	7,057	795	......	63,588	4,095	354	......	......	42
141,969	104,241	276,338	23,172	5,087	......	31	53,533	1,032	299	34	11	43
17,127	129,041	177,266	2,124	392	242	8,506	86,604	3,522	......	164	1,266	44
47,778	133,239	182,119	7,458	87	437	2,293	126,741	6,359	17	433	518	45
42,416	28,498	137,293	7,287	458	......	467	30,910	521	150	69	533	46
17,619	16,606	211,537	24,919	8,837	......	......	17,319	1,244	......	......	......	47
146,769	365,649	649,896	95,058	13,913	......	105	140,928	304	169	550	45	48
177,343	107,469	292,252	19,391	10	26	9,676	258,401	8,996	......	764	485	49
52,413	57,640	52,392	10,643	65	4,166	4,900	75,966	2,859	......	277	25	50
157,388	94,206	377,616	46,838	4,894	......	45	78,316	1,616	21	197	......	51
85,225	38,111	327,846	13,285	198	3	3,288	125,785	6,362	206	423	538	52
47,662	90,113	277,585	12,901	1,875	86	1,361	182,598	8,928	13	403	808	53
113,044	84,982	266,011	34,720	2,909	......	18	66,615	2,196	100	206	......	54
29,704	62,587	232,311	22,848	1,428	......	62	38,890	19	80	60	472	55
22,456	42,385	54,241	4,059	903	......	6,214	87,971	6,354	53	52	387	56
3,799	12,818	315,699	100,643	31,319	......	......	33,334	29	128	......	24	57
16,630	44,396	257,242	15,640	71	46	3,181	98,561	1,954	......	......	160	58
25,476	22,040	102,430	8,519	300	......	......	17,785	24	......	......	......	59
472,008	28,938	287,395	13,819	127	90	56	130,228	5,558	60	783	......	60
25,074	59,239	352,995	17,733	1,158	......	394	49,563	2,014	29	36	362	61
68,755	13,168	376,986	16,536	7,187	......	......	48,883	5	......	......	......	62
76,707	10,181	241,900	5,598	411	......	......	40,090	57	......	......	......	63
108,819	20,970	353,685	13,534	5,892	......	55	32,580	4	......	......	......	64
24,424	9,676	120,530	14,709	958	......	......	17,335	8	......	......	......	65
20,243	110,029	485,625	20,275	3,309	......	508	100,380	1,407	......	170	1,189	66
31,056	50,660	235,675	9,946	......	......	1,652	108,819	9,190	60	147	779	67
1,588	20,221	154,943	13,081	545	7	84	31,615	129	......	9	68	68
563,930	125,688	749,428	21,850	920	75	3,751	434,141	11,990	26	520	268	69
199,521	100,659	377,288	30,895	4,719	......	......	89,445	1,604	......	......	......	70
49,960	106,545	240,065	19,746	3,888	......	......	53,298	8	5	101	461	71
136,684	32,045	343,448	17,916	1,438	......	241	81,184	1,667	148	406	954	72
48,469	95,236	167,071	7,692	741	55	2,029	150,439	6,125	69	246	889	73
74,976	118,324	302,130	17,725	95	148	11,693	132,380	2,040	10	30	146	74
20,545	46,966	399,080	27,669	742	......	1,826	83,285	2,264	20	48	154	75
7,640	19,418	4,940	18,421	7,888	......	......	14,741	1,288	......	......	......	

	COUNTIES.	Agricultural products.									
		Flax, pounds.	Hemp, dew and water-rotted, tons.	Maple sugar, pounds.	Cane sugar, hhds. of 1,000 pounds.	Molasses, gallons.	Rice, pounds.	Tobacco, pounds.	Ginned cotton, bales of 400 pounds.	Wool, pounds.	Silk cocoons, pounds.
1	Accomac	9,159						140		20,029	1
2	Albemarle	9,215						1,456,300		50,407	
3	Alexandria										
4	Alleghany	3,434		8,933		359		19,216		7,207	12
5	Amelia	1,386						1,786,788	15	19,790	
6	Amherst	3,507	5					948,261		9,550	
7	Appomattox	14,034						964,100	36	14,652	
8	Augusta	11,771		380		28				42,004	
9	Barbour	33,063		70,454		2,536		400		33,264	2
10	Bath	4,130		6,188		6				12,271	
11	Bedford	29,244						1,955,436	8	27,614	52
12	Berkeley									34,517	
13	Boone	16,299		4,227		195		8,019		6,619	
14	Botetourt	42,521	5	140				156,183		22,081	
15	Braxton	7,699		17,721		654		3,743		13,479	41
16	Brooke			2,153		684				123,572	
17	Brunswick	180						2,155,017	108	17,253	5
18	Buckingham	9,434						2,342,987	2	24,077	
19	Cabell	2,833		5,464		374		8,947		11,264	
20	Campbell	13,063						2,534,730	6	20,275	
21	Caroline		23					663,155	89	18,312	
22	Carroll	15,285		71		9		5,526		15,357	
23	Charles City								2	5,144	
24	Charlotte	16,090						3,868,040		25,755	8
25	Chesterfied	85						218,562	212	10,880	
26	Clarke	40								42,595	
27	Culpeper	13,577						2,562		45,444	
28	Cumberland	12,130						2,476,135		18,610	
29	Dinwiddie	3						1,782,521	4	11,235	
30	Doddridge	4,912		9,912		560		1,690		7,192	
31	Elizabeth City									2,932	
32	Essex							999	191	14,260	
33	Fairfax									16,302	
34	Fauquier	9,079						2,565		72,825	
35	Fayette	3,392	1	4,705		45		170		10,862	16
36	Floyd	16,348		34				14,624		13,015	
37	Fluvanna	465						1,054,974		11,075	
38	Franklin	22,625	5			45		1,125,404		13,952	
39	Frederick	786		360		27				38,040	
40	Giles	19,997		10,298		549		1,022		23,591	
41	Gilmer	8,152		19,185		601		4,961		7,277	
42	Gloucester							575	62	11,934	
43	Goochland	342						924,208	1	12,014	
44	Grayson	20,980								28,169	
45	Greenbrier	10,931	6	93,313		2,842				42,574	2
46	Greene	4,471	6					200,714		6,783	
47	Greenville							138,000	715	5,667	
48	Halifax	6,521						6,485,762	26	32,708	
49	Hampshire	10,870		15,346		712				45,346	
50	Hancock	590		553		85				63,666	
51	Hanover							404,550	20	15,993	
52	Hardy	6,620	3	52,659		2,246		1,197		32,176	
53	Harrison	14,128		31,839		1,431		4,473		31,974	3
54	Henrico							400	338	3,615	
55	Henry	7,683						1,013,079	1	7,349	9
56	Highland	16,845	3	56,221		1,910		164		26,662	
57	Isle of Wight	1,276	30				205	44	9	7,904	
58	Jackson	13,617		18,826		459		7,832		31,028	196
59	James City									2,197	
60	Jefferson									47,456	
61	Kanawha	9,445	1	5,188				5,627		15,171	1
62	King and Queen							7,600	26	11,034	
63	King George									12,306	
64	King William								42	10,271	
65	Lancaster								7	3,343	
66	Lee	28,501		17,760		394		5,131		21,257	
67	Lewis	17,069		38,341		1,180		8,800		24,238	
68	Logan	2,936		3,677		42		8,353		8,202	
69	Loudon	1,213								60,228	2
70	Louisa							1,584,285		23,427	
71	Lunenburg	2,928						2,284,668	4	15,689	16
72	Madison	6,871	1	90				51,300		17,391	
73	Marion	17,548		45,304		2,117		1,096		34,916	
74	Marshall	4,600		6,792		61				38,144	
75	Mason	7,546		9,705		502		11,100		23,607	
76	Matthews									4,059	

AGRICULTURAL PRODUCTS.					MANUFACTURES.					
					Establishments.					
Beeswax and honey, pounds.	Value of animals slaughtered.	Value of produce of market gardens.	Value of orchard produce.	Wine, gallons.	Capital.	Hands employed.	Annual product.	Produced in families.	REMARKS.	
10,060	$132,607	$2,812	$14,531	......	$14,120	51	$19,830	$23,712	....	1
8,231	159,365	....	....	......	297,090	359	492,985	33,200	....	2
100	4,669	16,120	1,165	......	403,625	791	603,910	....	Belonged to Dist. of Co-	3
3,097	20,825	....	556	6	68,550	179	63,385	6,586	lumbia in 1840. Retroces-	4
2,628	56,164	49	56	......	17,100	21	44,800	13,856	sion accepted in 1847.	5
3,442	65,598	200	561	32	....	.....	....	14,982	[P. Edw'd, Charlotte, &c.	6
5,093	36,248	....	....	3	28,210	75	65,820	18,323	For'd '45 fr. Buckingham,	7
2,884	158,501	161	1,790	165	221,726	492	530,961	13,314	[&c. Div. '44 to fm. Taylor.	8
10,328	35,055	....	2	100	....	.....	....	26,111	F'd '43 fr. Harrison, Lewis,	9
4,779	21,442	....	97	23	23,800	40	43,136	10,360	Div. '47 to form Highland.	10
18,971	107,928	987	1,793	103	45,900	100	114,755	55,450	....	11
....	66,464	....	....	......	361,100	269	581,211	512	....	12
25,763	23,762	....	647	......	17,500	57	51,300	13,754	F'd '47 from Kanawha, Ca-	13
4,725	83,570	....	560	......	140,050	325	162,859	15,870	bell and Logan.	14
4,348	21,911	2,959	244	......	30,900	34	49,027	17,560	....	15
2,854	30,241	96	3,556	......	94,660	228	181,349	819	Div. '48 to form Hancock.	16
3,607	95,449	....	....	......	6,500	13	9,700	35,241	....	17
4,224	80,637	550	....	15	15,800	31	24,050	21,559	Div. '45 to fm Appomattox.	18
3,823	41,040	10	1,890	......	37,900	77	76,400	11,083	Div. 1842, 1847 and 1848.	19
20,068	132,289	735	1,290	......	816,700	1,717	1,839,307	21,122	Div. '45 to fm Appomattox.	20
6,097	80,044	....	....	......	88,970	126	170,569	36,292	....	21
10,854	29,731	240	700	......	14,270	19	21,706	18,389	Formed '42 from Grayson.	22
....	18,918	....	16	5	27,700	74	30,600	3,509	....	23
10,235	89,689	....	....	2	4,000	19	8,150	40,463	Div. '45 to fm Appomattox.	24
275	53,648	2,540	....	......	2,503,185	1,946	7,031,524	8,214	....	25
8,228	63,270	23	3,740	205	102,226	129	211,664	2,369	....	26
5,414	88,951	....	....	......	90,895	183	147,422	21,306	....	27
270	55,036	....	....	......	101,700	68	93,525	20,955	....	28
2,265	79,229	5,753	77	5	440,030	783	702,537	25,000	....	29
2,204	11,934	....	....	......	5,500	4	6,000	4,483	Formed in 1845 from Har-	30
....	24,801	1,424	379	......	14,920	47	38,690	....	rison, Tyler, Ritchie and	31
387	53,345	....	6,548	......	30,600	20	50,715	15,541	Lewis.	32
2,544	80,452	3,168	3,547	66	45,800	32	97,279	4,676	....	33
21,304	152,902	100	2,841	383	104,710	168	251,976	23,147	....	34
7,062	21,567	....	460	......	13,600	28	15,332	14,705	Div. 1850 to form Raleigh.	35
7,901	28,499	6	1,194	11	30,400	33	32,873	13,085	....	36
....	38,926	25	....	......	193,945	277	185,750	10,851	....	37
13,597	84,273	....	555	......	219,070	278	183,640	30,430	....	38
12,892	107,102	1,620	3,276	30	522,325	491	593,317	7,376	....	39
13,327	35,911	66	581	21	....	.....	....	21,274	....	40
6,649	12,427	....	2,926	......	1,800	4	4,000	8,877	Formed in 1845 from Lewis	41
1,480	70,817	....	228	.....	58,010	120	108,278	29,104	and Kanawha.	42
2,708	47,289	24	20	10	137,045	269	231,717	15,164	....	43
7,212	36,429	15	2,662	......	....	.....	....	20,324	Divided in 1842 to form	44
9,345	65,384	130	531	7	....	.....	....	22,526	Carroll.	45
1,750	26,770	140	1,100	155	18,575	51	38,804	8,033	....	46
208	46,835	....	....	......	8,000	8	10,000	7,641	....	47
8,005	157,815	....	5	10	103,050	149	182,720	104,946	....	48
21,705	85,000	630	5,295	105	88,650	174	195,275	31,839	....	49
3,737	15,047	145	1,478	......	104,665	130	113,245	1,294	For'd in 1848 from Brooke.	50
905	73,736	9,290	340	......	43,860	60	116,823	15,675	....	51
15,902	65,138	88	1,477	89	51,745	94	130,163	24,983	....	52
7,558	43,527	1,905	....	20	62,221	90	149,880	27,243	Divided. (See Counties	53
750	132,605	39,976	1,965	207	1,781,511	4,377	6,080,960	1,463	numbered 9, 30, 73, 111	54
5,799	44,956	....	5	3	21,750	172	84,213	15,743	and 124.)	55
10,962	22,862	5,373	1,267	5	13,500	10	21,000	12,049	Formed in 1847 from Pen-	56
3,632	82,517	6,565	2,293	145	45,300	102	49,550	8,882	dleton and Bath.	57
1,622	29,501	....	142	......	60,150	75	130,266	17,900	Divided in 1848 to form	58
24	14,339	365	....	......	....	.....	....	544	Wirt.	59
2,531	88,365	75	205	30	584,150	672	915,267	546	....	60
6,761	45,498	....	1,194	......	1,022,955	1,435	794,733	12,673	Divided. (See Counties	61
1,849	51,214	....	20	......	2,000	14	5,600	14,541	numbered 13, 41 and 106.)	62
....	16,373	....	2,005	......	12,800	25	28,625	5,432	....	63
2,190	39,112	....	....	......	30,215	27	50,900	6,671	....	64
115	28,024	....	322	......	2,800	16	4,350	3,265	....	65
16,196	51,358	....	....	......	7,600	22	10,315	28,060	[bered 9, 30, 41 and 111.)	66
6,823	29,997	....	....	......	28,360	68	33,168	18,700	Div. (See Counties num-	67
13,983	17,884	....	1,069	......	....	.....	....	13,301	Divided in 1847 and 1850 to	68
17,073	165,259	749	11,458	3	335,210	349	598,987	4,171	form Boone & Wyoming.	69
150	90,683	....	....	530	45,265	162	104,350	28,093	....	70
2,855	59,178	....	40	14	21,870	31	59,734	18,347	[1844 to form Taylor.	71
1,430	86,460	....	4,559	797	79,200	76	142,141	31,079	[and Harrison. Divided in	72
9,607	36,596	....	2,750	......	149,750	136	188,950	23,953	For'd '42 from Monongalia	73
11,485	45,261	2,295	3,353	380	36,30.	46	75,000	8,171	....	74
1,977	59,545	75	1,335	......	14,600	28	25,050	11,136	Divided in 1848 to form	75
222	3,069	5,520	2,084	100	10,500	34	18,000	5,097	Putnam	76

	COUNTIES.	POPULATION.								
		Whites.			Colored.		All classes.		Total population.	
		Male.	Female.	Total.	Free.	Slave.	Male.	Female.	1850.	1840.
77	Mecklenburg	3,611	3,645	7,256	912	12,462	10,480	10,150	20,630	20,724
78	Mercer	2,051	1,967	4,018	27	177	2,158	2,064	4,222	2,233
79	Middlesex	968	935	1,903	149	2,342	2,259	2,135	4,394	4,392
80	Monongalia	5,987	6,105	12,092	119	176	6,131	6,256	12,387	17,368
81	Monroe	4,585	4,477	9,062	81	1,061	5,175	5,029	10,204	8,422
82	Montgomery	3,451	3,371	6,822	66	1,471	4,201	4,158	8,359	7,405
83	Morgan	1,753	1,678	3,431	3	123	1,811	1,746	3,557	4,253
84	Nansemond	2,664	2,760	5,424	2,144	4,715	6,151	6,132	12,283	10,795
85	Nelson	3,274	3,204	6,478	138	6,142	6,417	6,341	12,758	12,287
86	New Kent	1,114	1,108	2,222	432	3,410	3,016	3,048	6,064	6,230
87	Nicholas	1,974	1,915	3,889	1	73	2,010	1,953	3,963	2,515
88	Norfolk	10,169	10,160	20,329	2,307	10,400	16,012	17,024	33,036	27,569
89	Northampton	1,534	1,571	3,105	745	3,648	3,689	3,809	7,498	7,715
90	Northumberland	1,530	1,542	3,072	519	3,755	3,726	3,620	7,346	7,924
91	Nottoway	1,144	1,090	2,234	153	6,050	4,278	4,159	8,437	9,719
92	Ohio	8,981	8,631	17,612	230	164	9,149	8,857	18,006	13,357
93	Orange	1,927	2,035	3,962	184	5,921	5,088	4,979	10,067	9,125
94	Page	3,186	3,146	6,332	311	957	3,845	3,755	7,600	6,194
95	Patrick	3,627	3,560	7,187	98	2,324	4,779	4,830	9,609	8,032
96	Pendleton	2,771	2,672	5,443	30	322	2,959	2,836	5,795	6,940
97	Pittsylvania	7,510	7,753	15,263	735	12,798	14,426	14,370	28,796	26,398
98	Pocahontas	1,675	1,628	3,303	28	267	1,816	1,782	3,598	2,922
99	Powhatan	1,229	1,284	2,513	383	5,282	4,197	3,981	8,178	7,924
100	Preston	6,943	4,619	11,562	59	87	7,019	4,689	11,708	6,866
101	Prince Edward	2,065	2,112	4,177	488	7,192	6,090	5,767	11,857	14,069
102	Prince George	1,311	1,359	2,670	518	4,408	3,884	3,712	7,596	7,175
103	Prince William	2,489	2,590	5,079	552	2,498	3,991	4,138	8,129	8,144
104	Princess Anne	2,208	2,072	4,280	259	3,130	4,016	3,653	7,669	7,285
105	Pulaski	1,790	1,823	3,613	34	1,471	2,630	2,488	5,118	3,739
106	Putnam	2,408	2,285	4,693	10	632	2,702	2,633	5,335	....
107	Raleigh	899	830	1,729	13	23	916	849	1,765	....
108	Randolph	2,561	2,442	5,003	39	201	2,677	2,566	5,243	6,208
109	Rappahannock	2,810	2,832	5,642	296	3,844	4,885	4,897	9,782	9,257
110	Richmond	1,722	1,741	3,463	708	2,277	3,188	3,260	6,448	5,965
111	Ritchie	1,983	1,903	3,886	....	16	1,987	1,915	3,902	....
112	Roanoke	2,935	2,877	5,812	155	2,510	4,329	4,148	8,477	5,499
113	Rockbridge	5,795	5,689	11,484	364	4,197	8,320	7,725	16,045	14,284
114	Rockingham	8,703	8,793	17,496	467	2,331	10,145	10,149	20,294	17,344
115	Russell	5,538	5,328	10,866	71	982	6,054	5,865	11,919	7,878
116	Scott	4,617	4,705	9,322	34	473	4,865	4,964	9,829	7,303
117	Shenandoah	6,203	6,362	12,565	292	911	6,829	6,939	13,768	11,618
118	Smyth	3,411	3,487	6,898	200	1,064	4,058	4,104	8,162	6,522
119	Southampton	2,807	3,133	5,940	1,826	5,755	6,667	6,854	13,521	14,525
120	Spottsylvania	3,271	3,623	6,894	536	7,481	7,137	7,774	14,911	15,161
121	Stafford	2,114	2,301	4,415	318	3,311	3,958	4,086	8,044	8,454
122	Surry	1,085	1,130	2,215	985	2,479	2,915	2,764	5,679	6,480
123	Sussex	1,486	1,600	3,086	742	5,992	4,981	4,839	9,820	11,229
124	Taylor	2,697	2,433	5,130	69	168	2,813	2,554	5,367	....
125	Tazewell	4,497	4,310	8,807	75	1,060	5,064	4,878	9,942	6,290
126	Tyler	2,778	2,678	5,456	4	38	2,794	2,704	5,498	6,954
127	Warren	2,288	2,205	4,493	366	1,748	3,353	3,254	6,607	5,627
128	Warwick	313	286	599	42	905	824	722	1,546	1,456
129	Washington	6,204	6,165	12,369	112	2,131	7,353	7,259	14,612	13,001
130	Wayne	2,450	2,114	4,564	7	189	2,532	2,228	4,760	....
131	Westmoreland	1,714	1,662	3,376	1,147	3,557	3,997	4,083	8,080	8,019
132	Wetzel	2,183	2,078	4,261	6	17	2,191	2,093	4,284	....
133	Wirt	1,695	1,624	3,319	2	32	1,710	1,643	3,353	....
134	Wood	4,664	4,344	9,008	69	373	4,876	4,574	9,450	7,923
135	Wyoming	811	772	1,583	1	61	842	803	1,645	....
136	Wythe	4,826	4,792	9,618	221	2,185	6,105	5,919	12,024	9,375
137	York	910	915	1,825	454	2,181	2,253	2,207	4,460	4,720

STATISTICS OF

1	Adams	122	65	187	....	....	122	65	187	....
2	Brown	3,580	2,590	6,170	45	....	3,603	2,612	6,215	2,107
3	Calumet	840	780	1,620	123	....	912	831	1,743	275
4	Chippewa	487	127	614	1	....	488	127	615	....
5	Columbia	5,200	4,347	9,547	18	....	5,212	4,353	9,564	....
6	Crawford	1,434	1,047	2,481	17	....	1,438	1,060	2,498	1,502
7	Dane	8,833	7,777	16,613	26	....	8,852	7,787	16,639	314
8	Dodge	10,334	8,792	19,126	12	....	10,341	8,797	19,138	67
9	Fond-du-lac	7,789	6,718	14,507	3	....	7,790	6,720	14,510	139

NATIVITIES, DWELLINGS, &c.				EDUCATION AND RELIGION.									
Born out of State.				Colleges, academies, and private schools.		Public Schools.							
United States.	Foreign countries.	Dwellings.	Families.	Pupils.	Annual income.	Pupils.	Annual income.	Total educational income.	White scholars during the year.	Whites 5 and under 20 years old.	Whites over 20 unable to read & write.	Accommodation of churches—persons.	
188	24	1,500	1,500	239	$2,625	574	$2,662	$5,287	809	2,773	506	10,405	77
72	13	655	655	...	...	400	800	800	639	1,675	578	1,100	78
33	4	401	401	74	908	152	805	1,713	233	674	117	3,600	79
2,231	118	2,124	2,127	109	3,334	907	2,139	5,473	2,317	4,793	1,204	12,310	80
114	73	1,576	1,576	75	888	498	3,452	4,340	1,684	3,576	880	8,575	81
114	17	1,121	1,124	20	1,000	350	3,250	4,250	693	2,729	436	4,700	82
407	147	606	606	...	...	645	411	411	646	1,399	436	2,150	83
261	4	1,523	1,523	174	3,700	298	4,439	8,139	562	2,036	1,004	5,250	84
51	132	1,217	1,217	30	...	347	1,322	1,322	822	2,333	502	6,670	85
9	...	535	535	...	...	300	247	247	333	833	190	2,300	86
72	47	602	602	...	...	189	230	230	402	1,611	52	2,650	87
2,774	1,260	3,906	4,052	363	21,152	1,926	9,535	30,687	3,018	7,143	1,699	18,435	88
57	9	693	693	...	525	622	4,815	5,340	620	1,163	252	4,700	89
22	...	639	639	...	...	279	2,420	2,420	304	1,274	408	2,880	90
11	8	492	492	16	400	260	3,760	4,160	228	810	63	5,350	91
5,005	4,015	3,097	3,178	400	5,265	3,529	24,247	29,512	2,292	6,316	145	9,150	92
42	28	756	764	...	...	253	3,132	3,132	586	1,439	299	3,200	93
84	59	1,089	1,089	35	250	463	2,252	2,502	943	2,402	993	4,200	94
215	6	1,248	1,301	...	...	826	4,710	4,710	734	2,957	884	3,500	95
71	16	891	891	...	...	225	...	...	1,007	2,109	1,131	3,300	96
261	20	2,804	2,804	142	793	667	3,527	4,320	743	5,965	776	14,950	97
28	42	553	557	40	...	200	...	...	524	1,315	100	2,700	98
40	20	517	517	...	...	305	...	...	175	935	...	4,850	99
1,881	2,628	1,664	1,664	70	600	840	675	1,275	1,399	3,858	846	4,500	100
35	...	805	808	237	15,340	406	387	15,727	764	1,595	98	10,250	101
54	30	661	661	23	202	175	2,032	2,234	328	1,391	381	4,200	102
374	51	998	998	...	...	316	675	675	777	1,916	784	4,650	103
267	8	893	906	...	...	819	6,977	6,977	816	1,537	970	5,000	104
125	14	585	606	...	...	292	...	...	584	1,399	492	7,200	105
168	20	788	819	...	1,600	115	1,090	2,690	531	1,837	838	3,900	106
32	...	296	296	...	...	...	...	...	117	711	102	...	107
132	42	844	844	...	...	380	750	750	378	2,017	601	2,450	108
58	36	990	990	30	600	437	4,305	4,905	763	2,176	428	3,450	109
12	15	805	805	...	...	220	972	972	205	1,325	573	3,100	110
416	51	649	649	...	...	376	196	196	410	1,539	307	1,200	111
96	38	925	925	137	5,278	185	1,467	6,745	507	2,351	299	3,900	112
348	345	1,908	1,972	309	96,010	430	6,681	102,691	1,479	4,316	236	8,800	113
419	94	3,047	3,064	...	...	1,970	1,496	1,496	1,678	6,724	2,580	9,500	114
1,301	7	1,786	1,786	40	318	557	1,290	1,608	1,329	4,581	1,728	4,350	115
1,287	10	1,523	1,523	...	...	1,000	652	652	1,270	3,956	860	6,075	116
266	180	2,143	2,163	...	...	130	1,033	1,033	1,487	4,621	279	5,700	117
705	5	1,146	1,157	...	...	600	5,584	5,584	1,313	2,803	462	2,400	118
195	6	1,572	1,572	68	2,810	288	4,580	7,390	627	2,188	1,085	10,100	119
275	107	1,416	1,416	461	12,475	300	4,580	17,055	773	2,538	113	12,450	120
75	13	922	922	...	...	245	424	424	219	1,604	210	4,200	121
3	6	650	650	30	1,000	150	256	1,256	229	769	262	5,300	122
23	9	751	751	99	...	150	...	...	415	1,114	284	7,300	123
226	278	818	823	100	500	...	...	500	702	2,084	107	4,350	124
597	19	1,449	1,449	...	...	654	546	546	694	3,708	1,506	3,000	125
1,276	104	949	949	...	...	145	381	381	747	2,202	578	3,000	126
118	88	828	919	...	...	484	385	385	530	1,670	435	3,500	127
5	...	132	138	...	...	58	445	445	84	229	50	350	128
510	39	2,137	2,137	324	7,300	1,512	7,712	15,012	536	5,070	393	7,000	129
849	12	749	790	...	...	203	472	472	740	1,895	493	2,300	130
96	4	869	869	...	...	300	6,000	6,000	367	1,330	398	3,150	131
1,192	29	716	716	...	...	78	20	20	780	1,755	633	...	132
253	24	528	528	...	...	600	1,074	1,074	416	1,419	65	2,050	133
2,167	186	1,554	1,554	130	10	293	82	92	1,333	3,554	251	6,275	134
192	...	248	248	...	...	...	...	...	53	672	277	260	135
676	115	1,631	1,631	...	...	494	6,565	6,565	1,051	3,911	1,673	15,600	136
38	4	442	442	...	...	150	40	40	252	723	108	8,700	137

WISCONSIN.

115	65	40	40	...	...	400	1,007	1,007	3	49	2	1,800	1
2,142	2,344	1,003	1,062	130	2,180	360	1,780	3,960	529	1,963	234	1,050	2
931	320	383	383	...	...	173	735	735	260	561	23	343	3
342	160	94	94	...	...	...	...	...	1	101	7	...	4
4,971	3,328	1,853	1,853	...	...	1,951	5,362	5,362	1,375	3,288	12	1,465	5
1,221	573	571	571	...	...	226	451	451	98	805	74	1,000	6
7,945	5,835	3,203	3,217	187	2,094	2,707	4,784	6,878	3,095	5,794	64	1,694	7
9,476	6,677	3,600	3,695	...	...	3,243	3,378	3,378	3,137	6,719	684	2,650	8
7,244	5,366	2,721	2,741	...	...	2,784	4,984	4,984	2,599	5,332	...	3,730	9

	COUNTIES.	LAND OCCUPIED OR IMPROVED.				LIVE STOCK UPON FARMS.			
		Farms.	Acres improved.	Acres unimproved.	Value with improvements and implements.	Horses, asses, and mules.	Neat cattle.	Sheep.	Swine.
77	Mecklenburg........	666	215,646	179,183	2,535,628	3,727	13,260	15.535	28,955
78	Mercer..............	472	20,552	137,333	400,474	1,127	5,587	6,210	9,138
79	Middlesex	280	34,828	37,645	905,408	580	3,576	2,281	5,696
80	Monongalia.........	727	58,536	68,047	1,620,331	2,730	8,516	13.015	8,121
81	Monroe..............	910	94,311	174,890	2,100,334	3,398	14,181	21,789	14,307
82	Montgomery.........	546	59,734	107,106	1,601,335	2,240	8,647	10,426	15,160
83	Morgan..............	300	29,628	66,156	468,906	931	3,174	3,318	3,835
84	Nansemond.........	731	62,308	117,968	1,717,090	1,388	7,710	4,845	26,822
85	Nelson..............	638	109,855	120,652	1,963,712	2,634	8,613	9,296	20,199
86	New Kent..........	313	45,067	63,077	761,596	914	3,187	2,553	8,366
87	Nicholas............	418	19,335	132,349	374,575	945	5,213	7,501	7,368
88	Norfolk.............	648	39,014	75,866	1,252,031	1,712	7,690	2,154	17,747
89	Northampton........	376	53,709	39,840	240,691	1,428	4,439	3,628	12,141
90	Northumberland.....	492	48,325	45,177	960,506	1,006	6,860	4,679	10,869
91	Nottoway...........	342	93,401	93,511	1,159,324	1,507	5,386	5,756	9,662
92	Ohio	376	44,311	15,473	2,025,951	1,531	3,267	46,847	6,753
93	Orange.............	335	95,196	67,036	1,914,084	1,805	5,702	7,564	11,436
94	Page...............	526	52,182	103,713	1,820,449	2,194	5,472	5,783	9,946
95	Patrick.............	748	38,192	184,034	734,771	1,689	7,188	4,699	20,987
96	Pendleton...........	693	52,141	170,040	1,076,111	2,561	11,109	14,903	7,324
97	Pittsylvania.........	1,524	210,580	300,295	2,850,908	4,776	16,409	14,954	34,382
98	Pocahontas.........	353	40,239	466,159	946,632	1,889	7,865	11,616	4,597
99	Powhattan...........	312	81,045	69,716	1,437,833	1,717	4,891	7,201	9,964
100	Preston.............	1,019	63,948	172,477	1,163,806	2,816	10,585	21,781	10,714
101	Prince Edward......	421	147,328	57,491	1,609,315	1,758	6,429	7,168	10,119
102	Prince George.......	336	57,603	175,313	1,175,024	1,274	3,515	1,786	8,392
103	Prince William......	579	104,424	72,343	1,499,886	1,801	6,624	8,215	9,431
104	Princess Anne	712	50,064	63,175	1,110,673	1,653	10,522	6,233	21,943
105	Pulaski.............	301	50,974	70,605	1,182,650	1,470	7,423	9,159	10,384
106	Putnam.............	455	20,239	31,522	506,086	1,136	4,187	6,159	9,868
107	Raleigh.............	216	7,325	43,178	157,854	445	2,018	2,845	4,416
108	Randolph...........	379	35,054	291,098	873,753	1,444	8,910	8,667	4,642
109	Rappahannock......	472	96,068	69,727	2,123,631	2,532	9,774	9,130	15,180
110	Richmond	336	46,607	46,901	585,537	806	5,131	2,491	8,397
111	Ritchie	385	17,993	80,062	464,434	906	3,461	7,622	5,231
112	Roanoke............	405	52,877	71,469	1,775,651	2,245	6,767	6,646	12,973
113	Rockbridge	666	104,638	155,233	3,306,376	3,760	10,809	1,262	20,937
114	Rockingham.........	1,213	203,530	119,234	6,062,655	5,732	19,521	17,612	33,356
115	Russell.............	942	28,150	175,419	1,124,904	3,638	19.969	21,442	24,645
116	Scott...............	614	44,911	104,374	727,813	2,283	9,215	12,187	18,697
117	Shenandoah	554	74,294	83,464	3,151,492	2,695	7,496	5,894	8,006
118	Smyth..............	460	54,735	95,271	1,628,473	2,940	10,296	13,207	11,792
119	Southampton	722	159,668	176,023	1,068,103	2,233	9,767	7,865	49,816
120	Spottsylvania	429	88,324	99,072	1,291,505	1,816	6,603	6,055	1,270
121	Stafford............	360	57,799	72,756	1,122,949	1,308	4,755	4,593	7,310
122	Surry..............	301	44,298	65,466	562,052	929	3,844	2,654	11,908
123	Sussex	472	91,408	98,677	600,096	1,612	6,513	5,729	22,633
124	Taylor..............	519	38,372	54,101	940,874	1,504	6,045	10,617	5,076
125	Tazewell...........	726	60,757	153,325	1,222,790	3,740	16,625	17,372	27,291
126	Tyler...............	417	24,413	94,762	620,740	1,130	4,260	7,944	5,976
127	Warren.............	397	53,992	52,615	1,545,191	1,916	4,907	5,862	7,308
128	Warwick............	91	10,929	19,180	258,107	286	1,688	788	3,720
129	Washington.........	1,148	100,362	136,123	2,017,708	5,022	15,424	22,170	26,248
130	Wayne..............	478	21,594	140,291	628,383	1,154	5,190	6,129	12,517
131	Westmoreland......	443	68,627	61,450	1,132,197	1,101	6,225	3,676	8,237
132	Wetzel.............	423	15,955	61,797	509,073	904	2,045	6,049	6,847
133	Wirt	309	14,217	83,499	411,166	738	2,855	5,109	4,709
134	Wood...............	640	39,206	106,534	1,352,404	1,729	5,529	12,785	8,304
135	Wyoming...........	188	5,930	22,080	120,820	427	3,206	1,789	4,092
136	Wythe	668	91,001	206,347	2,180,709	3,784	15,439	20,164	16,409
137	York...............	161	20,817	25,683	717,882	590	3,641	1,148	5,437

STATISTICS OF

1	Adams	245	10,795	33,415	295,847	339	2,949	2,176	2,251
2	Brown.............	190	5,936	45,027	319,310	586	2,355	39	963
3	Calumet...........	125	4,063	28,969	197,937	117	5,486	229	1,286
4	Chippewa...	See	Crawford.	....	....	....	....	....	....
5	Columbia..........	833	41,520	98,898	1,095,090	939	6,152	3,040	6,215
6	Crawford..........	80	4,068	10,630	70,000	233	747	262	945
7	Dane..............	1,501	73,067	139,251	1,709,447	2,056	14,493	8,122	13,585
8	Dodge.............	2,132	82,622	183,613	2,204,099	1,327	12,075	5,912	12,940
9	Fond-du-lac	921	43,712	116,268	1,302,288	943	8,072	4,583	7,948

AGRICULTURAL PRODUCTS.												
Wheat, bushels.	Rye & oats, bushels.	Indian corn, bushels.	Irish and sweet potatoes, bushels.	Peas and beans, bushels.	Barley, bushels.	Buckwheat, bushels.	Butter and cheese, pounds.	Hay, tons.	Hops, pounds.	Clover & other grass seeds, bushels.	Flaxseed, bushels.	
113,016	184,849	552,466	42,682	6,643	......	......	72,503	14	147	6	180	77
12,284	38,274	105,946	1,832	....	......	2,468	41,578	1,375	......	66	399	78
30,762	8,861	134,253	12,213	948	......	......	26,277	111	......	......	......	79
52,370	114,173	184,379	11,015	392	......	2,964	155,962	6,013	179	536	615	80
51,436	104,341	250,456	9,662	1,010	209	6,131	183,856	6,073	12	956	1,458	81
51,827	110,903	266,616	8,865	....	......	4,060	90,369	4,453	......	1,967	891	82
40,584	24,434	46,247	6,739	93	5	2,538	37,121	1,443	60	254	95	83
2,976	26,396	352,842	199,366	49,851	205	2	36,390	3,338	4	......	43	84
122,230	92,182	353,432	23,185	2,467	......	244	82,493	1,322	56	63	64	85
4,315	37,873	178,813	19,161	1,420	......	......	38,031	155	......	......	......	86
6,209	34,695	83,273	3,897	896	......	1,501	44,483	2,001	81	11	253	87
393	21,303	307,245	111,140	17,576	2,367	......	27,564	1,822	......	......	173	88
795	184,099	364,967	48,854	2,360	......	......	15,455	....	58	......	37	89
53,902	10,101	221,587	24,024	1,310	4	68	29,773	....	......	......	......	90
71,827	55,721	216,991	12,580	4,384	2	20	55,570	34	142	62	......	91
57,709	77,617	214,020	19,214	158	970	451	105,062	4,111	27	193	3	92
121,825	31,534	267,140	15,534	1,396	100	116	54,814	1,881	161	458	292	93
128,430	30,443	137,602	9,963	385	50	1,078	55,849	2,253	238	366	98	94
12,755	95,604	248,868	31,017	1,163	28	863	69,202	347	......	51	350	95
44,137	41,322	109,838	6,990	2,279	......	4,711	72,611	7,664	......	218	810	96
123,934	217,528	653,815	49,132	3,701	200	211	138,147	357	289	137	550	97
11,806	65,610	51,949	2,796	30	......	3,685	79,161	5,911	......	6	172	98
115,437	89,189	215,155	13,542	1,775	10	65	45,076	360	66	18	2	99
36,769	173,998	144,276	12,828	564	855	28,283	183,923	7,765	99	312	1,232	100
75,762	87,229	214,350	20,154	3,153	......	20	47,932	487	5	467	351	101
81,042	23,851	261,510	19,508	1,684	......	230	32,998	208	36	10	......	102
57,728	59,549	161,248	10,374	974	......	1,426	96,679	2,309	95	110	126	103
2,529	60,111	347,141	55,012	16,036	15	......	37,062	1,593	10	......	1,039	104
35,284	67,104	175,510	4,949	88	......	1,519	64,711	2,639	......	1,477	1,052	105
14,373	50,274	249,040	13,508	3,109	20	174	60,022	1,078	66	30	187	106
2,893	20,820	49,511	1,149	198	......	1,590	31,289	279	......	26	37	107
11,740	40,481	87,408	9,242	....	......	2,983	59,853	6,480	......	213	303	108
157,699	66,590	281,216	17,994	1,578	......	2,322	95,580	3,273	213	413	719	109
42,404	5,176	185,800	12,013	1,073	......	......	26,390	124	54	......	......	110
5,989	24,919	101,884	5,142	113	......	2,067	42,063	2,503	......	110	302	111
104,134	105,709	235,760	9,429	198	40	668	68,891	3,410	......	1,850	427	112
198,553	172,769	372,705	15,206	102	2,345	2,019	195,435	7,626	147	2,856	657	113
608,350	178,986	448,585	23,744	1,627	3,593	2,141	266,594	16,067	150	4,316	913	114
25,604	158,281	378,919	15,411	4,004	......	1,896	172,708	2,528	20	134	1,926	115
15,722	107,344	319,240	17,866	3,140	......	683	76,481	924	25	151	904	116
196,338	39,668	167,025	5,439	502	50	151	79,756	4,641	186	1,336	232	117
34,742	140,551	201,222	2,011	....	677	3,942	111,490	3,952	......	1,507	856	118
4,066	15,035	564,183	250,398	125,218	......	......	36,383	3,321	34	......	......	119
102,953	47,745	265,753	13,447	578	......	206	52,056	1,279	......	......	1	120
58,923	41,057	178,651	13,107	1,139	100	46	42,088	2,018	30	......	21	121
14,098	15,016	204,975	32,113	5,714	......	......	23,004	1,486	......	14	......	122
35,133	48,091	356,171	65,093	14,809	......	......	36,615	2,108	75	27	......	123
23,995	43,134	101,118	4,780	511	20	1,793	91,062	4,051	4	205	578	124
21,327	128,620	235,126	4,793	....	40	3,540	143,553	72	......	2,643	958	125
15,100	28,050	130,014	8,875	....	28	2,202	51,486	1,737	......	73	102	126
145,354	30,647	128,875	8,291	18	106	519	70,619	2,219	10	739	179	127
10,252	8,490	61,340	12,822	618	......	......	10,150	625	......	......	......	128
69,264	250,383	438,900	3,394	15	665	2,179	162,556	4,238	......	316	63	129
2,155	27,789	226,800	8,005	775	......	1,371	36,555	558	......	30	175	130
82,774	8,399	269,115	11,146	1,350	......	4,064	28,437	32	129	......	......	131
12,162	23,562	124,198	6,102	766	......	69	46,557	1,440	......	22	196	132
3,424	23,038	98,291	5,109	239	......	2,769	25,499	1,097	11	48	163	133
18,790	60,197	251,715	16,858	154	......	592	74,668	3,166	......	289	74	134
1,552	9,322	47,506	5,315	535	......	4,957	17,665	286	......	126	277	135
72,738	166,875	280,652	10,821	....	654	......	225,085	7,193	......	2,401	1,754	136
27,650	25,951	148,335	250	10	......	......	14,113	....	......	......	......	137

WISCONSIN.

Wheat, bushels.	Rye & oats, bushels.	Indian corn, bushels.	Irish and sweet potatoes, bushels.	Peas and beans, bushels.	Barley, bushels.	Buckwheat, bushels.	Butter and cheese, pounds.	Hay, tons.	Hops, pounds.	Clover & other grass seeds, bushels.	Flaxseed, bushels.	
30,533	47,055	23,149	18,272	284	2,522	115	37,633	3,051	......	......	......	1
6,212	19,127	11,462	25,262	1,987	255	870	17,774	2,486	......	5	......	2
7,827	8,541	10,532	9,116	80	887	286	24,965	846	27	6	......	3
....	....	....	....	....	......	......	....	....	......	......	......	4
169,369	120,317	77,380	51,369	827	2,836	1,197	180,615	13,497	......	40	......	5
9,522	16,922	9,655	8,688	136	535	1,142	6,650	1,302	......	......	......	6
347,250	243,786	122,290	106,387	907	19,089	1,464	294,938	21,705	120	352	27	7
327,936	209,723	127,672	158,228	1,087	13,772	3,977	374,239	25,384	8	142	13	8
166,718	103,504	74,361	85,748	3,481	5,414	5,769	144,786	14,065	45	282	40	9

	Counties.	Agricultural products.									
		Flax, pounds.	Hemp, dew and water-rotted, tons.	Maple sugar, pounds.	Cane sugar, hhds. of 1,000 pounds.	Molasses, gallons.	Rice, pounds.	Tobacco, pounds.	Ginned cotton, bales of 400 pounds.	Wool, pounds.	Silk cocoons, pounds.
77	Mecklenburg	4,790						4,863,184	34	25,655	
78	Mercer	11,559		18,610		477				12,949	
79	Middlesex								3	5,230	
80	Monongalia	12,293		52,716		2,403		3,750		29,129	
81	Monroe	11,547		62,992		2,030		4,017		44,282	51
82	Montgomery	10,055	2	1,257		64		46,100		21,539	
83	Morgan	1,611	5	1,249		57				8,185	2
84	Nansemond	3,978					2,365		109	8,671	
85	Nelson	2,096	12					1,433,730		17,056	
86	New Kent								12	5,233	
87	Nicholas	5,897		17,245		421		2,670		13,649	
88	Norfolk	3,725								2,634	
89	Northampton									7,756	
90	Northumberland									8,536	
91	Nottoway	70						2,109,314	46	10,691	
92	Ohio	100		375		368				98,590	
93	Orange	3,266						174,700		21,509	
94	Page	1,185						1,194		12,907	
95	Patrick	13,261		55				429,699		8,523	
96	Pendleton	11,145		59,109		1,931				26,107	
97	Pittsylvania	6.969						4,700,757	61	23.854	
98	Pocahontas	4,556		64,760		1,426				24,422	
99	Powhattan	56						1,000,490		14,671	
100	Preston	25,450		21,768		1,548		820		43,907	20
101	Prince Edward	3,715						2,571,850	41	16,189	
102	Prince George							16,550	2	4,314	
103	Prince William	2,867						795		25,978	
104	Princess Anne	19,389						15		12,115	
105	Pulaski	14,141		190		128				20,502	46
106	Putnam	7,011		3,721		329		37,122		10,468	1
107	Raleigh	3,790								4,929	
108	Randolph	5,026		62,773		939		1,844		18,395	
109	Rappahannock	8,079						2,785		24,948	
110	Richmond							3,741	27	6,458	5
111	Ritchie	6,873		11,522		739		4,295		15,207	
112	Roanoke	5,476	15	2,242		70		362,682		13,289	
113	Rockbridge	8,925	2	1,728		701		78,298		30,469	
114	Rockingham	12,992		3,225		143		1,800		46,013	
115	Russell	50,589		61,944		1,347		7,577		43,911	
116	Scott	20,528		22,433		411		4,440		19,356	
117	Shenandoah	1,465								16,009	
118	Smyth	12,849		24,455						26,882	
119	Southampton	12					14,584	971	869	11,739	
120	Spottsylvania	21	12					90,034		12,792	
121	Stafford	532								9,628	
122	Surry							50	32	4,565	
123	Sussex							56,392	780	10,979	
124	Taylor	11,361		25,370		1,435				18,240	
125	Tazewell	23,117		61,562		360		300		33,605	
126	Tyler	3,621		11,236		448		14,320		14,663	
127	Warren	2,853						1,512		17,371	
128	Warwick									2,218	
129	Washington	23,197		25,861						42,935	
130	Wayne	2,930		10				1,215		12,571	
131	Westmoreland							1,346	7	8,603	
132	Wetzel	8,218	1	15,675		502		3,000		12,369	
133	Wirt	6,176		8,027		349		2,122		9,758	21
134	Wood	6,149		6.932		464		53,170		23,854	
135	Wyoming	5,260		2,417				2,441		3,156	
136	Wythe	22,210	1	20,367		579				43,766	5
137	York									4,658	

STATISTICS OF

1	Adams			4,866		250		50		3,414	
2	Brown	50		32,290		52		200			
3	Calumet			14,761		553				685	
4	Chippewa, (see Crawford)										
5	Columbia	75						100		4,670	
6	Crawford	40		2,000		1,590				60	
7	Dane	967		145,922		4,160				16,630	
8	Dodge	462		32,922		21				8,926	
9	Fond-du-lac	100		2,756		178				4,323	

AGRICULTURAL PRODUCTS.					MANUFACTURES.					
					Establishments.				REMARKS.	
Beeswax and honey, pounds.	Value of animals slaughtered.	Value of produce of market gardens.	Value of orchard produce.	Wine, gallons.	Capital.	Hands employed.	Annual product.	Produced in families.		
2,153	$106,797	$40	....	......	$53,400	249	$191,231	$35,423	....	77
6,800	19,916	....	....	......	1,720	4	3,000	14,204	....	78
880	32,458	....	$95	......	37,950	21	39,655	7,092	....	79
8,118	35,116	198	301	......	231,730	185	358,634	17,946	Div. in '42 to form Marion.	80
10 889	62,872	....	2,226	73	51,595	69	64,130	33,408	....	81
4,990	53,764	....	179	......	22,827	112	46,250	13,871	....	82
861	20,260	364	6,119	......	29,000	19	30,200	2,226	....	83
6,038	92,913	....	13,090	162	340,040	362	152,810	15,941	....	84
240	81,133	235	110	181	71,650	149	99,110	13,981	....	85
173	25,889	1,625	9	......	23,000	14	53,552	6,330	....	86
4,255	18,676	....	953	......	1,000	1	500	11,533	....	87
....	72,745	53,512	385	......	619,140	1,541	1,409,757	2,837	....	88
3,617	53,521	40	1,898	50	7,150	43	30,480	13,067	....	89
....	43,735	113	2,446	60	2,500	10	4,300	7,802	....	90
2,425	44,118	10	....	28	44,250	31	61,206	10,005	....	91
5,323	26,037	6,167	2,187	......	1,184,111	2,493	2,401,434	1,120	....	92
4,067	58,896	....	110	......	57,645	131	114,770	12,766	....	93
4,248	48,847	....	3,769	......	92,300	75	175,472	13,200	....	94
29,440	52,297	30	1,091	......	81,250	247	119,370	20,802	....	95
19,328	31,531	....	1,387	......	44,535	8[illegible]	92,992	17,598	Div. '47 to form Highland.	96
29,084	124,610	231	6,514	......	168,810	977	827,409	51,251	....	97
18,722	22,378	95	50	......	6,660	9	6,439	17,941	....	98
1,376	49,312	75	338	10	....	......	....	8,065	....	99
18,445	48,912	463	2,041	......	12,600	15	12,700	20,813	....	100
3,024	45,815	....	20	254	184,350	458	301,920	3,794	Div. '45 to fm Appomattox.	101
2,026	31,932	3,336	....	10	1,500	86	22,276	5,067	....	102
6,111	40,140	....	379	30	144,880	96	142,296	5,213	....	103
5,585	87,771	1,529	1,520	......	9,475	25	23,350	9,987	....	104
7,322	42,463	....	240	......	39,980	54	30,962	17,202	[Cabell and Mason.	105
2,755	42,284	72	2,714	......	32,775	79	54,112	12,649	Formed '48 f'm Kanawha,	106
6,117	9,077	....	....	......	....	......	....	5,008	Formed '50 from Fayette.	107
10,773	18,362	....	614	......	....	......	....	13,872	Divided in 1843 to form	108
8,782	68,831	....	2,420	15	83,965	70	123,664	16,890	Barbour.	109
2,082	37,375	....	825	25	7,300	27	13,315	6,688	....	110
1,253	14,841	....	69	......	4,000	7	8,315	8,056	Formed in 1843 from Har-	111
2,475	55,000	....	67	......	31,000	37	74,000	10,451	rison, Lewis, and Wood;	112
6,298	89,525	153	851	257	195,540	432	307,842	22,018	divided in 1845 to form	113
8,426	152,067	....	459	142	321,595	382	620,795	26,584	Doddridge.	114
29,906	59,019	....	927	......	20,325	32	22,906	37,676	....	115
11,297	36,081	....	148	......	18,034	32	36,136	20,115	....	116
963	47,817	30	815	16	182,300	256	422,500	7,689	....	117
8,238	40,046	....	1,304	......	83,895	159	74,355	21,029	....	118
7,377	163,858	....	747	12	6,845	24	14,275	22,325	....	119
2,019	44,473	175	1,150	......	238,000	134	231,000	12,204	....	120
2,845	27,923	552	1,465	25	117,900	120	379,160	7,081	....	121
2,530	36,482	....	411	......	46,452	40	14,300	5,048	....	122
759	65,544	....	609	184	30,850	32	64,330	15,803	....	123
6,632	28,967	....	....	......	17,200	46	27,850	15,910	Formed '44 from Harrison,	124
20,095	48,872	....	....	......	12,850	33	18,500	32,969	Barbour, and Marion.	125
2,530	18,287	....	635	30	27,900	29	65,573	8,866	Divided in '45 & '46 to form	126
13,222	44,782	207	1,300	63	216,350	169	281,670	7,895	Doddridge and Wetzel.	127
350	13,392	....	....	......	....	......	....	1,032	....	128
9,534	75,315	....	864	......	348,190	264	211,887	31,545	....	129
4,624	31,369	....	129	......	10,000	29	17,290	15,565	Formed in '42 from Cabell.	130
3,700	41,740	26	512	2	3,300	19	16,300	7,843	....	131
4,730	18,675	....	910	.....	12,825	25	10,250	10,937	Formed in '46 from Tyler.	132
2,285	13,724	....	1,976	......	18,400	36	23,900	6,952	'48 fm Wood and Jackson.	133
2,972	38,028	765	1,309	......	62,160	108	70,314	13,077	Divided in '43 and '48.	134
11,272	8,410	....	1,200	......	....	......	....	6,320	Formed in '50 from Logan.	135
10,019	77,107	....	460	......	207,510	322	145,525	28,804	....	136
....	2,000	....	....	......	....	......	....	3,981	....	137

WISCONSIN.

Beeswax and honey, pounds.	Value of animals slaughtered.	Value of produce of market gardens.	Value of orchard produce.	Wine, gallons.	Capital.	Hands employed.	Annual product.	Produced in families.	Remarks.	
2,819	7,358	50	....	......	....	......	....	52	Formed '48 from Portage.	1
175	5,873	827	....	......	117,150	377	250,460	100	....	2
1,325	10,337	239	22	15	7,200	14	31,220	423	[not returned in 1840.	3
....	....	....	....	......	52,000	120	63,000	....	For. in '35 from Crawford;	4
185	34,580	602	3	......	35,100	54	160,260	1,163	Formed '46 from Portage.	5
....	3,483	....	....	......	46,700	65	46,130	....	Divided in 1835 and 1845	6
5,476	64,370	5,907	105	......	82,475	261	289,576	4,479	to form Chippewa and La	7
10,491	66,701	160	....	......	119,450	134	234,810	2,432	Pointe.	8
10,633	36.536	135	....	......	52,500	56	219,950	339	....	9

	COUNTIES.	POPULATION.								
		Whites.			Colored.		All classes.		Total population.	
		Male.	Female.	Total.	Free.	Slave.	Male.	Female.	1850.	1840.
10	Grant	8,851	7,288	16,139	30	....	8,865	7,304	16,169	3,926
11	Greene..............	4,557	4,009	8,566		....	4,557	4,009	8,566	933
12	Iowa................	5,086	4,410	9,496	29	....	5,104	4,421	9,525	3,978
13	Jefferson...........	8,084	7,230	15,314	3	....	8,086	7,231	15,317	914
14	Kenosha.............	5,586	5,130	10,716	18	....	5,600	5,134	10,734	....
15	Lafayette...........	6,241	5,276	11,517	14	....	6,247	5,284	11,531	....
16	La Pointe...........	258	225	483	6	....	262	227	489	....
17	Manitoowoc	2,157	1,545	3,702	....	....	2,157	1,545	3,702	235
18	Marathon	416	92	508	....	....	416	92	508	....
19	Marquette	4,811	3,823	8,634	7	....	4,816	3,825	8,641	18
20	Milwaukee	16,345	14,621	30,966	111	....	16,410	14,667	31,077	5,605
21	Portage.............	828	421	1,249	1	....	828	422	1,250	1,623
22	Racine	7,819	7,088	14,907	66	....	7,858	7,114	14,973	3,475
23	Richland	511	391	902	1	....	512	391	903	....
24	Rock................	11,234	9,493	20,727	23	....	11,251	9,499	20,750	1,701
25	St. Croix...........	433	186	619	5	....	434	190	624	809
26	Sauk................	2,338	2,032	4,370	1	....	2,339	2,032	4,371	102
27	Sheboygan	4,475	3,897	8,372	7	....	4,476	3,903	8,379	133
28	Walworth	9,400	8,459	17,859	3	....	9,402	8,460	17,862	2,611
29	Washington.........	10,380	9,105	19,485	....	....	10,380	9,105	19,485	343
30	Waukesha...........	10,296	8,917	19,213	45	....	10,322	8,936	19,258	....
31	Winnebago	5,623	4,524	10,147	20	....	5,635	4,532	10,167	135

STATISTICS OF

	Counties	Whites Male	Whites Female	Whites Total	Colored Free	Colored Slave	All classes Male	All classes Female	Total 1850	Total 1840
1	Benton..............	272	144	416	2	....	274	144	418	....
2	Dakotah.............	385	197	582	2	....	387	197	584	....
3	Itasca..............	55	42	97	....	....	55	42	97	....
4	Mankahta	130	28	158	....	....	130	28	158	....
5	Pembina	578	556	1,134	....	....	578	556	1,134	....
6	Ramsey	1,337	860	2,197	30	....	1,350	877	2,227	....
7	Wabashaw	139	103	242	1	....	140	103	243	....
8	Wahnahta..........	113	47	160	....	....	113	47	160	....
9	Washington........	686	366	1,052	4	....	689	367	1,056	....

STATISTICS OF

	Counties	Whites Male	Whites Female	Whites Total	Colored Free	Colored Slave	All classes Male	All classes Female	Total 1850	Total 1840
1	Bernalillo..........	3,960	3,789	7,749	2	....	3,962	3,789	7,751	....
2	Rio Arribo..........	5,278	5,389	10,667	1	....	5,279	5,389	10,668	....
3	Santa Anna.........	2,442	2,202	4,644	1	....	2,443	2,202	4,645	....
4	Santa Fé	4,119	3,580	7,699	14	....	4,129	3,584	7,713	....
5	San Miguel.........	3,719	3,351	7,070	4	....	3,722	3,352	7,074	....
6	Taos...............	4,814	4,693	9,507	....	....	4,814	4,693	9,507	....
7	Valencia...........	7,393	6,796	14,189	....	....	7,393	6,796	14,189	....

STATISTICS OF

	Counties	Whites Male	Whites Female	Whites Total	Colored Free	Colored Slave	All classes Male	All classes Female	Total 1850	Total 1840
1	Benton..............	456	354	810	4	....	457	357	814	....
2	Clackamus..........	1,106	730	1,836	23	....	1,122	737	1,859	....
3	Clark..............	495	97	592	51	....	533	110	643	....
4	Clatsop............	335	123	458	4	....	339	123	462	....
5	Lewis..............	344	113	457	101	....	393	165	558	....
6	Linn...............	557	437	994	....	....	557	437	994	....
7	Marion.............	1,603	1,137	2,740	9	....	1,608	1,141	2,749	....
8	Polk...............	575	471	1,046	5	....	576	475	1,051	....
9	Washington........	1,800	843	2,643	9	....	1,806	846	2,652	....
10	Yam Hill..........	867	644	1,511	1	....	867	645	1,512	....

STATISTICS OF

	Counties	Whites Male	Whites Female	Whites Total	Colored Free	Colored Slave	All classes Male	All classes Female	Total 1850	Total 1840
1	Davis..............	599	535	1,134	....	....	599	535	1,134	....
2	Iron...............	190	169	359	1	....	191	169	360	....
3	Salt Lake..........	3,115	3,027	6,142	15	....	3,126	3,031	6,157	....
4	San Pete	197	168	365	....	....	197	168	365	....
5	Tooele	86	66	152	....	....	86	66	152	....
6	Utah...............	1,122	870	1,992	8	*26	1,136	890	2,026	....
7	Weber	711	475	1,186	....	....	711	475	1,186	....

* *En route* for California.

NATIVITIES, DWELLINGS, &c.				EDUCATION AND RELIGION.									
Born out of State.				Colleges, academies, and private schools.		Public Schools.							
United States.	Foreign countries.	Dwellings.	Families.	Pupils.	Annual income.	Pupils.	Annual income.	Total educational income.	White scholars during the year.	Whites 5 and under 20 years old.	Whites over 20 unable to read and write.	Accommodation of churches—persons.	
7,924	4,054	2,861	2,899	140	$3,600	4,174	$6,615	$10,215	3,437	5,771	578	4,100	10
5,598	1,128	1,481	1,528	50	1,000	1,132	2,790	3,790	2,016	3,305	95	2,500	11
3,165	4,500	1,846	1,846	35	....	2,969	5,901	5,901	1,393	3,242	66	2,942	12
7,858	4,859	2,934	2,984	60	250	3,111	5,957	6,207	3,441	5,395	203	4,050	13
5,324	3,362	1,812	1,874	80	1,160	2,980	6,374	7,534	2,602	3,707	353	5,150	14
4,047	4,554	2,076	2,086	......	....	3,203	3,688	3,688	1,804	3,856	1,165	4,750	15
32	36	74	84	......	....	30	500	500	36	180	104	450	16
825	2,396	715	726	......	....	182	1,252	1,252	301	1,073	128	....	17
220	182	76	76	......	....	......	....	....	1	49	16	....	18
5,850	1,707	1,778	1,778	......	....	298	1,069	1,069	1,083	2,927	81	100	19
7,294	18,622	5,630	6,035	1,506	7,557	4,857	11,213	18,770	5,284	10,107	1,162	17,326	20
723	278	204	204	......	....	......	....	....	81	272	67	....	21
6,178	6,079	2,578	2,715	205	325	3,756	7,885	8,210	3,296	5,164	53	6,385	22
683	53	178	178	......	....	85	150	150	79	324	8	....	23
13,380	4,197	3,618	3,757	249	3,800	4,286	6,178	9,978	4,841	7,305	282	14,393	24
402	117	181	181	......	....	19	....	....	28	135	37	....	25
2,661	1,082	844	844	......	....	See	Adams.	....	778	1,527	17	see Adams	26
3,739	3,546	1,783	1,785	......	....	624	2,227	2,227	1,628	2,776	1	2,000	27
11,682	2,799	3,112	3,187	......	....	5,140	11,930	11,930	5,138	6,428	243	5,780	28
3,574	12,119	3,770	3,799	......	....	2,894	3,929	3,929	2,143	6,741	163	4,325	29
8,025	7,476	3,408	3,480	156	1,530	5,435	8,929	10,459	4,116	6,780	75	4,410	30
6,049	2,663	1,889	1,906	......	....	1,798	4,065	4,065	1,731	3,206	364	5,380	31

MINNESOTA TERRITORY.

United States.	Foreign countries.	Dwellings.	Families.	Pupils.	Annual income.	Pupils.	Annual income.	Total educational income.	White scholars during the year.	Whites 5 and under 20 years old.	Whites over 20 unable to read and write.	Accommodation of churches—persons.	
183	84	71	71	12	140	......	....	140	12	114	1	....	1
147	189	78	83	......	....	......	....	....	12	147	86	....	2
48	7	23	23	......	....	......	....	....	....	32	......	....	3
77	67	16	16	......	....	......	....	....	....	11	8	....	4
26	729	188	188	......	....	......	....	....	2	490	379	....	5
1,215	564	384	384	......	....	......	....	....	96	621	107	....	6
102	34	55	55	......	....	......	....	....	19	66	52	100	7
113	33	26	28	......	....	......	....	....	27	43	16	....	8
600	270	161	168	......	....	......	....	....	39	213	......	....	9

NEW MEXICO TERRITORY.

United States.	Foreign countries.	Dwellings.	Families.	Pupils.	Annual income.	Pupils.	Annual income.	Total educational income.	White scholars during the year.	Whites 5 and under 20 years old.	Whites over 20 unable to read and write.	Accommodation of churches—persons.	
82	172	1,684	1,684	......	....	......	....	....	122	2,919	3,163	4,500	1
15	6	2,413	2,413	......	....	......	....	....	....	4,279	4,317	4,100	2
13	....	973	973	......	....	......	....	....	12	1,591	2,099	3,500	3
314	538	1,561	1,561	......	....	......	....	....	165	2,623	3,027	8,950	4
57	53	1,731	1,731	......	....	......	....	....	....	2,573	2,763	6,400	5
66	34	2,214	2,214	......	....	......	....	....	24	3,602	3,695	400	6
225	1,348	2,877	2,926	40	....	......	....	....	143	5,187	6,021	800	7

OREGON TERRITORY.

United States.	Foreign countries.	Dwellings.	Families.	Pupils.	Annual income.	Pupils.	Annual income.	Total educational income.	White scholars during the year.	Whites 5 and under 20 years old.	Whites over 20 unable to read and write.	Accommodation of churches—persons.	
707	12	149	149	40	1,560	......	....	1,560	144	330	......	....	1
1,414	147	368	368	133	4,000	80	3,927	7,927	321	613	3	1,700	2
327	223	95	95	11	....	......	....	....	11	98	......	500	3
330	53	91	91	77	500	......	....	500	74	107	3	200	4
218	134	146	146	13	500	......	....	500	23	91	6	....	5
844	14	172	172	55	1,500	......	....	1,500	108	381	......	....	6
1,577	226	502	502	113	....	......	....	....	378	1,067	145	733	7
892	13	190	190	134	4,548	......	....	4,548	234	402	......	....	8
2,138	147	418	418	128	4,020	......	....	4,020	276	787	......	....	9
1,224	53	243	243	138	4,260	......	....	4,260	306	576	......	....	10

UTAH TERRITORY.

United States.	Foreign countries.	Dwellings.	Families.	Pupils.	Annual income.	Pupils.	Annual income.	Total educational income.	White scholars during the year.	Whites 5 and under 20 years old.	Whites over 20 unable to read and write.	Accommodation of churches—persons.	
877	153	215	215	......	600	......	....	600	184	423	8	....	1
243	57	86	86	......	150	......	....	150	75	115	8	....	2
4,125	1,362	1,288	1,288	......	....	......	11,200	11,200	1,009	2,185	64	....	3
277	43	62	62	......	....	......	312	312	147	142	2	....	4
98	41	33	33	......	....	......	....	....	28	55	......	....	5
1,574	234	414	414	......	800	......	....	800	434	724	54	....	6
943	154	227	227	......	500	......	....	500	158	413	17	....	7

	Counties.	Land occupied or improved.				Live stock upon farms.			
		Farms.	Acres improved.	Acres unimproved.	Value with improvements and implements.	Horses, asses, and mules.	Neat cattle.	Sheep.	Swine.
10	Grant	704	39,862	72,681	$886,793	2,695	7,722	4,517	14,120
11	Greene	763	47,307	87,774	1,113,388	1,782	5,963	5,764	8,026
12	Iowa	470	17,195	48,537	385,961	983	5,359	705	5,592
13	Jefferson	982	43,198	91,382	1,288,253	927	8,942	5,264	5,325
14	Kenosha	914	50,987	79,862	2,087,066	1,712	8,968	12,767	5,445
15	Lafayette	399	28,642	50,732	642.039	1,173	4,107	2,475	6,034
16	La Pointe	5	110	....	3,765	5	3,701	....	10
17	Manitoowoc	35	1,122	6,927	53,120	22	2,116	....	187
18	Marathon	7	226	....	5,245	2	33	....	1
19	Marquette	327	15,935	40,513	471,795	741	3,654	2,027	3,539
20	Milwaukee	935	35,589	63,945	1,918,151	1,500	4,620	4,702	6,560
21	Portage	5	370	150	5,510	4	3,389	....	13
22	Racine	971	63,338	82,947	1,901,591	1,671	7,005	10,093	5,007
23	Richland	58	2,106	20,664	92,934	155	5,583	183	887
24	Rock	1,965	143,235	137,111	3,323,276	3,426	11,020	13,456	14,455
25	St. Croix	4	178	480	3,296	3	5,556	....	29
26	Sauk	See	Adams.	....	....	....	....	....	....
27	Sheboygan	328	13,419	62,418	658,484	262	2,035	308	2,493
28	Walworth	1,884	116,750	149,905	3,197,706	3,352	14,189	22,744	12,984
29	Washington	1,353	42,963	108,335	1,402,397	400	11,922	1,253	10,217
30	Waukesha	1,703	105,269	128,486	3,059,694	2,362	9,970	12,415	10,098
31	Winnebago	338	11,915	42,239	475,649	618	5,250	1,860	2,121

STATISTICS OF

	Counties.	Farms.	Acres improved.	Acres unimproved.	Value with improvements and implements.	Horses, asses, and mules.	Neat cattle.	Sheep.	Swine.
1	Benton	20	405	4,540	36,745	59	246	....	42
2	Dakotah	......	....	....	....	....	....	....	....
3	Itasca	36	100	....	200	......	102	....	....
4	Mankahta	See	Wahnahta	....	....	....	....	....	....
5	Pembina	17	77	2,068	4.815	518	412	2	13
6	Ramsey	19	458	2,832	33,993	20	163	45	99
7	Wabashaw	8	439	560	9,775	107	264	26	227
8	Wahnahta	9	642	500	6,494	40	87	....	....
9	Washington	48	2,914	13,346	85,907	130	728	7	353

STATISTICS OF

	Counties.	Farms.	Acres improved.	Acres unimproved.	Value with improvements and implements.	Horses, asses, and mules.	Neat cattle.	Sheep.	Swine.
1	Bernalillo	164	13,436	806	153,815	2,505	4,349	153,048	880
2	Rio Arribo	472	30,417	2,644	429,932	2,739	4,645	54,998	1,585
3	Santa Anna	194	3,197	....	129,962	1,562	2,747	32,075	328
4	Santa Fé	713	19,081	82,206	181,738	1,504	3,155	23,770	329
5	San Miguel	177	42,880	....	207,804	1,115	4,104	26,726	381
6	Taos	651	10,469	11,608	197.325	2,209	3,975	23,755	2,329
7	Valencia	1,379	46,721	27,106	431,303	2,099	10,002	62,899	1,482

STATISTICS OF

	Counties.	Farms.	Acres improved.	Acres unimproved.	Value with improvements and implements.	Horses, asses, and mules.	Neat cattle.	Sheep.	Swine.
1	Benton	110	5,589	....	91,110	701	3,547	629	3,586
2	Clackamus	150	36,210	82,388	866,225	579	3,079	59	2,603
3	Clark	7	3,705	16,935	215,480	507	1,816	1,150	569
4	Clatsop	24	340	12,257	175,420	58	761	49	88
5	Lewis	55	13,441	35,804	287,285	866	5,577	10,208	937
6	Linn	13[illegible]	6,041	....	123,870	628	4,619	380	4,320
7	Marion	293	30,211	152,567	884,584	1,769	7,251	1,021	6,009
8	Polk	129	9,341	....	81,470	815	4,277	555	5,129
9	Washington	116	13,498	....	176,780	1,216	5,171	417	3,303
10	Yam Hill	142	14,481	....	130,369	1,327	5,631	914	3,692

STATISTICS OF

	Counties.	Farms.	Acres improved.	Acres unimproved.	Value with improvements and implements.	Horses, asses, and mules.	Neat cattle.	Sheep.	Swine.
1	Davis	112	2,115	5,639	56,509	413	1,522	756	210
2	Iron	54	1,325	1,766	43,895	156	639	122	28
3	Salt Lake	505	9,296	7,801	207,290	1,304	5,552	1,663	509
4	San Pete	51	592	712	9,187	124	443	45	8
5	Tooele	27	352	197	3,200	11	183	....	4
6	Utah	144	2,128	10,591	62,991	386	2,793	444	84
7	Weber	33	525	3,810	13,015	360	1,484	232	80

AGRICULTURAL PRODUCTS.												
Wheat, bushels.	Rye & oats, bushels.	Indian corn, bushels.	Irish and sweet potatoes, bushels	Peas and beans, bushels.	Barley, bushels.	Buckwheat, bushels.	Butter and cheese, pounds.	Hay, tons.	Hops, pounds.	Clover & other grass seeds, bushels.	Flaxseed bushels.	
127,164	206,731	200,585	46,299	265	10,342	1,572	130,635	8,834	14	266	27	10
148,997	153,027	133,595	16,634	152	4,365	987	122,284	10,588	13	287	30	11
50,747	110,174	81,108	29,039	76	2,013	282	53,430	8,128	.....	10	.....	12
182,545	120,512	81,079	60,934	257	7,260	2,397	224,620	14,296	1,800	105	100	13
318,051	231,038	100,046	68,817	1,047	10,020	7,125	342,064	24,229	34	622	32	14
63,283	176,238	91,491	18,829	792	4,161	320	77,881	9,196	34	99	21	15
.....	233	250	1,950	.....	5	.....	550	45	.....	.....	.....	16
214	5,444	287	7,297	85	96	.....	5,000	460	.....	.....	.....	17
.....	.....	1,510	2,075	5	.....	.....	.....	45	.....	.....	.....	18
85,614	66,197	43,052	36,724	738	1,488	1,083	71,364	5,495	15	76	1	19
61,147	136,095	39,299	71,950	3,083	3,102	3,985	162,706	11,246	196	504	7	20
100	3,400	75	1,300	.....	.....	130	.....	2	.....	.....	.....	21
218,149	176,543	78,847	58,279	1,158	6,322	8,642	253,006	14,551	133	491	214	22
1,683	2,515	11,095	1,956	47	100	300	9,445	1,132	.....	6	1	23
784,278	488,740	300,143	102,395	659	16,432	5,543	450,215	23,122	3	466	23	24
115	700	1,100	1,350	95	750	130	100	30	.....	.....	.....	25
.....	.....	.....	.....	.....	.....	.....	.....	.....	.....	.....	.....	26
29,437	42,506	7,331	37,206	172	2,141	559	55,010	1,757	.....	91	.....	27
655,704	378,549	215,242	100,437	1,417	31,599	15,826	386,432	27,193	279	608	51	28
123,866	145,048	34,524	123,352	727	10,078	3,406	172,122	3,261	.....	147	8	29
312,658	253,173	77,097	119,275	498	52,369	9,686	343,394	22,552	13,119	762	586	30
57,072	30,087	34,722	33,788	595	1,739	3,085	92,175	7,164	90	119	10	31

MINNESOTA TERRITORY.

Wheat, bushels.	Rye & oats, bushels.	Indian corn, bushels.	Irish and sweet potatoes, bushels	Peas and beans, bushels.	Barley, bushels.	Buckwheat, bushels.	Butter and cheese, pounds.	Hay, tons.	Hops, pounds.	Clover & other grass seeds, bushels.	Flaxseed bushels.	
.....	60	160	3,650	.....	.....	.....	.....	1,121	.....	.....	.....	1
.....	.....	.....	.....	.....	.....	.....	.....	.....	.....	.....	.....	2
10	.....	90	1,050	10	.....	.....	.....	43	.....	.....	.....	3
.....	.....	.....	.....	.....	.....	.....	.....	.....	.....	.....	.....	4
100	.....	60	.....	.....	.....	.....	.....	.....	.....	.....	.....	5
390	6,260	1,615	200	9,585	20	.....	.....	100	.....	.....	.....	6
200	1,100	1,855	7,105	250	.....	325	.....	.....	.....	.....	.....	7
150	.....	1,115	.....	.....	.....	.....	.....	.....	.....	.....	.....	8
551	23,287	11,830	9,340	157	1,196	190	1,100	755	.....	.....	.....	9

NEW MEXICO TERRITORY.

Wheat, bushels.	Rye & oats, bushels.	Indian corn, bushels.	Irish and sweet potatoes, bushels	Peas and beans, bushels.	Barley, bushels.	Buckwheat, bushels.	Butter and cheese, pounds.	Hay, tons.	Hops, pounds.	Clover & other grass seeds, bushels.	Flaxseed bushels.	
17,701	.....	39,303	3	2,300	.....	100	50	.....	.....	.....	.....	1
31,163	.....	56,483	.....	4,001	.....	.....	3,170	.....	.....	.....	.....	2
9,740	.....	24,373	.....	728	5	.....	547	.....	.....	.....	.....	3
11,499	5	26,962	.....	544	.....	.....	2,172	.....	.....	.....	.....	4
11,381	.....	33,862	.....	.....	.....	.....	.....	.....	.....	.....	.....	5
72,049	.....	26,633	.....	.....	.....	.....	.....	.....	.....	.....	.....	6
42,983	.....	157,795	.....	8,115	.....	.....	20	.....	.....	.....	.....	7

OREGON TERRITORY.

Wheat, bushels.	Rye & oats, bushels.	Indian corn, bushels.	Irish and sweet potatoes, bushels	Peas and beans, bushels.	Barley, bushels.	Buckwheat, bushels.	Butter and cheese, pounds.	Hay, tons.	Hops, pounds.	Clover & other grass seeds, bushels.	Flaxseed bushels.	
14,913	193	40	1,402	231	.....	.....	53,145	.....	.....	26	.....	1
16,281	6,970	216	18,893	630	.....	.....	3,810	353	.....	.....	.....	2
1,050	900	.....	5,550	.....	.....	.....	200	.....	.....	.....	.....	3
590	16	2,340	9,280	.....	.....	.....	8,250	20	.....	.....	.....	4
10,745	5,850	5	27,347	2,744	.....	.....	2,750	.....	8	.....	.....	5
21,893	1,694	165	3,366	356	.....	.....	37,965	.....	.....	.....	.....	6
86,165	34,172	.....	15,224	2,043	.....	.....	29,359	.....	.....	.....	.....	7
16,373	1,605	56	565	132	.....	.....	39,590	.....	.....	.....	.....	8
21,481	3,932	52	8,075	294	.....	.....	29,085	.....	.....	.....	.....	9
22,452	5,988	44	1,624	136	.....	.....	44,290	.....	.....	.....	.....	10

UTAH TERRITORY.

Wheat, bushels.	Rye & oats, bushels.	Indian corn, bushels.	Irish and sweet potatoes, bushels	Peas and beans, bushels.	Barley, bushels.	Buckwheat, bushels.	Butter and cheese, pounds.	Hay, tons.	Hops, pounds.	Clover & other grass seeds, bushels.	Flaxseed bushels.	
17,675	2,635	2,078	6,982	31	209	46	27,943	636	50	.....	.....	1
8,948	1,188	663	2,530	5	198	.....	5,020	312	.....	.....	5	2
58,492	5,066	5,220	25,919	102	1,123	143	47,025	2,205	.....	2	.....	3
3,210	262	47	967	38	164	43	2,523	439	.....	.....	.....	4
730	3	36	335	.....	.....	19	740	25	.....	.....	.....	5
13,142	1,376	1,460	5,882	111	95	39	22,910	1,127	.....	.....	.....	6
5,505	580	395	1,413	2	10	42	8,146	61	.....	.....	.....	7

	COUNTIES.	AGRICULTURAL PRODUCTS.									
		Flax, pounds.	Hemp, dew and water-rotted, tons.	Maple sugar, pounds.	Cane sugar, hhds. of 1,000 pounds.	Molasses, gallons.	Rice, pounds.	Tobacco, pounds.	Ginned cotton, bales of 400 pounds.	Wool, pounds.	Silk cocoons, pounds.
10	Grant	4,756		19,140		457				7,411	
11	Greene	1,293								14,858	
12	Iowa			81,316		45				656	
13	Jefferson	93		70						11,818	
14	Kenosha	42								33,429	
15	Lafayette	525		1,000						4,367	
16	La Pointe			46,006		969					
17	Manitoowoc			80							
18	Marathon										
19	Marquette	155		300		60		100		3,206	
20	Milwaukee	117		7,325		195				11,637	
21	Portage			5,520		81					
22	Racine	155		2,556		160				16,155	
23	Richland			60				740		479	
24	Rock	453						20		30,748	
25	St. Croix										
26	Sauk										
27	Sheboygan			61,135		136				90	
28	Walworth	582		1,050				58		49,256	
29	Washington	578		106,637		375				1,824	
30	Waukesha	57,950		37,709		443				25,492	
31	Winnebago			5,555		149				3,829	
	STATISTICS OF										
1	Benton										
2	Dakotah										
3	Itasca										
4	Mankahta										
5	Pembina										
6	Ramsey										
7	Wabashaw			2,950						75	
8	Wahnahta										
9	Washington									10	
	STATISTICS OF										
1	Bernalillo									8,500	
2	Rio Arribo					3,524				15,070	
3	Santa Anna							6,911		2,825	
4	Santa Fé					414		1,128		6,506	
5	San Miguel										
6	Taos										
7	Valencia					298		428			
	STATISTICS OF										
1	Benton	100						100		1,856	
2	Clackamus	200				24		225		150	
3	Clark										
4	Clatsop										
5	Lewis									18,150	
6	Linn	50								762	
7	Marion									3,093	
8	Polk	250								1,218	
9	Washington									1,156	
10	Yam Hill	40								3,301	
	STATISTICS OF										
1	Davis									1,818	
2	Iron	500								518	
3	Salt Lake					58		70		5,378	
4	San Pete									136	
5	Tooele										
6	Utah									1,207	
7	Weber	50								165	

AGRICULTURAL PRODUCTS.					MANUFACTURES.				REMARKS.	
Beeswax and honey, pounds.	Value of animals slaughtered.	Value of produce of market gardens.	Value of orchard produce.	Wine, gallons.	Establishments. Capital.	Hands employed.	Annual product.	Produced in families.		
17,134	$ 42,310	$ 1,231	$ 1,163	30	$ 134,474	208	$ 484,783	$ 4,635	....	10
11,585	34,288	40	484	......	71,450	80	111,742	9,039	....	11
140	13,328	360	57	......	64,620	121	600,804	119	Div. in '42 and '46 to form	12
6,832	41,430	....	....	......	209,400	252	403,117	2,522	Richland and Lafayette.	13
5,260	36,440	78	115	......	145,400	279	477,678	2,542	Formed in '50 from Racine.	14
7,464	17,746	562	1,819	68	58,675	90	411,309	2,962	Formed in 1846 from Iowa.	15
5,917	20	....	....	......	800	2	1,500	938	Formed '45 from Crawford.	16
2,853	1,946	....	....	......	134,687	171	112,123	894	....	17
....	163	100	....	......	101,000	125	98,900	....	Formed in '50 from Portage	18
....	17,746	110	....	......	51,700	24	145,500	....	....	19
....	183,331	8,644	237	......	587,175	1,583	1,871,661	....	Div. '46 to form Waukesha	20
7,827	27,366	....	....	......	58,400	117	80,320	1,240	Div. see counties 1, 5 & 18.	21
7,327	1,904	1,090	229	......	276,950	584	898,479	75	Div. in '50 to form Kenosha	22
3,214	73,883	25	....	......	5,100	17	9,650	2,281	Formed in 1842 from Iowa.	23
....	....	11,190	281	......	293,735	455	839,840	....	....	24
....	725	....	....	......	63,000	63	58,000	....	....	25
....	....	....	....	......	6,750	19	13,840	....	....	26
100	7,570	230	....	......	87,790	92	176,384	....	....	27
5,565	84,838	125	164	......	155,342	255	412,905	5,099	....	28
176	29,690	....	....	......	51,000	38	116,978	....	....	29
17,647	61,503	287	144	......	192,950	240	389,756	1,947	Formed '46 fr. Milwaukee.	30
860	14,710	150	....	......	119,175	193	282,393	343	....	31

MINNESOTA TERRITORY.

Beeswax and honey, pounds.	Value of animals slaughtered.	Value of produce of market gardens.	Value of orchard produce.	Wine, gallons.	Capital.	Hands employed.	Annual product.	Produced in families.	Remarks.	
....	....	....	....	......	7,000	12	10,000	....	....	1
....	....	....	....	......	....	......	....	....	....	2
....	....	....	....	......	....	......	....	....	....	3
....	....	....	....	......	....	......	....	....	....	4
....	....	....	....	......	....	......	....	....	....	5
....	....	....	....	......	....	......	....	....	....	6
75	1,950	....	....	......	....	......	....	....	....	7
....	....	....	....	......	....	......	....	....	....	8
5	890	150	....	......	87,000	51	47,500	....	....	9

NEW MEXICO TERRITORY.

Beeswax and honey, pounds.	Value of animals slaughtered.	Value of produce of market gardens.	Value of orchard produce.	Wine, gallons.	Capital.	Hands employed.	Annual product.	Produced in families.	Remarks.	
....	11,789	5,864	7,841	390	....	......	....	1,267	....	1
....	14,273	....	....	......	....	......	....	4,095	....	2
....	6,572	600	10	......	....	......	....	23	....	3
2	14,460	40	125	......	30,700	24	52,610	648	....	4
....	194	....	....	......	....	......	....	....	....	5
....	13,198	....	....	......	27,600	43	156,400	....	....	6
....	21,639	175	255	1,973	10,000	14	40,000	....	....	7

OREGON TERRITORY.

Beeswax and honey, pounds.	Value of animals slaughtered.	Value of produce of market gardens.	Value of orchard produce.	Wine, gallons.	Capital.	Hands employed.	Annual product.	Produced in families.	Remarks.	
....	15,045	5,987	16	......	2,500	2	43,200	....	....	1
....	8,621	9,865	350	......	465,000	92	681,500	....	....	2
....	....	500	....	......	110,000	40	251,500	....	....	3
....	11,965	27,494	....	......	50,000	28	260,000	....	....	4
....	8,000	13,100	....	......	80,000	29	71,200	....	....	5
....	8,455	5,300	75	......	11,400	18	189,440	....	....	6
....	41,256	....	630	......	48,000	42	285,000	....	....	7
....	21,055	9,405	....	......	14,200	7	118,800	....	....	8
....	23,575	10,045	....	......	46,000	17	202,900	....	....	9
....	26,558	8,545	200	......	16,500	10	133,100	....	....	10

UTAH TERRITORY.

Beeswax and honey, pounds.	Value of animals slaughtered.	Value of produce of market gardens.	Value of orchard produce.	Wine, gallons.	Capital.	Hands employed.	Annual product.	Produced in families.	Remarks.	
....	10,146	1,830	....	......	2,000	6	1,500	429	....	1
....	5,122	1,942	....	......	....	......	....	....	....	2
10	35,390	15,487	....	......	34,800	17	257,520	963	....	3
....	2,452	780	....	......	....	......	....	....	....	4
....	292	85	....	......	....	......	....	....	....	5
....	10,756	3,744	....	......	5,200	21	24,400	....	....	6
....	3,827	....	....	......	2,400	7	7,800	....	....	7

POPULATION

OF SUCH

CITIES, TOWNS, TOWNSHIPS, HUNDREDS, &c., IN THE UNITED STATES,

AS HAVE BEEN ASCERTAINED AT THE CENSUS OFFICE.

THE letter T affixed to a place designates the town in the township, &c. of the same name in the same county. "Bor." is an abbreviation of *borough*. The asterisk (*) is placed wherever the slave population cannot be defined, and is therefore not included; and the obelisk (†) wherever there is probability that slaves owned in, but not residents of, the town, are included.

Towns, the population of which is ascertained from other sources than the census schedules, are put in *italics*, and the figures are generally for 1853 or 1854.

Cities, towns, townships, &c.	County, district, or parish.	State.	Total Population.	Cities, towns, townships, &c.	County, district, or parish.	State.	Total Population.
Abbeville	Henry	Ala.	300	Albany	Carroll	N. H	455
Abbeville	Abbeville	S. C.	†1,252	Albany	Albany	N. Y.	50,763
Abbott	Piscataquis	Me	747	Albany	Berks	Pa	1,406
Aberdeen	Brown	Ohio	808	Albany	Bradford	Pa	1,043
Aberdeen	Monroe	Miss	5,000	Albany	Orleans	Vt.	1,052
Abingdon	Luzerne	Pa	2,886	Albany	Greene	Wis.	546
Abingdon	Washington	Va.	1,000	Albany	Marquette	Wis.	494
Abington	Knox	Ill.	210	*Albia*	Monroe	Iowa	500
Abington	Wayne	Ind.	1,042	Albion	Edwards	Ill.	365
Abington, T.	Wayne	Ind.	206	Albion	Kennebeck	Me.	1,604
Abington	Plymouth	Mass.	5,269	Albion	Calhoun	Mich.	1,665
Abington	Montgomery	Pa	1,836	Albion, T.	Calhoun	Mich.	*b*881
Aboite	Allen	Ind.	539	Albion	Orleans	N. Y.	*c*2,251
Acton	York	Me.	1,359	Albion	Oswego	N. Y.	2,010
Acton	Middlesex	Mass.	1,605	Albion	Dane	Wis.	817
Acworth	Cobb	Ga	118	*Albion*	Erie	Pa	300
Acworth	Sullivan	N. H	1,251	Albion Gore	Kennebeck	Me.	110
Ada	Kent	Mich.	593	Alburg	Grand Isle	Vt	1,568
Adams	Lasalle	Ill.	547	Alden	McHenry	Ill.	780
Adams	Allen	Ind.	1,012	Alden	Erie	N. Y.	2,520
Adams	Carroll	Ind.	671	Aleppo	Greene	Pa	1,176
Adams	Cass	Ind.	474	Alexander	Washington	Me	544
Adams	Decatur	Ind.	1,257	Alexander	Benton	Mo	*630
Adams	Hamilton	Ind.	861	Alexander	Genesee	N. Y.	1,927
Adams	Madison	Ind.	1,309	Alexander	Athens	Ohio	1,735
Adams	Morgan	Ind.	1,411	Alexander	Montgomery	Ohio	246
Adams	Parke	Ind.	879	*Alexandria*	Campbell	Ky.	1,000
Adams	Ripley	Ind.	1,524	Alexandria	Grafton	N. H	1,273
Adams	Keokuk	Iowa	29	Alexandria	Rapides	La	672
Adams	Berkshire	Mass.	6,172	Alexandria	Hunterdon	N. J.	3,811
Adams	Hillsdale	Mich.	1,129	Alexandria	Jefferson	N. Y.	3,178
Adams	Jefferson	N. Y.	3,106	Alexandria	Licking	Ohio	349
Adams	Champaign	Ohio	1,123	Alexandria	Huntingdon	Pa	601
Adams	Clinton	Ohio	869	Alexandria	De Kalb	Tenn	343
Adams	Coshocton	Ohio	1,419	Alexandria	Alexandria	Va	8,734
Adams	Darke	Ohio	1,416	Alford	Berkshire	Mass.	502
Adams	Defiance	Ohio	432	Alfred	York	Me.	1,319
Adams	Guernsey	Ohio	860	Alfred	Alleghany	N. Y.	2,679
Adams	Monroe	Ohio	1,182	Algansee	Branch	Mich.	609
Adams	Muskingum	Ohio	998	Algoma	Kent	Mich.	233
Adams	Seneca	Ohio	1,416	Algoma	Winnebago	Wis.	702
Adams	Washington	Ohio	1,293	Algodones	Santa Anna	N. M.	517
Adams	Greene	Wis.	275	Algonquin	McHenry	Ill	1,455
Adams	Sauk	Wis.	482	Allegan	Allegan	Mich.	752
Adamsburg	Westmoreland	Pa	263	Allegheny	Allegheny	Pa	21,262
Addison	Du Page	Ill.	818	Allegheny	Armstrong	Pa	2,506
Addison	Shelby	Ind.	1,917	Allegheny	Blair	Pa	2,352
Addison	Washington	Me.	1,152	Allegheny	Cambria	Pa	1,488
Addison	Oakland	Mich.	924	Allegheny	Potter	Pa	381
Addison	Steuben	N. Y.	3,721	Allegheny	Somerset	Pa	948
Addison	Gallia	Ohio.	924	Allegheny	Venango	Pa	1,174
Addison	Somerset	Pa	1,665	Allegheny	Westmoreland	Pa	3,329
Addison	Addison	Vt.	1,279	Allen	Noble	Ind	933
Addison	Washington	Wis.	1,144	Allen	Hillsdale	Mich.	1,033
Adelphi	Ross	Ohio.	412	Allen	Gentry	Mo.	*502
Adrian	Lenawee	Mich.	3,006	Allen	Alleghany	N. Y.	955
Aid	Lawrence	Ohio.	884	Allen	Darke	Ohio	290
Akron	Summit	Ohio.	*a*3,266	Allen	Hancock	Ohio	869
Alabama	Genesee	N. Y.	2,054	Allen	Union	Ohio	979
Alaiedon	Ingham	Mich.	377	Allen	Northampton	Pa	1,156
Alamo	Kalamazoo	Mich.	420	Allendale	Ottawa	Mich.	168
Albany	Baker	Ga.	1,000	Allenstown	Merrimack	N. H.	526
Albany	Oxford	Me.	747	*Allentown*	Monmouth	N. J.	600

a In 1853, 4,500. *b* In 1853, 1,200. *c* In 1853, 3,500.

Town	County	State	Population
Allentown	Lehigh	Pa.	a3,779
Alligator	Columbia	Fla.	131
Allison	Clinton	Pa.	411
Almena	Van Buren	Mich.	420
Almond	Alleghany	N. Y.	1,914
Almont	Lapeer	Mich.	1,452
Alna	Lincoln	Me.	916
Alpine	Kent	Mich.	618
Alsace	Berks	Pa.	2,697
Alstead	Cheshire	N. H.	1,425
Alto	Fond du Lac	Wis.	608
Alton	Madison	Ill.	3,585
Alton	Penobscot	Me.	252
Alton	Belknap	N. H.	1,795
Altoona	Blair	Pa.	2,500
Amanda	Allen	Ohio	607
Amanda	Fairfield	Ohio	1,788
Amanda, T.	Fairfield	Ohio	181
Amanda	Hancock	Ohio	1,162
Amboy	Lee	Ill.	540
Amboy	Hillsdale	Mich.	252
Amboy	Oswego	N. Y.	1,132
Amboy	Fulton	Ohio	460
Amenia	Dutchess	N. Y.	2,229
Americus	Sumter	Ga.	600
Ames	Athens	Ohio	1,482
Amesburg	Washington	Me.	126
Amesburg	Essex	Mass.	3,143
Amherst	Hancock	Me.	323
Amherst	Hampshire	Mass.	3,057
Amherst	Hillsborough	N. H.	1,613
Amherst	Erie	N. Y.	4,153
Amherst	Lorain	Ohio	1,399
Amity	Aroostook	Me.	256
Amity	Alleghany	N. Y.	1,792
Amity	Berks	Pa.	1,566
Amity	Erie	Pa.	739
Amsterdam	Montgomery	N. Y.	4,128
Amsterdam, T.	Montgomery	N. Y.	2,000
Amsterdam	Jefferson	Ohio	168
Amwell	Hunterdon	N. J.	2,505
Amwell	Washington	Pa.	1,754
Ancram	Columbia	N. Y.	1,569
Anderson	Clark	Ark.	201
Anderson	Madison	Ind.	1,357
Anderson, T.	Madison	Ind.	383
Anderson	Perry	Ind.	825
Anderson	Rush	Ind.	1,433
Anderson	Warrick	Ind.	392
Anderson	Hamilton	Ohio	3,048
Andes	Delaware	N. Y.	2,672
Andover	Tolland	Conn.	500
Andover	Oxford	Me.	710
Andover	Essex	Mass.	6,945
Andover	Merrimack	N. H.	1,220
Andover	Alleghany	N. Y.	1,476
Andover	Ashtabula	Ohio	963
Andover	Windsor	Vt.	725
Andrew	Jackson	Iowa	168
Angelica	Alleghany	N. Y.	1,592
Angola	Steuben	Ind.	226
Annapolis	Anne Arundel	Md.	3,011
Annapolis	Jefferson	Ohio	158
Ann Arbor	Washtenaw	Mich.	4,868
Annsville	Oneida	N. Y.	2,686
Anson	Somerset	Me.	848
Antalaway	Berks	Pa.	1,045
Antes	Blair	Pa.	2,452
Anthony	Lycoming	Pa.	1,076
Anthony	Montour	Pa.	962
Antioch	Lake	Ill.	1,192
Antioch	Monroe	Ohio	107
Antoine	Clark	Ark.	271
Antoine	Pike	Ark.	91
Antrim	Shiawassee	Mich.	282
Antrim	Hillsborough	N. H.	1,143
Antrim	Guernsey	Ohio	252
Antrim	Wyandott	Ohio	757
Antrim	Franklin	Pa.	3,005
Antwerp	Van Buren	Mich.	614
Antwerp	Jefferson	N. Y.	3,665
Apolacon	Susquehanna	Pa.	748
Apollo	Armstrong	Pa.	331
Appanoose	Hancock	Ill.	384
Appleton	Waldo	Me.	1,727
Appleton	Licking	Ohio	66
Appoquinimink	Newcastle	Del.	3,126
Aquaquenock	Passaic	N. J.	2,941
Arcadia	Wayne	N. Y.	5,145
Archer	Harrison	Ohio	875
Archibald	Luzerne	Pa.	1,500
Arena	Iowa	Wis.	402
Arenzville	Cass	Ill.	150
Argentine	Genesee	Mich.	436
Argyle	Penobscot	Me.	338
Argyle	Washington	N. Y.	3,274
Argyle	Lafayette	Wis.	421
Ariana	Grundy	Ill.	150
Arkadelphia	Clark	Ark.	248
Arkansas	Arkansas	Ark.	584
Arkwright	Chautauque	N. Y.	1,283
Arlington	Van Buren	Mich.	240
Arlington	Bennington	Vt.	1,084
Armada	Macomb	Mich.	1,146
Armagh	Indiana	Pa.	152
Armagh	Mifflin	Pa.	1,742
Armenia	Bradford	Pa.	310
Armstrong	Vanderburg	Ind.	849
Armstrong	Indiana	Pa.	1,185
Armstrong	Lycoming	Pa.	428
Arnheim	Brown	Ohio	61
Arrietta	Hamilton	N. Y.	108
Arrowsick	Lincoln	Me.	311
Ash	Monroe	Mich.	1,229
Ashby	Middlesex	Mass.	1,208
Ashborough	Randolph	N. C.	176
Ashburnham	Worcester	Mass.	1,875
Ash Creek	Oktibbeha	Miss.	280
Ashfield	Franklin	Mass.	1,394
Ashford	Windham	Conn.	1,295
Ashford	Cattaraugus	N. Y.	1,658
Ashford	Fon du Lac	Wis.	628
Ashland	Schuyler	Ill.	498
Ashland	Middlesex	Mass.	1,304
Ashland	Greene	N. Y.	1,290
Ashland	Ashland	Ohio	1,264
Ashley	Pike	Mo.	193
Ashley	Delaware	Ohio	500
Ashtabula	Ashtabula	Ohio	2,177
Ashtabula, T.	Ashtabula	Ohio	821
Ashville	Buncombe	N. C.	b†502
Asshuppan	Dodge	Wis.	1,017
Assyria	Barry	Mich.	336
Aston	Delaware	Pa.	1,558
Astoria	Fulton	Ill.	1,213
Astoria	Clatsop	Oreg'n.	252
Asylum	Bradford	Pa.	820
Athens	Limestone	Ala.	991
Athens	Clark	Ga.	*1,661
Athens	Somerset	Me.	1,460
Athens	Calhoun	Mich.	533
Athens	Gentry	Mo.	*1,428
Athens	Greene	N. Y.	2,986
Athens	Athens	Ohio	2,360
Athens, T	Athens	Ohio	898
Athens	Harrison	Ohio	1,416
Athens, Bor.	Bradford	Pa.	c706
Athens	Bradford	Pa.	2,127
Athens	Crawford	Pa.	928
Athens	Windham	Vt.	359
Athenstown	Gentry	Mo.	*165
Athol	Worcester	Mass.	2,034
Athol	Warren	N. Y.	1,590
Atkinson	Piscataquis	Me.	895
Atkinson	Rockingham	N. H.	600
Atlanta	De Kalb	Ga.	d2,572
Atlantic	Monmouth	N. J.	1,498
Atlas	Genesee	Mich.	1,207
Attica	Fountain	Ind.	1,500
Attica	Lapeer	Mich.	462
Attica	Wyoming	N. Y.	2,363
Attleborough	Bristol	Mass.	4,200
Attleborough	Bucks	Pa.	1,000
Atwater	Portage	Ohio	1,119
Aubbeewawbee	Fulton	Ind.	394
Auburn	Placer	Cal.	1,400
Auburn	Clark	Ill.	504
Auburn	De Kalb	Ind.	260
Auburn	Cumberland	Me.	2,840
Auburn	Worcester	Mass.	879
Auburn	Rockingham	N. H.	810
Auburn	Cayuga	N. Y.	e9,548
Auburn	Crawford	Ohio	951
Auburn	Fairfield	Ohio	626
Auburn	Geauga	Ohio	1,184
Auburn	Tuscarawas	Ohio	1,248
Auburn	Susquehanna	Pa.	1,837
Auburn	Fond du Lac	Wis.	248

a In 1853, 6,000. *b* In 1853, 1,000. *c* In 1853, 1,200. *d* In 1853, 4,000. *e* In 1853, 10,500.

Auburn & vicinity	Sutter	Cal.	1,302
Auglaize	Allen	Ohio	1,344
Auglaize	Paulding	Ohio	304
Augusta	Richmond	Ga	a11,753
Augusta	Des Moines	Iowa	496
Augusta	Bracken	Ky	*588
Augusta	Kennekeck	Me	b8,225
Augusta	Washtenaw	Mich	808
Augusta	Oneida	N. Y.	2,271
Augusta	Carroll	Ohio	1,297
Aurelius	Ingham	Mich	501
Aurelius	Cayuga	N. Y.	2,831
Aurelius	Washington	Ohio	1,251
Aurora	Kane	Ill.	1,895
Aurora	Dearborn	Ind.	c1,954
Aurora	Hancock	Me	217
Aurora, T.	Cayuga	N. Y.	600
Aurora	Erie	N. Y.	3,435
Aurora, T.	Erie	N. Y.	2,000
Aurora	Portage	Ohio	823
Ausable	Clinton	N. Y.	4,492
Austerlitz	Columbia	N. Y.	1,873
Austin	Travis	Texas	d629
Austinburg	Ashtabula	Ohio	1,285
Austintown	Mahoning	Ohio	1,174
Auxsable	Grundy	Ill.	370
Ava	Oneida	N. Y.	1,037
Averill	Essex	Vt.	7
Avery's Gore	Chittenden	Vt.	18
Avery's Gore	Franklin	Vt.	48
Avoca	Steuben	N. Y.	1,574
Avon	Hartford	Conn.	995
Avon	Lake	Ill.	1,010
Avon	Franklin	Me	778
Avon	Oakland	Mich.	1,456
Avon	Livingston	N. Y.	2,809
Avon	Lorain	Ohio	1,782
Avon	Rock	Wis.	579
Ayr	Fulton	Pa.	1,055
Aztalan	Jefferson	Wis.	597
Baileyville	Washington	Me	431
Bainbridge	Schuyler	Ill.	1,159
Bainbridge	Chenango	N. Y.	3,338
Bainbridge	Geauga	Ohio	1,014
Bainbridge	Ross	Ohio	626
Bainbridge	Lancaster	Pa	503
Baker	Martin	Ind	670
Baker	Morgan	Ind	335
Bakersfield	Franklin	Vt.	1,523
Bald Eagle	Clinton	Pa	683
Baldwin	Cumberland	Me	1,100
Baldwin	Allegheny	Pa.	1,610
Baldwinsville	Onondaga	N. Y.	1,200
Ball	Benton	Ark.	*422
Ballston	Saratoga	N. Y.	2,269
Ballston Spa	Saratoga	N. Y.	2,000
Ballsville	Sandusky	Ohio	1,556
Ballum	St. Louis	Mo.	84
Baltimore	Henry	Ind.	553
Baltimore	Baltimore	Md.	e169,054
Baltimore	Barry	Mich.	90
Baltimore	Fairfield	Ohio	492
Baltimore	Windsor	Vt.	124
Baltimore Hundred	Sussex	Del.	2,910
Bancroft	Aroostook	Me.	157
Bango	Elkhart	Ind.	587
Bangor	Penobscot	Me.	14,432
Bangor	Franklin	N. Y.	2,159
Banister	Halifax	Va	1,600
Banks	Carbon	Pa.	1,745
Baraboo	Sauk	Wis.	707
Baraboo T.	Sauk	Wis.	255
Barataria	Jefferson	La.	1,176
Barboursville	Knox	Ky.	184
Bardstown	Nelson	Ky.	2,000
Baresville	Monroe	Ohio	102
Baring	Washington	Me.	380
Barker	Broome	N. Y.	1,456
Barkhamsted	Litchfield	Conn.	1,524
Barkley	Jasper	Ind.	597
Barlow	Washington	Ohio	1,062
Barnard	Piscataquis	Me.	181
Barnard	Windsor	Vt	1,647
Barnesville	Belmont	Ohio	823
Barnegat	Ocean	N. J.	650
Barnet	Jefferson	Pa	579
Barnet	Caledonia	Vt.	2,521
Barnstable	Barnstable	Mass	4,901
Barnstead	Belknap	N. H.	1,848
Barr	Daviess	Ind.	1,802
Barre	Worcester	Mass.	2,976
Barre	Orleans	N. Y.	4,186
Barre	Huntingdon	Pa	1,271
Barre	Washington	Vt.	1,845
Barren	Independence	Ark.	341
Barrington	Cook	Ill.	676
Barrington	Strafford	N. H.	1,752
Barrington	Yates	N. Y.	1,550
Barrington	Bristol	R. I.	795
Barry	Pike	Ill.	400
Barry	Barry	Mich.	478
Barry	Schuylkill	Pa	689
Bart	Lancaster	Pa	2,337
Bartholomew	Desha	Ark	185
Bartholomew	Drew	Ark	394
Bartlet	Coos	N. H.	761
Barton	Gibson	Ind.	491
Barton	Tioga	N. Y.	3,522
Barton	Orleans	Vt	987
Basil	Fairfield	Ohio	200
Batavia	Kane	Ill.	892
Batavia	Branch	Mich.	724
Batavia	Genesee	N. Y.	4,461
Batavia	Clermont	Ohio	2,791
Bates	Crawford	Ark	212
Batesville	Independence	Ark	f848
Bath	Mason	Ill.	336
Bath	Franklin	Ind.	797
Bath	Lincoln	Me.	8,020
Bath	Clinton	Mich.	222
Bath	Grafton	N. H.	1,574
Bath	Steuben	N. Y.	6,185
Bath	Allen	Ohio	2,266
Bath	Greene	Ohio	2,079
Bath	Summit	Ohio	1,400
Batton Rouge	E. Baton Rouge	La.	g3,905
Battle Creek	Calhoun	Mich.	1,897
Battle Creek Village	Calhoun	Mich.	1,064
Baughman	Wayne	Ohio	1,727
Bay	Ottawa	Ohio	359
Bayou	Jackson	Ark	284
Bayou Baltholomew	Jefferson	Ark.	147
Bayou Mason	Chicot	Ark.	404
Bayou Metre	Pulaski	Ark.	342
Bayou Sara	W. Feliciana	La.	†523
Bazetta	Trumbull	Ohio	1,302
Beall	Juniata	Pa	744
Bealsville	Monroe	Ohio	276
Beal's Bar & Dead Man's Bar	Sutter	Cal.	42
Beal's Bar, Forkville	Sutter	Cal.	378
Bean Blossom	Monroe	Ind.	996
Bear Creek	Searcy	Ark	134
Bear Creek	Gallatin	Ill	462
Bear Creek	Jay	Ind.	737
Beardstown	Cass	Ill	1,583
Bearfield	Perry	Ohio	1,710
Beatie	Benton	Ark.	*668
Beaufort	Carteret	N. C.	h1,661
Beaufort	Beaufort	S. C.	*879
Beauvaistown	St. Genevieve	Mo.	*774
Beaver	Jasper	Ind.	224
Beaver	Pulaski	Ind.	168
Beaver	Guernsey	Ohio	1,991
Beaver	Mahoning	Ohio	2,144
Beaver	Pike	Ohio	520
Beaver	Beaver	Pa	2,054
Beaver	Clarion	Pa	2,804
Beaver	Columbia	Pa	672
Beaver	Crawford	Pa	672
Beaver	Jefferson	Pa	662
Beaver	Union	Pa	1,659
Beaver Creek	Greene	Ohio	2,063
Beaver Dam	Dodge	Wis	1,499
Beccaria	Clearfield	Pa	687
Becket	Berkshire	Mass	1,223
Beckmantown	Clinton	N. Y.	3,384
Bedford	Lawrence	Ind.	962
Bedford	Trimble	Ky	285
Bedford	Middlesex	Mass	975
Bedford	Calhoun	Mich.	747
Bedford	Monroe	Mich.	888
Bedford	Hillsborough	N. H	1,905

a In 1853, 12,000. *b* In 1853, 9,500. *c* In 1853, 2,500. *d* In 1853, 3,000. *e* In 1853, 195,000. *f* In 1853, 1,600. *g* In 1853, 4,500. *h* In 1853 2,000.

Bedford	West Chester	N.Y.	3,207	Benton	Hocking	Ohio	933
Bedford	Coshocton	Ohio	1,221	Benton	Ottawa	Ohio	54
Bedford	Cuyahoga	Ohio	1,853	Benton	Paulding	Ohio	61
Bedford	Meigs	Ohio	907	Benton	Luzerne	Pa	849
Bedford, Bor.	Bedford	Pa	1,203	Benton	Lafayette	Wis	2,227
Bedford	Bedford	Pa	1,831	Bentonville	Adams	Ohio	378
Bedington	Washington	Me	147	Benzinger	Elk	Pa	1,268
Bedminster	Somerset	N. J.	1,826	Bergen	Hudson	N. J.	2,758
Bedminster	Bucks	Pa	1,911	Bergen	Genesee	N. Y.	1,897
Bee Branch	Chariton	Mo	406	*Bergholtz*	Niagara	N. Y.	2,000
Beech Creek	Ashley	Ark	211	Berkley	Bristol	Mass	908
Beech Creek	Greene	Ind	1,181	Berkshire	Tioga	N. Y.	1,049
Beech Creek	Clinton	Pa	683	Berkshire	Delaware	Ohio	1,557
Beekman	Duchess	N. Y.	1,386	Berkshire	Franklin	Vt	1,955
Bel Air	Harford	Md	255	Berlin	Hartford	Conn	1,869
Belchertown	Hampshire	Mass	2,680	Berlin	Bureau	Ill	439
Belfast	Waldo	Me	5,051	*Berlin*	Worcester	Md	800
Belfast	Alleghany	N. Y.	1,679	Berlin	Worcester	Mass	866
Belfast	Fulton	Pa	764	Berlin	Ionia	Mich	391
Belgium	Washington	Wis	1,134	Berlin	St. Clair	Mich	533
Belgrade	Kennebeck	Me	1,722	Berlin	Coos	N. H.	173
Belin	Valencia	N. M.	510	Berlin	Rensselaer	N. Y.	2,005
				Berlin	Delaware	Ohio	1,151
Belin de los Chausel	Valencia	N. M.	402	Berlin	Erie	Ohio	1,582
				Berlin	Holmes	Ohio	1,452
Belin de los Gabalores	Valencia	N. M.	36	Berlin	Knox	Ohio	1,156
				Berlin	Mahoning	Ohio	1,376
Belin de los Jarales	Valencia	N. M.	329	Berlin	Somerset	Pa	665
				Berlin	Wayne	Pa	803
Belin de los Publitos	Valencia	N. M.	267	Berlin	Washington	Vt	1,507
Bell	Clearfield	Pa	489	Berlin	Marquette	Wis	1,061
Bell Brook	Greene	Ohio	502	Bernadotte	Fulton	Ill	787
Belle Centre	Logan	Ohio	153	Bernards	Somerset	N. J.	2,267
Bellefontaine	Logan	Ohio	a1,222	Bernardstown	Franklin	Mass	937
Bellefonte	Centre	Pa	1,179	Berne	Albany	N. Y.	3,441
Belleview	Calhoun	Ill	376	Berne	Athens	Ohio	819
Belleview	Jackson	Iowa	1,078	Berne	Fairfield	Ohio	2,656
Belleview, T.	Jackson	Iowa	362	Berne	Berks	Pa	1,734
Belleview	Washington	Mo	1,838	*Berrien*	Berrien	Mich	300
Belleville	St. Clair	Ill	b2,941	Berry	Dane	Wis	234
Belleville	Hendricks	Ind	201	Berwick	York	Me	2,121
Belleville	Essex	N. J.	3,514	Berwick	Adams	Pa	811
Belleville, T.	Essex	N. J.	1,800	Berwick	Columbia	Pa	486
Belleville	Richmond	Ohio	900	Bethany	New Haven	Conn	914
Belleville	Austin	Texas	93	Bethany	Genesee	N. Y.	1,904
Bellevue	Bossier	La	146	Bethany	Butler	Ohio	95
Bellevue	Eaton	Mich	769	Bethany	Wayne	Pa	295
Bellingham	Norfolk	Mass	1,281	Bethel	Posey	Ind	382
Belmont	Waldo	Me	1,486	Bethel	Oxford	Me	2,253
Belmont	Franklin	N. Y.	660	Bethel	Branch	Mich	679
Belmont	Belmont	Ohio	150	Bethel	Shelby	Mo	e*476
Belmont	Lafayette	Wis	325	Bethel	Sullivan	N. Y.	2,087
Beloit	Rock	Wis	c2,732	Bethel	Clark	Ohio	2,646
Belpre	Washington	Ohio	1,622	Bethel	Miami	Ohio	1,656
Belvidere	Boone	Ill	1,940	Bethel	Monroe	Ohio	1,028
Belvidere, T	Boone	Ill	1,003	Bethel	Berks	Pa	1,871
Belvidere	Warren	N. J.	1,001	Bethel	Delaware	Pa	426
Belvidere	Lamoille	Vt.	256	Bethel	Fulton	Pa	1,137
Bembridge	Dubois	Ind	1,491	Bethel	Lebanon	Pa	1,894
Benedicta	Aroostook	Me	325	Bethel	Windsor	Vt	1,730
Benezett	Elk	Pa	240	Bethlehem	Litchfield	Conn	815
Bengal	Clinton	Mich	143	Bethlehem	Cass	Ind	664
Benicia City	Solano	Cal	d480	Bethlehem	Clark	Ind	872
Bennett's Bayou	Fulton	Ark	375	Bethlehem	Grafton	N. H.	950
Bennington	Shiawassee	Mich	601	Bethlehem	Hunterdon	N. J.	2,746
Bennington	Hillsborough	N. H.	541	Bethlehem	Albany	N. Y.	4,102
Bennington	Wyoming	N.Y.	2,406	Bethlehem	Coshocton	Ohio	822
Bennington	Licking	Ohio	1,211	Bethlehem	Stark	Ohio	2,398
Bennington	Morrow	Ohio	1,265	Bethlehem, Bor.	Northampton	Pa	1,516
Bennington	Bennington	Vt	3,923	Bethlehem	Northampton	Pa	2,104
Bensalem	Bucks	Pa	2,239	Beverly	Adams	Ill	914
Benson	Rutland	Vt	1,305	Beverly	Essex	Mass	5,376
Benton	Conway	Ark	595	*Beverly*	Burlington	N. J.	1,000
Benton	Fulton	Ark	227	Biddeford	York	Me	6,095
Benton	Boone	Ill	801	Big Beaver	Beaver	Pa	922
Benton	Lake	Ill	730	Big Beaver	Lawrence	Pa	658
Benton	McHenry	Ill	333	Big Creek	Crawford	Ark	395
Benton	Elkhart	Ind	1,128	Big Creek	Greene	Ark	686
Benton	Monroe	Ind	622	Big Creek	Phillips	Ark	677
Benton	Des Moines	Iowa	650	Big Creek	Kane	Ill	496
Benton	Keokuk	Iowa	432	Big Creek	Henry	Mo	*623
Benton	Eaton	Mich	344	Big Creek	Taney	Mo	378
Benton	Knox	Mo	602	Big Flats	Chemung	N. Y.	1,709
Benton	Newton	Mo	*695	Bigger	Jennings	Ind	714
Benton	Osage	Mo	*1,213	Big Grove	Kendall	Ill	1,343
Benton	Taney	Mo	118	Big Grove	Johnson	Iowa	382
Benton	Grafton	N. H.	478	Big Island	Marion	Ohio	600
Benton	Yates	N. Y.	3,456	Big Lake	Mississippi	Ark	133
Benton	Brown	Ohio	37	Big Lick	Hancock	Ohio	1,008

a In 1853, 2,000. *b* In 1853, 5,000. *c* In 1853, 3,300. *d* In 1853, 2,000. *e* In 1853, 800.

Big North Fork	Fulton	Ark	450
Big Rock	Pulaski	Ark	972
Big Spring	Seneca	Ohio	1,932
Billerica	Middlesex	Mass	1,646
Biloxi	Harrison	Miss	1,700
Bingham	Somerset	Me	752
Bingham	Clinton	Mich	185
Bingham	Potter	Pa	584
Binghampton	Broom	N. Y.	5,000
Bird	Jackson	Ark	286
Birdsall	Alleghany	N. Y.	597
Birmingham	New Haven	Conn	1,800
Birmingham	Van Buren	Iowa	231
Birmingham	Guernsey	Ohio	174
Birmingham	Allegheny	Pa	3,732
Birmingham	Chester	Pa	328
Birmingham	Delaware	Pa	566
Birmingham	Huntingdon	Pa	266
Black	Posey	Ind	2,376
Blackberry	Kane	Ill	725
Black Brook	Clinton	N. Y.	2,525
Black Creek	Mercer	Ohio	490
Black Creek	Luzerne	Pa	425
Black Fish	Crittenden	Ark	300
Blackhawk	Jefferson	Iowa	322
Blacklick	Indiana	Pa	2,043
Black River	Independence	Ark	742
Black River	Lawrence	Ark	663
Black River	Lorain	Ohio	659
Black Rock	Erie	N. Y.	7,508
Blackstone	Worcester	Mass	4,391
Blackwater Village	Johnson	Mo	31
Bladensburg	Prince George	Md	500
Blair	Blair	Pa	991
Blairstown	Warren	N. J.	1,405
Blairsville	Indiana	Pa	1,135
Blakeley	Luzerne	Pa	1,703
Blanchard	Piscataquis	Me	192
Blanchard	Hancock	Ohio	1,051
Blanchard	Hardin	Ohio	252
Blanchard	Putnam	Ohio	1,395
Blandville	Ballard	Ky	*210
Blanford	Hampden	Mass	1,418
Bleeker	Fulton	N. Y.	510
Blendon	Franklin	Ohio	1,303
Blenheim	Schoharie	N. Y.	1,314
Blissfield	Lenawee	Mich	924
Blockly	Philadelphia	Pa	5,916
Bloom	Cook	Ill	785
Bloom	Fairfield	Ohio	2,289
Bloom	Morgan	Ohio	1,346
Bloom	Scioto	Ohio	1,648
Bloom	Seneca	Ohio	1,742
Bloom	Wood	Ohio	658
Bloom	Columbia	Pa	3,122
Bloomfield	Hartford	Conn	1,412
Bloomfield	Greene	Ind	234
Bloomfield	La Grange	Ind	934
Bloomfield	Clinton	Iowa	449
Bloomfield	Davis	Iowa	1,081
Bloomfield, T.	Davis	Iowa	287
Bloomfield	Nelson	Ky	500
Bloomfield	Somerset	Me	1,301
Bloomfield	Oakland	Mich	1,603
Bloomfield	Essex	N. J.	3,385
Bloomfield, T	Essex	N. J.	2,000
Bloomfield	Jackson	Ohio	1,402
Bloomfield	Jefferson	Ohio	184
Bloomfield	Logan	Ohio	671
Bloomfield	Trumbull	Ohio	789
Bloomfield	Crawford	Pa	838
Bloomfield	Perry	Pa	581
Bloomfield	Essex	Vt	244
Bloomfield	Walworth	Wis	879
Bloomingdale	Du Page	Ill	896
Bloomingdale	Van Buren	Mich	160
Bloomingdale	Winnebago	Wis	909
Blooming Grove	Franklin	Ind	1,276
Blooming Grove	Orange	N. Y.	2,184
Blooming Grove	Richland	Ohio	1,430
Blooming Grove	Dane	Wis	291
Bloomington	McLean	Ill	2,560
Bloomington (city)	McLean	Ill	1,594
Bloomington	Monroe	Ind	2,532
Bloomington, T.	Monroe	Ind	1,305
Bloomington	Muscatine	Iowa	199
Bloomington	Buchanan	Mo	*1,295
Bloomington	Macon	Mo	*194
Bloomingville	Hocking	Ohio	57
Bloss	Tioga	Pa	850
Blue	Jackson	Mo	6,458
Blue Ball	Lancaster	Pa	2,009
Blue Bayou	Sevier	Ark	566
Blue Creek	Adams	Ind	425
Blue Hill	Hancock	Me	1,939
Blue Mound	Dane	Wis	334
Blue Mountain	Izard	Ark	337
Blue River	Hancock	Ind	941
Blue River	Henry	Ind	868
Blue River	Johnson	Ind	964
Blue Rock	Muskingum	Ohio	1,476
Bluffton	Wells	Ind	477
Blythe	Marion	Ark	273
Blythe	Caldwell	Mo	*669
Blythe	Schuylkill	Pa	3,778
Boalsburg	Centre	Pa	400
Boardman	Clayton	Iowa	377
Boardman	Mahoning	Ohio	1,026
Bodcan	Hempstead	Ark	548
Bogard	Daviess	Ind	598
Bog Grove	Kendall	Ill	1,343
Boggs	Centre	Pa	1,923
Boggs	Clearfield	Pa	464
Bois Brule	Perry	Mo	*599
Bois d'Arc	Hempstead	Ark	351
Boke's Creek	Logan	Ohio	583
Bolivar	Jefferson	Ark	686
Bolivar	Poinsett	Ark	648
Bolivar	Polk	Mo	500
Bolivar	Alleghany	N. Y.	708
Bolivar	Tuscarawas	Ohio	302
Bolivar	Hardeman	Tenn	a626
Bolivar	Jefferson	Va	1,054
Bolton	Tolland	Conn	600
Bolton	Worcester	Mass	1,263
Bolton	Warren	N. Y.	1,147
Bolton	Chittenden	Vt	602
Bombay	Franklin	N. Y.	1,963
Bonaparte	Van Buren	Iowa	306
Bonham	Fannin	Texas	211
Bonne Homme	St. Louis	Mo	1,842
Bono	Lawrence	Ind	1,001
Bonus	Boone	Ill	874
Boone	Scott	Ark	725
Boone	Union	Ark	643
Boone	Boone	Ill	834
Boone	Cass	Ind	594
Boone	Crawford	Ind	406
Boone	Madison	Ind	299
Boone	Porter	Ind	541
Boone	Warrick	Ind	2,405
Boone	Greene	Mo	*974
Booneville	Warrick	Ind	196
Booneville	Cooper	Mo	2,326
Booneville	Oneida	N. Y.	3,306
Booneville, T	Oneida	N. Y.	700
Booneville	Brazos	Texas	70
Boonsborough	Washington	Md	943
Booth Bay	Lincoln	Me	2,504
Bordentown	Burlington	N. J.	2,725
Boscawen	Merrimack	N. H.	2,063
Boston	Franklin	Ark	338
Boston	Wayne	Ind	959
Boston	Suffolk	Mass	*136,881
Boston	Ionia	Mich	424
Boston	Erie	N. Y.	1,872
Boston	Belmont	Ohio	71
Boston	Summit	Ohio	1,180
Boston Corner	Berkshire	Mass	73
Boulware	Gasconade	Mo	1,050
Bourbonair	Will	Ill	1,719
Bovina	Delaware	N. Y.	1,316
Bow	Merrimack	N. H.	1,055
Bowdoin	Lincoln	Me	1,857
Bowdoinham	Lincoln	Me	2,382
Bower Bank	Piscataquis	Me	173
Bowling Green	Yuba	Cal	126
Bowling Green	Clay	Ind	318
Bowling Green	Warren	Ky	2,500
Bowling Green	Pike	Mo	319
Bowling Green	Licking	Ohio	1,538
Bowling Green	Marion	Ohio	448
Boxborough	Middlesex	Mass	395
Boxford	Essex	Mass	982
Boyle	Gentry	Mo	*336
Boylston	Worcester	Mass	918
Boylston	Oswego	N. Y.	661
Bozrah	New London	Conn	867

a In 1853, 1,200.

Place	County	State	Pop.	Place	County	State	Pop.
Braceville	Grundy	Ill.	93	Bristol	Morgan	Ohio	1,724
Braceville	Trumbull	Ohio	956	Bristol	Trumbull	Ohio	1,124
Bradford	Lee	Ill.	158	Bristol, Bor.	Bucks	Pa.	2,570
Bradford	Penobscot	Me.	1,296	Bristol	Bucks	Pa.	1,810
Bradford	Essex	Mass.	1,328	Bristol	Philadelphia	Pa.	2,230
Bradford	Merrimack	N. H.	1,341	Bristol	Bristol	R. I.	4,616
Bradford	Steuben	N. Y.	2,010	Bristol	Addison	Vt.	1,344
Bradford	Clearfield	Pa.	792	Bristol	Dane	Wis.	467
Bradford	McKean	Pa.	976	Bristol	Kenosha	Wis.	1,125
Bradford	Orange	Vt.	1,723	Broadalbin	Fulton	N. Y.	2,476
Bradford	Rock	Wis.	699	Broadkill Hundred	Sussex	Del.	3,617
Bradley	Penobscot	Me.	796	Broadtop	Bedford	Pa.	632
Bradleysvale	Caledonia	Vt.	107	*Brockport*	Monroe	N. Y.	1,500
Bradshaw	Greene	Ark.	298	Brockville	Steuben	Ind.	86
Brady	Kalamazoo	Mich.	578	Brockway	St. Clair	Mich.	731
Brady	Williams	Ohio	1,128	Broken Straw	Warren	Pa.	634
Brady	Clearfield	Pa.	1,083	Bronson	Branch	Mich.	713
Brady	Huntingdon	Pa.	1,020	Bronson	Huron	Ohio	1,220
Brady's Bend	Armstrong	Pa.	2,325	Brookfield	Fairfield	Conn.	1,359
Braintree	Norfolk	Mass.	2,969	Brookfield	Lasalle	Ill.	252
Braintree	Orange	Vt.	1,228	Brookfield	Worcester	Mass.	1,674
Braintrem	Wyoming	Pa.	836	Brookfield	Eaton	Mich.	255
Branch	Branch	Mich.	1,260	Brookfield	Carroll	N. H.	552
Branch	Schuylkill	Pa.	2,653	Brookfield	Madison	N. Y.	3,585
Branchburg	Somerset	N. J.	1,143	Brookfield	Morgan	Ohio	1,482
Branden	Jackson	Iowa	374	*Brookfield*	Stark	Ohio	500
Brandenburg	Meade	Ky.	700	Brookfield	Trumbull	Ohio	1,451
Brandon	Oakland	Mich.	893	Brookfield	Tioga	Pa.	741
Brandon	Rankin	Miss.	800	Brookfield	Orange	Vt.	1,672
Brandon	Franklin	N. Y.	590	Brookfield	Waukesha	Wis.	1,938
Brandon	Rutland	Vt.	2,835	Brookhaven	Suffolk	N. Y.	8,595
Brandt	Erie	N. Y.	1,028	Brooklin	Ogle	Ill.	522
Brandywine	Hancock	Ind.	837	Brooklin	Hancock	Me.	1,002
Brandywine	Shelby	Ind.	1,759	Brooklin	Hillsborough	N. H.	718
Branford	New Haven	Conn.	1,423	Brookline	Norfolk	Mass.	2,516
Brashear	St. Lawrence	N. Y.	2,582	Brookline	Windham	Vt.	285
Brattelborough	Windham	Vt.	3,816	Brooklyn	Windham	Conn.	1,514
Brawly	Bureau	Ill.	101	Brooklyn	Lee	Ill.	354
Brazeau	Perry	Mo.	*2,718	Brooklyn	McHenry	Ill.	1,006
Breckenridge	Jackson	Ark.	156	Brooklyn	Schuyler	Ill.	644
Brecknock	Berks	Pa.	876	*Brooklyn*	Campbell	Ky.	500
Brecknock	Lancaster	Pa.	1,366	*Brooklyn*	Jackson	Mich.	500
Bremen	Cook	Ill.	250	Brooklyn	Kings	N. Y.	a96,838
Bremen	Lincoln	Me.	891	Brooklyn	Cuyahoga	Ohio	6,375
Brenham	Washington	Texas	500	Brooklyn	Susquehanna	Pa.	1,082
Brentwood	Rockingham	N. H.	923	Brooklyn	Greene	Wis.	531
Breton	Washington	Mo.	1,352	Brooklyn	Marquette	Wis.	505
Brewer	Pike	Ark.	583	Brooklyn	Sauk	Wis.	429
Brewer	Penobscot	Me.	2,628	Brooks	Waldo	Me.	1,021
Brewster	Barnstable	Mass.	1,525	Brook's Grove	McLean	Ill.	135
Brick	Ocean	N. J.	1,558	Brookville	Ogle	Ill.	479
Bricksville	Cuyahoga	Ohio	1,116	Brookville	Franklin	Ind.	3,466
Bridesburgh	Philadelphia	Pa.	915	Brookville, T.	Franklin	Ind.	1,177
Bridgeport	Fairfield	Conn.	7,560	Brookville	Hancock	Me.	1,333
Bridgeport	Jackson	Iowa	42	Brookville	Jefferson	Pa.	763
Bridgeport	Saginaw	Mich.	374	*Brooksville*	Bracken	Ky.	500
Bridgeport	Fayette	Pa.	1,292	Broom	Schoharie	N. Y.	2,268
Bridgeport	Montgomery	Pa.	572	Brother's Valley	Somerset	Pa.	1,430
Bridgeton	Cumberland	Me.	2,710	Brown	Madison	Ark.	648
Bridgeton	Cumberland	N. J.	2,446	Brown	Union	Ark.	65
Bridgeville	Muskingum	Ohio	22	Brown	Hancock	Ind.	878
Bridgewater	Plymouth	Mass.	2,790	Brown	Hendricks	Ind.	1,469
Bridgewater	Washtenaw	Mich.	1,147	Brown	Martin	Ind.	631
Bridgewater	Grafton	N. H.	667	Brown	Montgomery	Ind.	1,957
Bridgewater	Somerset	N. J.	4,070	Brown	Morgan	Ind.	1,217
Bridgewater	Oneida	N. Y.	1,315	Brown	Ripley	Ind.	1,987
Bridgewater	Williams	Ohio	493	Brown	Washington	Ind.	1,636
Bridgewater	Susquehanna	Pa.	1,548	*Brown*	Athens	Ohio	2,360
Bridgewater	Windsor	Vt.	1,311	Brown	Carroll	Ohio	2,099
Bridport	Addison	Vt.	1,393	Brown	Darke	Ohio	684
Brier Creek	Columbia	Pa.	1,091	Brown	Delaware	Ohio	1,176
Brighton	Somerset	Me.	748	Brown	Franklin	Ohio	681
Brighton	Middlesex	Mass.	2,356	Brown	Knox	Ohio	1,535
Brighton	Livingston	Mich.	1,015	Brown	Miami	Ohio	1,397
Brighton, T.	Livingston	Mich.	500	Brown	Paulding	Ohio	368
Brighton	Monroe	N. Y.	3,117	Brown	Lycoming	Pa.	552
Brighton	Lorain	Ohio	669	Brown	Mifflin	Pa.	1,015
Brighton	Beaver	Pa.	1,111	Brownfield	Oxford	Me.	1,320
Brighton, T.	Beaver	Pa.	900	Brownhelm	Lorain	Ohio	1,080
Brighton	Essex	Vt.	193	Browning	Schuyler	Ill.	873
Brighton	Kenosha	Wis.	880	Brownington	Orleans	Vt.	613
Brimfield	Peoria	Ill.	350	Brownsburg	Hendricks	Ind.	132
Brimfield	Hampden	Mass.	1,420	Brownstown	Jackson	Ind.	1,732
Brimfield	Portage	Ohio	1,015	Brownstown	Wayne	Mich.	1,025
Bristol	Hartford	Conn.	2,884	Brownsville	Union	Ind.	1,443
Bristol	Kendall	Ill.	794	Brownsville, T.	Union	Ind.	293
Bristol	Lincoln	Me.	2,931	Brownsville	Jefferson	N. Y.	4,282
Bristol	Grafton	N. H.	1,103	Brownsville	Brown	Ohio	38
Bristol	Ontario	N. Y.	1,733	Brownsville	Licking	Ohio	480

a In 1853, 125,000.

Town	County	State	Pop.	Town	County	State	Pop.
Brownsville	Ross	Ohio	218	Burritt	Winnebago	Ill	591
Brownsville	Fayette	Pa	a2,369	Burr Oak	St. Joseph	Mich	658
Brownsville	Haywood	Tenn	971	Burton	Adams	Ill	1,226
Brownsville	Cameron	Texas	4,500	Burton	Cattaraugus	N. Y.	1,037
Brownville	Piscataquis	Me	787	Burton	Geauga	Ohio	1,063
Bruce	Lasalle	Ill	378	Burton	Pike	Ohio	639
Bruce	Macomb	Mich	1,555	Bushkill	Northampton	Pa	1,839
Brunersburg	Defiance	Ohio	169	Bushnell	Montcalm	Mich	66
Brunswick	Cumberland	Me	4,977	Bushwick	Kings	N. Y.	3,739
Brunswick	Chariton	Mo	2,116	Busti	Chautauque	N. Y.	1,990
Brunswick, T	Chariton	Mo	363	Butler	Winnebago	Ill	644
Brunswick	Rensselaer	N. Y.	3,146	Butler	De Kalb	Ind	651
Brunswick	Medina	Ohio	1,417	Butler	Franklin	Ind	1,037
Brunswick	Essex	Vt	119	Butler	Miami	Ind	840
Brush Creek	Washington	Ark	589	Butler	Jackson	Iowa	418
Brush Creek	Highland	Ohio	1,515	Butler	Branch	Mich	611
Brush Creek	Jefferson	Ohio	1,121	Butler	Wayne	N. Y.	2,272
Brush Creek	Muskingum	Ohio	1,392	Butler	Columbiana	Ohio	1,692
Brush Creek	Scioto	Ohio	650	Butler	Darke	Ohio	1,446
Brush Creek	Fulton	Pa	375	Butler	Knox	Ohio	763
Brush Run	Iowa	Iowa	113	Butler	Mercer	Ohio	220
Brush Valley	Indiana	Pa	1,481	Butler	Montgomery	Ohio	1,975
Brutus	Cayuga	N. Y.	3,046	Butler	Richland	Ohio	1,139
Buck	Hardin	Ohio	462	Butler	Adams	Pa	1,269
Buck	Tuscarawas	Ohio	1,326	Butler	Butler	Pa	d1,148
Buck	Luzerne	Pa	539	Butler	Luzerne	Pa	725
Buck Creek	Hancock	Ind	420	Butler	Schuylkill	Pa	400
Buckeye	Stephenson	Ill	1,271	Butlerville	Warren	Ohio	208
Buckhart	Fulton	Ill	1,115	Butternuts	Otsego	N. Y.	1,928
Buckingham	Bucks	Pa	2,767	Buxton	York	Me	2,995
Buckingham	Wayne	Pa	592	Byberry	Philadelphia	Pa	1,130
Buckland	Franklin	Mass	1,056	Byesville	Guernsey	Ohio	35
Buckle's Grove	McLean	Ill	755	Byram	Sussex	N. J.	1,340
Bucksfield	Oxford	Me	1,657	Byrd	Brown	Ohio	2,642
Buckskin	Ross	Ohio	2,104	Byron	McHenry	Ill	763
Bucksport	Hancock	Me	3,381	Byron	Ogle	Ill	644
Bucyrus	Crawford	Ohio	2,315	Byron	Oxford	Me	296
Buena Vista	Marion	Ga	530	Byron	Kent	Mich	309
Buena Vista	Schuyler	Ill	848	Byron	Genesee	N. Y.	1,566
Buena Vista	Saginaw	Mich	251	Byron	Fond du Lac	Wis	835
Buena Vista	Fayette	Ohio	107	Cabot	Caledonia	Vt	1,356
Buffalo	Ogle	Ill	1,134	Cache	Jackson	Ark	231
Buffalo	Morgan	Mo	*873	Cache	Monroe	Ark	526
Buffalo	Pike	Mo	3,163	Cache	St. Francis	Ark	287
Buffalo	Erie	N. Y.	b42,261	Cache Creek	Yolo	Cal	275
Buffalo	Guernsey	Ohio	1,053	Caddo	Clark	Ark	1,042
Buffalo	Butler	Pa	2,751	Caddo	Montgomery	Ark	286
Buffalo	Perry	Pa	782	Cadiz	Harrison	Ohio	2,453
Buffalo	Union	Pa	1,346	Cadiz, T	Harrison	Ohio	e1,144
Buffalo	Washington	Pa	1,210	Cadiz	Greene	Wis	459
Buffalo	Putnam	Va	400	Cadron	Conway	Ark	252
Buffalo	Henderson	Texas	45	Cadron	Van Buren	Ark	345
Buffalo	Marquette	Wis	565	Caernarvon	Berks	Pa	977
Buffalo Lick	Chariton	Mo	856	Caernarvon	Lancaster	Pa	1,551
Buffalo Fork	Marion	Ark	214	Caesar Creek	Dearborn	Ind	497
Bullskin	Fayette	Pa	1,428	Caesar Creek	Greene	Ohio	1,870
Buncombe	Independence	Ark	212	Cain	Fountain	Ind	1,008
Bunker Hill	Macoupin	Ill	166	Cairo	Greene	N. Y.	2,831
Bunker Hill	Ingham	Mich	374	Cairo City	Alexander	Ill	242
Burboise	Gasconade	Mo	504	Calais	Washington	Me	4,749
Bureau	Bureau	Ill	167	Calais	Monroe	Ohio	96
Burke	Franklin	N. Y.	2,477	Calais	Washington	Vt	1,410
Burke	Caledonia	Vt	1,103	Calamus	Dodge	Wis	413
Burkesville	Cumberland	Ky	†369	Caldwell	Appanoose	Iowa	303
Burlington	Hartford	Conn	1,161	Caldwell	Essex	N. J.	2,377
Burlington	Kane	Ill	664	Caldwell	Warren	N. Y.	752
Burlington	Carroll	Ind	846	Caledonia	Boone	Ill	715
Burlington, T	Carroll	Ind	164	Caledonia	Pulaski	Ill	284
Burlington (city)	Des Moines	Iowa	4,082	Caledonia	Kent	Mich	99
Burlington	Des Moines	Iowa	c1,219	Caledonia	Shiawassee	Mich	500
Burlington	Boone	Ky	*252	Caledonia	Livingston	N. Y.	1,804
Burlington	Penobscot	Me	481	Caledonia	Racine	Wis	1,090
Burlington	Middlesex	Mass	545	Calf Creek	Searcy	Ark	169
Burlington	Calhoun	Mich	811	*Calhoun*	Gordon	Ga	400
Burlington (city)	Burlington	N. J.	4,536	California	Stark	Ind	158
Burlington	Burlington	N. J.	863	California	Branch	Mich	473
Burlington	Otsego	N. Y.	1,835	Callicoon	Sullivan	N. Y.	1,981
Burlington	Licking	Ohio	1,389	Calumet	Pike	Mo	3,369
Burlington	Bradford	Pa	1,927	Calumet	Fond du Lac	Wis	1,764
Burlington	Chittenden	Vt	6,110	Calvin	Cass	Mich	624
Burlington, T	Chittenden	Vt	1,475	Camanche	Clinton	Iowa	454
Burlington	Racine	Wis	1,629	Cambria	Hillsdale	Mich	716
Burnett	Dodge	Wis	726	Cambria	Niagara	N. Y.	2,366
Burnham	Waldo	Me	784	Cambria	Cambria	Pa	1,400
Burns	Shiawassee	Mich	717	Cambridge	Wayne	Ind	1,217
Burns	Alleghany	N. Y.	943	Cambridge	Somerset	Me	487
Burnside	Clearfield	Pa	1,046	Cambridge	Middlesex	Mass	15,215
Burrillville	Providence	R. I.	3,538	Cambridge	Lenawee	Mich	973

a In 1853, 4,500. *b* In 1853, 60,000. *c* In 1854, 7,000. *d* In 1853, 1,500. *e* In 1853, 1,500.

Cambridge	Coos	N. H.	33
Cambridge	Washington	N. Y.	2,593
Cambridge	Guernsey	Ohio	2,488
Cambridge, T	Guernsey	Ohio	1,041
Cambridge	Lamoille	Vt.	1,849
Cambridge	Dane	Wis.	300
Camden	Kent	Del.	400
Camden	Wilcox	Ala	800
Camden	Ouachita	Ark.	894
Camden	Schuyler	Ill	426
Camden	Carroll	Ind	168
Camden	Jay	Ind	300
Camden	Ray	Mo	500
Camden	Waldo	Me	4,005
Camden	Hillsdale	Mich	594
Camden (city)	Camden	N. J.	9,479
Camden	Madison	Miss	215
Camden	Oneida	N. Y.	2,820
Camden	Lorain	Ohio	1,025
Camden	Kershaw	S. C.	1,133
Camden	Benton	Tenn	176
Cameron	Steuben	N. Y.	1,701
Camillus	Onondaga	N. Y.	3,105
Campbell	Searcy	Ark	684
Campbell	Jennings	Ind	731
Campbell	Warrick	Ind	1,157
Campbell	Greene	Mo	*1,820
Campbell	Taney	Mo	252
Campbell	Steuben	N. Y.	1,175
Campbellsville	Taylor	Ky	436
Campbellsville	Giles	Tenn	135
Campbellton	Campbell	Ga	146
Camp Creek	Pike	Ohio	389
Camp Point	Adams	Ill	588
Campton	Kane	Ill	875
Campton,	Grafton	N. H.	1,439
Canaan	Litchfield	Conn.	2,627
Canaan	Somerset	Me	1,696
Canaan	Gasconade	Mo	666
Canaan	Grafton	N. H.	1,682
Canaan	Columbia	N. Y.	1,941
Canaan	Athens	Ohio	1,142
Canaan	Madison	Ohio	685
Canaan	Morrow	Ohio	1,223
Canaan	Wayne	Ohio	1,922
Canaan	Wayne	Pa	1,938
Canaan	Essex	Vt	471
Canadian	Mississippi	Ark	353
Canadice	Ontario	N. Y.	1,075
Canajoharie	Montgomery	N. Y.	4,097
Canajoharie, T	Montgomery	N. Y.	2,000
Canal	Venango	Pa	870
Canal Winchester	Fairfield	Ohio	350
Canandaigua	Ontario	N. Y.	6,143
Canandaigua, T	Ontario	N. Y.	3,500
Candia	Rockingham	N. H.	1,482
Candor	Tioga	N. Y.	3,433
Canastota	Madison	N. Y.	1,000
Caneadea	Alleghany	N. Y.	1,477
Cane Creek	Gallatin	Ill	756
Cane Hill	Washington	Ark	1,082
Caneville	Cane	Ill	592
Canfield	Mahoning	Ohio	1,463
Canfield, T	Mahoning	Ohio	527
Canisteo	Steuben	N. Y.	2,030
Cannelton	Perry	Ind	2,500
Cannon	Kent	Mich	696
Cannon Creek	El Dorado	Cal	252
Canoe	Indiana	Pa	888
Canonsburg	Washington	Pa	627
Canterbury	Windham	Conn.	1,669
Canterbury	Merrimack	N. H.	1,614
Canton	Hartford	Conn.	1,986
Canton	Fulton	Ill	1,011
Canton	Jackson	Iowa	168
Canton	Oxford	Me	926
Canton	Norfolk	Mass	2,598
Canton	Wayne	Mich	1,333
Canton	Lewis	Mo	389
Canton	St. Lawrence	N. Y.	4,685
Canton, T	St. Lawrence	N. Y.	1,000
Canton	Stark	Ohio	4,322
Canton, T	Stark	Ohio	a2,603
Canton	Bradford	Pa	1,746
Canton	Washington	Pa	1,281
Canton City	Fulton	Ill	1,568
Cantwell's Bridge Hundred	New Castle	Del	501
Canuse	Hempstead	Ark	997

Cape Cinque Homme	Perry	Mo	*2,927
Cape Elizabeth	Cumberland	Me	2,082
Cape Island	Cape May	N. J.	600
Cape May C. H.	Cape May	N. J.	500
Cape Vincent	Jefferson	N. Y.	3,044
Carbondale, Bor	Luzerne	Pa	b4,945
Carbondale	Luzerne	Pa	459
Cardington	Morrow	Ohio	1,398
Cardington, T	Morrow	Ohio	c292
Carey	Will	Ill	214
Carlisle	Clinton	Ill	289
Carlisle	Nicholas	Ky	500
Carlisle	Middlesex	Mass	632
Carlisle	Schoharie	N. Y.	1,817
Carlisle	Brown	Ohio	114
Carlisle	Lorain	Ohio	1,512
Carlisle	Monroe	Ohio	114
Carlisle	Cumberland	Pa	4,581
Carlinville	Macoupin	Ill	433
Carlton	Barry	Mich	272
Carlton	Orleans	N. Y.	2,809
Carmel	Penobscot	Me	1,225
Carmel	Eaton	Mich	567
Carmel	Putnam	N. Y.	2,442
Caroline	Prairie	Ark	581
Caroline	Tompkins	N. Y.	2,537
Carondelet	St. Louis	Mo	3,354
Carondelet, T	St. Louis	Mo	1,201
Carothers	Clay	Ind	296
Carr	Jackson	Ind	1,001
Carroll	Ouachita	Ark	373
Carroll	Carroll	Ill	546
Carroll	Penobscot	Me	401
Carroll	Platte	Mo	2,216
Carroll	Coos	N. H.	396
Carroll	Chautauque	N. Y.	1,833
Carroll	Ottawa	Ohio	403
Carroll	Cambria	Pa	1,129
Carroll	Perry	Pa	1,169
Carroll	Washington	Pa	1,469
Carroll	York	Pa	807
Carrollton	Pickens	Ala	d394
Carrollton	Carroll	Ark	923
Carrollton	Carroll	Ga	750
Carrollton	Greene	Ill	e787
Carrollton	Carroll	Ind	694
Carrollton	Jefferson	La	1,470
Carrollton	Carroll	Miss	500
Carrollton	Carroll	Ky	1,105
Carrollton	Cattaraugus	N. Y.	515
Carrollton	Montgomery	Ohio	226
Carrollville	Tishemingo	Miss	150
Carryall	Paulding	Ohio	471
Carter	Ashley	Ark	82
Carter	Spencer	Ind	928
Carthage	Hancock	Ill	400
Carthage	Franklin	Me	420
Carthage	Athens	Ohio	1,087
Carthage	Leake	Miss	965
Carver	Plymouth	Mass	1,186
Casa Cabaroda	Valencia	N. M.	553
Cascade	Kent	Mich	358
Cascade	Lycoming	Pa	419
Cascade	Sheboygan	Wis	400
Casco	Cumberland	Me	1,046
Casco	St. Clair	Mich	134
Casey	De Kalb	Ga	797
Cass	Fulton	Ill	643
Cass	Clay	Ind	466
Cass	Greene	Ind	794
Cass	La Porte	Ind	337
Cass	Pulaski	Ind	84
Cass	Greene	Mo	*959
Cass	Taney	Mo	294
Cass	Hancock	Ohio	621
Cass	Richland	Ohio	1,431
Cass	Huntingdon	Pa	714
Cass	Schuylkill	Pa	4,115
Cassopolis	Cass	Mich	f379
Casstown	Miami	Ohio	395
Cassville	Barry	Mo	400
Castalia	Erie	Ohio	500
Castile	Wyoming	N. Y.	2,246
Castine	Hancock	Me	1,260
Castleton	Barry	Mich	324
Castleton	Richmond	N. Y.	5,389
Castleton	Rutland	Vt.	3,016
Castor	Stoddard	Mo	2,084

a In 1853, 3,000. *b* In 1853, 7,000. *c* In 1853, 500. *d* In 1853, 600. *e* In 1853, 1,500. *f* In 1853, 500.

Castroville	Medina	Texas..	366
Catasauqua	Lee	Pa	1,500
Catawissa	Columbia	Pa	1,143
Catharine	Chemung	N. Y.	3,096
Catharine	Blair	Pa	889
Catlin	Chemung	N. Y	1,474
Cato	Cayuga	N. Y.	2,247
Caton	Steuben	N. Y.	1,214
Catskill	Greene	N. Y.	5,454
Cattaraugus	Cattaraugus	N. Y.	1,633
Cavendish	Windsor	Vt	1,576
Cave Springs	Floyd	Ga	300
Cavetown	Washington	Md	167
Cayuga	Hinds	Miss	161
Cayuta	Chemung	N. Y.	1,035
Cazenovia	Madison	N. Y.	4,812
Cecil	Washington	Pa	1,008
Cedar	Clark	Ark	218
Cedar	Allen	Ind	814
Cedar	Lake	Ind	501
Cedar	Jefferson	Iowa	630
Cedar	Johnson	Iowa	145
Cedar	Muscatine	Iowa	291
Cedar	Van Buren	Iowa	608
Cedarburg	Washington	Wis	1,226
Cedar Creek	Madison	Ark	206
Cedar Creek Hund	Sussex	Del	2,326
Celina	Mercer	Ohio	222
Center	McHenry	Ill	1,139
Central Village	Windham	Conn	1,800
Centre	Polk	Ark	296
Centre	Cherokee	Ala	250
Centre	Bureau	Ill	383
Centre	Fulton	Ill	1,025
Centre	Dearborn	Ind	662
Centre	Delaware	Ind	541
Centre	Grant	Ind	1,991
Centre	Greene	Ind	1,314
Centre	Hancock	Ind	815
Centre	Hendricks	Ind	1,452
Centre	Howard	Ind	954
Centre	Lake	Ind	966
Centre	La Porte	Ind	853
Centre	Marion	Ind	9,774
Centre	Porter	Ind	1,014
Centre	Rush	Ind	1,252
Centre	St. Joseph	Ind	477
Centre	Stark	Ind	62
Centre	Union	Ind	1,674
Centre	Vanderburg	Ind	998
Centre	Wayne	Ind	2,822
Centre, No. 1	Appanoose	Iowa	473
Centre, No. 2	Appanoose	Iowa	183
Centre, No. 3	Appanoose	Iowa	416
Centre, No. 4	Appanoose	Iowa	65
Centre	Cedar	Iowa	1,233
Centre	Henry	Iowa	837
Centre	Buchanan	Mo	*1,092
Centre	Knox	Mo	736
Centre	St. Louis	Mo	1,133
Centre	Carroll	Ohio	1,190
Centre	Columbiana	Ohio	2,818
Centre	Guernsey	Ohio	1,066
Centre	Mercer	Ohio	491
Centre	Monroe	Ohio	2,943
Centre	Morgan	Ohio	1,439
Centre	Williams	Ohio	881
Centre	Wood	Ohio	357
Centre	Berks	Pa	1,346
Centre	Butler	Pa	1,495
Centre	Columbia	Pa	1,019
Centre	Greene	Pa	1,733
Centre	Indiana	Pa	1,193
Centre	Perry	Pa	944
Centre	Union	Pa	2,171
Centre	Lafayette	Wis	601
Centre	Rock	Wis	625
Centre Harbor	Belknap	N. H.	543
Centreville	Wayne	Ind	920
Centreville	Washington	Me	178
Centreville	Alleghany	N. Y.	1,441
Centreville	Butler	Pa	278
Centreville	Manitoowoc	Wis	215
Centreville and vicinity	El Dorado	Cal	84
Ceres	McKean	Pa	668
Ceresco	Fond du Lac	Wis	356
Cessna	Hardin	Ohio	303
Chagrin Falls	Cuyahoga	Ohio	1,250

Chalk Bluff	Greene	Ark	81
Chambersburg	Montgomery	Ohio	134
Chambersburg	Franklin	Pa	a3,335
Champagne	Dallas	Ark	168
Champagnolle	Ouachita	Ark	345
Champion	Jefferson	N. Y.	2,085
Champion	Trumbull	Ohio	1,070
Champlain	Clinton	N. Y.	5,067
Chanceford	York	Pa	1,614
Chandlersville	Muskingum	Ohio	203
Channahon	Will	Ill	617
Chapel Hill	Washington	Texas	600
Chaplin	Windham	Conn	796
Chapman	Clinton	Pa	542
Chapman	Union	Pa	1,501
Chardon	Geauga	Ohio	1,621
Chardon T.	Geauga	Ohio	b546
Chariton	Appanoose	Iowa	212
Chariton	Chariton	Mo	566
Chariton	Randolph	Mo	*924
Charlemont	Franklin	Mass	1,173
Charleston	Coles	Ill	2,262
Charleston T.	Coles	Ill	849
Charleston	Clark	Ind	3,902
Charleston	Lee	Iowa	500
Charleston	Penobscot	Me	1,283
Charleston	Kalamazoo	Mich	846
Charleston	Montgomery	N. Y.	2,216
Charleston	Tioga	Pa	1,470
Charleston	Washington	R. I.	994
Charleston City	Charleston	S. C.	42,985
Charleston	Orleans	Vt	1,008
Charleston	Kanawha	Va	1,050
Charlestown	Middlesex	Mass	17,216
Charlestown	Sullivan	N. H.	1,644
Charlestown	Portage	Ohio	809
Charlestown	Chester	Pa	979
Charlestown	Jefferson	Va	1,507
Charlotte	Washington	Me	718
Charlotte	Mecklenburg	N. C.	2,500
Charlotte	Chautauque	N. Y.	1,718
Charlotte	Chittenden	Vt	1,634
Charlottesville	Albemarle	Va	c†1,890
Charlton	Worcester	Mass	2,015
Charlton	Saratoga	N. Y.	1,902
Chartiers	Washington	Pa	1,677
Chateaugay	Franklin	N. Y	3,728
Chatfield	Crawford	Ohio	1,351
Chatham	Middlesex	Conn	1,525
Chatham	Barnstable	Mass	2,439
Chatham	Carroll	N. H.	516
Chatham	Morris	N. J.	2,469
Chatham	Columbia	N. Y.	3,839
Chatham	Licking	Ohio	208
Chatham	Medina	Ohio	1,167
Chatham	Tioga	Pa	1,208
Chattanooga	Hamilton	Tenn	3,500
Chautauque	Chautauque	N. Y.	2,622
Chazy	Clinton	N. Y.	4,324
Cheektowaga	Erie	N. Y.	3,042
Chelmsford	Middlesex	Mass	2,097
Chelsea	Suffolk	Mass	6,701
Chelsea	Orange	Vt	1,958
Cheltenham	Montgomery	Pa	1,292
Chemung	McHenry	Ill	928
Chemung	Chemung	N. Y.	2,673
Chenango	Broom	N. Y.	8,734
Cheney's Grove	McLain	Ill	251
Chepacket	Providence	R. I.	900
Chequest	Van Buren	Iowa	708
Cheraw	Chesterfield	S. C.	900
Cherry	Butler	Pa	970
Cherry	Sullivan	Pa	1,605
Cherry Creek	Chautauque	N. Y.	1,311
Cherryfield	Washington	Me	1,648
Cherry Grove	Carroll	Ill	261
Cherry Grove	Warren	Pa	63
Cherry Ridge	Wayne	Pa	614
Cherry Tree	Venango	Pa	930
Cherry Valley	Otsego	N. Y.	4,186
Cherry Valley	Ashtabula	Ohio	839
Chesapeake City	Cecil	Md	423
Cheshire	New Haven	Conn	1,625
Cheshire	Berkshire	Mass	1,298
Cheshire	Gallia	Ohio	1,410
Chesnut Hill	Monroe	Pa	1,029
Chest	Clearfield	Pa	397
Chester	Desha	Ark	189
Chester	Middlesex	Conn	992

a In 1853, 4,500. *b* In 1853, 1,000. *c* In 1853, 2,600.

Chester	Randolph	Ill	a985	Clark	Perry	Ind	673
Chester	Wabash	Ind	1,541	Clark	Chariton	Mo	717
Chester	Wells	Ind	510	Clark	Brown	Ohio	1,450
Chester	Penobscot	Me	340	Clark	Clinton	Ohio	1,654
Chester	Hampden	Mass	1,521	Clark	Coshocton	Ohio	833
Chester	Eaton	Mich	380	Clarksburgh	Berkshire	Mass	384
Chester	Ottawa	Mich	216	*Clarksburg*	Harrison	Va	1,200
Chester	Rockingham	N. H.	1,301	Clarksfield	Huron	Ohio	1,454
Chester	Burlington	N. J.	3,601	Clarkson	Monroe	N. Y.	4,555
Chester	Morris	N. J.	1,334	Clarkstown	Rockland	N. Y.	3,111
Chester	Orange	N. Y.	1,641	Clarksville	Johnson	Ark	398
Chester	Warren	N. Y.	1,850	Clarksville	Habersham	Ga	502
Chester	Clinton	Ohio	1,600	Clarksville	Pike	Mo	300
Chester	Geauga	Ohio	1,103	Clarksville	Coos	N. H.	187
Chester	Meigs	Ohio	1,598	Clarksville	Alleghany	N. Y.	668
Chester, T	Meigs	Ohio	189	*Clarksville*	Montgomery	Tenn	3,000
Chester	Morrow	Ohio	1,620	*Clarksville*	Mecklenburg	Va	1,000
Chester	Wayne	Ohio	2,235	Clay	Bradey	Ark	452
Chester, Bor	Delaware	Pa	1,667	Clay	Bartholomew	Ind	612
Chester	Delaware	Pa	1,553	Clay	Carroll	Ind	618
Chester	Chester	S. C.	982	Clay	Cass	Ind	642
Chester	Windsor	Vt	2,001	Clay	Dearborn	Ind	1,275
Chester	Dodge	Wis	829	Clay	Decatur	Ind	1,838
Chesterfield	Macoupin	Ill	37	Clay	Hamilton	Ind	1,106
Chesterfield	Hampshire	Mass	1,014	Clay	Hendricks	Ind	910
Chesterfield	Macomb	Mich	1,002	Clay	Howard	Ind	413
Chesterfield	Cheshire	N. H.	1,680	Clay	Kosciusko	Ind	975
Chesterfield	Burlington	N. J.	1,789	Clay	La Grange	Ind	464
Chesterfield	Essex	N. Y.	4,171	Clay	Miami	Ind	588
Chesterfield	Fulton	Ohio	539	Clay	Morgan	Ind	1,213
Chesterville	Franklin	Me	1,142	Clay	Owen	Ind	1,085
Chesterville	Morrow	Ohio	407	Clay	Pike	Ind	672
Chicago	Cook	Ill	b29,963	Clay	St. Joseph	Ind	659
Chichester	Merrimack	N. H.	997	Clay	Wayne	Ind	1,052
Chickalah	Yell	Ark	165	Clay	Jones	Iowa	445
Chickasawba	Mississippi	Ark	189	Clay	St. Clair	Mich	822
Chicktawaga	Erie	N. Y.	3,042	Clay	Dunklin	Mo	510
Chicopee	Hampden	Mass	8,291	Clay	Lafayette	Mo	1,732
Chili	Monroe	N. Y.	2,247	Clay	Onondaga	N. Y.	3,402
Chillicothe	Peoria	Ill	600	Clay	Auglaize	Ohio	840
Chillicothe	Ross	Ohio	7,100	Clay	Gallia	Ohio	949
Chillisquaque	Northumberland	Pa	1,344	Clay	Highland	Ohio	1,108
Chilmark	Dukes	Mass	747	Clay	Knox	Ohio	1,240
China	Lee	Ill	688	Clay	Montgomery	Ohio	1,905
China	Kennebeck	Me	2,769	Clay	Muskingum	Ohio	653
China	St. Clair	Mich	1,037	Clay	Ottawa	Ohio	293
China	Wyoming	N. Y.	1,961	Clay	Scioto	Ohio	872
Chippewa	Wayne	Ohio	2,637	Clay	Tuscarawas	Ohio	1,260
Chippewa	Beaver	Pa	908	Clay	Huntingdon	Pa	695
Chittenango	Madison	N. Y.	1,200	Claysville	Guernsey	Ohio	205
Chittenden	Rutland	Vt	675	Claysville	Washington	Pa	275
Chittenham	Montgomery	Pa	1,292	*Clayton*	Barbour	Ala	400
Choctaw City	Washington	Ala	100	Clayton	Adams	Ill	781
Choctaw Corner	Clarke	Ala	250	Clayton	Genesee	Mich	418
Choconut	Susquehanna	Pa	709	Clayton	Jefferson	N. Y.	4,191
Christ-Church	Charleston	S. C.	3,322	Clayton	Miami	Ohio	76
Christian	Independence	Ark	582	Clayton	Perry	Ohio	1,594
Christiana	Dane	Wis	1,054	Clayton	Winnebago	Wis	402
Christiana Hund'd	New Castle	Del	4,831	Claverack	Columbia	N. Y.	3,208
Christiansburg	Montgomery	Va	†532	Clear Creek	Sevier	Ark	233
Cibolletta	Valencia	N. M.	605	Clear Creek	Washington	Ark	677
Cicero	Tipton	Ind	890	Clear Creek	Clark	Ill	720
Cicero	Onondaga	N. Y.	2,989	Clear Creek	Cumberland	Ill	278
Cincinnati	Hamilton	Ohio	c115,435	Clear Creek	Monroe	Ind	946
Cincinnati and vicinity	El Dorado	Cal	168	Clear Creek	Johnson	Iowa	166
				Clear Creek	Keokuk	Iowa	242
Cincinnatus	Cortlandt	N. Y.	1,206	Clear Creek	Ashland	Ohio	1,205
Circleville	Pickaway	Ohio	3,842	Clear Creek	Fairfield	Ohio	1,739
Circleville, T	Pickaway	Ohio	d3,411	Clear Creek	Warren	Ohio	2,770
Citronelle	Mobile	Ala	250	Clearfield	Butler	Pa	1,924
Claiborne	Union	Ohio	919	Clearfield	Cambria	Pa	802
Clamo	Greene	Wis	715	Clearfield	Clearfield	Pa	503
Clara	Potter	Pa	89	Clear Lake	Steuben	Ind	191
Claremont	Sullivan	N. H.	3,606	Clear Spring	Hot Springs	Ark	*588
Clarence	Calhoun	Mich	485	Clear Spring	La Grange	Ind	674
Clarence	Erie	N. Y.	2,727	Cleaveland	Elkhart	Ind	419
Clarendon	Calhoun	Mich	669	Clermont	Columbia	N. Y.	1,130
Clarendon	Orleans	N. Y.	1,809	Cleveland	Cuyahoga	Ohio	f17,034
Clarendon	Rutland	Vt	1,477	*Cleveland*	Bradley	Tenn	500
Claridon	Geauga	Ohio	1,009	Cleves	Hamilton	Ohio	251
Claridon	Marion	Ohio	1,343	Clifford	Susquehanna	Pa	1,648
Clarington	Monroe	Ohio	341	Clifton	Penobscot	Me	306
Clarion	Bureau	Ill	537	Clifton	Greene	Ohio	258
Clarion, Bor	Clarion	Pa	e719	Clifton Park	Saratoga	N. Y.	2,868
Clarion	Clarion	Pa	1,798	Clifty	Bartholomew	Ind	945
Clark	Johnson	Ark	574	Climax	Kalamazoo	Mich	504
Clark	Lafayette	Ark	918	Clinton	Middlesex	Conn	1,344
Clark	Johnson	Ind	1,018	Clinton	De Kalb	Ill	350
Clark	Montgomery	Ind	1,301	Clinton	De Witt	Ill	367

a In 1853, 1,500. *b* In 1853, 60,000. *c* In 1853, 160,186. *d* In 1853, 4,500. *e* In 1853, 1,000. *f* In 1853, 41,196 including Ohio city, with 9,992 inhabitants.

Clinton	Cass	Ind	666
Clinton	Decatur	Ind	800
Clinton	Elkhart	Ind	804
Clinton	La Porte	Ind	698
Clinton	Putnam	Ind	1,231
Clinton	Vermillion	Ind	1,509
Clinton, T	Vermillion	Ind	321
Clinton	Hickman	Ky	300
Clinton	E. Feliciana	La	1,800
Clinton	Kennebeck	Me	1,743
Clinton	Worcester	Mass	3,113
Clinton	Lenawee	Mich	500
Clinton	Macomb	Mich	2,130
Clinton	Essex	N. J	2,508
Clinton	Hunterdon	N. J	2,369
Clinton, T	Hunterdon	N. J	800
Clinton	Clinton	N. Y	1,436
Clinton	Dutchess	N. Y	1,795
Clinton	Franklin	Ohio	1,186
Clinton	Fulton	Ohio	708
Clinton	Knox	Ohio	4,513
Clinton	Seneca	Ohio	4,398
Clinton	Shelby	Ohio	2,066
Clinton	Vinton	Ohio	886
Clinton	Wayne	Ohio	1,121
Clinton	Lycoming	Pa	851
Clinton	Wayne	Pa	840
Clinton	Wyoming	Pa	544
Clinton	De Witt	Texas	50
Clinton	Ohio	Va	313
Clinton	Rock	Wis	1,214
Clinton Gore	Kennebeck	Me	195
Clover	Jefferson	Pa	737
Cloverdale	Putnam	Ind	1,304
Cloverdale, T	Putnam	Ind	148
Cloverport	Breckenridge	Ky	700
Clyde	St. Clair	Mich	691
Clyde	Iowa	Wis	138
Clyman	Dodge	Wis	735
Clymer	Chautauque	N. Y	1,127
Coal	Northumberland	Pa	1,461
Coal Creek	Montgomery	Ind	1,517
Cobleskill	Schoharie	N. Y	2,229
Cohecton	Sullivan	N. Y	1,671
Coeymans	Albany	N. Y	3,050
Coffeeville	Yallabusha	Miss	700
Coganhouse	Lycoming	Pa	116
Cohassett	Norfolk	Mass	1,775
Cohansey	Cumberland	N. J	1,034
Cohocton	Steuben	N. Y	1,993
Cohoes	Albany	N. Y	4,229
Coitsville	Mahoning	Ohio	982
Cokesbury	Abbeville	S. C	†878
Colbath	Clark	Ark	300
Colchester	New London	Conn	2,468
Colchester	Delaware	N. Y	2,184
Colchester	Chittenden	Vt	2,575
Colden	Erie	N. Y	1,344
Cold Spring	Cattaraugus	N. Y	591
Cold Spring	Putnam	N. Y	1,200
Cold Spring	Jefferson	Wis	568
Cold Water	Branch	Mich	2,166
Cole	Benton	Mo	459
Colebrook	Litchfield	Conn	1,317
Colebrook	Coos	N. H	908
Colebrook	Ashtabula	Ohio	688
Colebrook	Clinton	Pa	326
Colebrookdale	Berks	Pa	1,102
Colerain	Franklin	Mass	1,785
Colerain	Belmont	Ohio	1,366
Colerain	Hamilton	Ohio	3,125
Colerain	Ross	Ohio	1,398
Coleraine	Bedford	Pa	1,281
Coleraine	Lancaster	Pa	1,602
Colesville	Broome	N. Y	3,061
College	Knox	Ohio	522
Colliersville	Shelby	Tenn	236
Collins	Erie	N. Y	4,001
Collins	Allegheny	Pa	1,324
Colon	St. Joseph	Mich	846
Colton	St. Lawrence	N. Y	506
Columbia	Tolland	Conn	876
Columbia	Monroe	Ill	378
Columbia	Dubois	Ind	752
Columbia	Fayette	Ind	889
Columbia	Gibson	Ind	1,184
Columbia	Jennings	Ind	947
Columbia	Martin	Ind	642

Columbia	Washington	Me	1,140
Columbia	Jackson	Mich	1,142
Columbia	Van Buren	Mich	265
Columbia	Boone	Mo	888
Columbia	Coos	N. H	762
Columbia	Herkimer	N. Y	2,000
Columbia	Hamilton	Ohio	2,413
Columbia	Meigs	Ohio	897
Columbia	Bradford	Pa	1,383
Columbia	Lancaster	Pa	*a*4,140
Columbia	Richland	S. C	6,060
Columbia	Maury	Tenn	†2,977
Columbiana	Columbiana	Ohio	650
Columbus	Muscogee	Ga	*b*5,942
Columbus	Adams	Ill	866
Columbus	Bartholomew	Ind	2,397
Columbus, T	Bartholomew	Ind	*c*1,008
Columbus	St. Clair	Mich	377
Columbus	Lowndes	Miss	*d*3,611
Columbus	Chenango	N. Y	1,381
Columbus	Franklin	Ohio	*e*17,882
Columbus	Lorain	Ohio	1,236
Columbus	Warren	Pa	1,278
Columbus	Columbia	Wis	960
Columbus, T	Columbia	Wis	288
Columbus, (city)	Louisa	Iowa	1,183
Columbus Grove	Putnam	Ohio	118
Columbus Village	Johnson	Mo	81
Comaltown	Comal	Texas	286
Commerce	Oakland	Mich	1,428
Comstock	Kalamazoo	Mich	1,202
Concord	Greene	Ark	50
Concord	Adams	Ill	764
Concord	Bureau	Ill	364
Concord	De Kalb	Ind	1,086
Concord	Elkhart	Ind	1,390
Concord	Somerset	Me	550
Concord	Middlesex	Mass	2,249
Concord	Jackson	Mich	983
Concord	Washington	Mo	815
Concord	Merrimack	N. H	8,576
Concord	Erie	N. Y	3,242
Concord	Champaign	Ohio	1,010
Concord	Delaware	Ohio	1,369
Concord	Fayette	Ohio	923
Concord	Highland	Ohio	1,501
Concord	Lake	Ohio	1,031
Concord	Miami	Ohio	3,409
Concord	Ross	Ohio	2,672
Concord	Delaware	Pa	1,049
Concord	Erie	Pa	882
Concord	Essex	Vt	1,153
Concord	Jefferson	Wis	725
Condemned Bar	Sutter	Cal	42
Conemaugh, Bor.	Cambria	Pa	854
Conemaugh	Cambria	Pa	3,027
Conemaugh	Indiana	Pa	1,748
Conemaugh	Somerset	Pa	1,434
Conestoga	Lancaster	Pa	3,616
Conesus	Livingston	N. Y	1,418
Conesville	Schoharie	N. Y	1,582
Conewango	Cattaraugus	N. Y	1,408
Conewango	Warren	Pa	884
Coney	Lancaster	Pa	1,035
Congress	Morrow	Ohio	1,651
Congress	Wayne	Ohio	2,336
Conklin	Broome	N. Y	2,232
Conneaut	Ashtabula	Ohio	2,695
Conneaut, T	Ashtabula	Ohio	*f*818
Conneaut	Crawford	Pa	1,807
Conneaut	Erie	Pa	1,942
Conneautville	Crawford	Pa	*g*787
Connellsville	Fayette	Pa	1,553
Connersville	Fayette	Ind	2,461
Connersville, T	Fayette	Ind	1,396
Connewago	Adams	Pa	775
Connewago	Dauphin	Pa	762
Connewago	York	Pa	1,270
Conois	Calhoun	Mich	621
Conquest	Cayuga	N. Y	1,863
Conshohocken	Montgomery	Pa	*h*727
Constable	Franklin	N. Y	1,447
Constantia	Oswego	N. Y	2,495
Constantine	St. Joseph	Mich	1,496
Constantine, T	St. Joseph	Mich	*i*760
Consumnes	El Dorado	Cal	1,092
Consumnes River	Sacramento	Cal	335
Conway	Franklin	Mass	1,831

a In 1853, 5,000. *b* In 1853, 7,000. *c* In 1853, 1,500. *d* In 1853, 3,000. *e* In 1853, 25,000. *f* In 1853, 1,500.
g In 1853, 1,000. *h* In 1853, 1,000. *i* In 1853, 1,200.

Conway	Livingston	Mich.	460	Croghan	Lewis	N. Y.	1,135
Conway	Carroll	N. H.	1,767	Cromwell	Huntingdon	Pa	1,297
Cookstown	Fayette	Pa	972	Crooked Creek	Carroll	Ark	539
Coolbaughs	Monroe	Pa	246	Crooked Creek	Jasper	Ill	658
Cool Spring	Laporte	Ind	394	Crosby	Hamilton	Ohio	2,488
Cool Spring	Mercer	Pa	2,760	Cross Creek	Jefferson	Ohio	1,912
Cooper	Washington	Me	562	Cross Creek	Washington	Pa	1,921
Cooper	Kalamazoo	Mich	733	Cross Plains	Dane	Wis	324
Cooper	Montour	Pa	322	*Crown Point*	Lake	Ind	400
Cooperstown	Otsego	N. Y.	1,600	Crown Point	Essex	N. Y.	2,378
Cooperstown	Manitoowoc	Wis	91	Croydon	Sullivan	N. H.	861
Copley	Summit	Ohio	1,541	*Crozierville*	Delaware	Pa	800
Copake	Columbia	N. Y.	1,652	Cuba	Lake	Ill	333
Coral	McHenry	Ill	980	Cuba	Alleghany	N. Y.	2,243
Corinna	Penobscot	Me	1,550	Cubiero	Valencia	N. M.	393
Corinth	Penobscot	Me	1,600	Cuivre	Pike	Mo	2,785
Corinth	Saratoga	N. Y.	1,501	Culloma	El Dorado	Cal	e588
Corinth	Orange	Vt	1,906	Culloma vicinity	El Dorado	Cal	42
Corning	Steuben	N. Y.	2,000	Cully	Sullivan	Pa	175
Cornish	York	Me	1,144	Cumberland	Clark	Ill	334
Cornish	Sullivan	N. H.	1,606	Cumberland	Marion	Ind	123
Cornplanter	Venango	Pa	693	Cumberland	Cumberland	Me	1,656
Cornville	Somerset	Me	1,260	Cumberland	Alleghany	Md	6,073
Cornwall	Litchfield	Conn	2,041	Cumberland	Guernsey	Ohio	431
Cornwall	Orange	N. Y.	4,471	Cumberland	Adams	Pa	1,408
Cornwall	Addison	Vt	1,155	Cumberland	Greene	Pa	2,143
Corpus Christi	Nueces	Texas	533	Cumberland	Providence	R. I.	6,661
Corrinna	Union	Ark	396	Cumberland Valley	Bedford	Pa	1,114
Cortland	Kent	Mich	406	*Cumming*	Forsyth	Ga	458
Cortlandt	Westchester	N. Y.	7,758	Cummings	Lycoming	Pa	505
Cortlandville	Cortlandt	N. Y.	4,203	Cummington	Macoupin	Ill	59
Cortsville	Clark	Ohio	48	Cummington	Hampshire	Mass	1,172
Corunna	Shiawassee	Mich	500	Cumru	Berks	Pa	3,853
Corydon	Harrison	Ind	462	Curran	Saline	Ill	1,061
Corydon	McKean	Pa	80	Curry	Sullivan	Ind	772
Corydon	Warren	Pa	228	Cushing	Lincoln	Me	807
Coshocton	Coshocton	Ohio	850	Cussawaga	Crawford	Pa	1,540
Cottage Grove	Dane	Wis	785	Cutler	Washington	Me	820
Cotton	Switzerland	Ind	1,872	Cynthiana	Pike	Ohio	134
Cottonwood	Cumberland	Ill	664	Cynthiana	Shelby	Ohio	797
Cottreville	St. Clair	Mich	913	Dagsborough Hun-			
Council	Crittenden	Ark	174	dred	Sussex	Del	2,668
Council Bluffs	Potawatomie	Iowa	3,000	Dahlonega	Lumpkin	Ga	735
Cove Creek	Washington	Ark	411	Dallas	Clinton	Mich	185
Coventry	Tolland	Conn	1,984	Dallas	Greene	Mo	*670
Coventry	Chenango	N. Y.	1,677	Dallas	Crawford	Ohio	406
Coventry	Summit	Ohio	1,299	Dallas	Luzerne	Pa	904
Coventry	Kent	R. I.	3,620	*Dallas*	Iowa	Wis	500
Coventry	Orleans	Vt	867	*Dalton*	Whitefield	Ga	2,000
Covert	Seneca	N. Y.	2,253	Dalton	Wayne	Ind	855
Covington	Fountain	Ind	a1,176	Dalton	Berkshire	Mass	1,020
Covington	Kenton	Ky	b9,408	Dalton	Coos	N. H.	751
Covington	Wyoming	N. Y.	1,385	*Dalton*	Wayne	Ohio	800
Covington	Miami	Ohio	451	Damascus	Henry	Ohio	223
Covington	Clearfield	Pa	448	Damascus	Wayne	Pa	1,602
Covington	Luzerne	Pa	650	Damariscotta	Lincoln	Me	1,328
Covington	Tioga	Pa	1,063	Dana	Worcester	Mass	842
Covington	Tipton	Tenn	375	Danbury	Fairfield	Conn	5,964
Covington	Alleghany	Va	500	Danbury	Grafton	N. H.	934
Cowanshanoc	Armstrong	Pa	1,318	Danbury	Ottawa	Ohio	501
Cowdersport	Potter	Pa	234	Danby	Ionia	Mich	262
Coxsackie	Greene	N. Y.	3,741	Danby	Tompkins	N. Y.	2,411
Coxsackie, T.	Greene	N. Y.	1,000	Danby	Rutland	Vt	1,535
Crab Orchard	Lincoln	Ky	500	*Dandridge*	Jefferson	Tenn	378
Craftsbury	Orleans	Vt	1,223	Dane	Dane	Wis	322
Craig	Van Buren	Ark	251	Danforth	Washington	Me	168
Craig	Switzerland	Ind	1,849	*Dansville*	Livingston	N. Y.	2,500
Cranberry	Middlesex	N. J.	600	Dansville	Steuben	N. Y.	2,545
Cranberry	Butler	Pa	2,256	Danube	Herkimer	N. Y.	1,730
Cranberry	Venango	Pa	1,317	Danvers	Essex	Mass	8,109
Cranberry Isle	Hancock	Me	283	Danville	Vermillion	Ill	736
Cranbury	Crawford	Ohio	1,042	Danville	Hendricks	Ind	386
Crane	Paulding	Ohio	287	Danville	Des Moines	Iowa	1,087
Crane	Wyandott	Ohio	1,544	*Danville*	Boyle	Ky	2,650
Cranston	Providence	R. I.	4,311	Danville	Cumberland	Me	1,636
Crawford	Washington	Me	324	Danville	Rockingham	N. H.	614
Crawford	Buchanan	Mo	*969	Danville	Knox	Ohio	160
Crawford	Osage	Mo	*1,025	Danville	Montour	Pa	3,302
Crawford	Orange	N. Y.	1,912	Danville	Caledonia	Vt	2,577
Crawford	Coshocton	Ohio	1,552	Danville	Pittsylvania	Va	1,514
Crawford	Wyandott	Ohio	1,306	Darby	Madison	Ohio	551
Crawford	Clinton	Pa	297	Darby	Pickaway	Ohio	1,166
Crawfordville	Taliaferro	Ga	400	Darby	Union	Ohio	881
Crawfordsville	Montgomery	Ind	c1,513	Darby	Delaware	Pa	1,310
Crete	Will	Ill	731	Dardanelle	Yell	Ark	477
Crittenden	Grant	Ky	250	Darien	Fairfield	Conn	1,454
Crockery	Ottawa	Mich	247	Darien	McIntosh	Ga	550
Crockett	Arkansas	Ark	230	Darien	Clark	Ill	1,343
Crockett	Houston	Texas	d150	Darien	Genesee	N. Y.	2,084

a In 1853, 1,500. *b* In 1853, 13,000. *c* In 1853, 2,500. *d* In 1853, 400. *e* In 1853, 2,000.

Darien	Walworth	Wis	1,013
Darlington	Beaver	Pa	1,160
Dartmouth	Bristol	Mass	3,868
Darwin	Clark	Ill	500
Darysaw	Jefferson	Ark	399
Dauphin	Dauphin	Pa	650
Davenport	Scott	Iowa	a1,848
Davenport	Delaware	N. Y.	2,305
Davidson	Sullivan	Pa	536
Davies	Caldwell	Mo	*378
Davis	Fountain	Ind	568
Davis	Lafayette	Mo	754
Davison	Genesee	Mich	367
Day	Saratoga	N. Y.	1,045
Dayton	Lasalle	Ill	630
Dayton, T.	Lasalle	Ill	168
Dayton	Tippecanoe	Ind	500
Dayton	Aroostook	Me	49
Dayton	Cattaraugus	N. Y.	1,448
Dayton (city)	Montgomery	Ohio	b10,977
Dearborn	Wayne	Mich	1,385
De Bastrop	Ashley	Ark	164
Decatur	Morgan	Ala	606
Decatur	De Kalb	Ga	744
Decatur	Macon	Ill	1,000
Decatur	Adams	Ind	231
Decatur	Marion	Ind	1,008
Decatur	Van Buren	Mich	386
Decatur	Otsego	N. Y.	927
Decatur	Brown	Ohio	171
Decatur	Lawrence	Ohio	1,052
Decatur	Washington	Ohio	807
Decatur	Clearfield	Pa	445
Decatur	Mifflin	Pa	990
Decatur	Greene	Wis	558
Decaturville	Decatur	Tenn	181
Deckertown	Sussex	N. J.	600
Dedham	Hancock	Me	546
Dedham	Norfolk	Mass	4,447
Deep Creek	Clinton	Iowa	132
Deep Water	Henry	Mo	*393
Deer Creek	Yuba	Cal	378
Deer Creek	Carroll	Ind	2,162
Deer Creek	Cass	Ind	664
Deer Creek	Miami	Ind	612
Deer Creek	Perry	Ind	710
Deer Creek	Madison	Ohio	583
Deer Creek	Pickaway	Ohio	1,354
Deerfield	Fulton	Ill	494
Deerfield	Lake	Ill	811
Deerfield	Randolph	Ind	121
Deerfield	Franklin	Mass	2,421
Deerfield	Livingston	Mich	882
Deerfield	Rockingham	N. H.	2,022
Deerfield	Cumberland	N. J.	927
Deerfield	Morgan	Ohio	1,325
Deerfield	Portage	Ohio	1,371
Deerfield	Ross	Ohio	1,315
Deerfield	Warren	Ohio	1,863
Deerfield, T.	Warren	Ohio	295
Deerfield	Tioga	Pa	721
Deerfield	Warren	Pa	1,022
Deerfield	Dane	Wis	639
Deering	Hillborough	N. H	890
Deer Isle	Hancock	Me	3,037
Deer Park	Lasalle	Ill	294
Deer Park	Orange	N. Y.	4,032
Deersfield	Oneida	N. Y.	2,287
Deerville	Harrison	Ohio	289
Defiance	Defiance	Ohio	1,281
Defiance, T	Defiance	Ohio	890
De Kalb	De Kalb	Ill	486
De Kalb	St. Lawrence	N. Y.	2,389
De Korra	Columbia	Wis	661
De Korra, T.	Columbia	Wis	81
Delafield	Waukesha	Wis	1,134
Delavan	Walworth	Wis	1,260
Delaware	Delaware	Ind	934
Delaware	Hamilton	Ind	867
Delaware	Ripley	Ind	1,274
Delaware	Camden	N. J.	2,577
Delaware	Hunterdon	N. J.	2,554
Delaware	Defiance	Ohio	445
Delaware	Delaware	Ohio	3,323
Delaware, T	Delaware	Ohio	2,074
Delaware	Hancock	Ohio	1,035
Delaware	Juniata	Pa	1,126
Delaware	Mercer	Pa	2,893
Delaware	Northumberland	Pa	1,908

Delaware	Pike	Pa	754
Delaware City	New Castle	Del	908
Delhi	Ingham	Mich	402
Delhi	Delaware	N. Y.	2,909
Delhi	Hamilton	Ohio	1,942
Delmar	Tioga	Pa	1,529
Delphi	Carroll	Ind	c1,381
Delphos	Allen	Ohio	374
Democrat	Carroll	Ind	681
Demopolis	Marengo	Ala	812
Denison	Luzerne	Pa	1,517
Denmark	Oxford	Me	1,203
Denmark	Lewis	N. Y.	2,824
Denmark	Ashtabula	Ohio	241
Denning	Ulster	N. Y.	447
Dennis	Barnstable	Mass	3,257
Dennis	Cape May	N. J	1,604
Dennysville	Washington	Me	458
Depere	Brown	Wis	d799
De Peyster	St. Lawrence	N. Y.	906
Deptford	Gloucester	N. J.	3,355
Derby	New Haven	Conn	3,824
Derby	Orleans	Vt	1,750
Derry	Rockingham	N. H.	1,850
Derry	Dauphin	Pa	1,843
Derry	Mifflin	Pa	1,342
Derry	Montour	Pa	853
Derry	Westmoreland	Pa	5,467
De Ruyter	Madison	N. Y.	1,931
Des Arc	White	Ark	272
Des Moines	Jefferson	Iowa	986
Des Moines	Van Buren	Iowa	683
Detroit	Somerset	Me	517
Detroit City	Wayne	Mich	e21,019
De Witt	Clinton	Iowa	459
De Witt	Clinton	Mich	706
De Witt	Onondaga	N. Y.	3,302
Dexter	Penobscot	Me	1,948
Dexter	Washtenaw	Mich	850
Diamond Grove	McLean	Ill	42
Diamond Springs	El Dorado	Cal	420
Diana	Lewis	N. Y	970
Dickinson	Franklin	N. Y	1,119
Dick Johnson	Clay	Ind	669
Dickson	Lee	Ill	1,073
Dighton	Bristol	Mass	1,641
Dillsburg	York	Pa	270
Dimmick	La Salle	Ill	378
Dimock	Susquehanna	Pa	1,056
Dingman	Pike	Pa	638
Dinsmore	Shelby	Ohio	701
District	Berks	Pa	842
District No. 2	St. Clair	Ill	588
District No. 3	St. Clair	Ill	1,008
District No. 4	St. Clair	Ill	799
District No. 5	St. Clair	Ill	1,764
District No. 6—American Bottom	St. Clair	Ill	2,384
District No. 7—Turkey Hill	St. Clair	Ill	882
District No. 8—12 Mile Prairie	St. Clair	Ill	882
District No. 9, High Prairie	St. Clair	Ill	1,202
District No. 10—Bellville	St. Clair	Ill	3,613
District No. 11—Centreville	St. Clair	Ill	2,646
Dix	Chemung	N. Y.	2,953
Dixfield	Oxford	Me.	1,180
Dixmont	Penobscot	Me	1,605
Dixon	Preble	Ohio	1,192
Dodgeville	Iowa	Wis	2,117
Dodson	Highland	Ohio	1,217
Doton's Bar and Long's Bar	Sutter	Cal	84
Donaldson	Schuylkill	Pa	1,477
Don Anna	Valencia	N. M.	498
Donegal	Butler	Pa	1,177
Donegal	Washington	Pa	1,679
Donegal	Westmoreland	Pa	2,527
Donnelsville	Clark	Ohio	196
Dorchester	Norfolk	Mass	7,969
Dorchester	Grafton	N. H.	711
Doro	Allegan	Mich	194
Dorrance	Luzerne	Pa	420
Dorset	Ashtabula	Ohio	236
Dorset	Bennington	Vt	1,700

a In 1853, 4,500. *b* In 1853, 16,562. *c* In 1853, 2,000. *d* In 1853, 1,200. *e* In 1853, 34,436.

Douglass	Arkansas	Ark	1,095
Douglass	Worcester	Mass	1,878
Douglass	Berks	Pa	1,018
Douglass	Montgomery	Pa	1,265
Dover	Bureau	Ill	742
Dover, T.	Bureau	Ill	103
Dover	Mason	Ky	600
Dover	Piscataquis	Me	1,927
Dover	Norfolk	Mass	631
Dover	Lenawee	Mich	1,223
Dover	Lafayette	Mo	1,405
Dover	Strafford	N. H	8,196
Dover	Ocean	N. J	2,385
Dover	Dutchess	N. Y	2,146
Dover	Athens	Ohio	1,232
Dover	Cuyahoga	Ohio	1,102
Dover	Fulton	Ohio	381
Dover	Tuscarawas	Ohio	3,248
Dover T.	Tuscarawas	Ohio	1,370
Dover	Union	Ohio	700
Dover	York	Pa	2,164
Dover	Stewart	Tenn	530
Dover	Windham	Vt	709
Dover	Racine	Wis	839
Dover	Walworth	Wis	1,268
Dover Hundred	Kent	Del	4,207
Downe	Cumberland	N. J	2,341
Downingtown	Chester	Pa	600
Downieville	Sierra	Cal	810
Downer's Grove	Du Page	Ill	957
Doylestown, Bor.	Bucks	Pa	1,006
Doylestown	Bucks	Pa	1,307
Dracut	Middlesex	Mass	3,503
Drakesville	Davis	Iowa	108
Dresden	Lincoln	Me	1,419
Dresden	Washington	N. Y	674
Dresden	Muskingum	Ohio	1,448
Dresden	Weakly	Tenn	†633
Driftwood	Jackson	Ind	602
Drumore	Lancaster	Pa	2,826
Dry Creek	El Dorado	Cal	210
Dryden	Lapeer	Mich	1,131
Dryden	Tompkins	N. Y	5,122
Dry Grove	McLean	Ill	294
Duane	Franklin	N. Y	222
Duanesburg	Schenectady	N. Y	3,464
Dublin	Wayne	Ind	713
Dublin	Cheshire	N. H	1,088
Dublin	Franklin	Ohio	274
Dublin	Mercer	Ohio	914
Dublin	Fulton	Pa	686
Dublin	Huntingdon	Pa	908
Dubuque	Dubuque	Iowa	a3,108
Duchouquet	Auglaize	Ohio	1,408
Duchess Creek	Yell	Ark	201
Duck Creek	Stoddard	Mo	716
Duck Creek Hundred	Kent	Del	4,682
Dudley	Henry	Ind	1,279
Dudley	Worcester	Mass	1,443
Dudley	Hardin	Ohio	529
Due West	Abbeville	S. C	†258
Dummer	Coos	N. H	171
Dummerston	Windham	Vt	1,645
Dunbar	Fayette	Pa	2,156
Dunbarton	Merrimack	N. H	915
Duncan's Falls	Muskingum	Ohio	196
Dundee	Kane	Ill	1,374
Dundee	Monroe	Mich	1,239
Dundee	Yates	N. Y	1,400
Dunkard	Greene	Pa	1,395
Dunkinsville	Adams	Ohio	91
Dunkirk	Chatauque	N. Y	3,000
Dunkirk	Dane	Wis	782
Dunmore	Luzerne	Pa	1,600
Dunn	Dane	Wis	330
Dunstable	Middlesex	Mass	590
Dunstable	Clinton	Pa	356
Du Page	Du Page	Ill	1,133
Du Page	Will	Ill	620
Duplain	Clinton	Mich	419
Duquesne	Allegheny	Pa	870
Durell	Bradford	Pa	1,202
Durham	Middlesex	Conn	1,026
Durham	Cumberland	Me	1,886
Durham	Strafford	N. H	1,497
Durham	Greene	N. Y	2,600
Durham	Bucks	Pa	948
Dutch Creek	El Dorado	Cal	504
Duxbury	Plymouth	Mass	2,679
Duxbury	Washington	Vt	845
Dyberry	Wayne	Pa	790
Eagle	Pulaski	Ark	891
Eagle	Gallatin	Ill	580
Eagle	Lasalle	Ill	336
Eagle	Monroe	Ill	1,331
Eagle	Ogle	Ill	623
Eagle	Clinton	Mich	521
Eagle	Wyoming	N. Y	1,381
Eagle	Brown	Ohio	1,279
Eagle	Hancock	Ohio	950
Eagle	Vinton	Ohio	476
Eagle	Sauk	Wis	336
Eagle	Waukesha	Wis	816
Eagle Creek	Lake	Ind	315
Eagle Harbor	Houghton	Mich	126
Eagle Harbor	Orleans	N. Y	500
Eagle Pass	Bexar	Texas	383
Earl	Lasalle	Ill	819
Earl	Berks	Pa	1,047
Earl	Lancaster	Pa	2,702
East	Carroll	Ohio	987
East Allen	Northampton	Pa	1,475
East Allentown	Lehigh	Pa	564
East Bethlehem	Washington	Pa	2,266
East Birmingham	Allegheny	Pa	1,624
East Bloomfield	Ontario	N. Y	2,262
East Bradford	Chester	Pa	1,330
East Brandywine	Chester	Pa	1,115
East Bridgewater	Plymouth	Mass	2,545
Eastbrook	Hancock	Me	212
East Brunswick	Schuylkill	Pa	1,337
East Buffalo	Union	Pa	970
East Caln	Chester	Pa	2,292
East Canon	El Dorado	Cal	42
East Chester	West Chester	N. Y	1,679
East Cleveland	Cuyahoga	Ohio	2,343
East Cocalico	Lancaster	Pa	2,117
East Connequenessing	Butler	Pa	1,142
East Coventry	Chester	Pa	1,288
East Deer	Allegheny	Pa	2,021
East Donegal	Lancaster	Pa	1,997
East Fallowfield	Chester	Pa	1,289
East Fallowfield	Crawford	Pa	739
East Finly	Washington	Pa	1,281
East Fishkill	Dutchess	N. Y	2,610
Eastford	Windham	Conn	1,127
East Genesee	Genesee	Mich	844
East Goshen	Chester	Pa	768
East Greenfield	La Grange	Ind	400
East Greenwich	Kent	R. I	2,358
East Haddam	Middlesex	Conn	2,610
Eastham	Barnstable	Mass	845
East Hampton	Hampshire	Mass	1,342
East Hampton	Suffolk	N. Y	2,122
East Hanover	Lebanon	Pa	1,815
East Hanover	Dauphin	Pa	1,658
East Hartford	Hartford	Conn	2,497
East Haven	New Haven	Conn	1,670
East Haven	Essex	Vt	94
East Hempfield	Lancaster	Pa	2,266
East Huntingdon	Westmoreland	Pa	1,873
East Indian	Penobscot	Me	193
East Kingston	Rockingham	N. H	532
East Lackawannock	Mercer	Pa	922
East Lampeter	Lancaster	Pa	1,980
East Liberty	Logan	Ohio	177
East Lima	La Grange	Ind	824
East Livermore	Kennebec	Me	891
East Liverpool	Columbiana	Pa	835
East Lyme	New London	Conn	1,382
East Machias	Washington	Me	1,905
East Mahoning	Indiana	Pa	869
East Marlboro'	Chester	Pa	1,425
East Maysville	Mason	Ky	416
East Montpelier	Washington	Vt	1,447
East Nantmeal	Chester	Pa	921
East Norwegian	Schuylkill	Pa	1,031
East Nottingham	Chester	Pa	2,412
Easton	Fairfield	Conn	1,432
Easton	Talbot	Md	1,413
Easton	Bristol	Mass	2,337
Easton	Ionia	Mich	397
Easton	Washington	N. Y	3,225
Easton	Northampton	Pa	7,250
East Penn	Carbon	Pa	688

a In 1853, 7,500.

East Pennsborough	Cumberland	Pa	1,605
East Pikeland	Chester	Pa	722
East Pike Run	Washington	Pa	1,358
Eastport	Washington	Me	4,125
East Providence	Bedford	Pa	991
East Saginaw	Saginaw	Mich	500
East Town	Chester	Pa	710
East Troy	Walworth	Wis	1,318
East Union	Williams	Ohio	1,940
East Van Buren	La Grange	Ind	298
East Vincent	Chester	Pa	1,505
East Whiteland	Chester	Pa	1,194
East Windsor	Hartford	Conn	2,633
East Windsor	Mercer	N. J	2,596
Eaton	Eaton	Mich	539
Eaton	Carroll	N. H	1,743
Eaton	Madison	N. Y	3,944
Eaton	Lorain	Ohio	1,111
Eaton	Preble	Ohio	*a*1,346
Eaton	Wyoming	Pa	914
Eaton Rapids	Eaton	Mich	1,525
Ebensburg	Cambria	Pa	600
Eckford	Calhoun	Mich	715
Ecofabra	Ouachita	Ark	342
Economy	Wayne	Ind	158
Economy	Beaver	Pa	1,390
Eddington	Penobscot	Me	696
Eddyville	Caldwell	Ky	700
Eden	Lasalle	Ill	504
Eden	Schuyler	Ill	806
Eden	La Grange	Ind	649
Eden	Hancock	Me	1,127
Eden	Erie	N. Y	2,494
Eden	Licking	Ohio	1,013
Eden	Seneca	Ohio	1,584
Eden	Wyandott	Ohio	646
Eden	Lamoille	Vt	668
Eden	Fond du Lac	Wis	840
Edenton	Chowan	N. C	†1,607
Edgartown	Dukes	Mass	1,990
Edgecombe	Lincoln	Me	1,231
Edgefield	Davidson	Tenn	1,621
Edgemont	Delaware	Pa	623
Edina	Knox	Mo	163
Edinborough	Erie	Pa	264
Edinburgh	Portage	Ohio	1,101
Edinburgh	Penobscot	Me	93
Edinburgh	Saratoga	N. Y	1,336
Edinburg	Cameron	Texas	500
Edmeston	Otsego	N. Y	1,885
Edmonds	Washington	Me	446
Edwards	St. Lawrence	N. Y	1,023
Edwardsburg	Cass	Mich	252
Eel, (Logansport)	Cass	Ind	2,251
Eel River	Allen	Ind	655
Eel River	Green	Ind	572
Eel River	Hendricks	Ind	1,346
Effingham	Carroll	N. H	1,252
Egg Harbor	Atlantic	N. J	2,688
Egypt	Ashley	Ark	94
Egremont	Berkshire	Mass	1,013
Ela	Lake	Ill	988
Elba	Lapeer	Mich	255
Elba	Genesee	N. Y	1,772
Elba	Dodge	Wis	727
Elbridge	Onondaga	N. Y	3,924
El Dorado	Union	Ark	1,925
El Dorado	Fond du Lac	Wis	504
Eldred	Jefferson	Pa	492
Eldred	McKean	Pa	527
Eldred	Warren	Pa	194
Elgin	Kane	Ill	2,359
Elida	Winnebago	Ill	499
Elington	Brown	Wis	64
Elizabeth	Essex	N. J	5,583
Elizabeth	Lawrence	Ohio	2,529
Elizabeth	Miami	Ohio	1,433
Elizabeth, Bor	Allegheny	Pa	1,120
Elizabeth	Allegheny	Pa	3,970
Elizabeth	Lancaster	Pa	2,309
Elizabeth City	Pasquotank	N. C	2,824
Elizabethtown	Essex	N. Y	1,635
Elizabethtown	Guernsey	Ohio	131
Elizabethtown	Licking	Ohio	170
Elizabethtown	Lancaster	Pa	600
Elizabethtown	Essex	N. J	4,000
Elizabethtown	Carter	Tenn	373
Elizaville	Fleming	Ky	166
El Jolla	Valencia	N. M	440

El Jollita	Valencia	N. M	186
Elk	Monroe	Ohio	955
Elk	Vinton	Ohio	1,645
Elk	Clarion	Pa	1,484
Elk	Warren	Pa	414
Elk Creek	Erie	Pa	1,535
Elk Grove	Cook	Ill	672
Elk Grove	Lafayette	Wis	624
Elkhart	Elkhart	Ind	1,035
Elkhart	Noble	Ind	621
Elkhorn	Walworth	Wis	42
Elkhorn Grove	Carroll	Ill	434
Elkins	Clark	Ark	230
Elkland	Sullivan	Pa	408
Elkland	Tioga	Pa	962
Elk Lick	Somerset	Pa	1,091
Elk River	Clinton	Iowa	426
Elk Run	Columbiana	Ohio	1,558
Elkton	Cecil	Md	1,099
Ellery	Chautauque	N. Y	2,104
Elletsville	Monroe	Ind	74
Ellenburg	Clinton	N. Y	1,504
Ellicott	Chatauque	N. Y	3,523
Ellicott's Mills	Howard	Md	847
Ellicottsville	Cattaraugus	N. Y	1,725
Ellington	Tolland	Conn	1,399
Ellington	Adams	Ill	1,451
Ellington	Chatauque	N. Y	2,001
Ellisburg	Jefferson	N. Y	5,524
Elliott	York	Me	1,803
Elliottsville	Piscataquis	Me	102
Ellsworth	Hancock	Me	4,009
Ellsworth	Grafton	N. H	380
Ellsworth	Mahoning	Ohio	954
Elmira	Chemung	N. Y	8,166
Elmore	Daviess	Ind	708
Elmore	Lamoille	Vt	504
El Pueblo de San Ildefonso	Santa Fe	N. M	139
El Pueblo de Nambo	Santa Fe	N. M	111
El Pueblo de Pajoaque	Santa Fe	N. M	48
El Pueblo de Tesuque	Santa Fe	N. M	119
Elsenborough	Salem	N. J	655
Elyria	Lorain	Ohio	2,658
Elyria, T	Lorain	Ohio	*b*1,482
Embden	Somerset	Me	971
Emmettsville	Randolph	Ind	37
Emmett	Calhoun	Mich	1,582
Emmett	Dodge	Wis	1,247
Emmitsburg	Frederick	Md	812
Empire Canon	El Dorado	Cal	84
Encorce	Wayne	Mich	653
Enfield	Hartford	Conn	4,460
Enfield	Penobscot	Me	396
Enfield	Hampshire	Mass	1,036
Enfield	Grafton	N. H	1,742
Enfield	Tompkins	N. Y	2,117
English River	Keokuk	Iowa	90
English River	Iowa	Iowa	142
Enoch	Monroe	Ohio	1,439
Enon	Clark	Ohio	294
Enosburg	Franklin	Vt	2,009
Ephratah	Fulton	N. Y	2,097
Ephratah	Lancaster	Pa	1,979
Epping	Rockingham	N. H	1,663
Epsom	Merrimack	N. H	1,366
Equality	Gallatin	Ill	794
Erie	Miama	Ind	420
Erie	Monroe	Mich	1,144
Erie	Ottawa	Ohio	292
Erie	Erie	Pa	5,858
Erin	Stephenson	Ill	886
Erin	Macomb	Mich	974
Erin	Washington	Wis	840
Erin	Chemung	N. Y	1,833
Errol	Coos	N. H	138
Erving	Franklin	Mass	449
Erwin	Steuben	N. Y	1,435
Esperance	Schoharie	N. Y	1,428
Esopus	Ulster	N. Y	2,900
Essex	Middlesex	Conn	*c*950
Essex	Porter	Ind	73
Essex	Essex	Mass	1,585
Essex	Clinton	Mich	410
Essex	Essex	N. Y	2,351
Essex	Chittenden	Vt	2,052

a In 1853, 1,600. *b* In 1853, 2,000. *c* In 1853, 1,200.

Etna	Huntington	Ind	105	Falls	Bucks	Pa	1,788
Etna	Penobscot	Me	802	Falls	Wyoming	Pa	798
Etna	Licking	Ohio	1,307	Fallsburg	Sullivan	N. Y.	2,626
Etna, T.	Licking	Ohio	293	Fallsburg	Licking	Ohio	1,206
Euclid	Cuyahoga	Ohio	1,447	Fallsington	Bucks	Pa	249
Eufaula	Barbour	Ala	3,000	Fallston	Beaver	Pa	571
Eugene	Vermillion	Ind	1,105	Fannet	Franklin	Pa	1,970
Eugene, T.	Vermillion	Ind	478	Farmer	Defiance	Ohio	894
Eulalie	Potter	Pa	288	Farmers	Fulton	Ill	830
Euphemia	Preble	Ohio	281	Farmersburg	Clayton	Iowa	241
Eureka	Trinity	Cal	55	Farmer's Creek	Jackson	Iowa	462
Eureka	Montcalm	Mich	461	*Farmerville*	Union	La	299
Eutaw	Greene	Ala	2,000	Farmersville	Cattaraugus	N. Y	1,554
Evans	Erie	N. Y.	2,182	Farmersville	Dane	Wis	206
Evansport	Defiance	Ohio	165	*Farmville*	Prince Edwards	Va	1,500
Evansville	Vanderburg	Ind	a3,235	Farmington	Hartford	Conn	2,630
Evesham	Burlington	N. J.	3,067	Farmington	Fulton	Ill	1,420
Ewing	Mercer	N. J.	1,480	Farmington	Van Buren	Iowa	2,074
Exeter	Penobscot	Me	1,853	Farmington, T.	Van Buren	Iowa	585
Exeter	Monroe	Mich	458	Farmington	Franklin	Me	2,725
Exeter	Rockingham	N. H.	3,329	Farmington	Oakland	Mich	1,844
Exeter	Otsego	N. Y.	1,526	Farmington	Strafford	N. H.	1,699
Exeter	Berks	Pa	2,074	Farmington	Ontario	N. Y.	1,876
Exeter	Luzerne	Pa	833	Farmington	Belmont	Ohio	45
Exeter	Wyoming	Pa	187	Farmington	Trumbull	Ohio	1,283
Exeter	Washington	R. I.	1,634	Farmington	Clarion	Pa	1,124
Exeter	Greene	Wis	450	Farmington	Tioga	Pa	903
Extra	Ashley	Ark	125	Farmington	Jefferson	Wis	736
Fabius	Davis	Iowa	427	Farmington	Washington	Wis	504
Fabius	St. Joseph	Mich	497	Farm Ridge	Lasalle	Ill	378
Fabius	Knox	Mo	782	Fawn	York	Pa	1,043
Fabius	Marion	Mo	2,739	Fawn River	Saint Joseph	Mich	472
Fabius	Onondaga	N. Y.	2,410	Fayette	Vigo	Ind	1,340
Fairbank	Sullivan	Ind	958	Fayette	Kennebeck	Me	1,085
Fairfax	Culpepper	Va	1,000	Fayette	Hillsdale	Mich	895
Fairfax	Franklin	Vt	2,111	*Fayette*	Jefferson	Miss	1,200
Fairfield	Fairfield	Conn	3,614	Fayette	Seneca	N. Y.	3,786
Fairfield	Bureau	Ill	205	Fayette	Lawrence	Ohio	1,111
Fairfield	Wayne	Ill	195	Fayette	Juniata	Pa	1,550
Fairfield	De Kalb	Ind	576	Fayette	Lafayette	Wis	753
Fairfield	Franklin	Ind	910	Fayetteville	Washington	Ark	e598
Fairfield	Tippecanoe	Ind	1,313	Fayetteville	Cumberland	N. C.	f4,646
Fairfield	Jackson	Iowa	210	Fayetteville	Brown	Ohio	317
Fairfield	Jefferson	Iowa	1,899	Fayston	Washington	Vt	684
Fairfield T.	Jefferson	Iowa	b909	Fearing	Washington	Ohio	1,254
Fairfield	Somerset	Me	2,452	Feesburg	Brown	Ohio	187
Fairfield	Lenawee	Mich	1,327	Fell	Huntingdon	Pa	983
Fairfield	Cumberland	N. J.	2,133	Fell	Luzerne	Pa	356
Fairfield	Herkimer	N. Y.	1,646	Fenner	Madison	N. Y	1,690
Fairfield	Butler	Ohio	5,978	Fennimore	Grant	Wis	325
Fairfield	Columbiana	Ohio	2,385	Fenton	Hot Springs	Ark	*630
Fairfield	Highland	Ohio	3,174	Fenton	Genesee	Mich	873
Fairfield	Huron	Ohio	1,594	Ferdinand	Dubois	Ind	546
Fairfield	Madison	Ohio	623	Ferguson	Centre	Pa	1,601
Fairfield	Tuscarawas	Ohio	871	Ferguson	Clearfield	Pa	337
Fairfield	Crawford	Pa	1,224	Fermanagh	Juniata	Pa	887
Fairfield	Lycoming	Pa	1,318	Ferrisburgh	Addison	Vt	2,075
Fairfield	Westmoreland	Pa	3,352	Fillmore	Allegan	Mich	527
Fairfield	Franklin	Vt	2,591	Fincastle	Brown	Ohio	145
Fairfield	Dodge	Wis	1,143	Findley	Hancock	Ohio	2,032
Fairhaven	New Haven	Conn	c1,317	Findley, T.	Hancock	Ohio	g1,256
Fairhaven	Bristol	Mass	4,304	Findley	Allegheny	Pa	1,318
Fairhaven	Rutland	Vt	902	Findley	Mercer	Pa	1,066
Fairlee	Orange	Vt	575	Fine	St. Lawrence	N. Y.	293
Fairmount	Marion	Va	d683	Finley	Greene	Mo	*1,640
Fairmount	Luzerne	Pa	958	Fishing Creek	Columbia	Pa	1,110
Fair Plain	Montcalm	Mich	229	Fishing River	Clay	Mo	1,987
Fairplay	Greene	Ind	447	Fishkill	Dutchess	N. Y	9,240
Fairview	Fulton	Ill	1,047	Fitchburg	Worcester	Mass	5,120
Fairview	Randolph	Ind	91	Fitchville	Huron	Ohio	1,178
Fairview	Jones	Iowa	721	Fitzwilliam	Cheshire	N. H	1,482
Fairview, T	Jones	Iowa	251	Flat	Taney	Mo	462
Fairview	Guernsey	Ohio	444	Flatbush	Kings	N. Y.	3,177
Fairview	Butler	Pa	1,078	Flatlands	Kings	N. Y.	1,155
Fairview	Erie	Pa	1,760	Flat Rock	Bartholomew	Ind	725
Fairview	York	Pa	2,164	Flat Rock	Henry	Ohio	406
Falmouth	Cumberland	Me	2,157	Fleming	Cayuga	N. Y.	1,193
Falmouth	Barnstable	Mass	2,621	Flemingsburg	Fleming	Ky	759
Fall Creek	Adams	Ill	948	*Flemington*	Hunterdon	N. J.	1,000
Fall Creek	Hamilton	Ind	1,240	Fletcher	Miami	Ohio	246
Fall Creek	Henry	Ind	1,242	Fletcher	Franklin	Vt	1,084
Fall Creek	Madison	Ind	2,128	Flinn	Lawrence	Ind	1,165
Fallowfield	Washington	Pa	1,132	Flint	Genesee	Mich	3,304
Fall River	Bristol	Mass	11,524	Flint, T.	Genesee	Mich	1,670
Fall River	Columbia	Wis	126	Flint River	Des Moines	Iowa	869
Falls	Hocking	Ohio	2,570	Flora	Sauk	Wis	239
Falls	Muskingum	Ohio	2,123	Florence	Lauderdale	Ala	h802

a In 1853, 8,000. *b* In 1853, 1,500. *c* In 1853, 3,000. *d* In 1853, 1,200. *e* In 1853, 1,200. *f* In 1853, 7,000. *g* In 1853, 2,500. *h* In 1853, 1,500.

Florence	Stephenson	Ill.	445	Franklin	Kosciusko	Ind.	1,201
Florence	Louisa	Iowa	776	Franklin	Marion	Ind	1,506
Florence	Boone	Ky	a*252	Franklin	Montgomery	Ind	1,487
Florence	St. Joseph	Mich	731	Franklin	Owen	Ind	1,153
Florence	Oneida	N. Y.	2,575	Franklin	Ripley	Ind	1,815
Florence	Erie	Ohio	1,491	Franklin	Washington	Ind	3,032
Florence	Williams	Ohio	669	Franklin	Wayne	Ind	1,362
Florence Village	Washington	Pa	318	Franklin	Putnam	Ind	1,218
Florida	Berkshire	Mass	561	Franklin	Des Moines	Iowa	1,106
Florida	Montgomery	N. Y.	3,571	*Franklin*	Simpson	Ky	400
Flowerfield	Saint Joseph	Mich	564	Franklin	St. Mary's	La	h891
Floyd	Putnam	Ind	1,386	Franklin	Hancock	Me	736
Floyd	Oneida	N. Y.	1,495	Franklin	Oxford	Me	188
Flushing	Genesee	Mich	708	Franklin	Norfolk	Mass	1,818
Flushing	Queens	N. Y.	5,376	Franklin	Lenawee	Mich	1,231
Flushing	Belmont	Ohio	1,811	*Franklin*	Holmes	Miss	80
Flushing, T.	Belmont	Ohio	325	Franklin	Merrimack	N. H	1,251
Fond du Lac	Fond du Lac	Wis	b2,014	Franklin	Bergen	N. J.	1,741
Forest	Genesee	Mich	178	Franklin	Gloucester	N. J.	2,948
Forest	Fon du Lac	Wis	1,256	Franklin	Hunterdon	N. J.	1,454
Forestburgh	Sullivan	N. Y.	715	Franklin	Somerset	N. J.	3,062
Forest Lake	Susquehanna	Pa	780	Franklin	Warren	N. J.	1,565
Forks	Northampton	Pa	2,321	Franklin	Delaware	N. Y	3,087
Forks	Sullivan	Pa	343	Franklin	Franklin	N. Y	724
Forkstown	Wyoming	Pa	694	Franklin	Adams	Ohio	1,963
Forsyth	Monroe	Ga	657	Franklin	Brown	Ohio	1,169
Fort Atkinson	Jefferson	Wis	334	Franklin	Clermont	Ohio	3,061
Fort Ann	Washington	N. Y.	3,383	Franklin	Columbiana	Ohio	1,164
Fort Covington	Franklin	N. Y.	2,641	Franklin	Coshocton	Ohio	966
Fort Des Moines	Polk	Iowa	502	Franklin	Darke	Ohio	551
Fort Edward	Washington	N. Y.	2,328	Franklin	Franklin	Ohio	1,851
Fort Gaines	Mankahta	Minn	143	Franklin	Fulton	Ohio	720
Fort Madison	Lee	Iowa	c1,509	Franklin	Harrison	Ohio	1,350
Fort Osage	Jackson	Mo	1,134	Franklin, T	Harrison	Ohio	151
Fort Plain	Montgomery	N. Y	1,500	Franklin	Jackson	Ohio	1,295
Fort Smith	Crawford	Ark	d964	Franklin	Licking	Ohio	1,059
Fort Valley	Houston	Ga	1,090	Franklin	Mercer	Ohio	357
Fort Wayne	Allen	Ind	e4,282	Franklin	Monroe	Ohio	1,588
Fort Winnebago	Columbia	Wis	1,674	Franklin	Morrow	Ohio	1,456
Fort Winnebago, T	Columbia	Wis	1,175	Franklin	Portage	Ohio	1,749
Foster	Providence	R. I	1,932	Franklin	Richland	Ohio	1,257
Fountain	Monroe	Ill	1,049	Franklin	Ross	Ohio	642
Fountain Prairie	Columbia	Wis	420	Franklin	Shelby	Ohio	788
Fourche	Pulaski	Ark	381	Franklin	Summit	Ohio	1,674
Fowler	St. Lawrence	N. Y	1,813	Franklin	Warren	Ohio	2,544
Fowler	Trumbull	Ohio	1,089	Franklin, T	Warren	Ohio	972
Fox	Kendall	Ill	846	Franklin	Wayne	Ohio	1,450
Fox	Davis	Iowa	677	Franklin	Adams	Pa	1,806
Fox	Carroll	Ohio	1,452	Franklin	Allegheny	Pa	1,327
Fox	Clearfield	Pa	50	Franklin	Armstrong	Pa	2,410
Fox	Elk	Pa	764	Franklin	Beaver	Pa	625
Fox	Sullivan	Pa	233	Franklin	Bradford	Pa	767
Foxborough	Norfolk	Mass	1,880	Franklin	Butler	Pa	1,119
Foxcroft	Piscataquis	Me	1,045	Franklin	Erie	Pa	687
Fox Lake	Dodge	Wis	500	Franklin	Fayette	Pa	1,432
Fraley	Schuylkill	Pa	649	Franklin	Greene	Pa	1,591
Framingham	Middlesex	Mass	4,252	Franklin	Huntingdon	Pa	1,401
Francistown	Hillsborough	N. H	1,114	Franklin	Luzerne	Pa	642
Franconia	Grafton	N. H	584	Franklin	Lycoming	Pa	1,059
Franconia	Montgomery	Pa	1,270	Franklin	Montour	Pa	738
Frankford	Sussex	N. J.	1,941	Franklin	Susquehanna	Pa	703
Frankford	Cumberland	Pa	1,241	Franklin	Venango	Pa	i936
Frankford	Philadelphia	Pa	5,346	Franklin	Westmoreland	Pa	2,560
Frankfort	Will	Ill	844	Franklin	York	Pa	897
Frankfort	Clinton	Ind	f582	Franklin	Williamson	Tenn	*891
Frankfort	Franklin	Ky	g†3,308	Franklin	Franklin	Vt	1,646
Frankfort	Waldo	Me	4,233	Franklin	Milwaukie	Wis	1,176
Frankfort	Herkimer	N. Y	3,023	*Franklin Mills*	Portage	Ohio	1,600
Frankfort	Ross	Ohio	553	*Franklinton*	Franklin	N. C	300
Franklin	Chicot	Ark	561	Franklinton	Erie	Ohio	596
Franklin	Desha	Ark	292	Franklinville	Cattaraugus	N. Y	1,706
Franklin	Fulton	Ark	212	Franks	St. Francis	Ark	849
Franklin	Izard	Ark	618	Frankstown	Blair	Pa	1,482
Franklin	Ouachita	Ark	288	Freco	Ouachita	Ark	436
Franklin	Sevier	Ark	402	Frederick	Schuyler	Ill	309
Franklin	Union	Ark	1,394	Frederick	Knox	Ohio	j712
Franklin	New London	Conn	895	Frederick	Montgomery	Pa	1,431
Franklin	Heard	Ga	265	*Fredericksburg*	Wayne	Ohio	573
Franklin	Crawford	Ill	504	Fredericksburg	Gillespie	Texas	754
Franklin	De Kalb	Ill	716	Fredericksburg	Spottsylvania	Va	4,061
Franklin	Kendall	Ill	357	Fredericktown	Frederick	Md	6,028
Franklin	De Kalb	Ind	900	Fredonia	Louisa	Iowa	369
Franklin	Floyd	Ind	758	Fredonia	Calhoun	Mich	623
Franklin	Henry	Ind	1,295	Fredonia	Licking	Ohio	141
Franklin	Hendricks	Ind	889	Fredonia	Washington	Wis	671
Franklin	Johnson	Ind	3,166	Freebourne	Dunkin	Mo	272
Franklin T.	Johnson	Ind	882	Freedom	Polk	Ark	175

a In 1853, 400. *b* In 1853, 4,000. *c* In 1853, 3,000. *d* In 1853, 1,500. Fort Smith is now in Sebastian county. *e* In 1853, 6,500. *f* In 1853, 700. *g* In 1853, 5,000. *h* In 1853, 1,400. *i* In 1853, 1,200. *j* In 1853, 1,000.

Place	County	State	Population
Freedom	Carroll	Ill.	332
Freedom	Lasalle	Ill.	908
Freedom	Waldo	Me.	948
Freedom	Washtenaw	Mich.	1,215
Freedom	Lafayette	Mo.	1,305
Freedom	Carroll	N. H.	910
Freedom	Cattaraugus	N. Y.	1,652
Freedom	Henry	Ohio	83
Freedom	Portage	Ohio	996
Freedom	Wood	Ohio	454
Freedom	Adams	Pa.	473
Freedom	Beaver	Pa.	524
Freehold	Monmouth	N. J.	2,642
Freehold	Warren	Pa.	1,162
Freeman	Franklin	Me.	762
Freeport	Stephenson	Ill.	a1,436
Freeport	Cumberland	Me.	2,629
Freeport	Harrison	Ohio	1,220
Freeport, T	Harrison	Ohio	288
Freeport	Armstrong	Pa.	1,073
Freetown	Bristol	Mass.	1,615
Freetown	Cortlandt	N. Y.	1,035
Frelinghuysen	Warren	N. J.	1,277
Fremont	Lake	Ill.	776
Fremont	Steuben	Ind.	539
Fremont	Hancock	Me.	1,425
Fremont	Sandusky	Ohio	1,464
Fremont Town	Yolo	Cal.	130
French	Adams	Ind.	344
French Canon	El Dorado	Cal.	168
French Creek	Chatauque	N. Y.	725
French Creek	Mercer	Pa.	691
French Creek	Venango	Pa.	962
French Lick	Orange	Ind.	1,243
Frenchtown	Monroe	Mich.	1,242
Frenchtown	Huntingdon	N. J.	800
Friendship	Lincoln	Me.	691
Friendship	Allegheny	N. Y.	1,675
Friendship	Fond du Lac	Wis.	412
Friendshipville	Susquehanna	Pa.	185
Fristo	Benton	Mo.	681
Front Royal	Warren	Va.	504
Fryeburg	Oxford	Me.	1,523
Fugit	Decatur	Ind.	1,763
Fulton	Polk	Ark.	219
Fulton	Fountain	Ind.	1,009
Fulton	Itawamba	Miss.	†275
Fulton	Oswego	N. Y.	2,344
Fulton, T	Oswego	N. Y.	2,000
Fulton	Schoharie	N. Y.	2,566
Fulton	Fulton	Ohio	625
Fulton	Hamilton	Ohio	3,224
Fulton	Lancaster	Pa.	1,797
Fulton	Ohio	Va.	266
Fulton	Rock	Wis.	828
Funk's Grove	McLean	Ill.	210
Funkstown	Washington	Md.	947
Funkstown	Franklin	Pa.	400
Gaines	Genesee	Mich.	286
Gaines	Kent	Mich.	319
Gaines	Orleans	N. Y.	2,722
Gaines	Tioga	Pa.	510
Gainsville	Sumter	Ala.	1,500
Gainesville	Hancock	Miss.	923
Gainesville	Wyoming	N. Y.	1,760
Galen	Wayne	N. Y.	4,609
Galena	Jo Daviess	Ill.	b6,004
Galena	Laporte	Ind.	551
Galesburg	Knox	Ill.	c882
Gallaher	Clinton	Pa.	210
Gallatin	Copiah	Miss.	203
Gallatin	Clay	Mo.	3,011
Gallatin	Columbia	N. Y.	1,586
Gallatin	Sumter	Tenn.	1,200
Galliopolis	Gallia	Ohio	2,228
Gallioplis, T	Gallia	Ohio	1,686
Galloway	Atlantic	N. J.	2,307
Gally Rock	Yell	Ark.	117
Galveston	Galveston	Texas.	d4,177
Galway	Saratoga	N. Y.	2,158
Gambia	Knox	Ohio	280
Ganges	Allegan	Mich.	246
Gap	Montgomery	Ark.	476
Gardiner	Kennebeck	Me.	6,486
Gardner	Worcester	Mass.	1,533
Garland	Penobscot	Me.	1,247
Garnaville	Clayton	Iowa	714

Place	County	State	Population
Garoga	Fulton	N. Y.	589
Garrettsville	Portage	Ohio	600
Gaskill	Jefferson	Pa.	603
Gaspar	Preble	Ohio	908
Gaston	Northampton	N. C.	†274
Gates	Monroe	N. Y.	2,005
Gayport	Blair	Pa.	590
Geddes	Onondaga	N. Y.	2,011
Geesecreek	Crawford	Ark.	572
Genesee	Alleghany	N. Y.	672
Genesee	Livingston	N. Y.	2,958
Genesee	Potter	Pa.	301
Genesee	Waukesha	Wis.	1,289
Genesee Falls	Wyoming	N. Y.	1,322
Geneva	Ontario	N. Y.	6,000
Geneva	Kane	Ill.	911
Geneva	Jennings	Ind.	1,770
Geneva	Ashtabula	Ohio	1,358
Geneva	Walworth	Wis.	1,557
Genoa	De Kalb	Ill.	605
Genoa	Livingston	Mich.	754
Genoa	Cayuga	N. Y.	2,503
Genoa	Delaware	Ohio	1,369
Gentryville	Gentry	Mo.	*126
Georges	Fayette	Pa.	2,536
Georgetown	Sussex	Del.	1,200
Georgetown	Washington	D. C.	8,366
Georgetown	Floyd	Ind.	1,198
Georgetown	Scott	Ky.	2,000
Georgetown	Lincoln	Me.	1,121
Georgetown	Essex	Mass.	2,052
Georgetown	Ottawa	Mich.	196
Georgetown	Madison	N. Y.	1,411
Georgetown	Brown	Ohio	e618
Georgetown	Harrison	Ohio	160
Georgetown	Georgetown	S. C.	1,628
Georgetown & vicinity	El Dorado	Cal.	462
Georgia	Franklin	Vt.	2,686
German	Bartholomew	Ind.	947
German	Saint Joseph	Ind.	614
German	Vanderberg	Ind.	1,084
German	Allen	Ohio	1,008
German	Auglaize	Ohio	2,242
German	Clark	Ohio	1,912
German	Darke	Ohio	1,501
German	Fulton	Ohio	982
German	Harrison	Ohio	1,357
German	Holmes	Ohio	1,517
German	Montgomery	Ohio	2,789
German	Fayette	Pa.	1,894
German Flats	Herkimer	N. Y.	3,578
Germantown	Wayne	Ind.	462
Germantown	Bracken	Ky.	f145
Germantown	Chenango	N. Y.	903
Germantown	Columbia	N. Y.	1,023
Germantown, Bor.	Philadelphia	Pa.	g6,209
Germantown	Philadelphia	Pa.	2,127
Germantown	Shelby	Tenn.	h245
Germantown	Washington	Wis.	1,714
Germany	Adams	Pa.	720
Gerry	Chautauque	N. Y.	1,332
Gettysburgh	Adams	Pa.	i2,180
Ghent	Columbia	N. Y.	2,293
Gibson	Washington	Ind.	1,095
Gibson	Mercer	Ohio	485
Gibson	Elk	Pa.	332
Gibson	Susquehanna	Pa.	1,459
Gilboa	Schoharie	N. Y.	3,024
Gilboa	Putnam	Ohio	378
Gilead	Calhoun	Ill.	553
Gilead	Oxford	Me.	359
Gilead	Branch	Mich.	503
Gilead	Morrow	Ohio	1,680
Giles	Van Buren	Ark.	415
Gilford	Belknap	N. H.	2,425
Gill	Sullivan	Ind.	1,241
Gill	Franklin	Mass.	754
Gillam	Jasper	Ind.	453
Gilman	Hamilton	N. Y.	101
Gilmanton	Belknap	N. H.	3,282
Gilmer	Upshur	Texas.	600
Gilmer	Adams	Ill.	1,051
Gilsum	Cheshire	N. H.	668
Girard	Russell	Ala.	748
Girard	Branch	Mich.	934
Girard	Clearfield	Pa.	286

a In 1853, 2,000. *b* In 1853, 8,000. *c* In 1853, 1,000. *d* In 1853, 7,000. *e* In 1853, 800. *f* In 1853, 500. *g* In 1853, 7,000. *h* In 1853, 400. *i* In 1853, 3,000.

Place	County	State	Population
Girard, Bor	Erie	Pa	400
Girard	Erie	Pa	2,443
Glade	Warren	Pa	420
Glasgow	Barren	Ky	933
Glasgow	Howard	Mo	1,200
Glassborough	Gloucester	N. J	1,300
Glastenbury	Hartford	Conn	3,390
Glastonbury	Bennington	Vt	52
Glen	Montgomery	N. Y	3,043
Glenburn	Penobscot	Me	905
Glonn's Falls	Warren	N. Y	2,717
Glenville	Barbour	Ala	900
Glenville	Schenectady	N. Y	3,409
Gloucester	Essex	Mass	7,786
Gloucester	Camden	N. J	2,371
Gloucoster	Providence	R. I	2,872
Gloucester City	Camden	N. J	2,188
Glover	Orleans	Vt	1,137
Goffstown	Hillsborough	N. H	2,270
Gold	Bureau	Ill	19
Golden Ridge	Aroostook	Me	194
Goldsborough	Wayne	N. C	1,500
Goodale	Lake	Ill	423
Goodfarm	Grundy	Ill	101
Goodhope	Hocking	Ohio	635
Gorham	Cumberland	Me	3,088
Gorham	Coos	N. H	224
Gorham	Ontario	N. Y	2,645
Gorham	Fulton	Ohio	906
Goshen	Litchfield	Conn	1,457
Goshen	Elkhart	Ind	a780
Goshen	Hampshire	Mass	512
Goshen	Sullivan	N. H	659
Goshen	Orange	N. Y	3,149
Goshen	Auglaize	Ohio	336
Goshen	Belmont	Ohio	2,017
Goshen	Champaign	Ohio	1,943
Goshen	Clermont	Ohio	1,937
Goshen	Hardin	Ohio	590
Goshen	Mahoning	Ohio	1,720
Goshen	Tuscarawas	Ohio	3,067
Goshen	Clearfield	Pa	160
Goshen	Addison	Vt	486
Goshen	Caledonia	Vt	215
Gosport	Clarke	Ala	500
Gosport	Owen	Ind	548
Gosport	Rockingham	N. H	102
Gosport, (Navy Yard)	Norfolk	Va	504
Gouldsboro	Hancock	Me	1,400
Gouverneur	St. Lawrence	N. Y	2,783
Grafton	Jersey	Ill	222
Grafton	McHenry	Ill	446
Grafton	Worcester	Mass	3,904
Grafton	Grafton	N. H	1,259
Grafton	Rensselaer	N. Y	2,033
Grafton	Loraine	Ohio	947
Grafton	Windham	Vt	1,241
Grafton	Washington	Wis	710
Graham	Jefferson	Ind	1,574
Granada	Yallobusha	Miss	1,590
Granby	Hartford	Conn	2,498
Granby	Hampshire	Mass	1,104
Granby	Oswego	N. Y	3,368
Granby	Essex	Vt	127
Grand	Marion	Ohio	353
Grand Blanc	Genesee	Mich	1,165
Grandchute	Brown	Wis	619
Grand de Tour	Ogle	Ill	378
Grand Gulf	Claiborne	Miss	b613
Grand Isle	Grand Isle	Vt	666
Grand Prairie	Marion	Ohio	474
Grand Rapids	Lasalle	Ill	336
Grand Rapids	Kent	Mich	c3,147
Grand Rapids, T	Kent	Mich	2,686
Grand Rapids	Portage	Wis	341
Grand River	Caldwell	Mo	*293
Grand River	Henry	Mo	*647
Grand View	Louisa	Iowa	1,028
Grandview	Washington	Ohio	1,154
Grandview & Embarrass	Edgar	Ill	1,337
Granger	Alleghany	N. Y	1,309
Granger	Medina	Ohio	1,317
Granite Creek	El Dorado	Cal	126
Grantham	Sullivan	N. H	784
Granville	Hampden	Mass	1,305
Granville	Washington	N. Y	3,434
Granville	Licking	Ohio	2,116
Granville, T	Licking	Ohio	771
Granville	Mercer	Ohio	564
Granville	Mifflin	Pa	1,052
Granville	Addison	Vt	603
Granville	Milwaukee	Wis	1,713
Granville	Bradford	Pa	1,033
Grass	Spencer	Ind	946
Grass Lake	Jackson	Mich	1,281
Grass Point	Wayne	Mich	1,392
Grass Valley	Yuba	Cal	454
Grassy Fork	Jackson	Ind	789
Gratiot	Lafayette	Wis	504
Gratiot	Muskingum	Ohio	1,444
Gratis	Preble	Ohio	2,107
Grattan	Kent	Mich	648
Grave Creek	Marshall	Va	1,200
Gravesend	Kings	N. Y	1,064
Gray	Pulaski	Ark	332
Gray	White	Ark	529
Gray	Cumberland	Me	1,788
Grayville	White	Ill	d334
Greasy Creek	Coles	Ill	453
Great Barrington	Berkshire	Mass	3,264
Great Bend	Susquehanna	Pa	1,150
Great Egg Harbor	Atlantic	N. J	2,689
Great Falls	Strafford	N. H	3,000
Great Valley	Cattaraugus	N. Y	1,638
Greece	Monroe	N. Y	4,219
Green	Howard	Ind	807
Green	Jay	Ind	362
Green	Morgan	Ind	1,330
Green	Noble	Ind	372
Green	Randolph	Ind	707
Green	St. Joseph	Ind	556
Green	Iowa	Iowa	181
Green	Kennebeck	Me	1,348
Green	Adams	Ohio	1,520
Green	Ashland	Ohio	1,902
Green	Brown	Ohio	669
Green	Clinton	Ohio	2,026
Green	Fayette	Ohio	1,058
Green	Gallia	Ohio	1,276
Green	Hamilton	Ohio	3,948
Green	Harrison	Ohio	1,527
Green	Hocking	Ohio	1,290
Green	Mahoning	Ohio	1,764
Green	Monroe	Ohio	1,226
Green	Ross	Ohio	1,994
Green	Scioto	Ohio	2,345
Green	Summit	Ohio	1,928
Green	Clinton	Pa	987
Green	Erie	Pa	1,542
Green	Pike	Pa	357
Green	Gentry	Mo	*168
Green Bay	Brown	Wis	e1,923
Greenbriar	Independence	Ark	676
Greenburgh	West Chester	N. Y	4,291
Greenbush	Penobscot	Me	457
Green Bush	Clinton	Mich	318
Greenbush	Rensselaer	N. Y	4,945
Green Camp	Marion	Ohio	383
Green Castle	Putnam	Ind	2,589
Greencastle, T	Putnam	Ind	1,382
Greencastle	Franklin	Pa	1,125
Green Creek	Sandusky	Ohio	1,289
Greene	Grant	Ind	373
Greene	Hancock	Ind	1,019
Greene	Madison	Ind	754
Greene	Parke	Ind	1,478
Greene	Wayne	Ind	1,532
Greene	Lawrence	Mo	*419
Greene	Platte	Mo	2,594
Greene	Sussex	N. J	823
Greene	Chenango	N. Y	3,763
Greene	Clark	Ohio	1,278
Greene	Shelby	Ohio	1,078
Greene	Trumbull	Ohio	958
Greene	Wayne	Ohio	2,060
Greene	Beaver	Pa	1,923
Greene	Franklin	Pa	3,154
Greene	Greene	Pa	667
Greene	Indiana	Pa	2,281
Greene	Mercer	Pa	933
Greenfield	Poinsett	Ark	706
Greenfield	Greene	Ill	237
Greenfield	Grundy	Ill	97
Greenfield	Orange	Ind	725
Greenfield	Jones	Iowa	168
Greenfield	Hancock	Me	305

a In 1853, 1,000. *b* In 1853, 800. *c* In 1853, 5,000. *d* In 1853, 600. *e* In 1853, 2,500.

Greenfield	Franklin	Mass.	2,580	Guilford	Piscataquis	Me.	834
Greenfield	Wayne	Mich.	1,674	Guilford	Chenango	N. Y.	2,600
Greenfield	Hillsborough	N. H.	716	Guilford	Medina	Ohio	1,800
Greenfield	Saratoga	N. Y.	2,890	Guilford	Franklin	Pa.	3,471
Greenfield	Fairfield	Ohio	2,113	Guilford	Windham	Vt.	1,389
Greenfield	Gallia	Ohio	952	Gull Lake	Mankahta	Minn.	15
Greenfield	Highland	Ohio	1,011	Gun Plains	Allegan	Mich.	587
Greenfield	Huron	Ohio	1,332	Gustavus	Trumbull	Ohio	1,226
Greenfield	Erie	Pa	731	Guyan	Gallia	Ohio	560
Greenfield	Luzerne	Pa	869	*Guyandotte*	Cabell	Va.	1,000
Greenfield	Washington	Pa	380	Gwynedd	Montgomery	Pa	1,571
Greenfield	Dane	Wis.	598	Hackensack	Bergen	N. J.	3,506
Greenfield	Milwaukie	Wis.	1,995	*Hackettstown*	Warren	N. J.	1,200
Greenfield	Blair	Pa	1,032	Haddam	Middlesex	Conn.	2,279
Greenford	Mahoning	Ohio	450	Haddenfield	Camden	N. J.	844
Green Lake	Marquette	Wis.	725	Haddon	Sullivan	Ind.	3,108
Greenland	Rockingham	N. H.	730	Hadley	Hampshire	Mass.	1,986
Green Oak	Livingston	Mich.	941	Hadley	Lapeer	Mich.	847
Greenport	Columbia	N. Y.	1,300	Hadley	Saratoga	N. Y.	1,003
Greenport	Suffolk	N. Y.	800	Hagerstown	Wayne	Ind	e606
Green River	Bureau	Ill.	75	Hagerstown	Washington	Md.	3,879
Greensborough	Greene	Ala.	2,500	Hague	Warren	N. Y.	717
Greentown	Stark	Ohio	261	Haines and Penn	Centre	Pa	2,454
Greenup	Cumberland	Ill	946	Halbert	Martin	Ind.	405
Greenville	Clark	Ark	300	Hale	Hardin	Ohio	428
Greenville	Bond	Ill	378	Half Moon	Saratoga	N. Y.	2,788
Greenville	Bureau	Ill	244	Half Moon	Centre	Pa	714
Greenville	Floyd	Ind	1,809	Halifax	Plymouth	Mass.	784
Greenville	Piscataquis	Me	326	Halifax, Bor	Dauphin	Pa	436
Greenville	Greene	N. Y.	2,242	Halifax	Dauphin	Pa	1,295
Greenville	Pitt	N. C.	1,150	Halifax	Windham	Vt.	1,133
Greenville	Darke	Ohio	3,417	Hall	Dubois	Ind	1,032
Greenville, T.	Darke	Ohio	1,045	Hallowell	Kennebeck	Me	4,769
Greenville	Somerset	Pa	723	Hamblin	Brown	Ind.	1,364
Greenville	Greenville	S. C.	1,305	Hamburg	Perry	Ala.	92
Greenville	Greene	Tenn.	660	Hamburg	Calhoun	Ill	f374
Greenville	Augusta	Va	300	Hamburg	Livingston	Mich.	895
Greenville	Brown	Wis.	98	Hamburg	Erie	N. Y.	5,219
Greenwich	Fairfield	Conn.	5,036	Hamburg	Berks	Pa	1,035
Greenwich	Hampshire	Mass.	838	Hamburg	Edgefield	S. C.	1,070
Greenwich	Cumberland	N. J.	1,158	Hamden	New Haven	Conn.	2,164
Greenwich	Gloucester	N. J.	3,067	Hamden	Delaware	N. Y.	1,919
Greenwich	Warren	N. J.	3,726	Hamer	Highland	Ohio	942
Greenwich	Washington	N. Y.	3,803	Hamersville	Brown	Ohio	131
Greenwich	Huron	Ohio	1,050	*Hamilton*	Harris	Ga	500
Greenwich	Berks	Pa	1,842	*Hamilton*	Boone	Ky	300
Greenwood	McHenry	Ill	844	Hamilton	Prairie	Ark.	249
Greenwood	Oxford	Me.	1,118	Hamilton	Lee	Ill.	316
Greenwood	Steuben	N. Y.	1,185	Hamilton	Delaware	Ind.	462
Greenwood	Columbia	Pa	1,260	Hamilton	Jackson	Ind.	1,151
Greenwood	Crawford	Pa	1,127	Hamilton	Sullivan	Ind.	1,610
Greenwood	Juniata	Pa	1,651	Hamilton	Essex	Mass.	889
Greenwood	Perry	Pa	995	Hamilton	Van Buren	Mich.	376
Greenwood	Abbeville	S. C.	†941	Hamilton	Mercer	N. J.	2,807
Greenwood Valley	El Dorado	Cal.	336	Hamilton	Madison	N. Y.	3,599
Greensboro'	Henry	Ind.	1,190	Hamilton	Butler	Ohio	g3,210
Greensborough	Orleans	Vt.	1,008	Hamilton	Franklin	Ohio	1,485
Greensburg	Decatur	Ind	a1,202	Hamilton	Jackson	Ohio	665
Greensburg	Putnam	Ohio	634	Hamilton	Warren	Ohio	2,068
Greensburgh	Westmoreland	Pa	b1,051	Hamilton	Adams	Pa	1,166
Green's Fork	Randolph	Ind	1,704	Hamilton, Bor	Adams	Pa	1,530
Gregg	Morgan	Ind	686	Hamilton	Franklin	Pa	1,924
Gregg	Centre	Pa	1,473	Hamilton	McKean	Pa	103
Greggs	Van Buren	Ark	259	Hamilton	Monroe	Pa	1,984
Greig	Lewis	N. Y.	1,074	Hamlin	McKean	Pa	118
Gretna	Jefferson	La	717	Hammond	Spencer	Ind	912
Griffin	Conway	Ark	480	Hammond	St. Lawrence	N. Y.	1,819
Griffin	Pike	Ga	c2,320	*Hammondsport*	Steuben	N. Y.	800
Griggsville	Pike	Ill	d585	Hammonton	Atlantic	N. J.	2,015
Griswold	New London	Conn.	2,065	Hampden	Penobscot	Me.	3,195
Groton	New London	Conn.	3,743	Hampden	Geauga	Ohio	919
Groton	Middlesex	Mass.	2,515	Hampden	Cumberland	Pa	1,273
Groton	Grafton	N. H.	776	Hampden	Columbia	Wis.	489
Groton	Tompkins	N. Y.	3,342	Hampshire	Kane	Ill.	759
Groton	Erie	Ohio	884	Hampsonville	Knox	Ill.	84
Groton	Caledonia	Vt.	895	Hampstead	Rockingham	N. H.	789
Grove	Davis	Iowa	456	Hampton	Monroe	Ark.	342
Grove	Alleghany	N. Y.	1,154	Hampton	Windham	Conn.	946
Grove	Clinton	Pa	258	Hampton	Saginaw	Mich.	546
Groveland	Essex	Mass.	1,286	Hampton	Rockingham	N. H.	1,192
Groveland	Oakland	Mich.	988	*Hampton*	Oneida	N. Y.	500
Groveland	Livingston	N. Y.	1,724	*Hampton*	Elizabeth City	Va	1,400
Groveport	Franklin	Ohio	483	Hampton	Washington	N. Y.	899
Guilderland	Albany	N. Y.	3,279	Hamptonburg	Orange	N. Y.	1,343
Guildhall	Essex	Vt.	501	Hampton Falls	Rockingham	N. H.	640
Guilford	New Haven	Conn.	2,653	Hamtramck	Wayne	Mich	1,628
Guilford	Winnebago	Ill.	917	Hancock	Aroostook	Me.	592
Guilford	Hendricks	Ind.	1,355	Hancock	Hancock	Me.	960

a In 1853, 1,600. *b* In 1853, 1,500. *c* In 1853, 3,500. *d* In 1853, 800. *e* In 1853, 900. *f* In 1853, 600. *g* In 1853, 5,000.

Town	County	State	Population
Hancock	Berkshire	Mass	789
Hancock	Hillsborough	N. H	1,012
Hancock	Delaware	N. Y	1,798
Hancock	Addison	Vt	430
Handy	Livingston	Mich	484
Hanging Rock	Lawrence	Ohio	800
Hannibal	Oswego	N. Y	2,857
Hannibal City	Marion	Mo	a2,020
Hanno	Lee	Ill	475
Hanover	Cook	Ill	672
Hanover	Jefferson	Ind	647
Hanover	Shelby	Ind	1,061
Hanover	Oxford	Me	266
Hanover	Plymouth	Mass	1,592
Hanover	Jackson	Mich	930
Hanover	Grafton	N. H	2,350
Hanover	Burlington	N. J	2,245
Hanover	Morris	N. J	3,614
Hanover	Chautauque	N. Y	5,144
Hanover	Ashland	Ohio	1,902
Hanover	Butler	Ohio	1,493
Hanover	Columbiana	Ohio	2,858
Hanover	Licking	Ohio	1,186
Hanover	Beaver	Pa	1,732
Hanover	Lehigh	Pa	2,375
Hanover	Luzerne	Pa	1,506
Hanover	Northampton	Pa	428
Hanover	Washington	Pa	1,803
Hanover	York	Pa	b1,210
Hanson	Plymouth	Mass	1,217
Harbor Creek	Erie	Pa	2,084
Hardin	Conway	Ark	168
Hardin	Calhoun	Ill	596
Hardingsburg	Breckenridge	Ky	1,000
Hardisten	Sussex	N. J	1,344
Hardwick	Worcester	Mass	1,631
Hardwick	Warren	N. J	727
Hardwick	Caledonia	Vt	1,402
Hardy	Holmes	Ohio	2,424
Harford	Cortlandt	N. Y	949
Harford	Susquehanna	Pa	1,258
Harlem	Carroll	Ill	392
Harlem	Winnebago	Ill	783
Harlem	Delaware	Ohio	1,182
Harley's Grove	McLean	Ill	42
Harmar	Washington	Ohio	c1,010
Harmony	Posey	Ind	1,886
Harmony	Union	Ind	848
Harmony	Somerset	Me	1,107
Harmony	Washington	Mo	700
Harmony	Warren	N. J	1,565
Harmony	Chatauque	N. Y	3,749
Harmony	Clark	Ohio	1,804
Harmony	Morrow	Ohio	1,041
Harmony	Butler	Pa	441
Harmony	Susquehanna	Pa	1,578
Harmony	Rock	Wis	840
Harper's Ferry	Jefferson	Va	1,747
Harpersfield	Delaware	N. Y	1,613
Harpersfield	Ashtabula	Ohio	1,278
Harpswell	Cumberland	Me	1,534
Harrietstown	Franklin	N. Y	181
Harrington	Washington	Me	963
Harrington	Bergen	N. J	1,195
Harris	Saint Joseph	Ind	437
Harris	Ottawa	Ohio	407
Harris	Centre	Pa	1,954
Harris	Caledonia	Vt	8
Harrisburg	Van Buren	Iowa	886
Harrisburg	Lewis	N. Y	1,367
Harrisburgh	Franklin	Ohio	109
Harrisburgh	Dauphin	Pa	d7,834
Harrison	Ouachita	Ark	534
Harrison	Union	Ark	804
Harrison	White	Ark	430
Harrison	Ogle	Ill	497
Harrison	Winnebago	Ill	449
Harrison	Bartholomew	Ind	607
Harrison	Blackford	Ind	746
Harrison	Cass	Ind	773
Harrison	Clay	Ind	684
Harrison	Daviess	Ind	692
Harrison	Dearborn	Ind	962
Harrison	Delaware	Ind	798
Harrison	Dubois	Ind	935
Harrison	Elkhart	Ind	840
Harrison	Fayette	Ind	1,544
Harrison	Hancock	Ind	500
Harrison	Henry	Ind	1,425
Harrison	Howard	Ind	912
Harrison	Kosciusko	Ind	780
Harrison	Miami	Ind	546
Harrison	Morgan	Ind	433
Harrison	Owen	Ind	375
Harrison	Pulaski	Ind	294
Harrison	Spencer	Ind	1,192
Harrison	Union	Ind	834
Harrison	Vigo	Ind	4,900
Harrison	Wayne	Ind	766
Harrison	Wells	Ind	1,460
Harrison	Cumberland	Me	1,416
Harrison	Macomb	Mich	483
Harrison	Scotland	Mo	*419
Harrison	Gloucester	N. J	1,984
Harrison	Hudson	N. J	1,345
Harrison	Westchester	N. Y	1,262
Harrison	Carroll	Ohio	1,268
Harrison	Champaign	Ohio	968
Harrison	Darke	Ohio	1,705
Harrison	Gallia	Ohio	1,008
Harrison	Hamilton	Ohio	940
Harrison	Henry	Ohio	516
Harrison	Knox	Ohio	751
Harrison	Licking	Ohio	1,447
Harrison	Logan	Ohio	987
Harrison	Montgomery	Ohio	2,059
Harrison	Muskingum	Ohio	1,533
Harrison	Paulding	Ohio	62
Harrison	Perry	Ohio	1,078
Harrison	Pickaway	Ohio	1,176
Harrison	Preble	Ohio	2,100
Harrison	Ross	Ohio	878
Harrison	Scioto	Ohio	1,102
Harrison	Van Wert	Ohio	513
Harrison	Vinton	Ohio	580
Harrison	Bedford	Pa	1,384
Harrison	Potter	Pa	718
Harrison	Hamilton	Tenn	500
Harrison	Grant	Wis	764
Harrisonburg	Catahoula	La	†326
Harrisonburg	Rockingham	Va	1,300
Harrisonville	Monroe	Ill	462
Harrisonville	Medina	Ohio	1,477
Harrisville	Butler	Pa	235
Harrisville	Harrison	Ohio	300
Harrodsburg	Mercer	Ky	e1,481
Harrodsburg Village	Johnson	Mo	25
Hart	Warrick	Ind	1,434
Hartford	Hartford	Conn	f13,555
Hartford	Adams	Ind	265
Hartford	Blackford	Ind	250
Hartford	Oxford	Me	1,293
Hartford	Van Buren	Mich	296
Hartford	Pike	Mo	789
Hartford	Washington	N. Y	2,051
Hartford	Guernsey	Ohio	113
Hartford	Licking	Ohio	1,426
Hartford, T	Licking	Ohio	251
Hartford	Trumbull	Ohio	1,258
Hartford	Windsor	Vt	2,159
Hartford	Washington	Wis	1,050
Hartland	Hartford	Conn	848
Hartland	McHenry	Ill	968
Hartland	Somerset	Me	960
Hartland	Livingston	Mich	996
Hartland	Niagara	N. Y	3,028
Hartland	Huron	Ohio	1,024
Hartland	Windsor	Vt	2,063
Hartley	Union	Pa	2,142
Hartsgrove	Ashtabula	Ohio	650
Hartsville	Steuben	N. Y	854
Hartwick	Otsego	N. Y	2,352
Hartzog's	Van Buren	Ark	252
Harvard	Worcester	Mass	1,630
Harveysburg	Warren	Ohio	329
Harwich	Barnstable	Mass	3,258
Harwinton	Litchfield	Conn	1,175
Hastings	Barry	Mich	554
Hastings	Oswego	N. Y	2,920
Hatfield	Hampshire	Mass	1,073
Hatfield	Montgomery	Pa	1,135
Havannah	Mason	Ill	g462
Haverford	Delaware	Pa	1,399
Haverhill	Essex	Mass	5,877
Haverhill, T	Essex	Mass	3,500

a In 1853, 3,500. *b* In 1853, 1,500. *c* In 1853, 1,500. *d* In 1853, 8,500. *e* In 1853, 3,000. *f* In 1853, 16,000. *g* In 1853, 1,000.

Haverhill	Grafton	N. H.	2,405
Haverstraw	Rockland	N. Y.	5,885
Havre-de-Grace	Harford	Md	*a*1,335
Haw	Bartholomew	Ind	1,572
Haw Creek	Morgan	Mo	*293
Hawley	Franklin	Mass	881
Hawley	Wayne	Pa	3,000
Haycock	Bucks	Pa	1,135
Hayfield	Crawford	Pa	1,723
Hayneville	Lowndes	Ala	800
Haynesville	Aroostook	Me	96
Haysville	Ashland	Ohio	441
Hazel	Luzerne	Pa	2,080
Hazel Green	Grant	Wis	1,840
Hazleton	Shiawassee	Mich	26
Heath	Franklin	Mass	803
Heath	Jefferson	Pa	203
Hebron	Tolland	Conn	1,345
Hebron	McHenry	Ill	731
Hebron	Oxford	Me	839
Hebron	Grafton	N. H.	565
Hebron	Washington	N. Y.	2,548
Hebron	Licking	Ohio	649
Hebron	Potter	Pa	337
Hebron	Jefferson	Wis	640
Hector	Tompkins	N. Y.	6,052
Hector	Potter	Pa	313
Heidleburg	Lebanon	Pa	2,085
Heidleburg	Lehigh	Pa	1,386
Heidleburg	York	Pa	1,616
Helen	Clarion	Pa	648
Helena	Phillips	Ark	614
Hellam	York	Pa	1,528
Helts	Vermillion	Ind	2,121
Hemlock	Columbia	Pa	1,087
Hempfield	Westmoreland	Pa	5,935
Hempstead	Queens	N. Y.	8,811
Henderson	Houston	Ga	1,429
Henderson	Henderson	Ky	1,175
Henderson	Jefferson	N. Y.	2,339
Henderson	Huntingdon	Pa	819
Hendersonville	Knox	Ill	378
Hendricks	Shelby	Ind	1,272
Hennepin	Putnam	Ill	430
Henniker	Merrimack	N. H.	1,688
Henrietta	Jackson	Mich	830
Henrietta	Monroe	N. Y.	2,513
Henrietta	Lorain	Ohio	1,042
Henry	Marshall	Ill	400
Henry	Fulton	Ind	952
Henry	Henry	Ind	1,936
Henry	Wood	Ohio	321
Henry Clay	Fayette	Pa	1,117
Hensley	Johnson	Ind	1,260
Hepburn	Lycoming	Pa	1,428
Hereford	Berks	Pa	1,244
Herkimer	Herkimer	N. Y.	2,601
Herman	Penobscot	Me	1,374
Herman	Gasconade	Mo	943
Herman	Dodge	Wis	918
Hermon	St. Lawrence	N. Y.	1,690
Hernando	De Soto	Miss	950
Herrick	Bradford	Pa	818
Herrick	Susquehanna	Pa	824
Hertford	Perquimans	N. C.	†369
Hester	Jackson	Ark	170
Hickman	Scott	Ark	787
Hickman	Fulton	Ky	401
Hickory	Fulton	Ill	764
Hickory	Schuyler	Ill	445
Hickory	Mercer	Pa	2,089
Hicksville	Defiance	Ohio	507
Higginsport	Brown	Ohio	535
Highgate	Franklin	Vt	2,653
Highland	Grundy	Ill	67
Highland	Madison	Ill	704
Highland	Franklin	Ind	1,625
Highland	Greene	Ind	847
Highland	Vermillion	Ind	1,505
Highland	Oakland	Mich	851
Highland	Defiance	Ohio	365
Highland	Muskingum	Ohio	956
Highland	Elk	Pa	33
Highland	Grant	Wis	597
Highland	Iowa	Wis	1,184
High Spire	Dauphin	Pa	291
Hilburn	Madison	Ark	551
Hill	Grafton	N. H.	954
Hilliar	Knox	Ohio	1,141
Hillsboro	Scott	Miss	†182
Hillsboro	Highland	Ohio	1,392
Hillsborough	Hillsborough	N. H.	1,685
Hillsborough	Somerset	N. J.	3,409
Hillsdale	Hillsdale	Mich	1,067
Hillsdale	Columbia	N. Y.	2,123
Hillstown	Bucks	Pa	2,301
Hinckley	Medina	Ohio	1,416
Hinesburgh	Chittenden	Vt	1,834
Hingham	Plymouth	Mass	3,980
Hinsdale	Berkshire	Mass	1,253
Hinsdale	Cheshire	N. H.	1,903
Hinsdale	Cattaraugus	N. Y.	1,302
Hiram	Oxford	Me	1,210
Hiram	Portage	Ohio	1,106
Hitesville	Coles	Ill	909
Hoadlin	Van Wert	Ohio	125
Hobert	Lake	Ind	240
Hoboken	Hudson	N. J.	*b*2,668
Hocking	Fairfield	Ohio	5,309
Hodgdon	Aroostook	Me	862
Hodgensville	La Rue	Ky	†246
Hohokus	Bergen	N. J.	2,274
Holden	Worceser	Mass	1,933
Holderness	Grafton	N. H.	1,744
Holland	Hampden	Mass	449
Holland	Ottawa	Mich	1,829
Holland	Erie	N. Y.	1,315
Holland	Orleans	Vt	669
Hollenbach	Luzerne	Pa	742
Hollidaysburg	Blair	Pa	2,430
Hollis	York	Me	2,683
Hollis	Hillsborough	N. H.	1,293
Holliston	Middlesex	Mass	2,428
Holly	Oakland	Mich	941
Holly Springs	Marshall	Miss	3,500
Holmes	Crawford	Ohio	1,238
Holmesville	Appling	Ga	19
Holyoke	Hampden	Mass	3,245
Homer	Champaign	Ill	120
Homer	Will	Ill	811
Homer	Claiborne	La	418
Homer	Calhoun	Mich	929
Homer	Cortlandt	N. Y.	3,836
Homer	Licking	Ohio	226
Homer	Medina	Ohio	1,102
Homer	Morgan	Ohio	1,590
Homer	Potter	Pa	140
Honesdale	Wayne	Pa	2,263
Honey Brook	Chester	Pa	1,937
Honey Creek	Adams	Ill	891
Honey Creek	Vigo	Ind	1,529
Honey Creek	Clinton	Ind	905
Honey Creek	Sauk	Wis	349
Hoodsville	Jefferson	Ark	178
Hooksett	Merrimack	N. H.	1,503
Hoosick	Rensselaer	N. Y.	3,724
Hope	La Salle	Ill	376
Hope	Waldo	Me	1,108
Hope	Barry	Mich	99
Hope	Warren	N. J.	1,755
Hope	Hamilton	N. Y.	789
Hopewell	Cumberland	N. J.	1,480
Hopewell	Mercer	N. J.	3,698
Hopewell	Ontario	N. Y.	1,923
Hopewell	Licking	Ohio	1,227
Hopewell	Mercer	Ohio	290
Hopewell	Muskingum	Ohio	2,378
Hopewell, T.	Muskingum	Ohio	110
Hopewell	Perry	Ohio	1,387
Hopewell	Seneca	Ohio	1,288
Hopewell	Beaver	Pa	1,025
Hopewell	Bedford	Pa	840
Hopewell	Cumberland	Pa	1,053
Hopewell	Huntingdon	Pa	788
Hopewell	Washington	Pa	1,748
Hopewell	York	Pa	2,432
Hopkinton	Middlesex	Mass	2,801
Hopkinton	Merrimack	N. H.	2,169
Hopkinton	Washington	R. I.	2,477
Hopkinton	St. Lawrence	N. Y.	1,476
Hopkinsville	Christian	Ky	3,500
Horicon	Warren	N. Y.	1,152
Hornby	Steuben	N. Y.	1,314
Hornellsville	Steuben	N. Y.	2,637
Horseham	Montgomery	Pa	1,336
Horsehead	Johnson	Ark	1,134
Horseshoe Bar	Sutter	Cal	125
Horton	Brown	Wis	192

a In 1853, 1,800. *b* In 1853, 5,527.

Hortontown	Comal	Texas	139
Hot Spring	Hot Springs	Ark.	*966
Houghton	Houghton	Mich.	456
Houlton	Aroostook	Me.	1,453
Houndsfield	Jefferson	N. Y.	4,136
Houston	Adams	Ill.	478
Houston	Clearfield	Pa.	230
Houston	Harris	Texas	2,396
Howard	Winnebago	Ill.	916
Howard	Howard	Ind.	636
Howard	Cass	Mich.	766
Howard	Gentry	Mo.	*336
Howard	Steuben	N. Y.	3,244
Howard	Knox	Ohio	1,002
Howard	Centre	Pa.	1,292
Howard	Brown	Wis.	567
Howell	Livingston	Mich.	1,155
Howell, T.	Livingston	Mich.	473
Howell	Monmouth	N. J.	4,058
Howland	Penobscot	Me.	214
Howland	Trumbull	Ohio	919
Hubbard	Trumbull	Ohio	1,272
Hubbard	Dodge	Wis.	874
Hubbardton	Worcester	Mass.	1,825
Hubbardton	Rutland	Vt.	701
Hudson	McLean	Ill.	336
Hudson	Laporte	Ind.	415
Hudson	Lenawee	Mich.	1,544
Hudson	Hillsborough	N. H.	1,312
Hudson	Columbia	N. Y.	6,286
Hudson	Summit	Ohio	1,457
Hudson	Walworth	Wis.	1,189
Hull	Spencer	Ind.	922
Hull	Plymouth	Mass.	253
Hume	Alleghany	N. Y.	2,159
Hummelstown	Dauphin	Pa.	619
Humphrey	Cattaraugus	N. Y.	824
Hunter	Greene	N. Y.	1,849
Huntersville	Miami	Ohio	225
Huntingdon	Adams	Pa.	1,408
Huntingdon	Huntingdon	Pa.	a1,470
Huntingdon	Luzerne	Pa.	1,747
Huntingdon	Carroll	Tenn.	383
Huntington	Fairfield	Conn.	1,301
Huntington	Huntington	Ind.	b594
Huntington	Suffolk	N. Y.	7,481
Huntington	Brown	Ohio	2,684
Huntington	Gallia	Ohio	1,308
Huntington	Lorain	Ohio	1,173
Huntington	Ross	Ohio	1,658
Huntington	Chittenden	Vt.	885
Huntsburg	Geauga	Ohio	1,007
Huntsville	Madison	Ala.	c2,863
Huntsville	Madison	Ark.	255
Huntsville	Schuyler	Ill.	513
Huntsville	Madison	Ind.	186
Huntsville	Randolph	Ind.	135
Huntsville	Logan	Ohio	214
Huntsville	Walker	Texas	1,200
Hurley	Ulster	N. Y.	2,003
Huron	Des Moines	Iowa	597
Huron	Wayne	Mich.	504
Huron	Wayne	N. Y.	1,966
Huron	Erie	Ohio	1,397
Hurricane	Bradley	Ark.	202
Hurricane	Cumberland	Ill.	539
Hustiford	Dodge	Wis.	635
Huston	Blair	Pa.	1,174
Huston	Centre	Pa.	375
Hyde Park	Dutchess	N. Y.	2,425
Hyde Park	Luzerne	Pa.	1,300
Hyde Park	Lamoille	Vt.	1,107
Iberia	Morrow	Ohio	208
Idatown	Monroe	Mich.	345
Illinois	Washington	Ark.	714
Illinois	Calhoun	Ill.	520
Illinois Canon	El Dorado	Cal.	84
Imley	Lapeer	Mich.	183
Independence	Phillips	Ark.	436
Independence	Van Buren	Ark.	282
Independence	Coles	Ill.	905
Independence	Warren	Ind.	248
Independence	Appanoose	Iowa	177
Independence	Kenton	Ky.	*182
Independence	Oakland	Mich.	1,279
Independence	Dunklin	Mo.	447
Independence	Jackson	Mo.	2,500
Independence	Warren	N. J.	2,621
Independence	Alleghany	N. Y.	1,701
Independence	Cuyahoga	Ohio	1,485
Independence	Washington	Ohio	728
Independence	Beaver	Pa.	799
Indianapolis	Marion	Ind.	d8,091
Indian Creek	Lawrence	Ind.	1,227
Indian Creek	Monroe	Ind.	1,202
Indian Creek	Pulaski	Ind.	420
Indian Creek	Pike	Mo.	588
Indian Grove	Livingston	Ill.	252
Indian Lake Settlement	Hamilton	N. Y.	46
Indian Lands	Marquette	Wis.	2,864
Indiana	Alleghany	Pa.	2,448
Indiana	Indiana	Pa.	963
Indianola	Calhoun	Texas	379
Indian River Hundred	Sussex	Del.	1,683
Indian Town	Bureau	Ill.	459
Industry	Franklin	Me.	1,041
Ingham	Ingham	Mich.	744
Ionia	Ionia	Mich.	774
Iowa	Cedar	Iowa	546
Iowa City	Johnson	Iowa	1,582
Iowa City, T.	Johnson	Iowa	e1,250
Ipswich	Essex	Mass.	3,349
Ira	St. Clair	Mich.	596
Ira	Cayuga	N. Y.	2,110
Ira	Rutland	Vt.	400
Irasburgh	Orleans	Vt.	1,034
Irish Creek	El Dorado	Cal.	252
Ironton	Lawrence	Ohio	1,600
Irondequoit	Monroe	N. Y.	2,397
Iroquois	Jasper	Ind.	374
Irvin	Howard	Ind.	847
Irwin	Venango	Pa.	1,504
Irving	Barry	Mich.	214
Isabella	Fulton	Ill.	539
Island	Desha	Ark.	177
Island Creek	Jefferson	Ohio	1,981
Island Grove	Jasper	Ill.	252
Isleboro	Waldo	Me.	984
Isle La Motte	Grand Isle	Vt.	476
Isle of Shoals	York	Me.	29
Islip	Suffolk	N. Y.	2,602
Israel	Preble	Ohio	1,641
Italy	Yates	N. Y.	1,627
Ithica	Tompkins	N. Y.	6,909
Ixonia	Jefferson	Wis.	1,109
Jacinto	Tishamingo	Miss.	360
Jacksborough	Campbell	Tenn.	117
Jackson	Crittenden	Ark.	312
Jackson	Dallas	Ark.	910
Jackson	Monroe	Ark.	339
Jackson	Newton	Ark.	484
Jackson	Sevier	Ark.	858
Jackson	Union	Ark.	796
Jackson	Calaveras	Cal.	1,200
Jackson	Will	Ill.	456
Jackson	Bartholomew	Ind.	343
Jackson	Blackford	Ind.	419
Jackson	Brown	Ind.	1,098
Jackson	Carroll	Ind.	895
Jackson	Cass	Ind.	488
Jackson	Clay	Ind.	735
Jackson	Clinton	Ind.	2,060
Jackson	Dearborn	Ind.	916
Jackson	Decatur	Ind.	1,349
Jackson	De Kalb	Ind.	726
Jackson	Elkhart	Ind.	991
Jackson	Fayette	Ind.	1,284
Jackson	Fountain	Ind.	1,170
Jackson	Greene	Ind.	1,146
Jackson	Hamilton	Ind.	1,800
Jackson	Hancock	Ind.	677
Jackson	Howard	Ind.	584
Jackson	Jackson	Ind.	625
Jackson	Jasper	Ind.	312
Jackson	Jay	Ind.	575
Jackson	Kosciusko	Ind.	851
Jackson	Madison	Ind.	950
Jackson	Miami	Ind.	546
Jackson	Morgan	Ind.	1,138
Jackson	Orange	Ind.	687
Jackson	Owen	Ind.	778
Jackson	Parke	Ind.	959
Jackson	Putnam	Ind.	1,218
Jackson	Randolph	Ind.	911
Jackson	Ripley	Ind.	887
Jackson	Rush	Ind.	887

a In 1853, 1,800. *b* In 1853, 1,000. *c* In 1853, 4,000. *d* In 1853, 12,000. *e* In 1853, 4,000.

Name	County	State	Population
Jackson	Shelby	Ind	1,310
Jackson	Spencer	Ind	744
Jackson	Steuben	Ind	594
Jackson	Sullivan	Ind	1,056
Jackson	Tippecanoe	Ind	966
Jackson	Washington	Ind	2,807
Jackson	Wayne	Ind	3,466
Jackson	Wells	Ind	633
Jackson	Henry	Iowa	555
Jackson	Jackson	Iowa	210
Jackson	Keokuk	Iowa	602
Jackson	Van Buren	Iowa	604
Jackson	East Feliciana	La	1,000
Jackson	Waldo	Me	833
Jackson	Jackson	Mich	4,147
Jackson, T	Jackson	Mich	2,363
Jackson	Hinds	Miss	a*1,881
Jackson	Adair	Mo	1,461
Jackson	Buchanan	Mo	*584
Jackson	Gentry	Mo	*336
Jackson	Greene	Mo	*742
Jackson	Johnson	Mo	2,256
Jackson	Newton	Mo	*327
Jackson	Osage	Mo	*943
Jackson	St. Genevieve	Mo	546
Jackson	Coos	N. H.	589
Jackson	Ocean	N. J.	1,333
Jackson	Washington	N. Y.	2,129
Jackson	Northampton	N. C.	†301
Jackson	Allen	Ohio	1,175
Jackson	Ashland	Ohio	1,532
Jackson	Brown	Ohio	1,262
Jackson	Champaign	Ohio	1,735
Jackson	Clermont	Ohio	1,241
Jackson	Coshocton	Ohio	2,037
Jackson	Crawford	Ohio	1,711
Jackson	Darke	Ohio	565
Jackson	Franklin	Ohio	1,550
Jackson	Guernsey	Ohio	1,192
Jackson	Hancock	Ohio	830
Jackson	Hardin	Ohio	530
Jackson	Highland	Ohio	1,449
Jackson	Jackson	Ohio	713
Jackson	Jackson	Ohio	480
Jackson	Knox	Ohio	1,080
Jackson	Licking	Ohio	256
Jackson	Mahoning	Ohio	1,142
Jackson	Monroe	Ohio	1,163
Jackson	Montgomery	Ohio	2,012
Jackson	Morgan	Ohio	1,249
Jackson	Muskingum	Ohio	1,233
Jackson	Muskingum	Ohio	45
Jackson	Paulding	Ohio	58
Jackson	Perry	Ohio	1,740
Jackson	Pickaway	Ohio	1,042
Jackson	Pike	Ohio	1,465
Jackson	Preble	Ohio	1,406
Jackson	Putnam	Ohio	221
Jackson	Richland	Ohio	1,093
Jackson	Sandusky	Ohio	1,092
Jackson	Seneca	Ohio	995
Jackson	Shelby	Ohio	705
Jackson	Stark	Ohio	1,517
Jackson	Union	Ohio	436
Jackson	Vinton	Ohio	835
Jackson	Wood	Ohio	74
Jackson	Wyandott	Ohio	395
Jackson	Cambria	Pa	832
Jackson	Columbia	Pa	374
Jackson	Dauphin	Pa	920
Jackson	Greene	Pa	1,252
Jackson	Huntingdon	Pa	1,431
Jackson	Lebanon	Pa	2,857
Jackson	Luzerne	Pa	592
Jackson	Lycoming	Pa	407
Jackson	Monroe	Pa	692
Jackson	Northumberland	Pa	1,935
Jackson	Perry	Pa	885
Jackson	Potter	Pa	51
Jackson	Susquehanna	Pa	978
Jackson	Tioga	Pa	1,419
Jackson	Venango	Pa	985
Jackson	Madison	Tenn	1,673
Jackson	Washington	Wis	1,038
Jacksonborough	Butler	Ohio	185
Jacksonville	Benton	Ala	716
Jacksonville	Tuolumne	Cal	1,000
Jacksonville	Duval	Fla	1,045
Jacksonville	Telfair	Ga	119
Jacksonville	Morgan	Ill	2,745
Jacobsburg	Belmont	Ohio	156
Jacobsport	Coshocton	Ohio	217
Jaffrey	Cheshire	N. H.	1,497
Jamaica	Queens	N. Y.	4,247
Jamaica	Windham	Vt	1,606
James	Taney	Mo	252
Jamestown	Steuben	Ind	415
Jamestown	Campbell	Ky	1,000
Jamestown	Ottawa	Mich	72
Jamestown	Chautauque	N. Y.	2,200
Jamestown	Greene	Ohio	337
Jamestown	Monroe	Ohio	90
Jamestown	Newport	R. I.	358
Jamestown	Grant	Wis	666
Janesville, east of Rock river	Rock	Wis	1,487
Janesville west of Rock river	Rock	Wis	b1,964
Jasper	Crawford	Ark	696
Jasper	Crittenden	Ark	420
Jasper	Dubois	Ind	700
Jasper	Hamilton	Fla	300
Jasper	Taney	Mo	84
Jasper	Steuben	N. Y.	1,749
Jasper	Fayette	Ohio	1,193
Jasper	Pike	Ohio	75
Jasper	Marion	Tenn	300
Jasper	Jasper	Texas	150
Java	Wyoming	N. Y.	2,245
Jay	Franklin	Me	1,733
Jay	Essex	N. Y.	2,688
Jay	Elk	Pa	327
Jefferson	Carroll	Ark	782
Jefferson	Independence	Ark	553
Jefferson	Jackson	Ark	465
Jefferson	Ouachita	Ark	720
Jefferson	Sevier	Ark	489
Jefferson	Jackson	Ga	380
Jefferson	Cook	Ill	744
Jefferson	Adams	Ind	297
Jefferson	Allen	Ind	563
Jefferson	Carroll	Ind	713
Jefferson	Cass	Ind	734
Jefferson	Clinton	Ind	254
Jefferson	Elkhart	Ind	707
Jefferson	Grant	Ind	1,029
Jefferson	Greene	Ind	470
Jefferson	Henry	Ind	816
Jefferson	Jay	Ind	717
Jefferson	Kosciusko	Ind	169
Jefferson	Miami	Ind	1,138
Jefferson	Morgan	Ind	874
Jefferson	Noble	Ind	722
Jefferson	Owen	Ind	1,191
Jefferson	Pike	Ind	1,638
Jefferson	Putnam	Ind	1,046
Jefferson	Switzerland	Ind	3,082
Jefferson	Tipton	Ind	787
Jefferson	Wayne	Ind	1,723
Jefferson	Wells	Ind	796
Jefferson	Clayton	Iowa	546
Jefferson	Henry	Iowa	758
Jefferson	Louisa	Iowa	646
Jefferson	Lincoln	Me	2,225
Jefferson	Frederick	Md	337
Jefferson	Cass	Mich	887
Jefferson	Hillsdale	Mich	763
Jefferson	Adair	Mo	1,502
Jefferson	Johnson	Mo	1,003
Jefferson	Osage	Mo	*492
Jefferson	Scotland	Mo	*1,024
Jefferson	Coos	N. H.	629
Jefferson	Morris	N. J.	1,358
Jefferson	Chemung	N. Y.	1,500
Jefferson	Schoharie	N. Y.	1,748
Jefferson	Adams	Ohio	1,530
Jefferson	Ashtabula	Ohio	1,064
Jefferson, T	Ashtabula	Ohio	439
Jefferson	Clinton	Ohio	810
Jefferson	Coshocton	Ohio	929
Jefferson	Fayette	Ohio	1,872
Jefferson	Franklin	Ohio	1,236
Jefferson	Guernsey	Ohio	857
Jefferson	Jackson	Ohio	1,036
Jefferson	Knox	Ohio	1,484
Jefferson	Logan	Ohio	2,042
Jefferson	Madison	Ohio	1,070
Jefferson	Mercer	Ohio	493

a In 1853, 3,500. *b* In 1853, 5,000, including Janesville, east of Rock River.

Town	County	State	Population
Jefferson	Montgomery	Ohio	1,808
Jefferson	Muskingum	Ohio	2,822
Jefferson	Preble	Ohio	2,258
Jefferson	Richland	Ohio	2,564
Jefferson	Ross	Ohio	845
Jefferson	Scioto	Ohio	840
Jefferson	Tuscarawas	Ohio	1,063
Jefferson	Williams	Ohio	1,015
Jefferson	Allegheny	Pa	1,138
Jefferson	Dauphin	Pa	710
Jefferson	Fayette	Pa	1,435
Jefferson	Greene	Pa	1,378
Jefferson	Luzerne	Pa	414
Jefferson	Somerset	Pa	775
Jefferson	Cass	Texas	1,500
Jefferson	Green	Wis	692
Jefferson	Jefferson	Wis	1,610
Jefferson, T	Jefferson	Wis	*a* 550
Jefferson Barracks	St. Louis	Mo	924
Jefferson City	Cole	Mo	3,000
Jeffersonville	Clark	Ind	3,847
Jeffersonville, T	Clark	Ind	2,122
Jenks	Jefferson	Pa	88
Jenner	Somerset	Pa	1,553
Jennings	Crawford	Ind	1,412
Jennings	Fayette	Ind	893
Jennings	Owen	Ind	458
Jennings	Scott	Ind	1,922
Jennings	Putnam	Ohio	336
Jennings	Van Wert	Ohio	201
Jericho	Chittenden	Vt	1,837
Jerman	Keokuk	Iowa	239
Jerome	Union	Ohio	1,249
Jerry	Jackson	Iowa	42
Jersey	Licking	Ohio	1,230
Jersey City	Hudson	N. J.	*b*6,856
Jersey Shore	Lycoming	Pa	632
Jerseyville	Jersey	Ill	760
Jerusalem	Yates	N. Y.	2,912
Jessup	Susquehanna	Pa	840
Jewett	Greene	N. Y.	1,452
Johnsburgh	Warren	N. Y.	1,503
Johnson	St. Francis	Ark	783
Johnson	Union	Ark	1,625
Johnson	Clark	Ill	672
Johnson	Brown	Ind	418
Johnson	Clinton	Ind	777
Johnson	Gibson	Ind	1,568
Johnson	Lagrange	Ind	878
Johnson	Porter	Ind	402
Jehnson	Ripley	Ind	2,141
Johnson	Scotland	Mo	*538
Johnson	Washington	Mo	462
Johnson	Champaign	Ohio	1,573
Johnson	Trumbull	Ohio	1,099
Johnson	Lamoille	Vt	1,381
Johnston	Providence	R. I	2,937
Johnstown	Barry	Mich	451
Johnstown	Fulton	N. Y.	6,131
Johnstown	Cambria	Pa	1,269
Johnstown	Rock	Wis	1,271
Johnsville	Morrow	Ohio	135
Joliet	Will	Ill	2,659
Jolly	Washington	Ohio	1,014
Jones	Hancock	Ind	670
Jones	Elk	Pa	235
Jonesboro	Washington	Me	466
Jonesborough	Union	Ill	584
Jonesport	Washington	Me	826
Jonesville	Hillsdale	Mich	565
Jordan	Jasper	Ind	262
Jordan	Warren	Ind	348
Jordan	Clearfield	Pa	612
Jordan	Green	Wis	391
Josco	Livingston	Mich	645
Joshua	Fulton	Ill	879
J. Q. Adams	Warren	Ind	539
Juniata	Blair	Pa	1,752
Juniata	Perry	Pa	1,435
Junius	Seneca	N. Y.	1,516
Kalamazoo	Kalamazoo	Mich	3,284
Kalamazoo, T	Kalamazoo	Mich	2,507
Kalamo	Eaton	Mich	429
Kalida	Putnam	Ohio	216
Kan	Jackson	Mo	2,529
Kanesville	Kane	Ill	592
Kankakee	Laporte	Ind	899
Kankanlin	Brown	Wis	704
Karthaus	Clearfield	Pa	316
Kaskaskia	Randolpb	Ill	513
Kahtahdin Iron Works	Piscataquis	Me	158
Kating	Clinton	Pa	225
Keating	McKean	Pa	1,181
Keeler	Van Buren	Mich	485
Keene	Adams	Ill	652
Keene	Ionia	Mich	737
Keene	Cheshire	N. H.	3,392
Keene	Essex	N. Y.	756
Keene	Coshocton	Ohio	1,078
Keithsburg	Mercer	Ill	252
Kelly's Island	Erie	Ohio	186
Kelly	Union	Pa	834
Kelsey's vicinity	El Dorado	Cal	714
Kelso	Dearborn	Ind	1,594
Kendall	Kendall	Ill	797
Kendall	Orleans	N. Y.	2,289
Kendall	Lafayette	Wis	333
Kennebunk	York	Me	2,650
Kennebunkport	York	Me	2,706
Kennett	Chester	Pa	1,706
Kenosha City	Kenosha	Wis	*c*3,455
Kensington	Rockingham	N. H.	700
Kensington	Philadelphia	Pa	46,744
Kent	Litchfield	Conn	1,848
Kent	Jefferson	Ind	133
Kent	Putnam	N. Y.	1,557
Kenton	Hardin	Ohio	1,065
Keokuk	Lee	Iowa	*d*2,478
Keosauqua	Van Buren	Iowa	705
Kerton	Fulton	Ill	308
Keytsville	Chariton	Mo	1,427
Key West	Monroe	Fla	*1,943
Kidder	Carbon	Pa	536
Kilbuck	Holmes	Ohio	1,244
Killingly	Windham	Conn	4,543
Killingworth	Middlesex	Conn	1,107
Kilmarnock	Piscataquis	Me	322
Kinderhook	Branch	Mich	356
Kinderhook	Columbia	N. Y.	3,970
Kingsbury	Piscataquis	Me	181
Kingsbury	Washington	N. Y.	3,032
Kingsessing	Philadelphia	Pa	1,778
Kingsfield	Franklin	Me	662
Kingsport	Sullivan	Tenn	†320
King's River	Madison	Ark	606
Kingston	Autauga	Ala	186
Kingston	De Kalb	Ill	601
Kingston	Plymouth	Mass	1,591
Kingston	Rockingham	N. H.	1,192
Kingston	Ulster	N. Y.	10,232
Kingston	Lenoir	N. C.	†455
Kingston	Delaware	Ohio	761
Kingston	Ross	Ohio	336
Kingston	Luzerne	Pa	2,454
Kingston	Roane	Tenn	386
Kingston	Marquette	Wis	536
Kingston	Sauk	Wis	435
Kingsville	Ashtabula	Ohio	1,494
Kingwood	Hunterdon	N. J.	1,799
Kinsman	Trumbull	Ohio	1,005
Kinzua	Warren	Pa	232
Kirby	Caledonia	Vt	509
Kirkland	Adams	Ind	190
Kirkland	Penobscot	Me	717
Kirkland	Oneida	N. Y.	3,421
Kirklin	Clinton	Ind	740
Kirklin, T.	Clinton	Ind	59
Kirkwood	Belmont	Ohio	2,208
Kirtland	Lake	Ohio	1,598
Kiskiminetas	Armstrong	Pa	2,430
Kittaning, Bor	Armstrong	Pa	1,561
Kittaning	Armstrong	Pa	1,175
Kittery	York	Me	2,706
Knight	Vanderburg	Ind	650
Knightstown	Henry	Ind	1,600
Knowlton	Warren	N. J.	1,366
Knox	Jay	Ind	271
Knox	Waldo	Me	1,102
Knox	Albany	N. Y.	2,021
Knox	Columbiana	Ohio	2,155
Knox	Guernsey	Ohio	755
Knox	Holmes	Ohio	1,210
Knox	Jefferson	Ohio	1,902
Knoxville	Knox	Ill	*e*798
Knoxville	Jefferson	Ohio	168
Knoxville	Knox	Tenn	*f*2,076
Kortwright	Delaware	N. Y.	2,181

a In 1853, 1,000. *b* In 1853, 18,456. *c* In 1853, 5,000. *d* In 1853, 5,000. *e* In 1853, 1,200. *f* In 1853, 4,000.

Place	County	State	Population
Koscinsko	Attala	Miss..	412
Koskonong	Jefferson	Wis...	1,143
Kossuth	Auglaize	Ohio..	76
Kossuth	Columbia	Wis...	394
Kutztown	Berks	Pa	640
Lack	Juniata	Pa	1,146
Lackawanna	Luzerne	Pa	*a*389
Lackawaxen	Pike	Pa	1,419
Lacon	Marshall	Ill	963
La Cuesta	San Miguel	N. M.	2,196
Lacy's Bar and vicinity, and Manhattan Bar	Sutter	Cal	420
Lafavor	Scott	Ark	175
Lafayette	Crawford	Ark	555
Lafayette	Ouachita	Ark	1,181
Lafayette	Scott	Ark	88
Lafayette	Walker	Ga	503
Lafayette	Fulton	Ill	965
Lafayette	Allen	Ind	524
Lafayette	Floyd	Ind	1,215
Lafayette	Madison	Ind	694
Lafayette	Owen	Ind	754
Lafayette	Jefferson	La	*14,190
Lafayette	Van Buren	Mich	1,143
Lafayette	Jefferson	Miss	*210
Lafayette	Sussex	N. J.	928
Lafayette	Onondaga	N. Y.	2,533
Lafayette	Coshocton	Ohio	1,040
Lafayette	Madison	Ohio	147
Lafayette	Medina	Ohio	1,332
Lafayette	McKean	Pa	183
Lafayette	Macon	Tenn	210
Lafayette	Walworth	Wis	1,048
Lafayette city	Tippecanoe	Ind	*b*6,129
Lafayette & Flagg	Ogle	Ill	616
La Grange	Lafayette	Ark	1,005
La Grange	Philips	Ark	462
La Grange	Troupe	Ga	1,523
La Grange	Brown	Ill	102
La Grange	Penobscot	Me	482
Lagrange	Cass	Mich	1,327
La Grange	Lewis	Mo	*c*439
La Grange	Dutchess	N. Y.	1,941
La Grange	Jefferson	Ohio	363
La Grange	Lorain	Ohio	1,402
La Grange	Fayette	Tenn	1,200
La Grange	Walworth	Wis	1,050
Lagro	Wabash	Ind	2,515
Lagro, T	Wabash	Ind	293
Lake	Cook	Ill	349
Lake	Allen	Ind	578
Lake	Buchanan	Mo	*378
Lake	Ashland	Ohio	880
Lake	Logan	Ohio	1,767
Lake	Stark	Ohio	2,228
Lake	Wood	Ohio	152
Lake	Luzerne	Pa	383
Lake	Milwaukee	Wis	1,474
Lake Mills	Jefferson	Wis	882
Lake Pleasant	Hamilton	N. Y.	305
Lamar	Marshall	Miss	224
Lamar	Clinton	Pa	1,182
Lamasco	Vanderburg	Ind	1,441
Lambertsville	Hunterdon	N. J.	*d*1,417
Lamartine	Fond du Lac	Wis	588
Lamoille	Bureau	Ill	462
Lancaster	Stephenson	Ill	835
Lancaster	Jefferson	Ind	1,381
Lancaster	Wells	Ind	795
Lancaster	Keokuk	Iowa	444
Lancaster, T	Keokuk	Iowa	95
Lancaster	Worcester	Mass	1,688
Lancaster	Coos	N. H.	1,559
Lancaster	Erie	N. Y.	3,794
Lancaster (city)	Lancaster	Pa	*e*12,369
Lancaster	Lancaster	Pa	811
Lancaster	Lancaster	S. C.	376
Lancaster (corporation)	Fairfield	Ohio	*f*3,483
Lance	Horton	Mich	126
Landaff	Grafton	N. H	948
Landgrove	Bennington	Vt	337
Landisburgh	Perry	Pa	416
Lanesborough	Berkshire	Mass	1,229
Langdon	Sullivan	N. H.	575
L'Anguelle	St. Francis	Ark	339
Lanier	Macon	Ga	217

Place	County	State	Population
Lanier	Preble	Ohio	1,694
Lansing	Ingham	Mich	1,229
Lansing	Tompkins	N. Y.	3,318
Lansing	Brown	Wis	209
Lansingburgh	Rensselaer	N. Y.	5,752
Laona	Winnebago	Ill	498
Lapeer	Lapeer	Mich	1,468
Lapeer	Cortlandt	N. Y.	822
Lapile	Union	Ark	542
Laporte	Laporte	Ind	1,824
Laporte	Sullivan	Pa	300
La Prairie	Rock	Wis	335
Lasalle	La Salle	Ill	3,201
La Salle	Monroe	Mich	1,100
Las Vegas	San Miguel	N. M.	1,550
Lathrop	Susquehanna	Pa	510
Lattimore	Adams	Pa	1,138
Laughery	Dearborn	Ind	1,092
Laughery	Ripley	Ind	868
Lauramie	Tippecanoe	Ind	1,611
Laurel	Sussex	Del	1,000
Laurel	Franklin	Ind	1,845
Laurel	Hocking	Ohio	1,126
Laurel Factory	Prince George	Md	1,000
Laurens	Otsego	N. Y.	2,168
Lausanne	Carbon	Pa	1,382
Lavacca	Calhoun	Texas	315
Lawrence	Marion	Ind	1,986
Lawrence	Essex	Mass	*g*8,282
Lawrence	Van Buren	Mich	510
Lawrence	Mercer	N. J.	1,138
Lawrence	Lawrence	Ohio	534
Lawrence	Stark	Ohio	2,287
Lawrence	Tuscarawas	Ohio	1,468
Lawrence	Washington	Ohio	814
Lawrence	Clearfield	Pa	1,173
Lawrence	Tioga	Pa	1,029
Lawrence	Brown	Wis	256
Lawrenceburg	Dearborn	Ind	836
LawrenceburgCity	Dearborn	Ind	*h*2,651
Lawrenceport	Lawrence	Ind	400
Lawrenceville	Lawrence	Ill	419
Lawrenceville	St. Lawrence	N. Y	2,214
Lawrenceville	Allegheny	Pa	1,746
Lawrenceville	Tioga	Pa	494
Lawrenceville	Brunswick	Va	400
Leaf River	Ogle	Ill	405
Leakesville	Rockingham	N. C.	300
Leasburg	Caswell	N. C.	300
Lebanon	Lawrence	Ark	182
Lebanon	New London	Conn	1,901
Lebanon	St. Clair	Ill	507
Lebanon	York	Me	2,208
Lebanon	Clinton	Mich	192
Lebanon	Grafton	N. H.	2,136
Lebanon	Hunterdon	N. J.	2,128
Lebanon	Madison	N. Y.	1,709
Lebanon	Meigs	Ohio	1,008
Lebanon	Warren	Ohio	2,088
Lebanon	Lebanon	Pa	2,184
Lebanon	Wayne	Pa	426
Lebanon	Wilson	Tenn	†1,554
Lebanon	Dodge	Wis	1,030
Lehœuf	Erie	Pa	990
Ledyard	New London	Conn	1,558
Ledyard	Cayuga	N. Y.	2,043
Lee	Fulton	Ill	333
Lee	Penobscot	Me	917
Lee	Berkshire	Mass	3,220
Lee	Calhoun	Mich	381
Lee	Platte	Mo	1,794
Lee	Strafford	N. H.	862
Lee	Oneida	N. Y.	3,033
Lee	Athens	Ohio	961
Lee	Carroll	Ohio	1,220
Lee Centre	Lee	Ill	292
Leeds	Kennebeck	Me	1,652
Leesburg	Kosciusko	Ind	217
Leesburg	Highland	Ohio	500
Leesburg	Union	Ohio	701
Leesburg	Loudon	Va	1,691
Lehigh	Northampton	Pa	2,343
Lehman	Luzerne	Pa	558
Lehman	Pike	Pa	869
Leicester	Worcester	Mass	2,269
Leicester	Livingston	N. Y	2,142
Leicester	Addison	Vt	596
Leidy	Clinton	Pa	263

a Now called Scranton; population in 1853, 3,000. *b* In 1853, 8,000. *c* In 1853, 600. *d* In 1853, 2,000. *e* In 1853, 14,000. *f* In 1853, 5,000. *g* In 1853, 12,000. *h* In 1853, 4,500.

Leighton	Allegan	Mich.	112
Leitersburg	Washington	Md	298
Lemington	Essex	Vt.	187
Lemon	Butler	Ohio	3,021
Lemon	Wyoming	Pa	284
Lemont	Cook	Ill	210
Lempster	Sullivan	N. H.	906
Lena	Miami	Ohio	105
Lenoir	Caldwell	N. C.	300
Lenox	Berkshire	Mass	1,599
Lenox	Macomb	Mich	652
Lenox	Madison	N. Y.	7,507
Lenox	Ashtabula	Ohio	731
Lenox	Susquehanna	Pa	1,443
Leominster	Worcester	Mass	3,121
Leon	Cattaraugus	N. Y.	1,340
Leoni	Jackson	Mich	1,290
Leonidas	St. Joseph	Mich	857
Leopold	Perry	Ind	485
Le Ray	Jefferson	N. Y.	3,654
Le Roy	Boone	Ill	919
Le Roy	McLean	Ill	210
Leroy	Calhoun	Mich	878
Le Roy	Ingham	Mich	254
Le Roy	Genesee	N. Y.	3,473
Le Roy	Lake	Ohio	1,128
Le Roy	Bradford	Pa	916
Leroy	Dodge	Wis	397
Leslie	Ingham	Mich	673
Letart	Meigs	Ohio	966
Letterkenny	Franklin	Pa	2,048
Levana	Brown	Ohio	175
Levant	Penobscot	Me	1,841
Leverett	Franklin	Mass	948
Lewes and Rehoboth Hundred	Sussex	Del	1,855
Lewis	Clay	Ind	574
Lewis	Essex	N. Y.	2,058
Lewis	Brown	Ohio	2,720
Lewis	Lycoming	Pa	596
Lewis	Northumberland	Pa	1,475
Lewisberry	York	Pa	245
Lewisborough	Westchester	N. Y.	1,608
Lewisburg	Champaign	Ohio	302
Lewisburgh	Preble	Ohio	355
Lewisburgh	Union	Pa	a2,012
Lewiston	Fulton	Ill	1,515
Lewiston	Lincoln	Me	3,584
Lewiston	Niagara	N. Y.	2,924
Lewistown	Mifflin	Pa	2,733
Lewisville	Henry	Ind	193
Lewisville	Monroe	Ohio	96
Lexington	Oglethorpe	Ga	650
Lexington	Scott	Ind	2,202
Lexington, T	Scott	Ind	273
Lexington	Fayette	Ky	†12,000
Lexington	Somerset	Me	538
Lexington	Middlesex	Mass	1,893
Lexington	Sanilac	Mich	1,176
Lexington	Holmes	Miss	†656
Lexington	Lafayette	Mo	b2,194
Lexington	Greene	N. Y.	2,263
Lexington	Stark	Ohio	1,996
Lexington	Rockbridge	Va	1,743
Lexington city	Lafayette	Mo	2,698
Leyden	Cook	Ill	756
Leyden	Franklin	Mass	716
Leyden	Lewis	N. Y.	2,253
Liberty	Ouachita	Ark	824
Liberty	St. Francis	Ark	150
Liberty	White	Ark	326
Liberty	Adams	Ill	1,077
Liberty	Crawford	Ind	545
Liberty	Delaware	Ind	1,171
Liberty	Fulton	Ind	657
Liberty	Grant	Ind	797
Liberty	Hendricks	Ind	1,955
Liberty	Henry	Ind	1,766
Liberty	Parke	Ind	1,234
Liberty	Porter	Ind	210
Liberty	St. Joseph	Ind	655
Liberty	Shelby	Ind	1,113
Liberty	Tipton	Ind	144
Liberty	Union	Ind	420
Liberty	Union	Ind	979
Liberty	Wabash	Ind	1,425
Liberty	Warren	Ind	900
Liberty	Wells	Ind	269
Liberty	Clinton	Iowa	215
Liberty	Jefferson	Iowa	1,209
Liberty	Johnson	Iowa	382
Liberty	Keokuk	Iowa	5
Liberty	Waldo	Me	1,116
Liberty	Jackson	Mich	891
Liberty	Clay	Mo	827
Liberty	Clay	Mo	2,730
Liberty	Marion	Mo	1,064
Liberty	Stoddard	Mo	424
Liberty	Washington	Mo	1,044
Liberty	Sullivan	N. Y.	2,612
Liberty	Adams	Ohio	1,498
Liberty	Butler	Ohio	1,501
Liberty	Clinton	Ohio	1,232
Liberty	Crawford	Ohio	1,782
Liberty	Delaware	Ohio	1,051
Liberty	Fairfield	Ohio	2,901
Liberty	Guernsey	Ohio	1,001
Liberty	Guernsey	Ohio	175
Liberty	Hancock	Ohio	874
Liberty	Hardin	Ohio	422
Liberty	Henry	Ohio	399
Liberty	Highland	Ohio	4,075
Liberty	Jackson	Ohio	1,017
Liberty	Knox	Ohio	1,320
Liberty	Licking	Ohio	1,190
Liberty	Logan	Ohio	1,262
Liberty	Mercer	Ohio	182
Liberty	Putnam	Ohio	322
Liberty	Ross	Ohio	1,126
Liberty	Seneca	Ohio	1,400
Liberty	Trumbull	Ohio	1,329
Liberty	Union	Ohio	1,257
Liberty	Van Wert	Ohio	424
Liberty	Washington	Ohio	1,223
Liberty	Wood	Ohio	236
Liberty	Adams	Pa	722
Liberty	Bedford	Pa	522
Liberty	Centre	Pa	387
Liberty	McKean	Pa	612
Liberty	Montour	Pa	1,233
Liberty	Susquehanna	Pa	833
Liberty	Tioga	Pa	1,472
Libertyville	Lake	Ill	756
Lick	Jackson	Ohio	1,501
Lick Creek	Davis	Iowa	547
Lick Creek	Van Buren	Iowa	830
Licking	Blackford	Ind	1,225
Licking	Licking	Ohio	1,371
Licking	Muskingum	Ohio	1,434
Licking Creek	Fulton	Pa	953
Lick Mountain	Conway	Ark	296
Ligonier, Bor	Westmoreland	Pa	378
Ligonier	Westmoreland	Pa	2,582
Lima	Adams	Ill	920
Lima	Carroll	Ill	198
Lima	Washtenaw	Mich	912
Lima	Livingston	N. Y.	2,433
Lima	Allen	Ohio	c757
Lima	Licking	Ohio	973
Lima	Grant	Wis	580
Lima	Rock	Wis	839
Limerick	York	Me	1,473
Limerick	Montgomery	Pa	2,165
Limestone	Clarion	Pa	1,461
Limestone	Lycoming	Pa	983
Limestone	Montour	Pa	763
Limestone	Union	Pa	807
Limestone	Warren	Pa	248
Limington	York	Me	2,116
Limitar	Valencia	N. M.	420
Lincoln	Penobscot	Me	1,356
Lincoln	Middlesex	Mass	719
Lincoln	Grafton	N. H.	57
Lincoln	Morrow	Ohio	891
Lincoln	Addison	Vt	1,057
Lincolnville	Waldo	Me	2,174
Lincolnton	Lincoln	Ga	166
Linden	Washtenaw	Mich	900
Linden	Perry	Tenn	500
Linden	Iowa	Wis	951
Lindley	Steuben	N. Y.	686
Lindsey	Benton	Mo	1,167
Linklean	Chenango	N. Y.	1,196
Linn	Cedar	Iowa	414
Linn	Osage	Mo	*1,176
Linn	Taney	Mo	504
Linn	Walworth	Wis	630
Linn City	Washington	Oregon	125

a In 1853, 2,500. b In 1853, 4,000. c In 1853, 1,000.

Place	County	State	Pop.	Place	County	State	Pop.
Linneus	Aroostook	Me	561	Londonderry	Windham	Vt	1,274
Linnville	Licking	Ohio	189	London Grove	Chester	Pa	1,425
Linton	Vigo	Ind	972	Long Creek	Carroll	Ark	294
Linton	Coshocton	Ohio	1,592	Long Lake	Hamilton	N. Y.	111
Lisbon	New London	Conn	938	Long Meadow	Hampden	Mass	1,252
Lisbon	Kendall	Ill	519	Long Point	Cumberland	Ill	512
Lisbon	Lincoln	Me	1,495	Long Prairie	Wahnahta	Minn	160
Lisbon	Grafton	N. H.	1,881	Long Swamp	Berks	Pa	1,868
Lisbon	St. Lawrence	N. Y.	5,295	Loramie	Shelby	Ohio	1,039
Lisbon	Waukesha	Wis	1,036	Lordstown	Trumbull	Ohio	1,329
Lisle	Broome	N. Y.	1,680	Loretto	Cambria	Pa	193
Litchfield	Litchfield	Conn	3,953	Lorion	Valencia	N. M.	242
Litchfield	Kennebeck	Me	2,100	Lorraine	Jefferson	N. Y.	1,511
Litchfield	Hillsdale	Mich	1,362	Los Angeles City	Los Angeles	Cal	1,610
Litchfield	Hillsborough	N. H.	447	Los Cruces	Valencia	N. M.	414
Litchfield	Herkimer	N. Y.	1,676	Los-en-Lames	Valencia	N. M.	180
Litchfield	Medina	Ohio	1,312	Los Lopis	Valencia	N. M.	191
Litchfield	Bradford	Pa	1,112	Los Lumas	Valencia	N. M.	226
Lithopolis	Fairfield	Ohio	386	Lost Creek	Vigo	Ind	1,232
Little Beaver	Lawrence	Pa	960	Lost Creek	Newton	Mo	*676
Little Britain	Lancaster	Pa	1,794	Lost Creek	Miami	Ohio	1,459
Little Canada Pre-				Loudon	Merrimack	N. H.	1,552
cinct	Ramsey	Minn	194	Loudon	Carroll	Ohio	840
Little Compton	Newport	R. I.	1,462	Loudon	Seneca	Ohio	1,781
Little Creek Hun-				Louisville	Jefferson	Ky	a43,194
dred	Kent	Del	2,315	*Louisville*	Blount	Tenn	430
Little Egg Harbor	Burlington	N. J.	2,020	Louisville	St. Lawrence	N. Y.	2,054
Little Falls	Herkimer	N. Y.	4,855	Louisville and vi-			
Little Mahoney	Northumberland	Pa	326	cinity	El Dorado	Cal	420
Little Rock	Pulaski	Ark	2,167	Loundesville	Abbeville	S. C.	†259
Little Rock	Kendall	Ill	906	Louisiana	Chicot	Ark	1,613
Littleton	Middlesex	Mass	987	Louisiana City	Pike	Mo	912
Littleton	Grafton	N. H.	2,008	Lovell	Oxford	Me	1,193
Littlestown	Adams	Pa	394	Lowell	Jackson	Iowa	84
Little Valley	Cattaraugus	N. Y.	1,383	Lowell	Penobscot	Me	378
Livermore	Oxford	Me	1,764	Lowell	Middlesex	Mass	b33 383
Liverpool	Fulton	Ill	674	Lowell	Kent	Mich	214
Liverpool	Columbiana	Ohio	1,581	Lowell	Orleans	Vt	637
Liverpool	Medina	Ohio	2,203	Lowell	Dodge	Wis	834
Liverpool, Bor.	Perry	Pa	606	Lower	Franklin	Ark	389
Liverpool	Perry	Pa	956	Lower	Cape May	N. J.	1,604
Livingston	Clark	Ill	672	Lower Allen	Cumberland	Pa	1,134
Livingston	Essex	N. J.	1,151	Lower Alloways			
Livingston	Columbia	N. Y.	2,020	Creek	Salem	N. J.	1,423
Livonia	Wayne	Mich	1,375	Lower All Saints	Georgetown	S. C.	6,690
Livonia	Livingston	N. Y.	2,627	Lower Augusta	Northumberland	Pa	2,019
Lloyd	Ulster	N. Y.	2,035	Lower Chanceford	York	Pa	1,637
Lock	Elkhart	Ind	171	Lower Chichester	Delaware	Pa	422
Lockbourne	Franklin	Ohio	218	Lower Dickenson	Cumberland	Pa	825
Locke	Ingham	Mich	321	Lower Dublin	Philadelphia	Pa	4,294
Locke	Cayuga	N. Y.	1,478	Lower Fourche	Yell	Ark	351
Lock Haven	Clinton	Pa	830	Lower Heidelburg	Berks	Pa	2,144
Lockport, T	Will	Ill	2,000	Lower Leacock	Lancaster	Pa	1,948
Lockport	Carroll	Ind	126	Lower Macungie	Lehigh	Pa	2,353
Lockport	St. Joseph	Mich	1,142	Lower Mahanoy	Northumberland	Pa	1,474
Lockport	Niagara	N. Y.	12,323	Lower Mahantan-			
Lockport	Licking	Ohio	164	go	Schuylkill	Pa	1,505
Lockport	Tuscarawas	Ohio	178	Lower Makefield	Bucks	Pa	1,741
Lockridge	Jefferson	Iowa	981	Lower Merion	Montgomery	Pa	3,517
Locust Bayou	Ouachita	Ark	545	Lower Mt. Bethel	Northampton	Pa	3,117
Locust Grove	Jefferson	Iowa	904	Lower Nazareth	Northampton	Pa	1,297
Lodi	Washtenaw	Mich	1,234	Lower Okaw	Coles	Ill	440
Lodi	Bergen	N. J.	1,114	Lower Oxford	Chester	Pa	1,341
Lodi	Seneca	N. Y.	2,269	Lower Paxton	Dauphin	Pa	1,573
Lodi	Athens	Ohio	1,336	Low. Penn's Neck	Salem	N. J.	1,429
Lodi	Columbia	Wis	317	Lower Providence	Montgomery	Pa	1,961
Lodomillo	Clayton	Iowa	273	*Lower Saginaw*	Saginaw	Mich	1,000
Logan	Dearborn	Ind	753	Lower Salford	Montgomery	Pa	1,207
Logan	Fountain	Ind	1,717	Lower St. Clair	Allegheny	Pa	5,930
Logan	Pike	Ind	820	*Lower Smithfield*	Monroe	Pa	1,283
Logan	Auglaize	Ohio	335	Lower Swatara	Dauphin	Pa	759
Logan	Hocking	Ohio	826	Lower Towamen-			
Logan, T	Hocking	Ohio	1,000	sing	Carbon	Pa	1,197
Logan	Clinton	Pa	712	Lower Turkeyfoot	Somerset	Pa	666
Logansport	Cass	Ind	3,500	Lower Windsor	York	Pa	1,923
Logansville	Logan	Ohio	82	Low Hill	Lehigh	Pa	1,021
Logtown & vicinity	Eldorado	Cal	420	*Lowndesborough*	Lowndes	Ala	500
Lomira	Dodge	Wis	653	Lowville	Lewis	N. Y.	2,377
London	Monroe	Mich	626	Lowville	Columbia	Wis	323
London	Madison	Ohio	513	Loyalhanna	Westmoreland	Pa	1,258
London Britain	Chester	Pa	680	Loyalsock	Lycoming	Pa	1,581
Londonderry	Rockingham	N. H	1,731	Lubec	Washington	Me	2,814
Londonderry	Guernsey	Ohio	1,548	Lucas	Crittenden	Ark	252
Londonderry, T.	Guernsey	Ohio	93	Luce	Spencer	Ind	1,042
Londonderry	Ross	Ohio	159	Ludlow	Hampden	Mass	1,186
Londonderry	Bedford	Pa	823	Ludlow	Washington	Ohio	1,051
Londonderry	Chester	Pa	643	Ludlow	Windsor	Vt	1,619
Londonderry	Dauphin	Pa	1,587	Luray	Licking	Ohio	88
Londonderry	Lebanon	Pa	1,849	Lumber	Clinton	Pa	136

a In 1853, 51,726. b In 1353, 37,000.

Lumberland	Sullivan	N. Y.	2,635
Lunenburgh	Worcester	Mass	1,249
Lunenburgh	Essex	Vt	1,123
Lurgan	Franklin	Pa	1,228
Luzerne	Warren	N. Y.	1,300
Luzerne	Fayette	Pa	1,869
Lycoming	Lycoming	Pa	1,275
Lykens	Crawford	Ohio	1,185
Lykens	Dauphin	Pa	1,371
Lyman	York	Me	1,376
Lyman	Grafton	N. H.	1,442
Lyme	New London	Conn	2,668
Lyme	Grafton	N. H.	1,617
Lyme	Jefferson	N. Y.	2,919
Lyme	Huron	Ohio	1,859
Lynchburg	Campbell	Va	a8,071
Lyndeborough	Hillsborough	N. H.	968
Lyndon	Washtenaw	Mich	901
Lyndon	Cattaraugus	N. Y.	1,092
Lyndon	Caledonia	Vt	1,752
Lynn	Posey	Ind	1,227
Lynn	Essex	Mass	14,257
Lynn	St. Clair	Mich	55
Lynn	Lehigh	Pa	1,997
Lynnfield	Essex	Mass	1,723
Lynnville	Ogle	Ill	168
Lyon	Oakland	Mich	1,134
Lyons	Cook	Ill	965
Lyons	Clinton	Iowa	453
Lyons	Ionia	Mich	850
Lyons	Wayne	N. Y.	4,925
Lyons	Sauk	Wis	68
Lysander	Winnebago	Ill	559
Lysander	Onondaga	N. Y.	5,833
McArthur	Logan	Ohio	1,376
McArthurstown	Vinton	Ohio	424
McCamorin	Martin	Ind	520
McConnelsburg	Fulton	Pa	477
McConnelsville	Morgan	Ohio	1,643
McDonald	Hardin	Ohio	582
McDonough	Chenango	N. Y.	1,522
McHenry	McHenry	Ill	1,176
McKean	Licking	Ohio	1,378
McKean	Erie	Pa	1,916
McKeesport	Allegheny	Pa	b1,392
McKinney	Collin	Texas	192
McLean	Shelby	Ohio	775
McLeansboro	Hamilton	Ill	221
McVeytown	Mifflin	Pa	c580
Macedon	Wayne	N. Y	2,384
Macia	Valencia	N. M.	688
Machias	Washington	Me	1,590
Machias	Cattaraugus	N. Y.	1,342
Machiasport	Washington	Me	1,266
Mackford	Marquette	Wis	520
Mackinaw	Michilimackinac	Mich	1,200
Mackintire	Lycoming	Pa	252
Macomb	McDonough	Ill	756
Macomb	Macomb	Mich	757
Macomb	St. Lawrence	N. Y	1,197
Macon	Bibb	Ga	d5,720
Macon	Bureau	Ill	74
Macon	Lenawee	Mich	1,030
Madawaska	Aroostook	Me	1,276
Madbury	Strafford	N. H.	483
Madison	Sevier	Ark	350
Madison	New Haven	Conn	1,837
Madison	Morgan	Ga	3,516
Madison	Allen	Ind	561
Madison	Carroll	Ind	558
Madison	Clinton	Ind	694
Madison	Daviess	Ind	919
Madison	Jay	Ind	645
Madison (city)	Jefferson	Ind	e8,012
Madison	Montgomery	Ind	651
Madison	Morgan	Ind	884
Madison	Putnam	Ind	1,199
Madison	St. Joseph	Ind	422
Madison	Tipton	Ind	778
Madison	Somerset	Me	1,769
Madison	Lenawee	Mich	2,404
Madison	Johnson	Mo	668
Madison	Madison	N. Y.	2,405
Madison	Butler	Ohio	2,242
Madison	Clark	Ohio	1,409
Madison	Columbiana	Ohio	1,406
Madison	Fairfield	Ohio	1,164
Madison	Fayette	Ohio	863
Madison	Franklin	Ohio	2,480
Madison	Guernsey	Ohio	1,519
Madison	Hancock	Ohio	667
Madison	Highland	Ohio	2,174
Madison	Jackson	Ohio	1,515
Madison	Lake	Ohio	2,986
Madison	Licking	Ohio	1,027
Madison	Montgomery	Ohio	1,668
Madison	Muskingum	Ohio	1,047
Madison	Perry	Ohio	988
Madison	Pickaway	Ohio	885
Madison	Richland	Ohio	5,135
Madison	Sandusky	Ohio	389
Madison	Scioto	Ohio	1,367
Madison	Williams	Ohio	227
Madison	Armstrong	Pa	1,151
Madison	Clarion	Pa	1,365
Madison	Columbia	Pa	712
Madison	Luzerne	Pa	579
Madison	Montour	Pa	1,255
Madison	Perry	Pa	1,292
Madison; C. H	Madison	Va	800
Madison	Dane	Wis	1,871
Madison, T	Dane	Wis	f1,525
Madrid	Franklin	Me	404
Madrid	St. Lawrence	N. Y.	4,856
Mad River	Champaign	Ohio	1,908
Mad River	Clark	Ohio	1,790
Mad River	Montgomery	Ohio	1,464
Magazine	Yell	Ark	571
Magnolia	Rock	Wis	630
Mahoning	Carbon	Pa	1,520
Mahoning	Lawrence	Pa	1,841
Mahoning	Montour	Pa	867
Maiden Creek	Berks	Pa	1,284
Maidstone	Essex	Vt	237
Maine	Cook	Ill	548
Maine	Broome	N. Y.	1,843
Maine	Columbia	Pa	581
Malaga	Monroe	Ohio	1,844
Malaga, T	Monroe	Ohio	138
Malaray	Clayton	Iowa	322
Malden	Middlesex	Mass	3,520
Malone	Franklin	N. Y	4,550
Malta	Saratoga	N. Y.	1,349
Malta	Morgan	Ohio	1,830
Malta, T	Morgan	Ohio	528
Mamakating	Sullivan	N. Y.	4,107
Mamaroneck	Westchester	N. Y.	928
Manalapan	Monmouth	N. J.	1,910
Manchester	Dallas	Ark	877
Manchester	Hartford	Conn	2,546
Manchester	Boone	Ill	869
Manchester	Dearborn	Ind	2,748
Manchester	Carroll	Md	517
Manchester	Essex	Mass	1,638
Manchester	Washtenaw	Mich	g1,275
Manchester	St. Louis	Mo	210
Manchester	Hillsborough	N. H	h13,932
Manchester	Passaic	N. J.	2,788
Manchester	Ontario	N. Y.	2,940
Manchester	Adams	Ohio	434
Manchester	Morgan	Ohio	1,337
Manchester	Allegheny	Pa	1,755
Manchester	Wayne	Pa	749
Manchester	York	Pa	2,603
Manchester	Chesterfield	Va	1,800
Manchester	Bennington	Vt	1,782
Manchester	Sauk	Wis	94
Manhatten	Lucas	Ohio	541
Manheim	Herkimer	N. Y.	1,902
Manheim	Lancaster	Pa	2,087
Manheim, Bor	Lancaster	Pa	778
Manheim	York	Pa	1,806
Manilla	Rush	Ind	199
Manitoowoc	Manitoowoc	Wis	i756
Manitoowoc rap'ds	Manitoowoc	Wis	969
Manlius	Lasalle	Ill	630
Manlius	Allegan	Mich	82
Manlius	Onondaga	N. Y.	6,298
Mannington	Salem	N. J.	2,187
Manor	Armstrong	Pa	775
Manor	Lancaster	Pa	3,329
Mansana	Valencia	N. M.	403
Mansfield	Tolland	Conn	2,517
Mansfield	Bristol	Mass	1,789
Mansfield	Burlington	N. J.	2,953
Mansfield	Warren	N. J.	1,615

a In 1853, 10,000. *b* In 1853, 2,500. *c* In 1853, 800. *d* In 1853, 7,000. *e* In 1853, 12,000. *f* In 1853, 3,500. *g* In 1853, 1,275. *h* In 1853, 20,000. *i* In 1853, 2,500.

Place	County	State	Population
Mansfield	Cattaraugus	N. Y.	1,057
Mansfield	Richland	Ohio	3,557
Mantua	Portage	Ohio	1,169
Manyunk	Philadelphia	Pa	6,158
Maple Grove	Barry	Mich	153
Maquon	Knox	Ill	84
Marathon	Lapeer	Mich	205
Marathon	Cortlandt	N. Y.	1,149
Marblehead	Essex	Mass	6,167
Marbletown	Ulster	N. Y.	3,839
Marcellon	Columbia	Wis	468
Marcellus	Cass	Mich	222
Marcellus	Onondaga	N. Y.	2,759
Marcus Hook	Delaware	Pa	492
Marcy	Oneida	N. Y.	1,857
Marengo	McHenry	Ill	1,030
Marengo	Iowa	Iowa	386
Marengo, T	Iowa	Iowa	50
Marengo	Calhoun	Mich	1,014
Margaretta	Erie	Ohio	1,537
Mariana	Jackson	Fla	377
Mariaville	Hancock	Me	374
Marietta	Fulton	Ill	442
Marietta	Washington	Ohio	5,254
Marietta, T	Washington	Ohio	a3,175
Marietta	Lancaster	Pa	b2,099
Marine Settlement	Madison	Ill	840
Marine Town	Madison	Ill	126
Marion	Crittenden	Ark	95
Marion	Perry	Ala	1,544
Marion	Crawford	Ark	623
Marion	Drew	Ark	951
Marion	Ouachita	Ark	859
Marion	White	Ark	404
Marion	Ogle	Ill	595
Marion	Allen	Ind	1,095
Marion	Decatur	Ind	1,595
Marion	Grant	Ind	703
Marion	Hendricks	Ind	1,270
Marion	Jasper	Ind	883
Marion	Jennings	Ind	1,260
Marion	Lawrence	Ind	2,025
Marion	Monroe	Ind	252
Marion	Owen	Ind	989
Marion	Putnam	Ind	1,320
Marion	Shelby	Iowa	786
Marion	Davis	Iowa	440
Marion	Henry	Iowa	494
Marion	Washington	Me	207
Marion	Livingston	Mich	883
Marion	Washington	Minn	114
Marion	Buchanan	Mo	*798
Marion	Newton	Mo	*327
Marion	Taney	Mo	294
Marion	Wayne	N. Y.	1,839
Marion	Allen	Ohio	1,046
Marion	Clinton	Ohio	995
Marion	Fayette	Ohio	841
Marion	Hancock	Ohio	904
Marion	Hardin	Ohio	452
Marion	Henry	Ohio	77
Marion	Hocking	Ohio	1,746
Marion	Marion	Ohio	2,291
Marion, T	Marion	Ohio	c1,311
Marion	Mercer	Ohio	1,428
Marion	Morgan	Ohio	1,764
Marion	Pike	Ohio	900
Marion	Beaver	Pa	494
Marion	Berks	Pa	1,530
Marion	Centre	Pa	595
Marion, (Waynesburg)	Greene	Pa	852
Marlboro	Hartford	Conn	832
Marlboro	Middlesex	Mass	2,941
Marlboro	Cheshire	N. H.	887
Marlboro	Monmouth	N. J	1,564
Marlboro	Ulster	N. Y.	2,406
Marlboro	Delaware	Ohio	587
Marlboro	Stark	Ohio	2,133
Marlboro	Montgomery	Pa	1,174
Marlboro	Windham	Vt	896
Marlow	Cheshire	N. H.	708
Marple	Delaware	Pa	876
Marquette	Marquette	Wis	246
Marrinett	Brown	Wis	243
Mars	Rosey	Ind	1,319
Marseilles	Wyandotte	Ohio	538
Marshall	Clark	Ill	1,341

Place	County	State	Population
Marshall	Calhoun	Mich	2,822
Marshall, T	Calhoun	Mich	d1,972
Marshall	Platte	Mo	2,243
Marshall	Oneida	N. Y.	2,115
Marshall	Highland	Ohio	1,187
Marshall	Harrison	Texas	1,189
Marshfield	Washington	Me	294
Marshfield	Plymouth	Mass	1,837
Marshfield	Washington	Vt	1,102
Mars Hill	Washington	Ark	660
Martin	Allegan	Mich	329
Martinicus Isle	Lincoln	Me	220
Martinsburg	Washington	Ind	166
Martinsburg	Lewis	N. Y.	2,677
Martinsburg	Fayette	Ohio	133
Martinsbusg	Blair	Pa	442
Martinsburg	Berkeley	Va	2,190
Martinsville	Clark	Ill	1,132
Martinsville	Morgan	Ind	1,000
Martinsville	Belmont	Ohio	500
Mary Ann	Licking	Ohio	999
Maryland	Otsego	N. Y.	2,152
Marysville	Yuba	Cal	8,000
Marysville	Union	Ohio	605
Marysville	Blount	Tenn	*388
Mascoutah	St. Clair	Ill	378
Mason	Oxford	Me	93
Mason	Cass	Mich	570
Mason	Ingham	Mich	600
Mason	Marion	Mo	2,557
Mason	Hillsborough	N. H.	1,626
Mason	Lawrence	Ohio	1,132
Mason	Warren	Ohio	431
Masonville	Delaware	N. Y.	1,550
Massena	St. Lawrence	N. Y.	2,870
Massillon	Stark	Ohio	4,009
Mastic	Lancaster	Pa	3,099
Matagorda	Matagorda	Texas	1,200
Matamoras	Dauphin	Pa	123
Mathinias	El Dorado	Cal	672
Mattawiscontis	Penobscot	Me	54
Mattison	Branch	Mich	475
Mauch Chunk	Carbon	Pa	3,727
Mauch Chunk, Bor	Carbon	Pa	2,557
Maumee	Allen	Ind	93
Maumee	Lucas	Ohio	1,465
Maumelle	Pulaski	Ark	389
Maurice River	Cumberland	N. J.	2,245
Maxatawny	Berks	Pa	1,740
Maxfield	Penobscot	Me	186
Mayfield	De Kalb	Ill	564
Mayfield	Somerset	Me	133
Mayfield	Fulton	N. Y.	2,429
Mayfield	Cuyahoga	Ohio	1,117
Mayville	Dodge	Wis	600
Maysville	Mason	Ky	e4,256
Maytown	Lancaster	Pa	634
Maywaketa	Jackson	Iowa	504
Maywaketa, T	Jackson	Iowa	168
Mazon	Grundy	Ill	469
Mead	Crawford	Pa	1,810
Mead	Warren	Pa	162
Meade	Belmont	Ohio	1,626
Mead Springs and vicinity	El Dorado	Cal	462
Meadville	Crawford	Pa	2,578
Meadville	Halifax	Va	500
Mecca	Trumbull	Ohio	872
Mechanic	Holmes	Ohio	1,647
Mechanicsburg	Sangamon	Ill	201
Mechanicsburg	Champaigne	Ohio	f682
Mechanicsburg	Cumberland	Pa	882
Mechanics' Village	Jefferson	La	*210
Medfield	Norfolk	Mass	966
Medford	Middlesex	Mass	3,749
Medford	Burlington	N. J	3,022
Media	Delaware	Pa	285
Medina	Warren	Ind	602
Medina	Lenawee	Mich	1,600
Medina, T	Orleans	N. Y.	2,500
Medina	Medina	Ohio	2,011
Medina, T	Medina	Ohio	g1,009
Medina	Dane	Wis	495
Medway	Norfolk	Mass	2,778
Medway	Clark	Ohio	69
Medybemps	Washington	Me	287
Meeme	Manitoowoc	Wis	199
Meford	Decatur	Ind	291

a In 1853, 4,000 *b* In 1853, 2,500. *c* In 1853, 1,600. *d* In 1853, 2,500. *e* In 1853, 6,500, *f* In 1853, 1,200
g In 1853, 1,400.

Mehoopany	Wyoming	Pa	767
Meigs	Adams	Ohio	1,438
Meigs	Muskingum	Ohio	1,680
Meigsville	Morgan	Ohio	1,512
Melmore	Seneca	Ohio	249
Melrose	Adams	Ill	1,541
Melrose	Clark	Ill	672
Melrose	Middlesex	Mass	1,260
Melrose	Nacogdoches	Texas	94
Memphis	Pickens	Ala	156
Memphis	Scotland	Mo	*183
Memphis	Shelby	Tenn	a8,841
Menallen	Adams	Pa	1,654
Menallen	Fayette	Pa	1,411
Menasha	Winnebago	Wis	1,200
Menden	Lasalle	Ill	378
Mendham	Morris	N. J	1,723
Mendon	Clayton	Iowa	355
Mendon	Worcester	Mass	1,300
Mendon	Monroe	N. Y	3,353
Mendon	Rutland	Vt	504
Menno	Mifflin	Pa	1,020
Menomonee	Waukesha	Wis	1,340
Mentor	Lake	Ohio	1,571
Mentz	Cayuga	N. Y	5,239
Mequon	Washington	Wis	2,100
Mercer	Somerset	Me	1,186
Mercer	Butler	Pa	1,296
Mercer	Mercer	Pa	1,004
Mercersburg	Franklin	Pa	1,179
Meredith	Belknap	N. H	3,521
Meredith	Delaware	N. Y	1,634
Meriden	New Haven	Conn	3,559
Meridian	Ingham	Mich	367
Merion	Montgomery	Pa	3,647
Merrimack	St. Louis	Mo	1,921
Merrimack	Hillsborough	N. H	1,250
Merton	Waukesha	Wis	966
Mesopotamia	Trumbull	Ohio	959
Metal	Franklin	Pa	1,221
Metamora	Franklin	Ind	865
Metamora	Lapeer	Mich	821
Methuen	Essex	Mass	2,538
Metomen	Fond du Lac	Wis	720
Metropolis city	Massac	Ill	427
Mexico	Oxford	Me	482
Mexico	Oswego	N. Y	4,221
Miami	Cass	Ind	669
Miami	Clermont	Ohio	2,690
Miami	Greene	Ohio	1,865
Miami	Hamilton	Ohio	1,556
Miami	Logan	Ohio	1,148
Miami	Montgomery	Ohio	3,457
Miamisburg	Montgomery	Ohio	1,095
Miami Town	Hamilton	Ohio	223
Micheltree	Martin	Ind	953
Michigan	Clinton	Ind	992
Michigan, T	Clinton	Ind	148
Michigan	Laporte	Ind	162
Michigan city	Laporte	Ind	999
Middle	Franklin	Ark	603
Middle	Hendricks	Ind	1,999
Middle	Cape May	N. J	1,884
Middleborough	Plymouth	Mass	5,336
Middleburg	Shiawassee	Mich	132
Middleburg	Schoharie	N. Y	2,967
Middleburg	Cuyahoga	Ohio	1,490
Middleburg	Knox	Ohio	1,092
Middlebury	New Haven	Conn	763
Middlebury	Elkhart	Ind	1,135
Middlebury	Wyoming	N. Y	1,799
Middlebury	Logan	Ohio	214
Middlebury	Tioga	Pa	1,096
Middlebury	Addison	Vt	3,517
Middle Creek	Union	Pa	614
Middlefield	Hampshire	Mass	737
Middlefield	Otsego	N. Y	3,131
Middlefield	Geauga	Ohio	918
Middle Fork of American river	El Dorado	Cal	1,722
Middle Paxton	Dauphin	Pa	1,204
Middleport	Iroquois	Ill	800
Middlesex	Yates	N. Y	1,385
Middlesex	Butler	Pa	2,262
Middlesex	Washington	Vt	1,365
Middle Smithfield	Monroe	Pa	1,478
Middleton	Essex	Mass	832
Middleton	Lafayette	Mo	889
Middleton	Strafford	N. H	476
Middleton	Columbiana	Ohio	1,570
Middleton	Wood	Ohio	331
Middleton	Dane	Wis	320
Middletown	Middlesex	Conn	4,230
Middletown (city)	Middlesex	Conn	4,211
Middletown	Newcastle	Del	368
Middletown	Henry	Ind	188
Middletown	Monmouth	N. J	3,251
Middletown	Delaware	N. Y	3,005
Middletown	Butler	Ohio	1,087
Middletown	Guernsey	Ohio	267
Middletown	Bucks	Pa	2,223
Middletown	Dauphin	Pa	900
Middletown	Delaware	Pa	1,972
Middletown	Susquehanna	Pa	1,140
Middletown	Marquette	Wis	359
Middletown	Newport	R. I	830
Middletown	Rutland	Vt	875
Middle Woodbury	Bedford	Pa	1,709
Mifflin	Ashland	Ohio	891
Mifflin	Franklin	Ohio	1,095
Mifflin	Pike	Ohio	546
Mifflin	Richland	Ohio	1,106
Mifflin	Wyandott	Ohio	570
Mifflin	Allegheny	Pa	2,693
Mifflin	Columbia	Pa	1,024
Mifflin	Cumberland	Pa	1,574
Mifflin	Dauphin	Pa	1,302
Mifflin	Lycoming	Pa	1,186
Mifflin	Iowa	Wis	640
Mifflinsburg	Union	Pa	783
Mifflintown	Juniata	Pa	485
Milan	Allen	Ind	361
Milan	Monroe	Mich	642
Milan	Coos	N. H	493
Milan	Dutchess	N. Y	1,764
Milan	Erie	Ohio	2,697
Milan, T	Erie	Ohio	2,000
Miles	Centre	Pa	1,306
Milesburg	Centre	Pa	478
Milford	New Haven	Conn	2,465
Milford	La Grange	Ind	806
Milford	Penobscot	Me	687
Milford	Worcester	Mass	4,819
Milford	Oakland	Mich	1,470
Milford, T	Oakland	Mich	800
Milford	Hillsborough	N. H	2,159
Milford	Otsego	N. Y	2,227
Milford	Butler	Ohio	2,068
Milford	Defiance	Ohio	645
Milford	Knox	Ohio	1,349
Milford	Bucks	Pa	2,527
Milford	Juniata	Pa	1,373
Milford	Pike	Pa	830
Milford	Jefferson	Wis	728
Milford Centre	Union	Ohio	211
Milford and Mispillion Hundreds	Kent	Del	5,895
Mill	Grant	Ind	1,537
Mill	Tuscarawas	Ohio	1,510
Millbridge	Washington	Me	1,170
Millbury	Worcester	Mass	3,081
Mill Creek	Ashley	Ark	542
Mill Creek	Franklin	Ark	286
Mill Creek	Clark	Ill	378
Mill Creek	Morgan	Mo	*637
Mill Creek	Coshocton	Ohio	872
Mill Creek	Hamilton	Ohio	6,287
Mill Creek	Union	Ohio	726
Mill Creek	Williams	Ohio	408
Mill Creek	Erie	Pa	3,064
Mill Creek	Lebanon	Pa	1,292
Mill Creek Hundr'd	Newcastle	Del	3,317
Mill Creek	Mercer	Pa	840
Milledgeville	Baldwin	Ga	2,216
Miller	Dearborn	Ind	1,122
Miller	Gentry	Mo	*1,924
Miller	Marion	Mo	1,298
Miller	Scotland	Mo	*666
Miller	Knox	Ohio	1,064
Millersburg	Mercer	Ill	100
Millersburg	Bourbon	Ky	214
Millersburg	Holmes	Ohio	837
Millersport	Fairfield	Ohio	149
Millerstown	Lebanon	Pa	798
Millerstown	Perry	Pa	389
Millersville	Marion	Ind	145
Millersville	Lancaster	Pa	498
Milford	Somerset	Pa	2,070

a In 1853, 12,000.

Mill Grove	Steuben	Ind	523	Monroe	Grant	Ind	777
Mill Hall	Clinton	Pa	492	Monroe	Howard	Ind	932
Millsborough	Washington	Pa	333	Monroe	Jefferson	Ind	1,090
Millstone	Monmouth	N. J	1,676	Monroe	Madison	Ind	1,246
Millville	Clayton	Iowa	293	Monroe	Morgan	Ind	1,496
Millville	Cumberland	N. J	2,332	Monroe	Pike	Ind	1,285
Millwood	Guernsey	Ohio	1,624	Monroe	Pulaski	Ind	545
Millwood, T	Guernsey	Ohio	216	Monroe	Putnam	Ind	1,255
Millwood	Knox	Ohio	240	Monroe	Randolph	Ind	735
Milo	Piscataquis	Me	932	Monroe	Washington	Ind	1,476
Milo	Yates	N Y	4,791	Monroe	Johnson	Iowa	254
Milton	Du Page	Ill	999	Monroe	Ouachita	La	435
Milton	Jefferson	Ind	1,544	Monroe	Waldo	Me	1,606
Milton	Wayne	Ind	765	Monroe	Franklin	Mass	254
Milton	Oxford	Me	166	Monroe	Monroe	Mich	837
Milton	Norfolk	Mass	2,241	Monroe (city)	Monroe	Mich	*h*2,813
Milton	Cass	Mich	611	Monroe	Middlesex	N. J	3,001
Milton	Caswell	N. C	1,200	Monroe	Orange	N. Y	4,280
Milton	Strafford	N. H	1,629	Monroe	Adams	Ohio	1,191
Milton	Saratoga	N. Y	4,220	Monroe	Allen	Ohio	924
Milton	Ashland	Ohio	1,432	Monroe	Ashtabula	Ohio	1,587
Milton	Jackson	Ohio	1,472	Monroe	Butler	Ohio	198
Milton	Mahoning	Ohio	1,123	Monroe	Carroll	Ohio	1,117
Milton	Miami	Ohio	398	Monroe	Clermont	Ohio	1,897
Milton	Wayne	Ohio	1,360	Monroe	Coshocton	Ohio	760
Milton	Wood	Ohio	244	Monroe	Darke	Ohio	918
Milton	Northumberland	Pa	*a*1,649	Monroe	Guernsey	Ohio	1,076
Milton	Chittendon	Vt	2,451	Monroe	Harrison	Ohio	1,154
Milton	Rock	Wis	1,032	Monroe	Holmes	Ohio	966
Milton City	Washington	Oreg'n	692	Monroe	Knox	Ohio	1,324
Miltonsburg	Monroe	Ohio	145	Monroe	Licking	Ohio	1,386
Miltonville	Butler	Ohio	249	Monroe	Logan	Ohio	1,435
Milwaukie	Milwaukie	Wis	1,351	Monroe	Madison	Ohio	403
Milwaukie City	Milwaukie	Wis	*b*20,061	Monroe	Miami	Ohio	2,035
Mina	Chautauque	N. Y	896	Monroe	Muskingham	Ohio	977
Minden	Claiborne	La	*c*533	Monroe	Perry	Ohio	1,429
Minden	St. Joseph	Mich	862	Monroe	Pickaway	Ohio	1,637
Minden	Montgomery	N. Y	4,623	Monroe	Preble	Ohio	1,343
Mine Creek	Hempstead	Ark	1,185	Monroe	Richland	Ohio	1,719
Mineral	Bureau	Ill	142	Monroe	Bedford	Pa	1,196
Mineral Point	Iowa	Wis	*d*2,584	Monroe	Bradford	Pa	1,436
Minersville	Schuylkill	Pa	*e*2,951	Monroe	Clarion	Pa	1,295
Minerva	Essex	N. Y	586	Monroe	Cumberland	Pa	1,772
Minisink	Orange	N. Y	4,972	Monroe	Wyoming	Pa	602
Minot	Cumberland	Me	1,734	Monroe	Greene	Wis	1,146
Minster	Auglaize	Ohio	428	Monroeville	Jefferson	Wis	101
Mishawaka	St. Joseph	Ind	*f*1,412	Monrovia	Morgan	Ind	196
Mission	Lasalle	Ill	840	Monson	Piscataquis	Me	654
Mississinewa	Darke	Ohio	378	Monson	Hampden	Mass	2,831
Mississinewa	Westmoreland	Pa	862	Montague	Franklin	Mass	1,518
Mississippi	Desha	Ark	683	Montague	Sussex	N. J	1,010
Mississippi	Pike	Mo	135	Montcalm	Montcalm	Mich	135
Mississippi Bar	Sacramento	Cal	168	Monterey, (city)	Monterey	Cal	1,092
Missouri	Clark	Ark	472	Monterey	Berkshire	Mass	761
Missouri	Hempstead	Ark	513	Monterey	Allegan	Mich	238
Missouri	Ouachita	Ark	730	Monterey	Putnam	Ohio	85
Missouri	Pike	Ark	434	Montgomery	Montgomery	Ala	*i*4,935
Missouri Canon	El Dorado	Cal	84	Montgomery	Desha	Ark	69
Mitchell	Poinsett	Ark	954	Montgomery	Monroe	Ark	317
Mitchell	Monroe	Ill	546	Montgomery	Gibson	Ind	2,248
Mobile	Mobile	Ala	20,515	Montgomery	Jennings	Ind	1,556
Mohawk	Montgomery	N. Y	3,095	Montgomery	Owen	Ind	987
Mohican	Ashland	Ohio	1,774	Montgomery	Hampden	Mass	393
Moira	Franklin	N. Y	1,340	Montgomery	Somerset	N. J	1,767
Moluncus	Aroostook	Me	199	Montgomery	Orange	N. Y	3,933
Momence	Will	Ill	573	Montgomery	Ashland	Ohio	3,192
Monaghan	York	Pa	997	Montgomery	Franklin	Ohio	1,331
Monday Creek	Perry	Ohio	1,124	Montgomery	Marion	Ohio	643
Money Creek	McLean	Ill	377	Montgomery	Wood	Ohio	922
Monkton	Addison	Vt	1,246	Montgomery	Franklin	Pa	3,235
Monmouth	Warren	Ill	797	Montgomery	Indiana	Pa	751
Monmouth	Jackson	Iowa	294	Montgomery	Montgomery	Pa	971
Monmouth	Kennebeck	Me	1,925	Montgomery	Franklin	Vt	1,001
Monona	Clayton	Iowa	332	Monticello	Jefferson	Fla	329
Monongahela	Greene	Pa	1,153	Monticello	Jones	Iowa	252
Monongahela City	Washington	Pa	*g*977	Monticello	Aroostook	Me	227
Monroe	Lafayette	Ark	714	Monticello	Lewis	Mo	222
Monroe	Mississippi	Ark	652	*Monticello*, T	Sullivan	N. Y	1,200
Monroe	Sevier	Ark	335	Monticello	Lafayette	Wis	198
Monroe	Fairfield	Conn	1,442	Montour	Columbia	Pa	409
Monroe	Walton	Ga	500	Montoursville	Lycoming	Pa	228
Monroe	Ogle	Ill	413	Montpelier	Muscatine	Iowa	378
Monroe	Saline	Ill	756	Montpelier	Washington	Vt	2,310
Monroe	Adams	Ind	347	Montrose	Lee	Iowa	1,723
Monroe	Allen	Ind	414	Montrose, T	Lee	Iowa	*j*484
Monroe	Carroll	Ind	588	Montrose	Genesee	Mich	52
Monroe	Clark	Ind	1,561	Montrose	Susquehanna	Pa	*k*917
Monroe	Delaware	Ind	720	Montrose	Dane	Wis	372

a In 1853, 2,000. *b* In 1853, 25,000. *c* In 1853, 1,000. *d* In 1853, 3,000. *e* In 1853, 4,000. *f* In 1853, 2,000. *g* In 1853, 1,500. *h* In 1853, 3,500. *i* In 1853, 7,000. *j* In 1853, 800. *k* In 1853, 1,500.

Name	County	State	Population
Montville	New London	Conn..	1,848
Montville	Waldo	Me....	1,881
Montville	Geauga	Ohio ..	702
Montville	Medina	Ohio ..	1,077
Monynagon	Wayne	Mich..	984
Moon	Allegheny	Pa....	1,383
Moon	Beaver	Pa	916
Mooney	Philips	Ark	335
Moore	Northampton	Pa	2,615
Moorefield	Clark	Ohio ..	1,214
Moorefield	Harrison	Ohio ..	1,265
Moorefield, T	Harrison	Ohio ..	244
Moores	Clinton	N. Y..	3,365
Moore's Hill	Dearborn	Ind....	206
Moorestown	Burlington	N. J...	1,000
Mooresville	Morgan	Ind....	550
Moquina	Valencia	N. M..	199
Moral	Shelby	Ind....	1,192
Moravia	Cayuga	N. Y..	1,876
Moreau	Morgan	Mo ..	*1,134
Moreau	Saratoga	N. Y..	1,834
Moredock	Monroe	Ill	630
Morehouse	Hamilton	N. Y..	242
Moreland	Lycoming	Pa	714
Moreland	Montgomery	Pa	2,348
Moreland	Philadelphia	Pa	492
Moretown	Washington	Vt	1,335
Morgan	Owen	Ind ...	951
Morgan	Porter	Ind....	373
Morgan	Ashtabula	Ohio ..	888
Morgan	Butler	Ohio ..	1,706
Morgan	Gallia	Ohio ..	1,128
Morgan	Knox	Ohio ..	823
Morgan	Morgan	Ohio ..	2,308
Morgan	Scioto	Ohio ..	280
Morgan	Greene	Pa	1,157
Morgan	Orleans	Vt....	486
Morgantown	Burke	N. C...	558
Morgantown	Monongalia	Va	1,000
Moriah	Essex	N. Y...	3,065
Mormon Bar	Sutter	Cal ...	42
Mormon Island	Sacramento	Cal ...	252
Moro	Bradley	Ark...	95
Moro	Dallas	Ark...	415
Morris	Grundy	Ill	627
Morris	Morris	N. J...	4,992
Morris	Otsego	N. Y..	2,155
Morris	Knox	Ohio ..	1,028
Morris	Clearfield	Pa	639
Morris	Greene	Pa	1,250
Morris	Huntingdon	Pa	787
Morris	Tioga	Pa	278
Morris	Washington	Pa	1,688
Morristown	Morris	N. J...	3,390
Morristown	St. Lawrence	N. Y..	2,274
Morristown	Belmont	Ohio ..	456
Morristown	Lamoille	Vt	1,441
Morrisville	Bucks	Pa	*a*565
Morrow	Warren	Ohio ..	459
Moscow	Muscatine	Iowa..	567
Moscow	Somerset	Me....	577
Moscow	Hillsdale	Mich..	942
Mosquito Canon	El Dorado	Cal ...	116
Moss	Lafayette	Ark...	203
Mottville	St Joseph	Mich..	611
Moulton	Auglaize	Ohio ..	450
Moultonborough	Carroll	N. H...	1,748
Mound	Warren	Ind ...	811
Mountain	Crawford	Ark...	566
Mountain	Montgomery	Ark...	436
Mountain	Scott	Ark...	304
Mountain	Washington	Ark...	909
Mount Auburn	Shelby	Ind....	129
Mount Carmel	Wabash	Ill	935
Mount Carmel	Fleming	Ky....	142
Mount Carmel	Covington	Miss...	108
Mount Carroll	Carroll	Ill	462
Mount Clemens	Macomb	Mich..	*b*1,302
Mount Desert	Hancock	Me....	782
Mount Ephraim	Guernsey	Ohio ..	121
Mount Gilead	Morrow	Ohio ..	*c*646
Mount Holly	Burlington	N. J...	2,000
Mount Holly	Rutland	Vt....	1,534
Mount Hope	Orange	N. Y..	1,512
Mount Joy	Adams	Pa	1,098
Mount Joy	Lancaster	Pa	2,626
Mount Lebanon	Bienville	La	360
Mount Morris	Ogle	Ill.....	1,092
Mount Morris	Livingston	N. Y..	4,531
Mount Morris, T.	Livingston	N. Y..	1,600
Mount Pleasant	Delaware	Ind ...	924
Mount Pleasant	Henry	Iowa..	758
Mount Pleasant	Lawrence	Mo ...	*474
Mount Pleasant	Scotland	Mo ...	*801
Mount Pleasant	Westchester	N. Y..	3,323
Mount Pleasant	Jefferson	Ohio ..	1,847
Mount Pleasant, T.	Jefferson	Ohio ..	755
Mount Pleasant	Adams	Pa	1,614
Mount Pleasant	Columbia	Pa	708
Mount Pleasant	Washington	Pa	1,254
Mount Pleasant	Wayne	Pa	1,551
Mount Pleasant	Westmoreland	Pa	2,576
Mount Pleasant, Bor	Westmoreland	Pa	534
Mount Pleasant	Charleston	S. C ..	657
Mount Pleasant	Maury	Tenn..	†367
Mount Pleasant	Greene	Wis...	579
Mount Pleasant	Racine	Wis...	1,086
Mount Pulaski	Logan	Ill	360
Mount Sterling	Brown	Ill	556
Mount Sterling	Montgomery	Ky....	*d*743
Mount Sterling	Madison	Ohio ..	118
Mount Sterling	Muskingum	Ohio ..	228
Mount Taber	Rutland	Vt....	308
Mount Tabor	Monroe	Ind ...	85
Mount Vernon	Jefferson	Ill	443
Mount Vernon	Posey	Ind ...	*e*1,120
Mount Vernon	Kennebeck	Me....	1,479
Mount Vernon	Lawrence	Mo ...	*1,579
Mount Vernon	Hillsborough	N. H..	722
Mount Vernon	Knox	Ohio ..	*f*3,711
Mount Washington	Berkshire	Mass..	351
Moyamensing	Philadelphia	Pa	26,979
Muddy	Coles	Ill.....	772
Muddy	Jasper	Ill.....	168
Muddy Bayou	Conway	Ark ...	210
Muddy Creek	Butler	Pa	1,142
Muhlenburg	Pickaway	Ohio ..	585
Mukwonago	Waukesha	Wis ..	1,094
Mulberry	Franklin	Ark...	534
Mulberry	Johnson	Ark ...	339
Mulberry Grove	Bond	Ill.....	84
Mullica	Atlantic	N. J...	918
Muncie Centre	Delaware	Ind....	666
Muncy	Lycoming	Pa	978
Muncy, Bor	Lycoming	Pa	901
Muncy Creek	Lycoming	Pa	1,250
Mundy	Genesee	Mich..	786
Munson	Geauga	Ohio ..	1,193
Murder Kill Hundred	Kent	Del ...	5,717
Murfreesborough	Rutherford	Tenn..	1,917
Murray	Orleans	N. Y..	2,520
Muscatine	Muscatine	Iowa..	*g*2,540
Muskeegan	Ottawa	Mich..	484
Muskeego	Waukesha	Wis...	1,111
Muskingum	Muskingum	Ohio ..	1,509
Myatt	Lawrence	Ark ...	357
Myerstown	Lebanon	Pa	*h*877
Naansay	Kendall	Ill	569
Nacogdoches	Nacogdoches	Texas.	468
Nankin	Wayne	Mich..	1,617
Nanticoke	Broome	N. Y..	576
Nanticoke Hundred	Sussex	Del ...	1,586
Nantucket	Nantucket	Mass..	8,452
Napa	Napa	Cal....	159
Naperville	Du Page	Ill	*i*1,628
Napier	Bedford	Pa	2,051
Naples	Cumberland	Me ...	1,025
Naples	Ontario	N. Y..	2,376
Napoleon	Desha	Ark....	239
Napoleon	Ripley	Ind....	500
Napoleon	Jackson	Mich..	1,208
Napoleon	Henry	Ohio ..	566
Napoli	Cattaraugus	N. Y..	1,233
Nashua	Ogle	Ill	703
Nashua	Hillsborough	N. H..	5,820
Nashville	Hillsborough	N. H..	3,122
Nashville	Davidson	Tenn..	*j*10,165
Nashville, South	Davidson	Tenn..	1,353
Nashville	Milan	Texas.	40
Nassau	Rensselaer	N. Y..	3,261
Natchez	Adams	Miss ..	4,434

a In 1853, 700. *b* In 1853, 2,500. *c* In 1853, 1,000. *d* In 1853, 1,500. *e* In 1853, 1,500. *f* In 1853, 4,500. *g* In 1853, 5,000. *h* In 1853, 1,000. *i* In 1853, 2,500. *j* In 1853, 15,000.

Natchitoches	Nachitoches	La	1,261
Natick	Middlesex	Mass.	2,744
Naugatuck	New Haven	Conn.	1,720
Nauvoo	Hancock	Ill.	*a*1,130
Nazareth	Northampton	Pa	408
Neave	Darke	Ohio	888
Needham	Norfolk	Mass.	1,944
Neenah	Winnebago	Wis.	1,413
Negro Bar	Sacramento	Cal	336
Nekama	Winnebago	Wis.	910
Nelson	Cheshire	N. H.	750
Nelson	Madison	N. Y.	1,965
Nelson	Portage	Ohio	1,383
Neosho	Newton	Mo.	*980
Neosho, T.	Newton	Mo	*221
Nepeuskun	Winnebago	Wis	403
Nescopeck	Luzerne	Pa	920
Neshannock	Lawrence	Pa	3,045
Nether Providence	Delaware	Pa	1,494
Nettle Creek	Grundy	Ill	318
Nettle Creek	Randolph	Ind	1,112
Nevada City	Yuba	Cal.	2,683
Nevans	Vigo	Ind	826
Neversink	Sullivan	N. Y.	2,281
New Albany	Coles	Ill	765
New Albany	Floyd	Ind	*b*9,895
New Albany	Franklin	Ohio	168
New Albany	Mahoning	Ohio	168
New Albany City	Floyd	Ind	8,181
New Albion	Cattaraugus	N. Y.	1,633
New Alexandria	Jefferson	Ohio	198
Newark	Allegan	Mich	246
Newark	Wayne	N. Y.	1,400
Newark	Tioga	N. Y.	1,983
Newark	Licking	Ohio	5,050
Newark, T.	Licking	Ohio	3,654
Newark	Caledonia	Vt	434
Newark	Rock	Wis	855
Newark City	Essex	N. J.	*c*38,894
New Ashford	Berkshire	Mass.	186
New Athens	Harrison	Ohio	331
New Baltimore	Greene	N. Y.	2,381
New Baltimore	Hamilton	Ohio	104
New Barbadoes	Bergen	N. J.	2,265
New Bedford	Bristol	Mass.	*d*16,443
New Berlin	Chenango	N. Y.	2,562
New Berlin	Starke	Ohio	221
New Berlin	Union	Pa	*e*741
New Berlin	Waukesha	Wis	1,293
Newbern	Craven	N. C.	4,681
Newberry	La Grange	Ind	503
Newberry	Merrimack	N. H.	738
Newberry	Miami	Ohio	2,217
Newberry	York	Pa	2,191
New Boston	Mercer	Ill	*f*229
New Boston	Hillsborough	N. H.	1,477
New Braintree	Worcester	Mass.	852
New Braumfels	Comal	Texas	1,298
New Bremen	Lewis	N. Y.	1,510
New Bremen	Auglaize	Ohio	344
New Brighton	Beaver	Pa	*g*1,443
New Britain	Hartford	Conn.	3,029
New Britain	Bucks	Pa	1,313
New Brunswick	Middlesex	N. J.	10,019
New Buffalo	Sauk	Wis	224
Newburg	Warwick	Ind	526
Newburg	Penobscot	Me	1,399
Newburg	Cass	Mich.	388
Newburg	Orange	N. Y.	11,415
Newburg	Cuyahoga	Ohio	1,542
Newburgh	Lewis	Tenn.	*79
Newbury	Essex	Mass	4,426
Newbury	Geauga	Ohio	1,253
Newbury	Orange	Vt	2,984
Newburyport	Essex	Mass.	*h*9,572
New California	Madison	Ohio	43
New Canaan	Fairfield	Conn.	2,600
New Carlisle	Clark	Ohio	*i*634
New Castle	New Castle	Del.	1,202
New Castle	Henry	Ky	1,000
New Castle	Fulton	Ind	657
New Castle	Henry	Ind	*j*666
New Castle	Lincoln	Me	2,012
New Castle	Rockingham	N. H.	891
New Castle	Westchester	N. Y.	1,800
New Castle	Coshocton	Ohio	1,229
New Castle	Lawrence	Pa	*k*1,614
New Castle	Schuylkill	Pa	2,140
New Castle Hundred	New Castle	Del.	1,886
Newcombe	Essex	N. Y.	277
Newcomerstown	Tuscarawas	Ohio	476
New Concord	Muskingum	Ohio	324
New Cumberland	Tuscarawas	Ohio	203
New Cumberland	Cumberland	Pa	315
New Design	Monroe	Ill	1,442
New Diggings	Lafayette	Wis	1,742
New Durham	Laporte	Ind	794
New Durham	Strafford	N. H.	1,049
New England, &c.	Sutter	Cal.	42
New Fairfield	Fairfield	Conn.	927
Newfane	Niagara	N. Y.	3,271
Newfaul	Windham	Vt	1,304
Newfield	York	Me	1,418
Newfield	Tompkins	N. Y.	3,816
New Frankfort	Scott	Ind	223
New Garden	Wayne	Ind	1.609
New Garden	Chester	Pa	1,391
New Germantown	Perry	Pa	69
New Glarus	Greene	Wis	311
New Gloucester	Cumberland	Me	1,848
New Gottengen	Guernsey	Ohio	54
New Hampton	Belknap	N. H.	1,612
New Hanover	Burlington	N. J.	2,245
New Hanover	Montgomery	Pa	1,635
New Harmony	Posey	Ind	400
New Hartford	Litchfield	Conn.	2,643
New Hartford	Oneida	N. Y.	4,847
New Haven	New Haven	Conn.	*l*20,345
New Haven	Gallatin	Ill	126
New Haven	Shiawassee	Mich.	150
New Haven	Oswego	N. Y.	2,015
New Haven	Hamilton	Ohio	141
New Haven	Huron	Ohio	1,398
New Haven	Addison	Vt	1,663
New Hope	Brown	Ohio	106
New Hope	Bucks	Pa	1,144
New Hudson	Alleghany	N. Y.	1,433
New Iberia	St. Martin's	La	306
Newington	Rockingham	N. H.	472
New Ipswich	Hillsborough	N. H.	1,877
New Lebanon	Columbia	N. Y.	2,300
New Lenox	Will	Ill	617
New Lexington	Perry	Ohio	406
New Liberty	Owen	Ky	385
New Limerick	Aroostook	Me	160
Newlin	Chester	Pa	738
New Lisbon	Otsego	N. Y.	1,773
New Lisbon	Columbiana	Ohio	2.500
New London	New London	Conn.	*m*8,991
New London	Henry	Iowa	1,358
New London	Merrimack	N. H.	945
New London	Huron	Ohio	1,329
New London	Chester	Pa	2,042
New Lyme	Ashtabula	Ohio	628
Newmanstown	Lebanon	Pa	233
New Market	Rockingham	N. H.	1,937
New Market	Highland	Ohio	1,528
New Marlborough	Berkshire	Mass.	1,847
New Martinsville	Wetzell	Va	228
New Milford	Litchfield	Conn.	4,058
New Milford	Winnebago	Ill	569
New Milford	Susquehanna	Pa	1,433
New Orleans	Orleans	La	*n*116,375
New Paltz	Ulster	N. Y.	2,729
New Philadelphia	Tuscarawas	Ohio	*o*1,413
Newport	Wakulla	Fla	300
Newport	Lake	Ill	964
Newport	Vermillion	Ind	328
Newport	Johnson	Iowa	301
Newport	Campbell	Ky	*p*5,895
Newport	Penobscot	Me	1,210
Newport	Sullivan	N. H.	2,020
Newport	Herkimer	N. Y.	2,125
Newport	Washington	Ohio	1,425
Newport	Luzerne	Pa	868
Newport	Perry	Pa	517
Newport	Newport	R. I.	*q*9,563
Newport	Cocke	Tenn.	151
Newport	Orleans	Vt	748
New Portland	Somerset	Me	1,460
New Providence	Essex	N. J.	1,216

a In 1853, 2,000. *b* In 1853, 14,000. *c* In 1853, 45,500. *d* In 1853, 17,500. *e* In 1853, 1,000. *f* In 1853, 600. *g* In 1853, 2,000. *h* In 1853, 11,000. *i* In 1853, 11,000. *j* In 1853, 1,200. *k* In 1853, 1,800. *l* In 1853, 23,000. *m* In 1853, 10,000. *n* In 1853, 145,449 *o* In 1853, 2,000.. *p* In 1853, 8,500 *q* In 1853, 10,000.

New Richmond	Clermont	Ohio	2,500	Northampton	Summit	Ohio	1,147
New Rochelle	Westchester	N. Y.	2,458	Northampton	Bucks	Pa	1,843
Newry	Oxford	Me	459	Northampton	Lehigh	Pa	332
New Salem	Franklin	Mass	1,253	North Anson	Somerset	Me	1,168
New Salem	Fairfield	Ohio	217	North Anville	Lebanon	Pa	2,119
New Scotland	Albany	N. Y.	3,459	North Beaver	Lawrence	Pa	2,404
New Sewickly	Beaver	Pa	2,131	North Bend	Stark	Ind	141
New Sharon	Franklin	Me	1,732	North Bend	Washington	Wis	672
New Shoreham	Newport	R. I.	1,262	North Bergen	Hudson	N. J.	3,578
Newstead	Erie	N. Y.	2,899	North Berwick	York	Me	1,593
Newton	Jasper	Ill	1,134	North Bloomfield	Morrow	Ohio	1,443
Newton	Jasper	Ind	435	Northborough	Worcester	Mass	1,535
Newton	Middlesex	Mass	5,258	North Branford	New Haven	Conn	998
Newton	Calhoun	Mich	569	Northbridge	Worcester	Mass	2,230
Newton	Taney	Mo	252	North Bridgewater	Plymouth	Mass	3,939
Newton	Rockingham	N. H.	685	North Brookfield	Worcester	Mass	1,939
Newton	Camden	N. J.	1,576	North Brown	Vinton	Ohio	439
Newton	Sussex	N. J.	3,279	North Buffalo	Armstrong	Pa	916
Newton	Licking	Ohio	1,364	North Butler	Butler	Pa	1,433
Newton	Miami	Ohio	1,447	North Castle	Westchester	N. Y.	2,189
Newton	Muskingum	Ohio	2,696	North Chelsea	Suffolk	Mass	935
Newton	Pike	Ohio	461	North Codorus	York	Pa	2,126
Newton	Trumbull	Ohio	1,678	North Coventry	Chester	Pa	985
Newton	Cumberland	Pa	1,666	North Dansville	Livingston	N. Y.	4,377
Newton	Luzerne	Pa	819	North East	Adams	Ill	499
Newton	Manitoowoc	Wis	545	North East	Orange	Ind	1,206
Newtonia	Wilkinson	Miss.	113	North East	Cecil	Md	338
Newton Hamilton	Mifflin	Pa	353	North East	Dutchess	N. Y.	1,555
Newtown	Yuba	Cal	336	North East, Bor.	Erie	Pa	387
Newtown	Fairfield	Conn	3,338	North East	Erie	Pa	2,379
Newtown	Queens	N. Y.	7,208	North Elba	Essex	N. Y.	210
Newtown, Bor.	Bucks	Pa	580	Northern Liberties	Philadelphia	Pa	47,223
Newtown	Bucks	Pa	842	North Fayette	Allegheny	Pa	1,430
Newtown	Delaware	Pa	823	Northfield	Cook	Ill	1,013
Newtrier	Cook	Ill	473	Northfield	Washington	Me	246
New Utrecht	Kings	N. Y.	2,129	Northfield	Franklin	Mass	1,772
Newville	De Kalb	Ind	396	Northfield	Washtenaw	Mich	1,116
Newville	Cumberland	Pa	*a*715	Northfield	Merrimack	N. H.	1,332
New Vineyard	Franklin	Me	635	Northfield	Richmond	N. Y.	4,020
New Windsor	Orange	N. Y.	2,457	Northfield	Summit	Ohio	1,474
New York	New York	N. Y.	515,547	Northfield	Washington	Vt	2,922
Niagara Falls	Niagara	N. Y.	2,200	North Fork	Izard	Ark	378
Nicholas	Tioga	N. Y.	1,905	North Fork	Marion	Ark	277
Nicholasville	Jessamine	Ky	1,000	North Fork	Gallatin	Ill	504
Nicholson	Fayette	Pa	1,353	North Fork	Jasper	Ill	588
Nicholson	Wyoming	Pa	727	North Hampton	Rockingham	N. H.	822
Nile	Scioto	Ohio	1,004	North Haven	New Haven	Conn	1,325
Niles	Cook	Ill	408	North Haven	Waldo	Me	806
Niles	Delaware	Ind	924	North Haven	Van Buren	Mich	220
Niles	Berrien	Mich	2,500	North Heidelburgh	Berks	Pa	844
Niles	Cayuga	N. Y.	2,053	North Hempstead	Queens	N. Y.	4,291
Nimishillen	Stark	Ohio	2,587	North Hero	Grand Isle	Vt	730
Nineveh	Bartholomew	Ind	720	North Hudson	Essex	N. Y.	561
Nineveh	Johnson	Ind	1,649	North Huntingdon	Westmoreland	Pa	2,570
Nippenose	Lycoming	Pa	351	North Kingston	Washington	R. I.	2,971
Niskayuna	Schenectady	N. Y.	783	North Lebanon	Lebanon	Pa	2,408
Noble	Cass	Ind	743	North Madison	Jefferson	Ind	992
Noble	Jay	Ind	745	North Mahoning	Indiana	Pa	840
Noble	La Porte	Ind	944	North Manheim	Schuylkill	Pa	3,006
Noble	Noble	Ind	595	North Middleton	Cumberland	Pa	2,235
Noble	Rush	Ind	1,386	North Norwich	Chenango	N. Y.	1,172
Noble	Shelby	Ind	1,313	North Penn	Philadelphia	Pa	2,687
Noble	Wabash	Ind	3,489	North Plains	Ionia	Mich	292
Noble	Branch	Mich	451	Nortport	Waldo	Me	1,260
Noble	Auglaize	Ohio	309	North Providence	Providence	R. I.	7,680
Noble	Defiance	Ohio	558	North Salem	Westchester	N. Y.	1,335
Noble	Morgan	Ohio	1,702	North Sewickly	Beaver	Pa	1,018
Nobleborough	Lincoln	Me	1,408	North Chenango	Crawford	Pa	825
Noblesville	Hamilton	Ind	2,308	North Slippery			
Noblesville, T	Hamilton	Ind	*b*664	Rock	Lawrence	Pa	2,254
Nockamixon	Bucks	Pa	2,445	North Stonington	New London	Conn	1,936
Nodaway	Adair	Mo	2,677	North Strabane	Washington	Pa	1,210
Nodaway City	Adair	Mo	139	Northumberland	Coos	N. H.	429
Norfolk	Litchfield	Conn	1,643	Northumberland	Saratoga	N. Y.	1,775
Norfolk	St. Lawrence	N. Y.	1,753	Northumberland	Northumberland	Pa	1,041
Norfolk	Norfolk	Va	*c*14,326	Northumberland	Wyoming	Pa	766
Norman	Grundy	Ill	56	Northville	Lasalle	Ill	951
Norridgewock	Somerset	Me	1,848	North West	Orange	Ind	1,245
Norristown, Bor.	Montgomery	Pa	6,024	North West	Williams	Ohio	343
Norristown	Montgomery	Pa	1,594	North Whitehall	Lehigh	Pa	2,955
North	Lake	Ind	97	Northwood	Rockingham	N. H.	1,308
North	Harrison	Ohio	1,123	North Woodbury	Blair	Pa	1,836
North Adams, T	Berkshire	Mass	3,000	North Yarmouth	Cumberland	Me	1,121
Northampton	Hampshire	Mass	5,278	Norton	Bristol	Mass	1,966
Northampton	Saginaw	Mich	122	Norton	Summit	Ohio	1,346
Northampton	Rockingham	N. H.	822	Norwalk	Fairfield	Conn	4,651
Northampton	Burlington	N. J.	3,031	Norwalk	Huron	Ohio	3,159
Northampton	Fulton	N. Y.	1,701	Norwalk, T	Huron	Ohio	1,437
Northampton	Clark	Ohio	147	Norway	Oxford	Me	1,963

a In 1853, 900. *b* In 1853, 1,500. *c* In 1853, 16,000.

Norway	Herkimer	N. Y.	1,052
Norway	Racine	Wis.	751
Norwegian	Schuylkill	Pa	2,642
Norwich	New London	Conn.	a10,265
Norwich	Hampshire	Mass.	756
Norwich	Chenango	N. Y.	3.615
Norwich, T	Chenango	N. Y.	2,000
Norwich	Franklin	Ohio	1,053
Norwich	Huron	Ohio	1,021
Norwich	Muskingum	Ohio	324
Norwich	McKean	Pa	265
Norwich	Windsor	Vt.	1,978
Nottaway	St. Joseph	Mich.	1,165
Nottingham	Wells	Ind.	523
Nottingham	Rockingham	N. H.	1,268
Nottingham	Mercer	N. J.	4,495
Nottingham	Harrison	Ohio	1,236
Nottingham	Washington	Pa	1,008
Novi	Oakland	Mich.	1,428
Nunda	Livingston	N. Y	3,128
Nyack	Rockland	N. Y	4,766
Oak Creek	Milwaukie	Wis.	1,259
Oakfield	Kent	Mich.	645
Oakfield	Genesee	N. Y.	1,457
Oakfield	Fond du Lac	Wis.	769
Oak Grove	Dodge	Wis.	1,143
Oakham	Worcester	Mass.	1,137
Oakland	Steuben	Ind.	141
Oakland	Oakland	Mich.	978
Oakland	Venango	Pa	837
Oakland	Jefferson	Wis.	806
Ocala	Marion	Fla	243
Occoquan	Prince William	Va	400
Ocean	Monmouth	N. J.	3,768
Oconomowock	Waukeska	Wis.	1,216
Oden	Chicot	Ark	1,173
Odessa	Ionia	Mich.	121
Ogden	Lenawee	Mich.	579
Ogden	Monroe	N. Y.	2.598
Ogdensburg	St. Lawrence	N. Y.	6.500
Oglethorpe	Macon	Ga	b*113
Ohio	Boone	Ill.	672
Ohio	Bureau	Ill.	183
Ohio	Bartholomew	Ind	293
Ohio	Crawford	Ind	779
Ohio	Spencer	Ind	1,930
Ohio	Warwick	Ind	1,448
Ohio	Herkimer	N. Y.	1,051
Ohio	Clermont	Ohio	4,479
Ohio	Gallia	Ohio	504
Ohio	Monroe	Ohio	1.664
Ohio	Allegheny	Pa	2.329
Ohio	Beaver	Pa	1,660
Oibolita	Valencia	N. M.	42
Oil	Perry	Ind	533
Oil Creek	Crawford	Pa	811
Old River	Arkansas	Ark	514
Old River	Chicot	Ark	867
Oldtown	Penobscot	Me	3,087
Olean	Cattaraugus	N. Y.	899
Oleana	Henderson	Ill.	47
Oley	Berks	Pa	1,799
Olive	Elkhart	Ind	337
Olive	St. Joseph	Ind	851
Olive	Clinton	Iowa	85
Olive	Clinton	Mich.	228
Olive	Ulster	N. Y.	2,710
Olive	Meigs	Ohio	924
Olive	Morgan	Ohio	2.013
Oliver	Mifflin	Pa	1,668
Oliver	Perry	Pa	870
Olmstead	Cuyahoga	Ohio	1,216
Oneco	Stephenson	Ill.	882
Oneida	Eaton	Mich.	492
Oneonta	Otsego	N. Y.	1,902
Onondaga	Ingham	Mich.	819
Onondaga	Onondaga	N. Y.	5.694
Ontario	Wayne	N. Y.	2,246
Ontwa	Cass	Mich.	781
Opelousas	St. Landry	La.	1,214
Ophir	Lasalle	Ill	210
Oppenheim	Fulton	N. Y.	2.315
Oquawka	Henderson	Ill.	c553
Orange	New Haven	Conn.	1,476
Orange	Fayette	Ind	1,129
Orange	Noble	Ind	607
Orange	Rush	Ind	1,672
Orange	Franklin	Mass.	1,701
Orange	Ionia	Mich.	378
Orange	Grafton	N. H.	451
Orange	Essex	N. J.	4.385
Orange	Rockland	N. Y.	4,769
Orange	Steuben	N. Y.	2,055
Orange	Ashland	Ohio	1,822
Orange, T	Ashland	Ohio	266
Orange	Carroll	Ohio	1,577
Orange	Cuyahoga	Ohio	1,063
Orange	Delaware	Ohio	1,150
Orange	Hancock	Ohio	704
Orange	Meigs	Ohio	948
Orange	Shelby	Ohio	922
Orange	Columbia	Pa	1.077
Orange	Orange	Vt	1,007
Orangeville	Barry	Mich.	364
Orangeville	Wyoming	N. Y.	1,438
Oregon	Ogle	Ill	540
Oregon	Schuyler	Ill	747
Oregon	Stark	Ind.	108
Oregon	Lapeer	Mich.	205
Oregon	Lucas	Ohio	436
Oregon	Seneca	Ohio	400
Oregon	Wayne	Pa	361
Oregon	Dane	Wis.	638
Oregon Bar and Rock Spring	Sutter	Cal.	42
Oregon Canon	El Dorado	Cal	126
Oregon City	Clackamus	Oregon	d697
Orien	Fulton	Ill.	527
Orient	Aroostook	Me	205
Orion	Oakland	Mich.	1,119
Orland	Cook	Ill.	504
Orland	Hancock	Me	1,579
Orleans	Orange	Ind	1.402
Orleans	Barnstable	Mass.	1,848
Orleans	Ionia	Mich.	491
Orleans	Jefferson	N. Y.	3,265
Orneville	Piscataquis	Me	424
Orono	Penobscot	Me.	2,785
Orrington	Penobscot	Me.	1,852
Orwell	Oswego	N. Y.	1,106
Orwell	Ashtabula	Ohio	825
Orwell	Bradford	Pa	1,241
Orwell	Addison	Vt.	1.470
Orwigsburg	Schuylkill	Pa	909
Osage	Carroll	Ark	719
Osage	Newton	Ark.	141
Osage	Morgan	Mo	*378
Osage	Osage	Mo	*492
Osage, including Bentonville	Benton	Ark	*1,454
Osceola	Livingston	Mich.	960
Osceola	Lewis	N. Y.	412
Oshkosh	Winnebago	Wis.	2,500
Oshtemo	Kalamazoo	Mich.	587
Oskaloosa	Mahaska	Iowa	e625
Osnaburg	Starke	Ohio	2,225
Osolo	Elkhart	Ind	471
Ossian	Alleghany	N. Y.	1.283
Ossining	Westchester	N. Y.	4,939
Ossipee	Carroll	N. H.	2,123
Oswayo	Potter	Pa	244
Oswegatchie	St. Lawrence	N. Y.	7.756
Oswego	Kendall	Ill	1,599
Oswego, T	Kendall	Ill.	1,000
Oswego	Kosciusko	Ind.	137
Oswego	Oswego	N. Y.	2,445
Oswego City	Oswego	N. Y.	12,205
Otego	Otsego	N. Y.	1,792
Otis	Hancock	Me	124
Otis	Berkshire	Mass.	1,224
Otisco	Ionia	Mich.	1.018
Otisco	Onondaga	N. Y.	1,804
Otisfield	Cumberland	Me.	1,171
Otsego	Steuben	Ind	541
Otsego	Allegan	Mich.	818
Otsego	Otsego	N. Y.	3,901
Otsego	Columbia	Wis.	412
Otselic	Chenango	N. Y.	1,800
Ottawa	Ottawa	Mich.	430
Ottawa	Putnam	Ohio	1,166
Ottawa, T	Putnam	Ohio	104
Ottawa	Waukesha	Wis.	793
Ottawa and South Ottawa	Lasalle	Ill.	3,219
Otter Creek	Ripley	Ind.	741
Otter Creek	Vigo	Ind.	789
Otter Creek	Jackson	Iowa	242
Otto	Cattaraugus	N. Y.	2,267

a In 1853, 11,500. *b* In 1853, 2,500. *c* In 1853, 1,000. *d* In 1853, 900. *e* In 1853, 1,500.

Town	County	State	Population
Ouachita	Bradley	Ark.	334
Ovid	Branch	Mich.	710
Ovid	Clinton	Mich.	172
Ovid	Seneca	N. Y.	2,248
Owasco	Cayuga	N. Y.	1,254
Owasso	Shiawassee	Mich.	392
Owego	Tioga	N. Y.	7,159
Owego, T	Tioga	N. Y.	4,000
Owen	Dallas	Ark.	366
Owen	Winnebago	Ill.	512
Owen	Clark	Ind.	680
Owen	Clinton	Ind.	634
Owen	Jackson	Ind.	1,257
Owen	Warwick	Ind.	728
Owensboro	Daviess	Ky.	a1,215
Owensville	Gibson	Ind.	b235
Oxford	New Haven	Conn.	1,564
Oxford	Lafayette	Miss.	1,200
Oxford	Oxford	Me.	1,233
Oxford	Worcester	Mass.	2,380
Oxford	Oakland	Mich.	1,019
Oxford	Grafton	N. H.	1,406
Oxford	Warren	N. J.	1,718
Oxford	Chenango	N. Y.	3,227
Oxford	Granville	N. C.	c1,978
Oxford	Butler	Ohio	3,139
Oxford, T.	Butler	Ohio	d1,111
Oxford	Coshocton	Ohio	1,112
Oxford	Delaware	Ohio	829
Oxford	Erie	Ohio	984
Oxford	Guernsey	Ohio	2,209
Oxford	Tuscarawas	Ohio	1,436
Oxford	Adams	Pa.	931
Oxford	Chester	Pa.	186
Oxford	Philadelphia	Pa.	1,787
Oyster Bay	Queens	N. Y.	6,900
Ozan	Hempstead	Ark.	1,547
Ozark	Franklin	Ark.	84
Ozark	Greene	Mo.	*569
Ozark	Lawrence	Mo.	*613
Packer	Carbon	Pa.	291
Paducah	McCracken	Ky.	e2,428
Pahaquary	Warren	N. J.	460
Painesville	Lake	Ohio	3,128
Paint	Fayette	Ohio	1,253
Paint	Highland	Ohio	2,678
Paint	Holmes	Ohio	1,618
Paint	Ross	Ohio	1,749
Paint	Wayne	Ohio	1,627
Paint	Clarion	Pa.	610
Paint	Somerset	Pa.	878
Painted Post	Steuben	N. Y.	4,372
Palatine	Cook	Ill.	617
Palatine	Montgomery	N. Y.	2,856
Palermo	Waldo	Me.	1,659
Palermo	Oswego	N. Y.	2,053
Palestine	Bradley	Ark.	154
Palestine	Anderson	Texas	f212
Palmer	Hampden	Mass.	3,974
Palmyra	Lee	Ga.	162
Palmyra	Lee	Ill.	588
Palmyra	Somerset	Me.	1,625
Palmyra	Lenawee	Mich.	1,098
Palmyra	Marion	Mo.	g1,284
Palmyra	Wayne	N. Y.	3,893
Palmyra	Portage	Ohio	1,093
Palmyra	Lebanon	Pa.	286
Palmyra	Pike	Pa.	447
Palmyra	Wayne	Pa.	2,015
Palmyra	Jefferson	Wis.	982
Palos	Cook	Ill.	336
Pamelia	Jefferson	N. Y.	2,528
Pampas	De Kalb	Ill.	1,038
Panola	Panola	Miss.	500
Panton	Addison	Vt.	559
Paoli	Orange	Ind.	2,023
Paoli, T.	Orange	Ind.	461
Paraclifta	Sevier	Ark.	144
Paradise	Lancaster	Pa.	1,828
Paradise	Monroe	Pa.	428
Paradise	York	Pa.	2,354
Pardeeville	Columbia	Wis.	81
Parida	Valencia	N. M.	168
Paris	Emanuel	Ga.	57
Paris	Edgar	Ill.	697
Paris	Bourbon	Ky.	h384
Paris	Oxford	Me.	2,882

Town	County	State	Population
Paris	Kent	Mich.	521
Paris	Oneida	N. Y.	4,281
Paris	Portage	Ohio	1,018
Paris	Stark	Ohio	2,740
Paris	Union	Ohio	1,587
Paris	Grant	Wis.	391
Paris	Kenosha	Wis.	956
Parish	Oswego	N. Y.	1,799
Parishville	St. Lawrence	N. Y.	2,132
Parkeman	Piscataquis	Me.	1,243
Parkeman	Geauga	Ohio	1,383
Parker	Butler	Pa.	769
Parkersburg	Chester	Pa.	400
Parkersburg	Wood	Va.	i1,218
Parks	Scott	Ark.	277
Parks	St. Joseph	Mich.	825
Parkville	Platte	Mo.	309
Parma	Monroe	N. Y.	2,947
Parma	Cuyahoga	Ohio	1,329
Parmer	Jackson	Mich.	1,081
Parsonsfield	York	Me.	2,322
Passadumkeag	Penobscot	Me.	295
Pass Christian	Harrison	Miss.	790
Passyunk	Philadelphia	Pa.	1,607
Paterson	Passaic	N. J.	j11,334
Patoca	Crawford	Ind.	937
Patoka	Dubois	Ind.	1,565
Patoka	Gibson	Ind.	3,385
Patoka, T.	Gibson	Ind.	99
Patoka, Madison, and Washington	Pike	Ind.	3,305
Patricktown	Lincoln	Me.	552
Pattenville	Grant	Wis.	2,171
Patterson	Putnam	N. Y.	1,371
Patterson	Darke	Ohio	319
Patterson	Beaver	Pa.	251
Patterson	Passaic	N. J.	17,615
Patterson	Juniata	Pa.	400
Patterson	Schuylkill	Pa.	500
Pattersonville	St. Mary's	La.	600
Patton	Penobscot	Me.	470
Patton	Allegheny	Pa.	881
Patton	Centre	Pa.	453
Paulding	Jasper	Miss.	335
Pavillion	Kalamazoo	Mich.	495
Pavillion	Genesee	N. Y.	1,640
Pawlet	Rutland	Vt.	1,843
Pawling	Dutchess	N. Y.	1,720
Paw Paw	De Kalb	Ill.	653
Pawpaw	Van Buren	Mich.	1,500
Pawtucket	Bristol	Mass.	3,753
Pawtuxet	Kent	R. I.	1,800
Paxton	Worcester	Mass.	820
Paxton	Ross	Ohio	930
Payson	Adams	Ill.	1,494
Peacham	Caledonia	Vt.	1,377
Peach Bottom	York	Pa.	1,409
Pearlington	Hancock	Miss.	110
Pease	Belmont	Ohio	3,515
Pecan	Mississippi	Ark.	267
Peebles	Allegheny	Pa.	2,168
Peekskill	Westchester	N. Y.	2,500
Peepee	Pike	Ohio	1,321
Pekin city	Taswell	Ill.	k1,678
Pelham	Hampshire	Mass.	983
Pelham	Hillsborough	N. H.	1,071
Pelham	Westchester	N. Y.	577
Pella	Marion	Iowa	500
Pemberton	Burlington	N. J.	2,866
Pembroke	Washington	Me.	1,712
Pembroke	Plymouth	Mass.	1,388
Pembroke	Merrimack	N. H.	1,733
Pembroke	Genesee	N. Y.	2,279
Pencada Hundred	Newcastle	Del.	2,614
Pendleton	Madison	Ind.	389
Pendleton	Niagara	N. Y.	2,166
Pendleton	Putnam	Ohio	180
Pendleton	Anderson	S. C.	634
Penfield	Monroe	N. Y.	3,185
Penfield	Lorain	Ohio	672
Penn	Jay	Ind.	810
Penn	St. Joseph	Ind.	3,034
Penn	Jefferson	Iowa	869
Penn	Johnson	Iowa	386
Penn	Cass	Mich.	698
Penn	Morgan	Ohio	1,370
Penn	Morrow	Ohio	876

a In 1853, 1,600. *b* In 1853, 400. *c* In 1853, 2,500. *d* In 1853, 2,200. *e* In 1853, 3,000. *f* In 1853, 1,000. *g* In 1853 2,000. *h* In 1853, 2,500. *i* In 1853, 3,500. *j* In 1853, 13,000. *k* In 1853, 2,000.

Penn	Berks	Pa	1,476
Penn	Chester	Pa	738
Penn	Clearfield	Pa	528
Penn	Huntingdon	Pa	839
Penn	Lancaster	Pa	1,909
Penn	Lycoming	Pa	578
Penn	Perry	Pa	1,109
Penn District	Philadelphia	Pa	8,939
Pennfield	Calhoun	Mich	598
Penn Forest	Carbon	Pa	415
Pennington	Bradley	Ark	1,216
Penns	Union	Pa	2,736
Pennsbury	Chester	Pa	761
Penn Yan	Yates	N. Y.	3,000
Peno	Pike	Mo	1,431
Penobscot	Hancock	Me	1,556
Pensacola	Escambia	Fla	2,164
Peoria city	Peoria	Ill	*a*5,095
Pepperell	Middlesex	Mass	1,754
Pequannock	Morris	N. J.	4,126
Peralto	Valencia	N. M.	588
Periquati	Valencia	N. M.	36
Perkins	Lincoln	Me	84
Perkins	Erie	Ohio	1,207
Perkinsville	Madison	Ind	115
Perkiomen	Montgomery	Pa	1,622
Perrin	Union	Pa	2,736
Perrinton	Monroe	N. Y.	2,891
Perry	Johnson	Ark	603
Perry	Houston	Ga	1,200
Perry	Pike	Ill	402
Perry	Allen	Ind	842
Perry	Clay	Ind	691
Perry	Clinton	Ind	893
Perry	Delaware	Ind	1,091
Perry	Lawrence	Ind	1,457
Perry	Marion	Ind	1,802
Perry	Martin	Ind	1,517
Perry	Miami	Ind	1,176
Perry	Monroe	Ind	1,008
Perry	Noble	Ind	1,104
Perry	Tippecanoe	Ind	1,036
Perry	Vanderburg	Ind	693
Perry	Wayne	Ind	868
Perry	Davis	Iowa	676
Perry	Jackson	Iowa	490
Perry	Washington	Me	1,324
Perry	Shiawassee	Mich	313
Perry	Wyoming	N. Y.	2,832
Perry, T	Wyoming	N. Y.	1,500
Perry	Allen	Ohio	923
Perry	Ashland	Ohio	1,788
Perry	Brown	Ohio	2,781
Perry	Carroll	Ohio	1,277
Perry	Columbiana	Ohio	2,371
Perry	Coshocton	Ohio	1,340
Perry	Fayette	Ohio	1,088
Perry	Franklin	Ohio	4,169
Perry	Gallia	Ohio	1,208
Perry	Hocking	Ohio	1,217
Perry	Lake	Ohio	1,131
Perry	Lawrence	Ohio	924
Perry	Licking	Ohio	1,254
Perry	Logan	Ohio	1,407
Perry	Monroe	Ohio	1,566
Perry	Montgomery	Ohio	1,906
Perry	Morrow	Ohio	1,150
Perry	Muskingum	Ohio	1,038
Perry	Pickaway	Ohio	1,120
Perry	Pike	Ohio	653
Perry	Putnam	Ohio	262
Perry	Richland	Ohio	924
Perry	Shelby	Ohio	899
Perry	Stark	Ohio	4,667
Perry	Tuscarawas	Ohio	1,396
Perry	Wood	Ohio	888
Perry	Armstrong	Pa	799
Perry	Berks	Pa	1,320
Perry	Clarion	Pa	1,394
Perry	Fayette	Pa	1,272
Perry	Greene	Pa	1,090
Perry	Jefferson	Pa	1,738
Perry	Lawrence	Pa	528
Perry	Union	Pa	1,341
Perry	Dane	Wis	121
Perrysburg	Cattaraugus	N. Y.	1,861
Perrysburg	Wood	Ohio	1,779
Perrysburg, T.	Wood	Ohio	*b*1,199

Perryville	Vermillion	Ind	1,505
Perryville	Perry	Mo	221
Perrysville	Decatur	Tenn	250
Persia	Cattaraugus	N. Y.	1,955
Perth	Fulton	N. Y.	1,140
Perth Amboy	Middlesex	N. J.	1,865
Peru	Miami	Ind	1,980
Peru, T	Miami	Ind	*c*1,266
Peru	Oxford	Me	1,109
Peru	Berkshire	Mass	519
Peru	Clinton	N. Y.	3,640
Peru, T	Clinton	N. Y.	900
Peru	Lasalle	Ill	4,500
Peru	Huron	Ohio	1,632
Peru	Bennington	Vt	567
Peru and vicinity	El Dorado	Cal	168
Peterborough	Hillsborough	N. H.	2,222
Peters	Franklin	Pa	2,310
Peters	Washington	Pa	924
Petersburg	Menard	Ill	714
Petersburg	Perry	Ind	386
Petersburg	Huntingdon	Pa	264
Petersburg	Dinwiddie	Va	*d*13,950
Petersburg	Pike	Ind	500
Petersburgh	Boone	Ky	*420
Petersburgh	Rensselaer	N. Y.	1,908
Petersburgh	Adams	Pa	356
Petersburgh	Perry	Pa	680
Petersburg, T	Perry	Pa	1,000
Petersham	Worcester	Mass	1,527
Pettis	Platte	Mo	2,953
Pewankee	Waukesha	Wis	1,106
Pharsalia	Chenango	N. Y.	1,185
Phelps	Ontario	N. Y.	5,542
Phelpstown	Ingham	Mich	393
Philadelphia	Jefferson	N. Y.	1,915
Philadelphia prop'r	Philadelphia	Pa	121,376
Philadelphia, including Kensington, Northern Liberties, Spring Garden, Southwark, & Moyamensing	Philadelphia	Pa	*e*340,045
Philips	Franklin	Me	1,673
Philipsburg	Beaver	Pa	473
Philipston	Worcester	Mass	809
Philipstown	Putnam	N. Y.	5,063
Philipsville, T.	Alleghany	N. Y.	800
Phippsburg	Lincoln	Me	1,805
Phœnix	Oswego	N. Y	872
Phœnixville	Chester	Pa	2,670
Pickaway	Pickaway	Ohio	1,425
Pickensville	Pickens	Ala	276
Pickerington	Fairfield	Ohio	157
Piermont	Rockland	N. Y	1,200
Piermont	Grafton	N. H.	948
Pierpont	St. Lawrence	N. Y	1,459
Pierpont	Ashtabula	Ohio	999
Pierson	Vigo	Ind	642
Pigeon	Vanderburg	Ind	5,305
Pigeon	Warrick	Ind	715
Pigeon Roost	Prairie	Ark	307
Pike	Jay	Ind	786
Pike	Marion	Ind	1,928
Pike	Warren	Ind	555
Pike	Muscatine	Iowa	265
Pike	Wyoming	N. Y	2,003
Pike	Brown	Ohio	1,022
Pike	Clark	Ohio	1,462
Pike	Coshocton	Ohio	1,081
Pike	Fulton	Ohio	485
Pike	Knox	Ohio	1,720
Pike	Madison	Ohio	423
Pike	Perry	Ohio	2,147
Pike	Stark	Ohio	1,447
Pike	Berks	Pa	883
Pike	Bradford	Pa	1,747
Pike	Clearfield	Pa	1,[illegible]49
Pike	Potter	Pa	200
Pike	Kenosha	Wis	680
Piketon	Pike	Ohio	690
Pikeville	Bledsoe	Tenn	136
Pile's Grove	Salem	N. J.	2,962
Pilot Hill and vicinity	El Dorado	Cal	420
Pinckney	Livingston	Mich	500
Pine	Warren	Ind	942
Pine	Allegheny	Pa	2,109

a In 1853, 8,000. *b* In 1853, 1,600. *c* In 1853, 1,700. *d* In 1853, 15,000. *e* Philadelphia, as now consolidated, contained in 1850 a population of 408,762.

Pine	Clarion	Pa	910
Pine	Armstrong	Pa	2,288
Pine	Crawford	Pa	702
Pine	Indiana	Pa	1,367
Pine	Jefferson	Pa	778
Pine Bluff	Jefferson	Ark	400
Pine Creek	Ogle	Ill	924
Pine Creek	Clinton	Pa	774
Pine Grove	Sierra	Cal	504
Pine Grove	Van Buren	Mich	62
Pine Grove, Bor.	Schuylkill	Pa	646
Pine Grove	Schuylkill	Pa	1,967
Pine Grove	Venango	Pa	690
Pine Grove	Warren	Pa	1,527
Pine Plains	Allegan	Mich	34
Pine Plains	Dutchess	N. Y	1,416
Piney	Johnson	Ark	290
Piney Fork	Lawrence	Ark	438
Pinkney	Lewis	N. Y	1,208
Pioneer	Cedar	Iowa	419
Pipe	Stoddart	Mo	1,053
Pipe Creek	Madison	Ind	1,512
Pipe Creek	Miami	Ind	504
Piqua	Miami	Ohio	3,277
Piscataway	Middlesex	N. J	2,975
Pitcairn	St. Lawrence	N. Y	503
Pitcher	Chenango	N. Y	1,403
Pitt	Wyandott	Ohio	886
Pitt	Allegheny	Pa	2,035
Pittsburg	Johnson	Ark	680
Pittsburg	Carroll	Ind	336
Pittsburg	Coos	N. H	425
Pittsburg	Allegheny	Pa	—46,601
Pittsfield	Pike	Ill	637
Pittsfield	Somerset	Me	1,166
Pittsfield	Berkshire	Mass	*a*5,872
Pittsfield	Washtenaw	Mich	1,232
Pittsfield	Merrimack	N. H	1,828
Pittsfield	Otsego	N. Y	1,591
Pittsfield	Lorain	Ohio	1,088
Pittsfield	Warren	Pa	756
Pittsfield	Rutland	Vt	512
Pittsfield	Brown	Wis	198
Pittsford	Hillsdale	Mich	1,223
Pittsford	Monroe	N. Y	2,061
Pittsford	Rutland	Vt	2,026
Pitts Grove	Salem	N. J	1,151
Pittston	Luzerne	Pa	4,049
Pittston, T.	Luzerne	Pa	2,000
Pittstown	Kennebec	Me	2,823
Pittstown	Rensselaer	N. Y	3,732
Placerville and vicinity	El Dorado	Cal	5,623
Plain	St. Francis	Ark	132
Plain	Kosciusko	Ind	868
Plain	Franklin	Ohio	1,561
Plain	Stark	Ohio	2,211
Plain	Wayne	Ohio	2,375
Plain	Wood	Ohio	492
Plainfield	Windham	Conn	2,732
Plainfield	Will	Ill	1,093
Plainfield	Hendricks	Ind	251
Plainfield	Hampshire	Mass	814
Plainfield	Kent	Mich	659
Plainfield	Sullivan	N. H	1,392
Plainfield	Essex	N. J	2,447
Plainfield	Otsego	N. Y	1,450
Plainfield	Northampton	Pa	1,753
Plainfield	Washington	Vt	808
Plaistow	Rockingham	N. H	748
Planters	Chicot	Ark	497
Planters	Philips	Ark	687
Plato	Kane	Ill	813
Platte	Adair	Mo	2,190
Platte	Buchanan	Mo	*881
Platte	Clay	Mo	1,176
Platte City	Platte	Mo	496
Plattekill	Ulster	N. Y	1,998
Platteville	Grant	Wis	2,171
Plattsburg	Clinton	N. Y	5,618
Pleasant	Fulton	Ill	964
Pleasant	Allen	Ind	658
Pleasant	Grant	Ind	1,082
Pleasant	Johnson	Ind	1,270
Pleasant	Laporte	Ind	632
Pleasant	Porter	Ind	311
Pleasant	Steuben	Ind	734
Pleasant	Switzerlend	Ind	2,211
Pleasant	Wabash	Ind	1,312

Pleasant	Brown	Ohio	2,074
Pleasant	Clark	Ohio	1,349
Pleasant	Fairfield	Ohio	2,011
Pleasant	Franklin	Ohio	1,071
Pleasant	Hancock	Ohio	522
Pleasant	Hardin	Ohio	2,124
Pleasant	Henry	Ohio	338
Pleasant	Knox	Ohio	909
Pleasant	Logan	Ohio	806
Pleasant	Madison	Ohio	1,184
Pleasant	Marion	Ohio	1,198
Pleasant	Putnam	Ohio	714
Pleasant	Seneca	Ohio	1,592
Pleasant	Van Wert	Ohio	619
Pleasant	Warren	Pa	240
Pleasant Grove	Des Moines	Iowa	802
Pleasant Hill or Shakertown	Mercer	Ky	342
Pleasant Hill and vicinity	El Dorado	Cal	378
Pleasant Mills	Adams	Ind	71
Pleasant Mount	Wayne	Pa	186
Plesant Prairie	Kenosha	Wis	959
Pleasant Run	Lawrence	Ind	1,342
Pleasant Spring	Dane	Wis	732
Pleasant Valley	Johnson	Iowa	287
Pleasant Valley	Dutchess	N. Y	2,226
Pleasant Valley	Madison	Ohio	168
Pleasant Valley	Potter	Pa	73
Pleasant Valley	Marquette	Wis	766
Plover	Portage	Wis	451
Plum	Allegheny	Pa	1,241
Plum	Venango	Pa	835
Plum Bayou	Jefferson	Ark	756
Plum Creek	Armstrong	Pa	2,220
Plumstead	Ocean	N. J	1,613
Plumstead	Bucks	Pa	2,300
Plunkett Creek	Lycoming	Pa	189
Plunket's Creek	Sullivan	Pa	199
Plymouth	Litchfield	Conn	2,568
Plymouth	Marshall	Ind	700
Plymouth	Penobscot	Me	925
Plymouth	Plymouth	Mass	6,024
Plymouth	Wayne	Mich	2,431
Plymouth	Grafton	N. H	1,290
Plymouth	Chenango	N. Y	1,551
Plymouth	Washington	N. C	951
Plymouth	Ashtabula	Ohio	753
Plymouth	Richland	Ohio	1,663
Plymouth	Luzerne	Pa	1,473
Plymouth	Montgomery	Pa	1,383
Plymouth	Windsor	Vt	1,226
Plymouth	Rock	Wis	581
Plympton	Plymouth	Mass	927
Poasttown	Butler	Ohio	126
Pocahontas	Bond	Ind	126
Pocono	Mercer	Pa	925
Pocopsin	Chester	Pa	592
Poestenkill	Rensselaer	N. Y	2,092
Point	Calhoun	Ill	812
Point	Posey	Ind	479
Point	Northumberland	Pa	876
Point Pleasant	Guernsey	Ohio	106
Point Remove	Conway	Ark	294
Pokagon	Cass	Mich	994
Poland	Cumberland	Me	2,660
Poland	Chautauque	N. Y	1,174
Poland	Mahoning	Ohio	2,126
Polk	Arkansas	Ark	322
Polk	Dallas	Ark	429
Polk	Montgomery	Ark	208
Polk	Newton	Ark	137
Polk	Monroe	Ind	431
Polk	Jefferson	Iowa	601
Polk	Greene	Mo	*732
Polk	Crawford	Ohio	1,318
Polk	Monroe	Pa	712
Polk	Washington	Wis	1,260
Polkton	Ottawa	Mich	268
Pomeroy	Meigs	Ohio	*b*1,638
Pomfret	Windham	Conn	1,848
Pomfret	Chatauque	N. Y	4,483
Pomfret	Windsor	Vt	1,546
Pompey	Onondago	N. Y	4,006
Pompton	Passaic	N. J	1,720
Pontiac	Livingston	Ill	27
Pontiac	Oakland	Mich	2,820
Pontiac, T.	Oakland	Mich	*c*1,681
Poplar Plains	Fleming	Ky	209

a In 1853, 6,500. *b* In 1853, 4,000. *c* In 1853, 2,500.

Name	County	State	Population
Poplin	Rockingham	N. H.	509
Portage	Porter	Ind	266
Portage	Saint Joseph	Ind	2,073
Portage	Kalamazoo	Mich	726
Portage	Livingston	N. Y.	2,478
Portage	Hancock	Ohio	614
Portage	Ottawa	Ohio	626
Portage	Summit	Ohio	4,426
Portage	Wood	Ohio	403
Portage	Potter	Ohio	34
Portage City	Columbia	Wis	2,000
Portage Prairie	Columbia	Wis	603
Port Byron	Cayuga	N. Y.	1,400
Port Carbon	Schuylkill	Pa	2,142
Port Clinton	Ottawa	Ohio	249
Port Deposit	Cecil	Md	1,008
Porter	Porter	Ind	768
Porter	Oxford	Me	1,208
Porter	Cass	Mich	1,259
Porter	Van Buren	Mich	443
Porter	Greene	Mo	*497
Porter	Niagara	N. Y.	2,455
Porter	Delaware	Ohio	1,037
Porter	Scioto	Ohio	1,674
Porter	Clarion	Pa	1,907
Porter	Clinton	Pa	968
Porter	Huntingdon	Pa	1,050
Porter	Jefferson	Pa	728
Porter	Lycoming	Pa	768
Porter	Schuylkill	Pa	305
Porter	Rock	Wis	882
Portersville	Butler	Pa	240
Port Gibson	Claiborne	Miss	1,037
Port Hope	Columbia	Wis	413
Port Huron	St. Clair	Mich	2,302
Port Huron, T.	St. Clair	Miss	1,584
Port Jefferson	Shelby	Ohio	286
Port Kennedy	Montgomery	Pa	449
Portland	Middlesex	Conn	2,836
Portland	Jefferson	Ky	800
Portland	Cumberland	Me	a20,815
Portland	Ionia	Mich	763
Portland	Chautauque	N. Y.	1,905
Portland	Washington	Oregon	b821
Portland	Dodge	Wis	513
Portland, Sandusky city	Erie	Ohio	5,087
Port Lawrence	Lucas	Ohio	134
Portsmouth	Rockingham	N. H.	c9,738
Portsmouth	Carteret	N. C.	510
Portsmouth	Scioto	Ohio	d4,011
Portsmouth	Dauphin	Pa	882
Portsmouth	Newport	R. I.	1,833
Portsmouth	Norfolk	Va	8,122
Port Penn	Newcastle	Del	273
Portville	Cattaraugus	N. Y.	747
Port Washington	Tuscarawas	Ohio	269
Port Washington	Washington	Wis	1,600
Posey	Clay	Ind	1,218
Posey	Fayette	Ind	1,184
Posey	Franklin	Ind	940
Posey	Rush	Ind	870
Posey	Switzerland	Ind	2,395
Posey	Washington	Ind	1,877
Post Oak	Johnson	Mo	908
Potosi	Grant	Wis	2,500
Potsdam	St. Lawrence	N. Y.	5,349
Potter	Yates	N. Y.	2,194
Potter	Centre	Pa	2,216
Pottsgrove	Montgomery	Pa	1,689
Pottstown	Montgomery	Pa	e1,664
Pottsville	Schuylkill	Pa	f7,515
Poughkeepsie	Dutchess	N. Y.	g13,944
Poultney	Rutland	Vt	2,329
Pound Ridge	Westchester	N. Y.	1,486
Powell	Greene	Ark	552
Pownal	Cumberland	Me	1,074
Pownal	Bennington	Vt	1,742
Prairie	Arkansas	Ark	338
Prairie	Carroll	Ark	1,131
Prairie	Franklin	Ark	502
Prairie	Hot Springs	Ark	*462
Prairie	Madison	Ark	836
Prairie	Marion	Ark	397
Prairie	Newton	Ark	176
Prairie	Prairie	Ark	696
Prairie	Washington	Ark	1,830
Prairie	Henry	Ind	1,340
Prairie	Kosciusko	Ind	987
Prairie	Tipton	Ind	722
Prairie	Davis	Iowa	369
Prairie	Chariton	Mo	936
Prairie	Randolph	Mo	1,764
Prairie	Taney	Mo	202
Prairie	Franklin	Ohio	1,043
Prairie	Holmes	Ohio	1,451
Prairie Creek	Vigo	Ind	875
Prairie du Long	Monroe	Ill	672
Prairie du Sauk	Sauk	Wis	798
Prairie du Sauk, T.	Sauk	Wis	168
Prairie Springs	Jackson	Iowa	209
Prairie Ronde	Kalamazoo	Mich	690
Prairieville	Barry	Mich	555
Prattsburgh	Steuben	N. Y.	2,786
Prattsville	Greene	N. Y.	1,989
Prattville	Autauga	Ala	h672
Preble	Adams	Ind	547
Preble	Cortlandt	N. Y.	1,312
Preble	Pike	Ohio	914
Prescott	Hampshire	Mass	737
Preston	New London	Conn	1,842
Preston	Platt	Mo	1,270
Preston	Chenango	N. Y.	1,082
Preston	Wayne	Pa	875
Price	Monroe	Pa	340
Primrose	Dane	Wis	334
Prince George	Georgetown	S. C.	12,329
Princeton	Dallas	Ark	1,163
Princeton	Bureau	Ill	778
Princeton	Gibson	Ind	i806
Princeton	Caldwell	Ky	1,500
Princeton	Washington	Me	280
Princeton	Worcester	Mass	1,318
Princeton	Mercer	N. J.	3,021
Princeton	Schenectady	N. Y.	1,031
Princeville	Peoria	Ill	500
Prince William	Beaufort	S. C.	9,994
Proctor	Crittenden	Ark	503
Prompton	Wayne	Pa	306
Prospect	New Haven	Conn	666
Prospect	Waldo	Me	2,467
Prospect	Marion	Ohio	848
Prospect	Butler	Pa	254
Providence	Saratoga	N. Y.	1,458
Providence	Lucas	Ohio	467
Providence, Bor.	Luzerne	Pa	465
Providence	Luzerne	Pa	4,467
Providence	Providence	R. I.	j41,513
Provincetown	Barnstable	Mass	3,157
Proviso	Cook	Ill	482
Puebla de Acuma	Valencia	N. M.	384
Puebla de Laguna	Valencia	N. M.	748
Puebla de Los Sentos	Valencia	N. M.	225
Puebla de Zuni	Valencia	N. M.	1,294
Pulaski	Jackson	Mich	760
Pulaski	Oswego	N. Y.	1,600
Pulaski	Williams	Ohio	760
Pulaski	Lawrence	Pa	1,721
Pulaski	Giles	Tenn	1,137
Pulaski	Panola	Texas	33
Pulaski	Iowa	Wis	181
Pultney	Steuben	N. Y.	1,815
Pultney	Belmont	Ohio	2,254
Pulvidera	Valencia	N. M.	363
Punxatawney and Young	Jefferson	Pa	1,891
Purdy	McNairy	Tenn	402
Pusheta	Auglaize	Ohio	1,008
Putnam	Livingston	Mich	977
Putnam	Washington	N. Y.	753
Putnam	Muskingum	Ohio	1,383
Putnam Valley	Putnam	N. Y.	1,626
Putnamville	Putnam	Ind	251
Putney	Windham	Vt	1,425
Pyatt	Pulaski	Ark	183
Pymatuning	Mercer	Pa	2,101
Quakertown	Bucks	Pa	242
Queensburg	Warren	N. Y.	2,597
Quemahonning	Somerset	Pa	878
Quincy	Gadsden	Fla	1,000
Quincy	Norfolk	Mass	5,017
Quincy	Branch	Mich	1,111
Quincy	Logan	Ohio	373
Quincy	Franklin	Pa	2,836
Quincy City	Adams	Ill	k6,902

a In 1853, 22,500. *b* In 1853, 6,000. *c* In 1853, 11,000. *d* In 1853, 5,000. *e* In 1853, 2,000. *f* In 1853, 10,000. *g* In 1853, 14,000. *h* In 1853, 1,000. *i* In 1853, 1,000. *j* In 1853, 47,500. *k* In 1833, 11,000.

Quinnebaugh	Windham	Conn.	1,500
Racine	Racine	Wis.	780
Racine City	Racine	Wis.	*a*5,107
Racoon	Gallia	Ohio	1,473
Racoon	Beaver	Pa.	1,023
Radnor	Delaware	Ohio	1,204
Radnor	Delaware	Pa.	1,334
Rahway	Essex	N. J.	*b*3,306
Rain	Indiana	Pa.	1,184
Raisin	Lenawee	Mich.	1,267
Raisinville	Monroe	Mich.	967
Raleigh	Saline	Ill.	1,092
Raleigh	Wake	N. C.	4,518
Raleigh	Shelby	Tenn.	300
Ramapo	Rockland	N. Y.	3,197
Randolph	Tippecanoe	Ind.	1,105
Randolph	Norfolk	Mass.	4,741
Randolph	Coos	N. H.	113
Randolph	Morris	N. J.	2,632
Randolph	Cattaraugus	N. Y.	1,606
Randolph	Montgomery	Ohio	1,883
Randolph	Portage	Ohio	1,732
Randolph	Crawford	Pa.	1,260
Randolph	Orange	Vt.	2,666
Randolph	Columbia	Wis.	616
Randolph's Grove	McLean	Ill.	1,176
Range	Madison	Ohio	988
Ransom	Hillsdale	Mich.	549
Ransom	Luzerne	Pa.	797
Raphoe	Lancaster	Pa.	3,160
Raritan	Hunterdon	N. J.	3,070
Raritan	Monmouth	N. J.	4,198
Raritan	Somerset	N. J.	900
Rathboneville	Steuben	N. Y.	500
Rattlesnake Bar	Sutter	Cal.	206
Ravenna	Ottawa	Mich.	77
Ravenna	Portage	Ohio	*c*2,240
Ravenswood	Jackson	Va.	200
Ray	Franklin	Ind.	1,231
Ray	Morgan	Ind.	1,153
Ray	Macomb	Mich.	1,232
Raymond	Cumberland	Me.	1,142
Raymond	Rockingham	N. H.	1,256
Raymond	Racine	Wis.	1,021
Raymond Cape	Cumberland	Me.	50
Raynham	Bristol	Mass.	1,541
Readfield	Kennebeck	Me.	1,985
Reading	Middlesex	Mass.	3,108
Reading	Hillsdale	Mich.	956
Reading	Steuben	N. Y.	1,434
Reading	Perry	Ohio	3,984
Reading	Adams	Pa.	1,252
Reading	Berks	Pa.	*d*15,743
Reading	Windsor	Vt.	1,171
Readington	Hunterdon	N. J.	2,836
Readsborough	Bennington	Vt.	857
Read's Creek	Lawrence	Ark.	567
Recovery	Mercer	Ohio	596
Redbank	Armstrong	Pa.	1,980
Redbank	Clarion	Pa.	1,225
Red Creek	Wayne	N. Y.	500
Redding	Fairfield	Conn.	1,754
Redding	Jackson	Ind.	1,325
Redfield	Oswego	N. Y.	752
Redford	Wayne	Mich.	1,645
Red Fork	Desha	Ark.	596
Red Hook	Dutchess	N. Y.	3,264
Red Land	Hempstead	N. Y.	516
Red Lion Hundred	New Castle	Del.	1,153
Red River	Lafayette	Ark.	623
Red River	Van Buren	Ark.	294
Red River	White	Ark.	190
Redstone	Fayette	Pa.	1,287
Reed	Will	Ill.	183
Reed	Dauphin	Pa.	408
Reeve	Daviess	Ind.	1,000
Rehoboth	Bristol	Mass.	2,104
Reid	Seneca	Ohio	1,494
Reiley	Butler	Ohio	1,716
Remsen	Oneida	N. Y.	2,407
Rensselaer	Jasper	Ind.	241
Rensselaerville	Albany	N. Y.	3,629
Republic	Seneca	Ohio	917
Republican	Jefferson	Ind.	1,538
Reserve	Allegheny	Pa.	1,160
Reynolds	Monroe	Ill.	756
Rhinebeck	Dutchess	N. Y.	2,816
Rice	Cattaraugus	N. Y.	906
Rice	Sandusky	Ohio	486

Rich	Cook	Ill.	168
Richfield	Adams	Ill.	820
Richfield	Genesee	Mich.	482
Richfield	Otsego	N. Y.	1,502
Richfield	Henry	Ohio	136
Richfield	Huron	Ohio	1,944
Richfield	Lucas	Ohio	399
Richfield	Summit	Ohio	1,268
Richfield	Washington	Wis.	1,134
Richford	Tioga	N. Y.	1,208
Richford	Franklin	Vt.	1,074
Rich Hill	Muskingum	Ohio	1,495
Rich Hill	Greene	Pa.	2,135
Richland	Crawford	Ark.	560
Richland	Desha	Ark.	216
Richland	Jefferson	Ark.	1,134
Richland	Madison	Ark.	736
Richland	Newton	Ark.	96
Richland	Phillips	Ark.	851
Richland	St. Francis	Ark.	547
Richland	Searcy	Ark.	126
Richland	Washington	Ark.	489
Richland	Clark	Ill.	924
Richland	De Kalb	Ind.	653
Richland	Fountain	Ind.	1,725
Richland	Fulton	Ind.	597
Richland	Grant	Ind.	878
Richland	Greene	Ind.	1,483
Richland	Jay	Ind.	349
Richland	Madison	Ind.	805
Richland	Miami	Ind.	1,176
Richland	Monroe	Ind.	966
Richland	Rush	Ind.	1,214
Richland	Steuben	Ind.	393
Richland	Jackson	Iowa	378
Richland	Jones	Iowa	414
Richland	Keokuk	Iowa	1,004
Richland, T.	Keokuk	Iowa	239
Richland	Kalamazoo	Mich.	795
Richland	Gasconade	Mo.	238
Richland	Morgan	Mo.	*882
Richland	Oswego	N. Y.	4,079
Richland	Allen	Ohio	989
Richland	Belmont	Ohio	4,376
Richland	Clinton	Ohio	1,975
Richland	Darke	Ohio	798
Richland	Defiance	Ohio	702
Richland	Fairfield	Ohio	1,776
Richland	Guernsey	Ohio	1,438
Richland	Holmes	Ohio	1,349
Richland	Logan	Ohio	1,169
Richland	Marion	Ohio	1,229
Richland	Vinton	Ohio	1,193
Richland	Wyandott	Ohio	615
Richland	Bucks	Pa.	1,733
Richland	Cambria	Pa.	1,273
Richland	Clarion	Pa.	1,360
Richland	Venango	Pa.	1,008
Richmond	Prairie	Ark.	165
Richmond	McHenry	Ill.	1,078
Richmond	Wayne	Ind.	*e*1,443
Richmond	Madison	Ky.	*f*411
Richmond	Lincoln	Me.	2,056
Richmond	Berkshire	Mass.	907
Richmond	Macomb	Mich.	1,000
Richmond	Ray	Mo.	1,000
Richmond	Cheshire	N. H.	1,128
Richmond	Ontario	N. Y.	1,852
Richmond	Ashtabula	Ohio	706
Richmond	Huron	Ohio	609
Richmond	Jefferson	Ohio	514
Richmond	Berks	Pa.	2,056
Richmond	Crawford	Pa.	1,139
Richmond	Philadelphia	Pa.	5,750
Richmond	Tioga	Pa.	1,231
Richmond	Washington	R. I.	1,784
Richmond	Fort Bend	Texas	323
Richmond	Chittenden	Vt.	1,453
Richmond	Henrico	Va.	27,570
Richmond	Walworth	Wis.	744
Richmond Dale	Ross	Ohio	286
Richmondville	Schoharie	N. Y.	1,666
Richwood	Izard	Ark.	334
Richwood	Lawrence	Ark.	343
Richwood	Washington	Mo.	839
Ridge	Van Wert	Ohio	400
Ridge	Wyandott	Ohio	501
Ridgebury	Bradford	Pa.	1,616
Ridgefield	Fairfield	Conn.	2,237

a In 1853, 7,500. *b* In 1853, 7,000. *c* In 1853, 3,500. *d* In 1853, 17,000. *e* In 1853, 3,800. *f* In 1853, 1,000.

Place	County	State	Population
Ridgefield	Huron	Ohio	1,944
Ridge Prairie District	St. Clair	Ill	3,527
Ridgeville	Cook	Ill	444
Ridgeville	Washington	Md	184
Ridgeville	Henry	Ohio	148
Ridgeville	Lorain	Ohio	1,212
Ridgeway	Lanawee	Mich	633
Ridgeway	Orleans	N. Y.	4,591
Ridgeway	Elk	Pa	*a*241
Ridgeway	Iowa	Wis	704
Ridley	Delaware	Pa	1,390
Ridotts	Stephenson	Ill	652
Rienzi	Tishamingo	Mich	217
Riga	Lenawee	Mich	208
Riga	Monroe	N. Y.	2,159
Riley	Yell	Ark	199
Riley	McHenry	Ill	445
Riley	Vigo	Ind	1,004
Riley	Clinton	Mich	191
Riley	St. Clair	Mich	311
Riley	Sandusky	Ohio	682
Riley	Putnam	Ohio	849
Rindge	Cheshire	N. H.	1,274
Ringgold	Jefferson	Pa	665
Ringgold and vicinity	El Dorado	Cal	253
Rio Grande City	Star	Texas	1,000
Ripley	Brown	Ill	232
Ripley	Montgomery	Ind	1,250
Ripley	Rush	Ind	1,908
Ripley	Somerset	Me	641
Ripley	Tippah	Miss	1,050
Ripley	Chautauque	N. Y.	1,732
Ripley	Brown	Ohio	1,780
Ripley	Holmes	Ohio	1,330
Ripley	Huron	Ohio	1,230
Ripton	Addison	Vt	567
Risdon	Seneca	Ohio	212
Rising Sun	Ohio	Ind	*b*1,674
Ritchieton	Ohio	Va	1,071
Riverhead	Suffolk	N. Y.	2,540
Rives	Jackson	Mich	518
Roane	Lafayette	Ark	989
Roaring Creek	Columbia	Pa	519
Roaring Creek	Montour	Pa	1,991
Roark	Gasconade	Mo	1,007
Robb	Posey	Ind	1,376
Robbinston	Washington	Me	1,028
Robeson	Berks	Pa	2,404
Robinson	Posey	Ind	1,619
Robinson	Crawford	Ill	294
Robinson	Greene	Mo	*1,157
Robinson	Allegheny	Pa	1,917
Robinson	Washington	Pa	843
Rochester	Fulton	Ind	1,401
Rochester	Cedar	Iowa	1,015
Rochester	Plymouth	Mass	3,808
Rochester	Adair	Mo	1,603
Rochester	Strafford	N. H.	3,006
Rochester	Monroe	N. Y.	*c*36,403
Rochester	Ulster	N. Y	3,174
Rochester	Lorain	Ohio	896
Rochester	Warren	Ohio	230
Rochester, Bor	Beaver	Pa	993
Rochester	Beaver	Pa	428
Rochester	Windsor	Vt	1,493
Rochester	Racine	Wis	1,672
Rock	Rock	Wis	546
Rockaway	Morris	N. J	3,139
Rock Creek	Bartholomew	Ind	819
Rock Creek	Wells	Ind	599
Rock Creek and Washington	Carroll	Ind	1,302
Rock Dale	Crawford	Pa	1,086
Rockford	Coosa	Ala	171
Rockford	Winnebago	Ill	*d*2,093
Rockford	Surry	N. C	639
Rockford	Caldwell	Mo	*840
Rock Grove	Stephenson	Ill	727
Rock Hill	Bucks	Pa	2,448
Rockingham	Windham	Vt	2,837
Rock Island	Rock Island	Ill	*e*1,711
Rockland	Lincoln	Me	5,052
Rockland	Sullivan	N. Y	1,175
Rockland	Berks	Pa	1,369
Rockland	Venango	Pa	1,409
Rockport	Spencer	Ind	*f*412
Rockport	Essex	Mass	3,274
Rockport	Cuyahoga	Ohio	1,441
Rockroe	Munroe	Ark	312
Rock Run	Stephenson	Ill	1,037
Rockton	Winnebago	Ill	1,010
Rockville	Will	Ill	514
Rockville	Parke	Ind	*g*726
Rocky Bayou	Izard	Ark	606
Rocky Hill	Hartford	Conn	1,042
Rodman	Jefferson	N. Y.	1,784
Rodney	Jefferson	Miss	*210
Rollin	Lenawee	Mich	1,080
Rollingsford	Strafford	N. H.	1,862
Rome	Floyd	Ga	3,000
Rome	Perry	Ind	600
Rome	Jones	Iowa	584
Rome	Kennebeck	Me	830
Rome	Lenawee	Mich	1,525
Rome	Oneida	N. Y.	7,918
Rome, Bor	Oneida	N. Y.	4,000
Rome	Ashtabula	Ohio	744
Rome	Lawrence	Ohio	1,134
Rome	Seneca	Ohio	469
Rome	Bradford	Pa	1,308
Rome	Crawford	Pa	940
Rome	Athens	Ohio	1,309
Romeo	Macomb	Mich	1,200
Romulus	Wayne	Mich	621
Romulus	Seneca	N. Y.	2,050
Ronald	Ionia	Mich	452
Rondout	Ulster	N. Y.	2,000
Root	Adams	Ind	1,099
Root	Montgomery	N. Y.	2,736
Rootstown	Portage	Ohio	1,308
Roscoe	Winnebago	Ill	1,050
Roscomb Manor	Berks	Pa	1,235
Rose	Oakland	Mich	886
Rose	Wayne	N. Y.	2,264
Rose	Carroll	Ohio	1,537
Rose	Jefferson	Pa	559
Rose Hill Village	Johnson	Mo	39
Rosendale	Ulster	N. Y.	2,418
Rosendale	Fond du Lac	Wis	714
Roseville	Franklin	Ark	25
Ross	Clinton	Ind	1,075
Ross	Lake	Ind	747
Ross	Kalamazoo	Mich	680
Ross	Butler	Ohio	1,648
Ross	Greene	Ohio	1,367
Ross	Jefferson	Ohio	1,144
Ross	Allegheny	Pa	1,442
Ross	Luzerne	Pa	709
Ross	Monroe	Pa	1,373
Rossie	St. Lawrence	N. Y.	1,471
Rossville	Clinton	Ind	160
Rossville	Butler	Ohio	*h*1,447
Rossville	Miami	Ohio	114
Rostraver	Westmoreland	Pa	2,087
Rotterdam	Schenectady	N. Y	2,446
Rough and Ready	Yuba	Cal	672
Roulette	Potter	Pa	222
Roundgrove	Marion	Mo	1,107
Roundhead	Hardin	Ohio	655
Roundhead, T.	Hardin	Ohio	135
Round Pond	Independence	Ark	346
Round Prairie	Jefferson	Iowa	786
Rowe	Franklin	Mass	659
Rowley	Essex	Mass	1,075
Roxana	Eaton	Mich	353
Roxborough	Philadelphia	Pa	2,660
Roxbury	Litchfield	Conn	1,114
Roxbury	Oxford	Me	246
Roxbury	Norfolk	Mass	*i*18,364
Roxbury	Cheshire	N. H.	260
Roxbury	Morris	N. J	2,269
Roxbury	Delaware	N. Y.	2,853
Roxbury	Washington	Ohio	1,093
Roxbury	Washington	Vt	967
Roxbury	Dane	Wis	274
Royal	White	Ark	224
Royal Oak	Oakland	Mich	1,092
Royalston	Worcester	Mass	1,546
Royalton	Niagara	N. Y.	4,024
Royalton	Cuyahoga	Ohio	1,253
Royalton	Fairfield	Ohio	252
Royalton	Fulton	Ohio	570
Royalton	Windsor	Vt	1,850
Rubicon	Dodge	Wis	827

a In 1853, 500. *b* In 1853, 2,000. *c* In 1853, 42,000. *d* In 1853, 3,500. *e* In 1853, 4,000. *f* In 1853, 800. *g* In 1853, 1,500. *h* In 1853, 2,500. *i* In 1853, 22,000.

Ruddell	Independence	Ark	1,174
Ruggles	Ashland	Ohio	1,084
Rumford	Oxford	Me	1,375
Rumley	Harrison	Ohio	1,088
Rumney	Grafton	N. H.	1,109
Rupert	Bennington	Vt	1,101
Rush	Buchanan	Mo	*557
Rush	Monroe	N. Y.	2,015
Rush	Champaign	Ohio	1,400
Rush	Tuscarawas	Ohio	1,373
Rush	Centre	Pa	371
Rush	Dauphin	Pa	325
Rush	Northumberland	Pa	1,178
Rush	Schuylkill	Pa	670
Rush	Susquehanna	Pa	1,159
Rush Creek	Fairfield	Ohio	1,218
Rush Creek	Logan	Ohio	1,458
Rushford	Alleghany	N. Y.	1,816
Rushford	Winnebago	Wis	514
Rushville	Schuyler	Ill	2,609
Rushville	Rush	Ind	2,340
Rushville, T	Rush	Ind	742
Rushville	Buchanan	Mo	14
Rushville	Yates	N. Y.	1,000
Rusk	Cherokee	Texas	355
Russell	Putnam	Ind	1,386
Russell	Hampden	Mass	521
Russell	St. Lawrence	N. Y.	1,808
Russell	Geauga	Ohio	1,083
Russellville	Clinton	Ind	77
Russellville	Logan	Ky	*a*1,272
Russellville	Brown	Ohio	386
Russia	Herkimer	N. Y.	2,349
Russia	Lorain	Ohio	2,061
Rutherford	Martin	Ind	603
Rutherfordton	Rutherford	N. C.	484
Rutland	Lasalle	Ill	630
Rutland	Worcester	Mass	1,223
Rutland	Barry	Mich	177
Rutland	Jefferson	N. Y.	2,265
Rutland	Meigs	Ohio	1,748
Rutland	Tioga	Pa	1,006
Rutland	Rutland	Vt	3,715
Rutland	Dane	Wis	759
Rutland	Kane	Ill	848
Rye	Rockingham	N. H.	1,295
Rye	West Chester	N. Y.	2,584
Rye	Perry	Pa	696
Ryegate	Caledonia	Vt	1,606
Sabina	Valencia	N. M.	232
Sabinal	Valencia	N. M.	602
Sabinetown	Sabine	Texas	104
Sabula	Jackson	Iowa	168
Sackett's Harbor	Jefferson	N. Y.	2,000
Saco	York	Me	5,798
Sacramento City	Sacramento	Cal	20,000
Sadsbury	Chester	Pa	2,767
Sadsbury	Crawford	Pa	982
Sadsbury	Lancaster	Pa	1,529
Saddle River	Bergen	N. J.	823
Saegerstown	Crawford	Pa	500
Sag Harbor	Suffolk	N. Y.	3,600
Saginaw	Saginaw	Mich	917
Saginaw City	Saginaw	Mich	1,200
Saint Albans	Somerset	Me	1,792
Saint Albans	Licking	Ohio	1,770
Saint Albans	Franklin	Vt	3,567
Saint Andrews	Charleston	S. C.	3,343
Saint Anthony	Ramsey	Minn	656
Saint Anthony, T.	Ramsey	Minn	*b*538
Saint Augustine	Saint Johns	Fla	1,934
Saint Armand	Essex	N. Y.	210
Saint Bartholomew	Colleton	S. C.	18,157
Saint Charles	Kane	Ill	*c*2,132
Saint Charles City	St. Charles	Mo	*d**1,498
Saint Clair	St. Clair	Mich	1,729
Saint Clair	Butler	Ohio	2,602
Saint Clair	Columbiana	Ohio	1,361
Saint Clair	Bedford	Pa	1,945
Saint Clair	Schuylkill	Pa	*e*2,016
Saint Clairsville	Belmont	Ohio	1,025
Saint Croix	Washington	Minn	253
Saint Croix, Falls of	Washington	Minn	68
Saint Francis	Crittenden	Ark	93
Saint Francis	Greene	Ark	453
Saint Francis	Phillips	Ark	1,276

Saint Francisville	West Feliciana	La	*405
Saint Genevieve	Saint Genevieve	Mo	2,258
Saint Genevieve City	Saint Genevieve	Mo	*f*872
Saint George	Lincoln	Me	2,217
Saint George	Colleton	S. C	4,694
Saint George	Chittenden	Vt	127
Saint George's Hundred	New Castle	Del	2,509
Saint Helena	Beaufort	S. C.	*245
Saint James, Goose Creek	Charleston	S. C	4,830
Saint James, Santee	Charleston	S. C	3,388
Saint John's	Lake	Ind	469
Saint John's	Colleton	S. C	11,039
Saint John's, Berkley	Charleston	S. C	9,555
Saint Johnsburg	Caledonia	Vt	2,758
Saint Johnsville	Montgomery	N. Y.	1,627
Saint Joseph	Berrien	Mich	800
Saint Joseph	Buchanan	Mo	5,000
Saint Joseph's	Allen	Ind	748
Saint Joseph's	Williams	Ohio	589
Saint Louis City	Saint Louis	Mo	*g*77,860
Saint Louis, south half	Saint Louis	Mo	*2,688
Saint Louisville	Licking	Ohio	109
Saint Luke's	Beaufort	S. C	8,841
Saint Maria	Jasper	Ill	420
Saint Mark's	Wakulla	Fla	†189
Saint Martinsville	Saint Martin's	La	*652
Saint Mary's	Camden	Ga	800
Saint Mary's	Adams	Ind	611
Saint Mary's	Auglaize	Ohio	1,567
Saint Mary's, T.	Auglaize	Ohio	873
Saint Michael's	Talbot	Md	863
Saint Omer	Decatur	Ind	336
Saint Paul	Ramsey	Minn	1,338
Saint Paul, T.	Ramsey	Minn	*h*1,112
Saint Paul's	Colleton	S. C	5,615
Saint Peter's	Beaufort	S. C	11,191
Saint Stephen's	Charleston	S. C	2,854
Saint Thomas	Franklin	Pa	1,957
Saint Thomas and Saint Dennis	Charleston	S. C	2,528
Salem	New London	Conn	764
Salem	Carroll	Ill	272
Salem	Marion	Ill	800
Salem	Delaware	Ind	843
Salem	Pulaski	Ind	168
Salem	Steuben	Ind	550
Salem	Washington	Ind	*i*1,223
Salem	Henry	Iowa	1,418
Salem	Franklin	Me	454
Salem	Essex	Mass	*j*20,264
Salem	Washtenaw	Mich	1,343
Salem	Forsyth	N. C	1,200
Salem	Tippah	Miss	800
Salem	Rockingham	N. H.	1,555
Salem	Salem	N. J.	*k*3,052
Salem	Washington	N. Y.	2,904
Salem	Auglaize	Ohio	476
Salem	Champaign	Ohio	1,634
Salem	Columbiana	Ohio	*l*1,960
Salem	Highland	Ohio	813
Salem	Jefferson	Ohio	2,191
Salem	Meigs	Ohio	1,415
Salem	Monroe	Ohio	1,652
Salem	Muskingum	Ohio	1,111
Salem	Ottawa	Ohio	187
Salem	Shelby	Ohio	1,496
Salem	Tuscarawas	Ohio	1,853
Salem	Warren	Ohio	3,525
Salem	Washington	Ohio	1,246
Salem	Wyandott	Ohio	738
Salem	Marion	Oreg'n	1,000
Salem	Luzerne	Pa	1,130
Salem	Mercer	Pa	2,206
Salem	Wayne	Pa	1,454
Salem	Westmoreland	Pa	2,065
Salem, Bor	Westmoreland	Pa	299
Salem	Orleans	Vt	455
Salem	Kenosha	Wis	1,123
Salesville	Guernsey	Ohio	71
Salina	Onondaga	N. Y.	2,142
Saline	Dallas	Ark	335

a In 1853, 1,600. *b* In 1853, 2,000. *c* In 1853, 3,500. *d* In 1853, 3,000. *e* In 1853, 3,000. *f* In 1853, 1,500. *g* In 1852, 94,819. *h* In 1853, 6,000. *i* In 1853, 2,000. *j* In 1853, 22,500. *k* In 1853, 4,000. *l* In 1853, 2,500.

Saline	Hempstead	Ark.	1,184	Saucon	Northampton	Pa.	2,905
Saline	Hot Springs	Ark.	*602	Saugerties	Ulster	N. Y.	8,041
Saline	Sevier	Ark.	400	Saugus	Essex	Mass.	1,552
Saline	Saline	Ill.	1,176	Saukville	Washington	Wis.	840
Saline	Washtenaw	Mich.	1,631	Sault de St. Marie	Chippewa	Mich.	898
Saline	St. Genevieve	Mo.	837	Savannah	Chatham	Ga.	b15,312
Saline	Jefferson	Ohio	1,090	Savannah	Carroll	Ill.	c658
Salisbury	Litchfield	Conn.	3,103	Savannah	Adair	Mo.	654
Salisbury	Coles	Ill.	1,426	Savannah	Wayne	N. Y.	1,700
Salisbury	La Salle	Ill.	2,911	Savannah	Hardin	Tenn.	d466
Salisbury, T.	La Salle	Ill.	1,279	Saville	Perry	Pa.	1,501
Salisbury	Somerset	Md.	1,500	Savoy	Berkshire	Mass.	955
Salisbury	Essex	Mass.	3,100	Say	Orleans	Vt.	371
Salisbury	Rowan	N. C.	2,000	Saybrook	Middlesex	Conn.	2,904
Salisbury	Merrimack	N. H.	1,228	Saybrook	Ashtabula	Ohio	1,374
Salisbury	Herkimer	N. Y.	2,035	Schaghticoke	Rensselaer	N. Y.	3,290
Salisbury	Meigs	Ohio	4,559	Scarborough	Cumberland	Me.	1,837
Salisbury	Lancaster	Ohio	3,646	Scarsdale	Westchester	N. Y.	342
Salisbury	Lehigh	Ohio	1,884	Schellsburgh	Bedford	Pa.	360
Salisbury	Addison	Vt.	1,027	Schenectady	Schenectady	N. Y.	8,921
Salmon Falls	El Dorado	Cal.	210	Schodack	Rensselaer	N. Y.	3,509
Salt	Monroe	Ind.	406	Schoharie	Schoharie	N. Y.	2,588
Salt Creek	Decatur	Ind.	774	Schoolcraft	Kalamazoo	Mich.	1,101
Salt Creek	Franklin	Ind.	807	Schroon	Essex	N. Y.	2,031
Salt Creek	Jackson	Ind.	1,105	Schrœpel	Oswego	N. Y.	2,386
Salt Creek	Davis	Iowa	726	Schuyler	Herkimer	N. Y.	1,696
Salt Creek	Hocking	Ohio	1,094	Schuyler's Falls	Clinton	N. Y.	2,110
Salt Creek	Holmes	Ohio	1,699	Schuylkill	Chester	Pa.	1,403
Salt Creek	Muskingum	Ohio	1,215	Schuylkill	Schuylkill	Pa.	1,742
Salt Creek	Pickaway	Ohio	1,844	Schuylkill Haven	Schuylkill	Pa.	2,071
Salt Creek	Wayne	Ohio	1,669	Scio	Alleghany	N. Y.	1,922
Salt Lake City	Salt Lake	Utah	10,000	Scio and Webster	Washtenaw	Mich.	3,555
Salt Lick	Perry	Ohio	1,747	Scioto	Shiawassee	Mich.	191
Salt Lick	Fayette	Pa.	879	Scioto	Delaware	Ohio	1,126
Salt River	Knox	Mo.	611	Scioto	Jackson	Ohio	1,347
Salt River	Pike	Mo.	312	Scioto	Pickaway	Ohio	1,347
Salt River	Randolph	Mo.	*692	Scioto	Ross	Ohio	8,696
Salt Rock	Marion	Ohio	347	Scipio	Allen	Ind.	173
Saltsburgh	Indiana	Pa.	623	Scipio	Laporte	Ind.	767
Salt Spring	Randolph	Mo.	*1,134	Scipio	Hillsdale	Mich.	864
Saluda	Jefferson	Ind.	1,335	Scipio	Cayuga	N. Y.	2,135
Salvisa	Mercer	Ky.	154	Scipio	Meigs	Ohio	1,405
San Antonio	Valencia	N. M.	228	Scipio	Seneca	Ohio	2,322
San Antonio	Bexar	Texas	a3,488	Scituate	Plymouth	Mass.	2,149
San Antonita	Valencia	N. M.	101	Scituate	Providence	R. I.	4,582
San Augustine	San Augustine	Texas	1,000	Scott	Mississippi	Ark.	157
Sandbornton	Belknap	N. H.	2,695	Scott	Ogle	Ill.	142
Sand Creek	Bartholomew	Ind.	1,071	Scott	Kosciusko	Ind.	255
Sand Creek	Decatur	Ind.	1,908	Scott	Montgomery	Ind.	1,209
Sand Creek	Jennings	Ind.	705	Scott	Steuben	Ind.	490
Sandgate	Bennington	Vt.	850	Scott	Vanderburg	Ind.	1,162
Sandisfield	Berkshire	Mass.	1,649	Scott	Johnson	Iowa	195
Sandiston	Sussex	N. J.	1,327	Scott	Cortlandt	N. Y.	1,290
Sand Lake	Rensselaer	N. Y.	2,559	Scott	Adams	Ohio	1,270
Sandown	Rockingham	N. H.	566	Scott	Brown	Ohio	1,036
Sandstown	Jackson	Mich.	823	Scott	Marion	Ohio	717
Sandusky	Crawford	Ohio	822	Scott	Sandusky	Ohio	792
Sandusky	Erie	Ohio	10,000	Scott	Luzerne	Pa.	1,268
Sandusky	Richland	Ohio	617	Scott	Wayne	Pa.	617
Sandusky	Sandusky	Ohio	2,504	Scott	Columbia	Wis.	433
Sandwich	Barnstable	Mass.	4,368	Scottville	Macoupin	Ill.	41
Sandwich	Carroll	N. H.	2,577	Scottville	Albemarle	Va.	e†666
Sandy	Stark	Ohio	1,270	Scottville	Bibb	Ala.	†301
Sandy	Tuscarawas	Ohio	1,227	Scottville	Allen	Ky.	400
Sandy Creek	Oswego	N. Y.	2,456	Scriba	Oswego	N. Y.	2,738
Sandy Creek	Mercer	Pa.	2,835	Scrub Grass	Venango	Pa.	1,143
Sandy Creek	Venango	Pa.	957	Seabrook	Rockingham	N. H.	1,296
Sandy Lake	Mercer	Pa.	1,100	*Seaford*	Sussex	Del.	800
Sandyville	Tuscarawas	Ohio	222	Seal	Pike	Ohio	2,210
Sanford	York	Me.	2,330	Searcy	Phillips	Ark.	573
Sanford	Broome	N. Y.	2,508	Searsburg	Bennington	Vt.	201
Sangerfield	Oneida	N. Y.	2,371	Searsmont	Waldo	Me.	1,693
Sangerville	Piscataquis	Me.	1,267	Searsport	Waldo	Me.	2,208
Sanilac	Sanilac	Mich.	335	Seaville	Hancock	Me.	139
San Francisco	San Francisco	Cal.	34,870	Sebago	Cumberland	Me.	850
San Jose	Santa Clara	Cal.	3,500	Sebasticook	Kennebeck	Me.	1,189
San Miguel	San Miguel	N. M.	2,008	Sebec	Piscataquis	Me.	1,223
San Pedro	Valencia	N. M.	166	Sebewa	Ionia	Mich.	247
Santa Anna	Santa Anna	N. M.	41	Section Ten	Van Wert	Ohio	402
Santa Fe	Santa Fe	N. M.	4,846	Sedgwick	Hancock	Me.	1,235
Sarahsville	Noble	Ohio	500	Seekonk	Bristol	Mass.	2,243
Saranac	Clinton	N. Y.	2,582	Segequa	Valencia	N. M.	420
Saratoga	Grundy	Ill.	200	Selma	Dallas	Ala.	1,728
Saratoga	Saratoga	N. Y.	3,492	Selma	Clark	Ohio	47
Saratoga Springs	Saratoga	N. Y.	4,650	Semple	Madison	Ill.	282
Sarcoxie	Jasper	Mo.	*1,009	Sempronius	Cayuga	N. Y.	1,266
Sardinia	Erie	N. Y.	1,761	Seneca	McHenry	Ill.	836
Sardinia	Brown	Ohio	198	Seneca	Lenawee	Mich.	1,092
Sardis	Monroe	Ohio	118	Seneca	Ontario	N. Y.	8,505

a In 1853, 6,000. *b* In 1853, 20,000. *c* In 1853, 800. *d* In 1853, 800. *e* In 1853, 1,200.

Seneca	Guernsey	Ohio	1,411	Shepherdstown	Belmont	Ohio	90
Seneca	Monroe	Ohio	2,078	Shepherdstown	Jefferson	Va	1,561
Seneca	Seneca	Ohio	1,662	Sherburne	Will	Ill	453
Seneca Falls	Seneca	N. Y.	4,296	Sherburne	Fleming	Ky	145
Seneca Falls, T	Seneca	N. Y.	3,600	Sherburne	Middlesex	Mass	1,043
Senecaville	Guernsey	Ohio	457	Sherburne	Chenango	N. Y.	2,623
Senora	Hancock	Ill	421	Sherburne	Rutland	Vt.	578
Serena	Lasalle	Ill	370	Sheridan	Calhoun	Mich	972
Sergeant	McKean	Pa	172	Sheridan	Chautauque	N. Y.	2,173
Sennet	Cayuga	N. Y.	2,347	Sherman	Fairfield	Conn	984
Settlements	Aroostook	Me	4,402	Sherman	St. Joseph	Mich	364
Settlements	Hancock	Me	1,175	Sherman	Chautauque	N. Y.	1,292
Settlements	Franklin	Me	1,169	Sherman	Huron	Ohio	1,134
Settlements	Lincoln	Me	321	*Shermanville*	Providence	R. I	400
Settlements	Oxford	Me	704	Sherwood	Branch	Mich	686
Settlements	Penobscot	Me	1,074	Shesheguin	Bradford	Pa	1,455
Settlements	Piscataquis	Me	148	Shiawassee	Shiawassee	Mich	810
Settlements	Somerset	Me	1,079	Shields	Lake	Ill	554
Settlements	Washington	Me	827	Shields	Dodge	Wis	590
Settlements	Coos	N. H.	158	Shieldsborough	Hancock	Miss	b†923
Seven Mile	Butler	Ohio	94	Shippen	McKean	Pa	369
Seventy-Six	Muscatine	Iowa	420	Shippen	Tioga	Pa	298
Sewanica	Brown	Wis	172	Shippensburg	Cumberland	Pa	198
Seward	Winnebago	Ill	330	Shippensburg, Bor	Cumberland	Pa	1,568
Seward	Schoharie	N. Y.	2,203	Shirland	Winnebago	Ill	353
Sewickly	Westmoreland	Pa	1,689	Shirley	Piscataquis	Me	250
Sewickleyville	Allegheny	Pa	800	Shirley	Middlesex	Mass	1,158
Seymour	New Haven	Conn	1,677	Shirley	Huntingdon	Pa	1,615
Shabbonas	De Kalb	Ill	360	Shirleysburgh	Huntingdon	Pa	361
Shade	Somerset	Pa	1,266	Shoal	Appanoose	Iowa	150
Shafferstown	Lebanon	Pa	616	Shoal Creek	Newton	Mo	*409
Shaftesbury	Bennington	Vt	1,896	Shokokan	Henderson	Ill	23
Shakerstown	Montgomery	Ohio	57	Shoreham	Addison	Vt	1,601
Shaler	Allegheny	Pa	2,002	Short Creek	Harrison	Ohio	1,950
Shallotte	Brunswick	N. C.	903	*Showstown*	Allegheny	Pa	1,000
Shalersville	Portage	Ohio	1,190	Shreveport	Caddo	La	c1,728
Shamokin	Northumberland	Pa	2,191	Shrewsbury	Worcester	Mass	1,596
Shandaken	Ulster	N. Y.	2,307	Shrewsbury	Lycoming	Pa	225
Shanesville	Tuscarawas	Ohio	382	Shrewsbury	Sullivan	Pa	195
Shannon	Muskingum	Ohio	104	Shrewsbury	York	Pa	1,659
Shapleigh	York	Me	1,348	Shrewsbury, Bor	York	Pa	472
Sharon	Litchfield	Conn	2,507	Shrewsbury	Monmouth	N. J	3,182
Sharon	Norfolk	Mass	1,128	Shrewsbury	Rutland	Vt	1,268
Sharon	Washtenaw	Mich	868	Shullsbury	Lafayette	Wis	d1,678
Sharon	Hillsborough	N. H	226	Shulesbury	Franklin	Mass	912
Sharon	Schoharie	N. Y.	2,632	Sidney	Delaware	N. Y.	1,807
Sharon	Franklin	Ohio	1,509	Sidney	Shelby	Ohio	e1,302
Sharon	Medina	Ohio	1,519	Sigourney	Keokuk	Iowa	698
Sharon	Richland	Ohio	1,950	Sigourney, T	Keokuk	Iowa	162
Sharon, Bor	Mercer	Pa	541	Silver Creek	Stephenson	Ill	603
Sharon	Potter	Pa	501	Silver Creek	Clark	Ind	880
Sharon	Windsor	Vt	1,240	Silver Creek	Cass	Mich	491
Sharon	Walworth	Wis	1,169	Silver Creek	Randolph	Mo	*1,300
Sharonville	Pike	Ohio	114	Silver Creek	Greene	Ohio	2,565
Sharpsburg	Bath	Ky	†329	Silver Lake	Susquehanna	Pa	1,213
Sharpsburg, Bor	Allegheny	Pa	1,229	Silver Spring	Cumberland	Pa	2,308
Shaumburg	Cook	Ill	489	Sims	Grant	Ind	552
Shawangunk	Ulster	N. Y.	4,036	Simsbury	Hartford	Conn	2,737
Shawnee	Fountain	Ind	1,103	*Sing Sing*	Westchester	N. Y.	3,000
Shawnee	Allen	Ohio	716	*Sisterville*	Tyler	Va	1,000
Shawneetown	Gallatin	Ill	1,764	Skaneateles	Onondaga	N. Y.	4,081
Shawswick	Lawrence	Ind	2,934	Skelton	Warrick	Ind	532
Sheboygan	Sheboygan	Wis	2,600	Skowhegan	Somerset	Me	1,756
Sheboygan Falls	Sheboygan	Wis	800	Slate Creek	El Dorado	Cal	42
Sheffield	Tippecanoe	Ind	1,549	*Slatersville*	Providence	R. I	1,500
Sheffield	Berkshire	Mass	2,769	Slippery Rock	Butler	Pa	1,490
Sheffield	Ashtabula	Ohio	845	Smackover	Ouachita	Ark	612
Sheffield	Lorain	Ohio	906	Smeltzen Grove	Grant	Wis	729
Sheffield	Warren	Pa	317	Smith	Bradley	Ark	697
Sheffield	Caledonia	Vt	797	Smith	Dallas	Ark	1,690
Shelburn	Coos	N. H.	480	Smith	Drew	Ark	727
Shelburne	Franklin	Mass	1,239	Smith	Saint Francis	Ark	484
Shelburne Falls	Franklin	Mass	1,000	Smith	Greene	Ind	313
Shelburne	Chittenden	Vt	1,257	Smith	Posey	Ind	765
Shelby	Jefferson	Ind	1,772	Smith	Gentry	Mo	*168
Shelby	Ripley	Ind	2,388	Smith	Belmont	Ohio	1,797
Shelby	Tippecanoe	Ind	741	Smith	Mahoning	Ohio	1,544
Shelby	Macomb	Mich	1,842	Smith	Washington	Pa	1,462
Shelby	Orleans	N. Y.	3,082	Smithfield	De Kalb	Ind	661
Shelbyville	Shelby	Ill	385	Smithfield	Somerset	Me	873
Shelbyville	Shelby	Ind	a995	Smithfield	Madison	N. Y.	1,669
Shelbyville	Shelby	Ky	2,000	Smithfield	Johnson	N. C.	329
Shelbyville	Shelby	Mo	359	Smithfield	Jefferson	Ohio	1,882
Shelbyville	Bedford	Tenn	†1,615	Smithfield, T	Jefferson	Ohio	425
Sheldon	Wyoming	N. Y.	2,527	Smithfield	Bradford	Pa	1,948
Sheldon	Franklin	Vt	1,814	Smithfield	Monroe	Pa	1,283
Shelter Island	Suffolk	N. Y.	386	Smithfield	Providence	R. I	—11,500
Shenango	Lawrence	Pa	2,476	Smithfield	Isle of Wight	Va	f733
Shenango	Mercer	Pa	1,574	Smithfield	Jefferson	Va	446

a In 1853, 1,500. *b* In 1853, 1,200. *c* In 1853, 3,000. *d* In 1853, 2,500. *e* In 1853, 2,000. *f* In 1853, 1,000.

Smithland	Livingston	Ky.	*882	South Hanover	Jefferson	Ind.	447
Smith's Bar	Sutter	Cal.	84	South Hanover	Dauphin	Pa.	736
Smithsburg	Washington	Md.	366	South Hero	Grand Isle	Vt.	705
Smithtown	Suffolk	N. Y.	1,972	South Huntingdon	Westmoreland	Pa.	1,470
Smithville	Chenango	N. Y.	1,771	Southington	Hartford	Conn.	2,135
Smithville	Brunswick	N. C.	1,464	Southington	Trumbull	Ohio	1,013
Smyrna	Kent	Del.	2,000	South Kingston	Washington	R. I.	3,807
Smyrna	Jefferson	Ind.	1,124	South Lebanon	Lebanon	Pa.	3,250
Smyrna	Aroostook	Me.	172	South Mahoning	Indiana	Pa.	1,138
Smyrna	Chenango	N. Y.	1,940	South Manheim	Schuylkill	Pa.	773
Smyrna	Harrison	Ohio	93	South Middleton	Cumberland	Pa.	2,252
Snake River	Ramsey	Minn.	39	*South Nashville*	Davidson	Tenn.	3,000
Sni Bar	Jackson	Mo.	1,386	South New Mar-			
Sni Bar	Lafayette	Mo.	612	ket	Rockingham	N. H.	516
Snowden	Allegheny	Pa.	1,225	Southold	Suffolk	N. Y.	4,723
Snow Hill	Worcester	Md.	1,200	South Pittsburg	Allegheny	Pa.	b1,883
Snowshoe	Centre	Pa.	432	*Southport*	Fairfield	Conn.	1,200
Snyder	Blair	Pa.	1,090	South Port	Lincoln	Me.	543
Snyder	Jefferson	Pa.	306	Southport	Chemung	N. Y.	3,184
Soap Creek	Davis	Iowa	533	Southport	Kenosha	Wis.	363
Socorro	Valencia	N. M.	543	South Reading	Middlesex	Mass.	2,407
Sodus	Wayne	N. Y.	4,598	South River	Marion	Mo.	757
Solebury	Bucks	Pa.	2,634	South Salem	Ross	Ohio	479
Solon	Somerset	Me.	1,415	South Scituate	Plymouth	Mass.	1,770
Solon	Cortlandt	N. Y.	1,150	South Shenango	Crawford	Pa.	1,664
Solon	Cuyahoga	Ohio	1,034	South Slippery			
Somers	Tolland	Conn.	1,508	Rock	Lawrence	Pa.	1,344
Somers	Westchester	N. Y.	1,722	South Strabane	Washington	Pa.	1,391
Somers	Preble	Ohio	2,085	South Thomaston	Lincoln	Me.	1,420
Somerset	Saline	Ill.	672	South Union	Logan	Ky.	245
Somerset	Pulaski	Ky.	412	South Valley	Cattaraugus	N. Y.	561
Somerset	Bristol	Mass.	1,166	Southwark	Philadelphia	Pa.	38,799
Somerset	Hillsdale	Mich.	913	South West	Warren	Pa.	390
Somerset	Niagara	N. Y.	2,154	South Whitehall	Lehigh	Pa.	2,913
Somerset	Belmont	Ohio	2,298	Southwick	Hampden	Mass.	1,120
Somerset	Perry	Ohio	1,240	South Windsor	Hartford	Conn.	1,638
Somerset	Somerset	Pa.	2,554	South Woodbury	Bedford	Pa.	1,122
Somerset, Bor.	Somerset	Pa.	866	Spadra	Johnson	Ark.	1,209
Somerset	Washington	Pa.	1,512	Spafford	Onondaga	N. Y.	1,903
Somerset	Windham	Vt.	321	Spanish Canon	El Dorado	Cal.	373
Somersworth	Strafford	N. H.	4,943	*Sparta*	Hancock	Ga.	1,024
Somerton	Belmont	Ohio	194	Sparta	Randolph	Ill.	510
Somerville	Morgan	Ala.	†217	Sparta	Dearborn	Ind.	1,598
Somerville	Middlesex	Mass.	3,540	Sparta	Noble	Ind.	590
Somerville	Somerset	N. J.	1,300	Sparta	Kent	Mich.	309
Somerville	Fayette	Tenn.	1,500	Sparta	Sussex	N. J.	1,919
Somonauk	De Kalb	Ill.	704	Sparta	Livingston	N. Y.	1,372
Sonora	Tuolumne	Cal.	4,000	Sparta	Morrow	Ohio	127
Soran	Stephenson	Ill.	654	Sparta	Crawford	Pa.	884
South Amboy	Middlesex	N. J.	2,266	Spartanburg	Spartanburg	S. C.	1,176
Southampton	Hampshire	Mass.	1,060	Spartansburg	Randolph	Ind.	165
Southampton	Burlington	N. J.	3,545	Spencer	Jennings	Ind.	1,390
Southampton	Suffolk	N. Y.	6,501	Spencer	Owen	Ind.	335
Southampton	Bedford	Pa.	1,347	Spencer	Worcester	Mass.	2,244
Southampton	Bucks	Pa.	1,416	Spencer	Pike	Mo.	1,037
Southampton	Cumberland	Pa.	1,651	Spencer	Tioga	N. Y.	1,782
Southampton	Franklin	Pa.	1,795	Spencer	Allen	Ohio	355
Southampton	Somerset	Pa.	1,326	Spencer	Guernsey	Ohio	1,847
South Anville	Lebanon	Pa.	887	Spencer	Hamilton	Ohio	1,656
South Beaver	Beaver	Pa.	1,115	Spencer	Lucas	Ohio	273
South Bend	St. Joseph	Ind.	a1,652	Spencer	Medina	Ohio	1,336
South Berwick	York	Me.	2,592	Sperry	Clayton	Iowa	210
South Bloomfield	Morrow	Ohio	1,395	Spiceland	Henry	Ind.	1,344
Southborough	Worcester	Mass.	1,347	Spice Valley	Lawrence	Ind.	946
Southbridge	Worcester	Mass.	2,824	Sprigg	Adams	Ohio	3,118
South Bristol	Ontario	N. Y.	1,129	Spring	Centre	Pa.	2,280
South Brown	Vinton	Ohio	648	Spring	Crawford	Pa.	1,836
South Brunswick	Middlesex	N. J.	3,368	Spring	Perry	Pa.	1,282
South Buffalo	Armstrong	Pa.	1,266	Spring Arbor	Jackson	Mich.	1,075
South Berry	New Haven	Conn.	1,484	Springborough	Warren	Ohio	454
South Butler	Butler	Pa.	1,209	Spring Creek	Philips	Ark.	483
South Charleston	Clark	Ohio	413	Spring Creek	Yell	Ark.	606
South Codorus	York	Pa.	1,135	Spring Creek	Miami	Ohio	1,588
South Coventry	Chester	Pa.	711	Spring Creek	Elk	Pa.	91
South Creek	Bradford	Pa.	709	Spring Creek	Warren	Pa.	601
South East	Orange	Ind.	1,501	Spring Dale	Dane	Wis.	344
Southeast	Putnam	N. Y.	2,079	*Springfield*	Effingham	Ga.	141
South Easton	Northampton	Pa.	1,511	Springfield	Sangamon	Ill.	c4,533
South Fayette	Allegheny	Pa.	1,118	Springfield	Allen	Ind.	702
Southfield	Oakland	Mich.	1,658	Springfield	Franklin	Ind.	1,657
Southfield	Richmond	N. Y.	2,709	Springfield	La Grange	Ind.	760
South Fork	Clark	Ark.	265	Springfield	Laporte	Ind.	430
South Fork	Fulton	Ark.	192	Springfield	Cedar	Iowa	314
South Fork	Jackson	Iowa	462	Springfield	Washington	Ky.	527
South Fork of				Springfield	Penobscot	Me.	583
American River	El Dorado	Cal.	1,386	Springfield	Hampden	Mass.	d11,766
South Grove	De Kalb	Ill.	147	Springfield	Oakland	Mich.	956
South Hadley	Hampshire	Mass.	2,495	Springfield, (city)	Greene	Mo.	e*415
South Hampton	Rockingham	N. H.	472	Springfield	Henry	Mo.	*553

a In 1853, 2,000. *b* In 1853, 2,500. *c* In 1853, 6,500. *d* In 1853, 14,000. *e* In 1853, 1,000.

Springfield	Sullivan	N. H.	1,270	Steuben	Washington	Me	1,122
Springfield	Burlington	N. J.	1,827	Steuben	Oneida	N. Y.	1,744
Springfield	Essex	N. J.	1,945	Steubenville	Jefferson	Ohio	7,224
Springfield	Otsego	N. Y.	2,322	Steubenville, T.	Jefferson	Ohio	6,140
Springfield	Clark	Ohio	7,314	Stephens' Point	Portage	Wis	458
Springfield, T.	Clark	Ohio	a5,108	Stewartson	Potter	Pa	58
Springfield	Gallia	Ohio	1,230	Stewartstown	Coos	N. H.	747
Springfield	Hamilton	Ohio	3,633	*Stewartsville*	Warren	N. J.	500
Springfield, T.	Jefferson	Ohio	216	Stillwater	Washington	Minn	c321
Springfield	Jefferson	Ohio	1,298	Stillwater	Sussex	N. J.	1,742
Springfield	Lucas	Ohio	782	Stillwater	Saratoga	N. Y.	2,967
Springfield	Mahoning	Ohio	2,385	Stock	Harrison	Ohio	888
Springfield	Muskingum	Ohio	2,975	Stockbridge	Berkshire	Mass	1,941
Springfield	Richland	Ohio	2,100	Stockbridge	Ingham	Mich	657
Springfield	Ross	Ohio	1,162	Stockbridge	Madison	N. Y	2,081
Springfield	Summit	Ohio	1,907	Stockbridge	Windsor	Vt	1,327
Springfield	Williams	Ohio	782	Stockholm	St. Lawrence	Vt	3,661
Springfield	Bradford	Pa	1,848	Stockport	Columbia	N. Y.	1,655
Springfield	Bucks	Pa	2,259	*Stockton*	San Joaquin	Cal	4,000
Springfield	Delaware	Pa	1,033	Stockton	Greene	Ind	840
Springfield	Erie	Pa	1,946	Stockton	Chatuauque	N. Y.	1,640
Springfield	Fayette	Pa	1,080	Stoddard	Cheshire	N. H.	1,105
Springfield	Huntingdon	Pa	593	Stokes	Logan	Ohio	489
Springfield	Mercer	Pa	1,275	Stokes	Madison	Ohio	591
Springfield	Montgomery	Pa	743	Stone Fort	Saline	Ill	831
Springfield	York	Pa	1,345	Stoneham	Oxford	Me	484
Springfield	Windsor	Vt	2,762	Stoneham	Middlesex	Mass	2,085
Springfield	Dane	Wis	295	Stone Lick	Clermont	Ohio	1,840
Spring Garden	Philadelphia	Pa	58,894	*Stone Mountain*	De Kalb	Ga	300
Spring Garden	York	Pa	2,435	Stonington	New London	Conn	5,431
Spring Grove	Greene	Wis	703	*Stonington*, Bor	New London	Conn	2,800
Spring Hill	Drew	Ark	627	Stony Creek	Henry	Ind	1,029
Spring Hill	Hempstead	Ark	362	Stony Creek	Madison	Ind	291
Spring Hill	Bradford	Pa	862	Stony Creek	Randolph	Ind	1,153
Springhill	Fayette	Pa	1,685	Stony Creek	Somerset	Pa	1,396
Springhill	Maury	Tenn	†245	Storrs	Hamilton	Ohio	1,676
Spring Lake	Ottawa	Mich	545	Stoughton	Norfolk	Mass	3,494
Springport	Jackson	Mich	759	Stoughton	Dane	Wis	70
Springport	Cayuga	N. Y.	2,041	Stout's Grove	McLean	Ill	839
Spring Prairie	Walworth	Wis	1,418	Stow	Oxford	Me	471
Spring River	Lawrence	Ark	966	Stow	Middlesex	Mass	1,455
Spring River	Lawrence	Mo	684	Stow	Summit	Ohio	1,701
Spring Rock	Clinton	Iowa	99	Stow Creek	Cumberland	N. J.	1,093
Spring Vale	Columbia	Wis	471	Stowe	Lamoille	Vt	1,771
Spring Vale	Fond du Lac	Wis	588	Stoystown	Somerset	Pa	321
Spring Valley	Rock	Wis	756	Strabane	Adams	Pa	1,433
Springville	Erie	N. Y.	1,000	Strafford	Strafford	N. H.	1,920
Springville	Chester	Pa	800	Strafford	Orange	Vt	1,540
Springville	Susquehanna	Pa	1,148	Strasburg	Tuscarawas	Ohio	109
Springwater	Livingston	N. Y.	2,670	Strasburg	Lancaster	Pa	1,724
Springwell	Wayne	Mich	b1,263	Strasburg, Bor	Lancaster	Pa	880
Squaw Grove	De Kalb	Ill	341	Stratford	Fairfield	Conn	2,040
Stafford	Tolland	Conn	2,940	Stratford	Coos	N. H	552
Stafford	De Kalb	Ind	372	Stratford	Fulton	N. Y.	801
Stafford	Greene	Ind	438	Stratham	Rockingham	N. H.	840
Stafford	Ocean	N. J.	1,384	Stratton	Windham	Vt	286
Stafford	Genesee	N. Y.	1,974	Strawberry	Lawrence	Ark	709
Stafford	Monroe	Ohio	124	Streetsborough	Portage	Ohio	1,108
Stamford	Fairfield	Conn	5,000	Stringtown	St. Louis	Mo	144
Stamford	Delaware	N. Y.	1,708	Strong	Franklin	Me	1,008
Stamford	Bennington	Vt	833	Strongsville	Cuyahoga	Ohio	1,199
Stamper's Creek	Orange	Ind	777	Stroud	Monroe	Pa	1,419
Standing Stone	Bradford	Pa	827	Stroudsburg, Bor	Monroe	Pa	811
Standish	Cumberland	Me	2,290	Sturbridge	Worcester	Mass	2,119
Stanford	Dutchess	N. Y.	2,158	Sturgis	St. Joseph	Mich	840
Stark	Coos	N. H.	418	*Sturgis*, T.	St. Joseph	Mich	700
Stark	Herkimer	N. Y.	1,576	Stuyvesant	Columbia	N. Y	1,766
Stark	Monroe	Ohio	1,223	Sudbury	Middlesex	Mass	1,578
Starkey	Yates	Ohio	2,675	Sudbury	Rutland	Vt	794
Starks	Somerset	Me	1,446	Suffield	Hartford	Conn	2,962
Starksborough	Addison	Vt	1,400	Suffield	Portage	Ohio	1,281
Starr	Hocking	Ohio	1,045	*Suffolk*	Nansemond	Va	1,500
Staunton	Fayette	Ohio	87	Sugar Creek	Benton	Ark	*580
Staunton	Miami	Ohio	1,475	Sugar Creek	Clinton	Ind	477
Staunton	Augusta	Va	2,500	Sugar Creek	Hancock	Ind	793
Steady Run	Keokuk	Iowa	467	Sugar Creek	Montgomery	Ind	777
Steele	Daviess	Ind	495	Sugar Creek	Parke	Ind	1,355
Stephenson	Rensselaer	N. Y.	2,622	Sugar Creek	Shelby	Ind	743
Sterling	Windham	Conn	1,025	Sugar Creek	Vigo	Ind	1,180
Sterling	Crawford	Ind	893	Sugar Creek	Randolph	Mo	*965
Sterling	Worcester	Mass	1,805	Sugar Creek	Allen	Ohio	756
Sterling	Macomb	Mich	876	Sugar Creek	Greene	Ohio	3,082
Sterling	Cayuga	N. Y.	2,808	Sugar Creek	Putnam	Ohio	550
Sterling	Brown	Ohio	981	Sugar Creek	Stark	Ohio	1,743
Sterling	Wayne	Pa	1,033	Sugar Creek	Tuscarawas	Ohio	1,400
Sterling	Lamoille	Vt	233	Sugar Creek	Wayne	Ohio	2,321
Stetson	Penobscot	Me	885	Sugar Creek	Armstrong	Pa	1,688
Steuben	Steuben	Ind	645	Sugar Creek	Venango	Pa	875
Steuben	Warren	Ind	741	Sugar Creek	Walworth	Wis	1,227

a In 1853, 7,000. *b* In 1853, 2,000. *c* In 1853, 1,500.

Sugar Grove	Kane	Ill	734	Talladaga	Jefferson	Ark	440
Sugar Grove	Warren	Pa	1,523	Talladega	Talladega	Ala	†1,320
Sugar Loaf	Carroll	Ark	226	Tallmadge	Ottawa	Mich	534
Sugar Loaf	Crawford	Ark	911	Tallmadge	Summit	Ohio	2,456
Sugar Loaf	Marion	Ark	343	Tamaqua	Schuylkill	Pa	3,080
Sugar Loaf	Van Buren	Ark	260	Tampa, including			
Sugar Loaf	Columbia	Pa	1,316	Fort Brook	Hillsborough	Fla	†974
Sugar Loaf	Luzerne	Pa	1,023	Tamworth	Carroll	N. H.	1,766
Sullivan	Hancock	Me	810	Taneytown	Carroll	Md	285
Sullivan	Cheshire	N. H	468	*Tarborough*	Edgecombe	N. C.	1,000
Sullivan	Madison	N. Y.	4,764	Tarentum	Allegheny	Pa	b509
Sullivan	Ashland	Ohio	1,101	*Tariffville*	Hartford	Conn	2,000
Sullivan	Tioga	Pa	1,757	Tarlton	Pickaway	Ohio	512
Sullivan	Jefferson	Wis	872	Tate	Clermont	Ohio	2,901
Sulphur Fork	Lafayette	Ark	218	Taunton	Bristol	Mass	c10,441
Sulphur Springs	Montgomery	Ark	552	Taycheeda	Fond du Lac	Wis	786
Sulphur Springs	Polk	Ark	247	Taylor	Ouachita	Ark	439
Summerfield	Monroe	Mich	472	Taylor	Greene	Ind	1,255
Summerfield	Monroe	Ohio	179	Taylor	Howard	Ind	572
Summerford	Madison	Ohio	755	Taylor	Owen	Ind	535
Summerford, T	Madison	Ohio	139	Taylor	Appanoose	Iowa	243
Summer Hill	Cambria	Pa	1,497	Taylor	Wayne	Mich	303
Summerhill	Cayuga	N. Y.	1,251	Taylor	Greene	Mo	*1,380
Summerhill	Crawford	Pa	1,160	Taylor	Cortlandt	N. Y.	1,252
Summerville	Chatooga	Ga	248	Taylor	Hardin	Ohio	531
Summit	Schoharie	N. Y.	1,800	Taylor	Union	Ohio	400
Summit	Cambria	Pa	406	Taylor	Centre	Pa	349
Summit	Crawford	Pa	1,074	Taylor	Fulton	Pa	514
Summit	Somerset	Pa	959	Taylor's Bay	Jackson	Ark	718
Summit	Waukesha	Wis	924	Taylorsville	Johnson	Tenn	118
Sumner	Oxford	Me	1,151	*Taylorsville*	Spencer	Ky	800
Sumpter	Wayne	Mich	434	*Taylorsville*	Muskingum	Ohio	1,000
Sumpterville	Sumter	S. C	†1,356	*Taylorsville*	Christian	Ill	1,000
Sunbury	Delaware	Ohio	337	Taymouth	Saginaw	Mich	58
Sunbury	Monroe	Ohio	1,533	*Tazewell*	Claiborne	Tenn	575
Sunbury	Northumberland	Pa	1,218	Tebo	Henry	Mo	*1,164
Sunderland	Franklin	Mass	792	Tecumseh	Lenawee	Mich	2,679
Sunderland	Bennington	Vt	479	Tekonsha	Calhoun	Mich	651
Sunfield	Eaton	Mich	122	Temperanceville	Belmont	Ohio	91
Sunfish	Pike	Ohio	371	*Temperanceville*	Alleghany	Pa	2,500
Sun Prairie	Dane	Wis	506	Temple	Franklin	Me	785
Superior	Washtenaw	Mich	1,127	Temple	Hillsborough	N. H.	579
Superior	Williams	Ohio	723	Templeton	Worcester	Mass	2,173
Surrounded Hills	Monroe	Ark	213	Terre Haute	Vigo	Ind	d4,051
Surry	Hancock	Me	1,189	Terre Noir	Clark	Ark	266
Surry	Cheshire	N. H	556	Tete Des Mort	Jackson	Iowa	572
Suspension Bridge	Niagara	N. Y.	800	Tewksbury	Middlesex	Mass	1,044
Susquehanna	Cambria	Pa	640	Tewksbury	Hunterdon	N. J.	2,301
Susquehanna	Dauphin	Pa	1,535	Texas	St. Francis	Ark	258
Susquehanna	Lycoming	Pa	406	Texas	Kalamazoo	Mich	410
Susquehanna	Susquehanna	Pa	1,500	Texas	Crawford	Ohio	545
Sutton	Worcester	Mass	2,595	Texas	Wayne	Pa	2,580
Sutton	Merrimack	N. H.	1,387	Theresa	Jefferson	N. Y.	2,342
Sutton	Meigs	Ohio	1,596	Theresa	Dodge	Wis	764
Sutton	Caledonia	Vt	1,001	Thetford	Genesee	Mich	303
Swain	Mississippi	Ark	198	Thetford	Orange	Vt	2,016
Swan	Noble	Ind	568	Thibodeauxville	Lafourche	La	1,242
Swan	Taney	Mo	946	Third Creek	Gasconade	Mo	588
Swan	Vinton	Ohio	1,154	Thomaston	Lincoln	Me	2,723
Swan Creek	Fulton	Ohio	621	Thompson	Pike	Ark	548
Swan Quarter	Hyde	N. C.	787	Thompson	Windham	Conn	4,638
Swansborough	Onslow	N. C.	801	Thompson	Sullivan	N. Y.	3,198
Swansey	Bristol	Mass	1,554	Thompson	Delaware	Ohio	732
Swanton	Franklin	Vt	2,824	Thompson	Geauga	Ohio	1,211
Swanville	Waldo	Me	944	Thompson	Seneca	Ohio	1,668
Swanzey	Cheshire	N. H	2,106	Thompson	Fulton	Pa	672
Swatara	Lebanon	Pa	1,843	Thompson	Susquehanna	Pa	509
Sweden	Oxford	Me	696	*Thompsonville*	Hartford	Conn	2,000
Sweden	Munroe	N. Y.	3,623	Thorn	Perry	Ohio	1,847
Sweden	Potter	Pa	254	Thorn Apple	Barry	Mich	336
Swedsburg	Montgomery	Pa	388	Thornburg	Delaware	Pa	876
Sweetland	Muscatine	Iowa	594	Thornbury	Chester	Pa	233
Switzerland	Monroe	Ohio	1,216	Thorndike	Waldo	Me	1,029
Sycamore	De Kalb	Ill	975	Thornton	Cook	Ill	369
Sycamore, T.	De Kalb	Ill	338	Thornton	Grafton	N. H.	1,011
Sycamore	Hamilton	Ohio	3,731	Thurston	Steuben	N. Y.	726
Sycamore	Wyandott	Ohio	880	Ticonderoga	Essex	N. Y.	2,669
Sydney	Kennebec	Me	1,955	Tiffin	Adams	Ohio	1,980
Sykesville	Anne Arundel	Md	127	Tiffin	Defiance	Ohio	709
Sylamore	Izard	Ark	241	Tiffin	Seneca	Ohio	e2,718
Sylvan	Washtenaw	Mich	924	*Tigerville*	Terre Bonne	La	69
Sylvania	Lucas	Ohio	751	Tinicum	Bucks	Pa	2,047
Sylvester	Greene	Wis	712	Tinicum	Delaware	Pa	178
Symmes	Hamilton	Ohio	1,115	Tinmouth	Rutland	Vt	717
Symmes	Lawrence	Ohio	487	Tioga	Tioga	N. Y.	2,839
Symmes Corner	Butler	Ohio	104	Tioga	Tioga	Pa	1,157
Syracuse	Onondaga	N. Y.	a22,271	Tionesta	Jefferson	Pa	106
Taghkanick	Columbia	N. Y.	1,539	Tionesta	Venango	Pa	1,185

a In 1853, 27,000. *b* In 1853, 1,200. *c* In 1853, 11,300. *d* In 1853, 7,000. *e* In 1853, 4,000.

Tippecanoe	Carroll	Ind	657
Tippecanoe	Kosciusko	Ind	620
Tippecanoe	Tippecanoe	Ind	1,273
Tippecanoe	Henry	Iowa	775
Tipton	Cass	Ind	837
Tipton	Tipton	Ind	197
Tipton	Cedar	Iowa	252
Tisbury	Dukes	Mass	1,803
Tittabawassee	Saginaw	Mich	341
Titusville	Crawford	Pa	243
Tiverton	Coshocton	Ohio	842
Tiverton	Newport	R. I	4,699
Tobin	Perry	Ind	1,725
Toboyne	Perry	Pa	707
Toby	Clarion	Pa	2,234
Tobyhanna	Monroe	Pa	550
Todd	Crawford	Ohio	578
Todd	Fulton	Pa	514
Todd	Huntingdon	Pa	1,222
Toledo	Lucas	Ohio	a3,829
Tolland	Tolland	Conn	1,406
Tolland	Hampden	Mass	594
Tom	Benton	Mo	462
Toms River	Ocean	N. J	800
Tomahawk	Searcy	Ark	296
Tome	Valencia	N. M	615
Tompkins	Jackson	Mich	623
Tompkins	Delaware	N. Y	3,022
Tonawanda	Erie	N. Y	2,072
Topsfield	Washington	Me	268
Topsfield	Essex	Mass	1,170
Topsham	Lincoln	Me	2,010
Topsham	Orange	Vt	1,668
Torrington	Litchfield	Conn	1,916
Toulon	Stark	Ill	377
Towamensing	Montgomery	Pa	904
Towanda, Bor	Bradford	Pa	1,171
Towanda	Bradford	Pa	1,138
Town Bluff	Tyler	Texas	60
Townsend	Middlesex	Mass	1,947
Townsend	Huron	Ohio	1,332
Townsend	Sandusky	Ohio	968
Townsend	Windham	Vt	1,354
Tredyffina	Chester	Pa	1,727
Tremont	Tazewell	Ill	461
Tremont	Will	Ill	240
Tremont	Henry	Iowa	1,000
Tremont, T	Schuylkill	Pa	1,000
Trenton	Hancock	Me	1,205
Trenton	Buchanan	Mo	*882
Trenton	Mercer	N. J	6,461
Trenton	Oneida	N. Y	3,540
Trenton	Butler	Ohio	220
Trenton	Delaware	Ohio	1,238
Trenton	Schuylkill	Pa	1,191
Trenton	Gibson	Tenn	732
Trenton	Dodge	Wis	997
Trenton	Washington	Wis	504
Trescott	Washington	Me	782
Triadelphia	Ohio	Va	242
Triangle	Broome	N. Y	1,728
Trimble	Athens	Ohio	924
Trinity	Catahoula	La	500
Trinity River	Trinity	Cal	204
Troupsburgh	Steuben	N. Y	1,754
Trowbridge	Allegan	Mich	313
Troy	Pike	Ala	600
Troy	Mississippi	Ark	419
Troy	La Salle	Ill	662
Troy	Will	Ill	338
Troy	De Kalb	Ind	392
Troy	Fountain	Ind	2,357
Troy	Perry	Ind	1,570
Troy	Waldo	Me	1,484
Troy	Oakland	Mich	1,427
Troy	Cheshire	N. H	759
Troy	Rensselaer	N. Y	28,785
Troy	Ashland	Ohio	849
Troy	Athens	Ohio	1,421
Troy	Delaware	Ohio	976
Troy	Geauga	Ohio	1,164
Troy	Miami	Ohio	1,956
Troy	Morrow	Ohio	640
Troy	Richland	Ohio	1,544
Troy	Wood	Ohio	559
Troy, Bor	Bradford	Pa	480
Troy	Bradford	Pa	1,418
Troy	Crawford	Pa	740
Troy	Obion	Tenn	†177

Troy	Orleans	Vt	1,008
Troy	Walworth	Wis	1,094
Trumbull	Fairfield	Conn	1,309
Truro	Barnstable	Mass	2,051
Truro	Franklin	Ohio	2,153
Truxton	Cortlandt	N. Y	3,623
Tuckelata	San Miguel	N. M	1,320
Tucker	Clark	Ark	267
Tuftonborough	Carroll	N. H	1,305
Tulip	Dallas	Ark	524
Tully	Lewis	Mo	309
Tully	Onondaga	N. Y	1,559
Tully	Marion	Ohio	736
Tully	Van Wert	Ohio	242
Tullytown	Bucks	Pa	234
Tulpehoccan	Berks	Pa	1,803
Tumlinson	Scott	Ark	350
Tunbridge	Orange	Vt	1,786
Tunkhannock, Bor	Wyoming	Pa	561
Tunkhannock	Wyoming	Pa	751
Turbett	Juniata	Pa	1,399
Turbot	Northumberland	Pa	1,047
Turin	Lewis	N. Y	1,826
Turkey Creek	Kosciusko	Ind	590
Turman	Sullivan	Ind	1,396
Turnback	Lawrence	Mo	*313
Turnbull	Ashtabula	Ohio	805
Turner	Oxford	Me	2,536
Turtle	Rock	Wis	1,005
Turtle Creek	Shelby	Ohio	792
Turtle Creek	Warren	Ohio	5,431
Tuscaloosa	Tuscaloosa	Ala	3,500
Tuscarawas	Coshocton	Ohio	1,593
Tuscarawas	Stark	Ohio	2,041
Tuscarora	Juniata	Pa	1,175
Tuscarora	Schuylkill	Pa	650
Tuscola	Livingston	Mich	544
Tuskegee	Macon	Ala	1,563
Twin	Preble	Ohio	1,942
Twin	Darke	Ohio	1,400
Twin	Ross	Ohio	2,239
Twin Grove	McLean	Ill	252
Twinsburg	Summit	Ohio	1,281
Two Rivers	Manitowoc	Wis	927
Tymochtee	Wyandott	Ohio	1,818
Tynsborough	Middlesex	Mass	799
Tyre	Seneca	N. Y	1,356
Tyringham	Berkshire	Mass	821
Tyrone	Livingston	Mich	867
Tyrone	Steuben	N. Y	1,894
Tyrone	Adams	Pa	891
Tyrone	Blair	Pa	1,068
Tyrone	Fayette	Pa	1,419
Tyrone	Perry	Pa	1,069
Tyrongee	Crittenden	Ark	132
Uhricksville	Tuscarawas	Ohio	576
Ulster	Bradford	Pa	1,082
Ulysses	Tompkins	N. Y	3,122
Ulysses	Potter	N. Y	699
Unadilla	Livingston	Mich	1,027
Unadilla	Otsego	N. Y	2,463
Underhill	Chittenden	Vt	1,599
Unincorporated Northern Liberties & Aramingo	Philadelphia	Pa	2,632
Union	Ashley	Ark	192
Union	Conway	Ark	319
Union	Fulton	Ark	363
Union	Greene	Ark	473
Union	Independence	Ark	256
Union	Izard	Ark	466
Union	Lafayette	Ark	550
Union	Lawrence	Ark	530
Union	Marion	Ark	543
Union	Newton	Ark	163
Union	St. Francis	Ark	600
Union	Van Buren	Ark	258
Union	White	Ark	244
Union	Tolland	Conn	728
Union	Fulton	Ill	916
Union	Adams	Ind	412
Union	Bartholomew	Ind	588
Union	Crawford	Ind	622
Union	De Kalb	Ind	778
Union	Delaware	Ind	1,012
Union	Elkhart	Ind	632
Union	Fulton	Ind	734
Union	Grant	Ind	544
Union	Hancock	Ind	522

a In 1853, 6,412.

Union	Johnson	Ind	1,227
Union	Laporte	Ind	808
Union	Madison	Ind	623
Union	Miami	Ind	812
Union	Montgomery	Ind	5,627
Union	Parke	Ind	1,188
Union	Perry	Ind	747
Union	Porter	Ind	487
Union	Rush	Ind	1,179
Union	St. Joseph	Ind	615
Union	Shelby	Ind	1,071
Union	Union	Ind	1,166
Union	Vanderburg	Ind	673
Union	Wells	Ind	567
Union	Appanoose	Iowa	266
Union	Clinton	Iowa	50
Union	Davis	Iowa	724
Union	Des Moines	Iowa	1,119
Union	Jackson	Iowa	420
Union	Van Buren	Iowa	969
Union	Lincoln	Me	1,972
Union	Branch	Mich	1,271
Union	Marion	Mo	988
Union	Benton	Mo	294
Union	Randolph	Mo	*504
Union	St. Genevieve	Mo	898
Union	Washington	Mo	1,761
Union	Camden	N. J.	1,095
Union	Essex	N. J.	1,662
Union	Ocean	N. J.	1,759
Union	Broome	N. Y.	2,143
Union	Auglaize	Ohio	1,008
Union	Belmont	Ohio	2,328
Union	Brown	Ohio	4,378
Union	Butler	Ohio	2,173
Union	Carroll	Ohio	804
Union	Champaign	Ohio	1,645
Union	Clermont	Ohio	1,800
Union	Clinton	Ohio	3,558
Union	Fayette	Ohio	2,392
Union	Hancock	Ohio	1,150
Union	Highland	Ohio	1,408
Union	Knox	Ohio	1,192
Union	Lawrence	Ohio	1,318
Union	Licking	Ohio	2,368
Union	Logan	Ohio	804
Union	Madison	Ohio	2,159
Union	Mercer	Ohio	746
Union	Miami	Ohio	2,625
Union	Monroe	Ohio	1,930
Union	Morgan	Ohio	1,795
Union	Muskingum	Ohio	1,559
Union	Pike	Ohio	564
Union	Putnam	Ohio	515
Union	Ross	Ohio	2,666
Union	Scioto	Ohio	605
Union	Tuscarawas	Ohio	944
Union	Union	Ohio	1,205
Union	Van Wert	Ohio	84
Union	Warren	Ohio	1,712
Union	Washington	Ohio	1,165
Union	Adams	Pa	952
Union	Bedford	Pa	1,291
Union	Berks	Pa	1,665
Union	Clearfield	Pa	262
Union	Erie	Pa	1,076
Union, Bor	Fayette	Pa	a2,333
Union	Fayette	Pa	2,873
Union	Huntingdon	Pa	631
Union	Jefferson	Pa	597
Union	Lebanon	Pa	1,590
Union	Luzerne	Pa	1,308
Union	Mifflin	Pa	1,284
Union	Schuylkill	Pa	1,064
Union	Tioga	Pa	825
Union	Union	Pa	1,452
Union	Washington	Pa	1,192
Union	Monroe	Va	500
Union	Rock	Wis	1,050
Union Town	Perry	Ala	290
Union Town	El Dorado	Cal	588
Union Town	Trinity	Cal	190
Union Town	Carroll	Md	365
Union Town	Belmont	Ohio	194
Union Town	Muskingum	Ohio	340
Union Town	Stark	Ohio	245
Union Vale	Dutchess	N. Y.	1,552
Union Village	Warren	Ohio	448
Unionville	Chester	Pa	300

Unionville	Union	S. C.	†554
Unity	Waldo	Me	1,557
Unity	Sullivan	N. H	961
Unity	Columbiana	Ohio	2,095
Unity	Westmoreland	Pa	4,152
Upper	Crawford	Ark	524
Upper	Cape May	N. J.	1,341
Upper	Lawrence	Ohio	2,494
Upper Allen	Cumberland	Pa	1,220
Upper Alton	Madison	Ill	1,309
Upper Alloway's Creek	Salem	N. J.	2,530
Upper Augusta	Northumberland	Pa	862
Upper Berne	Berks	Pa	1,747
Upper Chichester	Delaware	Pa	531
Upper Darby	Delaware	Pa	2,044
Upper Dickenson	Cumberland	Pa	2,219
Upper Dublin	Montgomery	Pa	1,380
Upper Fourche	Yell	Ark	530
Upper Freehold	Monmouth	N. J.	2,566
Upper Hanover	Montgomery	Pa	1,741
Upper Heidelburg	Berks	Pa	805
Upper Leacock	Lancaster	Pa	1,886
Upper Macungie	Lehigh	Pa	2,035
Upper Mehantango	Schuylkill	Pa	1,654
Upper Mahanoy	Northumberland	Pa	1,268
Upper Makefield	Bucks	Pa	1,701
Upper Milford	Lehigh	Pa	3,259
Upper Mt. Bethel	Northampton	Pa	2,855
Upper Nazareth	Northampton	Pa	708
Upper Okaw	Coles	Ill	657
Upper Oxford	Chester	Pa	1,021
Upper Paxton	Dauphin	Pa	1,690
Upper Peen's Neck	Salem	N. J	2,422
Upper Pitt's Grove	Salem	N. J.	1,656
Upper Providence	Delaware	Pa	778
Upper Providence	Montgomery	Pa	2,457
Upper Sandusky	Wyandott	Ohio	754
Upper Salford	Wyandott	Ohio	1,440
Upper Saucon	Lehigh	Pa	2,372
Upper St. Clair	Allegheny	Pa	1,626
Upper Swatara	Dauphin	Pa	1,239
Upp. Towamensing	Carbon	Pa	1,628
Upp'r Tulpehoccan	Berks	Pa	1,983
Upper Turkeyfoot	Somerset	Pa	952
Upperville	Fauquier	Va	700
Upton	Worcester	Mass	2,023
Urbana	Champaign	Ill	210
Urbana	Champaign	Ohio	3,414
Urbana, T	Champaign	Ohio	b2,020
Urbana	Steuben	N. Y.	2,079
Uwchland	Chester	Pa	1,528
Ursa	Adams	Ill	2,645
Utica	Fulton	Ill	700
Utica	Lasalle	Ill	252
Utica	Clark	Ind	1,538
Utica	Macomb	Mich	1,000
Utica	Oneida	N. Y.	c17,565
Utica	Licking	Ohio	422
Utica	Winnebago	Wis	669
Uxbridge	Worcester	Mass	2,457
Vallecito	Calaveras	Cal	1,600
Valencia	Valencia	N. M.	252
Valley	Montour	Pa	760
Valparaiso	Porter	Ind	522
Van Buren	Crawford	Ark	833
Van Buren, T	Crawford	Ark	d549
Van Buren	Newton	Ark	319
Van Buren	Union	Ark	1,242
Van Buren	Brown	Ind	717
Van Buren	Clay	Ind	867
Van Buren	Daviess	Ind	653
Van Buren	Fountain	Ind	1,296
Van Buren	Grant	Ind	525
Van Buren	Kosciusko	Ind	822
Van Buren	Madison	Ind	407
Van Buren	Monroe	Ind	1,026
Van Buren	Pulaski	Ind	336
Van Buren	Shelby	Ind	817
Van Buren	Jackson	Iowa	294
Van Buren	Keokuk	Iowa	283
Van Buren	Van Buren	Iowa	714
Van Buren	Aroostook	Me	1,050
Van Buren	Wayne	Mich	1,470
Van Buren	Jackson	Mo	1,485
Van Buren	Newton	Mo	*613
Van Buren	Onondaga	N. Y.	3,873
Van Buren	Darke	Ohio	780
Van Buren	Hancock	Ohio	536

a In 1853, 2,700. *b* In 1853, 3,000. *c* In 1853, 20,000. *d* In 1853, 1,600.

Van Buren	Hancock	Ohio	122
Van Buren	Montgomery	Ohio	1,400
Van Buren	Putnam	Ohio	172
Van Buren	Shelby	Ohio	629
Vandalia	Fayette	Ill	*a*419
Vandalia	Montgomery	Ohio	228
Van Rensselaer	Ottowa	Ohio	186
Van Vorst	Hudson	N. J.	4,617
Van Wert	Van Wert	Ohio	268
Varick	Seneca	N. Y	1,872
Vassalboro	Kennebeck	Me	3,099
Vaugine	Jefferson	Ark	1,122
Veale	Daviess	Ind	907
Veasey	Drew	Ark	576
Venango	Butler	Pa	1,473
Venango	Crawford	Pa	1,607
Venango	Erie	Pa	1,019
Venice	Shiawassee	Mich	183
Venice	Cayuga	N. Y.	2,028
Venice	Seneca	Ohio	1,830
Vergennes	Kent	Mich	876
Vergennes	Addison	Vt	1,378
Vermillion	Lasalle	Ill	458
Vermillion	Vermillion	Ind	1,679
Vermillion	Ashland	Ohio	2,459
Vermillion	Erie	Ohio	1,516
Vermont	Fulton	Ill	1,564
Vermontville	Eaton	Mich	324
Vernon	Tolland	Conn	2,900
Vernon	Lake	Ill	959
Vernon	Hancock	Ind	908
Vernon	Jackson	Ind	604
Vernon	Jennings	Ind	3,023
Vernon, T	Jennings	Ind	*b*690
Vernon	Washington	Ind	1,796
Vernon	Van Buren	Iowa	907
Vernon	Shiawassee	Mich	674
Vernon	Sussex	N. J.	2,619
Vernon	Oneida	N. Y.	3,093
Vernon	Clinton	Ohio	1,468
Vernon	Crawford	Ohio	1,276
Vernon	Scioto	Ohio	1,105
Vernon	Trumbull	Ohio	828
Vernon	Crawford	Pa	1,299
Vernon	Windham	Vt	821
Vernon	Waukesha	Wis	889
Verona	Oneida	N. Y.	5,570
Verona	Dane	Wis	364
Versailles	Brown	Ill	177
Versailles	Ripley	Ind	412
Versailles	Allegheny	Pa	1,659
Vershire	Orange	Vt	1,071
Vestal	Broome	N. Y.	2,054
Veteran	Chemung	N. Y	2,698
Vevay	Switzerland	Ind	1,800
Vevay	Ingham	Mich	781
Vicksburg	Warren	Miss	3,678
Victor	Clinton	Mich	277
Victor	Ontario	N. Y.	2,230
Victoria	Victoria	Texas	806
Victory	Cayuga	N. Y.	2,298
Victory	Essex	Vt	168
Vienna	Grundy	Ill	258
Vienna	Johnson	Ill	142
Vienna	Scott	Ind	1,761
Vienna, T	Scott	Ind	107
Vienna	Kennebeck	Me	851
Vienna	Genesee	Mich	390
Vienna	Ontario	N. Y.	1,600
Vienna	Oneida	N. Y.	3,393
Vienna	Trumbull	Ohio	1,007
Vienna	Dane	Wis	253
Village	Jackson	Ark	782
Village	Van Buren	Iowa	988
Vill'e of St. George	New Castle	Del	197
Villamont	Arkansas	Ark	162
Villanova	Chautauque	N. Y.	1,536
Vinalhaven	Waldo	Me	1,252
Vincennes	Knox	Ind	2,070
Vineyard	Washington	Ark	711
Vineyard	Lawrence	Mo	*529
Vinland	Winnebago	Wis	672
Vinton	Vinton	Ohio	460
Virgil	Kane	Ill	634
Virgil	Cortlandt	N. Y.	2,410
Virginia	Cass	Ill	462
Virginia	Coshocton	Ohio	1,226
Violot	Fairfield	Ohio	2,544
Volga	Clayton	Iowa	210
Volinia	Cass	Mich	607
Volney	Oswego	N. Y.	2,966
Voluntown	Windham	Conn	1,064
Wabash	Coles	Ill	746
Wabash	Cumberland	Ill	123
Wabash	Gallatin	Ill	462
Wabash	Adams	Ind	410
Wabash	Fountain	Ind	1,300
Wabash	Gibson	Ind	311
Wabash	Jay	Ind	345
Wabash	Tippecanoe	Ind	1,196
Wabash	Wabash	Ind	*c*966
Wabash	Darke	Ohio	309
Waddam	Stephenson	Ill	1,160
Wadesborough	Anson	N. C.	1,500
Waitsfield	Washington	Vt	1,021
Wahalak	Kemper	Miss	352
Wakefield	Carroll	N. H.	1,405
Wakeman	Huron	Ohio	704
Wakeshma	Kalamazoo	Mich	128
Walcott	Wayne	N. Y.	2,751
Walcott	Lamoille	Vt	909
Walden	Caledonia	Vt	910
Waldo	Waldo	Me	812
Waldo	Marion	Ohio	1,008
Waldo, T	Marion	Ohio	773
Waldoboro, Bor	Lincoln	Me	4,199
Waldron	Scott	Ark	90
Waldwick	Iowa	Wis	418
Wales	Kennebeck	Me	612
Wales	Hampden	Mass	711
Wales	St. Clair	Mich	189
Wales	Erie	N. Y.	2,124
Walker	Rush	Ind	1,229
Walker	Kent	Mich	823
Walker	Centre	Pa	1,221
Walker	Huntingdon	Pa	1,108
Walker	Juniata	Pa	1,493
Walkill	Orange	N. Y.	4,942
Wallace	Independence	Ark	480
Wallingford	New Haven	Conn	2,595
Wallingsford	Rutland	Vt	1,688
Walnut	Phillips	Ark	*541
Walnut	Bureau	Ill	71
Walnut	Montgomery	Ind	1,059
Walnut	Jefferson	Iowa	717
Walnut	Fairfield	Ohio	2,130
Walnut	Gallia	Ohio	905
Walnut	Pickaway	Ohio	1,840
Walnut Creek	Holmes	Ohio	1,077
Walpack	Sussex	N. J.	783
Walpole	Norfolk	Mass	1,929
Walpole	Cheshire	N. H.	2,034
Waltham	Lasalle	Ill	168
Waltham	Hancock	Me	304
Waltham	Middlesex	Mass	4,464
Waltham	Addison	Vt	270
Walton	Eaton	Mich	464
Walton	Delaware	N. Y.	2,271
Walworth	Wayne	N. Y.	1,981
Walworth	Walworth	Wis	987
Wantage	Sussex	N. J.	3,934
Wapausee	Grundy	Ill	217
Wapaukonetta	Auglaize	Ohio	504
Wapello	Louisa	Iowa	937
Wapello, T	Louisa	Iowa	336
Wappanocca	Chittenden	Ark	462
Wapsanonock	Muscatine	Iowa	477
Ward	Yell	Ark	124
Ward	Randolph	Ind	1,557
Ward	Hocking	Ohio	823
Wardsborough	Windham	Vt	1,125
Wadsworth	Medina	Ohio	1,622
Ware	Hampshire	Mass	3,785
War Eagle	Madison	Ark	985
War Eagle	Van Buren	Ark	248
Wareham	Plymouth	Mass	3,186
Warminster	Bucks	Pa	1,007
Warner	Merrimack	N. H.	2,038
Warren	Bradley	Ark	679
Warren	Litchfield	Conn	830
Warren	Henderson	Ill	92
Warren	Lake	Ill	1,007
Warren	Clinton	Ind	779
Warren	Huntington	Ind	169
Warren	Marion	Ind	1,733
Warren	Putnam	Ind	1,334
Warren	St Joseph	Ind	561
Warren	Warren	Ind	1,153

a In 1853, 1,000. *b* In 1853, 1,000. *c* In 1853, 1,800.

Warren	Keokuk	Iowa	287
Warren	Lincoln	Me.	2,428
Warren	Worcester	Mass.	1,777
Warren	Macomb	Mich.	700
Warren	Marion	Mo.	1,720
Warren	Grafton	N. H.	872
Warren	Somerset	N. J.	2,148
Warren	Herkimer	N. Y.	1,756
Warren	Belmont	Ohio	2,740
Warren	Jefferson	Ohio	1,918
Warren	Trumbull	Ohio	2,957
Warren	Tuscarawas	Ohio	1,140
Warren	Washington	Ohio	1,461
Warren	Bradford	Pa	1,573
Warren	Franklin	Pa	616
Warren	Warren	Pa	1,013
Warren	Bristol	R. I.	3,103
Warren	Washington	Vt	962
Warrensburg	Johnson	Mo.	1,210
Warrensburg	Warren	N. Y.	1,874
Warrensburg Village	Johnson	Mo	241
Warrensville	Cuyahoga	Ohio	1,410
Warrenton	Warren	Miss	178
Warrenton	Warren	N. C.	1,242
Warrenton	Fauquier	Va	1,500
Warrenton	Jefferson	Ohio	292
Warrington	Bucks	Pa	761
Warrington	York	Pa	1,580
Warrior's Mark	Huntingdon	Pa	1,188
Warsaw	Hancock	Ill	3,000
Warsaw	Kosciusko	Ind	304
Warsaw	Gallatin	Ky	1,000
Warsaw	Wyoming	N. Y.	2,624
Warsaw	Jefferson	Pa	870
Wartz	Wabash	Ind	1,856
Warwick	Franklin	Mass.	1,021
Warwick	Orange	N. Y.	4,902
Warwick	Tuscarawas	Ohio	1,195
Warwick	Bucks	Pa	1,234
Warwick	Chester	Pa	1,391
Warwick	Lancaster	Pa	2,252
Warwick	Kent	R. I.	7,740
Washburn	Scott	Ark	377
Washington	Conway	Ark.	325
Washington	Hempstead	Ark	469
Washington	Independence	Ark	465
Washington	Lawrence	Ark	519
Washington	Ouachita	Ark	409
Washington	Sevier	Ark	465
Washington	Yolo	Cal	320
Washington	Washington	D. C.	a40,001
Washington	Litchfield	Conn.	1,802
Washington	Wilkes	Ga	*462
Washington	Tazewell	Ill	712
Washington	Adams	Ind	548
Washington	Allen	Ind	1,305
Washington	Blackford	Ind	470
Washington	Brown	Ind	1,249
Washington	Carroll	Ind	1,302
Washington	Cass	Ind	822
Washington	Clark	Ind	1,101
Washington	Clay	Ind	1,744
Washington	Clinton	Ind	770
Washington	Daviess	Ind	2,578
Washington	Decatur	Ind	1,994
Washington	Delaware	Ind	757
Washington	Elkhart	Ind	810
Washington	Gibson	Ind	754
Washington	Grant	Ind	1,007
Washington	Greene	Ind	420
Washington	Hamilton	Ind	2,055
Washington	Hendricks	Ind	1,438
Washington	Jackson	Ind	856
Washington	Kosciusko	Ind	733
Washington	Marion	Ind	2,043
Washington	Miami	Ind	966
Washington	Monroe	Ind	740
Washington	Morgan	Ind	2,406
Washington	Noble	Ind	645
Washington	Owen	Ind	1,712
Washington	Parke	Ind	1,198
Washington	Porter	Ind	429
Washington	Putnam	Ind	2,129
Washington	Randolph	Ind	1,558
Washington	Ripley	Ind	1,195
Washington	Rush	Ind	1,075
Washington	Shelby	Ind	1,148
Washington	Starke	Ind	88
Washington	Tippecanoe	Ind	861
Washington	Warren	Ind	796
Washington	Washington	Ind	2,098
Washington, T.	Wayne	Ind	283
Washington	Wayne	Ind	2,305
Washington	Appanoose	Iowa	382
Washington	Johnson	Iowa	392
Washington	Jones	Iowa	423
Washington	Van Buren	Iowa	1,057
Washington	Lincoln	Me.	1,756
Washington	Berkshire	Mass.	953
Washington	Macomb	Mich.	1,541
Washington	Buchanan	Mo	*4,301
Washington	Clay	Mo.	1,428
Washington	Jackson	Mo	1,008
Washington	Johnson	Mo.	1,002
Washington	Lafayette	Mo.	2,101
Washington	Osage	Mo	*1,093
Washington	Taney	Mo	335
Washington	Sullivan	N. H.	1,053
Washington	Bergen	N. J.	1,807
Washington	Burlington	N. J.	2,010
Washington	Camden	N. J.	2,114
Washington	Morris	N. J.	2,502
Washington	Warren	N. J.	1,567
Washington	Dutchess	N. Y.	2,805
Washington	Beaufort	N. C.	2,015
Washington	Auglaize	Ohio	688
Washington	Belmont	Ohio	1,532
Washington	Brown	Ohio	1,185
Washington	Carroll	Ohio	1,020
Washington	Clermont	Ohio	2,540
Washington	Clinton	Ohio	1,216
Washington	Columbiana	Ohio	1,201
Washington	Coshocton	Ohio	998
Washington	Darke	Ohio	1,250
Washington	Defiance	Ohio	428
Washington	Fayette	Ohio	569
Washington	Franklin	Ohio	1,270
Washington	Guernsey	Ohio	972
Washington, T	Guernsey	Ohio	759
Washington	Hancock	Ohio	1,222
Washington	Hardin	Ohio	391
Washington	Harrison	Ohio	1,255
Washington	Henry	Ohio	532
Washington	Hocking	Ohio	1,640
Washington	Holmes	Ohio	1,468
Washington	Jackson	Ohio	756
Washington	Lawrence	Ohio	646
Washington	Licking	Ohio	1,361
Washington	Logan	Ohio	668
Washington	Lucas	Ohio	1,161
Washington	Mercer	Ohio	456
Washington	Miami	Ohio	4,258
Washington	Monroe	Ohio	944
Washington	Montgomery	Ohio	1,825
Washington	Morrow	Ohio	1,137
Washington	Muskingum	Ohio	1,380
Washington	Paulding	Ohio	155
Washington	Pickaway	Ohio	1,099
Washington	Preble	Ohio	3,060
Washington	Richland	Ohio	1,914
Washington	Sandusky	Ohio	1,499
Washington	Scioto	Ohio	706
Washington	Shelby	Ohio	1,261
Washington	Stark	Ohio	2,066
Washington	Tuscarawas	Ohio	1,091
Washington	Union	Ohio	333
Washington	Van Wert	Ohio	355
Washington	Warren	Ohio	1,566
Washington	Wood	Ohio	504
Washington	Berks	Pa	1,154
Washington	Butler	Pa	1,003
Washington	Cambria	Pa	1,691
Washington	Clarion	Pa	1,227
Washington	Dauphin	Pa	889
Washington	Erie	Pa	1,706
Washington	Fayette	Pa	1,276
Washington	Franklin	Pa	2,476
Washington	Greene	Pa	914
Washington	Indiana	Pa	1,111
Washington	Jefferson	Pa	646
Washington, Bor.	Lancaster	Pa	582
Washington	Lehigh	Pa	1,493
Washington	Lycoming	Pa	2,138
Washington	Union	Pa	1,238
Washington, Bor.	Washington	Pa	2,662
Washington	Westmoreland	Pa	2,076
Washington	Wyoming	Pa	1,675

a In 1853, estimated at 53,592.

Town	County	State	Population
Washington	York	Pa	1,339
Washington	Orange	Vt	1,348
Washington	Brown	Wis	171
Washington	Greene	Wis	307
Waterboro	York	Me	1,989
Waterbury	New Haven	Conn	a5,137
Waterbury	Washington	Vt	2,352
Waterford	New London	Conn	2,259
Waterford	Fulton	Ill	265
Waterford	Fayette	Ind	833
Waterford	Oxford	Me	1,448
Waterford	Oakland	Mich	1,085
Waterford	Camden	N. J.	1,638
Waterford	Saratoga	N. Y.	2,683
Waterford	Washington	Ohio	1,690
Waterford, Bor.	Erie	Pa	498
Waterford	Erie	Pa	1,546
Waterford	Caledonia	Vt	1,412
Waterloo	Monroe	Ill	791
Waterloo	Fayette	Ind	833
Waterloo	Jackson	Mich	1,090
Waterloo	Seneca	N. Y.	3,795
Waterloo	Athens	Ohio	1,016
Waterloo	Jefferson	Wis	807
Watertown	Litchfield	Conn	1,533
Watertown	Middlesex	Mass	2,837
Watertown	Clinton	Mich	315
Watertown	Jefferson	N. Y.	7,201
Watertown	Washington	Ohio	1,373
Watertown	Jefferson	Wis	2,778
Watertown, T.	Jefferson	Wis	b1,451
Waterville	Kennebeck	Me	3,964
Waterville	Grafton	N. H.	42
Waterville	Lucas	Ohio	958
Waterville	Lamoille	Vt	753
Watervliet	Albany	N. Y.	4,882
Watson	Allegan	Mich	313
Watson	Lewis	N. Y.	1,138
Watson	Lycoming	Pa	270
Watts	Perry	Pa	460
Wattsburgh	Erie	Pa	227
Wauconda	Lake	Ill	774
Waukegan	Lake	Ill	c2,949
Waukesha	Waukesha	Wis	d2,313
Waupun	Fond du Lac	Wis	880
Waushara	Dodge	Wis	856
Waverly	Van Buren	Mich	186
Waverly	Lafayette	Mo	350
Waverly	Pike	Ohio	725
Waverly	Humphries	Tenn	*174
Wawarsing	Ulster	N. Y.	6,459
Wawwatoso	Milwaukee	Wis	2,048
Wayland	Middlesex	Mass	1,115
Wayland	Allegan	Mich	404
Wayland	Steuben	N. Y.	2,067
Wayne	Du Page	Ill	857
Wayne	Stephenson	Ill	444
Wayne	Allen	Ind	5,282
Wayne	Bartholomew	Ind	789
Wayne	Fulton	Ind	590
Wayne	Hamilton	Ind	955
Wayne	Henry	Ind	2,075
Wayne	Jay	Ind	705
Wayne	Kosciusko	Ind	734
Wayne	Marion	Ind	2,323
Wayne	Montgomery	Ind	1,249
Wayne	Noble	Ind	624
Wayne	Owen	Ind	1,138
Wayne	Randolph	Ind	1,136
Wayne	Tippecanoe	Ind	1,597
Wayne	Wayne	Ind	4,959
Wayne	Henry	Iowa	201
Wayne	Kennebeck	Me	1,367
Wayne	Cass	Mich	682
Wayne	Buchanan	Mo	*336
Wayne	Passaic	N. J.	1,162
Wayne	Steuben	N. Y.	1,347
Wayne	Adams	Ohio	1,682
Wayne	Ashtabula	Ohio	899
Wayne	Auglaize	Ohio	671
Wayne	Belmont	Ohio	1,918
Wayne	Butler	Ohio	1,502
Wayne	Champaign	Ohio	1,429
Wayne	Clermont	Ohio	1,394
Wayne	Clinton	Ohio	1,435
Wayne	Columbiana	Ohio	977
Wayne	Darke	Ohio	1,162
Wayne	Fayette	Ohio	1,243
Wayne	Jefferson	Ohio	1,801
Wayne	Knox	Ohio	1,864
Wayne	Monroe	Ohio	1,177
Wayne	Montgomery	Ohio	1,090
Wayne	Muskingum	Ohio	1,440
Wayne	Pickaway	Ohio	644
Wayne	Scioto	Ohio	4,230
Wayne	Tuscarawas	Ohio	2,342
Wayne	Warren	Ohio	4,081
Wayne	Wayne	Ohio	2,079
Wayne	Armstrong	Pa	1,348
Wayne	Clinton	Pa	396
Wayne	Crawford	Pa	882
Wayne	Erie	Pa	1,122
Wayne	Greene	Pa	1,258
Wayne	Lawrence	Pa	756
Wayne	Mifflin	Pa	1,201
Wayne	Schuylkill	Pa	1,968
Wayne	Lafayette	Wis	336
Wayne	Washington	Wis	672
Waynesboro	Burke	Ga	196
Waynesboro	Franklin	Pa	1,019
Waynesburg	Greene	Pa	1,200
Waynesfield	Lucas	Ohio	2,371
Waynesville	De Witt	Ill	322
Waynesville	Warren	Ohio	744
Weare	Hillsborough	N. H.	2,435
Weathersfield	Trumbull	Ohio	1,717
Weathersfield	Windsor	Vt	1,851
Weaversville	Trinity	Cal	e210
Weaversville and vicinity	El Dorado	Cal	966
Webberville	Travis	Texas	200
Webster	Lincoln	Me	1,110
Webster	Worcester	Mass	2,371
Webster	Monroe	N. Y.	2,446
Webster	Wood	Ohio	237
Weisenburg	Lehigh	Pa	1,762
Welborne	Conway	Ark	644
Weller	Richland	Ohio	1,290
Wellfleet	Barnstable	Mass	2,411
Wellington	Piscataquis	Me	600
Wellington	Lorain	Ohio	1,556
Wells	Appanoose	Iowa	261
Wells	Franklin	Me	995
Wells	York	Me	2,945
Wells	Hamilton	N. Y.	486
Wells	Jefferson	Ohio	1,822
Wells	Bradford	Pa	1,113
Wells	Fulton	Pa	420
Wells	Rutland	Vt	804
Wellsborough	Tioga	Pa	620
Wellsburg	Brooke	Va	3,000
Wendell	Franklin	Mass	920
Wendell	Sullivan	N. H	787
Wenham	Essex	Mass	977
Wenlock	Essex	Vt	26
Wentworth	Grafton	N. H.	1,197
Wesley	Washington	Me	329
Wesley	Washington	Ohio	1,560
West	Columbiana	Ohio	2,110
West	Huntingdon	Pa	1,464
West	Potter	Pa	92
West Almond	Alleghany	N. Y.	976
West Bath	Lincoln	Me	603
West Beaver	Union	Pa	1,192
West Bend	Washington	Wis	672
West Bethlehem	Washington	Pa	2,114
West Bloomfield	Oakland	Mich	1,086
West Bloomfield	Ontario	N. Y.	1,698
Westborough	Worcester	Mass	2,371
West Boylston	Worcester	Mass	1,749
West Bradford	Chester	Pa	1,585
West Brandywine	Chester	Pa	771
West Bridgewater	Plymouth	Mass	1,447
West Brook	Middlesex	Conn	1,202
West Brook	Cumberland	Me	4,852
West Brookfield	Worcester	Mass	1,344
West Brownsville	Washington	Pa	477
West Brunswick	Schuylkill	Pa	1,693
West Buffalo	Union	Pa	1,007
West Caln	Chester	Pa	1,508
West Cambridge	Middlesex	Mass	2,202
West Chester	Porter	Ind	360
West Chester	West Chester	N. Y.	2,492
Westchester	Butler	Ohio	214
West Chester	Chester	Pa	f3,172
West Cocalico	Lancaster	Pa	1,966
West Connequenessing	Butler	Pa	1,376

a In 1853, 7,000. b In 1853, 4,000. c In 1853, 4,500. d In 1853, 4,000. e In 1853, 2,500. f In 1853, 4,500.

Place	County	State	Population
West Creek	Lake	Ind.	411
West Deer	Allegheny	Pa	1,716
West Donegal	Lancaster	Pa	1,382
West Earl	Lancaster	Pa	1,672
West Elizabeth	Allegheny	Pa	328
Westerly	Washington	R. I.	2,763
Westerlo	Albany	N. Y.	2,860
Western	Oneida	N. Y.	2,516
West Fairlee	Orange	Vt	696
Westfall	Pike	Pa	567
West Fallowfield	Chester	Pa	2,290
West Fallowfield	Crawford	Pa	654
West Farms	Westchester	N. Y.	4,436
Westfield	Hamilton	Ind.	215
Westfield	Hampden	Mass.	4,180
Westfield	Essex	N. J.	1,577
Westfield	Chautauque	N. Y.	3,100
Westfield	Richmond	N. Y	2,943
Westfield	Medina	Ohio	1,122
Westfield	Morrow	Ohio	1,414
Westfield	Tioga	Pa	1,348
Westfield	Orleans	Vt.	502
Westfield	Sauk	Wis.	210
West Finley	Washington	Pa	1,213
Westford	Middlesex	Mass.	1,473
Westford	Otsego	N. Y.	1,423
Westford	Chittenden	Vt.	1,458
West Fork	Washington	Ark	605
West Genesee	Genesee	Mich.	232
West Goshen	Chester	Pa	940
West Greenfield	La Grange	Ind.	457
West Greenville	Mercer	Pa	1,036
West Greenwich	Kent	R. I.	1,350
West Hampton	Hampshire	Mass.	602
West Hampton	Burlington	N. J.	1,507
West Hanover	Dauphin	Pa	897
West Hartford	Hartford	Conn.	4,411
West Haven	Rutland	Vt.	718
West Hemlock	Montour	Pa	193
West Hempfield	Lancaster	Pa	2,724
West Jefferson	Madison	Ohio	436
West Killingly	Windham	Conn.	2,500
West Lackawannock	Mercer	Pa	1,123
West Lampeter	Lancaster	Pa	1,605
Westland	Guernsey	Ohio	1,126
West Liberty	Ohio	Va	219
West Liberty	Logan	Ohio	643
West Lima	La Grange	Ind.	306
West Mahoning	Indiana	Pa	1,030
West Manchester	York	Pa	1,361
West Marlboro	Chester	Pa	1,130
West Meriden	New Haven	Conn.	1,500
West Middletown	Washington	Pa	326
West Milford	Passaic	N. J	2,624
Westminster	Carroll	Md.	884
Westminster	Worcester	Mass.	1,914
Westminster	Windham	Vt.	1,721
West Monroe	Oswego	N. Y.	1,197
Westmore	Orleans	Vt.	152
Westmoreland	Cheshire	N. H	1,678
Westmoreland	Oneida	N. Y.	3,291
West Nantimel	Chester	Pa	1,803
West Newbury	Essex	Mass.	1,746
West Newton	Westmoreland	Pa	771
West Nottingham	Chester	Pa	721
Weston	Fairfield	Conn.	1,056
Weston	Aroostook	Me	293
Weston	Middlesex	Mass.	1,205
Weston	Platte	Mo	3,775
Weston, T.	Platte	Mo	*a*1,915
Weston	Wood	Ohio	546
Weston	Windsor	Vt.	950
West Penn	Schuylkill	Pa	2,411
West Pennsborough	Cumberland	Pa	2,040
Westphalia	Clinton	Mich.	618
West Philadelphia	Philadelphia	Pa.	5,571
West Pikeland	Chester	Pa	881
West Pike Run	Washington	Pa.	1,166
West Point	Stephenson	Ill.	250
West Point	Lee	Iowa	1,248
West Point, T.	Lee	Iowa	*b*546
West Point	Columbia	Wis	197
Westport	Fairfield	Conn.	2,651
Westport	Lincoln	Me	761
Westport	Bristol	Mass.	2,795
Westport	Essex	N. Y	2,353
Westport	Dane	Wis.	202
West Providence	Bedford	Pa.	1,410
West River	Randolph	Ind.	1,357
West Salem	Mercer	Pa	2,481
West Sparta	Livingston	N. Y.	1,619
West Springfield	Hampden	Mass.	2,979
West Stockbridge	Berkshire	Mass.	1,713
Westtown	Chester	Pa	789
West Troy	Albany	N. Y.	7,564
West Turin	Lewis	N. Y	3,793
West Union	Steuben	N. Y.	950
West Union	Adams	Ohio	444
West Van Buren	La Grange	Ind.	434
Westville	New Haven	Conn.	*c*871
Westville	Franklin	N. Y.	1,301
West Vincent	Chester	Pa	1,350
West Wheeling	Belmont	Ohio	438
West Whiteland	Chester	Pa	1,141
West Windsor	Mercer	N. J.	1,596
West Windsor	Windsor	Vt.	1,002
West Zanesville	Muskingum	Ohio	324
Wethersfield	Hartford	Conn.	2,523
Wethersfield	Wyoming	N. Y.	1,489
Wetmore Isle	Hancock	Me	405
Wetumpka	Coosa	Ala.	3,824
Weverton	Frederick	Md	2,500
Weybridge	Addison	Vt.	804
Weymouth	Norfolk	Mass.	5,369
Weymouth	Atlantic	N. J.	1,032
Wharton	Fayette	Pa	1,853
Wharton	Potter	Pa	232
Whately	Franklin	Mass.	1,101
Wheatfield	Ingham	Mich.	231
Wheatfield	Niagara	N. Y.	2,650
Wheatfield	Indiana	Pa	2,387
Wheatfield	Perry	Pa	678
Wheatland	Will	Ill.	749
Wheatland	Hillsdale	Mich.	1,358
Wheatland	Monroe	N. Y.	2,916
Wheatland	Kenosha	Wis.	1,193
Wheeler	Steuben	N. Y.	1,471
Wheelersburg	Scioto	Ohio	504
Wheeling	Cook	Ill.	903
Wheeling	Belmont	Ohio	1,502
Wheeling	Guernsey	Ohio	1,159
Wheeling	Ohio	Va	11,435
Wheelock	Caledonia	Vt	855
Whetstone	Crawford	Ohio	1,657
Whiskey Run	Crawford	Ind.	930
White	Ashley	Ark	648
White	Newton	Ark	242
White	Pike	Ark	205
White	Polk	Ark	326
White	Benton	Mo	693
White	Cambria	Pa	667
White	Indiana	Pa	1,288
White Creek	Washington	N. Y.	2,994
White Deer	Union	Pa	1,537
White Eyes	Coshocton	Ohio	1,132
Whitefield	Lincoln	Me.	2,158
Whitefield	Coos	N. H.	857
Whitehall	Greene	Ill	246
Whitehall	Washington	N. Y.	4,726
Whitehall	Philadelphia	Pa	489
White Lake	Oakland	Mich.	905
Whitely	Greene	Pa	992
Whitemarsh	Montgomery	Pa	2,408
White Oak	Franklin	Ark	1,052
White Oak	Jefferson	Ark	512
White Oak	Ingham	Mich.	508
White Oak	Highland	Ohio	1,012
White Oak Grove	McLean	Ill.	252
White Oak Springs	Lafayette	Wis	453
White Pigeon	St. Joseph's	Mich.	795
White Plains	Westchester	N. Y.	1,414
White Post	Pulaski	Ind	168
White River	Benton	Ark.	*385
White River	Independence	Ark.	1,098
White River	Izard	Ark.	233
White River	Marian	Ark.	261
White River	Prairie	Ark.	99
White River	Washington	Ark.	695
White River	Gibson	Ind	830
White River	Hamilton	Ind	1,492
White River	Johnson	Ind	1,547
White River	Randolph	Ind	2,795
White Rock	Franklin	Ark.	159
White Rock	Ogle	Ill	145
White's Mills	Adams	Ohio	83
Whitestown	Oneida	N. Y.	6,810

a In 1853, 2,500. *b* In 1853, 1,000. *c* In 1853, 1,100.

Place	County	State	Population
White Water	Franklin	Ind	1,512
Whitewater	Hamilton	Ohio	1,567
Whitewater	Walworth	Wis	1,229
Whitford	Monroe	Mich	696
Whiting	Washington	Me	470
Whiting	Addison	Vt	629
Whittingham	Windham	Vt	1,380
Whitneyville	Washington	Me	519
Whitpaine	Montgomery	Pa	1,351
Wiconisco	Dauphin	Pa	1,316
Wilbraham	Hampden	Mass	2,127
Wildcat	Tipton	Ind	211
Wiley Cove	Searcy	Ark	568
Wilkesbarre, Bor.	Luzerne	Pa	2,723
Wilkesbarre	Luzerne	Pa	2,928
Wilkins	Allegheny	Pa	3,019
Wilkinson	Desha	Ark	265
Wilksville	Vinton	Ohio	1,037
Willet	Cortlandt	N. Y.	923
Williams	Benton	Mo	629
Williams	Northampton	Pa	2,634
Williamsburg	Wayne	Ind	219
Williamsburg	Piscataquis	Me	124
Williamsburgh	Hampshire	Mass	1,537
Williamsburg	Covington	Miss	100
Williamsburg	Kings	N. Y.	a30,780
Williamsburg	Clermont	Ohio	1,884
Williamsburg	Guernsey	Ohio	326
Williamsburgh	Blair	Pa	747
Williamsburg	James City	Va	877
Williamsfield	Ashtabula	Ohio	982
Williamson	Wayne	N. Y.	2,380
Williamsport	Warren	Ind	279
Williamsport	Washington	Md	1,091
Wiliamsport	Lycoming	Pa	b1,615
Williamsport	Maury	Tenn	†222
Williamstown	Grant	Ky	†317
Williamstown	Berkshire	Mass	2,626
Williamstown	Ingnam	Mich	600
Williamstown	Oswego	N. Y.	1,121
Williamstown	Orange	Vt	1,452
Williamstown	Dodge	Wis	914
Williamsville	Erie	N. Y.	1,000
Wilingsboro	Burlington	N. J.	1,596
Willimantic	Windham	Conn	3,500
Willington	Tolland	Conn	1,388
Williston	Chittenden	Vt	1,669
Willistown	Chester	Pa	1,463
Willoughby	Lake	Ohio	2,081
Willow Springs	Lafayette	Wis	615
Wills	La Porte	Ind	638
Wills	Guernsey	Ohio	2,216
Willsborough	Essex	N. Y.	1,932
Willshire	Van Wert	Ohio	1,053
Willshire, T	Van Wert	Ohio	147
Wilmington	Union	Ark	866
Wilmington	New Castle	Del	13,979
Wilmington	Will	Ill	1,346
Wilmington	Dearborn	Ind	287
Wilmington	De Kalb	Ind	800
Wilmington	Middlesex	Mass	874
Wilmington	Essex	N. Y.	1,218
Wilmington	New Hanover	N. C.	c7,264
Wilmington	Clinton	Ohio	1,238
Wilmington	Lawrence	Pa	1,478
Wilmington	Mercer	Pa	549
Wilmington	Windham	Vt	1,372
Wilmot	Merrimack	N. H.	1,272
Wilmot	Bradford	Pa	550
Wilmut	Herkimer	N. Y.	112
Wilna	Jefferson	N. Y.	2,993
Wilson	Will	Ill	269
Wilson, T	Niagara	N. Y.	800
Wilsons	Niagara	N. Y.	2,955
Wilton	Fairfield	Conn	2,066
Wilton	Franklin	Me	1,909
Wilton	Hillsborough	N. H.	1,161
Wilton	Saratoga	N. Y.	1,458
Wiltsburgh	St. Francis	Ark	50
Winchendon	Worcester	Mass	2,445
Winchester	Litchfield	Conn	2,179
Winchester	Scott	Ill	1,037
Winchester	Randolph	Ind	d532
Winchester	Middlesex	Mass	1,353
Winchester	Cheshire	N. H.	3,296
Winchester	Adams	Ohio	1,693
Winchester	Guernsey	Ohio	147
Winchester	Frederick	Va	3,857
Windham	Windham	Conn	4,503
Windham	Cumberland	Me	2,380
Windham	Rockingham	N. H.	818
Windham	Greene	N. Y.	2,048
Windham	Portage	Ohio	808
Windham	Bradford	Pa	957
Windham	Wyoming	Pa	549
Windham	Windham	Vt	763
Windsor	Hartford	Conn	3,294
Windsor	Kennebeck	Me	1,793
Windsor	Berkshire	Mass	897
Windsor	Eaton	Mich	495
Windsor	Hillsborough	N. H.	172
Windsor	Broome	N. Y.	2,645
Windsor	Ashtabula	Ohio	1,033
Windsor	Lawrence	Ohio	1,001
Windsor	Morgan	Ohio	1,592
Windsor	Berks	Pa	1,115
Windsor	York	Pa	1,711
Windsor	Windsor	Vt	1,928
Windsor	Dane	Wis	884
Windsor Locks	Hartford	Conn	1,200
Winfield	Du Page	Ill	1,149
Winfield	Lake	Ind	245
Winfield	Herkimer	N. Y.	1,481
Wing	Lucas	Ohio	261
Wingville	Grant	Wis	1,044
Winhall	Bennington	Vt	762
Winnebago	Winnebago	Wis	1,625
Winniconna	Winnebago	Wis	1,948
Winslow	Stephenson	Ill	384
Winslow	Kennebeck	Me	1,796
Winslow	Camden	N. J.	1,540
Winslow	Jefferson	Pa	507
Winstonville	Winston	Miss	150
Wintersville	Jefferson	Ohio	121
Winthrop	Kennebeck	Me	2,154
Winton	Butler	Ohio	77
Winton	Vinton	Ohio	460
Wiota	Lafayette	Wis	721
Wirt	Alleghany	N. Y.	1,544
Wiscasset	Lincoln	Me	2,332
Woburn	Middlesex	Mass	3,956
Wolcott	New Haven	Conn	603
Wolcott	Wayne	N. Y.	2,751
Wolcott	Lamoille	Vt	909
Wolcottville	Litchfield	Conn	1,200
Wolf	Lycoming	Pa	982
Wolfborough	Carroll	N. H	2,038
Wolf Creek	Mercer	Pa	2,048
Womelsdorf	Berks	Pa	947
Wood	Clarke	Ind	1,447
Woodbridge	New Haven	Conn	912
Woodbridge	Hillsdale	Mich	404
Woodbridge	Middlesex	N. J.	5.141
Woodburn	Macoupin	Ill	219
Woodbury	Litchfield	Conn	2,150
Woodbury	Cumberland	Ill	656
Woodbury	Gloucester	N. J.	1,000
Woodbury	Blair	Pa	1,450
Woodbury	Washington	Vt	1,070
Woodcock	Crawford	Pa	2,288
Woodford	Bennington	Vt	423
Woodhull	Shiawassee	Mich	259
Woodhull	Steuben	N. Y.	1,769
Woodland	Carroll	Ill	395
Woodland	Barry	Mich	377
Woodsfield	Monroe	Ohio	e393
Woodstock	Windham	Conn	3,381
Woodstock	McHenry	Ill	600
Woodstock	Schuyler	Ill	696
Woodstock	Oxford	Me	1,012
Woodstock	Lenawee	Mich	949
Woodstock	Grafton	N. H.	418
Woodstock	Ulster	N. Y.	1,650
Woodstock	Champaign	Ohio	205
Woodstock	Windsor	Vt	3,041
Woodstock, T.	Windsor	Vt	1,500
Woodstock	Shenandoah	Va	1,200
Woodville	Rappahannock	Va	300
Woodville	Morrow	Ohio	169
Woodville	Sandusky	Ohio	1,237
Woodward	Clearfield	Pa	390
Woodward	Clinton	Pa	476
Woolwich	Lincoln	Me	1,420
Woolwich	Gloucester	N. J.	3,265
Woonsocket	Providence	R. I.	6,696
Wooster	Scott	Ind	101
Wooster	Wayne	Ohio	4,122
Wooster, T	Wayne	Ohio	f2,797

a In 1853, 45,000. *b* In 185*k*, 2,500. *c* In 1853, 10,000. *d* In 1853, 1,200. *c* In 1853, 600. *f* In 1853, 4,000.

Worcester	Worcester	Mass..	a17,049	York	Clarke	Ill	840
Worcester	Otsego	N. Y..	2,047	York	Du Page	Ill	853
Worcester	Montgomery	Pa	1,453	York	Dearborne	Ind	1,013
Worcester	Washington	Vt	702	York	Elkhart	Ind	453
Worth	Cook	Ill	589	York	Noble	Ind	565
Worth	Hancock	Ind	718	York	Steuben	Ind	489
Worth	Sanilac	Mich..	600	York	Switzerland	Ind	1,523
Worth	Jefferson	N. Y..	326	York	York	Me	2,980
Worth	Centre	Pa	302	York	Washtenaw	Mich..	1,360
Worth	Mercer	Pa	1,015	York	Livingston	N. Y..	2,785
Worthington	Hampshire	Mass..	1,134	York	Athens	Ohio..	1,391
Worthington	Franklin	Ohio..	484	York	Belmont	Ohio..	1,312
Worthington	Richland	Ohio..	2,003	York	Darke	Ohio..	499
Wrentham	Norfolk	Mass..	3,037	York	Fulton	Ohio..	784
Wright	Greene	Ind	793	York	Jefferson	Ohio..	89
Wright	Hillsdale	Mich..	574	York	Medina	Ohio..	1,211
Wright	Ottawa	Mich..	521	York	Morgan	Ohio..	1,207
Wright	Schoharie	N. Y..	1,716	York	Sandusky	Ohio..	1,811
Wright	Guernsey	Ohio..	1,030	York	Tuscarawas	Ohio..	1,303
Wrightstown	Bucks	Pa	821	York	Union	Ohio..	831
Wrightsville	York	Pa	1,310	York	Van Wert	Ohio..	375
Wyaconda	Davis	Iowa..	602	York, T	York	Pa	6,863
Wyalusing	Bradford	Pa	1,275	York	York	Pa	1,960
Wyocena	Columbia	Wis	507	York	Dane	Wis	622
Wyocena, T	Columbia	Wis	101	York	Greene	Wis	191
Wyoming	Lee	Ill	808	Yorkshire,	Cattaraugus	N. Y..	2,010
Wyoming	Kent	Mich..	543	Yorktown	Westchester	N. Y..	2,273
Wyoming	Iowa	Wis	206	Yorkville	Pickens	Ala	96
Wysox	Carroll	Ill	636	Yorkville	York	S. C..	*511
Wysox	Bradford	Pa	1,167	Yorkville	Racine	Wis	998
Wytheville	Wythe	Va	900	Youghiogheny	Fayette	Pa	338
Xenia	Greene	Ohio..	7,055	Young	Niagara	Pa	1,513
Xenia, T	Greene	Ohio..	b3,024	*Youngstown*	Indiana	N. Y..	800
Yanceyville	Caswell	N. Y..	600	Youngstown	Mahoning	Ohio..	2,802
Yankee Springs	Barry	Mich..	292	Youngsville	Warren	Pa	363
Yarmouth	Cumberland	Me	2,144	Ypsilanti	Washtenaw	Mich..	3,051
Yarmouth	Barnstable	Mass..	2,595	Yuba and vicinity.	Sutter	Cal	336
Yates	Orleans	N. Y..	2,242	Zane	Logan	Ohio..	1,090
Yazoo City	Yazoo	Miss	c1,630	Zanesfield	Logan	Ohio..	317
Yellow Creek	Chariton	Mo	490	Zanesville	Muskingum	Ohio..	7,929
Yellow Creek	Columbiana	Ohio..	2,359	Zelianople	Butler	Pa	385
Yellow Spring	Des Moines	Iowa..	961	Zoar	Tuscarawas	Ohio..	249
Yellow Spring	Greeue	Ohio..	138	Zodiac	Gillespie	Texas.	160
Yonkers	Westchester	N. Y..	4,160				

a In 1853, 20,771. *b* In 1853, 3,500. *c* In 1853, 2000.

CALIFORNIA STATE CENSUS OF 1852.

TABLE I.—Population—Whites, Colored, Indians domesticated, and Foreigners.

COUNTIES.	WHITES.		Citizens of U. S. over 21 y'rs old.	BLACK.			MULATTO.			INDIANS DOMESTICATED.			FOREIGN RESIDENTS.			TOTAL POPULATION.
	Males	Fem.		M.	F.	Over 21 yrs.	M.	F.	Over 21 yrs.	M.	F.	Over 21 yrs.	M.	F.	Over 21 yrs.	
Butte	6,174	206	3,742	14	...	14	4	1	4	15	15	10	2,118	25	2,031	6,429
Calaveras	17,059	973	6,287	117	14	....	37	1	....	1,466	516	......	10,340	395	......	20,183
Colusi	400	63	......	*5		....	*3		....	*66		......	*21		......	537
Contra Costa	1,937	550	946	2	...	2	17	2	....	156	122	......	669	115	627	2,786
El Dorado—estimated at	......	......	......	...	...	....	....	....	....	......	......	......	......	......	......	40,000
Klamath	448	9	374	8	...	7	2	....	2	......	......	......	55	1	43	467
Los Angeles	2,494	1,597	1,173	23	11	36	6	5	5	2,778	1,415	1,864	236	59	245	8,329
Marin	652	160	350	*5		....	....	....	....	*218		......	85	8	......	1,035
Mariposa	*2,788		2,564	*82		69	*2		1	*4,533		2,748	......	......	1,359	7,405
Mendocino	169	28	111	...	...	....	....	....	....	84	103	86	32	......	31	384
Monterey	1,152	791	458	6	...	6	11	5	10	328	308	291	108	29	106	2,601
Napa	523	252	307	12	1	11	....	....	....	668	660	1,018	......	......	......	2,116
Nevada	12,448	920	11,585	76	26	....	....	1	....	1,445	1,781	2,175	721	61	......	†20,583
Placer	6,602	343	5,541	75	5	70	9	....	9	*730		......	562	72	479	‡10,783
Sacramento	9,457	1,739	7,431	195	45	218	80	18	84	62	18	38	971	291	1,015	§12,418
San Diego	397	140	274	7	...	7	....	....	....	1,249	1,024	1,474	91	7	90	2,817
San Joaquin	3,582	987	2,451	60	21	53	....	....	....	168	211	125	650	299	516	5,029
San Francisco	30,156	5,375	11,848	270	53	284	103	38	108	96	63	73	16,537	2,766	16,302	36,154
San Luis Obispo	331	163	143	4	4	4	....	....	....	......	......	......	85	36	77	502
Santa Clara	4,096	2,062	1,717	*53		47	....	3	....	388	162	198	1,059	276	1,081	6,764
Santa Cruz	723	374	279	3	1	4	....	8	8	63	47	37	33	......	30	1,219
Santa Barbara	834	682	301	...	...	....	4	5	5	......	......	......	110	10	106	1,525
Shasta	3,448	252	2,647	45	3	45	10	2	9	52	21	59	811	14	792	3,833
Sierra	3,630	62	3,463	*42		41	*7		7	......	......	......	1,033	34	976	3,741
Siskiyou	1,874	82	1,517	33	1	32	4	....	4	22	4	12	213	7	207	2,020
Solano	2,324	402	1,298	26	2	....	35	....	....	31	15	......	790	101	......	2,835
Sonoma	1,309	511	885	4	1	4	5	2	7	223	153	132	85	29	79	2,208
Sutter	590	85	527	8	3	11	....	....	....	262	252	414	7	3	10	1,200
Trinity	1,741	23	1,491	6	...	5	8	....	6	2	2	3	150	5	138	1,782
Tuolumne	15,967	958	6,904	96	4	95	39	3	40	*590		......	*8,663		8,600	17,657
Tulare	142	32	125	1	...	....	....	....	....	5,800	2,607	‖3,780	......	......	......	8,582
Yolo	1,085	189	1,016	11	...	10	3	....	3	109	43	90	83	3	51	1,440
Yuba	16,666	633	15,245	182	12	170	45	....	45	117	3	102	2,809	246	2,846	¶19,758
Total	171,841		......	1,678		....	528		....	31,266		......	54,803		......	**255,122

*Sex not given; included in the aggregate of counties.

† *Nevada County.*—" 3,886," " foreign residents over twenty-one years," are Chinese, not separated as to sex, included in the aggregate.

‡ *Placer County.*—The aggregate includes 3,019 Chinese, not given in preceding columns.

§ *Sacramento County.*—In the aggregate are included 804 Chinese, not in the other columns.

‖ It is not stated if these Indians are domesticated; as is also the case in some other instances.

¶ *Yuba County.*—The aggregate includes 2,100 Chinese, not given in the preceding columns.

** The aggregate, as published in the California State report, differs very much from the above, although the same detailed work was used in both cases. The following are the State figures: Total population of California, 224,435—county of Butte, 8,572; Calaveras, 20,192; Colusi, 620; Contra Costa, 2,745; *El Dorado, not returned; Klamath, 530; Los Angeles, 7,831; Marin, 1,036; Mariposa, 8,969; Mendocino, 416; Monterey, 2,728; Napa, 2,116; Nevada, 21,365; Placer, 10,784; Sacramento, 12,589; San Diego, 2,932; San Joaquin, 5,029; San Francisco, 36,151; San Luis Obispo, 984; Santa Clara, 6,664; Santa Cruz, 1,219; Santa Barbara, 2,131; Shasta, 4,050; Sierra, 4,855; Siskiyou, 2,240; Solano, 2,835; Sonoma, 2,337; Sutter, 1,207; Trinity, 1,764; Tuolumne, 17,657; Tulare, 8,575; Yolo, 1,307; Yuba, 22,005. There are many inconsistencies in the aggregates, and it has been almost impossible to frame a table from them.

* El Dorado is presumed to contain 40,000 inhabitants.

TABLE II.—Agriculture and Manufactures.

The aggregates of productions of agriculture and manufactures for California, as given by the Secretary of State, are as follows:

PRODUCTIONS AND CAPITAL OF THE STATE.

Number of horses	64,773
Number of mules	16,578
Number of cows	104,339
Number of beef cattle	315,392
Number of work oxen	29,065
Bushels of barley	2,973,734
Bushels of oats	100,497
Bushels of wheat	271,763
Bushels of potatoes	1,393,170
Bushels of corn	62,532
Acres of land under cultivation	110,748
Number of quartz mills	108
Capital invested in—	
Quartz mining	$5,871,405
Placer mining	4,174,419
Other mining operations	3,851,623
For other purposes	41,061,933

TABLE I.—*Age and Sex of the White and Free Colored Population in the leading Northern and Northwestern Cities.*—1850.

Cities.	Color and condition.	Sex.	Under 1 year old.	1 and under 5.	5 and under 10.	10 and under 15.	15 and under 20.	20 and under 30.	30 and under 40.	40 and under 50.	50 and under 60.	60 and under 70.	70 and over.	Age unknown.	Total.
Albany, N. Y.	White	M	710	2,811	3,090	2,509	2,139	4,787	3,851	2,413	1,171	469	232	5	24,187
		F	633	2,742	3,092	2,749	2,968	5,673	3,602	2,193	1,189	597	276	2	25,716
	Free col'd.	M	12	41	39	30	24	71	85	57	19	10	2	....	390
		F	10	35	46	48	50	99	72	55	27	16	12	....	470
	Total.	M	722	2,852	3,129	2,539	2,163	4,858	3,936	2,470	1,190	479	239	5	24,577
		F	643	2,777	3,138	2,797	3,018	5,772	3,674	2,248	1,216	613	290	2	26,186
Boston, Mass.	White	M	1,790	6,204	6,684	5,886	5,945	15,190	11,612	6,435	2,811	1,260	494	544	64,855
		F	1,937	6,256	6,826	6,130	7,190	17,892	11,453	6,280	3,440	1,727	831	65	70,027
	Free col'd.	M	24	74	79	69	58	187	199	120	53	25	7	24	919
		F	25	91	107	79	83	263	184	127	73	25	20	3	1,080
	Total.	M	1,814	6,278	6,763	5,955	6,003	15,377	11,811	6,555	2,864	1,285	501	568	65,774
		F	1,962	6,347	6,933	6,209	7,273	18,155	11,637	6,407	3,513	1,752	851	68	71,107
Burlington, Iowa.	White	M	91	297	276	214	175	497	414	168	59	28	3	....	2,222
		F	77	245	248	199	215	410	260	104	48	20	12	....	1,838
	Free col'd.	M	......	2	3	......	1	1	3	......	1	......	1	....	12
		F	......	1	1	......	1	2	1	1	2	......	1	....	10
	Total.	M	91	299	279	214	176	498	417	168	60	28	4	....	2,234
		F	77	246	249	199	216	412	261	105	50	20	13	....	1,848
Burlington, Vt.	White	M	76	287	339	271	331	706	471	250	142	73	31	....	2,977
		F	86	307	322	303	420	724	394	238	152	82	43	....	3,071
	Free col'd.	M	......	3	5	1	3	12	2	4	2	......	......	....	32
		F	......	1	4	......	1	12	4	1	5	1	1	....	30
	Total.	M	76	290	344	272	334	718	473	254	144	73	31	....	3,009
		F	86	308	326	303	421	736	398	239	157	83	44	....	3,101
Chicago, Ill.	White	M	487	1,590	1,664	1,439	1,384	4,209	3,148	1,477	486	186	47	2	16,119
		F	481	1,649	1,736	1,444	1,430	3,234	2,039	887	406	169	41	5	13,521
	Free col'd.	M	6	13	13	6	16	59	41	18	6	2	1	....	181
		F	2	14	23	16	7	46	24	5	4	1	......	....	142
	Total.	M	493	1,603	1,677	1,445	1,400	4,268	3,189	1,495	492	188	48	2	16,300
		F	483	1,663	1,759	1,460	1,437	3,280	2,063	892	410	170	41	5	13,663
Cincinnati, Ohio.	White	M	1,868	6,251	6,422	5,355	5,114	15,341	10,703	4,954	1,892	1,053	303	50	59,306
		F	1,813	6,128	6,154	5,221	6,110	12,991	7,426	3,645	1,978	1,004	385	37	52,892
	Free col'd.	M	42	144	181	145	105	391	316	145	47	33	13	....	1,562
		F	34	147	192	165	199	395	267	124	90	38	24	....	1,675
	Total.	M	1,910	6,395	6,603	5,500	5,219	15,732	11.019	5,099	1,939	1,086	316	50	60.868
		F	1,847	6,275	6.346	5,386	6,309	13,386	7.693	3,769	2,068	1,042	409	37	54,567
Cleveland, Ohio.	White	M	236	1,036	1,061	778	648	1,910	1,520	703	310	167	41	20	8,499
		F	252	980	1,072	873	880	1,962	1,250	566	272	145	50	9	8,311
	Free col'd.	M	4	14	19	4	5	23	21	10	3	......	1	....	104
		F	5	15	18	8	13	28	23	5	1	2	2	....	120
	Total.	M	240	1,050	1,080	782	653	1,942	1,541	773	313	167	42	20	8,603
		F	257	995	1,090	881	893	1,990	1,273	571	273	147	52	9	8,431
Columbus, Ohio.	White	M	222	1,140	1,006	833	729	2,168	1,530	719	297	154	50	....	8,848
		F	221	1,085	1,041	784	856	1,839	1,052	424	260	145	50	....	7,757
	Free col'd.	M	15	74	93	74	60	124	94	44	20	19	10	....	627
		F	13	83	79	68	86	176	75	40	11	13	6	....	650
	Total.	M	237	1,214	1,099	907	789	2,292	1,624	763	317	173	60	....	9,475
		F	234	1,168	1,120	852	942	2,015	1,127	464	271	158	56	....	8,407
Detroit, Mich.	White	M	322	1,167	1,355	1,066	877	2,334	1,787	1,004	425	147	72	....	10,556
		F	307	1,143	1,284	1,064	1,200	2,254	1,400	666	322	172	64	...	9,876
	Free col'd.	M	9	44	38	24	13	70	69	22	13	2	3	1	308
		F	9	44	36	30	21	63	42	14	10	3	6	1	279
	Total.	M	331	1,211	1,393	1,090	890	2,404	1,856	1,026	438	149	75	1	10,864
		F	316	1,187	1,320	1,094	1,221	2,317	1,442	680	332	175	70	1	10,155
Hartford, Conn.	White	M	145	537	595	457	687	1,679	1,132	553	275	149	71	....	6,280
		F	138	552	630	521	753	1,765	1,099	565	406	271	132	....	6,832
	Free col'd.	M	5	15	32	12	18	48	39	16	5	2	1	....	193
		F	6	28	17	17	25	54	51	18	21	10	3	....	250
	Total.	M	150	552	627	469	705	1,727	1,171	569	280	151	72	....	6,473
		F	144	580	647	538	778	1,819	1,150	583	427	281	135	....	7,082
Indianapolis, Ind.	White	M	125	430	518	424	425	990	580	330	160	55	3	3	4,043
		F	105	400	514	465	463	802	440	260	122	66	5	1	3,643
	Free col'd.	M	4	23	19	30	15	41	27	19	14	1	1	....	194
		F	3	21	33	28	26	52	22	12	11	3	......	....	211
	Total.	M	129	453	537	454	440	1,031	607	349	174	56	4	3	4,237
		F	108	421	547	493	489	854	462	272	133	69	5	1	3,854
Lowell, Mass.	White	M	376	1,183	1,390	1,325	1,310	3,360	2,101	1,235	558	237	76	1	13,152
		F	353	1,207	1,390	1,564	3,558	6,644	2,792	1,534	706	322	105	1	20,176
	Free col'd.	M	......	5	1	2	3	4	9	1	1	......	......	....	26
		F	1	2	2	4	1	6	10	2	1	......	......	....	29
	Total.	M	376	1,188	1,391	1,327	1,313	3,364	2,110	1,236	559	237	76	1	13,178
		F	354	1,209	1,392	1,568	3,559	6,650	2,802	1,536	707	322	105	1	20,205
Manchester, N. H.	White	M	98	432	536	509	664	1,739	893	502	251	88	26	....	5,738
		F	116	451	529	625	1,752	2,697	1,039	519	277	91	51	....	8,147
	Free col'd.	M	1	2	1	3	4	8	5	2	1	......	......	....	27
		F	......	4	1	1	......	8	4	......	1	......	1	....	20
	Total.	M	99	434	537	512	668	1,747	898	504	252	88	26	....	5,765
		F	116	455	530	626	1,752	2,705	1,043	519	278	91	52	....	8,167

TABLE I—*Continued.*

Cities.	Color and condition.	Sex.	Under 1 year old.	1 and under 5.	5 and under 10.	10 and under 15.	15 and under 20.	20 and under 30.	30 and under 40.	40 and under 50.	50 and under 60.	60 and under 70.	70 and over.	Age unknown.	Total.
Milwaukee, Wis.	White	M	336	1,238	1,221	914	806	2,435	2,050	910	363	117	43	....	10,433
		F	390	1,208	1,107	925	1,045	2,345	1,423	644	281	123	39	....	9,530
	Free col'd.	M	2	3	3	2	......	20	21	4	1	......	1	....	57
		F	......	4	3	4	6	11	9	2	1	......	1	....	41
	Total.	M	338	1,241	1,224	916	806	2,455	2,071	914	364	117	44	....	10,490
		F	390	1,212	1,110	929	1,051	2,356	1,432	646	282	123	40	....	9,571
Newark, N. J.	White	M	609	2,069	2,175	1,830	1,946	3,997	2,777	1,767	788	345	138	5	18,446
		F	587	2,060	2,225	1,972	2,093	4,308	2,629	1,707	903	490	239	5	19,218
	Free col'd.	M	14	57	69	54	45	97	93	50	38	21	5	....	543
		F	19	72	67	58	71	149	99	68	39	28	16	....	686
	Total.	M	623	2,126	2,244	1,884	1,991	4,094	2,870	1,817	826	366	143	5	18,989
		F	606	2,132	2,292	2,030	2,164	4,457	2,728	1,775	942	518	255	5	19,904
New Haven, Conn.	White	M	200	904	950	847	1,147	2,343	1,492	847	411	175	98	....	9,414
		F	172	232	956	940	1,137	2,311	1,529	914	531	332	188	....	9,942
	Free col'd.	M	6	36	50	46	41	88	80	54	27	11	5	....	444
		F	6	34	52	48	61	119	96	71	33	15	10	....	545
	Total.	M	206	940	1,000	893	1,188	2,431	1,572	901	438	186	103	....	9,858
		F	178	966	1,008	988	1,198	2,430	1,625	985	564	347	198	....	10,487
New York, N. Y.	White	M	7,250	25,369	26,903	21,790	21,486	62,452	43,738	23,089	10,126	4,230	1,533	42	248,008
		F	7,287	24,918	26,618	23,003	27,420	67,670	38,567	19,937	10,391	5,333	2,544	36	253,724
	Free col'd.	M	152	490	615	523	460	1,327	1,202	780	342	149	58	....	6,098
		F	118	572	645	609	693	1,918	1,447	929	451	203	132	....	7,717
	Total.	M	7,402	25,859	27,518	22,313	21,946	63,779	44,940	23,869	10,468	4,379	1,591	42	254,106
		F	7,405	26,490	27,263	23,612	28,113	69,588	40,014	20,866	10,842	5,536	2,676	36	261,441
Philadelphia as organized 1854.	White	M	5,357	20,661	23,100	19,536	17,720	39,824	28,820	17,749	8,940	4,225	1,853	171	187,956
		F	5,199	20,399	22,505	20,417	22,378	45,541	27,962	17,303	10,142	5,753	3,357	89	201,045
	Free col'd.	M	201	832	957	801	751	1,738	1,367	956	488	208	119	17	8,435
		F	260	853	1,058	952	1,137	2,706	1,805	1,257	691	345	248	14	11,326
	Total.	M	5,558	21,493	24,057	20,337	18,471	41,562	30,187	18,705	9,428	4,433	1,972	188	196,391
		F	5,459	21,252	23,563	21,369	23,515	48,247	29,767	18,560	10,833	6,098	3,605	103	212,371
Pittsburg, Pa.	White	M	683	2,594	2,700	2,225	2,235	5,374	3,351	1,981	916	389	143	15	22,606
		F	740	2,577	2,752	2,377	2,592	5,054	2,763	1,678	861	467	165	10	22,036
	Fres col'd.	M	26	87	99	81	85	222	152	95	36	18	6	....	907
		F	29	101	124	131	135	238	128	92	41	26	7	....	1,052
	Total.	M	709	2,681	2,799	2,306	2,320	5,596	3,503	2,076	952	407	149	15	23,513
		F	769	2,678	2,876	2,508	2,727	5,292	9,891	1,770	902	493	172	10	23,088
Portland, Me.	White	M	270	1,018	1,062	970	1,018	2,037	1,445	1,010	510	268	147	....	9,755
		F	250	899	1,083	1,078	1,287	2,322	1,468	1,051	629	366	232	....	10,665
	Free col'd.	M	5	19	17	23	16	40	33	24	13	7	8	....	205
		F	4	12	23	22	16	31	36	13	16	13	4	....	190
	Total.	M	275	1,037	1,079	993	1,034	2,077	1,478	1,034	523	275	155	....	9,960
		F	254	911	1,106	1,100	1,303	2,353	1,504	1,064	645	379	236	....	10,855
Portsmouth, N. H.	White	M	99	425	534	489	462	888	674	448	263	164	97	....	4,543
		F	100	429	522	520	593	1,048	707	521	317	210	178	....	5,145
	Free col'd.	M	......	......	5	1	1	3	2	5	2	......	2	....	21
		F	......	1	5	3	3	3	2	3	5	2	2	....	29
	Total.	M	99	425	539	490	463	891	676	453	265	164	99	....	4,564
		F	100	430	527	523	596	1,051	709	524	322	212	180	....	5,174
Providence, R. I.	White	M	531	2,035	1,963	1,821	1,794	4,570	3,205	1,800	905	435	208	....	19,267
		F	585	1,973	2,072	1,890	2,162	4,888	3,144	1,906	1,127	650	350	....	20,747
	Free col'd.	M	15	65	89	68	46	108	136	72	33	19	15	....	666
		F	12	79	78	80	66	164	153	90	40	37	34	....	833
	Total.	M	546	2,100	2,052	1,889	1,840	4,678	3,341	1,872	938	454	223	....	19,933
		F	597	2,052	2,150	1,970	2,228	5,052	3,297	1,996	1,167	687	384	....	21,580
Sacramento, Cal.	White	M	16	47	59	55	272	3,090	1,846	600	149	15	3	17	6,169
		F	10	48	47	43	45	142	82	34	6	2	1	....	460
	Free col'd.	M	......	......	......	3	11	64	54	31	11	3	......	....	177
		F	......	......	1	2	2	2	3	3	1	......	......	....	14
	Total.	M	16	47	59	58	283	3,154	1,900	631	160	18	3	17	6,346
		F	10	48	48	45	47	144	85	37	7	2	1	....	474
Springfield, Mass.	White	M	164	575	558	508	445	1,351	1,095	523	255	137	56	....	5,667
		F	154	596	586	480	546	1,506	930	489	290	174	77	....	5,828
	Free col'd.	M	1	6	13	7	14	28	15	16	6	2	1	....	109
		F	4	8	16	16	18	46	22	13	15	1	3	....	162
	Total.	M	165	581	571	515	459	1,379	1,110	539	261	139	57	....	5,776
		F	158	604	602	496	564	1,552	952	502	305	175	80	....	5,990
Syracuse, N. Y.	White	M	223	1,095	1,193	1,032	1,263	3,024	1,923	1,100	474	214	66	16	11,623
		F	277	1,235	1,172	1,100	1,321	2,358	1,455	730	388	154	82	6	10,278
	Free col'd.	M	4	17	24	15	13	35	26	25	12	6	3	....	180
		F	2	22	26	12	21	37	36	18	10	4	2	....	190
	Total.	M	227	1,112	1,217	1,047	1,276	3,059	1,949	1,125	486	220	69	16	11,803
		F	279	1,257	1,198	1,112	1,342	2,395	1,491	748	398	158	84	6	10,468
Troy, N. Y.	White	M	430	1,618	1,742	1,344	1,169	2,839	2,146	1,296	616	268	109	....	13,577
		F	394	1,583	1,681	1,428	1,735	3,489	2,076	1,214	631	310	158	....	14,699
	Free col'd.	M	3	22	21	22	20	50	46	18	10	6	5	....	223
		F	9	24	20	17	30	63	56	38	12	7	10	....	286
	Total.	M	433	1,640	1,763	1,366	1,189	2,889	2,192	1,314	626	274	114	....	13,800
		F	403	1,607	1,701	1,443	1,765	3,552	2,132	1,252	643	317	168	....	14,985

TABLE II.—*Age and Sex of the White, Free Colored and Slave Population in the leading Cities of the Slaveholding States*, 1850.

Cities.	Color and condition.	Sex.	Under 1 year old.	1 and under 5.	5 and under 10.	10 and under 15.	15 and under 20.	20 and under 30.	30 and under 40.	40 and under 50.	50 and under 60.	60 and under 70.	70 and over.	Age unknown.	Total.
Baltimore, Md.	White	M	2,275	7,761	8,253	6,863	6,505	16,180	12,034	6,189	2,860	1,310	643	....	70,873
		F	2,238	7,871	8,254	7,414	7,498	14,730	9,846	5,689	3,385	1,899	969	....	69,793
	Free col'd.	M	373	1,266	1,325	1,216	929	2,229	1,715	948	504	214	113	....	10,832
		F	366	1,296	1,486	1,485	1,615	3,304	2,280	1,293	791	415	279	....	14,610
	Slave.	M	20	81	120	182	172	179	91	49	37	9	6	1	947
		F	15	103	201	331	368	424	233	168	89	48	17	2	1,999
	Total.	M	2,668	9,108	9,698	8,261	7,606	18,588	13,840	7,186	3,401	1,533	762	1	82,652
		F	2,619	9,270	9,941	9,230	9,481	18,458	12,359	7,150	4,265	2,362	1,265	2	86,402
Charleston, S. C.	White	M	143	979	1,240	1,117	987	2,209	1,766	1,005	493	206	93	....	10,238
		F	130	889	1,207	1,153	1,026	2,049	1,468	862	543	286	161	....	9,774
	Free col'd.	M	14	169	248	228	110	170	181	124	66	27	18	....	1,355
		F	21	173	287	281	201	342	342	174	131	75	59	....	2,086
	Slave.	M	83	599	857	978	935	1,649	1,386	1,006	580	352	206	....	8,631
		F	92	682	1,127	1,142	1,113	1,818	1,850	1,260	927	600	290	....	10,901
	Total.	M	240	1,747	2,345	2,323	2,032	4,028	3,333	2,135	1,139	585	317	....	20,224
		F	243	1,744	2,621	2,576	2,340	4,209	3,660	2,296	1,601	961	510	....	22,761
Galveston, Texas.	White	M	49	191	186	185	145	355	398	205	73	32	6	....	1,825
		F	63	212	212	194	172	340	270	100	60	13	8	....	1,644
	Free col'd.	M	......	......	4	2	2	2	2	......	2	......	......	....	14
		F	......	1	2	......	1	2	5	2	2	......	1	....	16
	Slave.	M	6	42	33	41	25	79	40	17	16	9	1	....	309
		F	10	36	40	49	33	100	50	28	17	6	......	....	369
	Total.	M	55	233	223	228	172	436	440	222	91	41	7	....	2,148
		F	73	249	254	243	206	442	325	130	79	19	9	....	2,029
Little Rock, Ark.	White	M	17	105	90	88	55	180	165	79	33	8	5	1	826
		F	20	95	128	119	79	172	96	46	26	8	5	1	795
	Free col'd.	M	......	......	......	......	......	2	2	......	1	......	......	....	5
		F	......	......	1	1	5	2	1	1	2	......	3	....	16
	Slave.	M	3	23	31	39	20	39	36	20	13	6	......	....	230
		F	5	34	39	42	39	53	38	25	11	5	4	....	295
	Total.	M	20	128	121	127	75	221	203	99	47	14	7	1	1,061
		F	25	129	168	162	123	227	135	72	39	13	10	1	1,106
Louisville, Ky.	White	M	576	2,030	2,153	1,782	1,626	4,874	3,536	1,728	760	265	99	39	19,468
		F	578	1,882	2,224	1,840	1,749	3,784	2,307	1,245	686	297	133	31	16,756
	Free col'd.	M	13	60	85	61	45	118	102	84	67	30	33	....	698
		F	24	78	85	74	68	157	122	98	61	41	31	1	840
	Slave.	M	68	227	281	320	324	590	279	169	97	34	18	3	2,410
		F	74	266	286	428	423	592	400	317	143	64	23	6	3,022
	Total.	M	657	2,317	2,519	2,163	1,995	5,582	3,917	1,981	924	329	150	42	22,576
		F	676	2,226	2,595	2,342	2,240	4,533	2,829	1,660	890	402	187	38	20,618
Memphis, Tenn.	White	M	110	334	356	326	270	941	755	330	121	25	9	2	3,579
		F	99	370	357	335	300	626	411	160	69	34	14	1	2,776
	Free col'd.	M	......	11	5	5	3	11	10	3	2	1	......	....	51
		F	......	8	6	9	6	19	11	8	6	1	1	....	75
	Slave.	M	32	101	118	170	116	265	145	78	45	15	8	1	1,094
		F	39	116	131	175	137	276	190	110	64	24	4	....	1,266
	Total.	M	142	446	479	501	389	1,217	910	411	168	41	17	3	4,724
		F	138	494	494	519	443	921	612	278	139	59	19	1	4,117
Mobile, Ala.	White	M	208	659	750	554	437	1,585	1,693	769	265	66	34	2	7,022
		F	223	723	768	598	644	1,396	902	386	194	89	51	1	5,975
	Free col'd.	M	3	37	41	42	20	40	30	29	22	10	12	....	286
		F	8	42	41	41	47	94	47	46	25	13	25	....	429
	Slave.	M	20	316	349	336	277	682	628	316	167	79	42	....	3,212
		F	28	365	350	444	379	664	617	380	211	107	46	....	3,591
	Total.	M	231	1,012	1,140	932	734	2,307	2,351	1,114	454	155	88	2	10,520
		F	259	1,130	1,159	1,083	1,070	2,154	1,566	812	430	209	122	1	9,995
Nashville, Tenn.	White	M	86	411	436	389	378	1,082	639	335	165	65	30	2	4,016
		F	93	398	457	495	481	778	440	258	130	53	25	....	3,610
	Free col'd.	M	3	34	30	38	25	47	32	20	17	6	4	....	256
		F	3	26	33	25	29	53	30	27	15	8	6	....	255
	Slave.	M	13	105	134	144	107	221	115	52	61	16	9	....	977
		F	17	107	107	131	133	206	140	117	64	20	9	....	1,051
	Total.	M	102	550	600	571	510	1,350	786	407	243	87	43	2	5,249
		F	113	531	597	651	643	1,037	610	402	209	81	40	....	4,916
Natchez, Miss.	White	M	11	188	177	162	86	233	261	135	55	17	8	10	1,343
		F	15	177	188	204	133	259	202	91	48	20	15	15	1,367
	Free col'd.	M	......	13	14	18	14	19	7	6	2	3	4	....	100
		F	......	17	17	13	8	18	15	10	6	5	3	1	113
	Slave.	M	2	48	171	19	52	225	87	43	30	8	1	....	686
		F	2	45	152	20	54	308	125	71	32	16	......	....	825
	Total.	M	13	249	362	199	152	477	355	184	87	28	13	10	2,129
		F	17	239	357	237	195	585	342	172	86	41	18	16	2,305
New Orleans, including Lafayette and Algiers.	White	M	1,428	4,574	5,095	3,889	3,308	15,872	15,290	6,693	2,037	682	231	213	59,312
		F	1,448	4,623	5,068	4,100	4,643	12,035	7,261	3,094	1,252	619	256	32	44,431
	Free col'd.	M	129	451	628	557	384	625	567	402	213	84	48	16	4,104
		F	142	457	661	580	589	1,131	1,031	638	472	289	205	1	6,196

TABLE II.—*Continued.*

Cities.	Color and condition.	Sex.	Under 1 year old.	1 and under 5.	5 and under 10.	10 and under 15.	15 and under 20.	20 and under 30.	30 and under 40.	40 and under 50.	50 and under 60.	60 and under 70.	70 and over.	Age unknown.	Total.
New Orleans, including Lafayette and Algiers.	Slave.	M	152	757	941	892	751	1,856	1,374	779	331	116	56	7	8,012
		F	181	753	929	1,155	1,133	2,692	2,421	1,392	596	234	107	2	11,595
	Total.	M	1,709	5,782	6,664	5,338	4,443	18,353	17,231	7,874	2,581	882	335	236	71,428
		F	1,771	5,833	6,658	5,835	6,365	15,858	10,713	5,124	2,320	1,142	568	35	62,222
Norfolk, Va.	White	M	106	440	551	460	490	846	578	397	184	102	42	....	4,196
		F	114	463	577	563	557	983	707	432	279	125	79	....	4,879
	Free col'd.	M	10	53	50	49	44	56	35	29	21	7	10	....	364
		F	12	65	73	52	58	121	72	62	39	20	18	....	592
	Slave.	M	42	190	220	218	169	291	256	154	81	42	14	....	1,677
		F	39	230	343	340	273	432	295	305	195	100	66	....	2,618
	Total.	M	158	683	821	727	703	1,193	869	580	286	151	66	....	6,237
		F	165	758	993	955	888	1,536	1,074	799	513	245	163	....	8,089
Petersburg, Va.	White	M	68	331	400	389	360	607	500	292	136	63	31	....	5,177
		F	65	325	420	432	450	669	478	312	198	90	48	1	3,488
	Free col'd.	M	28	135	150	155	123	214	156	115	55	22	24	....	1,177
		F	26	140	155	167	152	279	196	141	80	48	55	....	1,439
	Slave.	M	31	215	233	306	252	426	330	315	153	71	44	....	2,376
		F	42	211	233	322	269	363	309	274	180	92	58	....	2,353
	Total.	M	127	681	783	850	735	1,247	986	722	344	156	99	....	6,730
		F	133	676	808	921	871	1,311	983	727	458	230	161	1	7,280
Richmond, Va.	White	M	156	836	945	750	735	1,694	1,347	731	379	152	56	2	7,783
		F	140	820	927	812	814	1,576	1,090	624	387	204	97	....	7,491
	Free col'd.	M	33	106	128	122	87	247	170	93	53	20	16	....	1,075
		F	20	110	134	132	142	274	231	114	74	35	28	....	1,294
	Slave.	M	56	401	380	662	578	1,010	1,064	678	300	126	52	....	5,307
		F	62	391	434	596	501	800	644	552	347	185	108	....	4,620
	Total.	M	245	1,343	1,453	1,534	1,400	2,951	2,581	1,502	732	298	124	2	14,165
		F	222	1,321	1,495	1,540	1,457	2,650	1,965	1,290	808	424	233	....	13,405
St. Augustine, Fla.	White	M	12	77	105	77	46	58	65	54	39	17	8	....	558
		F	12	75	93	82	78	103	74	54	33	40	11	....	655
	Free col'd.	M	......	1	9	7	2	1	2	2	......	3	4	....	31
		F	1	8	13	6	3	4	10	5	3	1	5	....	59
	Slave.	M	6	31	35	45	19	47	30	21	18	21	6	....	279
		F	4	29	52	53	39	52	42	37	25	10	9	....	352
	Total.	M	18	109	149	129	67	106	97	77	57	41	18	....	868
		F	17	112	158	141	120	159	126	96	61	51	25	....	1,066
St. Louis, Mo.	White	M	1,100	3,651	3,568	3,002	3,331	13,531	9,008	3,427	1,210	398	128	13	42,367
		F	981	3,455	3,607	3,251	3,830	8,169	4,582	2,066	972	416	104	6	31,439
	Free col'd.	M	13	47	61	57	69	231	144	74	25	13	5	3	742
		F	14	53	64	73	44	155	128	75	27	15	7	1	656
	Slave.	M	14	109	123	141	126	423	187	86	34	13	10	....	1,266
		F	18	104	136	220	178	299	209	144	49	26	7	....	1,390
	Total.	M	1,127	3,807	3,752	3,200	3,526	14,185	9,339	3,587	1,269	424	143	16	44,375
		F	1,013	3,612	3,807	3,544	4,052	8,623	4,919	2,285	1,048	457	118	7	33,485
Savannah, Ga.	White	M	93	389	433	387	394	1,097	923	416	169	78	30	....	4,409
		F	101	431	451	403	405	897	617	317	207	103	52	2	3,986
	Free col'd.	M	9	30	35	45	26	35	31	29	9	7	8	....	264
		F	8	40	55	44	29	71	51	39	37	21	27	....	422
	Slave.	M	50	226	300	368	250	626	480	318	179	117	35	....	2,949
		F	68	295	340	435	295	580	485	380	180	174	50	....	3,282
	Total.	M	152	645	768	800	670	1,758	1,434	763	357	202	73	....	7,622
		F	177	766	846	882	729	1,548	1,153	736	424	298	129	2	7,690
Washington, D. C.	White	M	385	1,661	1,889	1,629	1,403	2,806	2,169	1,323	787	349	123	2	14,526
		F	396	1,571	1,917	1,699	1,712	3,118	2,113	1,265	801	427	171	14	15,204
	Free col'd.	M	106	445	514	427	313	538	435	298	190	80	52	....	3,398
		F	106	401	534	486	538	944	664	497	289	154	146	1	4,760
	Slave.	M	20	78	104	129	122	129	67	42	22	17	3	....	733
		F	23	82	163	201	215	279	149	111	84	46	27	....	1,380
	Total.	M	511	2,184	2,507	2,185	1,838	3,473	2,671	1,663	999	446	178	2	18,657
		F	525	2,054	2,614	2,386	2,465	4,341	2,926	1,873	1,174	627	344	15	21,344
Wilmington, Del.	White	M	186	606	709	595	593	1,086	843	497	279	127	86	....	5,607
		F	179	588	704	626	751	1,349	883	530	320	180	122	....	6,232
	Free col'd.	M	35	126	134	85	80	129	125	95	57	40	25	....	931
		F	30	124	143	93	135	269	176	110	77	36	16	....	1,209
	Slave.	M	......	......	......	......	......	......	......	......	......	......	......	....	......
		F	......	......	......	......	......	......	......	......	......	......	......	....	......
	Total.	M	221	732	843	680	673	1,215	968	592	336	167	111	....	6,538
		F	209	712	847	719	886	1,618	1,059	640	397	216	138	....	7,441
Wilmington, N. C.	White	M	61	208	201	199	147	381	327	164	72	24	11	....	1,795
		F	54	205	236	200	157	375	263	154	73	41	28	....	1,786
	Free col'd.	M	8	40	37	46	24	51	40	20	7	7	5	....	285
		F	5	46	39	32	33	83	58	23	20	12	16	....	367
	Slave.	M	16	198	189	196	158	265	178	112	67	36	20	....	1,435
		F	26	172	216	230	158	272	207	135	91	59	30	....	1,596
	Total.	M	85	446	427	441	329	697	545	296	146	67	36	....	3,515
		F	85	423	491	462	348	730	528	312	184	112	74	....	3,749

TABLE III.—*Nativities of the Inhabitants of the Leading Cities of the United States*—1850.

Cities.	Born in the United States.																				
	In city or rest of same State.	Alabama.	Columbia, District of.	Connecticut.	Delaware.	Florida.	Georgia.	Illinois.	Indiana.	Kentucky.	Louisiana.	Maine.	Maryland.	Massachusetts.	Michigan.	Mississippi.	Missouri.	New Hampshire.	New Jersey.	New York.	N. Carolina.
Albany	28738	1	2	553	13	...	3	9	4	6	5	43	49	736	7	...	1	111	218	....	10
Baltimore	113583	26	1170	326	756	23	61	17	43	85	96	396	....	1192	11	121	51	215	723	2037	126
Boston	68687	17	47	575	29	9	82	17	3	12	32	7689	191	....	15	5	6	6628	118	1594	47
Charleston	16066	18	9	58	1	22	182	....	4	10	11	19	119	227	...	2	...	6	58	545	109
Chicago	5831	21	7	506	29	4	8	....	89	97	24	203	69	480	249	28	71	170	239	3870	24
Cincinnati	39322	52	127	527	215	1	105	147	1185	2096	378	220	1643	1079	87	189	126	225	1417	3142	169
Detroit	6323	6	15	224	9	2	13	25	10	98	6	70	34	296	...	4	19	80	83	2620	15
Hartford	8293	9	4	....	7	5	14	9	4	1	4	46	40	983	6	1	2	110	67	636	6
Louisville	16285	71	53	116	59	3	51	99	1255	....	195	45	742	219	8	69	148	39	206	777	109
Manchester	9555	...	....	11	....	1	1	2	13	....	...	197	1	1012	...	...	1	....	.....	82	1
Memphis	2134	187	18	36	4	10	96	67	94	360	56	21	100	56	4	164	79	16	20	160	351
Milwaukie	2641	1	1	263	14	...	1	91	33	19	5	156	30	350	122	5	26	83	80	2281	3
Mobile	5507	...	18	139	5	133	355	1	14	91	228	100	154	289	...	230	16	39	73	701	216
Nashville	4883	78	2	31	6	2	26	12	16	382	30	4	91	54	1	36	3	....	30	283	243
Newark	21477	4	12	533	31	1	16	12	2	7	16	46	111	277	9	2	1	45	.....	3239	20
New Haven	13775	21	9	....	13	15	92	6	6	15	34	79	57	551	5	12	8	35	270	1167	20
New Orleans	34101	620	92	228	44	139	249	147	118	1038	...	620	733	1178	52	842	431	155	274	4086	214
New York	234843	90	261	7784	393	54	277	72	41	122	303	1432	1852	5587	86	83	56	826	13255	....	284
Philadelphia	242681	55	394	829	8678	15	123	52	62	197	163	333	5760	1858	18	24	60	288	15570	4858	198
Portland	15110	5	15	43	8	1	6	7	1	....	8	....	35	1208	1	...	...	474	9	142	3
Portsmouth	7088	...	5	30	3	...	2	....	....	....	2	866	7	415	...	...	...	....	1	51	1
Providence	24368	6	35	989	22	9	29	5	3	9	6	326	218	4003	5	4	...	321	86	760	58
Richmond	14138	8	40	72	14	5	8	....	....	24	4	22	268	161	1	1	2	37	75	254	102
St. Augustine	1100	1	....	33	....	...	25	1	....	3	1	6	9	8	...	...	...	3	3	5	7
Savannah	4774	14	8	84	9	121	...	....	2	5	6	25	49	100	...	3	1	24	75	305	69
St. Louis	20321	82	109	325	79	10	73	1210	438	1846	360	112	841	603	94	234	...	137	270	2470	126
Washington	19237	18	....	122	66	23	60	23	26	78	23	79	7017	284	26	39	25	77	139	723	86
Wilm'ton, Del	8671	2	10	21	....	...	5	2	11	3	3	21	765	50	...	1	2	10	525	100	10
Wilm'ton, N.C	3527	9	3	55	3	17	13	2	....	5	...	16	26	42	...	1	1	2	8	97	....

Cities.	Born in the United States.							Foreign Born.									Aggregate.	
	Ohio.	Pennsylvania.	R. Island.	S. Carolina.	Tennessee.	Vermont.	Virginia.	England and Wales.	Ireland.	Scotland.	Germany.	Prussia.	Austria.	France.	Spain.	Italy.	Native.*	Foreign.*
Albany	26	154	92	21	1	322	31	2082	13079	540	2875	1	....	97	2	1	31162	16591
Baltimore	276	4986	181	122	26	211	3605	2133	12057	525	19274	164	16	346	16	67	130491	35492
Boston	69	393	584	94	6	1744	251	3213	35287	897	1777	39	....	225	67	134	88948	46677
Charleston	2	165	38	....	9	13	115	546	2369	323	1789	27	1	187	23	56	17809	4643
Chicago	390	545	46	5	18	456	119	1883	6096	610	5035	38	21	234	2	4	13693	15682
Cincinnati	....	5112	143	112	245	250	2178	4135	14393	718	33374	148	18	797	4	152	60558	54541
Detroit	305	276	21	12	24	281	161	1245	3289	474	2838	13	7	282	4	4	11055	9927
Hartford	25	66	67	7	3	114	12	235	2188	58	271	12	13	27	....	4	10551	2915
Louisville	1090	1365	22	72	306	42	1582	720	3105	162	7357	145	24	422	4	112	25079	12461
Manchester	....	1	15	....	....	1343	8	182	1193	31	......	....	....	1	....	....	12244	1688
Memphis	150	194	5	131	....	7	419	133	704	20	341	8	1	69	1	44	5026	1401
Milwaukie	334	314	35	16	4	225	42	1212	2816	245	6028	1243	16	129	....	....	7181	12782
Mobile	86	237	24	459	75	32	330	547	2009	205	513	22	17	303	144	65	9565	4086
Nashville	106	178	4	61	....	8	608	137	421	70	193	15	....	36	1	3	7185	948
Newark	41	504	38	25	1	45	43	2124	5564	265	3818	4	6	240	8	....	26561	12322
New Haven	57	212	47	21	4	63	39	371	2772	107	273	11	....	54	....	3	16641	3697
New Orleans	781	1515	174	502	484	133	1232	2670	20200	854	11220	205	129	7522	1150	658	50470	48601
New York	499	5283	961	535	26	953	1702	23671	133730	7660	55476	665	109	4990	303	708	277752	235733
Philadelphia	505	....	288	470	85	157	2602	17500	72312	3291	22750	270	84	1981	291	236	286346	121699
Portland	1	49	32	6	....	78	23	156	2301	50	22	14	2	14	....	6	17265	3512
Portsmouth	6	15	9	3	1	27	7	343	523	62	25	1	....	6	....	....	8540	1179
Providence	30	170	....	20	1	134	99	1119	7635	322	87	2	1	40	10	19	31755	9679
Richmond	12	206	9	43	11	16	....	268	685	183	740	18	2	68	5	34	15541	2102
St. Augustine	....	3	9	19	1	1	6	7	11	4	5	....	....	6	3	1	1244	56
Savannah	6	87	26	720	6	9	60	227	1555	60	383	3	7	37	13	15	6590	2434
St. Louis	1638	2684	45	73	380	176	1630	2957	9719	550	22340	231	13	682	36	101	36529	38397
Washington	114	1000	19	71	54	40	4046	585	2023	136	1246	10	1	69	22	49	33530	4282
Wilm'ton, Del.	15	1908	2	1	1	2	56	240	1215	24	157	26	....	16	1	....	12198	1763
Wilm'ton, N.C.	1	34	15	57	....	1	89	33	63	14	72	....	1	9	....	....	4025	208

NOTE.—Exclusive of 5 Arkansians in Baltimore, 25 in Cincinnati, 26 in Louisville, 80 in Memphis, 97 in New Orleans, and 39 in St. Louis, &c.; 4 Californians in New York; 19 Iowans in Chicago, 24 in Cincinnati, 10 in Louisville, 5 in Memphis, 6 in Milwaukie, 21 in New Orleans, 4 in New York, 7 in Philadelphia, and 77 in St. Louis; 19 Texans in Baltimore, 9 in Cincinnati, 8 in Hartford, 9 in Louisville, 10 in Mobile, 164 in New Orleans, 23 in New York, 8 in Philadelphia, 4 in Richmond, 21 in St. Louis, and 6 in Washington; 76 natives of Wisconsin in Chicago, 8 in Cincinnati, 21 in Detroit, 4 in New Haven, 28 in New York, 7 in Philadelphia, and 23 in St. Louis; 4 natives of the Territories in Louisville, 31 in New York, and 8 in Providence. Savannah cannot be defined on the returns.

* Exclusive of those unknown. The total foreign includes other countries not named in the table.

TABLE IV.—*Ages of Persons who died between June* 1, 1849, *and June* 1, 1850.

States and Territories.		Under 1.	1 and under 5.	5 and under 10.	10 and under 15.	15 and under 20.	20 and under 30.	30 and under 40.	40 and under 50.	50 and under 60.	60 and under 70.	70 and under 80.	80 and under 90.	90 and under 100.	100 and upwards.
Alabama	w	839	811	394	271	245	482	402	285	241	191	138	63	18	3
	c	1,184	1,279	343	202	232	429	286	262	190	166	62	44	19	22
Arkansas	w	390	453	212	106	134	264	224	168	96	67	30	13	1	2
	c	134	206	83	39	55	125	71	60	30	34	13	6	1	4
California	w	35	38	10	13	26	281	167	84	36	13	6	1	2	....
	c	1	....	....	....	....	9	1	5	1	2	....	....	....	....
Columbia, Dis. of	w	110	148	42	22	23	51	55	40	33	24	26	10	1	....
	c	44	39	21	10	16	31	26	22	15	18	12	4	2	1
Connecticut	w	684	905	282	138	223	591	487	423	406	479	490	390	79	5
	c	21	22	6	5	6	15	10	23	10	16	8	4	....	1
Delaware	w	186	184	60	37	32	74	91	69	77	61	53	17	6	....
	c	53	53	12	12	19	29	17	9	17	16	14	4	5	2
Florida	w	62	120	41	25	28	55	51	34	21	22	8	9	1	1
	c	85	128	34	17	27	49	21	23	24	15	12	6	5	2
Georgia	w	890	830	230	230	270	490	380	292	289	260	217	115	37	5
	c	1,393	1,330	296	238	330	466	315	252	199	234	132	76	49	43
Illinois	w	2,261	2,530	753	492	617	1,416	1,138	931	630	430	239	78	15	1
	c	9	10	4	3	4	13	5	5	6	3	2	....	1	....
Indiana	w	2,247	2,748	968	823	862	1,488	1,029	818	631	477	341	176	36	5
	c	22	21	14	6	11	20	11	8	10	7	....	2	1	....
Iowa	w	446	539	141	81	81	235	195	129	82	66	27	18	....	....
	c	....	3	....	....	....	1	....	....	....	....	....	....	....	....
Kentucky	w	1,743	2,074	655	456	618	1,359	1,006	748	623	540	445	251	60	6
	c	967	906	296	257	285	522	338	258	197	166	93	50	25	10
Louisiana	w	538	762	342	176	286	1,324	1,156	667	322	160	83	29	5	3
	c	737	1,302	435	279	326	851	778	535	320	237	90	62	38	25
Maine	w	910	1,584	519	260	454	921	631	497	403	459	462	350	82	4
	c	9	8	2	....	3	5	3	4	1	1	2	1	1	....
Maryland	w	1,536	1,555	454	475		579	473	492	412	383	352	151	22	5
	c	554	575	209	277		253	197	172	143	127	100	73	30	22
Massachusetts	w	2,833	4,380	1,064	584	725	2,203	1,802	1,309	1,070	1,138	1,078	793	174	7
	c	9	25	6	6	9	23	11	15	17	9	5	5	4	1
Michigan	w	851	995	293	177	198	493	408	312	280	227	165	61	8	2
	c	5	13	2	3	2	5	3	1	3	....	1	....	....	....
Mississippi	w	569	746	288	188	170	419	283	233	157	145	80	53	9	....
	c	1,270	1,502	375	248	256	543	408	296	164	152	62	36	16	26
Missouri	w	1,632	2,179	750	465	564	1,726	1,366	891	562	363	187	53	16	6
	c	322	309	100	92	91	188	120	75	51	39	29	8	11	3
New Hampshire	w	450	760	240	146	202	466	333	282	275	299	389	318	63	2
	c	1	1	1	1	....	....	....	1	....	....	....	....	....	....
New Jersey	w	1,040	1,282	344	185	232	592	472	469	421	438	366	245	40	....
	c	41	47	17	14	21	33	34	21	24	18	18	15	6	2
New York	w	6,628	9,758	2,889	1,387	1,834	5,404	4,369	3,534	2,608	2,351	2,098	1,341	243	15
	c	80	141	53	30	49	133	102	99	62	65	44	30	10	8
North Carolina	w	853	743	366	276	309	636	502	513	326	417	354	206	54	11
	c	1,059	1,147	264	217	272	415	294	216	243	234	192	140	62	36
Ohio	w	4,363	6,553	2,252	1,098	1,327	3,464	2,753	2,115	1,523	1,369	967	522	92	17
	c	57	97	27	19	33	65	32	29	24	13	15	2	2	1
Pennsylvania	w	4,835	6,683	1,978	838	1,079	2,663	2,146	1,779	1,543	1,590	1,425	838	165	15
	c	142	178	52	35	44	102	79	78	55	42	23	20	5	2
Rhode Island	w	340	437	104	36	102	249	206	152	148	127	147	78	24	....
	c	13	6	2	4	2	8	8	7	10	3	5	2	....	1
South Carolina	w	325	466	209	142	154	356	254	226	187	203	160	91	19	3
	c	1,091	1,261	320	272	269	462	304	244	242	300	173	99	49	34
Tennessee	w	1,517	1,318	499	369	443	992	594	489	428	350	318	241	62	13
	c	1,028	845	234	227	305	520	281	211	191	140	105	50	26	11
Texas	w	369	401	196	118	116	283	237	173	117	74	29	12	3	3
	c	186	235	59	46	56	94	70	51	36	12	9	6	3	3
Vermont	w	300	479	162	89	178	329	240	208	233	278	330	245	46	2
	c	1	2	....	....	....	....	1	1	1	1	....	....	....	....
Virginia	w	1,457	1,707	630	372	466	1,062	899	764	632	683	643	355	90	24
	c	1,693	1,918	513	464	492	892	611	571	591	531	434	271	121	58
Wisconsin	w	645	770	183	90	139	310	266	206	118	92	62	15	1	....
	c	....	....	....	....	....	2	....	....	....	....	....	....	....	....
Territ's. Minnesota	w	5	11	5	1	....	3	2	1	....	1	....	1	....	....
Territ's. New Mexico	w	207	240	67	45	78	158	99	66	52	55	37	29	11	3
Territ's. Oregon	w	5	11	3	2	1	9	9	3	2	2	....	....	....	....
Territ's. Utah	w	41	49	19	8	18	28	22	20	17	11	5	1	....	....

Ages.	White.	Colored.	Total.	Ages.	White.	Col'd.	Total.	Ages.	White.	Colored.	Total.
Under 1	42,142	12,211	54,353	30 and 40	24,747	4,437	29,184	90 and 100	1,504	473	1,977
1 and 5	55,249	13,609	68,858	40 and 50	19,422	3,554	22,976	Unknown	1,330	317	1,647
5 and 10	17,644	3,780	21,424	50 and 60	15,001	2,877	17,878	100 & over	163	318	481
10 and 15	10,221	3,023	13,244	60 and 70	13,845	2,601	16,446				
15 and 20	12,234	3,215	15,449	70 and 80	11,757	1,655	13,412				
20 and 30	31,455	6,303	37,758	80 and 90	7,169	1,016	8,185	Aggregate.	263,883	59,389	323,272

NOTE.—Average age of white deceased 25.45 yrs., colored 21.39, supposing those under 1 to have lived 6 mos., and those between 1 and 5, 3 years, &c. which is not true in point of fact, but sufficiently so for the comparison.

Free colored in Alabama 28, District of Columbia 204, Delaware 241, Florida 8, Georgia 46, Kentucky 184, Louisiana 165, Maryland 1,220, Mississippi 15, Missouri 83, New Jersey 304, North Carolina 462, South Carolina 81, Tennessee 125, Virginia 801. In Alabama 5 slaves died aged 105, 2 120; Arkansas 1 white 105, and 1 slave 110; District of Columbia 1 slave 103; Delaware 1 free colored 100, and 1 107; Georgia 1 white 105, 1 107, 3 slaves 103, 2 105, 1 120, 1 131; Michigan 1 white 103, 1 110; New Jersey 1 colored 114, 1 109; New York 1 white 102, 1 103, 1 free colored 104, 1 106, 2 110, 1 113; North Carolina 1 Indian female 140, 1 slave 120; Texas 1 slave 115.

www.ingramcontent.com/pod-product-compliance
Lightning Source LLC
La Vergne TN
LVHW020114110826
845151LV00001B/155

* 9 7 8 1 4 2 5 5 4 3 0 6 8 *